Canadian Health Law and Policy

FOURTH EDITION

General Editors

Jocelyn Downie, B.A., LL.B., M.A., M.Litt., LL.M., S.J.D., FCAHS, FRSC
Canada Research Chair in Health Law and Policy
Professor, Faculties of Law and Medicine
Dalhousie University

Timothy Caulfield, B.Sc., LL.B., LL.M., FCAHS, FRSC
Canada Research Chair in Health Law and Policy
Research Director, Health Law Institute
Professor, Faculties of Law,
Medicine and Dentistry
University of Alberta

Colleen M. Flood, B.A., LL.B. (Honours), LL.M., S.J.D.
Canada Research Chair in Health Law and Policy
Faculty of Law, School of Public Policy
and the Department of Health Policy,
Management and Evaluation
University of Toronto

Canadian Health Law and Policy, Fourth Edition
© LexisNexis Canada Inc. 2011
May 2011

Members of the LexisNexis Group worldwide

Canada	LexisNexis Canada Inc., 123 Commerce Valley Drive East, Suite 700, MARKHAM, Ontario
Australia	Butterworths, a Division of Reed International Books Australia Pty Ltd, CHATSWOOD, New South Wales
Austria	ARD Betriebsdienst and Verlag Orac, VIENNA
Czech Republic	Orac, sro, PRAGUE
France	Éditions du Juris-Classeur SA, PARIS
Hong Kong	Butterworths Asia (Hong Kong), HONG KONG
Hungary	Hvg Orac, BUDAPEST
India	Butterworths India, NEW DELHI
Ireland	Butterworths (Ireland) Ltd, DUBLIN
Italy	Giuffré, MILAN
Malaysia	Malayan Law Journal Sdn Bhd, KUALA LUMPUR
New Zealand	Butterworths of New Zealand, WELLINGTON
Poland	Wydawnictwa Prawnicze PWN, WARSAW
Singapore	Butterworths Asia, SINGAPORE
South Africa	Butterworth Publishers (Pty) Ltd, DURBAN
Switzerland	Stämpfli Verlag AG, BERNE
United Kingdom	Butterworths Tolley, a Division of Reed Elsevier (UK), LONDON, WC2A
USA	LexisNexis, DAYTON, Ohio

Library and Archives Canada Cataloguing in Publication

Canadian health law and policy / general editors: Jocelyn Downie, Timothy Caulfield, Colleen M. Flood. — 4th ed.

Includes index.
ISBN 978-0-433-46524-9

1. Medical laws and legislation—Canada. 2. Medical policy—Canada. I. Downie, Jocelyn Grant, 1962- II. Caulfield, Timothy A., 1963- III. Flood, Colleen M. (Colleen Marion), 1966-

KE3646.C343 2007   344.7104'1   C2007-903088-2
KF3821.C36 2007

Printed and bound in Canada.

FOREWORD

Health care, we are told, is the number one issue on the minds of Canadians. We have an array of studies, commissions, books and reports that reflect the extent of the debate.

Canadian Health Law and Policy is a little different because it reflects not only the policy debates that have surrounded us all, but speaks as well to the reality that whatever "system" is in place, a number of core legal issues will always be with us: what are the legal responsibilities of practitioners, and the rights of patients, dealing with the most difficult and emotional questions surrounding informed consent, negligence and decision-making about death itself? These are questions that need to be analyzed. They will, necessarily, lend themselves not to "the answers", but to a range of further questions and debates.

All of us need to be wiser on these questions, and wisdom will come only from the kind of informed discussion that is to be found in these pages. With new technologies come even more difficult issues, that is, those that the political process has notoriously been reluctant to deal with: reproductive questions and issues around genetics, stem cell therapies and other new technologies. These pose the fundamental moral dilemmas, which of necessity will lead to political and policy debates and eventually legislation.

It is crucial that policy and legislation reflect the complexity of the debates. While lawyers are often accused of making things more complicated and troubled than they really are, this is not the case here. Some might like a return to the easy certainties of another time, but it is clear to any thoughtful person that this is not possible. The users of the health care system rightly demand more information, more choices and more options; the old world of "doctor knows best" is gone forever. At the same time, physicians and other professionals are wrestling with the dilemmas associated with how to offer the best possible care when they see governments and other insurers more preoccupied with money than with health. These issues pose legal as well as personal and political challenges.

We are constantly testing what is known as "law's empire", to borrow Ronald Dworkin's well-known phrase. It is clear that the *Canadian Charter of Rights and Freedoms* has extended the boundaries of the justiciable. It is equally clear that a profound change in public attitudes and expectations, as well as revolutions in technology, make a return to a simple past impossible.

The chapters in this book are a vital contribution to a debate that can only become more critical and complex. There is no more room for snap judgments. Health care is too important to be left to the bumper sticker, and it is only right that rigorous legal analysis will be brought to bear on these vital questions.

The Right Honourable Bob Rae
January 2011

ACKNOWLEDGMENTS

Once again, our first and greatest debt is owed to the contributors to this collection for all their hard work. We thank them for their excellent and innovative contributions to health law and policy scholarship. They have made this an invaluable and enriching experience, and this is reflected in the scholarship found in the pages of this book.

We would like to thank all of the research assistants who helped with all four editions of the book. We would also like to thank all of our Faculty and Institute colleagues who provide us with stimulating and supportive intellectual homes, our wonderful and hard-working administrative staff, and finally our students, who represent the bright future of health law and policy in Canada. Finally, we would like to thank our families, who make it possible for us to pursue our dreams.

CONTRIBUTORS

PETER J. CARVER

Peter J. Carver, B.A. (U.B.C.), M.A. (Toronto), LL.B. (McGill), LL.M. (U.B.C.) is an Associate Professor at the Faculty of Law and Chairperson of the Centre for Constitutional Studies at the University of Alberta. He teaches in the area of Canadian public law, including constitutional, administrative, immigration and mental health law. Professor Carver has a joint appointment with the Faculty of Rehabilitation Medicine, which reflects his interests in health law and disability studies. Prior to joining the University of Alberta, Professor Carver practised law in Vancouver, worked with the Office of the Ombudsman of British Columbia, and served as a Member of the Immigration and Refugee Board.

TIMOTHY CAULFIELD

Timothy Caulfield has been Research Director of the Health Law Institute at the University of Alberta since 1993. In 2001, he received a Canada Research Chair in Health Law and Policy. He is also a Professor in the Faculty of Law and the School of Public Health and a Health Senior Scholar with the Alberta Heritage Foundation for Medical Research. He is currently the Principal Investigator for a number of large research initiatives, including a Genome Canada project on the regulation of genomic technologies and an AllerGen Network project on ethics, evidence and health policy research. He is the theme leader for the Stem Cell Network and has several other projects funded by the Canadian Institutes of Health Research. Professor Caulfield is and has been involved with a number of national and international policy and research ethics committees, including the Canadian Biotechnology Advisory Committee, Genome Canada's Science Advisory Committee and the Federal Panel on Research Ethics. He is a Fellow of the Royal Society of Canada and the Canadian Academy of Health Sciences. He teaches biotechnology in the Faculty of Law and is the editor for the *Health Law Journal* and *Health Law Review*.

JENNIFER CHANDLER

Jennifer Chandler, B.Sc. (University of Western Ontario), LL.B. (Queen's University), LL.M. (Harvard), of the Bar of Ontario, joined the University of Ottawa's Faculty of Law in 2002, after practising law as an associate lawyer with Stikeman Elliott and serving as a law clerk to the Honourable Mr. Justice John Sopinka of the Supreme Court of Canada. She is now an Associate Professor at the Faculty of Law, where she teaches health law, mental health law, tort law and a graduate level course called "Technoprudence", which addresses technology and legal theory. She has been a Visiting Associate Professor at the Centre for Biomedical Ethics at the National University of Singapore. Professor Chandler researches and writes about the legal and ethical challenges of advances in biomedical science and technology. Recently, she has written on the legal implications of advances in neuroimaging technologies; the ethical responses to legally coerced medical treatment; regulatory policy related to medical practices such as organ donation and transplantation; the proper limits on the governmental collection of personal health information; and the ethics and law of scientific inquiry. She is currently engaged in a project on the legal and social consequences of the developing neuroscientific understanding of memory and methods of memory modification.

BERNARD DICKENS

Bernard Dickens is the Professor Emeritus of Health Law and Policy at the Faculty of Law, cross-appointed to the Faculty of Medicine and Joint Centre for Bioethics at the University of Toronto. After qualifying at the English Bar, completing a Ph.D. degree in Law at the University of London and coming to the University of Toronto in 1974, he earned a higher doctorate (LL.D. degree) in Medical Jurisprudence. He has over 400 publications, primarily in medical law and bioethics, and many international collaborations. In 1990–1991, he was president of the American Society of Law, Medicine and Ethics, and is an Honorary Vice-President of the World Association for Medical Law. He has worked on several World Health Organization projects, particularly on human experimentation and organ transplantation. He is a Fellow of the Royal Society of Canada, and an Officer of the Order of Canada.

TRACEY EPPS

Tracey Epps has an LL.B./B.A. (Hons.) from the University of Auckland and an LL.M. and S.J.D. from the University of Toronto. Prior to undertaking doctoral studies, she worked as a solicitor with Cairns Slane and Buddle Findlay in Auckland, and as a consultant with IBM Business Consulting in Toronto. She is an active member of the International Economic Interest Law Group of the American Society for International Law and is currently working with the New Zealand Ministry of Foreign Affairs and Trade.

ELAINE GIBSON

Elaine Gibson is Associate Director of the Health Law Institute and Associate Professor of Law at the Schulich School of Law, Dalhousie University. She is cross-appointed to the Faculty of Health Professions. She has an LL.B. with distinction from the University of Saskatchewan and an LL.M. from the University of Toronto. She is a member of the Barristers' Societies of Nova Scotia and Saskatchewan. Her areas of expertise include health law, privacy and negligence. Her research focuses on legal issues surrounding health information and confidentiality, public health, medical malpractice and mental health law.

JOAN M. GILMOUR

Joan M. Gilmour, B.A., LL.B. (Toronto), J.S.M., J.S.D. (Stanford), of the Bar of Ontario, is a Professor at Osgoode Hall Law School, York University and the Director of Osgoode's Master's Program specializing in Health Law. She teaches Health Law, Legal Governance of Health Care, Torts and Disability and the Law in the J.D. program, and graduate courses on Professional Governance, and Legal Frameworks of the Canadian Health Care System. She is past Director of Osgoode's Institute for Feminist Legal Studies, and past Associate and Acting Director of York University's Centre for Health Studies (now the York Institute of Health Research). Current research projects include an examination of legal and ethical issues in decision-making about health care for children, studies of the effects of tort law on efforts to improve patient safety, and studies of the interrelation of disability, law, gender and inequality.

MICHAEL HADSKIS

Michael Hadskis is an Assistant Professor at the Schulich School of Law, Dalhousie University, and is a Faculty Member of the Health Law Institute. He has served on the IWK Health Centre Research Ethics Board and the Dalhousie University Health Sciences Research Ethics Board. In 2007, Dalhousie awarded Professor Hadskis the Health Sciences Research Ethics Board Distinguished Service Award. Currently, he sits on the Dalhousie Research Ethics Appeals Board. He teaches health law courses to law students, and oversees and delivers teaching in the Faculties of Medicine and Health Professions. Additionally, he oversees the health law curriculum in the Faculty of Dentistry. His research interests include neuroethics and the regulation of biomedical research.

IAN KERR

Ian Kerr holds the Canada Research Chair in Ethics, Law and Technology at the University of Ottawa, Faculty of Law, with cross-appointments to the Faculty of Medicine and the Department of Philosophy. In addition to his work on emerging health technologies, bioethics and the human-machine merger, Dr. Kerr has published books and articles on numerous topics at the intersection of ethics, law and technology, and is currently engaged in two large research projects: (i) On the Identity Trail, supported by one of the largest ever grants from the Social Sciences and Humanities Research Council, examining the impact of information and authentication technologies on our identity and our ability to be anonymous; and (ii) An Examination of Digital Copyright, supported by a large grant from Bell Canada and the Ontario Research Network in Electronic Commerce, examining various aspects of the current effort to reform Canadian copyright legislation. His devotion to teaching has earned him six awards and citations, including the Bank of Nova Scotia Award of Excellence in Undergraduate Teaching, the University of Western Ontario's Faculty of Graduate Studies' Award of Teaching Excellence, and the University of Ottawa's AEECLSS Teaching Excellence Award. Dr. Kerr sits as a member on numerous editorial and advisory boards and is co-author of *Managing the Law: The Legal Aspects of Doing Business*, a business law text published by Prentice Hall and used by thousands of students each year at universities across Canada.

ROBERT P. KOURI

Robert P. Kouri is a Professor of Law at the Faculté de droit of the Université de Sherbrooke, where he also served as Associate Dean of Law-Research and Director of the graduate programs in Health Law and Policy. After having obtained a licentiate in law, he went on to complete a Master's degree and a doctorate at McGill University. In addition to being co-author of three volumes on health law, *La responsabilité civile médicale* with Professor Alain Bernardot, *L'intégrité de la personne et le consentement aux soins* with Professor Suzanne Philips-Nootens and *Éléments de responsabilité civile médicale* with Professor Suzanne Philips-Nootens and Dr. Pauline Lesage-Jarjoura, he has published several articles in the fields of civil and health law. He has acted as consultant to the Department of Justice Canada, the Minister of Justice of Quebec, the Civil Code Revision Office and the Law Reform Commission of Canada. He is also a member of the Research Ethics Board of Health Canada.

WILLIAM LAHEY

William Lahey is an Associate Professor, Schulich School of Law, and Director, Dalhousie Health Law Institute. He holds a B.A. from Mount Allison, a B.A. (Jurisprudence) from Oxford and an LL.M. from Toronto. He teaches Public Law, Administrative Law, Health Systems Law and Policy, and Public Health Law. His research interests span law and medicare, professional self-regulation, administrative law, legal history, and regulatory governance in a range of sectors, including health and the environment. He is a member of the Nova Scotia Barristers' Society and a former Assistant Deputy Minister of Health and Deputy Minister of Environment and Labour for the Province of Nova Scotia.

CONSTANCE MACINTOSH

Constance MacIntosh is an Associate Professor with the Schulich School of Law at Dalhousie University, where she is a Faculty Associate with the Health Law Institute. She is also cross-appointed with the School of Resource Management, and the Leader of the Policing, Justice and Security Domain of the Atlantic Metropolis Centre of Excellence. Her health work focuses on the intersection between Indigenous health and Canadian laws and policies, with a considerable emphasis on environmental and political factors. Several recent publications have focused on identifying and understanding the reasons why First Nations reserves do not have safe and reliable drinking water, despite the extensive efforts that have been made over the past 20 years to rectify the situation. She has also recently published work on how internationally sourced bio-contaminants affect Indigenous health and well-being, and how domestic law can be brought to bear on remedying the situation. Forthcoming publications reflect work on how relational theory can inform laws and policies intended to support Indigenous health, and improve upon the social determinants approach.

ERIN NELSON

Erin Nelson is an Associate Professor in the Faculty of Law at the University of Alberta. She holds a B.Sc.PT and an LL.B. from the University of Alberta, and LL.M. and J.S.D. degrees from Columbia University. Professor Nelson clerked at the Supreme Court of Canada and completed her articles, then spent two years as Project Manager at the Health Law Institute at the University of Alberta. She joined the Faculty of Law in 2000, and teaches Tort Law, Health Care Ethics and the Law, Law and Medicine, and Health Law and Policy. Her research interests span the health law spectrum, and include women's health, reproductive health, end-of-life decision-making, organ and tissue donation, and the interface of health care law and ethics. She has published articles and book chapters on a number of health law related topics.

PATRICIA PEPPIN

Patricia Peppin, B.A. (Hons.), M.A., LL.B. (Queen's University) is a Professor of Law at Queen's University in Kingston, Ontario. She was a researcher in political studies and a political advisor before studying law; after being called to the Bar of Ontario in 1982, she worked in the Ontario Government on guardianship reform, deinstitutionalization of persons with disabilities, and rights of vulnerable adults. Since 1987, she has taught in the fields of health law and tort law, along with her current course in public health law and occasional teaching in drug and biotechnology law, advanced constitutional law, legal ethics, and law, gender and equality in the Faculty of Law at Queen's University. Professor Peppin has also taught courses in health law and policy and the *Canadian Charter of Rights and Freedoms* in the School of Policy Studies, has been Director of the Law program in the School of Medicine since 1991, and holds a cross-appointment to the Department of Family Medicine. She was appointed as Chair of the Developmental Consulting Program at Queen's during the 1990s, where she provided oversight to the programs of re-search, administration and consulting in the intellectual disabilities field. Professor Peppin's research has focused on drug advertising's construction of knowledge about pharmaceutical products and medical relationships; on the impact of health law on women's health; on the underlying problems of the drug regulation system; on inequities in clinical trials and health research; and on doctrinal strengths and weaknesses of products liability law. She has written recently about informed consent and substitute decision-making, vaccines, product liability from a feminist perspective, and access to drug information through the legal system. Currently, Professor Peppin is working with Australian and Canadian researchers on the regulation of the distribution of benefits and risks of clinical trials among those who will use the products, and is writing about the impact of drug imagery on women and its legal construction.

SUZANNE PHILIPS-NOOTENS

Suzanne Philips-Nootens is a physician trained in anaesthesiology and is a graduate of the Université de Louvain (Belgium). She also pursued legal studies at the Université de Sherbrooke and McGill University. Upon completing her baccalaureate and Master's degree in law, she commenced teaching at the Université de Sherbrooke, where she is presently a Professor of Health Law and holds the Chair of Health Law and Governance. Her research and publications deal with medical liability as well as various issues of modern medicine. She is co-author of three monographs, *Éléments de responsabilité civile médicale* (3rd edition) with Dr. Pauline Lesage-Jarjoura and Professor Robert Kouri, *L'intégrité de la personne et le consentement aux soins* (2nd edition) with Professor Robert Kouri and *Le mandat donné en prévision de l'inaptitude* with Professors L. Laflamme and Robert Kouri, and is co-editor of *La recherche en génétique et en génomique : droits et responsabilités* with B. Godard, B.M. Knoppers and M.-H. Régnier.

NOLA M. RIES

Nola M. Ries, B.A. (Hons.) (Alberta), LL.B. (Victoria), M.P.A. (Victoria), LL.M. (Alberta) is an Adjunct Professor at the University of Victoria, and a Research Associate at the Health Law Institute of the University of Alberta. She teaches and consults in the areas of health law, privacy law, research ethics, regulation of new health technologies, and legal aspects of health system reform. She has authored over 50 articles, book chapters and major reports, and is co-editor of *Public Health Law and Policy in Canada* (published by LexisNexis Canada). Professor Ries is a member of the Bar of British Columbia and has practised in the areas of constitutional, administrative and human rights law.

BARBARA VON TIGERSTROM

Barbara von Tigerstrom is an Associate Professor at the University of Saskatchewan College of Law. She holds an LL.B. from the University of Toronto and a Ph.D. in law from the University of Cambridge, and has worked at the Supreme Court of Canada, the University of Alberta Health Law Institute and the University of Canterbury. Professor von Tigerstrom's teaching and research are in the areas of health law, public health law and policy, administrative law, and international law. She has contributed chapters on tobacco control and (as co-author with Nola Ries) on obesity and the law in *Public Health Law and Policy in Canada*, and has recently published articles on food labelling, obesity prevention and the law, and cancer surveillance. Her current research projects focus on chronic disease prevention and the regulation of therapeutic products.

TABLE OF CONTENTS

Chapter 2: Regulation of Health Care Professionals
Tracey Epps

Chapter 3: Medical Negligence
Bernard Dickens

Chapter 13: Indigenous Peoples and Health Law and Policy: Responsibilities and Obligations
Constance MacIntosh

Chapter 14: Charter Challenges
Nola M. Ries

TABLE OF CASES

Table of Cases

INTRODUCTION:
THE BIG TENT THEORY OF HEALTH LAW

Timothy Caulfield, Colleen M. Flood and Jocelyn Downie

I.   CONTEXT: DEFINING HEALTH LAW

What is health law? When answering this question, the three of us have always taken a relatively expansive view. Our own research interests reside in very distinct areas, including health system policy, biotechnology and issues associated with the end of life. These are topics that draw on vastly different literatures, and engage separate communities of scholars, health care workers, scientists and policy-makers. Indeed, since the last edition of this book just a few years ago, the topics that we, the editors of this book, research have both enlarged in scope and moved farther apart, like galaxies in an expanding universe. But, despite the increasingly divergent nature of our own work, we still consider ourselves professors of health law. We see our work as separate but intimately related — residing in the same academic universe. Why is this so? Is health law really a distinct discipline that can be captured in a single textbook of this nature?

Even more so than when the previous editions of this book were published, the definition of "health law" remains elusive. But, this was not always the case; health law was once a small sub-topic of tort law, one that focused primarily on the issues associated with medical malpractice. Indeed, two decades ago, the entire field of study was often called "law and medicine" or "malpractice law". The field was centred on issues associated with the physician-patient relationship, the standards of care of health care professionals, and the nuts and bolts of informed consent. When the first health law courses emerged (in Canada, this was in the 1980s), these were the issues that were taught and, in general, these were the things students expected to learn.

Now, the scope of topics covered by the term "health law" is so broad that some commentators have suggested there is a coherence problem.[1] In the past few years, numerous academics, particularly in the United States, have sought to provide the field with a sharper definition or, at least, a limit to the territory of law that it can claim to cover.[2]

---

[1]   For an overview of the various perspectives associated with the coherence problem, see Theodore W. Ruger, "Health Law's Coherence Anxiety" (2008) 96 Geo. L.J. 625 at 627: "Health law flunks most of the classical attributes of field coherence. It is a mishmash of various legal forms, applied by divergent and often colliding institutions, and has developed much more often through external pressures and even historical accidents than from any determinate internal evolution or refinement."

[2]   See, for example, Mark Hall, "The History and Future of Health Care Law: An Essentialist View" (2006) 41 Wake Forest L. Rev. 347, and Paula Lobato De Faria, Wendy Mariner &

It is easy to see the problem. Health law engages almost every area of law, including contract, property, constitutional, criminal and tort law. It involves human rights, patenting and research ethics. It draws on and reacts to developments in innumerable other fields of study, such as philosophy, economics, sociology, genetics, neuroscience, cell biology and information technology, to name but a few. And, of course, it is a discipline that has relevance to a range of professionals: physicians, nurses, dentists, physical and occupational therapists, health management experts, health economists, and alternative medicine practitioners.

The growing scope — and, for that matter, popularity — is also reflected in the range of topics covered in the health law courses taught in law schools across this country. There are courses with titles like "health systems and the law", "health and bioethics", "mental disability and the law", "biotechnology law" and "reproductive and sexual health law". All of these classes are, rightly or not, considered to be part of the current health law curriculum, but they are vastly different in content from the original "law and medicine" course offerings that emerged three decades ago. Indeed, in some of the newer courses, medical malpractice is not even mentioned.

There is a similar breadth to the scholarly research done by those in the Canadian legal community who self-identify as health law academics. Since the last edition of this book, there have been two national health law conferences, one in Banff, Alberta and the other in Montreal, Quebec. The talks presented at these events serve as a perfect example of both the immensity of the field of health law and the degree to which it tackles some of the most pressing and topical social dilemmas. These conferences included presentations by leading health law experts on public health issues (*e.g.*, the relevance of the law in the context of the current obesity epidemic, and the use and implementation of novel vaccines), science and research policy challenges (*e.g.*, the regulation of stem cell research and genetics), and health care reform (*e.g.*, the reaction of the judiciary in cases focusing on access and the public funding of health care services).

But does all of this really fall within the ambit of "health law"? Is there a single sub-discipline of law that can encompass the study of, for instance, both the patenting of human genetic material and the rules of informed consent? Some commentators, such as Mark Hall, have argued that the answer to this question is no. For him, this is *not* all health law. Hall advocates for a more essentialist and narrow vision of the field, one that draws on its original foundations in the field of medicine. Health law, Hall argues, is "an academic sub-discipline that inquires how law should and does take account of the special features of medicine and treatment relationships".[3] Hall views this somewhat nar-

---

George Annas, "Defining Health Law or the Edgewood Syndrome" (2009) Número Especial 25 Anos 117.

[3] Mark Hall, "The History and Future of Health Care Law: An Essentialist View" (2006) 41 Wake Forest L. Rev. 347 at 362-63. Before Hall provides this concise definition, he narrows his inquiry

row concept as building on the discipline's history and allowing a focus of "future scholarship on the issues that are the most important and challenging".[4]

Other scholars have argued for a more expansive and inclusive approach. Wendy Mariner, for instance, has dispensed with the search for a single, constraining, definition.[5] For her, there is one unifying theme — health — and the primary goal of the field is to protect and enhance it "within the constraints of justice and human rights". She uses a rough framework — an "architecture" — to organize all the relevant laws and relationships that affect health. The architecture she proposes is built around notions of respect (*e.g.*, privacy and nondiscrimination), protection (*e.g.*, safety and quality of care) and fulfilment (*e.g.*, promotion of research, access to services).[6] Rather than as a definition, Mariner sees this framework as a tool used in the identification of laws and policies that affect health in a manner that recognizes the wide range of relevant relationships and institutions, be they financial, personal or professional. This approach to health law is necessary, Mariner suggests, because there is much more to health and healing than medical care:

> The range of social and environmental factors that affect health are often as or more important than medical care. The field of health continues to expand as more is learned about what affects health, especially socioeconomic factors, such as the distribution of income and wealth, political inequality, education, employment, housing, and the environment (known as the social determinants of health), as well as individual genetics, travel and migration, and climate change. Laws governing those factors should not be ignored.[7]

How then, do we, the editors of this textbook, understand health law? To be fair, our task is much easier than it is for our colleagues in the United States, where there is a larger and more disparate group of health law academics and practitioners. In Canada, the term "health law" is as much an organizing banner for a relatively small (but growing) and cohesive community of scholars as it is a description of a field of law. Indeed, in some respects, this vibrant academic community, which includes many of the individuals who have contributed to this and previous editions of this book, has done the defining for us. When Canadian health law academics gather — as we do at our national health law conferences — there is an intuitive understanding of what this field is about, and that is law and policy as it relates to health. Yes, this is a tautologically fraught response to the plea for a definition (health law is what health law scholars do), but, as noted by Mariner, a concern for human health is the arrow that cuts through all that we

---

by noting that he is concerned with health *care* law — thus excluding other "health" issues, such as public health. Of course, this seemingly minor adjustment to the title is not minor at all. If used as a selection criteria for our two national health law conferences, for example, it would necessitate the exclusion of perhaps 50 per cent of the presentations.

[4] *Ibid.*

[5] Wendy K. Mariner, "Toward an Architecture of Health Law" (2009) 35 Am. J. Law & Med. 67-87.

[6] *Ibid.*, at 73.

[7] *Ibid.*, at 77.

do as a legal and academic community. Without any explicit debate or referendum, the Canadian community seems to have rallied behind this expansive view.

As such, we, as part of Canada's wonderful health law community, find ourselves aligned with the more inclusive and flexible framework for health law as presented by Mariner.[8] It is much more than just the study of laws relevant to areas of medicine; it is a field of law that draws together *all* the legal and policy issues that are relevant to human health.

From a pedagogical perspective, this broad and inclusive approach creates some real challenges. Can one really master all the law and policy topics relevant to human health? Can they all be captured in one text?[9] The answer to both questions is, of course, no. And as the field continues to grow, as it seems likely to do, these challenges will intensify. But what we can provide to students, and all who want to learn about health law, is a foundation that both builds on the historic fundamentals of the field (such as the law relevant to consent, medical negligence, confidentiality, health systems and the regulation of health professionals) and offers a taste of the key elements of emerging topics. This is precisely what this book hopes to do. This approach provides students with an understanding of the law most often associated with this fascinating and challenging field, and a sense of the many ways in which this field is evolving. By doing so, this book seeks to introduce its readers to the area of health law and provide the groundwork for further study.

II.   ABOUT THIS EDITION

This fourth edition of *Canadian Health Law and Policy* offers the reader updates on the current law and a fresh perspective on a variety of topical and pressing issues. There is an entirely new chapter, which covers the critically important issues associated with health law and the Indigenous peoples of Canada, and some of the existing chapters (*e.g.*, emerging technologies and public health) have been significantly revised to include new social and scientific developments. All chapters have been updated to include an analysis of the most recent court decisions, legislation, policies and practices.

The book opens with William Lahey's chapter on Canadian Medicare. In addition to the continuing focus that Lahey places on the *Canada Health Act*, the provincial laws implementing the single-payer model and the role of the courts in reviewing health system governance, he now deals at greater length with the

---

8   Hank Greely has argued for a similarly broad approach. See Hank Greely, "Some Thoughts on Academic Health Law" (2006) 41 Wake Forest L. Rev. 391 at 392: "I believe health law should be defined very loosely, as encompassing all legal and public policy issues involving the provision of health care (medical or otherwise) or health status. Importantly, this includes policy questions about what the laws or, more broadly, the non-legal rules or standards as they affect health care should be and not just what they are." He goes on to argue for the inclusion of issues associated with public health, bioethics and biomedical research under the umbrella of health law.

9   See, for example, Lawrence E. Singer & Megan Bess, "Teaching Health Law: Combining Pedagogy and Practice: Creating a 21st Century Health Law Curriculum" (2009) 37 J.L. Med. & Ethics 852-56.

evolution in design and function of the legislative and institutional framework for health system governance. At the provincial level, some of the changes discussed include the creation of quality councils; the changing location of managerial and governance responsibility between provincial governments and regional health authorities; the liberalization of the rules that govern the boundaries between publicly and privately funded medicine; and the strengthening of regulatory frameworks that apply to health care organizations. At the national level, Lahey discusses the advent of a reliance on Health Care Accords as a quasi-legislative model of governance and the emergence over the past 10 to 15 years of a range of national institutions, including the Canadian Institute for Health Information, the Canadian Patient Safety Institute, the Canadian Mental Health Commission and the Health Council of Canada. At both levels of governance, the chapter suggests that the Canadian health system is placing increasing reliance on a mode of governance that is more regulatory than managerial.

Chapter 2, by Tracey Epps, focuses on the complex and ever-evolving area of regulation of health care professionals — both directly through statute and through self-regulation. She updates her chapter to convey recent changes aimed at improving quality, safety and accountability of care delivery in a range of health care settings and on the part of a broad spectrum of health care providers. Included, for example, is a discussion of Manitoba's new *Regulated Health Professions Act*; peer assessment practices and other systems of ensuring continued competency, including Ontario's *Excellent Care for All Act, 2010*; recent accountability measures, including amendments to Alberta's *Health Profession Act* in 2007 and the Royal Assent of Ontario's Bill 179 in 2009; expansion of the scope of practice of health professionals to promote inter-professional collaboration; developments in regulation of telepharmacy, complementary and alternative medicine; regulatory changes that encourage increased flexibility around delivery of health care services; and policy and other regulatory developments designed to address labour shortages.

Bernard Dickens' contribution provides a comprehensive overview of the legal landscape of medical negligence, an area that notwithstanding the broadened scope of the health law field we described earlier remains vitally important. In this edition, the chapter has been updated to include an analysis of the most recent cases and emerging policy issues, such as the liability of government for health policy decisions and actions, for example, in relation to public health threats such as SARS.

Chapter 4, written by Patricia Peppin, explores the complex area of informed consent. The chapter sets out the rationale behind existing doctrine and provides a summary and analysis of the relevant case law and legislation. Peppin tackles all of the key legal and policy challenges associated with consent, including the difficulties associated with the establishment of causation and the nature of the duty of disclosure in the context of medical errors.

The next chapter, by Robert Kouri and Suzanne Philips-Nootens, focuses on health law in the province of Quebec. While the chapter provides a wonderful and sweeping overview of the differences between Quebec and common law

Canada, its primary focus is medical liability. The chapter also includes a consideration of the most recent cases that touch on the issue of the division of powers between the federal and provincial governments in the context of health care.

Chapter 6, by Elaine Gibson, covers the myriad of issues associated with health information. This chapter touches on everything from the common law duty of healthcare practitioners to maintain patient confidentiality to the most recent federal and provincial privacy legislation. The chapter also includes an analysis of the most recent cases that deal with the "right" to privacy and the nature of interests in our own bodily tissue.

In Chapter 7, Erin Nelson tackles the complex issues associated with reproductive technologies. She looks at a number of hot topics associated with abortion law, including the licensing status of medical abortion and whether physicians have a duty to refer for abortion. Nelson also provides a significant update on the status of emergency contraception and the long-awaited and ultimately messy Supreme Court of Canada decision on the Quebec challenge to the federal *Assisted Human Reproduction Act*.

In Chapter 8, Peter Carver succinctly contextualizes the issues of mental health law in Canada. He explores the legal frameworks currently in place and discusses the numerous policy challenges that continually emerge in this area. In particular, after explaining such recent developments as the increasing number of jurisdictions using community treatment orders, the ongoing development of community and mental health courts, the increased attention being paid to the conditions being experienced by prison inmates with severe mental illness, and the active promotion of a human rights approach by the Mental Health Commission of Canada (among others), Carver concludes with reflections on the somewhat contrary trends in Canada to increase the scope for intervention in the lives of individuals with mental illness and to appreciate the human rights dimensions of social responses to mental illness and disability.

Chapter 9, authored by Joan Gilmour, addresses the many legal and policy challenges associated with the end of life. In addition to reviewing the basic law, the chapter provides an update on the extremely vigourous "futile treatment" debates and discussion of the development of "donation after cardiac death" protocols (*e.g.*, when is it permissible to proceed by way of determination of death by cardiopulmonary criteria rather than neurological criteria?).

The next chapter covers the law and policy issues associated with research involving humans. In this chapter, Michael Hadskis describes and critically engages with the full range of legal and extra-legal instruments used for the governance of research involving humans in Canada. He discusses such procedural and substantive issues as the composition of Research Ethics Boards, delegated vs. full REB review, consent, confidentiality, minimal risk, and incidental findings. Of particular note is the fact that this chapter reflects the new edition of the *Tri-Council Policy Statement: Ethical Conduct for Research Involving Humans*, which was released late in 2010. Interestingly, Hadskis concludes that, despite the new edition of the TCPS, there is still an urgent need for reform to the system of oversight of research involving humans in Canada.

In Chapter 11, which focuses on emerging technologies, Ian Kerr, Jennifer Chandler and Timothy Caulfield include updates in several key areas, including: a new discussion on the emerging uses for RFID technology in disease diagnosis and treatment; an investigation of recent legal developments aimed at preventing genetic discrimination in the United States and the possible causes for concern in Canada; an updated description of recent scientific developments in the field of stem cell research that may allow research to be carried on without the destruction of an embryo; and a discussion of the policy issues associated with nanomedicine technologies currently in use in Canada.

In Chapter 12, Barbara von Tigerstrom tackles the broad area of public health. She explores both the laws underlying and enabling our public health system as well as the most urgent and current public health issues, including the growing obesity problem and the challenges presented by events like the 2009–2010 H1N1 influenza pandemic.

As noted above, Chapter 13 is new. In this chapter, Constance MacIntosh provides an analysis of the law as it relates to the health issues of the Indigenous peoples of Canada. We feel this is a valuable chapter that provides a unique and needed contribution to both this edition and, more generally, to the Canadian health law literature. The health inequalities experienced by Indigenous peoples in Canada are extreme and shameful, and law and policy have played and continue to play a significant role in creating and perpetuating these inequalities. In this chapter, MacIntosh situates the health of Indigenous peoples in the causal chain of colonization to law, policy and practice, to social inequalities, and to health inequalities by describing the current health status of Indigenous peoples. She then explains the constitutional and legal framework through which health services are provided (or not) to Indigenous peoples. Next, she explains the various health policies, practices and protocols that are central to understanding the ways in which law and policy can be used to create, sustain or remove barriers to health — in particular, the Non-Insured Health Benefits program and the Health Transfer Policy. Finally, she gives examples of how positions taken on various health law issues such as consent to research participation and advance directives could serve the goal of adopting an ethic of enabling decolonization which, in the end, is the best path to redressing the health inequalities that continue to plague Indigenous populations in Canada.

The final chapter, authored by Nola Ries, builds on the discussion introduced in Chapter 1 by William Lahey concerning the many ways in which the *Canadian Charter of Rights and Freedoms* may be used to challenge various aspects of health care delivery and regulation in Canada. In updating this chapter, Ries provides commentary on the aftermath of the Supreme Court of Canada's decision of *Chaoulli v. Quebec (Attorney General)*, including the response of the Quebec government and subsequent developments in the supply of private care. She also provides a summary of pending constitutional litigation in other provinces (Alberta, British Columbia and Ontario) that challenge legislative restrictions on private care, which in turn, may unduly impede access to timely treatment. In addition, she discusses new cases that interpret Charter rights in the health context and the practical impact of successful Charter challenges — even where litigants have won their case, barriers to access to health care may persist due to budgetary limitations and political unresponsiveness.

From this brief summary of the chapters included in this fourth edition, it is clear that we have brought together some of Canada's leading health law scholars. Of course, many of our nation's top academics (some of whom were authors in previous editions) have not been included; there are simply too few chapters to go around. However, we hope they will appear (or reappear) in later editions. We were also not able to cover all the topics relevant to health law. As noted earlier in this introduction, this is a vast and growing field and the range of subjects that could reasonably be considered to fall under the umbrella of "health law" could not fit in one text. However, we believe this book provides an ideal foundation for the study of this dynamic area.

It should be noted that we have not sought to standardize the contributions. The variety of topics discussed in the chapters illustrates the variety of styles and perspectives — some are more doctrinal and others more policy-oriented. Indeed, this diversity of style reflects the diversity of health law more generally. It is an exciting, challenging and ever-changing field that draws together scholars from a wide range of backgrounds and disciplines. We believe that the chapters that follow provide a wonderful taste of the variety of perspectives found in this lively area of the law.

III. CONCLUSION

It has been an enormous privilege and pleasure to work with our colleagues across the country on this and previous editions of this book. We thank them for their enthusiasm, hard work and willingness to devote so much of their valuable time to this edition of this text. We hope that this edition, with its fresh perspectives and up-to-date revisions, will not only be useful to instructors as a text for health law courses, but will also serve as a valuable guide to those interested in exploring this constantly evolving field. Finally, we also hope that this book will inspire new scholars to take up health law and policy as an area of research or practice, and that these scholars will join us to tackle, debate, theorize and advance understanding in this exciting, challenging and rewarding field.

Chapter 1

MEDICARE AND THE LAW: CONTOURS OF AN EVOLVING RELATIONSHIP[*]

William Lahey

I.   INTRODUCTION

This chapter is about the role of law in the creation and operation of the Canadian health care system and the possible role of law in the evolution of that system. It is particularly about the relationship between law and the quasi-national program of public health insurance known as Medicare. Accordingly, it is about the branches of Canadian law that answer the basic questions of how the provision of health care services is financed and how the delivery of those services is organized, managed, regulated and governed.

In Canada, these questions lead directly to a discussion of the *Canada Health Act*.[1] Along with the laws, policies and administrative systems of the provinces and territories that operationalize its general principles, this legislation is the legal foundation for the distinguishing characteristic of the Canadian health care system. This is the single-payer system through which all Canadians are promised uniform and universal access to a comprehensive range of physician and hospital services at public expense. In Canada as elsewhere, patient health increasingly depends on access to drugs, home care, long-term care and a range of therapies that are not captured by the focus of the single-payer system on hospitals and physicians. Yet, that system and its underlying values and pragmatic logic are still the institutional core of Canada's health care system.

The study of the single-payer system by legal scholars is no longer in its infancy. Yet, health system law is still a relatively new branch of academic health law, probably because it has not been extensively litigated. It has been law for politicians, bureaucrats and administrators, rather than for lawyers and judges. As a result, it was once customary for those who wrote on the system from a legal perspective to explain the relevance and importance of law and of legal

---

[*] The previous version of this chapter was a revised version of a chapter previously published as "Chapter 2: The Legal Foundations of Canada's Health Care System" in Jocelyn Downie, Karen McEwen & William MacInnis, eds., *Dental Law in Canada* (Markham, ON: LexisNexis Canada, 2004) 29-90. The research assistance of Scott Nesbitt and Mary-Elizabeth Walker on the previous version of this chapter and of Pamela Johnson on the current version of this chapter, as well as the helpful editing of Colleen Flood, are gratefully acknowledged.
[1] R.S.C. 1985, c. C-6.

analysis to the broad issues of public policy that arise when Medicare is under discussion.[2] It is no longer necessary to begin this kind of chapter with that kind of explanation. On June 9, 2005, the Supreme Court of Canada dropped a bomb-shell onto Canada's ongoing debate on the future of Medicare. In *Chaoulli v. Quebec (Attorney General)*,[3] it ruled by a 4:3 majority that a Quebec law that prohibited contracts of private insurance applying to services available through public insurance was unconstitutional. Media and others jumped to the conclusion that the court had sided with those who advocate privatization to solve Medicare's difficulties, particularly the problem of waiting times.[4] For some, it seemed that the court was not only saying that privatization was constitutionally permissible. It was saying that greater privatization was constitutionally mandatory.

The precise meaning of *Chaoulli* for Medicare's future remains to be determined. Five years after the ruling, it has yet to be used to strike down the two legislative limitations on private medicine that have always been the most important ones in those provinces, including Quebec, that have either one or both of those limitations, the prohibition on billing under Medicare for services also provided for private payment, and the prohibition against charging private patients fees that are higher than those recoverable under Medicare. It is, however, already possible to conclude that the ruling shows that law will matter, possibly a great deal, to Medicare's future. Quebec responded by enacting legislation that liberalized the rules on private insurance, instituted guarantees of service within a specified time for hip and knee replacements and for cataract removals, and gave its Minister of Health direct authority and accountability for the management of waiting times, including designating procedures whereby the public system would be allowed to purchase from privately financed and operated surgical facilities.[5] In the latter aspect, Quebec was following the lead of Alberta, which adopted a legislative framework in 2000 that authorized private surgical facilities to provide publicly insured services for payment through Medicare and enhanced its services for private payment. British Columbia now seems poised to go in the same general direction. In Nova Scotia, a government-endorsed contract between the province's largest health district and a private for-profit surgical company allows the district to manage wait times by purchasing surgical procedures for its patients from the company. Thus, *Chaoulli* has helped to legitimize and, perhaps, encourage privatization of delivery within the public system across Canada.

---

2   Canadian Bar Association Task Force on Health Care, *What's Law Got to Do With It? Health Reform in Canada* (Ottawa: Canadian Bar Association, 1994); and Colleen M. Flood, "Chapter 1: The Anatomy of Medicare" in Jocelyn Downie, Timothy Caulfield & Colleen M. Flood, eds., *Canadian Health Law and Policy*, 2d ed. (Markham, ON: LexisNexis Canada, 2002) 1 at 1-2.

3   [2005] S.C.J. No. 33, [2005] 1 S.C.R. 791 (S.C.C.).

4   See, for example, Gregory P. Marchildon, "The *Chaoulli* Case: A Two-Tier Magna Carta?" (2005) 8:4 Healthcare Quarterly 49 and Lawrie McFarlane, "Supreme Court Slaps For-Sale Sign on Medicare" (2005) 173:3 CMAJ 269.

5   *An Act to amend the Act respecting Health Services and Social Services and Other Legislative Provisions*, S.Q. 2006, c. 43.

But, the fall-out of *Chaoulli* has not entirely been a steady march towards privitization. For example, in the wake of the ruling, Ontario adopted legislation that boldly strengthened the legal impediments that doctors in that province face if they want to earn a living providing care for private payment: they are now prohibited from charging privately for services that are included in Medicare.[6] More surprisingly, Alberta, the province that has long been most aggressive in testing the boundaries of federal government and citizen tolerance for privatization in health care, has passed the *Alberta Health Act*, which seeks to strengthen the province's health care system by increasing its commitment to, and reliance on, the principles and methods of public health care.[7]

The point is that *Chaoulli* is not only significant for what it says on the constitutionality of legislative limits on privately financed care or for the encouragement it may give to privatized delivery of care that is publicly financed. It is also significant for what it says about the role that constitutional law, as interpreted by the courts, may play in the future evolution of Medicare and of Canada's health care system more broadly. Other cases carry a similar implication for the role that administrative law may play, both in the realm of judicial review and in the functioning of the administrative tribunals that exist, in some provinces, to review government decisions on requests for funding of out-of-province treatments from residents who cannot get the care they need within their province. Together, such cases suggest that the law of Medicare will no longer be left as exclusively to legislatures, cabinets and ministers of health as it has been for much of its history.

Meanwhile, the legislative framework for Medicare is itself in a period of significant flux. From roughly the inception of Medicare as a quasi-national program in the late 1960s and early 1970s to the middle of the 1990s, its basic legislative framework and the broader health care system was both relatively stable and relatively consistent across the country, especially outside of Quebec. For the most part, Medicare was a funding program superimposed on the health care system of independent and lightly regulated hospitals and sole proprietor doctor offices that pre-existed Medicare. Provinces then used legislation, mostly in the 1990s, to impose the significant restructuring, generally called "regionalization", ostensibly to delegate responsibility for the management of health care to regional bodies that would be responsive to local population needs and regionally determined priorities. Restructuring is now occurring in several provinces implies a renewed legislative confidence in more centralized administrative structures. As indicated by the above discussion, provinces are altering the legislative boundaries between the public and private sectors; sometimes to relax these boundaries, sometimes to strengthen them. In multiple ways, strengthened accountability, specifically for improved performance, is being legislated. Examples include the national health accords (a kind of *quasi*-legislation) that try to stipulate provincial accountability for setting and meeting health system performance bench-

---

[6]   *Commitment to the Future of Medicare Act, 2004*, S.O. 2004, c. 5, s. 17.
[7]   S.A. 2010, c. A-19.5. This Act awaits proclamation.

marks; legislation in multiple provinces that establishes quality councils and mandates them to monitor and report on system performance; legislation that institutes more independent patient complaint processes (such as Quebec legislation that establishes a specialized ombudsmen's office for the health sector or British Columbia legislation that establishes patient care quality review board); and legislation that brings the management of health care organizations under tighter and more specific regulation by ministries of health (such as the Ontario legislation that requires health care institutions to develop a quality improvement plan and to tie executive compensation to its effective implementation).

These examples may suggest that governance in the Canadian health system is tentatively, if unevenly, headed in the more regulatory direction that other countries have embraced with greater enthusiasm.[8] Whether or not that is true, it is now clearer than it has ever been that law and legal processes matter greatly to the function and future of both Medicare and the broader health care system. It is therefore also clear that health law scholarship must embrace health *system* law just as it embraces more traditional subjects, such as medical malpractice law or professional regulation law. Equally, it is clear that health policy scholars must increasingly incorporate the significance of law and of the courts into their analysis and prescriptions for policy-making in Canadian health care. Conversely, if courts are to become increasingly active in health system issues, it is vitally important for health system lawyers to be conversant with other disciplines, including economics, political science and health services administration.

This chapter will develop some broader themes as a means to understanding and evaluating the influence that law, particularly through adjudicative processes, is having and may come to have on Medicare's future. One of these is how the system, as legally constructed, both addresses and fails to address the central question of the access of Canadians to health care services and treatments both in and outside of the single-payer system. Another is the question of how the design and operation of the system addresses (or raises) concerns about the cost of health care, the ongoing financial viability of the system and the availability of resources for society's other priorities. A third revolves around the demand for greater transparency, procedural inclusiveness and accountability at all levels of the system, including decision-making that defines the boundaries between public and private health care. A fourth is the relationship of the single-payer system to basic Canadian values of equality and liberty, particularly in light of the growing involvement of the courts and the centrality of these values not only to Medicare but also to the rights and freedoms that are protected under the *Canadian Charter of Rights and Freedoms*.[9]

---

[8]   William Lahey, "New Governance Regulation and Managerial Accountability for Performance in Canada's Health Care Systems" in Robert P. Kouri & Catherine Régis, eds., *Grand Challenges in Health Law and Policy* (Cowansville, QC: Éditions Yvon Blais, 2010) 243-78.

[9]   Part I of the *Constitution Act, 1982*, being Schedule B to the *Canada Act 1982* (U.K.), 1982, c. 11.

The balance of this chapter is divided into four parts. Part II aims to put the single-payer system into context. It does so by providing basic information that is critical to understanding the adoption of the single-payer system and to evaluating its continuing rationale and viability. Canadian health care spending, the health status of Canadians, some key aspects of the performance of the Canadian health care system, the basic organizational features of the systems that deliver service and the basic concepts and dynamics of health care insurance are each discussed.

With this background in place, Part III turns to the main concern of the chapter, the creation, operation and enforcement of the single-payer system. It begins with discussions of the role played by Canada's federal constitution in the design of the *Canada Health Act* and of the process of historical development that culminated in the Act's adoption and that continues to evolve through the dynamics of the federal-provincial process. It then focuses on unpacking the requirements that the Act places on the provinces in exchange for their eligibility for federal health funding. Part III then considers the implementation and enforcement of the *Canada Health Act* by overviewing the provincial laws and administrative systems that deliver public health insurance to Canadians. It then contrasts the lacklustre response of the federal government to clear or arguable provincial failures to abide by the principles of the Act with the growing willingness of Canadians to use the courts to protect, to extend and to challenge the essential premises of Medicare.

This leads to a discussion in Part IV of recent developments, at the national and provincial level, in Medicare's legislative and broader governance framework. After the discussion and evaluation of federal-provincial collaboration through political health accords — especially the Health Accord of 2004 — Part IV then considers the diverse patterns of legislative and institutional elaboration that are unfolding in the provinces.

Part V then offers some brief concluding remarks.

II.   GETTING ORIENTED: BASIC FACTS AND CONCEPTS

A.   WHAT AND WHO IT COSTS — HEALTH CARE SPENDING

In 2010, the total of public and private spending on health care in Canada was projected to be more than $190 billion.[10] This equates (in Canadian dollars) to $5,614 per capita. In contrast, as of 2008, spending on health care in the United States was (in U.S. dollars) $7,538 per capita, by far the highest level of per cap-

---

[10]   Except where otherwise indicated, the information contained in this section is from Canadian Institute for Health Information, *National Health Expenditure Trends, 1975 to 2010* (Ottawa: 2010) at 2, 4, 6, 8, 13, 17, 19, 22, 23, 32-33, 41, 54, 57, 60 and 65, online at: <http://secure.cihi.ca/cihiweb/products/NHEX_Trends_Report_2010_final_ENG_web.pdf> and Organisation for Economic Co-operation and Development, "OECD Health Data 2010 – How Does Canada Compare", online at: <http://www.oecd.org/dataoecd/46/33/38979719.pdf>.

ita spending in the world. In the same year, Canadian per capita spending ($4,079) ranked fifth among countries belonging to the Organisation for Economic Cooperation and Development (OECD) behind (in addition to the United States) Norway ($5,003), Switzerland ($4,627) and Luxembourg ($4,210).[11] As a percentage of Gross Domestic Product (GDP), Canadian spending was 10.4 per cent of GDP in 2008, ranking Canada sixth in the OECD behind the United States (16 per cent), France (11.2 per cent), Switzerland (10.7 per cent), and Austria and Germany (both at 10.5 per cent). Canadian spending as a percentage of GDP was ahead of that of Belgium (10.2 per cent), the Netherlands and Portugal (both 9.9 per cent), New Zealand (9.8 per cent) and Denmark (9.7 per cent). It was more significantly above that of the United Kingdom (8.7 per cent), Australia (8.5 per cent) and Japan (8.1 per cent).

Spending on health care is not the same across the country — in fact, it varies significantly. For the provinces, it was projected for 2010 to range (at the low end) from $5,096 per person in Quebec and $5,355 per person in British Columbia to (at the high end) $6,266 per person in Alberta and $6,249 in Manitoba. In public spending, Quebec and British Columbia were projected to spend the lowest per capita ($3,341 and $3,544 respectively), while Newfoundland and Labrador and Alberta were projected to spend the most per capita, at $4,564 and $4,295 respectively. In both total and public spending, per capita spending is higher in each of the three territories due to their large geographic areas and low population densities. Health care spending as a percentage of provincial GDP was projected to range from 8.2 per cent in Alberta to 17.4 per cent in Prince Edward Island, with most provinces above 12 per cent and, therefore, a projected national level for 2010 of 11.7 per cent.

Roughly 70 per cent of all Canadian spending on health care is public spending, with the balance obviously coming from private sources.[12] All but a very small fraction of the public spending is by governments and 92.3 per cent of that spending is by provincial and territorial governments. Private spending is largely divided between private health insurance (roughly 50 per cent) and out-of-pocket spending (roughly 40 per cent), with the other 10 per cent coming from other third party sources (such as workers' compensation schemes). The extent of reliance on public spending is much higher than that which prevails in the United States (where only 46.5 per cent of spending is public, though this may change under President Obama's reforms), but it is a lower rate of reliance on public funding than that which prevails in the United Kingdom, where a parallel private market for medical services functions without government restrictions. Indeed, Canada ranks only 18 out of 26 comparator OECD countries in its level of reliance on public spending, far behind Luxembourg, Denmark, Norway, Iceland, the Czech Republic, Sweden, Japan, New Zealand, France, Austria and Germany. In all of these countries, public spending accounts for more

---

[11]   All of these figures are in U.S. dollars.
[12]   Canadian Institute for Health Information, *Exploring the 70/30 Split: How Canada's Health Care System Is Financed* (Ottawa: 2005).

than 75 per cent of total spending, and, in a number of them, it ranks above 80 per cent of total spending. Thus, while Canada's reliance on public spending is very close to the OECD average of 72.8 per cent, it relies less on public financing than many countries said to share Canada's wealth and policy commitment to public health care.

In 2008, the programs and services included in Medicare (hospital and physician services) accounted for more than 40 per cent of total health care spending, more than half of all government spending and almost 60 per cent of health care spending by provincial and territorial governments. This reflects the fact that hospitals and doctors are the first and third largest items of total health care expenditure, and the fact that government funding accounts for 90 per cent of hospital spending and for 96 per cent of spending on doctors. But, in the same year, Canadian governments also spent more than $54 billion on other health care services, a figure equating to roughly 31 per cent of total health care spending. A large proportion of this non-Medicare spending is for home care, long-term care and prescription drugs. Spending in each of these other areas (overall and by governments) has increased steeply over the past decade or more.[13] Thus, whereas spending on Medicare (doctors and hospitals) in 2008 accounted for roughly 60 per cent of provincial and territorial spending, it accounted for 77 per cent of total provincial and territorial health spending in 1975. In the case of drugs, the second largest component of health expenditure after hospitals since the late 1990s, the reliance on private spending for prescription drugs taken outside of hospital has fallen from 80 per cent in 1975 to roughly 53 per cent in 2010. This of course means that access to prescription drugs continues to depend on private means for many Canadians.

The overall rate of growth in health care spending is often described as an existing or impending crisis, particularly when the aging of the population is taken into account. In 2002, when health care spending represented 9.6 per cent of GDP, the Commission on the Future of Health Care in Canada (the Romanow Commission) found that since Medicare's national implementation in the early 1970s, health care spending in Canada had grown at an average rate that was 2.5 per cent higher than the growth rate of the Canadian economy.[14] Since 2002, growth in health care spending has continued to grow faster than the Canadian economy, with the result that it was forecasted to be 11.7 per cent of GDP in 2010. Such a rate of growth in health care spending is fairly comparable to that experienced by other health care systems in the developed world, as evidenced by the fact that Canada's relative ranking in spending as a percentage of GDP

---

[13]   In 2002, Commissioner Romanow reported prescription drug costs as rising from 6 per cent of health care spending in 1975 to 12 per cent in 2001 and noted that provincial spending on home care has gone from $26 million in 1975 to $2.7 billion in 2001, that provincial spending on nursing homes has gone from $800 million to $6.8 billion and that provincial spending on non-physician professional health care services has gone from $120 million to $800 million: Roy J. Romanow, Q.C., *Building on Values: The Future of Health Care in Canada — Final Report* (Ottawa: Commission on the Future of Health Care in Canada, 2002) at 34.

[14]   *Ibid.*, at 39.

has remained very stable. Indeed, the OECD reports that the average ratio of health spending to GDP in OECD countries rose from 7.8 per cent in 2000 to 9.0 per cent in 2008.[15] It also reports that Canada's rate of growth in per capita health spending increased in real terms by 3.4 per cent per year between 2000 and 2008, whereas the average increase for OECD countries was 4.2 per cent. The outlier again is the United States, where the rate of growth in health care spending since the 1970s has been significantly higher than it has been in Canada: whereas both countries spent roughly 7 per cent of GDP on health in 1975, the United States was spending 15.3 per cent by 2005 when Canada was spending 9.8 per cent.[16] Also important is the fact that current health care spending as a percentage of GDP is not dramatically different from where it stood in 1992, at 10.2 per cent, especially when it is considered that the current bump to 11.7 per cent reflects the negative impact of the recession on economic growth as well as the unabated growth in health care spending. Facts such as these led the Standing Senate Committee on Social Affairs, Science and Technology (the Kirby Committee) to conclude that one of the myths about the Canadian system was that growth in spending was out of control.[17]

Yet, spending growth that is consistently higher than economic growth poses a significant long-term challenge for Canadians and their governments, particularly for provincial and territorial governments. Health care spending that accounted for 28 per cent of total provincial and territorial spending (and 32.8 per cent of program spending) in 1993, accounted for 35.9 per cent of total provincial and territorial spending and 39.2 per cent of provincial and territorial program spending in 2009. These averages include spending on health as a proportion of total spending as high as 45.7 per cent in Ontario and 43.7 per cent in Manitoba. These trends have raised the concern that spending on health care threatens spending in many other important areas of social and economic policy that are within provincial responsibility, including in areas that may be as vital to health as the delivery of health care services.[18] Scepticism often greets these worries, including from critics who point out that the increase in the proportion of government spending dedicated to health reflects not only the increases annually given to health departments, but also the decision of governments not to increase or maintain spending in other areas. This criticism may hold particular

---

[15] Organisation for Economic Co-operation and Development, "Growing health spending puts pressure on government budgets, according to OECD Health Data 2010", online at: <http://www.oecd.org/document/11/0,3343,en_2649_34631_45549771_1_1_1_37407,00.html>.

[16] Canadian Institute for Health Information, *National Health Expenditure Trends, 1975 to 2006* (Ottawa: 2006), online at: <http://secure.cihi.ca/cihiweb/dispPage.jsp?cw_page=AR_31_E>.

[17] Senate Standing Committee on Social Affairs, Science and Technology, "The Health of Canadians — The Federal Role — Volume One — The Story So Far" (Ottawa: March 2001) at 94. See also Canadian Health Services Research Foundation, "Myth: Canada's System of Healthcare Financing is Unsustainable" (December 2007), online at: <http://www.chsrf.ca/Migrated/PDF/MB_SystemOfHealthcare_Dec2007_e.pdf>.

[18] TD Bank Financial Group, "Charting a Path to Sustainable Health Care in Ontario: 10 Proposals to Restrain Cost Growth without Compromising Quality of Care" (TD Economics Special Reports: May 27, 2010), online at: <http://www.td.com/economics/special/db0510_health_care.pdf>.

water against governments that are more committed to tax cuts than to program spending.[19] Yet, it may also simply shift the concern for the sustainability of spending on health care to a concern about the sustainability of public spending overall. In the absence of a significant shift in public support for higher taxes and a general increase in government spending, it is difficult to deny the significance of the risk that growing health care spending poses to the ability of provincial and territorial governments to fund other programs, including those which positively affect the social determinants of health for all Canadians, particularly low-income Canadians.

B.   WHAT IT BUYS — THE HEALTH OF CANADIANS AND OF THEIR HEALTH CARE SYSTEM

Relatively speaking, Canada is generally a country of healthy people.[20] Two standard metrics for comparing the health of populations is average life expectancy and infant mortality. In 2010, the OECD reported that the Canadian life expectancy at birth (80.7 years) was 2.5 years higher than that of the United States, 1 year higher than the OECD average and fifth among OECD countries. Moreover, it is estimated that Canadians can expect to live the equivalent of 70 of their roughly 80 years of expected life in full health. Likewise, Canada's infant mortality rate of 5 deaths per 1,000 live births is in line with the OECD average of 4.7 and it is considerably lower than the United States' rate of 6.7. Thus, while both indicators obviously point to room for improvement, they show that Canadians enjoy an enviable level of general health.

There are, however, causes for concern. For example, Canadian life expectancy is not improving at the same rate as some other highly ranked countries, such as Japan (which has the highest life expectancy in the world) and Australia. Although infant mortality has gone from 27.3 deaths per 1,000 births in 1960 to 5.1 deaths per 1,000 births in 2007 and is very comparable to infant mortality in Australia and the United Kingdom, it is as far above the rate that pertains in Norway and Japan as it is below the American rate. In addition, the general picture includes negative trends that threaten the gains made over the past four decades as well as Canada's relative standing in health comparisons. For example, roughly 25 per cent of Canadians 18 and older are considered obese and an additional 34 per cent are considered "overweight", whereas the prevalence of obesity was 14 per cent in 1978-1979. Although this level of obesity is far below

---

[19]   See, for example, Irfan Dhalla, "Canada's Health Care System and the Sustainability Paradaox" (2007) 177:1 CMAJ 51 and Steven Lewis & Colleen Maxwell, "Decoding Mazankowski: A Symphony in Three Movements" (2002) 2:4 HealthcarePapers 20.

[20]   The information in this section is drawn largely from the following publications: Dr. David Butler-Jones, *The Chief Public Health Officer's Report on the State of Public Health in Canada 2008: Addressing Health Inequalities* (2008) at 19-33 and 35-40; Organisation for Economic Co-operation and Development, "OECD Health Data 2010 – How Does Canada Compare", online at: <http://www.oecd.org/dataoecd/46/33/38979719.pdf>; and Canadian Institute for Health Information, *Health Care in Canada 2009: A Decade in Review* (Ottawa: 2009) at 34-43.

that of the United States (33.8 per cent), it is 3-4 per cent higher than the OECD average.

The general healthiness of Canadians also conceals large inequalities in health status among Canadians. For example, life expectancy is lower and infant mortality is higher for Canadians living in poorer neighbourhoods than it is for Canadians living in more affluent neighbourhoods. In the case of differences in life expectancy, the gap is equivalent to increases in life expectancy that took many countries two decades to achieve. The measure of potential years of life lost to premature death also differs between low and higher income neighbourhoods as well as between regions of the country. For example, Canadians living in the north have a higher potential years of life lost to premature death than the national average. In Nunavut, it is 2.5 times higher than the national average. A more specific example is provincial differences in rates of hospitalization for heart attacks. Whereas the national rate is 217 for every 100,000 adults, the numbers for British Columbia, Newfoundland and Labrador, and Prince Edward Island are 169, 347 and 294 respectively. These differences correlate with underlying differences in population risk factors such as hypertension, diabetes, obesity and smoking levels.[21] They are part of a more general pattern in which lower health status generally prevails among northern and Atlantic Canadian populations, as well as in rural areas across the country.[22]

The most deplorable health status disparities are those that persist between Aboriginal and non-Aboriginal Canadians. The Kirby Committee described population health among Aboriginal Canadians as a "national disgrace", while Commissioner Romanow described it as "simply unacceptable".[23] Their indictments echoed those of the earlier Royal Commission on Aboriginal peoples.[24] Infant mortality levels, the prevalence of chronic disease, the suicide rate, the death and injury rate from accidents, the rate of substance addiction, obesity levels and HIV infection levels are all much higher among First Nation communities than among Canadians generally. Accordingly, life expectancy is substantially lower for Aboriginal Canadians.

These and other health status disparities reflect deeper disparities in socioeconomic conditions. Evidence shows that Canada does well compared to the United States in reducing health status disparities that arise from differential

---

[21] Statistics Canada and Canadian Institute for Health Information, *Health Indicators 2010* (Ottawa: Canadian Institute for Health Information, 2010) at 9.

[22] Roy J. Romanow, Q.C., *Building on Values: The Future of Health Care in Canada — Final Report* (Ottawa: Commission on the Future of Health Care in Canada, 2002) at 16-20. The pattern continues since being emphasized by Commissioner Romanow in 2002.

[23] Senate Standing Committee on Social Affairs, Science and Technology, "The Health of Canadians — The Federal Role: Volume Four — Issues and Options" (Ottawa: September 2001) at 130, online at: <http://www.parl.gc.ca/37/1/parlbus/commbus/senate/com-e/soci-e/rep-e/repintsep01-e.htm>. Romanow's characterization of the situation is found at 211 of *Building on Values* and a broader discussion about Aboriginal health status commences at 220.

[24] Royal Commission on Aboriginal Peoples, *Report of the Royal Commission on Aboriginal Peoples*, vol. 3: *Gathering Strength* (Ottawa: Minister of Supply and Services Canada, 1996) at 127.

access to health care services.[25] Yet, the stronger relationship between health status and broader socio-economic conditions raises the question of whether the health of Canadians might be better served by more spending on housing, nutrition, employment, economic development and social services rather than by higher (or even maintained) spending on the delivery of health care services.[26] This "determinants of health" perspective dovetails with the scepticism of many economists as to the benefits to be obtained from spending on health care services.[27] Such scepticism rests on the unavailability of evidence for the efficacy of many treatments;[28] on the positive evidence that exists of variation in treatment without discernable clinical justification or differing outcomes;[29] and on the *prima facie* plausibility, especially with fee-for-service compensation, that provider economic self-interest influences the volume of delivered treatment.[30]

Canadians may be convinced of the need for more action on health determinants, especially after events such as the Walkerton E.coli disaster and the growing attention that is paid to obesity, especially in children.[31] But, it is questionable whether they would accept a shift of resources or of effort from the delivery of medical and hospital services to make it happen. To the contrary, both analysis and general observation suggest that the consistently high focus of Canadians on health care is largely a focus on maintaining or improving access

---

[25] David Feeney, Mark S. Kaplan, Nathalie Huguet & Bentson H. McFarland, "Comparing Population Health in the United States and Canada" (2010) 8:8 Population Health Metrics, online at: <http://www.pophealthmetrics.com/content/pdf/1478-7954-8-8.pdf>.

[26] S. Mhatre & R. Deber, "From Equal Access to Health Care to Equitable Access to Health: A Review of Canadian Provincial Health Commissions Reports" (1992) 22 International Journal of Health Services 645; M.G. Marmot & R.G. Wilkinson, eds., *Social Determinants of Health* (Oxford: Oxford University Press, 1999).

[27] R.G. Evans & G.L. Stoddard, "Producing Health, Consuming Health Care" in R.G. Evans, M.L. Barer & T.R. Marmor, eds., *Why Are Some People Healthy and Others Not? The Determinants of Health of Populations* (New York: Aldine De Gruyter, 1994). For a critique of this amazingly influential article that is sympathetic to a determinants of health model, see B. Poland *et al.*, "Wealth, Equity and Health Care: A Critique of a 'Population Health' Perspective on the Determinants of Health" (1998) 46:7 Social Science and Medicine. 785. For a still broader critique, see T.L. Guidotti, "Commentary: 'Why Are Some People Healthy and Others Not?' A Critique of the Population − Health Model" (1997) 30:4 Annals of the Royal Society of Physicians and Surgeons 203.

[28] G.L. Stoddart, M.L. Barer, R.G. Evans & V. Bhatia, *Why Not User Charges? The Real Issues — A Discussion Paper* (Vancouver: University of British Columbia, 1993) at 6, online at: <http://www.chspr.ubc.ca/files/publications/1993/hpru93-12D.pdf>.

[29] As examples, see N.P. Roos & L.L. Roos, "Small Area Variations, Practice Style, and Quality of Care" in R.G. Evans, M.L. Barer & T.R. Marmor, eds., *Why Are Some People Healthy and Others Not? The Determinants of Health of Populations* (New York: Aldine De Gruyter, 1994) at 231 and J.V. Tu, C.L. Pashos & C.D. Naylor *et al.*, "Use of Cardiac Procedures and Outcomes in Elderly Patients with Myocardial Infarction in the United States and Canada" (1997) 336 New Eng. J. Med. 1501.

[30] R.G. Evans, *Strained Mercy: The Economics of Canadian Health Care* (Toronto: Butterworths, 1984).

[31] The Honourable Dennis R. O'Connor, Commissioner, *Report of the Walkerton Inquiry, Part 1: The Events of May 2000 and Related Issues* (Toronto: Queen's Printer for Ontario, 2002) [the Walkerton Inquiry].

to medical treatment.[32] They may be supported in this by the lack of evidence for the efficacy of some preventative or promotional measures and also by the common sense observation that the paucity of evidence for the connection between the availability of health care treatment and health outcomes does not prove the non-existence of such a connection.[33] But the importance of the determinants of health (as opposed to our ability to affect them with public programs) and the scepticism of the economist cannot be ignored. At a minimum, they establish the need for better monitoring of the efficacy of health services and for more precise targeting of available resources on treatments and preventive programs that are supported by evidence of effectiveness. This is a leading theme of all of the official studies of the health care system that have been completed, including the reports of the Kirby Committee and of the Romanow Commission.

Both of these studies recommended retention and even expansion of Canada's system of publicly financed health care. But they also recommended many changes and improvements. This is understandable, given that the system is alleged to be not as healthy as the Canadians it serves. For example, in 2000 the World Health Organization ranked Canada 30th among all nations in health system performance.[34] This put Canada behind many countries that spend less on health and that allow a greater range of hospital and physician services to be privately purchased. But, like Canada, these countries generally have a public policy commitment to ensuring all citizens have at least basic health insurance coverage. This has distinguished them (and Canada) from the system in the

---

[32] Roy J. Romanow, Q.C., *Building on Values: The Future of Health Care in Canada — Final Report* (Ottawa: Commission on the Future of Health Care in Canada, 2002) at 4, 31. The Kirby Committee reviewed a number of national polls on the attitudes of Canadians to health care and concluded: "When asked about spending priorities in health care, Canadians show a strong preference for 'bricks and mortar' infrastructure and research activities. Community-based activities are considered secondary, and activities that are seen as remote from front-line care are assigned the lowest priority for new health care funding"; Senate Standing Committee on Social Affairs, Science and Technology, "The Health of Canadians — The Federal Role — Interim Report: Volume One — The Story So Far" (Ottawa: March 2001) at 50.

[33] On the first point especially (that the evidence for the effectiveness of action on the broader determinants is also not good), see C.M. Flood, "Moving Medicare Home: The Forces Shifting Care Out of Hospitals and Into Homes" in T.A. Caulfield & B. von Tigerstrom, eds., *Health Care Reform and the Law in Canada: Meeting the Challenge* (Edmonton: University of Alberta Press, 2002) 131 at 139. On the second point (that spending on the delivery of health care services has a positive impact on general population health), see P.-Y. Cremieux, P. Ouellette & C. Pilon, "Health Care Spending as Determinants of Health Outcomes" (1999) 8 Health Economics 627.

[34] World Health Organization, *The World Health Report 2000: Health Systems — Improving Performance* (Geneva: World Health Organization, 2000), particularly at 200. The implications of this ranking for Canadian health care system reform, particularly relative to the first-place ranking of France, is drawn out in Sholom Glouberman & Brenda Zimmerman, "Discussion Paper No. 8: Complicated and Complex Systems: What Would Successful Reform of Medicare Look Like?" (July 2002).

United States (which ranked 37), where between 14 and 16 per cent of the population has had no health insurance.

The World Health Organization's ranking of Canada's system has been convincingly questioned.[35] Yet, the Canadian system has also not fared well in the annual survey-based comparisons that the Commonwealth Fund undertakes between the performance of the U.S. health care system and that of New Zealand, Australia, Germany, the Netherlands, the United Kingdom and Canada. In 2007, Canada's ranking in overall health system performance was fifth, ahead of the United States but behind (in this order) the United Kingdom, Germany, Australia and New Zealand.[36] Canada (along with the United Kingdom) had the highest number of patients experiencing long waits (a year or more) for elective surgery. Along with the United States and the United Kingdom, it stood out from other countries "with more than one in three saying that their doctor is not available outside of the nine-to-five workday". Canadians and Americans were found to be least likely to have same-day access to a doctor and most likely to have gone to an ER to receive care that they could have received from their doctor if their doctor had been available. Patients in Canada, the United States and the United Kingdom were least likely to report that they had enough time with their doctors. Finally, while the number of Canadians having access to primary care that had the attributes of a "medical home" was in the range for all countries (50-60 per cent), Canada was (at 48 per cent) at the very low end of this range. Moreover, Canada was the country after the United States where access to a medical home was most likely to depend on income levels. In 2009, the Netherlands had displaced the United Kingdom in the top spot and Canada's ranking was sixth, ahead of the United States in last spot.[37] It ranked seventh in "effective care measures" (encompassing effectiveness in prevention and treatment and management of chronic care); fifth in "safe care" and in "coordinated care measures"; fifth in "access measures" (including a last place showing on timeliness of care); and sixth in "efficiency measures". As with previous surveys, Canada did not even perform strongly in "equity", where it ranked fifth, partly because (despite Medicare) access to timely medical care depended more on income level in Canada than in all other countries except the United States, and partly because income-based differences in access to prescription drugs and dental care were high in Canada (and in Germany and New Zealand).

---

[35] Raisa Deber, "Why Did the World Health Organization Rate Canada's Health System as 30th? Some Thoughts on League Tables" (2004) 2:1 Longwoods Review 2-7.

[36] Cathy Schoen *et al.*, "Towards Higher-Performance Health Systems: Adults' Health Care Experiences in Seven Countries, 2007" (October 31, 2007) 26:6 Health Affairs w717.

[37] Karen Davis, Cathy Schoen & Kristoff Stremikis, "Mirror, Mirror on the Wall: How the Performance of the U.S. Health Care System Compares Internationally – 2010 Update" (Report of the Commonwealth Fund, June 2010), online at: <http://www.commonwealthfund.org/~/media/Files/Publications/Fund%20Report/2010/Jun/1400_Davis_Mirror_Mirror_on_the_wall_2010.pdf>.

Canadian public opinion runs strongly toward the view that the system has deteriorated significantly and is in perpetual crisis.[38] For roughly 15 years, the issues of waiting lists and waiting times and access to primary care (especially to family doctors) have been the dominate concerns.[39] In 2003 and again in 2004, the federal government entered into health accords with the provinces and territories, under which significant increases in federal health care funding were tied to wait time reductions and expanded access to primary care from interprofessional teams.[40] The 2004 Accord, which remains in effect until 2014, was more ambitious and specific on both objectives. For example, it committed provincial governments to developing benchmarks for acceptable days (or hours) of waiting for joint replacements, sight restoration (cataracts removal), cancer care oncology, bypass surgery and diagnostic imaging, and to the achievement of those benchmarks by ensuring 75 per cent compliance with them by December 31, 2007. Continued monitoring by the Canadian Institute for Health Information shows that some benchmarks (such as those requiring radiation therapy within 28 days, bypass surgery within 14, 42 or 182 days depending on acuity, or hip fracture repair within 48 hours) are being met or exceeded in most provinces.[41] But, it also shows that benchmarks for hip and knee replacements (within 182 days) are not being met in multiple provinces, and that data on waiting times for CT and MRI scans is simply unavailable from numerous provinces. Further, it shows that certain provinces are either behind or unable to report on multiple benchmarks. Meanwhile, concerns about waiting times for other services, many of which are still not rigorously or consistently tracked, remain unaddressed.[42] Indeed, there is a concern that undue focus on certain wait times can exacerbate problematic waiting in other areas.[43]

---

[38] See C.H. Tuohy, "The Costs of Constraint and Prospects for Health Care Reform in Canada" (2002) 21:3 Health Affairs 32, where Tuohy points out that in the late 1990s, Canadians went from being generally more satisfied with their health care system than the citizens of other countries were with their systems to being as displeased with their system as people in other countries were with theirs.

[39] In response, better information is finally being gathered as to the true nature and extent of the issue: see Canadian Institute for Health Information, *Waiting for Health Care in Canada: What We Know and What We Don't Know* (Ottawa: 2006).

[40] For the 2003 Accord, see First Minister's Meeting, "2003 First Ministers' Accord on Health Care Renewal", Doc. 800-039 (Ottawa: February 4-5, 2003), online at: <http://www.scics.gc.ca/pdf/800039004_e.pdf>. For the 2004 Accord, see First Ministers' Meeting, "A 10-Year Plan to Strengthen Health Care", Doc. 800-042 (Ottawa: September 13-16, 2004), online at: <http://www.scics.gc.ca/cinfo04/800042005_e.pdf>.

[41] Canadian Institute for Health Information, *Analysis in Brief: Wait Times Tables – A Comparison by Province*, 2010" (March 24, 2010), online at: <http://secure.cihi.ca/cihiweb/products/wait_times_tables_2010_e.pdf>.

[42] Canadian Wait Time Alliance, *Wait Time Alliance Report Card: No Time for Complacency – Report Card on Wait Times in Canada* (June 2010), online at: <http://www.waittimealliance.ca/media/2010reportcard/WTA2010-reportcard_e.pdf>.

[43] Pat Armstrong & Hugh Armstrong, *About Canada: Health Care* (Halifax & Winnipeg: Fernwood Publishing, 2008) at 97-101.

Another area of system performance that is receiving growing attention is patient safety. Estimates are that as many as 7.5 per cent of those who are treated in Canadian hospitals experience an "adverse result" — an unintended injury or complication that is caused by health care management rather than by the underlying disease and that leads to death, disability or prolonged hospital stays.[44] Almost 40 per cent of these events were judged to have been highly preventable, suggesting that between 9,250 and 23,750 deaths could have been prevented in the year 2000. These numbers are lower than, but comparable to, the alarming rates of adverse events reported for other countries.[45] They tell a story that is vividly reinforced by tragic events such as the misinterpretation of pathology tests for hundreds of women fighting cancer in Newfoundland; for hundreds of patients at the Miramichi Hospital in New Brunswick; and for women treated at the Hôtel-Dieu Grace Hospital in Windsor, Ontario, where erroneous pathology work is blamed for the performance of unnecessary mastectomies.[46]

It is therefore disconcerting that tackling the problem has, at least until recently, been less of a policy priority in Canada than in other countries, despite the occurrence in Canada of the sort of major events that have triggered wide-ranging reforms elsewhere.[47] For example, other countries have been more aggressive than Canada in establishing systems for mandatory reporting and centralized tracking and analysis of unsafe incidents by individual hospitals and/or

---

[44]   G. Ross Baker *et al.*, "The Canadian Adverse Events Study: The Incidence of Adverse Events Among Hospital Patients in Canada" (2004) 170 CMAJ 1678, online at: <http://www.cmaj.ca/cgi/reprint/170/11/1678>.

[45]   See G. Ross Baker & Peter G. Norton, "Adverse Events and Patient Safety in Canadian Health Care" (2006) 48:7 B.C. Medical Journal 326-328, which compares the Canadian numbers to those of other countries, online at: <http://www.bcmj.org/article/adverse-events-and-patient-safety-canadian-health-care>.

[46]   On the events in New Brunswick, see the Honourable Justice Paul S. Creaghan, "Commissioner's Report, vol. 1: Commission of Inquiry into Pathology Services at the Miramichi Regional Health Authority" (Fredericton, NB: 2008), online at: <http://leg-horizon.gnb.ca/e-repository/monographs/30000000048259/30000000048259.pdf>. For the events in Newfoundland, see the Honourable Margaret A. Cameron, "Commission of Inquiry on Hormone Receptor Testing" (St. John's, NL: 2009), online at: <http://www.cihrt.nl.ca>. For the events in Windsor, Ontario, see Sonja Puznic & Laura Stone, "Ontario woman to sue over having breast mistakenly removed" *National Post* (March 3, 2010).

[47]   U.K., The Bristol Royal Infirmary Inquiry, *Learning from Bristol: The Report of the Public Inquiry into Children's Heart Surgery at the Bristol Infirmary 1984-1995* (Norwich: The Stationary Office, 2001), online at: <http://www.bristol-inquiry.org.uk/>; Associate Chief Judge Murray Sinclair, "The Report of the Manitoba Pediatric Surgery Inquest: An Inquiry into Twelve Deaths at the Winnipeg Health Sciences Centre in 1994" (Winnipeg: Provinical Court of Manitoba, 2000), online at: <http://www.pediatriccardiacinquest.mb.ca/pdf/pcir_intro.pdf>. For overviews of what the Bristol Inquiry led to in the U.K., see A.C.L. Davies, "Don't Trust Me, I'm a Doctor — Medical Regulation and the 1999 NHS Reforms" (2000) 20:3 Oxford J. Legal Stud. 437 and C. Newdick, "NHS Governance After *Bristol*: Holding On, or Letting Go" (2002) 10 Med. L. Rev. 111.

physicians.[48] They have been ahead of Canada in the creation of independent complaints processes that ensure injured patients have an avenue of address other than the relatively inaccessible courts. In some cases, these processes supplement the investigation or adjudication of complaints by the self-regulating professions and the self-governing institutions against which the complaints are likely to be made.[49] In other cases, they displace these traditional and potentially self-serving processes or subject them to new levels of oversight and accountability. More broadly, other countries have done more than Canada has to frame the problem of patient safety as not only an issue of clinical practice and of individual or institutional responsibility, but also of system governance.[50]

As these examples show, law can be one of the instruments that governments can use to address concerns about patient safety.[51] It must, however, be used with prudence. Much of the work on medical error emphasizes the need for a shift from the culture of naming and blaming to one that emphasizes prevention and correction through the proactive identification, acknowledgement and discussion of error and its systemic roots.[52] Existing malpractice law and professional regulation law, with their heavy emphasis on individual responsibility and proximate causes, can be barriers to this shift. Additional law that simply accentuated these influences would be unhelpful. But, it is certain that improvements in patient safety will involve changes in law and legal processes, as demonstrated by Ontario's quick legislative response to the revelations of pathology errors and unnecessary surgery in Windsor, and by the recommendations of the Cameron Commission in Newfoundland and the Creaghan Inquiry in New Brunswick.[53]

---

[48]   See Jocelyn Downie *et al.*, "Patient Safety Law: From Silos to Systems: Final Report" (Halifax: Dalhousie Health Law Institute, 2006), online at: <http://www.energyk.com/healthlaw/documents/Patient_Safety_Main_Report_final.pdf>.

[49]   E. Bonney & G. Baker, "Current Strategies to Improve Patient Safety in Canada: An Overview of Federal and Provincial Initiatives" (2004) 7:2 Healthcare Quarterly 36; T.A. Briscoe, "New Zealand's Health Practitioner's Competence Assurance Act" (2004) 180:1 Med. J. Aust. 4; A.C.L. Davies, "Don't Trust Me I'm a Doctor: Medical Regulation and the 1999 N.H.S. Reforms" (2000) 20:3 Oxford J. Legal Stud. 437; B. Keogh *et al.*, "The Legacy of Bristol: Public Disclosure of Individual Surgeons' Results" (2004) 329:7463 BMJ 450; and C. Zhan *et al.*, "Assessing Patient Safety in the United States: Challenges and Opportunities" (2005) 43:3 Suppl. Med. Care I 42-I 47.

[50]   J. Braithwaite, J. Healy & K. Dwan, *The Governance of Health Safety and Quality: A Discussion Paper* (Canberra: Commonwealth of Australia, 2005); Michelle M. Mello, Carly N. Kelly & Troyen A. Brennan, "Fostering Rational Regulation of Patient Safety" (2005) 30 J. Health Pol. 375.

[51]   Tracey M. Bailey & Nola M. Ries, "Legal Issues in Patient Safety: The Example of Nosocomial Infection" (2005) 8 Healthcare Quarterly (Special Issue) 140.

[52]   G.P. Baker & P. Norton, "Making Patients Safer! Reducing Error in Canadian Healthcare" (2001) 2:1 HealthcarePapers 10.

[53]   Ontario enacted the *Excellent Care for All Act, 2010*, S.O. 2010, c. 14, which requires all errors to be reported directly to hospital administrators and the development and implementation of annual quality improvement plans in all health care organizations.

C.   HOW IT IS DELIVERED — BASIC ORGANIZATIONAL FEATURES OF THE CANADIAN SYSTEM

Canadian Medicare is not socialized medicine.[54] The vast majority of health care services in Canada are received from care providers who work either as independent professionals in private practice or as the employees of health care institutions or firms that are controlled and operated by independent corporate bodies, by partnerships or by sole proprietors. Doctors are obviously the leading examples of the former, while hospitals that are public but not government institutions are leading examples of the latter. Other examples of privately owned institutions or firms that employ care providers are nursing homes, various other kinds of continuing care organizations and private clinics.

The independence of doctors needs to be stressed. Not only are they not government employees, they are usually not the employees of hospitals or of other clinical institutions. Instead, the doctor relationship with hospitals is based on admitting privileges (held in accordance with hospital bylaws) and with the related membership in a medical staff that is essentially a distinct self-governing entity within the hospital.[55] In consequence, Canadians can be sure that they are treated according to the skill and judgment of their physician, not managerial direction.[56] On the other hand, this independence complicates management of the system in multiple ways. It may, for example, make a systemic approach to systemic challenges, such as unjustified variation in clinical practice or patient safety, more illusive than it might otherwise be.

The separateness of the delivery system from government is illustrated in *Stoffman v. Vancouver General Hospital*,[57] where doctors challenged a mandatory retirement policy under section 15 of the Charter, which prohibits age discrimination.[58] Having first ruled in another case[59] that the Charter only applied

---

[54]   See C.H. Tuohy, *Accidental Logics: The Dynamics of Change in the Health Care Arena in the United States, Britain and Canada* (New York: Oxford University Press, 1999) at 27-34 (where the Canadian collegial or accommodation model is distinguished from the American free market model and the British statist or hierarchical model) and 203-37 (where the essential accommodation between the Canadian state and the medical profession that shaped Medicare is described as one of exclusive state responsibility for financing in exchange for physician retention of clinical and entrepreneurial independence via the fee-for-service compensation system). See also R.B. Deber, "Getting What We Pay For: Myths and Realities About Financing Canada's Health Care System" (2000) 21:2 Health L. Can. 9 at 12-13 and Colleen M. Flood, "Chapter 1: The Anatomy of Medicare" in Jocelyn Downie, Timothy Caulfield & Colleen M. Flood, eds., *Canadian Health Law and Policy*, 2d ed. (Markham, ON: LexisNexis Canada, 2002) 1 at 3, 35-38 (with regard to physicians) and 40-42 (with regard to hospitals).

[55]   J.J. Morris, *Law for Canadian Health Care Administrators* (Toronto & Vancouver: Butterworths, 1996) and Lorne Rozovsky & Fay Rozovsky, *Canadian Health Facilities Law Guide* (Don Mills, ON: CCH Canadian, 1998), including 2010 updates.

[56]   The contrasting situation under managed care in the United States is illustrated dramatically by *Pegram v. Herdrich*, 530 U.S. 211, 120 S. Ct. 2143 (2000).

[57]   [1990] S.C.J. No. 125, [1990] 3 S.C.R. 483 (S.C.C.).

[58]   Section 15 of the Charter reads: "Every individual is equal before and under the law and has the right to the equal protection and equal benefit of the law without discrimination and, in particu-

to government or institutions controlled by government, the Supreme Court of Canada ruled that the Charter was not applicable in this case because the government of British Columbia could not be said to control the Vancouver General Hospital.

The functions that government does perform, in Canada and in other countries, can be divided into three categories. First, provincial governments are responsible for regulating the quality of health care services, whether or not it funds them.[60] For many health care professions, they do this through delegation of that responsibility to the profession itself. For institutional providers, provincial governments do the regulating directly.[61] For example, all provinces have legislation on hospitals that regulates public not-for-profit hospitals and one or more pieces of legislation that regulate nursing homes and other kinds of long-term care facilities. Some provinces also have legislation that regulates the licensing and operation of private clinics that are publicly financed.[62] Such clinics are also regulated through the contracts that they sign with hospitals, or regional or district health authorities. Of concern is the fact that private clinics that operate outside of the public system are generally not subject to institutional regulation, though the doctors and other regulated providers who work in them do so under the regulatory oversight of the regulators of their professions.[63]

Second, governments fund the delivery of health care services. As discussed in more detail below, this is a function that in Canada is shared by the federal and provincial governments. For "medically necessary" hospital and physician services, government funding is largely exclusive. For other services, including dental care, home care, long-term care and prescription drugs, the extent of government funding varies from province to province. Government funding for these non-medicare services can be subject to means testing, to co-payment and to deductibles that are not applied in any province to Medicare services. Across the country, private insurance starts, for those who can afford it and who are not otherwise excluded, where government funding ends.

The third function that government performs is more difficult to precisely label. It could broadly be characterized as system governance or stewardship. Whatever it is called, it includes responsibility for establishing the general objectives of the system, for monitoring and evaluating the system's success

---

lar, without discrimination based on race, national or ethnic origin, colour, religion, sex, age or mental or physical disability."

[59]   *McKinney v. University of Guelph*, [1990] S.C.J. No. 122, [1990] 3 S.C.R. 229 (S.C.C.).

[60]   See, for example, Marjorie A. Hickey & M. Michelle Higgins, "Chapter 6: Regulation of Dental Professionals" in Jocelyn Downie, Karen McEwen & William MacInnis, eds., *Dental Law in Canada* (Markham, ON: LexisNexis Canada, 2004) 161.

[61]   J.J. Morris, *Law for Canadian Health Care Administrators* (Toronto & Vancouver: Butterworths, 1996) and Lorne Rozovsky & Fay Rozovsky, *Canadian Health Facilities Law Guide* (Don Mills, ON: CCH Canadian, 1998).

[62]   See, for example, Ontario's *Independent Health Facilities Act*, R.S.O. 1990, c. I.3 and Saskatchewan's *Health Facilities Licensing Act*, S.S. 1996, c. H-0.02, as amended.

[63]   Dan Lett, "Private Health Clinics Remain Unregulated in Most of Canada" (2008) 178:8 CMAJ 986.

against those objectives, for ensuring coordination and continuity between the different parts of the system and for ensuring reasonable access to health care services either through public funding or other means.[64] In short, it is the general state responsibility of ensuring that there is a functioning health care system in place, capable of delivering to citizens the level of health care that most would agree should be, and that international law says must be, available to all people.[65] In Canada, Medicare is the core of the state's response to these obligations but it does not exhaust them, since the obligations extend to the services beyond Medicare, as well as to the relationship between the two.

The decision of the Supreme Court of Canada in *Eldridge v. British Columbia (Attorney General)*[66] aligns with this wider view of government's accountability for health care. The court applied section 15 of the Charter to a decision of British Columbia hospitals not to fund interpreter services for hearing impaired patients, despite the earlier finding in *Stoffman*[67] that the Charter did not apply to British Columbia's hospitals because they were not controlled by its government. The reason was that the decision on interpreter services (unlike the mandatory retirement policy) was a decision about access to services within Medicare, a government program that the hospitals provided on behalf of the British Columbia government.

An example of the ultimate responsibility of government for the design and functioning of the system as a whole is the process of regionalization that has been implemented in every province and territory, first in Quebec in the 1970s and then in most other provinces in the 1990s.[68] Through this legislatively defined process, governance and management responsibility was transferred from individual hospitals to regional boards of governance having responsibility for all (or most) of the hospitals in their legislatively defined regions.[69] Responsibil-

---

[64] See D. Longley, *Health Care Constitutions* (London: Cavendish Publishing, 1996), especially Chapter 1, "Core Principles", where the health care system is spoken of as a "social enterprise" that is legally constructed in ways that define the "immutable core principles" around which decisions about law, policies and structures get made.

[65] The reference to international law is to art. 12 of the *International Covenant on Economic, Social and Cultural Rights* (December 16, 1966), 933 U.N.T.S. 3, Can. T.S. 1976 No. 46. It provides that State parties "recognize the right of everyone to the enjoyment of the highest attainable standard of physical and mental health", and commit themselves to "[t]he creation of conditions which would assure to all medical service and medical attention in the event of sickness". See Barbara von Tigerstrom, "Human Rights and Health Care Reform" in T.A. Caulfield & B. von Tigerstrom, eds., *Health Care Reform and the Law in Canada: Meeting the Challenge* (Edmonton: University of Alberta Press, 2002) 157.

[66] [1997] S.C.J. No. 86, [1997] 3 S.C.R. 624 (S.C.C.).

[67] *Stoffman v. Vancouver General Hospital*, [1990] S.C.J. No. 125, [1990] 3 S.C.R. 483 (S.C.C.).

[68] Ontario established "Local Health Integration Networks" that will be structured and have comparable responsibilities to what other provinces (outside Quebec) call regional or district health boards. These are being established under the *Local Health System Integration Act, 2006*, S.O. 2006, c. 4.

[69] Prior to the current move to Local Health Integration Networks, Ontario pursued some of the rationalization objections of regionalization through a significant hospital consolidation process that saw many hospitals closed or merged into larger entities: see Health Services Restructuring

ity for the creation, governance and oversight of the broader continuum of care that encompassed non-hospital services, such as public health, long-term care and home care, was also devolved in varying degrees and configurations to these regional boards.[70] Finally, to varying degrees, the provinces devolved some health care planning and policy functions that the provinces had come to own primarily as an adjunct to the control that Medicare gave them over hospital operating and capital budgets.

The objectives of regionalization were to depoliticize governance by getting it out of the hands of politicians and bureaucrats; to democratize and improve decision-making by bringing it closer to affected communities; to reduce duplication and competition between communities; to improve coordination and integration of health care services across the full spectrum of the continuum of care; and to increase the focus on population health relative to the focus on acute care services.

The means chosen — imposed restructuring that coincided with significant spending reductions — caused great turmoil in the system. There is debate and uncertainty as to whether corresponding benefits have been achieved.[71] The policy pendulum has now started to swing in the opposite direction. Prince Edward Island has abandoned regionalization.[72] Alberta has replaced eight regional health boards with one province-wide entity (Alberta Health Services), while

---

Commission, *Looking Back, Looking Forward: The Ontario Health Services Restructuring Commission (1996-2000): A Legacy Report* (March 2000), online: <http://www.health.gov.on. ca/hsrc/HSRC.pdf>. See also Colleen M. Flood, Duncan Sinclair & Joanna Erdman, "Steering and Rowing in Health Care: The Devolution Option?" (2004) 30:1 Queen's L.J. 156-204.

[70] Regional health boards exercise this authority either through contractual relations with the public and private providers of these other services or by assuming direct responsibility for the delivery of these services, or through some combination of the two approaches; see, for example, *Regional Health Authorities Act*, C.C.S.M. c. R34, ss. 28, 29, 34, 36 and 44.1-44.6; *Nursing Home Act*, R.S.A. 2000, c. N-7, s. 2; *Health and Community Services Act*, S.N.L. 1995, c. P-37.1, s. 4.

[71] Government commissioned reviews of the system universally favour at least the retention of regionalization, and most have favoured a strengthening of it: see, for example, Commissioner Kenneth J. Fyke, *Caring for Medicare: Sustaining a Quality System* (Regina: 2001) at 55-60, online at: <http://www.health.gov.sk.ca/medicare-commission-final-report>; Commission d'étude sur les services de santé et les services sociaux, *Emerging Solutions: Report and Recommendations* (Quebec City: 2001) at 21-103; and Senate Standing Committee on Social Affairs, Science and Technology, "The Health of Canadians — The Federal Role — Volume Six: Recommendations for Reform — Highlights" (Ottawa: October 2002) at 8. In contrast, academic commentators are divided: compare Colleen Flood, Duncan Sinclair & Joanna Erdman, "Steering and Rowing in Health Care: The Devolution Option?" (2004) 30 Queen's L.J. 156 (both favourable) to Lawrie McFarlane & Carlos Prado, *The Best Laid Plans: Health Care's Problems and Prospects* (Montreal & Kingston: McGill-Queen's University Press, 2002) at 107; J. Church & P. Barker, "Regionalization of Health Services in Canada: A Critical Perspective" (1998) 28 Int'l J. of Health Services 467; and S. Glouberman & H. Mintzberg, "Managing the Care of Health and the Cure of Disease — Part I: Differentiation" (2001) 26 Health Care Management Review 56, all of whom are more sceptical.

[72] Donald J. Philippon & Jeffrey Braithwaite, "Health System Organization and Governance in Canada and Australia: A Comparison of Historical Developments, Recent Policy Changes and Future Implications" (2008) 4:1 Healthcare Policy, e168-e185, e178.

New Brunswick has replaced eight regions with two and otherwise opted for a managerial structure that is probably more centralized than the one that existed before regionalization. Even where regionalized governance remains in place, expectations seem greatly reduced as to what it will accomplish.[73] The point here, however, is not the value of regionalization but the fact that it occurred at all, since it dramatically demonstrated the extent to which governments have come to regard the health care system as theirs to organize and structure. In this regard it is ironic, given the decentralization that was intended, that regionalization actually confirmed the loss of local autonomy, as local hospital boards and administrative structures were displaced by larger regionalized ones that owed their existence, and much of their accountability, to government. In short, regionalization meant government imposition of a comprehensive and centrally planned organizational structure on a system that previously had been more or less indigenously organized in local communities. Regionalization legislation has tended to reinforce the implication of greater government control and accountability for the system by emphasizing the regionalized system's accountability to ministers of health, and by giving those ministers very broad, highly discretionary and essentially managerial powers of oversight and direction in very explicit and expansive terms.[74]

On the other hand, it has to be stressed that regionalization has not given legal control of hospitals to government but instead given it to regional (or district) boards that are as legally distinct from government as hospital boards were previously. Further, regionalization has not affected the legal or practical independence of doctors, who continue to have essentially the same relationship with regions as they had previously with hospitals, although the substance of that relationship (as opposed to its legal form) has been altered and complicated in many ways by the transfer of authority from hospital sites to regional "headquarters".

Understanding the organization of the health care system has always been challenging and regionalization has not made it less so. The boundaries that divide government's attributed authority and accountability from those of regionalized health authorities are shaped by perception and behaviour as much as by statutory law. They are fluid and subject to constant renegotiation. This may explain why some can describe the system as a command and control monopoly that is organized, funded and evaluated by government, and others can dismiss this description as nonsense that is completely at odds with the continuing clinical independence of doctors, the autonomy of the boards and of the administra-

---

[73] Katherine Fierlbeck & Martha Black, "Whatever Happened to Regionalization? The Curious Case of Nova Scotia" (2006) 49:4 Canadian Public Administration 506-26.

[74] See, for example, Nova Scotia's *Health Authorities Act*, S.N.S. 2000, c. 6. Such accountability may have also applied to the independent hospital boards that pre-dated the regionalized structures, but it was not expressed so explicitly in legislation.

tors who run hospitals, and the freedom of choice among doctors that is enjoyed by Canadians.[75]

D.   HEALTH CARE AND INSURANCE

To understand any legal framework for health care financing, it is helpful to have an understanding of the economics that any such framework must address.[76] The starting point is to recognize that access to health care demands access to third party health care insurance. Health care is expensive and needed unpredictably, putting comprehensive self-insurance beyond the capacity of all but the very wealthy. The shifting of the immediate cost of treatment to a third party, whether a private or public insurer, introduces cost escalation concerns. In the language of economics, this is a "moral hazard", where a user of a service has become indifferent to the cost of their utilization of that service because the cost accrues to others. In health care, the moral hazard implicates the physician or other provider, as well as the patient. The information asymmetry that exists between doctors and their patients means that utilization is often a consequence of decisions made by doctors on behalf of patients. It is the indifference of doctors to the cost of services and treatments, rather than the indifference of their patients, that is the true moral hazard.

The potential for cost escalation is reinforced by fee-for-service compensation, since it creates an incentive for physicians to provide more rather than less units of their services in order to increase their incomes. Together, moral hazard, information asymmetry and fee-for-service compensation create a strong pressure for cost escalation. The consequences of these interactions extend beyond the cost of services provided directly by physicians, since the cost of other services (particularly the cost of hospital services and prescription drugs) is largely a function of physician decision-making.

Many influences discourage physician-generated demand. The moral and ethical obligations of the profession require exclusive attention to the best interest of each patient. This precludes harmful or unnecessary treatment. But these and other counteracting influences still leave physicians with wide discretion to choose between courses of treatment and to choose ones that are more income beneficial, even if only of marginal clinical value. The real or perceived fear of

---

[75]   The view that Canadian health care is a government monopoly is accepted in *A Framework for Reform: Report of the Premier's Advisory Council on Health* (December 2001) (the so-called Mazankowski Report). See also Stanley Hartt, "Arbitrariness, Randomness and the Principles of Fundamental Justice" in Colleen M. Flood, Kent Roach & Lorne Sossin, eds., *Access to Care, Access to Justice: The Legal Debate Over Private Health Insurance in Canada* (Toronto: University of Toronto Press, 2005) 505. The alternative view is stated succinctly in Stephen Lewis & Colleen Maxwell, "Decoding Mazankowski: A Symphony in Three Movements" (2002) 2:4 HealthcarePapers 20 at 25.

[76]   The discussion in this section draws throughout upon C.M. Flood, *International Health Care Reform: A Legal, Economic and Political Analysis* (London: Routledge, 2000) and especially on Chapter 2, "Arguments in Economics and Justice for Government Intervention in Health Insurance and Health Service Markets" at 15-40.

malpractice allegations and of liability can push doctors towards providing more rather than less, especially of diagnostic services and prescription drugs. One estimate that is often cited is that physician-generated demand may be as high as between 30 and 40 per cent of total utilization.[77] Even if that figure is high, there are many studies that have documented wide variations in the use of particular treatments between populations that cannot be explained by differences in population need or justified by different outcomes.

Finding ways of eliminating or at least reducing unnecessary utilization is a leading preoccupation of health care policy. In Canada, the reintroduction of user fees for medical services (or their retention for other services) is invariably mentioned, even though the evidence is that they disproportionably discourage utilization by the poor (who may need more services) and may increase spending in the long run by discouraging preventive care.[78] Quebec reignited this debate with its proposal, now withdrawn, of a $25 deductible for every medical visit that would have been collected through the income tax process.[79] The other approach that has been applied on a massive scale is to simply reduce and then limit budgets, and therefore the resources that doctors are able to utilize, thus ostensibly forcing concentration on the delivery of truly necessary services. This has contributed to the waiting list phenomenon discussed above. In the United States, managed care has been the policy instrument of choice. It either uses rules to limit the circumstances in which various treatments can be provided or financial incentives that encourage physicians to withhold rather than to provide care in particular circumstances, or some combination of the two.[80]

The combined effect of information asymmetry, moral hazard and fee-for-service payment are problems for private as well as public insurance systems. Several other considerations go more directly to the choice between public and private insurance. All flow from the fact that private insurance is profit-driven, with the profit level being a function of the difference between premiums collected and administrative costs plus claims paid. Absent state intervention, the highest risk individuals will be charged premiums that are unaffordable or af-

---

[77] G.L. Stoddart, M.L. Barer, R.G. Evans & V. Bhatia, *Why Not User Charges? The Real Issues — A Discussion Paper* (Vancouver: University of British Columbia, 1993) at 6, online at: <http://www.chspr.ubc.ca/files/publications/1993/hpru93-12D.pdf>. For a review of more recent studies that put the figure at a lower level, see Michel Grignon *et al.*, "Discussion Paper No. 35 — Influence of Physician Payment Methods on the Efficiency of the Health Care System" (Ottawa: November 2002).

[78] Mark Stabile & Sevil N-Marandi, "C.D. Howe Institute Working Paper — Social Policy: Fatal Flaws: Assessing Quebec's Failed Health Deductible Proposal" (Toronto: C.D. Howe Institute, September 2010), online at: <http://www.cdhowe.org/pdf/Working _Paper_Stabile.pdf>.

[79] "Budget Speech 2010–2011" (read by Raymond Bachand, Minister of Finance, Gouvernement du Québec, March 30, 2010), online at: <http://www.budget.finances.gouv.qc.ca/ Budget/2010-2011/en/documents/BudgetSpeech.pdf>; Rheal Séguin, "Quebec stirs health-care debate with proposed user fee" *The Globe and Mail* (March 30, 2010); Andre Picard, "Medical user fees? They're so 1980" *The Globe and Mail* (April 8, 2010).

[80] A succinct history and description of managed care can be found in R. Adams Dudley & Harold S. Luft, "Managed Care in Transition" (2001) 344 New Eng. J. Med. 1087.

fordable only at a financially debilitating cost, or that they will be more directly denied coverage through explicit exclusionary rules. If insurers do not engage in perfect risk segregation, and either deliberatively or inadvertently pool relatively lower risk individuals with higher risk individuals, then "adverse selection" may occur. This is where individuals who can afford insurance nevertheless go without due to premiums that they regard as more expensive than is warranted by the likelihood of their need for insurance. Finally, independently of exclusions that are generated by risk selecting and risk pooling by insurers, private insurance will not reach people who cannot afford to pay any insurance premium.

The final concept to be considered is that of administrative and transaction costs. Private insurance systems obviously have multiple insurance companies that compete with one another to attract subscribers by providing good coverage at reasonable rates. They do this by paying careful attention to who they insure (risk selecting), by adjusting premiums to match likely claim experience (risk rating) and by managing claims to avoid unnecessary costs. All this is labour-intensive work that adds to the administrative cost of the health care system as a whole. These costs are also driven up by the additional burden that is imposed on providers if they are required to apply the different procedures and rules of different insurers.

The Canadian single-payer system responds to these challenges by making universal insurance under non-profit public administration available on uniform terms and conditions to all residents of each province. Together, universality and the prohibition on profit-taking eliminate risk selection and risk rating, and the associated administrative overhead. In consequence, Canada does not have a population of people without any health insurance and it has administrative costs that are thought to be much lower than in the American system. In addition, to the extent that the Canadian system is funded by a generally progressive income tax system, it redistributes the financial burden of illness from the lower to the upper rungs of the socio-economic ladder and therefore, in general, from the less healthy to the more healthy. Neither happens in an efficiently operating private insurance market.

Finally, an additional rationale for the single-payer system is the purchasing power it gives to the single payer (as a monopsony) to maintain the social affordability of health care by bargaining lower remuneration for providers and lower prices from suppliers than either might be able to demand in a system with multiple buyers. A current example of the cost control leverage that is given to government as purchaser in the Canadian system is the initiative of the provinces, led by Ontario, to dramatically lower the cost of generic drugs by 50 per cent by eliminating recovery, under public drug plans, of the cost of the professional allowance fees that generic drug manufacturers pay to pharmacies that dispense their product.[81] This example shows the kind of purchasing and cost

---

[81] These fees are estimated to be worth $750 million in Ontario; see Keith Leslie, "Drug stores demand millions Ontario told it will cost at least $260M a year to stop pharmacists' protests" *Kitchener-Waterloo Record* (May 8, 2010); "A bitter pill" *The Globe and Mail* (April 17, 2010)

control leverage that governments enjoy under a public health care system, even where the control over purchasing is not as comprehensive as it is under Medicare for hospital and physician services.

Over the course of Medicare, there can be little doubt that governments have used their consolidated purchasing power in negotiations with doctors, nurses and other health care workers to constrain wage growth.[82] The resulting criticism of governments tends to overlook that limits on provider compensation is one of the rationales for choosing the single-payer system over other options as the mechanism for health services financing.

E.   Financing and Accessing Services Outside the Single-Payer System

Part of the context for the more detailed discussion of the single-payer system that follows in Part III is an understanding of how access to health care services is financed in Canada where the single-payer system is not applicable. It is not necessary to refer to the experience of the United States, where roughly 16 per cent of the population until recently has had no health insurance, to demonstrate the outcomes that are produced when reliance is placed primarily on private insurance in health care markets. The same outcomes can be demonstrated by looking at the example of non-Medicare services in Canada.

Dentistry is a good example. One of the recommendations of the famous Hall Commission, which was adopted, was that Medicare should from its inception cover dental surgical services that needed to be performed in a hospital. However, to date, no province has extended the single-payer system to the rest of dental services and they are not required to do so by the *Canada Health Act*. In fact, public health insurance programs apply to only 6 per cent of Canadians, mostly to children for a limited range or quantity of services. Private insurance (usually provided as an employment benefit) applies to 62 per cent of Canadians, leaving 32 per cent of Canadians (and 53 per cent of those between 60 and 79, and 50 per cent of low-income Canadians) with no dental insurance.[83] Thus, a recent survey showed that 17 per cent of Canadians avoided going to the dentist because of the cost and 16 per cent avoided having recommended treatment for the same reason.[84] The same survey showed that Canadians from low-income or uninsured families avoid the dentist or recommended care three times

---

B4; and Lynne Taylor, "Another Canadian province cuts generic drug prices" *Pharma Times Online* (July 12, 2010), online at: <http://www.pharmatimes.com/Article/10-07-12/Another_Canadian_province_cuts_generic_drug_prices.aspx>.

[82]   Providers have fought back by unionizing, by constraining the numbers given entry to their professions and by using their control of the allocation of work among providers in ways that have maintained incomes.

[83]   Health Canada, *Summary Report on the Findings of the Oral Health Component of the Canadian Health Measures Survey, 2007-2009* (Ottawa: Minister of Health, 2010) at 6, online at: <http://www.fptdwg.ca/assets/PDF/CHMS/CHMS-E-summ.pdf>.

[84]   *Ibid.*, at 7.

more often than Canadians from high-income or insured families. These facts have implications for the linkages between socio-economic status and poor health, given the linkages of oral health to general health.

The situation is similar when it comes to prescription drugs, one of the fastest growing costs in Canadian health care.[85] The *Canada Health Act* covers these costs only if the drugs are taken on an in-patient basis. All provinces have programs that provide substantial public funding for prescription drugs taken outside of hospitals. This provincial spending accounts for most of the 44 per cent of the spending on prescription drugs that is public. But, this spending is not based on *Canada Health Act* principles. For example, in provinces that have universal programs (Quebec, Saskatchewan, Alberta and British Columbia), coverage depends on the payment of income-adjusted deductibles or premiums. In the Atlantic provinces and Ontario, public coverage is limited to certain groups (such as seniors, social assistance recipients or people suffering from specified illnesses) and is subject to deductibles, to co-payments or to a combination of the two.

The result is a patchwork of programs within and between provinces. This patchwork leaves as many as 10 per cent of Canadians with no drug insurance coverage and many with inadequate coverage, including for the high-cost drugs that are needed to fight diseases, such as cancer, and that can easily cause personal financial ruin.[86] It also means that Canadians have significantly different levels of access to necessary drugs depending on their province of residence and their socio-economic status. Thus, it has been documented that differences in pharmacare programs across the country means that many examples can be given of Canadians with exactly the same age and income profile and exactly the same need for drugs receiving substantially different levels of benefits from public insurance based on their province of residence. More broadly, a profile of those most likley to have no or inadequate drug coverage shows they are likely to live in the Atlantic provinces, Manitoba or Saskatchewan; to live in rural communities; to be under 34; to be self-employed or employed part-time; and to belong to households with incomes between $10,000 and $30,000.[87] For all these reasons, it is not surprising that 8 per cent of Canadians report that they

---

[85] The information contained in this paragraph comes from Canadian Institute for Health Information, "Drug Expenditure in Canada: 1985-2009" (Ottawa: 2010), online at: <http://secure.cihi.ca/cihiweb/products/dex_1985_to_2009_e.pdf> and from Marc-André Gagnon, "The Economic Case for Universal Pharmacare: Costs and Benefits of Publicly Funded Drug Coverage for all Canadians" (Ottawa: Canadian Centre for Public Policy Alternatives, 2010), online at: <https://s3.amazonaws.com/policyalternatives.ca/sites/default/files/uploads/publications/National%20Office/2010/09/Universal_Pharmacare.pdf>.

[86] Canadian Cancer Society, *Cancer Drug Access for Canadians* (September 2009), online at: <http://www.colorectal-cancer.ca/IMG/pdf/cancer_drug_access_report_en.pdf>.

[87] See V. Demers *et al.*, "Comparison of Provincial Prescription Drug Plans and the Impact on Patients' Annual Drug Expenditures" (2008) 178:4 CMAJ 405 and V. Kapur, "Drug Coverage in Canada: Who is at Risk?" (2005) 71:2 Health Policy 181-193.

have not filled a prescription or have skipped taking doses of their medication because of costs.[88]

As with dentistry and prescription drugs, there is variation across provinces and territories in the level of public funding for home care (where funding tends to be capped, status based or subject to co-payments) and for continuing care services, ambulance services and aspects of mental health services.[89]

Wherever they live, all Canadians are affected by the passive privatization that is enabled by the limitation of the single-payer model to hospital and physician services. This is the process whereby changes in medical science allow more treatment to be delivered on an extramural basis beyond the confines of the hospital or the doctor's office. Passive privatization has reduced the effectiveness of Medicare in meeting some of its key objectives. It addition to reducing protection against the financial burden of illness, it has also reduced the scope of the health benefit that is delivered through Medicare. In the health care system of the 1960s, the inclusion of hospital services meant there would be reasonably comprehensive coverage not only for physician services but also for the services through which the full benefit of physician expertise was obtained. It is the latter element of the Medicare deal that is being eroded by the occupational and locational limitations of the *Canada Health Act*. There has been corresponding erosion in the commitment of Canadian health care policy to the key rationale for Medicare, namely, that access to the full benefit of modern medicine should be based only on need and not on the ability to pay.

This has happened without there being any structural change in the single-payer system and without any amendment to the *Canada Health Act* or to the provincial and territorial laws that create and govern the programs of universal and comprehensive public health insurance that the *Canada Health Act* mandates. It has taken place not as deliberated public policy, but through acceptance and encouragement of incremental changes and the operation of impersonal system dynamics. Across the country, provincial and territorial governments have responded by increasing funding and programming in a host of areas, including pharmacare, home care, respite care, adult daycare and long-term care. Nevertheless, both the Romanow Commission and the Kirby Committee (and the National Health Forum before them) advocated a uniform national response with two elements: a national program to support Canadians facing catastrophic drug

---

[88] Cathy Schoen *et al.*, "Toward Higher-Performance Health Systems: Adults' Health Care Experiences in Seven Countries, 2007" (October 31, 2007) 26:6 Health Affairs w717 (web exclusive).

[89] Colleen M. Flood, "Moving Medicare Home: The Forces Shifting Care Out of Hospitals and Into Homes" in Timothy A. Caulfield & Barbara von Tigerstrom, eds., *Health Care Reform and the Law in Canada: Meeting the Challenge* (Edmonton: University of Alberta Press, 2002) at 131. Canadian Healthcare Association, "Home Care in Canada: From the Margins to the Mainstream" (2009), online at: <http://www.cha.ca/index.php?option=com_content&view= article&id=185& Itemid=101>.

expenses and the extension of the principles of the *Canada Health Act* into the acute care portion of home care.[90]

III. THE SINGLE-PAYER SYSTEM

A. CONSTITUTIONAL FOUNDATIONS

Canadians associate Medicare with the *Canada Health Act*. This makes sense, even though this law is not legally applicable to the provinces, the level of government that actually pays the doctors and funds hospitals and hospital-based providers who provide the care. Instead, it applies only to the federal government, authorizing it (through the federal Minister of Health) to make grants to the provinces upon being satisfied that they have met the criteria of eligibility spelled out in the Act. And yet, notwithstanding the Act's limited legal effect, it is more important to the access that Canadians have to health care than any provincial statute. Moreover, Canadians identify with the Act in much the same way as they identify with the *Canadian Charter of Rights and Freedoms*, as a document that defines and protects fundamental aspects of Canadian citizenship. Like the Charter, the Act is thought of as defining what it is to be Canadian. To understand how legislation that is so limited in its legal effect has come to have such a broad and fundamental effect on Canadian policy and identity, it is necessary to understand how the Canadian Constitution divides legislative power over health between the federal and provincial governments.[91]

As explained in Part II, jurisdiction over the delivery of health care services lies primarily with the provinces. Partly this is because the *Constitution Act, 1867*[92] gives to the provinces the exclusive authority to make (and administer) laws for the "establishment, maintenance, and management of hospitals, asylums, charities and eleemosynary institutions".[93] More broadly, it is because the more general provincial power to make laws on "property and civil rights" has been interpreted broadly by the courts to encompass most professional services and indeed, the buying and selling of most kinds of goods and services.[94] Thus, the provinces have authority to regulate the professional activities of doctors,

---

[90] Commissioner Romanow described home care as "The Next Essential Service" and recommended that home care services in three "priority" areas be brought under the umbrella of the *Canada Health Act*: mental health case management and intervention services, post-acute home care and palliative care.

[91] For broader discussions, see M. Jackman, "The Constitutional Basis for Federal Regulation of Health" (1996) 5:2 Health L. Rev. 3 and, by the same author, "Constitutional Jurisdiction Over Health in Canada" (2000) 8 Health L.J. 95. Recently, the Romanow Commission commissioned a number of discussion papers on federalism and health care, including one by André Braën, "Discussion Paper No. 2: Health and the Distribution of Powers in Canada" (Commission on the Future of Health in Canada, July 2002) and one by Howard Leeson, "Discussion Paper No. 12: Constitutional Jurisdiction Over Health and Health Care Services in Canada" (Commission on the Future of Health in Canada, August 2002).

[92] (U.K.), 30 & 31 Vict., c. 3, reprinted in R.S.C. 1985, App. II, No. 5.

[93] *Ibid.*, s. 92(7).

[94] *Ibid.*, s. 92(13).

nurses, dentists and physiotherapists on the same basis that they have authority to regulate lawyers, accountants and engineers. The exclusivity of provincial jurisdiction over the delivery of health care appears to have been reinforced by the reference opinion that the Supreme Court of Canada recently issued on the constitutionality of the federal government's *Assisted Human Reproduction Act*.[95] This Act was based on Parliament's jurisdiction over criminal law, a broad head of legislative power that can generally be said to encompass legislation that seeks to prevent harms by prohibiting the conduct that gives rise to the harm. Nevertheless, while all of the judges of the Court upheld the constitutionality of provisions that prohibited certain reproductive activities and services outright, a narrow majority of the Court struck down provisions that only prohibited beneficial activities and services to the extent they were not carried out in accordance with the conditions prescribed by the Act. For at least four of the judges in the majority, the key reason for this conclusion was their concern about the implications of the Act's intrusion into the regulation of the practice of medicine for provincial jurisdiction over that practice and the broader management of hospitals.

The jurisdiction to finance the delivery of health care services is a divided one. The provinces have the direct authority to make and administer laws that deal with financing under their more general authority over all programs of public insurance against social and economic hardship. This broad authority to deal with programs of social insurance, and the understanding that it includes health insurance, dates from court rulings in the 1930s that unemployment insurance (later allocated to the federal level by constitutional amendment) was a provincial rather than a federal responsibility.[96] However, later rulings recognized what has become known as the federal government's "spending power". It allows the federal government to indirectly fund programs of social insurance by making financial grants to the provinces that the provinces can then use to pay for the programs. It also allows the federal government to attach conditions to such grants, and thereby to exert influence over the provinces in the design and administration of the programs.

The legal correctness of the spending power is sometimes questioned by provinces and by academics because it has no explicit foundation in constitutional text and no definitive validation in judicial rulings.[97] But practically, the

---

[95] *Reference re Assisted Human Reproduction Act*, [2010] S.C.J. No. 61, 2010 SCC 61 (S.C.C.).

[96] See *Canada (Attorney General) v. Ontario (Attorney General); Reference re Employment and Social Insurance Act*, [1936] S.C.J. No. 30, [1936] S.C.R. 427 (S.C.C.) and *Reference re Employment and Social Insurance Act; Canada (Attorney General) v. Ontario (Attorney General)*, [1937] J.C.J. No. 6, [1937] A.C. 355 (J.C.P.C.) (affirming the Supreme Court of Canada). The amendment of the Constitution that reversed these rulings as regards the specific issue of unemployment insurance (but not the general holding that schemes of social insurance were provincial) came in 1940, through (U.K.) 3-4 Geo. VI, c. 36, which added s. 91(2A), "Unemployment Insurance", to enumerated federal powers.

[97] For example, see A. Petter, "Federalism and the Myth of the Federal Spending Power" (1989) 68 Can. Bar Rev. 448.

federal spending power has played a vital role in the development of Canadian federalism. It has allowed the federal government to play a role in ensuring some consistency across the country in provincial social programs and therefore in how Canadian social citizenship is defined. More broadly, the spending power has counteracted the imbalance that Canada's late 19th century Constitution creates by giving many of the governance responsibilities to the provinces and control of a large proportion of the resources to the federal government. The *Canada Health Act* is the prime example of how the spending power allows the federal government to do indirectly what it cannot do directly.

Before leaving the Constitution, it is worth noting that the federal role includes several direct service delivery responsibilities of tremendous and growing significance. The first is that the federal government is directly responsible for ensuring the delivery of health care services to Canada's First Nation communities.[98] The importance of this responsibility is obvious from the deplorable health status that is prevalent among these communities.[99] The second federal responsibility worth special mention here is the responsibility that the federal government shares with the provinces for the protection and promotion of public health.[100] As demonstrated dramatically by the experience of Ontario in 2003 with SARS and the broader experience with H1N1 in 2009, public health is becoming increasingly dependent on Canada's ability to deal with and respond to threats that have no regard for international or provincial boundaries.[101] This is leading to greater reliance by all Canadians and by all Canadian gov-

---

[98] *Constitution Act, 1867,* (U.K.), 30 & 31 Vict., c. 3, s. 91(24); see Constance MacIntosh, "Jurisdictional Roulette: Constitutional and Structural Barriers to Aboriginal Access to Health" in Colleen M. Flood, ed., *Just Medicare: What's In, What's Out, How We Decide* (Toronto: University of Toronto Press, 2006) 193.

[99] Auditor General of Canada, "Status Report of the Auditor General of Canada — May 2006, Chapter 5: Management of Programs for First Nations" at 141, online at: <http://www.oag-bvg.gc.ca/internet/docs/20060505ce.pdf>.

[100] Partly under the specific federal power to legislate on "Quarantine and the Establishment and Maintenance of Marine Hospitals", found at s. 91(11), and partly and more broadly under the more general federal power over criminal law, found at s. 91(27), and the general federal power to make laws for the "peace, order and good government of Canada", found in the preamble of s. 91. The latter power allows the federal government to deal with situations of national emergency or crisis and with other matters deemed to be of national dimensions or concern.

[101] See the report of the National Advisory Committee on SARS and Public Health (the Naylor Committee), *Learning from SARS: Renewal of Public Health in Canada* (Ottawa: Health Canada, 2003), online at: <http://www.phac-aspc.gc.ca/publicat/sars-sras/naylor/index.html>. In response to this report, the federal government adopted a public health strategy with three components: (1) a new federal Public Health Agency; (2) a Chief Public Health Officer for Canada; and (3) a pan-Canadian public health network; see online: <http://www.phac-aspc.gc.ca/about_apropos/federal_strategy_e.html>. Following discussions with the provinces and territories, the Public Health Agency of Canada was created in 2004; see online: <http://www.phac-aspc.gc.ca/about_apropos/index.html>. The role of the PHAC and of governments generally in dealing with H1N1 has been widely criticized but the response at least demonstrated a capacity for intergovernmental cooperation between public health professionals that was non-existent during the SARS crisis: see André Picard, "The H1N1 post-mortem: $2 billion, 428 deaths – and they still did the right thing" *The Globe and Mail* (May 13, 2010).

ernments on a robust, expanding and direct federal engagement with the health of Canadians.

B.   HISTORICAL DEVELOPMENT

Although public health care insurance has a Canadian history dating back at least to 1919, the story of Medicare can be said to start in 1944.[102] In that year, the Commonwealth Co-operative Federation (the CCF) was elected into office in Saskatchewan under the charismatic leadership of Tommy Douglas. In 1947, it introduced universal hospital insurance. Alberta and British Columbia quickly followed and Newfoundland brought a similar program into Confederation in 1949. In 1957, the Liberal government of St. Laurent offered 50/50 federal cost-sharing to these provinces and to any other province that adopted a comparable program through the *Hospital Insurance and Diagnostic Services Act*.[103] By the end of 1961, all provinces were participating.

The question then became whether physician services should be similarly financed. Organized medicine was opposed to universal access, arguing instead for limited state intervention and for publicly funded insurance only for those who were unable to purchase it for themselves. With provincial support, "voluntariness" became organized medicine's theme, which it contrasted with "socialized medicine". In 1960, the Canadian Medical Association asked for the appointment of a Royal Commission to study health care reform, expecting it to endorse public insurance only for those with low incomes. Within weeks, Conservative Prime Minister John Diefenbaker announced the creation of such a commission, eventually appointing Emmett Hall, then Chief Justice of Saskatchewan, as Chair.

The CCF then moved again in Saskatchewan. In November 1961, it introduced legislation creating a system of universal and comprehensive public insurance for physician services. The province's doctors responded with a three-week strike in July 1962 that ended with a mediated settlement that preserved the right of physicians to charge fees to patients in addition to those to be received under the new public plan and that gave physicians the options of partial and of non-participation in that plan.

---

[102] Full accounts are available in M. Taylor, *Health Insurance and Canadian Public Policy: The Seven Decisions That Created the Canadian Health Insurance System and Their Outcomes*, 2d ed. (Montreal: McGill-Queen's University Press, 1987); M.Taylor, *Insuring National Health Care: The Canadian Experience* (Chapel Hill, NC: University of North Carolina Press, 1990); and C.D. Naylor, *Private Practice, Public Payment: Canadian Medicine and the Politics of Health Insurance, 1911-1966* (Montreal: McGill-Queen's University Press, 1986). A version that pays particular attention to the interaction of federalism and party politics is Antonia Maioni, *Parting at the Crossroads: The Emergence of Health Insurance in the United States and Canada* (Princeton: Princeton University Press, 1998). A shorter and very accessible version that pays special attention to the position taken through the process by the organized medical profession can be found in Nuala P. Kenny, *What Good is Health Care? Reflections on the Canadian Experience* (Ottawa: CHA Press, 2002) at 46-59.

[103] S.C. 1957, c. 28.

These events set the stage for Hall's report, delivered in 1964.[104] It came down squarely on the side of national adoption of the Saskatchewan model. The rationale was equal parts social justice and sound financial management. On the one hand, Hall argued that access to needed medical attention should depend solely on need and be entirely independent of ability to pay. On the other hand, he argued that public insurance that covered everyone and all medical services on uniform terms and conditions would cost less (primarily because of lower administrative costs) than a mixed system with diverse and competing private insurers. The Hall Commission also followed Saskatchewan's example in recommending that public insurance be limited for the time being to hospital and physician services, with the expectation of future expansion to cover other services, including home care, out-of-hospital drugs and dental care.

In 1966, Lester Pearson's minority Liberal government largely adopted Hall's recommendations and embodied them in the *Medical Care Act*.[105] It offered 50/50 sharing of the cost of physician services to every province that made such services accessible to all by establishing a scheme of publicly administered insurance that ensured universal, portable and comprehensive coverage. By the end of 1971, all provinces had adopted a qualifying plan, despite stiff initial resistance to the federal legislation from Ontario, Alberta and British Columbia.[106]

The optimism that inspired the creation of Medicare dissipated quickly, once the bills started rolling in under the 50/50 cost-sharing arrangement. In 1977, the federal government of Pierre Trudeau ended its open-ended exposure by abandoning 50/50 cost-sharing of actual provincial expenditures. Instead, it instituted a system of block grants (the Established Program Financing, or EPF grant system) based on a formula linked to economic growth levels rather than health care spending levels.[107] This change also gave the provinces something they wanted: elimination of the requirement that they use federal health transfers only for Medicare. The block grants put federal contributions for health and higher education together and acknowledged the right of each province to use its grant in whatever way it saw fit. They also replaced 100 per cent annual cash transfers with a system consisting partly of annual cash transfers and partly of "tax points" that the federal government permanently relinquished to the provinces. Since the value of these tax points would change with the size of each provincial economy, the cash portion of the grants became residual: in each year, the cash payment made to each province was to be determined by first establishing the size of the general grant and then deducting from it the current

---

[104] Canada, *Royal Commission on Health Services*, vols. I and II (Ottawa: Queen's Printer, 1964-1965) (the Hall Report).

[105] S.C. 1966-67, c. 64.

[106] See Greg Marchildon, "Private Insurance for Medicare: Policy History and Trajectory in the Four Western Provinces" in Colleen M. Flood, Kent Roach & Lorne Sossin, eds., *Access to Care, Access to Justice: The Legal Debate Over Private Health Insurance in Canada* (Toronto: University of Toronto Press, 2005) at 429.

[107] *Federal-Provincial Fiscal Arrangements and Established Programs Financing Act, 1977*, S.C. 1976-1977, c. 10.

value of the transferred tax points. Finally, EPF included an escalator, at first applicable only to the cash portion of provincial grants but then to the entire grant. As the national economy grew, this escalator ensured corresponding increases in the size of EPF funding. This gave provinces protection against unfunded cost escalation and an incentive to keep growth in health care spending in line with growth in the economy.

Around the same time, provincial governments began to rely increasingly on user fees as a means of protecting their own treasuries, partly to discourage what was believed to be widespread abuse of a "free" service. Meanwhile, some doctors continued to "extra bill" their patients for services covered by Medicare, in accordance with the settlement that had ended the Saskatchewan strike of 1962 and that had not been disturbed in the design of the national program. These provincial trends led to the reappointment of Hall as a one-person committee of review by the Trudeau government and to the adoption in 1984 of the *Canada Health Act*, which combined the two earlier pieces of legislation into one comprehensive statute. It responded to growing concerns with physician extra billing and hospital user fees by stipulating dollar-for-dollar reductions from the federal transfer that would otherwise be payable to any province in which extra billing or user fees were allowed. The Act also placed Medicare within the framework of the wider public policy of protecting, promoting and restoring "the physical and mental well-being of residents of Canada". Optically at least, the legislation was about ends (health) and not merely means (doctor and hospital services). The replacement of the technocratic legislative nomenclature of 1957 and of 1969 with the bold *Canada Health Act* of 1984 symbolized how universal health insurance had become, in only 15 years, a defining part of the Canadian identity that fell within the protection of the federal government. At this symbolic level, the Act aligned closely with Trudeau's earlier success in having Canada's constitution repatriated with the enshrined *Canadian Charter of Rights and Freedoms*.

The history of Medicare as a national program through the 1980s and 1990s was largely one of continuing federal fiscal retrenchment and of federal-provincial bickering over the extent of that retrenchment.[108] The EPF escalator was reduced in 1986 and then eliminated in 1990, essentially freezing federal cash transfers while provincial spending continued to grow at a rate that was higher than the general rate of inflation. In 1995, the Chrétien government replaced the EPF with the Canada Health and Social Transfer (the CHST), which combined federal funding for health and higher education (until then under EPF) with federal social assistance program funding. As Commissioner Romanow put it, this made the exact size of the federal contribution to provincial health spending "extremely obscure to even the most informed". Simultaneously, staged reductions in the cash portion of this funding were initiated. Between 1995–1996

---

[108] This account draws heavily on Roy J. Romanow, Q.C., *Building on Values: The Future of Health Care in Canada — Final Report* (Ottawa: Commission on the Future of Health Care in Canada, 2002) at 35-41 and 65-73.

and 1998–1999 it fell from $18.5 to $12.5 billion, an amount that represented only 14.6 per cent of the cost of Medicare in 1998–1999. These decreases in cash occurred as growth in the value of the tax points continued, with the result that total federal contributions could be said to still account for 41 per cent of the cost of Medicare spending at the end of the 1990s, and for 27.5 per cent of total provincial and territorial health spending in 2001–2002. But, the growth in the tax points would have happened anyway, so the cuts in the cash contributions were, therefore, real cuts in the total federal contribution. At the end of the 1970s, the total federal contribution had covered 60 per cent of the cost of Medicare and 43 per cent of total provincial and territorial spending on health. Not surprisingly, the second half of the 1990s has been the only period since the beginning of Medicare during which public spending on health care declined, as provinces cut funding more or less in tandem with federal reductions in transfers. The proportion of spending that came from private sources increased. Waiting times and other indicators of decline emerged as indicators of a health care system in crisis.

Here, it is critical to note that the federal government's enforcement leverage depends entirely on the cash portion of federal funding. The only penalty that it can impose on provinces is to withhold some or all (depending on the breach) of the cash grant that would otherwise be made. It cannot reclaim, prevent or restrict the use of the tax points. Thus, the reduction in cash transfers that took place through the 1990s raised real concern that the ability of the federal government to insist on national compliance with the *Canada Health Act* was being seriously compromised. This concern, along with provincial demands for improved funding and citizen anger over a deteriorating system, set the stage for the federal-provincial health Accords of 2000, 2003 and 2004.[109]

These Accords are discussed further in Part IV. For now, three points are pertinent. First, in the name of enhanced transparency and accountability, the 2004 Accord called for the creation of the Canada Health Transfer (restricted to federal cash transfers for health) and the Canada Social Transfer (to deal with federal transfers for education and social services). Second, by 2009 the effect of the cumulative increases in federal cash transfers called for in the three Accords brought the level of federal cash transfers up to roughly 21 per cent of total provincial and territorial spending on health and to 33 per cent of provincial and territorial spending on Medicare.[110] Meanwhile, the provinces continue to be

---

[109] For the 2003 Accord, see First Minster's Meeting, "2003 First Ministers' Accord on Health Care Renewal", Doc. 800-039 (Ottawa: February 4-5, 2003), online at: <http://www.scics.gc.ca/pdf/800039004_e.pdf>. For the 2004 Accord, see First Minister's Meeting, "A 10-Year Plan to Strengthen Health Care, September 16, 2004", Doc. 800-042 (Ottawa: September 13-16, 2004), online at: <http://www.scics.gc.ca/cinfo04/800042005_e.pdf>.

[110] For a summary of total transfers agreed to in the three accords, see Department of Finance Canada, "Federal Transfers in Support of the 2000/2003/2004 First Ministers Accords", online at: <http://www.fin.gc.ca/fedprov/fmacc-eng.asp>. The calculations of the relative contribution of the federal government as of 2008 are based on federal government data on the CHT for 2009 and CIHI information on the level of provincial and territorial spending in 2009: see Department

substantially supported by the tax credits and (for the majority that are in receipt of them) equalization transfers. Third, the 2004 accord called for the reinstitution of an escalator, set at 6 per cent per annum, which is applicable from 2006 through to the end of the Accord in 2014. This escalator ensures that the relative level of federal cash contributions to provincial costs will be more or less maintained until the expiry of the Accord in 2014, provided the federal government continues to pass budgetary legislation in compliance with the Accord, as is highly likely.

C.   THE FIVE CRITERIA OF THE CANADA HEALTH ACT

The stated objective of the *Canada Health Act* is to "establish criteria and conditions in respect of insured health services and extended health care services provided under provincial law that must be met before a full cash contribution may be made".[111] In reality, the Act has little impact on the funding or delivery of "extended health care services" and so, these will not be discussed further.[112] Instead, the focus here will be on how the Act affects the funding and delivery of "insured health services"; that is, "medically necessary" hospital services, "medically required" physician services and dental-surgical services that must be performed in a hospital.[113]

The standards that the Act imposes on the provinces in respect of these services include the five criteria of public administration, universality, portability, comprehensiveness and accessibility. I will deal with the first three of these together and then separately with each of comprehensiveness and accessibility.

In addition to the five criteria, the Act also deals specifically with extra billing and user fees, mandating deductions from the federal contribution to the extent any province allows either, or both, to occur. These specific provisions (called "conditions" rather than criteria in the Act) are essentially specifications

---

of Finance Canada, "Federal Support to Provinces and Territories", online at: <http://www.fin.gc.ca/fedprov/mtp-eng.asp> and Canadian Institute for Health Information, *National Health Expenditure Trends, 1975 to 2010* (Ottawa: Canadian Institute for Health Information, 2010), online at: <http://secure.cihi.ca/cihiweb/products/NHEX_Trends_Report_2010_final_ENG_web.pdf>.

[111] R.S.C. 1985, c. C-6, s. 4.

[112] Section 2 of the *Canada Health Act* defines "extended health care services" to mean nursing home intermediate care, adult residential care, home care and ambulatory care, subject to further definition through regulation. Section 4 speaks of the purpose of the Act as being the establishment "of criteria and conditions in respect of insured health services and extended health services provided under provincial law that must be met before a full cash contribution may be made" from the federal government to any province. The reality, however, is that the criteria and conditions that are established by the Act apply only to the obligations of the province to fund and restrict user charges and extra billing in respect of insured health services. This means that provincial eligibility to a full cash contribution from the federal government is in no way dependent on provincial establishment of a comprehensive and universal scheme of publicly administered insurance that provides access to extended health care services. In other words, the *Canada Health Act* does not extend the single-payer model to extended health care services.

[113] *Canada Health Act*, R.S.C. 1985, c. C-6, s. 2.

of the "accessibility" criteria, and they will be discussed as elements of accessibility, rather than as distinct pre-conditions to provincial receipt of federal contributions.

1. Public Administration, Universality and Portability

Public administration is satisfied if the health care insurance plan of a province is administered and operated on a non-profit basis by a public authority that is appointed or designated by the government of the province.[114] In most provinces at most times, the public authority has been the Department of Health. But section 8(1) makes it clear that this is not the only arrangement that is acceptable. It clearly authorizes the utilization of an entity that is distinct from but accountable to the government of a province. Accordingly, the administration of provincial health insurance plans either has been or is entrusted in different provinces to arm's-length commissions. Section 8(2) contemplates that the public authority (be it the government itself or a commission) may be given the authority to designate another agency to receive payments on its behalf or to "carry out on its behalf any responsibility in connection with the receipt or payment of accounts rendered for insured health services". This second level delegation would therefore appear to be valid only if limited to certain functions rather than to a complete transfer of overall responsibility for plan administration.

The public administration requirement serves a number of functions. One is to maintain accountability through the political process for the administration of a health insurance plan that is to be operated in accordance with the other criteria. Another is to avoid unnecessary operating costs, whether in the guise of profit-taking, the additional operating overhead that comes with multiple and competing providers of physician and hospital insurance, or the cost of regulating private providers to deal with such dynamics as adverse selection or prohibitive premiums for high risk persons. Paying attention to the limited scope of these objectives is important — this criterion demands non-profit public administration of *health insurance*, not in *health care services delivery*. On the question of who can deliver service, neither this criterion nor any other provision of the *Canada Health Act* has any direct application, although, as seen below, arguments can be made that delivery arrangements that jeopardize equal access based on need conflict with the spirit if not the letter of the universality and accessibility criteria.

On universality, the *Canada Health Act* says that each province must insure all of its "insured persons ... on uniform terms and conditions".[115] The Act defines insured persons as all residents of a province with the exception of members of the Canadian Forces, members of the RCMP, inmates in federal penitentiaries and persons who have not completed a minimum residency re-

---

[114] *Ibid.*, s. 8(1).
[115] *Ibid.*, s. 10.

quirement that is not in excess of three months.[116] A separate definition of "resident" allows provinces to exclude tourists, transients or visitors but also makes clear that public insurance is to apply to everyone lawfully in Canada who makes a province his or her home. It is noteworthy that the standard that is adopted is actually a provincial one. The requirement is for universal coverage on terms and conditions that are uniform as between the residents of the insuring province. Variation between provinces seems to be acknowledged. In this way, the construction of the Act recognizes both the legal reality that constitutional authority over health care is largely provincial and (perhaps) the practical reality that different provinces may choose or be required to define uniformity differently.

The universality requirement exemplifies the difference between insuring health care services on social rather than on market principles. Unlike free market systems of private insurance, the provincial administrators of Medicare cannot reduce their costs by directly or indirectly excluding from coverage those who are high risk due, for example, to pre-existing conditions, medical history, age, occupation or personal choices (such as whether or not they smoke or eat or drink excessively). At the same time, universality ensures participation in the plan of higher income people whose higher premiums (in the form of taxes) subsidize the funding of health care for lower income people who are likely to require more of it. In this way, it eliminates the risk rating that inhibits such subsidization in a purely private market regime.

The leading challenge to the universality criterion is the increasing availability in Canada of private clinics that allow Canadians to purchase diagnostic and some surgical services and thereby circumvent waiting lists for obtaining the same service from publicly financed hospitals or clinics. Viewed narrowly, this advantageous access does not engage the universality criterion as long as access within the public system is inclusive and on uniform terms and conditions. But on a broader view, it is obvious that earlier diagnosis will mean early and therefore preferential access to treatment, including when that treatment is required from the publicly funded system. To deal with this problem, Romanow has recommended an amendment to the Act to clarify that it does apply to medically necessary diagnostic services, and the creation of dedicated federal funding to increase the diagnostic capacity of the publicly funded system.[117]

On portability, the Act says that qualifying health care insurance plans must not impose minimum residency requirements of more than three months on anyone moving into that province from elsewhere in Canada.[118] Conversely, each provincial plan is required to continue to cover its residents who move to another province during the receiving province's qualifying period. The Act also

---

[116] *Ibid.*, s. 2.

[117] Roy J. Romanow, Q.C., *Building on Values: The Future of Health Care in Canada — Final Report* (Ottawa: Commission on the Future of Health Care in Canada, 2002) at xxv, xxix, 64-65 and 139-41.

[118] The portability requirements are found in *Canada Health Act*, R.S.C. 1985, c. C-6, s. 11.

says that the health insurance plan of a province must provide for the payment of the cost of insured services provided to its residents when they are travelling in another province (unless it is elective surgery not approved in advance) at the rate payable under the plan of the service-providing province. In contrast, if services are provided outside Canada, the health insurance plan of the province of residence must (subject to some flexibility) pay for the services at the rates that would have applied if the work had been done in that province. Given the cost of medical treatment in the United States, this means that Canadians who receive treatment in that country can be left with substantial costs even after recovery of expenses in accordance with the Act.

2.   Comprehensiveness

The comprehensiveness criteria requires provinces to insure (that is, to fund 100 per cent of the cost of) "all insured health services" provided by hospitals, medical practitioners and dentists.[119] As mentioned previously, "insured health services" are defined as hospital services, physician services and (if they must be provided in a hospital) surgical-dental services. "Hospital services" are defined to be any item on a list of services when determined to be "medically necessary for the purpose of maintaining health, preventing disease or diagnosing or treating an injury, illness or disability".[120] "Physician services" are defined as "medically required services rendered by medical practitioners".

No definition is given for the governing concepts of "medical necessity" and "medically required". It may be that a general and definitive definition is simply not possible, or it may be that the Act's silence on the meaning of these critical concepts was necessary to physician cooperation with Medicare.[121] Whatever the reason for it, the absence of legislative definition means that the meaning of these terms has been largely left to doctors. Medically necessary hospital services are those ordered by doctors and medically required physician services are those provided by physicians. This lightness of the legislative hand assumes an essentially passive role for governments and a largely reactive role

---

[119] *Canada Health Act*, R.S.C. 1985, c. C-6, s. 9.

[120] Section 2 of the Act provides that "'hospital services' means any of the following services provided to in-patients or outpatients at a hospital, if the services are medically necessary for the purpose of maintaining health, preventing disease or diagnosing or treating an injury, illness or disability, namely, (a) accommodation and meals at the standard or public ward level and preferred accommodation if medically necessary, (b) nursing service, (c) laboratory, radiological and other diagnostic procedures, together with the necessary interpretations, (d) drugs, biologicals, and related preparations when administered in the hospital, (e) use of operating room, case room and anaesthetic facilities, including necessary equipment and supplies, (f) medical and surgical equipment and supplies, (g) use of radiotherapy facilities, (h) use of physiotherapy facilities, and (i) services provided by persons who receive remuneration therefore from the hospital, but does not include services that are excluded by the regulations".

[121] T. Caulfield, "Wishful Thinking: Defining 'Medically Necessary' in Canada" (1996) 4 Health L.J. 63. See also T.R. Marmor & D. Boyum, "Medical Care and Public Policy: The Benefits and Burdens of Asking Fundamental Questions" (1999) 49 Health Policy 27.

for the governors and administrators of hospitals. Medicare gave to government the role of funding the services that doctors either provided directly or that doctors decided needed to be provided by hospitals. It gave to hospitals the role of having in place (also largely through government funding) the staff, equipment, programs and support services needed to provide the clinical services that doctors decided were clinically indicated.

This understanding of comprehensiveness is subject to important qualification. First, provinces are required to insure only services that are provided because they are determined to be either medically necessary or required. Thus, in the case of hospitals, provinces must insure ward accommodation but are not required to insure semi-private or private accommodation, except where such accommodation is determined to be medically necessary. Second, decisions made at the provincial level place practical limits on the ability of physicians and their patients to access specific courses of treatment. These decisions include those relating to the acquisition and distribution of medical equipment and those relating to the addition of new drugs to the formulary that determines hospital eligibility for reimbursement.[122]

Third, the latitude that the *Canada Health Act* appears to leave with each treating physician to determine the meaning of medical necessity has been in every province limited by the processes that are used to determine the physician services that are assigned a fee code within the tariff of fees that allows physician to bill for their services. Across the country, this process involves a form of negotiation between the provincial government and the provincial medical association. For the most part, this process has resulted in steady expansion in the list of physician services that are covered under Medicare: as new services or new ways of providing service have emerged from technical and clinical developments they have been added to the fee code in most provinces. But there has been some "de-listing" of services from the tariff of fees in the various provinces as a budget reduction or control mechanism. Examples of services that have been de-listed are stomach stapling, wart removal, circumcision of newborns, tubal ligations, vasectomies and mammoplasty. In addition, various provinces have decided against providing full or any coverage for some new procedures. An example of this is the exclusion from coverage of certain procedures for the treatment of infertility, namely *in vitro* fertilization and intracytoplasmic sperm injection (ICSI).[123]

Thus, decisions made at a provincial level result in Medicare having a more constrained scope than the statutory reliance on the open-ended concept of medical necessity might suggest. This introduces access variation between provinces and between people within provinces based on ability to pay. It is ques-

---

[122] See Ontario Ministry of Health and Long-Term Care, "Ontario Drug Benefit: How Drugs Are Approved" (2002), online at: <http://www.health.gov.on.ca/english/public/pub/drugs/approved.html>.

[123] For the argument that other provinces should follow Quebec's lead in funding *in vitro* fertilization treatments, see Renda Bouzayen & Laura Eggertson, "In Vitro Fertilization: A Private Matter Becomes Public" (2009) 181:5 CMAJ 243.

tionable whether this makes sense, given that the underlying criteria is medical necessity. Federal acceptance of different answers to the question of what is medically necessary would seem to mean either the application of a variable standard across provinces or the consistent application of a lowest common denominator that is not mentioned in the Act.

The process that has been used to make decisions about comprehensiveness raises other sorts of questions. As mentioned, for physician services, it is a negotiating process that is constructed on collective bargaining lines.[124] Indeed, the *Canada Health Act* contemplates this.[125] Like other collective bargaining processes, this one has been conducted largely behind closed doors. It has been said that the process derives political legitimacy from the participation of governments and clinical legitimacy from the participation of medical associations.[126] But these sources of legitimacy are likely to be undermined by the primary focus of the process on physician incomes and by the pervasive concern of governments for cost-containment as an overriding policy objective.

Decisions about what is covered by Medicare are at the heart of the system. A truly public system of health insurance would be one that includes the public in decisions of such fundamental importance. The question is how to do this while addressing the concern that a more open process would be unlikely to make the tough decisions that are and will be needed to ensure the ongoing sustainability of the system. It is possible to believe, as others argue, that greater openness and transparency are part of the answer to this question, either because they will lead either to greater acceptance of the need for tough decisions that limit the list of insured services to match available resources, or because they will lead to greater acceptance of the higher taxes needed to increase Medicare's capacity to fund a longer list of insured services.[127] A worry, however, is the past tendency of the system to be better at adding new programs and services than it has been at removing old ones, even when the new was intended to replace the old. Another concern is the difficulty the system has had in achieving true engagement and participation by the general public, as opposed to the organizations who purport to represent them. A third worry is the risk that decisions on the scope of Medicare will not be connected to decisions on rates of taxation made through the electoral process. A casualty could be funding for other social programs, without the powerful constituency that health care holds.

---

[124] For example, see Nova Scotia's *Medical Society Act*, S.N.S. 1995-96, c. 12, ss. 7, 8 and 9 and its *Health Services and Insurance Act*, R.S.N.S. 1989, c. 197, ss. 13, 13A and 13B.

[125] Clause 12(1)(c) of the Act requires each province to pay "reasonable compensation for all insured health services rendered by medical practitioners or dentists". Section 12(2) then says that this requirement is satisfied if the province commits itself to negotiating physician compensation with "provincial organizations" that represent doctors and accepts the resolution of disputes through conciliation or binding arbitration.

[126] C. Tuohy, *Accidental Logics: The Dynamics of Change in the Health Care Arena in the United States, Britain and Canada* (New York: Oxford University Press, 1999) at 260.

[127] Colleen M. Flood, Mark Stabile & Carolyn Tuohy, "What Is In and Out of Medicare? Who Decides?" in Colleen M. Flood, ed., *Just Medicare: What's In, What's Out, How We Decide* (Toronto: University of Toronto Press, 2006) 15 at 23.

Modest reform to allow greater transparency and openness can be seen in the creation of administrative tribunals in Ontario, Alberta, British Columbia and Quebec that are mandated to hear appeals where health insurance administrators decide not to fund out-of-country treatment where the treatment in question is not available in Canada.[128] Whereas Quebec's tribunal is a general administrative appeal tribunal that hears appeals on decisions from across government, the tribunals in Ontario, Alberta and British Columbia are more specialized bodies that focus on the issue of out-of-country treatment or (in the case of Ontario) a broader range of health system issues. The Ontario tribunal (called the Ontario Health Services Appeal and Review Board) is the most elaborate of these, differentiated from the others by its independence from government and the formality of its proceedings. It has been criticized for the narrowness of its mandate, its dependency on the opinion of physicians, its slowness and its inaccessibility, including the unavailability of its jurisprudence.[129] It has recently moved to respond to, at least, the latter criticism by making its decisions available online.[130]

The availability of such avenues of review enhances the legitimacy of the overall process by which decisions on comprehensiveness are made.[131] In other provinces, a similar review may be available through an ombudsmen's office, but such offices do not have the authority to issue binding rulings. Another option may be a complaint under human rights law, but only where the decision not to fund is aligned with a prohibited ground of discrimination. This may be more difficult to establish in the wake of the decision of the Supreme Court of Canada in *Auton (Guardian ad litem of) v. British Columbia (Attorney General)*,[132] discussed below and in Chapter 14 in this volume. Finally, whether or not decisions to fund out-of-country treatments are subject to an administrative review; they are open to review by the courts under administrative law princi-

---

[128] Caroline Pitfield & Colleen M. Flood, "Section 7 'Safety Valves': Appealing Wait Times Witihin a One-Tier System" in Colleen M. Flood, Kent Roach & Lorne Sossin, eds., *Access to Care, Access to Justice: The Legal Debate Over Private Health Insurance in Canada* (Toronto: University of Toronto Press, 2005) at 477.

[129] *Ibid.*, at 485-488, 490-496. The legislative framework for Ontario's Board consists of the following Acts and regulations: *Ministry of Health and Long-Term Care Appeal and Review Boards Act, 1998*, S.O. 1998, c. 18, Sched. H; *Health Insurance Act*, R.S.O. 1990, c. H.6, s. 21(1) and *General Regulation*, R.R.O. 1990, Reg. 552, s. 28.4.

[130] See the web page of the Health Services Appeal and Review Board, announcing the availability of decisions online through the Canadian Legal Information Institute as of August 2, 2010: <http://www.hsarb.on.ca/scripts/english/default.asp>.

[131] Colleen M. Flood, Mark Stabile & Carolyn Tuohy, "What Is In and Out of Medicare? Who Decides?" in Colleen M. Flood, ed., *Just Medicare: What's In, What's Out, How We Decide* (Toronto: University of Toronto Press, 2006) 15; Caroline Pitfield & Colleen M. Flood, "Section 7 'Safety Valves': Appealing Wait Times Within a One-Tier System" in Colleen M. Flood, Kent Roach & Lorne Sossin, eds., *Access to Care, Access to Justice: The Legal Debate Over Private Health Insurance in Canada* (Toronto: University of Toronto Press, 2005) 477.

[132] [2004] S.C.J. No. 71, [2004] 3 S.C.R. 657 (S.C.C.).

ples, as illustrated by the decision in *Stein v. Québec (Régie de l'Assurance-maladie)*,[133] discussed below.

The limited scope for recourse that is available through nationally available mechanisms highlights the importance of the step that has been taken in the four largest provinces to establish more specialized administrative review processes. But even where such processes are put in place, they do not fully address the underlying problem, which is that the decisions that *de facto* define comprehensiveness are often initially taken out of the public eye, within health care bureaucracies and in physician negotiations, without much clarity either as to the criteria or the evidence on which they are based.

An improved process would be one built differently from the ground up, where decisions on the scope of Medicare are initially made. It would establish a greater separation between the questions of what services should be covered and the question of what fees should be paid to doctors for providing those services. It would be one that, with or without this separation, was flexibly guided by criteria that would be defined in advance of their application to specific facts but that would be subject to revision in the course of the decision-making process. Opportunities for participation would extend into the application of the criteria to specific cases. Decisions would include not only the outcome, but also the rationale that explained the outcome. Finally, an improved process would reduce the institutionalized advantage that services already on the list might have over new services yet to be added. It would be more than a gatekeeper process, limited to reviewing new treatments or new ways of doing established things. It would have the broader responsibility of ensuring that the list of funded services generally included the services, both new and old, that meet the criteria for inclusion.

3.   Accessibility

In discussions about the current status and the reform of the Canadian health care system, concerns about access invariably figure prominently. The relevant provisions are section 12 (dealing with the accessibility criteria) and sections 18 and 19 (dealing respectively with user charges and extra billing). Working together, these provisions deal with accessibility on two levels. First, they create a general and open-ended requirement of accessibility. Second, they deal specifically with two elements of accessibility, one being the compensation of physicians and the funding of hospitals and the other being point-of-service charges (banning user charges and extra billing).

The first and broader requirement says that a provincial plan "must provide for insured health services on uniform terms and conditions and on a basis that does not impede or preclude, either directly or indirectly, whether by charges made to insured persons or otherwise, reasonable access to those services by

---

[133] [1999] Q.J. No. 2724, [1999] R.J.Q. 2416 (Que. S.C.).

insured persons".[134] In the *Canada Health Act*, "reasonableness" means that the Act can be applied with sensitivity to the particular circumstances and factors of relevance to the standard of access that is needed, possible or desired in each province. Such flexibility was and is important in achieving and maintaining provincial participation in Medicare as a quasi-national program.

Having said that, the requirement for reasonable access implies an objective standard that must be capable of accomplishing the Act's larger objectives — protecting, promoting and restoring the physical and mental well-being of residents of Canada. The accessibility requirement therefore demands more than accessibility on terms and conditions that are uniform. It demands access on terms and conditions that ensure the general adequacy of access, as measured against these objectives.

What adequacy means will depend on many complex questions about (for example) what is a health care need, the ranking of needs, the efficacy of alternative courses of treatment and the priority that should be given to health over other social goods. The *Canada Health Act* does not purport to answer these questions. But it does seem to contemplate that they will be asked. In doing so, the Act demands more of the provinces than the creation of a system of public funding that covers all medically necessary hospital and physician services. It demands that the provinces ensure a level of access to these services that is consistent with the objectives spelled out in the Act.

One implication is that funding must not just be public but adequate when measured against the need for service. But the implications go farther, since access can be affected by many other factors in the organization and operation of the health care system, including the allocation of funding among providers. There is nothing in the language of the *Canada Health Act* that establishes the irrelevance of these other factors. Clause 12(1)(*a*) does specify a concern with financial barriers, but it also goes beyond financial barriers. It speaks of barriers that impede or preclude reasonable access, "either directly or indirectly whether by charges made to insured persons *or otherwise*" [emphasis added].

In this aspect, the accessibility criterion demands a deeper level of interest by provincial and territorial governments in the delivery of services than is called for by the other criteria. Conversely, the accessibility criterion can be seen as authorizing the federal government to find provinces in non-compliance where reasonable access is "impeded or precluded" by the level of funding that a province provides to its health care system or by the choices the province makes in organizing, managing and regulating its health care system.

For example, the problem of waiting lists and of waiting times would seem to be one that could obviously bring a province into violation of the accessibility criteria, whether the cause of the problem was the inadequacy of public funding, sub-optimal allocation of funding or the failure to manage waiting lists and waiting times in a coordinated and coherent fashion. More ambitiously, it has been argued that the accessibility criterion could potentially be engaged by a provin-

---

[134] *Canada Health Act*, R.S.C. 1985, c. C-6, s. 12(1)(*a*).

cial plan (such as that instituted in Alberta under the *Health Care Protection Act of 2000*) to allow the private purchase of a greater range of surgical services from for-profit clinics.[135] This would require showing that the implementation of the plan was diverting physicians, nurses and other human and non-human resources from the public system, thereby reducing access to the services that continue to be publicly funded.

As with comprehensiveness, accessibility can be enhanced by adjudicative mechanisms that are empowered to review the decisions of health systems officials who have the responsibility to deal with accessibility issues. In Ontario and Quebec, as in other provinces, bureaucrats are called upon to make decisions on requests for funding for out-of-country care where treatments that are part of Medicare cannot be made available on a timely basis to particular patients in-province. In both provinces, appeals from these decisions can be taken to the same tribunals that hear appeals from decisions about funding where the request is to receive funding to obtain a treatment outside Canada that is not included within Medicare. Such review mechanisms are referred to as "safety valves" in the literature.[136] In *Chaoulli*, the dissenting judges suggested that their availability weighed in favour of judicial deference to legislative decisions such as the decision of Quebec (and of other provinces) to protect public health care by banning private insurance for medical services available through Medicare. This deference is certain to be contingent. It is for example, less likely to be forthcoming where the administrative review process lacks independence from government, does not observe the principles of procedural fairness and does not have the authority to give such remedies as are demanded by the merits of the case.

The specific accessibility requirements of the *Canada Health Act* can be quickly dealt with. Clause 12(1)(*b*) requires payments to physicians for the delivery of insured health services, "in accordance with a tariff or system of payment authorized by the law of the province". The reference to a "tariff" indicates the underlying assumption that fee-for-service arrangements (with the incentive structure that they imply) would continue to be the standard method of physician compensation. In this line, it is interesting that the Act requires each province to pay reasonable compensation for all insured services rendered by doctors (as well as those rendered by dentists).[137] In contrast, it simply requires that pay-

---

[135] The argument is made by Sujit Choudhry, "Bill 11, the *Canada Health Act* and the Social Union: The Need for Institutions" in T.A. Caulfield & B. von Tigerstrom, eds., *Health Care Reform and the Law in Canada: Meeting the Challenge* (Edmonton: University of Alberta Press, 2002) 37 at 68-72. For the legislation, see the *Health Care Protection Act*, R.S.A. 2000, c. H-1.

[136] There is much discussion of the "safety valve" concept in the wake of *Chaoulli v. Quebec (Attorney General)*, [2005] S.C.J. No. 33, [2005] 1 S.C.R. 791 (S.C.C.), where the dissenting judges portrayed the availability of such mechanisms as a rationale for non-intervention under the *Canadian Charter of Rights and Freedoms*. See Caroline Pitfield & Colleen M. Flood, "Section 7 'Safety Valves': Appealing Wait Times Within a One-Tier System" in Colleen M. Flood, Kent Roach & Lorne Sossin, eds., *Access to Care, Access to Justice: The Legal Debate Over Private Health Insurance in Canada* (Toronto: University of Toronto Press, 2005) 477.

[137] *Canada Health Act*, R.S.C. 1985, c. C-6, s. 12(1)(*c*).

ments be made to hospitals, "in respect of the cost of insured health services".[138] Thus, while it is a condition of federal funding that doctors be paid "reasonable compensation", all that is by implication required in the funding of hospitals is that they receive payments in consideration for the services they provide.

Finally, a discussion of accessibility under the *Canada Health Act* must include the section 18 requirement that deductions must be made from the federal contribution to any province to the extent that it allows extra billing to occur, and section 19, which specifies the same consequence for any province that allows the levying of user charges. Contrary to the suggestion of some, Quebec's decision (now rescinded) to adopt a \$25 "deductible" for medical visits that would have been collected through the income tax process rather than by doctors, seems clearly contrary to the latter provision, since section 19 does not turn on the method of collection.[139]

Sections 18 and 19 are what set Canada's health care system apart from all others. No other system goes quite as far in making the state the exclusive source of financing for medical services, although other countries do employ other forms of regulation to fetter the growth of the privately financed sector.[140] Sections 18 and 19 are often criticized based on the assumption that such charges could deter inappropriate utilization of services that are regarded as "free". As mentioned above, this critique rests on highly debatable premises.[141]

D.   THE IMPLEMENTATION AND ENFORCEMENT OF THE CANADA HEALTH ACT

We now have a picture of what the *Canada Health Act* requires of the provinces. In this section, the question is whether the health care systems of the provinces satisfy these requirements. We look first at the legislation, administrative frameworks and policies through which the provinces establish and operate the scheme of publicly administered health insurance that is mandated by the *Canada Health Act*. We will then consider the enforcement of the Act in situations where the provincial reality arguably has departed from the ideal that is envisaged in the *Canada Health Act*.

---

[138] *Ibid.*, s. 12(1)(*d*).

[139] Robert Silver, "The *Canada Health Act* is dead" *The Globe and Mail* (April 9, 2010), commenting on the apparent unwillingness of the federal government or of federal politicians to recognize that the deductible is a user fee.

[140] Colleen Flood & Amanda Haugan, "Is Canada Odd? A Comparison of European and Canadian Approaches to Choice and Regulation of the Public/Private Divide in Health Care" (2010) 5 Health Economics, Policy and Law 319-41.

[141] For a relatively current empirical perspective on these issues, see Noralou P. Roos *et al.*, "Does Universal Comprehensive Insurance Encourage Unnecessary Use? Evidence from Manitoba Says 'No'" (2004) 170 CMAJ 209.

1. Provincial Implementation

As outlined above, the stronger view is that only the provinces can enact public health insurance for the general population. It follows that for the single-payer model to be a functioning reality for the residents of any province, the laws of that province must translate the general principles of the *Canada Health Act* into operating reality. Every province (and each of the territories) has in place a framework of laws that do exactly this by establishing a scheme of public health insurance that encompasses most physician and hospital services.[142] In contrast to the almost breathtaking brevity of the *Canada Health Act*, these provincial frameworks are quite detailed, technical and complex. Moreover, although their basic objectives are very consistent, they differ considerably in how they go about achieving those objectives.

Thankfully, we do not have to deal with all this complexity. What is important to know is what is accomplished by the legislation of each of the provinces, no matter how differently organized, structured or written. In all provinces, health insurance legislation establishes a plan for the funding of doctor and hospital services; delegates the responsibility for administering that plan to a minister of health, government official or government agency; defines insured services in such a way as to generally encompass the services that doctors and hospitals provide; gives all residents of the province a right to receive these services on uniform terms and conditions and (in compliance with the prohibitions on user fees and extra billing) without being charged any fee; and entitles doctors to compensation and hospitals to funding in place of the charges that each would otherwise levy to patients or their private insurers. In all these essential respects, all of the provinces have in place the legislative framework that the *Canada Health Act* mandates.

In fact, provincial legislation goes beyond what is required by the *Canada Health Act*. It has not only ensured the availability of publicly funded medical care, but also made the alternative of privately funded care largely unavailable within Canada, thereby greatly reinforcing the single-payer model.[143] In Quebec and several other provinces, private insurance for services that are included within the public scheme have been prohibited, but of course, this is the provision of Quebec law struck down in *Chaoulli v. Quebec (Attorney General)*.[144] More indirect but effective mechanisms are relied upon in other provinces, as well as in Quebec and in the other provinces that banned overlapping private insurance. For example, in all jurisdictions physicians are required to elect between delivering "medically necessary" service under the public scheme or outside of it. The consequence of an election to offer service privately is to make the cost of the service the full responsibility of the patient (or of his or her pri-

---

[142] Laurel Montrose, *Medicare in Ontario: A Legal Reference Guide* (Markham, ON: LexisNexis Canada, 2008).

[143] C.M. Flood & T. Archibald, "The Illegality of Private Health Care in Canada" (2001) 164 CMAJ 825.

[144] [2005] S.C.J. No. 33, [2005] 1 S.C.R. 791 (S.C.C.).

vate insurer). In some provinces, doctors are also prohibited from charging more in private for providing a medical service than they would receive for providing the same service under Medicare. Essentially, this extends the *Canada Health Act* prohibition against extra billing to the provision of services outside Medicare.

For much of the history of Medicare, these types of restrictions have helped to make the private delivery and purchase of most medical services that are included in Medicare an unattractive business proposition for doctors and patients, except in limited circumstances. The rationale for this relatively absolute approach has been threefold: first, to prevent the private ability to pay from becoming a determinant of relative access to treatment; second, to prevent taxpayer subsidization of a parallel private system (and the preferential access it may provide); and third, to prevent the diversion of human and other resources from the public to the private system. Yet, in recent years, the number of private diagnostic and surgical clinics has grown significantly. In the name of reduced waiting times, provincial governments are moving to give these clinics a role inside Medicare as a provider of services that are paid for by Medicare. Concern has been expressed that these arrangements are a slippery slope that will subsidize investment in a private system, a system that will eventually be given as the rationale for reduced investment in the public system.[145] A distinct concern is the enforcement of the restrictions described above, including the prohibition on providing services both in and outside of Medicare and the prohibition on billing at rates above those payable under Medicare. Some enforcement appears to be taking place in British Columbia, where the owners of private clinics have sought to use *Chaoulli* to challenge the legislative restrictions under which they must function.[146]

Provincial actions that can be said to be clear violations of the *Canada Health Act* relate to the more specific requirements of the Act. For example, the refusal of governments in Atlantic Canada to cover the "facility fees" for abortion services provided via private clinics where the service was otherwise funded publicly and the decision of an Alberta clinic to directly charge patients from other provinces for cataract surgery both run contrary to the stipulation that user fees and extra billing should not be allowed. The refusal of Quebec to reimburse other provinces (except Ontario) at the rates of the other province for services provided to Quebec residents, the decision of various provinces to reimburse residents who receive service in the United States at rates that are below the rates that apply to the service if received in province, and the decision once made by Alberta to refuse to give dialysis to visitors from other provinces, all seem obviously contrary to the portability requirements.

---

[145] Marie-Claude Premont, "Wait-time Guarantees for Health Services: An Analysis of Quebec's Reaction to the *Chaoulli* Supreme Court Decision" (2007) 15 Health L.J. 43.

[146] Pamela Fayerman, "Province files health countersuit: Private medical centres accused of unlawful billing, refusing records access" *The Vancouver Sun* (March 11, 2009) A10.

2.   Federal Enforcement

The enforcement mechanism provided to the federal government by the Canada *Health Act* is financial penalization of the offending province. If the violation is of one of the five criteria, the federal government is given the discretion to decide for or against penalization and a further discretion to decide on the amount of the penalty. In contrast, if the violation is of the prohibitions on user fees or extra billing, the Act stipulates dollar-for-dollar reductions in the cash transfer that would otherwise go to the offending province. The Act also stipulates the payment of the withheld amount once the charging of user fees or the extra billing ceases. In addition, since 1991 other federal legislation has authorized the federal government to enforce the *Canada Health Act* by withholding or reducing payments due to the offending province under any other federal statute, program or federal-provincial arrangement.[147]

The most important point is that the federal government has never exercised its discretionary power to financially penalize a province for breach of any of the general criteria. The only enforcement action that has ever been taken is in respect of user fees and extra billing, where the *Canada Health Act* obligates matching reductions in the federal transfers. Initial provincial (and physician) resistance to the *Canada Health Act* (particularly to the bans on user fees and extra billing) resulted in a total amount of approximately $245 million being withheld from seven provinces between 1984 and 1987, all of which was later paid once the user charges or extra billing had been ended. Between November 1995 and 1999, a total of approximately $6 million had been withheld from four provinces that had permitted (or rather, had refused to pay for) a so-called "facility fee" at clinics that provided abortion services as an insured service.

The larger story is the federal inaction on possible violations of the five criteria, including on rather straightforward violations of the portability requirement. The lack of any federal action on the accessibility front in the face of prevalent concern about waiting times and waiting lists is particularly noteworthy, given the breadth of the concern for accessibility that is displayed in the drafting of the *Canada Health Act*. On the other hand, it is clear that waiting lists and waiting times are complex phenomena that are caused by many factors, many of which are not easily influenced by the kinds of tools governments, especially the federal government, have at their disposal in the Canadian system.[148] This complexity encompasses the basic structural features of the system, including the independence of hospitals and of other health care institutions and the autonomy of physicians, both within hospitals and from governments. Under these circumstances, it is hard to see how the blunt instrument of financial pe-

---

[147] *Budget Implementation Act, 1991*, S.C. 1991, c. 51, s. 4, amending *Federal-Provincial Fiscal Arrangements Act*, R.S.C. 1985, c. F-8, s. 23.2.

[148] S. Lewis, M.L. Barer, C. Sanmartin, S. Ships, S.E.D. Short & P.W. MacDonald, "Ending Waiting-List Mismanagement: Principles and Practice" (2000) 162 CMAJ 1297. See also Health Canada, *Final Report of the Federal Advisor on Wait Times by Brian Postl, M.D.* (Ottawa: Minister of Health, 2006).

nalization could be applied by the federal government with sufficient sensitivity to cause and effect so as to improve matters. Conversely, it is easy to see how it could make matters worse wherever funding was either a contributing cause to the waiting times or a necessary ingredient in their improvement.

Still, the difficulties and practical implications of enforcement do not justify the failure of the federal government to conduct rigorous assessments of the nature and degree of provincial compliance with the criteria on which federal funding is supposed to depend. Past inquiries indicate that the federal government does not even gather the kind of information that would be necessary for this kind of assessment, but instead relies on "field reports" from Health Canada staffers and on very general reports from the provinces.[149] These concentrate on describing the formal elements of health insurance legislation and administration, but include little or no detail on the actual operation of each provincial health care system. Although the *Canada Health Act* authorizes regulations that would require more detailed and operational reports from the provinces, no such regulations have been adopted.[150]

Why the federal passiveness? The prominence of the national unity file has undoubtedly been a factor with violations attributed to Quebec. This factor (along with political calculation) seems once again at play in the unwillingness of federal politicians in the opposition as well as in the government to question the consistency of Quebec's proposed income tax charge of $25 per medical visit (now withdrawn) with the prohibition on user fees.[151] It seems equally obvious that the federal cuts in cash transfers that took place in the 1990s and the ensuing argument about whether or not the federal government was doing its share did not create ideal conditions for assertions of federal power, especially on what might be regarded as debatable interpretations of the *Canada Health Act*. The growth in waiting lists and waiting times that occurred in the provinces followed cuts in provincial levels of funding to hospitals (both for operations and equipment), which in turn paralleled the cuts that the federal government imposed on the provinces. It seems likely that the federal government was not anxious to point fingers for fear that its own contribution to the problems would become more obvious. For some, this shows the hopelessness of a sysem in which the interests of government as funding agent conflict with its responsibilities as the guarantor of performance and quality.[152] For others, it points to the need for independent institutions, such as a Medicare Commission, that can monitor the performance of the system with the mandate and the credibility to report, not only to governments but directly to Canadians.[153]

---

[149] Auditor General of Canada, *Report of the Auditor General of Canada to the House of Commons* (Ottawa: 1999), c. 29 at 29-14 to 29-20, inclusive.

[150] R.S.C. 1985, c. C-6, s. 22(1)(*c*).

[151] Robert Silver, "The *Canada Health Act* is dead" *The Globe and Mail* (April 9, 2010).

[152] Brian Crowley & David Zitner, *Public Health, State Secret* (Halifax: Atlantic Institute for Market Studies, 2002).

[153] Colleen M. Flood & Sujit Choudhry, "Strengthening the Foundations: Modernizing the *Canada Health Act*" in Tom McIntosh, Pierre-Gerlier Forest & Gregory P. Marchildon, eds., *The Gov-*

Finally, it is important for lawyers to recognize that the influence of the federal government continues to be substantial despite the absence of an aggressive enforcement posture. The best evidence of this is the continuing adherence of all provinces and territories to the core design principles of the single-payer system. While it can be said that this reflects the influence of provincial and territorial voters more than it does the influence of the federal government, it has to be acknowledged that the federal government plays an important role every time it is called upon to speak publicly about the consistency of provincial reform proposals with the *Canada Health Act*. In recent years, it has been required to do this most frequently with respect to proposals put forward by Alberta. The emphasis that Alberta has put on intergovernmental dispute resolution mechanisms, even though federal action has never gone beyond the expression of ministerial opinion, would suggest that Ottawa carries a fairly large stick when it comes to protecting Medicare, even though it has been reluctant to wield it.

E.   MEDICARE AND THE COURTS

Against this background of limited federal enforcement of the *Canada Health Act*, questions arise on the extent to which Canadians can take matters into their own hands by seeking redress from the courts when Medicare fails to deliver the benefits that the Act promises. In considering this question, it is useful to distinguish between direct judicial enforcement of the *Canada Health Act* and judicial scrutiny of the financing, governing and managing of health care delivery under the provincial and territorial laws that implement the single-payer system. A related question relates to the circumstances in which Canadians can challenge the limitation of the single-payer system on hospital and physician services in the courts.

1.   Judicial Enforcement of the *Canada Health Act* and Its "Principles"

The prospects for success in proceedings that seek direct enforcement of the *Canada Health Act* by the courts are quite limited. As explained above, a province or territory cannot be taken to court for violating the *Canada Health Act*. This is because the Act does not in strict law even apply to the provinces, but only to the federal government in the exercise of its spending power.

There are, however, two other routes for judicial enforcement of the Act, or at least of the criteria and conditions established by the Act. The first is an action against the federal government alleging a failure to penalize a province or provinces for their failure to abide by the Act.[154] Such an action would be heard as an

---

ernance of Health Care in Canada: Romanow Papers, Volume 3 (Toronto: University of Toronto Press, 2004) at 346.

[154] Sujit Choudhry, "The Enforcement of the *Canada Health Act*" (1996) 41 McGill L.J. 461. See also Canadian Bar Association Task Force on Health Care, *What's Law Got To Do With It? Health Care Reform in Canada* (Ottawa: Canadian Bar Association, 1994).

administrative law case, where the question for the court is essentially whether the failure to take action is authorized by the governing statute. If successful, such an action could result in a declaration that the failure to act was unlawful and perhaps even a direction to take the action that the court determines should have been taken, such as deducting certain amounts from the payments being made to certain provinces. But that kind of outcome would be highly unlikely. In administrative law cases, the more usual outcome is a quashing of the reviewed decision and its referral back to the administrative authority for reconsideration in accordance with the applicable statute and with the benefit of whatever the court has said on the interpretation of the statute or on the procedures that should be followed in the administration of the statute. More importantly, such a proceeding is unlikely to be successful in the first place. The *Canada Health Act* places broad discretion into the hands of the federal Minister of Health and the federal cabinet, two political decision-makers. The courts are generally reluctant to interfere with the exercise of such powers by government ministers, particularly where the decisions being made are of a broad policy nature affecting the interests of many as opposed to the specific rights of specific individuals.[155] The exception to this might be where the issue was the failure of the federal government to make mandatory deductions from federal transfers where a province permitted extra billing or user fees.

The second possibility (only available in some provinces) is for an action against provincial authorities where the *Canada Health Act* criteria have been written directly into provincial law, as they have been in British Columbia.[156] In these provinces, individuals can ask the courts to review provincial government decisions or policies for consistency with the criteria as adopted in provincial law and, in that way, challenge provincial actions under the substance if not the letter of the *Canada Health Act*. Such legislation makes provincial compliance with the criteria legally mandatory and this gives the courts the ability to strike down provincial decisions that are in violation of the criteria, again, on administrative law principles. Thus, although the hurdle of establishing that a violation has occurred remains, the additional hurdle that exists in litigation against the federal government of convincing a court that it should interfere with the exercise of discretionary powers is either avoided or minimized, depending on how the provincial legislation is structured. This litigation, where available, opens

---

[155] For a review of the jurisprudence, see William Lahey & Diana Ginn, "After the Revolution: Being Pragmatic and Functional in Canada's Trial Courts and Courts of Appeal" (2002) 25 Dalhousie L.J. 259.

[156] *Medicare Protection Act*, R.S.B.C. 1996, c. 286. This Act delegates the provincial government's responsibility to operate a plan of health insurance that accords with the *Canada Health Act* to the Medical Services Commission. Section 2 defines the purpose of the Act to be the preservation of "a publicly managed and fiscally sustainable health care system for British Columbia in which access to necessary medical care is based on need and not an individual's ability to pay". More importantly, s. 5(1) lays out the responsibilities and powers of the Commission and then says (in s. 5(2)): "The commission must not act under subsection (1) in a manner that does not satisfy the criteria described in section 7 of the *Canada Health Act* (Canada)." See also the *Regional Health Authorities Act*, C.C.S.M. c. R34, s. 2(2).

avenues for greater individual enforcement of the principles of the single-payer system through the courts. It is interesting however that the leading example of a successful claim of this sort is the case of *Waldman v. British Columbia (Medical Services Commission)*.[157] There doctors successfully argued that a provincial policy that limited the compensation of physicians relocating to British Columbia to 50 per cent of their billings unless they located in underserviced areas violated the part of the accessibility criterion that requires payment of "reasonable compensation" to physicians. It therefore dealt more directly with doctor rights than it did with patient rights to treatment, although it is easy to see how the former can have negative implications for the latter.

2.   Judicial Scrutiny Under Tort or Administrative Law

Broader judicial scrutiny of the financing, governing and managing of the delivery of health care services under provincial and territorial laws can take place under several branches of law. For example, where decisions about the level and distribution of funding cause harm or loss to a patient by constraining the system's capacity to provide quality services on a timely basis, liability in negligence could extend beyond the doctors, nurses and other providers who treated the patient to those (including government) who made the financing and allocation decisions. The law of negligence is discussed extensively elsewhere in this volume and will therefore not be further considered here. It suffices to say that while such liability is a possibility, establishing it in particular cases will face significant barriers, including the difficulties of proving causation and the general limits that the law places on liability when governments act in a policy-making capacity.[158]

The other branch of law that is potentially applicable is administrative law, whether or not *Canada Health Act* criteria have been written into provincial law. Here again, a large part of the story is the challenges that plaintiffs are likely to face in obtaining judicial intervention, due to the deference that the courts usually extend to administrative decisions that have a significant policy element. An example of this deference is the refusal of the courts to overturn decisions of the Health Services Restructuring Commission, which was mandated by Ontario to review the hospital and nursing homes sectors in the 1990s and decide which institutions should be "rationalized" (*i.e.*, closed).[159] This deference does, however, have limits where the exercise of statutory discretion gives inadequate weight to basic values of the legal system, such as the unwritten constitutional principle of respect for, and promotion of, minorities. Thus, where the Health Services Restructuring Committee ordered the closure of a hospital that pro-

---

[157]   [1999] B.C.J. No. 2014, 177 D.L.R. (4th) 321 (B.C.C.A.).

[158]   Timothy A. Caulfield, "Malpractice in the Age of Health Care Reform" in T.A. Caulfield & B. von Tigerstrom, eds., *Health Care Reform and the Law in Canada: Meeting the Challenge* (Edmonton: University of Alberta Press, 2002) at 11.

[159]   *Pembroke Civic Hospital v. Ontario (Health Services Restructuring Commission)*, [1997] O.J. No. 3142, 36 O.R. (3d) 41 (Ont. Div. Ct.).

vided service in French without considering the impact on Ontario's French-language minority, the Ontario courts ordered the Commission to reconsider its decision.[160] As a result, the Montfort Hospital survived.

The Quebec case of *Stein v. Québec (Régie de l'Assurance-maladie)* shows another kind of limit to judicial deference in administrative law, where the decision-making becomes specific to individual and identifiable patients.[161] Stein had colon cancer, which metastasized to his liver and required complex surgical intervention and chemotherapy treatment. He became frustrated with waiting his turn to receive this treatment in Quebec and proceeded to have it done in the United States. His subsequent application to the Régie de l'Assurance-maladie du Québec (the RAMQ) for reimbursement was refused. Stein challenged this refusal in court as being administratively unreasonable and was successful. The Quebec Superior Court ordered the RAMQ to reimburse Stein.

So applied, administrative law gets at compliance with the principles of the *Canada Health Act*, especially as regards access, from the bottom up. It engages at the level of decisions that are made in particular cases, where the general principles are applied to specific patients, rather than at the level of decision-making about the general design, structure or capacity of a province's health care system. At the former level, as *Stein* demonstrates, judicial intervention is more likely. And equally importantly, such interventions can drive systemic responses from governments and their officials.

The *Stein* case can be read straightforwardly as a garden-variety administrative law case where the court found a decision to be "patently unreasonable" and therefore unauthorized by statute. But *Stein* can also be read as an example of how the frustration, anxiety and anger over the inaccessibility of publicly insured services can make their way into court. It shows the question of waiting lists being transformed from a technocratic question about the management and organization of structures, processes, and systems into a question about the consequences for an individual Canadian of the movement of these broad and impersonal forces. With the question so transformed, *Stein* also shows at least one judge willing, against the grain of traditional judicial deference to government allocation activities, to impose standards of individual fairness and justice on a decision-making process that is all too likely to focus primarily on aggregate outcomes. To put it another way, it might be said that *Stein* indicates an emerging willingness in the courts to demand that health care policy-makers more tightly connect their decisions to an understanding (and a justification) of the consequences of those decisions for real flesh-and-blood citizens.

---

[160] *Lalonde v. Ontario (Commission de restructuration des services de santé)*, [2001] O.J. No. 4767, 56 O.R. (3d) 505 (Ont. C.A.).

[161] [1999] Q.J. No. 2724, [1999] R.J.Q. 2416 (Que. S.C.). This case is analyzed in M.A. Somerville, "The Ethics and Law of Access to New Cancer Treatments" (1999) 6:3 Current Oncology 161.

3.   Constitutional Scrutiny

The final area of law that needs to be mentioned is human rights law, particularly in the form of the *Canadian Charter of Rights and Freedoms*. This topic is the subject of Chapter 14 in this volume, which readers should refer to for greater detail. Here, the focus is on the policy implications of two important Charter decisions, *Auton (Guardian ad litem of) v. British Columbia (Attorney General)* and *Chaoulli v. Quebec (Attorney General)*, particularly with regard to the accountability of governments for health system policy-making and governance.[162]

Each of these cases concerned one of the two Charter provisions that are likely to have the greatest potential significance for Medicare. The *Auton* case dealt with section 15 (the equality guarantee) in the context of a challenge of the decision of the British Columbia government not to fund a form of applied behavioural therapy for children with autism (Lovaas therapy) that is generally provided by non-physician therapists. The *Chaoulli* case dealt with waiting times, Quebec's ban on private insurance for services available under Medicare, and the constitutional right to security of the person (encompassed by section 7 of the Canadian Charter and by section 1 of the Quebec *Charter of Human Rights and Freedoms*[163]), as well as the right to life (also encompassed by section 7 of the Canadian Charter). At this broad level, each case can be seen to have dealt with a Charter right that has significant alignment with the objectives and fundamental values of Medicare. This is most obviously true with the guarantee of equality, since equality of access is at the core of the single-payer model. But it is also true of the section 7 guarantees, since Medicare was intended not only to ensure equality of access but to give Canadians access to a level and quality of medical care that would be effective in saving lives, preserving health and advancing well-being.

In *Auton*, the Supreme Court of Canada unanimously ruled that British Columbia did not violate section 15 in deciding not to fund Lovaas therapy.[164] It ruled, in effect, that the scope of Medicare was a matter for governments and legislatures, not for the courts, provided that governments maintained equality of access (in accordance with the ruling in *Eldridge*) to the services that it does decide to include in Medicare.[165] Cutting through the technicalities of the constitutional analysis, this reflected the court's desire to leave responsibility for allocating limited resources with governments and legislatures. In reaching this outcome, the Court rejected the proposed comparison between autistic children

---

[162] *Auton (Guardian ad litem of) v. British Columbia (Attorney General)*, [2004] S.C.J. No. 71, [2004] 3 S.C.R. 657 (S.C.C.); *Chaoulli v. Quebec (Attorney General)*, [2005] S.C.J. No. 33, [2005] 1 S.C.R. 791 (S.C.C.). The decision of the British Columbia Court of Appeal, which found for Auton, can be found at [2002] B.C.J. No. 2258, 220 D.L.R. (4th) 411 (B.C.C.A.), affg [2001] B.C.J. No. 215, 197 D.L.R. (4th) 165 (B.C.S.C.).

[163] R.S.Q., c. C-12.

[164] For a comprehensive discussion of s. 15 in the health care context, see Martha Jackman, "Health Care and Equality: Is There a Cure?" (2007) 15 Health L.J. 87.

[165] *Eldridge v. British Columbia (Attorney General)*, [1997] S.C.J. No. 86, [1997] 3 S.C.R. 624 (S.C.C.).

denied public funding for Lovaas therapy and non-disabled persons provided access to medical servcies through Medicare on the basis that it did not take account of the fact that the therapy (unlike the medical services) was "emergent and only recently becoming recognized as medically required".[166]

In *Chaoulli*, a bitterly divided court ruled 4:3 that Quebec's ban on private insurance was, in light of the waiting lines that existed in the public system, a violation of the right to personal inviolability under section 1 of the Quebec *Charter of Human Rights and Freedoms*, which parallels section 7 of the Canadian Charter. Three judges, including McLachlin C.J.C., were prepared to reach the same conclusion on a national basis under section 7. Under both Charters, the underlying reasoning was the same: that waiting times in Quebec had become so dangerous to physical health and to psychological integrity as to make it constitutionally impermissible for Quebec to continue to deny Quebecers the option of seeking access through the alternative of private insurance. In effect, the majority seemed to be telling Canadian governments that they could not prevent Canadians from buying medical care privately if they were not providing acceptable access through the public system.

The activism of *Chaoulli* stands in marked contrast to the deference of *Auton*. An obvious interpretation is that the judges empathized more readily with patients waiting for potentially life-saving medical procedures (assumed to be at issue in *Chaoulli*) than they did with autistic children seeking access to a controversial therapy of uncertain efficacy. It is also possible to conclude that the difference reveals a more fundamental issue: the priority that the Charter gives to individual freedom — the right to be left alone by government — over the interests of those who stand to benefit from positive state action to address social and economic inequality.[167] This interpretation aligns with the failure of the *Chaoulli* majority to recognize that the interests of those who would have no alternative to the public system were deeply implicated in the constitutionality of legislative efforts to control the growth of privately financed medicine. This of course assumes that the *Chaoulli* majority understood that an expanded private system would threaten the public system, particularly by attracting away scarce human resources. In fact, the majority dismissed this concern out of hand, despite the availability of plenty of supporting evidence and the conclusions of almost all of the independent studies that have been completed of the Canadian health care system. In this, *Chaoulli* raises serious questions about the capacity of the courts to adjudicate questions of health system design.[168]

---

[166] *Auton (Guardian ad litem of) v. British Columbia (Attorney General)*, [2004] S.C.J. No. 71, [2004] 3 S.C.R. 657 at para. 55 (S.C.C.).

[167] See Allan C. Hutchinson, "'Condition Critical': The Constitution and Health Care" and Andrew Petter, "Wealthcare: The Politics of the *Charter* Revisited" in Colleen M. Flood, Kent Roach & Lorne Sossin, eds., *Access to Care, Access to Justice: The Legal Debate Over Private Health Insurance in Canada* (Toronto: University of Toronto Press, 2005) at 101 and 116, respectively.

[168] Sujit Choudhry, "Worse than *Lochner*?" in Colleen M. Flood, Kent Roach & Lorne Sossin, eds., *Access to Care, Access to Justice: The Legal Debate Over Private Health Insurance in Canada* (Toronto: University of Toronto Press, 2005) 75. In Lawrie McFarlane, "Supreme Court Slaps

Still, it is very important from a policy-making perspective to keep a sense of proportion in reacting to *Chaoulli*, as the government of Quebec has arguably done.[169] This is partly warranted by the fact that *Chaoulli* is a decision that applies only in Quebec and that has a very uncertain future, independently of what governments do in response. This is not only due to the narrowness of Chaoulli's victory by a 4:3 majority and the impact that changing membership of the court may have on that division. It is also due to the number of points of constitutional doctrine on which *Chaoulli* arguably departs from earlier case law or takes section 7 and Charter analysis in new and expansive directions, both within and beyond health care.[170]

A measured response to *Chaoulli* is also warranted by a careful analysis of what the case does and does not decide on the issue before it — the constitutionality of a prohibition of private insurance for services covered by Medicare.[171] The ruling does not create a constitutional right to free market medicine, despite the hints of this in the opinion authored by McLachlin C.J.C. and Major J. It also did not decide that Canadian governments could not act to protect the public health care system by using law to discourage or even block the development of a competing private system. Again, it is true that the opinion of McLachlin C.J.C. and Major J. suggests otherwise. But this is only the opinion of three judges of a nine-member court. What is important is what is said in the swing opinion of Deschamps J. Her ruling that the prohibition on private insurance was not a justified infringement of individual rights was based on her conclusion that other options for guarding the public system, including a legislative cap on the fees that could be charged in the private system, were available to Quebec. It

---

For-Sale Sign on Medicare" (2005) 173 CMAJ 269, *Chaoulli* is compared to the *Dred Scott* decision.

[169] Minister of Health and Social Services, *Guaranteeing Access: Meeting the Challenges of Equity, Efficiency and Quality — Consultation Document* (Quebec: 2006).

[170] In addition to the chapters of critique available in Colleen M. Flood, Kent Roach & Lorne Sossin, eds., *Access to Care, Access to Justice: The Legal Debate Over Private Health Insurance in Canada* (Toronto: University of Toronto Press, 2005), see Robert G. Evans, "Baneful Legacy: Medicare and Mr. Trudeau" (2005) 1:1 Healthcare Policy 20; Colleen M. Flood, "Just Medicare: The Role of Canadian Courts in Determining Health Care Rights and Access" (2005) 33:4 J.L. Med. & Ethics 669; David Hadorn, "The *Chaoulli* Challenge: Getting a Grip on Waiting Lists" (2005) 173 CMAJ 271; Gregory R. Hagen, "Personal Inviolability and Public Health Care: *Chaoulli v. Quebec*" (2005) 14:2 Health L. Rev. 34; Martha Jackman, "Misdiagnosis or Cure? *Charter* Review of the Health Care System" in Colleen M. Flood, ed., *Just Medicare: What's In, What's Out, How We Decide* (Toronto: University of Toronto Press, 2006) 58; Antonia Maioni & Christopher Manfredi, "When the Charter Trumps Health Care — A Collision of Canadian Icons" (2005) 26:7 Policy Options 52; Colleen Flood, "*Chaoulli*'s Legacy for the Future of Health Care Policy" (2006) 44 Osgoode Hall L.J. 273; Martha Jackman, "The Last Line of Defence for [Which?] Citizens" (2006) 44 Osgoode Hall L.J. 349-375; Colleen Flood & Sujith Xavier, "Health Care Rights in Canada: The *Chaoulli* Legacy" (2008) 27 Med. & L. 617-644.

[171] See Peter Russell, "*Chaoulli*: The Political versus the Legal Life of a Judicial Decision" and Bernard Dickens, "The *Chaoulli* Decision: Less than Meets the Eye — or More?" in Colleen M. Flood, Kent Roach & Lorne Sossin, eds., *Access to Care, Access to Justice: The Legal Debate Over Private Health Insurance in Canada* (Toronto: University of Toronto Press, 2005) at 5 and 19, respectively.

was clearly premised on the legitimacy of state action to protect the integrity of the public system by controlling the growth of a competing private system. It therefore seems very likely that in future cases, where the challenge may be to these other measures, Deschamps J. would join the dissenting justices (Binnie, LeBel and Fish JJ.) in upholding them. In fact, her *Chaoulli* opinion suggests that she might, like them, be more likely to uphold these measures the stronger the evidence of their effectiveness is in preventing the growth of a parallel private system.

But even if *Chaoulli* does indeed put all legislative restraints on private medicine at risk, this does not necessarily spell the end of Canadian Medicare. Private medicine has never been illegal in Canada. The most that the law has done is to discourage its growth by making it difficult, uncertain or uneconomic. It may be true that the historically slow pace at which private medicine has grown shows that these soft limitations have been very effective,[172] but there is no way to tell. It seems equally plausible that the real explanation for the limited growth of private medicine has been that Medicare has, for most of its history, offered a deal to Canadians (and to Canadian doctors) that private medicine could not match. The early history of Medicare would seem to support this explanation.[173] Even when governments were forced (as in Saskatchewan) to tolerate, or tried mightily (as in the other western provinces) to preserve room for a parallel private system, the private alternative soon withered due to its inability to compete.

Thus, if *Chaoulli* is an attack on Medicare, it is an attack on an ancillary element, not the essential core. Accordingly, a proportionate response, like the original response to the original resistance to Medicare, would focus primarily on the capacity of the public system to provide Canadians with consistently dependable access within reasonable time frames to quality care. As to whether or not governments can pull this off, the key question is probably not going to be whether or not they will be prevented from doing so by judicial intermeddling. Instead, the question is more likely to be whether governments have the capacity to make Medicare as successful in the 21st century as it was for most of the late 20th century, when public funds were perceived to be more unlimited, medicine was more simple and expectations more modest.

Having said all that, *Chaoulli* is surely a milestone in the involvement of law and our judiciary in the ongoing development of our health care system. It establishes that, in the age of the Charter, health care policy is no more immune than any other area of public policy from the pervasive influence of Canada's shift from a constitutional order based unequivocally on legislative supremacy to one based on entrenched individual rights. In consequence, the right of Canadi-

---

[172] C.M. Flood & T. Archibald, "The Illegality of Private Health Care in Canada" (2001) 164 CMAJ 825.

[173] Greg Marchildon, "Private Insurance for Medicare: Policy History and Trajectory in the Four Western Provinces" in Colleen M. Flood, Kent Roach & Lorne Sossin, eds., *Access to Care, Access to Justice: The Legal Debate Over Private Health Insurance in Canada* (Toronto: University of Toronto Press, 2005) 429.

ans to health care is in the process of transitioning from a right that is defined by governments through their legislative and administrative processes to a right that Canadians will be able, still to an uncertain extent, to demand from governments through the adjudicative process.

Whatever else this may mean, it certainly means a new kind of accountability that requires governments to explain the rationale for their legislative and policy choices to the overseeing courts. It is therefore critical that the policy response take the case seriously because the outcome in future cases will partly depend on what governments do — or do not do — in response to *Chaoulli*. The court's adjudication of future cases could depend on whether it comes to understand (as some of the judges seemed not to understand) that the elimination of all waiting is probably not a reasonable or desirable objective. The credibility with which governments can provide this education to the court will partly depend on the success they can demonstrate in documenting and eliminating the truly unreasonable wait times that undoubtedly do exist.

Accountability is also at issue in *Auton*. But there, the Supreme Court possibly does not go far enough in reinforcing the accountability on governments and legislatures to base their decisions on sound evidence and on equal concern for the health and well-being of all citizens. From a policy perspective, the outcome in *Auton* respects the difficulty governments unquestionably face in funding a health care system characterized by escalating costs while preserving fiscal capacity to address other public policy priorities. For some, it is an outcome that might also be supported by the lack of evidence for the efficacy of the particular autism treatment that was at issue in *Auton*. This argument, heavily relied upon by British Columbia, was very influential with the court, which grouped Lovaas therapy together with other "novel" therapies that were "emergent and only recently becoming recognized as medically required".[174] On this view, the facts of *Auton* demonstrate why questions about the scope of Medicare need to be decided within Medicare where clinical criteria can be appropriately evaluated and applied.

Scepticism about Lovaas treatment may be valid. But it needs to be remembered that similar criticism can be directed at the various services that are provided by doctors and hospitals. Yet, law requires those services to be publicly funded largely because they are offered by physicians or in hospitals. In con-

---

[174] Donna Greschner & Steven Lewis, "*Auton* and Evidence-Based Decision-Making: Medicare in the Courts" (2003) 82 Can. Bar Rev. 501-534. See also Donna Greschner, "*Charter* Challenges and Evidence-Based Decision-Making in the Health Care System: Towards a Symbiotic Relationship" in Colleen M. Flood, ed., *Just Medicare: What's In, What's Out, How We Decide* (Toronto: University of Toronto Press, 2006) 42. For a broader consideration of the role of courts as health system policy-makers, see Christopher P. Manfredi & Antonia Maioni, "Courts and Health Policy: Judicial Policy Making and Publicly Funded Health Care in Canada" (2002) 27 J. Health Pol. 213 and Christopher P. Manfredi, "Déjà Vu All Over Again: *Chaoulli* and the Limits of Judicial Policy-making" in Colleen M. Flood, Kent Roach & Lorne Sossin, eds., *Access to Care, Access to Justice: The Legal Debate Over Private Health Insurance in Canada* (Toronto: University of Toronto Press, 2005) 139.

trast, British Columbia, and every other province, deals on a more individualized basis with health care services provided outside hospitals by other providers (including the therapists who provide Lovaas treatment). Some are funded and some are not. This can depend on relatively objective factors such as the availability of resources, the supporting therapeutic evidence and the understood nature of the need. But, it can also depend on more subjective factors such as the perceived credibility of the providers or therapy and the nature and extent of power (or of powerlessness) of the requesting group. Either way, the decision for or against funding is likely to have a certain "black box" quality. The decision would not, as it appears not to have in *Auton*, flow from a decision-making process that is laid out in law. Instead, as in *Auton*, such decisions are often made within and between bureaucracies, with uneven and uncertain participation by affected and interested persons.

Even if the final outcome in *Auton* is the right one because it leaves policy questions to governments and legislatures, the sheer breadth of the latitude that it leaves to governments (not only in health care but more broadly as well) is questionable. More demanding scrutiny under section 15 would impose a higher standard of accountability to at least validate that decisions on funding that are potentially discriminatory are indeed based on genuine concerns about clinical efficacy. This would provide greater protection for people, such as those living with autism, against the risk of having their needs ignored due to the institutionalized priority that is given to the needs of those who (for the most part) only require periodic attention during episodic periods of illness. Instead, what *Auton* arguably does is extend this institutionalized preference from the *Canada Health Act* and parallel provincial statutes into constitutional law.

The point here is to illustrate through *Auton* how the legal compartmentalization of our health care system obscures the nature of the premises and assumptions on which we implicitly rely when we make choices about (for example) funding for treatments that are outside the scope of Medicare. These include a premise that medicine is generally superior to other responses to illness, suffering and disability; that curing is more important than caring (as well as prevention); that dealing with the episodic illness of the healthy is more important than dealing with chronic illness and disability; and that physical health takes priority over other dimensions of health, including mental health. Seen in this broader light, the *Auton* case is a manifestation of a decision-making dynamic that cuts across the Canadian health care system. As with Lovaas therapy, the question of public funding for drugs taken outside hospitals, for care received in the home, for long-term care, for palliative and hospice care, and for various forms of established and emerging therapy is decided by each province and outside the constraining influence of national standards or principles. In contrast, the funding of physician and hospital services is largely treated as decided by virtue of their status as "insured services" that fall under the protective framework of the *Canada Health Act*. Under *Auton*, this institutionalized asymmetry seems destined to remain largely outside of judicial scrutiny.

There is a legitimate concern that judicially imposed accountability will unavoidably focus attention on specific circumstances instead of general conditions and give more importance to the rights of individuals than to collective interests. *Chaoulli* gives considerable weight to these concerns. But, on the other hand, the opportunity that was missed in *Auton* perhaps suggests that there is also something to be said for an accountability that is unavoidable and that focuses attention on the impact on individual citizens of macro-level decision-making, especially given the tendency to "black box" decision-making in Canadian health care.

IV. DIRECTIONS IN HEALTH SYSTEMS GOVERNANCE

The past decade has been a decade of significant change in the governance framework of the Canadian health care system, at both the national and the provincial/territorial levels. There is much diversity and some contradiction in the direction and nature of this change. For example, as already noted, some provinces have abandoned regionalization or greatly centralized authority within regionalization while others have retained regionalization in its decentralized form. Quebec has liberalized its rules on private health care insurance, but Ontario has strengthened the inhibitions it places on private payment medicine. Nevertheless, some broad patterns of commonality can be observed.

One is the increased attention in health system governance to the performance and therefore the management of the delivery system. The search for "value for money" or for a high performing health care system, and for the policies, structures and mechanisms that will achieve them have become a dominant governance theme that embraces the search for sustainability, the battle against waiting, access to emergency care, patient safety, patient-centered care and so on.[175] In some contexts, this has meant an expansion of the direct involvement of governments in the delivery system. In others, it has meant the delegation of governance functions related to managerial performance to new arm's-length agencies. But, in both manifestations, it has meant government providing much of the directional leadership and shouldering much of the accountability for the quality of essentially managerial work that regionalization was supposed to have delegated to health regions or districts or (in Ontario) local integration networks.

A related pattern of commonality is in the development of health care's institutional framework. Governments are establishing new types of agencies and additional layers of governance that generally function with a system-wide mandate and that intersect with lines of authority that operate inside buildings, regions or sectors (*i.e.*, primary, acute or continuing care). These do many different kinds of things; some manage, others coordinate and enable, and still

---

[175] See Health Council of Canada, "Value for Money: Making Canadian Health Care Stronger" (Toronto: February 2009), online at: <http://www2.infoway-inforoute.ca/Documents/HCC_VFMReport_WEB.pdf> and Ontario Health Quality Council (2007) "QMonitor: 2007 Report on Ontario's Health System" (Toronto: 2007) 3-13 and 67-75, online at: <http://www.ohqc.ca/pdfs/final_ohqc_report_2007.pdf>.

others provide oversight and accountability. The common feature is that they reflect a general understanding that the governance and institutional framework needed for high-performing health care requires more than an optimal division of responsibilities between government and regions or a simple and all-encompassing choice between centralized and decentralized managerial structures.

The theme of institutional development relates to a third pattern that can be discerned — the growing reliance on processes that seek to drive change in policy-making, and in managerial and clinical practice through accountability regimes. More specifically, there is growing reliance on institutions and processes that seek to enhance accountability by creating institutional separation between the accountability process and the functions and activities to which accountability applies. In this sense, it can be said that Canadian health system governance appears to be headed in a more regulatory direction, perhaps following the path established by other public health systems, such as that of the United Kingdom, that have gone farther in this direction.

A.   NATIONAL HEALTH SYSTEM GOVERNANCE

Intergovernmental conferences resulted in health accords between the federal government and the provinces and territories in 2000, 2003 and 2004. Each committed the federal government to substantially increasing the transfers it would make over the life of each accord to the general revenues of the provinces and territories in respect of health care. Both the 2000 and the 2003 Accords covered five years, whereas the more ambitious 2004 Accord covered 10 (2004–2014). As already discussed, the cumulative impact of these increases has gone some way to restoring the financial partnership between Ottawa and the provinces that made Medicare possible. In addition, each of the accords committed the federal government to more targeted funding of specific priorities. For example, in the 2003 Accord the federal government agreed to create the Health Reform Fund, worth $16 billion over five years, to fund provincial efforts in the reform of primary care and in wait time reduction. In the 2004 Accord, it agreed to create a Wait Times Reduction Fund, worth $4.5 billion over six years.

In exchange for increases in federal funding, the provinces can be said to have agreed, with increasing explicitness, on both the need for health care reform and their accountability to make it happen. In the 2000 Accord, they did so only in very general terms. In the 2003 and 2004 Accords, the provinces agreed to the need for specific action in specific areas, including improved access to reformed primary care through interprofessional teams, expanded access to acute care home care and improved catastrophic drug coverage. They also agreed, in both Accords, on the need for action to address wait times. In all these respects however, the commitments made were to provincial voters, not to the federal government.

Within this general pattern, the 2004 Accord was by far the most significant and ambitious document. It committed governments to the development of a national pharmaceuticals strategy, with a report on progress by June 30, 2006; to first dollar coverage for all Canadians of certain home care services, again by 2006; to 24/7 access to primary care through interprofessional teams by 50 per cent of Canadians by 2011; to ensuring that 50 per cent of Canadians have an electronic health record by 2010; and to the development (by December 31, 2005) and implementation (by March 2007) of evidence-based benchmarks for medically acceptable wait times for joint replacement, sight restoration (cataracts removal), diagnostic imaging, and cancer and cardiac care.

For the federal government, the 2004 Accord was, like the 2003 Accord, about the implementation of the recommendations of the Romanow Commission. It was an attempt to "buy change". But, despite the bold claim of Prime Minister Martin that the Accord was "the fix for a generation", the 2004 Accord shared the same fundamental limitation of the earlier and more modest efforts. It was a political accord that was not legally binding on the governments that negotiated it. This reflects the basic fact that Canada's decentralized federalism — under which each level of government is as sovereign as the other in its own jurisdictional sphere — was the point of departure for the Accord and its predecessors.

So as law, the 2004 Accord was, like the other Accords, only "soft" law. Moreover, it is asymmetrical soft law that contains demanding and specific commitments to funding from the federal government in exchange for more general commitments from the provinces to use the money to make the system better. This reflects the surrounding dynamics of the negotiations: the pervasive concern to avoid the triggering of national unity debates; the limited leverage of the federal government after decades of retrenchment from the equal financial partnership originally promised in the 1960s; and the political weakness of the Martin government due to its minority government status. It probably also reflects a federal unwillingness to accept the responsibility for holding the provinces accountable to hard obligations, which is roughly commensurate with the provincial resistance to the very notion of such accountability.

Indeed, the commitments contained in the Accords only become legally binding to the extent that the level of government to which they apply enacts them into law through its own legislative process. Parliament has done so with all of the federal funding commitments, as indeed it was required to do so before money could flow to the provinces. But the commitments given by the provinces have not been incorporated into provincial legislation. This no doubt reflects their diffuse nature and the fact that it is easier to legislate funding levels than it is to legislate reductions in wait times or the availability of primary care from interprofessional teams. Clearly, the hope of the federal government was that the very making of commitments in legally sounding "accords" would invest the accords, especially the 2004 Accord, with some of the normative weight that they lacked as mere political agreements that relied on loosely coordinated effort across 14 independent jurisdictions. More concretely, the federal government relied on the general mandate that both the 2003 and 2004 Accords gave to the Health Council of Canada (created under the 2003 Accord) to monitor and report on accord implementation, and on the more specific mandate that the 2004 Accord gave to the Canadian Institute of Health Information (CIHI) to track and report on provincial and territorial progress in meeting waiting times benchmarks. To reinforce this informational regulation, the 2004 Accord stated that all funding arrangements required provinces to report the data on which the mandates of the CIHI and the Health Council depended. In these respects, the 2003 and 2004 Accords contributed to the further development of a national governance framework for the health care system that included the Canadian Blood Agency, the Public Health Agency of Canada, the Canadian Patient Safety Institute (created under the 2003 Accord), the Canadian Mental Health Commission, and the process for avoiding and resolving disputes under the *Canada Health Act* (originally established by an exchange of letters between ministers of health in 2002, but "formalized" by the 2004 Accord).[176]

Initial optimism about what the 2004 Accord might accomplish has largely turned to disappointment and concern that massive increases in federal funding have bought peace but not much, or enough, change. The qualified nature of the progress on waiting times in targeted areas has been discussed above. Meanwhile, there is concern about the extent to which other waiting times, including those affecting vulnerable populations such as young people living with mental illness, have persisted or worsened. The story on other promised improvements is worse. The National Pharmaceuticals Strategy has never materialized and interprovincial variation on the accessibility of home care continues to prevail. Progress on the availability of interprofessional primary care teams has moved ahead, particularly in some provinces, but Canada as a whole seems still to lag behind comparator countries on the accessibility and continuity of primary care. Meanwhile, the broader promise of continuing intergovernmental work on a more accountable health care system seems to have been delegated by default back to the provinces. In its 2008 report, the Health Council of Canada cited nine areas of health care renewal where "action has been slower, less comprehensive, and less collaborative than First Ministers originally envisaged in their 2003 Accord".[177] More specifically, noting the discontinuation of the intergovernmental committee that was mandated by the 2003 Accord to work on accountability, the Council concluded that "Information about how governments spend targeted funds is not easily accessible or, in some cases, not available at all".[178] Somewhat ironically, the Health Council now seems to have redirected its efforts away from monitoring and reporting on implementation of the 2004 Accord and towards the more innocuous role of supporting "the pursuit of a sus-

---

[176] The Health Canada description of the process, as well as the letter that was sent to provincial ministers of health by the federal minister in 2002, can be found online at: <http://www.hc-sc.gc.ca/hcs-sss/pubs/cha-lcs/2008-cha-lcs-ar-ra/page3-eng.php#AnC>. The Province of Quebec is not a party to this dispute resolution process.

[177] Health Council of Canada, *Rekindling Reform: Health Care Renewal in Canada, 2003-2008* (Toronto: 2008) at 34-37, online at: <http://www.healthcouncilcanada.ca/docs/rpts/2008/HCC%205YRPLAN%20(WEB)_FA.pdf>.

[178] *Ibid.*, at 35.

tainable and high-performing health care system that recognizes its role in improving the health of Canadians".[179] The Council says this means improving public understanding of sustainable high-performance, supporting the health care community, and monitoring and reporting "on successes and challenges in achieving a sustainable high-performing health care system".[180] In short, the Council, which was never very threatening to governments in the first place, has been largely domesticated.

These developments set the stage for the intergovernmental negotiations that are anticipated as the expiry of the 2004 Accord in 2014 approaches. As always, much of the focus will be on funding adequacy and stability. But, from a governance perspective, it is clear, based on experience, that much of the attention needs to be on mechanisms that will ensure effective utilization of resources to make the system better. The soft law model applied in 2004 — money for commitment to broad objectives under gentle informational accountability — clearly needs reconsideration. The model might have been more strongly implemented by a federal government that was more inclined than the Harper government has been since its election in 2005 to view health care as a realm of federal concern. Nevertheless, experience under the 2003 and 2004 Accords demonstrates the wisdom of the recommendation of Romanow (and of the Kirby Committee) for a stronger health council and a more robust accountability process than was agreed to by governments in 2003 or 2004.[181] More fundamentally, it demonstrates the rationale for Romanow's recommendation to add a principle on accountability to the *Canada Health Act*.[182] This would make increased federal cash transfers conditional on the action of provincial governments to strengthen their own accountability and that of their health care systems.

Yet, as pointed out above, the federal government has never withheld funding for violation of any of the existing principles of the Act. Even if the federal government had been willing to pay the price in its relations with the provinces that adding accountability to the Act would have entailed, it seems unlikely that the new principle would have been enforced any more rigorously than the existing principles. Thus, experience under the 2004 Accord may actually show that measures even stronger than those recommended by Romanow are needed. For example, it may confirm that real intergovernmental accountability depends, as Flood and Choudhry argued, on the transfer of much of the monitoring and evaluation work that the *Canada Health Act* assigns to Health Canada to arm's-

---

[179] Health Council of Canada, *Strategic Plan 2008/2009 – 2012/2013: Taking the Pulse Toward Improved Health and Health Care in Canada* (Toronto: 2008) at 7, online: <http://www. healthcouncilcanada.ca/docs/rpts/2008/HCCStratplan2008to2013.pdf>.

[180] *Ibid.*

[181] Roy J. Romanow, Q.C., *Building on Values: The Future of Health Care in Canada – Final Report* (Ottawa: Commission on the Future of Health Care in Canada, 2002) 45-59.

[182] *Ibid.*, at 59-65.

length institutions that would be independent from, but accountable to, both levels of government.[183]

The need for independent institutions may go beyond the intergovernmental level. Although improvement through strengthened accountability is often equated with the accountability of governments, the reality is that provincial governments are constrained in their ability to achieve health care reform through their direct management of the delivery system. The reasons include their inherent weakness as managers and the inherent complexity of management (relative to other directional forces) in the health care system. Accountability therefore needs to be cast more broadly, encompassing the organizations, managers, providers and networks that determine the functioning of the delivery system from the ground up.[184] But, provincial governments are also constrained in their ability to apply this accountability with consistency and dependability, including by their level of interest and implication in the decision-making and conduct to which the accountability must be applied. This argues for a second level of arm's-length institutions focused on accountability *within* provincial health care systems. Indeed, the argument of Flood and Choudhry is that the creation and demonstrated effectiveness of such institutions should be a core element of provincial accountability at the intergovernmental level.

Of course, it is easy to say that since the Romanow recommendations did not fly in 2003 or 2004 (when federal finances were very strong), these more ambitious proposals are unlikely to be realistic in 2014 (when federal finances will still be recovering from recession), particularly if the federal government maintains its disinterest in governance of health care from the centre. On the other hand, the national institutional framework that now exists would have seemed unrealistic in the middle of the fractious federal-provincial health care relations of the 1990s. At a minimum, the existence of this framework establishes the point that there is a place for national institutions that function outside of government and that use that independence to support and to push the efforts of governments and, more indirectly, of the broader health care system, to achieve health care reform. In this context it may not be unreasonable to think that future negotiations might develop this institutional framework in directions that will strengthen its capacity to more strongly insist on accountability for implementation of politically determined policy commitments, thereby contributing to more effective governance at the national, intergovernmental, provincial and system levels.

---

[183] Colleen M. Flood & Sujit Choudhry, "Strengthening the Foundations: Modernizing the Canada Health Act" in Tom McIntosh, Pierre-Gerlier Forest & Gregory P. Marchildon, eds., *The Governance of Health Care in Canada: Romanow Papers, Volume 3* (Toronto: University of Toronto Press, 2004) 346.

[184] William Lahey, "New Governance Regulation and Managerial Accountability for Performance in Canada's Health Care Systems" in Robert P. Kouri & Catherine Régis, eds., *Grand Challenges in Health Law and Policy* (Cowansville, QC: Éditions Yvon Blais, 2010) 243-78.

B.   PROVINCIAL HEALTH SYSTEM GOVERNANCE

National health system governance is important. But the governance that matters most to health system performance happens in the provinces and territories. That is the level at which governance must grapple directly with the tension that exists between the need to manage costs, to meet or manage public expectations, to harness or counteract provider influence, and to marshal and apply evolving knowledge of the best methodologies to ensure dependable delivery of high-quality health care to patients. There are many examples of how all this is done successfully in particular institutions, in particular localities, between particular groups of providers or in certain clinical programs at varying geographic scales. The governance question is how to enable and, where necessary, require wider replication of these successes and extension of the best practices on which they are based in other opportunities for performance improvement.[185]

Provincial and territorial governments and health care systems are taking a far greater variety of approaches to this question than can be reviewed here. One general area receiving attention is the flexibility that the single-payer system offers on two key questions: who is funded to provide service and how they are funded to provide service. As noted above, there is a growing openness to the contracting of the delivery of specific services to private clinics that occupy a space between the traditional for-profit doctors' office and the not-for-profit and publicly governed hospital. Adopting an idea that the Kirby Committee recommended and that others such as the Canadian Medical Association have advocated, British Columbia is implementing a funding system for hospitals and private clinics under which funding will no longer determine the number of procedures performed, but will instead be determined *by* the number of procedures performed.[186] The goal is to create incentives for efficiency. Meanwhile, alternatives to the traditional fee-for-service compensation model for doctors that go somewhat in the opposite direction are now widely in place, particularly in primary care. Increasingly, these are linked to efforts to organize doctors and other primary care providers into interprofessional teams. They generally seek to give doctors incentives to spend time with patients, to assist patients in managing their chronic conditions, to provide health promoting advice and to assist patients in navigating the wider system.

At the same time, provincial and territorial governance is giving increased emphasis to centralized direction in the organization and management of the delivery of health care services. Sometimes, this either means or comes close to meaning direction from provincial ministries of health. As mentioned already, Prince Edward Island has abandoned regionalization while New Brunswick and Alberta have opted for more centralized versions of regionalization. In Prince

---

[185] See, for example, Brian Hutchinson, Julia Abelson & John Lavis, "Primary Care in Canada: So Much Innovation, So Little Change" (2001) 20:3 Health Affairs 116.

[186] British Columbia, Ministry of Health Services, News Release, "B.C. Launches Patient-Focused Funding Provincewide" (April 12, 2010), online: <http://www2.news.gov.bc.ca/news_releases _2009-2013/2010HSERV0020-000403.htm>.

Edward Island, managerial responsibilities have been repatriated to government and the same has happened in New Brunswick for non-clinical functions. In Alberta, regional health boards that were governed on behalf of local communities have been replaced by the province-wide board that governs Alberta Health Services. No doubt this Board functions independently of Alberta Health. But, unlike its predecessors, it does so with only one line of accountability to citizens, which is through Alberta's Minister of Health. In some of the provinces where managerial responsibilities are being left with regional boards, ministries of health are not only providing oversight but also direction as to how those responsibilities are to be discharged. Examples include Saskatchewan's province-wide adoption of the Lean approach to organizational and program management and Nova Scotia's development of a province-wide "models of care" framework.[187]

The assertion of significant managerial authority from the centre is more widely seen in the range of initiatives that have been implemented across the country to track and manage waiting times. Now, all provinces centrally track and report on waiting times.[188] Most have a range of initiatives under way to ensure effective management of waiting times, often through centralized processes that wield the authority that previously belonged solely to institutions or regions. In Ontario, these include the creation of a province-wide "Wait Time Strategy" that monitors and directs local waiting time reduction efforts. As already discussed, in Quebec this includes legislation that imposes wait time management duties on local and regional units of the health care system and that empowers the Minister of Health to supervise the implementation of those duties and, assume direct control of particular waiting times when they exceed the standards defined by government. Much can legitimately be made of the fact that the Ontario approach functions within strengthened legislative restrictions on private medicine, whereas Quebec's legislation now contemplates the reduction or avoidance of wait times by the purchase of services from private clinics in a province where the law has been liberalized to allow private health insurance that overlaps with public insurance. But, these differences function within a broader commonality: both provinces have instituted a legislative framework that acknowledges waiting times as a government policy priority that is too important to be left to the persons or institutions who have general responsibility for operational management. This perhaps reflects an interesting implication of the 2003 and 2004 Accords; that they confirmed provincial and territorial gov-

---

[187] Saskatchewan, Ministry of Health, *09-10 Annual Report* (Regina: 2010) 12, online: <http://www.finance.gov.sk.ca/PlanningAndReporting/2009-10/200910HealthAnnualReport.pdf>; Nova Scotia, Department of Health, "Nova Scotia's New Collaborative Care Model: What it Means for You" (Halifax: Province of Nova Scotia Health Transformation: A Partnership of the Department of Health, District Health Authorities and the IWK Health Centre, 2008), online at: <http://www.gov.ns.ca/health/MOCINS/MOCINS_What_it_Means_For_You.pdf>.

[188] Health Council of Canada, *Wading Through Wait Times: What Do Meaningful Reductions and Guarantees Mean?* (Toronto: 2007).

ernment accountability for the effectiveness of management in their largely devolved health care systems.

The tendency towards centralized direction does not always mean increased instruction directly from government. Especially in the larger provinces, governments are delegating a range of policy-making, managerial and oversight functions to specialized agencies that operate at arm's-length from government and from the organizations to which more generic responsibility for the management of health care have been delegated. For example, multiple provinces have handed province-wide coordination and management of cancer care to specialized bodies that function as a layer of clinical governance that cuts across the boundaries that define regions or that divide primary, acute and continuing care into distinct sectors of care. A provincial disease management model has also been applied to cardiac care (for example, in Ontario and Nova Scotia) and to orthopaedic care (for example, in Alberta). Similarly, the development, management and governance of health information systems have generally been handed to specialized agencies with province-wide and (to some extent) multi-sector mandates.

These examples reflect the complex realities of health care, where factors such as increasing clinical specialization, technological complexity, interprofessional interdependency and the growing population of patients living with chronic disease, all make horizontal governance at least as important as governance within the component units of the system. In other words, they reflect the need for integration and for governance mechanisms that can make it happen. They may also reflect public expectations of the governmental accountability for effective management of the system as a whole that the enthusiasm of the 1990s for regionalized governance may have overlooked or ignored. Whether driven by the need for integration or public demands for performance, the growing use of specialized agencies that provide horizontal governance in priority functions can be said to take advantage of the opportunity that Medicare creates for this kind of governance, precisely because of the comprehensive mandate it implies for the state (in contrast to the residual role that is reserved for the state under the American model).

Provincial governance frameworks are also undergoing change and development designed to strengthen the accountability of those to whom managerial and clinical functions are assigned, however the scope of their mandate is defined. Sometimes this is through delegation of accountability functions to arm's-length agencies. Examples include the creation of quality councils in at least six provinces,[189] the institution of a multi-layered complaint process under the

---

[189] These provinces include Ontario, Saskatchewan, Alberta and New Brunswick. See *Commitment to the Future of Medicare Act, 2004*, S.O. 2004, c. 5, ss. 1-8, as amended by *Excellent Care for All Act, 2010*, S.O. 2010, c. 14, ss. 10-13; *Health Quality Council Act*, S.S. 2002, c. H-0.04; Health Quality Council of Alberta Regulation, Alta. Reg. 130/2006; *Health Council Act*, S.N.B. 2008, c. N-5.105.

authority of the Office of the Ombudsman in Quebec,[190] and the creation of a patient safety agency in British Columbia to oversee the creation and function of a province-wide system of complaint processes at the institutional and regional levels.[191] Another approach is exhibited by the recent Ontario legislation, discussed earlier, that imposes a duty on health care organizations to develop and implement annual quality improvement plans, and to tie the compensation of their Chief Executive Officer to the success of these plans in achieving their objectives.

Provincial governance is heading — or being pulled — in this direction partly by the confidence that is pervasive in policy circles that enhanced accountability will mean improved and more consistent performance. More specifically, it is being pushed in this direction by the growing concern for patient safety and quality more broadly. More processes of external oversight and accountability are likely to be promoted and supported as both research and tragic events continue to increase public and official awareness of the consequences for vulnerable patients of ineffective management and oversight of care. This trend may be reinforced by the tendency of *post hoc* inquiries, in Canada and elsewhere, to conclude that adverse consequences arise from systemic problems that internal management or self-regulation did not identify or address. These problems have adverse consequences beyond the threat they pose to safety. This therefore means either that improvements in safety can improve overall performance or that safety can be improved by broader attention to the determinants of quality and high performance more generally. Either way, both the need and the demand for accountability mechanisms that ensure external oversight of managerial and clinical processes is likely to increase as Canadian governments continue to tolerate the operation of for-profit clinics, purchase more Medicare services from for-profit clinics, and adopt funding approaches for public hospitals that are of a broadly commercial nature.

The further driver for accountability that is more rigorous, in part because it is applied by dedicated and independent agencies, may be the example of other countries that have gone farther than Canada in both performance-based financ-

---

[190] For an overview of the jurisdiction of the Office, see Le Protecteur du citoyen : Assemblée nationale Québec, "Health and Social Services Network Agencies and Authorities", online at: <http://www.protecteurducitoyen.qc.ca/en/filing-a-complaint/concerning-the-health-and-social-services-network/index.html>.

[191] British Columbia, Ministry of Health Services, News Release, "B.C. Launches Patient Care Review Process" (October 21, 2008), online at: <http://www2.news.gov.bc.ca/news_releases_2005-2009/2008HSERV0097-001594.pdf>; British Columbia, Ministry of Health, "Patient Care Quality Review Boards", online at: <http://www.patientcarequalityreviewboard.ca/>; *Patient Care Quality Review Board Act*, S.B.C. 2008, c. 35. Meanwhile, in Nova Scotia and more dramatically in Ontario, provincial ombudsmen have started to exercise their jurisdictions to investigate and make recommendations on allegations of maladministration in publicly funded health care; see, for example, André Marin, Ombudsman of Ontario, *The LHIN Spin: Investigation into the Niagara Haldimand Brant Local Health Integration Network's Use of Community Engagement in Its Decision-making Process* (August 2010), online: <http://www.ombudsman.on.ca/media/151950/lhinreport-en.pdf>.

ing and in third party oversight. The experience of England's National Health Service (NHS) stands out. Through the 1970s and 1980s, it personified the association of public health care with poor health care, providing a level of service into the 1990s that Canadians would probably never have tolerated. Now, at least according to the Commonwealth Fund, it is a system that outperforms the Canadian system on many metrics of quality, including equity of access. The fact that the United Kingdom now spends much more on health than it did historically undoubtedly explains part of the change. But, the United Kingdom still spends much less as a percentage of GDP or per capita than Canada does. What the United Kingdom has done much more extensively than Canada is to leverage performance (or at least efficiency) with funding while applying a comprehensive framework of external accountability to the delivery component of the NHS. This framework includes institutions that are responsible for the kind of general system-level oversight that is provided (to some extent) by Canadian quality councils. But, it also includes institutions that bring accountability to bear on specific NHS players through league tables, strengthened and expanded patient complaint processes, and processes of independent inspection and audit that are increasingly guided by independently established standards on clinical and managerial practice.

In a word, the NHS has used regulation by independent agencies, as well as financial and organizational restructuring, to drive change and improvement. The same can be said in some degree of other countries, like New Zealand, that also outperform Canada in Commonwealth Fund comparisons. In the United Kingdom, New Zealand and various Australian states, a core institution in the accountability framework is a variously named health care commission that has a broad jurisdiction to take complaints on the service that people receive (or do not receive) and (in the United Kingdom at least) to conduct broadly gauged audits and inspections.[192] In this regard, it is worth note that Alberta has passed (but not yet proclaimed) the *Alberta Health Act* that, along with confirming Alberta's commitment to the *Canada Health Act*, calls for the adoption of a "Health Charter" and the appointment of a "health advocate" who would have the role, among others, of determining complaints of non-compliance with that charter.[193]

V.   CONCLUSION

This overview of the Canadian health care system has concentrated on the design and functioning of the legal framework that created and that governs the

---

[192] An overview of the Australian commissions is found in Fiona McDonald, "Chapter 15: The Regulation of Health Professionals" in Ben White, Fiona McDonald & Lindy Willmott, *Health Law in Australia* (Sydney: Thomson Reuters, 2010) 547-48.

[193] Minister's Advisory Committee on Health, "Putting People First: Part One – Recommendations for an *Alberta Health Act*" (Edmonton: September 2010), online at: <http://www.health.alberta.ca/documents/Alberta-Health-Act-Report-2010.pdf>; *Alberta Health Act*, S.A. 2010, c. A-19.5 [not yet in force].

single-payer system that is the core of Canada's quasi-national health care system. It has tried to develop some larger themes that can provide the basis for the critical evaluation of the system's current structure and performance, the growing role of the courts as arbiters and perhaps makers of health system policy, and evolving approaches to governance at the national and the provincial levels.

One of these themes is the role of law, legal institutions and legal ideas in shaping the uneven success of the system in delivering access to quality health care services. The chapter has tried to show how federal and provincial law work together to provide all Canadians with "no questions asked" access to most doctor and hospital services, without regard to their ability to pay and with minimal intrusion into the physician-patient relationship. This happens against the backdrop of the division of responsibilities that are created by the 1867 Constitution. The federal-provincial bickering that is produced by this division of responsibilities gets most of the attention, for understandable reasons. But a more balanced picture would include the positive impact that Canada's federalism has had, and continues to have, on the Canadian health care system. This includes the very existence of Medicare and the continuing potential of a "system of systems" to generate innovation and experimentation that might not be possible in a more monolithic public system. New national institutions, such as the Health Council for Canada, the Canadian Patient Safety Institute and the Canadian Institute for Health Information, can be regarded as limited by the restrictive parameters of Canada's federalism. Alternatively, they can be regarded as vehicles for encouraging and harnessing this potential for innovation and beneficial imitation.

At the same time, this chapter has explored how access is not addressed by the laws that define and govern the single-payer system. For example, the law does not provide Canadians with options for ensuring accountability from governments for effective and robust implementation of the *Canada Health Act* through government-to-government mechanisms. It does not provide much scope for citizen-initiated enforcement as an alternative mechanism for ensuring that system level action is taken to address systemic barriers to access. Canadian law provides only limited "safety valve" protection that would allow Canadians to take personal access difficulties to independent and accountable decision-makers who have the authority to implement case-specific solutions. Although administrative tribunals that provide this kind of personalized redress have been established in some provinces, citizens in other provinces are unduly dependent on bureaucratically internalized processes that lack transparency, accountability and independence of action.

This theme of the need for institutional development also emerges from the discussion of the access of Canadians to services that are not covered by the single-payer system. Canadians do not have adequate opportunities for participation in the fundamentally important decisions that are made about what physician and hospital services are in and out of the public system of universal health insurance. But the larger story is perhaps that they also do not have adequate opportunities for involvement with the decisions that are made about the extent and terms of public funding that is provided to address health needs that are not met by doctors and hospitals. These Canadians overwhelmingly belong to vulnerable groups who obviously benefit from Medicare as it is currently structured and legally protected. Yet, the chapter has suggested that the asymmetry of Canada's single-payer system can produce consequences that are inconsistent with the broader objective of the *Canada Health Act*, "to protect, promote and restore the physical and mental well-being of residents of Canada". This calls for an intensified attention to the question of essentiality, not only in relation to physician and hospital services, but more broadly as well. Broadened public engagement in these deliberative processes is called for by the values that underlie Medicare and by the values that infuse Canadian public law. In *Auton*, the Supreme Court may have missed an opportunity to encourage and structure this engagement.

Another theme to emerge is the closely related one of the extent and nature of government's involvement in, and responsibility for, the system and its performance. This chapter has suggested that the role of government in the Canadian system is in a period of transition. The implication to be drawn from the overall direction in Canadian health system governance, including from the imposed process of regionalization, is that provincial governments have assumed more direct responsibility for the system's organizational configuration, for mandating priorities and objectives, and for monitoring and evaluating performance. To some extent, they are doing so by establishing independent and specialized institutions to manage specific diseases (such as cancer), to monitor more pervasive problems (such as patient safety), or to be responsible for the general accountability of the system for quality and high and dependable performance. The direct involvement of governments in the management of waiting lists, pushed by the health accords, by *Chaoulli* and, more importantly, by voters, is an example of this.

At the same time however, physician autonomy both from government and from regional authorities has remained intact. One consequence is that the allocation of resources and thus the priorities of the system continue to be determined largely by physicians, notwithstanding all the talk of community empowerment through regional health authorities. From one direction, the concern is that this leaves the tendencies to cost-escalation that are produced under fee-for-service compensation undisturbed. From another direction, it causes concern that the system continues to emphasize the interests of particular patients in curative procedures and therapies over the broader interest of the community in preventive care. These dynamics push toward the rationale for greater management of physician clinical practice. But, this invites a counter-response that physician autonomy is as much a pillar of the Canadian system as is the government's responsibility for the costs; not only because this is, and has been, good for physicians. It is also because it gives freedom of choice to the patient and reassurance to the patient that medical advice is at least that, whatever else its deficiencies. At the same time, Canadians should appreciate that there is a cost to be paid for preserving this traditional level of physician autonomy, including the poor quality that derives from differences in clinical practice that are not supported by evidence. It may be a price worth paying, but whether it is or is not, it is important to recognize it is a price caused by how we have structured our publicly funded and publicly governed system, not by the decision to have a publicly funded and publicly governed system.

Finally, the chapter has explored how unresolved issues and the consequences of policy decisions are creating openings for the broader engagement of the courts with health care policy, guided primarily but not exclusively by the *Canadian Charter of Rights and Freedoms*. It is far too early in this process to confidently predict how far the courts will go or in what ways their intervention will change the system. Nevertheless, it does seem reasonable to regard recent cases as harbingers.

Whether one thinks this is a good thing or a bad thing will depend on many factors, including one's general opinions about what are and what are not appropriate matters for the courts, and one's level of confidence in the capacity of governments and other health systems actors to do what needs to be done to make Medicare effective and sustainable. It will depend on one's reading of *Auton* and of *Chaoulli* and of the response of governments to both decisions, but especially to the latter. While neither decision is satisfactory, the larger concern is with *Chaoulli*. The remedy given by the majority in that case is a remedy that could only make sense as one that would give wealthier Canadians preferential access to medical care. This seems to rank individual liberty over collective equality, contrary to Canada's historic health care commitment to equal access based on need alone. Thus, Canadians are confronted with an apparent tension between the judicial understanding of Canadian values as manifested through the Charter and what has been the understanding of those values articulated by legislatures through the *Canada Health Act* and the provincial laws that make it operational. In some commentary, this is portrayed as a collision between the Charter and Canadian values as represented by Medicare. But the reality of the situation is more complex than that, for the attachment that Canadians have continuously expressed to the *Canada Health Act* as a symbol of their citizenship is more or less equally matched by the attachment they have demonstrated for the same reason to the Charter. What is at stake then is potentially something even larger than Canada's commitment to public health care. At stake is the understanding of collective values and their relationship to one another that makes a commitment to public health care possible and truly sustainable.

Chapter 2

REGULATION OF HEALTH CARE PROFESSIONALS

Tracey Epps

I. INTRODUCTION

Provincial and territorial governments in Canada delegate a large measure of responsibility for governance of health professionals to the professions themselves. This chapter explores how these self-regulatory regimes operate and considers the implications of the policy choice to delegate governance to members of the professions themselves. Section Two provides a general overview of regulation as a tool in the health care sector. Section Three examines the types of regulation that operate to govern health professionals, drawing a distinction between *input* regulation (who may be admitted to the profession) and *output* regulation (performance by those in the profession). Section Four looks at sources of regulation, paying particular attention to the predominant source of regulation in Canada, namely, self-regulation. Section Five provides an overview of current regulation of health professionals in Canada, while Section Six discusses how regulation of health professionals can help to achieve greater accessibility to health care services.

II. OVERVIEW OF REGULATION

The term "regulation" describes "any process or set of processes by which norms are established, the behaviour of those subject to the norms monitored or fed back into the regime, and for which there are mechanisms for holding the behaviour of regulated actors within the acceptable limits of the regime (whether by enforcement action or by some other mechanism)".[1] In the health sector, regulation is a tool that allows policy-makers to establish norms to which health professionals must adhere. For example, regulations may specify the scope of practice of a certain profession and establish standards of practice. Through regulation, legislators may also hold health professionals accountable for adhering to norms through mechanisms such as complaints and discipline procedures.

---

[1] C. Scott, "Analysing Regulatory Space: Fragmented Resources and Institutional Design" (2001) P.L. 329 at 331, cited in Bettina Lange, "Regulatory Spaces and Interactions: An Introduction" (2003) 12 Soc. & Leg. Stud. 411 at 411.

Regulatory intervention is considered necessary in the health sector in order to correct market failure arising from imperfect information and information asymmetries.[2] Health care markets are characterized by imperfect information due largely to uncertainty concerning the incidence of disease and the efficacy of treatment.[3] Information asymmetries arise between consumers and health professionals because consumers typically do not have the information needed to evaluate the competence of medical professionals, and the complexity of medical practice means that consumers are often unable to understand information they do have.[4]

Given that the consequences of error in the practice of medicine are high and potentially irreversible, regulatory intervention is also required to protect public safety by helping people make knowledgeable choices[5] and ensuring that professionals have the necessary qualifications and competencies.[6]

The professions themselves also receive benefits from regulation and, recognizing this, have long supported the legislation accordingly. In the United States, for example, the American Medical Association and its constituent state societies were proactive from the beginning in the development of professional licensure through which they hoped to eliminate competition from "unorthodox" schools of medicine.[7] Early supporters of licensure for the professions were also concerned with protecting trained medical practitioners from graduates of substandard medical institutions or from untrained lay healers.[8] As Jost notes, regulation of health professionals has, in this manner, served to maintain professional identity and orthodoxy, economic power, and social and educational elitism.[9]

Like any regulatory activity, the regulation of health professionals risks being captured by the demand of private interests.[10] This tendency can be seen in

---

[2]   See, generally, K.J. Arrow, "Uncertainty and the Welfare Economics of Medical Care" (1963) 53 American Economic Review 941 (making the presumption that health care markets will not reach a competitive equilibrium without non-market intervention).

[3]   *Ibid.*, at 941.

[4]   Margot Priest, "The Privatization of Regulation: Five Models of Self-Regulation" (1997-1998) 29 Ottawa L. Rev. 233 at 253.

[5]   *Ibid.*

[6]   Tim Jost, ed., *Regulation of Healthcare Professions* (Chicago: Health Administration Press, 1997) at 2. See also J. Lieberman, *The Tyranny of the Experts* (New York: Walker & Co., 1970) at 246. (Lieberman argues that "performance of some occupations without due regard for professional standards of technical competence could result in death, serious bodily injury, catastrophic destruction or deprivation of legal rights".) See also D. Irvine, "The Performance of Doctors: The New Professionalism" (1999) 353 The Lancet 1174 and A. Donabedian, "Evaluating Physician Competence" (2000) 78 Bulletin of the World Health Organization 857.

[7]   J.G. Burrow, *Organized Medicine in the Progressive Era: The Move Toward Monopoly* (Baltimore, MD: Johns Hopkins University Press, 1977), cited in Tim Jost, ed., *Regulation of Healthcare Professions* (Chicago: Health Administration Press, 1997) at 2.

[8]   *Ibid.*

[9]   *Ibid.*

[10] Robert Baldwin & Martin Cave, *Understanding Regulation: Theory, Strategy, and Practice* (New York: Oxford University Press, 1999) at 21.

the noted example of medical professions in the United States seeking to eliminate competition from "unorthodox" schools of medicine, as well as more recent cases of professions seeking to maintain control over their practice areas.[11] The American Society for Gastrointestinal Endoscopy and the American College of Gastroenterology undertook a national campaign in the early 1990s to convince hospitals that allowing family practitioners to perform endoscopies would be tantamount to condoning malpractice.[12] In Canada, dentists in Ontario opposed efforts by dental hygienists to obtain the right to practise independently. As Adams writes, this situation is explicable by the fact that dental hygienists cannot attain greater professional status and autonomy, except at the expense of the dental profession's own claims to status and jurisdiction.[13]

The possibility of capture by certain groups aside, legislative intent in Canada is that regulation of health professionals serves the public interest, a concept which may be seen as encompassing protection from harm, quality of care, accountability, accessibility, equity and equality.[14] In Ontario, a report prepared prior to the 1991 implementation of the *Regulated Health Professions Act, 1991*[15] (RHPA) recommended that:

> The important principle underlying each of the criteria [for regulation] is that the sole purpose of professional regulation is to advance and protect the public interest. The public is the intended beneficiary of regulation, not the members of the profession. Thus the purpose of granting self-regulation to a profession is not to enhance its status or to increase the earning power of its members by giving the profession a monopoly over the delivery of particular health services. Indeed, although these are common results of traditional regulatory models, they are undesirable results, and the model of regulation we recommend [the RHPA] aims to minimize them.[16]

Following these recommendations, Ontario's legislation was designed to advance the "public interest" in four ways: (1) protecting the public, to the extent possible, from unqualified, incompetent and unfit health care providers; (2)

---

[11] See, generally, Frederic W. Hafferty & Donald W. Light, "Professional Dynamics and the Changing Nature of Medical Work" (1995) 35 Journal of Health and Social Behaviour 132; S. Clark, *State and Status: The Rise of the State and Aristocratic Power in Western Europe* (Montreal and Kingston: McGill-Queen's University Press, 1995).

[12] Frederic W. Hafferty & Donald W. Light, "Professional Dynamics and the Changing Nature of Medical Work" (1995) 35 Journal of Health and Social Behaviour 132 at 136.

[13] Tracey L. Adams, "Inter-professional Conflict and Professionalization: Dentistry and Dental Hygiene in Ontario" (2004) 58 Social Science and Medicine 2243 at 2243.

[14] Douglas Alderson & Deanne Montesano, "Regulating, De-Regulating, and Changing Scopes of Practice in the Health Professions — A Jurisdictional Review" (a report prepared for the Health Professions Regulatory Advisory Council, Ottawa, 2003) at 4 and 7. In some provinces, legislation also notes the explicit goal of protecting the integrity of the health profession and its professionals. See, for example, the statement by the Yukon Government, Press Release #03-203, "Omnibus Act Proposed for Health Professions" (September 25, 2003).

[15] S.O. 1991, c. 18.

[16] Health Professions Legislation Review, *Striking a New Balance: A Blueprint for the Regulation of Ontario's Health Professions* (Toronto: Queen's Printer, 1989) at 9.

developing mechanisms to encourage the provision of high quality care; (3) permitting the public to exercise freedom of choice of health care provider within a range of safe options; and (4) promoting evolution in the roles played by individual professions and flexibility in how individual professions can be utilized, so that health services are delivered with maximum efficiency.[17]

Section 3 of the RHPA imposes a duty on the Minister of Health and Long-Term Care to, *inter alia*, "ensure that the health professions are regulated and coordinated in the public interest . . .". The Act contains a Health Professions Procedure Code that expressly states that the regulatory Colleges, in carrying out their corporate objects, have a "duty to serve and protect the public interest".[18] Similar public interest legislative objectives are found in other Canadian jurisdictions.[19]

On one hand, self-regulation may be seen as based on a "social contract" between the profession and the public.[20] That is, in exchange for a grant of authority to self-regulate, professionals are expected to maintain high standards of competence and moral responsibility.[21] The social contract rests upon the concept of professionalism, whereby it is understood that professionals will devote themselves to serving others rather than themselves.[22] That is, there is an argument that regulated professionals are motivated not simply by private interests, but also by ideals, principles and values. On the other hand, self-interest undoubtedly exists among health professions. The concept of professionalism carries with it an inherent conflict of interest as professionals have a biased interest in the outcome of regulation, and consequent motivation to enact policies that promote the professions' own goals rather than those that serve the interests of the public. In other words, self-regulatory regimes embody contrary tendencies — the push of self-serving economic (or political) interests and the pull of moral aspirations.[23]

It is not apparent that Canadian regulatory regimes always result in the optimal fulfilment of the public interest mandate. Numerous instances of self-interest in self-regulatory schemes have been evidenced in Canada. Alderson refers to: (1) "turf" battles waged between various professions; (2) the monopolistic implications and impact of regulation, including the creation of artificial barriers to entry to practice, reduced competition and restricted access to ser-

---

[17] *Ibid.*, at 2.

[18] RHPA, Sched. 2, s. 3(2).

[19] See, for example, British Columbia, *Health Professions Act*, R.S.B.C. 1996, c. 183, s. 10(1) and (2); Alberta, *Health Professions Act*, R.S.A. 2000, c. H-7, s. 26(1); and Manitoba, *Regulated Health Professions Act*, S.M. 2009, c. 15, s. 10(1) [the latter has received Royal Assent but is yet to be proclaimed].

[20] William M. Sullivan, "Medicine under Threat: Professionalism and Professional Identity" (2000) 162 CMAJ 673 at 673.

[21] *Ibid.*

[22] Margaret Somerville, ed., *Do We Care? Renewing Canada's Commitment to Health* (Montreal: McGill-Queen's University Press, 1999) at 34.

[23] Neil Gunningham & Joseph Rees, "Industry Self-Regulation: An Institutional Perspective" (1997) 19 Law & Pol'y 363 at 372.

vices; (3) lack of coordination between health professions; (4) regulatory regimes that are unable to adapt to changing technological/scientific innovations and advancements, which in turn have an impact upon the efficient and effective delivery of health care services; (5) economic/political self-interest of the professions and regulators, which are supported and encouraged though regulation; and (6) insufficient integration and/or coordination with other public and private consumer protection processes such as criminal or civil remedies.[24] However, as will be discussed later in this chapter, provinces are continuing to make legislative changes to address these kinds of issues. Some provinces have done more than others, and those that have yet to focus on these issues can learn from those that have.

It is helpful to heed the advice of Gunningham and Rees, who argue that the opposing tendencies of self-regulated bodies ought to put us on guard against analyzing institutions in terms only of self-interest or only normative expectations. Rather than choosing one perspective over the other, they suggest that we ought to ask about the different circumstances under which each is true. That is, when does self-regulation tend to result in self-serving standards and under what conditions might it become a real force for moral constraint and an aspiration to protect the public?[25]

III. TYPES OF REGULATION

Regulatory controls on health professionals belong to one of two broad categories: *output* regulation or *input* regulation.[26] Input regulation focuses on who is entitled to provide health services while output regulation focuses on the quality of the services provided. The key distinction between the two forms of regulation is that output regulation tends to be reactive in nature, while input regulation is more proactive.[27] Both forms of regulation share the broad common goal of protecting the public.[28]

A. OUTPUT REGULATION

Output regulation has traditionally taken two key forms. First, civil liability; and second, monitoring and discipline of professionals in accordance with profes-

---

[24] Douglas Alderson & Deanne Montesano, *Regulating, De-Regulating, and Changing Scopes of Practice in the Health Professions — A Jurisdictional Review* (a report prepared for the Health Professions Regulatory Advisory Council, Ottawa, 2003) at 5.

[25] Neil Gunningham & Joseph Rees, "Industry Self-Regulation: An Institutional Perspective" (1997) 19 Law & Pol'y 363 at 373.

[26] A.D. Wolfson, M.J. Trebilcock & C.J. Tuohy, "Regulating the Professions: A Theoretical Framework" in S. Rottenberg, ed., *Occupational Licensure and Regulation* (Washington, DC: American Enterprise for Public Policy Research, 1980) 180 at 180.

[27] M.J. Trebilcock, C.J. Tuohy & A.D. Wolfson, *Professional Regulation: A Staff Study of Accountancy, Engineering and Law in Ontario: Prepared for the Professional Organization Committee* (Toronto: Ministry of the Attorney General, 1979) at 69.

[28] *Ibid.*, at 66.

sional standards. More recently, a third form of regulation has emerged, involving external assessment of health care services. While used more in the context of assessing institutions, there are indications that this method of regulation may also be used in the case of individual health professionals in the future.

Civil liability plays an ostensibly important role in Canada as a mechanism to ensure quality of health services. Civil liability may act as a constraint on health professionals and may be perceived as more objective than disciplinary action by the professions themselves. It has the advantage of imposing penalties to compensate consumers, and deterring incompetent and unethical practice. It is also relatively flexible and capable of evolving to reflect changing practices and norms. However, civil liability has significant drawbacks as a means of ensuring quality of care and protecting the public. Litigation is expensive and beyond the means of many Canadians. The practice that costs follow the event means that an unsuccessful plaintiff must pay a proportion of the defendant's costs. This may deter all but those with claims that are very likely to be successful. The burden of proof can be difficult for plaintiffs to meet, necessitating (expensive) expert assistance. Another drawback of civil liability is what Trebilcock refers to as "claim consciousness";[29] that is, many consumers are ignorant of their legal rights and are unaware that they have a legal claim. Given the complexities of medical practice, it may also be difficult for consumers to detect instances of malpractice. Emotional barriers may also exist to adopting an adversarial position towards physicians to whom they have entrusted their care. Finally, it should be noted that physicians in Canada are relatively sheltered from the impact of malpractice litigation. Most are insured through the Canadian Medical Protective Association. Not only are the Association's insurance costs heavily subsidized, but premiums do not increase in light of adverse events.

The available evidence suggests that only a small proportion of negligently injured patients initiate malpractice claims. Between 1971 and 1990, the number of medical malpractice claims filed per 100 Canadian doctors increased from 0.55 to 1.7.[30] The number of malpractice claims peaked in 1996. However, over the last 10 years, there has been a decrease in the number of legal actions brought annually against Canadian physicians. Physicians are half as likely to be involved in legal actions resulting from medical practice as they were 10 years ago. In 2000, there were 22.2 claims per 1,000 physicians, but in 2009 this had come down to 11.6 claims.[31]

---

[29]   M.J. Trebilcock, D. Dewees & D. Duff, *Exploring the Domain of Accident Law: Taking the Facts Seriously* (New York: Oxford University Press, 1996) at 96.

[30]   *Ibid.*, at 120.

[31]   Canadian Medical Protective Association, *CMPA Annual Report 2009* (Ottawa: released August 2010) at 11. The CMPA suggests that this decline is indicative of the many efforts across the country to improve the safety of medicine. It must be noted, however, that other factors are also likely to be at play such as the significant barriers that people face in bringing malpractice claims, including the high costs of litigation, as well as restraints on damages that may be awarded, and the low success rate of litigation.

The relatively low number of legal actions is not unique to Canada. A study in New York in 1991 found that only 2 per cent of patients who were negligently injured in that state initiated malpractice claims.[32] A more recent study found that of patients negligently injured in Utah and Colorado, only 3 per cent initiated claims.[33] Further, the Utah/Colorado study found that the tort system is unequal in its protection of patients, with the poor and the elderly particularly likely to suffer negligent injury without taking legal action.

The other main form of output regulation in professional markets is referred to as "professional monitoring" or discipline. In general, the advantages and disadvantages of discipline are similar to those for civil liability. Unlike civil liability, the disciplinary process is administered by the professional's peers.[34] This lends credibility to the process from the profession's perspective and may assist in promoting compliance with standards. It may arguably also lead to fewer errors in adjudication than in the civil liability system.[35]

However, because the process is administered by the profession itself, it is prone to being managed in a self-serving manner and may not be trusted by the public.[36] Like civil liability, the system is activated largely based on victim complaints, which may prevent a barrier to the hearing of complaints. Further, the professional discipline process does not provide compensation for victims, resulting in a lack of economic incentive to pursue their complaints.

Recent years have seen an increase in a third form of output regulation, where governments are focusing on quality of outcomes by using external assessment of health care services. This form of regulation has tended to concentrate on assessment of institutions rather than individual professionals, however, there is scope for greater use of it in the latter case. Health quality councils in some provinces have legislative mandates mostly aimed at measuring and reporting on the quality of care and promoting quality improvement.[37] The Health

---

[32] A.R. Localio, A.G. Lawthers & T.A. Brennan, "Relation between Malpractice Claims and adverse Events due to Negligence: Results of the Harvard Medical Practice Study III" (1991) 325 New Eng. J. Med. 245.

[33] D.M. Studdert *et al.*, "Negligent Care and Malpractice Claiming Behavior in Utah and Colorado" (2000) 38:3 Medical Care 250.

[34] See M.J. Trebilcock, "Regulating Service Quality in Professional Markets" in D.N. Dewees, ed., *The Regulation of Quality: Products, Services, Workplaces and the Environment* (Toronto: Butterworths, 1983) at 90-91; and M.J. Trebilcock, C.J. Tuohy & A.D. Wolfson, *Professional Regulation: A Staff Study of Accountancy, Engineering and Law in Ontario: Prepared for the Professional Organizations Committee* (Toronto: Ministry of the Attorney General, 1979) at 71.

[35] M.J. Trebilcock, "Regulating Service Quality in Professional Markets", *ibid.*, at 91; M.J. Trebilcock, C.J. Tuohy & A.D. Wolfson, *Professional Regulation: A Staff Study of Accountancy, Engineering and Law in Ontario: Prepared for the Professional Organizations Committee, ibid.*, at 69 and 77.

[36] M.J. Trebilcock, C.J. Tuohy & A.D. Wolfson, *Professional Regulation: A Staff Study of Accountancy, Engineering and Law in Ontario: Prepared for the Professional Organizations Committee, ibid.*, at 71-72.

[37] See, for example, Saskatchewan's *Health Quality Council Act*, S.S. 2002, c. H-0.04; in Manitoba, the Manitoba Institute for Patient Safety (<http://www.mbips.ca>); in Alberta, the Health Quality Council (<http://www.hqca.ca>); in New Brunswick, the New Brunswick Health Coun-

Quality Council of Saskatchewan is responsible for developing quality indicators and publishes results of evaluations in its own publications as well as in
peer-reviewed journals. The Council has initiated a number of projects to improve health outcomes, including to improve chronic disease management,
asthma care, cancer care, as well as patient care and safety in Intensive Care
Units. These types of projects make recommendations regarding the practice of
individual professionals.[38]

A private initiative, the Fraser Institute Initiative, involves the publication
of report cards for hospitals. The aim is to contribute to the improvement of
health care by providing quality of care information directly to patients and the
general public. The Initiative aims to make people more informed about their
care and to improve hospital performance through enhanced transparency and
accountability.[39]

B.   INPUT REGULATION

Three main modes of regulation fall under the heading of input regulation. First,
licensure gives a profession a monopoly on the activity regulated. This may be
done through profession-specific practice legislation, where licensed practitioners gain an exclusive right to deliver certain services. Licensure limits licensed
professionals to performing certain types of procedures. In most cases, licensing
regimes are controlled by a regulatory body with the delegated power to control
entry into the profession. For example, in Nova Scotia a physician cannot practise unless he or she is licensed by the College of Physicians and Surgeons of
Nova Scotia, while a nurse must be a member of the College of Registered
Nurses of Nova Scotia. Under a licensing regime, there are usually strict admission requirements, often with competency tests and educational qualifications
attached.

Second, *certification* is less restrictive than licensing and involves giving
designated recognition to individuals who have met predetermined qualifications
set by a regulatory agency or professional body. Non-certified individuals may
still offer services but they may not use the term "certified" or the designated
title. Certification is not as strict as licensing in the sense of creating a monopoly
over the occupation as a whole. It may also be referred to as "title restriction" or
"title reservation" and is a form of shorthand or credentialing signal for the public, indicating a certain background or educational level.[40] For example, the
Massage Therapists Association of Nova Scotia requires massage therapists to

---

cil (<http://www.nbhc.ca>); and in Quebec, the Commissaire à la santé et au bien-être Québec.
In Ontario, see the *Excellent Care for All Act, 2010*, S.O. 2010, c. 14.

[38]   See Health Quality Council of Saskatchewan, online at: <http://www.hqc.sk.ca>.

[39]   See online at: <http://www.hosptialreportcards.ca>. Ontario previously ran an initiative for hos-
       pital reporting that was a joint initiative of the Ontario Hospital Association and the Government
       of Ontario.

[40]   Margot Priest, "The Privatization of Regulation: Five Models of Self-Regulation" (1997-1998)
       29 Ottawa L. Rev. 233 at 252.

fulfil certain educational requirements in order to join the Association. The Association holds the Official Marks in Nova Scotia for various titles including "massage therapist".[41]

Third, *registration* is the least restrictive mode of input regulation and simply requires an individual to register their particulars with a designated agency.[42] All members of an occupational group who register may offer their services to the public; for example, in Kansas, the Board of Healing Arts maintains a register of individuals who are "physicians' assistants".[43] Of the three forms of regulation, registration is the most limited in the protection it can provide against incompetence, offering little more than a means to identify a practitioner so that an aggrieved patient can pursue legal redress using general principles of civil liability.[44]

IV. SOURCES OF REGULATION

Regulatory regimes range from direct state control through to self-regulation.[45] Where there is direct state control (classic "command and control" regulation), the state is responsible for all aspects of regulation and administration; however, this form of regulation is rarely used in the context of health professionals. Combinations of government and self-regulation are possible where a profession has authority to govern itself but relies on a state agency to carry out certain functions, such as administration and adjudication of complaints. Self-regulation describes a situation where at least 51 per cent of the governing entity is comprised of members of the profession. The governing entity is responsible for all decisions, both administrative and profession-specific, such as clinical standard setting, ethical, investigative and disciplinary matters. This is the predominant mechanism used to regulate health professionals in Canada.

Even when a profession is self-regulated, the regime will usually, at some level, acknowledge the legislature's and executive's ultimate authority. Priest argues that self-regulation works best when it operates "in the shadow" of government intervention, receiving its impetus from the prospect of government action.[46] Similarly, Gunningham and Rees suggest that self-regulatory mecha-

---

[41]   Massage Therapists Association of Nova Scotia, online at: <http://www.mtans.com>.

[42]   Douglas Alderson & Deanne Montesano, *Regulating, De-Regulating, and Changing Scopes of Practice in the Health Professions — A Jurisdictional Review* (a report prepared for the Health Professions Regulatory Advisory Council, Ottawa, 2003) at 12.

[43]   *Ibid.*

[44]   M. Christine Cagle, J. Michael Martinez & William D. Richardson, "Privatizing Professional Licensing Boards: Self-Governance or Self-Interest?" (1999) 30 Administration and Society 734 at 737.

[45]   Neil Gunningham & Joseph Rees, "Industry Self-Regulation: An Institutional Perspective" (1997) 19 Law & Pol'y 363 at 366.

[46]   Margot Priest, "The Privatization of Regulation: Five Models of Self-Regulation" (1997-1998) 29 Ottawa L. Rev. 233 at 238.

nisms underpinned by some form of state intervention are more resilient and effective than self-regulation in isolation.[47]

While self-regulatory schemes usually grant a large degree of autonomy to professional bodies to regulate their members (through rulemaking, monitoring, enforcement and sanctions), government control is usually found in the structuring of the statute that delegates power to the body, and is often found in the power to approve regulations or bylaws established by the body.[48] Self-regulatory bodies are also subject to judicial review,[49] and may be subject to the *Canadian Charter of Rights and Freedoms.*[50]

A.   GROUNDS FOR SELF-REGULATION

Several advantages are commonly claimed for self-regulation. First, self-regulatory bodies have a greater degree of expertise and technical knowledge of practices in their particular area than independent agencies. The involvement of a professional's peers in the disciplinary process arguably assists in *promoting compliance* with standards and thus leads to fewer errors in adjudication than in tort law. As Cory J. stated in *Milstein v. Ontario College of Pharmacy*: "The peers of the professional person are deemed to have and, indeed, they must have special knowledge, training and skill that particularly adapts them to formulate their own professional standards and to judge the conduct of a member of their profession. No other body could appreciate as well the problems and frustrations that beset a fellow member."[51] Peer pressure is also arguably a benefit of self-regulation as professionals feel pressure to adhere to the standards set by their profession. Priest refers to the "psychological buy-in" to regulation that individuals have had a hand in developing and for which they are responsible.[52]

---

[47]   Neil Gunningham & Joseph Rees, "Industry Self-Regulation: An Institutional Perspective" (1997) 19 Law & Pol'y 363 at 366.

[48]   Margot Priest, "The Privatization of Regulation: Five Models of Self-Regulation" (1997-1998) 29 Ottawa L. Rev. 233 at 252. Also see the discussion in Section V(C) below.

[49]   *Khan v. College of Physicians and Surgeons of Ontario*, [1992] O.J. No. 1725, 9 O.R. (3d) 641 (Ont. C.A.).

[50]   Part I of the *Constitution Act, 1982*, being Schedule B to the *Canada Act 1982* (U.K.) 1982, c. 11. See *Knutson v. Saskatchewan Registered Nursing Assn.*, [1990] S.J. No. 603, [1991] 2 W.W.R. 327 (Sask. C.A.). It should be noted, however, that some bodies will not be subject to the Charter. For example, an Ontario court recently ruled that Canadian Blood Services is not subject to the Charter, since it is a private corporation and its policy development and operational activities are not controlled by government: *Canadian Blood Services v. Freeman*, [2010] O.J. No. 3811, 2010 ONSC 4885 (Ont. S.C.J.).

[51]   [1976] O.J. No. 2277 at para. 42, 13 O.R. (2d) 700 (Ont. Div. Ct.), vard [1978] O.J. No. 3434, 20 O.R. (2d) 283 (Ont. C.A.).

[52]   Margot Priest, "The Privatization of Regulation: Five Models of Self-Regulation" (1997-1998) 29 Ottawa L. Rev. 233 at 270, citing also E. Bardach & R.A. Kagan, *Going by the Book: The Problem of Regulatory Unreasonableness* (Philadelphia: Temple University Press, 1982) at 65-66; and J. Braithwaite, "Enforced Self-Regulation: A New Strategy for Corporate Crime Control" (1982) 80 Mich. L. Rev. 1466.

Second, the expertise of self-regulating bodies arguably results in *lower costs* with respect to the formulation and interpretation of standards, as well as monitoring and enforcement. Administrative costs tend to be internalized in the profession rather than passed directly on to taxpayers.[53] Whether or not the self-regulatory system is supervised by government, the costs to government are likely to be less than they would be if government took on the majority of regulatory responsibilities.[54]

Third, self-regulatory regimes benefit from *greater flexibility* due to the use of less formal rules and processes. Rules can be more easily adjusted to meet changing circumstances than if they were subject to the time-consuming process of legislative reform.[55] Self-regulatory bodies also have the advantage of being able to hire staff as needed and pay competitive salaries to retain expertise.

Finally, it is argued that because self-regulation contemplates *ethical standards* of conduct, which extend beyond the letter of the law, it has the capacity to raise standards of behaviour.[56]

B. CRITICISMS OF SELF-REGULATION

Self-regulation of health professionals is subject to several criticisms. Most notably, it has been criticized for failing to ensure professional competence and to protect patients. Some commentators in Canada have argued that public confidence in physicians is waning, in part because of a high frequency of adverse events, of reports of hospital and professional mismanagement, and of professional malfeasance.[57] Critics charge that self-regulatory standards are usually weak, enforcement is ineffective, and punishment is secret and mild. These failures can be related back to the tension inherent in self-regulatory regimes between, on the one hand, the public interest, and on the other, private interests that would otherwise be threatened by regulation.[58] Where regulatory powers are delegated to the professions, the members of those professions no longer have to seek to influence regulators to serve their interests, but are in an optimal position to profit from rent-seeking. Priest argues that self-regulation is the ultimate form of regulatory agency capture and is incapable of being impartial and fair. She describes it as tantamount to "putting the fox to guard the henhouse".[59] Self-

---

[53] Anthony Ogus, "Rethinking Self-Regulation" (1995) 15 Oxford J. Legal Stud. 97 at 98. It is arguable, however, that taxpayers are being charged indirectly through higher prices.

[54] Margot Priest, "The Privatization of Regulation: Five Models of Self-Regulation" (1997-1998) 29 Ottawa L. Rev. 233 at 270.

[55] *Ibid.*, at 269.

[56] Neil Gunningham & Joseph Rees, "Industry Self-Regulation: An Institutional Perspective" (1997) 19 Law & Pol'y 363 at 366.

[57] Editorial, "Can Physicians Regulate Themselves?" (2005) 172 CMAJ 717.

[58] Neil Gunningham & Joseph Rees, "Industry Self-Regulation: An Institutional Perspective" (1997) 19 Law & Pol'y 363 at 370.

[59] Margot Priest, "The Privatization of Regulation: Five Models of Self-Regulation" (1997-1998) 29 Ottawa L. Rev. 233 at 271, citing M.G. Cochrane, "Buyer beware: The new regulatory reality in Canada" *Law Times* (September 1996).

interest may result in "under-regulation" due to lack of enthusiasm on the part of members of the group. To use the fox/chicken analogy, "foxes may be more interested in the chickens than they are in controlling the other foxes".

Self-regulatory regimes are also vulnerable to "over-regulation", where the organization becomes similar to a government bureaucracy with rigid hierarchies, desire to expand territory and placement of the interests of the organization before its mandate.[60] The resulting over-regulation, especially the artificial inflation of entry requirements, can result in an overall reduction in access to, or increase in the cost of, services available to the public. Prices might be increased where self-regulatory bodies create professional "cartels" and block the substitution of lower-cost for higher-cost services of equivalent quality.[61] When the number of practitioners is reduced or the price increased, some consumers will do without the service, obtain it from unqualified practitioners or do it themselves.[62]

Over-regulation may also be to the detriment of those wanting to enter the profession. Jost notes that self-regulated health professions have tended to block entry into those professions by minorities and foreign-trained professionals, and that they have sought to restrict the development of alternative forms of medicine.[63] In Prince Edward Island, for example, physicians have opposed the integration of nurse practitioners into the health care system, raising arguments that they are not qualified to practice. In 2005, they reportedly took action that effectively shut down a pilot project that would have enabled nurse practitioners to make certain services more accessible to the public.[64]

Self-regulation is also criticized for lacking many of the advantages of conventional government regulation "in terms of visibility, credibility, accountability, compulsory application to all ... greater likelihood of rigorous standards being developed, cost spreading ... and availability of a range of sanctions".[65]

---

[60] Margot Priest, "The Privatization of Regulation: Five Models of Self-Regulation" (1997-1998) 29 Ottawa L. Rev. 233 at 273.

[61] Tim Jost, ed., *Regulation of Healthcare Professions* (Chicago: Health Administration Press, 1997) at 3.

[62] Manitoba Law Reform Commission, *Discussion Paper: The Future of Occupational Regulation in Manitoba* (Winnipeg: Law Reform Commission, 1993); Margot Priest, "The Privatization of Regulation: Five Models of Self-Regulation" (1997-1998) 29 Ottawa L. Rev. 233 at 273.

[63] Tim Jost, ed., *Regulation of Healthcare Professions* (Chicago: Health Administration Press, 1997) at 3.

[64] C. Morris, "Nurse Practitioners Say They Face Barrier" (October 11, 2005), online at: Nurse Practitioners Canada <http://www.npcanada.ca/portal>. Note that regulations enabling nurse practitioners to practice were subsequently passed in New Brunswick: Janis Hass, "Nurse Practitioners Now Able to Work Across Canada" (2006) 174:7 CMAJ 911-12.

[65] Kernaghan Webb & Andrew Morrison, "The Legal Aspects of Voluntary Codes" (paper presented to Voluntary Codes Symposium, Office of Consumer Affairs, Industry Canada and Regulatory Affairs, Treasury Board, 1996), cited in Neil Gunningham & Joseph Rees, "Industry Self-Regulation: An Institutional Perspective" (1997) 19 Law & Pol'y 363 at 370. See also Margot Priest, "The Privatization of Regulation: Five Models of Self-Regulation" (1997-1998) 29 Ottawa L. Rev. 233 at 273 (arguing that accountability and transparency can get lost in the self-regulatory process).

There may also be a breach of the separation of powers doctrine where the self-regulated profession has control over policy formulation, interpretation of the rules, adjudication and enforcement as well as rule-making.[66]

Finally, while the flexibility of self-regulatory regimes is often cited as an advantage, it may also have negative results for the public interest if self-regulated bodies focus on their own interests rather than those of the public.[67]

In sum, self-regulation of health professionals has both positive and negative aspects. In Canada, governments have considered the positives sufficient to outweigh the negatives and thus self-regulation is the primary means of regulating health professionals. However, it remains important that legislatures provide checks and balances to guard against self-interested action, and ensure adequate accountability and transparency.[68] The finely tuned balance of a self-regulatory regime is vulnerable to being upset by undue influence from the profession. Further, experience suggests that governments risk capitulating to the interests of the regulated profession where that profession enjoys a strong bargaining position due to the essential nature of the service provided or through public support for the profession.[69]

V. REGULATION OF HEALTH PROFESSIONALS IN CANADA

Regulation of health professionals in Canada dates back to 1778 when British-governed Quebec passed an Act allowing British-educated "scientific" practitioners to set and pass licensing requirements.[70] However, it was not until the mid-19th century that the state set up a blueprint for professional licensing, which

---

[66] Anthony Ogus, "Rethinking Self-Regulation" (1995) 15 Oxford J. of Legal Stud. 97 at 99.

[67] Margot Priest, "The Privatization of Regulation: Five Models of Self-Regulation" (1997-1998) 29 Ottawa L. Rev. 233 at 274.

[68] Andrew Green & Roy Hrab, *Self-Regulation and the Protection of the Public Interest* (paper prepared for the Panel on the Role of the Government, Toronto: University of Toronto, 2003) at 4. See also discussion below at Section V(C).

[69] See discussion in Section III(B) of Chapter 1 by Bill Leahy of the strikes organized by physicians in Saskatchewan in 1962 in response to the introduction of legislation creating a system of universal and comprehensive public insurance for physician services. The strikes ended with a mediated settlement that preserved the right of physicians to charge fees to patients in addition to those to be received under the plan and the right of physicians to choose partial- or non-participation in the plan. See also Tom Archibald & Allison Jeffs, "Physician Fee Decisions, the Medicare Basket and Budgeting: A Three-Province Survey", a paper presented at a Conference presenting results from the CHRSF-funded project "Defining the Medicare Basket", in collaboration with the Institute for Research on Public Policy (Toronto: November 30, 2004). The paper discusses the negotiating process for physician fees in Ontario, Alberta and British Columbia, and discusses the influence of the medical profession and the importance of maintaining labour peace as between physicians and the government.

[70] This Act, along with others that followed in Upper Canada, were either inconsistently applied, repealed, never enforced or flaunted by those they had excluded. The first licensing board in Upper Canada was not appointed until 1818. See Patricia O'Reilly, *Health Care Practitioners: An Ontario Case Study in Policy Making* (Toronto: University of Toronto Press, 2000) at 15 and footnote 3.

allowed health professions to select and govern their own members, as well as prosecute those outside the profession who attempted to work within the exclusive area of the profession.

The regulation of occupations and professions in Canada is a provincial responsibility under section 92(13) of the *Constitution Act, 1867*.[71] This section will first discuss input regulation (focusing on licensure), followed by output regulation (focusing on discipline and monitoring).

A.   INPUT REGULATION: LICENSURE, CERTIFICATION AND REGISTRATION

Provincial and territorial legislation delegates competence for input regulation, with varying degrees of discretion, to self-governing professional bodies. Legislation principally sets out qualifications for (compulsory) membership in colleges and outlines required standards of practice. There are two main approaches in use across Canada. The first is a "framework" or "umbrella" legislative approach. The provinces and territories that use this approach have one piece of legislation that provides a single regulatory framework for all self-governing health professions. This is the more modern approach and is in part a response to criticisms during the 1990s that traditional systems of occupational regulation in the health professions were fragmented, complex and inconsistent.[72] The second approach is the more traditional one where individual statutes deal with each profession separately.

A framework approach has been adopted by Ontario,[73] British Columbia,[74] Alberta,[75] Manitoba[76] and the Yukon.[77] Typically, the framework legislation regulates the scope of practice of a number of health professions, which are covered by individual regulatory colleges. The most recent province to have introduced a framework approach is Manitoba, where each of the health professions' statutes is to be repealed over time as the professions become regulated under the framework legislation. This legislation (which has received Royal Assent but is yet to be proclaimed) was introduced with the goals, *inter alia*, of offering more protection for the public by regulating actions or clinical procedures that may present a risk of harm if performed by someone who is not adequately

---

[71]   (U.K.), 30 & 31 Vict., c. 3, reprinted in R.S.C. 1985, App. II, No. 5.

[72]   See, for example, British Columbia Royal Commission on Health Care and Costs, *Closer to Home: The Report of the British Columbia Royal Commission on Health Care and Costs*, vol. 2 (Victoria: The Commission, 1991) at D-30; Alberta Workforce Rebalancing Committee, "New Directions for Legislation Regulating the Health Professions in Alberta: A Discussion Paper" (August 19, 1994) at 6; and Manitoba Law Reform Commission, *Discussion Paper: The Future of Occupational Regulation in Manitoba* (Winnipeg: Law Reform Commission, 1993) at 6.

[73]   *Regulated Health Professions Act, 1991*, S.O. 1991, c. 18.

[74]   *Health Professions Act*, R.S.B.C. 1996, c. 183.

[75]   *Health Professions Act*, R.S.A. 2000, c. H-7.

[76]   *Regulated Health Professions Act*, S.M. 2009, c. 15, s. 10(1) [this Act has received Royal Asset but is yet to be proclaimed in force].

[77]   *Health Professions Act*, S.Y. 2003, c. 24.

trained; strengthening accountability between the regulatory bodies and the government; and fostering greater confidence in the province's health care delivery system.[78]

A common characteristic of the framework approach is that the legislation outlines the manner in which the colleges are to operate. In Ontario, the *Regulated Health Professions Act, 1991* contains a Health Professions Procedural Code that establishes the structure of the regulatory colleges.[79] The Procedural Code gives the colleges responsibility for, *inter alia*, regulating the practice of the relevant health profession; developing and maintaining standards of qualification for those who apply for certificates of registration; and developing and maintaining standards of professional practice, knowledge, skill and professional ethics for their members.[80] It also sets out procedures for registration, complaints, discipline, reporting of health professionals, quality assurance and the like. The Code is deemed to be part of each of the individual specific health profession Acts.[81] In this manner, it ensures that procedures are uniform across the regulated health professions. Similarly, in Alberta, the *Health Professions Act* requires all health professional colleges to follow common rules to investigate complaints and to set educational and practice standards for registered members. However, Alberta's legislation grants the professional colleges less discretion than Ontario. While the colleges administer licensure and registration, the legislation sets out detailed provisions as to the qualifications required for each profession.

Where framework legislation is employed, "new" professions may apply to obtain designation as a profession. For example, under the British Columbia *Health Professions Act*, where an application is made and it is considered to be in the public interest to do so, the Lieutenant Governor in Council may, by regulation, make an order designating a health profession, in which he or she can prescribe various matters for a profession such as the scope of service.[82] On designation of a health profession, section 15 of the Act provides for establishment of a college.

These jurisdictions typically regulate scope of practice in more than one way. First, scope of practice statements describe what the profession does.[83] Second, they have a system of reserved activities. Under this system they list so-called "reserved activities". These are higher risk, invasive activities that medical practitioners may perform in the course of providing the services described in their respective scope of practice statements. The same reserved activities

---

[78] "Health Professions Regulatory Reform Consultation Document, Proposed Umbrella Health Professions Legislation: The Regulated Health Professions Act" (Government of Manitoba: January 2009) 90.

[79] RHPA, Sched. 2.

[80] Section 3 of the Health Professions Procedural Code.

[81] RHPA, s. 4.

[82] R.S.B.C. 1996, c. 183, s. 12.

[83] Scope of practice statements are usually prescribed in regulations. In Alberta, scope of practice statements are prescribed in the *Government Organization Act*, R.S.A. 2000, c. G-10, Sched. 7.1.

may be granted to more than one profession. This represents a departure from
the traditional practice whereby each profession had exclusivity in respect of
certain services or procedures. It is intended to promote enhanced multidisciplinary practice and consumer choice.[84]

Relatedly, it is common for provinces to restrict the use of given titles to
registrants of a regulatory college.[85] This prevents patients from being misled
into thinking that the professional whom they are seeing is regulated by a college and qualified and subject to disciplinary procedures.[86]

In provinces and territories that take a more traditional approach to regulation, each health profession is regulated by an independent and separate piece of
legislation. For example, in Saskatchewan 21 statutes regulate different health
professions. Each of these statutes grant the respective professional body self-
governing competence. Quebec takes a slightly different approach. It has a *Professional Code* that entrusts 45 "professional orders" with the right and responsibility to supervise and administer their professions.[87] Health professions are
included along with other professions such as accountants, social workers, archi-
tects and engineers. There are two types of professions: those with reserved titles only, and professions with reserved titles *and* an exclusive right to practise.
A number of health professions are included in each category, for example, physicians and nurses. The professional orders are responsible for ensuring professional competence, which they do by establishing standards regarding admission
to practise. They are responsible for controlling the title and the right to practise
a profession; verifying the competence and integrity of candidates to the profession; ensuring that competence and integrity are maintained throughout the
member's professional life; and punishing offences against the *Professional
Code*, specific laws and related regulations.[88] In this manner, self-regulated bodies in Quebec seem to have more discretion with regard to licensure and standard setting than similar bodies in other provinces and territories.

---

[84] In British Columbia, the Minister may prescribe restricted activities in regulations under s.
55(2)(g) of the *Health Professions Act*; in Alberta, the *Health Professions Act*, s. 131(1) provides
that a council may make regulations respecting who may perform restricted activities under
Schedule 7.1 to the *Government Organization Act*; in Ontario, the *Regulated Health Professions
Act* provides in s. 27(1) that no person shall perform a "controlled act" as defined in s. 27(2)
unless they are authorized by a health profession Act to perform the said act, or the act has been
delegated to the person by someone who is so authorized; in Manitoba, the *Regulated Health
Professions Act* [not yet in force] provides for restrictions on the performance of "reserved acts"
in s. 5.

[85] See, for example, British Columbia, *Health Professions Act*, s. 12; Manitoba, *Regulated Health
Professions Act* [not yet in force], Part 6, ss. 77-81; Ontario, *Regulated Health Professions Act*, s.
33; and Alberta, *Health Professions Act*, Part 7, s. 128.

[86] For example, until the enactment of recent legislation, physicians in Ontario were able to hold
themselves out as cosmetic surgeons.

[87] R.S.Q., c. C-26.

[88] Quebec Interprofessional Council, "The Professional System — Control of the Practice of a Profession", online at: <http://www.professions-quebec.org/index.php/en/element/visualiser/id/78>.

B. OUTPUT REGULATION: MONITORING AND DISCIPLINING HEALTH PROFESSIONALS

1. Monitoring Standards and Ongoing Competence

Across the provinces and territories, self-regulated bodies are responsible for various activities that fall under the rubric of monitoring and disciplining health professionals. Where provinces have adopted framework legislation, the provisions for monitoring and discipline will be the same for all professions covered by the legislation. For example, in Ontario, the *Health Professions Procedural Code* sets out procedures for monitoring and discipline that cover all 23 professions regulated under the RHPA.[89] In provinces where each profession is subject to specific legislation, that legislation governs issues concerning monitoring and discipline. A key disadvantage of this approach compared to the framework approach is a lack of consistency across the health professions, resulting in potential confusion for both the public and professionals themselves.

The primary monitoring activity carried out by self-regulated professional bodies is the discipline of members who do not meet the standards set by the profession. Discipline is the means by which health professions enforce their standards, and its goal is to prevent actions that threaten public well-being.[90] Professional bodies generally sanction, or discipline, three types of unacceptable behaviour on the part of their members: (1) misconduct, (2) incompetence, and (3) conduct unbecoming a member of the profession.[91] In general, "professional misconduct" refers to unacceptable conduct within the scope of the professional's practice. "Conduct unbecoming a member" usually relates to conduct outside the professional's practice which may bring the profession into disrepute. "Incompetence" describes conduct or a pattern of practice falling below a generally accepted minimum level.[92] Incompetence may arise from incapacity (such as that caused by addiction or illness), and licensing bodies generally have the power to sanction a practitioner who is incapacitated, even where there have been no complaints or acts of misconduct.[93]

Various kinds of behaviour have been found to constitute unbecoming or unprofessional behaviour. For the most part, the definition of these terms has been left to disciplinary bodies and the courts, although some statutes provide guidance. For example, in section 46 of the *Medical Profession Act, 1981*, Saskatchewan provides examples of behaviour that is considered "unbecoming,

---

[89] *Regulated Health Professions Act, 1991*, S.O. 1991, c. 18, Sched. 2.

[90] Manitoba Law Reform Commission, "The Future of Occupational Regulation in Manitoba" (Discussion Paper of the Manitoba Law Reform Commission, Winnipeg, 1993) at 51.

[91] Linette McNamara, Erin Nelson & Brent Windwick, "Regulation of Health Care Professionals" in J. Downie, T. Caulfield & C.M. Flood, eds., *Canadian Health Law and Policy*, 2d ed. (Markham, ON: LexisNexis Canada, 2002) 55 at 77.

[92] *Ibid.*, citing K.R. Hamilton, *Self-governing Professions: Digests of Court Decisions* (Aurora, ON: Canada Law Book, 1995) at 11-1.

[93] *Ibid.*

improper, unprofessional, or discreditable conduct", including betraying a professional secret, alcohol addiction, employing an assistant not registered to administer the services being provided, and performing a service that is not justifiable on reasonable grounds.[94] A variety of behaviours have been found to constitute professional misconduct, including a physician's fraudulent overbilling of a provincial health plan,[95] sexual misconduct between professionals and their patients,[96] incompetent practice,[97] breaching patient confidentiality[98] and in one case, intermixing Scientology and medical practice.[99]

Another key aspect of monitoring is to ensure continuing competence of regulated health professionals. Processes for ensuring continuing competence are determined by individual professional colleges, with no oversight by government. Some colleges have mandatory requirements for participation in educational programs (for example, the provincial Colleges of Physicians and Surgeons in Ontario, Quebec and Saskatchewan), while others rely on feedback from patients and peers. A common mechanism is a committee structure, which allows inspection of health practices in order to ensure competence. For example, section 50 of Alberta's *Health Professions Act* provides that each college must establish a "continuing competence program" in order to maintain competence and enhance the provision of professional services.[100] Competence committees may make a referral to the complaints director for various reasons including if, on the basis of information obtained from a practice visit or continuing competence program, they are of the opinion that a regulated member is incompetent or has engaged in conduct unbecoming of the profession.[101] In Saskatchewan, the *Medical Profession Act* provides that where the council or executive committee has reasonable grounds to believe a practitioner may not have

---

[94]   S.S. 1980-81, c. M-10.1.

[95]   *Alberta (College of Physicians and Surgeons) v. Moosa*, [1986] A.J. No. 1014, 68 A.R. 9 (Alta. C.A.). See also *Golomb v. College of Physicians and Surgeons of Ontario*, [1976] O.J. No. 1707, 68 D.L.R. (3d) 25 (Ont. Div. Ct.).

[96]   See, generally, James T. Casey, *The Regulation of Professions in Canada* (Toronto: Thomson Carswell, 2005 – Release 2). See, for example, *College of Physicians and Surgeons of Ontario v. Boodoosingh*, [1990] O.J. No. 921, 73 O.R. (2d) 478 (Ont. Div. Ct.), affd [1993] O.J. No. 859, 12 O.R. (3d) 707*n* (Ont. C.A.), leave to appeal refused [1993] S.C.C.A. No. 273, 69 O.A.C. 159*n* (S.C.C.); and *McKee v. College of Psychologists of British Columbia*, [1992] B.C.J. No. 207, [1992] 4 W.W.R. 197 (B.C.S.C.), revd on other grounds [1994] B.C.J. No. 1778, 116 D.L.R. (4th) 555 (B.C.C.A.).

[97]   See, for example, *Green v. College of Physicians and Surgeons of Saskatchewan*, [1986] S.J. No. 723, 51 Sask. R. 241 at 258-59 (Sask. C.A.): "The medical profession has been granted a status which gives the public the right to expect that it will take reasonable measure to assure that reasonable skills will be exhibited by a doctor who is held out by the profession through the College as possessing the ability to practise medicine."

[98]   *Shulman v. College of Physicians and Surgeons of Ontario*, [1980] O.J. No. 3627, 111 D.L.R. (3d) 689 (Ont. Div. Ct.).

[99]   *Taams v. College of Physicians and Surgeons of British Columbia*, [1977] B.C.J. No. 1232, 79 D.L.R. (3d) 377 (B.C.S.C.).

[100] R.S.A. 2000, c. H-7.

[101] *Ibid.*, s. 51.

adequate skill and knowledge to practise, they may appoint a competency committee to investigate.[102] In Ontario, this system is known as "peer assessment". The College of Physicians and Surgeons runs a Peer Assessment Program aimed at improving practice (as opposed to detecting poor practice).[103] Physicians are randomly selected for assessment and are also assessed on a regular basis once they reach the age of 70. In addition, the College's Quality Assurance Committee can require a physician to be peer assessed if clinical concerns have been identified. Minor problems tend to be addressed through further education, while for more significant problems, a physician may be sent on a general or specialty review program. Reviews of the program are mixed: some find the process expensive and invasive, while others have found it valuable.[104] In Quebec, the Collège des médecins du Québec runs a system of monitoring and improving professional practice. The Professional Inspection Committee organizes professional inspection visits to ensure that physicians are practising competently and in accordance with relevant standards.[105] Selection of physicians for inspection visits is made under several programs established by the Professional Inspection Committee, including those chosen at random and those who completed their medical degree over 35 years ago.[106]

Current systems of ensuring continuing competency have been criticized for a lack of rigour, accountability and transparency. One concern is that while colleges run continuing competency programs, they tend not to follow up to provide evidence of whether physicians have actually put their knowledge and skills into practice.[107] This has been contrasted with the United States, where the American Board of Internal Medicine's Maintenance of Certification is reported to be a demanding process whereby physicians must participate in a practice-improvement exercise and a secure examination. Data are submitted to the American Board of Internal Medicine and physicians receive feedback compared with established standards and their peers. They must also submit a quality-improvement plan.[108]

Undoubtedly, ensuring ongoing competence is a critical aspect of ensuring the quality of health care that is delivered. However, anecdotal evidence suggests that the self-regulatory system is not performing as well as it should, with

---

[102] S.S. 1980-81, c. M-10.1, s. 45.

[103] Note, however, that the Peer Assessment Program has been criticized for being more concerned about detecting poor practice: Judith Allsop & Kathryn Jones, "Quality Assurance in Medical Regulation in an International Context" (report for the Chief Medical Officer, Department of Health, UK, 2006) at 52, online at: <http://www.lincoln.ac.uk/socialsciences/psrc/docs/CMO Report.pdf>.

[104] *Ibid.*, at 54.

[105] See *Professional Code*, R.S.Q., c. C-26, s. 112. See also Collège des médecins du Québec, "The Professional Inspection Visit" (leaflet) (Montreal: April 2010).

[106] Collège des médecins du Québec, *ibid.*

[107] Wendy Levinson, "Revalidation of Physicians in Canada: Are We Passing the Test?" (2008) 179:10 CMAJ 979.

[108] *Ibid.*

poor performance often going unchecked.[109] Further, it has been noted that health professionals perceive regulatory bodies as more focused on removing "bad apples" than improving practice, and that the regulatory process should place greater emphasis on continuous improvement through education and remediation rather than blame and punishment.[110]

Institutions may also play a role in identifying problems within the health professions. In Ontario, the *Excellent Care for All Act, 2010*[111] requires every health care organization[112] to establish and maintain a quality committee.[113] These committees' mandate is to monitor and report on quality issues and on the overall quality of services provided in the organization, and to make recommendations regarding quality improvement initiatives.[114] The Act also requires health care organizations to conduct an annual survey of people who have received services, as well as their caregivers, and employees/health care providers within the organization. The purpose of the surveys is to collect information regarding satisfaction with services provided by the organization.[115] Health organizations are required under the Act to develop Annual Quality Improvement Plans, which must contain, *inter alia*, annual performance improvement targets and justification for those targets, with executive compensation linked to the achievement of those targets.[116] This legislation is a positive step toward recognizing the important role of institutions in ensuring quality of care and patient safety. Institutions may also take certain actions where professionals are found to be incompetent or to have engaged in misconduct. For example, under Ontario's *Public Hospitals Act*, hospitals may restrict or cancel a physician's privileges[117] by reason of their incompetence, negligence or misconduct.[118] A recent

---

[109] It is difficult to find comprehensive documented evidence of the extent to which poor performance is a problem. See, for example, Robert Cribb, "The unkindest cut" *The Toronto Star* (March 17, 2007). Cribb investigated allegations against Toronto obstetrician and gynecologist, Dr. Richard Austin. Cribb found — by searching public records at a Toronto court house — that 14 women had filed lawsuits against Dr. Austin between 1991 and 2007. Cribb reports that hospital documents he obtained showed Austin had complication rates — or unexpected problems related to a procedure — for total abdominal hysterectomies of 30 per cent in 2000, 30 per cent in 2001, 9 per cent in 2002 and 10 per cent in 2003. Cribb reported that Dr. Austin retained hospital privileges despite the lawsuits and complication rates.

[110] National Steering Committee on Patient Safety, "Building a Safer System: A National Integrated Strategy for Improving Patient Safety in Canadian Health Care" (Ottawa: 2002) at 15, online at: <http://rcpsc.medical.org/publications/building_a_safer_system_e.pdf>.

[111] S.O. 2010, c. 14.

[112] "Health care organization" includes publicly funded hospitals and other organizations that are provided for in the regulations and receive public funding.

[113] *Excellent Care for All Act, 2010*, S.O. 2010, c. 14, s. 3(1).

[114] *Ibid.*, s. 4(1) and (2).

[115] *Ibid.*, s. 5.

[116] *Ibid.*, s. 8(3).

[117] Privileges define the role that a physician (or other health professional) is entitled to perform in a particular institution. See the International Association of Medical Regulatory Authorities (IAMRA), online at: <http://www.iamra.com/glossary.asp#pv>.

decision by the Health Professions Appeal and Review Board of Ontario upheld the 2009 revocation of privileges of a physician in part due to his "repeated and disruptive behaviour" towards administrative staff, colleagues and patients. This was found to be contrary to hospital by laws and policies, and prompted the hospital to take action in respect of the physician's privileges. Such behaviour may not amount to incompetency as such, but would nevertheless threaten patient safety and the delivery of quality care.[119] Hospital powers to restrict or cancel privileges, therefore, also have a potentially useful role to play in ensuring patient safety and quality care. It is not at all clear, however, that they currently play a significant role.[120]

2.   The Discipline Process

Discipline processes usually consist of four stages: detection, investigation, hearing and appeal.[121] The most common way of detecting a problem that warrants investigation is through consumer complaints. This has been criticized because consumers may not always be in a position to recognize that a situation warrants a complaint; may feel uncomfortable in complaining about a health professional to whom they had entrusted their care;[122] and may fear jeopardizing their access to needed care (indeed, in areas with a shortage of medical personnel).

Some provinces require members to report situations where an inquiry may be warranted. For example, in British Columbia the *Health Professions Act* requires that a registered member report to the registrar any member believed not to be competent to practise the designated health profession, or to be suffering from a physical or mental ailment, emotional disturbance or addiction to alcohol or drugs that impairs their ability to practise.[123] Also, a member must report if they suspect that another has engaged in sexual misconduct.[124] In addition, some provinces afford discretion to college registrars or the like to instigate investigations. In Alberta, the *Health Professions Act* gives college "complaints direc-

---

[118] *Public Hospitals Act*, R.S.O. 1990, c. P.40. Where they do so, hospitals must provide notice of the restriction or cancellation, and a detailed report, to the College of Physicians and Surgeons of Ontario (s. 33).

[119] Lad Kucis, Gardiner Roberts LLP, "A New Era of Accountability for Hospitals and Physicians – The Impact of the *Rosenhek v Windsor Regional Hospital* Decisions" (May 2010), online at: <http://www.gardinerroerts.com/documents/articles/Commentary%20re%20Rosenhek%20v.%20Windsor%20Regional%20Hospital%20Cases.pdf>.

[120] See footnote 109 above.

[121] See *Stephen v. College of Physicians and Surgeons of Saskatchewan*, [1990] S.J. No. 536, 89 Sask. R. 25 (Sask. Q.B.); and *Khosla v. Alberta*, [1993] A.J. No. 640, 12 Alta. L.R. (3d) 325 (Alta. Q.B.).

[122] Linette McNamara, Erin Nelson & Brent Windwick, "Regulation of Health Care Professionals" in Jocelyn Downie, Timothy Caulfield & Colleen M. Flood, eds., *Canadian Health Law and Policy*, 2d ed. (Markham, ON: LexisNexis Canada, 2002) 55 at 78.

[123] R.S.B.C. 1996, c. 183, ss. 32.1, 32.2 and 32.3. See also Manitoba, *Regulated Health Professions Act*, S.M. 2009, c. 15, s. 136 [not yet proclaimed in force].

[124] British Columbia, *Health Professions Act*, R.S.B.C. 1996, c. 183, s. 32.4.

tors" the power not only to act on complaints, but also to act on information they obtain themselves. Where, *inter alia*, they have reasonable grounds to believe that the conduct of a regulated member constitutes unprofessional conduct, they may treat the information as if a complaint had been made and take action accordingly.[125]

Once a problem has been detected, an investigation is initiated. Generally, investigations are mandatory and the powers of investigators established statutorily. The purpose of investigations is to eliminate or resolve some charges as quickly as possible, and to gather evidence about charges that will proceed to the next stage of the process.

If an investigation determines that a complaint has merit, typically the complaint will proceed to a hearing, where a panel will hear evidence and decide whether or not the professional's conduct was inappropriate and deserving of sanction. Hearings tend to be strongly adversarial in nature, with parties represented by lawyers. At the conclusion of the hearing, the panel will determine what (if any) penalty should be imposed; for example, reprimand, suspension, loss of licence, conditions on a licence, mandatory remedial education, a fine, costs or a combination of these options. A right to appeal the decision may be explicit or implicit in governing legislation.

Governing bodies have a legal duty to act fairly and observe the principles of "natural justice" in their investigation and prosecution of a complaint.[126] What will be considered a fair and satisfactory process in each case will depend on the particular statutes governing each profession in each province, other provincial statutes that apply (for example, those concerning evidence) and general administrative law principles.[127]

In some cases, mediation and settlement are encouraged as an alternative to a formal hearing process. The idea is that an informal process such as mediation may be preferable to the adversarial nature of disciplinary hearings, as it allows both the complainant patient and the respondent physician to have an input into the final outcome. Examples include section 57 of Nova Scotia's *Medical Act*, which provides that after a matter is referred to a hearing committee, the member complained of may tender a settlement agreement that includes admission of a violation and the member's consent to a specified disposition.[128] Prince Ed-

---

[125] R.S.A. 2000, c. H-7, s. 56.

[126] K.R. Hamilton, *Self-Governing Professions: Digests of Court Decisions* (Aurora, ON: Canada Law Book, 1995) at 5. See also G. Sharpe, *The Law and Medicine in Canada*, 2d ed. (Toronto: Butterworths, 1987) at 243; J.J. Morris, *Law for Canadian Health Care Administrators* (Toronto: Butterworths, 1996) at 55.

[127] A full discussion of what constitutes fairness at all of the stages of the process is beyond the scope of this chapter. For a general discussion of how administrative law principles have been applied to physicians, nurses and other health care professionals, see G. Sharpe, *The Law and Medicine in Canada*, 2d ed., *ibid.*, at 234; J.J. Morris, *Law for Canadian Health Care Administrators, ibid.*, at 67. For a general discussion of the principles of administrative law which would apply to the discipline process, see D.P. Jones & A.S. de Villars, *Principles of Administrative Law*, 2d ed. (Toronto: Carswell, 1994).

[128] S.N.S. 1995-96, c. 10.

ward Island's *Medical Act* states that wherever it is appropriate, the complaint should be referred to mediation, thus eliminating the need for either an investigation or disciplinary action.[129]

In British Columbia, the Health Professions Review Board (which reviews various decisions of college committees[130]) uses mediation as an initial step before proceeding to a formal review. The Board notes that a benefit of mediation is that it allows an applicant to participate in a "direct and respectful" meeting in respect of college processes that they have perceived to be "less than transparent and responsive". In some cases, colleges are exposed to new information that causes them to re-evaluate the decisions of college committees under review.[131] In its first year of operation, the Review Board conducted 16 mediations, 75 per cent of which were reported to be successful in resolving the case.[132]

A key criticism directed towards college disciplinary systems is that they do not do enough to ensure quality of care. In the United States, a recent study found that even when medical boards exercise their disciplinary discretion, they tend to focus on character-related misconduct, including criminal misconduct, that may bear little relationship to clinical quality and patient care.[133] While great caution must be exercised in extrapolating lessons from the United States to the Canadian setting, this issue at least warrants further exploration in Canada. To what extent do disciplinary proceedings actually focus on matters that are of the greatest concern when it comes to ensuring quality of care and patient safety?

C.   ACCOUNTABILITY AND TRANSPARENCY

In recent years, provincial governments have sought to improve accountability and transparency of regulation of health professionals through various mechanisms including new forms of government control over the self-regulating professions, increased levels of public representation on the governing councils of professional colleges and the introduction of public discipline hearings.

One of the most basic accountability mechanisms is provision for the review of decisions made by college committees, including Registration Committees, as well as Complaints/Discipline Committees. In Ontario, the Health Professions Review and Appeal Board reviews, *inter alia*, decisions of the Colleges Complaints Committees and orders of the Registration Committees to ensure that they fulfil their duties in the public interest and as mandated by relevant legislation. The Review Board provides a neutral forum for members of

---

[129]   R.S.P.E.I. 1988, c. M-5, s. 32.6.
[130]   See discussion at footnote 135.
[131]   British Columbia, *Health Professions Review Board, 2009 Annual Report* (Victoria: 2010) at 13.
[132]   *Ibid.*
[133]   Nadia N. Sawicki, "Character, Competence, and the Principles of Medical Discipline" (2010) 13 J. Health Care L. & Pol'y 285 at 287.

the public as well as for health professionals.[134] Similar bodies exist in other provinces.[135]

Other newer accountability measures have tended to pit the professions against government, with the professions resistant to legislative changes that increase government oversight of their activities. A controversial amendment was passed to Alberta's *Health Professions Act* in 2007, which allows the Minister to direct a college council to adopt standards of practice or amendments to its standards of practice; to make bylaws or regulations as set out in the order; or to carry out any power or duty of a council under the Act or a bylaw in the manner set out in the order. Direction can only be made following consultation with the affected college.[136]

The Alberta Medical Association called the amendment "draconian" and a "threat to self-regulation", while the Government countered that the amendments would simply allow the Minister to step in and make changes where necessary, working collaboratively with the health profession bodies.[137] The legislation was drafted in response to outbreaks of antibiotic-resistant bacteria in medical facilities in 2007. In response to the outbreaks, Alberta Health and Wellness conducted a review that called for new standards of practice by all health professionals in infection prevention and control.[138] The review noted that during the outbreaks, the Minister did not have any legal authority to step in and make changes.

However, this type of provision does not necessarily give the Minister unfettered power. Ontario has a provision in its legislation that allows the Minister to require a council to make, amend or revoke a regulation under a health profession Act,[139] but a court ruling has imposed a check on this power. In the case in question, the Ontario Minister of Health asked Cabinet to pass a regulation making it an act of professional misconduct for a physician to charge a block or annual fee for all uninsured services a physician may provide to a patient. The

---

[134] *Ministry of Health and Long-Term Care Appeal and Review Boards Act, 1998*, S.O. 1998, c. 18, Sched. H; *Health Professions Procedural Code*, Sched. 2 to the Ontario *Regulated Health Professions Act, 1991*, S.O. 1991, c. 18.

[135] See, for example, British Columbia's Health Professions Review Board, which may, on request, review registration decisions, as well the timeliness of college inquiry committee complaint dispositions or investigations and review certain dispositions of complaints by the committee. The Board may also develop and publish guidelines and recommendations to help colleges establish and employ disciplinary procedures that are transparent, objective, impartial and fair. The purpose is to provide a neutral forum for the public and health professionals to resolve issues or seek review of the colleges' decisions: British Columbia, *Health Professions Act*, R.S.B.C. 1996, c. 183, s. 50.53.

[136] *Health Professions Act*, R.S.A. 2000, c. H-7, s. 135.1.

[137] Deborah Jones, "Alberta to Limit Self-Regulation" (2007) 177:11 CMAJ 1342.

[138] Alberta Health and Wellness, "Provincial Review of Infection Prevention and Control" (Calgary: August 2007), online at: <http://www.health.alberta.ca/documents/IPC-Review-2007.pdf>.

[139] Section 5(1)(c) of the *Regulated Health Professions Act, 1991*, S.O. 1991, c. 18. See also s. 95 of the *Health Professions Procedural Code*, being Schedule 2 to the *Regulated Health Professions Act, 1991*, S.O. 1991, c. 18, which contains a list of a regulatory body's rule-making powers which are subject to Cabinet approval.

College of Physicians and Surgeons of Ontario (CPSO) had earlier refused to make such a regulation. The regulation was challenged by the CPSO in court, and it was struck down on the grounds that the Government had exceeded its powers to make regulations. The court found that the Lieutenant Governor in Council's power was not unfettered. Rather, the power must be exercised with due regard for the purpose and intent of the statute. The court found that the Government's purpose in enacting the regulation (to ensure accessibility and prevent abuses of "extra-billing") was not consistent with the purposes of the *Medical Practitioners Act*. The court stated that "when the Minister sees fit to override a determination made by a self-governing body of professionals authorized by the legislature to determine such issues, the views of the self-governing body of the profession should be taken into consideration by the court in determining whether the Minister pushed the definition of 'professional misconduct' beyond permissible limits, given that the term is peculiarly defined by the standards of the profession".[140]

Ontario has recently strengthened government oversight of the regulated professions. Bill 179 (which received Royal Assent in 2009) amended the *Regulated Health Professions Act, 1991* to empower Cabinet, on the recommendation of the Minister, to appoint a College Supervisor to ensure, *inter alia*, that the college is performing the duties and powers imposed on it by legislation.[141] The Minister may consider any matter that he or she considers relevant in deciding whether to make a recommendation about the appointment of a College Supervisor, including the quality of the administration and management of the college, and the performance of the college respecting its statutory duties under the *Regulated Health Professions Act, 1991*. The College Supervisor will have all the powers of a college Council and any other college official or employee.

Ontario's provision was introduced as an accountability mechanism prompted by concern about patient safety, and it is reportedly only to be used as a last resort if patient safety is compromised.[142] However, the provision has attracted significant criticism from the regulated professions. The Ontario College of Physicians and Surgeons has suggested that there are already adequate oversight mechanisms in place to ensure the accountability of health regulatory colleges[143] and that the move fundamentally undermines professional self-regulation in Ontario.

---

[140] *Szmuilowicz v. Ontario (Minister of Health)*, [1995] O.J. No. 1699, 24 O.R. (3d) 204 (Ont. Div. Ct.).

[141] *Regulated Health Professions Act, 1991*, S.O. 1991, c. 18, s. 5.0.1.

[142] Ann Silversides, "Governments Make Inroads into Medical Self-Regulation" (2009) 181:11 CMAJ 784.

[143] See "The College of Physicians and Surgeons of Ontario's Submission on Bill 179 – The Regulated Health Professions Statute Law Amendment Act, 2009" (September 25, 2009), online at: <http://www.cpso.on.ca/uploadedFiles/policies/positions/Bill179Submission_Sep09.pdf>. They refer to, *inter alia*, public representation on governing councils; the requirement to circulate proposed regulations for public comment before they are approved by council; the requirement for regulations to be approved by Cabinet, the fact that council meetings and disciplinary hearings are open to the public; the fact that registration practices are reviewed by and audited for the

A similar means of accountability focuses on the making of college bylaws. Section 19(3) of British Columbia's *Health Professions Act*[144] provides that a regulatory body's bylaws do not take effect until they are approved by the Lieutenant Governor in Council. Section 19 also permits the Minister to request a board to amend or repeal an existing bylaw or to make a new bylaw for its college. Where a board does not comply with such a request, the Lieutenant Governor in Council may amend or repeal the existing bylaw, or make the new bylaw.[145] The medical and nursing professions have both argued that this unilateral right to impose a rule weakens the independence of professions and the credibility of self-governing bodies. It argues that requirements for public representation on governing bodies, annual reports and a provision that rules be approved by the Lieutenant Governor are adequate to ensure accountability.[146]

As discussed earlier in this chapter, public safety is the number one priority in the regulation of health professionals. Therefore, to the extent that government oversight of colleges can help to ensure that public safety is front and centre, provisions such as those discussed above are positive. However, there is always a risk that ministers (and/or their advising officials) will not be the most well-equipped to make decisions concerning clinical and ethical standards. In particular, there is a risk of hasty decisions being made in response to a crisis or adverse event in order to respond to public concerns. It will be important not only that the power is exercised as a last resort, but that any decisions made are based on sound research and evidence.

A different form of government involvement is used in British Columbia, where the legislation allows the Minister to refer questions concerning the duties of the colleges and the training and regulation of health professionals to an advisory panel.[147] Similarly, Manitoba's pending *Regulated Health Professions Act* permits the Government to appoint a person to inquire into the functioning of a college, and make recommendations about its administration or operation, or the state of practice of a regulated health professional.[148] Following an inquiry, the Minister may issue a directive to the college if it is in the public interest to do so, or it would provide for matters related to health, safety or quality assurance in the practice of the regulated health professional.[149]

Office of the Fairness Commissioner to ensure that they are transparent, objective, impartial and fair; the fact that registration and complaints decisions are subject to external appeal by the Health Professions Appeal and Review Board; the fact that quality assurance and patient relations programs are subject to the scrutiny of the Health Professions Regulatory Advisory council.

[144] R.S.B.C. 1996, c. 183.

[145] *Ibid.*, s. 19(6).

[146] Health Professions Council, "Safe Choices: A New Model for Regulating Health Professions in British Columbia" (Vancouver: Government of British Columbia, Ministry of Health, 2001) at para. E.1.

[147] *Health Professions Act*, R.S.B.C. 1996, c. 183, s. 6.3(1).

[148] S.M. 2009, c. 15, s. 155(1) [not yet proclaimed in force].

[149] *Ibid.*, s. 156(1) [not yet proclaimed in force]. This provision is similar to those existing in Ontario, Quebec, Alberta and British Columbia. It excludes clinical practice standards.

Some provinces require public appointees on councils of professional colleges and to various committees (*e.g.*, disciplinary committees).[150] Some provinces also require disciplinary hearings to be public, although there tend to be exceptions for certain cases. For example, the British Columbia *Health Professions Act* provides an exception where the complainant or the respondent requests that the hearing be held in private, and the discipline committee is satisfied that a private hearing would be appropriate in the circumstances.[151] In contrast, other provinces, such as Saskatchewan, do not require disciplinary hearings to be made public at all.

There is inadequate research to determine how successful public representation requirements have been in Canada, while studies from the United States show mixed results. Studies there have found that simply placing citizen members on self-regulatory bodies does not ensure that the public interest is protected, although improved protection is one possible outcome.[152] Unfortunately, another possible outcome is that the public member might feel accountable to the professional group rather than to the "public interest".[153] As Graddy and Nichols argue, health professionals "enjoy a certain mystique and can intimidate those not in their profession".[154] A study by Broscheid found that the presence of public members on licensing boards leads to an emphasis on licensing requirements that can be better justified with quality control arguments. That is, strong consumer interests increase education-related licensing requirements, while professional interests are associated with licensing requirements whose purpose does not seem to go beyond entry restriction.[155]

Still another aspect of accountability and transparency is making information about health practitioners available to the public. In Manitoba, for example, the *Regulated Health Professions Act* (which, as noted previously, has not yet entered into force at the time of writing) enables councils to create and make available to the public individual practitioner profiles of members who hold a certificate of practice.[156] Members may be required to provide information that includes a description of any offence that is reasonably related to the member's competence or to the safe practice of the regulated profession; a description of

---

[150] See, for example, Alberta *Health Professions Act*, s. 12; Manitoba *Regulated Health Professions Act*, S.M. 2009, c. 15, ss. 13(2), 81(1)(c) and 105(1)(c) [not yet proclaimed in force]. See also Health Professions Regulatory Advisory Council, "Regulation of Health Professionals in Ontario: New Directions" (Ottawa: 2006) at 77.

[151] R.S.B.C. 1996, c. 183, s. 38(3).

[152] M. Christine Cagle, J. Michael Martinez & William D. Richardson, "Privatizing Professional Licensing Boards: Self-Governance or Self-Interest?" (1999) 30 Administration and Society 734 at 759.

[153] *Ibid.*

[154] Elizabeth Graddy & Michael E. Nichol, "Public Members on Occupational Licensing Boards: Effects on Legislative Regulatory Reforms" (1989) 55:3 Southern Economic Journal 610.

[155] Andreas Broscheid & Paul E. Teske, "Public Members on Medical Licensing Boards and the Choice of Entry Barriers" (2003) 114 Public Choice 445 at 456.

[156] S.M. 2009, c. 15, s. 129(1) [not yet proclaimed in force].

any final disciplinary action taken against the member by a regulating body; and a description of any malpractice court judgments.[157]

VI. REGULATING TO ENSURE ACCESSIBILITY OF CARE

The Canadian health care system continues to face many challenges as provinces strive to meet the principles of the *Canada Health Act*: accessibility, universality, comprehensiveness, public administration and portability. This final section focuses on the principle of *accessibility* and the role that regulation of health professionals can play in helping to achieve access to care for all Canadians. Accessibility of care can be enhanced through various means, including changing methods of service delivery, uptake of new technologies, facilitating access to a broader range of services, and more effective and efficient use of health professionals.

A.   CHANGING METHODS OF SERVICE DELIVERY: INTERDISCIPLINARY AND COLLABORATIVE CARE

A significant change to health service delivery over recent years has been a growth in interdisciplinary care. Interdisciplinary care involves the participation of health professionals from various disciplines, such as medicine, occupational therapy, psychology and social work. It relies on professionals interacting and coordinating with each other in order to develop intervention and treatment plans for patients. Interdisciplinary care is about more than just receiving services from multiple providers. Interdisciplinary care is based on the interaction of providers to deliver complementary services in a jointly collaborative manner. It is also different from multidisciplinary care, where patients receive simultaneous care from several disciplines but there is no significant degree of interaction among the various professions.[158] Interdisciplinary care aims to ensure close collaboration among a team of professionals to meet patient needs. Its advantages lie in its potential to bring a variety of professional staff together around a continuum of care, and in so doing, to foster the promotion of health and prevention of illness. Interdisciplinary care has the potential to respond to health care needs and provide a better quality of care; to increase organizational capacity to respond to overall care needs of individuals; to increase the appropriateness of care (due to collaboration among providers during their interactions with the patient); and to better coordinate care.[159]

---

[157] *Ibid.*, s. 129(3)(a) [not yet proclaimed in force].

[158] The Health and Welfare Commissioner, "2009 Appraisal Report on the Performance of Québec's Health and Social Services System, Building on Primary Healthcare Renewal: Recommendations, Issues and Implications" at 30, online at: <http://csbe.gouv.qc.ca/fileadmin/www/RapportAppreciation/version_anlaise_Volume_4/CSBE_AppraisalReportBuildingPrimaryCare.pdf>.

[159] *Ibid.*, at 31. See also HealthForceOntario "Interprofessional Care: A Blueprint for Action in Ontario" (report of HealthForceOntario submitted by the Interprofessional Care Steering Committee,

This model of service delivery requires that physicians and other members of the team receive appropriate training. It also requires regulation that allows experimentation and innovative approaches in human resources utilization and management.[160] In some cases, legislation prevents such approaches, for example, by forbidding registered members of a college to practise in association with a non-member. As well, some legislation prohibits professionals from being affiliated with or establishing a partnership with non-registrants. In British Columbia, for example, the now-repealed *Medical Practitioners Act* made it an offence for a physician to practise medicine in partnership with a non-member of the College of Physicians and Surgeons of British Columbia without the written consent of the Executive Committee.[161] Such provisions have the potential to create unnecessary barriers to interdisciplinary practice. Other barriers to interdisciplinary practice may take the form of restrictions on dual licensure, such as preventing chiropractors from practising physical therapy in addition to chiropody.[162] When it comes into force, Manitoba's *Regulated Health Professions Act* is intended to remove barriers to interdisciplinary practice through provisions regarding "practice in association" that minimize barriers to practitioners working together, including members of different professions.[163] In Quebec, amendments were made to the Professional Code in the early 2000s that contributed to the growth of interdisciplinary care by redefining various medical professions such as nursing, physiotherapy and pharmacy. Fields of practice were expanded so that certain services were no longer exclusively reserved to physicians but could be shared among various professions.[164]

Growth in interdisciplinary care also requires regulatory changes to the scope of practice for health professionals who work with physicians.[165] In Ontario, amendments to the *Health Professions Regulation Act* in 2009 expanded the scope of practice of certain regulated health professions in order to promote greater collaboration amongst professions and to enable them to provide more

---

2007), online at: <http://www.healthforceontario.ca/upload/en/whatishfo/ipc%20blueprint%20final. pdf>; and Health Professions Regulatory Advisory Council, "Critical Links: Transforming and Supporting Patient Care" (report to the Ontario Minister of Health and Long-Term Care, January 2009).

[160] Health Professions Regulatory Advisory Council, "Regulation of Health Professionals in Ontario: New Directions" (Ottawa: 2006) at 11.

[161] R.S.B.C. 1996, c. 285, repealed by *Health Professions Amendment Act, 2003*, S.B.C. 2003, c. 57, s. 58, effective June 1, 2009 (B.C. Reg. 423/2008).

[162] *Chiropractors Act*, R.S.B.C. 1996, c. 48, s. 21(1), repealed by *Health Professions Amendment Act, 2003*, S.B.C. 2003, c. 57, s. 58, effective March 1, 2009 (B.C. Reg. 423/2008).

[163] S.M. 2009, c. 15, s. 65(2) [not yet proclaimed in force]. See also "Proposed Umbrella Health Professions Legislation: The *Regulated Health Professions Act*" (Health Professions Regulatory Reform Consultation Document, Government of Manitoba: January 2009) at 70.

[164] The Health and Welfare Commissioner, "2009 Appraisal Report on the Performance of Québec's Health and Social Services System, Building on Primary Healthcare Renewal: Recommendations, Issues and Implications" at 30, online at: <http://csbe.gouv.qc.ca/fileadmin/www/Rapport Appreciation/version_anlaise_Volume_4/CSBE_AppraisalReportBuildingPrimaryCare.pdf>.

[165] See discussion in British Columbia Medical Association, Policy Statement, "Multidisciplinary Primary Care" (May 2010).

services. Under the amended rules, some professions (including chiropody, podiatry, respiratory therapy and pharmacy) are able to administer, by inhalation, certain substances that are designated under regulation. Other health professions are given an expanded role in managing patient care. For example, physiotherapists are permitted to order X-rays and diagnose patients' conditions.[166]

B. UPTAKE OF NEW TECHNOLOGIES: TELEHEALTH

The terms "telehealth", "telemedicine" and "e-health" are used interchangeably and may be broadly defined as "the use of communications and information technologies to overcome geographic distances between health care practitioners or between practitioners and service users for the purposes of diagnosis, treatment, consultation, education and health information transfer".[167] Telehealth encompasses Internet or web-based "e-health" solutions, as well as video-based applications. There are an increasing number of telehealth initiatives in place across Canada, covering a wide range of areas from the provision of health information and advice via telephone to diagnostic services utilizing electronic technologies and robotic surgery from a distance.

Despite the growing potential of telehealth applications, regulation in Canada remains in its infancy. Telehealth raises a number of issues with respect to regulation and licensure where health professionals provide services to patients located outside of the professional's jurisdiction. Two aspects of input regulation are particularly important: qualification and locus of accountability. Regarding qualification, if different provinces impose divergent requirements for entry into practice, it may be difficult for physicians in one province to get permission to practise in another province. Locus of accountability is key to determining which jurisdiction has the authority to investigate and discipline health professionals providing telehealth services.

There are essentially two options for determining the locus of accountability. First, it may be stipulated as being the physician's location. Where this happens, the patient is "virtually transported" to the physician's location and the physician does not need any additional licences to treat the patient.[168] This approach arguably does not afford out-of-province/territory patients sufficient protection, because the regulatory agency in the patient's home province is generally considered to be the agency best able to ensure protection of patients. As well, there may be practical problems involved in investigating complaints

---

[166] See McMillan LLP Health Law Bulletin, "A Prescription for Better Access: Bill 179 Receives Royal Assent" (January 2010), online at: <http://www.mcmillan.ca/Files/Bill179_ReceivesRoyal Assent_0110.pdf>.

[167] R.W. Pong & J.C. Hogenbirk, "Licensing Physicians for Telehealth Practice: Issues and Policy Options" (1999) 8 Health L. Rev. 3 at 3.

[168] Sabrina Hasham, Rajen Akalu & Peter G. Rossos, "Medico-Legal Implications of Telehealth in Canada" (2003-2004) 4:2 Telehealth Law 9 at 12. They note that the G-8 Global Healthcare Applications Subproject recommends establishing the locus of accountability as the physician's location to reduce licensure obstacles.

where the physician providing services is regulated in a jurisdiction different from that of the patient. For example, a patient may have difficulty participating in discipline proceedings in another province.[169]

The second option is to take a patient-centric approach, where the locus of accountability is the patient's location. This means that the physician providing the service must be authorized to practise in the jurisdiction where the patient is located.[170] Advantages cited for this approach are that provinces ought to have the most control possible over the health care services received by their residents, and that it will help to both ensure higher practice standards and control the behaviour of health professionals through the threat of licence suspension or revocation.[171] However, there are also downsides. On a practical level, it will be difficult to develop a process for telehealth practitioners to obtain dual or multiple licences. The scenario of having physicians obtain licences on a province-by-province basis may constrain the growth of telehealth and, thus, accessibility of care.

The Federation of Medical Regulatory Authorities of Canada has developed a policy on telehealth that emphasizes patient safety. It recommends that each Medical Regulatory Authority should make it known to its members that it expects registered physicians to comply with the licensing or registration requirements of any jurisdiction where they provide telemedicine services (that is, a patient-centric approach).[172]

One aspect of telehealth that has been described as particularly promising is telepharmacy.[173] This involves the provision of pharmaceutical care through the use of telecommunications and information technologies to a patient at a distance.[174] Telepharmacy can help to improve access to pharmacist services, especially for patients in rural and remote areas. However, telepharmacy requires a supporting regulatory environment that does not currently exist across Canada. Many provinces have regulations requiring pharmacists to provide direct and personal supervision throughout the dispensing process and provide the final verification of the drug before it is given to the patient.[175]

In 2005, British Columbia became the first province to allow telepharmacy, while amendments to Ontario's *Regulated Health Professions Act, 1991* in 2009

---

[169] R.W. Pong & J.C. Hogenbirk, "Licensing Physicians for Telehealth Practice: Issues and Policy Options" (1999) 8 Health L. Rev. 3 at 8.

[170] Sabrina Hasham, Rajen Akalu & Peter G. Rossos, "Medico-Legal Implications of Telehealth in Canada" (2003-2004) 4:2 Telehealth Law 9 at 12.

[171] R.W. Pong & J.C. Hogenbirk, "Licensing Physicians for Telehealth Practice: Issues and Policy Options" (1999) 8 Health L. Rev. 3 at 8.

[172] Federation of Medical Regulatory Authorities of Canada, "Policy on Telemedicine" (updated June 2010), online at: <http://www.fmrac.ca/policy/telemedicine.html>.

[173] For example, Health Canada, "Commission on the Future of Health Care in Canada: The Romanow Commission" (2002) highlighted telepharmacy's potential benefits. See also David Huston, "Considering Telehealth Regulation in Canada" (Paper Submission #1 for CHE Designation, Canadian College of Health Service Executives: November 2009).

[174] *Ibid.*, at 2.

[175] *Ibid.*, at 4-5.

removed the requirement that a pharmacist be physically present in a pharmacy with respect to "remote dispensing locations".[176] Where pharmacy regulation is the domain of self-regulated professions (such as the Ontario College of Pharmacists), those professions will — where enabled by legislation — be able to design the manner in which telepharmacy operates. In Ontario, the College of Pharmacists approved revisions to the consolidated *Drug and Pharmacies Regulation Act* Regulations in June 2010. These revisions permit remote dispensing either through an automated pharmacy system or a remote dispensing location staffed by a regulated Pharmacy Technician. The Regulations make provision for public safety including, for example, requiring accreditation of remote dispensing locations; assigning responsibilities for safety and security to the designated manager of the pharmacy that operates the remote location; and requiring that remote dispensing locations where a pharmacist is not present be equipped with a live, two-way, audio-visual link that permits dialogue between the patient and the remote pharmacist.

C.   ACCESS TO A BROADER RANGE OF SERVICES: COMPLEMENTARY AND ALTERNATIVE MEDICINE

While there is no exclusive list of what constitutes complementary and alternative medicine (CAM) therapies, a starting definition is a broad domain of healing resources that encompasses all health systems, modalities, and practices and their accompanying theories and beliefs, other than those intrinsic to the politically dominant health system of a particular society or culture in a given historical period. CAM includes all such practices and ideas self-defined by their users as preventing or treating illness or promoting health and well-being. Boundaries within CAM and between the CAM domain and the domain of the dominant system are not always sharp or fixed.[177]

There has been an increase in the demand for CAM since the 1990s,[178] which has led to an increase in the number of CAM practitioners and the use of

---

[176] See s. 146 of the *Drug and Pharmacies Regulation Act*, R.S.O. 1990, c. H.4. A certificate of accreditation must have been issued permitting the operation of the remote dispensing location, and said location must be operated in accordance with the regulations.

[177] Linette McNamara, Erin Nelson & Brent Windwick, "Regulation of Health Care Professionals" in Jocelyn Downie, Timothy Caulfield & Colleen M. Flood, eds., *Canadian Health Law and Policy*, 2d ed. (Markham, ON: LexisNexis Canada, 2002) 55 at 86, citing, among other sources, Theodore de Bruyn, "Taking Stock: Policy Issues Associated with Complementary and Alternative Health Care" in *Perspectives on Complementary and Alternative Health Care: A Collection of Papers Prepared for Health Canada* (Ottawa: Public Works and Government Services Canada, 2001) at II.18; and N.I.H. Panel on Definition and Description, "Defining and Describing Complementary and Alternative Medicine" (1997) 3:2 Alternative Therapies 49.

[178] See, for example, Lynda Buske, "Popularity of Alternative Health Care Providers Continues to Grow" (2002) 166 CMAJ 366.

alternative therapies by mainstream medical practitioners.[179] However, regulation of CAM in Canada remains patchy and minimal; for example, only chiropractors are regulated in all provinces, and in some provinces, professions allow non-traditional medicine to be practised without regulation. Slowly, professional colleges, entry to practice requirements, standards of practice and disciplinary systems are being established for these new professions. Ontario will be the first province to regulate homeopathy,[180] while British Columbia was the first province to regulate practitioners of traditional Chinese medicine and acupuncture.[181] Acupuncturists are regulated in Alberta and Quebec, and will be covered by Ontario's new regulations for traditional Chinese medicine. Massage therapy is only regulated in British Columbia, Ontario, and Newfoundland and Labrador. Naturopathic medicine is regulated in five provinces, with Alberta planning to introduce regulations in 2011.[182]

Increasingly, CAM practitioners have sought to engage in a process of "professionalization" whereby they transition from "occupation" to self-regulated "profession". This process affords practitioners greater legitimacy, and benefits such as enhanced income, status and power.[183] However, not all CAM practitioners want to be regulated. The Canadian Society of Homeopaths, for example, has opposed regulation in Ontario, arguing that there is not a sufficient number of homeopaths in order to fund a professional college.[184] There has also traditionally been opposition from many mainstream physicians who benefit from a restrictive regulatory regime that does not recognize the status of CAM practitioners.

It has sometimes been suggested that regulation of CAM is not necessary because it is not "real" medicine and does not work. Therefore, the argument goes, there is no safety issue as there is with respect to conventional medicine.[185]

---

[179] In Ontario at least, a key reason for this increase is demographic change as consumers and practitioners of CAM therapies arrive from countries where these approaches are accepted parts of health care. Health Professions Regulatory Advisory Council, "Regulation of Health Professionals in Ontario: New Directions" (Ottawa: 2006).

[180] *Traditional Chinese Medicine Act, 2006,* S.O. 2006, c. 27.

[181] Traditional Chinese Medicine Practitioners and Acupuncturists Regulation, B.C. Reg. 385/2000, repealed by B.C. Reg. 290/2008, effective October 17, 2008. The current regulation is the Traditional Chinese Medicine Practitioners and Acupuncturists Regulation, B.C. Reg. 290/2008, effective October 17, 2008.

[182] Lauren Vogel, "'Hodge-podge' Regulation of Alternative Medicine in Canada" (2010) 182:12 CMAJ E569, online at: <http://www.cmaj.ca/cgi/content/full/182/12/E569>.

[183] Sandy Welsh *et al.,* "Moving Forward? Complementary and Alternative Practitioners Seeking Self-regulation" (2004) 26:2 Sociology of Health and Illness 216 at 217, citing A. Abbott, *The System of Professions: An Essay on the Division of Expert Labor* (Chicago: The University of Chicago Press, 1988); S. Cant & U. Sharma, "Demarcation and Transformation within Homeopathic Knowledge: A Strategy of Professionalisation" (1996) 42 Social Science and Medicine 579; M. Saks, *Professions and the Public Interest: Medical Power, Altruism and Alternative Medicine* (London: Routledge, 1995).

[184] Lauren Vogel, "'Hodge-podge' Regulation of Alternative Medicine in Canada" (2010) 182:12 CMAJ E569, online at: <http://www.cmaj.ca/cgi/content/full/182/12/E569>.

[185] See discussion in Lauren Vogel, "'Hodge-podge' Regulation of Alternative Medicine in Canada", *ibid.*

Others argue, however, that despite the relative safety of some of the therapies, CAM practitioners can still cause harm to their patients (for example, by failing to refer them to another profession). Further, issues such as sexual impropriety are just as pertinent to CAM as to other medical professions.[186]

Without regulation, anyone can set up practice; therefore, regulation becomes important to ensure that patients have some certainty that the person from whom they are seeking treatment has an appropriate level of training, that there is some system of quality assurance, and that patients have a forum for complaints. Ultimately, lines will have to be drawn in order to determine which practitioners are regulated and which are not. The line will never be an easy one to draw, and judgments will need to be made in the interests of public safety as well as feasibility for the practitioners concerned.

D.   MORE EFFICIENT AND EFFECTIVE USE OF HEALTH PROFESSIONALS

1.   Increasing Flexibility Around Delivery of Health Care Services

One of their stated objectives of the amendments made to Ontario's *Regulated Health Professions Act, 1991* in 2009 is to ensure that Ontarians have access to the right number and mix of qualified health care providers.[187] The amendments, therefore, seek to better utilize regulated health care professionals and reduce barriers to their practice. To this end, they introduce greater flexibility around prescribing and dispensing drugs and around remote dispensing. Prescribing and dispensing drugs are acts that have traditionally been reserved for physicians and pharmacists, respectively. The amendments to the legislation include these acts in the practice of a number of other health professionals, including naturopaths, dental hygienists, nurse practitioners and midwives. Nurse practitioners will be able to prescribe, dispense, compound or sell drugs that are designated in the regulations (previously, nurse practitioners could not compound or sell drugs). Pharmacists will be allowed to prescribe drugs that are specified in the regulations. Pharmacists will also be entitled to promote health and to prevent and treat disease through the management of therapy, as well as adapt, modify and extend an existing prescription. These changes recognize that pharmacists are experts in medication management therapy and that being able to fully utilize this expertise will enhance the care available to patients. Similarly, the expansion of scope for dental hygienists allows them to work independently of dentists in new practice settings, such as long-term care facilities, schools, mobile clinics, and remote and rural locations.[188]

---

[186] *Ibid.*

[187] "Compendium, Regulation Health Professions Statute Law Amendment Act, 2009", online at: <http://www.health.gov.on.ca/english/public/legislation/regulated/compendium_regulated_health.pdf>.

[188] McMillan LLP Health Law Bulletin, "A Prescription for Better Access: Bill 179 Receives Royal Assent" (January 2010), online at: <http://www.mcmillan.ca/Files/Bill179_ReceivesRoyal Assent_0110.pdf>.

Concerns have been raised about the adequacy of some of these amendments. For example, the Ontario College of Nurses has argued that nurse practitioners require access to drugs in countless clinical situations that cannot possibly be predicted by a list of drugs and substances, and that this access is critical to reducing fragmentation of care and ensuring that the health care system meets patients' needs. They argue that the drug list should be eliminated altogether so as to enable nurse practitioners to have immediate access to appropriate drug therapy as needed. They note that system resources required to "work around" the legislative restrictions could more helpfully be redirected to other patient care priorities if the list was eliminated. For these and other reasons, they consider that eliminating the list would facilitate more timely and equitable access to drug therapies for patients with limited access to resources.[189]

Any reforms aimed at facilitating new means of delivering health care services must ensure that patient safety is first and foremost. This will require ensuring that the expanded scope of practice falls within the parameters of the profession's knowledge and skills.[190] Inevitably, there will be disagreement as to what scope of practice is appropriate, with vested interests promoting designations that best serve those interests. Each case will have to be decided on its merits, with patient safety and the objectives and interests of the health care system as a whole being the overriding considerations.

2. Designating New Professions

Designations of "new" professions can help to ensure access to health care services where regulation of the new profession enables safe delivery of services and a more efficient spread of the skills of health professionals. A notable case of new designations with the potential to improve accessibility to health care services is the pharmacy profession. Pharmacists have been identified as having a key role to play in delivering (and improving) health care.[191] To this end, the profession of "pharmacy technician" is gradually being regulated across Canada.[192] Pharmacy technicians undertake technical functions related to prescrip-

---

[189] "The College of Nurses of Ontario, Submission to: the Standing Committee on Social Policy, Bill 179, *Regulated Health Professions Law Statute Amendment Act, 2009*" (September 25, 2009), online at: <http://www.cno.org/Global/docs/policy/Bill179SubmissionStandingCommittee_Final_CouncilApproved.pdf>. Other provinces allow for broader prescriptive authority for nurse practitioners: see "Executive Director's Dispatch: Government Must Remove Regulatory Handcuffs that Limit NP Practice", online at: Registered Nurses' Association of Ontario <http://www.rnao.org/Page.asp?PageID=924&ContentID=2951>.

[190] See "The College of Physicians and Surgeons of Ontario's Submission on Bill 179 – The Regulated Health Professions Statute Law Amendment Act, 2009" (September 25, 2009), online at: <http://www.cpso.on.ca/uploadedFiles/policies/positions/Bill179Submission_Sep09.pdf>.

[191] Saskatchewan College of Pharmacists, "Pharmacy Technician Regulation in Saskatchewan – Concept Paper for Regulatory Framework" (September 18, 2009) at 3.

[192] In Alberta, a voluntary register for pharmacy technicians was established in 2008 and regulation was provided for in an amendment to the *Health Professions Act*, R.S.A. 2000, c. H-7 in 2009; in Ontario, the Health Professions Review and Advisory Council approved the regulation of phar-

tion preparation and processing. The purpose of regulating pharmacy technicians is to free pharmacists from technical and administrative tasks (such as counting and preparing a medication) that take up much of their time, by allocating these to pharmacy technicians instead. Pharmacists would then have more time to spend with patients, undertaking health promotion, disease prevention and chronic disease management.[193] Pharmacists have traditionally been reluctant to delegate even technical tasks to technicians because of limitations and variations in training, and concern for public safety.[194] However, regulation provides the possibility for standardization in training and competencies. It can also offer quality assurance and a transparent discipline process.

Alberta was the first province to regulate pharmacy technicians and has been followed by British Columbia and Ontario.[195] Pharmacy technicians will be governed by the Alberta College of Pharmacists, but will have their own register separate and distinct from the pharmacist register.[196] British Columbia is taking a voluntary approach, where pharmacy technicians may choose whether or not they wish to be regulated. Where they do become regulated, they will have independent authority, responsibility and liability relating to the preparation, processing and compounding of prescriptions.[197]

In Ontario, the *Health Systems Improvement Act, 2007* enabled the regulation of pharmacy technicians.[198] This followed a 2006 report by the Health Professions Advisory Council, which concluded that regulation would contribute to a higher and more consistent level of patient safety.[199]

---

macy technicians in 2005 and legislation was passed in 2007; in British Columbia, the transition to regulating pharmacy technicians is under way; in Manitoba, the Manitoba Pharmaceutical Association Pharmacy Technician sub-committee recommended that pharmacy technicians should be regulated under the *Pharmaceutical Act*, R.S.M. 1987, c. P60, as Regulated Pharmacy Technicians; in Nova Scotia, a Pharmacy Technician Task Force was established in 2008 to develop a plan to achieve regulation of pharmacy technicians; and in Saskatchewan, the Pharmacy Technician Regulation Advisory Working Group released a report in September 2009 supporting the regulation of pharmacy technicians in Saskatchewan. For details, see Saskatchewan College of Pharmacists, "Pharmacy Technician Regulation in Saskatchewan – Concept Paper for Regulatory Framework" (September 18, 2009).

[193] *Ibid.*, at 3.

[194] *Ibid.*

[195] Lauren Vogel, "'Hodge-podge' Regulation of Alternative Medicine in Canada" (2010) 182:12 CMAJ E569, online at: <http://www.cmaj.ca/cgi/content/full/182/12/E569>.

[196] Alberta College of Pharmacists, *The Transition Times* (Spring 2010), online at: <https://pharmacists.ab.ca/downloads/documentloader.ashx?id=6014>.

[197] See background regarding regulation at College of Pharmacists of British Columbia, "Pharmacy Technician Regulation", online at: <http://www.bcpharmacists.org/about_us/key_initiatives/index/articles27.php#Background>.

[198] S.O. 2007, c. 10. This Bill (No. 171) received Royal Assent on June 4, 2007. Pharmacy technicians are regulated under the *Pharmacy Act, 1991*, S.O. 1991, c. 36 (as amended) by Bill 171.

[199] Health Professions Advisory Council, "Regulation of Health Professionals in Ontario: New Directions" (Ottawa: 2006) at 136-141.

3.   Addressing Labour Shortages

Provinces are experiencing labour shortages across a number of health professions. One solution is reliance on internationally trained practitioners. This means that labour mobility is becoming an increasingly relevant factor in meeting the health care needs of Canadians.[200] This raises some difficult regulatory challenges that are borne out in the number of foreign-trained physicians in Canada who are not approved to practise. A study based on the 2001 Census found that of 5,400 foreign-trained physicians in Canada aged between 32 and 54, only 55 per cent were working as physicians.[201] Boyd argues that one way of interpreting this data is as an indication that Canadian medical boards tend to exclude foreign-trained physicians. She finds that the ability of provinces to bring in more international physicians has been constrained by the complex systems of multiple licensing and certifying authorities that are in place, and by the medical schools' power to determine the number and accessibility of residency slots.[202] Internationally trained physicians are required to pass the Medical Council of Canada's Evaluating Examination, which assesses the candidate's general medical knowledge in comparison with graduates of Canadian medical schools. Following this baseline examination, most provinces require graduates of foreign medical schools to undertake two years of postgraduate medical training in Canada in order to practise family medicine and four to five years of training for other specialties. They must also pass certification examinations of the College of Physicians of Canada or the Royal College of Physicians and Surgeons of Canada.

The Health Professions Review Board of British Columbia has noted a number of potential challenges for the registration of internationally trained applicants. These challenges include ensuring protection of the public and comparing different programs that vary in important aspects, such as course content and teaching standards, different scopes of practice, and differing expectations as to how people ought to be treated or handled by health care providers. In addition, registration of international applicants requires significant resources to determine the legitimacy or equivalency of an international applicant.[203] Various approaches are being trialled in the case of internationally trained health professionals in British Columbia. These include bridging programs that recruit health professionals on behalf of employers in the province, and differentiated registration either through "tiered" titles of practice based on objective indica-

---

[200] British Columbia Health Professions Review Board, "Best Practices Pilot Study on Health Professions Registration" (April 2010) at para. 24, online at: <http://www.hprb.gov.bc.ca/publications/Best_Practices_Pilot_Study.pdf>.

[201] Monica Boyd & Grant Schellenberg, "Re-accreditation and the Occupations of Immigrant Doctors and Engineers" (Statistics Canada, Catalogue No. 11-008) at 4, online at: <http://www.statcan.gc.ca/pub/11-008-x/2007004/10312-eng.htm>.

[202] Cited in Miriam Shuchman, "Searching for Docs on Foreign Shores" (2008) 178:4 CMAJ 379.

[203] British Columbia Health Professions Review Board, "Best Practices Pilot Study on Health Professions Registration" (April 2010) at para. 27, online at: <http://www.hprb.gov.bc.ca/publications/Best_Practices_Pilot_Study.pdf>.

tors of achievement, skill or experience, or through provisional registration whereby an applicant may apply for provisional status while they obtain any necessary further qualifications. The Board suggests that international registration ought to meet certain best practices. They refer to: flexibility so as to avoid unfair restrictions based on the unique situation of an otherwise acceptable application; transparency of registration practices; fairness (procedural and substantive) to all qualified candidates; impartiality such that decisions about applicants are based on objective criteria and are without bias, prejudice or favouritism; and objectivity in the sense that decisions are made on the basis of clear, understandable criteria. This is a challenging area and patient safety must come first. However, it is also important that the challenges are not used as a disguise for prejudice and turf protection of locally trained professionals.

E.   PRIVATE HEALTH CARE

Recent years have seen an increase in the numbers of privately owned, for-profit independent health facilities that operate both within and outside the public health care system.[204] Regulation has been slow to keep pace with the developments. Only three provinces — Ontario, Alberta and British Columbia — have regulatory and monitoring systems that encompass private health clinics.

Many private facilities, such as those offering physiotherapy and laboratory testing services, rely largely on physician referrals for patients. Choudhry *et al.* suggest that this fact raises two serious issues. First, the facilities may compensate physicians for referrals (a kickback), a practice that can potentially distort clinical judgments.[205] Second, physicians can make referrals to facilities that they themselves own (self-referral), which raises similar concerns.[206] Choudhry *et al.* have examined and found wanting the rules established by self-regulatory bodies in Canada that govern financial relationships between physicians and private for-profit clinics. They found that many of the rules governing kickbacks and self-referrals are inadequate and require reform. For example, only five provinces prohibit physicians from paying or offering to pay kickbacks, an action that represents a conflict of interest by seeking to induce referrals regardless of patient health status. Regarding self-referrals, regulation is often inadequate, particularly where restrictions only relate to investments held by immediate family (given the ease of circumventing the restrictions by placing investments in the name of extended family members), and where only disclosure is required.[207]

---

[204]   Sujit Choudhry, Niteesh K. Choudhry & Adalsteinn D. Brown, "Unregulated Private Markets for Health Care in Canada? Rules of Professional Misconduct, Physician Kickbacks and Physician Self-referral" (2004) 170 CMAJ 1115 at 1115.

[205]   See, for example, recent allegations of kickbacks to physicians referring clients to a chiropractic clinic with locations in Ontario, Nova Scotia and Manitoba: Yoni Freedhoff, "Chiropractic Clinic Offered Referred Kickbacks" (2010) 182:11 CMAJ E522.

[206]   *Ibid.*

[207]   *Ibid.* See also Moe Litman, "Self-Referral and Kickbacks: Fiduciary Law and the Regulation of 'Trafficking in Patients'" (2004) 170 CMAJ 1119 at 1119-1120.

However, while the practices of kickbacks and referrals may be undesirable, Saver sounds a cautionary note with respect to Choudhry *et al.*'s call for stricter regulation. He argues that overly broad bans could result in unintended consequences whereby regulation could prevent financing and delivery innovations such as gainsharing programs (a reward and participation system where organizations and workers share the financial gains arising through reforms such as increased productivity, quality enhancement and cost reduction).[208]

VII. CONCLUSION

Regulation of health professionals is complicated by competing public and provider interests.[209] Public interest dictates that the regulatory system protect the public from harm by ensuring that professionals are suitably qualified to perform services and that those services are of an appropriate quality. Professional interests, on the other hand, suggest that those being regulated will seek to advance their own economic welfare.

Tension arises between public and self-interest in all aspects of Canada's regulatory system. On the input side, self-interest of professionals leads to efforts to restrict entry into their profession in order to maintain exclusivity and increase rent. They may also attempt to restrict designation of other professions (for example, physicians resisting the designation of nurse practitioners). On the other hand, the public is interested in ensuring that entry restriction is based on factors relevant only to qualification and competency, so as to ensure affordability and quality of care.

Tension also arises in the realm of output regulation, where self-interest leads to a perception that health professionals tend to protect their colleagues in disciplinary matters. Public interest, on the other hand, dictates that individuals have a right to have their complaints heard and to seek appropriate redress. Often in Canada, professional bodies have been accused of failing to enforce standards of professional conduct or rendering inappropriate disciplinary action against physicians guilty of incompetence. These tensions — and the ability of professional groups to capture the regulatory system to advance their interests — have been recognized by provincial legislators, who have taken steps to increase transparency and public accountability of self-regulating bodies. Increasingly, there are requirements for public representatives on the councils of self-regulating bodies, for disciplinary hearings to be open to the public and for governments to have some level of control over the regulated professions. Reforms, such as those in Ontario, to develop an umbrella approach for regulation of professions have sought to enhance consistency of regulation across professions. These developments are welcome but must be evaluated and strengthened to

---

[208] Richard S. Saver, "The Costs of Avoiding Physician Conflicts of Interest: A Cautionary Tale of Gainsharing Regulation" in C.M. Flood, ed., *Just Medicare: What's In, What's Out, How We Decide* (Toronto: University of Toronto Press, 2006) 281 at 282.

[209] Andreas Broscheid & Paul E. Teske, "Public Members on Medical Licensing Boards and the Choice of Entry Barriers" (2003) 114 Public Choice 445 at 447.

ensure not only that the public is adequately protected, but that regulation acts as an enabler for the delivery of high-quality health care.

This chapter concluded with a discussion of the ways in which provinces are seeking to improve accessibility of health care services and the role that regulation of health professionals plays in these developments and initiatives. In all aspects of regulation, provincial legislatures must be proactive in reviewing mechanisms and institutional designs, and in designing adequate incentives in order to ensure that regulation serves its intended purpose of public protection and enabling progress in the health care sector. The ever-present human tendency to act in one's own self-interest is too strong to trust that self-regulated professions will wholeheartedly seek to advance the public interest in the absence of such government actions.

Chapter 3

MEDICAL NEGLIGENCE

Bernard Dickens[*]

I.   INTRODUCTION

The area of legal study once modestly described as Law and Medicine or Medical Law, approached as a specialized division of tort law addressing battery and negligence, has evolved as Health Law, and its historic and prospective contexts are addressed by linkage with health policy. As now understood, health law and policy embrace not only the human life span but such areas as medical research, genetics, drug development, artificially assisted reproduction and biotechnology. The pedagogical constraint to contain the potential range of health law and policy within a teaching curriculum often requires that public health law and policy be addressed separately, because legal principles apply differently. For instance, the emphasis on individual consent characteristic of clinical health care may be replaced by democratic or legislative consent, sometimes at the sacrifice of individual liberties and preferences.[1]

Despite its mature richness, however, health law and policy continue to be centred on medical negligence. The exclusion or minimization of medical negligence may be crucial to patients' health, enjoyment of life and very survival. Not every medical error is avoidable or a result of negligence (see Section III(B)(2), "Error of Judgment", below), but many errors are negligent. The volume of medical errors justifies concern about the proportion of errors that are due to medical negligence. It was estimated that in fiscal year 2000, from 9,250 to 23,750 Canadians admitted to acute care hospitals died as a result of preventable adverse events.[2] It is apparent, therefore, that the avoidance of and the response to negligent errors in medical care warrant critical legal attention, and that the law of medical negligence remains a core issue in the study of Canadian health law and policy.

---

[*]   I am indebted to Professor Gerald Robertson, Q.C., for his preparation of this topic in the first and second editions of this book. Much of his scholarship and research are reflected in this chapter.
[1]   T.M. Bailey, T. Caulfield & N.M. Ries, *Public Health Law & Policy in Canada*, 2d ed. (Markham, ON: LexisNexis Canada, 2008).
[2]   G.R. Baker *et al.*, "The Canadian Adverse Events Study: The Incidence of Adverse Events Among Hospital Patients in Canada" (2004) 170 CMAJ 1678; see also S.B. McIver, *Medical Nightmares: The Human Face of Errors* (Toronto: Chestnut Publishing, 2001).

II. NEGLIGENCE AND MALPRACTICE

It is common to treat "medical negligence" and "malpractice" as synonymous terms, or to regard negligence as a major form of malpractice. However, legislation and regulations may distinguish negligence from malpractice. For instance in Ontario, when the limitation period under section 17 of the former *Health Disciplines Act* was superseded by the *Regulated Health Professions Act*, s. 89(1) of the Health Professions Procedural Code retained the historical provision regarding any action arising out of "negligence *or* malpractice".[3] This raises the question of what forms of medical conduct can constitute actionable malpractice without regard to negligence.

Touching a person without appropriate consent or other legal authorization constitutes a battery in tort law, and may be an assault in criminal law. If a health care provider has battered or assaulted a patient, it is no defence that the battery or assault was done carefully. The Supreme Court of Canada has held, however, that treating a patient with consent that is not adequately informed (see Chapter 4, "Informed Consent") is actionable not in battery, since even inadequately informed consent negates battery, but only in negligence if legal requirements, such as damage, are satisfied.[4]

When there is a contract between a health care provider and a patient, an action for breach of contract may be brought separately from or in the alternative to an action for negligence and/or battery. Surgery performed for instance by reading an X-ray plate the wrong way round, or on the wrong limb or organ,[5] may be actionable on all three grounds. Breach of fiduciary duty may found an equitable claim against a physician, whether or not a relationship with a patient is contractual. This may arise not only when a physician acts unconscionably or takes advantage of a patient,[6] such as by succumbing to a conflict of interest, but also when disregarding a patient's interests.[7] Courts may be disposed to develop jurisprudence on fiduciary duties as physicians move towards a salaried and away from a fee-for-service basis of remuneration that in the past would have afforded contractual remedies.

Malpractice liability may also arise for false arrest and imprisonment, such as through negligent or otherwise improper employment of powers of involuntary detention under mental health legislation,[8] and for other torts including defamation, such as by writing libellous reports regarding patients, or for instance making slanderous statements about them, or about colleagues. However, legislation may afford protection when reports or statements are made in good faith and without gross negligence, such as in reporting child abuse or neglect.

---

[3]   *Regulated Health Professions Act, 1991*, S.O. 1991, c. 18, Sched. 2, s. 89(1) [emphasis added], now superseded by the *Limitations Act, 2002*, S.O. 2002, c. 24, Sched. B, s. 4.

[4]   *Reibl v. Hughes*, [1980] S.C.J. No. 105, 114 D.L.R. (3d) 1 (S.C.C.).

[5]   *Urbanski v. Patel*, [1978] M.J. No. 211, 84 D.L.R. (3d) 650 (Man. Q.B.).

[6]   *Norberg v. Wynrib*, [1992] S.C.J. No. 60, 92 D.L.R. (4th) 449 (S.C.C.).

[7]   *McInerney v. MacDonald*, [1992] S.C.J. No. 57, 93 D.L.R. (4th) 415 (S.C.C.).

[8]   *Mullins v. Levy*, [2005] B.C.J. No. 1878, 258 D.L.R. (4th) 460 (B.C.S.C.).

Technical developments are introducing a relatively new aspect to medical negligence law, namely Private International Law, often called Conflict of Laws. With telemedicine and robotic surgery, physicians acting in one jurisdiction may cause effects on patients in other jurisdictions. This raises questions of whether they would be liable for negligence where they are located, where their patients are located, or in both jurisdictions. Related questions concern duties of care owed by the decision-making physicians and distant caregivers following their instructions in direct patient care, locations by reference to which standards of care have to be determined and, for instance, where physicians have to be licensed to provide treatment to cross-border patients.

III. THE ELEMENTS OF NEGLIGENCE

At common law, the customary elements of tort liability for negligence are that the plaintiff must show, on a balance of probability, that:

(1) the defendant owed the plaintiff a legal duty of care;

(2) the defendant breached that duty of care;

(3) the plaintiff suffered legally recognized damage; and

(4) the damage was caused by the defendant's breach of the duty of care.

A. DUTY OF CARE

1. Duty to Patients

Much legal initiative goes into plaintiffs' attempts to show that those they select to sue for negligence owed them legal duties of care, as opposed to mere moral or conscientious duties, but it is rarely contested that physicians owe legal duties of care to their patients. It may be contested that those suing physicians actually were their patients. Since physicians usually may decline to accept persons as their patients, in the ordinary course of practice, no one has a general right to be the patient of any particular physician. If physicians discriminate against persons who want to be their patients on grounds of race, age or other prohibited grounds, they may violate provincial human rights laws,[9] but for instance pediatricians can decline to accept adults as patients, and geriatricians can decline to accept younger patients.

Emergency instances may constitute an exception to this rule. In Quebec, the provincial *Charter of Human Rights and Freedoms* requires physicians and others to attempt within reason to rescue those in peril[10] and jurisprudence in common law provinces is showing some sympathy for the same duty, of reason-

---

[9]   *Korn v. Potter*, [1996] B.C.J. No. 692, 134 D.L.R. (4th) 437 (B.C.S.C.).

[10] L.R.Q., c. C-12, art. 2; see S. Rodgers-Magnet, "The Right to Emergency Medical Assistance in the Province of Quebec" (1980) 40 R du B. 373.

able medical rescue.[11] The *Code of Ethics* of the Canadian Medical Association (CMA)[12] directs a physician in section 18 to "[p]rovide whatever appropriate assistance you can to any person with an urgent need for medical care". Courts may be willing to convert this professional ethical duty into a legal duty of care, if physicians are seen less as independent professionals than as a public resource.[13]

In some circumstances, physicians may have a duty of care not to treat their patients, but promptly to refer them to colleagues whose skills are more suited to the patients' needs.[14] That is, physicians have no duty, outside emergency cases, to undertake treatment they know or reasonably should know to be beyond their capacities, but should propose appropriate referrals. Physicians are not responsible for negligence of those to whom they properly refer their patients, but they are responsible for negligent acts by those whose treatment of their patients they supervise, if supervision falls short of legally required standards.

The duty to refer also applies regarding procedures in which physicians conscientiously object to participate.[15] Physicians' duties of care, owed to both their actual and prospective patients, include disclosure of procedures within the ordinary scope of practice undertaken by colleagues in the same style of practice, that they decline to undertake on grounds of conscience. Abortion is an obvious example, and other items of reproductive health care are similar, but there may also be related objection for instance to forms of end of life care. Disclosure forewarns patients that, for such care, they will be referred to other providers, and spares both patients and physicians the discomfort of patients' requests for procedures in which the physicians will decline to participate. This accommodation of conscience does not allow physicians not to inform patients, when they are medically indicated, that such procedures are legitimate options for the patients to consider. Failure to disclose options for patients' treatment would violate the duty of care, and may constitute negligence, depending on satisfaction of the other conditions of legal liability. Failure of adequately informed consent can be actionable in negligence,[16] and may be found if a practitioner refuses or fails to disclose a legitimate choice of patient care because of the practitioner's conscientious objection to participation in that choice.

Once the physician-patient relationship is established, the physician cannot terminate it arbitrarily, because abandonment of patients is a form of negli-

---

[11] *Egedebo v. Bueckert*, [1993] B.C.J. No. 298, (*sub nom. Egedebo v. Windermere District Hospital Assn.*) (1993), 78 B.C.L.R. (2d) 63 (B.C.C.A.).

[12] Canadian Medical Association, *Code of Ethics* (Ottawa: CMA, 2004).

[13] However, in *Terra Energy Ltd. v. Kilborn Engineering Alberta Ltd.*, [1999] A.J. No. 221, 170 D.L.R. (4th) 405 (Alta. C.A.), the Alberta Court of Appeal held that compliance with a professional engineer's code of professional ethical conduct was not an implied term of a contract for services, but was a matter for the governing body of the profession.

[14] *Jaglowska v. Kreml*, [2002] M.J. No. 344, 167 Man. R. (2d) 71 (Man. Q.B.).

[15] See *Zimmer v. Ringrose*, [1981] A.J. No. 596, 124 D.L.R. (3d) 215 (Alta. C.A.) on the duty to refer in cases where practitioners are obliged to decline to perform services; see also CMA, *Code of Ethics* (Ottawa: CMA, 2004), ss. 12, 19.

[16] *Reibl v. Hughes*, [1980] S.C.J. No. 105, 114 D.L.R. (3d) 1 (S.C.C.).

gence.[17] This common law and fiduciary duty is embodied in section 19 of the CMA *Code of Ethics*, which directs a physician that "[h]aving accepted professional responsibility for a patient, [you should] continue to provide services until they are no longer required or wanted; until another suitable physician has assumed responsibility for the patient; or until the patient has been given reasonable notice that you intend to terminate the relationship". This applies for instance to retirement from practice, office relocation, conscientious objection, change of practice pattern such as to concentrate in a specialty and ending professional responsibility for a refractory patient.

As private corporations, hospitals *per se* are not licensed to practise medicine, but they bear both direct corporate and often vicarious liability for the medical and other care they accommodate and facilitate (see Section V(A), "Hospitals", below).[18] Perhaps more than physicians, they are subject to the "holding out" principle of tort law, in that they hold themselves out, either expressly or impliedly, as being willing and capable to provide assistance.

In *Bateman v. Doiron* it was noted that:

> A hospital has an obligation to meet standards reasonably expected by the community it serves in the provision of competent personnel and adequate facilities and equipment and also with respect to the competence of physicians to whom it grants privileges to provide medical treatment. It is not responsible for negligence of physicians who practice in the hospital, but it is responsible to ensure that doctors or staff are reasonably qualified to do the work they might be expected to perform.[19]

By operating emergency care departments, hospitals induce their relevant communities to rely upon them, and they assume a duty of care to provide adequate personnel, equipment and resources to manage reasonably anticipated emergencies. There may be limits to the non-delegable duty of care they owe for the negligent acts of their staff, such as physicians who are not salaried staff members but who practice only within their facilities by billing health services insurers or patients on a fee-for-service basis,[20] but hospitals' direct and vicarious liability must be addressed when negligence within their scope of operation causes injury. If hospitals intend to close or limit opening hours of emergency departments, for instance, they must give adequate prior notice to their appropriate communities and ambulance services, and indicate to which other facilities emergency cases should go.[21]

---

[17]   *Zimmer v. Ringrose*, [1981] A.J. No. 596, 124 D.L.R. (3d) 215 (Alta. C.A.).

[18]   See E. Picard & G. Robertson, *Legal Liability of Doctors and Hospitals in Canada*, 4th ed. (Toronto: Thomson Carswell, 2007).

[19]   [1991] N.B.J. No. 714, 8 C.C.L.T. (2d) 284 at 290 (N.B.Q.B.), affd [1993] N.B.J. No. 598, 18 C.C.L.T. (2d) 1 (N.B.C.A.).

[20]   *Yepremian v. Scarborough General Hospital*, [1980] O.J. No. 3592, 110 D.L.R. (3d) 513 (Ont. C.A.); but see *Jaman Estate v. Hussain*, [2002] M.J. No. 283, 166 Man. R. (2d) 51 (Man. C.A.), finding the Ontario Court of Appeal decision unpersuasive.

[21]   *Baynham v. Robertson*, [1993] O.J. No. 2838, 18 C.C.L.T. (2d) 15 (Ont. Gen. Div.).

Further, unlike natural persons whose human rights of conscientious objection should be respected as far as reasonably possible, the artificial legal personality that hospital corporations enjoy for pragmatic purposes does not allow hospitals as such to decline information or services on grounds of religious or other conscience.

2.   Duty to Non-Patients

In treating their patients negligently, physicians may incur liability not only to the patients but also to third parties foreseeably at risk of suffering injury. For instance, negligent treatment of a patient's infection may create liability to family members and partners to whom the patient may transmit the infection. A physician who failed to disclose to a husband that he may have contracted HIV infection from a blood transfusion, for instance, was held liable when the man subsequently infected his wife.[22] Similarly, a surgeon who negligently removed a patient's only healthy kidney was held liable to her father who donated one of his kidneys to aid her survival, because it was held foreseeable that a parent would donate in these circumstances.[23]

Courts are increasingly hearing claims on behalf of children born with disabilities attributed to negligent medical care of their mothers. Physicians' liability to women patients' subsequently born children relates to what physicians should know and disclose about the effects that treatment options may have on such patients' children. Women do not bear legal liability for the choices they make that affect their own unborn children.[24] If physicians disclose risks to fetuses[25] that women patients give informed consent to take, physicians bear no legal liability to the patients' children born with consequent injuries. However, if physicians do not recognize or disclose risks to fetuses that are later born alive with injuries the children would have been spared with physicians' due anticipation and disclosure, liability may arise to the parents, and also to the children themselves. Mothers, unlike the children, may even succeed on the claim that physicians' failure to disclose denied them the opportunity to abort their pregnancies.[26]

The courts have long recognized physicians' duties of care owed to fetuses *in utero*, which may become actionable when the children are born alive.[27] This does not entitle physicians to impose treatments on their pregnant patients to which the patients do not freely give their informed consent. The women duly

---

[22]   *Pittman Estate v. Bain*, [1994] O.J. No. 463, 112 D.L.R. (4th) 257 (Ont. Gen. Div.).

[23]   See *Urbanski v. Patel*, [1978] M.J. No. 211, 84 D.L.R. (3d) 650 (Man. Q.B.).

[24]   *Dobson (Litigation guardian of) v. Dobson*, [1999] S.C.J. No. 41, 174 D.L.R. (4th) 1 (S.C.C.); see also *Winnipeg Child and Family Services (Northwest Area) v. G. (D.F.)*, [1997] S.C.J. No. 96, 152 D.L.R. (4th) 193 (S.C.C.).

[25]   Meaning products of human conception at any time before live birth, *i.e.*, including embryos.

[26]   See the discussion in *Arndt v. Smith*, [1997] S.C.J. No. 65, 148 D.L.R. (4th) 48 (S.C.C.).

[27]   *Montreal Tramways Co. v. Léveillé*, [1933] S.C.J. No. 40, [1933] 4 D.L.R. 337 (S.C.C.); *Duval v. Seguin*, [1973] O.J. No. 2185, 40 D.L.R. (3d) 666 (Ont. C.A.).

informed may exercize choice without liability to a subsequently born child.[28] Similarly, physicians are not liable if a patient who is not pregnant gives informed consent to a form of treatment, such as for acne, that affects a subsequently conceived and born child.[29] This is so even if the treatment anticipates pregnancy, such as prescription of a fertility drug that increases the likelihood of twin or greater pregnancy and its associated complications.[30] This does not justify a conclusion, however, that physicians bear no legal liability to conceived unborn children,[31] but leaves open liability to children not yet conceived, and duties to inform patients who are not pregnant of the harmful effects they and subsequently conceived children may bear, in consequence of proposed procedures.

Injured children's rights to sue for negligent care of their mothers while they were *in utero* are not recognition of "fetal rights" or of their pre-born status as "fetal patients". Canada adheres to the historical common law "born alive" rule. Therefore, individuals' rights accrue only upon their live birth,[32] meaning that fetuses are no longer fetuses but have become what the law recognizes as "human beings" or "persons".[33] Once live births occur, however, the born persons may bring claims on the basis that negligent genetic or other diagnosis of their parents before they were born or even conceived denied them therapeutic care *in utero*, such as maternal dietary management or fetal surgery.

It is interesting to speculate on whether Canadian courts would follow an Illinois court that awarded damages to a child born severely disabled eight years after its mother was transfused with negligently mislabelled blood.[34] The jaundice and related disabilities affecting the child became actionable only on the child's live birth, but the case may be seen as the negligent mislabelling and transfusion creating a continuing wrong. This became apparent only when, in prenatal monitoring of the former patient, fetal blood incompatibility with the mother's blood was traced back to the negligent mislabelling of the transfused blood, resulting in the born child's impairments. The analogy would be with the foreseeability of a negligently designed or constructed wall standing for 10 years, and collapsing onto a two-year-old child. However, the *Paxton* and

---

[28] *Dobson (Litigation guardian of) v. Dobson*, [1999] S.C.J. No. 41, 174 D.L.R. (4th) 1 (S.C.C.).

[29] *Paxton v. Ramji*, [2008] O.J. No. 3964, 299 D.L.R. (4th) 614 (Ont. C.A.), leave to appeal refused [2008] S.C.C.A. No. 508 (S.C.C.).

[30] *Bovingdon v. Hergott*, [2008] O.J. No. 11, 290 D.L.R. (4th) 126 (Ont. C.A.), leave to appeal refused [2008] S.C.C.A. No. 92 (S.C.C.).

[31] *Liebig (Litigation guardian of) v. Guelph General Hospital*, [2010] O.J. No. 2580, 321 D.L.R. (4th) 378 (Ont. C.A.).

[32] *Winnipeg Child and Family Services (Northwest Area) v. G. (D.F.)*, [1997] S.C.J. No. 96, 152 D.L.R. (4th) 193 (S.C.C.); compare *R. v. Sullivan*, [1991] S.C.J. No. 20, 63 C.C.C. (3d) 97 (S.C.C.) on criminal negligence.

[33] *Winnipeg Child and Family Services (Northwest Area) v. G. (D.F.)*, [1997] S.C.J. No. 96, 152 D.L.R. (4th) 193 (S.C.C.).

[34] *Renslow v. Mennonite Hospital*, 367 N.E.2d 1250 (1977).

Bovingdon decisions[35] suggest that disclosure to the patient before conception and her informed consent to treatment would exclude the physician's liability.

A further area of physicians' potential liability to third parties concerns the duty to protect them, such as by warning them or others of possible sources of harm. For instance, plaintiffs who were injured in motor vehicle accidents have succeeded in claims against physicians who failed to discharge their duty to warn vehicle-licensing authorities of their patient's unfitness to drive.[36] This is a variant of the widely discussed *Tarasoff* case in California,[37] in which a campus clinic, through its psychotherapist and supervising psychiatrist, failed to act protectively when a student was found liable to kill or injure a young woman he knew. The student arranged to share accommodation with her brother, and killed her when she returned to town. His conviction for second degree murder was set aside on the ground that he suffered from mental disorder. Her family sued the university on the claim that it owed her a duty of care, such as to warn her or them of the danger its clinic personnel foresaw. The claim succeeded, on the basis of the principle of tort law that when, in a special relationship, a person anticipates or reasonably should anticipate that a third party is in peril, the person is obliged to take reasonable protective action.

In this case, the psychotherapist-patient relationship was found to be special, and the protective duty could be discharged by warning the potential victim or those guarding her interests if known[38] or, if unknown, such as in the case of unfitness to drive, of warning police or comparable authorities whose vigilance would be liable to prevent the harm. Prevention would not only spare victims' injuries, but would also prevent patients from causing injuries and so becoming offenders. This duty does not arise, however, when both patients and third parties are joint victims of a predisposition to suffer harm, such as from common genetic inheritance.

B.   BREACH OF DUTY — THE STANDARD OF CARE

1.   General Principles

The general principle governing the standard of care that medical practitioners are legally required to observe was expressed by the Ontario Court of Appeal, and affirmed by the Supreme Court of Canada, in 1956. Written in the gendered language of its time, it provides that:

---

[35]   *Paxton v. Ramji*, [2008] O.J. No. 3964, 299 D.L.R. (4th) 614 (Ont. C.A.), leave to appeal refused [2008] S.C.C.A. No. 508 (S.C.C.); *Bovingdon v. Hergott*, [2008] O.J. No. 11, 290 D.L.R. (4th) 126 (Ont. C.A.), leave to appeal refused [2008] S.C.C.A. No. 92 (S.C.C.).

[36]   *Toms v. Foster*, [1994] O.J. No. 1413, 7 M.V.R. (3d) 34 (Ont. C.A.); *Spillane (Litigation guardian of) v. Wasserman*, [1998] O.J. No. 2470, 41 C.C.L.T. (2d) 292 (Ont. C.A.).

[37]   *Tarasoff v. Regents of the University of California*, 551 P.2d 334 (1976).

[38]   See Elaine Gibson, Chapter 6, "Health Information: Confidentiality and Access" on "Confidentiality" and "Privacy" aspects.

Every medical practitioner must bring to his task a reasonable degree of skill and knowledge and must exercise a reasonable degree of care. He is bound to exercise that degree of care and skill which could reasonably be expected of a normal, prudent practitioner of the same experience and standing, and if he holds himself out as a specialist, a higher degree of skill is required of him than of one who does not profess to be so qualified by special training and ability.[39]

It does not follow from this proposition that the medical profession can it-self set the standards to which its members are legally required to perform. If the profession could set the standard failure to satisfy which would constitute negligence, the profession might succumb to a self-serving temptation to set low standards. Standards are judicially set as a matter of law, under judicial powers and duties to separate tortious from non-tortious conduct and, for instance, to interpret and apply the usually implied terms of contracts for delivery of medical care. The Supreme Court of Canada has noted that:

[W]hile conformity with common practice will generally exonerate physicians of any complaint of negligence, there are certain situations where the standard practice itself may be found to be negligent. However, this will only be where the standard practice is "fraught with obvious risks" such that anyone is capable of finding it negligent, without the necessity of judging matters requiring diagnostic or clinical expertise.[40]

The principle that specialists are held to the standard of specialists has some refinements. Under the "holding out" rule, those who hold themselves out as possessing specialist skills, although they have no specialist qualification or training, will be held to the standard they profess.[41] Psychiatrists who practise by psychoanalysis will, however, be held only to standards of psychoanalytical practice, not to those of psychiatrists whose practice is based on psychopharmacology.

In both general and specialist medical practice, there may be more than a single standard. Under the "respected minority" rule, a practitioner may be found to have complied with a legally acceptable standard even if the practice in issue is not followed by the mainstream of practitioners, but only by a respected minority of them. This rule accommodates evolution in professional practice. When more recently qualified practitioners may conform to more modern techniques and convictions, some may retain the style of practice of former times. They cannot pursue discredited or obsolete methodologies, but may adhere to more traditional practices and conventional remedies. Similarly, pioneering practice may be accepted as it becomes established on the basis of modern research and scientific study. For instance, the findings of evidence-based medicine may be introduced into clinical care before they are widely adopted by the

---

[39] *Crits v. Sylvester*, [1956] O.J. No. 526, 1 D.L.R. (2d) 502 at 508 (Ont. C.A.), *per* Schroeder J.A., affd [1956] S.C.J. No. 71, [1956] S.C.R. 991 (S.C.C.).

[40] *ter Neuzen v. Korn*, [1995] S.C.J. No. 79 at para. 41, 127 D.L.R. (4th) 577 (S.C.C.); see also *Nattrass v. Weber*, [2010] A.J. No. 424, 316 D.L.R. (4th) 666 (Alta. C.A.).

[41] *Poole v. Morgan*, [1987] A.J. No. 1414, [1987] 3 W.W.R. 217 (Alta. Q.B.).

profession, and new genetic understanding may be applied in advance of its widespread adoption. This does not accommodate eccentric, maverick or unproven practice, but permits both traditional and more innovative practitioners defences against negligence claims based on their non-mainstream practice. Expert witnesses will be called to testify as to whether a minority style of practice is adequately respected.

Limitation Acts require plaintiffs to initiate complaints within a given time from when they actually knew or reasonably should have known that they have a cause of action.[42] Limitation periods may also be suspended during plaintiffs' disability.[43] Action may therefore be initiated some time after the procedure complained of was performed. Further, the process of litigation may be prolonged, so that a case is presented at trial several years after the allegedly negligent procedure was undertaken. Justice requires, as Sopinka J. observed in the Supreme Court of Canada, that "the conduct of physicians must be judged in the light of the knowledge that ought to have been reasonably possessed at the time of the alleged act of negligence".[44] Accordingly, findings of fault based on knowledge only subsequently available cannot stand.[45]

Historically, Canadian law applied the so-called "locality rule", by which a physician's conduct was measured against the standard of like practitioners in the area. The Supreme Court of Canada adopted this rule, observing in *Wilson v. Swanson* that "the medical man must possess and use that reasonable degree of learning and skill ordinarily possessed by practitioners in similar communities in similar cases".[46] This rule was adopted from the United States, where the practice of rural medicine was and to an extent remains something of a medical specialty. However, in Canada, the locality rule has become discredited.[47] With development of Canadian Medicare[48] funded by taxpayers' close to equal liability to pay, and support under the *Canada Health Act*[49] for everyone's reasonable access to medically necessary care, it appears inequitable that residents of one locality may have less entitlement to a given standard of care than residents of other localities in the same province.[50] The rule was also objectionable even in earlier times for insulating pockets of substandard practice.

Accepting everyone's entitlement to at least the same minimum standard of care unavoidably raises the Orwellian specter among equals that some are more

---

42   *Patterson v. Anderson*, [2004] O.J. No. 3619, 72 O.R. (3d) 330 (Ont. S.C.J.).
43   See *E. (D.) (Guardian ad litem of) v. British Columbia*, [2005] B.C.J. No. 492, 252 D.L.R. (4th) 689 (B.C.C.A.).
44   *ter Neuzen v. Korn*, [1995] S.C.J. No. 79, 127 D.L.R. (4th) 577 at 589 (S.C.C.).
45   *Grass (Litigation guardian of) v. Women's College Hospital*, [2005] O.J. No. 1403, 75 O.R. (3d) 85 (Ont. C.A.).
46   [1956] S.C.J. No. 58, 5 D.L.R. (2d) 113 at 124 (S.C.C.), *per* Abbott J.
47   See *Sunnucks (Litigation guardian of) v. Tobique Valley Hospital*, [1999] N.B.J. No. 344, 216 N.B.R. (2d) 201 (N.B.Q.B.).
48   See Chapter 1 on the Canadian health system.
49   R.S.C. 1985, c. C-6.
50   For the example of Quebec, see the discussion in *Chaoulli v. Quebec (Attorney General)*, [2005] S.C.J. No. 33, 2005 SCC 35 (S.C.C.).

equal than others. Residents in the catchment area of university-affiliated medical centres and centres of medical excellence may indeed receive a higher standard of care than residents of more remote areas, certainly for treatment of conditions whose sufferers cannot practicably be referred or transported to such centres. Despite the demise of the locality rule, the standard of care must be applied realistically with regard to the resources and facilities available to physicians and patients. Physicians cannot be legally faulted for not using equipment or resources where none is available.[51] This applies not only to high-technology equipment that requires services of skilled medical technicians, but also to delivery of basic care by skilled nursing and related personnel. The standard of care may accordingly be higher in urban than rural localities for treatment of some emergency and routine conditions, and higher in urban localities with medical schools than in urban localities without schools.

Physicians' dilemmas in use of available but scarce resources are aggravated by pressures of cost-containment.[52] Their ethical and legal duties may be in conflict, since the CMA *Code of Ethics*, on Responsibilities to Society, requires practitioners to "[r]ecognize the responsibility of physicians to promote equitable access to health care resources", and to "[u]se health care resources prudently",[53] by applying scarce public resources to most equitable and beneficial effect, while the law requires each practitioner to serve fiduciary and perhaps implied contractual obligations to each individual patient.

The dilemma was brought into focus in *Law Estate v. Simice*,[54] where a patient died following the physician's decision not to order an available diagnostic CT scan due to pressure from hospital and provincial medical association authorities to be economic in use of this costly tool. Allowing the family's negligence claim, the trial judge, later upheld by the British Columbia Court of Appeal, observed that:

> [I]f it comes to a choice between a physician's responsibility to his or her individual patient and his or her responsibility to the medicare system overall, the former must take precedence in a case such as this. The severity of the harm that may occur to the patient who is permitted to go undiagnosed is far greater than the financial harm that will occur to the medicare system if one more CT scan procedure only shows the patient is not suffering from a serious medical condition.[55]

---

[51] *Rodych Estate v. Krasey*, [1971] M.J. No. 106, [1971] 4 W.W.R. 358 (Man. Q.B.) recognized the constraints on a physician examining a patient at a remote roadside on a cold December morning.

[52] See T.A. Caulfield, "Malpractice in the Age of Health Care Reform" in T.A. Caulfield & B. von Tigerstrom, eds., *Health Care Reform and the Law in Canada: Meeting the Challenge* (Edmonton: University of Alberta Press, 2002) 11-36.

[53] CMA, *Code of Ethics* (Ottawa: CMA, 2004), ss. 43-44.

[54] [1994] B.C.J. No. 979, 21 C.C.L.T. (2d) 228 (B.C.S.C.), affd (*sub nom. Law Estate v. Ostry*) [1995] B.C.J. No. 2596, [1996] 4 W.W.R. 672 (B.C.C.A.).

[55] *Ibid.*, at 240 (B.C.S.C.).

Hospital authorities may limit each physician's power to order "one more CT scan procedure" for each of their patients whose diagnosis a scan may assist by denying physicians the choice, immunizing them from legal liability for negligence, at the cost of making the hospital itself a defendant in litigation.[56]

A physician's lack of resources, like a lack of specialist or other skill, may trigger the legal duty to refer a patient to a more suitably equipped practitioner or facility. It may be negligent to fail to refer, since physicians are expected to be aware of the limits of their own skills, and to recognize the general limits of the facilities in which they practice, although not necessarily on a case-by-case basis. For instance, they should recognize when they should refer their patients to specialists, and refer them promptly, such as when diagnosis shows the need of specialist referral or when a patient fails to respond to treatment the physician was legally entitled to initiate. For life-threatening conditions, even a short delay in referral can constitute negligence.[57]

It is not clear how far the duty to refer may extend, since a particular patient's circumstances may have to be considered. Referral to another conveniently accessible practitioner or hospital may be expected, but a patient's access to a more distant source of care may not be practically feasible. A single parent with young dependent children, for instance, may not be able to take a day or more to travel. Patients should not be tantalized with information of treatments that are beyond their reach. In contrast, patients with the capacity and resources to travel might have to be informed of where they may access services from which they may benefit in other towns, provinces, or countries. Although provincial residents should not have to travel out of their locality or province for timely access to the care indicated for their medical conditions,[58] physicians may have at least to inquire whether travel for care is an option. For services not covered by provincial health insurance plans, for instance, such as resort to reproductive technologies, Canadian specialist practitioners may be expected to be aware of resources available in the United States and perhaps elsewhere. Indeed for some conditions, such as HIV/AIDS, patients may expect to be informed of where they may enter research studies of new but unproven products or combinations of products.[59]

With growth of patients' access to cross-border services (which should not be trivialized as "tourism"), physicians may be required to know where to advise patients to travel for many forms of safe and reliable care. They should also advise patients about the caution they should exercise in seeking cross-border care, especially by experimental, unproven means, and the need to ensure that they return home with information of the products, means and dosages used in their treatment that may be required for their continuing medical care on return.

---

[56]   See *Bateman v. Doiron*, [1991] N.B.J. No. 714, 8 C.C.L.T. (2d) 284 (N.B.Q.B.).

[57]   See *Dillon v. LeRoux*, [1994] B.C.J. No. 795, [1994] 6 W.W.R. 280 (B.C.C.A.).

[58]   See *Chaoulli v. Quebec (Attorney General)*, [2005] S.C.J. No. 33, 2005 SCC 35 (S.C.C.).

[59]   See Michael Hadskis, Chapter 10, "The Regulation of Human Biomedical Research in Canada" on "Research".

An aspect of measuring physicians' compliance with the legally required standard of care is to assess whether treatment conformed to medically approved practice or professionally set guidelines. Proven departure from such practice or guidelines may leave a practitioner vulnerable to liability for negligence, unless, for instance, a deliberate departure can be shown to fall under the "respected minority" rule. The burden of proof of this is liable to fall on the defendant practitioner. On the other hand, conformity to the approved practice or guidelines will not necessarily constitute a sound defence. It has been seen that, in general, when a physician acts according to recognized and respected professional practice, negligence will not be found, but that standards are set as a matter of law, and professional practice that is "fraught with obvious risks" will not be legally approved.[60] Further, where non-technical matters are concerned that do not require the assessment of medical specialists, triers of fact, whether judges or juries, may determine whether physicians acted reasonably or were negligent.

2. Error of Judgment

Lawyers are perhaps more familiar than physicians with recognizing that many matters cannot be determined accurately, but call for determination by an exercise of judgment; legal officers who are required to judge and resolve conflicting evidence are accordingly named "judges". Any exercise of judgment is liable to prove incorrect. Trial judgments are liable to be reversed on appeal, and appeal courts may decide by slender majorities, since differences of opinion are common. Reversed or dissenting judgments are not necessarily "wrong", even though they do not prevail. Similarly with an exercise of medical judgment, it is not necessarily flawed or negligent even though it may prove erroneous. That is, liability to be erroneous is often inherent in an exercise of judgment.[61] For instance, physicians prescribing drugs for children that have been tested only on adults may have to guess what dosage is appropriate, and may accordingly prescribe an overdose, or a dosage too low to be effective.

Physicians sometimes claim that the legal requirement that they make decisions, for instance about patients' capacity to understand information, about offer of optimal care to patients and, for instance, about appropriate use of scarce resources, is impossible to satisfy, because they cannot be certain to be right. The legal response is that physicians are not legally required to make correct decisions, but only to make decisions correctly. That is, they should take account of all factors properly to be considered, and exclude factors that should have no bearing. In the *Law Estate* case,[62] for instance, the requirement of economy in use of resources was not a matter the physician was legally entitled to

---

[60] *ter Neuzen v. Korn*, [1995] S.C.J. No. 79, 127 D.L.R. (4th) 577 (S.C.C.).

[61] A. Merry & R.A. McCall Smith, *Errors, Medicine and the Law* (Cambridge: Cambridge University Press, 2001); see also O. Quick, "Outing Medical Errors: Questions of Trust and Responsibility" (2006) 14 Med. Law. Rev. 22.

[62] *Law Estate v. Simice*, [1994] B.C.J. No. 979, 21 C.C.L.T. (2d) 228 at 240 (B.C.S.C.), affd (*sub nom. Law Estate v. Ostry*) [1995] B.C.J. No. 2596, [1996] 4 W.W.R. 672 (B.C.C.A.).

consider. In the U.S. *Tarasoff* case,[63] although the prediction that the patient would kill proved tragically correct, the defence was that psychotherapists and psychiatrists cannot predict dangerousness accurately, and so cannot ensure protection. The judicial response was that professionals are not legally required to make correct predictions, but are required to act appropriately in light of the predictions they actually make.

The law distinguishes between negligence and error of judgment. A proven mistake does not in itself prove negligence, even though its consequences may be tragic, such as in failure accurately to diagnose breast cancer when it is at a treatable stage.[64] It must also be shown that a reasonable physician, in the same material circumstances, would not have made this mistake. The principle has been stated in the Supreme Court of Canada that:

> An error in judgment has long been distinguished from an act of unskillfulness or carelessness or due to lack of knowledge. Although universally-accepted procedures must be observed, they furnish little or no assistance in resolving such a predicament as faced the surgeon here. In such a situation a decision must be made without delay based on limited known and unknown factors; and the honest and intelligent exercise of judgement has long been recognized as satisfying the professional obligation.[65]

Error of judgment is most often apparent in misdiagnosis. Illustrations of non-negligent misdiagnoses are diagnosing infant meningitis as chicken pox,[66] and bowel obstruction as gastroenteritis,[67] failure to diagnose acute vascular insufficiency,[68] and causing a lung collapse injury (pneumothorax) when performing a fine needle aspiration on a breast lump.[69] Initial diagnostic error may be non-negligent when it is reasonable in light of the patient's presenting symptoms, but the patient's failure to respond to treatment based on that diagnosis may create a legal duty to reconsider the diagnosis, and rediagnose the patient. Failure to reconsider the initial diagnosis may violate the required standard of care, and constitute a negligent breach of that standard. For instance, when a patient suffered a ruptured appendix, she was misdiagnosed as having pelvic inflammation. When she failed to respond to treatment for that condition and steadily deteriorated, the physicians did not reconsider their diagnosis. After four days in hospital, she died of the ruptured appendix. The physicians were

---

[63] *Tarasoff v. Regents of the University of California*, 551 P.2d 334 (1976).
[64] See *Report of the Commission of Inquiry on Hormone Receptor Testing* (St. John's, NL: Office of the Queen's Printer, 2009).
[65] *Wilson v. Swanson*, [1956] S.C.J. No. 58, [1956] S.C.R. 804 at 812 (S.C.C.), *per* Rand J.
[66] *Siddle (Guardian ad litem of) v. Poole*, [1990] B.C.J. No. 2691 (B.C.C.A.).
[67] *Davies v. Gabel Estate (Public Trustee of)*, [1994] S.J. No. 605, [1995] 2 W.W.R. 35 (Sask. Q.B.), affd [1997] S.J. No. 138, [1997] 6 W.W.R. 459 (Sask. C.A.).
[68] *Smith v. Aggarwal*, [1991] A.J. No. 221, 114 A.R. 361 (Alta. Q.B.).
[69] *Comeau v. Fenzl*, [2000] N.B.J. No. 254 (N.B.Q.B.).

held negligent not for their original error of judgment, but for not appropriately reviewing whether that diagnosis was erroneous.[70]

Although neither a physician nor a hospital may be legally liable for an error of judgment, an individual practitioner should review the basis of an erroneous decision and learn from the experience. Hospitals and the medical profession should attempt to dispel the atmosphere of fault, blame and shame that has often surrounded recognition of error, and pursue its origins openly, in order to reduce the risk of repetition and advance the education of practising members of the profession. Medical journals are publishing case studies of errors,[71] and more are being opened to discussion at medical Grand Rounds. Audit of practitioners' practice should identify abnormally high levels of error, not for purposes of discipline but as a feature of institutional quality assurance. Identification of origins of error can result in improved procedures, such as by information sharing among medical team members responsible for care of the same patient, clear labelling with perhaps colour-coding of drugs delivered in similar packaging and double-checking of prescribed dosage levels of drugs. Further, errors attributable to hospital staff work exhaustion can be addressed by regulation of work hours and mandatory rest periods.

Hospitals that fail to monitor the incidence of physicians' and other staff members' errors, including both negligent and non-negligent errors, may themselves be liable to be held negligent. Courts may reinforce institutional vigilance by their disposition to find hospitals negligent that do not monitor and introduce strategies to reduce rates of error, much as courts enforced instrument and sponge counts before completion of invasive surgery by holding surgeons and hospitals inescapably negligent in their absences, if instruments or sponges were left inside patients. Reciprocating judicial requirements of hospital inquiry into origins of error is the privilege and inadmissibility in evidence of reports of such inquiries, so that hospitals that compel staff members' disclosure of error and analyze the causes will not furnish ammunition to be available in litigation brought against them or their staff members.

Studies in cognitive psychology and human-factors engineering indicate that safety often requires more than reliance on individual carefulness. The concept of "latent" errors has been developed,[72] meaning deficiencies in the design, organization, maintenance, training and management of systems, such as institutional health care systems, that create conditions in which individuals are more likely to make errors.[73] Management decisions that create excessive workloads,[74] for instance, or that designate tasks to improperly trained or equipped personnel, make errors more likely, such as emergency room physicians or

---

[70]   *Bergen Estate v. Sturgeon General Hospital No. 100*, [1984] A.J. No. 2575, 52 A.R. 161 (Alta. Q.B.).

[71]   See The Lancet, "Uses of Error", named contribution in each number.

[72]   J.T. Reason, *Human Error* (Cambridge: Cambridge University Press, 1990).

[73]   See L. Leake & A.M. Epstein, "A Series on Patient Safety" (2002) 347 New Eng J. Med. 1272.

[74]   See D.M. Gaba & S.K. Howard, "Fatigue among Clinicians and the Safety of Patients" (2002) 347 New Eng. J. Med. 1249.

nurses not having time to check that they are administering the right drugs or dosages. Correcting systemic defects in institutional management may offer the most effective way to reduce human error,[75] and may be the most relevant focus of preventive strategies. Litigation against individual physicians, though understandable from a patient's perspective, may systemically be a distraction.

When a physician and/or hospital recognizes that an error has occurred, the issue arises of whether there is a legal duty to disclose this to the patient.[76] Guidance may be found in the jurisprudence on disclosure for informed consent, where the Supreme Court of Canada requires disclosure of material risks to patients.[77] Accordingly, errors that do not affect patients or their care may not have to be disclosed. For instance, if a surgeon or surgical team member drops an instrument on the floor, which then has to be inspected for damage and resterilized, and the surgery is prolonged by no more than a few minutes or a less suitable instrument is effectively used, it is not clear that, on recovery, the patient needs to be informed. How instruments are handled and exchanged during surgery may have to be reviewed for avoidance of repetition, but, since the outcome and risks of the surgery were not affected, and no injury to the patient resulted, no disclosure may be required, even under fiduciary duties. Similarly, if a decimal point is erroneously misplaced in a prescription, but prescription double-checking exposed and corrected the risk of the patient receiving one-tenth or 10 times the intended dosage, the self-correcting procedure has worked and the patient need not be informed of the initial error, even if it presented a "near miss".

The focus of the professional ethical duty is on harm. The CMA *Code of Ethics*[78] provides in section 14 that an ethical physician shall "[t]ake all reasonable steps to prevent harm to patients; should harm occur, disclose it to the patient". Further, several provincial Colleges of Physicians and Surgeons require similar disclosure, as do practices in many hospitals. Failure to observe such requirements is a disciplinary offence.[79] The ethical duty relates more to fiduciary duties than to negligence law.

Perhaps the earliest Canadian judgment acknowledging the duty of disclosure was *Stamos v. Davies*,[80] in which a surgeon punctured the plaintiff's spleen in attempting a lung biopsy. As a result of the error, the spleen had to be removed by subsequent surgery. The lung biopsy was unsuccessful, and had to be

---

[75]   J.T. Reason, *Managing the Risks of Organizational Accidents* (Aldershot, U.K.: Ashgate, 1997).

[76]   M. Waite, "To Tell the Truth: The Ethical and Legal Implications of Disclosure of Medical Error" (2005) 13 Health L.J. 1.

[77]   See *Reibl v. Hughes*, [1980] S.C.J. No. 105, 114 D.L.R. (3d) 1 (S.C.C.); and Patricia Peppin, Chapter 4, "Informed Consent" on "Consent".

[78]   CMA, *Code of Ethics* (Ottawa: CMA, 2004).

[79]   See Tracey Epps, Chapter 2, "Regulation of Health Care Professionals" on the medical profession.

[80]   [1985] O.J. No. 2625, 52 O.R. (2d) 10 (Ont. H.C.J.); see also *Kueper v. McMullin*, [1986] N.B.J. No. 89, 30 D.L.R. (4th) 408 (N.B.C.A.) and *Kiley-Nikkel c. Danais*, [1992] J.Q. no 1836, 16 C.C.L.T. (2d) 290 (Que. S.C.).

repeated at the same time. The physician failed to inform the patient of the erroneous puncture, but advised the patient only that the biopsy had not been successful and had to be repeated, which was true. The court applied informed consent law, and found breach of the legal duty to disclose the error. However, since the repeat surgery was necessary in any event, the court found that the patient had suffered no additional injury occasioned by the error, and awarded no damages for the breach of disclosure. While this finding applies principles of negligence law, the court did not address fiduciary duty or punitive damages, nor, since with due disclosure the patient might have declined to allow this physician to undertake the repeat surgery, possible liability for battery. If none of these alternative bases of claim was pleaded, of course, the judge would have been justified in not addressing them.

If a court finds an error of judgment not to have been negligent, failure to disclose it to the patient it harmed may still be actionable for breach of fiduciary duty. If the error was negligent, however, and was deliberately concealed, an action may succeed for negligence, and attract punitive damages. For instance, in *Gerula v. Flores*,[81] the defendant surgeon operated on the wrong disc in the patient's back, and later altered the hospital record to conceal the error before undertaking further surgery on the disc that should have been operated on initially. The Court of Appeal held that $40,000 in punitive damages should be paid because of the physician's dishonesty. The English Court of Appeal has indicated that a hospital is also obliged to disclose negligent errors,[82] but there seems to be no Canadian authority on the point.

Due disclosure of harmful errors, and giving apologies, may be deterred by the fear that, since error and apology are associated with wrongdoing, they will increase the chances of patients bringing legal actions. This intuitive apprehension has little if any empirical support, however, and evidence exists that physicians' honesty, apology and sincere expressions of regret for the patients' discomfort and inconvenience may disincline patients from litigation.[83]

C. DAMAGE

Unlike the tort of, for instance, battery, which is actionable *per se*, negligence is actionable only when the plaintiff has suffered damage, or injury. In most cases, the injury is obvious, such as organ or tissue damage, the pain and inconvenience of repetition of medical procedures,[84] adverse consequences of use of pharmaceutical products or medical devices, or of failures to undertake indicated interventions that prolong the patients' pain, discomfort and suffering. Beyond physical injuries are equally demonstrable losses of, for instance, employment income and business opportunities. Courts are also able to quantify future losses,

---

[81]　[1995] O.J. No. 2300, 126 D.L.R. (4th) 506 (Ont. C.A.).

[82]　*Lee v. South West Thames Regional Health Authority*, [1985] 2 All E.R. 385 (C.A.).

[83]　See M. Waite, "To Tell the Truth: The Ethical and Legal Implications of Disclosure of Medical Error" (2005) 13 Health L.J. 1 at 27-28.

[84]　See, for instance, *Bonfoco v. Dowd*, [2000] O.J. No. 3799, 136 O.A.C. 339 (Ont. C.A.).

such as rehabilitation costs, and costs of future care, such as in the *Yepremian* case where, in an agreed structured settlement, the court determined annuity payments dependent on the severely disabled plaintiff's years of survival.[85] Similarly, estimated forfeited years of life, and lost enjoyment of companionship and family life or opportunities, or *solatium*, can be financially assessed, as can lost means of family financial support, both support children may have received from their parents, and that aged parents may have received from their adult children.

For instance in *Bowlby v. Oosterhuis*,[86] the plaintiff, the mother of a child, had her family physician insert an intrauterine device (IUD) for contraceptive purposes. He recommended replacement in two years' time, and she therefore returned to him for replacement. On examining her, the physician could not find the IUD inserted before, and may have supposed its spontaneous expulsion. He inserted a second IUD. The plaintiff suffered significant pain and bleeding. She had another physician remove the second IUD, and in the following 10 or so years unsuccessfully tried to have another child, but eventually stopped trying and decided to have tubal ligation for contraceptive purposes. Four years later, it was found that the first IUD inserted had remained in her body. When the family physician was held negligent in failing to trace the first IUD, damages were awarded for her pain. Further, she and her husband received assessed compensation for the emotional suffering of involuntary infertility, on the finding that the first IUD was the proximate cause of her failure to conceive.

In some cases, however, there is a legal issue whether what is claimed as an injury can be judicially recognized as such. The historical instance concerned mental suffering or psychological pain and suffering. Courts were skeptical of such claims unless they were shown to follow from physical injury. According to the "impact rule", courts would be willing to recognize a head of claim for mental suffering only as an adjunct to a claim for physical injury. They were fearful, however, that, in the absence of demonstrable physical injury, mental suffering would be simulated for self-serving purposes, such as to gain compensation or to support vexatious litigation brought by angry, resentful, humiliated, or jealous litigants. In a historical concession perhaps to social stratification, however, persons of social or professional status could succeed in defamation actions for loss of reputation and for being lowered in the estimation of right-thinking members of their communities.[87]

The impact of medical negligence can have material, psychological and other dimensions. For instance in *Udeschini v. Juma*,[88] the plaintiff was negligently misdiagnosed by a cardiologist as suffering from a generalized, progressive incurable heart disease, and followed the cardiologist's advice to take early

---

[85]   *Yepremian v. Scarborough General Hospital (No. 2)*, [1981] O.J. No. 2889, 120 D.L.R. (3d) 341 (Ont. H.C.J.).

[86]   [2003] O.J. No. 1130, 63 O.R. (3d) 748 (Ont. S.C.J.).

[87]   See S.M. Waddams, *The Law of Damages*, looseleaf (Aurora, ON: Canada Law Book), 4.10-4.220.

[88]   [1998] O.J. No. 580 (Ont. Gen. Div.).

retirement. The plaintiff did not learn that the diagnosis was erroneous for 10 years. The defendant was held liable in negligence for the plaintiff's loss of income due to his early retirement, but also for the severe depression he suffered due to worry about his heart condition. It may be questioned whether, had the plaintiff continued in his employment despite his concern about a heart condition, his depression alone would have founded a successful negligence claim.

A matter on which modern law remains unclear concerns claims for what is described, somewhat unevenly, as "wrongful birth" and "wrongful life". The former arises when parents sue for the births of children they intended not to conceive or to carry to term, due for instance to negligently conducted genetic counselling, contraceptive care or sterilization procedures, or to negligent prenatal diagnosis. The latter arises when action is taken by or on behalf of children claiming that, had their parents been treated without negligence, they would not have been conceived, or if conceived, would not have been born. The law is more clear that "wrongful conception" is actionable by patients, such as when negligently conducted tubal ligation or vasectomy results in unplanned pregnancy that ends in induced or spontaneous abortion.

However, when a child is born, even of an unwanted and negligently induced pregnancy, the historical attitude that it is a "blessing" that transcends all detriments can be found to persist in some judicial rulings. The "blessing" approach is supported by religiosity such as is seen in a 2004 report of the U.S. President's Council on Bioethics, which urges that all children be received in submissive gratitude as "gifts".[89] Two contemporaneous 1978 trial judgments show the contrast. In *Doiron v. Orr*,[90] where in fact a sterilization procedure was found not to have been negligently performed, the Ontario trial judge considered it "grotesque" that parents should seek compensation for a child's birth. However, in *Cataford v. Moreau*,[91] a Quebec trial judge considered the claim routine, and assessed damages, as reduced by the off-setting financial benefits to the parents of the provincial child-support policy.

In *Kealey v. Berezowski* in 1996, the Ontario trial court noted the change in approach since 1978, and proposed a structure to determine the quantum of damages.[92] In her analysis to clarify the law, however, the judge observed that:

> Courts have struggled with the novel question at issue in this case [damages for wrongful birth claims] because, in the absence of legislative guidelines for assessing damages of this kind, they are driven back on standard principles of negligence law or public policy. Both may be inadequate for the task.[93]

In a scholarly judgment reviewing, comparing and contrasting Canadian, British and U.S. jurisprudence, the judge distinguished different approaches and

---

[89] President's Council on Bioethics, *Beyond Therapy: Biotechnology and the Pursuit of Happiness* (New York: HarperCollins, 2003) at 70.
[90] [1978] O.J. No. 3388, 86 D.L.R. (3d) 719 (Ont. H.C.J.).
[91] [1978] J.Q. no 302, 114 D.L.R. (3d) 585 (Que. S.C.).
[92] [1996] O.J. No. 2460, 136 D.L.R. (4th) 708 (Ont. Gen. Div.).
[93] *Ibid.*, at 731, *per* Lax J.

bases of claim. On the facts of the case, a married woman with two boys requested contraceptive sterilization, which the court found was performed negligently. She gave birth to a healthy daughter, and stated that her family was quite happy with this, and could afford the costs of childcare. The court accordingly assessed damages to cover costs only of confinement and delivery, and those associated with repetition of a sterilization procedure.

However, the court added that had sterilization been requested to prevent birth of a foreseeably handicapped child, and negligence resulted in birth of such a child, damages would include the additional costs of caring for the child's needs due to the handicap, during the years when parents are legally obliged to supply their children's necessaries of life, which include medically indicated care.[94] Further, had sterilization been requested because the family could not afford the costs of childrearing, and those costs had arisen due to medical negligence, whether the child was handicapped or healthy, damages would include childcare costs.

In a British case in the House of Lords, as the Supreme Court of the United Kingdom was then called, involving birth of a healthy child, the Law Lords considered *Kealey*, and rejected it,[95] apparently reversing earlier jurisprudence.[96] However, the House of Lords subsequently approved modest damages for care of a healthy child because the mother was visually impaired.[97] Accordingly, as in Canada, the jurisprudence appears unsettled, some judges and courts applying a "blessing" approach, others invoking perceptions of public policy ranging from policy opposition to physicians becoming responsible for costs of families rearing their children, to opposition to immunizing medical negligence if it results in birth of a possibly severely handicapped child. Similarly, some judges and courts reject a distinction between healthy and handicapped children, because of fear of stigmatizing the latter, and between affluent and impoverished families, on the grounds of everyone's equality under the law.

In the U.S., the courts were seen to "bust the blessing balloon"[98] in a 1971 Michigan case. A pharmacist negligently misread a woman's prescription for a contraceptive drug (Norinyl) and instead provided her with a tranquilizer (Nardil), resulting in birth of her eighth child. Her claim for negligence required proof of damage, but the trial judge followed precedent to rule that a child's birth could not be regarded in law as a species of damage. The Michigan Court of Appeals reversed this judgment, invoking a democratic perception of public sentiment. It observed that:

---

94 *R. v. Brooks*, [1902] B.C.J. No. 4, 5 C.C.C. 372 (B.C.S.C.); *R. v. Lewis*, [1903] O.J. No. 123, 7 C.C.C. 261 (Ont. C.A.).

95 *McFarlane v. Tayside Health Board*, [2000] 2 A.C. 59 (H.L.).

96 See *Udale v. Bloomsbury Area Health Authority*, [1983] 1 W.L.R. 1098 (Q.B.D.).

97 *Rees v. Darlington Memorial Hospital N.H.S. Trust*, [2003] 4 All E.R. 987 (H.L.).

98 J.S. Ranous & J.J. Sherrin, "Busting the Blessing Balloon: Liability for the Birth of an Unplanned Child" (1975) 39 Alb. L. Rev. 221.

To say that for reasons of public policy contraceptive failure can result in no damage as a matter of law ignores the fact that tens of millions of persons use contraceptives daily to avoid the very result which the defendant would have us say is always a benefit, never a detriment. Those tens of millions of persons, by their conduct, express the sense of the community.[99]

The court accordingly awarded damages to the woman, and modest amounts to her husband and existing seven children, recognizing that the latter would have less of their mother's time and attention.

There is widespread agreement in the U.S., Canada and beyond, that the general legal duty of plaintiffs to mitigate their damages should not disentitle plaintiffs to recovery of damages because they declined to abort an unplanned pregnancy, or on birth to surrender a child for adoption.[100] This is consistent with "eggshell skull" reasoning that, if physicians have wronged their patients, they cannot claim relief from paying compensation because the patients are the sort of people who reject abortion or adoption.

Highly objectionable, not only to religiously based opponents of abortion, may be the very description given to so-called "wrongful life" claims, brought by or on behalf of disabled children. The description arose as a dismissive parody of the Fatal Accident Acts, which founded claims for "wrongful death". The concept that a child's life is an injury to the child itself may induce a visceral rejection.

Canadian jurisprudence tends not to accept wrongful life claims,[101] and children's lawyers try to frame litigation on their behalf in terms that avoid the wrongful life description.[102] Some courts have allowed claims so described to proceed,[103] but the prevailing opinion appears to be that claims by disabled children that their injuries are legally attributable to negligence that resulted in their parents conceiving them, or to their mothers gestating them to birth, can be successfully resisted by characterizing them as wrongful life claims.

This is generally the position in U.S. jurisdictions, although in 1980 Californian courts found children's disabilities shown in wrongful life claims to be compensable,[104] on the grounds that the bases of damage awards in tort are not confined to restoration of conditions had injuries not occurred, and that the philosophical difficulty can be overcome by plaintiffs' lawyers' resourcefulness and judicial responsiveness. Indeed, in 2000, the New Jersey Supreme Court

---

[99] *Troppi v. Scarf*, 187 N.W.2d 511 at 517 (1971).

[100] See the discussion in *McFarlane v. Tayside Health Board*, [2000] 2 A.C. 59 (H.L.).

[101] See *Arndt v. Smith*, [1995] B.C.J. No. 1416, 126 D.L.R. (4th) 705 (B.C.C.A.), revd on other grounds [1997] S.C.J. No. 65, 148 D.L.R. (4th) 48 (S.C.C.).

[102] See *McDonald-Wright (Litigation guardian of) v. O'Herlihy*, [2005] O.J. No. 1636, 75 O.R. (3d) 261 (Ont. S.C.J.).

[103] *Cherry (Guardian ad litem of) v. Borsman*, [1992] B.C.J. No. 1687, 94 D.L.R. (4th) 487 (B.C.C.A.), leave to appeal refused [1992] S.C.C.A. No. 472, 99 D.L.R. (4th) vii (S.C.C.); *Bartok v. Shokeir*, [1998] S.J. No. 645 (Sask. C.A.).

[104] *Curlender v. Bio-Science Laboratories*, 106 Cal. App. 3d 811 (1980); see also *Harbeson v. Parke-Davis, Inc.*, 656 P.2d 483 (1983).

reversed a 1967 decision and admitted wrongful life actions.[105] Canadian courts have approved token compensation for a plaintiff who suffered a battery without which she might have died, when a Jehovah's Witness was wrongly given a blood transfusion,[106] and the award of $20,000 is now commonly accepted as appropriate when no scales exist for compensation assessment.

If a child that would otherwise have been born in good health is born with disability, due to medical negligence in its mother's prenatal care or counselling, it is not contested that it is entitled to recover damages. Whether it offends public policy that it should recover because negligence denied its parents the choice not to conceive, or to conceive a different child in better circumstances, or to terminate the pregnancy, is a matter on which judgment or guidance of the Supreme Court of Canada is still to be provided. The judges might refer to the jurisprudence of the U.K., U.S. and, for instance Australia,[107] as well as to the evolution of Canadian court decisions, to resolve an issue that many find beyond their direct interests, but at the centre of values that are important to them.

D.   CAUSATION

A plaintiff cannot succeed in a negligence claim simply by showing that the defendant owed the plaintiff a legal duty of care, was negligent in failing to satisfy the legal standard of care, and that the plaintiff suffered a legally recognized injury. Success requires the plaintiff also to show, on a balance of probability, that the defendant's negligence caused the injury. The usual test of causation is the "but for" test,[108] meaning that the plaintiff must show that, but for the defendant's negligence, the plaintiff would not have suffered the injury.

The Supreme Court of Canada, in a leading judgment, confirmed the "traditional principles in the law of torts that the plaintiff must prove on a balance of probabilities that, but for the tortious conduct of the defendant, the plaintiff would not have sustained the injury complained of".[109] An illustrative scenario is life-saving emergency surgery on a patient at high risk of death. When, following surgery, the patient dies, it may be shown on behalf of dependants or the patient's estate, or admitted by the defendant, that negligent errors occurred in the conduct of the surgery or in after-care. The negligence claim will not succeed, however, unless the plaintiff can show that, but for the negligence, it was more likely than not that the patient would have survived. If there is a high mortality rate associated with the patient's condition, which explained why the surgery was attempted, the plaintiff may be unable to discharge the burden of proof.

For instance, in a case in which a patient in his 30s died from colon cancer, his estate sued two physicians, Dr. O and Dr. H, for negligence. The defendants

---

[105]   *Procanik v. Cillo*, 478 A.2d 755 (1984).
[106]   *Malette v. Shulman*, [1990] O.J. No. 450, 67 D.L.R. (4th) 321 (Ont. C.A.).
[107]   *Cattanach and the State of Queensland v. Melchior* (2003), 77 A.L.J.R. 1312 (H.C.A.).
[108]   *Resurfice Corp. v. Hanke*, [2007] S.C.J. No. 7, 278 D.L.R. (4th) 643 (S.C.C.).
[109]   *Snell v. Farrell*, [1990] S.C.J. No. 73, 72 D.L.R. (4th) 289 at 293-94 (S.C.C.).

denied negligence, but argued in the alternative that the cancer was highly unusual and aggressive, rapidly evolving into a lethal form. The action was allowed against Dr. O in negligence and breach of contract, but dismissed against Dr. H on the ground that, although that physician's professional negligence was established, the patient's cancer was so advanced that, even with Dr. H's management of the patient's treatment that met the standard of care, he would not have survived.[110]

Similarly, in the *Yepremian* case,[111] a physician standing in for a family physician conducted an insufficient examination of a patient, whose family later took him to a local hospital emergency department when his condition deteriorated. He was admitted to hospital and seen the next morning by an endocrinologist, who initially missed his symptoms of diabetic coma, and then overprescribed medication. The family physician's replacement was held not liable because, although providing substandard care, no injury would have resulted had the endocrinologist acted appropriately. That is, the replacement physician's negligence did not cause the injury the patient suffered. The acts of the endocrinologist were new intervening acts that broke the chain of causation between the first physician's conduct and the injury.

Since *Reibl v. Hughes*,[112] many negligence claims allege negligent (non)disclosure of material information that caused plaintiffs to make choices of care that they would not have made if adequately informed. Unlike claims that involve complex physiological, biological or, for instance, pharmaceutical evidence of causation presented by expert witnesses, these cases turn on understanding of human psychology and disposition, and may be tried by juries. The claim is that, even if procedures undertaken complied with the standard of care and the plaintiff was exposed to no more than the irreducible minimum risk inherent in a particular form of treatment, had due disclosure been made, the plaintiff would have chosen a different treatment option, and so not been exposed to that risk; that is, that but for the negligent (non)disclosure, the plaintiff would not have accepted to run that risk.

Plaintiffs must satisfy the double test of showing that, with due disclosure, they would not have consented to the treatments they received, and also that a prudent or reasonable person in their circumstances would not have consented. For instance, a patient convinced a court that, with due disclosure of the risks of the sterilization procedure she underwent, she would have not proceeded. She was a sincere Roman Catholic, and was troubled about the procedure because it was contrary to her religion. Due disclosure of risks of the procedure might well have persuaded her not to proceed. She failed in her claim, however, because

---

[110] *Lindahl Estate v. Olsen*, [2004] A.J. No. 967, 360 A.R. 310 (Alta. Q.B.).

[111] *Yepremian v. Scarborough General Hospital*, [1980] O.J. No. 3592, 110 D.L.R. (3d) 513 (Ont. C.A.); but see *Jaman Estate v. Hussain*, [2002] M.J. No. 283, 166 Man. R. (2d) 51 (Man. C.A.), finding the Ontario Court of Appeal decision unpersuasive.

[112] [1980] S.C.J. No. 105, 114 D.L.R. (3d) 1 (S.C.C.).

many prudent, reasonable women in her circumstances, properly informed, consented to that procedure.[113]

In contrast, in *Arndt v. Smith*,[114] a woman who went to considerable medical lengths to achieve the pregnancy she keenly wanted, was exposed to rubella (German measles). She asked her physician if this presented any risk to the pregnancy, and was incorrectly told that it did not, although the physician should have informed her that it posed a low risk of causing severe fetal damage. She sued for negligence when she gave birth to a child that suffered from such damage, claiming that, if properly informed, she would have terminated the pregnancy. Evidence showed that many pregnant women exposed to rubella choose abortion. She failed in her action, however, because she was unable to show that, if properly informed, she would have made that choice. She had a history of discounting medical information, and had pursued her chance of achieving pregnancy with determination, so she could not show that she would more likely than not have terminated the pregnancy.

Causation includes failure to prevent a reasonably foreseeable consequence that there is a duty of care to anticipate and prevent. In a case in which a father of two children underwent a vasectomy, he later fathered a healthy third child. He and his wife sued the physician for negligent misrepresentation due to the physician's misreading of the urologist's report. The report disclosed that, following the procedure, the plaintiff continued to have motile sperm, but the defendant physician advised the plaintiff that his sperm count was zero. He and his wife then discontinued contraceptive precautions. It was held that the physician's misreading was negligent, and that this negligence was the legal cause of the third child's birth.[115]

Some earlier jurisprudence suggested that medical negligence cases differ from other negligence claims in that, once a plaintiff has shown an association between the defendant's breach of the standard of care and an injury, the evidentiary burden shifts to the defendant, usually a medical specialist with particular understanding of physiological, biological or other scientific knowledge of cause-and-effect relationships, to disprove causation. The Supreme Court of Canada has now rejected a shift to the defendants of the burden of proof, but not necessarily to the plaintiffs' disadvantage.

In the leading case on causation, *Snell v. Farrell*,[116] the patient lost the sight of an eye following an operation performed by the defendant, an ophthalmic surgeon. He was held negligent in continuing the surgery after noticing a haemorrhage in the eye. The issue the Supreme Court of Canada addressed was whether the surgeon's negligence caused the patient's partial blindness. The trial judge applied the House of Lord's decision in *McGhee v. National Coal*

---

[113] *Videto v. Kennedy*, [1981] O.J. No. 3054, 125 D.L.R. (3d) 127 (Ont. C.A.).

[114] [1997] S.C.J. No. 65, 148 D.L.R. (4th) 48 (S.C.C.).

[115] *Bevilacqua v. Altenkirk*, [2004] B.C.J. No. 1473, 242 D.L.R. (4th) 338 (B.C.S.C.).

[116] [1990] S.C.J. No. 73, 72 D.L.R. (4th) 289 at 293-94 (S.C.C.).

Board,[117] and found causation established if the defendant's negligence was shown to have "materially increased the risk" of the injury. The Supreme Court rejected this reasoning, holding that *McGhee* does not support the proposition that a material increase in risk of injury is in itself proof of causation, nor does it result in the onus of proof shifting to the defendant.[118]

However, the Supreme Court emphasized that trial judges, particularly in medical negligence cases, should not be reluctant to adopt a "robust and pragmatic approach", and may draw an inference of causation from the evidence presented. As Sopinka J. said for the Court:

> The legal or ultimate burden remains with the plaintiff, but in the absence of evidence to the contrary adduced by the defendant, an inference of causation may be drawn, although positive or scientific proof of causation has not been adduced.[119]

If some evidence to the contrary is adduced by the defendant, the trial judge is entitled to take a robust and pragmatic approach to it. Sopinka J. added, however, that:

> It is not, therefore, essential that the medical experts provide a firm opinion supporting the plaintiff's theory of causation. Medical experts ordinarily determine causation in terms of certainties whereas a lesser standard is demanded by the law.[120]

That is, while certainty in medical science and expertise approaches a 100 per cent standard, "reasonable" certainty in civil law need be only at a 51 per cent standard. The language of Sopinka J. has been applied in numerous cases, with the effect that plaintiffs in medical negligence cases have not been held to fastidious standards of proof that medical defendants' negligence was the cause of patients' injuries.

A claim of loss of a chance of cure or relief is measured by this standard of proof. For a plaintiff to show that denial or delay of a treatment option caused injury, the plaintiff must show that, had the chance of that treatment been taken, it is more likely than not that the injury would not have occurred. For instance, a plaintiff who suffered from diabetes for many years developed a sore between toes of her left foot. The defendant physician did not examine her but promised to make an appointment for her to see a skin specialist. He failed to do this, and gave her no further instructions or warnings. The sore became infected and gangrene set in, resulting in below the knee amputation.

At trial for negligence, both the plaintiff's and defendant's expert witnesses testified that, had the plaintiff received an aggressive form of treatment, her leg

---

[117] [1972] 3 All E.R. 1008 (H.L.).

[118] Nevertheless, *McGhee* has retained an impact in Canadian medical malpractice cases; see *Webster v. Chapman*, [1997] M.J. No. 646, [1998] 4 W.W.R. 335 (Man. C.A.), leave to appeal refused [1998] S.C.C.A. No. 45, 227 N.R. 395*n* (S.C.C.).

[119] *Snell v. Farrell*, [1990] S.C.J. No. 83 at para. 33, 72 D.L.R. (4th) 289 (S.C.C.).

[120] *Ibid.*, at para. 34.

might have been saved. However, in light of her pre-existing medical condition, of severe atherosclerosis, no witness was prepared to say that it was more likely than not that with proper treatment amputation would have been unnecessary. The trial judge found for the plaintiff because the defendant had denied her a "window of opportunity" to save her leg. However, the Ontario Court of Appeal allowed an appeal and reversed this finding.[121] The plaintiff had failed to show that, on a balance of probability, but for the loss of the chance of treatment, she would have avoided amputation. She established no more than the loss of a less than 50 per cent chance of saving her leg had the defendant not been negligent.[122]

In special circumstances, the law allows an exception to the basic "but for" test of causation. If the test is applicable and the patient fails to satisfy it, causation is unproven.[123] If for reasons outside the plaintiff's control the test cannot be applied, however, such as the limits of scientific knowledge, a court may apply the "material contribution" test. This may be applied where it is clear that the defendant breached a duty of care owed to the plaintiff, and thereby exposed the plaintiff to an unreasonable risk of injury, which the plaintiff actually suffered. That is, "the plaintiff's injury must fall within the ambit of the risk created by the defendant's breach. In ... exceptional cases ... liability may be imposed, even though the 'but for' test is not satisfied, because it would offend basic notions of fairness and justice to deny liability by applying a 'but for' approach."[124]

IV. DEFENCES

The overwhelming majority of physicians practising in Canada, and perhaps all, including those who have retired, are members of the Canadian Medical Protective Association (CMPA).[125] Many hospitals require physicians' membership as a condition of appointing them to their staffs, and of allowing physicians privileges to practice under their auspices. Indeed, a hospital may even contribute to physicians' membership fees, which in high risk specialties, such as neurosurgery and obstetrics and gynecology, in more litigious provinces, can be several tens of thousands of dollars annually.[126] Hospitals require membership because, should hospitals incur legal liability due to physicians' misconduct, which can

---

[121] *Cottrelle v. Gerrard*, [2003] O.J. No. 4194, 67 O.R. (3d) 737 (Ont. C.A.).

[122] Compare *Gregg v. Scott*, [2005] UKHL 2; see V. Black, "Ghost of a Chance: *Gregg v. Scott* in the House of Lords" (2005) 14 Health L. Rev. 38; and contrast *Chester v. Afshar*, [2005] 1 A.C. 134 (H.L.).

[123] *Bohun v. Segal*, [2008] B.C.J. No. 97, 289 D.L.R. (4th) 614 (B.C.C.A.).

[124] Chief Justice McLachlin in *Resurfice Corp. v. Hanke*, [2007] S.C.J. No. 7, 278 D.L.R. (4th) 643 at para. 25 (S.C.C.).

[125] See Canadian Medical Protective Association (CMPA), online at: <http://www.cmpa.org>.

[126] For instance in Ontario for 2006, membership fees for obstetricians exceeded $78,000. General practitioners' fees outside Ontario and Quebec in contrast were $1,644 if no obstetrics, anaesthesia, emergency care or surgery are undertaken.

run into millions of dollars,[127] they want to ensure that they can claim indemnities against physicians that can be met, if necessary through the resources of the CMPA.

The CMPA is not an insurance company, but a professional self-defence organization. Commercial insurance companies may assess each claim to determine whether it is cheaper to settle than to fight. The CMPA in contrast considers the impact of each case on the overall interests of the medical profession. It does not waste resources defending claims its own medical personnel and consultants find indefensible, but will pursue contentious claims and matters of principle to the highest possible level, including taking matters of principle to the Supreme Court of Canada even when plaintiffs discontinue their involvement.[128] Accordingly, claims for medical negligence are liable to be vigorously defended when the CMPA considers a defence feasible on the facts, or on a matter of legal principle important to the profession.

Because of the years usually taken to resolve litigation, for instance by adjudication, settlement or discontinuation, CMPA Annual Report statistics for a given year are unreliable to show the volume of suits brought and their outcomes. With over 78,500 members in 2009, the CMPA Annual Report recorded:

	2005	2006	2007	2008	2009
Legal actions (civil) resolved	1,275	1,151	982	1,003	942
Trial outcome — judgment for plaintiff	38	21	25	13	19
Trial outcome — Judgment for physician	97	81	70	75	82
Settled	386	385	312	341	319
Dismissed/discontinued/abandoned	754	664	575	574	522[129]

Terms of successful plaintiffs' awards and of settlements vary, of course, from case to case. However, in 2009 the CMPA paid about $163 million in awards and settlements, an increase from about $142 million in 2008.

What can be concluded from these figures is how relatively few cases initiated against physicians get to trial. Because the CMPA realistically settles cases its medical experts advise it cannot successfully defend, its trials largely result in judgments for its members. More instructive than the trials successfully defended, however, are cases the CMPA does not settle, and loses at trial.

The most common defence is that the claim has been brought out of time. Limitation Acts may vary from province to province, setting times within which a writ must be issued, such as two years[130] or less,[131] and sometimes depending

---

[127] See *Yepremian v. Scarborough General Hospital (No. 2)*, [1981] O.J. No. 2889, 120 D.L.R. (3d) 341 (Ont. H.C.J.).

[128] See, for instance, *McInerney v. MacDonald*, [1992] S.C.J. No. 57, 93 D.L.R. (4th) 415 (S.C.C.), where the plaintiff took no further action in the case following discovery of documents, but the CMPA, for the defendant physician, took the case to trial, and provincial and federal appeal courts.

[129] *CMPA Annual Report 2009* (Ottawa: CMPA, 2010) at 11.

[130] See, for instance, Alberta's *Limitations Act*, R.S.A. 2000, c. L-12, s. 2.

on whether the claim is for negligence, breach of fiduciary duty and/or for assault and battery,[132] or whether the defendant is a physician, a hospital or other health care professional.[133] Further, time begins to run from different starting points, including from when the plaintiff actually knew, or reasonably should have known, a cause of action may exist,[134] or from when professional services terminated in respect of the matter about which the complaint arose, whether or not the plaintiff knew or reasonably could have known of the cause of action. With the increasing sophistication of medical interventions and, for instance, long-term adverse effects of use of interventions, drugs and medical devices, it appears oppressive and unjust that patients may be time-barred before they can be aware that they have been negligently treated, or negligently informed.[135]

The Supreme Court of Canada has explained what is known as the "discoverability rule", according to which the limitation period does not start to run until the plaintiff discovers, or ought to have discovered, the material facts on which the cause of action is based.[136] However, Courts of Appeal in some provinces, notably Alberta,[137] Manitoba,[138] and Newfoundland and Labrador,[139] have held the discoverability rule inapplicable in medical malpractice actions. In such provinces, negligently injured patients and related plaintiffs may lose their claims to compensation if evidence of negligence and the injury it caused failed to materialize within the limitation period. Further, some legislation sets absolute limits, such as 10 years in Alberta.[140] However, fraudulent concealment of negligence or injury will suspend running of the limitation period until the fraud becomes apparent. In a case where a physician deceived family members as to the treatment program in which a patient died, for instance, and created a false set of notes to conceal details of the care delivered, the strict wording of the limitation legislation was held inapplicable. The court held that an unscrupulous defendant who stood in a special relationship with the injured party could not be allowed to use a limitation provision as an instrument of fraud.[141]

---

[131] See, for instance, six months, P.E.I.'s *Dental Profession Act*, R.S.P.E.I. 1988, c. D-6, s. 16(2).

[132] *H. (B.) v. Dattani*, [2010] S.J. No. 7, 315 D.L.R. (4th) 705 (Sask. C.A.).

[133] Contrast two years under P.E.I.'s *Medical Act*, R.S.P.E.I. 1988, c. M-5, s. 49.

[134] *Brooks v. Jackson*, [2009] B.C.J. No. 659, 310 D.L.R. (4th) 564 (B.C.C.A.).

[135] See G. Robertson, "*Scott v. Birdsell*: Limitation Periods in Medical Malpractice Cases" (1994) 32 Alta. L. Rev. 181.

[136] *Kamloops (City) v. Nielsen*, [1984] S.C.J. No. 29, [1984] 2 S.C.R. 2 (S.C.C.); *Central Trust Co. v. Rafuse*, [1986] S.C.J. No. 52, [1986] 2 S.C.R. 147 (S.C.C.); *M. (K.) v. M. (H.)*, [1992] S.C.J. No. 85, [1992] 3 S.C.R. 6 (S.C.C.); *Murphy v. Welsh; Stoddart v. Watson*, [1993] S.C.J. No. 83, [1993] 2 S.C.R. 1069 (S.C.C.); *Peixeiro v. Haberman*, [1997] S.C.J. No. 31, [1997] 3 S.C.R. 549 (S.C.C.).

[137] *Czyz v. Langenhahn*, [1998] A.J. No. 432, [1998] 10 W.W.R. 235 (Alta. C.A.).

[138] *Fehr v. Jacob*, [1993] M.J. No. 135, [1993] 5 W.W.R. 1 (Man. C.A.); *J. (A.) v. Cairnie Estate*, [1993] M.J. No. 351, [1993] 6 W.W.R. 305 (Man. C.A.).

[139] *Snow (Guardian ad litem of) v. Kashyap*, [1995] N.J. No. 15, 125 Nfld. & P.E.I.R. 182 (Nfld. C.A.).

[140] *Limitations Act*, R.S.A. 2000, c. L-12, s. 3(1)(b).

[141] *Giroux Estate v. Trillium Health Centre*, [2005] O.J. No. 226, 249 D.L.R. (4th) 662 (Ont. C.A.).

A more complicated case arose when, following her treatment of injuries suffered in a vehicle accident, a patient received written reports from her family practitioner and from her surgeon that she would fully recover. When treatment involving the family physician to overcome injury-related infertility failed, she sued both physicians for negligent advice. The Alberta *Limitation of Actions Act* provided a limitation period for physicians of one year from the termination of services, but the plaintiff commenced her action over two years after she received the medical reports. The trial judge found both physicians liable for negligent misrepresentation. The Court of Appeal allowed the surgeon's appeal, since action was taken out of time. However, the action against the family practitioner was not statute-barred, because it was commenced within one year of that practitioner attempting to treat the patient's inability to conceive.[142]

Under general principles, Limitation Acts do not apply their limitation periods during a potential plaintiff's incapacity, due for instance to minority age or mental disability. If injury is claimed to have arisen before or at birth, therefore, and the prevailing age of majority is, for instance, 18 years, action may be taken within the limitation period after majority age is reached. Taking account of how long a case may take to reach trial, judgment may not be delivered until over two decades after a negligent incident. Damages awarded at a rate of compound interest from the date of injury may be significant. The chance of liability being found, or even of litigation being commenced, so long after an alleged negligent incident encourages retired physicians to maintain membership in the CMPA, although under the membership contract the CMPA may be liable to consider defence of a claim dating back to a physician's earlier period of membership even though membership has not been retained.

An uncommon but complete basis of defence is that the plaintiff waived the right to sue for medical negligence. In *Hobbs v. Robertson*,[143] a hospital requested a Jehovah's Witness patient asking for a hysterectomy to sign a refusal of blood document that stated that she accepted the consequences of refusing a blood transfusion that might become medically indicated in the course of surgery. There was no discussion of whether she would be treated if she refused to sign. Against the operating physician's advice, she opted for a method of procedure that entailed greater risk of bleeding, despite receiving information that if excessive bleeding occurred, she might die. She signed a release document that provided that the hospital, its agents and personnel and the attending doctors, were released "from any responsibility whatsoever for unfavourable reactions or complications or any untoward results" due to her refusal of blood or its derivatives.

---

[142] *Kelly v. Lundgard*, [2001] A.J. No. 906, 202 D.L.R. (4th) 385 (Alta. C.A.).

[143] [2004] B.C.J. No. 1689, 243 D.L.R. (4th) 700 (B.C.S.C.). Note [2006] B.C.J. No. 266, 265 D.L.R. (4th) 537 (B.C.C.A.), where the B.C. Court of Appeal ordered a re-trial, on issues of contract law, *volenti* and *Canadian Charter of Rights and Freedoms* rights, so that the hospital's position could be clarified.

The patient suffered excessive bleeding, was not transfused, and died. Her husband and children sued, alleging negligent conduct of the surgery, and that the release covered only the usual risk inherent in the surgery when properly performed, not negligent performance. However, the judge ruled that, had negligence caused the excessive bleeding, it would have been remedied by blood transfusion, but for the patient's informed refusal. The plaintiffs accepted that blood transfusion would have saved the patient's life. Referring to *Malette v. Shulman*,[144] where damages were awarded for battery for transfusing a Jehovah's Witness who carried evidence of refusal of blood, the judge found that the patient accepted every risk of excessive bleeding, and that "her death was 'due to' her refusal to permit the administration of blood products".[145] This afforded a physician proven to have been negligent a full defence if there would have been no injury to a patient who received a blood transfusion.

A defence that may reduce rather than eliminate a negligent defendant's liability to pay compensation is contributory (sometimes called "comparative") negligence, meaning that a patient's own negligence contributed to the damage suffered. For instance, a patient who failed to use crutches following a bone biopsy, and fell and broke her leg, was held to be 20 per cent responsible for her injury.[146] A common form of patients' contributory negligence is that they fail to arrange, or to keep, follow-up appointments. A patient has been held 25 per cent liable for failing to revisit her doctor when she suffered continuing chest pains,[147] and in a wrongful birth case the patient was found 100 per cent at fault for failing to attend a follow-up appointment for an ultrasound examination, resulting in birth of a child with spina bifida.[148]

If physicians warn patients that, following medical procedures, they should not drink alcohol or, for instance, smoke tobacco[149] or drive vehicles, and the patients' failure to follow such warnings aggravates injuries they suffer due to medical negligence, courts will take their own negligence into account in assessing defendants' financial responsibility for injuries they suffer. Courts are looking more critically at patients' own responsibility for the extent of injuries they suffer due to medical negligence. This is a counterpoint to the greater autonomy patients have achieved in recent decades. As Picard and Robertson have observed:

> As patients strive for (and achieve) a more equal role in their medical care and in the doctor-patient relationship, it is predictable and just that there will be

---

[144] [1990] O.J. No. 450, 67 D.L.R. (4th) 321 (Ont. C.A.).

[145] *Hobbs v. Robertson*, [2004] B.C.J. No. 1689, 243 D.L.R. (4th) 700 at 716 (B.C.S.C.); see also [2004] B.C.J. No. 2402, 246 D.L.R. (4th) 380 (B.C.S.C.), holding that a request to sign a waiver is not a violation of freedom of religion, contrary to the *Canadian Charter of Rights and Freedoms*, ss. 2(*a*), 7 or 15(1).

[146] *Brushett v. Cowan*, [1990] N.J. No. 145, 69 D.L.R. (4th) 743 (Nfld. C.A.).

[147] *Anderson (Litigation guardian of) v. Nowaczynski*, [1999] O.J. No. 4485 (Ont. S.C.J.).

[148] *Patmore (Guardian ad litem of) v. Weatherston*, [1999] B.C.J. No. 650 (B.C.S.C.).

[149] *Dumais v. Hamilton*, [1998] A.J. No. 761 (Alta. C.A.).

more patients found to be contributorily negligent, with a consequential reduction in the compensation awarded.[150]

That is, if patients want to achieve more responsibility for their medical care, they must take more responsibility for their own behaviour that aggravates any injuries caused by the negligence of their health care providers.

V. INSTITUTIONAL NEGLIGENCE

A. HOSPITALS[151]

It has been seen that, though individual health service providers are often the named defendants in Canadian medical negligence litigation, the circumstances conditioning errors are often to be found in failures of institutional management.[152] Accordingly, suing hospitals instead of or in addition to doctors who practise in their facilities is sometimes an appropriate strategy for plaintiffs. Indeed in the U.K., hospital-based physicians enjoy a Crown immunity in some circumstances, and negligence litigation involving National Health Service (NHS) hospitals and health authorities is handled by the NHS Litigation Authority.[153]

An important legal distinction concerns the tort liability that hospitals bear for their own institutional negligence, that is, their direct liability, and their vicarious liability for acts of their personnel arising as a matter of legal policy. There can at times be uncertainty about whether a potential claim is better pursued as direct or vicarious liability, and each may be alleged in the alternative. When hospitals bear vicarious liability, they may be disposed to seek indemnities against those for whose acts they are held so liable. If plaintiffs elect to sue hospitals rather than their employees, the defendant hospitals may initiate third party proceedings against their employees to bring them into the litigation. For this reason, hospitals may be unable to represent their employees in litigation, and may for instance require that those who are eligible must join the CMPA for representation and ability to satisfy hospitals' indemnity claims.

Hospitals and their medical staff members are not necessarily in an adversarial relationship, however, and may collaborate in agreement with such agencies as the CMPA. Further, though hospitals frequently have the legal status of private corporations, their infrastructure is almost invariably strongly, if not entirely, financially supported by provincial Ministries of Health, under global budgetary arrangements and sometimes supplementary funding. Because provincial health authorities depend on hospitals for discharge of their responsibili-

---

[150] E. Picard & G. Robertson, *Legal Liability of Doctors and Hospitals in Canada*, 4th ed. (Toronto: Thomson Carswell, 2007) at 369.

[151] See, generally, E. Picard & G. Robertson, *ibid.*

[152] James Reason, *Managing the Risks of Organizational Accidents* (Aldershot, U.K.: Ashgate, 1997).

[153] See J.K. Mason & G.T. Laurie, *Law and Medical Ethics*, 7th ed. (Oxford: Oxford University Press, 2006) 303-305.

ties,[154] they cannot passively allow hospital corporations to become insolvent or bankrupt, and are usually obliged to ensure their financial viability. In the out-of-court settlement of the *Yepremian* case,[155] for instance, the Ontario Ministry of Health and the CMPA contributed to payment, the latter perhaps to obviate the hospital's third-party or indemnity claim against the responsible physician, whom the plaintiff had not sued.

1.   Vicarious Liability

Hospitals are governed by the general rule of tort law that employers are vicariously liable for the torts of their employees committed in the course of employment. If a hospital employee, such as a nurse or radiology technician is negligent and causes injury to the hospital's patient, the hospital will be held legally liable. The patient is not required to prove that the hospital itself was at fault in any way, such as in recruiting, training or equipping the employee. Vicarious liability arises automatically from the employer-employee relationship, based on the negligence of the employee alone. The negligent act must have been undertaken, however, in the course of employment. For instance, a hospital will not be vicariously liable if an employee with no record of previous misconduct takes advantage of a vulnerable patient to commit sexual abuse, although a health care clinic has been held vicariously liable for the sexually abusive acts of an employee that were sufficiently related to authorized conduct to justify the imposition of liability. The clinic significantly increased the risk of harm from sexual abuse by putting the employee in his position and requiring him to perform assigned tasks in the course of which the abuse occurred.[156]

Arguably the key legal principle in this context is that, as a general rule, doctors who work in hospitals, whether on a full-time or a part-time basis, are not employees of the hospital, but only independent contractors. The hospital is accordingly not vicariously liable for their negligent acts.[157] The typical physician-hospital relationship is that physicians are given hospital privileges, usually for 12-month renewable periods, which entitle them to admit and treat patients. They are paid not by the hospital, but by billing the provincial health insurance plan on a contractual fee-for-service basis. In contrast to their status as independent contractors, is the status of physicians salaried as hospital staff members, interns and residents, who are regarded as hospital employees and for whose negligent acts the hospitals may be vicariously liable.

An evolving tendency is for physicians to move towards salaried employment by hospitals, being paid by provincial governments or by regional health

---

[154] *Eldridge v. British Columbia (Attorney General)*, [1997] S.C.J. No. 86, 151 D.L.R. (4th) 577 (S.C.C.).

[155] *Yepremian v. Scarborough General Hospital (No. 2)*, [1981] O.J. No. 2889, 120 D.L.R. (3d) 341 (Ont. H.C.J.).

[156] *W. (T.) v. Seo*, [2005] O.J. No. 2467, 256 D.L.R. (4th) 1 (Ont. C.A.).

[157] See the full discussions in *Yepremian v. Scarborough General Hospital*, [1978] O.J. No. 3457, 88 D.L.R. (3d) 161 (Ont. H.C.J.), revd [1980] O.J. No. 3592, 110 D.L.R. (3d) 513 (Ont. C.A.).

authorities. Provinces often prefer this system of pre-set annual funding to the open-ended principle of fee-for-service billing, in which physicians may, for instance, increase their incomes 50 percent by requiring patients' follow-up visits at four-, eight- and twelve-month intervals rather than at six- and twelve-month intervals. Salaried employment also allows physicians to undertake teaching responsibilities and unfunded research without loss of income derived from patient care. Legal implications are that the contractual relationship between patients and physicians no longer exists, perhaps encouraging courts to develop jurisprudence binding physicians to patients through fiduciary duties, and that hospitals may bear vicarious liability for salaried physicians' negligence.

2. Direct Liability

In contrast to hospitals' no-fault vicarious liability is their direct liability for faults in patients' care and treatment attributable to them, usually through acts and omissions of their senior administrative officers, under principles of corporate responsibility. The duties that hospitals owe their patients in particular and their communities in general include the duties to:

(1) select and maintain competent, adequate staff;

(2) provide proper instruction and supervision of staff;

(3) provide and maintain proper and adequate equipment and facilities for patients and staff; and

(4) establish systems necessary for the safe operation of the hospital.

Instances in which hospitals have been found in breach of their own duty of care include failure to have a proper system to ensure that an X-ray report from a radiology department was sent to the emergency room physician in time, which resulted in a patient's fracture being misdiagnosed;[158] misdirection in receipt of pap test results causing harmful delay in diagnosis of cervical cancer;[159] and failure to have a necessary drug in an emergency room to save the life of a patient suffering an asthma attack.[160]

Whether a hospital's level of staffing and equipment is reasonable is increasingly measured against a determination of "community expectations". It has been judicially observed that a hospital "has an obligation to meet standards reasonably expected by the community it serves in the provision of competent personnel and adequate facilities and equipment".[161] By this criterion of reasonable community expectations, a Moncton, New Brunswick hospital was found not negligent in staffing its emergency department with part-time family physi-

---

[158] *Osburn v. Mohindra and St. John General Hospital* (1980), 29 N.B.R. (2d) 340 (N.B.Q.B.).
[159] *Braun Estate v. Vaughan*, [2000] M.J. No. 63 (Man. C.A.).
[160] *Lahey Estate v. St. Joseph's Hospital*, [1993] N.B.J. No. 617, 351 A.P.R. 366 (N.B.C.A.).
[161] *Bateman v. Doiron*, [1991] N.B.J. No. 714, 8 C.C.L.T. (2d) 284 at 290 (N.B.Q.B.), affd [1993] N.B.J. No. 598, 18 C.C.L.T. (2d) 1 (N.B.C.A.).

cians rather than with experienced emergency room physicians. The judge observed that:

> [T]o suggest that the defendant Moncton Hospital might be reasonably expected by the community to staff its emergency department with physicians qualified as expert in the management of critically ill patients does not meet the test of reality, nor is it a reasonably expected community standard. The non-availability of trained and experienced personnel, to say nothing of the problems of collateral resource allocation, simply makes this standard unrealistic, albeit desirable.[162]

As provinces face growing needs for economy in expenditure on health care services, but also pressure to reduce waiting times for necessary care, the concept of community expectations may be developed by courts adjudicating hospitals' claims that less than ideal provision of care nevertheless satisfies community standards, and patients' claims that they are reasonably entitled to expect more than hospitals have been able to provide.

B.   GOVERNMENTS AND QUASI-GOVERNMENTAL AGENCIES

The *Chaoulli* case,[163] successfully challenging the legal basis of governmental limits on private provision of health care insurance and services,[164] shows how governmental policies and practices have become targets of patients' litigation based on complaints of inadequate and negligent medical services. In this case, the Supreme Court of Canada reversed provincial courts' rejection of claims expressing dissatisfaction with governmental services. Some lower courts have allowed such negligence claims to proceed to trial. However, in *Mitchell Estate v. Ontario*, where an infant died in a health centre emergency department, and the plaintiffs alleged that delayed care and overcrowding causing death were attributable to government funding reductions and health facility restructuring decisions, the Divisional Court held that the province owed no private law duty of care for its policy decisions on funding or restructuring.[165]

The outbreak of severe acute respiratory syndrome (SARS) in Toronto in 2003 triggered several claims against governmental authorities. In *Williams v. Canada (Attorney General)*,[166] a class action alleged operational negligence against the federal Crown, the provincial Crown, and the City of Toronto. Motions brought by the federal Crown and the City of Toronto to strike out the claim were granted, but the motion by the provincial Crown was dismissed. Neither the federal Crown nor the City of Toronto were found to owe a private law

---

[162] *Ibid.*, at 292 (N.B.Q.B.).

[163] *Chaoulli v. Quebec (Attorney General)*, [2005] S.C.J. No. 33, 2005 SCC 35 (S.C.C.) [*Chaoulli*].

[164] See C.M. Flood, K. Roach & L. Sossin, eds., *Access to Care, Access to Justice: The Legal Debate over Private Health Insurance in Canada* (Toronto: University of Toronto Press, 2005).

[165] [2004] O.J. No. 3084, 242 D.L.R. (4th) 560 (Ont. Div. Ct.).

[166] [2005] O.J. No. 3508, 257 D.L.R. (4th) 704 (Ont. S.C.J.).

duty of care to the plaintiff class.[167] However, Cullity J. allowed claims to go to trial alleging negligence of the provincial government in premature lifting of SARS emergency measures, and in advice to hospitals to ease their infection control procedures, which were claimed to have exposed some class members to preventable infection.

The same judge also allowed claims for negligence brought by infected nurses against the provincial government to proceed to trial,[168] and by family members of a nurse who died from SARS infection and had infected them.[169] The judge made no findings of liability on these claims, but found that they warranted trial based on a full record of the facts, because it was not plain and obvious at that time on the governmental motions to dismiss them that they had no prospect of success. However, by addressing these claims together, the Ontario Court of Appeal decisively ruled that it was indeed plain and obvious that the province owed no private law duty of care to such plaintiffs for its management of the infection.[170] The same court had previously ruled similarly that Health Canada owed no private law duty of care to recipients of silicone breast implants[171] or of devices used in mandibular joint implants.[172]

Provincial governments have delegated or devolved many of their responsibilities for health care to quasi-governmental agencies, such as regional health authorities and health professional licensing authorities. Even when agencies to which governments have delegated their responsibilities, such as hospitals, are not bound by the *Canadian Charter of Rights and Freedoms* in their day-to-day administration, for instance in hiring staff and contracting for supplies,[173] they are required to comply with Charter provisions in exercise of their delegated functions.[174] Accordingly, when, for instance, regional health authorities, which exist in every Canadian jurisdiction except Nunavut, Ontario and the Yukon, make decisions on resource allocation that patients or prospective patients find disadvantageous, such individuals acting alone or in class action suits, may sue. They may claim on grounds of negligence and, for instance, under section 15(1) of the Charter, alleging "discrimination based on ... religion, sex, age or mental or physical disability".

---

[167] See also *St. Elizabeth Home Society v. Hamilton (City)*, [2010] O.J. No. 1515, 319 D.L.R. (4th) 74 (Ont. C.A.).

[168] *Abarquez v. Ontario*, [2005] O.J. No. 3504, 257 D.L.R. (4th) 745 (Ont. S.C.J.).

[169] *Laroza Estate v. Ontario*, [2005] O.J. No. 3507, 257 D.L.R. (4th) 761 (Ont. S.C.J.).

[170] *Williams v. Canada (Attorney General)*, [2009] O.J. No. 1819, 310 D.L.R. (4th) 710 (Ont. C.A.); *Abarquez v. Ontario*, [2009] O.J. No. 1814, 310 D.L.R. (4th) 726 (Ont. C.A.); *Laroza Estate v. Ontario*, [2009] O.J. No. 1820, 310 D.L.R. (4th) 743 (Ont. C.A.).

[171] *Attis v. Canada (Minister of Health)*, [2008] O.J. No. 3766, 300 D.L.R. (4th) 415 (Ont. C.A.).

[172] *Drady v. Canada (Minister of Health)*, [2008] O.J. No. 3772, 300 D.L.R. (4th) 443 (Ont. C.A.).

[173] *Stoffman v. Vancouver General Hospital*, [1990] S.C.J. No. 125, 76 D.L.R. (4th) 700 (S.C.C.).

[174] *Eldridge v. British Columbia (Attorney General)*, [1997] S.C.J. No. 86, 151 D.L.R. (4th) 577 (S.C.C.).

An increasing willingness of courts to allow negligence claims against governments to proceed to trial[175] may indicate an equal or greater willingness to find regional health authorities bound by a legal duty of care, because they are created to be closer, more responsive and more accountable than province-wide ministries to their community members in setting priorities for resource management. Whether they are liable for inadequate health system design and/or negligent provision of care, such as in causing delays in access to treatment, may depend on how, or whether, courts distinguish between their policy and operational decisions.

The Supreme Court of Canada has recognized that governmental authorities should not necessarily be held accountable in negligence law in the same way as private individuals and bodies, because in matters of policy, they bear democratic rather than judicial accountability. The Court recognized that the executive branch of government, acting within constitutional limits,

> ... must be free to govern and make true policy decisions without becoming subject to tort liability as a result of those decisions. On the other hand, complete Crown immunity should not be restored by having every government decision designated as one of "policy". Thus, the dilemma giving rise to the continuing judicial struggle to differentiate between "policy" and "operation" ....

> The dividing line between "policy" and "operation" is difficult to fix, yet it is essential that it be done.[176]

Accordingly, while policy decisions are open to judicial scrutiny to ensure compliance with constitutional, including Charter, values, they will not be measured according to the standards of negligence law. In contrast, methods of implementation of policy choices may be subject to observance of a standard of care.

In 1984, the Supreme Court of Canada addressed the contrast between public law and private law relevant to governmental duties to private persons and bodies. It proposed that:

> ... in order to decide whether or not a private law duty of care existed, two questions must be asked:
>
> (1) is there a sufficiently close relationship between the parties ... so that, in the reasonable contemplation of the [governmental] authority, carelessness on its part might cause damage to that person? If so,
>
> (2) are there any considerations which ought to negative or limit (a) the scope of the duty and (b) the class of persons to whom it is owed or (c) the damages to which a breach of it may give rise?[177]

---

[175] *Decock v. Alberta*, [2000] A.J. No. 419, 186 D.L.R. (4th) 265 (Alta. C.A.); contrast *Mitchell (Litigation administrator of) v. Ontario*, [2004] O.J. No. 3084, 71 O.R. (3d) 571 (Ont. Div. Ct.).

[176] *Just v. British Columbia*, [1989] S.C.J. No. 121, 64 D.L.R. (4th) 689 at 704 (S.C.C.). The Court cited with approval Mason J. in *Sutherland Shire Council v. Heyman* (1985), 60 A.L.R. 1 (H.C.A.).

[177] *Kamloops (City) v. Nielsen*, [1984] S.C.J. No. 29, 10 D.L.R. (4th) 641 at 662-63 (S.C.C.).

If a decision is operational rather than of policy,[178] it therefore is credible although not authoritative to claim that regional health authorities are liable to patients for negligent breach of a duty of care that is owed to them, in the same way that a police authority has been held liable to individuals injured through its failure to conduct proper inquiries and enforce police discipline.[179]

Regional health authorities are not empowered to control conduct of physicians, since provincial governments have delegated that responsibility to Colleges of Physicians and Surgeons. In *McClelland v. Stewart*,[180] plaintiffs who were sexually assaulted by a treating physician sued the provincial College for negligence and misfeasance in public office in failing to investigate their allegations. The motions judge allowed a motion to strike out the latter claim, but dismissed a motion to strike out the negligence claim. On the College's appeal of the decision to permit the negligence claim to proceed, the Court of Appeal relied upon a Supreme Court of Canada decision under the *Civil Code of Québec*[181] to find that, at Common law too, regulatory bodies might bear the private law liability to individuals claimed by the plaintiffs. The College's appeal was therefore dismissed, and action allowed to proceed on its merits.

---

[178] The policy/operational distinction has more recently been rejected by the highest courts in the U.K. and U.S.A. and doubted in Australia. Its effectiveness and reliability were also questioned by Sopinka J. in *Brown v. British Columbia (Minister of Transportation and Highways)*, [1994] S.C.J. No. 20, 112 D.L.R. (4th) 1 at 3-4 (S.C.C.).

[179] *Odhavji Estate v. Woodhouse*, [2003] S.C.J. No. 74, 233 D.L.R. (4th) 193 (S.C.C.).

[180] [2004] B.C.J. No. 1852, 245 D.L.R. (4th) 162 (B.C.C.A.).

[181] *Finney v. Barreau du Québec*, [2004] S.C.J. No. 31, 240 D.L.R. (4th) 410 (S.C.C.) (*sub nom. McCullock-Finney v. Barreau du Québec*).

Chapter 4

INFORMED CONSENT

Patricia Peppin[*]

I. INTRODUCTION

The doctrine of informed consent plays a central role in the health law field as it protects patient choice about their bodies. Common law has long protected the individual's interest in physical inviolability and, in that context, individuals have the right to self-determination. The right to make treatment decisions is set out in two ways in the law of torts. First, patients are entitled to protect their bodily integrity through giving consent to or refusing to permit contact with their body by another person. Second, health practitioners have a duty to disclose relevant information about treatments so that patients may make informed decisions about whether to proceed with a proposed treatment.

Participation in decision-making provides the opportunity to exercise choice according to one's own values and beliefs rather than receiving treatment through paternalistic imposition of another's treatment decisions. As well, patients' rights to decide have also been extended to wishes made by capable persons in advance. In *Malette v. Shulman*, Robins J.A., for the Ontario Court of Appeal, expressed the principle in this way:

> The doctrine of informed consent has developed in the law as the primary means of protecting a patient's right to control his or her medical treatment. ... The right of self-determination, which underlies the doctrine of informed consent, also obviously encompasses the right to refuse medical treatment. ... The doctrine of informed consent is plainly intended to ensure the freedom of individuals to make choices concerning their medical care. For this freedom to be meaningful, people must have the right to make choices that accord with their own values, regardless of how unwise or foolish those choices may appear to others.[1]

[*]   I am grateful to Brittany Sargent and Michael Edmonds for their research assistance on this chapter and to the Law Foundation of Ontario and Queen's University Faculty of Law for financial assistance. I would also like to acknowledge the contributions of Bernard Dickens and Erin Nelson in their chapters in the first two editions of this book.

[1]   [1990] O.J. No. 450, 72 O.R. (2d) 417 at 423-24 (Ont. C.A.), affg [1987] O.J. No. 1180, 64 O.R. (2d) 243 (Ont. H.C.J.). This judgment was applied and this passage cited by the majority in *C. (A.) v. Manitoba (Director of Child and Family Services)*, [2009] S.C.J. No. 30 at paras. 41-45, (S.C.C.), *per* Abella J., while Binnie J., dissenting, also adopted the judgment at para. 196.

The doctrine of informed consent changed radically in 1980 when the Supreme Court of Canada decided *Hopp v. Lepp* and *Reibl v. Hughes*, moving most actions to negligence law and finding that doctors owed a duty of disclosure to their patients.[2] As La Forest J., for the majority of the Supreme Court of Canada in *Hollis v. Dow Corning Corp.*, stated subsequently:

> The doctrine of "informed consent" dictates that every individual has a right to know what risks are involved in undergoing or foregoing medical treatment and a concomitant right to make meaningful decisions based on a full understanding of those risks. ...
>
> The doctrine of "informed consent" was developed as a judicial attempt to redress the inequality of information that characterizes a doctor-patient relationship.[3]

As these decisions have been implemented, a shift to greater patient involvement in decision-making has been discernible. At the same time, courts, including the Supreme Court itself, have engaged in critical assessment of the doctrine, and particularly of the modified objective test of causation. These doctrines are analyzed in Parts II and III of this chapter. The extent to which the patient's role has been enhanced by the changes in informed consent and the doctrinal implications of the Supreme Court of Canada's judgments on this issue are examined in the concluding sections of Part III. Some legislatures have taken steps to codify and expand the frameworks applying to consent to treatment, while others have confined their reforms to advance directives. These developments are examined briefly in Part IV. Since 1980, profound changes in the provision of health care and availability of knowledge have had an impact on implementation of the doctrines, affecting disclosure of information, perception of treatment information and patients' abilities to participate in decision-making. The context within which medical treatment decisions are made has altered radically in the intervening decades as practice has shifted to collaborative care provided by a variety of health practitioners, patients have been deinstitutionalized to community settings, the range of treatment alternatives has expanded and, with it, risks and benefits have increased, while spiralling costs accompanied by planning lag have led to significant delays in access to care. The final section critically assesses the extent to which the law has promoted the achievement of greater equality in the doctor-patient relationship, understanding of health information and participation in decision-making.

---

[2]   *Hopp v. Lepp*, [1980] S.C.J. No. 57, [1980] 2 S.C.R. 192 (S.C.C.); *Reibl v. Hughes*, [1980] S.C.J. No. 105, [1980] 2 S.C.R. 880 (S.C.C.).

[3]   [1995] S.C.J. No. 104, [1995] 4 S.C.R. 634 at paras. 24-25 (S.C.C.).

II. INFORMED CONSENT IN BATTERY

A. NATURE AND EFFECT OF CONSENT IN BATTERY

Nature of consent: The action in battery continues to protect patients' autonomy interests even though most actions are now litigated in negligence. Following the Supreme Court of Canada's decision in *Reibl v. Hughes*, battery continues to be the appropriate action in situations where there is no consent at all or where the act exceeds the consent.[4] Negligence law applies in other circumstances, where disclosure has been inadequate. The battery action has descended from the early common law doctrine of trespass *vi et armis*, which protected the interest in freedom from direct and forcible bodily intrusions.[5] Battery takes place when an actor intentionally touches another without his or her consent. Intent is inferred from knowledge or substantial certainty that the physical action will lead to such contact, as, for example, when a person pulls the trigger of a gun pointed at another. Intent is distinguishable from motive, as the well-intentioned guard, a former prize fight manager, found when he manipulated the arm of the protesting woman injured by a fall at the New Dreamland Roller Skating Rink.[6] Significantly, the battery action requires no proof of actual physical injury to the plaintiff. The harm is inherent in the invasion of the bodily integrity and as a result the award of damages reflects this injury to the individual's dignitary interest. Situations where there was no consent at all or consent was exceeded include wrong limb surgery, a procedure such as sterilization performed after consent to abdominal surgery, absence of a requirement for a valid consent (capacity, informed, voluntary, without fraud or misrepresentation) as described below, and refusal of the procedure.

Effect of consent: Consent relates to a specific act by a specific person. For example, one consents to be kissed by one person but not by another. Consent is a defence to a battery action.[7] For example, in *Toews (Guardian ad litem of) v. Weisner*, the vaccination of a minor without the consent of the parents was held to be a battery even though Weisner, the community health nurse, held an honest

---

[4]   [1980] S.C.J. No. 105, [1980] 2 S.C.R. 880 (S.C.C.).

[5]   John G. Fleming, *The Law of Torts*, 7th ed. (Sydney: The Law Book Co., 1987) at 23-24.

[6]   *Clayton v. New Dreamland Roller Skating Rink, Inc.*, 82 A.2d 458 (Sup. Ct. N.J. 1951), *cert.* denied 100 A.2d 567 (1953).

[7]   Consent is a defence provable by the defendant rather than an element of the tort requiring proof by the plaintiff. The Supreme Court of Canada affirmed this view in the four-judge majority judgment by McLachlin J. in *Non-Marine Underwriters, Lloyd's of London v. Scalera*, [2000] S.C.J. No. 26, [2001] 1 S.C.R. 551 (S.C.C.). The three minority judges, while concurring in the result, took a position dramatically at odds with battery's goal of protecting autonomy, dignity and bodily integrity, in positing that the plaintiff had the onus of proving the harmful or offensive nature of the contact by proving that the defendant knew that she was not consenting or that a reasonable person in the defendant's position would have known that the plaintiff was not consenting.

belief that the students' parents had consented.[8] Actual consent, whether express or implied, must exist and not simply an honest belief.[9]

Validity of consent: To be valid, consent must meet certain requirements.[10] It must be informed, capable and voluntary. The nature and quality of the act must be disclosed. Capacity refers to the mental ability to make the decision in addition to any legal capacity established by statute or common law. Consent must be given by a capable person or by a person legally entitled to decide on an incapable person's behalf. The complexity of the meaning and role of capacity is not considered in this chapter. Rather, the reader is referred to the discussion of capacity in the contexts in which it most frequently arises: that is, for individuals rendered incapable by psychiatric illness (in Chapter 8, "Mental Health Law in Canada") and for minors (in Chapter 9, "Death, Dying and Decision-Making about End of Life Care"). Voluntary acts are those free of coercion or duress. In addition, consent must be free from fraud or misrepresentation, which vitiate consent. The doctrine of unconscionability, an exploitation of the power imbalance between the parties, is another possible basis for consent to be undermined.[11]

Manifestations of consent: Consent may be expressed, orally or in writing, or consent may be implied from behaviour. Express consent must refer clearly to the act to be performed and the actor. Implied consent may be given where the behaviour indicates it, as when a person offers his or her limb for vaccination. In an 1891 Massachusetts case arising out of mass smallpox vaccination provided on board ship since immunization was required prior to entry into the United States, a woman discussed with the doctor whether she needed it and then lifted her arm. She was found to have implied her consent: "In determining whether she consented, he could be guided only by her overt acts and the manifestations of her feelings."[12] Hospital forms and similar documents may not reflect the nature of the transaction underneath, particularly since they may be created for other purposes, such as hospital management or protection from liability. These documents are evidence and must be examined to determine whether they accurately reflect what transpired between the parties, the true basis for consent. In *Tremblay v. McLauchlan*, the patient had signed a consent form without reading

---

8   [2001] B.C.J. No. 30 (B.C.S.C.).
9   *Allan v. New Mount Sinai Hospital*, [1980] O.J. No. 3095, 28 O.R. (2d) 356 (Ont. H.C.J.), revd [1981] O.J. No. 2874, 33 O.R. (2d) 603 (Ont. C.A.), applied in *Toews (Guardian ad litem of) v. Weisner*, [2001] B.C.J. No. 30 at paras. 18, 20 (B.C.S.C.).
10 These requirements have been incorporated into statutes in some of the provinces and territories, as discussed in Part IV below.
11 In *Norberg v. Wynrib*, [1992] S.C.J. No. 60, [1992] 2 S.C.R. 226 (S.C.C.), additional reasons at [1992] S.C.J. No. 109, [1992] 2 S.C.R. 318 (S.C.C.), three judges in the plurality found for the plaintiff on the basis of battery because of the unconscionable behaviour of the defendant, Dr. Wynrib, of obtaining sexual acts in return for prescriptions for the barbiturate to which Laura Norberg was addicted. The other three judges found that she had consented to the sexual acts. Two judges found a breach of fiduciary duty and one found for her in negligence. Five of six judges found for the plaintiff on the basis of inequality analysis.
12 *O'Brien v. Cunard S.S. Co.*, 28 N.E. 266 at 266 (Mass. 1891).

it and the court found that the form did not preclude him from suing since the form was "only as good as the degree of material disclosure".[13] Similarly, in *Coughlin v. Kuntz*, the court stated that no protection was provided to the defendant by a form unless the risks were explained.[14]

When there is no consent at all: A battery action is appropriate if there is no consent at all or the consent has been exceeded.[15] Since consent refers to a specific act by a specific person, consent is absent where a procedure has been performed on another body part, such as the wrong arm, where another person has performed the procedure, or where a different non-emergency procedure has been performed than the one expected.[16] Situations where there is no consent at all include refusals as well as those where one of the requirements for valid consent is missing — the consent is not informed as to the nature and quality of the act or the actor who will perform it,[17] or is not made with capacity, or is not voluntary, or the consent has been vitiated through fraud or inactivated through unconscionability.

Since consent is specific to acts and actors, its boundary does not extent to collateral matters including the consequences of the act, such as acquiring an STD after consenting to sex, as discussed in the paragraph below. For example, in *Halkyard v. Mathew*, a case involving the physician's non-disclosure of his epilepsy, the trial judge found no fraud or misrepresentation, no evidence that the physician was covering up in order to obtain consent to the surgery, no obligation to disclose, no materiality of the risk and no battery, since the patient consented to the surgery she received.[18] In *Bradaric v. Dr. B.B.K. Pirani Inc.*, where the patient had consented to a hysterectomy for a fibroid condition that she did not have, and where the physician knew she wanted her fertility preserved, her consent was found not to have extended to the removal of her uterus when another severe diagnosis was made.[19]

As noted above, fraud or misrepresentation may vitiate consent. For example, in *Gerula v. Flores*, the doctor performed surgery on the wrong spinal vertebrae and was liable for performing this procedure without consent.[20] He failed

---

[13] [2001] B.C.J. No. 1403 at para. 28 (B.C.C.A.).

[14] [1987] B.C.J. No. 1869 (B.C.S.C.), affd [1990] B.C.J. No. 2365 (B.C.C.A.), and the denial of the defendant's attempt to reopen the case at [1997] B.C.J. No. 1624 (B.C.S.C.).

[15] *Reibl v. Hughes*, [1980] S.C.J. No. 105, [1980] 2 S.C.R. 880 (S.C.C.), discussed below.

[16] For example, consenting to toe surgery and having a spinal fusion (*Schweizer v. Central Hospital*, [1974] O.J. No. 2205 (Ont. H.C.J.)) and wrong limb surgery, a common enough problem that quality assurance programs now require the correct part to be marked with a magic marker and initialled by the attending physician. As the Ontario Court of Appeal stated in *Gerula v. Flores*, a case involving representation of the need for second surgery after an error in the first surgery, choice of the individual to provide one's medical care is "not to be lightly disregarded": [1995] O.J. No. 2300 at para. 71 (Ont. C.A.).

[17] The wrongful sterilization of Leilani Muir, *Muir v. Alberta*, [1996] A.J. No. 37 (Alta. Q.B.), is one such case.

[18] [1998] A.J. No. 986 (Alta. Q.B.), affd [2001] A.J. No. 293 (Alta. C.A.).

[19] [2006] B.C.J. No. 1683 (B.C.S.C.), affd [2008] B.C.J. No. 1445 (B.C.C.A.).

[20] [1995] O.J. No. 2300 (Ont. C.A.).

to reveal his error and misrepresented the need for a second surgery, and this constituted a second battery because consent was vitiated by misrepresentation and constituted a breach of fiduciary duty. Fraud or misrepresentation as to collateral matters may not undermine consent, however, as in the old Irish case where fraud as to the consequences of having sex with someone with a sexually transmitted disease was found not to have undermined the consent, since the woman consented to the act itself, even if not to the collateral matter of the STD.[21] The case of *R. v. Cuerrier*, a non-disclosure of HIV-positive status case, provided the opportunity to visit this doctrine under the *Criminal Code* sexual assault provision, whose fraud definition had been amended to remove mention of the nature and quality of the act.[22] Justice Cory, with three judges concurring, declined to find the defence of consent successful where the defendant had concealed his status, finding fraud where the failure to disclose is dishonest and results in deprivation by putting the complainant at risk of serious bodily harm.[23] Since tort and criminal law are related areas, the action in battery may expand its conceptual boundaries to include consequences and incorporate risk analysis in a similar fashion, although a change more in keeping with intentional tort doctrine would recast the nature of the act to include an STD, to acknowledge that consent to sex with an STD differs from consent to sex without one. The Court in *R. v. Williams* did not regard the seriousness as essential but cited the judgment of Cory J. in *Cuerrier* and followed it:

> Without disclosure of HIV status there cannot be a true consent. The consent cannot simply be to have sexual intercourse. Rather it must be consent to have intercourse with a partner who is HIV-positive. True consent cannot be given if there has not been a disclosure by the accused of his HIV-positive status. A consent that is not based upon knowledge of the significant relevant factors is not a valid consent.[24]

B.   EMERGENCY EXCEPTION

Emergency treatment is an exception to the common law requirement of informed consent. In an emergency situation, it is permissible to provide treatment without consent to "save the life or preserve the health" of the person.[25] The basis for the emergency exception has been debated but the better opinion finds

---

[21]   *Hegarty v. Shine* (1878), 4 L.R. Ir. 288 (C.A.). The *ex turpi causa* doctrine barred recovery since the plaintiff had participated in the "illegal or immoral act" of having sex outside marriage.

[22]   [1998] S.C.J. No. 64 (S.C.C.); *Criminal Code*, R.S.C. 1985, c. C-46.

[23]   Justice L'Heureux-Dubé focused on inducement to consent, regardless of risk, while Gonthier and McLachlin JJ. confined fraud to the nature of the act or identity of the partner, a traditional approach, but considered sexually transmitted diseases an exception so that inducing consent on this basis would vitiate consent. See Mary Anne Bobinski, "HIV/AIDS and Public Health Law" in Tracey M. Bailey, Timothy Caulfield & Nola M. Ries, eds., *Public Health Law and Policy in Canada*, 2d ed. (Markham, ON: LexisNexis Canada, 2008) 179, esp. at 238-44.

[24]   [2003] S.C.J. No. 41 at para. 39 (S.C.C.), citing [1998] S.C.J. No. 64 at para. 127 (S.C.C.).

[25]   *Marshall v. Curry (No. 2)*, [1933] 3 D.L.R. 198 (N.S.C.A.). The criteria for emergencies have been expanded in some provincial consent statutes.

its foundation not in an imagined implied consent but in a loose notion of necessity.[26]

Exceptions to informed consent are also found in legislation, such as public health statutes.[27]

C. WITHDRAWAL OF CONSENT

In *Ciarlariello v. Schacter*, the Supreme Court of Canada also protected the individual's right to withdraw their consent during a procedure, unless stopping it would endanger the patient's life or threaten immediate and serious health problems.[28] Justice Cory began his analysis with the patient's right to decide what is done to his or her own body, including the right to be free of procedures to which consent has not been given, and found that this right must include the right to stop a procedure.[29] The doctor has the onus to determine whether consent has been withdrawn. Once consent has been withdrawn, consent must be given again before the procedure continues, along with disclosure of material changes in the risks if circumstances have changed but without repeated disclosure if circumstances have not altered. The scope of the original consent becomes relevant in these cases, as in *McNeil v. Yamamoto*, where the patient's consent to excision of a vaginal nodule was held to extend to a larger nodule than expected whose excision required penetration of the vaginal wall.[30]

D. REFUSAL BY PRIOR CAPABLE WISH

The right to refuse a treatment is a corollary of the right to decide what is done with one's body. Refusal is not usually considered controversial for capable persons making current decisions. More complex are those situations involving persons who are currently incapable and unable to participate in decision-making but who, when capable, had expressed their wishes to refuse treatment. Some provinces have put into place legislation governing such prior capable wishes, as noted in Part IV below. The common law position was set out in 1990 in *Malette v. Shulman*, in which the Ontario Court of Appeal affirmed the trial judge's finding of battery in an emergency situation involving a blood transfu-

---

[26] Lord Goff in *In re F. (Mental Patient: Sterilisation)*, [1989] 2 W.L.R. 1021 at 1084-85 (H.L. (E.)) characterized it as a third category of necessity cases, in addition to public and private necessity, concerned with actions in necessity taken "to preserve the life, health or well-being of another who is unable to consent to it". This necessity principle is broader than emergencies, applying to situations where it is not possible to communicate with the person, as in cases of mental incapacity. Canadian substitute decision-making legislation, in those provinces where it has been enacted, would govern the mental incapacity situation.

[27] Ellen I. Picard & Gerald B. Robertson, *Legal Liability of Doctors and Hospitals in Canada*, 4th ed. (Toronto: Thomson Carswell, 2007) at 53-56.

[28] [1993] S.C.J. No. 46, [1993] 2 S.C.R. 119 (S.C.C.).

[29] *Ibid.*, at para. 42.

[30] [2004] M.J. No. 457 (Man. Q.B.).

sion to an unconscious woman who had expressed a prior wish to refuse blood.[31] Dr. Shulman provided a blood transfusion to save the life of the unconscious Mme. Malette, although he had been made aware of a signed printed card in her wallet stating her refusal to accept blood or blood products in any circumstance, based on her Jehovah's Witness belief. This case raised the issue of the effect of a prior capable wish to refuse an emergency treatment necessary to save the person's life. The Ontario Court of Appeal found the signed card carried in her wallet was a valid expression of her wish. They considered four state interests — in the protection of life, the prevention of suicide, the prevention of harm to innocent third parties and the preservation of the ethical integrity of the medical profession. Although they incorporated them[32] without constitutional analysis in a case involving a fundamental individual right, the Ontario Court of Appeal found that the state's interest in the protection of life would not override the individual's autonomy interest and, in reaching this conclusion, strongly affirmed the individual's right to express, and have respected, prior capable wishes about treatment.

The Ontario Court of Appeal rejected the argument that the emergency exception applied, since the prior capable wish constituted an express refusal. They also rejected the defence's argument that the requirement to disclose and ensure comprehension must have a parallel requirement of informing prior to "informed refusal", a requirement that would have been impossible to meet in the circumstances, commenting on the fact that no prior relationship existed. Refusal would never be possible in this situation otherwise. It could also be argued that the defence argument reflects an understanding of informed decision-making that exists only in negligence. The Court found that the card was valid, laying emphasis on the fact that she carried it in her wallet and finding the concerns raised about it entirely speculative. Mme. Malette's card was a printed card prepared by her church, the Jehovah's Witnesses, stating that blood substitutes were acceptable but that blood and blood products were not acceptable in any circumstances. The card had been signed but had not been dated or witnessed. The daughter's presence affirming her mother's belief was considered irrelevant.[33] Dr. Shulman questioned relying on the card in the absence of witnesses to affirm it or a date to indicate current adherence. No evidence of involuntariness was present and Robins J.A. rejected these speculative positions, finding that the fact that she carried it in her wallet indicated that it reflected her views. Providing a sense of certainty for health practitioners about the existence

---

[31]   [1990] O.J. No. 450, 72 O.R. (2d) 417 (Ont. C.A.), affg [1987] O.J. No. 1180, 63 O.R. (2d) 243 (Ont. H.C.J.).

[32]   These were first set out as "countervailing" interests in the end of life case of an incapable intellectually disabled man, *Supt. of Belchertown State School v. Saikewicz*, 373 Mass. 728, 370 N.E.2d 417 (1977), and were subsequently considered in American guardianship and end of life cases. See also *Rodriguez v. British Columbia (Attorney General)*, [1993] S.C.J. No. 94, [1993] 3 S.C.R. 579 (S.C.C.).

[33]   At this time, provisions to transfer authority to substitute decision-makers were poorly defined or required cumbersome, expensive and stigmatizing guardianship proceedings.

of prior capable wishes is important, particularly when decisions with profound consequences are being made without time to examine the issues in depth. As discussed in Part IV, some provincial/territorial legislatures have codified the common law and have set out with greater clarity the legal requirements in particular circumstances. This case strongly affirmed the individual's right to autonomy.

Subsequently, in *Fleming v. Reid*, the Ontario Court of Appeal reached the same conclusion with respect to prior capable wishes to refuse treatment with neuroleptic drugs in a psychiatric facility to which the appellants, Reid and Gallagher, had been involuntarily confined under a Lieutenant Governor's Warrant.[34] They struck down the Ontario *Mental Health Act* provision authorizing the area review board to override an involuntarily committed individual's wish if the Board decided treatment was in the person's best interests.[35] The section 7 Charter right to security of the person had been infringed by the statutory provision, the infringement was not in accordance with the principles of fundamental justice because no hearing had been held, and it was not saved by section 1.[36] Justice Robins relied on the *Malette v. Shulman* case for the statement of the common law principle of informed consent affirming that the patient's right is paramount to any societal interest and found that the individual's common law right to decide what may be done to his or her body was "co-extensive" with the constitutional right to security of the person, "both of which are founded on the belief in the dignity and autonomy of each individual".[37]

A difficult case followed the death of a member of the Jehovah's Witness faith, Daphine Hobbs, who had signed a hospital form in which she refused blood and absolved the hospital and any attending doctors from responsibility for any effects, including death, from the refusal of blood. The British Columbia Court of Appeal ordered a retrial because they found the facts insufficient given the case's far-reaching implications, which included public policy and Charter questions.[38] At trial, Dr. Robertson was found to have performed a hysterectomy using a vaginal method assisted by laporoscopy and to have delayed switching to the abdominal method for almost an hour after he should have when Ms.

---

[34]   [1991] O.J. No. 1083, 4 O.R. (3d) 74 (Ont. C.A.).

[35]   *Mental Health Act*, R.S.O. 1980, c. 262, as am. 1987, c. 37, s. 12.

[36]   *Canadian Charter of Rights and Freedoms*, ss. 1, 7, Part I of the *Constitution Act, 1982*, being Schedule B to the *Canada Act 1982* (U.K.), 1982, c. 11. *R. v. Parker*, [2000] O.J. No. 2787 (Ont. C.A.) upheld the stay of charges for medical marijuana use, declaring the provision of no force or effect under the Charter, finding a broad criminal prohibition preventing access to necessary treatment inconsistent with the principles of fundamental justice, citing Robins J.A. in *Fleming v. Reid*, [1991] O.J. No. 1083, 4 O.R. (3d) 74 (Ont. C.A.) on the principle of informed consent as "fundamental and deserving of the highest order of protection" (at para. 102) and finding informed consent doctrine the "closest analogue", in the right to self-determination, to the entitlement to drug therapy (at para. 135).

[37]   *Fleming v. Reid*, [1991] O.J. No. 1083 at para. 39, 4 O.R. (3d) 74 (Ont. C.A.).

[38]   *Hobbs v. Robertson*, [2006] B.C.J. No. 266 at para. 34 (B.C.C.A.), sending for retrial [2004] B.C.J. No. 1689 (B.C.S.C.). The case had previously been sent for retrial by [2002] B.C.J. No. 2021 (B.C.C.A.).

Hobbs began to bleed critically. No transfusion was administered since she had refused it and her husband also refused on her behalf when told of her critical situation. Ms. Hobbs died as a result. The defendant admitted to negligence in performing the surgery and to the negligence causing her death.[39] The trial judge found that Ms. Hobbs assumed the risks associated with blood loss through her refusal and found for the defendant.[40] On appeal the court pointed to the particular need for evidence about whether the hospital would have denied admission if she had declined to sign the form, as part of a determination of whether such a document would be contrary to public policy. A further important issue raised by the plaintiffs is whether a refusal and release can insulate a doctor from responsibility for the very negligence that led to the need for the blood transfusion.

Through the period before 1980, the battery action provided the legal basis for patients to sue doctors for failure to provide treatment information and it continues in its more limited form. From a tactical point of view, the action in battery has significant advantages for the plaintiff. The defendant has the onus of proving informed consent. Causation is not an element of the tort. Battery requires no proof of harm and so damages are available to compensate for the infringement of the plaintiff's bodily integrity. Fraud, misrepresentation and unconscionability may all be available to vitiate the consent. Significantly, the loss of autonomy is compensated, although likely with a lower damage award.

III.   INFORMED DECISION-MAKING IN NEGLIGENCE

Since the 1980 Supreme Court decisions in *Hopp v. Lepp* and *Reibl v. Hughes*, most actions for failure to inform patients have been litigated in negligence.[41] These negligence actions focus on inadequate disclosure by a health professional who owes a duty of care. As in all negligence actions, the plaintiff must prove the elements of the action — a duty of care owed by the health practitioner to the patient, a breach of the standard of care, causation linking the defendant's negligence to the plaintiff's harm, remoteness and actual harm to the plaintiff.

A.   DUTY OF DISCLOSURE

In declaring that a doctor had a duty to disclose information about a proposed procedure, the Supreme Court of Canada took a significant step in the direction of patient participation in decision-making. The *Hopp v. Lepp* case, the first 1980 decision, arose out of spinal surgery that required a second neurosurgeon to operate to remove extruded disc material that would not have been apparent in the first operation, a procedure that resulted in nerve damage and permanent disabilities.[42] Chief Justice Laskin said that the underlying principle is the right

---

[39]   *Hobbs v. Robertson*, [2006] B.C.J. No. 266 at para. 2 (B.C.C.A.).
[40]   *Hobbs v. Robertson*, [2004] B.C.J. No. 1689 at para. 93 (B.C.S.C.).
[41]   *Hopp v. Lepp*, [1980] S.C.J. No. 57, [1980] 2 S.C.R. 192 (S.C.C.); *Reibl v. Hughes*, [1980] S.C.J. No. 105, [1980] 2 S.C.R. 880 (S.C.C.).
[42]   *Hopp v. Lepp*, *ibid.*

of patients to decide what if anything should be done with their bodies and found that the doctor owed a duty of disclosure to the patient.[43] He stated the duty as follows:

> In summary, the decided cases appear to indicate that, in obtaining the consent of a patient for the performance upon him of a surgical operation, a surgeon, generally, should answer any specific questions posed by the patient as to the risks involved and should, without being questioned, disclose to him the nature of the proposed operation, its gravity, any material risks and any special or unusual risks attendant upon the performance of the operation. However, having said that, it should be added that the scope of the duty of disclosure and whether or not it has been breached are matters which must be decided in relation to the circumstances of each particular case.[44]

Further, "even if a certain risk is a mere possibility which ordinarily need not be disclosed, yet if its occurrence carries serious consequences, as for example, paralysis or even death, it should be regarded as a material risk requiring disclosure".[45] The Court clearly established a broad standard of disclosure based on patients' need to know. In doing so, it rejected the alternative professional disclosure standard based on customary disclosure of the profession. The Supreme Court of Canada found medical evidence important but "at most" only one factor to be considered since it is a particular patient and particular treatment that are at issue in the decision.[46] "Materiality connotes an objective test, according to what would reasonably be regarded as influencing a patient's consent", they decided.[47] Probable risks need to be disclosed and possible risks with grave consequences may well be material.[48] Scope and breach "are matters which must be decided in relation to the circumstances of each particular case".[49] Significantly, the Supreme Court required that informed decision-making be assessed in an individualized way by taking account of the context.[50] Finding that there was nothing in the record to indicate that there were possible risks beyond those in any operation, to which Mr. Lepp had consented, the Court found no breach of the duty of disclosure. As a result, there was no need to proceed to the causation analysis.

---

[43] *Ibid.*, at 196.

[44] *Ibid.*, at 210.

[45] *Reibl v. Hughes*, [1980] S.C.J. No. 105, [1980] 2 S.C.R. 880 at 884-85 (S.C.C.), summarizing their earlier position.

[46] *Hopp v. Lepp*, [1980] S.C.J. No. 57, [1980] 2 S.C.R. 192 at 209 (S.C.C.).

[47] *Ibid.*

[48] *Ibid.*

[49] *Ibid.*, at 210.

[50] In considering the definition of material risks, Laskin C.J.C. made reference to the standard adopted in *Canterbury v. Spence*, 464 F.2d 772 (D.C. Cir. 1972), *cert.* denied, 409 U.S. 1064n, which found materiality when a reasonable person in what the doctor knew or should know to be the patient's position would likely attach significance to the risk in deciding whether to proceed with the proposed treatment.

In *Reibl v. Hughes*, John Reibl was diagnosed with hypertension and a specialist, Dr. Hughes, recommended a carotid endarterectomy to surgically remove a blockage in his left carotid artery.[51] As a result of the "very poor communication"[52] by Dr. Hughes, Mr. Reibl mistakenly believed that his headaches would be cured and did not understand the risks of the procedure, including the risk of non-fatal stroke, which could occur in 10 per cent of cases, and death from stroke of under 4 per cent, for a cumulative risk of 14 per cent.[53] The Supreme Court noted that Mr. Reibl's first language was Hungarian but that he was intelligent and capable of understanding the information, had it been provided. A risk of having a stroke would also have existed if he had postponed the surgery but it would have been postponed and was indeterminate, unlike the surgical risk. Mr. Reibl suffered a massive stroke as a result of the surgery and became paralyzed on one side and impotent.

The standard of care for disclosure includes the nature of the treatment and its gravity; the material risks, including probability and gravity, grave consequences even if they have a low probability, and what the doctor knows or should know the patient deems relevant; special or unusual risks; the alternatives and their risks, including the risk of not proceeding with the treatment; and the answers to any questions asked by the patient.[54] The elements, apart from questions, are what reasonable patients would want to know about these factors. The measure of material risk involves not only a risk-benefit calculation. In addition, they found, "What the doctor knows or should know that the particular patient deems relevant to a decision whether to undergo prescribed treatment goes equally to his duty of disclosure as do the material risks recognized as a matter of required medical knowledge."[55] Doctors and other health practitioners are not aware of all the personal circumstances that might be relevant to the patient's decision but disclosure of the risks should either trigger a discussion of those factors by the patient or enable the patient to make the decision without discussion.

Alternatives must also be disclosed. Chief Justice Laskin considered the issue of alternatives to the proposed treatment in a passage referring to *Canterbury v. Spence* which indicated that disclosure included "alternative means of treatment and their risks".[56] Later courts have considered the requirement in a variety of circumstances. In *Van Mol (Guardian ad litem of) v. Ashmore*, the British

---

51   [1977] O.J. No. 2289 at paras. 5-6 (Ont. H.C.J.), revd [1978] O.J. No. 3502, 21 O.R. (2d) 14 (Ont. C.A.), affd [1980] S.C.J. No. 105, [1980] 2 S.C.R. 880 (S.C.C.).

52   Ellen I. Picard, *Legal Liability of Doctors and Hospitals in Canada* (Toronto: Carswell, 1977) at 71-72.

53   *Reibl v. Hughes*, [1977] O.J. No. 2289 at paras. 12, 21 (Ont. H.C.J.).

54   Chief Justice Howland provided a useful — and often-quoted — summary of the Supreme Court's conclusions in *Videto v. Kennedy*, [1981] O.J. No. 3054 (Ont. C.A.).

55   *Reibl v. Hughes*, [1980] S.C.J. No. 105, [1980] 2 S.C.R. 880 at 894 (S.C.C.).

56   *Ibid.*, at 895; *Canterbury v. Spence*, 464 F.2d 772 (D.C. Cir. 1972), *cert.* denied 409 U.S. 1064n. Justice Krever noted later in *Ferguson v. Hamilton Civic Hospitals* that the obligation to disclose alternatives to the procedure and its risks was "implicit" in the quotation: [1983] O.J. No. 2497, 40 O.R. (2d) 577 (Ont. H.C.J.), affd [1985] O.J. No. 2538 (Ont. C.A.).

Columbia Court of Appeal found that the full range of alternatives, including the alternative methods of carrying out the cardiac surgery, should have been disclosed to the 16-year-old patient.[57] The Ontario Court of Appeal considered these cases recently in *Van Dyke v. Grey Bruce Regional Health Centre* and concluded that it is the patient's decision and so the doctor must equip the patient with the information necessary to make an informed choice.[58] Where more than one medically reasonable treatment exists and the risk/benefit analysis engaged by the alternatives involves different considerations, a reasonable person would want to know about the alternatives and would want the assistance of the doctor's risk/benefit analysis of the various possible treatments before deciding whether to proceed with a specific treatment.[59]

Where a divergence of views exists in the profession and the physician disagrees with an option, some cases have indicated that the physician needs to disclose only those alternatives considered advantageous to the patient. Picard and Robertson thought the duty should extend beyond this to alternatives considered inappropriate by the doctor, who should provide an explanation of this opinion.[60] The existence of alternatives outside the scope of the profession, for instance in the area of complementary medicine or treatments by other health professions, poses a particular problem of expertise and it seems unlikely that a court would find an obligation to disclose those alternatives falling below the standard of care or requiring expertise beyond the scope of practice of the health practitioner. Caulfield and Feasby have commented helpfully about complementary medicine that the expansive disclosure obligations in Canada indicate that physicians are likely to be required to disclose known risks, to counsel about the existence of risks, to discuss efficacy and to consider the possible application of the broader research standard of disclosure.[61] The requirement to disclose alternatives should be held to the standard of care of the profession to protect patients from untested therapies until they are able to meet the standard of care.[62] In *Dickson v. Pinder*, for example, Yamauchi J. found, in a case involving a chiropractor proposing spinal manipulation therapy who disclosed the risk of stroke but did not explain the consequences, that a medical practitioner should "disclose reasonable alternatives to any therapy they propose" including disclo-

---

57   [1999] B.C.J. No. 31 (B.C.C.A.), leave to appeal refused [1999] S.C.C.A. No. 117 (S.C.C.).

58   [2005] O.J. No. 2219 (Ont. C.A.), leave to appeal refused [2005] S.C.C.A. No. 335 (S.C.C.).

59   *Ibid.*, at para. 57.

60   Ellen I. Picard & Gerald B. Robertson, *Legal Liability of Doctors and Hospitals in Canada*, 4th ed. (Toronto: Thomson Carswell, 2007) at 153.

61   Timothy Caulfield & Colin Feasby, "Potions, Promises and Paradoxes: Complementary and Alternative Medicine and Malpractice Law in Canada" (2001) 9 Health L.J. 183 at paras. 18-21.

62   Hunter Prillaman commented that:

>   Under such a standard, a physician could avoid the danger of having to describe the theories of quacks or to explain treatments too new to have a track record, but could still be held to have a duty to keep up with the relevant literature and other sources of information, and to inform patients of new treatments as they met the criteria of acceptance.

Hunter L. Prillaman, "A Physician's Duty to Inform of Newly Developed Therapy" (1990) 6 J. Contemp. Health L. & Pol'y 43 at 58.

sure of the consequences of reasonable alternatives or inaction.[63] The trial judge discussed several cases in support and relied on *Seney v. Crooks*, in which the Alberta Court of Appeal advised that a "fringe alternative" or "alternative medicine practices" might not be required to be disclosed where the practitioner believes that they are not reasonable options.[64]

Erin Nelson has raised the issue of whether disclosure might be required for perceptions of risks, where there are posited but unproven risks that are subsequently disproved as causal links, such as the abortion-breast cancer or vaccine-autism links.[65] We might consider such posited links on a continuum from the largely speculative to the soundly established indication, with her two examples falling into the category of the weakly examined (or politically motivated). A case that would fit into the category of soundly documented risk was the pertussis vaccine which was once linked by reputable scientific evidence to brain damage through the U.K. National Childhood Encephalopathy Study (NCES), leading the trial judge in *Rothwell v. Raes* to find a manufacturer's duty to disclose during that period, while also finding that such a scientific link between the vaccine and the injury could not be established on the balance of probabilities at the time of trial, since other causes had been found for the brain damage of some of the children in the NCES, so that the plaintiff was unable to establish general scientific causation.[66] Recently, in *Gerelus v. Lim*, the trial judge found that the health practitioner did not have to disclose the risk of intracranial haemorrhage during the baby's delivery, based on what was known or ought to have been known at the time, and the Manitoba Court of Appeal upheld this decision, finding little or no evidence that it was a known risk and no expert evidence that indicated that it was a known risk.[67] Similarly, in *Morgan v. Metropolitan Toronto (Municipality)*, the Ontario Court of Appeal upheld the trial judgment in which the judge had found that concerns about the risk of serious neurological damage from the hepatitis B vaccine had not reached the level of knowledge and did not require disclosure by the nurse, also finding that the plaintiff would have had the vaccine in any event.[68]

The disclosure obligation is intended to create a degree of understanding sufficient for the patient to make an informed choice. For example, the Supreme Court of Canada stated that because of Mr. Reibl's language difficulties, Dr. Hughes should have ensured that he comprehended the information, and simi-

---

[63]   [2010] A.J. No. 445 at para. 81 (Alta. Q.B.).

[64]   *Ibid.*, at para. 79, citing [1998] A.J. No. 1060 at paras. 57-58 (Alta. C.A.).

[65]   Erin L. Nelson, "Informed Consent: Reasonableness, Risk and Disclosure" in Jocelyn Downie & Elaine Gibson, eds., *Health Law at the Supreme Court of Canada* (Toronto: Irwin Law, 2007) 145.

[66]   [1988] O.J. No. 1847 (Ont. H.C.J.), affd [1990] O.J. No. 2298 (Ont. C.A.). The earlier epidemiological evidence in the NCES, discussed at paras. 142-228, indicated that the pertussis vaccine would lead one child to suffer brain damage out of 330,000 doses, but the initially "fragile" conclusion was "so diluted by the subsequent follow-up investigations that one cannot accept them as convincing evidence of causal relationship" (at para. 228).

[67]   [2008] M.J. No. 240 (Man. C.A.).

[68]   [2008] O.J. No. 3433 (Ont. C.A.).

larly in *Ciarlariello v. Schacter* stated this duty broadly by requiring that the burden be met by the doctor to show the patient's comprehension particularly where language is an issue.[69] Picard and Robertson have expressed reservations about this level of responsibility, finding it too onerous and impractical for the physician, and instead suggested that reasonable steps be taken to ensure understanding, noting that doctors may need to look for signs of misunderstanding or repeat explanations or call for a translator, depending on the circumstances.[70] In *Byciuk v. Hollingsworth*, McMahon J. found that the physician must take reasonable steps to determine whether the patient understood, agreeing with the Picard and Robertson critique, but also found that if the physician discloses remotely, as with videos and pamphlets about gastroplasty and the brief office visit without disclosure in person in this case, then there is a higher burden to ensure understanding, which the defendant had not met as he had not made sure that the plaintiff understood the risks.[71] Justice McMahon usefully noted the factors of deference and intimidation that can confound interaction between doctor and patient. In the recent case of *Martin v. Findlay*,[72] the Alberta Court of Appeal found it unnecessary to disclose the mechanism of the resulting harm — the stroke — and considered it unnecessary to ensure understanding, citing the cases above and limiting the requirement to persons with language difficulties, or for others such as elderly patients, those with unsophisticated understanding or distress — in effect, those with vulnerabilities, citing *Schanczl v. Singh*.[73] In *Reibl*, the Court stated that Mr. Reibl could have understood, if Dr. Hughes had disclosed sufficiently, since his intellectual abilities were sufficient, and this seems to be the critical issue in this part of the judgment. This same point is made later in the majority judgment in *Starson v. Swayze*,[74] discussed below, where the Supreme Court of Canada, in its interpretation of the capacity test, focused on the *ability* of the person to understand information and appreciate the consequences, rather than on the fact of understanding, noting that a patient might not understand because of the professional's non-disclosure. With the understanding of the power imbalance between doctors and patients reflected in the Supreme Court's decisions in *Hollis v. Dow Corning Corp.* and *Norberg v. Wynrib*, it would be surprising if the Court were to retrench from its position that understanding, and not simply describing, lies at the core of informed decision-making.[75]

---

[69] *Reibl v. Hughes*, [1980] S.C.J. No. 105, [1980] 2 S.C.R. 880 at 895 (S.C.C.); *Ciarlariello v. Schacter*, [1993] S.C.J. No. 46 at para. 36, [1993] 2 S.C.R. 119 at 140 (S.C.C.).

[70] Ellen I. Picard & Gerald B. Robertson, *Legal Liability of Doctors and Hospitals in Canada*, 4th ed. (Toronto: Thomson Carswell, 2007) at 161-64.

[71] [2004] A.J. No. 620 (Alta. Q.B.).

[72] [2008] A.J. No. 462 (Alta. C.A.).

[73] [1987] A.J. No. 1126, 56 Alta. L.R. (2d) 303 (Alta. Q.B.).

[74] [2003] S.C.J. No. 33, [2003] 1 S.C.R. 722 (S.C.C.).

[75] *Hollis v. Dow Corning Corp.*, [1995] S.C.J. No. 104, [1995] 4 S.C.R. 634 (S.C.C.); *Norberg v. Wynrib*, [1992] S.C.J. No. 60, [1992] 2 S.C.R. 226 (S.C.C.), additional reasons at [1992] S.C.J. No. 109, [1992] 2 S.C.R. 318 (S.C.C.).

Elective procedures generally require a broader scope of disclosure and some courts have described this as a higher standard of disclosure. In *White v. Turner*, a case that raised the issue in the context of reconstructive breast surgery, Linden J. found that it was necessary to disclose even the minimal risks of reconstructive breast surgery, including box-like appearance and asymmetrical nipples, and the nature of the scarring with mammoplasty, which were found to be special or unusual risks.[76] "Where an operation is elective, as this one was, even minimal risks must be disclosed to patients, since 'the frequency of the risk becomes much less material when the operation is unnecessary for his medical welfare'."[77] Although this view of a broader standard of disclosure has not been universally accepted, Picard and Robertson have explained this difference by pointing out that the scope differs as courts are more likely to find the risk material, special or unusual.[78] The disclosure duty applies broadly, not only to material risks but also to other aspects of the procedure about which the reasonable patient would want information. For instance, in *Skeels Estate v. Iwashkiw*, the physician should have disclosed the safety limitations of the particular facility that the doctor had promoted as a safe place to have the patient's baby, as well as the risk of shoulder dystocia that required a higher level of care than could be provided there during the delivery.[79] This case also illustrated the greater scope of disclosure required for elective procedures as the court commented that since it was an elective decision concerning where to have the delivery, the "information component must be very high, as the patient had other viable and easily exercisable options".[80] Another difference emerged in *Hill v. Victoria Hospital Corp.*,[81] a case involving procedures to remedy incontinence. The Ontario Court of Appeal indicated that a doctor is not obliged to recommend whether an elective procedure such as the surgery is advisable, because of the heightened importance of personal factors when procedures are elective, although they determined in the end that it was not clear that Dr. Allen had not recommended the surgery.[82]

The duty to disclose is a continuing duty that applies to risks discovered after treatment has begun. Although the act of disclosure is often delegated to others, the non-delegable nature of the obligation requires the treating physician to determine that the standard of care is met. As collaborative care becomes more

---

[76] [1981] O.J. No. 2498, 31 O.R. (2d) 773 (Ont. H.C.J.), affd [1982] O.J. No. 3097 (Ont. C.A.).

[77] *Ibid.*, at para. 69 (H.C.J.), quoting Grange J. in *Videto v. Kennedy*, [1980] O.J. No. 3538 at para. 25 (Ont. H.C.J.).

[78] Ellen I. Picard & Gerald B. Robertson, *Legal Liability of Doctors and Hospitals in Canada*, 4th ed. (Toronto: Thomson Carswell, 2007) at 145.

[79] [2006] A.J. No. 666 at para. 149 (Alta. Q.B.).

[80] *Ibid.*, at para. 161.

[81] [2009] O.J. No. 300, 2009 ONCA 70 (Ont. C.A.).

[82] They relied on the court's earlier decision in *Zamparo v. Brisson*, [1981] O.J. No. 10, 32 O.R. (2d) 75 (Ont. C.A.), in which Wilson J.A., Brooke J.A. concurring, discussed the point that while the surgeon might have the duty to assess the relative risks, only the patient could evaluate the subjective factors.

common, responsibilities among team members will need to be carefully deline-ated.

The Institute of Medicine's report on patient safety, *To Err is Human*, raised awareness about the extent of systemic error in North American health institutions, with the death toll of such adverse events exceeding such common conditions as breast cancer and AIDS.[83] Over the following decade, much more attention has been paid to developing better practices, to creating a culture of safety and to creating measures to prevent such system errors as prescription errors, inadequate transmission of information, and flawed inter-professional communication.

Courts have found a duty to disclose medical errors such as leaving a drill bit inside a patient's mouth after a dental procedure, piercing the spleen or oper-ating on the wrong vertebrae.[84] Gerald Robertson has noted that the duty to dis-close medical error has been well established through these cases, based on informed consent doctrine and breach of fiduciary duty, while its precise scope remains to be determined.[85] Adoption of policy statements by the medical pro-fession, accepting the legal analysis and promoting disclosure of error as an im-portant dimension in achieving trust and openness in the doctor-patient relationship, are important steps in achieving acceptance in practice.[86] Enact-ment of Apology Acts in a number of provinces has enhanced the acceptability of apologizing since the legislation protects an apology extended outside legal proceedings from being used in subsequent litigation.[87] Since many patients sue because they want to find out what happened and want the person who has erred

---

[83] Institute of Medicine, Committee on Quality of Health Care in America, *To Err is Human: Building a Safer Health System* (Washington, DC: National Academy Press, 2000).

[84] *Kueper v. McMullin*, [1986] N.B.J. No. 89 (N.B.C.A.), finding that the duty arose after the drill bit broke and that the alternatives should have been discussed, although the plaintiff lost on cau-sation; *Stamos v. Davies*, [1985] O.J. No. 2625, 52 O.R. (2d) 10 (Ont. H.C.J.), where Krever J. found a duty to disclose the doctor's negligence in performing a lung biopsy; and *Vasdani v. Sehmi*, [1993] O.J. No. 44 (Ont. Gen. Div.) and *Gerula v. Flores*, [1995] O.J. No. 2300 (Ont. C.A.), both involving disc surgery, with the court in the latter case finding a battery for the sur-gery based on the doctor's "deliberate and flagrant disregard for the appellant's rights" (at para. 72), along with a breach of fiduciary duty for the second surgery.

[85] Gerald B. Robertson, "The Legal Duty of Physicians to Disclose Medical Errors" in Hon. Justice Margaret A. Cameron, Commissioner, *Report of the Commission of Inquiry on Hormone Recep-tor Testing*, vol. 2, "'Looking Forward…' Policy Papers" (St. John's, NL: Office of the Queen's Printer, 2009) at 65-80. See also Gerald Robertson, "When Things Go Wrong" (2002) 28 Queen's L.J. 353; Michael Waite, "To Tell the Truth: The Ethical and Legal Implications of Dis-closure of Medical Error" (2005) 13 Health L.J. 1; Joan Gilmour, "Duty of Care and Standard of Care: Understanding the Standard of Care in Laboratory Testing" in Hon. Justice Margaret A. Cameron, Commissoner, *Report of the Commission of Inquiry on Hormone Receptor Testing*, vol. 2, "'Looking Forward…' Policy Papers", *ibid.*, at 35-63, especially at 53-55, assessing the duty to test or re-test to reveal the truth to individuals.

[86] College of Physicians and Surgeons of Ontario, Policy #5-10, "Disclosure of Harm" (updated May 2010), online at: <http://www.cpso.on.ca>; Canadian Medical Association, *Code of Ethics* (Ottawa: CMA, 2004), s. 14, online at: <http://policybase.cma.ca/PolicyPDF/PD04-06.pdf>.

[87] *Apology Act*, S.B.C. 2006, c. 19; *Apology Act*, C.C.S.M. c. A98; *Apology Act, 2009*, S.O. 2009, c. 3; *Apology Act*, S.N.L. 2009, c. A-10.1; *Apology Act*, S.N.S. 2008, c. 34.

to say they are sorry, the likely result is a sense of justice being satisfied for injured plaintiffs and their families, as well as a diminished need to bring legal actions.

Errors that have occurred on a widespread basis raise further dimensions of the issue. Denise Dudzinski and colleagues have examined why institutions may be reluctant to disclose widespread events to their patients, particularly for those "near-miss" patients who have not suffered physical harm but may suffer mentally from the knowledge.[88] For example, insufficient cleaning of prostate-biopsy equipment in a Toronto hospital meant that hundreds of men had potentially been exposed to pathogens. The hospital disclosed the error and offered testing, which found no evidence of harm. A class-action suit for psychological harm from the disclosure and the wait led to a settlement of $1.2 million, a sum much lower than the $150 million claimed.[89] They concluded that while the circumstances have important implications for disclosure, the norm should be disclosure, based on the duty and the need to remedy any harm, and arguing that ultimately this should lead to a greater level of trust in the institutions.[90]

The Goudge Inquiry analyzed the series of serious errors committed by Dr. Charles Smith, Director of the Ontario Pediatric Forensic Pathology Unit at the Hospital for Sick Children from 1992 to 2005.[91] Concerns had arisen even before his promotion to that position, but it was not until 2005 that a review by five external forensic pathologists of 45 of his cases found serious failures, with questions raised about his testimony or his report in 20 of them, 12 of which had resulted in guilty verdicts. Justice Goudge identified Dr. Smith's lack of training in forensic pathology as a cause of great harm, and outlined a series of failures that included misunderstanding his role as an expert witness, failing to prepare, overstating his expertise, failing to provide a balanced view of the evidence and unscientific testimony. He also analyzed the system errors including lack of oversight and the "institutional and organizational weaknesses that made oversight difficult".[92] Wrongful convictions have been overturned in some cases and others are still being litigated, while settlements have been made or are under consideration by the Ontario government.[93]

---

[88]   Denise M. Dudzinski, Philip C. Hebert, Mary Beth Foglia & Thomas H. Gallagher, "The Disclosure Dilemma — Large-Scale Adverse Events" (2010) 363 N. Eng. J. Med. 978.

[89]   *Ibid.*, at 978, and notes 2-4 citing court documents in *Farkas v. Sunnybrook and Women's College Health Sciences Centre*, [2004] O.J. No. 5134 (Ont. S.C.J.), settlement approved [2009] O.J. No. 3533 (Ont. S.C.J.).

[90]   *Ibid.*, at 984.

[91]   Hon. Stephen T. Goudge, Commissioner, *Report of the Inquiry into Pediatric Forensic Pathology in Ontario* (Toronto: Ministry of the Attorney General, 2008), online at: <http://www.attorneygeneral.jus.gov.on.ca/inquiries/goudge/report/v1_en.html>.

[92]   *Ibid.*, at 21.

[93]   CBC News reported on the Ontario Government's offer of compensation for individuals of up to $250,000 plus payments to affected family members in "Dr. Charles Smith: The man behind the public inquiry", online at: <http://www.cbc.ca/news/canada/story/2009/12/07/f-charles-smith-goudge-inquiry.html>.

The breast cancer testing of estrogen receptors performed by Eastern Health for the Newfoundland and Labrador health care system was carried out to determine whether particular hormonal treatments were advisable. It was found to have been fundamentally deficient over an eight-year period, with almost 40 per cent of patients receiving incorrect information. When the errors first became apparent, retesting was done at an out-of-province laboratory, but patients were not made aware of the problems. The flawed testing raised systemic issues of the training and certification of pathologists, the need for continuing education, and shortages of trained pathologists, as well as internal organizational issues.[94] The Newfoundland and Labrador Commission of Inquiry on Hormone Receptor Testing, conducted by Justice Margaret A. Cameron, examined the sources of the errors in light of the legal responsibilities of care and disclosure and assessed the duties to inform of the errors and the need for retesting.[95] The class action for 2,000 women and men affected by the testing, including claims for 425 who allegedly received incorrect results, led to a mediated settlement in 2009 of $17.5 million, an apology, a memorial, and participation in a new panel to make changes to the breast cancer testing protocol.[96]

The duty to disclose has not been extended to personal characteristics of the physician, such as the epilepsy status in *Halkyard v. Mathew*, or the fact that it was his first such surgery after certification as a fully qualified specialist in *Hopp v. Lepp*.[97] The question of whether disclosure is required for procedures that are unavailable due to funding shortfalls has received some attention. Courts have also found that the risk that should have been disclosed was the one that arose, and not simply that the procedure would have been avoided if proper disclosure had been made. This issue arose in *Brito (Guardian ad litem of) v. Woolley*, where the risk of cord compression and the alternative of a Cesarean section were not disclosed and one twin was injured by cord compression during a vaginal delivery.[98]

Conscientious objection to a particular procedure, such as performing an abortion or providing contraceptive services, permits the physician to avoid performing the procedure but requires the physician to disclose information and refer the patient to providers who will perform the procedure. As Rebecca Cook

---

[94] Karyn Hede, "Breast Cancer Testing Scandal Shines Spotlight on Black Box of Clinical Laboratory Testing" (2008) 100 J. Natl. Cancer Inst. 836.

[95] Hon. Justice Margaret A. Cameron, Commissioner, *Report of the Newfoundland Commission of Inquiry on Hormone Receptor Testing* (St. John's, NL: Office of the Queen's Printer, 2009).

[96] Jon Hood, "Breast Cancer Lawsuit Alleged Needless Suffering, Death" Consumer Affairs (November 2, 2009), online at: <http://www.consumeraffairs.com/news04/2009/11/breast_cancer_suit.html>.

[97] *Halkyard v. Mathew*, [1998] A.J. No. 986 (Alta. Q.B.), aff'd [2001] A.J. No. 293 (Alta. C.A.); *Hopp v. Lepp*, [1980] S.C.J. No. 57, [1980] 2 S.C.R. 192 (S.C.C.). See also Barry R. Furrow, "Must Physicians Reveal Their Wounds?" (1996) 5 Cambridge Q. of Healthcare Ethics 204; Brenda J. Johnson, "Recent Decisions: Must Doctors Disclose Their Own Personal Risk Factors? *Halkyard v. Mathew*" (2001) 10 Health L. Rev. 18.

[98] [2003] B.C.J. No. 1539 at paras. 23-25 (B.C.C.A.), leave to appeal refused [2003] S.C.C.A. No. 418 (S.C.C.).

and Bernard Dickens have stated, "Physicians' rights to refuse to participate in medical procedures that offend their conscience may be incompatible with patients' rights to receive lawful, medically indicated treatment."[99] This conflict, they argued, may be resolved by referring patients to others to provide the care, in the same manner as physicians refer patients in other circumstances where they are unable to provide care.[100] Rebecca Cook and Susannah Howard have observed that conscientious objection poses a fundamental challenge to professionalism since it conflicts with the obligation to place the patient first.[101] Bernard Dickens made a powerful argument in favour of disclosure of certain kinds of information when physicians disagree with a procedure based on their own values or conscientious beliefs.[102] As he noted, participation in such procedures is not normally expected but a duty still exists, to their own patients and to those likely to seek their care, to disclose which procedures they are unwilling to provide, and to give reasonable advice on available services of these types, along with access to it. Emergency contraception, which must be provided within 72 hours, provides an important instance of these principles. Dickens noted that failure to disclose the option to those to whom the duty is owed may lead to civil liability, breach of fiduciary duty, negligence for failure to refer, breach of contract for fraudulent misrepresentation, criminal liability for criminal negligence causing bodily harm and contravention of a provincial human rights code provision, since non-disclosure may be seen as discrimination against women and as inhuman and degrading treatment. Some refusals may also contravene provisions in international documents. He concluded, "Accordingly, the right to object to perform or immediately to participate in medical procedures on grounds of conscience carries no parallel right to refuse to inform those eligible to receive these procedures where or how they are practically accessible."[103] This issue has become highly politicized in the United States, where conscientious objection or refusal statutes have been increasing in scope, including providers such as pharmacists and institutions, along with a range of procedures.[104]

---

[99] Rebecca J. Cook & Bernard M. Dickens, Op-Ed, "The Growing Abuse of Conscientious Objection" (May 2006) 8 Virtual Mentor 337 at 337 (Ethics Journal of the American Medical Association), online at: <http://virtualmentor.ama-assn.org/2006/05/oped1-0605.html>.

[100] The duty to refer exists generally where the physician is unable to provide care to their patients, whether for personal reasons such as holidays or their beliefs, or because they lack the expertise to fulfill the duty.

[101] Rebecca Cook & Susannah Howard, "Accommodating Women's Differences under the Women's Anti-Discrimination Convention" (2007) 56 Emory L.J. 1039, especially at 1085-87.

[102] Bernard Dickens, "Informed Consent" in Jocelyn Downie, Timothy Caulfield & Colleen Flood, eds., *Canadian Health Law and Policy*, 2d ed. (Markham, ON: LexisNexis Canada, 2002) at 148-49. See, *inter alia*, Bernard Dickens, "Legal Protection and Limits of Conscientious Objection: When Conscientious Objection is Unethical" (2009) 28 Med. & L. 337; Bernard Dickens, Op-Ed, "Unethical Protection of Conscience: Defending the Powerful against the Weak" (September 2009) 11 Virtual Mentor 725.

[103] Bernard Dickens, "Informed Consent", *ibid.*, at 149.

[104] Mary K. Collins, "Conscience Clauses and Oral Contraceptives: Conscientious Objection or Calculated Obstruction?" (2006) 15 Annals Health L. 37. In Canada, the issue of emergency contraception has proceeded through a number of phases focused on its prescription status, as it was

In analyzing the materiality of risks, Laskin C.J.C. noted several exceptions to the duty to disclose: therapeutic privilege, common risks and waiver.[105] These exceptions are rarely raised in the case law, have been omitted from the consent legislation adopted in some provinces, discussed in Part IV below, with the exception of waiver in Prince Edward Island, arguably removing the exception through legislative occupation of the disclosure field, and appear to have limited scope for application. Common risks are considered as exceptions to disclosure obligations owed by manufacturers and retailers regarding risks of which people would generally be aware. For example, the extremely small — one in a million — risk of streptococcus A infection and even lower risk of necrotizing fasciitis, did not need to be disclosed to a kidney donor because it was within the public domain and general knowledge about infections.[106] Determining the level of common knowledge may be problematic, although a degree of scepticism is warranted about the level of knowledge that can be attributed to anyone, especially in light of the strength of the duty to disclose.

Waiver is the right to forgo something to which one would otherwise be entitled. The Supreme Court of Canada found that voluntary assumption of risk includes assumption of both the physical risks and the legal risks and that a waiver signed without knowledge and intent does not support the voluntary assumption of risk defence or act as a contractual defence.[107] In the context of disclosure, waiver is problematic since it leaves a capable patient without information to make the decision and exposes a doctor to a conflict of roles if the doctor takes on the patient's proper role. It is clearly impossible for a health practitioner to ensure comprehension of information that the patient has declined to receive. The doctor may need to discuss frankly with the patient the doctor's legal requirement to disclose and the patient's role as decision-maker. The solution of informing supportive family members is one that may work well in practice since the information may reach the individual who may then make the decision with such personal assistance, even though actual transfer of decision-making authority would remain problematic without legislative change or judicial consideration of the relative rights and duties.

Therapeutic privilege, another of Laskin C.J.C.'s proposed exceptions, is based on the idea that it is better in some circumstances for the patient not to know the information. If available at all, it has a very limited scope. The rationale, as described in the early case of *Videto v. Kennedy*, was the emotional state of the patient, but such a broad exception is in direct opposition to the principles

---

granted behind-the-counter status, which removed physician prescription, and then over-the-counter status, removing the requirement of a pharmacist.

[105] *Reibl v. Hughes*, [1980] S.C.J. No. 105, [1980] 2 S.C.R. 880 at 895 (S.C.C.).

[106] *Kovacich v. St. Joseph's Hospital*, [2004] O.J. No. 4471 at paras. 144-47 (Ont. S.C.J.). The trial judge also thought that a reasonable person with his characteristics would not be deterred from the treatment. A similar conclusion was reached in another necrotizing fasciitis case, *Best v. Hoskins*, [2006] A.J. No. 48 (Alta. Q.B.).

[107] *Crocker v. Sundance Northwest Resorts Ltd.*, [1988] S.C.J. No. 60, [1988] 1 S.C.R. 1186 at 1201-1203 (S.C.C.).

of autonomy and physical inviolability.[108] Further, the fiduciary duty between doctor and patient applies to patient information so as to require disclosure of the patient's own information except in a narrow set of circumstances where disclosure poses serious risks,[109] and, as Caulfield and Feasby have argued, it should be limited to situations of serious mental distress.[110] It has been mentioned or applied in only a few cases and generally given a narrow scope, as in *Pittman Estate v. Bain*,[111] where Lang J. found such a privilege existed when a patient is unwilling to hear bad news or where his or her health is precarious enough that the news would trigger unnecessary harm, but that it did not apply in the circumstances, and it has been excluded in one, *Meyer Estate v. Rogers*, which found that no such therapeutic privilege existed because of its potentially erosive effect on informed consent.[112] As a result, all three exceptions noted *obiter* by Laskin C.J.C. appear to exist, if they do at all, on narrow and shaky grounds.

The Ontario courts have recently considered the multi-faceted nature of risk and the disclosure obligation that results. In *Matuzich v. Lieberman*, Ferrier J. found that three significant elements were involved in disclosing material risks: the explanation of the procedure and the injury that might result, explanation of the probability of the risk arising, and explanation of the consequence of the risk if it arose.[113] The trial judge in *Revell v. Heartwell* applied these three elements in a case involving delayed wound healing following breast reconstruction, finding that Dr. Chow had explained the procedure and possible injury, but had failed to explain the likelihood of the harm arising or the possible consequences of delayed wound healing, which included a delay in chemotherapy.[114] The defendant had made an argument about limiting the requirement to ensure understanding to the types of language difficulties and vulnerabilities accepted by the Alberta Court of Appeal in *Martin v. Findlay*,[115] discussed above. On appeal, the Ontario Court of Appeal adopted the three-element risk analysis.[116] The court found that the trial judge's determination that the patient lacked understanding meant that Dr. Chow's inadequate disclosure led to Ms. Revell's lack of appreciation of the probability of the risks and of the consequences of that happening,

---

[108] *Videto v. Kennedy*, [1981] O.J. No. 3054 at para. 11 (Ont. C.A.).

[109] As Picard and Robertson have noted, therapeutic privilege has been acknowledged by the Supreme Court in the analogous situation of access to patient's records in *McInerney v. MacDonald*, [1992] S.C.J. No. 57 at paras. 28-31 (S.C.C.): Ellen I. Picard & Gerald B. Robertson, *Legal Liability of Doctors and Hospitals in Canada*, 4th ed. (Toronto: Thomson Carswell, 2007) at 174n.

[110] Timothy Caulfield & Colin Feasby, "Potions, Promises and Paradoxes: Complementary and Alternative Medicine and Malpractice Law in Canada" (2001) 9 Health L.J. 183 at para. 23.

[111] [1994] O.J. No. 463 at paras. 700-713 (Ont. Gen. Div.), supp. reasons [1994] O.J. No. 3410 (Ont. Gen. Div.).

[112] [1991] O.J. No. 139 (Ont. Gen. Div.).

[113] [2002] O.J. No. 2811 at para. 53 (Ont. S.C.J.).

[114] [2008] O.J. No. 5948 (Ont. S.C.J.).

[115] [2008] A.J. No. 462 (Alta. C.A.).

[116] [2010] O.J. No. 1992 at paras. 43, 47-49 (Ont. C.A.).

and dismissed this ground of appeal. Adoption of a multi-faceted analysis of risk provides the opportunity to take a more subtle approach to the analysis of risk perception and patients' understanding.

B. CAUSATION

The second major element in a negligence action is causation. Several questions of causation exist simultaneously in negligent disclosure actions. First, the plaintiff must prove factual causation between the procedure and the harm, by applying the but-for test and if proof is impossible, then those alternatives, particularly the material contribution test, that supplement it.[117] For example, Mr. Reibl's surgery led to the stroke that caused his physical harm. In the medical and scientific field, causation may be particularly difficult to prove. As Sopinka J. found for the Court in *Snell v. Farrell*, legal proof is distinguishable from scientific proof and an inference of causation may be drawn on the basis of very little affirmative evidence where positive or scientific proof has not been made, in the absence of rebuttal evidence by the defendant.[118] Uncertainty is particularly troublesome where multiple actors engage in conduct that might contribute to the harm, additively or in combination with the other factors. Courts have responded to this dilemma by relying on a variety of alternative tests.[119]

Second, it is necessary to prove decision causation, to connect the inadequate disclosure to the harm.[120] This application of the but-for test would require examination of whether the harm would have been avoided if adequate disclosure had been made. The test employed by the Supreme Court added a further objective element to this analysis. The plaintiff must prove that if the health practitioner had disclosed adequately, the reasonable patient in the position of the plaintiff would have declined the procedure that the plaintiff accepted (or would have accepted the procedure that the plaintiff declined, as in the U.S. case of *Truman v. Thomas*, where the patient declined a pap smear[121]). This "modified objective" test of causation was adopted by the Court instead of a subjective

---

[117] *Resurfice Corp. v. Hanke*, [2007] S.C.J. No. 7 (S.C.C.). See also *Aristorenas v. Comcare Health Services*, [2006] O.J. No. 4039 (Ont. C.A.), which was also cited in *Hill v. Victoria Hospital Corp.*, [2009] O.J. No. 300 (Ont. C.A.), leave to appeal refused [2009] S.C.C.A. No. 143 (S.C.C.), where the issue to be raised was the need to assess the modified objective test in light of *Resurfice*.

[118] [1990] S.C.J. No. 73, [1990] 2 S.C.R. 311 (S.C.C.).

[119] *Bonnington Castings Ltd. v. Wardlaw*, [1956] 1 All E.R. 615 (H.L.); *McGhee v. National Coal Board*, [1972] 3 All E.R. 1008 (H.L.); *Athey v. Leonati*, [1996] S.C.J. No. 102 (S.C.C.); *Webster v. Chapman*, [1997] M.J. No. 646 (Man. C.A.), leave to appeal refused [1998] S.C.C.A. No. 45 (S.C.C.); *Fairchild v. Glenhaven Funeral Services Ltd.*, [2002] 3 W.L.R. 89 (H.L.); and *Resurfice Corp. v. Hanke*, [2007] S.C.J. No. 7 (S.C.C.).

[120] Alan Meisel & Lisa D. Kabnick, "Informed Consent to Medical Treatment: An Analysis of Recent Legislation" (1980) 41 U. Pitt. L. Rev. 407 at 438-39 used the terms "injury causation" and "decision causation".

[121] 611 P.2d 902 (Cal. 1980).

test of causation because of its concern about the "hindsight and bitterness" it thought that plaintiffs would inevitably bring to court in the aftermath of injury, that would make it problematic for judges to separate what they would have done from what they say they would have done.[122] The reasonable person in Mr. Reibl's shoes, the Court decided, would have postponed the procedure, based in large part on the fact that in just over a year and a half Mr. Reibl would have been entitled to disability benefits through a work-based pension. They also considered the determinate risks of surgery as opposed to the risk of postponing the surgery to an indeterminate time. Although the Court was unanimous in its decision, the modified objective test has provoked significant concern among commentators and, more recently, among the minority members of the Supreme Court itself, in *Arndt v. Smith*,[123] discussed below.

C.   CRITIQUE

The modified objective test can be criticized on multiple dimensions. Although the but-for test of causation determines whether the negligence makes a difference by comparing what happened with the negligence and what would have happened "but-for" the negligence, the modified objective test requires more. Its hypothetical comparison is combined with the need to prove what a hypothetical reasonable patient in the patient's circumstances would have done. As Gerald Robertson noted, this combination of the hypothetical and the negative makes it difficult for the plaintiff to prove causation in general and creates an impossible situation for the onus-bearing plaintiff in situations where it is equally reasonable both to proceed and to decline.[124]

Second, the reasonableness standard has been subject to the criticism of bias. Feminist scholars have criticized the "reasonable man" standard in tort law for its normative bias.[125] Far from being a neutral and universally applicable standard, the reasonableness standard hides a gendered and class-ridden notion of appropriate behaviour that fails to take account of others' experiences and views. Only the man on the Clapham omnibus can meet the standard. Twerski and Cohen have made another argument — that the psychological literature has indicated that most decisions are illogical.[126] If there is no such thing as a reasonable person, or only one version that only some people can meet, then the plaintiff should not be required to meet that standard.

---

[122] Chief Justice Laskin in *Reibl v. Hughes*, [1980] S.C.J. No. 105, [1980] 2 S.C.R. 880 at 897-99 (S.C.C.), quoted a Comment "Informed Consent — A Proposed Standard for Medical Disclosure" (1973) 48 N.Y.U.L. Rev. 548 at 550.

[123] [1997] S.C.J. No. 65 (S.C.C.).

[124] Gerald B. Robertson, "Overcoming the Causation Hurdle in Informed Consent Cases: The Principle in *McGhee v. N.C.B.*" (1984) 22 U.W.O. L. Rev. 75.

[125] Leslie Bender, "Changing the Values in Tort Law" (1990) 25 Tulsa L.J. 759; Lucinda Finley, "A Break in the Silence: Including Women's Issues in a Torts Course" (1989) 1 Yale J.L. & Feminism 41.

[126] Aaron D. Twerski & Neil B. Cohen, "Informed Decision Making and the Law of Torts: The Myth of Justiciable Causation" [1988] U. Ill. L. Rev. 607.

Third, another problem lies in demonstrating that the reasonable patient would have declined the treatment proposed by the doctor, which is likely to have been a reasonable proposal. Chief Justice Laskin considered this problem but thought that the particular situation and the balance of subjective and objective factors would reduce its force. Having said that, however, he thought that the patient's particular concerns must be reasonably based so that fears unrelated to the treatment would not be causative but economic considerations could be.[127] Another formulation of this thought is that reasonable patients do what their doctors recommend. The mistrust of patient's reports may more properly be seen as an evidentiary concern that could be addressed through close assessment of credibility. The Supreme Court itself recognized this later in the manufacturer-consumer relationship in *Hollis v. Dow Corning Corp.*, where it stated that the problem could be handled through cross-examination and the trial judge's weighing of the testimony; however, the Court did not disturb the modified objective test for the doctor-patient relationship and set out differences between the manufacturer-consumer and doctor-patient relationship that would justify using a subjective test in the pharmaceutical company disclosure situation.[128]

Fourth, and most fundamentally, the test does not protect autonomy. The imposition of the reasonableness standard requires that the decision be reasonable. Autonomy does not require reasonable decisions. On the contrary, the principle of autonomy supports a patient's right to make decisions based on whatever values and beliefs and idiosyncratic ideas the patient holds. For example, the Supreme Court of Canada in *Starson v. Swayze*, the case interpreting Ontario's statutory capacity test, supported the right of patients "knowingly" to be foolish.[129] This possibility is not protected by the modified objective test.

Fifth, a subjective standard would fit the logic of causation analysis more clearly since it would connect the fault of the defendant to the harm experienced by the plaintiff without the distracting and unjust embellishment of a reasonable patient. A modified test of causation may be unjust to both parties in certain circumstances. Consider a variation in which the real patient, unlike the reasonable patient in the patient's shoes, would have proceeded. The plaintiff still wins. This result — where the patient who would have acted just the same regardless of the doctor's disclosure wins the action — seems unjust to the doctor. In the reverse situation, where the reasonable patient would have proceeded with the treatment, but the actual patient would have declined the procedure and avoided the injury as a result, the plaintiff loses and the resulting lack of compensation seems unjust to the patient. In both cases, the tort requirement that the defendant's fault be connected to the actual plaintiff's harm through the medium of causation is unmet.[130] Only when the behaviour of both the reasonable and

---

127 *Reibl v. Hughes*, [1980] S.C.J. No. 105, [1980] 2 S.C.R. 880 at 899-900 (S.C.C.).

128 [1995] S.C.J. No. 104, [1995] 4 S.C.R. 634 at para. 46 (S.C.C.).

129 *Starson v. Swayze*, [2003] S.C.J. No. 33, [2003] 1 S.C.R. 722 at para.76 (S.C.C.), quoting Quinn J. in *Re Koch*, [1997] O.J. No. 1487, 33 O.R. (3d) 485 at para. 21 (Ont. Gen. Div.). Later events were litigated in *Starson v. Pearce*, [2009] O.J. No. 21 (Ont. S.C.J.).

130 Ernest Weinrib, "A Step Forward in Factual Causation" (1975) 38 Mod. L. Rev. 518.

subjective patients is consonant is the required connection made, and then the reasonable patient is superfluous.

The dissonance problem would be resolved if a subjective test were applied in addition to the reasonable patient test. The injustice to the doctor would be removed, but only when both the hypothetical reasonable patient and the actual patient would decline the procedure that the patient had accepted would the plaintiff win. The possibility of both tests applying was considered in the American case of *Truman v. Thomas.*[131] This 4:3 decision supported the action of Mrs. Thomas' children for wrongful death in a case involving a physician's failure to warn of the material risks of *not* consenting to a recommended pap smear and expanding the duty of disclosure to include the risks of not undergoing the procedure. The majority found that the fiduciary duty in the doctor-patient relationship meant that the patient should have been given all the information material to her decision, including not only the risks of the procedure but also the risks of not undergoing it and the probability of a successful outcome. The majority noted that the reasonable person test of causation is necessary but not sufficient, stating, "If the jury were to reasonably conclude that Mrs. Truman would have unreasonably refused a pap smear in the face of adequate disclosure, there could be no finding of proximate cause."[132]

The proposition that causation requires a dual test has not been decided in a Canadian court, although several courts have given the matter consideration. Justice Lambert referred to statements by Linden J. in *White v. Turner* and Robins J.A. in *Buchan v. Ortho Pharmaceutical (Canada) Ltd.* to the effect that the Court had required not merely the subjective test but also the reasonableness test, as indicating that they thought both tests needed to be met, but their statements are equally consistent with an interpretation that the *Reibl* test was simply more onerous in adding the element of reasonableness.[133] In *Baksh-White v. Cochen*, Snowie J. applied a subjective test, finding that if she had been informed of the material risk of bowel perforation — material in part because she had an increased risk because of three previous surgeries — the plaintiff would have proceeded with the hysterectomy because she had a self-directed and focused approach to having the procedure, had research knowledge and was a nurse.[134] Because of the finding on subjective causation, Snowie J. decided that it was unnecessary to consider what the reasonable person in her shoes would have

---

[131] 611 P.2d 902 (Cal. 1980).

[132] *Ibid.,* at 907.

[133] *Arndt v. Smith,* [1995] B.C.J. No. 1416 at paras. 34-42 (B.C.C.A.); *White v. Turner,* [1981] O.J. No. 2498, 31 O.R. (2d) 773 at paras. 58, 67-69 (Ont. H.C.J.); *Buchan v. Ortho Pharmaceutical (Canada) Ltd.,* [1986] O.J. No. 2331, 54 O.R. (2d) 92 at para. 69 (Ont. C.A.); *Reibl v. Hughes,* [1980] S.C.J. No. 105, [1980] 2 S.C.R. 880 (S.C.C.). He referred as well to Southin J.A.'s comment in *Hollis v. Dow Corning Corp.,* [1993] B.C.J. No. 1363, 16 C.C.L.T. (2d) 140 at 177 (B.C.C.A.) about the separate issue of what would happen if the reasonable person would opt against the treatment while the patient would opt for it.

[134] [2001] O.J. No. 3397 (Ont. S.C.J.).

done. The analysis in *Reibl v. Hughes*[135] does not support a two-tiered test since the court conceptualized and chose between dichotomous options.[136] It remains to be seen what will be decided when the risk-taking plaintiff is paired with the prudent reasonable person in the patient's shoes.[137]

D.   REVISITING CAUSATION IN ARNDT V. SMITH

The *Arndt v. Smith* case provided the Supreme Court of Canada with the opportunity to revisit the causation test.[138] Carole Arndt sued Dr. Margaret Smith for breach of the duty of disclosure, arguing that if she had been adequately warned of the risk of chronic varicella syndrome during her pregnancy, she would have had an abortion. Ms. Arndt became ill with chicken pox and asked her family physician, Dr. Smith, about the risks to the fetus during the 12th week of her pregnancy. Dr. Smith said she would find the answers and, after doing research, Dr. Smith told her in the 14th week of some risks but not the risk of chronic varicella syndrome. The probability of chronic varicella syndrome was 0.23 per cent, about a quarter of 1 per cent, but if it arises, it causes seriously disabling results. The trial judge, Hutchison J., found that Dr. Smith did not disclose this risk because it was a very low risk statistically, she did not want Ms. Arndt to worry about this risk, and she thought that abortion would not have been medically defensible. At the time these events took place in 1986, the *Morgentaler* case had not been decided and Ms. Arndt would have had to apply to a Therapeutic Abortion Committee to obtain permission for an abortion; in addition, she would have been at increasing risk during the second trimester.[139] Her daughter Miranda was born with chronic varicella syndrome, which caused brain damage requiring tube feeding for her lifetime, surgery for breathing difficulties and severely diminished quality of life.[140]

---

[135] [1980] S.C.J. No. 105, [1980] 2 S.C.R. 880 at 895 (S.C.C.).

[136] Justice Lambert reached this conclusion, agreeing with Southin J.A., that it does not give "a considered answer to that question" and that the "general tenor" of the analysis eliminates the subjective question: *Arndt v. Smith*, [1995] B.C.J. No. 1416 at para. 39 (B.C.C.A.).

[137] This problem is distinguishable from the evidentiary issue posed in *Jaskiewicz v. Humber River Regional Hospital*, [2001] O.J. No. 6 (Ont. S.C.J.). The trial judge applied the modified objective test but commented *obiter* on the absence of connecting evidence because of the plaintiff's lack of testimony on what she would have done, saying that it was an essential part of the process since the modified objective test acts as a test of credibility of the subjective statement. In *Hartjes v. Carman*, [2003] O.J. No. 3344 at paras. 29-31 (Ont. S.C.J.), affd [2004] O.J. No. 5597 (Ont. Div. Ct.), a breast uplift surgery case in which the plaintiff was not asked whether she would have proceeded, the trial judge confined *Jaskiewicz* to its own facts and found it unnecessary to ask the self-serving question. Affirming the decision, the Divisional Court respectfully disagreed with disentitling a plaintiff for failing to testify that she would not have had the procedure if warned, and stated that a trial judge may determine the causal connection on other evidence.

[138] [1997] S.C.J. No. 65 (S.C.C.).

[139] *R. v. Morgentaler*, [1988] S.C.J. No. 1, [1988] 1 S.C.R. 30 (S.C.C.).

[140] *Arndt v. Smith*, [1995] B.C.J. No. 1416 at para. 6 (B.C.C.A.).

At trial, Hutchison J. found negligent disclosure but no causation. The trial judge took into account two main points: Ms. Arndt's strong desire for a child and her scepticism of mainstream medicine, based on wanting a midwife along with the doctor and the fact that she did not want to have an ultrasound. The last factor was considered to indicate "less concern with risks in foresight than in hindsight" and, based on the two factors of her desire and her mistrust, the trial judge concluded that she would have carried the pregnancy to term if she had been informed.[141] Whether the trial judge applied a subjective or an objective test of causation was a matter of dispute in the higher courts. The British Columbia Court of Appeal found that the trial judge had applied the wrong test and ordered a new trial.[142] These judgments raised important issues about the modified objective test and threw the matter wide open for Supreme Court consideration.

The Supreme Court of Canada decided on a 6:3 basis to retain the modified objective test of causation. In doing so, however, the majority judgment by Cory J. stated that the court must take into account any "specific concerns" and any "special considerations" of the patient and that the reasonable patient must be taken to have the patient's reasonable beliefs, fears, desires and expectations.[143] A purely subjective fear unrelated to material risks should not be considered.[144] Justice Cory stated the test in this way:

> The test enunciated [in *Reibl*] relies on a combination of objective and subjective factors in order to determine whether the failure to disclose *actually* caused the harm of which the plaintiff complains. It requires that the court consider what the reasonable patient in the circumstances of the plaintiff would have done if faced with the same situation. The trier of fact must take into consideration any "particular concerns" of the patient and any "special considerations affecting the particular patient" in determining whether the patient would have refused treatment if given all the information about the possible risks."
>
> . . . . .
>
> He went on and stated that "special considerations" affecting the particular patient should be considered, as should any "specific questions" asked of the physician by the patient. In my view this means that the "reasonable person" who sets the standard for the objective test must be taken to possess the patient's reasonable beliefs, fears, desires and expectations. Further, the patient's expectations and concerns will usually be revealed by the questions posed.[145]

By highlighting the *Reibl* subjective elements as the bases for these points, Cory J. has provided them with further legitimacy today and given direction in a situation in which competing interpretations have flourished.[146] Chief Justice

---

[141] *Arndt v. Smith*, [1994] B.C.J. No. 113 at paras. 59-60 (B.C.S.C.).
[142] *Arndt v. Smith*, [1995] B.C.J. No. 1416 at para. 105 (B.C.C.A.).
[143] *Arndt v. Smith*, [1997] S.C.J. No. 65 at para. 9 (S.C.C.).
[144] *Ibid.*, at paras. 12, 14.
[145] *Ibid.*, at paras. 6, 9.
[146] For example, McLachlin J. noted at para. 64 that it has been read in different ways.

Laskin had stated that the patient's concerns in the modified objective test must be reasonably based. As examples, he cited matters that would affect causation — fears related to undisclosed risks or economic concerns that relate to an undisclosed risk.[147] It posed a relatively easy case in which to identify the "in the shoes of" elements, since the pension and the indeterminacy of the risk are factors clearly within the context of the plaintiff's life.

In contrast, the list that Cory J. outlined — of beliefs, fears, desires and expectations — consists of factors that are clearly internal values and beliefs and are much more clearly identifiable as matters relevant to autonomous decision-making.[148] If these factors, which must still be reasonable, are to be based on the individual rather than drawn from a hypothetical reasonable person, then the test has clearly become more subjective and the "shoes" have gone inside. A more subjective test of this sort may reduce to some extent the potential for norm-based and biased analysis, but the continued constraint of unreasonable beliefs indicates that the loss of fully autonomous decision-making is not being compensated and the belief in logical decision-making remains strong. As well, Cory J. remained concerned about the evidentiary problem. Justice Cory's judgment, for Lamer C.J.C., and La Forest, L'Heureux-Dubé, Gonthier and Major JJ., concluded that there was no causation since the reasonable person in Ms. Arndt's shoes would not have had an abortion, taking into account the same factors as the lower courts, and restoring the trial judgment.

Drawing on the statement of Cory J., the trial judge and the Ontario Court of Appeal in *Hill v. Victoria Hospital Corp.* have approached the issue by listing and reviewing individually both the subjective and the objective features.[149] Such an approach may heighten the importance of the particular features of such decisions, potentially respecting the concerns of the patient to a greater degree.

The minority judges in *Arndt v. Smith* all supported use of the subjective test of causation. Justice McLachlin, finding that the trial judge correctly applied the subjective test, concurred in the dismissal of the appeal based on the finding of no causation. She reasoned that the subjective test is preferable since it fits negligence principles better than the modified objective test, it is fair to both plaintiff and defendant, and it

> takes into account the plaintiff's right of choice, rather than presuming that choice on the basis of a hypothetical reasonable person. And it permits serious consideration of the plaintiff's evidence as to what that choice would have been. ... At the same time, it is fair to the physician, who may introduce evi-

---

[147] *Reibl v. Hughes*, [1980] S.C.J. No. 105, [1980] 2 S.C.R. 880 at 899-900 (S.C.C.).

[148] In *Felde v. Vein and Laser Medical Centre*, [2003] O.J. No. 4654 (Ont. C.A.), Moldaver J.A. found that the timing of the surgical procedure may or may not be a significant factor in assessing the modified objective test and it was significant in this case, and Borins J.A., concurring, found it "significant that both Reibl and Arndt recognize that 'special considerations affecting the particular patient' may play a significant role in the causation analysis" (at para. 29).

[149] [2009] O.J. No. 300 at paras. 23-24 (Ont. C.A.), leave to appeal refused [2009] S.C.C.A. No. 143 (S.C.C.).

dence of what the reasonable patient would have done as it bears on the choice the particular patient at bar would have made.[150]

She also thought that the subjective test could accommodate cases of two equally reasonable choices since it focuses on the choice that the plaintiff would have made, determined on the balance of probabilities and based on an examination of all the evidence. In contrast, the objective test "depreciates the plaintiff's personal choice in such situations and deprives her testimony of any weight".[151]

Justice McLachlin rejected the theory advanced by Lambert J.A. in the Court of Appeal that the plaintiff had lost the opportunity to decide, and that the loss of choice should itself be compensable, pointing out that Laskin C.J.C. had rejected this battery theory.[152] For the same reason, she rejected the fiduciary obligation argument, and said that recovery becomes "virtually automatic" on proof of breach of disclosure and she saw no reason to depart from the existing law in negligence.[153] As Philip Osborne noted, Lambert J.A. used fiduciary duty analysis, which has been a developing area in Canadian medical law, to alter the causation analysis.[154] The theories are similar in doing away with the requirement of causation and compensating the lost right itself. Justice Lambert would have chosen the fiduciary obligation only after applying the modified objective test to determine whether "some reasonable patients in the plaintiff's position would have taken a different course than the uninformed plaintiff actually took", regardless of whether another group of people would have decided the same way as the uninformed plaintiff.[155] While such an approach would resolve some problems, it would continue to place weight on what others would do and require reasonableness.

The fact that six of nine judges upheld the modified objective test of causation is significant in that it requires adherence to a test that has been resoundingly criticized and has now been supported by three of nine judges.[156] At the same time, the majority judges have made the test somewhat more subjective both in emphasizing the *Reibl* elements of subjectivity and in making the "in the shoes of" test a more interior and particularized one. When put to the test in this most subjective of situations, however, the weight was given to the reasonable person with her scepticism. The dissenting judges, Sopinka and Iacobucci JJ., expressed a concern that Ms. Arndt's own statement that she would have had an abortion was not considered adequately. It is worth recalling that neither position would have been exceptional at the time, when midwifery had achieved acceptance and when ultrasound had just been introduced into practice. Her

---

[150] *Arndt v. Smith*, [1997] S.C.J. No. 65 at para. 66 (S.C.C.).
[151] *Ibid.*, at para. 67.
[152] *Ibid.*, at para. 37.
[153] *Ibid.*, at para. 38.
[154] Philip H. Osborne, "Annotation to *Arndt v. Smith*" (1995) 25 C.C.L.T. (2d) 264.
[155] *Arndt v. Smith*, [1995] B.C.J. No. 1416 at paras. 49-54 (B.C.C.A.), where Lambert J.A. set out four options.
[156] Erin Nelson & Timothy Caulfield, "You Can't Get There From Here: A Case Comment on *Arndt v. Smith*" (1999) 32 U.B.C. L. Rev. 353.

scepticism about mainstream medicine and opposition to ultrasound may be viewed as a concern to protect her fetus in the face of new technologies and it is not apparent how care to avoid injury automatically translates into a desire to carry a potentially injured fetus to term. Erin Nelson and Timothy Caulfield have commented that, "It could be argued that the Court allowed an idiosyncratic concern (distrust of mainstream medicine) to outweigh an objectively reasonable fear (fear of the potential impact of chicken pox on the fetus)."[157] As Wood J.A. stated in the British Columbia Court of Appeal:

> The fact that a woman prefers a natural form of childbirth, with a minimum of medical intervention and the assistance of a midwife, cannot by itself reasonably support the inference that she would knowingly disregard or take lightly the risk of serious birth defects resulting from an illness contracted during her pregnancy.[158]

Determining risk-bearing behaviour is a difficult enterprise at any time since people vary widely in their assessments of risk and in their willingness to assume them. Determining the choice that an abstract reasonable person would make about such a personal and difficult matter as terminating a pregnancy seems like an illegitimate exercise.

Reproductive matters, involving ethical and personal questions of an intimate nature, are particularly difficult to second-guess through a requirement of objectivity. Do judicial views on pregnancy and its termination have a place in such an intimate and far-reaching decision? Justice Wood stated that:

> As Mr. Justice Lambert has pointed out, the rule in *Reibl v. Hughes* is inadequate to the point where injustice can surely result from its application. That is particularly so in cases such as this, where any treatment decision involves a delicate balancing of overlapping personal, ethical, and medical considerations which can lead to more than one "reasonable" choice.[159]

In *Buchan v. Ortho Pharmaceutical (Canada) Ltd.*,[160] the Ontario Court of Appeal rejected the modified objective test for the test of causation for the manufacturer's failure to disclose action. Justice Robins said that where the manufacturer had failed to warn physicians of the risks of stroke in taking birth control pills and the patient would not have proceeded:

> [w]hether a so-called reasonable woman in the plaintiff's position would have done likewise is beside the point. The selection of a method of preventing unwanted pregnancy in the case of a healthy woman is a matter, not of medical treatment, but of personal choice ... . So long as the court is satisfied that the plaintiff herself would not have used the drug if properly informed of the risks,

---

[157] *Ibid.*, at 359.
[158] *Arndt v. Smith*, [1995] B.C.J. No. 1416 at para. 87 (B.C.C.A.).
[159] *Ibid.*, at para. 91.
[160] [1986] O.J. No. 2331, 54 O.R. (2d) 92 (Ont. C.A.).

this causation issue should be concluded in her favour regardless of what other women might have done. [161]

This position sustains the argument in favour of a subjective test, particularly in situations involving wide ranges of choice that are highly dependent on the patients' own — possibly unreasonable — values and beliefs.[162] The analysis of Feldman J.A. for the Ontario Court of Appeal in *Bovingdon v. Hergott*, a preconception duty case, takes a useful step since it takes the position of the plaintiff as central and uses the assessment of the reasonable person in her shoes to assess the reliability of the subjective statement.[163] This application effectively adopts the position of McLaughlin J., but without adopting her preference for the subjective test. It resolves the "hindsight and bitterness" problem by testing the subjective statement yet preserves the central importance of the subjective statement.

E.   ACHIEVING THE PURPOSE OF INFORMED CONSENT

The Supreme Court of Canada established a duty of disclosure that required physicians to provide the information necessary for patients to act as autonomous decision-makers. The decision reflected the concerns from the consumer and feminist movements for a greater role for patients in their own health care decisions and a desire to move away from the paternalistic approach that had previously characterized the doctor-patient relationship. In his classic book, *The Silent World of Doctor and Patient*, Jay Katz analyzed how patient participation in decision-making was "an idea alien to the ethos of medicine", reflecting deeply held views about the role of silence in creating trust.[164] This trust, he argued, was unidirectional, and needed to be replaced by mutual trust. Resistance among physicians existed during the period following the decision, but by 2000, the duty appeared so well-established — through attrition, generational change and acceptance — as to be uncontroversial.

Empowerment of patients through disclosure was the foundation of the Supreme Court's decision and its most enduring accomplishment. To the extent that patients possess information as the basis of their choices about treatment, they may act as autonomous individuals. The patient needs sufficient understanding to be able to assess the proposed treatment in light of the patient's val-

---

[161] *Ibid.*, at para. 77.

[162] The Supreme Court of Canada, in the leading case of *Hollis v. Dow Corning Corp.*, [1995] S.C.J. No. 104, [1995] 4 S.C.R. 634 (S.C.C.), adopted the subjective test of causation for the manufacturer. Justice La Forest found that the manufacturer had a greater likelihood of devaluing risk and overvaluing benefit than the doctor and found much in the inequality of information and resources between manufacturer and patient to counter such a modification. Although the Court retained the modified objective test for the doctor-patient relationship, his concern for lack of information extended to that relationship and might have provided a basis for such a modification to a subjective test of causation.

[163] *Bovingdon v. Hergott*, [2008] O.J. No. 11 at paras. 66-67 (Ont. C.A.).

[164] Jay Katz, *The Silent World of Doctor and Patient* (New York: The Free Press, 1984).

ues, beliefs, goals and circumstances — all of which may or may not be disclosed to the doctor.

The Supreme Court counter-balanced the power given to patients at the duty stage by providing doctrinal protection to physicians through adoption of the "reasonable patient in the position of the patient" test of causation. As Cory J. expressed it in *Arndt v. Smith*:

> ... its modified objective test for causation ensures that our medical system will have some protection in the face of liability claims from patients influenced by unreasonable fears and beliefs, while still accommodating all the reasonable individual concerns and circumstances of plaintiffs.[165]

This doctrine undermines the autonomy of the patient by preventing unreasonable and idiosyncratic views — or those perceived as such — from being actionable. It is not clear how many claims would have been won if a subjective test of causation had been in place. In his review of litigation at the 20-year mark, Gerald Robertson found that plaintiffs were still losing on causation, as they had been 10 years after the 1980 decisions but, surprisingly, a shift on the part of some judges to a more subjective application made it even harder for plaintiffs to win.[166] *Brito (Guardian ad litem of) v. Woolley* illustrates such a loss in a case finding breach of the disclosure of a low risk/grave consequences Cesarean section alternative to vaginal delivery that deprived a woman of important health information, but which the Court of Appeal found she would not have chosen because her doctors would have recommended against it and she trusted her physicians.[167] He concluded that, in part, this results from contradictory reasoning about the same factors in different courts and questionable inferences drawn from other risk-taking behaviours.[168] His most encouraging conclusion relates to an increased level of disclosure: patients still lose badly on causation "but increasingly because the required information has in fact been disclosed by the physician, which may be an indication that the legal standard is having a positive impact on medical practice".[169] The most important legacy of the 1980 cases may be the enhancement of patient participation in decision-making. Sadly though, failure to reveal needed information remains an uncompensated loss.

F.   DOCTRINAL IMPLICATIONS

The causation test prevents recovery in many circumstances. Twerski and Cohen argued that what we know about decision-making is that it is in fact illogical

---

[165] [1997] S.C.J. No. 65 at para. 15 (S.C.C.).

[166] Gerald B. Robertson, "Informed Consent 20 Years Later" [2003] Health L.J. Special Edition 153 at 157-59.

[167] [2003] B.C.J. No. 1539 at paras. 40-47 (B.C.C.A.), leave to appeal refused [2003] S.C.C.A. No. 418 (S.C.C.).

[168] Gerald B. Robertson, "Informed Consent 20 Years Later" [2003] Health L.J. Special Edition 153 at 158.

[169] *Ibid.*, at 159.

rather than reasonable, that it depends on presentation of the information, and that it is affected by prior idiosyncratic information. The uncertainties created by these factors undermine the credibility of the legal analysis.[170] The literature on semiotics provides support for their view on presentation, as it indicates how meaning is constructed based on the viewer's values and beliefs, which are anticipated and called upon by presentation in forms such as advertising. The creation of knowledge about diseases, treatments and patients for physicians and patients affects the acceptance of certain treatments. Power and profits are secured through presentation of information, and medical judgments reflect these perceptions and values.

As an alternative to the negligence action, recovery could be given for the failure to disclose *per se* in the absence of any proof of resulting harm. As Marjorie Maguire Schultz has argued, informed consent doctrine "embeds protection of patient choice within the interest in physical well-being" and out of fear of false claims, diminishes protection for the patient's right to choose.[171] If choice were protected as an independent interest, "the factual cause issue would be narrower and simpler — whether the patient's right to choose had been encroached upon as a result of a doctor's failure to disclose".[172] This approach appears to have been forestalled — at least temporarily — by the division between battery and negligence actions and by McLachlin J.'s rejection, and the other judges' implicit rejection, of the Lambert J.A. approach in *Arndt v. Smith*.[173] As noted in Part II, the battery approach has advantages for plaintiffs although the dignitary tort approach or valuation of lost choice approach produces lower damage awards than the negligence action.

Short of this solution, better protection would be provided to the plaintiff if the court were to presume the reasonableness of the plaintiff's position and reverse the onus to require the defendant health practitioner to rebut this presumption, as has happened in the products liability failure to warn cases. Justice Robins for the Ontario Court of Appeal in *Buchan v. Ortho Pharmaceutical (Canada) Ltd.* created a rebuttable presumption that the doctor would have disclosed the risks to the patient if the manufacturer had disclosed the product risks to the doctor and La Forest J. in *Hollis v. Dow Corning Corp.* declined to require proof by the plaintiff of the hypothetical and denied access to the learned intermediary defence to non-disclosing manufacturers, since both courts found a fundamental lack of fairness in requiring proof of such an element.[174] Justice La

---

[170] Aaron D. Twerski & Neil B. Cohen, "Informed Decision Making and the Law of Torts: The Myth of Justiciable Causation" [1988] U. Ill. L. Rev. 607.

[171] Marjorie Maguire Shultz, "From Informed Consent to Patient Choice: A New Protected Interest" (1985) 95 Yale L. J. 219 at 232 [capitalization removed].

[172] *Ibid.*, at 251.

[173] [1997] S.C.J. No. 65 (S.C.C.).

[174] *Buchan v. Ortho Pharmaceutical (Canada) Ltd.*, [1986] O.J. No. 2331, 54 O.R. (2d) 92 at paras. 59, 63-66 (Ont. C.A.); *Hollis v. Dow Corning Corp.*, [1995] S.C.J. No. 104, [1995] 4 S.C.R. 634 at paras. 60-61 (S.C.C.). Justice La Forest saw only one situation where the manufacturer could

Forest, drawing a "close analogy" to *Cook v. Lewis*, stated that the plaintiff's power of proof, if not destroyed, had been seriously undermined by the hypothetical proof requirement and because of her "position of great information inequality" in relation to both manufacturer and doctor, she was uninvolved in the causal chain.[175] Similarly, a doctor who has destroyed the patient's possibility of proof could appropriately be required to rebut the presumption of causation.

As another partial remedy, the negligence action could compensate a loss by valuing elements other than the purely physical loss experienced by the plaintiff. The model for this valuation would be the Supreme Court of Canada's analysis in *Laferrière v. Lawson* of the losses arising out of Dr. Lawson's failure to disclose to Mme. Fortier-Dupuis for five years that she had breast cancer.[176] The action failed to prove that timely disclosure would have made a difference to her life expectancy and no liability was imposed for loss of the chance of living, with La Forest J. dissenting on this point. The Court fashioned a different remedy and awarded damages for the psychological harm experienced during the period after discovering her diagnosis and the deprivation caused by the denied benefit of earlier treatment, which would likely have improved her condition. These losses had clearly been caused by the defendant's negligence sufficiently to ground injury causation. This method provides a helpful way to avoid problems in finding injury causation where survival cannot be proven on the balance of probabilities and where a court is reluctant to compensate for loss of a chance. By changing the way the harm is conceptualized, the decision causation test will also be subtly altered to a test of whether the contextualized reasonable patient, if adequately informed of the risk of the reconceptualized loss, would have gone ahead. Because the loss is valued differently, the nature of disclosure changes, and with it, the nature of the decision that would have been made. For example, if the loss is conceptualized as the lost opportunity to be injury-free for a longer period of time in *Reibl*, or the lost opportunity to make a decision whether to take care of a child with a disability in *Arndt*, then the decision itself may be seen differently, even from a reasonable point of view.[177]

In the related product liability disclosure action, Berger and Twerski have suggested compensating the deprivation of informed choice without proof of

---

be absolved, "in cases where some extraneous conduct by the doctor would have made the failure to give adequate warning irrelevant" (at para. 59).

[175] *Cook v. Lewis*, [1951] S.C.J. No. 28, [1951] S.C.R. 830 (S.C.C.), *per* Rand J.; *Hollis v. Dow Corning Corp.*, [1995] S.C.J. No. 104, [1995] 4 S.C.R. 634 at paras. 57-60 (S.C.C.). See Bernard J. Garbutt III & Melinda E. Hofmann, "Recent Developments in Pharmaceutical Products Liability Law: Failure to Warn, the Learned Intermediary Defense, and Other Issues in the New Millennium" (2003) 58 Food & Drug L.J. 269 for discussion of recent U.S. developments.

[176] [1991] S.C.J. No. 18, [1991] 1 S.C.R. 541 (S.C.C.).

[177] Sanda Rodgers made a similar argument with respect to valuing the real losses experienced by women, including care for the child and the home, in wrongful birth actions where the reproductive injury results in the birth of a child and also suggested that the loss of reproductive autonomy itself should be compensable: Sanda Rodgers, "Taking Care of Baby: Denying Legal Recovery for the Birth of a Child" (1999-2000) 1 J. Women's Health & L. 235.

injury causation in those toxic tort cases involving lifestyle drugs where the causal link between product and harm is problematic and unresolved when litigation commences, where information about the alleged link was known or could have been revealed through testing, and where the information has not been disclosed to patients.[178] In cases such as these involving non-therapeutic lifestyle drugs, decision causation would be resolved in favour of the plaintiff since the lifestyle enhancement would be clearly outweighed by the material risk.[179] They recommended that the emotional distress of the lost choice be the basis for the damage award. Such a protection for negligent infliction of emotional distress would be consistent with the Supreme Court's view in *R. v. Morgentaler* that infringements of security of the person include psychological stress.[180]

IV. STATUTES GOVERNING INFORMED CONSENT

A. STATUTES

Some provinces and territories have enacted fully developed health care consent legislation while others have legislated in the personal directives area and regarding some aspects of consent to treatment. Legislation grew out of the need to provide methods to transfer treatment decision-making authority to substitute decision-makers in short-term circumstances in which guardianship legislation would be inadequate. The *Canadian Charter of Rights and Freedoms* provided an impetus for change in the area of guardianship for mentally incompetent persons.[181] Some reforms involved guardianship and delegation of authority through advance directives or powers of attorney for personal care. As a general matter, comprehensive consent legislation provides a framework for disclosure of information to meet informed consent standards; establishes processes for capacity determination in circumstances such as treatment, admission to care facilities and everyday care where long-term guardianship would be unnecessary or cumbersome; sets out standards to determine who should make a substitute decision for an incapable person; establishes the standards to be applied in making a substitute decision; and provides legal processes for reviews and procedures to deal with specific circumstances. Such comprehensive statutes have been enacted in Ontario, British Columbia, Prince Edward Island and the Yukon.[182] Provisions for proxy decision-making and/or advance directives have

---

[178] Margaret A. Berger & Aaron D. Twerski, "Uncertainty and Informed Choice: Unmasking *Daubert*" (2005) 104 Mich. L. Rev. 257.

[179] *Ibid.*, at 149*n*.

[180] [1988] S.C.J. No. 1, [1988] 1 S.C.R. 30 (S.C.C.).

[181] *Canadian Charter of Rights and Freedoms*, s. 7, Part I of the *Constitution Act, 1982*, being Schedule B to the *Canada Act 1982* (U.K.), 1982, c. 11.

[182] British Columbia: *Health Care (Consent) and Care Facility (Admission) Act*, R.S.B.C. 1996, c. 181. Unproclaimed portions of this Act were repealed in 2006 by the *Supplements Repeal Act*, S.B.C. 2006, c. 33, s. 1 in force May 18, 2006, ss. 2, 4-18 not in force. This statute affects or will

been specified in legislation in Alberta, Manitoba, Newfoundland and Labrador, the Northwest Territories, Nova Scotia, Nunavut and Saskatchewan.[183] New Brunswick governs this issue under two separate statutes, covering infirm persons generally and those persons institutionalized under the mental health legislation.[184] In another development, several jurisdictions have added co-decision-making provisions to their guardianship jurisdiction, creating a form of supported decision-making for incapable persons with their guardians.[185]

B. LITIGATION

Litigation concerning the Ontario legislation has resulted in several important precedents.[186] *Re Koch* was an early case involving evaluations of incapacity after allegations of incapacity by one marital partner against the other while they were engaged in a separation dispute.[187] Justice Quinn identified the "formidable" power of the incapacity determination, noted that persons are entitled to be unreasonable in their decision-making as long as the decision is reasoned, and found that the evaluators of incapacity should have been alert to the compromising impact of the separation and should have protected her process rights:

---

affect the *Adult Guardianship Act*, R.S.B.C. 1996, c. 6; *Representation Agreement Act*, R.S.B.C. 1996, c. 405; *Public Guardian and Trustee Act*, R.S.B.C. 1996, c. 383. Ontario: *Health Care Consent Act, 1996*, S.O. 1996, c. 2, Sched. A; *Substitute Decisions Act, 1992*, S.O. 1992, c. 30. Prince Edward Island: *Consent to Treatment and Health Care Directives Act*, R.S.P.E.I. 1988, c. C-17.2. Yukon: *Adult Protection and Decision Making Act*, S.Y. 2003, c. 21, Sched. A; *Care Consent Act*, S.Y. 2003, c. 21, Sched. B; *Public Guardian and Trustee Act*, S.Y. 2003, c. 21, Sched. C.

[183] *Personal Directives Act*, R.S.A. 2000, c. P-6; *Health Care Directives Act*, C.C.S.M. c. H27; *Infirm Persons Act*, R.S.N.B. 1973, c. I-8; *Advance Health Care Directives Act*, S.N.L. 1995, c. A-4.1; *Personal Directives Act*, S.N.W.T. 2005, c. 16; *Personal Directives Act*, S.N.S. 2008, c. 8; *Hospitals Act*, R.S.N.S. 1989, c. 208; *Involuntary Psychiatric Treatment Act*, S.N.S. 2005, c. 42; *Powers of Attorney Act*, S.Nu. 2005, c. 9; *Adult Guardianship and Co-decision-making Act*, S.S. 2000, c. A-5.3; *Health Care Directives and Substitute Health Care Decision Makers Act*, S.S. 1997, c. H-0.001.

[184] *Infirm Persons Act*, R.S.N.B. 1973, c. I-8; *Mental Health Act*, R.S.N.B. 1973, c. M-10.

[185] Doug Surtees, "The Evolution of Co-Decision-Making in Saskatchewan" (2010) 73 Sask L. Rev. 75 at para. 20 has stated that:

Today some form of supported or assisted decision-making legislation, for some types of decisions, is in force in several jurisdictions, including Alberta, Saskatchewan, Quebec, the Yukon and Manitoba. Strangely the Manitoba legislation applies only to so-called "vulnerable persons" who are statutorily defined as adults living with a mental disability. British Columbia has passed similar provisions, although they are not yet in force. Internationally, countries including Norway, Denmark, Sweden, Germany, Japan and England and Wales have introduced or proposed some provision for supported or assisted decision making with respect to some types of decisions. [footnotes omitted]

[186] *Health Care Consent Act, 1996*, S.O. 1996, c. 2, Sched. A; *Substitute Decisions Act, 1992*, S.O. 1992, c. 30.

[187] [1997] O.J. No. 1487, 33 O.R. (3d) 485 (Ont. Gen. Div.).

The right knowingly to be foolish is not unimportant; the right to voluntarily assume risks is to be respected. The State has no business meddling with either. The dignity of the individual is at stake.[188]

M. (A.) v. Benes was a case in which a constitutional argument was made about the amount of information provided to substitute decision-makers about the nature of their responsibilities under the Act.[189] Substitute decision-makers (SDMs) must decide on the basis of prior capable wishes expressed when at least 16 years of age, or, if no such wish exists, on the basis of the best interests, as defined in the *Health Care Consent Act, 1996*.[190] If the health practitioner determines that the substitute decision-maker has failed to decide according to this requirement, the matter may be sent to the Consent and Capacity Board, to give directions to the SDM or make the decision on its own.[191] The Ontario Court of Appeal found that this provision did not contravene the section 7 Charter rights of the incapable person in failing to give substitute decision-makers notice of their responsibilities.[192] Instead the court found a statutory obligation to ensure that they understood their responsibilities in the provision that no treatment shall be given unless the health practitioner has formed the opinion that the person is incapable and the substitute decision-maker has consented "in accordance with" the Act.[193] This decision is highly significant since it fills a gap created when advocates and rights advisers were removed from the system, except those in mental health facilities. It is important to ensure that health practitioners are able to carry out this responsibility, through educating them about their roles and responsibilities under the statute. Further, it adds another dimension to the duty to ensure comprehension discussed in Part III.

In *Starson v. Swayze*, a case involving an appeal of a mental incapacity finding, the Supreme Court of Canada reached a 6:3 decision that the reviewing judge had correctly determined the standard on review to be reasonableness and had correctly applied it in finding the Board unreasonable.[194] The Board's decision on capacity had been based on their view that Starson denied his mental disorder and failed to appreciate the consequences of his decision, but these views were not founded on evidence. Second, the Board incorrectly applied the definition of capacity, which requires a finding that the person lacks the *ability*

---

188   *Ibid.*, at 521, cited with approval in *Starson v. Swayze*, [2003] S.C.J. No. 33, [2003] 1 S.C.R. 722 at para. 76 (S.C.C.), as noted in Part III above.
189   [1999] O.J. No. 4236 (Ont. C.A.).
190   S.O. 1996, c. 2, Sched. A, s. 21.
191   *Ibid.*, s. 37.
192   *Canadian Charter of Rights and Freedoms*, s. 7, Part I of the *Constitution Act, 1982*, being Schedule B to the *Canada Act 1982* (U.K.), 1982, c. 11.
193   *Health Care Consent Act, 1996*, S.O. 1996, c. 2, Sched. A, s. 10(1)(b).
194   [2003] S.C.J. No. 33, [2003] 1 S.C.R. 722 (S.C.C.). In *D'Almeida v. Barron*, [2010] O.J. No. 3647 at paras. 19-21 (Ont. C.A.), affg [2008] O.J. No. 2945 (Ont. S.C.J.), leave to appeal refused [2010] S.C.C.A. No. 511 (S.C.C.), a constitutional challenge to Ontario's *Health Care Consent Act, 1996, ibid.*, s. 4 capacity test on grounds of vagueness was rejected and the Board's application of *Starson* upheld.

to understand the information and appreciate the consequences of the decision and not simply a finding that the person does not understand the information or appreciate the consequences. Further, their view of the patient's best interests was irrelevant to their mandate to decide the capacity issue. The dissenting judges, in a decision written by McLachlin C.J.C., considered the Board's decision to have been within the range of reasonable conclusions and the conclusions amply based on the evidence. The majority protected individuals from Board actions that rely more on Board members' views about treatment need than on the range of individuality that autonomy is supposed to protect.

Legislative requirements for informed consent in Ontario, British Columbia, Prince Edward Island and the Yukon combine both the criteria for valid consent in battery and the criteria for disclosure in negligence. Since negligence imposes a duty, it is not much of a stretch to find that consent without fulfilment of the duty would be invalid, but negligence law operates on different principles. Gerald Robertson concluded that this requirement of negligence disclosure to make consent valid as informed is an effective repudiation of Laskin C.J.C.'s separation of battery and negligence in *Reibl v. Hughes* and, hopefully, that proceeding in battery again would remove the obstacles posed by the modified objective test of causation.[195] The provisions have not yet led to such a revolutionary result, although they continue to be anomalous. The Ontario Court of Appeal commented recently that the Ontario statutory definition of informed consent, which was not in force when the case before them began, contains "many of the same principles found in the common law of informed consent. The extent, if any, to which the statute departs from the common law will have to be addressed if and when that issue arises."[196]

V.   EMERGING ISSUES IN INFORMED CONSENT

Has informed consent doctrine succeeded in enabling patients to participate in decision-making? Cathy Jones was a participant observer in a hospital for six months while she studied these interactions.[197] She identified four features that doctors cited in the late 1980s as objections to informed consent: (1) "Patients neither understand nor remember what they're told"; (2) "Testing patients' understanding is too resource intensive"; (3) "Patients want physicians to make decisions for them"; and (4) "Physicians can convince almost any patient to do what the physician believes is best for the patient".[198] After making suggestions to deal with these objections, she concluded that shifting the power balance was

---

[195] Gerald B. Robertson, "Ontario's New Informed Consent Law: Codification or Radical Change?" (1994) 2 Health L.J. 88; *Reibl v. Hughes*, [1980] S.C.J. No. 105, [1980] 2 S.C.R. 880 at 891-92 (S.C.C.).

[196] *Van Dyke v. Grey Bruce Regional Health Centre*, [2005] O.J. No. 2219 at para. 63 (Ont. C.A.), leave to appeal refused [2005] S.C.C.A. No. 335 (S.C.C.).

[197] Cathy J. Jones, "Autonomy and Informed Consent in Medical Decision-Making: Toward a New Self-Fulfilling Prophecy" (1990) 47 Wash. & Lee L. Rev. 379.

[198] *Ibid.*, at 409-25.

necessary to achieve informed consent. Patients need to trust themselves more and this self-trust comes through others trusting them more.[199] Vulnerable patients are not autonomous and more power produces less vulnerability but also a position of not having to take responsibility. Cathy Jones argued that if we are serious about patient autonomy and decision-making, we must render a patient's shifting of responsibility to the physician unacceptable, and we must insist that patients take primary responsibility for making decisions relating to their health care.[200]

The question remains whether the current system is able to provide an environment in which patients' desires for the doctor-patient relationship — such as mutual trust, listening skills, truthfulness in disclosure, openness, respect, discussion of uncertainties, and confidentiality — can be achieved.

Today, medicine is practised in a way that differs significantly even from its 1980 counterpart, in the involvement of a bigger range of health practitioners, the increasing acceptance of collaborative care, shorter periods of hospitalization, the wide availability of sophisticated technology for diagnostics and treatment, dramatically increased prescription drug usage and rapid information-processing. From the perspective of patients, much more information is available. Internet access, media coverage, consumer groups (some funded by the pharmaceutical industry) and direct-to-consumer advertising provide information in forms that vary greatly in their degree of reliability. The doctor-patient dyad is no longer the sole, or even perhaps primary, source of patient information, as it had been in the period leading up to the 1980 decisions when medicine had achieved primacy over other health care providers and family members and when technology continued to promise progress in care. At the same time the economics of patient care have changed dramatically, so that timely access can no longer be guaranteed. Because the service system is fragmented, higher degrees of sophistication are required for patients to make their way effectively to the needed care. Because there are few patient advocates available to counsel patients about services or legal rights, health practitioners often advise patients and their families about these issues, sometimes as a legal requirement. Unless health professionals are educated in legal issues early in their education and are supported in continuing education in this area, they will lack the expertise to put into effect their own responsibilities and to ensure that patients' rights are respected in the decision-making process. At the same time, deficiencies in product information arising out of inadequate testing in the populations who will use it and a rush to get products to market to maximize profits before patent protection expires has led to increased adverse effects.

Through this period, the pharmaceutical industry has vastly expanded its influence over the sources of information available to physicians, controlling to a greater extent the structuring of information that reaches physicians and then patients. They have done this by increasing the percentage of research funded by

---

[199] *Ibid.*, at 427.
[200] *Ibid.*, at 421.

industry, by expanding their ties to medical journals, government regulators and physician assessors, and by increasing the funding allocated to promotional activities such as direct-to-consumer advertising, and promotion to physicians through detailers, print advertising and educational seminars.[201] Preparation of articles by industry representatives and researchers connected to industry has permitted the industry to sell their products and construct product knowledge under the guise of peer-reviewed authorship. Unless independent and reliable sources of information are available to physicians, they will be unable to exercise professional judgment about proposed treatment alternatives and unable to convey reliable knowledge to patients. Informed consent rests on the premise that the information is adequate. This expectation is undermined by biases that exist throughout the process of knowledge construction.

Empowerment of patients depends as well on contextual elements such as race, age, gender and class. These social factors form part of the inquiry into dominance and equality in the health practitioner-patient relationship. Jocelyn Downie and Jennifer Llewellyn have observed that relational theory, which "is grounded in a shared core belief that the object/subject of attention should be understood in relation to others and as *being in* relation *to* others", enables us to conceptualize the self as constructed, connected and embodied.[202]

Attending to the context leads us to examine variations in the degree to which individuals can access and evaluate Internet information, depending on a range of factors including literacy, geography, poverty, availability of resources, level of education and critical awareness of sources. These power relationships among the participants need to be taken into account in the attempt to secure participation in decision-making. Susan Sherwin argued that creating personal control over health care requires examining context including medical structures themselves as sources of power and status that have contributed to women's inequality.[203] The myth of autonomy incorrectly perceives patients as empowered to act when they are not; understanding this point requires us to take account of the medicalization of women's bodies and sexist, racist and paternalistic norms.[204] Jennifer Nedelsky has pointed out that a liberal notion of autonomy focuses on atomistic individuals and fails to reflect "the inherently social nature of human beings", beings whose social context is "literally consti-

---

[201] Jerry Avorn, *Powerful Medicine: The Benefits, Risks, and Costs of Prescription Drugs* (New York and Toronto: Vintage Books, 2005); John Abramson, *Overdosed America: The Broken Promise of American Medicine* (New York: HarperCollins, 2004); Jerome P. Kassirer, *On The Take: How Medicine's Complicity With Big Business Can Endanger Your Health* (New York: Oxford University Press, 2005).

[202] Jocelyn Downie & Jennifer Llewellyn, "Relational Theory & Health Law and Policy" (2008) Special Ed. Health L.J. 193 at 195, 196 [emphasis in original].

[203] Susan Sherwin, "Feminist and Medical Ethics: Two Different Approaches to Contextual Ethics" (1989) 4 Hypatia 57.

[204] Erin Nelson, "Reconceiving Pregnancy: Expressive Choice and Legal Reasoning" (2004) 49 McGill L.J. 593 at 614.

tutive of us".[205] She suggested that autonomy consists not only of self-determination but also probably of "comprehension, confidence, dignity, efficacy, respect, and some degree of peace and security from oppressive power".[206]

Autonomy is enabled by relationships that provide experience and guidance in autonomy. The doctrine of informed decision-making can encourage the capacity to be autonomous through enhancing the individual's power in the relationship. Participation in decision-making is critical to achieving autonomy and respect for individuals' values and beliefs. In global health it is increasingly recognized that such human rights interact with health so that improving the rights of citizens to make decisions about themselves and their dependent family members is a means to achieve better health status. Improving access to accurate information, and educating people so that they can understand and assess the information are vital steps toward achieving autonomy.

---

[205] Jennifer Nedelsky, "Reconceiving Autonomy: Sources, Thoughts and Possibilities" (1989) 1 Yale J.L. & Feminism 7 at 8.

[206] *Ibid.*, at 9.

Chapter 5

CIVIL LIABILITY OF PHYSICIANS UNDER QUEBEC LAW

Robert P. Kouri
Suzanne Philips-Nootens

I.   INTRODUCTION

The gradual evolution of the Quebec health care system to its present state has occurred in a very similar fashion to that of its sister provinces. From depending on religious communities, charitable foundations and other non-profit entities, it has become, for the most part, the responsibility of the province.[1] As in the rest of Canada, Quebec has adhered to the guiding principles of the *Canada Health Act*[2] which enunciates what is expected of a publicly funded and publicly administered system. Nevertheless, a general acceptance of these principles has not led to a willingness to pursue uniformity in all legal aspects relating to health care. This rejection of a transsystemic harmonization is most evident in two areas: the refusal to tolerate the encroachment by the federal government upon jurisdictions reserved to the provinces and the need to safeguard the integrity of the civil law.

The desire to resist federal intrusion into provincial health law is evidenced by the partially successful contestation of the *Assisted Human Reproduction Act*[3] as an encroachment upon the jurisdiction of the provinces.[4] As for protecting the

---

[1]   See, generally, Michelle Giroux, Guy Rocher & Andrée Lajoie, « L'émergence de la *Loi sur les services de santé et les services sociaux*; une chronologie des événements » (1999) 33 R.J.T. 659.

[2]   R.S.C. 1985, c. C-6.

[3]   S.C. 2004, c. 2.

[4]   In *Renvoi fait par le gouvernement du Québec en vertu de la Loi sur les renvois à la Cour d'appel, L.R.Q. ch. R-23, relativement à la constitutionnalité des articles 8 à 19, 40 à 53, 60, 61 et 68 de la Loi sur la procréation assistée, L.C. 2004 ch. 2*, [2008] J.Q. no 5489, [2008] R.J.Q. 1551 at 1557 (Que. C.A.), the Court of Appeal stated:

   [The federal statute] is intended to control a medical activity, in both its clinical and its research aspects because this would favour a certain uniformity deemed desirable. The suitability of a single law regulating for all of Canada an accepted and recognized activity is not an objective which would fall within the competence of the criminal law. [our translation]

   However, the Supreme Court decided (*Reference re Assisted Human Reproduction Act*, [2010] S.C.J. No. 61, 2010 SCC 61 (S.C.C.)) that ss. 8 (consent to the use of reproductive material), 9 (obtaining and utilizing sperm or ova from minor donors), 12 (reimbursement of costs of donors,

coherence of the civil law system, it is important to bear in mind that the statement by Mignault J. in *Desrosiers v. Canada*[5] that "the civil law constitutes a complete system in itself and it must be interpreted according to its own rules" has attained the status of dogma in Quebec. Indeed, it is generally held that the law is a reflection of the history, language, mores and economy of a people. Although drawing inspiration from another jurisdiction can enrich the law, ill-considered borrowings between legal systems can disturb the philosophical cohesion of a body of law. In this regard, one cannot gloss over the fundamental dichotomy between the common law, where jurisprudence is the primary source of law, and the civil law, based upon Roman law, in which the judge applies the law rather than creates it.

Quebec civil law *has* on occasion adopted certain principles from the common law. The Supreme Court of Canada "trilogy"[6] on the evaluation of damages for personal injury serves as a perfect example. Yet in the area of medical liability, even William Campbell James Meredith, a Quebec writer who was far from adverse to looking to the common law for possible solutions, felt constrained to write:

> It must be emphasized, however, that common law decisions should be applied in Quebec civil law only when the principles underlying the particular subject matter are the same under both systems. Even then they should be treated merely as "persuasive" precedents and not as binding authorities.[7]

But Professor Paul-André Crépeau, writing the same year as Meredith (1956), set in motion forces which are still strongly felt today in Quebec medical malpractice law. Crépeau argued that problems must be resolved only according to civil law principles, contrary to what had been, up to then, a far from exceptional practice.[8]

In this chapter we will describe the state of the law in Quebec relating to medical liability[9] and provide several illustrations of legal reasoning which may

---

surrogate mothers), 19 (information and privacy considerations) and 60 (enforcement provisions) were a valid exercise of the federal criminal law power under s. 91(27) of the *Constitution Act, 1867*. The Attorney General of Quebec had conceded that ss. 5-7 of the *Assisted Human Reproduction Act* were *intra vires*. Four judges (LeBel, Deschamps, Abella and Rothstein JJ.) held, *inter alia*, that ss. 8-19 went beyond the scope of the criminal law power of Parliament.

5   [1920] S.C.J. No. 5, 60 S.C.R. 105 at 126 (S.C.C.).

6   *Andrews v. Grand & Toy Alberta Ltd.*, [1978] S.C.J. No. 6, [1978] 2 S.C.R. 229 (S.C.C.); *Thornton (Next friend of) v. Prince George School District No. 57*, [1978] S.C.J. No. 7, [1978] 2 S.C.R. 267 (S.C.C.); *Arnold v. Teno*, [1978] S.C.J. No. 8, [1978] 2 S.C.R. 287 (S.C.C.).

7   William Campbell James Meredith, *Malpractice Liability of Doctors and Hospitals* (Toronto: Carswell, 1956) at xi of the introduction.

8   Paul-André Crépeau, *La responsabilité civile du médecin et de l'établissement hospitalier* (Montreal: Wilson & Lafleur, 1956) at 249.

9   Jean-Louis Baudouin & Patrice Deslauriers, *La responsabilité civile*, vol. II: *Responsabilité professionnelle*, 7th ed. (Cowansville, QC: Éditions Yvon Blais, 2007) at 27*ff.* and 2-20*ff.* Alain Bernardot & Robert P. Kouri, *La responsabilité civile médicale* (Sherbrooke, QC: Éditions Revue de Droit Université de Sherbrooke, 1980) at 9 n. 15.

or may not be analogous to solutions proposed under the common law, but which are, we submit, consonant with the spirit of the civil law.

First we will review the general principles of civil liability, and then describe the major obligations inherent in the physician-patient relationship, namely, the duty to obtain informed consent, and the duty to treat, which includes the related obligations to attend and to respect professional secrecy.

II.   BRIEF OVERVIEW OF THE GENERAL PRINCIPLES GOVERNING CIVIL LIABILITY

Paul-André Crépeau had occasion to affirm over half a century ago that medical civil liability evolved in an empirical and random fashion, relying essentially upon litigation brought before the courts.[10] It was dealt with as any other form of civil responsibility. Even today, medical liability is not afforded special treatment by the *Civil Code of Québec* even though since 1994, several articles of Book One of the Code — generally under Title Two dealing with Certain Personality Rights — establish rights devoted to the integrity of the person, to medical care, to psychiatric evaluations and to confinement in an establishment.[11] The liability of a physician arising from his or her relationship with a patient is thus governed by the general principles of civil responsibility as set out in the Third Chapter of Book Five dealing with Obligations.[12] The liability of hospitals, which will be alluded to in the course of this discussion but not otherwise dealt with, also falls under these general principles.

A.   BASIC CONDITIONS OF CIVIL LIABILITY

From an etymological point of view, "to be liable" is to be bound to answer for one's actions or to be held to make reparation for the injury caused to another. The obligation to indemnify does not arise unless the person has committed a fault that actually caused the injury complained of by the victim. These fundamental conditions must be met whether the juridical relationship between the parties is contractual or extracontractual. Despite many attempts to add to the legal burden assumed by physicians,[13] the courts have generally refused to go

---

[10]   Paul-André Crépeau, *La responsabilité civile du médecin et de l'établissement hospitalier* (Montreal: Wilson & Lafleur, 1956) at 42.

[11]   *Civil Code of Québec*, S.Q. 1991, c. 64, arts. 26 to 31 [hereafter sometimes referred to as the Code or C.C.Q.].

[12]   Arts. 1457 to 1481 C.C.Q.

[13]   Notably through presumptions or through the "loss of a chance". The ongoing debate whether victims of medical error should be indemnified under a no-fault system similar to the auto insurance scheme in Quebec resurges periodically in the literature; see generally Thierry Bourgoignie, ed., *Accidents thérapeutiques et protection du consommateur : vers une responsabilité médicale sans faute au Québec?* (Cowansville, QC: Éditions Yvon Blais, 2006) and more particularly the chapter written by Robert Tétrault, « Esquisse d'un régime québécois d'indemnisation des victimes d'accidents thérapeutiques » at 251.

down this road, feeling that any fundamental changes should more properly be effected by legislation rather than by judicial activism.

1.   Fault

In law, a fault can be defined as the failure to fulfil a duty or the violation of an obligation.[14] The duty in question may be imposed by law (for example, specific rules or standards relating to safety), it can result from a personal undertaking (within the framework of a contract),[15] and it may also be inherent in a general duty of abiding by the rules of conduct so as not to cause harm to others.[16] The celebrated French jurist, Demogue, introduced the concept of the intensity of obligations, a distinction which determines the scope of an undertaking, whether voluntarily assumed or imposed by law.[17] Under Quebec law, an obligation involves one of three levels of intensity. In the case of an *obligation of means* or *of diligence*, the debtor must do all that is in his or her power, given the circumstances and the means available, to attain the desired result. Therefore, an individual will have a defence to an action if there exists factors or risks beyond one's control resulting in the failure of a particular act or intervention. An *obligation of result* presupposes that a specific anticipated outcome lies within the debtor's control, and thus the failure *per se* to attain the result promised constitutes a fault. Although this type of obligation is more frequently encountered in contractual relationships, it can also occur in an extracontractual context because of certain presumptions of liability of legislative origin.[18] For its part, an *obligation of warranty* imposes a duty to assume, under all circumstances including superior force, the legal consequences of non-performance. This type of obligation can be found in certain types of contracts as well as in particular cases of extracontractual liability, such as the responsibility of principals for injury caused by the fault of servants or employees in the performance of their duties.[19]

---

[14]   Jean-Louis Baudouin & Patrice Deslauriers, *La responsabilité civile*, vol. I: *Principes généraux*, 7th ed. (Cowansville, QC: Éditions Yvon Blais, 2007) at 151*ff.* nn. 1-160*ff.*; Alain Bernardot & Robert P. Kouri, *La responsabilité civile médicale* (Sherbrooke, QC: Éditions Revue de Droit Université de Sherbrooke, 1980) at 9 n. 15.

[15]   Art. 1458, para. 1 C.C.Q.: "Every person has a duty to honour his contractual undertakings."

[16]   Art. 1457, para. 1 C.C.Q.: "Every person has a duty to abide by the rules of conduct which lie upon him, according to the circumstances, usage or law, so as not to cause injury to another." Consequently, the "duty" under the civil law is not to cause harm to others, and not whether a duty of care was owed to a particular plaintiff as is the rule under the common law: see Ellen Picard & Gerald B. Robertson, *Legal Liability of Doctors and Hospitals in Canada*, 4th ed. (Toronto: Thomson Carswell, 2007) at 212-13.

[17]   Paul-André Crépeau, *L'intensité de l'obligation juridique ou des obligations de diligence, de résultat et de garantie*, Centre de Recherche en Droit Privé et Comparé du Québec (Cowansville, QC: Éditions Yvon Blais, 1989); Jean-Louis Baudouin, Pierre-Gabriel Jobin & Nathalie Vézina, *Les obligations*, 6th ed. (Cowansville, QC: Éditions Yvon Blais, 2005) at 36 n. 33.

[18]   For example, the liability of the custodian of an animal, art. 1466 C.C.Q.

[19]   Art. 1463 C.C.Q. See also Paul-André Crépeau, *L'intensité de l'obligation juridique ou des obligations de diligence, de résultat et de garantie*, Centre de Recherche en Droit Privé et Comparé du Québec (Cowansville, QC: Éditions Yvon Blais, 1989) at 59 n. 104.

In Quebec law, the distinction between these different types of obligations determines the burden of proof imposed upon plaintiffs and the means of exoneration available to defendants depend upon this classification. In the case of an obligation of means, the plaintiff must prove by a preponderance of the evidence that the debtor was at fault and thus the debtor may seek exoneration by proving an absence of fault on his or her part. In the case of obligation of result, the plaintiff's burden is much easier to fulfil since fault resides in the mere fact of not having attained the result promised. In this situation, the only means of avoiding liability is by proving that non-fulfilment of the obligation results from superior force.[20] As for obligations of warranty, once the plaintiff has established non-performance of the undertaking, the right to indemnification is virtually ensured, since even superior force cannot obviate the defendant's liability.[21]

Generally speaking, most duties inherent in medical practice are viewed as obligations of means.[22] Jurisprudence and doctrine are unanimous in this regard.[23] This being the case, how must one proceed in order to determine whether a physician has acted in conformity with the standards of conduct expected of a member of the medical profession? On this point also there is unanimity in that "the criterion applicable is that of a normally prudent and competent practitioner"[24] acting in conformity with current standards of medical science. An *in abstracto* or objective approach is thus retained.[25] Accordingly, in the evaluation of a person's conduct, one must take into account certain circumstances relative to the individual, which normally include the level of training or specialization. "It would be abnormal that a medical specialist, performing an act falling within his or her field of specialization, be compared to that which a general practitio-

---

[20] Art. 1470 C.C.Q.

[21] *Ibid.*

[22] Unless the physician was reckless enough to guarantee a result, in which case liability would lie if the result was not attained: *Fiset c. St-Hilaire*, [1976] C.S. 994 (Que. S.C.). A promise of this nature is contrary to the Code of Ethics of Physicians, R.R.Q., c. M-9, r. 17, s. 83: "A physician must refrain from guaranteeing, explicitly or implicitly, the effectiveness of an examination, investigation or treatment, or the cure of a disease."

[23] See the doctrine and cases cited by Suzanne Philips-Nootens, Pauline Lesage-Jarjoura & Robert P. Kouri, *Éléments de responsabilité civile médicale — le droit dans le quotidien de la médecine*, 3d ed. (Cowansville, QC: Éditions Yvon Blais, 2007) at 45 n. 55 and footnote 24, at 258-260 nn. 290-292 and footnotes 4 to 8.

[24] *Cloutier c. Hôpital le Centre Hospitalier de l'Université Laval*, [1990] J.Q. no 294, [1990] R.J.Q. 717 at 721 (Que. C.A.) [our translation]. Suzanne Philips-Nootens, Pauline Lesage-Jarjoura & Robert P. Kouri, *Éléments de responsabilité civile médicale — le droit dans le quotidien de la médecine*, 3d ed. (Cowansville, QC: Éditions Yvon Blais, 2007) at 45 n. 55, at 258-260 nn. 290-292 and footnotes 4 to 8.

[25] Jean-Louis Baudouin & Patrice Deslauriers, *La responsabilité civile*, vol. I: *Principes généraux*, 7th ed. (Cowansville, QC: Éditions Yvon Blais, 2007) at 171 n. 1-192; Suzanne Philips-Nootens, Pauline Lesage-Jarjoura & Robert P. Kouri, *Éléments de responsabilité civile médicale — le droit dans le quotidien de la médecine*, 3d ed. (Cowansville, QC: Éditions Yvon Blais, 2007) at 50-54 nn. 62-66; *Abitbol c. Weiswall*, [1998] J.Q. no 7, [1998] R.R.A. 31 (Que. C.A.).

ner would have done under similar circumstances."[26] One thus compares a generalist to a generalist and a specialist to a specialist.

One must also take into account the external circumstances under which the medical acts in question are performed. Is the physician working in a large city or close to a university medical centre where he or she can easily consult with specialists and have recourse to sophisticated diagnostic procedures, or is his or her practice situated in a remote area and with limited resources? Although the courts will likely be more frequently faced with these issues due to growing demands on the health system, as matters stand there would appear to be no clear position adopted in the jurisprudence.[27]

The burden of proof, in medical liability cases as elsewhere, rests upon the plaintiff and unless this standard is met, the defendant will be exonerated.[28] In a field as complex as medicine, the testimony of experts is generally indispensable for determining fault.[29]

A physician is not expected to be infallible. Provided the standard of a reasonable professional has been met, a physician who makes an error in diagnosis or in treatment will not be held liable even though an injury is sustained.[30] As the Quebec Court of Appeal pointed out in *Léveillé c. Blanchette*, a case involving maxillofacial surgery, "[in] the absence of proof [that current standards of medical practice have not been met], one cannot infer that appellant is liable by the mere fact that abnormalities appeared a few days after the intervention, performed under the circumstances described".[31] The Supreme Court of Canada has also formally acknowledged this principle.[32]

---

[26] Alain Bernardot & Robert P. Kouri, *La responsabilité civile médicale* (Sherbrooke, QC: Éditions Revue de Droit Université de Sherbrooke, 1980) at 13 n. 22 [our translation]. The Supreme Court of Canada expressed its approval of this approach in the case of *ter Neuzen v. Korn*, [1995] S.C.J. No. 79, [1995] 3 S.C.R. 674 (S.C.C.) (case originating in British Columbia). See also *Harewood c. Spanier*, [1995] J.Q. no 2825, [1995] R.R.A. 147 (Que S.C.), affd on the question of liability [2000] J.Q. no 4500, [2000] R.R.A. 864 at para. 42 (Que. C.A.); *Abitbol c. Weiswall*, [1998] J.Q. no 7, [1998] R.R.A. 31 at 36 (Que. C.A.).

[27] See Section IV(A), "The Duty to Treat", below.

[28] Art. 2803 C.C.Q.

[29] The depth of knowledge and the qualifications of an expert obviously play a major role in establishing his or her credibility before the courts. See *Ratelle c. Hôpital Cité de la Santé de Laval*, [2000] R.R.A. 697 (Que. S.C.), affd B.E. 2005BE-17 (Que. C.A.): expert congratulated by the court for his objectivity. *Contra*, *F. (L.) c. Villeneuve*, [1999] J.Q. no 6498, [1999] R.R.A. 854 (Que. S.C.), affd [2002] J.Q. no 1057, [2002] R.R.A. 296 (Que. C.A.): expert severely criticized by the court for excessive partiality towards the party that retained his services.

[30] *L. (P.) c. Benchetrit*, [2010] J.Q. no 8067, 2010 QCCA 1505 at para. 41 (Que. C.A.). In *Holz c. Greentree*, [2006] J.Q. no 15047, 2006 QCCS 6219 at paras. 81, 83 and 84 (Que S.C.): to decide that the unintentional cannulation of the carotid artery resulting from the installation of a Swan-Ganz catheter as well as the remedial measures undertaken immediately were faulty, would have the effect of retrospectively converting the physician's obligation of means into one of result.

[31] [1998] J.Q. no 1257 at para. 28, [1998] R.R.A. 385 at 390 (Que. C.A.) [our translation].

[32] *St-Jean v. Mercier*, [2002] S.C.J. No. 17 at para. 53, [2002] 1 S.C.R. 491 at 511 (S.C.C.), affg [1999] J.Q. no 2584, [1999] R.J.Q. 1658 (Que. C.A.) and [1998] J.Q. no 234 (Que. S.C.); *Lapointe v. Hôpital Le Gardeur*, [1992] S.C.J. No. 11 at para. 31, [1992] 1 S.C.R. 351 at 363

Under certain circumstances, direct proof of fault may not be available, in which case legislation provides for the possibility of establishing fault by invoking presumptions of fact,[33] an indirect means of proof having a certain resemblance to the common law notion of *res ipsa loquitur*.[34] Presumptions of fact are conclusions that can be drawn by the court provided they are "serious, precise and concordant".[35] They must not be confused with legal presumptions or presumptions created by legislation.[36] In offering proof by presumption of fact, the plaintiff must convince the trier of fact that only through an inference of fault on the part of the defendant can the injury to the victim be explained. According to the Quebec Court of Appeal, the conditions to be met for applying presumptions of fact "allow for a significant measure of judicial discretion".[37] In order to avoid altering the fundamental nature of an obligation of means, one must not confuse proof of fault by presumptions of fact with failure to attain the anticipated results of a medical act. A lack of success in treatment does not necessarily imply medical fault. Only through a thorough analysis of all pertinent elements and circumstances can an inference of fault be drawn.[38]

2. Injury

The establishment of harm or injury is intrinsic to medical liability since, as already pointed out, the notion of liability relates to the duty of indemnifying the victim. The injury suffered may be "bodily, moral or material" according to article 1607 of the *Civil Code of Québec*. Any injury, whether present or future, must be certain[39] (as opposed to being merely hypothetical or eventual). It must also be an immediate and direct consequence of the defendant's fault. Bodily or mental injury usually includes patrimonial (*e.g.*, temporary or permanent inability to work, costs of present and future care) and extrapatrimonial (*e.g.*, loss of physical integrity, pain and suffering, loss of enjoyment of life) aspects. While a

---

(S.C.C.). See also, *inter alia*, *Mathieu c. Vigneault*, [1991] J.Q. no 1079, [1991] R.J.Q. 1607 (Que. C.A.); *Tremblay c. Claveau*, [1990] J.Q. no 278, [1990] R.R.A. 268 (Que. C.A.).

[33] Art. 2846 C.C.Q. states: "A presumption is an inference established by law or the court from a known fact to an unknown fact."

[34] Although the Supreme Court of Canada decided in *Fontaine v. British Columbia (Official Administrator)*, [1997] S.C.J. No. 100, [1998] 1 S.C.R. 424 (S.C.C.) that *res ipsa loquitur* is no longer applied in the common law courts, this would have no effect on the application of presumptions of fact under the *Civil Code of Québec* according to the Quebec Court of Appeal in *Ferland c. Ghosn*, [2008] J.Q. no 3351, 2008 QCCA 797 at para. 53 (Que. C.A.).

[35] Art. 2849 C.C.Q.

[36] Art. 2847 C.C.Q.: "A legal presumption is one that is especially attached by law to certain facts; it exempts the person in whose favour it exists from making any other proof." Thus, it suffices to establish that the conditions giving rise to the presumption are met in order for the presumption to take effect.

[37] *Chabot c. Roy*, [1997] J.Q. no 3096 at para. 53, [1997] R.R.A. 920 at 929 (Que. C.A.) [our translation].

[38] See more particularly *Mathieu c. Vigneault*, [1991] J.Q. no 1079, [1991] R.J.Q. 1607 (Que. C.A.); *Liberman c. Tabah*, [1990] J.Q. no 802, [1990] R.J.Q. 1230 (Que. C.A.).

[39] Art. 1611 C.C.Q.

discussion of the means of evaluating injury and the payment of damages goes beyond the scope of this chapter,[40] we do note that an injury resulting from a medical fault can be of a purely moral nature.[41]

In addition, the Quebec *Charter of Human Rights and Freedoms* provides for awarding punitive damages in cases of unlawful and intentional interference with a fundamental right or freedom[42] which includes, *inter alia*, the right of inviolability of the person. The *Civil Code of Québec* also alludes to this type of damages.[43] However, the Supreme Court has set out a stringent intent requirement: the person must have "a desire or intent to cause the consequences of his or her wrongful conduct", or act "with full knowledge of the immediate and natural or at least extremely probable consequences that his or her conduct will cause".[44] Consequently, the awarding of punitive damages in medical liability cases is, in fact, very rare.[45]

3. Causal Relationship Between Fault and Injury

In the words of Baudouin J., the injury suffered must be the "logical, direct and immediate consequence of fault",[46] a determination which the courts treat as a question of fact left entirely to the appreciation of the trial judge.[47] The trier of

---

[40]   See the detailed analysis of Jean-Louis Baudouin & Patrice Deslauriers, *La responsabilité civile*, vol. I: *Principes généraux*, 7th ed. (Cowansville, QC: Éditions Yvon Blais, 2007) at 464*ff*. nn. 1-456*ff*. and jurisprudence cited; see arts. 1614 to 1620 C.C.Q.; and more generally, Daniel Gardner, *Le préjudice corporel*, 3d ed. (Cowansville, QC: Éditions Yvon Blais, 2009).

[41]   *Massinon c. Ghys*, [1996] J.Q. no 5632, [1996] R.J.Q. 2258 (Que. S.C.): breast cancer undetected by a specialist in the field.

[42]   R.S.Q., c. C-12, s. 49.

[43]   Art. 1621 C.C.Q.

[44]   *Québec (Public Curator) v. Syndicat national des employés de l'hôpital St-Ferdinand*, [1996] S.C.J. No. 90 at para. 121, [1996] 3 S.C.R. 211 at 262 (S.C.C.).

[45]   One could add that as a general rule, in the few cases where punitive damages were awarded, they tended to be fairly modest. See, *e.g.*, *Bédard c. Gauthier*, [1996] R.R.A. 860 (Que. S.C.), where an orthopaedic surgeon on call who refused to attend a patient was condemned to pay $2,000 as compensatory and punitive damages for the physical, psychological and moral harm caused. In *Jagura-Parent c. Dvorkin*, B.E. 99BE-442 (Que. C.Q.), the plaintiff was awarded punitive damages to the amount of $5,000 because a physician refused to correct an erroneous medical report which stated that the patient was epileptic and thus should not be allowed to drive a motor vehicle. On the other hand, in *Soccio c. Leduc*, [2004] J.Q. no 2485, [2004] R.J.Q. 1254 (Que. S.C.), revd [2007] J.Q. no 1137 (Que. C.A.), the Superior Court granted $100,000 as punitive damages in addition to compensatory damages because the defendant psychiatrist had drafted a supplementary report in conformity with an employer's wishes in order to facilitate discharging an employee. The Court of Appeal reversed this decision, stating that the trial judge's finding of fact was erroneous.

[46]   Jean-Louis Baudouin & Patrice Deslauriers, *La responsabilité civile*, vol. I: *Principes généraux*, 7th ed. (Cowansville, QC: Éditions Yvon Blais, 2007) at 624 n. 1-622 [our translation].

[47]   In *St-Jean v. Mercier*, [2002] S.C.J. No. 17 at para. 104, [2002] 1 S.C.R. 491 at 528 (S.C.C.), Gonthier J. wrote: "In contrast, in the determination of causation one is inquiring into whether something happened between the fault and the damage suffered so as to link the two. That link must be legally significant in an evidentiary sense, but it is rendered no less a question of fact."

fact must be convinced of the existence of a direct relationship between the defendant's fault and the victim's situation. However, a review of the jurisprudence reveals that the issue of causation is rarely discussed unless it lies at the very heart of the dispute, usually involving contradictory expert testimony, difficulties of proof of causation or defences based on a lack of causation. As is also the case in proving fault, the plaintiff may seek to establish causation indirectly through presumptions of fact.[48] For instance, although the Supreme Court in *Morin v. Blais*[49] concluded that a presumption of causation existed due to the particular circumstances of the case, this presumption was, by the very nature of these circumstances, one of fact and not of law since it was based solely on inference.[50] In medical liability cases in general, many decisions have clearly reaffirmed that no legal presumptions against physicians exist.[51] One must therefore be very wary when certain judges make overly generalized statements seemingly to the contrary, if the affirmations are not explicitly supported by the facts.[52]

A physician whose fault is established can attempt to seek exoneration by proving a lack of causation. The defendant can do this by arguing that what occurred was an "unforeseeable and irresistible event";[53] in other words, a case of superior force over which, due to its very nature, he or she had no control — or that it resulted from the act or fault of either the victim or of a third person. Each of these elements constitutes a *novus actus interveniens*, which interrupts the causal connection between the physician's fault and the victim's injuries, provided, according to the courts, that its gravity or importance is at least equal, if

---

This point of view was followed in *Labonté c. Tanguay*, [2003] J.Q. no 6539 at para. 19, [2003] R.R.A. 774 at 775 (Que. C.A.), affg [2002] R.R.A. 62 (Que. S.C.).

[48] Alain Bernardot & Robert P. Kouri, *La responsabilité civile médicale* (Sherbrooke, QC: Éditions Revue de Droit Université de Sherbrooke, 1980) at 77 n. 115; Jean-Louis Baudouin & Patrice Deslauriers, *La responsabilité civile*, vol. I: *Principes généraux*, 7th ed. (Cowansville, QC: Éditions Yvon Blais, 2007) at 638-639 n. 1-644.

[49] [1977] S.C.J. No. 128, [1977] 1 S.C.R. 570 (S.C.C.).

[50] Robert P. Kouri, "From Presumptions of Fact to Presumptions of Causation: Reflections on the Perils of Judge-Made Rules in Quebec Medical Malpractice Law" (2001) 32 R.D.U.S. 213. The Supreme Court reiterated this principle in *Laferrière v. Lawson*, [1991] S.C.J. No. 18, [1991] 1 S.C.R. 541 at 609 (S.C.C.): "In some cases where a fault presents a clear danger and where such a danger materilaizes, it may be reasonable to presume a causal link unless there is a demonstration or indication to the contrary."

[51] For example, *Camden-Bourgault c. Brochu*, [1996] J.Q. no 4586, [1996] R.R.A. 809 (Que. S.C.), affd [2001] J.Q. no 1327, [2001] R.R.A. 295 (Que. C.A.), leave to appeal refused [2001] C.S.C.R. no. 279 (S.C.C.); *Zanchettin c. De Montigny*, [1994] J.Q. no 1163, [1995] R.R.A. 87 (Que. S.C.), affd [2000] J.Q. no 2640, [2000] R.R.A. 298 (Que. C.A.), leave to appeal refused [2000] C.S.C.R. no 418 (S.C.C.); *Bérubé c. Samson*, [2000] J.Q. no 1452, [2000] R.R.A. 484 (Que. S.C.), affd (*sub nom. Bérubé c. Hôpital Hôtel-Dieu de Levis*) [2003] J.Q. no 3068, [2003] R.R.A. 374 (Que. C.A.).

[52] See, *e.g.*, in *St-Jean c. Mercier*, [1999] J.Q. no 2584, [1999] R.J.Q. 1658 at 1666 (Que. C.A.), affd [2002] S.C.J. No. 17, [2002] 1 S.C.R. 491 (S.C.C.): "the court may thus presume the existence of a causal link" [our translation].

[53] Art. 1470 C.C.Q.

not superior to, the fault committed by the physician.[54] In other circumstances, several faults may cause the harm, in which case the court will apportion liability, including that of the victim if the situation so indicates, in proportion to the seriousness of the fault of each person involved.[55]

A victim may be faced with a complex situation in which each of several persons (for example, a team of physicians and nurses) committed a fault capable of causing the injury, only one fault caused the injury, and it cannot be established with a sufficient degree of certainty which person actually caused the harm.

In order to avoid the inequity involved in depriving the patient of his or her recourse, article 1480 of the *Civil Code of Québec* provides a solution of jurisprudential origin: all persons who have committed a fault that may have caused the injury are to be held solidarily liable unless they can discharge a reverse onus of proof that there was no causal connection between each individual fault and the injury.

An obvious and simple means of defence available to the defendant in appropriate circumstances is that of extinctive prescription, according to which an action in damages for bodily injury must be brought within three years.[56] Sometimes, the appearance of injury resulting from a medical fault will not materialize instantaneously as, for instance, when a compress is forgotten in an abdominal cavity[57] or when there has been only a partial removal of an organ.[58] In such situations, the prescriptive period will run from the day the damage appears for the first time.[59]

B.   NATURE OF THE PHYSICIAN-PATIENT RELATIONSHIP

The basis of this relationship, whether contractual or extracontractual, in fact has relatively little influence on the physician's obligations and consequently on his

---

[54]   More particularly *Liberman c. Tabah*, [1990] J.Q. no 802, [1990] R.J.Q. 1230 (Que. C.A.): fault of the nursing staff and of an intern following a thyroidectomy; *Boulet c. Léveillé*, [1990] R.R.A. 412 (Que. S.C.): fault of members of the family and of another hospital. In order to constitute a *novus actus interveniens*, there must also be an interval or time lag between the first and second fault: see Jean-Louis Baudouin & Patrice Deslauriers, *La responsabilité civile*, vol. I: *Principes généraux*, 7th ed. (Cowansville, QC: Éditions Yvon Blais, 2007) at 632 n. 1-632. See also *Chouinard c. Robbins*, [2001] J.Q. no 6081 at para. 32, [2002] R.J.Q. 60 at 65 (Que. C.A.).

[55]   Art. 1478 C.C.Q.

[56]   Art. 2925 C.C.Q. Whether the regime is contractual or extracontractual.

[57]   *Thomassin c. Hôpital de Chicoutimi*, [1990] J.Q. no 1247, [1990] R.J.Q. 2275 (Que. S.C.), affd [1997] J.Q. no 2748, [1997] R.J.Q. 2121 (Que. C.A.); *Trottier v. Rajotte* (1936), 74 C.S. 569 (Que. S.C.), affd (1938), 64 Q.B. 484 (Que. C.A.), revd [1939] S.C.J. No. 41, [1940] S.C.R. 203 (S.C.C.) on a question as to whether the patient, a married woman, had capacity to sue for damages in her own name.

[58]   *Drolet c. Côté*, [1983] C.S. 719 (Que. S.C.), but reversed on the issue of liability [1986] J.Q. no 206, [1986] R.R.A. 11 (Que. C.A.).

[59]   Art. 2926 C.C.Q. It is difficult to demand of the victim that he or she act before even knowing the condition from which he or she is suffering. To decide otherwise would be contrary to common sense.

or her liability, except in regard to civil liability for the act of another. The differences which *do* exist play a role on a more technical level relating to modalities of the recourse in damages.

1.   Contractual Relationship

The notion that an *intuitu personae* contract exists between the physician and his or her patient has formed part of Quebec law since the end of the 1950s.[60]

Despite the importance of access to medical services in our society, a physician does not have to enter into a contractual relationship with all those who would wish to do so. He or she enjoys the right not to contract under the *Act Respecting Health Services and Social Services*[61] and, in deference to his or her religious or moral sensibilities, can refuse to treat for reason of conscience according to the Code of Ethics of Physicians.[62] This right of refusal is not without certain limitations. For example, the refusal to contract cannot be based on discrimination prohibited by the Quebec *Charter of Human Rights and Freedoms*[63] and by the Code of Ethics of Physicians.[64] The refusal cannot arise out of a certain sentiment of vengeance,[65] nor can it violate a legal obligation such as the duty of coming to the assistance of a person whose life is in danger, as set out in the *Charter of Human Rights and Freedoms*,[66] the *Act Respecting Health Services and Social Services*,[67] the *Act Respecting Medical Laboratories, Organ, Tissue, Gamete and Embryo Conservation, and the Disposal of Human Bodies*[68] and the Code of Ethics of Physicians.[69] It is open to debate whether certain innovative ways of organizing health care in Quebec, such as the regrouping of

---

[60]   *X. c. Mellen*, [1957] B.R. 389 (Que. C.A.). Paul-André Crépeau, *La responsabilité civile du médecin et de l'établissement hospitalier* (Montreal: Wilson & Lafleur, 1956). Although the therapeutic relationship is based on confidence, one cannot help but notice that due to various modern phenomena such as changes in the manner of practising medicine (*e.g.*, the growing popularity of group practice and walk-in clinics), the lack of medical personnel, the multiplication of specialties and the exponential growth of medical technology, this particular aspect of the medical contract, regrettably, is being constantly eroded. See Alain Bernardot & Robert P. Kouri, *La responsabilité civile médicale* (Sherbrooke, QC: Éditions Revue de Droit Université de Sherbrooke, 1980) at 166 n. 246. See also Code of Ethics of Physicians, R.R.Q., c. M-9, r. 17, s. 18.

[61]   R.S.Q., c. S-4.2, s. 6.

[62]   R.R.Q., c. M-9, r. 17, s. 24.

[63]   R.S.Q., c. C-12, s. 10: race, sexual orientation or handicap. *Hamel c. Malaxos*, [1993] J.Q. no 2114, [1994] R.J.Q. 173 (Que. C.Q.): dentist who refused to continue treating a patient who was HIV-positive.

[64]   R.R.Q., c. M-9, r. 17, s. 23: the nature of the illness or for moral reasons, modification added to the Code in 1994.

[65]   *Comité-médecins-2*, [1988] D.D.C.P. 160, [1990] D.D.C.P. 334 (T.P.): refusal to treat a patient and her family by all physicians of a clinic for reasons of resentment.

[66]   R.S.Q., c. C-12, s. 2. This duty is imposed on all citizens. *Zuk c. Mihaly*, [1989] R.R.A. 737 (Que. S.C.).

[67]   R.S.Q., c. S-4.2, s. 7.

[68]   R.S.Q., c. L-0.2, s. 43.

[69]   R.R.Q., c. M-9, r. 17, s. 38.

family physicians to serve a particular segment of the population, will still afford physicians some latitude in the enrolment of patients they wish to serve.[70]

A contractual relationship gives rise to certain reciprocal rights and obligations. Over and above the four facets of the doctor-patient relationship alluded to in the introduction lies the principle that a treating physician undertakes to personally care for the patient. He or she cannot delegate fulfilment of these duties to someone else without the express or tacit consent of the person being treated. The following case illustrates this rule. A surgeon convinced a young woman of the importance of undergoing surgery to correct a patent *ductus arteriosus* (a fetal blood vessel connecting the left pulmonary artery to the aorta) which failed to close at birth. In the course of the operation, the surgeon decided to have his surgical resident perform the actual surgery under his direct supervision. Serious complications occurred and a malpractice action was brought. The decision to delegate a key part of the operation to an assistant was severely criticized by the court, which held that the patient had the right to expect that the physician whose services she retained would actually perform the surgery.[71]

As for the patient, his or her principal obligation is to collaborate with the physician in order to contribute as much as possible to a successful treatment outcome. Accordingly, the patient must provide all pertinent information necessary in order to facilitate an accurate diagnosis, respect all directives and recommendations made by the physician,[72] and accept, if indicated, recourse to consultants or a transfer of his or her case to another doctor. The patient must also keep the physician informed of all developments and undertake appropriate initiatives indicated by circumstance and by common sense. As other scholars note, this duty of compliance imposed upon the patient devolves from that patient's right of autonomy.[73] In one instance, a 43-year-old pregnant woman refused to undergo genetic screening by amniocentesis as recommended by her physician and subsequently gave birth to a child with Down's Syndrome. In her suit, the patient was unable to prove that her obstetrician failed to properly advise her of this precaution. Indeed, the facts established quite the contrary. As a result, she had to assume, in the words of the court, the dramatic consequences of her own decision.[74] In cases of this nature, the suit is usually dismissed due to

---

[70]   Suzanne Philips-Nootens, Pauline Lesage-Jarjoura & Robert P. Kouri, *Éléments de responsabilité civile médicale — le droit dans le quotidien de la médecine*, 3d ed. (Cowansville, QC: Éditions Yvon Blais, 2007) at 19 n. 21.

[71]   *Currie c. Blundell*, [1992] J.Q. no 331, [1992] R.J.Q. 764 (Que. S.C.).

[72]   *St-Cyr c. Fisch*, [2003] J.Q. no 4707 at para. 34, [2003] R.J.Q. 1582 at 1591 (Que. S.C.), affd on this point [2005] J.Q. no 9876 at para. 94, [2005] R.J.Q. 1944 at 1956 (Que. C.A.), leave to appeal granted [2005] C.S.C.R. no 430 (S.C.C.), notice of discontinuance filed September 1, 2006.

[73]   Alain Bernardot & Robert P. Kouri, *La responsabilité civile médicale* (Sherbrooke, QC: Éditions Revue de Droit Université de Sherbrooke, 1980) at 221 n. 325.

[74]   *Bouchard c. Villeneuve*, [1996] J.Q. no 2288, [1996] R.J.Q. 1920 (Que. S.C.) (appeal rejected on motion). To the same effect, *Bergeron c. Faubert*, [1996] J.Q. no 5469, [1996] R.R.A. 820 (Que. S.C.), affd [2000] J.Q. no 6184 (Que. C.A.): a veterinarian who had surgery in both hands and who refused to follow orders concerning restrictions on the use of his hands.

the fault of the "victim", provided of course that the physician has indeed been sufficiently clear and precise in fulfilling the duty to inform.

2.   Extracontractual Relationship

Various circumstances can prevent a patient from contracting for medical care, such as unconsciousness following an accident, a pre-existing state of incapacity or sudden incapacity due to illness. Notwithstanding the absence of a contractual relationship, physicians on call and those who provide care in emergency situations do not have the right to withdraw from a case and must provide care even though no contractual relationship has been entered into.[75]

If a capable patient, without having previously retained the services of a particular physician with admitting privileges, goes to a hospital to receive care, the patient is deemed to have contracted with the institution itself and not with any physician, nor indeed with the other members of staff who are called upon, under the terms of their employment, to actually provide the services offered by the hospital.[76] In such a case, the hospital would be obliged not only to provide hospital services but also medical care.[77] Should the patient suffer injury in the course of treatment, the hospital would be contractually liable for the fault of

---

[75]   Code of Ethics of Physicians, R.R.Q., c. M-9, r. 17, s. 34: "A physician who treats a patient requiring emergency care must ensure the medical management required by the patient's condition until the transfer is accepted by another physician."

[76]   The so-called "hospital contract" in Quebec has undergone an evolution similar to that of the medical contract. See Paul-André Crépeau, *La responsabilité civile du médecin et de l'établissement hospitalier* (Montreal: Wilson & Lafleur, 1956); Paul-André Crépeau, « La responsabilité médicale et hospitalière dans la jurisprudence québécoise récente » (1960) 20 R. du B. 433; Jean-Louis Baudouin & Patrice Deslauriers, *La responsabilité civile*, vol. II: *Responsabilité professionnelle*, 7th ed. (Cowansville, QC: Éditions Yvon Blais, 2007) at 32 and 33 nn. 2-28 to 2-30, at 84-86 nn. 2-98 to 2-100. Certain writers have gone so far as to suggest that the obligations of a hospital can only be extracontractual in nature since hospitals cannot refuse to treat patients. See Andrée Lajoie, Patrick A. Molinari & Jean-Louis Baudouin, « Le droit aux services de santé : légal ou contractuel? » (1983) 43 R. du B. 675. *Contra*, Suzanne Nootens, « La remise en cause du contrat hospitalier » (1984) 44 R. du B. 625. Indeed, the ascendancy of the state over hospitals has increased dramatically and their autonomous status has in fact become somewhat more illusory. Formally, however, they remain distinct legal entities and as such are free to enter into contractual relationships with persons requiring their services, according to an opinion generally held until recently by the Quebec Court of Appeal. See *Côté c. Houde*, [1987] J.Q. no 282, [1987] R.J.Q. 723 (Que. C.A.); *Lapointe c. Hôpital Le Gardeur*, [1989] J.Q. no 1660, [1989] R.J.Q. 2619 (Que. C.A.). The Supreme Court did not express any opinion on this point since it decided there was no fault on the part of the physician: *Lapointe v. Hôpital Le Gardeur*, [1992] S.C.J. No. 11, [1992] S.C.R. 351 (S.C.C.). See also François Tôth, « Contrat hospitalier moderne et ressources limitées : conséquences sur la responsabilité civile » (1990) 20 R.D.U.S. 313.

[77]   In which case the physician-patient relationship is extracontractual. Suzanne Philips-Nootens, Pauline Lesage-Jarjoura & Robert P. Kouri, *Éléments de responsabilité civile médicale — le droit dans le quotidien de la médecine*, 3d ed. (Cowansville, QC: Éditions Yvon Blais, 2007) at 33-36 n. 43-44.

another, namely for those members of its staff who have been designated to fulfil its obligations.[78]

A fairly recent judgment of the Quebec Court of Appeal appears to dispute this approach. Justice Rochon held that a hospital could not undertake to provide actual medical services on the grounds that the administration of medical care, as opposed to hospital care, is the exclusive prerogative of health professionals.[79] A finding of this nature is very difficult if not impossible to justify, since the exclusion of the hospital's liability for errors in treatment would logically encompass *all* specialized professional acts (nursing, radiology, hemodynamics, physical therapy, *etc.*) performed within its walls.[80] It is hoped that the Court of Appeal will soon have occasion to reconsider its position on this point.

When a patient, due to his or her incapacity, is not able to actually contract with the hospital, the traditional approach to extracontractual responsibility would make the institution liable only for those persons considered its agents and servants according to article 1463 of the *Civil Code of Québec*. The requirement that there exist a master-servant relationship between the person at fault and the hospital renders somewhat problematic the potential liability of institutions for physicians practising within its walls, due precisely to the absence of a relationship of subordination or dependency between the hospital and doctors with hospital privileges in the exercise of their profession.[81] This difference in remedies afforded victims, which results from the distinction between contractual and extracontractual hospital liability, has caused some debate in legal writing.[82] Like others,[83] we are inclined to believe that the very existence of a recourse in damages must not be subject to the vagaries of the juridical relationship binding the parties. Since hospitals have the legal obligation to provide health care, they must be held liable to the patient for the non-fulfilment of this duty

---

[78]   Art. 1458(1) C.C.Q.

[79]   *Camden-Bourgault c. Brochu*, [1996] J.Q. no 4586, [1996] R.R.A. 809 (Que. S.C.), revd [2001] J.Q. no 1325, [2001] R.J.Q. 832 (Que. C.A.). For a critique of this position, see Robert P. Kouri, « L'arrêt *Hôpital de l'Enfant-Jésus c. Camden-Bourgault* et le contrat hospitalier occulté : aventurisme ou évolution? » (2004) 35 R.D.U.S. 307.

[80]   François Tôth, « Contrat hospitalier moderne et ressources limitées : conséquences sur la responsabilité civile » (1990) 20 R.D.U.S. 313.

[81]   *Act Respecting Health Services and Social Services*, R.S.Q., c. S-4.2, s. 236: "A physician, dentist or midwife other than a member of the managerial staff of the instititution is deemed not to be a member of the staff of the institution."

[82]   See on this point Suzanne Philips-Nootens, Pauline Lesage-Jarjoura & Robert P. Kouri, *Éléments de responsabilité civile médicale — le droit dans le quotidien de la médecine*, 3d ed. (Cowansville, QC: Éditions Yvon Blais, 2007) at 36 n. 44 and the authorities cited in footnote 135 of their text.

[83]   François Tôth, « Contrat hospitalier moderne et ressources limitées : conséquences sur la responsabilité civile » (1990) 20 R.D.U.S. 313. To the same effect: Jean-Louis Baudouin & Patrice Deslauriers, *La responsabilité civile*, vol. II: *Responsabilité professionnelle*, 7th ed. (Cowansville, QC: Éditions Yvon Blais, 2007) at 85-86 n. 2-100.

through application of the *qui agit per alium agit per se* rule,[84] which does not rely on a master-servant relationship.

C. LIABILITY FOR THE ACT OF ANOTHER AND FOR THE MATERIAL UTILIZED

A physician may be held liable not only for his or her own fault but also for the acts of medical auxiliaries and for the material utilized. With regard to medical auxiliaries, two elements must be considered, namely the nature of the acts performed as well as the nature of the relationship between the physician and the patient. Nursing care and other so-called "hospital acts" fall under the authority of the institution. Medical acts, as defined in the *Medical Act*,[85] are reserved to physicians, although certain of them may be delegated under specific conditions to other care providers on staff.[86]

Medical residents, trainees and interns are also viewed as agents or servants of the institution.[87] However, if they perform a medical act under the supervision or direction of a physician, the physician becomes liable to the patient for the acts so performed. In cases where there is a medical contract, it becomes a question of contractual liability for the act of another. A physician may have certain of his or her professional obligations fulfilled by another[88] (which often happens in a university hospital setting) provided, of course, certain precautions are taken. But the physician will consequently assume the risks resulting from the non-fulfilment of these obligations,[89] as occurred when a particular manipulation performed by a resident under supervision in order to close a *ductus arteriosus* ended disastrously.[90] In the absence of a contract with the patient, in order to apply arti-

---

[84]   Albert Mayrand, *Dictionnaire de maximes et locutions latines utilisées en droit*, 3d ed. (Cowansville, QC: Éditions Yvon Blais, 1994) at 421: "He who acts through another acts for himself" [our translation]. Paul-André Crépeau, « La responsabilité civile de l'établissement hospitalier en droit civil canadien » (1981) 26 McGill L.J. 673 at 733-34.

[85]   R.S.Q., c. M-9, s. 31.

[86]   Regulation respecting the activities contemplated in section 31 of the Medical Act which may [be] engaged in by classes of persons other than physicians, R.R.Q., c. M-9, r. 13 (for example, first surgical assistant nurses and specialized nurse practitioners); Regulation respecting the professional acts that may be performed by persons other than physicians, R.R.Q., c. M-9, r. 12.1 (medical students). More generally, see Michelle Giroux, "Medical Law: Québec" in R. Blanpain, General Editor, M. Colucci, Associate Editor, *International Encyclopedia of Laws* (Netherlands: Kluwer Law International, 2009) at 41-44 nn. 81-86.

[87]   *Act Respecting Health Services and Social Services*, R.S.Q., c. S-4.2, s. 236. Jean-Pierre Ménard & Denise Martin, *La responsabilité médicale pour la faute d'autrui* (Cowansville, QC: Éditions Yvon Blais, 1992) at 85.

[88]   *Murray-Vaillancourt c. Clairoux*, [1989] J.Q. no 2524, [1989] R.R.A. 762 at 771 (Que. S.C.).

[89]   Art. 1458 C.C.Q. Alain Bernardot & Robert P. Kouri, *La responsabilité civile médicale* (Sherbrooke, QC: Éditions Revue de Droit Université de Sherbrooke, 1980) at 342 and 344 nn. 521 and 526; Suzanne Nootens, « La responsabilité civile du médecin anesthésiste », Part 2 (1989) 19 R.D.U.S. 317 at 373.

[90]   *Currie c. Blundell*, [1992] J.Q. no 331, [1992] R.J.Q. 764 (Que. S.C.). In this case, there was fault resulting from the decision to delegate itself.

cle 1463 of the *Civil Code of Québec*, which establishes an absolute presumption of liability against the principal for injury caused by an agent or servant in the performance of his or her duties, the medical auxiliary must indeed be under the physician's control. Control in this context implies the power to give orders and instructions on the manner of fulfilling the work assigned.

The liability of a physician for the act of another does not apply to fellow physicians when they are acting on an equal footing. Each must assume responsibility for his or her own acts according to an agreed-upon division of tasks (as occurs for example, between a surgeon and an anaesthetist).[91] Otherwise when acting in concert, they may all be held liable since, in the presence of common obligations, liability is solidary.[92]

The Code does not specifically address liability resulting from harm caused by the material or products utilized in treatment and thus this is left to the general rules of contract. If there is no contract between the parties, article 1465 of the Code provides for the extracontractual liability of the person having custody of a thing for damages resulting from its autonomous act. In the hospital environment, the institution is generally responsible for the condition and the good working order of appliances and devices. The physician may, however, be answerable for harm resulting from the inadequate supervision or improper operation of certain equipment.[93] In private clinics on the other hand, the physicians assume full liability for any injury caused by their equipment.[94]

Having reviewed the general rules governing civil liability, we now turn to the principal duties of physicians.

III. THE DUTY TO INFORM AND TO OBTAIN CONSENT

The fundamental goal of the duty to inform is to ensure respect of the patient's right to autonomy, expressed through the patient's free and informed consent, always bearing in mind that consent is an ongoing process rather than a simple formality or a signature on a consent form. However, overwhelming the patient with a plethora of detail in the name of providing full information can be as in-

---

[91] Suzanne Philips-Nootens, Pauline Lesage-Jarjoura & Robert P. Kouri, *Éléments de responsabilité civile médicale — le droit dans le quotidien de la médecine*, 3d ed. (Cowansville, QC: Éditions Yvon Blais, 2007) at 123-124 nn. 154-156.

[92] Art. 1523 C.C.Q. Jean-Louis Baudouin & Patrice Deslauriers, *La responsabilité civile*, vol. I: *Principes généraux*, 7th ed. (Cowansville, QC: Éditions Yvon Blais, 2007) at 1109 n. 1-1321. In *Marcoux v. Bouchard*, both surgeons were exonerated: [2001] S.C.J. No. 51, [2001] 2 S.C.R. 726 (S.C.C.), affg [1999] J.Q. no 3055, [1999] R.R.A. 447 (Que. C.A.), affg [1995] J.Q. no 2325, [1995] R.R.A. 1149 (Que. S.C.).

[93] *S. (L.) c. Centre hospitalier affilié universitaire de Québec, Hôpital de l'Enfant-Jésus*, [2009] J.Q. no 3325, 2009 QCCS 1622 (Que. S.C.): physician performing cerebral angiography injects isopropyl alcohol instead of the contrast medium Visipaque from a syringe prepared by an X-ray technician, thus causing the death of the patient.

[94] Suzanne Philips-Nootens, Pauline Lesage-Jarjoura & Robert P. Kouri, *Éléments de responsabilité civile médicale — le droit dans le quotidien de la médecine*, 3d ed. (Cowansville, QC: Éditions Yvon Blais, 2007) at 130*f.* n. 167*ff.*

imical to patients' rights as untoward reticence. Ideally, the information provided must suffice in order to enable a person to make the best decision possible. In reality, it must provide the means for the patient to arrive at a decision which may or may not necessarily be reasonable, but will at least be enlightened.[95]

Arriving at informed consent is a two-stage process: informing the patient and then getting consent.

A.   The Duty to Inform

Generally speaking, the duty to inform exists towards the patient and not towards others unless, of course, they represent the patient or are authorized to decide on the patient's behalf. In other words, information is provided to the person to whom the treatment decision devolves. In practice, this means to a capable adult, or to a minor patient directly in the case of a minor 14 years of age or more when the care is required by the minor patient's state of health.[96] For adults incapable of giving consent, information is given to the lawfully appointed representative of the patient, who may be, under Quebec law, a mandatary, tutor to the person or curator. If a patient lacks formal representation, information is provided to the married, civil union or *de facto* spouse, to a close relative or to a person who shows a special interest in the patient.[97] For minors under 14 years of age, the person having parental authority or the tutor must be informed.[98]

The Quebec Code of Ethics of Physicians specifically provides that a physician cannot reveal a serious prognosis to the family without the consent of the patient unless there is "just grounds".[99] Consultation with the family is advised but is not a duty.[100] There is no obligation to arrive at a consensus amongst the relatives with regard to therapeutic choice.

The duty to inform rests upon the person who will carry out the diagnostic test or treatment.[101] The treating physician will be held liable for having failed to inform if he or she erroneously takes for granted that information was provided by someone else such as the referring physician, a nurse or an assistant. Never-

---

[95]   Alain Bernardot & Robert P. Kouri, *La responsabilité civile médicale* (Sherbrooke, QC: Éditions Revue de Droit Université de Sherbrooke, 1980) at 117 n. 172.

[96]   Arts. 11 and 14, para. 2 C.C.Q. See also *Labbé c. Laroche*, [2000] J.Q. no 5652, [2001] R.R.A. 184 (Que. S.C.), in which the information was provided to a minor aged 14 years and two months, as well as to the Youth Protection authorities who had custody of the minor.

[97]   Art. 15 C.C.Q.

[98]   Art. 14, para. 1 C.C.Q.

[99]   R.R.Q., c. M-9, r. 17, s. 20(5).

[100] Alain Bernardot & Robert P. Kouri, *La responsabilité civile médicale* (Sherbrooke, QC: Éditions Revue de Droit Université de Sherbrooke, 1980) at 132 n. 198.

[101] *Lamarre c. Hôpital du Sacré-Coeur*, [1996] J.Q. no 663, [1996] R.R.A. 496 (Que. S.C.); *Chartier c. Sauvé*, [1997] J.Q. no 258, [1997] R.R.A. 213 at 215 (Que. S.C.); *Currie c. Blundell*, [1992] J.Q. no 331, [1992] R.J.Q. 764 at 775 (Que. S.C.).

theless, the courts have held that a physician is not liable if the patient has indeed been adequately informed through some other source.[102]

In advising the patient, the physician must impart technical knowledge of a medical nature to a person often lacking a scientific background. For this reason, a reductionist approach usually becomes necessary; the information should be presented in simple and clear terms best adapted to the patient's level of comprehension[103] and not, we submit, to the standard of the reasonable patient as proposed by the Supreme Court in *Reibl v. Hughes*[104] and *Hopp v. Lepp.*[105] Although physicians enjoy a certain latitude in communicating information, this flexibility relates to the terminology utilized and the mode of presentation rather than to the actual content. Indeed, language barriers[106] or a physical impairment such as deafness[107] could require adjustments in the manner of communicating information, but would not excuse dispensing with the duty to inform. As will be explained below, due to jurisprudence since *Reibl* and *Hopp*, the general tendency is toward offering more complete information in order to ensure respect for the patient's rights. The specific manner in which information is provided is left to the discretion of the physician although in most cases, it will be verbal. The use of information sheets, pamphlets, video cassettes or other such means, while valid, cannot, in all cases, suffice in fulfilling the duty to inform since the information to be imparted must be adapted to each particular patient and he or she must be afforded the opportunity to raise and obtain responses to questions.[108] Moreover, the duty to inform goes beyond merely presenting information in an objective, dispassionate manner. The physician has an affirmative duty to advise or counsel[109] even though the Quebec Code of Ethics of Physicians[110] is silent on this point. Since the physician-patient relationship is based on confidence,[111] loyalty and trust,[112] advising the patient to opt for a particular

---

102 *Mainville c. Hôpital Général de Montréal*, [1992] R.R.A. 579 (Que. S.C.).

103 *Morrow c. Royal Victoria Hospital*, [1972] C.S. 549 (Que. S.C.), affd [1989] J.Q. no 2239, [1990] R.R.A. 41 (Que. C.A.); *Dunant c. Chong*, [1985] J.Q. no 523, [1986] R.R.A. 2 (Que. C.A.).

104 [1980] S.C.J. No. 105, [1980] 2 S.C.R. 880 (S.C.C.).

105 [1980] S.C.J. No. 57, [1980] 2 S.C.R. 192 (S.C.C.). See *Schierz c. Dodds*, [1986] J.Q. no 1801, [1986] R.J.Q. 2623 at 2630 (Que. C.A.) (opinion of Monet J.A.); *Chouinard c. Landry*, [1987] J.Q. no 1625 at paras. 97, 98, [1987] R.J.Q. 1954 at 1968, 1969 (Que. C.A.) (opinion of LeBel J.A.), leave to appeal refused [1988] C.S.C.R. no 15, [1988] 1 S.C.R. vii (S.C.C.).

106 *Ciarlariello v. Schacter*, [1993] S.C.J. No. 46 at para. 54, [1993] 2 S.C.R. 119 at 140 (S.C.C.). See also *Soltani v. Desnoyers*, [2008] Q.J. No. 3627, 2008 QCCS 1720 at para. 64 (Que. S.C.) and *Batoukaeva c. Fugère*, [2006] J.Q. no 3341, 2006 QCCS 1950 (Que. S.C.): the patient who, because of language difficulties, does not understand the information provided, has a duty to so inform the person and to request a translator.

107 *Eldridge v. British Columbia (Attorney General)*, [1997] S.C.J. No. 86 at para. 55, [1997] 3 S.C.R. 624 at 677 (S.C.C.).

108 *Daigle c. Lafond*, [2006] J.Q. no 18098, [2006] R.R.A. 1071 at para. 70 (Que. S.C.).

109 *Bolduc c. Lessard*, [1989] J.Q. no 737 at para. 85, [1989] R.R.A. 350 at 358 (Que. S.C.), affd [1993] J.Q. no 605, [1993] R.R.A. 291 (Que. C.A.); *Lauzon c. Taillefer*, [1991] R.R.A. 62 at 72 (Que. S.C.).

110 R.R.Q., c. M-9, r. 17.

111 *Johnson c. Harris*, [1990] J.Q. no 1467 at para. 75, [1990] R.R.A. 832 at 841 (Que. S.C.).

alternative or expressing a bias in favour of a particular treatment choice is acceptable provided the physician is motivated solely by the patient's best interests.

1.   Content of the Duty to Inform

The *Civil Code of Québec* speaks of "care" in the broadest sense at article 11; care includes "examination, specimen taking, removal of tissue, treatment or any other act". It would appear that care encompasses not only situations where the care is absolutely necessary for the health of the person but also those cases where the care would be conducive to improving well-being, avoiding health deterioration or providing comfort and relief from pain and suffering. In establishing specific rules governing consent, certain nuances are, however, introduced by the *Civil Code of Québec* in that it distinguishes "care required by the state of health" from "care not required by the state of health".[113]

This fundamental distinction set out in the *Civil Code of Québec* has significant consequences for both the extent of the duty to inform and the capacity to consent.

(a) Care Required by One's State of Health

As a general rule, the following elements are relevant to fulfilling the duty to inform.

(i)   The Diagnosis

Before being advised of the various therapeutic options available, the patient must be made aware of his or her affliction or illness. In order to arrive at a proper diagnosis, it may be necessary to perform certain invasive or risky diagnostic procedures. Each such procedure, which otherwise could constitute an infringement of one's integrity, has to be the object of specific consent based upon adequate information.

The failure to reveal a diagnosis can prevent a patient from pursuing appropriate treatment. In *Laferrière v. Lawson*,[114] the Supreme Court awarded damages resulting from a surgeon's failure to inform his patient that the lump he had removed from her breast was cancerous. Even though, according to expert testimony, the patient was unlikely to survive her illness, her estate was indemnified for the psychological distress suffered resulting from the fact that she was unaware of her true situation and thus deprived of the possibility of pursuing active treatment in the hope of obtaining a remission. However, the Court refused to grant damages for the "loss of a chance" of recovery since the causal

---

[112] *Bolduc c. Lessard*, [1989] J.Q. no 737 at para. 88, [1989] R.R.A. 350 at 358 (Que. S.C.), aff'd [1993] J.Q. no 605, [1993] R.R.A. 291 (Que. C.A.).

[113] See, for example, arts. 13 to 18 C.C.Q.

[114] [1991] S.C.J. No. 18, [1991] 1 S.C.R. 541 (S.C.C.), modifying [1988] J.Q. no 2245, [1989] R.J.Q. 27 (Que. C.A.).

relationship between the physician's fault and the patient's death could not be established by a preponderance of the evidence.

(ii) The Nature of the Treatment Proposed and Its Chances of Success

The physician must reveal the type of treatment recommended, its necessity and its intended result. In order to be properly informed of the outcome of an intervention, the patient should be advised of the chances of success or failure,[115] and made aware of the repercussions of a negative outcome.[116] It is reasonable that the chances of success be revealed since only the individual concerned can truly decide whether the degree of risk of failure is worth authorizing an intrusion upon his or her integrity. When a physician glosses over the possibility of failure of a medical act or projects an exaggerated sense of optimism unrepresentative of the true situation, the risks which are normally borne by a sufficiently enlightened patient will be assumed by the health professional. Indeed, in *Fiset c. St-Hilaire*,[117] a surgeon who assured his patient suffering from Madelung's Disease that surgery would certainly improve her condition, was held liable in damages even without proof of any fault in the performance of the surgery. Because the surgeon promised an improvement, his obligation of diligence or of means in treating the patient became an obligation of result.[118]

(iii) The Risks of Treatment

In *Hopp v. Lepp*[119] and *Reibl v. Hughes*,[120] the Supreme Court affirmed that one must disclose to the patient the gravity of the operation and any material, special and unusual risks attendant upon its performance. It also underlined in *Reibl*[121] that "if a certain risk is a mere possibility which ordinarily need not be disclosed, yet if its occurrence carries serious consequences, as for example, paralysis or even death, it should be regarded as a material risk requiring disclosure".

On this question of risk, Baudouin J.A., concurring with the majority of the Court of Appeal panel in *Drolet c. Parenteau*,[122] expressed the opinion that one had to take into account two factors in evaluating the hazards of treatment: the probability of the hazard occurring, and the severity of the injury if it occurs.

In setting out a standard to be applied in relation to probability, one writer, Margaret A. Somerville, has proposed a fixed percentage:

---

[115] *Faucher-Grenier c. Laurence*, [1987] R.J.Q. 1109 at 1114 (Que. S.C.) (concerning the success rate of tubal ligations).

[116] Jean-Louis Baudouin & Patrice Deslauriers, *La responsabilité civile*, vol. II: *Responsabilité professionnelle*, 7th ed. (Cowansville, QC: Éditions Yvon Blais, 2007) at 50 n. 2-52.

[117] [1976] C.S. 994 (Que. S.C.).

[118] See also *Gingues c. Asselin*, [1990] J.Q. no 731 at para. 52, [1990] R.R.A. 630 at 636 (Que. S.C.).

[119] [1980] S.C.J. No. 57, [1980] 2 S.C.R. 192 at 210 (S.C.C.).

[120] [1980] S.C.J. No. 105, [1980] 2 S.C.R. 880 at 884-85 (S.C.C.).

[121] *Ibid.*

[122] [1994] J.Q. no 167, [1994] R.J.Q. 689 (Que. C.A.), revg in part [1991] J.Q. no 2583, [1991] R.J.Q. 2956 (Que. S.C.).

... [It] is suggested that any risk greater than one percent probability of causing irreversible morbidity should be disclosed. Risks of death with a lesser probability of occurring should also be disclosed, but for this most serious risk, it is difficult to state a minimum level.[123]

At first glance, this approach appears not to have received the endorsement of the courts in Quebec and indeed, on occasion, has been formally disavowed. For example, Baudouin J.A. stated in *Drolet c. Parenteau*:[124]

I do not think, however, that in a purely abstract, one could even say arbitrary manner, it is possible to decide mathematically and state for example that a risk of 1%, of 0.04% or of 0.001% is negligible and that its divulgation can be systematically avoided.[125]

However, notwithstanding Baudouin J.A.'s rejection of a single standard, an examination of Quebec jurisprudence indicates a clear inclination on the part of the courts to retain one per cent of probability of risk as a benchmark, at least in cases of therapeutic treatment.[126]

It is worth noting that the duty to inform relates not only to "immediate risks linked to the intervention itself, but also to potential consequences which may manifest themselves during the post-operative phase or even beyond".[127] In addition, the extent of the duty to inform will vary according to the nature of care required by the patient's state of health.

An intervention or treatment can also affect certain functions such as a person's mobility, ability to pursue various activities, and even comfort. The importance or gravity of this type of risk will vary according to the particular circumstances of each patient.[128]

(iv) Therapeutic Alternatives

When there exists a choice between various therapeutic approaches, the physician must indicate the alternatives available and set out the risks and advantages of each.[129] In accordance with this principle, the Supreme Court in *McCormick v. Marcotte*[130] held a physician liable for failing to reveal the advantages and disadvantages of two methods for reducing a fracture, especially since he re-

---

[123] Margaret A. Somerville, "Structuring the Issues in Informed Consent" (1981) 26 McGill L.J. 740 at 757.

[124] [1994] J.Q. no 167, [1994] R.J.Q. 689 (Que. C.A.), revg in part [1991] R.J.Q. 2583 (Que. S.C.).

[125] *Ibid.*, at para. 71 [our translation].

[126] Robert P. Kouri & Suzanne Philips-Nootens, *L'intégrité de la personne et le consentement aux soins*, 2d ed. (Cowansville, QC: Éditions Yvon Blais, 2005) at 292-93 n. 315 and cases cited.

[127] *Drolet c. Parenteau*, [1994] J.Q. no 167 at para. 70, [1994] R.J.Q. 689 at 706 (Que. C.A.) [our translation].

[128] *Binette c. Éthier*, J.E. 79-972 (Que. S.C.): medication administered to a young woman which had the effect of promoting the growth of facial hair.

[129] *Chouinard c. Landry*, [1987] J.Q. no 1625 at para. 101, [1987] R.J.Q. 1954 at 1969 (Que. C.A.), *per* LeBel J.A., leave to appeal refused [1988] C.S.C.R. no 15, [1988] 1 S.C.R. vii (S.C.C.).

[130] [1971] S.C.J. No. 83, [1972] S.C.R. 18 (S.C.C.), revg [1969] B.R. 454 (Que. C.A.).

fused to utilize the method recommended by a specialist called in for consultation.[131]

The patient must also be informed of the consequences should the proposed treatments be refused, even when the patient is asymptomatic and the operation is not urgent.[132] Each individual is certainly free to decline treatment, but he or she must be apprised of all pertinent facts.

(v) Answer Questions

The duty of responding to specific questions raised by the patient has been upheld by the Supreme Court in *Hopp v. Lepp*.[133] A patient's questions can signify that he or she has misunderstood the information received, or that he or she would like additional information concerning certain aspects of treatment which would not normally require revelation or elucidation. In the first case, a lack of comprehension could indicate a need for the physician to better adapt the description of particular aspects of the proposed intervention to the patient's powers of comprehension. In the second case, by expressing a greater need for information, the patient is unilaterally extending or expanding the physician's duty to inform since the mere fact of raising a question creates a correlative duty to adequately respond to it.[134]

It should be noted that failing to raise questions or to query aspects of treatment which should have been revealed spontaneously by the physician does not constitute an implicit renunciation by the patient to the right to information regarding these points.

(vi) The Behaviour Expected of the Patient

The patient must often play an active role in his or her treatment.[135] This may require performing specific acts or avoiding certain behaviours. The physician must take the initiative and indicate to the patient the manner in which he or she must collaborate during treatment and convalescence. The patient should also be made aware of certain signs or symptoms which may signal a complication or aggravation of the condition for which treatment has been administered.[136] The

---

[131] See also *Tremblay c. Boyer*, [1977] C.S. 622 (Que. S.C.) (concerning treatment choice involving breast implants); *Sunne c. Shaw*, [1981] C.S. 609 (Que. S.C.) (failure to advise patient of a more conservative course of action to treat a malocclusion); *O'Shea c. McGovern*, [1989] R.R.A. 341 at 345-46 (Que. S.C.), affd [1994] Q.J. No. 601, [1994] R.R.A. 672 (Que. C.A.) (surgical removal of a portion of the colon rather than merely removing a rectal polyp).

[132] *Currie c. Blundell*, [1992] J.Q. no 331, [1992] R.J.Q. 764 (Que. S.C.).

[133] [1980] S.C.J. No. 57, [1980] 2 S.C.R. 192 at 210 (S.C.C.).

[134] Margaret A. Somerville, "Structuring the Issues in Informed Consent" (1981) 26 McGill L.J. 740 at 774.

[135] *St-Cyr c. Fisch*, [2005] J.Q. no 9876, [2005] R.J.Q. 1944 (Que. C.A.), modifying [2003] J.Q. no 4707, [2003] R.J.Q. 1582 (Que. S.C.): failure to inform the physician of certain symptoms such as a lump in the breast and of not undergoing a recommended post-menstrual breast examination.

[136] *Drolet c. Parenteau*, [1994] J.Q. no 167 at para. 75, [1994] R.J.Q. 689 at 707 (Que. C.A.).

average patient cannot be presumed to possess this type of knowledge and must be advised accordingly.

Once he or she has been properly informed, the non-compliance of the patient can be then be raised as a defence to a malpractice action, as occurred in the case of *Dame Cimon c. Carbotte.*[137] Complaining of a mass in her breast, the patient was diagnosed as suffering from breast dysplasia. As a precaution, her physician taught the patient how to perform a breast self-examination and advised her to return immediately should she detect any change. About one year later, another physician discovered that the breast tumour was now cancerous, and a mastectomy had to be performed. In answer to her suit alleging an error in diagnosis, the defendant successfully argued that she had failed to follow his instructions to monitor the state of her breast and to advise him of any changes.

(b) Care Not Required by the Patient's State of Health

Although not intended to improve one's health or ensure one's comfort, the care to which reference is made under this heading nonetheless relates to treatment administered in the interest of the patient. Quebec jurisprudence appears to establish a significantly higher standard when the treatment is non-therapeutic and elective as opposed to therapeutically indicated. As Crépeau J. stated in *Kimmis-Patterson c. Rubinovich,*[138] in matters of non-therapeutic surgery, the duty of divulging risks is comprehensive whereas in cases of necessary surgery, only serious, normally foreseeable risks must be revealed to the patient. The most obvious examples of purely elective interventions include cosmetic surgery and sterilizations for purely contraceptive purposes.[139] The opinion of Rothman J. in *Hamelin-Hankins c. Papillon,*[140] involving dermabrasion to eliminate hyperpigmentation of the skin, accurately reflects the attitude of the courts in situations of this type:

> In cases of plastic surgery, however, where the decision to be made by the patient is more subjective and personal than therapeutic, I believe the doctor has a duty to be especially careful to disclose completely all material risks and, certainly, any special risks, as well as the consequences for the patient should such risks materialize. In matters of this kind, there is normally no urgency, the relevant problems can be explained to the patient, and the patient can weigh the medical risks against his own non-medical desires and priorities. Since there is no therapeutic need for the operation, a patient might well decide that he would prefer to live with a blemish rather than take the risk.[141]

---

[137] [1971] C.S. 622 (Que. S.C.).

[138] [1996] J.Q. no 5470, [1996] R.R.A. 1123 at 1129 (Que. S.C.), revd on other grounds [1999] J.Q. no 5574, [2000] R.R.A. 26 (Que. C.A.).

[139] *Stevens c. Ackman,* [1989] R.R.A. 109 at 110 (Que. S.C.) (dealing with the risks of a vasectomy). For the purposes of this discussion, we exclude altruistic medical acts such as the gift of organs and tissue for purposes of transplantation, as well as participation in experimentation as a research subject.

[140] [1980] C.S. 879 (Que. S.C.).

[141] [1980] C.S. 879 at 881 (Que. S.C.).

Justice Vallerand in *Dulude c. Gaudette*[142] is even more categorical. In matters relating to plastic surgery, he feels that the physician has the duty to "reveal all risks inherent in this type of undertaking, without any reservations".[143]

The potential *sequelae* of treatment may be temporary or permanent and the patient must be so informed.[144] For instance, a physician was found liable when a young female patient was not informed that injections to treat alopecia carried a foreseeable risk of provoking the growth of facial hair.[145] Likewise in *Blais c. Dion*,[146] a surgeon performing a facelift failed to inform the patient that there could be scarring, and was obliged to pay damages when, in fact, scars remained.

2.   Exceptions or Limitations to the Duty to Inform

A physician's duty to inform is attenuated when therapeutic privilege can be invoked or when, under certain circumstances, a state of emergency exists. The duty to inform is obviated when the patient renounces his or her right to information.

(a) Therapeutic Privilege

In addition to the possibility of concealing "a fatal or grave prognosis" from a patient, as provided for by the Code of Ethics of Physicians,[147] Quebec jurisprudence[148] has generally recognized the right of a physician to downplay or even gloss over certain truths which, in the opinion of a reasonable physician, could have a significant adverse physical or psychological effect on the patient.

Despite these clear authorities acknowledging its acceptance, the principle of therapeutic privilege is not totally devoid of controversy. For instance, if the patient asked specific questions concerning risks which, under normal circumstances, a physician would be entitled to conceal, would the privilege lapse? The

---

[142] [1974] C.S. 618 at 621 (Que. S.C.).

[143] *Ibid.* [our translation].

[144] Jean-Louis Baudouin & Patrice Deslauriers, *La responsabilité civile*, vol. II: *Responsabilité professionnelle*, 7th ed. (Cowansville, QC: Éditions Yvon Blais, 2007) at 52 n. 2-53.

[145] *Binette c. Éthier*, J.E. 79-972 (Que. S.C.).

[146] J.E. 85-934 (Que. S.C.).

[147] R.R.Q., c. M-9, r. 17, s. 57.

[148] *Brunelle c. Sirois*, [1974] C.S. 105 (Que. S.C.), revd [1975] C.A. 779 (Que. C.A.) involved a patient having to undergo bilateral cerebral arteriography because of a suspected aneurysm. The patient was not advised of the risk of loss of vision which could result from the arteriography because this information would have increased his blood pressure, thus aggravating the risk of rupturing the aneurysm. In *Dunant c. Chong*, [1985] J.Q. no 523, [1986] R.R.A. 2 (summary) (Que. C.A.), the patient became blind as a result of an operation for the removal of a brain tumour. The Court of Appeal approved the trial judge's finding that the surgeon had acted properly in not informing the patient of this risk since it would have provoked a state of anguish or distress which would have compromised the outcome of the operation. For a detailed description of the conditions for invoking therapeutic privilege, see Suzanne Philips-Nootens, Pauline Lesage-Jarjoura & Robert P. Kouri, *Éléments de responsabilité civile médicale — le droit dans le quotidien de la médecine*, 3d ed. (Cowansville, QC: Éditions Yvon Blais, 2007) at 165 n. 201.

Court of Appeal in *O'Hearn c. Estrada*[149] appears to suggest that if a patient so requested, an obligation to be completely candid would exist and he or she would assume the consequences of being told the unvarnished truth.

(b) Emergency Situations

The *Civil Code of Québec* provides that consent to medical care is not required in cases of emergency when it cannot be obtained in due time.[150] Consequently, the duty to inform may be similarly set aside. In *Boyer c. Grignon*,[151] the surgeon was exonerated for having operated on a patient suffering from an aortic aneurism that was discovered during surgery originally intended to remove what was thought to be a benign tumour. Given the gravity of the situation, it was decided that since the patient's life was in danger, the surgeon was not bound to inform him of the risk of losing his voice as a result of the operation.

In different situations, and while not eliminating it entirely, an emergency may limit the extent of the duty to inform where certain constraints such as insufficient time do not allow all pertinent information to be provided to the patient.[152]

(c) Renunciation of the Right to Information

It may occur that the patient will express a refusal to be informed of the particulars concerning treatment. In this eventuality, it is logical to state that obtaining a consent that is truly informed would be highly unlikely given the state of ignorance in which the patient has willingly placed himself or herself. This raises the question of whether a patient can indeed renounce so fundamental a right when the repercussions for one's integrity could be far from negligible. Would such a renunciation be contrary to public order?

In an *obiter* relating to therapeutic care, the Supreme Court in *Reibl v. Hughes* affirmed that:

> It is, of course, possible that a particular patient may waive aside any question of risks and be quite prepared to submit to the surgery or treatment, whatever they be. Such a situation presents no difficulty.[153]

In matters of care not required by the state of health,[154] opinions are not as clear; most writers favour that there can be no waiver of this right.[155] Unfortu-

---

[149] [1984] J.Q. no 533, J.E. 84-449 at 16 (Que. C.A.).

[150] Art. 13 C.C.Q.

[151] [1988] J.Q. no 327, [1988] R.J.Q. 829 (Que. S.C.).

[152] Jean-Louis Baudouin & Patrice Deslauriers, *La responsabilité civile*, vol. II: *Responsabilité professionnelle*, 7th ed. (Cowansville, QC: Éditions Yvon Blais, 2007) at 54 n. 2-55.

[153] [1980] S.C.J. No. 105, [1980] 2 S.C.R. 880 at 895 (S.C.C.).

[154] This term, which is used in the *Civil Code of Québec*, refers to non-therapeutic care and should not be confused with elective treatment or surgery. Elective treatment is not essential and is intended to correct a non life-threatening condition.

[155] Margaret A. Somerville, "Structuring the Issues in Informed Consent" (1981) 26 McGill L.J. 740 at 773; Suzanne Philips-Nootens, Pauline Lesage-Jarjoura & Robert P. Kouri, *Éléments de res-*

nately, these writers do not explain why one cannot renounce the right to information.

One should not lose sight of the fact that the rule of inviolability requires that any interference with a person's integrity must be authorized by law or consented to by the individual involved.[156] In all logic, there is no reason for the validity of a waiver of the right to information to depend on the purpose of the act to be performed; a renunciation is either valid or invalid. Obviously, consent to any medical act can be enlightened only if the person involved has been provided with or possesses adequate information. Yet while informing the patient is a duty imposed upon the physician, receiving the information is not an obligation on the part of the patient — it is a right intended for his or her protection. Why then could not the subject forgo this right? If the law permits a person to renounce his or her inviolability, it would seem coherent to conclude that the right to information should be governed by the same considerations.

B.   THE DUTY TO OBTAIN CONSENT

According to the *Private Law Dictionary and Bilingual Lexicons — Obligations*,[157] consent is the "assent of a person to an act that another cannot accomplish without this formality". The requirement acknowledges the fact that a capable person remains the best judge of his or her interests.

As a matter of law, one must distinguish consent required for entering into a medical contract from consent which must be given prior to each medical act other than routine care in the context of a medical contract that has already been formed. The failure to consent to a contract of care places the question of liability within the realm of extracontractual responsibility. But once a medical contract has been validly entered into, any unauthorized medical intervention constitutes a violation of this contract and any resulting liability will lie in contract.

As to the modalities of consent, it may be given either expressly or tacitly. Except for anaesthesia, medical interventions and other treatment provided in an establishment governed by the *Act Respecting Health Services and Social Services*,[158] care not required by the patient's state of health, the alienation of a part of one's body, or participation in an experiment,[159] there is no formal requirement that consent be provided in writing. Although consent is often given verbally, there is no bar to consent by gesture or sign of assent. However, Quebec

---

ponsabilité civile médicale — le droit dans le quotidien de la médecine, 3d ed. (Cowansville, QC: Éditions Yvon Blais, 2007) at 164 n. 200; Louise Potvin, *L'obligation de renseignement du médecin* (Cowansville, QC: Éditions Yvon Blais, 1984) at 72.

[156] Art. 10 C.C.Q.

[157] *Private Law Dictionary and Bilingual Lexicons — Obligations* (Cowansville, QC: Éditions Yvon Blais, 2003) at 56.

[158] R.S.Q., c. S-4.2. According to s. 79 of the legislation, these establishments would include local community service centres, hospital centres, child and youth protection centres, residential and long-term care centres and rehabilitation centres.

[159] Art. 24 C.C.Q.

courts have held that the burden of proving lack of consent rests on the plaintiff.[160]

1. The Principle of Consent

Article 10 of the *Civil Code of Québec* enunciates two principles, the first reiterating the rule of inviolability, and the second affirming that any interference with a person can take place only with the free and enlightened consent of that person unless otherwise authorized by law. In order to be valid, consent must be provided by an informed person having the capacity to act and who, in fact, is acting freely and without constraint.

The Code clearly distinguishes between incapacity as it relates to the legal status of a person requiring protection and the situation of an individual who is *de facto* incapable of providing consent. Capacity is a juridical notion which describes the faculty of enjoying and of exercising rights.[161] Inaptitude to consent may exist independently of the institution of protective supervision, just as a person under protective supervision due to insanity may be considered factually capable during an interval of lucidity.[162] As Baudouin J.A. has had occasion to point out, "the mere fact that a person is under protective supervision does not create a presumption of inaptitude to consent to medical care".[163]

Quebec legislation does not define the notion of incapacity (in French "inaptitude"), nor does it set out criteria for determining whether a person is incapable of giving consent. Article 258 of the *Civil Code of Québec* does, however, describe a number of situations in which inaptitude could be encountered, such as "illness, deficiency or debility due to age which impairs the person's mental faculties or physical ability to express his or her will".

Due to the silence of the law, Quebec courts have had to develop criteria to be applied in determining incompetency. In the case of *Institut Philippe-Pinel de Montréal c. Blais*[164] involving a mental patient's refusal of treatment, LeBel J. proposed that due to their persuasiveness, the standards established by the *Hospitals Act*[165] of Nova Scotia be retained as guidelines.[166] This approach has since been confirmed by subsequent jurisprudence.[167]

---

[160] *Chouinard c. Landry*, [1987] J.Q. no 1625 at para. 49, [1987] R.J.Q. 1954 at 1962 (Que. C.A.); *Dulude c. Gaudette*, [1974] C.S. 618 at 622 (Que. S.C.).

[161] Jean Pineau, Danielle Burman & Serge Gaudet, *Théorie des obligations*, 4th ed. (Montreal: Éditions Thémis, 2001) at 228 n. 108.

[162] See the decision of LeBel J. in *Institut Philippe-Pinel de Montréal c. Blais*, [1991] J.Q. no 5241, [1991] R.J.Q. 1969 at 1973 (Que. S.C.): "Capacity to consent to or to refuse treatment is not evaluated in light of the situation of the individual but according to his or her decisional autonomy and capacity to comprehend and appreciate the issues involved" [our translation].

[163] *W. (J.M.) v. W. (S.C.)*, [1996] J.Q. no 65 at para. 40, [1996] R.J.Q. 229 at 235 (Que. C.A.) [our translation].

[164] [1991] J.Q. no 5241, [1991] R.J.Q. 1969 (Que. S.C.).

[165] R.S.N.S. 1989, c. 208, s. 52(2) [now s. 52(2A), (2B)].

[166] According to these criteria, one must determine whether the person "(a) understands the condition for which treatment is proposed; (b) understands the nature and purpose of the treatment; (c)

In situations where the patient is incapable of giving or refusing consent to care, consent must be provided by someone authorized by law to act on his or her behalf.[168] When acting for another, the person so authorized "is bound to act in the sole interest of that person, taking into account, as far as possible, any wishes the latter may have expressed".[169] Moreover, if the person authorized indeed gives consent, he or she must "ensure that the care is beneficial notwithstanding the gravity and permanence of certain of its effects, that it is advisable in the circumstances and that the risks incurred are not disproportionate to the anticipated benefit".[170]

In keeping with the categories set out in the *Civil Code of Québec*, our examination of the law of consent will deal first with care required by the state of health and second with non-therapeutic care,[171] examining in each case the situation of adults who are incapable of consenting and that of minors.

(a) Consent to Care Required by the State of Health of the Person

(i) Adults Incapable of Consenting

The incapable adult does not lose the enjoyment of his or her rights, but merely the exercise of them. A person's incapacity must not serve as a pretext to deny fundamental rights, which explains why legislation grants certain powers to legal representatives or, in specified cases, to persons in the patient's circle of friends or family to provide consent. For medical care in particular, the *Civil Code of Québec* stipulates:

> 15. ... consent is given by his or her mandatary, tutor or curator. If the person of full age is not so represented, consent is given by his or her married, civil union or *de facto* spouse or, if the person has no spouse or his or her spouse is prevented from giving consent, it is given by a close relative or a person who shows a special interest in the person of full age.[172]

In the absence of a legal representative, one must follow the order set out in the Code. Although this hierarchy seems relatively simple, the reality of human relationships can complicate the choice of the person authorized to consent. It is surprising to note, for instance, the lack of specific rules of antecedence between the various close relatives or between close relatives and a person showing a

---

understands the risks involved in undergoing the treatment; (d) understands the risks involved in not undergoing the treatment; and (e) whether or not his ability to consent is affected by his condition" (*Institut Philippe-Pinel de Montréal v. Blais*, [1991] J.Q. no 5241 at para. 22, [1991] R.J.Q. 1969 at 1974 (Que. S.C.)).

[167] *Hôpital Charles-Lemoyne c. Forcier*, [1992] R.D.F. 257 (Que. S.C.); *Institut Philippe-Pinel de Montréal c. Gharavy*, [1994] J.Q. no 837 at para. 72, [1994] R.J.Q. 2523 at 2534 (Que. C.A.).

[168] Art. 11 C.C.Q.

[169] Art. 12, para. 1 C.C.Q.

[170] Art. 12, para. 2 C.C.Q.

[171] We will not discuss experimentation nor the gift of organs and tissue, since certain of these questions are dealt with in other parts of this book.

[172] Art. 15 C.C.Q.

special interest in the incapable person. Even the expression "special interest" remains fairly vague and would appear to include a close friend, a *de facto* custodian of the patient, an in-law, a spiritual advisor, *etc.*

In certain situations involving incapable adults, it may be necessary to have recourse to the court. Specifically provided for in article 16 of the Code, three sets of circumstances render judicial intervention obligatory when the care involved is required by the person's state of health: when the person who may consent on behalf of the incapable adult is prevented from doing so, when he or she unjustifiably refuses to give consent, or when the patient "categorically refuses to receive care, except in the case of hygienic care or emergency".[173] Paradoxically, article 23, para. 2 requires that the refusal of the person concerned be respected "unless the care is required by his state of health". Thus, recourse to the court in this type of situation must be viewed as a form of verification that the care is indeed required for the patient because once this condition is met, the authorization of the court must be given. In practice, authorizations of this nature have usually involved the administration of antipsychotic medication to mental patients.[174]

(ii) Unemancipated Minors

For purposes of medical treatment, the *Civil Code of Québec* distinguishes between minors 14 years of age and older and minors under 14 years of age. It should be pointed out that the age of 14 retained by legislation for consenting to medical care, does not necessarily take into account the maturity or even the discernment of the minor, which, as experience often indicates, is not always proportional to age.

According to article 14, para. 2 of the Code, a minor 14 years of age or more may consent alone to care required by his or her state of health. Should the minor's condition necessitate hospitalization for over 12 hours, the person having parental authority[175] or the tutor shall merely be informed of that fact, without any other information being divulged. The intent of this legislation is to facilitate access to medical care for adolescents, including abortion services, treatment of sexually transmitted diseases, and problems related to drug and alcohol abuse. As the law presently stands, it would appear to suggest that access to contraceptive services can only be provided for therapeutic reasons.

---

[173] Art. 16 C.C.Q. In deciding whether or not to authorize treatment, the court must obtain the opinion of experts, of the mandatary, of the tutor or the curator and of the tutorship council. It may also obtain the opinion of any person who shows a special interest in the person concerned by the application (art. 23, para. 1 C.C.Q.).

[174] See, for example, *Institut Philippe-Pinel de Montréal c. Blais*, [1991] J.Q. no 5241, [1991] R.J.Q. 1969 (Que. S.C.); *Hôpital Charles-Lemoyne c. Forcier*, [1992] R.D.F. 257 (Que. S.C.); *Cité de la Santé de Laval c. Lacombe*, [1992] R.J.Q. 58 (Que. S.C.); *Institut Philippe-Pinel de Montréal c. Gharavy*, [1994] J.Q. no 837, [1994] R.J.Q. 2523 (Que. C.A.). See also Robert P. Kouri & Suzanne Philips-Nootens, « Le majeur inapte et le refus catégorique de soins de santé : un concept pour le moins ambigu » (2003) 63 R. du B. 3 at 26-27.

[175] Under art. 600 C.C.Q., the father and mother exercise parental authority together.

Unless one is prepared to conclude that as a general principle, the tender age of a young girl is a contraindication for pregnancy, then any medical act intended to prevent conception should be viewed as care not required by the state of health of young women, and the conditions of article 17 of the Code would then apply.[176] It seems counterintuitive however, to ban access to birth control products and services while authorizing abortion due to the youthfulness of a pregnant child.

Article 16, para. 2 of the Code requires the authorization of the court in cases where the minor aged 14 or more refuses care except in cases of emergency where one's life is in danger or one's integrity is threatened. In this situation, the consent of the person having parental authority or of the tutor suffices. When the court is called upon to rule, article 23 of the Code indicates that it would not be held to respect the minor's refusal.[177] As regards consent to care required by the state of health of a minor less than 14 years old, the codal provisions are very clear: consent is given by the person having parental authority or by the tutor.[178] An unjustified refusal by the parents or tutor would give rise to recourse to the courts under article 16.[179] Any consent or refusal on behalf of the minor would have to respect the criteria of article 12.[180]

---

[176] Article 17 of the Code states:

   17. A minor fourteen years of age or over may give his consent alone to care not required by the state of his health; however, the consent of the person having parental authority or the tutor is required if the care entails a serious risk for the health of the minor and may cause him grave and permanent effects.

[177] *Protection de la Jeunesse — 884*, [1998] R.J.Q. 816 (Que. S.C.) (a child refused an operation on religious grounds, believing that her scoliosis would be corrected by prayer). In this regard, the Supreme Court's decision in *C. (A.) v. Manitoba (Director of Child and Family Services)*, [2009] S.C.J. No. 30, [2009] 2 S.C.R. 181 (S.C.C.) would appear to have some pertinence in that the Manitoba legislation (*Child and Family Services Act*, C.C.S.M. c. C80) authorizes medical treatment which is considered in the best interests of the child (s. 25(8)) unless the child is 16 years of age and is able to understand the information relative to making a decision and is able to appreciate the reasonably foreseeable consequences of a decision to consent or not consent to treatment (s. 25(9)). Although under Quebec law, the age of consent to medical treatment is set at 14, the court must, as in Manitoba, first consult the minor child (art. 34 C.C.Q.) if his or her power of discernment so permits, and decide whether a refusal of treatment is in the child's best interests (arts. 12, 23 C.C.Q.). As indicated in the *C. (A.)* decision, the more dangerous the situation for the child's security, the more intense the degree of scrutiny by the court (*C. (A.) v. Manitoba (Director of Child and Family Services)* at paras. 86, 133). See generally, Robert P. Kouri, « Le mineur et les soins médicaux, *A.C. c. Manitoba* : de l'autonomie au meilleur intérêt, une limite bien floue » (2010) 4 McGill J. of Law and Health/Revue de droit & santé de McGill 65.

[178] Art. 14, para. 1 C.C.Q.

[179] *In Re Goyette: Centre de Services Sociaux du Montréal Métropolitain*, [1983] C.S. 429 (Que. S.C.); *Montreal Children's Hospital v. Couture-Jacquet*, [1986] Q.J. No. 258, [1986] R.J.Q. 1221 (Que. C.A.); *Protection de la Jeunesse — 332*, [1988] R.J.Q. 1666 (Que. S.C.).

[180] Article 12 reads in part as follows: "A person who gives his consent to or refuses care for another person is bound to act in the sole interest of that person, taking into account, as far as possible, any wishes the latter may have expressed." To which one must add the words of art. 33 C.C.Q., which include factors such as "the moral, intellectual, emotional and material needs of

(b) Consent to Care Not Required by the State of Health of the Person

A straightforward reading of the *Civil Code of Québec* provisions governing care not required by the state of health of the person indicates that the rules pertaining to non-therapeutic care administered in the sole interest of the person (purely contraceptive sterilization, cosmetic surgery, *etc.*) differ from those relating to medical acts of an altruistic nature (organ donations, experimentation). We will limit our examination of the law of consent to care administered in the exclusive interest of the patient. Since no specific rules govern consent by capable adults to this type of care, other than requiring that it be provided in writing, our analysis will deal with incapable adults and with minors who, as vulnerable persons, are protected by additional safeguards.

(i) Incapable Adults

Article 18 of the *Civil Code of Québec* states that consent to non-therapeutic care for incapable adults is provided by the mandatary, tutor or curator. In addition, the authorization of the court is necessary "if the care entails a serious risk for health or if it might cause grave and permanent effects".

Two aspects of article 18 should be emphasized. Firstly, the law requires that the incapable adult be represented by a mandatary, tutor or curator. Since close relatives, spouses and others who have not otherwise been designated as representatives are excluded from the list,[181] it follows that non-therapeutic care cannot be administered to an incapable person unless he or she has designated a mandatary in anticipation of his or her incapacity,[182] or has been placed under a regime of protective supervision.[183]

Secondly, the representative's consent alone will suffice provided the care does not entail a serious risk for health or cause grave and permanent effects. The stringency of these conditions would appear to limit the representative's authority to authorizing only minor medical acts such as the elimination of a birthmark for aesthetic reasons, orthodontia or the prescription of certain forms of contraception, such as an intrauterine device. If, on the other hand, the care indeed involves a serious risk for health or grave and permanent effects, approval of the court becomes necessary. Since the care in question is not required by the patient's state of health, his or her refusal will constitute an absolute bar to any such authorization.[184] The inconsistency inherent in this situation is that if

---

the child ... the child's age, health, personality and family environment, and to the other aspects of his situation".

[181] In contradistinction to art. 15 C.C.Q. concerning therapeutic care which allows relatives, spouses and others who are not representatives, to consent to care required by the state of health.

[182] Art. 2166 C.C.Q.

[183] Art. 256 C.C.Q.

[184] Art. 23, para. 2 C.C.Q. states: "The court is also bound to obtain the opinion of the person concerned unless that is impossible, and to respect his refusal unless the care is required by his state of health."

the patient is so incapable as to be unable to express an opinion for or against the intervention, the patient's power to refuse disappears.

Obviously, the most controversial intervention which falls within the purview of article 18 is the non-therapeutic sterilization of mentally challenged women. While the risks inherent in this type of surgery are fairly minimal, by its very nature, the operation will produce "grave and permanent effects" for the individual.

In the Supreme Court of Canada case of *E. (Mrs.) v. Eve*,[185] a widow sought court authorization to have her daughter sterilized, fearing the negative emotional impact of a pregnancy for her daughter, as well as the inability of her daughter to care for a child, who would then become Mrs. E.'s responsibility. Speaking on behalf of the Supreme Court panel, La Forest J. felt that the courts exercising their *parens patriae* powers could authorize only those acts which were necessary for the person under protection. Since Eve's mother failed to establish the advantages of surgery for Eve herself as opposed to the convenience of others, the court declined the requested authorization. At first blush, La Forest J. appears to have issued a blanket condemnation of sterilization for the mentally incompetent:

> The grave intrusion on a person's rights and the certain physical damage that ensues from non-therapeutic sterilization without consent, when compared to the highly questionable advantages that can result from it, have persuaded me that it can never safely be determined that such a procedure is for the benefit of that person. Accordingly, the procedure should never be authorized for non-therapeutic purposes under the *parens patriae* jurisdiction.[186]

Further on, however, he writes:

> If sterilization of the mentally incompetent is to be adopted as desirable for general social purposes, the legislature is the appropriate body to do so. It is in a position to inform itself and it is attuned to the feelings of the public in making policy in this sensitive area.[187]

Even though this type of operation is not specifically mentioned in the *Civil Code of Québec*, arguably the Code provisions meet the standard set out by La Forest J., as the patient's representative must consent, and the patient, the tutorship council and experts must be consulted before the court can authorize any sterilization.[188] It should also be noted that unlike the conditions for enabling the courts to act under their *parens patriae* powers, the Code requires that any act must be undertaken in the "sole interest of that person".[189] Refusing a mentally incompetent person access to certain birth control methods available to the general population, all in the name of "protecting" her rights, can be as morally

---

[185] [1986] S.C.J. No. 60, [1986] 2 S.C.R. 388 (S.C.C.).
[186] *Ibid.*, at 431.
[187] *Ibid.*
[188] Art. 23 C.C.Q.
[189] Art. 12 C.C.Q.

blameworthy as sterilization for the convenience of those close to the mentally challenged person. Nevertheless, due to the potential for abuse, we feel that the Code provisions would permit the sterilization of incompetents only in highly exceptional circumstances.[190]

(ii) Minors

As is the case with therapeutic care, the *Civil Code of Québec* distinguishes between minors 14 years of age or more and those less than 14 in matters relating to consent to non-therapeutic care. Article 17 states the principle that "[a] minor 14 years of age or over may give his consent alone to care not required by the state of his health". But it places restrictions on the exercise of this capacity:

> 17. [The] consent of the person having parental authority or of the tutor is required if the care entails a serious risk for the health of the minor and may cause him grave and permanent effects.

Contrary to one's initial impression, the limitations placed by article 17 on the minor's powers of consent do not unduly restrict his or her autonomy since the conditions imposed by the Code are cumulative and as such, would not concern acts that a minor would likely wish to undertake alone. For example, as the law stands, a minor can consent to non-surgical forms of contraception,[191] to an early abortion for non-therapeutic reasons, or to being provided with the "morning after" pill.

When the minor is less than 14 years of age, article 18 stipulates that the person having parental authority or the tutor may consent alone provided there is no serious risk for health nor any grave and permanent effects. If the intervention proposed indeed involves a serious risk for health or grave and permanent effects, authorization of the court becomes necessary. In this situation, the minor child has a right to be consulted. If he or she expresses a refusal, then the court

---

[190] In *T. (N.) c. N.-T. (C.)*, [1999] R.J.Q. 223 (Que. S.C.), the court refused to authorize the sterilization by tubal ligation of a mentally challenged adult, stating that there was no evidence that the surgery was in the girl's best interest as opposed to other factors such as the burden for her mother, the risk of transmission of her condition to her offspring and the social cost (at para. 225). The court suggested that instead, Depo-Provera or the Norplant method could be used, thus avoiding the risks and the irreversibility of surgery (at para. 227). Likewise, the court in *Centre de santé et de services sociaux de Beauce — services hospitaliers c. G. (M.)*, [2008] J.Q. no 3997, 2008 QCCS 1907 (Que. S.C.) rejected the application of a hospital for permission to surgically sterilize an adult schizophrenic drug addict of limited intellect, as recommended by her psychiatrist, and ordered instead that in her best interest (at para. 10), hormonal contraception by injection be administered. On the other hand, in *Centre de santé et de services sociaux Pierre-Boucher c. T. (J.)*, [2008] J.Q. no 8176, 2008 QCCS 3867 (Que. S.C.), the court refused to order contraception by injection or by installation of an intrauterine device (IUD), holding that this did not constitute care required by the state of health of the 40-year-old paranoid-schizophrenic patient.

[191] Suzanne Philips-Nootens, Pauline Lesage-Jarjoura & Robert P. Kouri, *Éléments de responsabilité civile médicale — le droit dans le quotidien de la médecine*, 3d ed. (Cowansville, QC: Éditions Yvon Blais, 2007) at 235 n. 277.

is bound to respect this refusal since the care is not required by the patient's state of health.[192]

2.   Corollary: The Right to Refuse Treatment

It is generally admitted in Quebec law that a capable patient has the right to refuse treatment even at the risk of putting his or her life in danger.[193] An important issue which remains to be resolved in this regard is whether this refusal of treatment must be informed.

In two cases of common law origin, the Supreme Court appears to have posited a symmetrical approach to both consent and refusal: both must be informed. In *Hollis v. Dow Corning Corp.*, La Forest J., speaking for the Court, stated:

> The doctrine of "informed consent" dictates that every individual has a right to know what risks are involved in undergoing or foregoing medical treatment and a concomitant right to make meaningful decisions based on a full understanding of those risks. [194]

In *Reibl v. Hughes*,[195] Laskin C.J.C. affirmed that the fundamental issue relating to consent involves the "patient's right to know what risks are involved in undergoing or foregoing certain surgical or other treatment".[196]

A right to be informed does not include a duty or obligation to be informed. If a capable patient refuses to be informed, he or she must assume the consequences of this refusal. Nonetheless, the physician must offer to provide the relevant information.

Even if consent to care is given prior to a medical intervention, it remains an ongoing process.[197] The patient is free to authorize an interference with his or her integrity, and the patient is just as free to withdraw this authorization at any time. Indeed, it may occur that during treatment, fear, pain or discomfort will provoke a reaction that could be interpreted as a withdrawal of consent. In order to distinguish an involuntary reaction to pain or discomfort from an actual refusal of further treatment, one's only recourse is to rely on the standard of a reasonable person's appreciation of the event. If, in the eyes of a reasonable person, the patient's protestations are more likely the manifestation of discomfort than an actual refusal, the medical act can be continued. However, since the patient's right to autonomy and inviolability are involved, the burden of proof in this type of situation will have to be assumed by the physician. In *Courtemanche c. Potvin*,[198] for instance, a patient undergoing a myelogram

---

[192] Art. 23, para. 2 C.C.Q.

[193] *B. (N.) v. Hôtel-Dieu de Québec*, [1992] Q.J. No. 1, [1992] R.J.Q. 361 (Que. S.C.); *Manoir de la Pointe Bleue (1978) Inc. c. Corbeil*, [1992] J.Q. no 98, [1992] R.J.Q. 712 (Que. S.C.).

[194] [1995] S.C.J. No. 104 at para. 24, [1995] 4 S.C.R. 634 at 656 (S.C.C.).

[195] [1980] S.C.J. No. 105, [1980] 2 S.C.R. 880 (S.C.C.).

[196] *Ibid.*, at 895.

[197] Suzanne Philips-Nootens, Pauline Lesage-Jarjoura & Robert P. Kouri, *Éléments de responsabilité civile médicale — le droit dans le quotidien de la médecine*, 3d ed. (Cowansville, QC: Éditions Yvon Blais, 2007) at 180 n. 215.

[198] [1996] R.R.A. 829 (Que. S.C.).

claimed to have begged the neurologist to stop the procedure. The court rejected the plaintiff's action in damages, taking into consideration the exceptionally low tolerance to discomfort of the patient in question who suffered from hypochondria. It was felt that his protestations were cries of pain.

As a general rule, when consent has been withdrawn, the physician must interrupt treatment, subject to the *caveat* put forward by Cory J. in *Ciarlariello v. Schacter*:

> Thus, if it is found that the consent is effectively withdrawn during the course of the proceeding then it must be terminated. This must be the result except in the circumstances where the medical evidence suggests that to terminate the process would be either life threatening or pose immediate and serious problems to the health of the patient.[199]

3. The Emergency Exception to the Requirement of Consent

An emergency situation constitutes more than a simple means of exoneration for having proceeded with treatment without authorization; it in fact replaces consent. According to article 13, para. 1 of the *Civil Code of Québec*: "Consent to medical care is not required in case of emergency if the life of the person is in danger or his integrity is threatened and his consent cannot be obtained in due time."

As a result, in order to justify an intrusion upon one's inviolability without the consent of the person or of a third party authorized to consent on his or her behalf, the patient or the third party must in fact be incapable of being informed, of expressing consent and the situation must be of such a gravity that the patient's life or integrity is in peril. It should be noted that this exception to the requirement of consent cannot be invoked in cases where "the care is unusual or has become useless or where its consequences could be intolerable for the person".[200] There are thus three exceptions to the emergency exception!

The first exception deals with unusual treatment: physicians cannot impose extraordinary or experimental interventions on patients (such as artificial heart implants).[201] The second exception states that treatment cannot have become useless; in other words, heroic or futile treatment cannot be imposed upon a terminally ill patient.[202] As for the third exception involving the consequences of

---

[199] [1993] S.C.J. No. 46 at para. 42, [1993] 2 S.C.R. 119 at 136 (S.C.C.).

[200] Art. 13, para. 2 C.C.Q.

[201] A hypothesis actually raised during parliamentary commission hearings by Dr. Augustin Roy, president of the Corporation Professionnelle des Médecins du Québec, *Journal des Débats : Commissions Parlementaires*, 4e session, 32e législature, p. B-1661.

[202] In *Centre de santé et services sociaux Richelieu-Yamaska c. L. (M.)*, [2006] J.Q. no 3578, EYB 2006-104015 (Que. S.C.), application was made to the court to obtain permission for the cessation of treatment. Paradoxically, the physicians involved had already determined that the patient was irreversibly brain-dead (at para. 14). Thus, it would appear that permission was sought to stop ventilating a corpse. See also *Centre hospitalier affilié universitaire de Québec c. B. (L.) et Curateur public du Québec*, EYB 2006-103837 (Que. S.C.): suspending active treatment of a seriously injured victim of a criminal assault.

care which could be intolerable for the person, it would appear to apply to those who, for philosophical or religious reasons, would not have consented to care had they been able to express an opinion.[203]

C. VIOLATION OF THE DUTY TO INFORM AND CAUSATION

A patient inadequately informed as to the risks, advantages and disadvantages of medical treatment and who, on the basis of this lack of information, has authorized a medical act which gives rise to injury, may claim damages provided, of course, the physician's failure to advise actually caused the harm. Must the patient prove that had he or she known the truth, consent to treatment would not have been forthcoming (the "subjective standard"), or must the patient go further and establish that had a reasonable person in the patient's situation been aware of the truth, treatment would have been refused (the "modified objective standard")?

Traditionally, the issue of causation in cases of violation of the duty to inform was not a source of controversy in Quebec law, since the courts have tended to rely on a subjective standard of appreciation. The case of *Dulude c. Gaudette*,[204] in which a plastic surgeon was sued for not having advised his patient of the risks of augmentation mammoplasty surgery, is a classic example of this approach. While finding that the surgeon had indeed inadequately advised his patient, Vallerand J. nonetheless rejected the claim on the basis of a lack of causal relationship between the physician's fault and the plaintiff's injuries:

> Plaintiff avers that had she known of the slightest possibility of that which took place actually occurring, she would never have undergone the operation. I do not have any doubt as to her sincerity coloured by hindsight. I must, however, point out that as a pretty and coquettish young woman anxious to remain such, she preferred corrective surgery to a fur coat offered by her husband.
>
> I cannot believe that evoking the highly unlikely possibility of the complications from which she eventually suffered, would have deterred her from pursuing her plan.[205]

However, following the Supreme Court decision in the Ontario case of *Reibl v. Hughes*[206] proposing a "modified objective criterion",[207] the courts in

---

[203] The Ontario case of *Malette v. Shulman*, [1987] O.J. No. 1180, 47 D.L.R. (4th) 18 (Ont. H.C.J.), affd [1990] O.J. No. 450, 67 D.L.R. (4th) 321 (Ont. C.A.) would likely have had the same outcome in Quebec.

[204] [1974] C.S. 618 (Que. S.C.).

[205] *Ibid.*, at 622 [our translation].

[206] [1980] S.C.J. No. 105, [1980] 2 S.C.R. 880 (S.C.C.).

[207] *Ibid.*, at 898-900 At 899-900. Laskin C.J.C. writes: "In saying that the test is based on the decision that a reasonable person in the patient's position would have made, I should make it clear that the patient's particular concerns must also be reasonably based; otherwise, there would be more subjectivity than would be warranted under an objective test."

Quebec began to adapt this standard.[208] But then, the Court of Appeal entered the fray and became divided on this particular question,[209] which inevitably led to a certain amount of confusion in the courts of first instance.[210]

At this point, a compromise of sorts between the modified objective and subjective standard was broached at the appellate level. In *Pelletier v. Roberge*,[211] the Court of Appeal employed the expressions "rational subjectivity" and "subjective reasonableness" for the first time apparently in order to bridge the gulf. Speaking on behalf of the panel, Brossard J.A. introduced this new approach in the following terms:

> Appellant rightly submits that Quebec jurisprudence has not retained the strictly objective test laid down by the Supreme Court in the case of *Reibl v. Hughes*. This, however, is only partially true. In effect, our jurisprudence is made up of a duality of opinions on this subject, and it is only in our last three decisions ... that this Court has settled on a test that one could describe as based on "rational subjectivity" or "subjective reasonableness," which consists of determining and appreciating, in light of the nature of the risk and the evidence, what would have been the reasonable probable response of that particular patient, as opposed to the response of a reasonable person in the abstract sense as set out in *Reibl v. Hughes*.[212]

Justice Baudouin further elucidated the parameters of this test in *Drolet c. Parenteau*:[213]

> The civil liability of a physician is not however automatically engaged by the mere fact of having wrongfully fulfilled the duty of informing. According to our jurisprudence, one must apply a test which, in our opinion, is essentially a subjective test and consists of evaluating if the patient, in the circumstances in question, would still have consented to the intervention if he or she had been adequately informed. This appreciation is usually made in light of the patient's testimony. Obviously, this testimony must be evaluated with care and other factors must be considered. It is for this reason that often, the courts ask them-

---

208 See, *e.g.*, *Barette c. Lajoie*, J.E. 85-853 (Que. S.C.); *Dionne c. Ferenczi*, [1987] R.R.A. 420 (Que. S.C.).

209 *O'Hearn c. Estrada*, [1984] J.Q. no 533, J.E. 84-449 (Que. C.A.); *Dunant c. Chong*, [1985] J.Q. no 523, [1986] R.R.A. 2 (summary) (Que. C.A.); *Chouinard c. Landry*, [1987] J.Q. no 1625, [1987] R.J.Q. 1954 (Que. C.A.), leave to appeal refused [1988] C.S.C.R. no 15, [1988] 1 S.C.R. vii (S.C.C.).

210 *Weiss c. Solomon*, [1989] J.Q. no 312, [1989] R.J.Q. 731 (Que. S.C.); *Stevens c. Ackman*, [1989] R.R.A. 109 (Que. S.C.); *O'Shea c. McGovern*, [1989] R.R.A. 341 (Que. S.C.); *Masson c. De Koos*, [1990] R.R.A. 818 (Que. S.C.); *Lacharité c. Waddell*, [1998] J.Q. no 4753, [1998] R.R.A. 459 (Que. S.C.). However, in *Rafferty v. Kulczycky*, [1989] Q.J. No. 1708, [1989] R.R.A. 582 (Que. S.C.) and in *Murray-Vaillancourt c. Clairoux*, [1989] J.Q. no 2524, [1989] R.R.A. 762 (Que. S.C.) the objective standard was applied.

211 [1991] J.Q. no 1624, [1991] R.R.A. 726 (Que. C.A.).

212 *Ibid.*, at 734 R.R.A. [our translation].

213 [1994] J.Q. no 167, [1994] R.J.Q. 689 (Que. C.A.) The Quebec Court of Appeal confirmed its adherence to the "rational subjectivity" test in *Ferland c. Ghosn*, [2008] J.Q. no 3351, 2008 QCCA 797 at para. 49 (Que. C.A.).

selves what a normally prudent and diligent person would have decided in that particular case, a so-called "objective" test, but one which, in my opinion, relates essentially to the credibility of this testimony. This objective test does not replace the subjective test. It merely completes it.[214]

It is undeniable that the modified objective test, the subjective test and the "rational subjectivity" or "subjective reasonableness" test each present certain advantages and shortcomings. The challenge is to adopt the test most in keeping with the fundamental principles of the civil law. In our opinion, both the modified objective test and the standard of "subjective reasonableness" fail to respect the genius of Quebec liability law.

Without question, the greatest merit inherent in the modified objective test is to discount testimony based on bitterness and hindsight. Yet, in the guise of substantive law, its role is essentially evidentiary[215] and would appear to circumscribe the trier of fact's function in evaluating testimony. In at least two cases on appeal from Quebec in matters unrelated to medical law, the Supreme Court reaffirmed the trial judge's sovereign powers of appreciation of the evidence. Reasserting a principle previously acknowledged in *W.T. Rawleigh Co. v. Dumoulin*,[216] Lamont J. wrote in *Montreal Tramways Co. v. Léveillé*,[217] a celebrated case involving proof through testimony of a causal relationship between harm caused to a child born with club feet and a fall suffered by her mother during pregnancy:

> It was urged that to so hold would open wide the door to extravagance of testimony and lead, in all probability, to perjury and fraud. I am not apprehensive on this point for, although in certain cases special care will be required on the part of the judge ... I feel quite confident that the rules of evidence are adequate to require satisfactory proof of responsibility and that the determination of the relation of cause and effect will not involve the court in any greater difficulty than now exists in many of our cases.[218]

There are many other reservations regarding the adoption of the modified objective test. For instance, in the exercise of fundamental rights under the Quebec *Charter of Human Rights and Freedoms*,[219] including the right to inviolability and freedom,[220] a person has the right to refuse care even if this refusal is not in his or her best interests and could not, by any stretch of the imagination, be considered reasonable according to an objective standard. This being the case,

---

214 *Ibid.*, at 707 R.J.Q. [our translation]. Adoption of the "subjective rationality" or "rational subjectivity" test was later confirmed by the Court of Appeal in *Baum c. Mohr*, [2006] J.Q. no 4561, [2006] R.R.A. 1008 (Que. S.C.), affd [2008] Q.J. No. 2978, [2008] R.R.A. 285 (Que. C.A.), leave to appeal refused [2008] S.C.C.A. No. 277 (S.C.C.).

215 Ellen I. Picard & Gerald B. Robertson, *Legal Liability of Doctors and Hospitals in Canada*, 4th ed. (Toronto: Thomson Carswell, 2007) at 199.

216 [1926] S.C.J. No. 35, [1926] S.C.R. 551 (S.C.C.).

217 [1933] S.C.J. No. 40, [1933] S.C.R. 456 (S.C.C.).

218 *Ibid.*, at 465 S.C.R.

219 R.S.Q., c. C-12.

220 *Ibid.*, s. 1.

then how can anyone presume to judge one's personal choice in light of what a reasonable person in the plaintiff's situation would have decided?[221] Moreover, in cases of therapeutic privilege, how can this exception to the duty of fully informing, based on the sensibilities or the precarious state of health of a particular patient — a subjective appreciation — be reconciled with the notion that the presumed reaction of this patient would necessarily conform to that of a reasonable person in similar circumstances?

The most telling objection to the *Reibl* test of causation occurs when the proposed intervention does not have a therapeutic purpose, as in the case of cosmetic surgery. How can one compare the reaction of a particular individual to that of a reasonable person since in this type of situation, most reasonable people would arguably forgo the risks of surgery under general anaesthesia just to correct a minor or imagined imperfection? In *Dulude c. Gaudette*,[222] did not Vallerand J. find that given the choice by her husband, the plaintiff nonetheless expressed a preference for risky breast enhancement surgery rather than receive the gift of a fur coat? Likewise in *Johnson c. Harris*,[223] involving cosmetic surgery to remove an abdominal scar, Macerola J. felt impelled to write:

> This is a case involving purely elective plastic surgery. All depends upon the patient's choice. In effect, the circumstances would lead one to believe that an ordinary person would prefer to live with an aesthetic imperfection than run the risk of physical harm as a result of an operation.[224]

In proposing a so-called "rational subjectivity" test, the Quebec Court of Appeal has undoubtedly sought to reaffirm the principles of the civil law while protecting health professionals from "hindsight and bitterness".[225] In addition, this criterion would at least seem to be an expression of deference towards the moral and persuasive authority of the Supreme Court by appearing to incorporate objective elements in the evaluation of testimony. As a compromise between the modified objective and subjective tests however, this proposed solution suffers from one major weakness in that it fails to distinguish the fundamental difference between substantive and adjective law. In deciding *Reibl*, the Supreme Court intended to restructure the law governing consent in medical malpractice,[226] an aspect of substantive tort law, whereas through "rational subjectivity" or "subjective reasonableness", the Quebec Court of Appeal appears to be proposing criteria relating exclusively to proof. This nuance is far from academic because as a general rule, in appreciating the evidence and more particularly evidence adduced through testimony, the Court of Appeal must avoid substituting

---

221 *Reibl v. Hughes*, [1980] S.C.J. No. 105, [1980] 2 S.C.R. 880 at 899-900 (S.C.C.).

222 [1974] C.S. 618 (Que. S.C.).

223 [1990] J.Q. no 1467, [1990] R.R.A. 832 (Que. S.C.).

224 *Johnson c. Harris*, [1990] J.Q. no 1467 at para. 77, [1990] R.R.A. 832 at 841 (Que. S.C.) [our translation].

225 *Reibl v. Hughes*, [1980] S.C.J. No. 105, [1980] 2 S.C.R. 880 at 898 (S.C.C.).

226 Ellen I. Picard & Gerald B. Robertson, *Legal Liability of Doctors and Hospitals in Canada*, 4th ed. (Toronto: Thomson Carswell, 2007) at 131.

its opinion on the credibility of witnesses for that of the trier of fact.[227] But when the issue involves application of a substantive rule, the revisionary powers of an appellate court take full effect. One must also avoid confusing actual corroboration of the plaintiff's testimony with a determination of what a reasonable person would have decided in similar circumstances. The testimony of a person corroborated by the factual circumstances of the case will invariably be closer to the truth than the application of an objective standard which must, by its very nature, remain conjectural. Even if one were to favour application of the "rational subjectivity" or "subjective reasonableness" criterion as a rule of prudence in matters of proof, one would have to do so with much circumspection in order to avoid imposing upon the trier of fact, directives which could hinder his or her appreciation of the victim's testimony.

IV. THE DUTY TO TREAT AND CORRELATIVE OBLIGATIONS

While the duty to treat the patient is at the very heart of the physician-patient relationship, the duty to attend the patient in light of the evolution of the illness or condition becomes a natural extension of the more fundamental duty to provide care. The greatest number of suits against physicians have generally arisen from violations of these two obligations. The general principles of civil liability having been set out in the first part of this chapter, that which follows deals essentially with the determination of fault with respect to the duties to treat and to attend. We will then turn to duties of professional secrecy and confidentiality of medical records.

A. THE DUTY TO TREAT

As has already been pointed out, the duty to treat is considered an obligation of diligence or of means; the physician must utilize all means at his or her disposal to ensure proper diagnosis, treatment or relief for the patient. Due to the risks inherent in this type of activity, the physician cannot be held to an obligation of result. In their approach to this fundamental distinction, the courts have tended to differentiate the realization of risks inherent in medical practice from actual civil fault resulting from negligence or imprudence.

1. Extent of the Duty to Treat

In the words of the Quebec Court of Appeal in a landmark 1957 decision, the physician must "provide his patient with conscientious, attentive care in conformity with accepted standards of medical science".[228] In applying this stan-

---

[227] *Beaudoin-Daigneault v. Richard*, [1984] S.C.J. No. 2, [1984] 1 S.C.R. 2 at 8-9 (S.C.C.); *Lapointe v. Hôpital Le Gardeur*, [1992] S.C.J. No. 11 at para. 15, [1992] 1 S.C.R. 351 at 358 (S.C.C.).

[228] *X. c. Mellen*, [1957] B.R. 389 at 416 (Que. C.A.) [our translation].

dard, a physician's professional conduct is compared to that which a prudent, diligent, competent colleague enjoying similar training and placed in the same circumstances would have done. The assessment is thus *in abstracto*, according to objective criteria.

Fault may occur at any stage of the duty to treat, whether in the course of diagnosis or during treatment itself. The best way to illustrate this is through the presentation of actual illustrations drawn from jurisprudence.

(a) Conscientious and Attentive Care

It is important that a physician listen to the patient and take into account his or her complaints in order to arrive at an accurate diagnosis. Thus, a physician who concluded that a patient was suffering from cataracts whereas the presence of pain would have tended to indicate glaucoma, was held liable for his failure to properly diagnose the condition.[229] Moreover, a physical examination, an examination of the back of the eye and the measurement of ocular pressure, all of which was indicated in cases of this nature, would have enabled the physician to properly diagnose the illness.[230] In another decision, an intern discharged a patient who, following an accident, still had a metal particle under the eyelid. The resulting infection caused the loss of the eye. The court criticized the intern, *inter alia*, for having failed to conform to the most basic of precautions.[231] In yet another, older case, an anaesthetist forgot to ensure that the pipes or tubing to his medical apparatus were properly connected and consequently deprived the patient of oxygen. The patient emerged from surgery in a neurovegetative state and died months later. The physician was found to be at fault for having acted "without due thought in preparing for the intervention, for omitting a fundamental precaution and for lacking vigilance in the administration of the anaesthesia itself".[232]

The failure to have recourse to certain specific procedures can also become a source of liability if it leads to an inaccurate diagnosis, as for example when a fracture has not been detected because an X-ray examination was not performed.[233] Similarly, good medical practice would require that a spermogram be performed in order to verify the success of a vasectomy,[234] that renal and auditory functions be verified when certain antibiotics are prescribed,[235] and that the pathologist's report be consulted following a tubal ligation.[236] A physician who fails to inform a patient that a breast biopsy established the presence of cancer

---

[229] *Lauzon c. Taillefer*, [1991] R.R.A. 62 (Que. S.C.).

[230] *Ibid.*

[231] *Boies c. Hôtel-Dieu de Québec*, [1980] C.S. 596 at 603 (Que. S.C.), revd in part on another point (*sub nom. Bois c. Plamondon*) [1985] J.Q. no 537, J.E. 85-976 (Que. C.A.).

[232] *Covet c. Jewish General Hospital*, [1976] C.S. 1390 at 1394 (Que. S.C.) [our translation].

[233] *Hôpital Notre-Dame de l'Espérance c. Laurent*, [1974] J.Q. no 73, [1974] C.A. 543 (Que. C.A.), revd in part on another point [1977] S.C.J. No. 66, [1978] 1 S.C.R. 605 (S.C.C.).

[234] *Engstrom c. Courteau*, [1986] R.J.Q. 3048 (Que. S.C.).

[235] *Gburek c. Cohen*, [1988] J.Q. no 1693, [1988] R.J.Q. 2424 (Que. C.A.).

[236] *Suite c. Cooke*, [1995] J.Q. no 696, [1995] R.J.Q. 2765 (Que. C.A.).

must answer for damages resulting from having prevented the patient from pursuing active treatment for several years.[237]

On the other hand, an error in diagnosis will not give rise to liability if the physician has acted, given the circumstances, in a competent, diligent fashion. For example, a child diagnosed by the treating physician with having a viral infection following vaccination was in reality suffering from meningitis. In this case, two other physicians had arrived at the same conclusion. As a result, the treating physician was exonerated.[238] A similar finding occurred in the case of *Gendron c. Leduc*, where the physician, relying on the patient's statement that she had already undergone a hysterectomy, performed surgery for a cervical polyp and discovered in the course of the operation, an intact but atrophied uterus.[239]

When an error occurs, a conscientious physician must so inform the patient as soon as possible so that the diagnosis or treatment can be revised and physical or psychological harm can be avoided.[240]

It has been previously pointed out that fault is determined by taking into account the actual circumstances, including those of time and place, in which the physician is providing care. An immediate danger for the patient's life — an emergency in the strictest sense — may justify acts or omissions which, under different circumstances, would be totally unacceptable. This is illustrated in a case involving a patient in severe respiratory distress due to an asthma attack who had to be intubated in order to be saved. The perforation of the esophagus which resulted from the intubation did not lead to liability.[241]

---

[237] *Laferrière v. Lawson*, [1991] S.C.J. No. 18, [1991] 1 S.C.R. 541 (S.C.C.). The physician was held liable for the injury resulting from the moral suffering of the patient when she learned the truth, but not for her death since there was no proof that on a balance of probabilities his error had caused her death.

[238] *Tremblay c. Claveau*, [1990] J.Q. no 278, [1990] R.R.A. 268 (Que. C.A.).

[239] [1989] J.Q. no 304, [1989] R.R.A. 245 (Que. C.A.). See also other cases cited by Suzanne Philips-Nootens, Pauline Lesage-Jarjoura & Robert P. Kouri, *Éléments de responsabilité civile médicale — le droit dans le quotidien de la médecine*, 3d ed. (Cowansville, QC: Éditions Yvon Blais, 2007) at 47-48, para. 57, nn. 32-33 of their text.

[240] *Kiley-Nikkel c. Danais*, [1992] J.Q. no 1836, [1992] R.J.Q. 2820 (Que. S.C.): a woman underwent a mastectomy following the pathologist's error in diagnosis. The surgeon never told her the truth and she not only underwent unnecessary surgery, she also suffered the anguish of thinking she had cancer. Indeed, there is a duty to report any incident, accident or complication that may have a significant impact on the patient's state of health. See *Code of Ethics of Physicians*, R.R.Q., c. M-9, r. 17, s. 56. See also *Act Respecting Health Services and Social Services*, R.S.Q., c. S-4.2, s. 8.

[241] But there would be liability for having failed to attend the patient: *Harewood c. Spanier*, [1995] J.Q. no 2825, [1995] R.R.A. 147 (Que. S.C.), aff'd on the question of liability [2000] J.Q. no 4500, [2000] R.R.A. 864 (Que. C.A.).

Work in an emergency room has its own set of difficulties,[242] including and most notably, unfamiliarity with the patients. The courts take this fact into account, as illustrated in the case of *Bouchard c. Bergeron* in which it was readily acknowledged that: "The emergency room physician does not know the patient who seeks out his services; ... . He is not familiar with his habits, his character."[243] Yet the fact of practising in a university setting "with all the investigative equipment necessary, [a] hospital where there can be found physicians of all specialities"[244] will tend to impose a higher standard regarding the quality of care provided.

(b) Care in Keeping with Current Standards

The Code of Ethics of Physicians is clear: "A physician must practise his profession in accordance with the highest possible current medical standards; to this end, he must, in particular, develop, perfect and keep his knowledge and skills up to date."[245]

A surgeon practised a cholecystectomy on a female patient and later had occasion to reoperate on the patient in order to correct some adhesions. Following the second operation, the patient suffered an arterial thrombosis which left her hemiplegic. Not only was she a smoker, she was also on anovulants and the surgeon failed to advise her to stop smoking and taking the pill before the operation. A special committee created by the Government of Canada to study vascular complications linked to birth control pills had recommended that anovulants be discontinued prior to major surgery and this report had been distributed to all physicians. The defendant surgeon was thus unable to plead ignorance of its existence and was held liable for failing to have met current medical standards of practice.[246]

---

[242] *Savard (Succession de) c. Houle*, [2009] J.Q. no 1552, 2009 QCCS 795 at para. 165 (Que. S.C.): "... the primary function of an emergency physician is not to establish a final diagnosis but to ensure that the patient's life is not in danger. With this in mind, he must always assume the worst and eliminate the more serious pathologies before discharging the patient" [our translation].

[243] [1994] R.R.A. 967 at 979 (Que. S.C.) [our translation]. The physician did not recognize a rare neurological condition due especially to problems of communication with the patient.

[244] *Harewood c. Spanier*, [1995] J.Q. no 2825 at para. 159, [1995] R.R.A. 147 at 167 (Que. S.C.) [our translation], affd on the question of liability [2000] J.Q. no 4500, [2000] R.R.A. 864 (Que. C.A.). The physicians were liable for having failed to diagnose a perforation of the esophagus since they did not go further in the pursuit of a diagnosis. In *St-Jean c. Mercier*, [1999] J.Q. no 2584, [1999] R.J.Q. 1658 (Que. C.A.), affd [2002] S.C.J. No. 17, [2002] 1 S.C.R. 491 (S.C.C.), an orthopedist did not act in a conscientious manner when he neglected to perform a proper examination of a patient suffering from a spinal fracture. It is only due to a lack of causation that the physician was exonerated because the damage had already been suffered as a result of an accident.

[245] R.R.Q., c. M-9, r. 17, s. 44. According to *Aubin c. Moumdjian*, EYB-110126 at para. 23 (Que. S.C.), the standard to be followed is that generally in use in North America (affd [2006] Q.J. No. 12186, 2006 QCCA 1264 (Que. C.A.)).

[246] *Poulin c. Prat*, [1995] J.Q. no 1665, [1995] R.J.Q. 2923 (Que. S.C.), affd on the question of liability [1997] J.Q. no 3125, [1997] R.J.Q. 2669 (Que. C.A.).

In another tragic case, a physician specialized in the screening and treatment of breast cancer tended to utilize diagnostic techniques qualified as experimental such as "diaphanoscopy" and "thermography". In addition, he erroneously interpreted not only the standard tests to which he had recourse but also the more obvious clinical signs indicative of the presence of cancer. When his patient, who demanded a closer follow-up due to her fears regarding this particular type of cancer, finally decided to consult another surgeon, it was too late since her cancer was by then inoperable. For obvious reasons, her original physician was held liable.[247]

A physician is not required to systematically employ the most modern examinations or advanced treatment techniques. Only those which are considered part of standard practice at the time of the events in question are to have been applied. A gynaecologist who failed to propose that the patient undergo an alpha-fetoprotein test then considered experimental, was exonerated from all liability when her baby was born suffering from the same congenital defects (*hydrocephalus* and *meningocele*) as an older sibling.[248]

A physician, however, cannot rely on the defence of customary practice. A case in point involved a dentist who, like the majority of this profession at the time,[249] did not utilize a dental dam and thus failed to prevent the patient from accidentally swallowing a needle during surgery. He was found liable in damages due to this oversight. Thus a court may decide that an existing practice within a profession is not sufficiently secure.

There may exist a lack of unanimity within the medical profession regarding what constitutes best practice when several alternative approaches are available. In order to be recognized, the method adopted by the physician must be accepted by a significant proportion of the medical profession. As normally occurs in situations of this nature, courts must rely upon expert opinion. If the experts called are all credible but unable to reach a consensus, then the physician defendant will normally not be found liable as the plaintiff has failed to meet the burden of proof by a preponderance of the evidence.[250] The courts' role does not extend to resolving purely scientific controversies.

It is interesting to note that while very few decisions have actually found physicians liable for a simple lack of knowledge, the courts have instead tended to impute civil responsibility on the basis of negligence relating to what should or should not have been done in a particular case. In this regard, the issue of

---

[247] *Massinon c. Ghys*, [1996] J.Q. no 5632, [1996] R.J.Q. 2258 (Que. S.C.).

[248] *Bérard Guillette c. Maheux*, [1989] J.Q. no 841, [1989] R.J.Q. 1758 (Que. C.A.), leave to appeal refused [1989] C.S.C.R. no 344 (S.C.C.).

[249] *Boudreau-Gingras c. Gilbert*, J.E. 82-446 (Que. S.C.): 57 per cent of the practitioners did not install them.

[250] Alain Bernardot & Robert P. Kouri, *La responsabilité civile médicale* (Sherbrooke, QC: Éditions Revue de Droit Université de Sherbrooke, 1980) at 198 n. 290; Suzanne Philips-Nootens, Pauline Lesage-Jarjoura & Robert P. Kouri, *Éléments de responsabilité civile médicale — le droit dans le quotidien de la médecine*, 3d ed. (Cowansville, QC: Éditions Yvon Blais, 2007) at 55-58 nn. 69-70, at 269 n. 304 and cases cited.

professional incompetence *per se* seems to figure more often in disciplinary proceedings brought by the College of Physicians.[251]

(c) Care Provided within the Physician's Area of Competence

(i) The General Rule

The Code of Ethics of Physicians states:

> A physician must, in the practice of his profession, take into account his capacities, limitations and the means at his disposal. He must, if the interest of his patient requires it, consult a colleague, another professional or any competent person, or direct him to one of these persons.[252]

Since patients are entitled to receive the best care possible under the circumstances, a physician must not undertake treatment or interventions which exceed his or her personal qualifications or skills relative to the setting in which he or she is practising. Generally, the courts will compare a generalist to a generalist in light of current medical practice.[253] But if a general practitioner were to go beyond his or her field of practice, there is a strong possibility that he or she would be compared to a specialist to whom the patient should normally have been referred. In one case, a general practitioner, in attempting to treat a leg fracture, utilized an outdated technique contrary to the advice of a specialist called in for consultation. The Supreme Court refused to accept his plea that he was unfamiliar with the technique recommended.[254] Likewise, when a dentist undertook to provide treatments which obviously exceeded his level of competence, the court evaluated his professional behaviour in light of the standard expected of a specialist.[255] For their part, specialists sued in malpractice must prove that they possess the level of skill consonant with specialty practice and indeed, patients who consult specialists are entitled to expect a higher standard of competence. This point is emphasized in jurisprudence, particularly in the cases of *Rouillier c. Chesney*[256] and *Gordon c. Weiswall*.[257]

---

[251] Suzanne Philips-Nootens, Pauline Lesage-Jarjoura & Robert P. Kouri, *Éléments de responsabilité civile médicale — le droit dans le quotidien de la médecine*, *ibid.*, at 269 n. 303 and examples cited.

[252] R.R.Q., c. M-9, r. 17, s. 42.

[253] This point of view is changing over time since the custom of quickly referring patients to specialists has given way to a tendency of extending the scope of activities of general practitioners.

[254] *McCormick v. Marcotte*, [1972] S.C.J. No. 83, [1972] S.C.R. 18 (S.C.C.). Alain Bernardot & Robert P. Kouri, *La responsabilité civile médicale* (Sherbrooke, QC: Éditions Revue de Droit Université de Sherbrooke, 1980) at 179 n. 265.

[255] *Baker c. Silver*, [1998] J.Q. no 808, [1998] R.R.A. 321 (Que. C.A.).

[256] [1993] R.R.A. 528 (Que. S.C.).

[257] [1992] R.R.A. 815 (Que. S.C.).

(ii) Consultations

A physician may simply wish to benefit from another doctor's insight in order to receive guidance in a situation presenting certain difficulties, or a patient may desire the reassurance of a second opinion. In Quebec, it is unacceptable for a treating physician to refuse the patient's request. If a greater level of expertise than that possessed by the primary physician is required, or if the treating physician lacks the investigative tools necessary (radiology, gastroscopy, catheterization, *etc.*), there would have to be a consultation with a more competent or experienced colleague. By failing to do so or by refusing to transfer the patient to someone more qualified to provide the requisite care, the treating physician risks being held liable should complications arise.

The decision in *Camden-Bourgault c. Brochu*[258] is illustrative. After having fallen from a ladder, a male patient with a history of diabetes and vascular problems was taken to emergency. Despite suffering severe pain and being unable to put weight on his legs, the patient, diagnosed as having suffered a torn muscle, was provided with analgesics and then discharged. Two days later, the appearance of tissue necrosis led to the eventual amputation of both feet. The emergency physician was held to blame, not for an initial error in diagnosis but for having failed to consult specialists present in the hospital who were familiar with the patient, and for having inadequately provided for patient follow-up, given the circumstances. In another case, liability was attached to a defendant-physician who insisted on treating a patient with severe headache as a case of migraine, instead of immediately transferring the case to neurology, where the patient was eventually diagnosed as suffering from an aneurysm.[259]

In determining the liability of the parties involved, how should one analyze the relationship between the treating physician and the consultant? Obviously, it is important that there be a clear understanding between them not only so that their respective roles can be properly fulfilled but also in order to determine who will actually be in charge of the patient. Unless a patient has entered into a special agreement with the consultant, it is generally held that the physician of record will assume the duty to treat and to attend the patient.[260] Since the treating physician ultimately decides whether or not to follow the recommendations of

---

[258] [1996] J.Q. no 4586, [1996] R.R.A. 809 (Que. S.C.), affd [2001] J.Q. no 1327, [2001] R.R.A. 295 (Que. C.A.), leave to appeal refused [2001] C.S.C.R. no. 279 (S.C.C.).

[259] *Montpetit c. Léger*, [2000] J.Q. no 3119, [2000] R.J.Q. 2582 (Que. S.C.). To the same effect: *Chouinard c. Robbins*, [1998] J.Q. no 3507, [1999] R.R.A. 65 (Que. S.C.), revd on other grounds [2001] J.Q. no 6081, [2002] R.J.Q. 60 (Que. C.A.) (diagnosis that the patient was psychotic but failure to refer the case to a psychiatrist). Other physicians have been sanctioned by the disciplinary committee of the College of Physicians of Quebec; see more particularly the cases cited in Suzanne Philips-Nootens, Pauline Lesage-Jarjoura & Robert P. Kouri, *Éléments de responsabilité civile médicale — le droit dans le quotidien de la médecine*, 3d ed. (Cowansville, QC: Éditions Yvon Blais, 2007) at 285 n. 322.

[260] The mere fact of authorizing an interference with one's right of inviolability when permission is granted to a consultant to examine the patient does not *per se* constitute the conclusion of a new contract.

the consultant, traditional doctrine posits that the physician of record alone will assume liability for errors committed by the consultant.[261] Some argue, however, that this point of view must be qualified in light of current medical practices characterized by an information explosion and by the development of very advanced fields of specialization. How can one expect a treating physician who consults a more competent colleague, precisely in order to benefit from his or her greater knowledge, to be in a position to evaluate the opinion advanced by the specialist? Could it not be argued that each physician enjoys a certain independence within his or her own sphere of activity and would logically assume liability only for medical acts performed within that realm? According to this point of view, the physician of record would be liable for coordinating the care provided by himself or herself in light of the recommendations of the consultant, whereas each consultant would answer only for examinations or treatments personally administered[262] or for treatment recommendations expressed to the treating physician. Beyond being responsible for his or her own acts, the physician of record would also be liable, along with the specialist, for any error which could have been detected by both of them such as an improperly taken X-ray or a grossly erroneous medication dosage.

In cases of disagreement between the treating physician and the consultant, the physician of record is free to follow or to disregard the recommendations of the physician called in for consultation, but would do so at his or her own risk since no part of the blame could be passed on to the consultant.[263] If need be, in case of uncertainty as to treatment options, nothing would prevent seeking an additional opinion from, for example, an *ad hoc* medical committee struck for this purpose.[264]

The courts have not yet had occasion to express an opinion on the division of tasks and of liability between the treating physician and the consultant. As can be seen from the jurisprudence cited above, the decided cases appear to deal mainly with issues such as the failure to consult, of not following the opinion of the consultant or of failure to provide adequate follow-up.

The traditional physician-patient relationship may undergo certain transformations resulting from the fact that diagnosis and treatment may be provided by a person who is not physically present. We refer, of course, to telemedicine.

---

[261] Alain Bernardot & Robert P. Kouri, *La responsabilité civile médicale* (Sherbrooke, QC: Éditions Revue de Droit Université de Sherbrooke, 1980) at 179 n. 265; Jean-Pierre Ménard & Denise Martin, *La responsabilité médicale pour la faute d'autrui* (Cowansville, QC: Éditions Yvon Blais, 1992) at 40.

[262] See *Therrien c. Launay*, [2005] J.Q. no 5303 at para. 466, [2005] R.R.A. 349 at 403 (Que. S.C.), affd [2005] J.Q. no 9043, J.E. 2005-1345 (Que. C.A.), leave to appeal refused [2005] C.S.C.R. no 427 (S.C.C.).

[263] Jean-Pierre Ménard & Denise Martin, *La responsabilité médicale pour la faute d'autrui* (Cowansville, QC: Éditions Yvon Blais, 1992) at 45; Suzanne Philips-Nootens, Pauline Lesage-Jarjoura & Robert P. Kouri, *Éléments de responsabilité civile médicale — le droit dans le quotidien de la médecine*, 3d ed. (Cowansville, QC: Éditions Yvon Blais, 2007) at 291 n. 331.

[264] *Tremblay c. Claveau*, [1990] J.Q. no 278, [1990] R.R.A. 268 (Que. C.A.).

2.   A New Way of Practising: Telemedicine

As a new phenomenon, telemedicine is assuming greater importance in medical practice and is undoubtedly changing the traditional manner of providing care.[265] Due to its various applications, this notion can be defined in several ways. Telehealth in general is said to apply to all diagnostic, therapeutic and consultative medical services provided from a distance through modern technology[266] whereas telemedicine involves the practice of medicine from a distance by means of telecommunication.[267]

These definitions thus emphasize an important aspect of telemedicine or telehealth, which one may call the "delocalization" of medical practice. The physician and the patient are not in the same physical location. This occurs for instance in cases of telesurgery, or when the treating physician consults a specialist in another location through transmission of radiological images or other data for interpretation. There can also be telesurveillance or telemonitoring of a patient at home or elsewhere, or "telementoring" by an experienced surgeon of a less experienced colleague, *etc.* Since the rules governing civil liability[268] are usually determined by the place where the injurious act occurred, where in reality would each medical act be deemed to have been performed in cases such as these? There is a disquieting lack of unanimity on this question.[269] Certain American states have decided that the act will be considered as having been performed where the patient is located. This opinion, while being held by the Federation of Medical Regulatory Authorities of Canada, is not generally adhered to in all provinces. Indeed, in the Province of Quebec, the *Act Respecting Health Services and Social Services* stipulates that "telehealth services are considered provided at the place where the health or social services professional who was consulted practises".[270] We feel however that since medical acts necessarily have

---

[265] Agency for Health Services and Technology Assessment, *Télésanté et télémédecine au Québec — état de la question* (Montreal: CÉTS, 1998).

[266] *Act Respecting Health Services and Social Services*, R.S.Q., c. S-4.2, s. 108.1, para. 3, telehealth services include "a healthy or social services-related activity, service or system that is practised, provided or delivered in Québec from a distance for educational, diagnostic or treatment purposes or for purposes of research, clinical management or training, using information aned communications technologies".

[267] The College of Physicians of Quebec, *Telemedicine, Background Paper*, online at: <http://www.cmq.org/en/Public/Profil/Commun/AProposOrdre/Publications/~/media/624CD6B 46CC94CA2B0B374790B888209.ashx?sc_lang=en&21119> at 2.

[268] As well as permits to practise and all related aspects such as hospital privileges, *etc.*

[269] See, generally, Robert P. Kouri & Sophie Brisson, « Les incertitudes juridictionnelles en télémédecine, où est posé l'acte médical? » (2005) 35 R.D.U.S. 521; Frédéric Pérodeau, « La télémedecine: enjeux juridiques et déontologiques » in Service de formation permanente, Barreau du Québec, *Tendances en droit de la santé*, vol. 287 (Cowansville, QC: Éditions Yvon Blais, 2008) 43 at 56*ff.*; Mylène Beaupré, « Réflexions sur l'encadrement juridique de la télésanté après la loi 83 » in Service de formation continue, Barreau du Québec, *Après le projet de loi 83 : un nouveau réseau de la santé*, vol. 260 (Cowansville, QC: Éditions Yvon Blais, 2006) 85.

[270] R.S.Q., c. S-4.2, s. 108.2.

only one focal point, namely the patient, the patient's location should have been retained as determinant.

Issues concerning the *situs* of the act notwithstanding, the specific standards established for each branch of telemedicine must also be taken into consideration in establishing fault. In his or her utilization of this new medical tool, has the physician acted in conformity with standard practices? Moreover, given the opportunities afforded by telemedicine, it could even be possible to fault a physician for not having had recourse to these tools if the required equipment were indeed available and if he or she possessed the skills and training to benefit therefrom.[271]

Teleconsultations are presently the most often utilized forms of telemedicine. We have already described the nature of the relationship between the treating physician and the consultant under normal circumstances, but in consultations through telecommunication, the process is not quite the same since the consultant does not actually meet the patient but can, on occasion, ask him or her questions. The necessity of providing the consultant with all pertinent information in the possession of the physician of record assumes greater importance, as does the decision to follow or disregard the recommendations of the consultant. For his or her part, the consultant must decline to offer an opinion if there are insufficient elements necessary to make a proper evaluation of the case. Otherwise, the consultant could be deemed to have acted negligently and thus held liable. In attributing fault, one would have to analyze the nature of the acts performed by each participant according to the type of consultation. An act falling within the specialty of the consultant (radiology or tissue analysis, for example) would engage only his or her liability, unless, here also, there was negligence on the part of the treating physician in communicating information or in taking certain decisions following the consultation. One should note that Quebec courts have not yet been called upon to decide these issues.

What would occur if the equipment used proved defective? In matters of teleconsultation, the equipment itself cannot directly cause harm to the patient since it serves only as a means of exchanging information between two or more physicians. These physicians must thus refrain from issuing opinions on the basis of images or data of inferior quality. On the other hand, in cases such as surgical operations performed from a distance, or home-surveillance, should a device injure the patient, liability for the act of a thing could come into play.[272]

Obviously, the whole field of telemedicine requires the elaboration of specific rules in order to answer these and similar questions,[273] especially with regard to international or cross-border practices.

---

[271] College of Physicians of Quebec, online at: <http://www.cmq.org/en/Public/Profil/Commun/AproposOrdre/Publications/~/media/624CD6B46CC94CA2B0B374790B888209.ashx?sc_lang=en&21119> at 5.

[272] Arts. 1465, 1468-1469 C.C.Q.

[273] Sabrina Hasham, Rajen Akalu & Peter Rossos, "Medico-legal Implications of Telehealth in Canada" (2003-2004) 4 Telehealth Law 9.

B.   THE DUTY TO ATTEND

1.   Nature of the Duty

The duty to attend falls within the purview of the duty to treat. Section 5 of the *Act Respecting Health Services and Social Services*[274] establishes the right to continuity in the provision of services. Likewise, the Code of Ethics of Physicians states:

> A physician who can no longer provide the required medical follow-up of a patient must, before ceasing to do so, ensure that the patient can continue to receive the required care and contribute thereto to the extent necessary.[275]

In essence, this obligation is founded upon the duty not to abandon the patient once treatment has been initiated, whether the duty to treat results from contract or by sole operation of law in the absence of a contractual relationship. A number of disciplinary decisions have sanctioned physicians for failing to respect this fundamental obligation.[276] Emergency practice, the custodial role of institutions, a proliferation in the number of consultations requested and the shortening of hospital stays have all produced a need to pay greater attention to this aspect of the doctor-patient relationship. Is it acceptable for a hospitalized patient to be unable to identify his or her treating physician?

As in the case of the duty to treat, the duty to attend must, as a rule, be assumed personally by the treating physician. Yet it is a well-known common practice in university settings that post-operative follow-up, for example, is generally provided by the surgical residents who remain under the control and responsibility of the surgeon having actually performed the operation. Since it is the surgeon's duty that is being fulfilled by others, this calls into play the principles of liability for the act of another to which we have alluded above. The same general rule applies to developments occurring in the course of treatment: the physician must respond to calls from medical personnel or from residents who feel that the treating physician's intervention is required. The same principle

---

[274] R.S.Q., c. S-4.2, s. 5: "Every person is entitled to receive, with continuity and in a personalized and safe manner, health services and social services which are scientifically, humanly and socially appropriate." For a striking illustration of a violation of this duty in a hospital setting, see *Lacombe c. Hôpital Maisonneuve-Rosemont*, [2004] J.Q. no 423 at paras. 37 and 38, [2004] R.R.A. 138 at 142 (Que. S.C.) (an elderly woman suffering respiratory problems was left unattended on a stretcher in a hospital corridor for four hours during the night).

[275] R.R.Q., c. M-9, r. 17, s. 35.

[276] *Girard c. Ordre professionnel des médecins du Québec*, [1995] D.T.P.Q. no 106, [1995] D.D.O.P. 259 (T.P.): a detainee in a police station deemed a malingerer by the physician who refused to administer treatment even though the patient was in shock; *Collège des médecins du Québec c. Blitte*, [1998] D.T.P.Q. no 154, [1998] D.D.O.P. 321 (T.P.): a cardiologist leaves for two months, merely leaving a message on his answering machine; *Ordre professionnel des médecins c. Pelletier*, [2005] D.D.O.P. 160 (C.D. Méd.): a rheumatologist who agreed to provide a patient with a written evaluation failed to do so despite promises to this effect and who also failed to keep numerous appointments. Fortunately, these are rare examples.

applies to specialists on call who must be available to provide support to general practitioners or emergency physicians who are in need of assistance.[277]

Ensuring an attentive follow-up implies that the physician must provide the patient, or those within the patient's entourage, sufficient indication of what is expected of them such as, for example, the medication to be taken or the signs and symptoms which could signal a complication or deterioration. The particular complaints and anxieties of the patient must also be given serious consideration, as is illustrated in the case of *Drolet c. Parenteau*.[278] A female patient lost the sight in one eye following plastic surgery on her eyelids (bilateral blepharoplasty). The surgeon disregarded certain symptoms which presented in the hours and days following surgery and thus overlooked the incipient indications of a rare but serious and well-known complication. Moreover, due to the insufficiency of instructions given to those close to the patient who were physicians in their own right, they failed to react in time.[279] In another case, a woman called the attention of her gynaecologist to a birthmark on her right buttock but he did not attach any importance to the presence of this lesion. She died three years later as a result of a generalized melanoma for which her gynaecologist was held liable, the court refusing to lend credence to his argument that it was the duty of his patient to have reminded him of her problem![280]

Because it is impossible to be available at all times, physicians tend to practise as a group. In this type of situation, even if the patient has a regular physician, he or she could, at any time, be attended by another member of the group who would have access to the medical record and to all other pertinent information relating to that patient. Arrangements of this kind greatly facilitate the organization and division of work and thus provide a greater sense of security to the client. On the other hand, should complications arise in the course of treatment, group practice may make it more difficult to establish the liability of those involved when the patient has in fact been seen by various members of the group. In order to establish solidary liability under these circumstances, each debtor of the duty to care for the patient must have committed a prejudicial fault[281] or, more clearly stated, must actually have been involved in administering treatment.[282] Under article 1525, para. 3 of the *Civil Code of Québec*, the exploitation of a group practice clinic constitutes the carrying on of "an organ-

---

[277] The sanctions imposed in these cases are most often disciplinary, dealt with at a local level in the institution. Nevertheless, see *Bédard c. Gauthier*, [1996] R.R.A. 860 (Que. C.Q.), in which a specialist, pleading fatigue, refused to answer calls from his colleagues.

[278] [1994] J.Q. no 167, [1994] R.J.Q. 689 (Que. C.A.), revg in part [1991] J.Q. no 2583, [1991] R.J.Q. 2956 (Que. S.C.): found liable only for having failed to attend and not for any fault in treatment.

[279] *Ibid.*, at 701 (Que. C.A.).

[280] *Stunell c. Pelletier*, [1999] J.Q. no 4992, [1999] R.J.Q. 2863 (Que. S.C.).

[281] Art. 1523 C.C.Q.; Suzanne Philips-Nootens, Pauline Lesage-Jarjoura & Robert P. Kouri, *Éléments de responsabilité civile médicale — le droit dans le quotidien de la médecine*, 3d ed. (Cowansville, QC: Éditions Yvon Blais, 2007) at 340 n.395.

[282] Suzanne Philips-Nootens, Pauline Lesage-Jarjoura & Robert P. Kouri, *Éléments de responsabilité civile médicale — le droit dans le quotidien de la médecine, ibid.*

ized economic activity" and on this basis legal solidarity exists between its members. Since the summer of 2001, the Quebec government has adopted a policy of actively encouraging family practitioners to engage in group practice as one of its priorities within a more general approach to reforming the health care system.[283]

Walk-in clinics established through private initiative also constitute an alternative means of offering health services. They enable persons suffering from less serious conditions to avoid having to attend hospital emergency rooms. However, by their very nature, they raise certain legal dilemmas including the determination of who is the actual treating physician and who will ensure adequate follow-up of the patient. If the physician practising in this type of setting is responsible for the medical acts performed, he or she is working in conditions quite analogous to that of an emergency room physician since in both settings, neither usually knows the patient. It is felt that the courts will tend to take these circumstances under consideration in order to determine whether or not a medical fault has occurred.[284]

Another recent phenomenon in relation to the provision of health services — the development of home care — involves opportunities resulting from advances in technology and a concomitant desire on the part of the government to reduce the costs of these services. It is obviously more comforting for a patient to be treated in his or her home provided this environment is conducive to adequate care and does not impose an excessive burden on the family. The system of follow-up must ensure that given the situation of the patient and his or her entourage, adequate care can be provided.[285] This type of determination concerns not only the physician; nursing, social services, and local community health centres must also be involved. In cases of injury in the home care setting, one must prove the fault of one or several of these persons as well as a causal link with the injury in order to establish liability.

2.   Suspension and Termination of the Duty to Attend

A physician cannot always be at the beck and call of a patient. He or she is entitled to a personal and family life, to enjoy holidays and even to be indisposed on occasion. Consequently, there must be a system established in order to ensure adequate coverage of patients. Under certain circumstances, it may become necessary to transfer the patient to the care of a more specialized practitioner or to a physician who is in a better position to provide proper treatment. Greater spe-

---

[283] Quebec, Commission of Study on Health and Social Services, *Emerging Solutions — Report and Recommendations* (Quebec: Ministère de la Santé et des Services Sociaux, Direction des Communications, 2001) [Clair Report].

[284] See Section IV(A)(1)(a), "Conscientious and Attentive Care", which was discussed earlier.

[285] See more particularly Jean-Pierre Ménard, « Virage ambulatoire et responsabilité médicale et hospitalière » in Service de la Formation Permanente du Barreau du Québec, *Développements récents en responsabilité médicale et hospitalière 1999*, vol. 125 (Cowansville, QC: Éditions Yvon Blais, 1999) at 109.

cialization in medicine, various modalities of practice in the hospital setting and walk-in clinics all give rise to situations where the replacement of physicians or the transfer of patients may occur.

(a) Temporary Replacement

When the replacement of a physician is only temporary, the physician who is replaced normally reassumes responsibility for the patient upon his or her return. The patient must be properly informed of the fact that the treating physician will be temporarily replaced, the duration of this replacement, the identity and quali-fications of the replacing physician and the possibility of retaining the services of another physician if the patient so desires. In the context of individual prac-tice, the physician must be diligent in the choice of a replacement so that in his or her absence, the patient will receive uninterrupted adequate care. The physi-cian must provide the replacement with all necessary information in order that the latter can properly fulfil his or her tasks. In this regard, the medical record must be clear and complete. As for the replacing physician or *locum tenens*, he or she assumes all the duties of the physician replaced and must ensure continu-ity of care in a diligent and competent manner. The replacement must refrain from undertaking new initiatives unless the condition of the patient so requires since it is not for him or her to unduly interfere with treatment already initiated unless an obvious error has been discovered. When the period of replacement has come to an end, the replacing physician must in turn provide the original physi-cian with all pertinent information arising from his or her attendance upon the patient.

There are very few cases dealing with replacement *per se*. A less recent Quebec decision found that a physician was liable for the injury caused to a pa-tient as a result of his replacement's failure to respond to a patient's calls.[286] Certain writers have sought to justify this point of view,[287] whereas other have raised doubts as to its validity, arguing that each physician involved should be answerable only for his or her own fault because the contract existing between the treating physician and the patient should be deemed suspended during the interval of replacement. Interestingly enough, this approach has received some measure of support. In the case of *De Bogyay c. Royal Victoria Hospital*,[288] for example, the Court of Appeal held that the replacing physician, and not the treating physician who was on vacation, would be liable for the suicide of a pa-tient. This decision even held that a second contract had been concluded be-tween the patient and the physician acting as a replacement.

---

[286] *Bergstrom c. G.*, [1967] C.S. 513 (Que. S.C.).

[287] Alain Bernardot & Robert P. Kouri, *La responsabilité civile médicale* (Sherbrooke, QC: Éditions Revue de Droit Université de Sherbrooke, 1980) at 186 n. 276.

[288] [1987] J.Q. no 1413, [1987] R.R.A. 613 (Que. C.A.). In this case, the replacement physician was exonerated since there had been no fault on his part. See also *Drapeau-Gourd c. Power*, J.E. 82-424 (Que. S.C.).

(b) Permanent Transfer

There can be no possible doubt in the case of a permanent transfer that the relationship between the treating physician and the patient is terminated and a new legal relationship is entered into with the physician to whom the patient is transferred, provided of course the second physician is willing to assume responsibility for this patient. A simple request for a transfer in itself is insufficient; the doctor approached must agree to take on the patient:

> A physician who wishes to refer a patient to another physician must assume responsibility for that patient until the new physician takes responsibility for the latter.[289]

All pertinent information must be provided to the new physician in order that he or she can properly treat the patient and ensure continuity of care. One must be particularly careful in cases where the actual transfer poses risks for the patient in light of his or her health status. For example, one must ensure that the patient can be transported safely. The case of *Lapointe v. Hôpital Le Gardeur*[290] is very eloquent in this connection. A four-year-old child suffered an injury to her arm and was bleeding profusely. She was transported to a first hospital, Le Gardeur, where the physician on call administered first aid and decided to transfer the patient to a pediatric hospital because of a lack of resources necessary to perform the required surgery. A certain amount of confusion arose during the actual transfer. The child suffered a cardio-respiratory arrest, was resuscitated but sustained significant permanent *sequelae*. The Supreme Court of Canada overturned the Court of Appeal and re-established the decision of the trial judge exonerating the first physician since he was found not to have committed any fault under the circumstances.[291]

C.   PROFESSIONAL SECRECY AND MEDICAL RECORDS

We will allude briefly to these two elements inherent in the physician-patient relationship for purposes of information only since no exceptional rules of civil liability are involved.

1.   Professional Secrecy

Professional secrecy has always been a cornerstone of medical deontology. As the present Code of Ethics of Physicians provides: A physician "must keep confidential the information obtained in the practice of his profession".[292] As a corollary to the right of privacy and respect of human dignity, this duty is specifically recog-

---

[289] Code of Ethics of Physicians, R.R.Q., c. M-9, r. 17, s. 33.
[290] [1992] S.C.J. No. 11, [1992] 1 S.C.R. 351 (S.C.C.).
[291] Likewise: *Green (Curator to) v. Surchin*, [1993] Q.J. No. 1865, [1993] R.R.A. 821 (Que. S.C.), affd [1997] Q.J. No. 198, [1997] R.R.A. 39 (Que. C.A.), leave to appeal refused [1997] C.S.C.R. no 122 (S.C.C.).
[292] R.R.Q., c. M-9, r. 17, s. 20(1).

nized by the Quebec *Charter of Human Rights and Freedoms*,[293] and as such is considered a fundamental right. Its scope is extensive, encompassing all information having come to the physician's knowledge in the course of his or her professional activities.

Since the right to secrecy is vested in the patient, he or she has the right to expressly or tacitly allow certain confidential information to be released. For instance, a patient may request that the physician communicate pertinent information to a colleague for purposes of consultation or for effecting a transfer. Similarly, the information can be included in a medical certificate or report intended for an employer or an insurance company in furtherance of a claim. A tacit renunciation to confidentiality in favour of close family members may be inferred from their presence during consultation or treatment, unless, of course, the patient objects. One cannot, however, presuppose a tacit renunciation by the mere fact that the patient is obliged to provide information to clerical staff at a reception desk within the hearing of others in facilities poorly designed to ensure privacy.

Certain situations, by their very nature, allow for the divulgation of confidential information without the patient's authorization. Indeed, several laws provide for this possibility.[294] Likewise, by the mere fact of initiating a malpractice suit against a physician, pertinent medical information may be revealed since everyone has the right to a full defence. The trial judge enjoys, in this regard, broad discretionary powers concerning the admissibility of information normally protected.[295] On the other hand, when a physician is summoned to testify in judicial proceedings other than in a malpractice suit brought by his or her patient, the legal situation remains far from clear. Certain judgments have held that the decision to breach confidentiality falls within the sole discretion of the physician. We feel that the better approach would be for the judge to decide what information is essential for the proper administration of justice within the framework of the litigation pending before the court.[296]

The Code of Ethics of Physicians itself provides that in addition to the reasons alluded to above, it is not possible to reveal confidential information "except when the patient or the law authorizes him to do so, or when there are compelling and just grounds related to the health or safety of the patient or of others".[297] Since the Code of Ethics of Physicians specifically states "may not reveal", this implies that the decision to reveal is left to the physician's discretion in certain cases where, for example, there may be a need to ensure proper

---

[293] R.S.Q., c. C-12, s. 9.

[294] See, for example, *Youth Protection Act*, R.S.Q., c. P-34.1; *Public Health Act*, R.S.Q., c. S-2.2; *Highway Safety Code*, R.S.Q., c. C-24.2.

[295] *Goulet c. Lussier*, [1989] J.Q. no 1204, [1989] R.J.Q. 2085 (Que. C.A.).

[296] Suzanne Philips-Nootens, Pauline Lesage-Jarjoura & Robert P. Kouri, *Éléments de responsabilité civile médicale — le droit dans le quotidien de la médecine*, 3d ed. (Cowansville, QC: Éditions Yvon Blais, 2007) at 369-370 nn. 420-421; *Société d'habitation du Québec v. Hébert*, [2004] J.Q. no 3192, [2004] R.R.A. 446 (Que. S.C.).

[297] R.R.Q., c. M-9, r. 17, s. 20(5). See also s. 21.

surveillance by the family of a depressive patient or of a patient requiring special monitoring following surgery. Moreover, legislation undoubtedly inspired
by the Supreme Court's decision in *Smith v. Jones*[298] allows professionals governed by the *Professional Code*[299] to "communicate information that is protected
by professional secrecy, in order to prevent an act of violence, including a suicide, where ... there is an imminent danger of death or serious bodily injury to a
person or to an identifiable group of persons". The question is much more difficult when it becomes necessary to go against the wishes of a non-violent patient
who represents nonetheless a risk for persons close to him or her due to a particular medical condition such as a sexually transmitted disease, HIV or the danger of a genetically transmissible condition. A physician could be faced with the
choice of either actually warning third parties and being exposed to a suit by a
patient whose right to secrecy has been violated, or else remaining silent and
being sued by those close to the patient who may have suffered harm due to the
physician's failure to warn. We feel that as the better of two alternatives, doctors
should choose in favour of protecting the life and health of others.[300]

2.   The Medical Record

As an indispensable component of good medical practice, as well as a means of
evaluating the quality of care, physicians are obliged to keep accurate records in
accordance with several statutory and regulatory provisions that deal with the
drafting and maintaining of medical records. These provisions include the *Act*

---

[298] [1999] S.C.J. No. 15, [1999] 1 S.C.R. 455 (S.C.C.), involving the issue whether a psychiatrist
retained by defendant's counsel in order to assist in preparing an accused's defence, would be allowed to reveal the fact that the individual was a sexual sadist likely to commit future offences of
a violent nature.

[299] R.S.Q., c. C-26, s. 60.4.

[300] Suzanne Philips-Nootens, Pauline Lesage-Jarjoura & Robert P. Kouri, *Éléments de responsabilité civile médicale — le droit dans le quotidien de la médecine*, 3d ed. (Cowansville, QC: Éditions
Yvon Blais, 2007) at 377 n. 426. Indeed, in the recent decision of *Liss v. Watters*, [2010] Q.J.
No. 7176, 2010 QCCS 3309 (Que. S.C.), presently under appeal (involving the duty of physicians to warn close relatives of the danger of transmitting Pelizaeus-Merzbacher Disease, a sex-
linked disorder affecting the brain and spinal cord of male offspring), the court went beyond affirming that a physician may ethically and legally inform third persons who could be affected by
critical genetic information. It held (at paras. 65 and 69):

> Based on general civil law principles, it seems obvious that where a physician has
> personal knowledge of and some form of contact with third persons affected by critical
> genetic information, he is manifestly within a radius of contact that would impose the ob-
> ligation to inform on him, particularly where there is only a small number of third per-
> sons involved. What reasonable person, physician or not, would not feel the need to warn
> such persons in those circumstances? ...
>
>   . . . . .
>
> [The physician] cannot rest until he has done everything reasonable to ensure that his pa-
> tient comprehends both the hereditary nature of the illness and the absolute need to share
> the information with other family members who might also be affected. Failure to take
> the necessary steps to that end constitutes a negligent omission and a civil fault.

Respecting Health Services and Social Services[301] and its regulations, the *Act Respecting Access to Documents Held by Public Bodies and the Protection of Personal Information*[302] and the *Act Respecting the Protection of Personal Information in the Private Sector.*[303] Quebec has, in effect, tended to focus on the need to safeguard privacy in its approach to legislation in this regard.

The question of ownership of medical records has been the subject of some debate in the past, but the Supreme Court of Canada appears to have resolved this issue in *McInerney v. MacDonald*[304] by deciding that while medical records, as repositories of information for purposes of treatment, should belong to the physician, the clinic or the hospital establishment, the patient has a vital interest in and a right of access to the information contained therein. As beneficiary of the right to confidentiality, the patient can waive this right and allow others to take cognizance of the medical file. At first glance, the Supreme Court of Canada, in *Frenette v. Metropolitan Life Insurance Co.*,[305] appears to have broadly interpreted authorizations of this kind in favour of insurance companies.[306] However, in its more recent decision in *Glegg v. Smith & Nephew Inc.*,[307] the Court narrowed the ambit of this holding. It held that by initiating a malpractice action involving issues of pain and suffering, shock and nervousness, the patient had granted an implied waiver of confidentiality regarding production of her psychiatric record. According to LeBel J.:

> [*Frenette v. Metropolitan Life Insurance Co.*] did not establish a principle that an express or implied waiver would authorize unlimited and uncontrolled access to a patient's medical record. On the contrary, the limits on secrecy are reflected in the principle of relevance, which applies at all stages of a civil action.[308]

Accordingly, the pertinence of the information to which access is requested, in light of the specific purposes for which it is intended, shall determine the extent to which access will in fact be provided, notwithstanding the generality of the terms in which the authorization is couched. The issue is thus reduced to one of ensuring, as much as possible given the circumstances, the protection of a fundamental right, while favouring a just outcome between the parties.

---

[301] R.S.Q., c. S-4.2.

[302] R.S.Q., c. A-2.1.

[303] R.S.Q., c. P-39.1.

[304] [1992] S.C.J. No. 57, [1992] 2 S.C.R. 138 (S.C.C.).

[305] [1992] S.C.J. No. 24, [1992] 1 S.C.R. 647 (S.C.C.).

[306] According to L'Heureux-Dubé J., writing on behalf of the Court: "A patient's right to the confidentiality of his medical records is a relative right which a patient may waive without restriction as to scope or time" (*ibid.*, at 695). In addition, when a clear waiver has been given, "the holder of the right has, of his own accord, put aside his privacy [... and therefore] no balancing of interests in necessary" (*ibid.*, at 678).

[307] [2005] S.C.J. No. 29, [2005] 1 S.C.R. 724 (S.C.C.).

[308] *Ibid.*, at para. 21.

V.   CONCLUSION

The liability of physicians is governed by the general rules of civil responsibility as set out by the *Civil Code of Québec* and its interpretation by jurisprudence and doctrine. Certain trends have emerged, transforming the physician-patient relationship, and making doctors more conscious of patient's rights. The development of the notion of informed consent by the courts is a case in point. By its nature, the medical contract will always remain an association built essentially on trust.

Despite a readily discernible tendency to treat the patient as an active participant in what has become a collaborative and egalitarian relationship, successfully suing a hospital or physician remains a very expensive and a highly unpredictable undertaking. Certain simplistic solutions such as attenuating the burden of proof in medical malpractice cases or imposing a much higher standard of conduct on the members of one of the most extensively regulated occupations in Canada would be highly inequitable. It is undeniable that pressures are building in Quebec to institute a no-fault system of indemnification for victims of medical misadventure. For the moment, the economic burden of such a system would appear to be the primary obstacle to its implementation.

Chapter 6

HEALTH INFORMATION: CONFIDENTIALITY AND ACCESS

Elaine Gibson

I. INTRODUCTION

The Canadian prototype for health information has been physician notes, recorded on paper in the course of or following a face-to-face interaction with a patient, and stored in cardboard files in large metal filing cabinets either in physicians' offices or in hospitals. The body of jurisprudence and legislation developed over time for such a circumstance was, if not straightforward, at least reasonably coherent. But the health information world has changed dramatically over the past 50 years. Not only is the physician-patient model no longer the dominant model, it has been eclipsed by such developments as multiplication of types of health professions, team-based practice, digitized billing records, electronic health records, telehealth, telerobotics and telesurgery, tissue samples rich in genetic information, commercial practice and research. Each of these developments presents challenges with which the law must grapple. As we shall see in this chapter, sometimes laws are more successful than at other times in coping with the brave new world of modern health information.

Most of the legal protections for health information are based in statute. There are, however, some significant areas carved out in common law.

This chapter commences with a discussion of confidentiality, and then of ownership, custodianship and the right of access to one's own information. The *Canadian Charter of Rights and Freedoms*[1] has had a strong influence on law in this area, particularly but not exclusively in the area of criminal law. A discussion of the Charter is followed by an overview of the types of legislation, both federal and provincial, as well as jurisdictional issues in the areas of health and of information.

Next I examine consensual and non-consensual collection, use and disclosure of health information. A number of exceptions to confidentiality have been carved out to satisfy the apparent requirements of various sectors of society, such as child protection and legal proceedings. In some circumstances there is a duty to disclose and in others, disclosure is permitted but not mandated.

---

[1] Part 1 of the *Constitution Act, 1982*, being Schedule B to the *Canada Act 1982* (U.K.), 1982, c. 11 [Charter].

The last part of the chapter briefly highlights a number of contemporary areas of controversy, including electronic health information, globalization trends, use of newborn blood spots for research, and personalized medicine. These areas push the limits in terms of our traditional conceptions of health information, and give rise to questions as to whether particular uses, often without the consent of the subjects of such information, are legitimate.

II. CONFIDENTIALITY

The duty of confidentiality in the context of provision of health care services has a long and venerable history in ethics and in law. In 1928, the Supreme Court of Canada in *Halls v. Mitchell* incorporated into common law the essence of the Hippocratic Oath, ruling in the context of physician-patient relations that:

> Nobody would dispute that a secret [acquired in the course of a medical practitioner's practice] is the secret of the patient and, normally, is under his control, and not under that of the doctor. Prima facie, the patient has the right to require that the secret shall not be divulged; and that right is absolute, unless there is some paramount reason which overrides it.[2]

Specifically, the Hippocratic Oath states that "whatsoever I shall see or hear in the course of my profession … if it be what should not be published abroad, I will never divulge".[3] Thus, in the case of personal information garnered in the course of physician practice, one commences with the premise that this information is to be kept confidential.[4] The principle underlying this practice was discussed in *Halls v. Mitchell* as follows:

> It is, perhaps, not easy to exaggerate the value attached by the community as a whole to the existence of a competently trained and honourable medical profession; and it is just as important that patients, in consulting a physician, shall feel that they may disclose the facts touching their bodily health, without fear that their confidence may be abused to their disadvantage.[5]

The same logic underlying this principle applies to personal information acquired not just by physicians but throughout the health care system, in that trust that one's information will not be broadcast indiscriminately is

---

[2]   [1928] S.C.J. No. 1, [1928] S.C.R. 125 at 136 (S.C.C.). Note that, despite the strong language, the majority finds that the information at issue was not in fact confidential, having been conveyed to an official in order to obtain information. The reference to confidentiality of personal health information was being used in contrast and is therefore *obiter*.

[3]   *Hippocrates*, W.H.S. Jones, trans. (Cambridge: Harvard University Press, 1923). Cited in M. Marshall & B. von Tigerstrom, "Health Information" in Jocelyn Downie, Timothy Caulfield & Colleen Flood, eds., *Canadian Health Law and Policy*, 2d ed. (Markham, ON: LexisNexis Canada, 2002) at 190.

[4]   Confidentiality is the obligation of the third party holder of information to respect its secrecy. Privacy is more difficult to define in that it is nuanced and subject to multiple interpretations, but there is general agreement that it focuses on the individual or group and not on a third party.

[5]   [1928] S.C.J. No. 1, [1928] S.C.R. 125 at 138 (S.C.C.).

fundamental to patients feeling comfortable in revealing deeply personal and private facts and beliefs to their health care providers.

Legal and ethical duties of confidentiality operate in rough parallel. A health professional practises under a Code of Ethics,[6] which may in turn be incorporated under her or his professional governing legislation.[7] In the case of a self-governing profession, breach of an ethics code provides grounds for discipline by the governing body, for example, the College of Physicians and Surgeons.

The Quebec *Charter of Human Rights and Freedoms* protects confidential information as follows:

> Every person has a right to non-disclosure of confidential information.
>
> No person bound to professional secrecy by law and no priest or other minister of religion may, even in judicial proceedings, disclose confidential information revealed to him by reason of his position or profession, unless he is authorized to do so by the person who confided such information to him or by an express provision of law.
>
> The tribunal must, *ex officio*, ensure that professional secrecy is respected.[8]

Information does not lose its confidential nature by sole virtue of the fact that someone has already broadcast it to third parties. In *Calgary Regional Health Authority v. United Western Communications Ltd. (c.o.b. Alberta Report Magazine)*,[9] a nurse supplied the *Alberta Report* magazine editor with copies of internal hospital documents discussing the performance of late-term abortions, including the names of some of the doctors and nurses participating. At a hearing an injunction was sought restraining the magazine from publishing an article containing information internal to the hospital. One of the arguments of the editor was that they had already distributed these documents to others and so the interlocutory injunction being sought should not be granted. Justice Hawko for the Alberta Court of Queen's Bench disagreed, stating:

> The fact that the defendants, or some other person, have already sent this information on to others does not make it knowledge in the public domain. The

---

[6] See Canadian Medical Association, *CMA Code of Ethics* (updated 2004) at ss. 31-37, online at: <http://policybase.cma.ca/PolicyPDF/PD04-06.pdf>; Canadian Nurses Association, *Code of Ethics for Registered Nurses* (June 2008) at 15, online at: <http://www.cna-nurses.ca/CNA/documents/pdf/publications/Code_of_Ethics_2008_e.pdf>; National Association of Pharmacy Regulatory Authorities, *The Model Standards of Practice for Canadian Pharmacists* (March 2009), online at: <http://129.128.180.43/Content_Files/Files/Model_Standards_of_Prac_for_Cdn_Pharm_March09.pdf>; Canadian Dental Association, *CDA Code of Ethics* at Art. 9, online at: <http://www.cda-adc.ca/en/cda/about_cda/code_of_ethics/index.asp>.

[7] Quebec *Code of Ethics of Dentists*, R.R.Q. 1981, c. D-3, r. 4, s. 3.06.01; Nova Scotia *Code of Ethics Regulations (Regulation 3)*, N.S. Reg. 165/93, s. 1.

[8] R.S.Q., c. C-12, s. 9. Section 5 of the Quebec Charter also provides the right to respect for one's private life.

[9] [1999] A.J. No. 805, 75 Alta. L.R. (3d) 326 (Alta. Q.B.).

defendants cannot by their actions take something which is confidential and turn it into something which is not. It still retains its protection.[10]

Confidentiality is, however, never considered so sacrosanct that competing forces may not be seen to override it. In fact, as we shall see, most of the discussion in law and in this chapter consists of the numerous circumstances in which it has been deemed appropriate to set aside the duty of confidentiality in favour of some other, apparently compelling, cause.

III. CUSTODIANSHIP, OWNERSHIP AND ENTITLEMENT TO ACCESS

Both common law and statute have adopted the concept of custodianship when a patient's health information is being held by another party, whether health care provider, hospital, long-term care facility, research centre or department of health. The property or ownership model has been considered at common law and ultimately rejected by the Supreme Court of Canada.[11] Interestingly, we have recently seen its resurgence in the form of a claim by the National Aboriginal Health Organization of ownership over health information of Aboriginal people,[12] but no court has substantiated this claim as of yet. The patient's entitlement to access this information may be seen as corollary to questions of ownership or custodianship.

The Supreme Court of Canada weighed into the matter of ownership and custodianship of health information in its 1992 judgment in *McInerney v. Mac-Donald*,[13] a case involving a patient's right to access her own health information.[14] Mrs. MacDonald sought from her family physician Dr. McInerney not only copies of health records drafted and tests ordered by Dr. McInerney, but

---

[10]   *Ibid.*, at para. 18.

[11]   Note that in two recent American cases, the courts have rejected arguments of ownership by the individual source of bodily tissues supplied for research purposes. However, both cases were narrowly determined based on the facts at hand. In *Greenberg v. Miami Children's Hospital Research Institution*, 264 F. Supp. 2d 1064 at 1074 (S.D. Fla. 2003), the court found that the plaintiffs had voluntarily donated their tissues, and most recently in *Washington University v. William Catalona*, 437 F. Supp. 2d 985 (E.D. Mo. 2006), affd 490 F.3d 667 (8th Cir. 2007), the court ruled that the patients had turned control over to the University as to where samples could be sent on the basis that they had signed valid consent forms. According to one scholar, *Washington University* expands the tissue ownership doctrine by holding that whoever pays to house the samples "owns" them: Lisa C. Edwards, "Tissue Tug-of-War: A Comparison of International and U.S. Perspectives on the Regulation of Human Tissue Banks" (2008) 41 Vand. J. Transnat'l L. 639 at 659. On the other hand, R. Alta Charo in "Body of Research — Ownership and Use of Human Tissue" (2006) 355 New Eng. J. Med. 1517 argues that these cases still do not answer the simple question of whether we own our bodily tissue.

[12]   Valerie Gideon, "Understanding OCAP (Ownership, Control, Access, Possession) and its Ties to Privacy" (2002) NAHO Network News at 4, online at: <http://www.naho.ca/english/pdf/summer2002.pdf>.

[13]   [1992] S.C.J. No. 57, [1992] 2 S.C.R. 138 (S.C.C.).

[14]   Note that this case was decided in the absence of New Brunswick legislation speaking to the issue of access.

also those that had been compiled from previous treating physicians. Dr. McInerney was willing to provide copies of the records she had drafted but took the position that Mrs. MacDonald would need to approach the former physicians for copies of records they had compiled. All three levels of court found in favour of Mrs. MacDonald, albeit for different reasons. Justice Turnbull for the New Brunswick trial court ruled that patients have a proprietary interest in their own information. A majority of the Court of Appeal decided that the question was not ownership, but that there was an implied contract between physician and patient for information ancillary to treatment. Part of this contract was an entitlement to access that information.

A unanimous Supreme Court of Canada ruled that neither of these approaches — proprietary or contractual — was necessary for the disposition of the case. The Court found that the physical file belonged to the physician but that the patient was entitled to access the file contents, barring unusual circumstances that would make such access inappropriate or dangerous. Justice La Forest indicated that, while the information contained therein "remains, in a fundamental sense, one's own",[15] it is not necessary to "reify"[16] this to a property interest. Rather, a trust-like relationship in the nature of a fiduciary duty develops when a patient imparts information to a physician.[17]

Health information legislation is constructed around the concept of a "health information custodian"[18] or "trustee",[19] which may include a multitude of organizations, corporations and facilities as well as health care practitioners. In Ontario, anyone whose primary function is to provide health care services in exchange for payment, whether or not such services are publicly funded, is included in the definition of "health care practitioner", although interestingly, Aboriginal healers and midwives are explicitly excluded along with faith healers.[20] Agents of the custodian, providers of information technology services, and persons who receive personal health information from a custodian are all assigned responsibilities pursuant to the statute. It would appear that insurance companies that receive information such as prescription claims directly from individuals as opposed to from custodians are excluded from the Ontario legisla-

---

[15]   *Ibid.*, at para. 22.

[16]   *Ibid.*, at para. 25.

[17]   Note that the Australian High Court in *Julie Breen v. Cholmondeley W Williams* (1996), 186 C.L.R. 71 ruled otherwise — *i.e.*, that the patient does not have a right to access her or his health information. The Australian Court was highly critical of the Supreme Court of Canada judgment in *McInerney v. MacDonald*, [1992] S.C.J. No. 57, [1992] 2 S.C.R. 138 (S.C.C.), denying that the physician-patient relationship gives rise to a fiduciary duty, and finding that the records belong to the physician. In the context of implementation of electronic health records, it has been suggested that health organizations continue to have a culture of ownership rather than custodianship: David Wiljer *et al.*, "Patient Accessible Electronic Health Records: Exploring Recommendations for Successful Implementation Strategies" (2008) 10:4 J. Med. Internet Res. e34.

[18]   *Personal Health Information Protection Act, 2004*, S.O. 2004, c. 3, Sched. A, s. 3.

[19]   *Personal Health Information Act*, C.C.S.M. c. P33.5, s. 1(1); *Health Information Protection Act*, S.S. 1999, c. H-0.021, s. 2(t).

[20]   *Personal Health Information Protection Act, 2004*, S.O. 2004, c. 3, Sched. A, s. 3(4).

tion, as they do not fall within the definition of a "custodian".[21] This is a curious exception given the quantity and sensitivity of personal health information handled by these companies.

IV. THE CANADIAN CHARTER OF RIGHTS AND FREEDOMS

Is there a right to informational privacy under the *Canadian Charter of Rights and Freedoms*? The answer is unequivocally affirmative in the area of criminal law, and qualifiedly affirmative in other areas of law.

One of the first cases decided by the Supreme Court of Canada under the Charter, *Hunter v. Southam Inc.*,[22] involved a search of documents authorized by a warrant issued under authority of the *Combines Investigation Act*. The Court found that the procedures for issuance of a warrant violated Charter section 8, protection against unreasonable search and seizure, in that the person authorized to issue the warrant was not an impartial arbiter and the statute failed to set an appropriate standard for such issuance, given the privacy interest engaged.

A string of cases followed in which bodily substances had been taken or turned over to the police without consent. In *R. v. Dyment*,[23] a blood sample taken for medical purposes had been handed over to the police at their request and resulted in a conviction for driving while intoxicated. Justice La Forest, writing for the majority, stated:

> [T]he sense of privacy transcends the physical. The dignity of the human being is equally seriously violated when use is made of bodily substances taken by others for medical purposes in a manner that does not respect that limitation. In my view, the trust and confidence of the public in the administration of medical facilities would be seriously taxed if an easy and informal flow of information, and particularly of bodily substances from hospitals to the police, were allowed.[24]

The fact that a warrant was not sought was found to be "a flagrant breach of personal privacy"[25] in violation of section 8 of the Charter and not salvageable under section 24(2), as the admission of the evidence in these circumstances "would bring the administration of justice into disrepute".[26]

In *R. v. Dersch*,[27] the treating physician took a blood sample from the unconscious accused despite his earlier refusal, and in turn provided the test results to the police in response to their warrantless request. The conduct of the police

---

21 Ann Cavoukian, Information and Privacy Commissioner (IPC) of Ontario, "A Guide to the *Personal Health Information Protection Act*" (Toronto: IPC, 2004) at 11, online at: <http://www.ipc.on.ca/images/Resources/hguide-e.pdf>.
22 [1984] S.C.J. No. 36, [1984] 2 S.C.R. 145 (S.C.C.).
23 [1988] S.C.J. No. 82, [1988] 2 S.C.R. 417 (S.C.C.).
24 *Ibid.*, at para. 38.
25 *Ibid.*
26 *Ibid.*, at para. 2, quoting the Charter, ss. 8 and 24(2).
27 [1993] S.C.J. No. 116, [1993] 3 S.C.R. 768 (S.C.C.).

was found to constitute unreasonable search and seizure, again not admissible due to section 24(2).[28]

R. v. B. (S.A.)[29] involved a pregnant 14-year-old who indicated she was a victim of sexual assault by the accused. Fetal tissue was seized following her abortion, and a blood sample was taken from the accused pursuant to a warrant granted *ex parte* in accordance with sections 487.04 to 487.09 of the *Criminal Code*.[30] The DNA matched and the accused claimed a violation of his Charter rights in the taking of the sample. The Supreme Court of Canada upheld the impugned sections under section 8 in that they require a warrant, at which point the interest in law enforcement is balanced against privacy interests, and they limit the issuance of DNA warrants to designated offences.

A presentencing report by a psychologist in *R. v. Shoker*[31] recommended that the accused be subjected to random urinalysis, blood or breathalyzer tests as part of his conditions for probation, and the sentencing judge so ordered. This order was struck down by the Supreme Court of Canada as violating section 8 of the Charter in the absence of a governing regulatory or statutory framework.

In *R. v. Rodgers*,[32] the Crown applied *ex parte* under *Criminal Code* section 487.055(1)(*c*) for authorization for the taking of a blood sample from the accused for entry into the national DNA data bank. A majority of the Supreme Court of Canada upheld the constitutionality of the section, finding as follows:

> Society's interest in using this powerful new technology to assist law enforcement agencies in the identification of offenders is beyond dispute. The resulting impact on the physical integrity of the targeted offenders is minimal. The potential invasive impact on the right to privacy has carefully been circumscribed by legislative safeguards that restrict the use of the DNA data bank as an identification tool only. As convicted offenders still under sentence, the persons targeted by s. 487.055 have a much reduced expectation of privacy. Further, by reason of their crimes, they have lost any reasonable expectation that their identity will remain secret from law enforcement authorities.[33]

The Supreme Court of Canada has ruled that where an item of information does not on its own convey something about an individual, but must first be combined with other information in order to draw inferences about the individual, it does not likely attract protection under Charter section 8. An infrared device used by police to take pictures of heat patterns on the exterior of the defendant's house in *R. v. Tessling* was found given the present state of technology not to generate information about the defendant that touched on a bio-

---

[28] But see *R. v. Colarusso*, [1994] S.C.J. No. 2, [1994] 1 S.C.R. 20 (S.C.C.), in which a majority of the Court found on similar facts a violation of s. 8 but upheld the seizure under s. 24(2).

[29] [2003] S.C.J. No. 61, [2003] 2 S.C.R. 678 (S.C.C.).

[30] R.S.C. 1985, c. C-46.

[31] [2006] S.C.J. No. 44, [2006] 2 S.C.R. 399 (S.C.C.).

[32] [2006] S.C.J. No. 15, [2006] 1 S.C.R. 554 (S.C.C.).

[33] *Ibid.*, at para. 5.

graphical core of personal information or revealed intimate details of his life-style.[34]

The above cases all revolved around section 8 of the Charter. Section 7 has also been examined concerning privacy of health information, primarily concerning the special circumstance wherein persons accused of sexual assault seek access to their victims' counselling records. For a period of time this was so routine that L'Heureux-Dubé J. was moved to state that "[f]rom a quick perusal of lower court judgments, it would appear as if a request for therapeutic records in cases of sexual assault is becoming virtually automatic, with little regard to the actual relevancy of the documents".[35] In response to the striking down of previous *Criminal Code* provisions, sections 278.1 to 278.91 were enacted and subsequently upheld by a majority of the Supreme Court of Canada in *R. v. Mills.*[36] The victim's Charter section 7 security interest was found to be engaged in the circumstances:

> This Court has on several occasions recognized that security of the person is violated by state action interfering with an individual's mental integrity ... Therefore, in cases where a therapeutic relationship is threatened by the disclosure of private records, security of the person and not just privacy is implicated.[37]

In balancing the accused's right to make full answer and defence against the victim's right against unreasonable search and seizure, the Court stated:

> The values protected by privacy rights will be most directly at stake where the confidential information contained in a record concerns aspects of one's individual identity or where the maintenance of confidentiality is crucial to a therapeutic, or other trust-like, relationship.[38]

In addition to the section 7 right to security, the right to liberty has been found to cover aspects of privacy; indeed, La Forest J. has commented that "privacy is at the heart of liberty in a modern state".[39] And in *R. v. O'Connor,* L'Heureux-Dubé J. stated that when one's personal information is exposed to others against one's wishes, "it is an invasion of the dignity and self-worth of the individual, who enjoys the right to privacy as an essential aspect of ... liberty in a free and democratic society".[40]

---

[34] [2004] S.C.J. No. 63, [2004] 3 S.C.R. 432 at paras. 62-63 (S.C.C.).
[35] *R. v. Carosella*, [1997] S.C.J. No. 12 at para. 147, [1997] 1 S.C.R. 80 (S.C.C.) (in dissent). In this case the therapeutic records had been destroyed by the sexual assault crisis centre to prevent their use in judicial proceedings, leading a majority of the Court to order a stay of proceedings as the accused's right to make full answer and defence had been compromised.
[36] [1999] S.C.J. No. 68, [1999] 3 S.C.R. 668 (S.C.C.).
[37] *Ibid.*, at para. 85.
[38] *Ibid.*, at para. 89.
[39] *R. v. Dyment*, [1988] S.C.J. No. 82 at para. 17, [1988] 2 S.C.R. 417 (S.C.C.), drawing on the work of Alan Westin, *Privacy and Freedom* (New York: Athenium, 1970).
[40] [1995] S.C.J. No. 98 at para. 119, [1995] 4 S.C.R. 411 (S.C.C.).

Finally, section 15 is implicated in attempting to balance sexual assault victims' right to privacy in their counselling records against the rights of the accused:

> Equality concerns must also inform the contextual circumstances in which the rights of full answer and defence and privacy will come into play. In this respect, an appreciation of myths and stereotypes in the context of sexual violence is essential to delineate properly the boundaries of full answer and defence. ... The accused is not permitted to "whack the complainant" through the use of stereotypes regarding victims of sexual assault.[41]

Note that all of the above cases have arisen in the criminal law context. There has been considerably less discussion of a Charter right to privacy of information in civil law. In *Canadian AIDS Society v. Ontario*,[42] the plaintiffs argued that notification to blood donors of their HIV-positive status many years after the blood had been collected and without any indication to the donors that such testing would be done constituted a violation of their sections 7 and 8 rights. Justice Wilson for the Ontario Court of Justice (General Division) found that the right to security of the person would indeed be violated by such notification, as the donors' psychological integrity would be shaken, but that there was no violation of the principles of fundamental justice.[43]

In a more recent case, Belobaba J. found a violation of privacy rights under Charter section 7 in the enactment of legislation by the government of Ontario designed to open up confidential adoption records in the absence of consent.[44] On his analysis, there is an informational privacy interest enshrined in the right to liberty, and the legislation in question was not in accordance with the principles of fundamental justice. Finding no justification under Charter section 1, he struck down provisions in the legislation that would have made available confidential personal information without consent of the adoptee or birth parent.

Despite this interesting development, we have yet to see the Supreme Court of Canada make such a finding. Its most recent pronouncement on the matter of section 7 protection of information privacy appears to have been in *Ruby v. Canada (Solicitor General)*.[45] The appellant argued that his right to access information held by the government was corollary to the right to privacy under section 7 and was violated by provisions of the *Privacy Act*. The Court chose not to rule on this argument, and decided that even if such a violation was present, the provisions were in accordance with principles of fundamental justice.

---

[41] *R. v. Mills*, [1999] S.C.J. No. 68, [1999] 3 S.C.R. 668 at para. 90 (S.C.C.).

[42] [1995] O.J. No. 2361, 25 O.R. (3d) 388 (Ont. Gen. Div.), affd [1996] O.J. No. 4184, 31 O.R. (3d) 798 (Ont. C.A.), leave to appeal refused [1997] S.C.C.A. No. 33 (S.C.C.).

[43] The claim under s. 8 was that the "seizure" of the donated blood for testing, which had been conducted in order to notify recipients of their possible receipt of tainted blood, was unreasonable. The court disagreed, finding the seizure reasonable in light of the public health imperative at stake.

[44] *Cheskes v. Ontario (Attorney General)*, [2007] O.J. No. 3515, 87 O.R. (3d) 581 (Ont. S.C.J.).

[45] [2002] S.C.J. No. 73, [2002] 4 S.C.R. 3 (S.C.C.).

V.   OVERVIEW OF LEGISLATIVE LANDSCAPE

Laws governing health information might politely be described as smorgasbord in nature. Some protections have developed in common law; for instance, the entitlement in certain circumstances to access records for purposes of judicial proceedings. The great majority, however, have been legislated due to *lacunae* in development of the common law. This section commences with a brief discussion of the constitutional division of powers in the areas of health and of information. The lion's share of legislation is provincial/territorial, leading to significant differences in coverage depending on one's jurisdiction. Nova Scotia, Prince Edward Island and the Territories are at present the only jurisdictions without provincial legislation that at least to some extent governs information in the private sector, and every jurisdiction has public sector legislation. Not all is provincial; for example, since 1983 there has been federal legislation governing personal information held by government and its agencies. And the federal government has stepped into the scene in major fashion in recent years with its enactment of the *Personal Information Protection and Electronic Documents Act* (PIPEDA).[46] This section introduces the various major pieces of legislation, both federal and provincial, and discusses their scope. Details of the legislation regarding permitted collection, use and disclosure, as well as remedial provisions, will be covered in later sections of this chapter.

A.   CONSTITUTIONAL DIVISION OF POWERS

Jurisdiction is divided for matters both of health and of information, with the provinces/territories responsible for the lion's share of each. The *Constitution Act, 1867* allocated marine hospitals and quarantine to the federal government,[47] whereas the provinces were assigned power over "the Establishment, Maintenance, and Management of Hospitals, Asylums, Charities, and Eleemosynary Institutions in and for the Province, other than Marine Hospitals".[48] Most health matters were assumed by the provinces pursuant to this power over hospitals as well as power over property and civil rights and matters of a local or private nature. This division still exists, with federal jurisdiction over quarantine being interpreted to apply only to ingress and egress into and out of Canada.[49] The *Canada Health Act*[50] was not an assertion of federal jurisdiction over health matters; rather, it invoked federal spending power to gain the participation of the provinces/territories in a program of Medicare for hospitals and medically necessary physician services.[51]

---

[46]   S.C. 2000, c. 5.
[47]   (U.K.), 30 & 31 Vict., c. 3, s. 91(11).
[48]   *Ibid.*, s. 92(7).
[49]   See, *e.g.*, *Quarantine Act*, S.C. 2005, c. 20.
[50]   R.S.C. 1985, c. C-6.
[51]   For more extensive discussion, see Chapter 1.

As to information, the federal government was granted jurisdiction over census and statistics.[52] However, the topic of information *per se* was likely not in the minds of the drafters of the *Constitution Act, 1867,* and certainly was not mentioned in the document. As information has become a commodity of considerable import in recent years, it has been interpreted to fall primarily under the provincial power over property and civil rights[53] and matters of a local or private nature.[54] However, the fact that jurisdiction over both health and information rests primarily with the provincial governments has not deterred the federal government from enacting legislation governing information management, most notably PIPEDA.[55] Because the legislation only applies to information collected, used or disclosed in the course of commercial activity, the government has relied on its trade and commerce power in asserting its constitutionality.[56]

The fact that PIPEDA also applies to commercial activities which are solely intraprovincial has raised concern and controversy. In 2003, the Attorney General for Quebec launched a challenge to the constitutionality of PIPEDA before the Court of Appeal.[57] The claim was that PIPEDA trenches on Quebec's constitutional competence with respect to property and civil rights, and that a provision in the statute giving the federal government the right to review a provincial statute to ensure substantial similarity is incompatible with principles of federalism. However, the action has since been discontinued.[58]

B. FEDERAL LEGISLATION

1. *Personal Information Protection and Electronic Documents Act*

The *Personal Information Protection and Electronic Documents Act*[59] was brought into force in a number of stages between 2001 and 2004.[60] Since Janu-

---

[52] *Constitution Act, 1867* (U.K.), 30 & 31 Vict., c. 3, s. 91(6).

[53] *Ibid.,* s. 92(13).

[54] *Ibid.,* s. 92(16).

[55] Additional federal legislation that touches on health information includes the *Food and Drugs Act,* R.S.C. 1985, c. F-27; the *Controlled Drugs and Substances Act,* S.C. 1996, c. 19; and the *Quarantine Act,* S.C. 2005, c. 20.

[56] *Constitution Act, 1867* (U.K.), 30 & 31 Vict., c. 3, s. 91(2).

[57] Reference to the Court of Appeal relating to the Law on the protection of the personal information and electronic documents (L.C. 2000, c. 5), O.I.C. 1368-2003, G.O.Q. 2003.II.184.

[58] Also see *State Farm Mutual Automobile Insurance Co. v. Canada (Privacy Commissioner),* [2010] F.C.J. No. 889, 2010 FC 736 (F.C.), in which one of the arguments was that since insurance is a provincially regulated industry, PIPEDA's incursion into the area violates the division of powers. The Federal Court ruled that because the activity under review, *i.e.,* defence of a civil action in tort, did not constitute a commercial activity (see discussion *infra* at footnote 80 on this aspect of the case), PIPEDA did not apply. The court therefore declined to rule on its constitutionality.

[59] S.C. 2000, c. 5.

[60] PIPEDA came into force in three stages: January 2001 for interprovincial transfers of information, with the exception of health information, and for the operation of federal works, undertak-

ary 1, 2004, it has been in force both for information crossing provincial boundaries and also intra-provincially in provinces that do not have legislation declared by the Governor in Council to be "substantially similar"[61] to PIPEDA in providing information protection. In other words, in provinces with legislation declared "substantially similar", PIPEDA applies only to information going into and out of the province and to information collected, used or disclosed in connection with the operation of a federal work, undertaking or business, but not to other information kept within the province. The Ontario *Personal Health Information Protection Act, 2004*[62] is the first health information-specific legislation to have been declared substantially similar.[63] General private sector information legislation in Quebec,[64] British Columbia[65] and Alberta[66] has been declared substantially similar.[67] Alberta is in a unique and curious position in that only its health information legislation has not been deemed substantially similar. Thus, information in the private sector within Alberta is subject to PIPEDA only if it is health information; such information is subject also to the *Health Information Act* so long as it is collected, used, held or disclosed by a health services provider.[68] In all provinces, PIPEDA still applies to information that crosses provincial/territorial or federal borders.

PIPEDA covers solely personal information, defined as "information about an identifiable individual, but does not include the name, title or business address or telephone number of an employee of an organization".[69] Thus, information pursuant to which there is no reasonable potential for identification of an

---

ings and businesses; January 2002 for interprovincial transfers of health information; and January 2004 for the former plus intraprovincial transfers of information.

[61] PIPEDA, S.C. 2000, c. 5, s. 26(2)(*b*). To be declared substantially similar, the provincial legislation must comply with three requirements: it must be based on the 10 principles of fair practices of collection, use and disclosure of personal information that PIPEDA is built upon; it must restrict collection, use and disclosure to purposes that are appropriate or legitimate; and it must have a mechanism for independent oversight and remedy when rights have been violated: Robert Weist, "Process for the Determination of 'Substantially Similar' Provincial Legislation by the Governor in Council" (2002) 136:31 Can. Gaz. I, 2385 at 2388.

[62] S.O. 2004, c. 3, Sched. A.

[63] Health Information Custodians in the Province of Ontario Exemption Order, SOR/2005-399.

[64] *An Act respecting the protection of personal information in the private sector*, R.S.Q., c. P-39.1.

[65] *Personal Information Protection Act*, S.B.C. 2003, c. 63.

[66] *Personal Information Protection Act*, S.A. 2003, c. P-6.5.

[67] Organizations in the Province of Quebec Exemption Order, SOR/2003-374; Organizations in the Province of British Columbia Exemption Order, SOR/2004-220; Organizations in the Province of Alberta Exemption Order, SOR/2004-219.

[68] R.S.A. 2000, c. H-5, s. 1(1)(n).

[69] PIPEDA, S.C. 2000, c. 5, s. 2(1). For a critique of PIPEDA in the context of health research, see Canadian Institutes of Health Research (CIHR), "Draft recommendations for the interpretation and application of the *Protection of Personal Information and Electronic Documents Act* in health research" (discussion document from the CIHR Consultation Session, Ottawa: June 2001), online at: <http://www.cihr-irsc.gc.ca/e/documents/pipeda_discussion_e.pdf>.

individual appears to fall outside its mandate.[70] There is a lengthy and detailed definition of "personal health information", as follows:

> "personal health information", with respect to an individual, whether living or deceased, means
>
> (a) information concerning the physical or mental health of the individual;
>
> (b) information concerning any health service provided to the individual;
>
> (c) information concerning the donation by the individual of any body part or any bodily substance of the individual or information derived from the testing or examination of a body part or bodily substance of the individual;
>
> (d) information that is collected in the course of providing health services to the individual; or
>
> (e) information that is collected incidentally to the provision of health services to the individual.[71]

Note the breadth, which at times could be seen to contradict the definition of "personal information". For example, "information collected in the course of providing health services to an individual" could include non-individually-identifiable items of information, yet they would appear to be covered. Note also that the definition of "personal health information" is broad enough to include information regarding a deceased individual, and information as to body parts or substances, but does not include the samples themselves.[72]

PIPEDA only applies to personal information collected, used or disclosed "in the course of commercial activit[y]", which is "any particular transaction, act or conduct or any regular course of conduct that is of a commercial character, including the selling, bartering or leasing of donor, membership or other fund-raising lists".[73] This rather tautological definition was at least mildly elucidated

---

[70] An issue raised by this definition is what degree of anonymization is required to render information no longer "about an identifiable individual". A finding by the Office of the Privacy Commissioner holds that "[i]nformation will be about an identifiable individual if there is a serious possibility that someone could identify the available information" and that "de-identified data will not constitute 'truly anonymous information' when it is possible to subsequently link the de-identified data back to an identifiable individual": *PIPEDA Case Summary #2009-018*, 2009 CanLII 84472 (P.C.C.). In the context of DNA information, research has shown that absolute anonymization may not be feasible: Bradley Malin, David Karp & Richard Scheuermann, "Technical and Policy Approaches to Balancing Patient Privacy and Data Sharing in Clinical and Translational Research" (2010) 58:1 J. Investig. Med. 11.

[71] PIPEDA, S.C. 2000, c. 5, s. 2(1).

[72] For a *contra* view, *i.e.*, arguing that tissues, bodily substances and samples are included in the definition, see L. Rozovsky & N. Inions, *Canadian Health Information: A Practical Legal and Risk Management Guide*, 3d ed. (Markham, ON: LexisNexis Canada, 2002) at 19.

[73] PIPEDA, S.C. 2000, c. 5, ss. 4(1)(a) and 2(1) "commerical activity", respectively.

in *Rodgers v. Calvert*,[74] in which the court found that the profit or non-profit character of an organization is not conclusive as to whether or not PIPEDA applies, and that the mere exchange of consideration in providing personal information and a membership fee in exchange for membership in an organization does not in and of itself constitute commercial activity. Likewise, the court found that the production of a membership list by an organization, short of trading or selling such a list, does not constitute a commercial activity.[75]

Is the provision of health care services a commercial activity? The most substantial guidance to date on this topic has been a document produced by Industry Canada[76] which addresses various issues surrounding PIPEDA's applicability to the health care services community. Industry Canada suggests that PIPEDA does apply to the activities of pharmacies, laboratories and health care providers in private practice. On the other hand, in its view, PIPEDA does not apply to provincially funded hospitals as "their core activities are not commercial in nature".[77] Engaging in some activity such as charging a fee for a cast or for a private room does not bring PIPEDA into play, in its view, as this only happens in connection with the hospital's core activity, which is non-commercial.

This interpretation is dubious, as the phrase "core activity" is found nowhere in PIPEDA itself, nor, arguably, is the concept. Also, this interpretation contradicts the fact that the Act focuses on a specific activity and not on the nature of an organization. Further, the application of a "preponderant purpose" test has been rejected by the Ontario Superior Court in its interpretation of "commercial activity" under PIPEDA.[78] This "preponderant purpose" test, under which one looks to whether the main purpose of an activity is the making of profit, had been adopted by the Supreme Court of Canada in the context of whether an activity constitutes a business for the purpose of taxation under the *Assessment Act*.[79] However, the Ontario Superior Court ruled that this test is not applicable to PIPEDA, given the different purposes of the two statutes.

In a recent case, the State Farm Mutual Automobile Insurance Company argued before the Federal Court that the collection of evidence in order to facilitate the defence of a civil tort claim falls outside the definition of "commercial

---

[74] *Ibid.*, s. 2(1); *Rodgers v. Calvert*, [2004] O.J. No. 3653, 244 D.L.R. (4th) 479 (Ont. S.C.J.). For further discussion of the meaning of "commercial activity", see *Ferenczy v. MCI Medical Clinics*, [2004] O.J. No. 1775 (Ont. S.C.J.), affd [2005] O.J. No. 2076, 198 O.A.C. 254 (Ont. C.A.) without discussion of this point.

[75] *Rodgers v. Calvert, ibid.,* at para. 56.

[76] Industry Canada, not the Office of the Privacy Commissioner or Health Canada, is the federal Department under whose auspices PIPEDA falls, since its aim is commerce and not health care services *per se*.

[77] Industry Canada, "PIPEDA Awareness Raising Tools (PARTs) Initiative for the Health Sector: Questions and Answers" at No. 24, online at: <http://www.ic.gc.ca/eic/site/ecic-ceac.nsf/eng/gv00235.html>.

[78] *Rodgers v. Calvert*, [2004] O.J. No. 3653 at para. 50, 244 D.L.R. (4th) 479 (Ont. S.C.J.).

[79] *Ontario (Regional Assessment Commissioner) v. Caisse populaire de Hearst Ltée*, [1983] S.C.J. No. 8, [1983] 1 S.C.R. 57 (S.C.C.).

activity" under PIPEDA.[80] The court accepted State Farm's argument, applying the concept of "primary activity" in deciding that the activity under review did not constitute a commercial activity. Justice Mainville indicated that "[t]he primary characterization of the activity or conduct in issue is thus the dominant factor in assessing the commercial character of that activity or conduct under PIPEDA, not the incidental relationship between the one who seeks to carry out the activity or conduct and third parties".[81] This analysis may be seen to affirm the notion that one looks to the specific activity under review, and not to the core function or activity of an organization, in applying the definition of "commercial activity" under PIPEDA. However, clearly there is much analysis of the scope of the commercial activity provision yet to come, given the relative infancy of this statute.

Where PIPEDA applies, then, what does it actually do? It lays out a number of principles for the handling of personal information, including the following: collecting,[82] using,[83] disclosing[84] and retaining only the minimum information necessary for the purpose;[85] identifying this purpose[86] and, subject to a number of exceptions, obtaining the consent of the information source individual;[87] and seeking further consent if the information is to be used or disclosed for other purposes.[88] The legislation also provides the individual with a right of access, and to have incorrect information amended.[89] Other rules attempt to ensure transparency,[90] accuracy,[91] accountability[92] and the safeguarding of information being held.[93] Details of these provisions will be examined in later sections of this chapter.

2.   *Privacy Act* and *Access to Information Act*

The *Privacy Act*[94] and its companion *Access to Information Act*[95] apply to personal information collected, used, retained or disclosed by the federal public sector. Personal information is defined as "information about an identifiable

---

[80]   *State Farm Mutual Automobile Insurance Co. v. Canada (Privacy Commissioner)*, [2010] F.C.J. No. 889, 2010 FC 736 (F.C.).
[81]   *Ibid.*, at para. 106.
[82]   PIPEDA, S.C. 2000, c. 5, Sched. 1, s. 4.4.
[83]   *Ibid.*, Sched. 1, s. 4.5.
[84]   PIPEDA, S.C. 2000, c. 5, s. 5(3).
[85]   *Ibid.*, Sched. 1, s. 4.5.2.
[86]   *Ibid.*, Sched. 1, ss. 4.2, 4.2.5.
[87]   *Ibid.*, Sched. 1, s. 4.3.
[88]   *Ibid.*, Sched. 1, s. 4.3.1.
[89]   *Ibid.*, Sched. 1, s. 4.9.
[90]   *Ibid.*, Sched. 1, s. 4.8.
[91]   *Ibid.*, Sched. 1, s. 4.6.
[92]   *Ibid.*, Sched. 1, s. 4.1.
[93]   *Ibid.*, Sched. 1, s. 4.7.
[94]   R.S.C. 1985, c. P-21.
[95]   R.S.C. 1985, c. A-1.

individual that is recorded in any form".[96] It is widely acknowledged that there is a need for review and updating, in particular because electronic and digital forms of information were not but should now be explicitly included in their purview, and also because of the need to reconcile these statutes with other federal legislation.[97]

3. Other Federal Legislation

In addition to PIPEDA and the *Privacy Act* and *Access to Information Act*, there are a number of other federal statutes relevant to the handling of personal information. The *Statistics Act* authorizes the collection of information "to collect, compile, analyse, abstract and publish statistical information relating to the commercial, industrial, financial, social, economic and general activities and condition of the people".[98] Health information is included in its purview.

The *Controlled Drugs and Substances Act* provides for the collection of personal information regarding controlled drug prescriptions to attempt to stop "double doctoring" or attending on more than one health care provider to obtain multiple prescriptions for a controlled drug within 30 days.[99] The *Criminal Code*[100] contains numerous provisions regarding personal information, some of which are discussed in the Charter and judicial proceedings sections of this chapter. The *Quarantine Act* authorizes the collection of personal information regarding travellers from the person in charge of a conveyance,[101] and places a duty on travellers to provide any information reasonably required by a screening or quarantine officer.[102]

C. PROVINCIAL AND TERRITORIAL LEGISLATION

There are a number of different kinds of provincial/territorial legislation impacting directly on health information. Some provinces have enacted health-information-specific legislation. Others have legislation that covers personal information in the private sector,[103] including health information. All have legis-

---

[96] *Privacy Act*, R.S.C. 1985, c. P-21, s. 3.

[97] See Office of the Privacy Commissioner of Canada, "Governmental Accountability for Personal Information: Reforming the *Privacy Act*" (June 2006), online at: <http://www.priv.gc.ca/information/pub/pa_reform_060605_e.cfm> and David H. Flaherty, "Reflections on Reform of the Federal *Privacy Act*" (2008) 21 Can. J. Admin. L. & Prac. 271.

[98] R.S.C. 1985, c. S-19, s. 3(*a*).

[99] S.C. 1996, c. 19.

[100] R.S.C. 1985, c. C-46.

[101] S.C. 2005, c. 20, ss. 34 and 38.

[102] *Ibid.*, s. 15(1).

[103] The distinction between public and private that is reflected in privacy laws has been critiqued as being "out of step with the realities of research and health care delivery" such as public-private partnerships and research consortia: Matthew Herder, "Toward Personalized Medicine in Canada: Legal & Ethical Frameworks, Opportunities for Policy Innovation" at 15 (report commissioned by Health Canada, March 2010) [unpublished, on file with author].

lation governing information in the public sector, which may include hospitals and extended care facilities.

Another kind of legislation enacted by a number of provinces creates a statutory form of redress specifically for violations of privacy, which may include the misuse of personal health information. There are also multiple pieces of legislation aimed at the governance of members of the health professions, as well as hospitals, nursing homes and extended care facilities, which include provisions on confidentiality and disclosure of information. Finally (but not exhaustively), there are statutes aimed at protection of vulnerable individuals, such as children and disabled adults. Each will be introduced in this section, and elaborated upon in subsequent discussion.

1.   Health-Information-Specific Legislation

A number of provinces have enacted legislation that deals exclusively with health information, in the belief that the area is both complex and worthy of specific and focused protection. In ascending order of recency of legislation in force, these provinces are Manitoba, Alberta, Saskatchewan, Ontario, Newfoundland and Labrador (partly in force), and New Brunswick.[104] The Ontario legislation is the most lengthy and arguably the most complex, as the government was able to draw upon lessons from its previous abortive attempts to legislate in this area[105] and on the experience of other provinces with health information legislation already in place.

The primary aim of these statutes is to provide for the protection of personal health information being collected, used, stored or disclosed by an entity other than the individual who is the information source. Personal health information or, in the case of Alberta, individually identifying information, is defined in various ways in the legislation. Basically, the legislation tends to provide wide scope to the types of information that fall under its rubric. Thus, it may include information with respect to the donation of body parts or body substances;[106] health card number;[107] genetic information;[108] payment information;[109] family

---

[104] *Personal Health Information Act*, C.C.S.M. c. P33.5; *Health Information Act*, R.S.A. 2000, c. H-5; *Health Information Protection Act*, S.S. 1999, c. H-0.021; *Personal Health Information Protection Act, 2004*, S.O. 2004, c. 3, Sched. A; *Personal Health Information Act*, S.N.L. 2008, c. P-7.01; *Personal Health Information Privacy and Access Act*, S.N.B. 2009, c. P-7.05. The *E-Health (Personal Health Information Access and Protection of Privacy) Act*, S.B.C. 2008, c. 38 is also health-information-specific, albeit applying to very limited circumstances, and will be discussed below.

[105] *Personal Health Information Protection Act, 1997* (draft); *Personal Health Information Privacy Act, 2000* (Bill 159), 1st Sess., 37th Leg., Ontario, 2000 (First Reading December 7, 2000, referred to the Standing Committee on General Government December 11, 2000).

[106] *Health Information Act*, R.S.A. 2000, c. H-5, s. 1(1)(i)(iii); *Health Information Protection Act*, S.S. 1999, c. H-0.021, s. 2(m)(iii); *Personal Health Information Protection Act, 2004*, S.O. 2004, c. 3, Sched. A, s. 4(1)(e); *Personal Health Information Privacy and Access Act*, S.N.B. 2009, c. P-7.05, s. 1.

[107] *Personal Health Information Protection Act, 2004*, *ibid.*, s. 34(2).

health history;[110] and an individual's substitute decision-maker.[111] The Manitoba definition includes only recorded information, whereas those in Ontario and New Brunswick include information in oral form.[112] In Alberta, Saskatchewan and Manitoba the personal health information of a deceased individual is protected;[113] in Ontario and New Brunswick it is protected for the first 50 years after death, or until the expiration of 120 or 100 years, respectively, after the creation of the record containing the information;[114] Saskatchewan protects it for the first 30 years after death or until the record is 120 years old.[115]

(a) Non-Directly-Identifying Information

One of the interesting aspects of scope of coverage relates to information that is not directly identifying but may in combination with other information provide identification of an individual. Manitoba excludes from the statute information that, when combined with other information available to the holder, does not permit individuals to be readily identified; New Brunswick does the same but omits "readily".[116] Ontario and Saskatchewan similarly acknowledge the risk of identification through combining non-directly-identifying information, but add a reasonableness component — for example, in the case of Saskatchewan, the information is protected under the statute if it can *reasonably* be expected to permit identification.[117] Ontario defines identifying information as "information that identifies an individual or for which it is reasonably foreseeable in the circumstances that it could be utilized, either alone or with other information, to identify an individual".[118]

The Alberta legislation takes a very different approach. It does not exclude non-identifying information but permits its collection, use and disclosure, the

---

[108] *Personal Health Information Act*, C.C.S.M. c. P33.5, s. 1(1); *Personal Health Information Privacy and Access Act*, S.N.B. 2009, c. P-7.05, s. 1.

[109] *Health Information Act*, R.S.A. 2000, c. H-5, s. 1(1)(i)(vi); *Personal Health Information Act*, C.C.S.M. c. P33.5, s. 1(1); *Personal Health Information Protection Act, 2004*, S.O. 2004, c. 3, Sched. A, s. 4(1)(d); *Personal Health Information Privacy and Access Act*, S.N.B. 2009, c. P-7.05, s. 1.

[110] *Personal Health Information Protection Act, 2004, ibid.*, s. 4(1)(a); *Personal Health Information Privacy and Access Act, ibid.*, s. 1.

[111] *Personal Health Information Protection Act, 2004, ibid.*, s. 4(1)(g); *Personal Health Information Privacy and Access Act, ibid.*, s. 1.

[112] *Personal Health Information Act*, C.C.S.M. c. P33.5, s. 1(1); *Personal Health Information Protection Act, 2004, ibid.*, s. 4(1); *Personal Health Information Privacy and Access Act, ibid.*, s. 1.

[113] *Health Information Act*, R.S.A. 2000, c. H-5; *Health Information Protection Act*, S.S. 1999, c. H-0.021, s. 2(m) — the definition of "personal health information" includes an individual living or deceased; *Personal Health Information Act*, C.C.S.M. c. P33.5, s. 60(1)(f).

[114] *Personal Health Information Protection Act, 2004*, S.O. 2004, c. 3, Sched. A, s. 9(1); *Personal Health Information Privacy and Access Act*, S.N.B. 2009, c. P-7.05, s. 3(2)(b).

[115] *Health Information Protection Act*, S.S. 1999, c. H-0.021, s. 3(2)(b) and (c).

[116] *Personal Health Information Act*, C.C.S.M. c. P33.5, s. 3; *Personal Health Information Privacy and Access Act*, S.N.B. 2009, c. P-7.05, s. 3(2)(a).

[117] *Health Information Protection Act*, S.S. 1999, c. H-0.021, s. 3(2).

[118] *Personal Health Information Protection Act, 2004*, S.O. 2004, c. 3, Sched. A, s. 4(2).

latter subject to minor conditions. Its definition of non-identifying health information is problematically over-broad, in that it "means that the identity of the individual who is the subject of the information cannot be readily ascertained from the information".[119] "Ready ascertainment" is a much more lax standard than that of "reasonable expectation". Also, while the legislation does discuss "data matching", the protections against data matching do not apply unless two or more electronic databases are being merged. By deduction, then, other pieces of individually non-identifying information, so long as they are not electronic, may be merged to provide identification but are not subject to statutory protection in Alberta.[120]

(b) Non-Individually-Identifying Information

Another striking feature of the Alberta *Health Information Act* (HIA) is that, along with individuals' personal health information, protection is granted for health services provider information.[121] This form of protection came under scrutiny when physicians in Alberta protested the passing of information by pharmacists to IMS Health which identified physicians' prescribing habits, to be used by pharmaceutical corporations for targeted individual marketing purposes.[122] A similar case under PIPEDA had failed in that prescribing patterns were found to be a work product and hence not to fall under the definition of "personal information".[123] However, the explicit inclusion of health services provider information in the definition of "personal information" in HIA resulted in a finding by the Alberta Information and Privacy Commissioner that this practice violated the statute.[124] This finding was then set aside on judicial review on the basis that, of the information disclosed by pharmacies to IMS, only the prescribers' names came within the definition of "health services provider" information, and names could be disclosed without consent under the (since repealed) business card exception.[125] HIA has now been amended such that information about a health services provider "is deemed to be individually identifying health information about the individual who received the health service from the health services provider and not individually identifying health information about the health services provider".[126] In contrast, Ontario and New

---

[119] *Health Information Act*, R.S.A. 2000, c. H-5, s. 1(1)(p).

[120] For more thorough discussion of this point, see Barbara von Tigerstrom, "Alberta's *Health Information Act* and the *Charter*: A Discussion Paper" (2000) 9:2 Health L. Rev. 3.

[121] R.S.A. 2000, c. H-5, s. 1(1)(k).

[122] *IMS Health Canada, Ltd. v. Alberta (Information and Privacy Commissioner)*, [2005] A.J. No. 1293, 53 Alta. L.R. (4th) 201 (Alta. C.A.).

[123] *Finding #2001-15*, 2001 CanLII 21546 (P.C.C.).

[124] See Alberta, Office of the Information and Privacy Commissioner, "Alberta Pharmacists and Pharmacies" Order H2002-003, File No. H0036 (March 19, 2003), online at: <http://www.oipc.ab.ca/ims/client/upload/H2002-003.pdf>.

[125] *IMS Health Canada, Ltd. v. Alberta (Information and Privacy Commissioner)*, [2008] A.J. No. 358, 2008 ABQB 213 (Alta. Q.B.).

[126] *Health Information Act*, R.S.A. 2000, c. H-5, s. 1(4) as amended by *Health Information Amendment Act, 2009*, S.A. 2009, c. 25, s. 2(b).

Brunswick include information that identifies an individual's health care provider within their definition of "personal health information".[127]

With health care budgets exploding, the delivery of health care services has come more and more under scrutiny for efficiency and cost-savings purposes. This scrutiny has meant the identification and comparison of the outcomes ratings of specific practitioners, departments, institutions and regional health authorities. This in turn has led to concerns being raised about the privacy rights of these individuals and groups. The Government of Manitoba has established a physician profile website that identifies any practice restrictions or terms or conditions on registration, final disciplinary actions by the College of Physicians and Surgeons, medical malpractice judgments and criminal convictions against the physician.[128] Its potentially strong effects are seriously weakened by the fact that it is based primarily on self-reporting, and only final disciplinary actions, judgments and convictions are reportable. Nevertheless, it is an interesting development in Canadian health law and policy, as historically, a physician's record of practice has been in a practical sense off-limits to the general public. The facilitation of access to physician profiles was one of the measures recommended by Sinclair J. in the report of an inquiry following the deaths of infants at the pediatric cardiac surgery unit of the Winnipeg Health Sciences Centre.[129]

2. Private Sector Personal Information Legislation

Quebec,[130] British Columbia[131] and Alberta[132] have enacted legislation that protects personal information in the private sector. The Alberta *Personal Information Protection Act* does not apply to "health information as defined in the Alberta *Health Information Act* to which that Act applies".[133] The definition of "personal information" in this legislation is less encompassing than in health-information-specific legislation, referring to "information about an identifiable

---

[127] *Personal Health Information Protection Act, 2004*, S.O. 2004, c. 3, Sched. A, s. 4(1)(b); *Personal Health Information Privacy and Access Act*, S.N.B. 2009, c. P-7.05, s. 1.

[128] *Medical Amendment (Physician Profiles and Miscellaneous Amendments) Act*, S.M. 2002, c. 34, amending *Medical Act*, C.C.S.M. c. M90; Physician Profile Regulation, Man. Reg. 104/2005.

[129] Associate Chief Judge Murray Sinclair, Provincial Court of Manitoba, *The Report of the Manitoba Pediatric Cardiac Surgery Inquest: An Inquiry into Twelve Deaths at the Winnipeg Health Sciences Centre in 1994* (Winnipeg, MB: Provincial Court of Manitoba, 2001), online at: <http://www.pediatriccardiacinquest.mb.ca>. For further discussion of this issue, see M. Marshall & B. von Tigerstrom, "Health Information" in Jocelyn Downie, Timothy Caulfield & Colleen Flood, eds., *Canadian Health Law and Policy*, 2d ed. (Markham, ON: LexisNexis Canada, 2002) at 174-76.

[130] *An Act respecting the protection of personal information in the private sector*, R.S.Q., c. P-39.1.

[131] *Personal Information Protection Act*, S.B.C. 2003, c. 63.

[132] *Personal Information Protection Act*, S.A. 2003, c. P-6.5.

[133] *Ibid.*, s. 4(3)(f).

individual"[134] or that "allows that person to be identified"[135] without acknowledgment of issues regarding indirect identifiers.

3. Public Sector Personal Information Legislation

Every province and territory in Canada has legislation that aims to protect personal information held by governments and other public sector bodies. This type of legislation is of foremost importance in provinces and territories without other forms of information legislation in that often hospitals and other health care facilities fall under its rubric.[136]

4. Provincial Privacy Acts

British Columbia, Manitoba, Newfoundland and Labrador, and Saskatchewan have enacted legislation purporting to protect individuals against invasions of privacy, including informational privacy.[137] Their scope is seriously limited in that the actions of the defendant must have been wilful or, in the case of Manitoba, the violation of privacy must have been committed "substantially, unreasonably and without claim of right".[138] Indeed, despite the egregious nature of the violation in *Peters-Brown v. Regina District Health Board*,[139] there was found to be no violation of the Saskatchewan *Privacy Act*. This case concerned Ms. Peters-Brown, an employee of a correctional institution who had been successfully treated for hepatitis B. Five years later, a list of names of individuals for whom bodily fluid precautions should be taken, which included the name of Ms. Peters-Brown, was circulated at her workplace and caused her considerable distress. While the court found that the hospital had been negligent in its management of the list such that it could fall into the hands of employees of the correctional institution, no violation of the *Privacy Act* was found in that the violation had not been not "wilful". There was no evidence before the court as to how the list had made its way from the hospital to the correctional facility.

On the other hand, a British Columbia court has indicated that it would have found a violation of their *Privacy Act vis-à-vis* health information in the context

---

[134] *Personal Information Protection Act*, S.B.C. 2003, c. 63, s. 1; *Personal Information Protection Act*, S.A. 2003, c. P-6.5, s. 1(i)(k).

[135] *An Act respecting the protection of personal information in the private sector*, R.S.Q., c. P-39.1, s. 2.

[136] *Access to Information and Protection of Privacy Act*, S.N.W.T. 1994, c. 20; *Freedom of Information and Protection of Privacy Act*, S.N.S. 1993, c. 5.

[137] *Privacy Act*, R.S.B.C. 1996, c. 373; *Privacy Act*, C.C.S.M. c. P125; *Privacy Act*, R.S.N.L. 1990, c. P-22; *Privacy Act*, R.S.S. 1978, c. P-24.

[138] *Privacy Act*, C.C.S.M. c. P125, s. 2(1).

[139] [1995] S.J. No. 609, [1996] 1 W.W.R. 337, 136 Sask. R. 126 (Sask. Q.B.), affd [1996] S.J. No. 761, [1997] 1 W.W.R. 638, 148 Sask. R. 248 (Sask. C.A.). The hospital was found liable for negligence and breach of contract.

of the videotaping and television airing of baldness correction surgery.[140] The reporter was falsely advised by a contractor with the clinic that the subject had consented to use of the videotape, which showed the plaintiff's face. Default judgment was issued, but the court also indicated it would have found that there was a violation of the *Privacy Act*.

5. Other Provincial Legislation

Provincial legislation governing specific aspects of health care services, such as hospitals, nursing homes and mental health services, often includes provisions regarding the handling of personal health information.[141] Public health legislation addresses disclosure of health information.[142] Some jurisdictions have legislation establishing a cancer registry.[143] Every province has legislation making mandatory the reporting of child abuse,[144] and some also have mandatory reporting of adult abuse.[145]

VI. CONSENSUAL COLLECTION, USE AND DISCLOSURE

The health information statutes as well as PIPEDA operate on the basic model of consent to collection of information, and use and disclosure are also premised on consent, but with multiple exceptions. What constitutes consent, however, differs from statute to statute; so too do the circumstances wherein consent may be waived.

PIPEDA permits different forms of consent, depending on the sensitivity of the type of information being collected. However, it also indicates that medical records would almost always be considered sensitive, implying that explicit consent is likely required.[146] Under Ontario's *Personal Health Information Protection Act, 2004* (PHIPA), consent must be knowledgeable, which is inferred "if it is reasonable in the circumstances to believe that the individual knows, (a) the purposes of the collection, use or disclosure, as the case may be; and (b) that the

---

[140] *Hollinsworth v. BCTV, a Division of Westcom TV Group Ltd.*, [1996] B.C.J. No. 2638, 34 C.C.L.T. (2d) 95 (B.C.S.C.), affd [1998] B.C.J. No. 2451, 59 B.C.L.R. (3d) 121 (B.C.C.A.). Appeal dismissed and British Columbia Court of Appeal found no liability on the part of BCTV.

[141] See, *e.g.*, *Hospitals Act*, R.S.N.S. 1989, c. 208, s. 71 (confidentiality of hospital records); *Continuing Care Act*, R.S.B.C. 1996, c. 70, s. 11 (confidentiality of client information).

[142] For more detail, see E. Gibson, "Public Health Information Privacy and Confidentiality" in Tracey M. Bailey, Timothy Caulfield & Nola M. Ries, eds., *Public Health Law & Policy in Canada* (Markham, ON: LexisNexis Canada, 2005) at 89.

[143] See, for example, *Cancer Agency Act*, S.S. 2006, c. C-1.1, Part IV. For further discussion of cancer registries, see Barbara von Tigerstrom & Nola M. Ries, "Cancer Surveillance in Canada: Analysis of Legal and Policy Frameworks and Tools for Reform" (2009) 17 Health L.J. 1.

[144] *Child and Family Services Act*, C.C.S.M. c. C80, s. 18.

[145] *Adult Protection Act*, R.S.N.S. 1989, c. 2, s. 5(1).

[146] *Personal Information Protection and Electronic Documents Act*, S.C. 2000, c. 5, Sched. 1, s. 4.3.4.

individual may give or withhold consent".[147] Note that the individual therefore, by implication, need not necessarily be aware of the actual content of the information in order to proffer a knowledgeable consent.

Saskatchewan's *Health Information Protection Act* (HIPA), similarly to other jurisdictions, provides a list of exceptions to the need for collection directly from the subject individual.[148] Following are the most salient:

> (a) the individual consents to collection of the information by other methods;
>
> (b) the individual is unable to provide the information;
>
> (c) the trustee believes, on reasonable grounds, that collection directly from the subject individual would prejudice the mental or physical health or the safety of the subject individual or another individual;
>
> (d) the information is collected, and is necessary, for the purpose of:
>
> > (i) determining the eligibility of the individual to participate in a program of the trustee or receive a product or service from the trustee ... or
> >
> > (ii) verifying the eligibility of the individual who is participating in a program of the trustee or receiving a product or service from the trustee;
>
> (e) the information is available to the public ...[149]

The only information that is to be collected is that reasonably necessary for the purpose for which it is being collected,[150] and the source individual is to be notified of that purpose.[151] For other uses and disclosures, consent of the individual is to be obtained unless the circumstance falls within one of the many exceptions permitted by statute.[152] Manitoba's legislation was recently amended to provide explicitly for the withdrawal of consent by an individual through notification of the trustee.[153]

Under the Ontario legislation, consent may be inferred where the sharing of information is to another custodian for health care purposes, unless the individual has expressly indicated a lack of consent.[154] In the circumstance wherein the custodian is disclosing personal health information for a health care purpose, and believes that the absence of consent means that he or she is not disclosing all the information considered reasonably necessary for the purpose, the custo-

---

[147] S.O. 2004, c. 3, Sched. A, s. 18(5).

[148] S.S. 1999, c. H-0.021.

[149] *Ibid.*, s. 25(1).

[150] *Personal Health Information Act*, C.C.S.M. c. P33.5, s. 13(2).

[151] *Personal Information Protection and Electronic Documents Act*, S.C. 2000, c. 5, Sched. 1, s. 4.2.3; *Health Information Act*, R.S.A. 2000, c. H-5, s. 22(3).

[152] *Health Information Protection Act*, S.S. 1999, c. H-0.021, ss. 26, 27.

[153] *Personal Health Information Act*, C.C.S.M. c. P33.5, ss. 19.1(7)-19.2 (in force May 2010).

[154] *Personal Health Information Protection Act, 2004*, S.O. 2004, c. 3, Sched. A, s. 20(2).

dian is required to inform the person to whom the information is being conveyed of this limitation.[155]

In the context of confidential adoption records, the court in *Cheskes v. Ontario (Attorney General)* strongly affirmed the importance of consent in use and disclosure of personal information, indicating that "[w]here an individual has a reasonable expectation of privacy in personal and confidential information, that information may not be disclosed to third parties without his or her consent".[156]

VII. NON-CONSENSUAL USE AND DISCLOSURE

The reader will recall that in the initial quote from *Halls v. Mitchell*,[157] the right of confidentiality is referred to as absolute in the absence of a paramount reason to set it aside. What could constitute such a reason? Further guidance is provided in the following quote:

> Such reasons may arise, no doubt, from the existence of facts which bring into play overpowering considerations connected with public justice; and there may be cases in which reasons connected with the safety of individuals or of the public, physical or moral, would be sufficiently cogent to supersede or qualify the obligations prima facie imposed by the confidential relation.[158]

The requirement of consent to use and disclosure of personal health information is subject to a number of exceptions. These may include the provision of health care services, disclosure to relatives and other interested parties, warning third parties of risk of serious harm, protection from abuse, judicial and quality review proceedings, public health, governmental purposes and the conduct of research. Following is discussion of these exceptions.

A.   PROVISION OF HEALTH CARE SERVICES

There is a general presumption that information may be shared among health care services providers rendering care to a particular patient, referred to by Industry Canada as the "circle of care".[159] This occurs under the umbrella of "implied consent".[160] Ontario, Manitoba and New Brunswick allow for an opting out from this implied consent, sometimes referred to as a "lock box". Manitoba's legislation incorporates this concept as follows:

---

[155]   *Ibid.*, s. 38(2).
[156]   [2007] O.J. No. 3515, 87 O.R. (3d) 581 at para. 107 (Ont. S.C.J.).
[157]   [1928] S.C.J. No. 1, [1928] S.C.R. 125 (S.C.C.).
[158]   *Ibid.*, at 136.
[159]   Patricia Kosseim & Megan Brady in "Policy by Procrastination: Secondary Use of Electronic Health Records for Health Research Purposes" (2008) 2 McGill J.L. & Health 5 at 31 review the concept of "circle of care" and define it as referring to individuals or institutions directly connected to an individual's health care.
[160]   Industry Canada, "PIPEDA Awareness Raising Tools (PARTs) Initiative for the Health Sector: Questions and Answers" at 3 and 6, online at: <http://www.ic.gc.ca/eic/site/ecic-ceac.nsf/eng/h_gv00207.html>.

A trustee may disclose personal health information without the consent of the individual the information is about if the disclosure is

> (a) to a person who is or will be providing or has provided health care to the individual, to the extent necessary to provide health care to the individual, unless the individual has instructed the trustee not to make the disclosure ...[161]

Ontario's PHIPA states that a custodian may disclose personal health information to another health information custodian where reasonably necessary for the provision of health care and where the individual's consent cannot be obtained in a timely manner. However, this is not to occur if the individual objects to such disclosure.[162] In this circumstance, if the custodian or trustee believes that not all the information is being conveyed that is necessary for the provision of health care to the individual, he or she must advise the recipient of this fact.[163] The Manitoba legislation contains no such requirement.

B.   DISCLOSURE TO RELATIVES AND OTHER INTERESTED PARTIES

Personal health information may be disclosed under Ontario legislation in order to contact a relative, friend or other potential substitute decision-maker to seek consent on behalf of an incapacitated individual.[164] Saskatchewan permits disclosure regarding current health services to next-of-kin and others with whom the individual has a close personal relationship provided that the individual has not expressed a contrary wish regarding such disclosure.[165] In Ontario, a facility may disclose that an individual is a patient or resident, the individual's general health status in broad terms, and the location of the individual within the facility, unless the individual objects to such disclosure.[166]

Disclosure may be made about a deceased individual for identification purposes and also for informing any person "it is reasonable to inform in the circumstances" that the individual is deceased,[167] "to a relative of a deceased individual if the trustee reasonably believes that disclosure is not an unreasonable invasion of the deceased's privacy"[168] and of the circumstances of death where appropriate.[169] Also, in Ontario, the individual's spouse, partner, sibling or child may receive information concerning the deceased reasonably that would impact on their own or

---

[161]   *Personal Health Information Act*, C.C.S.M. c. P33.5, s. 22(2).
[162]   *Personal Health Information Protection Act, 2004*, S.O. 2004, c. 3, Sched. A, s. 38(1)(a).
[163]   *Ibid.*, s. 38(2). New Brunswick's provision contains requirements similar to Ontario's: *Personal Health Information Privacy and Access Act*, S.N.B. 2009, c. P-7.05, s. 37(2) and (3).
[164]   *Ibid.*, s. 38(1)(c).
[165]   *Health Information Protection Act*, S.S. 1999, c. H-0.021, s. 27(2)(c)(ii).
[166]   *Personal Health Information Protection Act, 2004*, S.O. 2004, c. 3, Sched. A, s. 38(3).
[167]   *Personal Health Information Act*, C.C.S.M. c. P33.5, s. 22(2)(c).
[168]   *Ibid.*, s. 22(2)(d).
[169]   *Personal Health Information Protection Act, 2004*, S.O. 2004, c. 3, Sched. A, s. 38(4).

their children's health care.[170] Of special note is the fact that this could occur even if the individual had indicated, prior to death, that he or she did not wish family members to have access to his or her health information.

C.   DUTY OR RIGHT TO WARN THIRD PARTIES

An appreciation of a potential duty to warn has developed in Canada based on principles outlined by the Supreme Court of California in *Tarasoff v. Regents of the University of California.*[171] In this case, the facts as alleged were that a man told his psychologist that he was planning to kill his former girlfriend. The psychologist advised campus police but did not warn the woman, who was indeed subsequently murdered by the former boyfriend. On a preliminary motion, the California Supreme Court ruled that the psychologist, in the circumstances of an imminent plausible threat to the life of an identifiable individual or group of individuals, had a duty to try to prevent the occurrence of harm. This duty supersedes any duty of confidentiality, and is described as follows:

> When a therapist determines, or pursuant to the standards of his profession should determine, that his patient presents a serious danger of violence to another, he incurs an obligation to use reasonable care to protect the intended victim against such danger. The discharge of this duty may require the therapist to take one or more of various steps, depending upon the nature of the case. Thus it may call for him to warn the intended victim or others likely to apprise the victim of the danger, to notify the police, or to take whatever other steps are reasonably necessary under the circumstances.[172]

While not yet squarely adopted by Canadian courts, several courts have cited *Tarasoff* with approval. Most notable is the Supreme Court of Canada case of *Smith v. Jones.*[173] A psychiatrist hired by the defence to perform an assessment of the accused came to the view that the accused had developed an intricate plan to murder prostitutes in Vancouver and, if released, was likely to actualize this plan. The psychiatrist sought judicial guidance as to whether he was entitled to warn the prosecution and the court of this plan, thereby potentially influencing whether or not the accused would be released. A majority of the Supreme Court of Canada ruled that solicitor-client privilege could be set aside in favour of warning the court of this clear, serious and imminent threat. Note, however, that unlike in *Tarasoff*, the Court did not identify a *duty* to warn in these circumstances; rather, it was left to the discretion of the psychiatrist. Since solicitor-client privilege is the strongest privilege in Canadian law, the confidentiality of health information obtained in a trust relationship would reasonably fall under such an exception also. However, it is not accurate to call it

---

[170]   *Ibid.*, s. 38(4)(c).
[171]   551 P.2d 334, 17 Cal. 3d 425 (Cal. 1976).
[172]   *Ibid.*, at 340.
[173]   [1999] S.C.J. No. 15, [1999] 1 S.C.R. 455 (S.C.C.).

an obligation or duty to warn, but rather a permission on the part of the health care provider to do so in law.

Each of the health information statutes has included this developing common law right to warn third parties.[174] Manitoba's PHIA states that disclosure may be made without consent if the disclosure is:

> (b) to any person if the trustee reasonably believes that the disclosure is necessary to prevent or lessen a serious and immediate threat to
>
> (i) the health or safety of the individual the information is about or another individual, or
>
> (ii) public health or public safety;[175]

In Ontario, where a custodian believes on reasonable grounds that a disclosure "is necessary for the purpose of eliminating or reducing a significant risk of serious bodily harm to a person or group of persons",[176] he or she may disclose personal health information without consent. Note that this provision applies regardless of whether the individual has explicitly indicated the information is not to be disclosed.

D. PROTECTION FROM ABUSE

Every province and territory in Canada has legislation that aims to protect children in case of abuse. There rests an obligation on professionals, and in some cases on all individuals, to report suspected or known child abuse.[177]

In addition, some provinces have mandatory reporting in case of adult abuse, if a person is subjected to physical or sexual abuse or inadequate care and is incapable of protecting herself or himself from such abuse due to a physical or mental disability.[178]

E. JUDICIAL AND QUALITY REVIEW PROCEEDINGS

The sensitivity of much personal health information has resulted in a fair amount of review by both courts and legislatures to establish proper circumstances for its disclosure for purposes of judicial proceedings, whether civil or criminal. There has also been much discussion regarding the obtaining of bodily substances, such as blood and tissue samples, for testing for alcohol levels and

---

[174] *Health Information Act*, R.S.A. 2000, c. H-5, s. 35(1)(m); *Health Information Protection Act*, S.S. 1999, c. H-0.021, s. 27(4)(a); *Personal Health Information Privacy and Access Act*, S.N.B. 2009, c. P-7.05, s. 39(1).

[175] C.C.S.M. c. P33.5, s. 22(2).

[176] *Personal Health Information Protection Act, 2004*, S.O. 2004, c. 3, Sched. A, s. 40(1).

[177] The Nova Scotia *Children and Family Services Act*, S.N.S. 1990, c. 5, for example, contains two standards for reporting: a higher standard that applies to professionals and officials (s. 24) and a standard that applies to everyone (s. 23(1)).

[178] *Adult Protection Act*, R.S.N.S. 1989, c. 2; *Protection for Persons in Care Act*, S.A. 2009, c. P-291.

DNA matching in light of the *Canadian Charter of Rights and Freedoms*. And internal incident reviews by hospitals and other health care institutions have become increasingly important in response to concerns regarding patient safety, meriting their own sets of rules. Each of these matters will be discussed in turn.

1.   Civil

Are health records admissible in civil proceedings? The short answer is yes, in some circumstances. It will depend in large part on whether a class privilege attaches to the records, or whether privilege is to be sought on a case-by-case basis, and on whether the person who is the subject of the information contained in the records has either explicitly or implicitly waived his or her right to confidentiality.

The hearsay rule prevents statements made by persons other than the witness before the court from being introduced as evidence of the truth of the information contained therein, but it is subject to a series of exceptions. The Supreme Court of Canada decided in 1970 that hospital records were indeed one of these exceptions, provided they were "made contemporaneously by someone having a personal knowledge of the matters then being recorded and under a duty to make the entry of record".[179] This means that patient charts may be introduced as *prima facie* proof of their contents, but may be challenged for accuracy. A number of provinces also have provisions to this effect in their Evidence Acts.[180]

But there remains the question of whether patient records should be introduced in a given proceeding because of their confidential nature. The Supreme Court of Canada affirmed in 1997 in *M. (A.) v. Ryan*[181] that, generally speaking, there is no class privilege in the case of records held by a health professional on behalf of a patient.[182] Privilege must therefore be argued on a case-by-case basis under the Wigmore principles.[183] Thus, it is up to the party seeking to prevent disclosure to establish that the communication originated in confidence, that it is

---

[179] *Ares v. Venner*, [1970] S.C.J. No. 26, [1970] S.C.R. 608 at 626 (S.C.C.).

[180] L. Rozovsky & N. Inions, *Canadian Health Information: A Practical Legal and Risk Management Guide*, 3d ed. (Markham, ON: LexisNexis Canada, 2002) at 54.

[181] [1997] S.C.J. No. 13, [1997] 1 S.C.R. 157 (S.C.C.). Class privilege in the form of solicitor-client privilege did apply in the case of *Smith v. Jones*, [1999] S.C.J. No. 15, [1999] 1 S.C.R. 455 (S.C.C.). A psychiatrist examined the accused in preparation of a pre-sentencing report on behalf of the accused. The report was found to be covered by solicitor-client privilege, but an exception was made in the circumstances. For further discussion, see Section VII(C) of this chapter, "Duty or Right to Warn Third Parties". Class privilege also applied to protect the names of police informants in *Canada (Solicitor General) v. Ontario (Royal Commission of Inquiry into the Confidentiality of Health Records)*, [1981] S.C.J. No. 95, [1981] 2 S.C.R. 494 (S.C.C.) regardless of the fact that the physicians and hospital employees concerned were in breach of their duty of confidentiality in passing patient information on to the police.

[182] Interestingly, the United States Supreme Court decided earlier in the same year that class privilege does indeed attach in the context of psychotherapist-patient communications: *Jaffee v. Redmond*, 518 U.S. 1 (1996).

[183] *M. (A.) v. Ryan*, [1997] S.C.J. No. 13, [1997] 1 S.C.R. 157 at para. 20 (S.C.C.).

essential to the relationship that this confidence be protected, that the protection of this relationship is in the public interest, and that the privacy interest outweighs the probative value of the information. The onus is still on the party seeking production to establish the relevance of the information contained therein, as per the applicable rules of court.

In *Frenette v. Metropolitan Life Insurance Co.*,[184] the insurer of the deceased paid the basic indemnity for death but refused to pay the additional accidental death benefit, believing that death was caused by suicide and therefore excluded. The deceased, when applying for insurance, had signed a statement authorizing access to his records by the insurer "for the purposes of risk assessment and loss analysis".[185] When the hospital that had treated the deceased two days prior to his death refused to share his hospital record with the insurer, the insurer launched a lawsuit to receive the record. The Supreme Court of Canada ruled that the agreement by the insured to have his records reviewed for purposes of loss analysis constituted an explicit waiver, thus entitling the insurance company to his entire record held by the hospital.

Waiver of one's right to confidentiality may also be implicit. In *Glegg v. Smith & Nephew Inc.*,[186] the plaintiff suffered an allergic reaction to an implant following fracture of her femur. She had the implant removed and sued the manufacturer and attending physicians. The defendants sought access to medical records held by a psychiatrist she had consulted following the first surgery, but access was denied due to confidentiality. A unanimous Supreme Court of Canada ruled that by bringing a civil action claiming physical and psychiatric injury due to the actions of the manufacturer and physicians, the plaintiff in effect placed her medical history directly on trial. Thus, she had implicitly waived her right to have her information kept confidential by her psychiatrist.

2. Criminal

The Crown is obliged to reveal to the accused all relevant information in its possession unless the information is privileged.[187] If the accused wishes to access third party information not in the hands of the Crown, he or she may apply for issuance of a subpoena. In light of the particular sensitivity of sexual assault victim records, the *Criminal Code* now contains a detailed three-step procedure that determines whether such records will be provided to the accused.[188] The first question is whether the record is likely relevant to an issue at trial or to the competence of a witness to testify. Second, without having actually viewed the record, the judge is to balance the accused's ability to make full answer and defence against the complainant's right to privacy and equality. If the scale is in

---

[184] [1992] S.C.J. No. 24, [1992] 1 S.C.R. 647 (S.C.C.).
[185] *Ibid.*, at para. 18.
[186] [2005] S.C.J. No. 29, [2005] 1 S.C.R. 724 (S.C.C.).
[187] *R. v. Stinchcombe*, [1991] S.C.J. No. 83, [1991] 3 S.C.R. 326 (S.C.C.) as cited in *R. v. O'Connor*, [1995] S.C.J. No. 98 at para. 4, [1995] 4 S.C.R. 411 (S.C.C.).
[188] R.S.C. 1985, c. C-46, ss. 278.1-278.91.

favour of the accused, the judge then reviews the record in light of a number of factors to determine whether it is appropriate to provide them to the accused. These provisions have been upheld by the Supreme Court of Canada in *R. v. Mills*.[189]

If the Crown wishes to gain access to patient records for purposes of prosecution, it may apply for a search warrant under the *Criminal Code*.[190] Where the justice hearing the application is satisfied on reasonable grounds that evidence regarding the commission of an offence will be acquired, a warrant is issued authorizing the police to undertake a search and seizure.[191] A warrantless search is *prima facie* a violation of section 8 of the *Canadian Charter of Rights and Freedoms*, the right to be protected against unreasonable search and seizure.[192] If section 8 is violated, the court turns to section 24(2) of the Charter to determine whether use of the information gained through the illegal search would bring the administration of justice into disrepute; if so, the evidence is not permitted to be used at trial.[193]

The trial court in *R. v. Serendip Physiotherapy Clinic*[194] ruled that at common law, the high degree of confidentiality of patient records required that section 487 of the *Criminal Code* have read into it a number of additional protections similar to those for sexual assault victim records. The trial decision was overturned by the Ontario Court of Appeal and leave to appeal to the Supreme Court of Canada was denied.[195]

3.   Obtaining of Bodily Substances

The taking of blood or tissue samples for purposes of testing for intoxication or DNA banking and matching is authorized by a number of sections of the *Criminal Code*.[196] However, it is recognized as highly invasive of one's privacy and bodily integrity. Major cases involving a violation of the Charter have been discussed in Part IV of this chapter, "The Canadian Charter of Rights and Freedoms". The case of *R. v. C. (R.)*,[197] however, did not involve the Charter. In this case a 13-year-old boy stabbed his mother in the foot with a pen and struck her in the face. The young offender pleaded guilty to assault with a weapon, which is a designated offence, and breach of an undertaking. Section 487.051(2) of the *Criminal Code* requires that the court order the taking of a DNA sample if a person is convicted of a designated offence unless the effect of such an order be

---

[189] [1999] S.C.J. No. 68, [1999] 3 S.C.R. 668 (S.C.C.).

[190] R.S.C. 1985, c. C-46, s. 487(1)(*b*).

[191] *Canadian Broadcasting Corp. v. New Brunswick (Attorney General)*, [1991] S.C.J. No. 88, [1991] 3 S.C.R. 459 (S.C.C.).

[192] *Hunter v. Southam Inc.*, [1984] S.C.J. No. 36, [1984] 2 S.C.R. 145 (S.C.C.).

[193] *R. v. Collins*, [1987] S.C.J. No. 15, [1987] 1 S.C.R. 265 at para. 19 (S.C.C.).

[194] [2004] O.J. No. 4653, 73 O.R. (3d) 241 (Ont. C.A.), leave to appeal refused [2004] S.C.C.A. No. 585 (S.C.C.).

[195] *Ibid.*

[196] R.S.C. 1985, c. C-46, ss. 487.05, 487.051(2).

[197] [2005] S.C.J. No. 62, [2005] 3 S.C.R. 99 (S.C.C.).

"grossly disproportionate to the public interest". The Supreme Court of Canada restored the finding of the trial judge that given these facts, including the age of the accused, the taking and retention of a DNA sample was not sufficiently in the public interest to warrant the serious intrusion on the accused's personal and informational privacy.

4.   Quality/Incident Review

Patient safety has become a major focus both in Canada and internationally. This has led to an increasing focus on risk management, peer review, incident review and quality assurance, both to allay concerns regarding patient safety and to reduce costs of litigation. Patients seek access to review documents, while health care institutions attempt to keep such documents out of the hands of prospective plaintiffs. Governments at present appear to empathize with institutions, accepting the argument that health care providers will be more willing to openly disclose information regarding adverse events and near-misses if they do not fear that legal proceedings will result therefrom. In turn, greater openness is intended to lead to prevention of subsequent adverse incidents. Thus, legislated protection for disclosure of such reviews may be found in various types of legislation, the most recent of which, the *Quality of Care Information Protection Act, 2004*[198] of Ontario, is stand-alone legislation protecting against all but criminal and other federal proceedings.

A number of provinces have addressed this issue in either their Evidence Act[199] or their Medical Act.[200] In Nova Scotia, additional protection for health professionals has been provided through an addition to the *Freedom of Information and Protection of Privacy Act*, which reads as follows:

> The head of a local public body that is a hospital may refuse to disclose to an applicant a record of any report, statement, memorandum, recommendation, document or information that is used in the course of, or arising out of, any study, research or program carried on by or for the local public body or any committee of the local public body for the purpose of education or improvement in medical care or practice.[201]

Medical and hospital records pertaining to the patient are excluded;[202] in other words, patients are still entitled to access such records.

The health information statutes of Alberta, Manitoba, Saskatchewan and New Brunswick have addressed this topic in differing ways. In each case, disclosure of personal information to a review committee may be without consent of the individual. In Alberta, the custodian must refuse to disclose the findings

---

[198]   S.O. 2004, c. 3, Sched. B.
[199]   See, for example, *Evidence Act*, R.S.N.S. 1989, c. 154, ss. 60-61.
[200]   *Medical Act*, R.S.P.E.I. 1988, c. M-5.
[201]   S.N.S. 1993, c. 5, s. 19D(1).
[202]   *Ibid.*, s. 19D(2).

of a review committee to the individual;[203] in Manitoba, Saskatchewan and New Brunswick, the trustee or custodian is entitled but not mandated to refuse disclosure.[204]

In conjunction with its *Personal Health Information Protection Act, 2004*, the province of Ontario has chosen to enact stand-alone legislation to protect this type of information from judicial scrutiny. The *Quality of Care Information Protection Act, 2004*[205] is designed to protect quality of care information prepared by or for a quality of care committee. It is intended to facilitate disclosure to a committee reviewing the quality of services delivered by an organization by rendering the information not subject to disclosure for other purposes, especially legal proceedings.[206] However, criminal proceedings or other matters under federal jurisdiction are not included in the exemption — in other words, disclosures to the quality of care committee are not protected from production for criminal matters. This Act overrides PHIPA in that it permits any person to disclose personal health information to a quality of care committee, even if it would otherwise be a violation of PHIPA.[207] Information that is "contained in a record that is maintained for the purpose of providing health care to an individual" — in other words, what we would normally describe as a patient record — is excluded from protection under the *Quality of Care Information Protection Act, 2004*.[208] Interestingly, it also excludes "facts contained in a record of an incident involving the provision of health care to an individual", unless these facts are also fully included in the patient record.[209] Thus, the individual is entitled to disclosure of all facts concerning his or her care that are revealed before the quality of care committee. The Act also contains an exception where disclosure of quality of care information is required to reduce the significant risk of serious bodily harm to one or more persons.[210] The Information and Privacy Commissioner is not granted jurisdiction over the Act.

F.   PUBLIC HEALTH

Each province and territory has legislation dealing with public health matters, and the federal government has passed *An Act respecting the establishment of the Public Health Agency of Canada*.[211] Provincial legislation differs greatly in its content. All, however, cover aspects of duty on individuals to self-report, mandatory reporting by third parties, duty of confidentiality of public health

---

[203] *Health Information Act*, R.S.A. 2000, c. H-5, s. 11(2)(b).

[204] *Personal Health Information Act*, C.C.S.M. c. P33.5, s. 11(1)(d); *Health Information Protection Act*, S.S. 1999, c. H-0.021, s. 38(1)(d); *Personal Health Information Privacy and Access Act*, S.N.B. 2009, c. P-7.05, s. 14(1)(*d*).

[205] S.O. 2004, c. 3, Sched. B, s. 5.

[206] *Ibid.*

[207] *Ibid.*, s. 3.

[208] *Ibid.*, s. 1 "quality of care information" (c).

[209] *Ibid.*, s. 1 "quality of care information" (e).

[210] *Ibid.*, s. 4(4).

[211] *Public Health Agency of Canada Act*, S.C. 2006, c. 5.

authorities, contact notification, public notification, surveillance, epidemiology and research.[212] Not all cover information sharing outside the province. Ontario's new PHIPA has addressed this topic, allowing for disclosure to medical officers of health within Ontario and to public health authorities throughout Canada, including at the federal level, to facilitate health protection and promotion.[213]

G. GOVERNMENT

As explained in the section on freedom of information and protection of privacy legislation, these statutes outline the conditions under which governments may collect, use and disclose information. Health information legislation also contains provisions for custodians or trustees to share personal health information with government. Generally, these include for purposes of determining eligibility for funding, funding services, auditing, planning and management, and keeping a registry of disease or body parts or fluids. In Ontario, at the request of the Minister of Health and Long-Term Care, disclosure for monitoring or verifying claims for payment for publicly funded health care goods and services is mandatory.[214]

PHIPA contains detailed provisions for the sharing of information with a "prescribed entity" in order to facilitate the management and evaluation of the health system.[215] A health information custodian may disclose to a prescribed entity personal health information for the purpose of analysis or compiling statistical information with respect to the management of, evaluation or monitoring of, the allocation of resources to or planning for all or part of the health system, including the delivery of services, if the entity meets the requirements under section 45(3) of the Act. PHIPA also outlines the creation and governance of an intermediate body referred to as a "health data institute"[216] for the purpose of analysis of the health system on behalf of the Minister of Health. Such institutes are to be reviewed on a periodic basis by the Access and Privacy Commissioner to ensure that information is being de-identified and confidentiality is being protected.[217]

---

[212] For further details, see Elaine Gibson, "Public Health Information Privacy and Confidentiality" in Tracey M. Bailey, Timothy Caulfield & Nola M. Ries, eds., *Public Health Law & Policy in Canada* (Markham, ON: LexisNexis Canada, 2005).

[213] *Personal Health Information Protection Act, 2004*, S.O. 2004, c. 3, Sched. A, s. 39(2). Justice Archie Campbell in his Second Interim Report on SARS and Public Health Legislation has criticized this section for its lack of clarity and, in particular, for not making mandatory such information sharing: see Justice Archie Campbell, "SARS Commission Second Interim Report: SARS and Public Health Legislation" (2005) at 213-15, online at: <http://www.health.gov.on.ca/english/public/pub/ministry_reports/campbell05/campbell05.pdf>.

[214] *Personal Health Information Protection Act, 2004, ibid.*, s. 46(1).

[215] *Ibid.*, s. 45. The Institute for Clinical Evaluative Sciences has been approved under these provisions.

[216] *Ibid.*, s. 47. To date, no health data institutes have been approved.

[217] *Ibid.*, s. 47(10).

H.   RESEARCH

The Tri-Council Policy Statement (TCPS)[218] constitutes an agreement between the three major federal research funding agencies — Canadian Institutes of Health Research, Social Sciences and Humanities Research Council, and National Sciences and Engineering Research Council — to a set of principles intended to guide the conduct of research at institutions receiving funding from these agencies. Its second edition, released in December 2010, identifies that "[t]he articles in this Policy are intended to provide guidance, and in some cases, to set out certain requirements".[219] Its provisions on confidentiality and research uses of health information have been somewhat revised. Researchers have a specific ethical duty of confidentiality assigned to them; Article 5.1 states that "[r]esearchers shall safeguard information entrusted to them and not misuse or wrongfully disclose it".[220] Second, there is a more nuanced appreciation of information falling along a scale of identifiability. There appears to be contradiction, however, between the definition of "anonymized information" and its later use in the same document. The second edition of TCPS defines "anonymized information" as information stripped of direct identifiers and absent a code to allow future re-linkage.[221] Later on the same page, though, there is a discussion of circumstances wherein a researcher is "proposing to link anonymized ... datasets",[222] which would seem to not be possible on the basis of the earlier definition (*i.e.*, the requirement of absence of a code to allow re-linkage). This apparent contradiction should be clarified.

Factors to be considered when proposing to utilize information include:

(a)   the type of information to be collected;

(b)   the purpose for which the information will be used, and the purpose of any secondary use of identifiable information;

(c)   limits on the use, disclosure and retention of the information;

(d)   risks to participants should the security of the data be breached, including risks of re-identification of individuals;

(e)   appropriate security safeguards for the full life cycle of information;

(f)   any recording of observations (e.g., photographs, videos, sound recordings) in the research that may allow identification of particular participants;

---

[218] Canadian Institutes of Health Research, Natural Sciences and Engineering Research Council of Canada, Social Sciences and Humanities Research Council of Canada, *Tri-Council Policy Statement: Ethical Conduct for Research Involving Humans* (December 2010), online at: <http://www.pre.ethics.gc.ca/eng/policy-politique/initiatives/tcps2-eptc2/Default/>.

[219] *Ibid.*, at 13.

[220] *Ibid.*, at 58.

[221] *Ibid.*, at 57.

[222] *Ibid.*

(g) any anticipated uses of personal information from the research; and

(h) any anticipated linkage of data gathered in the research with other data about participants, whether those data are contained in public or personal records. ...[223]

While these are identified as factors to be considered, there is not a great deal of specific guidance as to the weighting of the various factors. Further, the legal status of the TCPS is weak in that it is not a statutory instrument but rather was drafted primarily as an ethical framework. Thus, each of the provinces with health information legislation has included further guidance for the conduct of research utilizing identifiable personal information.[224] Manitoba's PHIA establishes a health information privacy committee, which is tasked with the review of health research project proposals seeking to utilize information held by government and its agencies.[225] One-fourth of the composition of the committee is to be persons who are not health professionals, researchers or government employees.[226] The committee is authorized to approve projects that require access to personal health information in identifiable form without the consent of individuals if it is not practical to obtain consent, it is necessary to use identifiers, and sufficient confidentiality safeguards are in place such that the benefits of the research outweigh the risks. Where a research proposal requires direct contact with individuals, the trustee is permitted to release names and addresses to the researcher without consent; for release of any further information, the trustee requires the consent of the individual.[227]

Ontario's PHIPA contains detailed provisions regarding the disclosure of health information pursuant to the conduct of research: the researchers must submit a completed application, a research plan and the documented approval of a research ethics board. Interestingly, the research ethics board must be somewhat differently constituted than what is required by the Tri-Council Policy Statement[228] in that it requires a member knowledgeable in privacy issues.[229] The research plan must identify the affiliation of all persons involved in the re-

---

[223] *Ibid.*, at 60-61.

[224] *Health Information Act*, R.S.A. 2000, c. H-5, ss. 49-56; *Personal Health Information Act*, C.C.S.M. c. P33.5, ss. 24-24.1, 59; *Personal Health Information Protection Act, 2004*, S.O. 2004, c. 3, Sched. A, s. 44; *Health Information Protection Act*, S.S. 1999, c. H-0.021, s. 29; *Personal Health Information Privacy and Access Act*, S.N.B. 2009, c. P-7.05, s. 43.

[225] *Personal Health Information Act, ibid.*, ss. 24, 59.

[226] *Ibid.*, s. 59(2).

[227] *Ibid.*, s. 24(5).

[228] Canadian Institutes of Health Research, Natural Sciences and Engineering Research Council of Canada, and Social Sciences and Humanities Research Council of Canada, *Tri-Council Policy Statement: Ethical Conduct for Research Involving Humans* (December 2010), online at: <http://www.pre.ethics.gc.ca/eng/policy-politique/initiatives/tcps2-eptc2/Default/>. The newly revised Statement does suggest that the representative knowledgeable in the law should alert research ethics boards regarding legal matters, including privacy issues.

[229] General Regulation, O. Reg. 329/04, s. 15, para. 1(iv).

search,[230] the reason individual consent is not being sought, the necessity for any planned linkage of databases and a description of all persons who will have access to the information.[231] Finally, the researcher must enter an agreement with the custodian that attempts to ensure that information is kept confidential,[232] including commitments not to publish identifying information, not to contact the individual except through the custodian and to notify the custodian of any breach.[233]

VIII. OVERSIGHT

Federal and provincial privacy commissioners generally are not vested with authority to make binding decisions. There are, however, exceptions: the British Columbia Information and Privacy Commissioner's orders are enforceable,[234] and both the Alberta and Ontario Commissioners make binding orders under their health information legislation.[235] Commissioners are empowered to investigate pursuant to a complaint, and may also launch an investigation where there are reasonable grounds to believe there has been a contravention of the statute. There are provisions for mediation and alternate dispute resolution.

Under PIPEDA, decisions of the federal Privacy Commissioner are non-binding, but a dissatisfied complainant may seek a binding judgment in the Federal Court.[236] Recourse in the provinces is to the Superior Court; in Ontario, for instance, even though the order of the Commissioner is binding, where damages are sought, the individual must proceed to the Superior Court of Justice. It is necessary at this stage that the applicant establish "actual harm", which may include an award of up to $10,000 for mental anguish.[237]

IX. CONTEMPORARY CONTROVERSIES

A.   ELECTRONIC HEALTH INFORMATION

One of the areas providing the greatest challenge to our notions of health information is the electronicization of health information. Legal conceptions of privacy and confidentiality have been structured around the model of paper records stored in manila folders in filing cabinets in physician offices and hospitals. However, the world is shifting in this regard. Commissioner Romanow dedicated a chapter of the final report of the Commission on the Future of Health

---

[230] *Personal Health Information Protection Act, 2004*, S.O. 2004, c. 3, Sched. A, s. 44(2).

[231] General Regulation, O. Reg. 329/04, s. 16.

[232] *Personal Health Information Protection Act, 2004*, S.O. 2004, c. 3, Sched. A, s. 44(5).

[233] *Ibid.*, s. 44(6).

[234] *Freedom of Information and Protection of Privacy Act*, R.S.B.C. 1996, c. 165, s. 59; *Personal Information Protection Act*, S.B.C. 2003, c. 63, s. 53.

[235] *Health Information Act*, R.S.A. 2000, c. H-5, s. 81; *Personal Health Information Protection Act, 2004*, S.O. 2004, c. 3, Sched. A, s. 61.

[236] *Personal Information Protection and Electronic Documents Act*, S.C. 2000, c. 5, s. 14(1).

[237] *Personal Health Information Protection Act, 2004*, S.O. 2004, c. 3, Sched. A, s. 65(2), (3).

Care in Canada to this topic,[238] and developments continue apace, with Alberta rolling out the first province-wide integrated electronic health record.[239] Once records are in electronic form, their potential for various uses, including research, public health, accounting, quality assessment and even law enforcement, makes them a valuable asset. And when different databases (*e.g.*, social assistance and health) are merged, their value for such uses increases dramatically. However, control is required so that personal health information is not indiscriminately made available to multiple users without consent of the source individual.[240]

Alberta, Ontario, New Brunswick, and Newfoundland and Labrador have responded to the challenge with provisions in their health information legislation. A separate Part has been added to Alberta's *Health Information Act* (HIA) in order "to enable the sharing and use, via the Alberta EHR, of prescribed health information among authorized custodians".[241] The Alberta HIA also contains extensive provisions on "data matching", defined as "the creation of individually identifying health information by combining individually identifying or non-identifying health information or other information from 2 or more electronic databases",[242] and permits such matching without consent under certain conditions.[243] Ontario has developed by regulation a set of standards

> with which a health information custodian is required to comply when using electronic means to collect, use, modify, disclose, retain or dispose of personal health information, including standards for transactions, data elements for transactions, code sets for data elements and procedures for the transmission and authentication of electronic signatures ...[244]

New Brunswick provides that an individual cannot refuse or withdraw consent to the collection, use or disclosure of personal health information by a custodian if it is for the purpose of creation or maintenance of an electronic health record (EHR).[245] In addition, a custodian is required to disclose personal health infor-

---

[238] R.J. Romanow, *Building on Values: The Future of Health Care in Canada – Final Report* (Saskatoon: Commission on the Future of Health Care in Canada, 2002). For a critique of the Romanow recommendations regarding electronic health records, see E. Gibson, "Jewel in the Crown? The Romanow Commission Proposal to Develop a National Electronic Health Record System" (2003) 66 Sask. L. Rev. 647.

[239] Government of Alberta, Alberta Netcare, "Welcome to Alberta Netcare", online at: <http://www.albertanetcare.ca>.

[240] For extensive discussion of issues concerning longitudinal research databases, and especially the thorny issue of consent, see Timothy Caulfield & Nola Ries, "Consent, Privacy and Confidentiality in Longitudinal, Population Health Research: The Canadian Legal Context" (2004) Health L.J. Supplement 1.

[241] R.S.A. 2000, c. H-5, Part 5.1, s. 56.2 (in force September 1, 2010); Alberta Electronic Health Record Regulation, Alta. Reg. 118/2010.

[242] *Health Information Act*, R.S.A. 2000, c. H-5, s. 1(1)(g).

[243] *Ibid.*, ss. 68-72.

[244] *Personal Health Information Protection Act, 2004*, S.O. 2004, c. 3, Sched. A, s. 73(1)(h); General Regulation, O. Reg. 329/04, s. 6.

[245] *Personal Health Information Privacy and Access Act*, S.N.B. 2009, c. P-7.05, s. 22(1)(c).

mation without consent to or via an information network designated by the Minister in which the information is stored for the purpose of facilitating the EHR.[246] Newfoundland and Labrador has enacted a similar provision that requires disclosure without consent to or via a designated information network for purposes of facilitating an integrated electronic record of personal health information.[247]

British Columbia is unique in having enacted stand-alone legislation, the *E-Health (Personal Health Information Access and Protection of Privacy) Act*,[248] that enables the Minister to designate databases housed within health care bodies which contain personal health information as health information banks. The terms of a designation order must set out in detail the types of personal health information that the database may contain, who may collect, use or disclose it, and for which purposes among a limited menu that ranges from facilitating an individual's care to planning and research.[249] If a person is authorized by a designation order to collect personal health information into a health information bank, it is mandatory for a health care body to provide it, subject to other legislation that prohibits disclosure.[250] The Act sets out a procedure for individuals whose personal health information is contained in a health information bank to make a disclosure directive that limits collection, use or disclosure of certain classes of information, for certain purposes, by certain classes of person.[251] The Act also establishes a data stewardship committee to manage disclosure of information from health information banks or ministry databases for planning or research purposes.[252]

The federal government has invested over one and a half billion dollars into an electronic health record system in which just over one-third of general practitioners are participating.[253] There is much debate surrounding the relative merits of such an initiative and its incidental effects on privacy. Although legislation normally requires consent for the use of personal information, there is growing concern about secondary uses of electronic records.[254] For example, a great deal of research and surveillance is conducted relying on administrative databases originally created for health care billing purposes without consent of the source individuals and without awareness on the part of the public that such activities

---

[246] *Personal Health Information Privacy and Access Act, ibid.*, s. 37(6)(*c*)(iii); General Regulation — *Personal Health Information Privacy and Access Act*, N.B. Reg. 2010-112, ss. 14-15.
[247] *Personal Health Information Act*, S.N.L. 2008, c. P-7.01, s. 39(4)(c)(iii).
[248] S.B.C. 2008, c. 38.
[249] *Ibid.*, ss. 3-5.
[250] *Ibid.*, s. 6.
[251] *Ibid.*, Part 2, Division 2; Disclosure Directive Regulation, B.C. Reg. 172/2009.
[252] *Ibid.*, Part 2, Division 3.
[253] Kimberlyn McGrail, Michael Law & Paul C. Hébert, "No More Dithering on E-Health: Let's Keep Patients Safe Instead" (2010) 182 CMAJ 535.
[254] Patricia Kosseim & Megan Brady, "Policy by Procrastination: Secondary Use of Electronic Health Records for Health Research Purposes" (2008) 2 McGill J.L. & Health 5.

are occurring.[255] Surveys show that members of the public support the use of their personal health information for research purposes, but a majority want to retain a degree of control over such use.[256] As electronic health records come onstream, there will be a wealth of opportunities for secondary use (in addition to the provision of health care services), and decisions regarding the appropriateness of such uses without consent are certain to vex the custodians of such information.

B. GLOBALIZATION

Pressures of globalization are revealed in our economic, social and cultural systems, and information flow is a not insignificant part of these systems. Indeed, PIPEDA was enacted in response to an edict by the European Union (EU), which specified that EU countries would discontinue the trade of information for commercial purposes with countries that could not promise similar levels of protection of personal information as that in force within the EU. The Canadian government drafted legislation framed around a voluntary code of Fair Information Practices that had been developed by the Canadian Standards Association. This resulted in a peculiar piece of legislation in that the code is attached to the legislation as a "Schedule", yet much of the substance is contained in this schedule. It is also rather unique in legislative circles in that it contains phrases such as "should" rather than the mandatory "shall".[257]

Another development has been the adoption by the World Health Organization of new *International Health Regulations* (IHRs),[258] which aim to facilitate international trade and travel while minimizing the risk of the spread of infectious diseases. Canada is a signatory to the IHRs, yet presently lacks the ability to compel provinces and territories to provide the information needed to comply. This was noted to be a serious problem during SARS, with the federal government not receiving the information it needed to report in turn to the World Health Organization.[259] In September 2009, the federal/provincial/territorial ministers of health signed a memorandum of understanding creating a frame-

---

[255] Donald Willison, "Use of Data from the Electronic Health Record for Health Research — Current Governance Challenges and Potential Approaches" (produced for Office of the Privacy Commissioner of Canada, March 2009) at 25, online at: <http://www.priv.gc.ca/information/pub/ehr_200903_e.cfm>.

[256] Donald Willison, Elaine Gibson & Kim McGrail, "A Roadmap to Research Uses of Electronic Health Information" in Colleen Flood, ed., *Data Data Everywhere: Access and Accountability?* (Montreal and Kingston: Queen's Policy Studies Series, McGill-Queen's University Press, forthcoming 2011).

[257] See, *e.g.*, *Personal Information Protection and Electronic Documents Act*, S.C. 2000, c. 5, Sched. 1, ss. 4.2.3, 4.2.5 and 4.5.2.

[258] World Health Organization, *International Health Regulations* (58th World Health Assembly, WHA58.3, Geneva, Switzerland: May 16, 2005), online at: <http://www.who.int/mediacentre/events/2005/wha58/en/>

[259] Health Canada, *Learning From SARS: Renewal of Public Health in Canada* (October 2003) at 39, online at: <http://www.phac-aspc.gc.ca/publicat/sars-sras/pdf/sars-e.pdf>.

work intended to facilitate information sharing in case of a public health emergency. The next step will be to enter into a detailed information-sharing agreement if the various players can agree as to its terms.[260]

C. USE OF NEWBORN BLOOD SPOTS FOR RESEARCH

Researchers in British Columbia, among other provinces, are using newborn "blood spots" stored in hospitals for secondary purposes. Blood spot samples are extracted following delivery of babies in order to screen for conditions such as cystic fibrosis and hypothyroidism that would benefit from early diagnosis and treatment.[261] However, after these tests are conducted, the blood spot samples are being stored and used for research and testing purposes without parental knowledge or consent. A class action lawsuit has been filed in British Columbia,[262] with the plaintiffs arguing that this practice contravenes the *Freedom of Information and Protection of Privacy Act* and the *Privacy Act* as well as constituting a breach of section 8 rights under the Charter. This lawsuit squarely frames the controversy between the individual's privacy rights, including the right to make decisions concerning uses of information, as against the perceived needs of the research community for access to this valuable resource without being required to gain consent of the subject individual.

D. PERSONALIZED MEDICINE

The concept of personalized medicine incorporates the idea that health care should be targeted to the extent possible to an individual's profile. More specifically, it is often considered to focus on the use of genomic and molecular data to select the best medications and other forms of treatment for an individual patient.[263] The promise is improvement in disease prevention, early-stage management of illness and prediction of response to various treatments on an

---

[260] See Pan-Canadian Public Health Network, "Federal/Provincial/Territorial Memorandum of Understanding (MOU) on the Sharing of Information During a Public Health Emergency", online at: <http://www.phn-rsp.ca/pubs/mou-is-pe-pr/index.html>. In September 2007, the Public Health Agency of Canada and Ontario signed an information sharing agreement for all nationally notifiable infectious diseases: Office of the Auditor General of Canada, *Report of the Auditor General of Canada to the House of Commons*, "Chapter 5 — Surveillance of Infectious Diseases — Public Health Agency of Canada" (May 2008) at 5.37, online at: <http://www.oag-bvg.gc.ca/internet/English/parl_oag_200805_05_e_30701.html>.

[261] K. Wilson *et al.*, "Developing a National Newborn Screening Strategy for Canada" (2010) 18:2 Health L. Rev. 31; see also Beth Potter, Denise Avard & Brenda Wilson, "Newborn Blood Spot Screening in Four Countries: Stakeholder Involvement" (2008) 29 Journal of Public Health Policy 121 at 121.

[262] See the Statement of Claim, online at: <http://www.bccla.org/pressreleases/10DNA_Statement.pdf>.

[263] A. Jamie Cuticchia, *Genetics: A Handbook for Lawyers* (Chicago: ABA Publishing, 2009) at 112-13, referencing the Genomics and Personalized Medicine Act of 2007, S. 976, which was never enacted.

individualized basis. As a first step, advances in genetic research have led to routine tests that screen for genetic mutations.

The privacy threat posed by personalized medicine stems from its requirement for prospective population-based research, the need for the amassing of large databases of health information and repositories of biosamples,[264] and an unprecedented scale of information-sharing.[265] Matthew Herder identifies three main challenges resulting from the application of the current legal and ethical framework to personalized medicine.[266] First is the fact that information will flow between the public and private sectors. Health research and health care delivery in personalized medicine straddle the public/private sector divide around which privacy legislation is framed, as information is conveyed back and forth between these sectors. Uncertainty as to which type of legislation will therefore apply, to what types of activities, and in what circumstances, is inevitable. There will also be confusion as to applicability of the Tri-Council Policy Statement.

Second, true anonymization of genetic materials is not possible. Even if samples are de-identified, various techniques permit re-identification due to the uniqueness of DNA. The large-scale biobanks required for personalized medicine therefore carry the potential for re-identification, which in turn brings to light questions of the need for consent, about which there is no consensus, and more broadly how best to protect privacy and confidentiality.

And third, consent of the research subjects is difficult to obtain and manage when large-scale databases are being created and maintained, with multiple uses contemplated. Further, law and policy give little guidance as to the balancing of privacy as against other interests such as data sharing. This leads to a lack of consensus as to the need for consent, with some arguing that the obtaining of consent is impractical and should be waived. Privacy may be sacrificed at the altar of personalized medicine.

X. CONCLUSION

This chapter has covered a number of salient aspects of protection of health information at common law and in legislation as well as under the *Canadian Charter of Rights and Freedoms*. It has highlighted a number of emerging issues, in particular the electronicization of health information, globalization, the use of newborn blood spots for research purposes, and personalized medicine. Other major issues *vis-à-vis* information collection, use, storage and disclosure include broader issues surrounding genetics, Aboriginal health, employees,

---

[264] See Timothy Caulfield & Bartha Maria Knoppers, "Consent, Privacy & Research Biobanks" (report produced for Genome Canada: January 26, 2010) for an overview of the challenges posted by the creation of biobanks in light of traditional consent norms and current laws.

[265] Matthew Herder, "Toward Personalized Medicine in Canada: Ethical & Legal Frameworks, Opportunities for Policy Innovation" (report commissioned by Health Canada: March 2010) [unpublished, on file with author] at 10.

[266] *Ibid.*, at 15.

mental health and HIV/AIDS, to name but a few. The ultimate pressure faced by legislators and courts is to affirm privacy, autonomy and freedom of choice while facilitating low-risk and high-value uses of health information, as well as other interests such as criminal law prosecution and protection of the public. Needless to say, the answers are not clear and this topic will continue to present challenges in the foreseeable future.

Chapter 7

REGULATING REPRODUCTION

Erin Nelson

I.   INTRODUCTION

Reproductive decision-making takes place in a web of overlapping public and private concerns — political and ideological, socio-economic, health and health care — all of which engage the public and involve strongly held opinions and attitudes about appropriate conduct on the part of individuals and the state. Decisions about reproducing are deeply meaningful to us as individuals and are of profound consequence to society. And, it is now possible to actively make decisions about childbearing in ways which would not have been open in the past. We now can make choices about aspects of the reproductive process that, in the past, were matters of chance; we routinely see evidence of the social concerns that these choices raise in the popular press[1] and popular culture.[2]

The shift from reproduction as a matter of chance to an opportunity for deliberate choice has led to greater state involvement in reproductive activity. The introduction of medical products and procedures to prevent conception, to terminate pregnancy and to initiate pregnancies *in vitro* have yielded regulation aimed at consumer protection and quality control, much as is the case with other medications, medical devices and procedures. But the complexities introduced by increased choice in reproduction go beyond issues of safety and quality, in that they also introduce new policy challenges. Reproductive choices, controversial as they sometimes are, demand a carefully balanced response from law and policy. This is particularly the case given that the history of reproductive regulation is a history of discounting women's needs and interests and burdening the exercise of their reproductive autonomy.

---

[1]   See, *e.g.*, Carl Laskin & David Mortimer, "Government should fund fertility therapy" *The Vancouver Sun* (October 1, 2010), online at: Infertilità <http://infertilita.forumfree.it/?t=51143341>; Nicole Baute, "Clinic offers 'social' egg freezing: If you need more time, consider putting your biological clock on ice, LifeQuest says" *The Hamilton Spectator* (October 1, 2010), online at: <http://www.thespec.com/living/healthfitness/article/263604-clinic-offers-socia-egg-freezing>; Kenyon Wallace, "Doctor sued as wrong sperm alleged in fertility cases" *National Post* (September 15, 2010), online at: <http://www.nationalpost.com/news/canada/Doctor+sued+wrong+sperm+alleged+fertility+cases/3525349/story html#ixzz117wK6Ry5>.

[2]   See, *e.g.*, *The Backup Plan* (2010); *My Sister's Keeper* (2009); *Baby Mama* (2008); *Godsend* (2004).

Women's role in reproduction demands that regulation be grounded in respect for women's reproductive autonomy and concern for women's reproductive health. But a tension exists between the need for state involvement to ensure access to reproductive health services and the need to ensure that women are free to make their own reproductive decisions. While a full discussion of the scope and meaning of reproductive autonomy cannot be undertaken here, it is a theme that underlies this discussion of reproductive regulation.

The aim of this chapter is to provide an overview of reproductive law and policy in Canada. It is not possible to address all of the issues in detail here, given the scope of the topic; instead, I will highlight issues of current importance and controversy. In the public law context, I will consider abortion, contraception, non-consensual sterilization, state intervention in the lives of pregnant women and the regulation of assisted reproductive technologies (ARTs). In the private law context, I will examine wrongful birth, wrongful conception and wrongful life claims, and tort duties owed by pregnant women to their fetuses.

Although much has changed since this chapter was originally published in 2007, many of the issues and concerns identified then remain unresolved, as do the fundamental tensions around the scope of reproductive autonomy,

II.   ABORTION IN LAW AND POLICY

Abortion was criminalized in Canada in the 19th century.[3] In 1969, the abortion provisions in the *Criminal Code*[4] were modified to make it possible for women to obtain legal abortions; section 251 of the *Criminal Code* permitted therapeutic abortions where the woman received the approval of a hospital therapeutic abortion committee (made up of three physicians) on the basis that continuation of the pregnancy would endanger her life or health. While permitting abortion in some circumstances, the provisions instituted a rigid administrative structure which could impede a woman's ability to obtain abortion services. Pro-choice advocates therefore continued to lobby for legislative change.[5]

---

[3]   Prior to the 19th century, expertise around pregnancy and childbirth rested with midwives, usually women. In the 19th century, as part of the drive to wrest control over obstetrical care from midwives, physicians campaigned to criminalize abortion. See Reva Siegel, "Reasoning from the Body: A Historical Perspective on Abortion Regulation and Questions of Equal Protection" (1992) 44 Stan. L. Rev. 261; Janine Brodie, Shelley A.M. Gavigan & Jane Jenson, *The Politics of Abortion* (Toronto: Oxford University Press, 1992).

[4]   R.S.C. 1985, c. C-46.

[5]   See Sanda Rodgers, "The Legal Regulation of Women's Reproductive Capacity in Canada" in Jocelyn Downie, Timothy Caulfield & Colleen Flood, eds., *Canadian Health Law and Policy*, 2d ed. (Markham, ON: LexisNexis Canada, 2002) at 334-35; see also Canada, Department of Justice, Committee on the Operation of the Abortion Law, *Report* (Ottawa: Minister of Supply and Services Canada, 1977) for an itemization of concerns with the operation of s. 251 of the *Criminal Code*.

In 1988, section 251 of the *Criminal Code* was struck down by the Supreme Court of Canada in *R. v. Morgentaler*,[6] on the ground that it violated women's constitutionally enshrined right to security of the person. The abortion provision was found to violate section 7 of the *Canadian Charter of Rights and Freedoms*,[7] not because it prohibited abortion in all but limited circumstances, but because the administrative process that it put into place could deprive women of security of the person in a manner that did not accord with the principles of fundamental justice.[8] In other words, the Court struck down the law not because criminal prohibition of abortion is impermissible under the Charter, but because the law created an arbitrary and unfair decision-making process.[9]

One year after the *Morgentaler* decision, the federal government introduced a new restrictive abortion Bill.[10] The Bill was passed in the House of Commons, but was defeated by a vote of 44:43 in the Senate. Since then, no new federal law governing abortion has been introduced, although several provinces have enacted legislation or regulations purporting to govern the provision of abortion services.[11] The provincial statutes have generally either attempted to restrict

---

[6]   [1988] S.C.J. No. 1, [1988] 1 S.C.R. 30 (S.C.C.) [*Morgentaler*].

[7]   Part I of the *Constitution Act, 1982*, being Schedule B to the *Canada Act 1982* (U.K.), 1982, c. 11 [Charter].

[8]   *R. v. Morgentaler*, [1988] S.C.J. No. 1, [1988] 1 S.C.R. 30 (S.C.C.).

[9]   For example, different committees took different approaches to the interpretation of what constituted a threat to a woman's health. Some hospitals did not have therapeutic abortion committees, which meant that some jurisdictions did not have any legal access to abortion. *R. v. Morgentaler*, *ibid.*

[10] Bill C-43 was introduced by Justice Minister Doug Lewis. The Bill recriminalized abortion, except in situations where a woman's doctor thought the woman's life or health was threatened. Health was defined to include mental, physical and psychological health. See Sanda Rodgers, "The Legal Regulation of Women's Reproductive Capacity in Canada" in Jocelyn Downie, Timothy Caulfield & Colleen Flood, eds., *Canadian Health Law and Policy*, 2d ed. (Markham, ON: LexisNexis Canada, 2002) at 331.

[11] British Columbia passed a regulation pursuant to the *Medical Services Act*, R.S.B.C. 1979, c. 255; B.C. Reg. 54/88, which provided that the only insured abortion services were those provided in a hospital in cases where continuing the pregnancy posed a significant threat to a woman's life. The regulation was struck down as *ultra vires* the province: *British Columbia Civil Liberties Assn. v. British Columbia (Attorney General)*, [1988] B.C.J. No. 373, 24 B.C.L.R. (2d) 189 (B.C.S.C.). In Manitoba, a regulation excluding non-hospital abortions from the province's health insurance plan was also ruled *ultra vires*: see *Lexogest Inc. v. Manitoba (Attorney General)*, [1993] M.J. No. 54, 101 D.L.R. (4th) 523 (Man. C.A.). The Province of New Brunswick amended its *Medical Act*, S.N.B. 1981, c. 87 to provide the penalty of licence suspension for any physician who performed (or was likely to perform) abortion services outside a hospital; this amendment was found to be *ultra vires* the province: *Morgentaler v. New Brunswick (Attorney General)*, [1995] N.B.J. No. 40, 121 D.L.R. (4th) 431 (N.B.C.A.). New Brunswick has since amended the legislation and regulations to remove the penalty of licence suspension for the performance of abortions in private clinics, but maintains the prohibition on paying for clinic abortions. The prohibition is not a straightforward refusal to fund clinic abortions; instead, the regulation in issue states that abortion is not an "entitled service" under the *Medical Services Payment Act*, R.S.N.B. 1973, c. M-7 "unless the abortion is performed by a specialist in the field of obstetrics and gynaecology in a hospital facility approved by the jurisdiction in which the hospital facility is located and two medical practitioners certify in writing that the abortion was

funding for abortion services to those provided in hospitals, or to preclude the provision of abortion outside a hospital setting; most of these statutes have been found to be *ultra vires* provincial jurisdiction (or beyond the scope of their parent legislation) and therefore unconstitutional.

Canada is the sole Western nation without any criminal (or direct governmental) control over the provision of abortion services. Under current Canadian law, a woman may have an abortion at any time, for any reason. The absence of a criminal prohibition against abortion, however, has not translated into readily accessible abortion services. Currently, pregnancy termination is governed in diverse ways across the country, with significant variations among jurisdictions. Timing, site and methods of pregnancy termination are governed in part by provincial physician regulatory bodies,[12] and provincial governments control access to and funding for abortion services pursuant to their jurisdiction over the delivery of health care.

The implication of this approach to regulation of abortion services is enormous variability in access to these services across the country. For example, of the seven provinces with freestanding abortion clinics, only six provinces cover

---

medically required" (N.B. Reg. 84-20, Sched. 2 (*a.*1)). In its Statement of Defence to a lawsuit initiated by Dr. Morgentaler to challenge these provisions, the Province of New Brunswick asserted that Dr. Morgentaler did not have standing to bring the claim. The New Brunswick courts have declared that Dr. Morgentaler does indeed have public interest standing to challenge the regulation. The province has said that it will not appeal this decision and that the claim, which was commenced in July 2003, will continue to go forward. See "N.B. will not appeal Morgentaler decision" CBC News (August 18, 2009), online at: <http://www.cbc.ca/canada/new-brunswick/story/2009/08/18/nb-morgentaler-appeal-206.html>. See *Morgentaler v. New Brunswick*, [2008] N.B.J. No. 279, 2008 NBQB 258 (N.B.Q.B.), affd [2009] N.B.J. No. 139, 2009 NBCA 26 (N.B.C.A.). Nova Scotia enacted legislation creating significant penal sanctions for anyone providing health care services outside a hospital; this, too, was struck down as *ultra vires*: *R. v. Morgentaler*, [1993] S.C.J. No. 95, 107 D.L.R. (4th) 537 (S.C.C.). Prince Edward Island enacted regulations under the *Health Services Payment Act*, R.S.P.E.I. 1988, c. H-2 that permitted coverage by the province's health care insurance plan for only those abortions performed in a hospital, and only where a committee of five doctors authorized the abortion. The P.E.I. Court of Appeal upheld these regulations as being authorized by the *Health Services Payment Act* (*Morgentaler v. Prince Edward Island (Minister of Health and Social Services)*, [1996] P.E.I.J. No. 75, 139 D.L.R. (4th) 603 (P.E.I.C.A.)). As Sanda Rodgers notes, the decision of the P.E.I.C.A. is anomalous and is arguably wrongly decided. See Sanda Rodgers, "The Legal Regulation of Women's Reproductive Capacity in Canada", *ibid.*, at 341. Between 1999 and 2005, the Province of Quebec required women to pay for part of the cost of abortion procedures performed in private clinics. Recently, the Quebec Superior Court ordered the Province to pay $13 million to reimburse these women: see *Association pour l'accès à l'avortement c. Québec (Procureur général)*, [2006] J.Q. no 8654, 2006 QCCS 4694 (Que. C.S.). The Government of Quebec elected not to appeal the decision.

12   See, for example, College of Physicians & Surgeons of Alberta, *Termination of Pregnancy: Standards & Guidelines* (February 2008), online at: <http://www.cpsa.ab.ca/Libraries/Pro_QofC_Non-Hospital/NHSF_-_Termination_of_Pregnancy.sflb.ashx>; College of Physicians and Surgeons of British Columbia, *Resource Manual* (rev. September 2009), online at: <https://www.cpsbc.ca/files/u6/Abortion.pdf>.

the cost of clinic abortions.[13] Three provinces and all three territories lack non-hospital abortion facilities,[14] and the number of hospitals that provide abortion services apparently continues to decline. A 2003 report by the Canadian Abortion Rights Action League (CARAL) notes that only 17.8 per cent of Canadian hospitals perform abortion services,[15] while a similar report issued by Canadians For Choice (CFC) in 2006 puts the figure at 15.9 per cent.[16] In addition to the declining availability of abortion in Canadian hospitals, the exclusion of therapeutic abortion services from the interprovincial reciprocal billing agreement[17] creates a further constraint on access for women who are temporarily living away from their home province (such as university students), or those who live in an area where the nearest abortion provider is in a different province. Other barriers to access also exist. As noted in the CFC study, these include: the need to travel outside one's community;[18] anti-choice physicians who refuse to refer women to those who provide abortion services; lack of availability of information about abortion services; long waiting periods; hospital gestational limits on

---

[13] British Columbia, Alberta, Manitoba, Ontario, Quebec, and Newfoundland and Labrador (see Laura Eggertson, "News: Abortion Services in Canada: A Patchwork Quilt with Many Holes" (2001) 164:6 CMAJ 847). In Manitoba and Quebec, full funding for non-hospital abortion services is now paid as a result of successful litigation. In Manitoba, see *Jane Doe 1 v. Manitoba*, [2004] M.J. No. 456, 2004 MBQB 285 (Man. Q.B.) (granting the applicants' motion for summary judgment and declaring the offending provision of the Manitoba *Health Services Insurance Act*, C.C.S.M. c. H35, s. 116(1)(h), 116(2), Excluded Services Regulation, Man. Reg. 46/93, s. 2(28) of no force and effect), revd in part [2005] M.J. No. 335, 2005 MBCA 109 (Man. C.A.); *Jane Doe 1 v. Manitoba*, [2005] M.J. No. 335, 2005 MBCA 109 (Man. C.A.) (allowing the government's appeal from the summary judgment in favour of the plaintiffs); *Jane Doe 1 v. Manitoba*, [2005] S.C.C.A. No. 513 (S.C.C.) (dismissing the applicants' motion for leave to appeal to the Supreme Court of Canada); and in Quebec, see *Association pour l'accès à l'avortement c. Québec (Procureur général)*, [2006] J.Q. no 8654, 2006 QCCS 4694 (Que. C.S.). The *Jane Doe* case differs from *Lexogest Inc. v. Manitoba (Attorney General)*, [1993] M.J. No. 54, 101 D.L.R. (4th) 523 (Man. C.A.), in that the Charter issues were not decided in *Lexogest*.

[14] Saskatchewan, Nova Scotia and Prince Edward Island. See National Abortion Federation, "Access to Abortion in Canada: Abortion Coverage by Region", online at: <http://www.prochoice.org/canada/regional.html>.

[15] See Canadian Abortion Rights Action League, "Protecting Abortion Rights in Canada" (2003), online at: Canadian For Choice <http://canadiansforchoice.ca/caralreport.pdf>.

[16] Jessica Shaw, "Reality Check: A Close Look at Accessing Abortion Services in Canadian Hospitals" (2006), online at: <http://www.canadiansforchoice.ca/report_english.pdf>.

[17] Canadian Institute for Health Information, *Reciprocal Billing Report, Canada, 2004–2005, Revised August 2007* (Ottawa: CIHI, 2007) at F-1.

[18] *Ibid.* See also Christabelle Sethna & Marion Doull, "Far From Home? A Pilot Study Tracking Women's Journeys to a Canadian Abortion Clinic" (2007) 27:8 Journal of Obstetrics and Gynaecology Canada 640; Ingrid Peritz, "Despite being legal, abortions still not accessible for all Canadians" *The Globe and Mail* (June 18, 2010), online at: <http://www.theglobeandmail.com/news/national/despite-being-legal-abortions-still-not-accessible-for-all-canadians/article1610254/>; Laura Eggertson, "News: Abortion Services in Canada: A Patchwork Quilt with Many Holes" (2001) 164:6 CMAJ 847. In P.E.I., women must travel outside their home jurisdiction in order to obtain abortion services. See Jessica Shaw, "Reality Check: A Close Look at Accessing Abortion Services in Canadian Hospitals" (2006), online at: Canadians For Choice <http://www.canadiansforchoice.ca/report_english.pdf>.

abortion services; and anti-choice "counselling" centres.[19] In 2003, the executive director of the CARAL noted the significant implications of funding policy on the availability of abortion services: "Ironically, it seems to be getting worse rather than better since the Morgentaler decision in 1988. There are a number of barriers and the [number is increasing]."[20]

Medical abortion — where pregnancy is terminated as a result of the ingestion of pharmaceutical agents — is an option that many women prefer over surgical abortion. Studies from France and the United Kingdom show that when given the choice, more than half of women opt for medical rather than surgical abortion.[21] It can be argued that medical abortion is not only preferable to many women, but is clinically superior to surgical abortion early in pregnancy.[22] Medical abortion using mifepristone and misoprostol "can make abortion earlier, more accessible, safer, less traumatic, less medicalised and less expensive".[23] Up to nine weeks gestation, medical abortion can take place at home if the woman prefers that option to waiting in the clinic, and need only involve two visits to the clinic.[24] There is evidence of its safety, efficacy and acceptability as an alternative to surgical abortion, at least in the early part of pregnancy.[25] However,

---

[19]   Jessica Shaw, "Reality Check: A Close Look at Accessing Abortion Services in Canadian Hospitals", *ibid.*

[20]   As quoted in Laura Eggertson, "News: Abortion Services in Canada: A Patchwork Quilt with Many Holes" (2001) 164:6 CMAJ 847 at 847.

[21]   Victoria Jane Davis, "Induced Abortion Guidelines" (November 2006) 184 Journal of Obstetrics and Gynaecology Canada 1014 at 1018; see also Ellen Wiebe *et al.*, "Comparison of Abortions Induced by Methotrexate or Mifepristone Followed by Misoprostol" (2002) 99:5 Obstetrics & Gynecology 813.

[22]   There is also some preliminary evidence suggesting that the incidence of miscarriage and postpartum hemorrhage in the next pregnancy is significantly lower after first-trimester medical (as opposed to surgical) abortion. See Changping Gana *et al.*, "The Influence of Medical Abortion Compared with Surgical Abortion on Subsequent Pregnancy Outcome" (2008) 101 International Journal of Gynecology & Obstetrics 231.

[23]   Marge Berer, "Medical Abortion: Issues of Choice and Acceptability" (2005) 13 Reproductive Health Matters 25 at 26.

[24]   Janice Raymond has argued that medical abortion using mifepristone and misoprostol is highly medicalized, time consuming and painful: see Janice G. Raymond, "RU 486: Progress or Peril" in Joan C. Callahan, ed., *Reproduction, Ethics and the Law: Feminist Perspectives* (Indianapolis: Indiana University Press, 1995) at 286. As Marge Berer points out, however, it need not be so highly medicalized — as with surgical abortion, there need only be two clinic visits: one to prescribe the drug and give instructions on use as well as on complications, and one follow-up visit to ensure that the abortion is complete and that there are no complications. This is identical to the clinical schedule with surgical abortion. Berer also notes that most women who have experienced medical abortion have been satisfied with the procedure and would choose it again. See Marge Berer, "Medical Abortion: Issues of Choice and Acceptability", *ibid.*, at 26, 29.

[25]   In the United States, concerns have been voiced about the safety of mifepristone, but the data indicates that medical abortion is a safe and effective option. See, *e.g.*, Eric Schaff, "Mifepristone: Ten Years Later" (2010) 81:1 Contraception 1; Association of Reproductive Health Professionals, "What You Need to Know: Mifepristone Safety Overview", online at: <http://www.arhp.org/uploadDocs/mifepristonefactsheet.pdf#search=%22mifepristone%22>; Jillian T. Henderson *et al.*, "Safety of Mifepristone Abortions in Clinical Use" (2005) 72:3 Contraception 175; Susan Dudley & Stephanie Mueller, "Fact Sheet: What is Medical Abortion?" (Washington, DC: Na-

medical abortion is not readily available in Canada. The only medication indicated for use in medical abortion is mifepristone, and it is not available in Canada. Another medication, methotrexate, can be and is used for medical abortion but this use is "off-label", in that the drug has not been approved for the termination of pregnancy. Methotrexate is an effective abortifacient, but methotrexate abortions take longer to complete than those induced using mifepristone and mifepristone is therefore preferred.[26] The Society of Obstetricians and Gynaecologists of Canada has urged Health Canada to work with industry and with professional organizations to ensure the availability of mifepristone in Canada and noted that "[t]he use of such medication for terminating early pregnancy constitutes a significant medical and public health gain and has received medical acceptability in Europe and the USA".[27]

Another barrier to access faced by women seeking abortion services relates to the availability of health care providers able and willing to perform the procedure. Concerns have been raised about the insufficiency of training in abortion procedures offered by medical schools,[28] as well as in relation to the scope of conscientious objection to the provision of abortion services.[29] From a Canadian legal perspective, the scope of conscientious objection to the provision of abortion services is unsettled.[30] There is no Canadian case law or legislation that

---

tional Abortion Federation, 2008), online at: <http://www.prochoice.org/pubs_research/publications/downloads/about_abortion/medical_abortion.pdf>.

[26] Joanna N. Erdman, Amy Grenon & Leigh Harrison-Wilson, "Medication Abortion in Canada: A Right-to-Health Perspective" (2008) 98:10 American Journal of Public Health 1764 at 1767; Ellen Wiebe *et al.*, "Comparison of Abortions Induced by Methotrexate or Mifepristone Followed by Misoprostol" (2002) 99:5 Obstetrics & Gynecology 813.

[27] Society of Obstetricians and Gynaecologists of Canada, "SOGC Policy Statement: Mifepristone" (2009) 31:12 Journal of Obstetrics and Gynaecology Canada 1180.

[28] See Abortion Rights Coalition of Canada, "Position Paper # 6: Training of Abortion Providers/Medical Students for Choice" (October 2005), online at: <http://www.arcc-cdac.ca/postion papers/06-Training-Abortion-Providers-MSFC.PDF>; Atsuko Koyama & Robin Williams, "Abortion in Medical School Curricula" (2005) 8:2 McGill Journal of Medicine 157; Laura Eggertson, "News: Abortion Services in Canada: A Patchwork Quilt with Many Holes" (2001) 164:6 CMAJ 847 at 848; Laura Shanner, "Pregnancy Intervention and Models of Maternal-Fetal Relationship: Philosophical Reflections on the Winnipeg C.F.S. Dissent" (1998) 36 Alta. L. Rev. 751 at 764; Bonnie Steinbock, "Symposium: Opening Remarks" (1999) 62 Alb. L. Rev. 805 at 806.

[29] See, *e.g.*, Sanda Rodgers & Jocelyn Downie, "Guest Editorial: Abortion: Ensuring Access" (2006) 175:1 CMAJ 9; Bernard M. Dickens & Rebecca J. Cook, "The Scope and Limits of Conscientious Objection" (2000) 71 International Journal of Gynecology & Obstetrics 71 at 73; Bernard M. Dickens, "Informed Consent" in Jocelyn Downie, Timothy Caulfield & Colleen Flood, eds., *Canadian Health Law and Policy*, 2d ed. (Markham, ON: LexisNexis Canada, 2002) at 148.

[30] Indeed, the scope of conscientious objection is somewhat unclear in ethical and other legal contexts as well. See Julie Cantor & Ken Baum, "The Limits of Conscientious Objection — May Pharmacists Refuse to Fill Prescriptions for Emergency Contraception?" (2004) 351:19 New Eng. J. Med. 2008; R. Alta Charo, "The Celestial Fire of Conscience — Refusing to Deliver Medical Care" (2005) 352:24 New Eng. J. Med. 2471; Sanda Rodgers & Jocelyn Downie, "Guest Editorial: Abortion: Ensuring Access", *ibid.*

clearly delineates the rights or responsibilities of providers who object to abortion for moral reasons.

In an attempt to enshrine protection for "conscience rights" in the *Criminal Code*, a Private Members' Bill was introduced in Parliament in 2008.[31] The Bill sought to "[p]rotect the right of health care practitioners and other persons to refuse, without fear of reprisal or other discriminatory coercion, to participate in medical procedures that offend a tenet of their religion, or their belief that human life is inviolable". The Bill defined human life as beginning at fertilization, and made it a criminal offence to refuse to employ or promote, or to dismiss, a health care practitioner who refuses to participate in medical procedures that offend their religion or their belief that human life is inviolable. Similarly, it would be criminal offence under this Bill to refuse to admit to study, to grant accreditation to or to refuse to admit (or exclude from membership) a health care practitioner to a professional association on this basis. The Bill generated significant discussion and debate. Due to the dissolution of Parliament in September 2008, it did not get past first reading stage; to date, the Bill has not been reintroduced.

Although it seems clear that the law of negligence requires providers to refer their patients to non-objecting practitioners, there is significant opposition to this claim within the medical profession, as is clear from the vocal reaction to a Guest Editorial published in the CMAJ in 2006.[32] In response to the Guest Editorial, which stated that physicians who "fail to provide appropriate referrals ... are committing malpractice and risk lawsuits and disciplinary proceedings", the CMA provided a "clarification" of its own policy on Induced Abortion.[33] The clarification suggests that physicians are not obligated to provide referrals where participating in the termination of a pregnancy violates their moral beliefs.[34] The CMA policy actually states, *inter alia*:

- The provision of advice and information on family planning and human sexuality is the responsibility of practising physicians; however, educational institutes and health care agencies must share this responsibility.

- The patient should be provided with the option of full and immediate counselling services in the event of unwanted pregnancy.

---

[31] Bill C-537, *An Act to amend the Criminal Code (protection of conscience rights in the health care profession)*, 2d Sess., 39th Parl., 2008 (first reading April 16, 2008).

[32] See Sanda Rodgers & Jocelyn Downie, "Guest Editorial: Abortion: Ensuring Access" (2006) 175:1 CMAJ 9.

[33] Jeff Blackmer, "Letter: Clarification of the CMA's Position Concerning Induced Abortion" (2007) 176:9 CMAJ 1310.

[34] See Bernard M. Dickens & Rebecca J. Cook, "The Scope and Limits of Conscientious Objection" (2000) 71 International Journal of Gynecology & Obstetrics 71; Bernard M. Dickens, "Informed Consent" in Jocelyn Downie, Timothy Caulfield & Colleen Flood, eds., *Canadian Health Law and Policy*, 2d ed. (Markham, ON: LexisNexis Canada, 2002) at 148. Dickens notes that fiduciary law also protects patients from their physicians' failure to disclose options or to refer due to the provider's moral convictions.

- Since the risks of complications of induced abortion are lowest in early pregnancy, early diagnosis of pregnancy and determination of appropriate management should be encouraged.

- There should be no delay in the provision of abortion services.[35]

While Dr. Blackmer (who authored the clarification) is correct in saying that the policy does not explicitly require referrals to an abortion provider, the policy can certainly sustain the interpretation asserted in the Guest Editorial.

Similar opposition was elicited[36] when the College of Physicians & Surgeons of Alberta published its *Health Professions Act Standards of Practice* in 2010.[37] Section 25 of the *Standards of Practice* precludes physicians from withholding information about "the existence of a procedure or treatment because providing that procedure or giving advice about it conflicts with their moral or religious beliefs". The section further provides that

> When moral or religious beliefs prevent a physician from providing or offering access to information about a legally available medical or surgical treatment or service, that physician must ensure that the patient who seeks such advice or medical care is offered timely access to another physician or resource that will provide accurate information about all available medical options.

Whether or not physician codes of ethics or standards of practice clearly articulate a requirement to refer, it does seem clear that the law of negligence demands that providers make appropriate referrals when they refuse to participate in procedures on the basis of moral or religious objection. As Bernard Dickens puts it:

> The equilibrium between physicians rights and those of patients is maintained through objecting physicians' legal and ethical duty to refer their patients who request lawful services to physicians who do not object. Religiously based claims of complicity in procedures, conducted by physicians to whom patients are referred, have neither legal nor ethical substance. Referral does not constitute participation in any discussions that referred physicians have with patients, or in any procedures upon which such physicians and patients agree. Physicians do not share in any fees paid to the physicians to whom they refer their patients, nor in any liability that physicians may incur for any form of malpractice.[38]

---

[35] Canadian Medical Association, *CMA Policy: Induced Abortion* (December 1988) at 1, online at: <http://policybase.cma.ca/PolicyPDF/PD88-06.pdf>.

[36] "Edmonton physician opposes mandatory referrals for abortion" CBC News (February 23, 2009), online at: <http://www.cbc.ca/canada/edmonton/story/2009/02/22/edm-abortion-referrals.html>.

[37] College of Physicians & Surgeons of Alberta, *Health Professions Act Standards of Practice* (January 1, 2010), online at: <http://www.cpsa.ab.ca/Libraries/Res_Standards_of_Practice/HPA_Standards_of_Practice_Consolidatation_Issued_Jan_1_2010.pdf>.

[38] Bernard M. Dickens, "Conscientious Objection and Professionalism" (2009) 4:2 Expert Review of Obstetrics & Gynecology 97 at 97; see also Bernard M. Dickens, "Legal Protection and Limits of Conscientious Objection: When Conscientious Objection is Unethical" (2009) 28 Med. & L. 337.

III.   CONTRACEPTION AND STERILIZATION

A.   CONTRACEPTION

Contraceptive services were criminally prohibited in Canada between 1892 and 1969. Contraceptives are now generally available in Canada, but, as in the case of abortion services, barriers to access continue to exist. These barriers are largely financial and regulatory, but also encompass the issue of provider conscientious objection, especially in relation to emergency contraception (EC).

Financial barriers to contraceptive access pose a complex problem. Canada's health care system provides universal coverage of physician and hospital services, but most provincial health care plans do not include prescription drug coverage,[39] nor do they include non-prescription contraceptives such as condoms, spermicides, the contraceptive sponge and intrauterine devices.[40] As a result of the organization and structure of the health care system around physician and hospital services, the most affordable contraceptive option may also be the most permanent — surgical sterilization.[41] While the provision of tubal ligation or vasectomy without charge[42] is clearly not coercive, it may nonetheless be cause for concern. If women are led to choose sterilization even where it is not an optimal method of contraception in their particular circumstances (that is, they may wish to have more children in the future) because it is more affordable than non-permanent options, then the autonomous quality of the choice becomes questionable. Poor women who wish to avoid pregnancy in the short term may be led to the most permanent contraceptive option, due to the costs of other methods. While this is a point I cannot argue fully here, a potential answer to this concern seems clear: the health care system should provide funding for a wide range of contraceptive options.[43] Not only would this approach lead to a

---

[39]   Some provinces have "pharmacare" programs that provide some prescription drug coverage. See, for example, Manitoba Health, "Manitoba Pharmacare Program: About the Manitoba Pharmacare Program", online: <http://www.gov.mb.ca/health/pharmacare/index.html>; British Columbia, Ministry of Health Services, "Welcome to Pharmacare", online: <http://www.health. gov.bc.ca/pharmacare/index.html#>.

[40]   Some contraceptive methods are available without charge to certain individuals (for example, those who attend sexual health or university health clinics) or in certain jurisdictions (where prescription drugs are covered), but availability is variable and unpredictable, depending on the specific contraceptive an individual seeks to use, and where in Canada the individual lives.

[41]   Tubal ligation and vasectomy procedures are provided as insured services in most Canadian provinces. Intrauterine device insertion is also covered under health care insurance plans, but the devices themselves must be purchased from a pharmacy.

[42]   Note that this is not the case in all Canadian jurisdictions.

[43]   There are many points in a woman's life at which her reproductive health needs are identical to her basic health needs, and reproductive services play a "critical role ... in primary health care for women". As such, it seems at least arguable that reproductive health care, including contraception, should be funded by the health care system. See Canadian Women's Health Network, National Coordinating Group on Health Care Reform and Women, *Reading Romanow: The Implications of the Final Report of The Commission on the Future of Health Care in Canada for Women*, revised and updated edition (Winnipeg: Centre for Health Studies, 2003) at 53, online at: <http://www.womenandhealthcarereform.ca/publications/reading-romanow.pdf>.

better range of options for women, it would also help to reduce the incidence (and associated costs) of abortion as well as the social costs created by unwanted and mistimed pregnancies.

A significant non-financial barrier to access requires attention as well, and that is the Canadian regulatory environment. In a study comparing the availability of contraceptive methods in Canada to availability in other countries,[44] researchers found that Canadian women have access to a significantly smaller range of hormonal contraceptive products than women in the U.S., France, Sweden, Denmark and the U.K.[45] In relation to newer contraceptive products, Canadian women have access to the fewest options.[46] The study also points out that, while regulatory approval for new drug products in Canada tends to lag approximately six months behind the United States, as of January 1, 2004, Canada was 29.6 months behind for six contraceptive products seeking regulatory approval.[47] The authors conclude that:

> Canada appears to be lagging behind other countries with respect to the availability of hormonal contraceptive options. A wider choice of contraceptive options, including a variety of dosage forms, routes of administration and chemical entities, can improve access to effective contraception ... [and] reduce the number of unplanned and unwanted pregnancies.[48]

Emergency contraception has also been the subject of much recent concern in both Canada and the U.S.[49] When used within 72 hours after unprotected sex-

---

[44] Dianne Azzarello & John Collins, "Canadian Access to Hormonal Contraceptive Drug Choices" (2004) 26:5 Journal of Obstetrics and Gynaecology Canada 489 at 490.

[45] Canadian women have access to 35 per cent of contraceptive products available worldwide, and 37 per cent of hormonal contraceptives. Figures for the other countries studied are as follows: U.S. 58 per cent and 59 per cent; U.K. 52 per cent and 54 per cent; France 44 per cent and 54 per cent; Denmark 46 per cent and 41 per cent; Sweden 44 per cent and 50 per cent. Dianne Azzarello & John Collins, "Canadian Access to Hormonal Contraceptive Drug Choices", *ibid.*, at 495-97.

[46] Canadian women have access to 22 per cent of available contraceptive products. Women in Denmark have the greatest number of options (67 per cent of available products). Dianne Azzarello & John Collins, "Canadian Access to Hormonal Contraceptive Drug Choices", *ibid.*, at 496. As the authors note, "[d]ifferent dose regimens and routes of hormonal contraceptive administration offer a range of efficacy, side-effect profiles and advantages and disadvantages that allow each woman to make an optimal choice". In addition, wider choice may improve compliance with drug regimens, leading to more effective use of hormonal contraceptives (at 496-97).

[47] Dianne Azzarello & John Collins, "Canadian Access to Hormonal Contraceptive Drug Choices", *ibid.*, at 495. The authors note that hormonal contraceptive products and hormone replacement therapy products all required longer review times than Viagra, a drug used in erectile dysfunction. The shortest approval time for an HRT product was 111 days longer than the approval time required for Viagra. It is unclear why this is the case, because information is not readily available due to restrictions in the *Access to Information Act*, R.S.C. 1985, c. A-1. See 495, 498.

[48] Dianne Azzarello & John Collins, "Canadian Access to Hormonal Contraceptive Drug Choices", *ibid.*, at 499.

[49] See, *e.g.*, Joanna N. Erdman & Rebecca J. Cook, "Protecting Fairness in Women's Health: The Case of Emergency Contraception" in Colleen M. Flood, ed., *Just Medicare: What's In, What's Out, How We Decide* (Toronto: University of Toronto Press, 2006) 137, Joanna N. Erdman &

ual intercourse, EC[50] prevents 89 per cent of expected pregnancies. It is most effective when used within 24 hours of unprotected sex (when it prevents 95 per cent of expected pregnancies), and least effective when taken more than 49 hours post-intercourse (when it prevents 58 per cent of expected pregnancies).[51] It is abundantly clear that timely access to EC is essential. Until fairly recently, EC was only available in most Canadian jurisdictions with a physician's pre-scription.[52] In 2005, EC was changed to non-prescription status across Canada meaning that it could be kept "behind the counter" in pharmacies and obtained by women upon direct request to the pharmacist. While this meant that the im-pediment to access created by the need for a physician's prescription was cleared away, other potential obstacles emerged. Concerns were raised around cost — pharmacies were charging a counselling fee in addition to the cost of the drug[53] — and around privacy concerns arising from the information collection practices of many pharmacists who dispense EC.[54]

The privacy concerns centred on a form recommended for use by the Cana-dian Pharmacists Association (CPhA). The form asked for "personal data, in-cluding the woman's name, address, the date of her last menstrual period, when

---

Rebecca J. Cook, "Morning after pill still faces hurdles" (May 21, 2004) *National Post* A18. See also: Editorial, "Emergency Contraception Moves Behind the Counter" (2005) 172:7 CMAJ 845; Laura Eggertson & Barbara Sibbald, "Privacy Issues Raised Over Plan B: Women Asked for Names, Addresses, Sexual History" (2005) 173:12 CMAJ 1435; and Alastair J.J. Wood, Jeffrey M. Drazen & Michael F. Greene, "A Sad Day for Science at the FDA" (2005) 353 New Eng. J. Med. 1197 at 1198.

[50] There are two primary methods of EC. One uses a high dose of combination oral contraceptive pills containing both estrogen and progesterone/levonorgestrel (the Yuzpe method); the other is levonorgestrel alone, which is marketed under the brand name "Plan B". See, *e.g.*, Rebecca J. Cook, Bernard M. Dickens & Mahmoud F. Fathalla, *Reproductive Health and Human Rights: Integrating Medicine, Ethics, and Law* (Oxford: Oxford University Press, 2003) at 289. The effi-cacy rates given here are for levonorgestrel: see D.A. Grimes *et al.*, "Randomised Controlled trial of Levonorgestrel versus the Yuzpe Regimen of Combined Oral Contraceptives for Emer-gency Contraception" (1998) 352:9126 Lancet 428.

[51] Rebecca J. Cook, Bernard M. Dickens & Mahmoud F. Fathalla, *Reproductive Health and Hu-man Rights: Integrating Medicine, Ethics, and Law, ibid.*, at 289.

[52] Prior to April 2006, EC was available without a prescription in Quebec, Saskatchewan and Brit-ish Columbia. See Barbara Sibbald, "Nonprescription Status for Emergency Contraception" (2005) 172:7 CMAJ 861.

[53] See, *e.g.*, Joanna N. Erdman & Rebecca J. Cook, "Morning after pill still faces hurdles" *National Post* (May 21, 2004) A18. See also: Editorial, "Emergency Contraception Moves Behind the Counter" (2005) 172:7 CMAJ 845; and Laura Eggertson & Barbara Sibbald, "Privacy Issues Raised Over Plan B: Women Asked for Names, Addresses, Sexual History" (2005) 173:12 CMAJ 1435, noting that the fee charged is approximately $20.

[54] See Laura Eggertson & Barbara Sibbald, "Privacy Issues Raised Over Plan B: Women Asked for Names, Addresses, Sexual History", *ibid.* In an especially interesting turn of events, these stories around Plan B played a part in the emergence of serious concerns over the editorial independ-ence of the Canadian Medical Association Journal, Canada's well-respected generalist medical journal. See, *e.g.*, International Committee of Medical Journal Editors, "Canadian Medical Asso-ciation Journal Announcement", online at: <http://www.icmje.org/update_cmaj.html>; CMAJ, Press Release, "CMAJ Acting Editor-in-Chief Accepts Editorial Board Resignations" (March 16, 2006), online at: <http://www.cmaj.ca/misc/press/cmaj_release_mar16.pdf>.

she had unprotected sex, and her customary method of birth control, [and] ... the reason for dispensing the medication".[55] Objections were raised to the practice, as it could deter women from seeking access to EC because of their fears around the collection and storage of sensitive information. Privacy commissioners in a number of Canadian jurisdictions articulated concerns about the CPhA form, noting that personal information is not normally collected by pharmacists when they dispense Schedule II drugs.[56]

Another appreciable roadblock to access in the contraceptive context is conscientious objection by health care professionals.[57] Like physicians who object to participating in the provision of abortion services, Canadian pharmacists assert a right to conscientiously object to the provision of services that they find morally or religiously offensive.[58]

The proposed solution to these remaining barriers to access was to make EC available without the need for pharmacist intervention at point of sale.[59] In May 2008, the National Association of Pharmacy Regulatory Authorities (NAPRA) recommended that EC could be sold off-the-shelf.[60] In theory, this means that women should be able to purchase EC without pharmacist involvement, just as they would purchase any other number of items at the pharmacy. However, the scheduling change recommended by NAPRA is not binding on provincial and territorial regulators, and at least two provinces have declined to make the change.[61]

---

[55] Laura Eggertson & Barbara Sibbald, "Privacy Issues Raised Over Plan B: Women Asked for Names, Addresses, Sexual History", *ibid.*

[56] Laura Eggertson, "Ontario Pharmacists Drop Plan B Screening Form" (2006) 174:2 CMAJ 149.

[57] As has been noted by others, conscientious objection to the provision of hormonal contraceptives (including emergency contraception) can create significant barriers to access for women, particularly low-income women and those who live in rural areas. See Holly Teliksa, "Recent Development: Obstacles to Access: How Pharmacist Refusal Clauses Undermine the Basic Health Care Needs of Rural and Low-Income Women" (2005) 20 Berkeley Journal of Gender Law & Justice 229; Tania Khan & Megan Arvad McCoy, "Sixth Annual Review of Gender and Sexuality Law: VI. Healthcare Law Chapter: Access to Contraception" (2005) 6 Geo. J. Gender & L. 785.

[58] See Mike Mastromatteo, "Alberta pharmacist wins concessions in right-to-refuse case" *The Interim* (December 2003), online at: <http://www.theinterim.com/2003/dec/02alberta.html>. See also The Protection of Conscience Project, online at: <http://www.consciencelaws.org/>. In addition, like their physician counterparts, some pharmacists object to the provision of referrals to those who will furnish the requested service.

[59] Joanna N. Erdman & Rebecca J. Cook, "Protecting Fairness in Women's Health: The Case of Emergency Contraception" in Colleen M. Flood, ed., *Just Medicare: What's In, What's Out, How We Decide* (Toronto: University of Toronto Press, 2006) at 137.

[60] Laura Eggertson, "Plan B Comes Out from Behind the Counter" (2008) 178:13 CMAJ 1645.

[61] Once a drug is no longer under federal government control (as is now the case with levonorgestrel), it is up to provincial and territorial regulatory bodies to determine how the drug may be sold. Provincial and territorial regulatory authorities act on the basis of recommendations made by the NDSAC. See Joanna N. Erdman & Rebecca J. Cook, "Protecting Fairness in Women's Health: The Case of Emergency Contraception" in Colleen M. Flood, ed., *Just Medicare: What's In, What's Out, How We Decide* (Toronto: University of Toronto Press, 2006) at 138-39. In Saskatchewan, EC is kept behind the counter and in Quebec, EC can be obtained by prescription

The phenomenon of conscientious objection in Canada has not been thoroughly studied, meaning that it is difficult to ascertain the frequency with which it poses a problem for contraceptive access.[62] Ideally, health care professionals should not be required to participate in procedures or services they find morally objectionable. But there must be limits to the protection of provider conscience where such protection threatens women's health and well-being. To date, no Canadian court has explicitly addressed the issue of provider obligations and the role of conscience,[63] meaning that it is left to policy-makers and regulators to address the question of conscientious objection.[64]

---

from a pharmacist (O.C. 964-2001, August 23, 2001, G.O.Q. 2, 6198). See Plan B, online at: <http://www.planb.ca/where.php>.

[62] But it is clear that women do face difficulty accessing contraceptives due to provider objection. See, *e.g.*, Mike Mastromatteo, "Alberta pharmacist wins concessions in right-to-refuse case" *The Interim* (December 2003), online at: <http://www.theinterim.com/2003/dec/02alberta.html>; Barbara Sibbald, "Nonprescription Status for Emergency Contraception" (2005) 172:7 CMAJ 861; Barbara W., "Counter Attack" (2006) 174:2 CMAJ 211.

[63] As noted earlier (see notes 29, 34 and accompanying text), there are signals that lead to the fairly safe conclusion that Canadian law requires physicians who object to participating in certain procedures for reasons of conscience to refer their patients to a provider who does not similarly object. See, *e.g.*, Rebecca J. Cook & Bernard M. Dickens, "Access to Emergency Contraception" (2003) 25:11 Journal of Obstetrics and Gynaecology Canada 914. Cook & Dickens cite *Zimmer v. Ringrose*, [1981] A.J. No. 596, 124 D.L.R. (3d) 215 (Alta. C.A.), where the Alberta Court of Appeal held that the physician's failure to refer his patient to a local physician who would facilitate an abortion amounted to negligence (for failure to provide appropriate follow-up care). While this case does not deal with a refusal to refer because of conscientious objection (indeed, the physician's reason for referring his patient to a U.S. practitioner rather than a local physician was to ensure the abortion took place as soon as possible), it does indicate that the courts are likely to see a failure to provide an appropriate referral as negligence tantamount to abandonment. Cook & Dickens also refer to *McInerney v. MacDonald*, [1992] S.C.J. No. 57, [1992] 2 S.C.R. 138 (S.C.C.), which holds that physicians owe fiduciary duties to their patients, and note that this surely requires that physicians must place their patients' well-being ahead of their own personal convictions.

[64] Most Canadian Colleges of Pharmacists have policies or ethical guidelines that outline pharmacist responsibilities in the context of conscientious objection. See, for example, College of Pharmacists of British Columbia, *Framework of Professional Practice* (Vancouver: College of Pharmacists of British Columbia, 2006), online at: <http://www.bcpharmacists.org/legislation_standards/provincial_legislation/framework_of_professional_practice.php> at Appendix I: Code of Ethics. The Code of Ethics states that pharmacists are "not ethically obliged to provide requested pharmacy care when compliance would involve a violation of his or her moral beliefs" (at 31), but goes on to state that there is a professional obligation to refer to a willing pharmacist and that pharmacists shall provide the requested care where there is no other pharmacist "within a reasonable distance or available within a reasonable time willing to provide the service". The Ontario College of Pharmacists has adopted a position statement on "Refusal to Fill for Moral or Religious Reasons" which also permits a pharmacist to decline the provision of care that conflicts with his or her moral or religious beliefs, but again requires that an alternate source must be "insured". Ontario College of Pharmacists, "Position Statement: Refusal to Fill for Moral or Religious Reasons", online at: <http://www.ocpinfo.com/client/ocp/OCPHome.nsf/web/Position+Statement+on+Refusal+to+Fill+for+Moral+or+Religious+Reasons>. See also Nova Scotia College of Pharmacists, *Code of Ethics*, online at: <http://www.nspharmacists.ca/ethics/index.html> (Value V); Saskatchewan College of Pharmacists, "Statement Regarding Pharmacists' Refusal to Provide Products or Services for Moral or Religious Reasons" (June 23, 2000), online at:

B.   STERILIZATION

Sterilization is the most common form of contraception worldwide.[65] It is, for the most part, uncontroversial that sterilization should be available to those who would choose it as a method of contraception,[66] but its use in some contexts provides cause for significant concern.[67] Specifically of interest here is the issue of consent to sterilization by or on behalf of those who may, by reason of intellectual disability or mental illness, lack the immediate capacity to make such decisions.[68] Most commonly, this occurs when intellectually disabled or mentally ill women (or men) are sterilized without their consent.

The leading Canadian case on non-consensual sterilization is *E. (Mrs.) v. Eve.*[69] In this case, the Supreme Court of Canada held that a third party may not authorize the non-therapeutic sterilization of an individual who is incapable of consenting for himself or herself, nor may the Court do so under its *parens patriae* jurisdiction. The decision in *Eve* has been harshly criticized in both academic and judicial opinion,[70] and at least one author has raised questions about

---

<http://www.napra.org/Content_Files/Files/Saskatchewan/PFM/Pharmacists_Refusal_to_Provide_Products_for_Moral_Reaons.pdf>.

[65]   John Cleland, "Contraception in Historical and Global Perspective" (2008) 23 Best Practice & Research Clinical Obstetrics and Gynaecology 165; Emily Jackson, *Regulating Reproduction: Law, Technology, Autonomy* (Oxford: Hart Publishing, 2000) at 19.

[66]   Recently, however, the board of a Catholic hospital in Saskatchewan modified its existing policy, deciding that sterilization procedures would no longer be available at the hospital. The policy change was made in order to improve compliance with the Catholic Health Care Ethics Guide. See Kiply Lukan Yaworski, "Catholic hospital wrestles with ethics of, stops tubal ligations" *Canadian Catholic News* (September 25, 2006), online at: Catholic Online <http://www. catholic.org/international/international_story.php?id=21391>.

[67]   For example, the "emergency" in India in the late 1970s, and involuntary sterilization of indigent women in Latin American countries (see, *e.g.*, Rebecca J. Cook, Bernard M. Dickens & Mahmoud F. Fathalla, *Reproductive Health and Human Rights: Integrating Medicine, Ethics, and Law* (Oxford: Oxford University Press, 2003) at 315-22).

[68]   Mental health law and policy is a complex area of the law; a detailed discussion is beyond the scope of this chapter.

[69]   [1986] S.C.J. No. 60, [1986] 2 S.C.R. 388 (S.C.C.) [*Eve*]. While it is arguable that the Supreme Court's decision in *Eve* leaves room for physicians to characterize non-therapeutic sterilization procedures as therapeutic and thereby avoid the prohibition, La Forest J. was clear that while sterilization might sometimes "be necessary as an adjunct to treatment of a serious malady, ... I would underline that this, of course, does not allow for subterfuge" (at para. 93). See also: The Canadian Medical Protective Association, "The Legal Limits of Sterilizing the Mentally Incapable, What Physicians Need to Know" (Ottawa: The Canadian Medical Protective Association, April 2010), online at: <http://www.cmpa-acpm.ca/cmpapd04/docs/resource_files/web_sheets/ com_w10_001-e.cfm>; Ellen I. Picard & Gerald B. Robertson, *Legal Liability of Doctors and Hospitals in Canada*, 4th ed (Toronto: Thomson Carswell, 2007) at 116-20.

[70]   In *Re B (A Minor) (Wardship: Sterilisation)*, [1987] 2 All E.R. 206, [1988] 1 A.C. 199 (H.L.), the House of Lords authorized the sterilization of a mentally disabled 17-year-old girl, holding that the procedure was in her "best interests". Lord Hailsham refers to La Forest J.'s decision in *Eve* as follows (at 213):

> . . . I find, with great respect, his conclusion ... that the procedure of sterilisation "should never (*sic*) be authorised for non-therapeutic purposes" totally unconvincing and

its continued persuasiveness.[71] Clearly, a balance needs to be struck between the potential advantages and disadvantages of the various methods of contraception and the desire to preserve an individual's fertility when there may be no real likelihood that it will ever matter to the individual whether or not he or she can bear children. However, given the fluidity of capacity,[72] the historical willingness of decision-makers to take a pessimistic view of the facts of these cases,[73] and "[t]he grave intrusion on a person's rights and the certain physical damage"[74] occasioned by non-consensual sterilization, this restrictive approach seems preferable to one which might permit sterilization in anticipation of problems which might never materialize.[75] Such an approach seems particularly appropriate now, in light of the developments in reproductive technology such as long-acting injectable and implantable hormonal contraceptives, safer intrauterine devices, emergency contraception and medical abortion, and contraceptive pills that are intended to suppress menstruation as well as ovulation.[76]

---

in startling contradiction to the welfare principle which should be the first and paramount consideration in wardship cases. Moreover, for the purposes of the present appeal, I find the distinction he purports to draw between "therapeutic" and "non-therapeutic" purposes of this operation in relation to the facts of the present case above as totally meaningless and, if meaningful, quite irrelevant to the correct application of the welfare principle. To talk of the "basic right" to reproduce of an individual who is not capable of knowing the causal connection between intercourse and childbirth, the nature of pregnancy, what is involved in delivery, unable to form maternal instincts or to care for a child appears to me wholly to part company with reality.

[71] Dwight Newman, "An Examination of Saskatchewan Law on the Sterilization of Persons with Mental Disabilities" (1999) 62 Sask. L. Rev. 329-46 at para. 16: "When combined with the criticism it faces in Canadian academic and law reform writing, the judgment is of rather uncertain persuasive force. While the case may articulate a rule, one might wonder to what extent this rule can stand in its present form when it has been the subject of such criticism."

[72] For a discussion of the evolving nature of children's capacity acknowledged in law and ethics, see generally, *C. (A.) v. Manitoba (Director of Child and Family Services)*, [2009] S.C.J. No. 30, 2009 SCC 30, [2009] 2 S.C.R. 181 (S.C.C.); Joan M. Gilmour, "Death, Dying and Decision-making about End of Life Care" in Jocelyn Downie, Timothy Caulfield & Colleen Flood, eds., *Canadian Health Law and Policy*, 3d ed. (Markham, ON: LexisNexis Canada, 2007) 437 at 441-45, 453-55; Ellen I. Picard & Gerald B. Robertson, *Legal Liability of Doctors and Hospitals in Canada*, 4th ed. (Toronto: Thomson Carswell, 2007) at 81-86; American Association of Pediatrics, Committee on Bioethics, "Informed Consent, Parental Permission and Assent in Pediatric Practice" (1995) 95:2 Pediatrics 314; and Christine Harrison *et al.*, "Bioethics for Clinicians: 9. Involving Children in Medical Decisions" (1997) 156 CMAJ 825-28.

[73] See, *e.g.*, Jonathan Montgomery, "Rhetoric and 'Welfare'" (1989) 9 Oxford J. Legal Stud. 395 at 397-99.

[74] [1986] S.C.J. No. 60 at para. 86, [1986] 2 S.C.R. 388 (S.C.C.).

[75] See Danny Sandor, "Sterilisation and Special Medical Procedures on Children and Young People: Blunt Instrument? Bad Medicine?" in I. Freckelton & Kerry Petersen, *Controversies in Health Law* (Sydney: Law Federation Press, 2000) at 16.

[76] See, for example, SOGC Clinical Practice Guideline, "Canadian Consensus Guideline on Continuous and Extended Hormonal Contraception, 2007" (2007) 29:7 (Supplement 2) Journal of Obstetrics and Gynaecology Canada S1.

IV. RECOVERY OF DAMAGES FOR CHILDBEARING AND CHILDREARING

As reproductive technology has become increasingly sophisticated, expectations about the level of control one has over one's reproductive capacity have shifted. Individuals now routinely seek to control the number and timing of their children, as well as the health and developmental attributes of the children they bear. When these aims are frustrated by medical negligence, parents may seek compensation for costs related to the pregnancy and birth, including costs of childrearing. Children who are born with disabilities resulting from medical negligence may also seek compensation for their injuries. Parental claims are variously referred to as wrongful conception, wrongful pregnancy and wrongful birth claims,[77] while the label "wrongful life" is applied to the claim by a child that "but for" the physician's negligence he or she would not have been born.[78]

In general, the wrongful birth claim involves a claim for the negligent failure of a physician to inform a pregnant woman of circumstances that might lead her to terminate the pregnancy. Such cases usually involve the birth of a child with illness or disability,[79] and the claim for damages reflects the increased childrearing costs resulting from the child's illness or disability. Wrongful conception (or wrongful pregnancy) claims are brought where a provider is said to have been negligent in giving contraceptive advice or performing a sterilization procedure and, as a result, an unwanted pregnancy occurs. Wrongful life cases are those in which the child alleges that, absent the physician's negligence, he or she would not have been conceived, or that the pregnancy would have been terminated and he or she would not have been born. These categories are somewhat

---

[77] See Ellen I. Picard & Gerald B. Robertson, *Legal Liability of Doctors and Hospitals in Canada*, 4th ed (Toronto: Thomson Carswell, 2007) at 260-67. In *Krangle (Guardian ad litem of) v. Brisco*, [1997] B.C.J. No. 2740, 154 D.L.R. (4th) 707 (B.C.S.C.), affd [2002] S.C.J. No. 8, 2002 SCC 9 (S.C.C.), the Court categorized the cases as follows:
  • unwanted conception following a failed medical sterilization procedure performed on either parent;
  • unwanted birth following a failed medical abortion;
  • loss of opportunity to have an abortion following failure to be provided with necessary medical information or advice; and
  • physical damage to the fetus resulting from a medical procedure during pregnancy.

[78] In spite of the differing terminology used in these cases, it is clear that these are all negligence claims where the injury relates to the birth of a child. Indeed, it has been argued that the very fact of the distinctive vocabulary used to describe these claims indicates the unwillingness of judges to recognize and compensate women's losses related to childbearing and childrearing. As Sanda Rodgers has noted, "[tort] actions for wrongful birth, wrongful pregnancy and wrongful life ... show a remarkably unsettled, variable and fundamentally resistant jurisprudential and legislative life both in common law and in civil law jurisdictions". See Sanda Rodgers, "A Mother's Loss Is the Price of Parenthood: The Failure of Tort Law to Recognize Birth as Compensable Reproductive Injury" in Sanda Rodgers, Rakhi Ruparelia & Louise Bélanger-Hardy, *Critical Torts* (Markham, ON: LexisNexis Canada, 2009) 161 at 162.

[79] This group of cases also includes unsuccessful abortion procedures, among others. See Ellen I. Picard & Gerald B. Robertson, *Legal Liability of Doctors and Hospitals in Canada*, 4th ed. (Toronto: Thomson Carswell, 2007) at 260-61.

slippery — sometimes wrongful conception cases concern the birth of a child with disabilities — and the case law can justly be described as confused (and confusing). Recently, for example, two Alberta trial judges came to opposing conclusions on damages in factually similar cases.[80] What follows is an attempt to distill some general ideas about this species of negligence claim.

Initially, wrongful birth and wrongful conception claims met with reluctance on the part of Canadian judges, but they are now fairly well established in Canadian jurisdictions.[81] The courts have awarded damages for the "inconveniences" and any lost income caused by pregnancy and childbirth, but have been inconsistent when it comes to awarding the costs of childrearing. Courts are loath to award the full costs of childrearing in wrongful conception cases, although they appear to be less so where the claim is for the additional costs of raising a child born with disabilities.[82]

Several approaches to damage assessment in wrongful conception cases have been considered by courts in Canada, the United States, the United Kingdom and Australia. Some courts have taken the position that, as the birth of a child is occasion for joy even where it is the result of provider negligence, no damages can be awarded to parents.[83] Others have taken the opposite approach, holding that a principled approach to tort law demands full recovery of all losses flowing from the pregnancy and birth, including the full costs of childrearing.[84]

---

[80] In *S. (M.) v. Baker*, [2001] A.J. No. 1579, 100 Alta. L.R. (3d) 124 (Alta. Q.B.), Moreau J. would have awarded damages for the costs of raising the unplanned child to age 18 (if she had found the defendant physician negligent), on the theory articulated in *Kealey v. Berezowski*, [1996] O.J. No. 2460, 136 D.L.R. 4th 708 (Ont. Gen. Div.) that the motivation for the sterilization governs the recovery of such damages. Justice Moreau concluded that financial circumstances were an important consideration in the plaintiffs' decision to proceed with sterilization, and therefore would have awarded damages for childrearing. In *Y. (M.) v. Boutros*, [2002] A.J. No. 480, 2 Alta. L.R. (4th) 153 (Alta. Q.B.), Rawlins J. would not have awarded childrearing costs, even if she had found the physician to be negligent. Justice Rawlins disagreed with the approach adopted in *Kealey* and *Baker*, and instead followed the ruling of the U.K. House of Lords in *McFarlane v. Tayside Health Board*, [2000] 2 A.C. 59, [1994] 4 All E.R. 961 (H.L.), although it is not clear on what basis she did so. She found that the Law Lords were unanimous in declining to award the costs of raising a healthy child, although all five arrived at this result for different reasons. Justice Rawlins then went on to consider the "offset-benefits" approach to considering whether damages for childrearing should be awarded, and concluded (at para. 158) that although this approach was not adopted in *McFarlane*, she "[accepted] that the benefits a child brings to a family outweigh the costs of that child to a family".

[81] *Doiron v. Orr*, [1978] O.J. No. 3388, 86 D.L.R. (3d) 719 (Ont. H.C.J.); *Colp v. Ringrose* (1976), 3 Med. Q. 72 (Alta. T.D.); *Pozdzik (Next friend of) v. Wilson*, [2002] A.J. No. 450, 2002 ABQB 351 (Alta. Q.B.).

[82] *Cherry (Guardian ad litem of) v. Borsman*, [1991] B.C.J. No. 315, 75 D.L.R. (4th) 668 (B.C.S.C.), var'd [1992] B.C.J. No. 1687, 94 D.L.R. (4th) 487 (B.C.C.A.); *Joshi (Guardian ad litem of) v. Woolley*, [1995] B.C.J. No. 113, 4 B.C.L.R. (3d) 208 (B.C.S.C.).

[83] See *Roe v. Dabbs*, [2004] B.C.J. No. 1485 at paras. 189-193, 2004 BCSC 957 (B.C.S.C.) for a description of the various approaches taken to awarding damages in wrongful conception cases.

[84] This is the common law position in Australia (see *Cattanach v. Melchior*, [2003] H.C.A. 38, 215 C.L.R. 1 (H.C.A.)). The common law has been overruled by statute in three jurisdictions. See

Still other courts have attempted to offset the benefits of the child's presence in the parents' lives against the costs of raising that child in arriving at an award of damages.[85] Finally, and most commonly, courts have awarded limited damages to compensate women for the pregnancy and childbirth, and both parents for "start-up" costs relevant to the newborn, but have stopped short of awarding any additional rearing costs.[86] Complete recovery for the costs of raising the child is rare,[87] meaning that parents are generally compensated for little if any of the actual costs that result from the provider's negligence.

Various policy arguments have been deployed in rationalizing the departure from principle marked by the refusal to award the full measure of damages to parents who have established provider negligence leading to the birth of an (at least initially) unwanted child. Most of these arguments boil down to essentially the same premise — that "it is morally offensive to regard a normal, healthy baby as more trouble and expense than it is worth".[88] Less troubling to courts is the reality that this approach leaves parents — especially women — who have been negligently deprived of their right to limit the size of their family without compensation for the most significant part of their loss.[89]

Civil Liability Act 2003 (Qld.), s. 49; *Civil Liability Act 2002* (N.S.W.), s. 71; and *Civil Liability Act 1936* (S.A.), s. 67.

[85] This is often referred to as the "offset-benefits" approach. See *Suite c. Cooke*, [1995] J.Q. no 696, [1995] R.J.Q. 2765 (Que. C.A.) and *Chaffee v. Seslar*, 786 N.E.2d 705 at 707-708 (Ind. 2003), in which the Supreme Court of Indiana clearly and concisely explains the state of play in American jurisdictions. For cases adopting this approach, see *Univ. of Arizona Health Sciences Ctr. v. Superior Court*, 136 Ariz. 579, 667 P.2d 1294 at 1299 (1983); *Ochs v. Borrelli*, 187 Conn. 253, 445 A.2d 883 at 886 (1982); *Sherlock v. Stillwater Clinic*, 260 N.W.2d 169 at 175-76 (Minn. 1977).

[86] *McFarlane v. Tayside Health Board*, [2000] A.C. 59, [1994] 4 All E.R. 961 (H.L.); *Rees v. Darlington Memorial Hospital NHS Trust*, [2003] U.K.H.L. 52, [2003] 4 All E.R. 987 (H.L.) (in which the majority of the House of Lords acknowledged the wrong to parents from violation of their reproductive autonomy and awarded a conventional sum of £15,000). Like the House of Lords in *Rees*, the British Columbia Supreme Court awarded non-pecuniary damages to the parents in *Bevilacqua v. Altenkirk*, [2004] B.C.J. No. 1473, 2004 BCSC 945 (B.C.S.C.) and *Roe v. Dabbs*, [2004] B.C.J. No. 1485, 2004 BCSC 957 (B.C.S.C.). In *Mummery v. Olsson*, [2001] O.J. No. 226, [2001] O.T.C. 43 (Ont. S.C.J.) and *Y. (M.) v. Boutros*, [2002] A.J. No. 480, 11 C.C.L.T. (3d) 271 (Alta. Q.B.), the courts refused to award any damages for childrearing, while in *Kealey v. Berezowski*, [1996] O.J. No. 2460, 136 D.L.R. (4th) 708 (Ont. Gen. Div.) and *S. (M.) v. Baker*, [2001] A.J. No. 1579, [2002] 4 W.W.R. 487 (Alta. Q.B.), the courts held that childrearing damages may be awarded where the motivation for sterilization is financial.

[87] See, *e.g.*, *Cattanach v. Melchior*, [2003] H.C.A. 38, 215 C.L.R. 1 (H.C.A.); *Custodio v. Bauer*, 251 Cal. App. 2d 303, 59 Cal. Rptr. 463 (Cal. Ct. App. 1967); *Lovelace Med. Ctr. v. Mendez*, 111 N.M. 336, 805 P.2d 603 (N.M. 1991); *Zehr v. Haugen*, 318 Ore. 647, 871 P.2d 1006 (Ore. 1994); and *Marciniak v. Lundborg*, 153 Wis. 2d 59, 450 N.W.2d 243 (Wis. 1990).

[88] Lord Millet in *McFarlane v. Tayside Health Board*, [2000] 2 A.C. 59 at 113, [1999] 4 All E.R. 961 (H.L.).

[89] See Elizabeth Adjin-Tettey, "Claims of Involuntary Parenthood: Why the Resistance?" (paper presented at Emerging Issues in Tort Law, University of Western Ontario, June 2006) [copy on file with the author]; Nicolette Priaulx, "Joy to the World! A (Healthy) Child is Born! Reconceptualizing 'Harm' in Wrongful Conception" (2004) 13:1 Soc. & Leg. Stud. 5; Ben Golder, "From

Women are generally the primary caregivers for their young children and, where couples choose to have one of them take time out of the labour force in order to raise children, it is almost exclusively the female member of the couple.[90] Thus, the impact of judicial policy favouring limited (or no) recovery for wrongful conception is largely borne by women. And physicians (and society) are told, in effect, that violating women's reproductive autonomy bears few consequences. Arguably, the effects of denying claims for childrearing damages in wrongful conception cases go well beyond the confines of tort law. The gendered impact of decisions to reject these claims undermines women's reproductive autonomy and hence their ability to participate fully in social, economic and political life.

Wrongful birth claims, in which parents are generally asking for costs of childrearing related to the child's disability, have been approached much more generously than have those related to the birth of a healthy child.[91] In the genetics context, the cases have dealt with negligence in failing to provide or to refer parents for genetic counselling, resulting in the birth of two children with Duchenne muscular dystrophy,[92] and negligence in failing to inform parents of the availability of prenatal genetic testing, resulting in the birth of a child with Down's Syndrome.[93] Recently, the British Columbia Supreme Court decided a case involving a claim for damages respecting a child who was born with spina bifida.[94] The child's mother claimed that her physician was negligent in failing to refer her for an ultrasound. In this case, the physician also successfully claimed contributory negligence on the part of the child's mother for failing to follow medical advice.[95] The physician did not order an ultrasound because the

---

McFarlane to *Melchior* and Beyond: Love, Sex, Money and Commodification in the Anglo-Australian Law of Torts" (2004) 9 Torts Law Journal 1.

[90] See, *e.g.*, Reva Siegel, "Reasoning from the Body: A Historical Perspective on Abortion Regulation and Questions of Equal Protection" (1992) 44 Stan. L. Rev. 261 at 375; Arlie Hochschild, *The Second Shift* (New York: London Books, 1989); Sylvia Ann Hewlett & Carolyn Buck Luce, "Off-Ramps and On-Ramps: Keeping Talented Women on the Road to Success" (2005) 83:3 Harvard Bus. Rev. 43 at 44; and Sandra Fredman, *Women and the Law* (Oxford: Oxford University Press, 1997) at 180.

[91] There are also "wrongful conception" cases where the child was born with disabilities and the additional costs of rearing attributable to the disabilities have been compensated: *Parkinson v. St James and Seacroft University Hospital NHS Trust*, [2001] 3 All E.R. 97, [2001] 3 W.L.R. 376 (C.A. (Civ. Div.)); *Joshi (Guardian ad litem of) v. Woolley*, [1995] B.C.J. No. 113, 4 B.C.L.R. (3d) 208 (B.C.S.C.).

[92] *H. (R.) v. Hunter*, [1996] O.J. No. 4477, 32 C.C.L.T. (2d) 44 (Ont. Gen. Div.).

[93] *Krangle (Guardian ad litem of) v. Brisco*, [2002] S.C.J. No. 8, [2002] 1 S.C.R. 205 (S.C.C.); *Jones (Guardian ad litem of) v. Rostvig*, [1999] B.C.J. No. 647, 44 C.C.L.T. (2d) 313 (B.C.S.C.).

[94] *Patmore (Guardian ad litem of) v. Weatherston*, [1999] B.C.J. No. 650, 86 A.C.W.S. (3d) 981 (B.C.S.C.).

[95] *Ibid*. See also *Zhang v. Kan*, [2003] B.C.J. No. 164, 15 C.C.L.T. (3d) 1 (B.C.S.C.), where the British Columbia Supreme Court assessed the plaintiff's contributory negligence at 50 per cent. The plaintiff sought a referral for amniocentesis from the defendant physician. He informed her that it was too late in her pregnancy for amniocentesis; his advice on this point was held to be negligent. The court noted that the plaintiff doubted the defendant's advice, but did not seek a second opinion, or seek to have the test elsewhere.

mother did not return to the physician's office for a second prenatal visit office until later in pregnancy than such testing would normally be offered.

Damages do not seem to pose the same moral difficulty in the wrongful birth context as in wrongful conception claims,[96] but wrongful birth claims do give rise to interesting causation problems. In *Arndt v. Smith*, the plaintiff contracted chicken pox in the twelfth week of her pregnancy with her daughter, Miranda, and was assured by her physician, Dr. Smith, that the risk of harm to the fetus was minimal, though she did note the chance of limb and skin abnormalities. Although Dr. Smith was aware of more serious risks, including intellectual disabilities and cortical atrophy, she did not inform Ms. Arndt of these risks on the basis that she did not wish to "unduly worry an expectant mother about an improbable risk and one for which she would not advise therapeutic abortion".[97]

Miranda was born with congenital varicella syndrome, which led to multiple disabilities. After Miranda's birth, Ms. Arndt sued Dr. Smith, alleging failure to inform her of the risks of infection with chicken pox while pregnant and further alleging that, had she been properly informed of the risks, she would have terminated the pregnancy. The trial judge found that Dr. Smith had breached her duty to inform, but went on to conclude that even if she had been told of the very small risk of serious deformities, Ms. Arndt would not have terminated the pregnancy. In other words, Ms. Arndt's action failed on the question of causation. The decision was appealed to the British Columbia Court of Appeal and to the Supreme Court of Canada, a majority of which ultimately upheld the trial judge's decision.[98]

---

[96] Some authors have noted the distinction being made on the basis of disability as a significant cause for concern. See, *e.g.*, *Cattanach v. Melchior*, [2003] H.C.A. 38 at para. 164, 199 A.L.R. 131 (H.C.A.), *per* Kirby J.: "Apart from the arbitrariness of this exception it has a further flaw. It reinforces views about disability and attitudes towards parents and children with physical or mental impairments that are contrary to contemporary Australian values reinforced by the law."

[97] *Arndt v. Smith*, [1994] B.C.J. No. 1137 at para. 54, 21 C.C.L.T. (2d) 66 (B.C.S.C.), affd [1997] S.C.J. No. 65, [1997] 2 S.C.R. 539 (S.C.C.). This concern around "unduly worrying" an expectant mother is actually something of a delicate issue. Obviously, a robust approach to reproductive autonomy would recognize the significance of the pregnant woman of having this information. Without it, she is not in a position to decide whether or not to continue the pregnancy and risk having a severely, multiply disabled child (which, in turn, will have immense significance for her own life). Yet it is not entirely clear that informing a pregnant woman that she runs a minimal risk of her child being born with multiple, severe disabilities and health issues is helpful to a woman's ability to make choices. See Barbara Katz Rothman, *The Tentative Pregnancy: Prenatal Diagnosis and the Future of Motherhood* (New York: Viking, 1986) at 180-81:

> The whole thing about the new technology they are offered is that it gives choice. That is what it is all about, after all, the opening up of new reproductive choices. But for most women the choices are all so dreadful that trying to find one she can live with is terribly hard. Taking the least awful choice is not experienced as "choosing"...

[98] This decision, as well as the decision in *Mickle v. Salvation Army Grace Hospital Windsor Ontario*, [1998] O.J. No. 4683, 166 D.L.R. (4th) 743 (Ont. Gen. Div.), illustrates one of the significant difficulties that courts have in wrongful birth cases — some reasonable women might choose to carry a pregnancy to term, in spite of warnings of possible fetal ill-health or disability;

Wrongful life claims are for damages associated with the pain and suffering that arises from living with a disability, as well as for costs of future care. Unlike the claims for wrongful birth and wrongful conception, these claims have met with no success in Canadian courts.[99] Claims made by children born with disabilities have been characterized as falling into one of two categories.[100] The first — cases in which the disabilities or injuries were caused by the wrongful act or omission of a third party — have long been considered valid claims,[101] while claims in the second category — cases in which the negligence led to the birth of the child — have been labelled wrongful life claims and uniformly rejected.[102]

In two recent judgments, the Ontario Court of Appeal has raised doubt about the above-described approach to cases in which a child born with disabili-

---

other reasonable women might choose to terminate the pregnancy under those circumstances. The test for causation in Canadian common law is whether a reasonable person in the position of the patient, having been properly informed of the risks, would have taken a different approach with respect to treatment. Given that two equally reasonable choices exist, the test seems unworkable in these circumstances. In its decision in *Arndt v. Smith*, the British Columbia Court of Appeal specifically invited the Supreme Court of Canada to deal with this point, but the decision of the Supreme Court does not address the issue. See Erin Nelson & Timothy Caulfield, "You Can't Get There from Here: A Case Comment on *Arndt v. Smith*" (1998) 32 U.B.C. L. Rev. 353; see also Vaughn Black & Dennis Klimchuk, "Case Comment: *Hollis v. Dow Corning*" (1996) 75 Can. Bar Rev. 355 at 363 (explaining problems with the test for causation).

[99] Nor have they met with success in the courts of Australia, England or most of the United States. A small minority of American states recognize wrongful life claims — see *Curlender v. Bioscience Laboratories*, 106 Cal. App. 3d 811, 165 Cal. Rptr. 477 (Cal. 1988); *Turpin v. Sortini*, 643 P.2d 954, 31 Cal. 3d 220 (Cal. 1982); *Procanik v. Cillo*, 478 A.2d 755, 97 N.J. 339 (N.J. 1984); and *Harbeson v. Parke-Davis*, 656 P.2d 483, 98 Wn. 2d 460 (Wash. 1983) — but the majority do not, and a number of states have statutes barring wrongful life claims (see, *e.g.*, Sanda Rodgers, "A Mother's Loss Is the Price of Parenthood: The Failure of Tort Law to Recognize Birth as Compensable Reproductive Injury" in Sanda Rodgers, Rakhi Ruparelia & Louise Bélanger-Hardy, *Critical Torts* (Markham, ON: LexisNexis Canada, 2009) 161 at 172).

[100] *Lacroix (Litigation guardian of) v. Dominique*, [2001] M.J. No. 311, 2001 MBCA 122 (Man. C.A.), leave to appeal refused [2001] S.C.C.A. No. 477, 389 N.R. 202 (S.C.C.).

[101] *Duval v. Seguin*, [1972] O.J. No. 1781, 26 D.L.R. (3d) 418 (Ont. H.C.J.); *Montreal Tramways Co. v. Léveillé*, [1933] S.C.J. No. 40, [1933] S.C.R. 456 (S.C.C.).

[102] *Jones (Guardian ad litem of) v. Rostvig*, [1999] B.C.J. No. 647, 44 C.C.L.T. (2d) 313 (B.C.S.C.); *Patmore (Guardian ad litem of) v. Weatherston*, [1999] B.C.J. No. 650, 86 A.C.W.S. (3d) 981 (B.C.S.C.); *Mickle v. Salvation Army Grace Hospital Windsor Ontario*, [1998] O.J. No. 4683, 166 D.L.R. (4th) 743 (Ont. Gen. Div.); *Lacroix (Litigation guardian of) v. Dominque*, [2001] M.J. No. 311, 2001 MBCA 122 (Man. C.A.); *Cataford v. Moreau*, [1978] J.Q. no 302, 114 D.L.R. (3d) 585 (Que. S.C.). In a few such cases, courts have denied the defendant's motion for summary judgment on the basis that it is not plain and obvious that the claim discloses no reasonable cause of action; see, *e.g.*: *Bartok v. Shokeir*, [1998] S.J. No. 645, 168 Sask. R. 280 (Sask. C.A.); *Petkovic v. Olupona*, [2002] O.J. No. 1269, [2002] 11 C.C.L.T. (3d) 91 (Ont. S.C.J.), affd [2002] O.J. No. 3411, 30 C.C.L.T. (3d) 266 (Ont. Div. Ct.); *Bovingdon v. Hergott*, [2006] O.J. No. 3594, 42 C.C.L.T. (3d) 119 (Ont. S.C.J.); *McDonald-Wright (Litigation guardian of) v. O'Herlihy*, [2005] O.J. No. 135, [2005] O.T.C. 37 (Ont. S.C.J.).

ties brings a negligence claim against a physician.[103] In *Paxton v. Ramji*, the trial judge considered and rejected the possibility that the claim was one for wrongful life.[104] Instead, she concluded that the child's claim was more properly framed as being based on the defendant physician's duty not to prescribe Accutane to a woman of childbearing potential. The claim was ultimately unsuccessful because the trial judge found that the defendant met the standard of care expected of him and thus did not breach his duty to the infant plaintiff.

The plaintiff appealed the trial judge's decision, and the Court of Appeal took the view that in "asking whether or not the claim before the court should be characterized as one for wrongful life, Canadian courts have asked the wrong question".[105] Instead, the court held that the appropriate analysis in such cases is a first-principles duty of care analysis based on the reasoning of the House of Lords in *Anns v. Merton London Borough Council*,[106] and expounded upon by the Supreme Court of Canada in several negligence cases.[107] The court stated that there is no "settled jurisprudence in Canada on the question whether a doctor can be in a proximate relationship with a future child who was not yet conceived or born at the time of the doctor's impugned conduct".[108] Accordingly, the court went on to apply the *Anns* test, holding that no duty of care is owed by a physician to a child that is not yet born or conceived at the time of the negligent act. The primary reason for the rejection of a duty of care was the "proximity" analysis, which demands consideration of whether the defendant doctor and the future child are in such a "close and direct relationship" that the court would be justified in imposing a duty of care. The court ultimately concluded that no duty of care is owed to the future child of a female patient because of the potential for the physician to owe conflicting duties to "a female patient and to her future child (whether conceived or not yet conceived)".[109]

Because of the court's references to the child being "conceived or not yet conceived" at the time of the physician's negligent act, the Ontario Court of Appeal's reasoning in both *Paxton* and *Bovingdon v. Hergott*[110] immediately gave rise to a great deal of concern about the long line of cases in which it had always been assumed that a duty of care is owed by physicians (and other health

---

[103] *Paxton v. Ramji*, [2008] O.J. No. 3964, 2008 ONCA 697 (Ont. C.A.), leave to appeal refused [2008] S.C.C.A. No. 508 (S.C.C.); *Bovingdon v. Hergott*, [2008] O.J. No. 11, 2008 ONCA 2 (Ont. C.A.), leave to appeal refused [2008] S.C.C.A. No. 92 (S.C.C.).

[104] [2006] O.J. No. 1179 (Ont. S.C.J.).

[105] *Paxton v. Ramji*, [2008] O.J. No. 3964 at para. 29, 2008 ONCA 697 (Ont. C.A.).

[106] [1978] A.C. 728, [1977] 2 All E.R. 492 (H.L.).

[107] Including: *Kamloops (City) v. Nielsen*, [1984] S.C.J. No. 29, [1984] 2 S.C.R. 2 (S.C.C.); *Cooper v. Hobart*, [2001] S.C.J. No. 76, 2001 SCC 79, [2001] 3 S.C.R. 537 (S.C.C.); *Edwards v. Law Society of Upper Canada*, [2001] S.C.J. No. 77, 2001 SCC 80, [2001] 3 S.C.R. 562 (S.C.C.); *Childs v. Desormeaux*, [2006] S.C.J. No. 18, 2006 SCC 18, [2006] 1 S.C.R. 643 (S.C.C.); *Syl Apps Secure Treatment Centre v. D. (B.)*, [2007] S.C.J. No. 38, 2007 SCC 38, [2007] 3 S.C.R. 83 (S.C.C.); and *Holland v. Saskatchewan*, [2008] S.C.J. No. 43, 2008 SCC 42 (S.C.C.).

[108] *Paxton v. Ramji*, [2008] O.J. No. 3964 at para. 53, 2008 ONCA 697 (Ont. C.A.)

[109] *Ibid.*, at para. 76.

[110] [2008] O.J. No. 11, 2008 ONCA 2 (Ont. C.A.).

care providers) to an unborn child. The so-called "labour and delivery" cases[111] follow the reasoning of the early cases that held that a child, once born alive, may sue a third party for damages caused by negligence while the child was "en ventre sa mère".[112] The use of the words "conceived or not yet conceived" and "not yet conceived or born" in the Court of Appeal's reasons understandably led to uncertainty about the potential scope of the decision. Recently, the Ontario Court of Appeal clarified its comments in *Paxton* and *Bovingdon*, noting that:

> We do not read those passages as governing the issue raised on this appeal. In accordance with the tradition of the common law and the doctrine of precedent, *Paxton* and *Bovingdon* must be read in the light of their precise facts, the issues they addressed, and in a proper legal context ... In our view, the authority of the labour and delivery cases remains intact and is unaffected by *Bovingdon* and *Paxton*.[113]

The Court of Appeal's comments are welcome to the extent that they foreclose any doubt about whether a physician owes a duty of care to a fetus in the labour and delivery context. But there is more than just this to be concerned about in the reasoning of the court in *Paxton*. The court's decision on the duty of care turned largely on the perception that to recognize that coextensive duties are owed by a physician to both her female patient and the unborn child will inevitably lead to situations in which the two duties conflict. The worry is that such a conflict could have "an undesirable chilling effect on doctors", in that they might refuse to "offer treatment to some female patients in a way that might deprive them of their autonomy and freedom of informed choice in their medical care".[114]

This perception of conflicting duties is illusory and, as explained by Holmes J. of the British Columbia Supreme Court, to the extent any such conflict exists, "it is answered by the simple reality that mothers make decisions — both as to medical care and in other areas — for their unborn children. As to the conflict of interests (mother's versus unborn child's) implicated in that decision, it is for the mother, and not the physician, to resolve".[115] The Ontario Court of Appeal's

---

[111] See, *e.g., Crawford (Litigation guardian of) v. Penney*, [2003] O.J. No. 89, 14 C.C.L.T. (3d) 60 (Ont. S.C.J.), affd [2004] O.J. No. 3669, 26 C.C.L.T. (3d) 246 (Ont. C.A.); *Commisso (Litigation guardian of) v. North York Branson Hospital*, [2000] O.J. No. 1866, 48 O.R. (3d) 484 (Ont. S.C.J.), affd [2003] O.J. No. 20, 168 O.A.C. 100 (Ont. C.A.).

[112] *Duval v. Seguin*, [1972] O.J. No. 1781, 26 D.L.R. (3d) 418 (Ont. H.C.J.); *Montreal Tramways Co. v. Léveillé*, [1933] S.C.J. No. 40, [1933] S.C.R. 456 (S.C.C.).

[113] *Liebig (Litigation guardian of) v. Guelph General Hospital*, [2010] O.J. No. 2580 at para. 13, 2010 ONCA 450 (Ont. C.A.).

[114] *Paxton v. Ramji*, [2008] O.J. No. 3964 at para. 68, 2008 ONCA 697 (Ont. C.A.), leave to appeal refused [2008] S.C.C.A. No. 508 (S.C.C.).

[115] *Ediger (Guardian ad litem of) v. Johnston*, [2009] B.C.J. No. 564 at para. 186, 2009 BCSC 386 (B.C.S.C.). Justice Holmes declined to find that *Paxton* and *Bovingdon* "require reconsideration of the law in this province that a physician's duty of care to a pregnant woman encompasses her fetus". *Ibid.*, at para. 213. Justice Holmes' reasoning has been followed in other B.C. cases: see *Steinebach (Litigation guardian of) v. Fraser Health Authority (c.o.b. Surrey Memorial Hospital)*, [2010] B.C.J. No. 1129, 2010 BCSC 832 (B.C.S.C.); *Cojocaru (Guardian ad litem of) v.*

comments about conflicting duties are interesting in that they demonstrate an awareness of the need to respect pregnant women's "autonomy and freedom of informed choice" in medical care, and because they are made in the context of a line of cases in which women's reproductive autonomy is largely, if not completely, disregarded.

Given the ongoing difficulty that Canadian courts have with wrongful life cases, it is safe to say that health law scholars and the practising bar alike would welcome a decision on point from the Supreme Court of Canada.

V. TORT DUTIES OF PREGNANT WOMEN

To what extent is a pregnant woman's choice of activities circumscribed by the fact of her decision to reproduce? Is she free to engage in risky conduct while pregnant? Can a woman be sued by her child for conduct during pregnancy that results in her child being born with disabilities?[116] In *Dobson (Litigation guardian of) v. Dobson*,[117] the Supreme Court of Canada held that she cannot.

The *Dobson* case involved a claim by a child against his mother (or, more accurately, his mother's insurer) for her allegedly negligent driving. Ms. Dobson was involved in a collision, and her fetus was delivered prematurely that same day. Ryan Dobson was born with permanent mental and physical impairments, including cerebral palsy. The case advanced to the Supreme Court of Canada on the preliminary question of whether a pregnant woman owes a tort law duty of care to her fetus.

The lower courts held that the narrow issue requiring consideration in this case was the potential liability of a pregnant woman for negligent driving causing injuries to her born alive child.[118] Therefore, any policy considerations that might arise in cases involving negligence in "lifestyle choices"[119] were, in the

---

British Columbia Women's Hospital, [2009] B.C.J. No. 731, 2009 BCSC 494 (B.C.S.C.). For an interesting discussion of *Paxton* and *Bovingdon*, see Richard Halpern, "Birth Trauma and the Duty of Care", online at: Thomson Rogers <http://www.thomsonrogers.com/birth-trauma-and-duty-care>.

[116] In *Winnipeg Child and Family Services (Northwest Area) v. G. (D.F.)*, [1997] S.C.J. No. 96, 152 D.L.R. (4th) 193 (S.C.C.) [*Winnipeg*], the Supreme Court of Canada considered the potential liability of a woman for her conduct during pregnancy, in the context of an application to detain (and treat) a pregnant woman who was addicted to sniffing glue. The purpose of the proceedings was to obtain authority to detain the woman so that she could receive treatment for her addiction. Therefore, the Court was not asked to determine whether a woman could be liable to her child for her conduct prior to the child's birth. The Court concluded that tort law does not permit the granting of such an order with the aim of protecting the fetus from potential harm. The Court went on to hold that tort law should not be extended to allow a fetus to assert a claim against its mother, in part due to the implications of such a finding with respect to the ability of pregnant women to make autonomous lifestyle choices.

[117] [1999] S.C.J. No. 41, 174 D.L.R. (4th) 1 (S.C.C.) [*Dobson*].

[118] *Dobson (Litigation guardian of) v. Dobson*, [1997] N.B.J. No. 232, 148 D.L.R. (4th) 332 (N.B.C.A.), revd [1999] S.C.J. No. 41, 174 D.L.R. (4th) 1 (S.C.C.).

[119] By this, Hoyt C.J.N.B. seems to have meant such things as cigarette smoking, consumption of alcohol and other legal or illegal substances, and the taking of or refusal to take medication.

courts' view, irrelevant.[120] The Court of Appeal concluded that the duty of a pregnant woman toward her unborn fetus in the context of driving a motor vehicle is a part of her "general duty to drive carefully", and that if a child suffers injury as a result of the mother's negligent driving during pregnancy, the child should be able to sue for compensation.[121] To hold otherwise would constitute a partial exception to a pregnant woman's general duty to drive with care.

A majority of the Supreme Court of Canada allowed Cynthia Dobson's appeal, holding that "[t]he public policy concerns raised in this case are of such a nature and magnitude that they clearly indicate that a legal duty of care cannot, and should not, be imposed by the courts upon a woman towards her foetus or subsequently born child".[122] The policy concerns articulated by the Court fall into two primary categories: those relating to the privacy and autonomy rights of women,[123] and the difficulties inherent in articulating a judicial standard of conduct for pregnant women. With respect to the privacy and autonomy rights of women, the Court refused to impose a duty of care upon pregnant women, because "[t]o do so would result in very extensive and unacceptable intrusions into the bodily integrity, privacy and autonomy rights of women".[124]

In its reasons in *Dobson*, the Court invited legislative intervention in this area of private law, and at least one province has taken up that invitation.[125] In

---

[120] The Court made reference to the fact that this distinction has been employed in legislation in the United Kingdom: the *Congenital Disabilities (Civil Liability) Act 1976* (U.K.), c. 28. The Act provides that mothers cannot be sued by their children for prenatal injuries, with the exception of injuries caused by motor vehicle accidents. The specific reason for this exception is the existence of a mandatory insurance regime with respect to motor vehicles; the U.K. Law Commission that recommended the enactment of this legislation was of the view that permitting recovery by the child (to the extent of the policy limits) in this situation would decrease the anxiety pregnant women feel in relation to driving: see Law Commission (U.K.), Law Commission Report No. 60, "Report on Injuries to Unborn Children" Cmnd. 5709 in *Law Commission Reports*, vol. 5 (Oxford: Professional Books, 1979).

[121] The Court of Appeal found support for its decision in an Australian case (*Lynch v. Lynch (By Her Tutor Lynch)* (1991), 25 N.S.W.L.R. 411 (N.S.W.C.A.)) and in some of the U.S. jurisprudence. It should be noted, however, that there is no consistency among U.S. decisions as to whether a pregnant woman does owe a duty of care toward her fetus. In part, the development of the law on this point in the U.S. seems to have been confounded by the existence of what is known as the doctrine of "parental immunity".

[122] *Dobson (Litigation guardian of) v. Dobson*, [1999] S.C.J. No. 41 at para. 76, 174 D.L.R. (4th) 1 (S.C.C.).

[123] *Ibid.*, at para. 78. While Cory J. refers at length in his decision to such "privacy and autonomy rights", which he refers to at one point as "fundamental rights" (at para. 30), he does not explain the derivation or character of those rights.

[124] *Ibid.*, at para. 23. Although the facts of the case related solely to the question of negligent driving during pregnancy, the Court was concerned about the broader implications of any decision they might make, given the common law process; as Cory J. noted at para. 28: "There is no rational and principled limit to the types of claims which may be brought if such a ... duty of care were imposed upon pregnant women."

[125] *Ibid.*, at para. 76: "However, unlike the courts, the legislature may, as did the Parliament of the United Kingdom, enact legislation in this field, subject to the limits imposed by the *Canadian Charter of Rights and Freedoms.*"

November 2005, the Alberta Legislature passed the *Maternal Tort Liability Act*,[126] which provides that:

> 4. A mother may be liable to her child for injuries suffered by her child on or after birth that were caused by the mother's use or operation of an automobile during her pregnancy if, at the time of that use or operation, the mother was insured under a contract of automobile insurance evidenced by a motor vehicle liability policy.

Section 5(1) of the Act provides that the liability created by section 4 is limited in quantum to the automobile insurance policy limits.

In introducing the Bill to the legislature, the government indicated that its intent was to create a limited exception to the common law position set out in *Dobson*.[127] According to the Bill's sponsor, "[t]he proposed provision relates only to motor vehicle accidents and does not change tort law in any way other than to provide a limited exception to the common law concept of maternal tort immunity".[128] Further, the government's stated objective in passing this legislation was to provide a means of accessing insurance funds to benefit the child, the mother and the family as a whole.[129] It has now been almost five years since the passage of this legislation, and it seems that the *Maternal Tort Liability Act* has played a limited, if any, role in relation to tort liability for pregnant women. At least to date, it seems safe to say that the Alberta government can be taken at its word as to its limited objective in passing this legislation.

VI. COERCIVE TREATMENT OF PREGNANT WOMEN

In the previous section, issues of private law related to the behaviour of pregnant women were considered; here, I am concerned with state action that threatens

---

[126] S.A. 2005, c. M-7.5.

[127] *Dobson (Litigation guardian of) v. Dobson*, [1999] S.C.J. No. 41, 174 D.L.R. (4th) 1 (S.C.C.).

[128] Alberta, Legislative Assembly, *Hansard* (November 16, 2005) at 1681 (Mr. Oberle).

[129] *Ibid.* The government's reasons for proceeding with the *Maternal Tort Liability Act* are intriguing. In addressing the Bill, the government stated that situations requiring legislation of this nature arise infrequently. Why, then, did the government decide to pursue this route? In the spring of 2004, a Private Bill was introduced to the Private Bills Committee of the Alberta Legislature in an attempt to create an exception to the applicability of the *Dobson* case for Brooklynn Rewega. Brooklynn was born blind and suffering from cerebral palsy allegedly as a result of a motor vehicle accident caused by her mother, who was five months pregnant with Brooklynn at the time (see Alberta, Legislative Assembly, *Private Bills Committee Transcripts* (April 20, 2004), online at: <http://www.assembly.ab.ca/ISYS/LADDAR_files/docs/committees/pb/legislature_25/session_4/20040420_1200_01_pb.pdf>). Before the Private Bills Committee made a determination about whether to introduce the Bill to the Legislature, an election was called and the Legislature dissolved. In November 2005, both the *Maternal Tort Liability Act* and the *Brooklynn Hannah George Rewega Right of Civil Action Act*, S.A. 2005, c. 51 were debated and passed by the Alberta Legislature. In his comments on the *Maternal Tort Liability Act*, the Minister of Justice and Attorney General of Alberta stated that the Private Bill relating to Brooklynn Rewega addressed an issue of public policy, and that a Private Bill was not the appropriate place to deal with issues of public policy (Alberta, Legislative Assembly, *Hansard* (November 21, 2005) at 1772 (Mr. Stevens)).

the ability of pregnant women to act autonomously, and with state responses to reproduction by certain classes of women.[130]

The type of state action that is of concern here is the legal imposition of medical care or other treatment intended to protect the fetus from the actions or decisions of the pregnant woman. Where a pregnant woman refuses medically recommended care, state intervention can take the form of coercive medical treatment. In cases where the pregnant woman is addicted to substances alleged to be harmful to the fetus, state intervention is potentially wide-ranging and can include criminal prosecution, sentencing practices intended to restrict the woman's access to the substance she is addicted to, and the use of child welfare and/or mental health legislation to attempt to constrain the behaviour of pregnant addicts.

All forms of state intervention in pregnancy purportedly serve the same aim — to protect the fetus who may suffer harm as a result of the pregnant woman's behaviour, whether that consists in refusing recommended medical interventions or ingesting a potentially feto-toxic substance. Commendable though that objective may be, all of these interventions involve, to a greater or lesser degree, violations of the pregnant woman's bodily integrity and reproductive autonomy. If a woman is required to submit to a Cesarean section because, in her physician's opinion, the baby cannot be safely delivered otherwise, the violation is particularly profound. The same goes for detention in a health care facility or incarceration. But even in the case of less invasive measures, it must be borne in mind that the woman's bodily integrity is implicated. Respect for women's reproductive autonomy in this context thus requires that the state proceed with great caution.

There are few reported Canadian cases concerning coercive medical treatment in pregnancy (although similar issues were raised in *Winnipeg Child and Family Services (Northwest Area) v. G. (D.F.)*, as will be discussed below),[131] but lower court decisions indicate that these matters have received judicial consideration. In *Children's Aid Society Belleville (City) Hastings (County) v.*

---

[130] Numerous commentators have noted that state intervention in the lives of pregnant women is almost exclusively directed at women who are addicted to drugs, poor women and women of colour. See, *e.g.*, Lynn M. Paltrow, "Punishment and Prejudice: Judging Drug Using Pregnant Women" in Julia E. Hanigsberg & Sara Ruddick, eds., *Mother Troubles: Rethinking Contemporary Maternal Dilemmas* (Boston: Beacon Press, 1999) at 59; Dorothy E. Roberts, "Racism and Patriarchy in the Meaning of Motherhood" (1993) 1 Am. U. J. Gender & L. 1; Dorothy E. Roberts, "Punishing Drug Addicts Who Have Babies: Women of Color, Equality and the Right of Privacy" (1991) 104 Harv. L. Rev. 1419; Sanda Rodgers, "The Legal Regulation of Women's Reproductive Capacity in Canada" in Jocelyn Downie, Timothy Caulfield & Colleen Flood, eds., *Canadian Health Law and Policy*, 2d ed. (Markham, ON: LexisNexis Canada, 2002) at 331; and Françoise Baylis, "Dissenting with the Dissent: *Winnipeg Child and Family Services (Northwest Area) v. G. (D.F.)*" (1998) 36 Alta. L. Rev. 785.

[131] But see Rachel Roth, *Making Women Pay: The Hidden Costs of Fetal Rights* (Ithaca: Cornell University Press, 2000) at 94-95, who notes that it is not possible to ascertain the full extent of court-ordered medical intervention in pregnancy. Roth's work suggests that by no means all such cases are reported in law reports (or elsewhere, for that matter).

T. (L.),[132] the Ontario Provincial Court held that a fetus can be a "child in need of protection" under the *Child and Family Services Act*[133] where a pregnant woman refuses obstetrical care. Accordingly, the court granted an order making the "child" a ward of the Children's Aid Society for a period of three months. The court also issued an order under the *Mental Health Act,*[134] for assessment of the pregnant woman by a physician, on the basis that her behaviour posed a danger to both herself and the "child".

In *Re Baby R.*, the Superintendent of Child and Family Services apprehended a fetus during labour after the pregnant woman refused to consent to delivery via Cesarean section. Ms. R. was never notified of the apprehension and, ultimately, consented to the surgery "practically at the door of the operating room".[135] The child was apprehended immediately following its birth, and the Provincial Court judge held that the apprehension was justified. On appeal by the mother, the British Columbia Supreme Court overturned the order of the Provincial Court, on the basis that the *Family and Child Service Act*[136] gave the Superintendent the power to apprehend only "living children that have been delivered".[137]

In *Re A.*, the Children's Aid Society of Hamilton-Wentworth sought an order subjecting Mrs. A.'s fetus to the supervision of the Society, and requiring Mrs. A. to seek prenatal care from a physician whose name was to be provided to the Society. In addition, Society asked the court to order Mrs. A. to make "immediate plans" for a hospital birth, to advise the Society of the name of the hospital and to attend at the hospital for the child's birth.[138] The Society also requested that the court grant a further order "requiring P.A. to be detained in hospital until the birth of the child and to undergo all necessary medical procedures for the well-being of the unborn child", in the event that Mrs. A. refused to comply with the original order.[139] The order was sought on the basis of the court's jurisdiction under the *Child and Family Services Act*[140] or, in the alternative, its jurisdiction *parens patriae*. The court concluded, albeit "reluctantly",[141] that it had no jurisdiction to make an order that would require the forcible confinement of the pregnant woman in order to protect the fetus.

In *Winnipeg*, the Supreme Court of Canada considered the broad question of whether there is any foundation in law to support the detention of a pregnant woman for the purpose of protecting her fetus. When Ms. G. was five months

---

[132] [1987] O.J. No. 2606, 59 O.R. (2d) 204 (Ont. Prov. Ct.).
[133] S.O. 1984, c. 55, s. 37.
[134] R.S.O. 1980, c. 262, s. 10(1).
[135] *Re Baby R.*, [1988] B.C.J. No. 2986, 53 D.L.R. (4th) 69 at 73 (B.C.S.C.).
[136] S.B.C. 1980, c. 11.
[137] *Re Baby R.*, [1988] B.C.J. No. 2986, 53 D.L.R. (4th) 69 at 80 (B.C.S.C.).
[138] *Re A. (In Utero)*, [1990] O.J. No. 1347, 72 D.L.R. (4th) 722 at 723-24 (Ont. U.F.C.).
[139] *Ibid.*, at 723-24.
[140] S.O. 1984, c. 55.
[141] *Re A. (In Utero)*, [1990] O.J. No. 1347, 72 D.L.R. (4th) 722 at 728 (Ont. U.F.C.). The court thus overruled *Children's Aid Society Belleville (City) Hastings (County) v. T (L.)*, [1987] O.J. No. 2606, 59 O.R. (2d) 204 (Ont. Prov. Ct.).

pregnant with her fourth child,[142] and addicted to sniffing glue, Winnipeg Child and Family Services sought an order for mandatory detention so that Ms. G. could be kept at a place of safety (and required to undergo treatment for her addiction). The order was granted by the Manitoba Court of Queen's Bench, which held that both the *Mental Health Act*[143] and the court's inherent jurisdiction could be invoked in support of the order.[144] The Manitoba Court of Appeal struck down the order, holding that Ms. G. was not incompetent (as required before the issuance of an order under the *Mental Health Act*), and concluding that the lower court erred in relying on the *parens patriae* jurisdiction.[145] In spite of the invalidity of the court order, Ms. G. voluntarily remained at the Winnipeg Health Sciences Centre until her discharge a number of weeks later. Ultimately, Ms. G. gave birth to a healthy baby who remained in her custody.

The Supreme Court of Canada granted leave to appeal and, ultimately, concluded that an order of the type granted in this case could not be supported by statute, tort law or the court's inherent jurisdiction *parens patriae*. The Court noted the significant policy issues that arise in the context of contemplating the extension of the common law in this way[146] — in particular, the Court noted the dramatic impact on women's fundamental liberties that would result from extending the common law to permit an order for the detention and treatment of a pregnant woman to prevent harm to the fetus — as well as the ramifications of such a change for other areas of tort law.[147] As in the case of tort law duties of pregnant women, the Supreme Court took the view that "[t]he changes to the law sought on this appeal are best left to the wisdom of the elected legislature".[148]

Other cases on point have dealt with the removal of a child after birth based on the mother's conduct during pregnancy.[149] In *Re Children's Aid Society for*

---

[142] Her three children were all wards of the state.

[143] C.C.S.M. c. M110.

[144] *Winnipeg Child and Family Services (Northwest Area) v. G. (D.F.)*, [1996] M.J. No. 386, 138 D.L.R. (4th) 238 (Man. Q.B.).

[145] *Winnipeg Child and Family Services (Northwest Area) v. G. (D.F.)*, [1996] M.J. No. 398, 138 D.L.R. (4th) 254 (Man. C.A.).

[146] *Winnipeg Child and Family Services (Northwest Area) v. G. (D.F.)*, [1997] S.C.J. No. 96 at paras. 30-45, 152 D.L.R. (4th) 193 (S.C.C.).

[147] *Ibid.*, at paras. 18-57.

[148] *Ibid.*, at para. 59. Indeed, McLachlin J. refers repeatedly to the possibility of legislative action throughout her judgment.

[149] See also *J. (A.) v. Yukon Territory (Family and Children Services, Director)*, [1986] Y.J. No. 40, 1 Y.R. 169 (Y.T.S.C.), striking down a provision of the Yukon *Children's Act*, S.Y.T. 1984, c. 2. Section 134(1) of the Act permitted the Director of Family and Children Services — acting on reasonable and probable grounds to believe that a fetus was at serious risk of suffering from fetal alcohol syndrome or some other congenital injury attributable to the pregnant woman's consumption of addictive or intoxicating substances — "to apply to a judge for an order requiring the woman to participate in such reasonable supervision or counselling as the order specifies in respect of her use of addictive or intoxicating substances". The section was found to be unconstitutionally vague. In spite of this ruling, the section remained on the books in the *Children's Act*, R.S.Y. 2002, c. 31 as s. 135(1). The section has since been repealed: see *Child and Family Ser-*

the District of Kenora and L. (J.),[150] the child suffered from fetal alcohol syndrome resulting from the mother's alcohol abuse during her pregnancy. The Ontario Provincial Court held that a fetus was entitled to protection under the *Child Welfare Act.* In *British Columbia (Superintendent of Child and Family Services) v. M. (B.),*[151] a baby born addicted to methadone (whose mother had been advised by her physician to continue to take methadone during pregnancy) was apprehended, and an order of permanent custody was made in favour of the child welfare authorities. In upholding the order, Proudfoot J. stated that "it would be incredible to come to any other conclusion than that a drug-addicted baby is born abused".[152] Finally, in *Ackerman v. McGoldrick,*[153] a baby apprehended after her father absconded with her was returned to her mother's care, as there was no evidence that she was in need of protection. The baby's mother had ingested drugs on one or two occasions during her pregnancy, but at the time of the hearing, the baby was developing normally.

State intervention in the lives of pregnant women can take a variety of forms. Arguably, and depending heavily on what is meant by intervention, state intervention in the lives of pregnant women might sometimes be very desirable. If we take intervention to mean, for example, the positive involvement of the state in the lives of pregnant women in seeking out and helping those who need assistance with prenatal care, addiction treatment, nutrition, care of other children, or protection from a violent spouse, then there is clearly an important role for intervention. If, on the other hand, we take it to mean what it seems to mean now — forced obstetrical treatment, incarceration, detention or other forms of punishment — intervention in pregnancy is misguided and unlikely to further the alleged goal of healthy mothers and healthy children.[154]

In the case of medical treatment, respect for women's bodily integrity clearly requires that women's decisions about what medical treatment they will or will not accept must be deferred to, even where it appears that this decision might lead to a less than desirable outcome for the pregnant woman and/or the fetus. Health care providers may attempt to persuade a woman to change her mind about treatment, they may advise her about all of the concerns they have for her potential child should she refuse the treatment, but they may not coerce her to agree to the procedure, either physically or through the use of threats.

---

vices Act, S.Y. 2008, c. 1, s. 199(6), repealing Part 4 — Child Protection of the *Children's Act.* The *Children's Act* has also been renamed the *Children's Law Act* — see *Child and Family Services Act,* s. 199(1).

[150] (1981), 134 D.L.R. (3d) 249 (Ont. Prov. Ct.).

[151] [1982] B.C.J. No. 468, 135 D.L.R. (3d) 330 (B.C.C.A.).

[152] *Ibid.,* at 335.

[153] [1990] B.C.J. No. 2832 (B.C. Prov. Ct.).

[154] See John Seymour, *Childbirth and the Law* (New York: Oxford University Press, 2000) at 230, 238; Sanda Rodgers, "The Legal Regulation of Women's Reproductive Capacity in Canada" in Jocelyn Downie, Timothy Caulfield & Colleen Flood, eds., *Canadian Health Law and Policy,* 2d ed. (Markham, ON: LexisNexis Canada, 2002) at 354.

But what about the pregnant drug addict? Is she capable of exercising autonomy? If not, do her decisions deserve respect? The situation of substance-addicted pregnant women is complex. Clearly, addictions have great potential to interfere with autonomy.[155] But to treat addicts as being completely incapable of exercising autonomy is misguided. Take, for example, Ms. G.,[156] the pregnant woman whose behaviour was at issue in the *Winnipeg* case. A social worker learned that Ms. G. was pregnant and was addicted to sniffing glue.[157] Ms. G. expressed an interest in getting help for her addiction, and agreed to enter a treatment facility. When the social worker returned to accompany Ms. G. to the treatment centre, Ms. G. was high and refused to go. Instead of waiting until Ms. G. was sober, Winnipeg Child and Family Services sought an order compelling Ms. G. to remain "in a place of safety", and requiring treatment for her addiction.[158]

These facts illustrate that, if not fully autonomous, Ms. G. was nonetheless capable of exercising autonomy, at least while not under the influence of the substance to which she was addicted. While her decision not to accompany the social worker to the treatment centre was not autonomous[159] and arguably need not be respected, seeking a court order to compel her to enter addiction treatment shows utter contempt for the autonomy she was capable of exercising in the minimally longer term. In any case, pregnant women who are addicted to harmful substances are not likely to be helped by mandatory treatment, given the "general consensus in the field of addiction treatment ... that many of the addict's beliefs and attitudes must change if she is to modify her behavior, and this change will not occur in treatment if she is there unwillingly".[160] In addition to being ineffective, mandatory treatment is also likely to further undermine the limited autonomy these women can claim.[161]

VII. ASSISTED REPRODUCTIVE TECHNOLOGIES

The Canadian response to the flourishing science of assisted reproduction has a long and complex history, beginning with the appointment of the Royal Com-

---

[155] See, *e.g.*, Carolyn McLeod, "Women's Autonomy and the 'G' Case" (May 1998) 3:2 Canadian Bioethics Society Newsletter.

[156] *Winnipeg Child and Family Services (Northwest Area) v. G. (D.F.)*, [1997] S.C.J. No. 96, 152 D.L.R. (4th) 193 (S.C.C.).

[157] As noted earlier, Ms. G. had three children, all of whom were wards of the state. See *Winnipeg Child and Family Services (Northwest Area) v. G. (D.F.)*, *ibid*.

[158] *Winnipeg Child and Family Services (Northwest Area) v. G. (D.F.)*, *ibid*.

[159] This is borne out by her decision to remain in the addiction treatment program even after the order of the Manitoba Court of Queen's Bench mandating treatment was stayed two days later, pending appeal. See *Winnipeg Child and Family Services (Northwest Area) v. G. (D.F.)*, *ibid*.

[160] Carolyn McLeod & Susan Sherwin, "Relational Autonomy, Self-Trust and Health Care for Patients Who Are Oppressed" in Catriona Mackenzie & Natalie Stoljar, eds., *Relational Autonomy: Feminist Perspectives on Autonomy, Agency and the Social Self* (Oxford: Oxford University Press, 2000) at 271.

[161] Carolyn McLeod & Susan Sherwin are particularly concerned about addicted women who lack self-trust, since imposing treatment simply further diminishes their decision-making power. See "Relational Autonomy, Self-Trust and Health Care for Patients Who Are Oppressed", *ibid.*, at 273-74.

mission on New Reproductive Technologies in 1989.[162] The political discussion around regulating reproductive technologies in Canada has been ongoing since the Royal Commission's final report in 1993,[163] and continues despite the enactment of legislation aimed at comprehensively governing research and clinical applications of assisted reproductive technologies (ARTs). In 2004, after 11 years of debate, discussion[164] and failed attempts at legislating, the *Assisted Human Reproduction Act*[165] (AHR Act) received Royal Assent.

The AHR Act, as currently structured,[166] creates categories of prohibited and controlled activities, regulates privacy and access to information, establishes the Assisted Human Reproduction Agency of Canada (known as Assisted Human Reproduction Canada, or AHRC), and sets out provisions relating to administration, inspection and enforcement of the provisions of the AHR Act and Regulations.[167] In short, the AHR Act designates ART-related activities as either prohibited or controlled; the majority of the AHR Act is devoted to the regulation of the controlled activities. Several sections of the AHR Act (those concerning prohibited and controlled activities)[168] are now in force, but the remainder of the Act (dealing with the regulatory framework) has not yet been implemented,

---

[162] The Ontario Law Reform Commission and the Law Reform Commission of Canada also studied reproductive and genetic technologies: see Ontario Law Reform Commission, *Report on Human Artificial Reproduction and Related Matters* (Toronto: Ontario Law Reform Commission, 1985); Law Reform Commission of Canada, *Medically Assisted Procreation (Working Paper 65)* (Ottawa: Minister of Supply and Services Canada, 1992).

[163] Royal Commission on New Reproductive Technologies, *Proceed with Care: Final Report of the Royal Commission on New Reproductive Technologies* (Ottawa: Minister of Supply and Services Canada, 1993).

[164] See, *e.g.*, Timothy Caulfield, "Bill C-13: The *Assisted Human Reproduction Act*: Examining the Arguments Against a Regulatory Approach" (2002) 11 Health L. Rev. 20; Timothy Caulfield, "Clones, Controversy and Criminal Law: A Comment on the Proposal for Legislation Governing Assisted Human Reproduction" (2001) 39 Alta. L. Rev. 335; Alison Harvison Young & Angela Wasunna, "Wrestling with the Limits of Law: Regulating New Reproductive Technologies" (1998) 6 Health L.J. 239; Francoise Baylis, "Human Cloning: Three Mistakes and an Alternative" (2002) 27:3 Journal of Medicine and Philosophy 319.

[165] S.C. 2004, c. 2.

[166] The impact of the recent Supreme Court of Canada decision on a reference involving the Act is as yet undetermined. See notes 174-180 and accompanying text.

[167] According to s. 66 of the AHR Act, the Minister of Health must present proposed regulations to both the House of Commons and the Senate. The "relevant committees" of each House will then have an opportunity to consider and report on the regulations, and the Minister is to take into account these reports and, in the event that the regulation is not modified to incorporate recommendations of the committees, the Minister "shall lay before that House a statement of the reasons for not incorporating [them]" (s. 66(4)). The only exceptions to the requirement of presenting proposed regulations to Parliament are found in s. 67, and occur: (1) where the changes made by the regulation to existing regulation are, in the opinion of the Minister, "so immaterial or insubstantial that s. 66 should not apply in the circumstances" (s. 67(1)(*a*)); and (2) in situations where the regulation must be made immediately "to protect the health or safety of any person" (s. 67(1)(*b*)).

[168] Prior to the coming into force of the Act, a voluntary moratorium was in place to deal with concerns around the prohibited activities. See Health Canada, "A Chronology of the *Assisted Human Reproduction Act*", online at: <http://www.hc-sc.gc.ca/hl-vs/reprod/hc-sc/general/chronolog-eng.php>.

as the requisite regulations have not been adopted. The regulation-making process commenced in 2007 and, to date, one set of regulations has been approved — the consent regulations came into force on December 1, 2007.[169] In spite of the years of debate and the political and legislative efforts, assisted reproduction remains largely unregulated in most of the country, with the notable exception of Quebec, where provincial legislation was recently enacted "to regulate clinical and research activities relating to assisted procreation in order to ensure high-quality, safe and ethical practices".[170]

In part at least, the delay in implementing of the AHR Act can be attributed to litigation commenced by the Government of Quebec; the litigation essentially stalled the regulation-making process.[171] In 2007, the Quebec Court of Appeal heard a reference made by the Government of Quebec as to the constitutional validity of most of the AHR Act.[172] The challenge was to the "controlled activities" and the regulatory aspects of the AHR Act; the criminal prohibitions were not challenged. The Court of Appeal held that the impugned sections of the Act are indeed *ultra vires* federal jurisdiction.[173] Despite the assertion of the Attorney General of Canada that the Act represents a legitimate use of the federal criminal law power, the Court of Appeal held that the legislative intent of the AHR Act is the regulation of both clinical practice and research involving assisted reproductive technologies, and that its aim is to create a national, uniform approach to such regulation.

The Government of Canada appealed the decision to the Supreme Court of Canada, which heard arguments on April 24, 2009 and rendered its decision on December 22, 2010.[174] The reasons reveal a deeply divided Court, which might

---

[169] Assisted Human Reproduction (Section 8 Consent) Regulations, SOR/2007-137.

[170] *An Act respecting clinical and research activities relating to assisted procreation*, R.S.Q., c. A-5.01, s. 1. An Expert Panel on Infertility and Adoption convened by the Ontario Government has recommended that Ontario do likewise. See Government of Ontario Expert Panel on Infertility and Adoption, *Raising Expectations: Recommendations of the Expert Panel on Infertility and Adoption* (Ontario Ministry of Children and Youth Services, 2009) at 100, online at: <http://www.children. gov.on.ca/htdocs/English/documents/infertility/RaisingExpectationsEnglish.pdf>.

[171] While this reference was before the Supreme Court of Canada, Health Canada indicated that it would not pre-publish draft regulations pending the outcome of the reference. Health Canada indicated at the time that "work continues unabated to develop proposed regulations". See Health Canada, "Publication of Proposed Assisted Human Reproduction Regulations Delayed Until Supreme Court Appeal is Decided", online at: <http://www.hc-sc.gc.ca/hl-vs/reprod/hc-sc/legislation/delay-interruption-eng.php>.

[172] *Orders in Council Reference to the Court of Appeal re Assisted Human Reproduction Act*, O.C. 1177-2004, December 15, 2004, G.O.Q. 2005.II.62 and *Amendment to Order in Council 1177-2004 concerning a Reference to the Court of Appeal re the Assisted Human Reproduction Act*, O.C. 73-2006, February 14, 2006, G.O.Q. 2006.II.1290, made pursuant to the *Court of Appeal Reference Act*, R.S.Q., c. R-23. The impugned sections are ss. 8 to 19, 40 to 53, 60, 61 to 68.

[173] *Renvoi fait par le gouvernement du Québec en vertu de la Loi sur les renvois à la Cour d'appel, L.R.Q. ch. R-23, relativement à la constitutionnalité des articles 8 à 19, 40 à 53, 60, 61 et 68 de la Loi sur la procréation assistée, L.C. 2004, ch. 2 (Dans l'affaire du)*, [2008] J.Q. no 5489, 2008 QCCA 1167 (Que. C.A.).

[174] *Reference re Assisted Human Reproduction Act*, [2010] S.C.J. No. 61, 2010 SCC 61 (S.C.C.).

explain the lengthy interval between the hearing and the release of the reasons. The Court split 4:4:1, with Cromwell J.'s vote determining the majority. Chief Justice McLachlin, writing for one of the groups of four justices, would have upheld the AHR Act as a valid exercise of the federal criminal law power, stating that "[t]aken as a whole, the Act seeks to avert serious damage to the fabric of our society by prohibiting practices that tend to devalue human life and degrade participants".[175] Justices LeBel and Deschamps, who authored the reasons for the other group of four, found all of the impugned provisions to be *ultra vires* Parliament on the basis that the regulation of clinical uses of assisted reproductive technologies and related research activities fall within provincial jurisdiction.[176] Justice Cromwell agreed with LeBel and Deschamps JJ. as to their characterization of the majority of the impugned sections of the Act, stating that these provisions are aimed at "regulation of virtually every aspect of research and clinical practice in relation to assisted human reproduction".[177] He did uphold several sections of the Act, however, on the basis that they fall within the "traditional ambit of the federal criminal law power"[178] or are sufficiently related to sections of the Act that are constitutionally valid.

The practical impact of the Supreme Court's decision remains to be seen. References are advisory judicial opinions and, as such, are not binding on the government. While these decisions are ordinarily treated just as any other judicial opinion,[179] no specific remedial action is recommended or demanded by the Court's decision. Thus, and bearing in mind that the majority of the AHR Act is not in force, unless and until the federal government takes action in response to the Supreme Court's decision, the Act remains the law on assisted reproduction in Canada.[180] It could well be the case that the legislation will remain on the books for some time to come, as the current federal government has shown little interest in taking any steps on this file — the Act is more than two years overdue for Parliamentary review.[181] In light of this reality, and given that some sections of the Act were held to be within the authority of Parliament, it is useful to articulate some general observations about the structure and aims of the legislation. In what follows, the Act is described as it currently stands, and the accompanying footnotes indicate how the particular section(s) fared in the Supreme Court's decision.

---

[175] *Ibid.*, at para. 61.

[176] In particular, provincial jurisdiction over hospitals, property and civil rights in the province and matters of a merely local nature. See *ibid.*

[177] *Ibid.*, at para. 285.

[178] *Ibid.*, at para. 291.

[179] Peter Hogg, *Constitutional Law of Canada*, 5th ed., vol. 1, looseleaf (Toronto: Thomson Reuters, 2007) at 8-18.

[180] Health Canada has not yet officially responded to the decision, meaning that all we can do at this point is speculate as to the intentions of the federal government.

[181] Based on s. 70 of the Act, this review was due in January 2009. *Assisted Human Reproduction Act*, S.C. 2004, c. 2, s. 70.

Rather than setting out broad legislative goals in a preamble, the "overriding principles" of the Act are set out in a declaratory section.[182] These principles include the paramountcy of the health and well-being of children born through ART procedures, the acknowledgment of the fact that ART practice affects women more "directly and significantly" than it does men, and that measures must be taken to ensure the protection of women's health and well-being, reference to the importance of informed consent and non-discrimination in the provision of ART services, and identification of the fact that health and ethical concerns are raised by the commercialization of reproductive capacity.[183]

A number of ART-related clinical and research practices are prohibited by the AHR Act; as these sections were not among those contested by Quebec, this will not change as a result of the Supreme Court's decision unless the government decides to repeal the entire Act. Maximum penalties for the commission of prohibited activities are a fine of $500,000 or a 10-year term of imprisonment, or both.[184] Prohibited activities include:

- cloning;[185]

- creating an embryo for research purposes (other than the narrow research purpose of improving or providing instruction in ART procedures);[186]

- creating an embryo from an embryo or fetus;[187]

- maintaining an embryo *in vitro* for more than 14 days;[188]

- sex selection for non-medical purposes;[189]

- commercial surrogacy;[190]

- purchase of gametes or embryos;[191] and

- use of reproductive material without consent.[192]

---

[182] *Ibid.*, s. 2. This section is unaffected by the Supreme Court's decision.

[183] The other governing principles relate to the need for measures to safeguard human health, safety, dignity and rights in the use of ARTs, and a reference to the importance of human diversity, individuality and the integrity of the human genome.

[184] *Assisted Human Reproduction Act*, S.C. 2004, c. 2, s. 60.

[185] *Ibid.*, s. 5(1)(*a*).

[186] *Ibid.*, s. 5(1)(*b*).

[187] *Ibid.*, s. 5(1)(*c*).

[188] *Ibid.*, s. 5(1)(*d*).

[189] *Ibid.*, s. 5(1)(*e*). Other prohibitions under s. 5 are: germ line alteration (s. 5(1)(*f*)); transfer of non-human gametes, embryos or fetuses into a human being (s. 5(1)(*g*)); use (for reproductive purposes) of any human gametes reproductive material that is or was transplanted into a non-human animal (s. 5(1)(*h*)); creation of a chimera or hybrid (s. 5(1)(*i*)); and advertising (s. 5(2)) or paying (s. 5(3)) for the performance of prohibited activities.

[190] *Ibid.*, s. 6. This includes prohibitions on payment to the surrogate mother herself or an intermediary, and also prohibits the acceptance of payment by an intermediary.

[191] *Ibid.*, s. 7.

The AHR Act also creates a class of controlled activities — use of human gametes or embryos,[193] transgenic research in certain situations,[194] reimbursement of expenses incurred by gamete or embryo donors or surrogate mothers,[195] and the use of premises to carry out controlled activities[196] — which may only be carried out in accordance with the regulations and a licence.

As noted above, the AHR Act also deals with privacy and access to information. Key provisions here include a section that requires AHRC to maintain a personal health information registry about gamete and embryo donors, persons undergoing ART procedures and those conceived through the use of such procedures.[197] In addition, the Act gives AHRC the power to disclose, upon request by a person conceived by means of ART procedures, health reporting information relating to a gamete or embryo donor. Identifying information about the donor cannot be disclosed without the consent of the donor.[198] Moreover, where two persons who have reason to believe that they may be related[199] submit a request in writing, the Act authorizes AHRC to inform them "whether it has information that they are genetically related and, if so, the nature of the relationship".[200]

Arguably, the most significant feature of the legislation is the creation of the regulatory body, AHRC.[201] AHRC operates at arm's length from the federal government, but is accountable to Parliament through the Minister of Health.[202] The objectives of AHRC are clearly spelled out in the legislation. They centre on the protection and promotion of the health, safety, human dignity and human rights of Canadians, and seek to foster the application of ethical principles in

---

[192] *Ibid.*, s. 8.

[193] *Ibid.*, s. 10. This section was found by the Supreme Court of Canada to be *ultra vires* Parliament.

[194] *Ibid.*, s. 11. This section was found by the Supreme Court of Canada to be *ultra vires* Parliament.

[195] *Ibid.*, s. 12 [not yet in force].

[196] *Ibid.*, s. 13. This section was found by the Supreme Court of Canada to be *ultra vires* Parliament.

[197] *Ibid.*, s. 17 [not yet in force]. This section was found by the Supreme Court of Canada to be *ultra vires* Parliament.

[198] *Ibid.*, s. 18(3) [not yet in force]. This section was found by the Supreme Court of Canada to be *ultra vires* Parliament. The issue of donor anonymity is contentious and has been abolished in many jurisdictions (see, *e.g.*, Eric Blyth, "Davina and Goliath: The Personal Cost of Seeking Justice" (October 29, 2010) 582 Bionews, online at: <http://www.bionews.org.uk/page_80623.asp>). A lawsuit has been commenced in British Columbia asserting that the Province and the College of Physicians and Surgeons have "failed to protect her right to know the identity of her biological father". See *Pratten v. British Columbia (Attorney General)*, [2010] B.C.J. No. 2012 at para. 4, 2010 BCSC 1444 (B.C.S.C.).

[199] Where one or both were conceived by means of an ART procedure involving human reproductive material from the same donor.

[200] *Assisted Human Reproduction Act*, S.C. 2004, c. 2, s. 18(4) [not yet in force]. This section was found by the Supreme Court of Canada to be *ultra vires* Parliament.

[201] *Ibid.*, s. 21. For an in-depth discussion of the role and structure of the Agency, see Erin L. Nelson, "Comparative Perspectives on the Regulation of Assisted Reproductive Technologies in the United Kingdom and Canada" (2006) 43 Alta. L. Rev. 1023-1048.

[202] Health Canada, "Backgrounder: The Assisted Human Reproduction Agency of Canada", online at: <http://www.hc-sc.gc.ca/hl-vs/reprod/hc-sc/legislation/agenc_e.html>.

relation to ART practice.[203] AHRC's role is, in essence, regulation of ART techniques used both in the clinical and research settings. Its mandate includes powers in relation to licensing,[204] inspection and enforcement,[205] and the provision of advice to the Minister of Health on matters integral to the AHR Act.[206] AHRC also has legislative authority to monitor and evaluate national and international developments in ART practice,[207] consult with persons and organizations both within and outside Canada,[208] and collect, analyze and maintain health reporting information relating to controlled activities.[209] Finally, AHRC is empowered to provide information to the public and relevant professions respecting ART practice and regulation and risk factors for infertility.[210] AHRC's Board of Directors is to be made up of members reflecting "a range of backgrounds and disciplines relevant to the Agency's objectives",[211] and may not include a licensee or applicant for a licence, or a director, officer, shareholder or partner of a licensee or applicant.[212]

AHRC, like its parent legislation, has been beleaguered by controversy and opposition. The President and Board of Directors of AHRC were appointed in December 2006, in a process that commenced under the Liberal government and concluded after the election of the Conservative party in January 2006. In 2005, the Liberal government had convened an expert panel to develop a list of potential Directors for AHRC, but the federal election took place before the government could act on the panel's recommendations. According to those involved in the 2005 process, the list of appointees announced in December 2006 included only two of the 25 recommended candidates, and many of those who were appointed to the AHRC Board were not on the list of candidates reviewed by the expert panel.[213] Concerns were raised at the time about the lack of broad representation on the Board of Directors; the absence of stem cell researchers, obstetrician/gynecologists and patient representatives was particularly notable.[214]

Not only was the initial appointment process of the Board problematic; recently, several members of the Board of Directors resigned their positions.[215]

---

[203] *Assisted Human Reproduction Act*, S.C. 2004, c. 2, s. 22.

[204] *Ibid.*, s. 24(1)(*a*) [not yet in force].

[205] *Ibid.*, s. 24(1)(*g*) [not yet in force].

[206] *Ibid.*, s. 24(1)(*b*).

[207] *Ibid.*, s. 24(1)(*c*).

[208] *Ibid.*, s. 24(1)(*d*).

[209] *Ibid.*, s. 24(1)(*e*) [not yet in force].

[210] *Ibid.*, s. 24(1)(*f*).

[211] *Ibid.*, s. 26(2).

[212] *Ibid.*, s. 26(8).

[213] Laura Eggertson, "New Reproductive Technology Board Belies Expert Selection Process" (2007) 176:5 CMAJ 611.

[214] *Ibid.* See also Sam Solomon, "Reproduction Agency Appointments Spark Controversy" (2007) 4:2 National Review of Medicine, online at: <http://www.nationalreviewofmedicine.com/issue/2007/01_30/4_policy_politics02_2.html>. Ms. Irene Ryll, a patient/consumer representative, was later appointed to the Board of Directors.

[215] See Antony Blackburn-Starza, "Another Member Leaves Canada's AHRC" (June 7, 2010) 561 Bionews, online at: <http://www.bionews.org.uk/page_62469.asp>.

One of those who resigned apparently did so because of unease related to AHRC's "prudence and diligence in managing public funds".[216] Another "cited 'Group dynamics' on the board, limits on the expert advice provided to directors and a lack of regulations"[217] as factors leading to her resignation. The Board, which can have a maximum of 13 Directors, currently has seven members.

In addition to the worries generated by these resignations, one Canadian Member of Parliament has suggested that AHRC should be shut down because of its lack of action, in spite of having an annual budget of $10 million.[218] And, fertility experts have now suggested that the prohibitions in the Act, which have been in force since 2004, are being ignored by some fertility clinics.[219]

It is difficult to be optimistic about the future of the regulation of assisted human reproduction in Canada at this point, given the history of the legislation and the problems at the fledgling AHRC. In the months since the Supreme Court of Canada published its decision on the constitutionality of the AHR Act, the federal government has been silent as to its plans for the legislation and AHRC (at the time of writing this chapter). Specifically in respect of the AHRC, the provisions that create AHRC and give it authority to enforce the various other aspects of the Act were successfully defended by the Attorney General of Canada. This means that even if the federal government decides to repeal all of the sections of the legislation that were found to be beyond federal jurisdiction, AHRC would still exist and would have much the same legislative mandate. What would actually do, however, is very much in question, as its primary function was to be the enforcement of the regulatory aspects of the Act.

More globally, the Supreme Court's decision creates a number of concerns. It is beyond the scope of this chapter to delve into broader questions about how the Supreme Court understands the federal criminal law power, but LeBel and Deschamps JJ. are exactly right in noting that many advances in medical technology and practice give rise to concerns around "ethics, morality, safety and public health",[220] but that this alone does not justify regulation of those technologies on the basis of the federal criminal law power.[221] While it may be very

---

[216] Tom Blackwell, "Fertility spending at issue: Letter" *National Post* (June 2, 2010), online at: <http://www.nationalpost.com/news/canada/toronto/Fertility+spending+issue+letter/3100561/story.html>.

[217] *Ibid.*

[218] Gabrielle Samuel, "Canada's Fertility-Industry Watchdog Under Scrutiny Again" (June 21, 2010) 563 Bionews, online at: <http://www.bionews.org.uk/page_64674.asp>.

[219] Tom Blackwell, "Fertility law leaves us in limbo, doctors say: Oversight of burgeoning industry a 'farce'" *National Post* (April 30, 2010), online at: <http://www.canada.com/health/Fertility+leaves+limbo+doctors/2970981/story.html>; Alison Motluk, "The Human Egg Trade: How Canada's Fertility Laws Are Failing Donors, Doctors, and Parents" *The Walrus* (April 2010), online at: <http://www.walrusmagazine.com/articles/2010.04-health-the-human-egg-trade/>.

[220] *Reference re Assisted Human Reproduction Act,* [2010] S.C.J. No. 61 at para. 255, 2010 SCC 61 (S.C.C.).

[221] Another concern respecting the Court's reasoning (and this applies particularly to McLachlin C.J.C.'s reasons) is the role of or need for evidence of a legitimate criminal law purpose. The Chief Justice's reasons are replete with comments about the "public health evils" sought to be

desirable to have national standards for regulating clinical and research uses of assisted reproductive technologies, it seems fairly clear that the federal government simply does not have the constitutional authority to legislate such standards.[222] Unfortunately, we are now left with a great deal of uncertainty as to the future regulatory landscape for assisted reproduction in Canada. The provinces do have legislative authority to regulate in this area, but it is highly doubtful that all provinces (or even most) will do so. Alberta, for example, has two fertility treatment clinics, and a number of other provinces have only one clinic. Does it make sense for those provinces to expend the time, energy and political capital demanded by a full debate and discussion of assisted reproduction to create laws that will be relevant to such a narrow group of medical practitioners? On a more optimistic note, perhaps we will now see cooperation among provinces in crafting a regulatory regime for assisted reproductive technologies.

Although the full implications of the Supreme Court's decision may not be clear for some time yet, it seems safe to say that it is highly unlikely that the AHR Act will ever come fully into force. In any case, the Act does not completely occupy the field in regulating reproductive technologies. As a result, it is necessary to consider as well the regulatory environment outside the scope of the legislation, in order to get a clear picture of the regulatory landscape in Canada. The current picture involves some regulation of ARTs, but regulation is neither comprehensive nor integrated, nor is it uniformly applied or enforced.[223]

---

avoided by the AHR Act. See, for example, *ibid.*, at paras. 32, 47, 90, 116-118. Here is one example of the Chief Justice's concerns (at para. 100):

> These developments raise the prospect of novel harms to society, as the Baird Report amply documents. The "commodification of women and children" (p. 718); sex-selective abortions (p. 896); cross-species hybrids; ectogenesis with the potential to "dehumanize motherhood"; "baby farms" (p. 637); saviour siblings (a child whose primary purpose is to cure another child suffering from a genetic disorder); devaluation of persons with disabilities; discrimination based on ethnicity or genetic status (p. 28); and exploitation of the vulnerable — these are but some of the moral concerns raised in the Report. While the ethical acceptability of these techniques is, of course, debatable ... it cannot be seriously questioned that Parliament is able to prohibit or regulate them.

It is troubling to see the extent to which concerns (many of which were completely speculative) that were raised in a Report that was published 18 years ago are being relied on to justify current criminal prohibitions and regulation of a widely used medical technology. I do not mean to suggest that none of these concerns were then (or are now) valid, simply that it seems counter-intuitive to rely on the Baird Commission's articulation of these worries without explaining or expanding on the current status of these issues.

222 Arguably, this was acknowledged by the Baird Commission, who noted that the provinces have broad legislative jurisdiction over health. The Commission asserted, however, that the regulation of reproductive technologies could be accomplished by the federal government pursuant to the federal power to legislate for peace, order and good government, as the matter is one of "genuine national concern". See Royal Commission on New Reproductive Technologies, *Proceed with Care: Final Report of the Royal Commission on New Reproductive Technologies* (Ottawa: Minister of Supply and Services Canada, 1993) at 18-22.

223 Including, for example, the status of gametes and embryos. See, *e.g.*, Roxanne Mykitiuk & Albert Wallrap, "Regulating Reproductive Technologies in Canada" in Jocelyn Downie, Timothy Caulfield & Colleen Flood, eds., *Canadian Health Law and Policy*, 2d ed. (Markham, ON: Lex-

A number of Canadian jurisdictions have legislation concerning the status of children born as a result of ARTs,[224] but in most provinces, the common law governs on this issue.[225] Processing, testing and distribution of semen for donor insemination[226] is governed by the *Food and Drugs Act*.[227] In addition, all provinces have human tissue legislation.[228] There are also professional guidelines and policies in place to help guide medical practice involving some aspects of assisted human reproduction. In particular, the Society of Obstetricians and Gynecologists of Canada and the Canadian Fertility and Andrology Society have produced a joint policy statement on ethical issues in assisted reproduction,[229] which sets out ethical guidelines in relation to sperm sorting for non-medical reasons, preconception arrangements, oocyte donation, disposition of frozen embryos, research on human embryos, intracytoplasmic sperm injection (ICSI), preimplantation genetic diagnosis (PGD), social screening and participation in reproductive technologies, and medical and genetic screening of gamete and embryo donors.

Finally, research involving ARTs is governed by the *Tri-Council Policy Statement: Ethical Conduct for Research Involving Humans* (TCPS),[230] which has rules in place as to ethically appropriate uses of human genetic material,

---

isNexis Canada, 2002) at 399-408. See also *C. (C.) v. W. (A.)*, [2005] A.J. No. 428, 2005 ABQB 290 (Alta. Q.B.), where Sanderman J. treats embryos and gametes as property.

[224] The legislation is not uniform. Alberta has passed a new *Family Law Act* (S.A. 2003, c. F-4.5, s. 12 (surrogacy) and s. 13 (assisted conception)). In the Yukon, the *Children's Act*, R.S.Y. 2002, c. 31, s. 13 (renamed *Children's Law Act* by S.Y. 2008, c. 1, s. 199(1), which was proclaimed in force as of April 30, 2010) provides for determination of paternity in the case of artificial insemination (as does Newfoundland and Labrador's legislation: *Children's Law Act*, R.S.N.L. 1990, c. C-13, s. 12 and Prince Edward Island's legislation: *Child Status Act*, R.S.P.E.I. 1988, c. C-6, s. 9). In Manitoba, the *Vital Statistics Act*, C.C.S.M. c. V60, s. 3(6) speaks to birth registrations in cases involving artificial insemination.

[225] For a discussion of the case law on point, see Angela Campbell, "Conceiving Parents Through Law" (2007) 21 Int'l J.L. Pol'y & Fam. 242; Roxanne Mykitiuk, "Beyond Conception: Legal Determinations of Filiation in the Context of Assisted Reproductive Technologies" (2001) 39 Osgoode Hall L.J. 771 at 791-814; see also Simon R. Fodden, *Family Law* (Toronto: Irwin Law, 1999), c. 5, "6. A Note on Reproduction Technology".

[226] Processing and Distribution of Semen for Assisted Conception Regulations, SOR/96-254, as am.

[227] R.S.C. 1985, c. F-27.

[228] For example, *Human Tissue and Organ Donation Act*, S.A. 2006, c. H-14.5. While the Alberta legislation specifies that the Act does not apply to zygotes, oocytes, embryos, sperm, semen and ova (s. 2(c)), some such statutes, although they deal generally with organ transplantation, do not define "tissue" narrowly, and therefore could be involved in the regulation of some aspects of ARTs; see, *e.g.*, *Human Tissue Act*, R.S.N.W.T. 1988, c. H-6; *Human Tissue Gift Act*, R.S.S. 1978, c. H-15; *Human Tissue Gift Act*, R.S.B.C. 1996, c. 211.

[229] Canadian Fertility and Andrology Society & Society of Obstetricians and Gynaecologists of Canada, "Joint Policy Statement: Ethical Issues in Assisted Reproduction" (1999) 21:1 Journal of Obstetrics and Gynaecology Canada 1. See also Jason K. Min *et al.*, "Joint SOGC-CFAS Clinical Practice Guideline: Elective Single Embryo Transfer Following In Vitro Fertilization" No. 241 (April 2010) Journal of Obstetrics and Gynaecology Canada 363; Erin Nelson *et al.*, "SOGC Clinical Practice Guideline: Informed Consent to Donate Embryos for Research Purposes" No. 215 (September 2008) Journal of Obstetrics and Gynaecology Canada 824.

[230] Canadian Institutes of Health Research, Natural Sciences and Engineering Research Council of Canada & Social Sciences and Humanities Research Council of Canada, *Tri-Council Policy Statement: Ethical Conduct for Research Involving Humans* (December 2010), online at: <http://www.pre.ethics.gc.ca/pdf/eng/tcps2/TCPS_2_FINAL_Web.pdf>.

gametes, embryos and fetuses. In general, these rules echo (and refer to) the AHR Act provisions respecting the use of gametes and embryos. Chapter 13 of the TCPS, which governs human genetic material, refers to the prohibition on germ line genetic alteration found in the AHR Act.[231] Chapter 12, which considers ethical issues involving human biological (including reproductive) materials states that commercially obtained human reproductive materials shall not be used in research.[232] The TCPS also notes that the AHR Act prohibits the creation of human embryos specifically for use in research,[233] as well as certain activities related to the creation of hybrids and chimeras.[234]

Another piece of the regulatory puzzle in this context is funding for ART services. Until very recently, only one Canadian jurisdiction provided funding for *in vitro* fertilization (IVF) treatment, and only in very limited circumstances[235] (although all cover related investigative and diagnostic procedures).[236]

---

[231] TCPS, Chapter 13, Section G (Gene Transfer) notes that the issue of germ-line alteration is addressed in s. 5(1)(*f*) of the AHR Act.

[232] TCPS, art. 12.6(b).

[233] The use of embryos created for reproductive (or other permitted) purposes is permitted once the embryos are no longer needed for the original purpose, provided that the following conditions are met (see TCPS, art. 12.8):

    (a)   the ova and sperm from which they were formed are obtained in accordance with Article 12.7;

    (b)   consent was provided by the gamete donors;

    (c)   embryos exposed to manipulations not directed specifically to their ongoing normal development will not be transferred for continuing pregnancy; and

    (d)   research involving human embryos will take place only during the first 14 days after their formation by combination of the gametes, excluding any time during which embryonic development has been suspended.

Article 12.10 directs that researchers who use embryos "to derive or use pluripotent stem cells shall follow the *Guidelines for Human Pluripotent Stem Cell Research*, as amended from time to time". The current version of the CIHR Guidelines for Human Pluripotent Stem Cell Research can be found online at: <http://www.cihr-irsc.gc.ca/e/42071.html>.

[234] TCPS, art. 12.10 refers researchers to the AHR Act for prohibitions on the use of chimeras and hybrids (see AHR Act, S.C. 2004, c. 2, s. 5(1)(i) and (j)).

[235] The Province of Ontario provides coverage for up to three cycles of IVF in cases where a woman's fallopian tubes are completely occluded. If a live birth is achieved after IVF treatment, another three cycles may be provided. See Edward G. Hughes & Mita Giacomini, "Funding In Vitro Fertilization Treatment for Persistent Subfertility: the Pain and the Politics" (2001) 76:3 Fertility and Sterility 431; Sharon Ikonomidis & Bernard Dickens, "Ontario's Decision to Defund In Vitro Fertilization Treatment Except for Women with Bilateral Fallopian Tube Damage" (1995) 21:3 Can. Pub. Pol'y 379. While it did not cover IVF treatment in the public health care system prior to August 2010, since 2002 the Province of Quebec has allowed persons undergoing IVF treatment to claim a 30 per cent refundable tax credit. See Beverly Hanck & Katharina Böcker, *Access to IVF with Reduced Multiple Birth Risks: A Public Health Strategy for Assisted Reproduction in Canada*, online at: Infertility Awareness Association of Canada <http://www.iaac.ca/print/427>. One province's refusal to cover infertility treatment under its health care insurance plan was the subject of an unsuccessful Charter challenge: see *Cameron v. Nova Scotia (Attorney General)*, [1999] N.S.J. No. 297, 177 D.L.R. (4th) 611 (N.S.C.A.), leave to appeal refused [1999] S.C.C.A. No. 531 (S.C.C.). The denial of coverage for ICSI and IVF was initially challenged on the basis of ss. 7 and 15 of the Charter. The trial judge gave short shrift to the s. 7 claim, which was not pursued before the Court of Appeal. As to the plaintiffs'

In August 2010, the Province of Quebec amended its health insurance plan to cover the costs of three cycles of IVF (and related procedures),[237] and in October 2010, the Province of Manitoba initiated a tax credit program to help families with some of the costs of fertility treatment.[238] In addition, an Expert Panel on Infertility and Adoption has recommended that the Ontario government fund assisted reproduction services.[239]

---

s. 15 claim, the trial judge found that the government had not discriminated against the plaintiffs as infertile persons in deciding not to cover infertility treatment services; he found it unnecessary to consider whether infertility amounts to a disability (*Cameron v. Nova Scotia (Attorney General)*, [1999] N.S.J. No. 33, 172 N.S.R. (2d) 227 (N.S.S.C.)). In the Court of Appeal, the plaintiffs were successful in their assertion that infertility is a physical disability and that the province's failure to fund infertility treatment services drew a discriminatory distinction between the infertile and the fertile (who receive full coverage for reproduction-related health care needs). The court concluded, however, that the exclusion of IVF and ICSI from coverage was justified under s. 1 of the Charter, in that it was related (and proportional) to the pressing objective of delivering the best possible health care coverage in the context of limited financial resources. In its decision in *Auton (Guardian ad litem of) v. British Columbia (Attorney General)*, [2004] S.C.J. No. 71, 2004 SCC 78 (S.C.C.), the Supreme Court of Canada held (at para. 35) that the denial of a "non-core" medically necessary service does not amount to discrimination under s. 15 of the Charter, as "the legislative scheme does not promise that any Canadian will receive funding for all medically required treatment"; rather, it leaves non-core services to the discretion of the provinces. Taken together with the Court's refusal to hear the *Cameron* case, it seems that *Auton* suggests that any future s. 15 claim to funding for infertility treatment will be an uphill battle.

[236] It has been noted that Canada is one of the few jurisdictions with a publicly funded health care system that excludes funding for IVF and related procedures: see Laura Shanner & Jeffrey Nisker, "Bioethics for Clinicians: Assisted Reproductive Technologies" (2001) 164:1 CMAJ 1589 at 1591. See also Beverly Hanck & Katharina Böcker for the Infertility Awareness Association of Canada, *Access to IVF with Reduced Multiple Birth Risks: A Public Health Strategy for Assisted Reproduction in Canada*, online at: <http://www.iaac.ca/print/427>.

[237] *An Act respecting clinical and research activities relating to assisted procreation*, R.S.Q., c. A-5.01; *Regulation to amend the Regulation respecting the application of the Health Insurance Act*, O.C. 645-2010, July 7, 2010. See also Santé et services sociaux Québec's website at: <http://www.msss.gouv.qc.ca/en/sujets/santepub/assisted-procreation.php>; William Buckett, "Assisted Reproductive Technologies: Moving Toward Universal Access: Québec Government to Provide Public Funding" (Spring 2010), online at: Infertility Awareness Association of Canada <http://www.iaac.ca/print/453>.

[238] See Manitoba, News Release, "New Fertility Treatment Tax Credit Takes Effect Oct. 1" (October 1, 2010), online at: <http://news.gov.mb.ca/news/index.html?archive=2010-10-01&item=9845>; Manitoba Finance, "Personal Tax Credits", online at: <http://residents.gov.mb.ca/reference.html?d=details&program_id=5060>.

[239] Government of Ontario Expert Panel on Infertility and Adoption, *Raising Expectations: Recommendations of the Expert Panel on Infertility and Adoption* (Ontario Ministry of Children and Youth Services, 2009), online at: <http://www.children.gov.on.ca/htdocs/English/documents/infertility/RaisingExpectationsEnglish.pdf> at 118-19. See also Jeff Nisker, "Socially Based Discrimination Against Clinically Appropriate Care" (2009) 181:10 CMAJ 764; Jennifer MacMillan, "Report calls on Ontario to foot fertility bill" *The Globe and Mail* (August 26, 2009), online at: <http://www.theglobeandmail.com/news/national/report-calls-on-ontario-to-foot-fertility-bill/article1264580/>. A human rights complaint has been made against the Ontario government alleging that the government's policy on funding infertility treatment is discriminatory (Jennifer MacMillan, "Report calls on Ontario to foot fertility bill", *ibid.*).

One final noteworthy issue that bears mention here is the role of tort law in the ART context. As noted in Section IV, recent case law out of the Ontario Court of Appeal suggests that no duty of care is owed by a physician to a future child who is "conceived or not yet conceived" at the time of the health care provider's negligent act. In *Liebig (Litigation guardian of) v. Guelph General Hospital*, the Ontario Court of Appeal clarified that this statement does not disturb the well-established authority of the "labour and delivery cases" where it is clear that providers owe a duty to the not-yet born child. The court also said that "[b]oth *Bovingdon* and *Paxton* hold that there is no duty of care to a future child if the alleged negligence by a health care provider took place prior to conception".[240] It is interesting to consider the potential effect of the Court of Appeal's statement on provider liability in the ART context — does this mean that a child harmed due to negligence in this context could not successfully claim damages from the negligent providers? Will such cases be approached as "wrongful life" cases, or will the distinct context of assisted reproduction and the specific harms that can be claimed lead the courts to treat the cases differently? While a "wrongful life" claim is typically one in which the child is alleging that but for the physician's negligence, he or she would not have been born, it is certainly possible that the harm claimed in the ART context could be much more direct and specific, including injuries caused to the child as a result of negligence in creating, manipulating or testing the embryo prior to implantation. Likewise, if parental claims are also made, will these be handled as wrongful birth cases or, again, will the specific factual context lead the courts toward a different approach? Wrongful birth cases are those in which a provider has negligently denied the woman or couple a choice as to whether to proceed with the pregnancy. What if the harm caused to the embryo prior to implantation could not be detected early enough in pregnancy to permit parents to make such a choice? We might not have to wait long for answers to some of these questions, as two lawsuits have been commenced against an Ottawa fertility specialist alleging that provider negligence led to the use of sperm from someone other than the intended donor.[241]

---

[240] *Liebig (Litigation guardian of) v. Guelph General Hospital*, [2010] O.J. No. 2580 at para. 11, 2010 ONCA 450 (Ont. C.A.). In both *Paxton* and *Bovingdon*, the alleged negligence revolved around the provision of medication to women who were not pregnant at the time (in *Bovingdon*, the medication was Clomid, a fertility drug; in *Paxton*, the medication was Accutane, an acne treatment that is known to have serious teratogenic potential and which is, as a result, not prescribed to pregnant women). In neither case was the physician negligent in prescribing the medication to the woman. See *Paxton v. Ramji*, [2008] O.J. No. 3964, 2008 ONCA 697 (Ont. C.A.); *Bovingdon v. Hergott*, [2008] O.J. No. 11, 2008 ONCA 2 (Ont. C.A.).

[241] Indeed, the plaintiffs have asked the court to order that the defendant physician undergo a blood test to rule out the possibility that he used his own sperm for their procedures. See Amber Kanwar, "Doctor sued over allegedly mixing up sperm samples" *The Globe and Mail* (September 10, 2010), online at: <http://donorsiblingregistry.com/globeandmail910.pdf>; Kenyon Wallace, "Doctor sued as wrong sperm alleged in fertility cases" *National Post* (September 15, 2010), online at: <http://www.nationalpost.com/news/canada/Doctor+sued+wrong+sperm+alleged+fertility+cases/3525349/story.html>.

VIII. CONCLUSION

The time is long past when reproduction was chiefly a matter of chance — when heterosexual intercourse was the only mode of conception, and when the outcome of each pregnancy was unpredictable. The introduction of reproductive technologies — including contraception, medical and surgical abortion, prenatal and preimplantation diagnosis, and assisted reproductive technologies — has ushered in a new era in reproductive decision-making, an era of complex and complicated choices. With these choices has come increasing state involvement in reproduction.

Developing legal and policy strategies aimed at regulating reproduction is a complex task that requires consideration of conflicting needs, rights and interests. The most recent example of the challenge posed by this task is the Canadian government's announcement of, and international reaction to, its maternal and child health program.[242] The Canadian initiative targets improving maternal and child health and reducing maternal, newborn and child mortality. It calls for action by the G8 nations on interventions that comprehend the continuum of care. The scope of such interventions has been acknowledged to include "antenatal care; post-partum care; family planning, which includes contraception; reproductive health; treatment and prevention of diseases; prevention of mother-to-child transmission of HIV; immunizations; and nutrition",[243] as well as initiatives focused on water sanitation and equality for women. There is no disagreement as to the urgency of the need or the potential benefits of taking comprehensive action to improve maternal and child health. Yet, almost as quickly as the initiative was announced by the Harper government, questions were raised as to whether the government's notion of "family planning" included access to abortion.[244] The initiative drew criticism for the exclusion of abortion from its definition of family planning, on the basis that maternal health cannot be achieved without reproductive health and that, in turn, entails access to legal and safe abortion.[245]

While reproductive law and policy have clear significance to men and women alike, they have particular significance for women, not only because of the unique role women play in the process of reproduction, but because of the reality of the consequences of reproduction on all aspects of women's lives. Decisions about whether, when and with whom to reproduce, about how many children to have and about what kind of children to bear shape women's lives to a much greater (and more specific) extent than they do men's lives. Women's

---

[242] See Paul Christopher Webster, "Nutrition and Integrated Health Care to Highlight Canadian Plan to Fight Child and Maternal Mortality, Minister Says" (2010) 182:9 CMAJ e397-98.

[243] See "G8 Development Ministers Meeting: Chair's Summary" (April 28, 2010), online at: Canadian International Development Agency <http://www.acdi-cida.gc.ca/acdi-cida/ACDI-CIDA. nsf/eng/ANN-428145532-Q7R>.

[244] "No abortion in Canada's G8 maternal health plan" CBC News (April 26, 2010), online at: <http://www.cbc.ca/news/canada/story/2010/04/26/abortion-maternal-health.html>.

[245] "G8 maternal health initiative draws flak" (June 23, 2010) CBC News, online at: <http://www. cbc.ca/world/story/2010/06/23/g8-maternal-health-initiative.html>.

career paths and, by implication, financial security may be determined by their ability to make reproductive decisions. Reproduction can have significant effects on women's health, both during and after pregnancy. And, women are frequently the primary caregivers of the children they bear.[246] Assisted reproductive technologies are currently a focal point for law, policy and public discussion but, as this chapter illustrates, there is work to be done in all areas of reproductive decision-making in order to ensure that law and policy respect women's reproductive autonomy and safeguard their reproductive health.

---

[246] See, *e.g.*, Joan Williams, *Unbending Gender: Why Family and Work Conflict and What to Do About It* (Oxford: Oxford University Press, 2000) at 48, 156-57.

Chapter 8

MENTAL HEALTH LAW IN CANADA

Peter J. Carver

I. INTRODUCTION

A. RECENT DEVELOPMENTS

Several important developments have taken place in Canadian mental health law in the four years since the publication of the third edition of this book.[1] Alberta amended the committal criteria in its *Mental Health Act* and became the fifth provincial jurisdiction to adopt the mechanism of the community treatment order.[2] The Supreme Court of Canada made significant rulings on the state's authority to override a refusal of treatment by a competent minor[3] and on the jurisdiction of Forensic Review Boards to grant remedies under the *Canadian Charter of Rights and Freedoms*.[4] The federal Investigator of Corrections released a critical report about the inadequacy of programs for the growing proportion of inmates with serious mental illness.[5] Community and mental health courts continued to develop as a response to related concerns about persons with mental illness ending up in the criminal justice system. Canada ratified the United Nations *Convention on the Rights of Persons with Disabilities*.[6] The

---

[1] Peter J. Carver, "Mental Health Law in Canada" in T. Caulfield, J. Downie & C. Flood, eds., *Canadian Health Law and Policy*, 3d ed. (Markham, ON: LexisNexis Canada, 2007) 399. See also H. Archibald Kaiser, "Mental Disability Law" in T. Caulfield, J. Downie & C. Flood, eds., *Canadian Health Law and Policy*, 2d ed. (Markham, ON: LexisNexis Canada, 2002) 251. The latter chapter provides a broad overview of mental disability, and includes excellent discussions of such issues as the legacy of abuse, poverty and institutionalization.

[2] *Mental Health Act*, R.S.A. 2000, c. M-13, as amended by *Mental Health Amendment Act, 2007*, S.A. 2007, c. 35 (proclaimed in force January 1, 2010). For commentary on the amendments, see papers in (2010) 19 Health L. Rev. See discussion in Sections III(C) and IV(F), below.

[3] *C. (A.) v. Manitoba (Director of Child and Family Services)*, [2009] S.C.J. No. 30, [2009] 2 S.C.R. 181 (S.C.C.), and see discussion in Section IV(A), below.

[4] Part I of the *Constitution Act, 1982*, being Schedule B to the *Canada Act 1982* (U.K.), 1982, c. 11 [Charter]. See *R. v. Conway*, [2010] S.C.J. No. 22, [2010] 1 S.C.R. 765 (S.C.C.), and see discussion in Section V(B), below.

[5] "Under Warrant: A Review of the Implementation of the Correctional Service of Canada's 'Mental Health Strategy'" (Ottawa: Office of the Correctional Investigator of Canada, September 2010), online at: <http://www.oci-bec.gc.ca/rpt/oth-aut/oth-aut20100923-eng.aspx>, and see discussion at Section V(C), below.

[6] A/RES/61/611 (2006), in force May 3, 2008; ratified by Canada March 11, 2010. See discussion at Section VI(A), below.

Mental Health Commission of Canada, established in 2006, continued work directed at reducing the stigma of mental illness and extending a human rights approach to mental health services across the country.

Before getting to the details of these developments and what they say about the direction of mental health law in Canada, it is helpful to locate this area of legal concern within the broader contexts of social response to mental disability and of Canadian law.

B.   MENTAL DISABILITY AND THE LAW

Why is mental disability a category of interest or attention in law?[7] After all, to describe and use the term seems to admit of a making of differences, a marginalizing, that seems inconsistent with general concepts of equality before the law. Can this differentiation be justified? Two possible justifications can be given.

The first is that the phenomena captured by the term "mental disability" have significance with respect to several of the standard assumptions which underlie legal relationships in our society. One such assumption is that of the autonomous individual, conceived as a person capable of exercising legal rights and responsibilities by acting with intention, making agreements and giving consent to actions by other persons that affect him or her. On the basis of this assumption, we hold individuals responsible in law for their decisions and actions. We include in this the responsibility of individuals for their own well-being. To the extent that mental disability interferes with individual autonomy and responsibility, the law must respond with alternative solutions.

A second reason for law to take cognizance of mental disability has more to do with the historical socioeconomic experience of persons with mental disabilities in Canada. That reality was recognized by the Supreme Court in the 1991 case, *R. v. Swain*:

> The mentally ill have historically been the subjects of abuse, neglect and discrimination in our society. The stigma of mental illness can be very damaging. The intervener, [the Canadian Disability Rights Council], describes the historical treatment of the mentally ill as follows:
>
>> For centuries, persons with a mental disability have been systematically isolated, segregated from mainstream of society, devalued, ridiculed, and excluded from participation in ordinary social and political processes.
>
> The above description is, in my view, unfortunately accurate and appears to stem from an irrational fear of the mentally ill in our society.[8]

---

[7]   The best single reference dealing with the various different aspects of mental disability in Canadian law remains G. Robertson, *Mental Disability and the Law in Canada*, 2d ed. (Toronto: Carswell, 1994). See also the collection of papers on the subject of law and mental disability in (2008) 25 Windsor Rev. Legal Soc. Issues 117 ("Special Volume: Perspectives on Law and Psychiatry: Exploring the Legal and Social Issues Surrounding Mental Disability").

[8]   [1991] S.C.J. No. 32 at para. 39, [1991] 1 S.C.R. 933 (S.C.C.), *per* Lamer C.J.C.

Related to these two justifications, it is possible to identify five areas or "dimensions" through which Canadian law plays a role in the social response to mental disability. Each dimension speaks to a different set or regime of laws. The first three dimensions respond to problems caused by the undermining of reason and autonomy. The last two dimensions respond to problems of social disadvantage and discrimination on grounds of mental disability.

1. Public Safety Dimension

(a) The problem: the risk of harm to third persons posed by conduct of a person with a mental impairment for which they are not responsible, and which is viewed as not being amenable to the "deterrence" of penal law.

(b) Response: laws governing committal under the *Criminal Code*[9] for persons found not criminally responsible by reason of mental disorder, and civil committal laws.

This dimension turns largely on making predictions of dangerousness based on diagnoses of mental condition. This is a famously difficult endeavour.[10]

2. Therapeutic Dimension

(a) The problem: the need to facilitate the providing of health care responsive to diagnosed mental disability, including overcoming barriers caused by interference with the individual's ability to seek out or consent to needed therapy.

(b) Response: civil mental health laws relating to treatment and consent; laws establishing therapeutic programs for persons seeking and qualifying for therapy.

3. Individual Autonomy Dimension

(a) The problem: interference with the individual's capacity or competence to make autonomous decisions with legal effect concerning one's property or person.

(b) Response: adult guardianship laws, and laws providing for appointment and guidance of substitute decision-makers.

The response to that reality has given rise to two further encounters between law and mental disability, as follows.

---

[9] R.S.C. 1985, c. C-46.

[10] A useful analysis and critique of predictions of dangerousness in the mental health field is given by H. Archibald Kaiser, "Mental Disability Law" in T. Caulfield, J. Downie & C. Flood, eds., *Canadian Health Law and Policy*, 2d ed. (Markham, ON. LexisNexis Canada, 2002) 251.

4. Social Welfare Dimension

(a) The problem: social disadvantages in income and other social goods experienced by persons as a consequence of mental dysfunction or impairment, principally related to underemployment or unemployment.

(b) Response: laws establishing social benefits programs, turning in whole or in part on describing the "target" group(s) through eligibility criteria drawn in terms of functional impairments interfering with work performance. Such laws would include disability benefits programs, disability insurance plans, housing programs, *etc.*

5. Human Rights Dimension

(a) The problem: to protect individuals with mental disabilities, or those perceived to have disabilities, from the harmful effects of stigma, disrespect and exclusion from mainstream social goods and activities.

(b) Response: equality rights in section 15 of the *Canadian Charter of Rights and Freedoms*, and provisions in federal and provincial human rights legislation against discrimination on grounds of mental disability.

Which of the five dimensions outlined above is viewed as most needing attention depends both on events occurring in Canadian society, and on the political perspectives that interested parties bring to the subject. In very general terms, Canadian law tended in the past to place emphasis on the dimensions above in order from headings 1 to 5. This continues to be true for advocacy groups comprising families of persons with mental illness and the psychiatric community. Patients and patients' rights advocates have tended, by contrast, to emphasize legal recourses in the opposite order, from 5 to 1. Until the adoption of the Charter and for several years thereafter, Canadian law appeared to be moving in the same direction. It seems fair to suggest that in recent years, the pendulum has shifted back.

Most of this chapter concerns itself with mental health law, an area of law in which the dimensions of public safety, treatment and individual autonomy have predominated. Following that discussion, the chapter returns to a consideration of human rights issues involving mental disability. Before going further, however, it may be helpful to say a few words about terminology, a matter that the human rights perspective on disability has greatly impacted. "Mental disability" in the human rights context is understood in a broad and non-medical fashion. The term is associated more with disadvantage caused by social response to actual or perceived variations from cognitive or emotional norms than with particular impairments. The Supreme Court has stated that "disability" can include a subjective component of being *perceived* as having a disability:

> Whatever the wording of the definitions used in human rights legislation, Canadian courts tend to consider not only the objective basis for certain exclusionary practices (i.e. the actual existence of functional limitations), but also the

subjective and erroneous perceptions regarding the existence of such limitations. Thus, tribunals and courts have recognized that even though they do not
result in functional limitations, various ailments such as congenital physical
malformations, asthma, speech impediments, obesity, acne and, more recently,
being HIV positive, may constitute grounds of discrimination.[11]

In this respect, Canada's equality rights law has departed markedly from the
model adopted by the U.S. Supreme Court in interpreting the *Americans with
Disabilities Act* (ADA).[12] Claimants qualify for that statute's protection only on
the basis of proving that they have an impairment that substantially interferes
with activities of daily living.[13]

Like the statutes of several other provinces, the *Alberta Human Rights Act*
employs a broad definition of "mental disability" saying that it encompasses
"any mental disorder, developmental disorder or learning disorder, regardless of
the cause or duration of the disorder".[14] As this implies, "mental disorder", a
term commonly used to describe what is generally understood as "mental illness", is viewed in Canada as a subset of the broader term "mental disability".

C. THE STRUCTURE OF CANADIAN MENTAL HEALTH LAW

The principal characteristic of mental health law[15] is that it is a law based on
legal compulsion or coercion. In this respect, Nova Scotia's statute, the *Involuntary Psychiatric Treatment Act*,[16] is aptly titled. Common law principles governing health care assume a standard model in which patients seek treatment for
illness, and enter into voluntary arrangements with clinicians. To the extent that
persons with mental health problems seek assistance in the same fashion, those
common law principles apply to the care they receive. The fact that the presenting problem manifests itself in psychological rather than physiological symptoms makes no difference, and would not itself necessitate a separate legal
regime.

The two principal means of compulsory intervention have been involuntary
committal to a psychiatric hospital facility, and the provision of psychiatric
treatment in the absence of the individual patient's consent. These measures
require statute law both to grant the authority to intervene in a coercive fashion,
and to limit the scope of this authority. While provincial mental health statutes

---

[11] *Québec (Commission des droits de la personne et des droits de la jeunesse) v. Montreal (City)*,
      [2000] S.C.J. No. 24 at para. 48, [2000] 1 S.C.R. 665 (S.C.C.), *per* L'Heureux-Dubé J.
[12] 42 U.S.C. 1210. For extensive discussion of the U.S. experience with the ADA and for compara-
      tive issues in mental disability and mental health law, see M.L. Perlin, A.S. Kanter, M.P.
      Treuthart, E. Szeli & K. Gledhill, *International Human Rights and Comparative Mental Disabil-
      ity Law* (Durham, NC: Carolina Academic Press, 2006).
[13] See *Sutton v. United Air Lines Inc.*, 527 U.S. 471 (U.S.S.C. 1999).
[14] R.S.A. 2000, c. A-25.5, s. 44(1)(h).
[15] For differing perspectives on the subject, see H. Savage & C. McKague, *Mental Health Law in
      Canada* (Toronto: Butterworths, 1987) and J. Gray, M. Shone & P. Liddle, *Canadian Mental
      Health Law and Policy* (Markham, ON: LexisNexis Canada, 2000).
[16] S.N.S. 2005, c. 42.

deal with various other matters in the delivery of mental health services, their *raison d'être* remains this framework of lawful coercion.

A striking fact about Canada's mental health law in the early 21st century is that Canada's provinces and territories have adopted quite different approaches to the issues of involuntary hospitalization and treatment. There are two reasons for the variation in mental health law across provinces and territories. The first is Canada's constitutional architecture, which places the greater part of health care within provincial jurisdiction. Consequently, there can be several answers at any one time to the question, "How does mental health law operate in Canada?" Ultimately, there is no substitute for consulting the legislation of the particular jurisdiction with which one is concerned.[17]

Parliament and provincial legislatures both have jurisdiction in the area of mental health law under the Canadian Constitution. Provincial jurisdiction is broader, lying in the general authority of provinces over health care based in jurisdiction over "matters of a merely local and private nature" in section 92(16) of the *Constitution Act, 1867*[18] and over hospitals in section 92(7). The principal source of federal jurisdiction is located in its authority over criminal law in section 91(27). The rough division in mental health laws and services set out by the Constitution is between civil mental health, a matter of provincial jurisdiction, and the forensic system governing criminal conduct caused by mental disorder, a matter of federal jurisdiction.

More specifically, federal jurisdiction has been found to relate to laws directed at protecting public safety, while provincial jurisdiction relates to laws directed at treatment of illness. The two domains overlap. For example, provincial jurisdiction over health and the federal jurisdiction over public safety both support involuntary detention, but for different purposes. In *Schneider v. British Columbia*, the Supreme Court of Canada upheld provincial legislation that provided for the involuntary detention of heroin addicts for purposes of treatment.[19]

---

17   The 10 provincial and three territorial mental health statutes are the following: *Mental Health Act*, R.S.A. 2000, c. M-13; *Mental Health Act*, R.S.B.C. 1996, c. 288; *Mental Health Act*, C.C.S.M. c. M110; *Mental Health Services Act*, S.N.B. 1997, c. M-10.2; *Mental Health Care and Treatment Act*, S.N.L. 2006, c. M-91; *Involuntary Psychiatric Treatment Act*, S.N.S. 2005, c. 42 and *Hospitals Act*, S.N.S. 1989, c. 208; *Mental Health Act*, R.S.O. 1990, c. M.7; *Mental Health Act*, R.S.P.E.I. 1988, c. M-6.1; *Civil Code of Québec*, S.Q. 1991, c. 64, ss. 10-31, and *An Act respecting the Protection of Persons Whose Mental State Presents Danger to Themselves or to Others*, R.S.Q., c. P-38.001; *Mental Health Services Act*, S.S. 1984-85-86, c. M-13.1; *Mental Health Act*, R.S.N.W.T. 1988, c. M-10; *Mental Health Act*, R.S.N.W.T. (Nu.) 1988, c. M-10; *Mental Health Act*, R.S.Y. 2002, c. 150. Hereinafter, these statutes will frequently be referred to as "the statute" or "mental health statute" of the specified province(s).

18   (U.K.), 30 & 31 Vict., c. 3, reprinted in R.S.C. 1985, App. II, No. 5.

19   [1982] S.C.J. No. 64, [1982] 2 S.C.R. 112 (S.C.C.). Referring to involuntary detention under B.C.'s *Heroin Treatment Act* (then S.B.C. 1978, c. 24), Dickson J. said (at 138):

> This intervention is necessarily provincial. The compulsory aspects of this intervention are incidental to the effectiveness of the treatment, narcotic addiction by its very nature being a compulsive condition over which the individual loses control. Although coercion will obviously play a significant role it seems to me that the dominant or most important characteristic of the *Heroin Treatment Act* is the treatment and not the coercion. The Leg-

Similarly, both jurisdictions support laws governing treatment and consent to treatment. Federal power over the latter has to date been limited to requiring assessment and treatment of individuals found "not fit for trial due to mental disorder". Section 672.58 of the *Criminal Code* authorizes psychiatric treatment on an involuntary basis for unfit accused, for the limited purpose of restoring them to fitness.[20]

The second reason for variety is generational. Provinces have drafted and amended their mental health legislation at different times, and depending when this has been done, the laws have been influenced by different thinking about the appropriate balance between individual rights, public safety and therapeutic interests. To sketch this history in broad strokes, we can see three "generations" of thinking at work. The first, running from the early 20th century to the late 1960s, emphasized public safety and institutionalization. From the late 1960s to approximately the mid-1990s, a shift in emphasis to greater protection of individual rights took place. This coincided with the introduction of the Charter in 1982, and a dramatic reduction in institutional populations. The third phase is ongoing. Since the mid-1990s, several provinces, including Saskatchewan, British Columbia, Ontario, Nova Scotia and Alberta have engaged in extensive revisions of their mental health statutes. This period has seen a lowering of the legal standards for involuntary admission to hospital, and an extension of the reach of compulsory treatment to community services. At the same time, procedures for assessing treatment competency of patients, and for facilitating substitute decision-making for incapable patients, have received considerable attention. These changes coincide with increased concern in society over the role of untreated mental illness in such issues as homelessness, and the growing strength of organizations representing families of persons with mental illness in political advocacy.

The Charter provides further constitutional context within which mental health laws operate. The Charter places limits on the powers of the state to intervene in individuals' lives. As such, the compulsory aspects of mental health law encounter several Charter rights and are subject to the limits they impose. The most significant Charter rights in this regard are sections 7 and 15(1). Section 7 protects rights of "liberty" and "security of the person", which are precisely the interests compromised by involuntary hospitalization and treatment without consent, respectively. Section 15(1) guarantees equality before and under the law and equal benefit and protection of the law without discrimination on several enumerated grounds, including "mental disability". Differential legislative treatment accorded persons with mental disorders should and does raise

---

islature of British Columbia in my view has sought to treat persons found to be in a state of psychological or physical dependence on a narcotic as sick and not criminal. The Legislature is endeavouring to cure a medical condition, not to punish a criminal activity.

[20] The Supreme Court of Canada recognized that Parliament's jurisdiction over criminal law, and specifically over the law of criminal procedure, extended to provisions governing persons deemed unfit to stand trial for a criminal offence in *R. v. Demers*, [2004] S.C.J. No. 43, [2004] 2 S.C.R. 489 (S.C.C.) (LeBel J. dissenting).

section 15(1) issues. Since the Charter and the standards it imposes apply both to federal and provincial laws, it is an interesting question why these have not had the effect of creating greater uniformity in mental health laws across Canada. The answer is, in part, because of the leeway which the justification clause in section 1 allows with respect to "reasonable limits" that can be placed on Charter rights. It is also because of the difficulty patients face in trying to bring Charter issues before Canadian courts. In addition to problems with the lack of resources needed to pursue the difficult issues involved in Charter challenges, the very changeability of mental conditions and of individual patients' status under mental health law creates a further barrier. Many potential cases become "moot" before they can be raised in a formal setting. Despite the fact that relatively few Charter challenges to civil mental health laws have made their way to courts across the country, the Charter plays an important role in structuring mental health laws. Several Charter issues are discussed in Parts III through VI of this chapter.

II.   CONTEMPORARY UNDERSTANDING OF MENTAL DISORDER AND ITS TREATMENT

The May 2006 Report, *Out of the Shadows at Last*, by the Senate's Standing Committee on Social Affairs, Science and Technology provides a good overview of contemporary approaches to the treatment of mental illness.[21] Building on several recent provincial reports on mental health service systems,[22] *Out of the Shadows at Last* summarized much of the current Canadian and international thinking on the subject. The Report emphasized the social determinants of mental illness,[23] and community-based treatment and support services. The Committee described the preferred approach to mental health as the idea of "Recovery":

> *Recovery* is not the same thing as being cured. For many individuals, it is a way of living a satisfying, hopeful, and productive life even with limitations caused

---

[21]   *Out of the Shadows at Last: Transforming Mental Health, Mental Illness and Addiction Services in Canada*, Final Report of the Standing committee on Social Affairs, Science and Technology (Ottawa: Senate of Canada, May 2006).

[22]   See, for example, *Plan d'action en santé mentale 2005-2010 — La force des liens* (Quebec: Ministère de la santé et des services sociaux, 2005); *Community Mental Health Evaluation Initiative: Making a Difference* (Toronto: Ontario Community Mental Health Initiative, 2004).

[23]   *Out of the Shadows at Last: Transforming Mental Health, Mental Illness and Addiction Services in Canada*, Final Report of the Standing Committee on Social Affairs, Science and Technology (Ottawa: Senate of Canada, May 2006), Section 3.1.3 at 41:

> In particular, the Committee believes it is extremely important to stress the significance of what are called the social determinants of health in understanding mental illness and in fostering recovery from it. The Committee was repeatedly told that factors such as income, access to adequate housing and employment, and participation in a social network of family and friends, play a much greater role in promoting mental health and recovery from mental illness than is the case with physical illness. As well, it is important to see that the direction of causality goes both ways, from the mental (psychological, emotional, etc.) to the physical (neurobiological) as well as from the physical to the mental.

by the illness; for others, recovery means the reduction or complete remission of symptoms related to mental illness.[24]

The Committee's work led to the creation of the Mental Health Commission of Canada (MHCC) in March 2007.[25] The MHCC has continued to promote the recovery concept with its emphasis on community-based services and integration of persons with mental illness into the community.[26] These goals reflect the concerns of clients of the system, family and other caregivers, and ministry officials who have recognized the cost savings in moving care from hospital facilities to the community. In a sense, however, this emphasis avoids dealing with the precise issues that are the principal concerns of mental health law. It is doubtful that a distinct body of law is needed to facilitate delivering community mental health services. The core of mental health law, its coercive aspects, play only a limited role in community-based services and supports.

This goes to another distinction within the field of mental health: that between serious mental disorders, and less serious disorders. *Out of the Shadows at Last* recognized this distinction:

> Epidemiological data indicate that, each year, roughly 3% of the population will experience a serious mental illness, and that another 17% or so will experience mild to moderate illness. The full range of services must be available therefore to address the needs of both broad categories of people.[27]

Serious disorders, those which predominate among involuntarily hospitalized populations, generally include schizophrenia,[28] bipolar disorder[29] and severe depression. Estimates place the prevalence of schizophrenia among the Canadian population at 1 per cent. A common symptom of schizophrenia is auditory hallucination; that is, the hearing of voices. Other common symptoms include believing that one's thoughts are broadcast to others or that one's actions are under the control of another. Bipolar disorder also affects approximately 1 per cent of the population. In the manic phase, persons with bipolar disorder may also experience delusions. Persons with severe depression are at serious risk of suicide.

For contemporary psychiatry, the principal mode of treatment for schizophrenia is antipsychotic medication. This coincides with the growing acceptance of schizophrenia as having biological rather than social causes. Antipsychotics

---

[24] *Ibid.*, Section 3.2 at 42.

[25] The website for the Commission can be found online at: <http://www.mentalhealthcommission. ca/English/Pages/default.aspx>.

[26] See *Toward Recovery and Well-being: A Framework for a Mental Health Strategy for Canada* (Ottawa: Mental Health Commission of Canada, November 2009), online at: <http://www.mental healthcommission.ca/SiteCollectionDocuments/boarddocs/15507_MHCC_EN_final.pdf>.

[27] *Out of the Shadows at Last: Transforming Mental Health, Mental Illness and Addiction Services in Canada*, Final Report of the Standing Committee on Social Affairs, Science and Technology (Ottawa: Senate of Canada, May 2006), Section 3.4 at 50.

[28] See E. Fuller Torrey, *Surviving Schizophrenia* (New York: Quill, 2001).

[29] See E. Fuller Torrey, *Surviving Manic Depression* (New York: Basic Books, 2002).

are generally divided into first-generation and second-generation drugs. First-generation drugs were introduced in the 1950s, and included chloropromazine and haloperidol. While many people with schizophrenia experience improvement when taking these medications, the medications also frequently cause potentially severe side effects, the most common of which is tardive dyskinesia,[30] whose symptoms include involuntary movements of the tongue and mouth. Other side effects of medication include sedation, dry mouth, blurred vision, stiffness, tremor and restlessness. The second generation of antipsychotic drugs was introduced in the 1990s and include clozapine and respiradone. Second-generation drugs appear to cause fewer side effects than the first-generation drugs. There are newer drugs being introduced for schizophrenia, and of course there are many others for other mental illnesses.

The Senate Committee emphasized that even for persons with serious mental illnesses, treatment and rehabilitation is best accomplished in the community, and not in institutional facilities. The Report acknowledged the success of programs such as Assertive Community Treatment Teams and Intensive Case Management in working closely and on an interdisciplinary basis with individuals with serious mental illness in maintaining their health in the community.[31] Five provinces — Ontario, Saskatchewan, Nova Scotia, Newfoundland and Labrador, and Alberta — have introduced "Community Treatment Orders" into their mental health laws to support interventions of this kind. Their utility is considered in Part IV, below.

III. INVOLUNTARY HOSPITALIZATION

Every Canadian province and territory has laws that provide for involuntary committal on grounds of mental disorder. Committal provides lawful authority to detain an individual in hospital premises. This includes the authority to employ security measures to prevent patients from leaving hospital without permission, and authority to issue warrants to apprehend and return an involuntary patient to hospital.

Civil committal has both procedural and substantive dimensions. The procedural dimension includes all the steps which must be taken to effect and continue committal, including identifying who may complete certificates stating an opinion concerning an individual's mental condition,[32] how many certificates

---

[30] For a description of tardive dyskinesia, and its causation by exposure over time to antipsychotic medications, see the website of the National Alliance on Mental Illness (NAMI), online at: <http://www.nami.org/Content/ContentGroups/Helpline1/Tardive_Dyskinesia.htm>.

[31] *Out of the Shadows at Last: Transforming Mental Health, Mental Illness and Addiction Services in Canada*, Final Report of the Standing Committee on Social Affairs, Science and Technology (Ottawa: Senate of Canada, May 2006), Section 5.6.

[32] All Canadian jurisdictions grant this authority to physicians, or in certain cases, to psychiatrists (*e.g.*, Nova Scotia's *Involuntary Psychiatric Treatment Act*, S.N.S. 2005, c. 42). This approach can be contrasted with that of many U.S. states, in which committal orders are made by "mental health courts" (administrative tribunals), which conduct hearings, generally in psychiatric hospital facilities, within 72 hours of a patient's initial involuntary admission. For an overview of U.S.

are needed to effect committal, the period for which the certificates remain effective, and review processes by which patients may challenge certificates.

Substantive criteria for committal go to the facts which the law requires to be present in order to hospitalize an individual on an involuntary basis. Nova Scotia's *Involuntary Psychiatric Treatment Act*[33] (IPTA) incorporates virtually all of the substantive criteria cumulatively employed in the statutes of other provinces. This statute can therefore serve as a template to examine each of the substantive criteria. Section 17 of IPTA provides for involuntary hospitalization on the basis of opinions of two psychiatrists stating that:

(a) the person has a mental disorder;

(b) the person is in need of the psychiatric treatment provided in a psychiatric facility;

(c) the person as a result of the mental disorder,

(i) is threatening or attempting to cause serious harm to himself or herself or has recently done so, has recently caused serious harm to himself or herself, is seriously harming or is threatening serious harm towards another person or has recently done so, or

(ii) is likely to suffer serious physical impairment or serious mental deterioration, or both;

(d) the person requires psychiatric treatment in a psychiatric facility and is not suitable for inpatient admission as a voluntary patient; and

(e) as a result of the mental disorder, does not have the capacity to make admission and treatment decisions,

the psychiatrist may admit the person as an involuntary patient by completing and filing with the chief executive officer a declaration of involuntary admission in the form prescribed by the regulations.

A.   PRESENCE OF A MENTAL DISORDER

Terms and definitions of the underlying mental conditions supporting committal vary widely. Several provinces use the term "mental disorder". The Alberta statute reads:

"mental disorder" means a substantial disorder of thought, mood, perception, orientation or memory that grossly impairs

(i) judgment,

(ii) behaviour,

(iii) capacity to recognize reality, or

---

law on civil committal, see Paul S. Appelbaum, *Almost a Revolution: Mental Health Law and the Limits of Change* (New York: Oxford University Press, 1994) at 20.

[33] S.N.S. 2005, c. 42.

(iv) ability to meet the ordinary demands of life.[34]

Ontario defines "mental disorder" as "any disease or disability of the mind".[35] Both capture the major mental illnesses of schizophrenia and serious mood disorders, which comprise the great preponderance of diagnosed conditions among committed patients across Canada. They likely do not capture developmental disabilities. No province expressly lists intellectual disability as a basis for committal. British Columbia removed the phrase "mentally retarded" from its definition of "person with a mental disorder" in 1998. Prince Edward Island is the only province to cite mental disorder resulting from alcohol or drug abuse in its committal criteria.[36] The Nova Scotia IPTA defines "mental disorder" as a "substantial disorder of behaviour, thought, mood, perception, orientation or memory that severely impairs judgement, behaviour, capacity to recognize reality or the ability to meet the ordinary demands of life, *in respect of which psychiatric treatment is advisable*".[37] The latter phrase makes treatability part of the definition of "mental disorder".

Ontario authorities have used the open-ended definition of "mental disorder" in that province's statute to effect the committal of a pedophile nearing the end of a criminal sentence on the basis that he continued to pose a danger to the community.[38]

B.   NEED FOR PSYCHIATRIC TREATMENT

To the extent that treatment is a justification for the coercive features of mental health law, it would seem to follow that only persons who have disorders amenable to psychiatric treatment should be subject to committal. Like Nova Scotia, British Columbia makes treatability a requirement for committal:

> "[p]erson with a mental disorder" means a person who has a disorder of the mind that requires treatment and seriously impairs the person's ability
>
> (a)   to react appropriately to the person's environment, or
>
> (b)   to associate with others.[39]

---

[34] R.S.A. 2000, c. M-13, s. 1(g).

[35] R.S.O. 1990, c. M-7, s. 1.

[36] Section 1(k) of the P.E.I. statute, R.S.P.E.I. 1988, c. M-6.1, reads:

"mental disorder" means a substantial disorder of thought, mood, perception, orientation or memory that seriously impairs judgment, behaviour, capacity to recognize reality or ability to meet the ordinary demands of life and *includes a mental disorder resulting from alcohol or drug addiction or abuse*, but a mental handicap or learning disability does not, of itself, constitute mental disorder. [emphasis added]

[37] S.N.S. 2005, c. 42, s. 3(q) [emphasis added].

[38] *Starnaman v. Penetanguishene Mental Health Centre*, [1995] O.J. No. 2130, 24 O.R. (3d) 701 (Ont. C.A.). See also J. Andres Hannah-Suarez, "Psychiatric Gating of Sexual Offenders under Ontario's *Mental Health Act*: Illegality, *Charter* Conflicts & Abuse of Process" (2005-2006) 37 Ottawa L. Rev. 71.

[39] *Mental Health Act*, R.S.B.C. 1996, c. 288, s. 1.

"Treatment" is then defined as "safe and effective psychiatric treatment".[40] A requirement of treatability implies that a mental condition for which no known treatment is available cannot serve as the basis for civil committal. Arguably, personality disorder of the nature of psychopathy falls in this category. Notoriously difficult to treat, and associated by many in the psychiatric community with disruptive conduct harmful to a therapeutic environment, the B.C. definition may serve to exclude this group from the civil system.

C. HARM CRITERIA

The degree of "harm" caused by mental disability needed to support civil committal is the most controversial issue in this area of legal concern. Every Canadian jurisdiction makes imminent, serious bodily harm directed to self or others a basis for committal. This level of harm is known as the "dangerousness" standard, and certainly extends to risks of non-trivial physical harm to third parties, and of suicidal and serious self-mutilating behaviour. Judicial interpretations of the words "danger" or "dangerous" suggested that the harm must be imminent, not merely a consequence of a deterioration in condition to a point of dangerousness likely to occur over several weeks.[41] Other decisions suggested that anticipated negative consequences of a patient's ceasing to take medications is sufficient for a finding of danger.[42]

Ontario's statutory criteria specify that the requisite harm must be physical in nature. Prior to 2000, Ontario's statute used these criteria:

[that the person] is suffering from a mental disorder of a nature or quality that likely will result in

(d) serious bodily harm to that person,

(e) serious bodily harm to another person, or

(f) imminent and serious bodily impairment of that person.[43]

While this phrasing appears to embody a dangerousness standard, Ontario courts interpreted the wording to support the continued committal of a patient because, if released, she would return to poor eating habits that might result in a stroke.[44] This is much closer to a welfare standard approach. In 2000, Ontario nevertheless removed the word "imminent" from this provision.[45]

However, most Canadian jurisdictions have moved away from the dangerousness standard in favour of what might be termed a well-being standard that authorizes involuntary hospitalization where there is a risk of mental deteriora-

---

[40] *Ibid.* Treatability also appears in the committal criteria, which state in s. 22(3)(c)(i) of the B.C. statute that the person "requires care, supervision and control in or through a designated facility".
[41] *M. v. Alberta*, [1985] A.J. No. 915, 63 A.R. 14 (Alta. Q.B.).
[42] See, for example, *T. (B.) v. Alberta Hospital*, [1997] A.J. No. 894 (Alta. Q.B.).
[43] *Mental Health Act*, R.S.O. 1990, c. M.7, s. 20(5) (am. 2000, c. 9, s. 7).
[44] *B. (I.) v. O'Doherty*, 38 A.C.W.S. (2d) 152 (Ont. Dist. Ct.).
[45] S.O. 2000, c. 9, s. 7(2).

tion if a person is not treated. Alberta amended its mental health legislation in 2010 in order to make this change. Where the *Mental Health Act* formerly stated that physicians could certify only on the basis of a "condition presenting or likely to present a danger to the person or others", the statute now refers to "substantial mental or physical deterioration". The Ontario *Mental Health Act* goes further and creates a class of persons subject to civil commitment that might be termed the "treatable, chronically mentally ill". For members of this class, the history of their mental disorder and of its previous treatment serve as predictors of harm. This largely replaces the need for the observation of present harmful behaviour.[46]

D.   NOT SUITABLE FOR VOLUNTARY ADMISSION

This requirement appears to ensure that certification for involuntary hospitalization occurs only in the last resort, when an individual cannot be admitted to a psychiatric facility on a voluntary basis. This may not necessarily mean that an individual can avoid involuntary committal by agreeing to voluntary admission to hospital. In certain provinces (see below), involuntary status permits treating an individual without his or her consent. The perceived need to facilitate treatment may serve as a basis for certification.[47]

E.   CAPACITY TO CONSENT TO TREATMENT

Nova Scotia and Saskatchewan require as part of a hospital committal that the individual be incapable of giving or withholding consent to treatment.[48] This means that only persons for whom substituted consent will be needed can be

---

[46]   The *Mental Health Act*, R.S.O. 1990, c. M.7, s. 20(1.1) reads:

  The attending physician shall complete a certificate of involuntary admission or a certificate of renewal if, after examining the patient, he or she is of the opinion that the patient,

  (a)   has previously received treatment for mental disorder of an ongoing or recurring nature that, when not treated, is of a nature or quality that likely will result in serious bodily harm to the person or to another person or substantial mental or physical deterioration of the person or serious physical impairment of the person;
  (b)   has shown clinical improvement as a result of the treatment;
  (c)   is suffering from the same mental disorder as the one for which he or she previously received treatment or from a mental disorder that is similar to the previous one;
  (d)   given the person's history of mental disorder and current mental or physical condition, is likely to cause serious bodily harm to himself or herself or to another person or is likely to suffer substantial mental or physical deterioration or serious physical impairment ...

[47]   For a discussion of this requirement for committal, see Gerald Robertson, "Civil Commitment and the 'Unsuitable' Voluntary Patient" (2010) 19 Health L. Rev. 5.

[48]   *Mental Health Services Act*, S.S. 1984-85-86, c. M-13.1, s. 24(2)(a):

  (a)   ... [the physician] has probable cause to believe that:

          . . . . .

      (ii)   as a result of the mental disorder the person is unable to fully understand and to make an informed decision regarding his need for treatment or care and supervision ...

subject of involuntary hospitalization. This approach avoids the kind of dilemma posed by situations like that of Scott Starson in Ontario (see Part IV, "Consent to Treatment in Mental Health Law", below): a hospitalized but treatment-capable individual who refuses recommended psychiatric treatment. That situation, much criticized by the psychiatric community, can result in housing an individual without providing treatment. The Nova Scotia approach ensures that involuntary committal is closely connected to active treatment of mental disorder. Of course, having such a requirement means that committal will not be available for some persons whose mental condition otherwise meets the requisite harm standard, including dangerousness, but who have treatment capacity. It also permits involuntary hospitalization of an individual who is presently incapable, but who expressed prior capable wishes concerning treatment.

F.   COMMITTAL CRITERIA AND THE CANADIAN CHARTER OF RIGHTS AND FREEDOMS

Section 7 of the Charter reads:

> Everyone has the right to life, liberty and security of the person, and the right not to be deprived thereof except in accordance with the principles of fundamental justice.

Section 7 is the first of the Charter's "legal rights", which include the right to be free from "arbitrary detention" in section 9. These sections provide relevant constitutional protections against the interference by the state with individual liberty, including freedom of movement. This protection is understood to extend both to the procedure, or "due process", by which the state may take away an individual's liberty, and to the substantive criteria for doing so.[49]

Despite the fact that sections 7 and 9 of the Charter apply to civil committal and create constitutional boundaries within which these laws operate, only two significant Charter challenges on this issue have come before our courts. In *Thwaites v. Health Sciences Centre Psychiatric Facility*,[50] the Manitoba Court of Appeal struck down statutory criteria that stated a person could be certified when, in the opinion of a physician, he or she "should be confined as a patient in a psychiatric facility". The court ruled that by failing to establish objective criteria related to mental condition and risk of harm, this provision exposed individuals to arbitrary detention and so breached section 9 of the Charter. Justice Philp stated: "I do not think it can be said that, in the absence of a 'dangerousness' or like standard, the provisions impair as little as possible the right of a person 'not to be arbitrarily detained'."[51] The Manitoba Legislature then

---

[49]   *Reference re Motor Vehicle Act (British Columbia), Section 94(2)*, [1985] S.C.J. No. 73, [1985] 2 S.C.R. 486 (S.C.C.).

[50]   [1988] M.J. No. 107, 40 C.R.R. 326 (Man. C.A.).

[51]   *Ibid.*, at 332.

amended the statute to include the standard of a "likelihood of serious harm". This standard was subsequently upheld.[52]

The committal criteria in British Columbia's *Mental Health Act* were challenged in 1993 in *McCorkell v. Riverview Hospital*.[53] The petitioner argued that the statute violated sections 7 and 9 of the Charter by authorizing committal where a person "requires care, supervision and control in a Provincial mental health facility for his own protection or for the protection of others". He argued that only criteria based strictly on dangerousness could be justified under the Charter as the standard for restriction of an individual's liberty. Justice Donald of the British Columbia Supreme Court rejected this argument. In particular, he rejected the plaintiff's attempt to draw an analogy between criminal law, in which the state's power to restrict liberty is circumscribed by extensive substantive and procedural protections for accused persons, and mental health law:

> Statutes dealing with criminal law are penal in nature; incarceration is a punishment of culpable individuals and serves the objectives of public safety and denunciation of crime. The *Mental Health Act* involuntarily detains people only for the purpose of treatment; the punitive element is wholly absent.[54]

Citing the Manitoba cases, Donald J. continued:

> In the Manitoba legislation, "serious harm" is not qualified; it can include harms that relate to the social, family, vocational or financial life of the patient as well as to the patient's physical condition. The operative word in the British Columbia act is "protection" which necessarily involves the notion of harm. ... The Manitoba cases dealt initially with a statute that had no criteria at all, then with an amended statute with criteria remarkably like British Columbia's act which passed a Charter examination.[55]

The decisions in *Thwaites* and *McCorkell* have binding force only in Manitoba and British Columbia, respectively. Taken together, and in the absence of other decisions, they describe the following situation: while mental health statutes must set out objective harm criteria for committal, and not leave this as a mere matter of medical judgment, considerable leeway exists with respect to the kinds of harm which will justify committal.

IV.   CONSENT TO TREATMENT IN MENTAL HEALTH LAW

The question of whether competent involuntary patients should have the right in law to refuse psychiatric treatment is the most disputed issue in mental health law. Patients' rights advocates argue that the right to refuse treatment should be available to persons with mental illnesses on the same basis that it is for every-

---

52   *Bobbie v. Health Sciences Centre*, [1988] M.J. No. 485, 49 C.R.R. 376 (Man. Q.B.).
53   [1993] B.C.J. No. 1518 (B.C.S.C.).
54   *Ibid.*, at para. 45.
55   *Ibid.*, at para. 58.

one with respect to non-psychiatric health care. Many family group advocates and psychiatrists believe that permitting involuntary patients to refuse psychiatric treatment not only imposes a barrier to restoring patients to health, but also results in having persons detained in hospital without being able to be treated.

In legal terms, the consent to treatment issue concerns this question: does statute law permit the state to override a *competent refusal* of psychiatric treatment? If an individual lacks capacity to give or withhold consent to treatment in the first place, then a process for substitute decision-making is necessary and the individual will not himself or herself be able to refuse treatment. Much of the debate over the consent issue is really a disagreement over whether there is ever such a thing as a *competent* refusal by an involuntary patient. Many people who oppose recognition of a right to refuse treatment believe that major mental illness makes it impossible for an individual to understand and appreciate that he or she is ill and in need of treatment. In their view, only a naive or shallow understanding of mental illness would suggest otherwise. Certainly, many persons who meet the criteria for involuntary admission to a psychiatric facility will lack treatment competence. Canadian law, however, rejects global assumptions about decision-making capacity. It views competence as a mutable quality that must be assessed with respect to the specific activity in question. A person may be incompetent for one purpose, such as making a will, but competent with respect to another, such as health care. As a consequence, and as a matter of principle, competence to consent to treatment must be assessed independently from the issue of whether the individual otherwise meets statutory criteria for involuntary status. A further complicating factor related to the consent issue is that a person may, during a period of competence, express a wish to refuse psychiatric treatment should he or she later become incompetent. Several provinces have sought to encourage pre-planning for periods of incompetence with respect to health care decisions generally, through instruments such as personal directives[56] and representation agreements.[57] The status of pre-expressed refusals poses a particular challenge to law governing decision-making in mental health settings.[58] Given the episodic nature of much mental illness, the availability of legal techniques for pre-planning treatment choices has particular significance.

In Canada, four distinct approaches to the question of consent to treatment can be identified. Only one of these approaches, that employed in Ontario, recognizes a right to refuse treatment for involuntary patients that corresponds to the common law right to refuse medical treatment. The approaches are:

---

[56] *Personal Directives Act*, R.S.A. 2000, c. P-6.

[57] *Representation Agreement Act*, R.S.B.C. 1996, c. 405.

[58] For an example of the kind of complications that can follow from a pre-expressed wish to refuse treatment, see the litigation in *Conway v. Jacques*, [2002] O.J. No. 2333, 59 O.R. (3d) 737 (Ont. C.A.), leave to appeal refused [2002] S.C.C.A. No. 341 (S.C.C.), in which the Ontario Court of Appeal found grounds for rejecting the patient's wishes due to changed circumstances, but three years later the issue of competency was still being disputed ([2005] O.J. No. 400, 250 D.L.R. (4th) 178 (Ont. S.C.J.)).

(a) a right to refuse treatment (Ontario);

(b) no right to refuse treatment (British Columbia);

(c) a right to refuse, subject to a "best interests" override (Alberta, Manitoba); and

(d) excluding capable individuals from committal (Saskatchewan, Nova Scotia).

A.   RIGHT TO REFUSE TREATMENT: ONTARIO, NORTHWEST TERRITORIES AND NUNAVUT[59]

Ontario law on this question was established by the decision of the province's Court of Appeal in *Fleming v. Reid*,[60] a Charter case from 1991. The *Fleming* case concerned a previously expressed competent refusal. An individual who had experienced several involuntary admissions in his life stated a wish to refuse medications should he be committed again. When this occurred, the treating psychiatrist proposed that the patient take medications covered by the refusal. The substitute decision-maker for the now incompetent patient was the Public Trustee. Acting under a statutory obligation to abide by the individual's previously expressed competent wish, the Public Trustee refused to consent to the treatment plan. The treating psychiatrist applied to the province's Review Board to override the refusal. The Board did so, on the basis that the *Mental Health Act* obliged the Board to make a treatment decision based on the patient's best interests, not on his or her wishes. The Ontario Court of Appeal ruled this to be invalid as a violation of "security of the person" under section 7 of the Charter. The court concluded that the statute denied the patient's right to refuse treatment by making it subject to a best interests test. Moreover, the statute did this without requiring that any hearing be held into whether the patient's competent wishes should be honoured, irrespective of what might be thought to be in his best interests.[61]

A narrow reading of *Fleming* might focus on this last point and suggest that a statutory scheme that balances a patient's competent wishes against his or her therapeutic best interests (without holding either to be determinative in every case) would be constitutional. However, the Court of Appeal's ruling implied a broader understanding of the individual's right to refuse treatment when it said of the issues relevant to a hearing into a previously expressed refusal of treatment:

> [T]here may be questions as to the clarity or currency of the wishes, their applicability to the patient's present circumstances, and whether they have been re-

---

[59] This section discusses in detail the law of Ontario, particularly in light of jurisprudence that has confirmed the right of competent individuals to refuse treatment. This right is also recognized in the statutes of the Northwest Territories and Nunavut: see *Mental Health Act*, R.S.N.W.T. 1988, c. M-10, s. 21 and *Mental Health Act*, R.S.N.W.T. (Nu.) 1988, c. M-10, s. 21.

[60] [1991] O.J. No. 1083, 4 O.R. (3d) 74 (Ont. C.A.).

[61] *Ibid.*, at paras. 51-56.

voked or revised by subsequent wishes or a subsequently accepted treatment program. The resolution of questions of this nature is patently a matter for legislative action. But, in my respectful view, it is incumbent on the legislature to bear in mind that, as a general proposition, psychiatric patients are entitled to make competent decisions and exercise their right to self-determination in accordance with their own standards and values and not necessarily in the manner others may believe to be in the patients' best interests.[62]

Ontario statute law incorporates the *Fleming* principles.[63] The Consent and Capacity Board, created after *Fleming* to replace the former Review Board, has no power to override a competent treatment refusal by an involuntary patient. In 2003 the Supreme Court of Canada rendered judgment in *Starson v. Swayze*,[64] a case that demonstrated how the law established in *Fleming* operates in practice.

Scott Starson had been hospitalized involuntarily pursuant to the mental disorder provisions of the *Criminal Code*.[65] He was diagnosed with bipolar disorder. His psychiatrists recommended treatment involving various medications, including antipsychotics. Starson refused. He stated that his great and only passion in life was physics. While Starson had never been employed or affiliated with an educational institution, he had co-authored at least one paper with a leading physicist, and was recognized among physicists as a good and creative thinker. Starson said that he was familiar with the medications proposed for his treatment and with their side effects, which included the dulling of his thinking processes.

The principal issue before the Supreme Court was whether Starson had capacity to give or withhold consent to treatment. The Ontario *Health Care Consent Act, 1996* (HCCA) sets out the following test for competence in section 4(1):

> A person is capable with respect to a treatment, admission to a care facility or a personal assistance service if the person is able to understand the information that is relevant to making a decision about the treatment, admission or personal assistance service, as the case may be, and able to appreciate the reasonably foreseeable consequences of a decision or lack of decision.[66]

In Ontario, determinations of whether a person meets this test of capacity are made by the Consent and Capacity Board, a statutory tribunal empowered

---

[62] *Ibid.*, at para. 55.

[63] Provisions on consent, the obligations of substitute decision-makers with respect to consent, and the applications which can be made to the Consent and Capacity Board are found in the *Health Care Consent Act, 1996*, S.O. 1996, c. 2, Sched. A.

[64] [2003] S.C.J. No. 33, [2003] 1 S.C.R. 722 (S.C.C.). In 2001, the film *A Beautiful Mind* won the Academy Award for Best Picture. Based on true events, it told the story of Nobel Prize-winning mathematician John Nash, a person with schizophrenia who managed to maintain a long career at Princeton University despite refusing pharmaceutical treatment for his condition. The facts of *Starson* were strikingly similar in outline.

[65] See Part V, "The Forensic Psychiatric System"; see also R.S.C. 1985, c. C-46, Part XX.1, s. 672.54(C).

[66] S.O. 1996, c. 2, Sched. A.

under the HCCA. Starson testified before the Board that while he understood he had mental "problems", he did not acknowledge the diagnosis of bipolar disorder. He said at one point that his work in physics would contribute to the building of spaceships. He rejected the idea that antipsychotic medications could ever resolve his "problems". He was not asked, and never said, whether he understood that if his condition did not change, he might continue to be detained in hospital indefinitely. The Board concluded that he lacked sufficient understanding and appreciation of his condition and the proposed treatment to be capable of making a treatment decision. A majority of six Supreme Court Justices disagreed. All nine Justices agreed that the test set out in the HCCA corresponds with the common law's understanding of capacity and requires an assessment of the individual's *ability* to understand and appreciate his or her circumstances, not merely of the individual's *actual* understanding of those circumstances. The majority concluded that the evidence before the Board failed to demonstrate that Starson lacked capacity in this sense. Writing for the majority, Major J. stated:

> In my view, the Board's reasons, as stated earlier, appear to be overly influenced by its conviction that medication was in Professor Starson's best interest. The Board arrived at its conclusion by failing to focus on the overriding consideration in this appeal, that is, whether that adult patient had the mental capacity to choose whether to accept or reject the medication prescribed. The enforced injection of mind-altering drugs against the respondent's will is highly offensive to his dignity and autonomy, and is to be avoided unless it is demonstrated that he lacked the capacity to make his own decision.[67]

Starson represents strong support for the principle of individual autonomy. Nevertheless, the case did not address any constitutional issues, and dealt only with interpretation of the Ontario statute on capacity. It was also highly dependent on its facts. These are all reasons to think that its implications are limited. Of interest in *Starson* is what the Court implicitly says about the issue of whether legislatures may override competent refusals of psychiatric treatment. While the Supreme Court majority did not comment specifically on whether *Fleming* represents good law on the Charter status of the right to refuse treatment, it twice referred approvingly to the case in more general terms.[68]

---

[67] *Starson v. Swayze*, [2003] S.C.J. No. 33 at para. 91, [2003] 1 S.C.R. 722 (S.C.C.). The majority acceded to Starson's request to be referred to as "Professor Starson" despite the fact that he had never been employed by a post-secondary institution in Canada or elsewhere.

[68] *Ibid.*, at para. 75, where Major J. said:

> The right to refuse unwanted medical treatment is fundamental to a person's dignity and autonomy. This right is equally important in the context of treatment for mental illness: see *Fleming v. Reid* (1991), 4 O.R. (3d) 74 (C.A.). ..:
>
>> Few medical procedures can be more intrusive than the forcible injection of powerful mind-altering drugs which are often accompanied by severe and sometimes irreversible adverse side effects.
>
> Unwarranted findings of incapacity severely infringe upon a person's right to self-determination.

The combined effect of *Fleming* and *Starson* in Ontario has been the subject of harsh criticism. The authors of the article "Treatment Delayed — Liberty Denied"[69] argue that Ontario faces a situation in which it is obliged to warehouse in its psychiatric facilities seriously ill individuals who refused treatment at a time of competence and cannot now be treated:

> ... rather than promoting the rights of involuntary psychiatric patients, the Ontario law results in many patients being subject to prolonged periods of detention, physical and chemical restraint, and solitary confinement.[70]

The authors propose that the legislation be amended to include an override of a patient's prior competent refusal if following that refusal would "endanger his or her physical or mental health".[71] The particular instances of long-term hospitalization outlined in "Treatment Delayed" raise concerns that deserve attention. At the same time, however, it should be remembered that there may be many more unreported cases in which the law's respecting of a competent refusal, including where the refusal was stated in previous wishes, may serve the subtler purpose of facilitating a negotiation between patient and treatment team that results in a better treatment plan.

Developments in legal areas outside the domain of civil committal may shed further light on the consent to treatment issue. In *C. (A.) v. Manitoba (Director of Child and Family Services)*,[72] the Supreme Court of Canada dealt with the constitutionality of a statutory provision authorizing a judge to order medical treatment of a minor under the age of 16 in her best interests, even where the minor apparently met the test for a "mature minor" and had refused treatment. Justice Abella, writing for the majority, upheld the statute on the basis that a best interests test could be reconciled with respect for an adolescent's emerging autonomy by taking the minor's level of maturity and wishes into account. Nevertheless, the uncertainty over when a minor under 16 could be found to reach a mature competence justified placing decision-making authority in the hands of a court. Only Binnie J. was prepared to rule that where evidence establishes that a person (of whatever age) has treatment capacity, then section 7 of the Charter forbids overriding his or her refusal or treatment.

While the *C. (A.)* case deals with the issue of health care decision-making by and for minors, the majority's decision echoes the narrow interpretation of *Fleming*, whereby the constitutional problem lies more in paying too little atten-

---

At para. 101, Major J. added:

> In *Fleming v. Reid* ... Robins J.A. observed ... that neuroleptic medication carries with it "significant, and often unpredictable, short term and long term risks of harmful side effects". Professor Starson clearly appreciated the extent of these risks. However, it was the intended purpose of the medication that he primarily objected to. [emphasis omitted]

[69] Robert Solomon, Richard O'Reilly, John Gray & Martina Nikolic, "Treatment Delayed — Liberty Denied" (2008) 87 Can. Bar Rev. 679.

[70] *Ibid.*, at 681.

[71] *Ibid.*, at 718.

[72] [2009] S.C.J. No. 30, [2009] 2 S.C.R. 181 (S.C.C.).

tion to the individual's competent wishes than in the ultimate overriding of those wishes. The majority's view also implies that competence is not an either/or proposition — circumstances may cast doubt on the ability to measure or rely on measures of competence.

In *Deacon v. Canada (Attorney General)*,[73] the Federal Court of Appeal ruled that the National Parole Board acted constitutionally in imposing a term of release that a pedophile take medications intended to reduce his libido. The court found this to be a justifiable violation of the accused's security of person in the interest of public safety. The court preferred the narrow reading of *Fleming*, but also sought to distinguish it on the basis that the parolee in *Deacon* could refuse treatment, so long as he was prepared to accept the consequence of not being released from prison.

B.   NO RIGHT TO REFUSE TREATMENT: BRITISH COLUMBIA

British Columbia stands at the opposite end of the spectrum from Ontario on the issue of consent. The province maintains an approach that was long used in Canada: the directors of psychiatric facilities may authorize treatment for involuntarily committed patients without obtaining their consent. Section 31 of the British Columbia statute states that "treatment authorized by the director is deemed to be given with the consent of the patient". Further, the *Health Care (Consent) and Care Facility (Admission) Act*, which essentially codifies the common law on consent to treatment, is expressly stated not to apply to involuntary patients in psychiatric hospitals.[74] This legislative distinction between psychiatric patients and all other individuals with respect to the right to consent would appear to raise an issue of discrimination under section 15(1) of the Charter. Such a claim would, of course, be subject to the government's seeking to justify the distinction under section 1, or even on the basis that it "corresponds to the needs" of psychiatric patients.[75]

Under this model, there is no requirement to assess an involuntary patient's treatment competency, nor is there any role for a substitute decision-maker to make treatment decisions on the patient's behalf. This does not mean, of course, that informal practices of assessing competence, respecting patients' treatment wishes and working with family members cannot be employed.

This approach ensures that treatment can be provided to involuntary patients with a minimum of procedural delay. Given that it involves the clearest denial of a right to consent to treatment, it might seem the most vulnerable to Charter challenge on *Fleming*-like grounds. However, the decision in *McCorkell*

---

[73]   [2006] F.C.J. No. 1153, [2007] 2 F.C.R. 607 (F.C.A.), leave to appeal refused [2006] S.C.C.A. No. 319 (S.C.C.).

[74]   R.S.B.C. 1996, c. 181, s. 2.

[75]   In *Law v. Canada (Minister of Employment and Immigration)*, [1999] S.C.J. No. 12, [1999] 1 S.C.R. 497 (S.C.C.), "correspondence to need" is identified by the Court as one of four contextual issues that might show that a distinction in law is not, in fact, discriminatory for purposes of s. 15(1). See paras. 69-71.

v. Riverview Hospital (Director)[76] dealing with committal criteria, with its emphasis on the therapeutic purposes of mental health law, may signal a different judicial view in British Columbia.

C. "BEST INTERESTS" OVERRIDE: ALBERTA AND MANITOBA

The mental health statutes of Alberta and Manitoba recognize the distinction between treatment competence and incompetence, and the right of a competent patient to refuse proposed treatment. However, in Alberta, the hospital board or attending physician may apply to the Review Panel for a review of the refusal. The Review Panel must act in what it believes to be the patient's best interests, and on that basis may override the refusal and order that the proposed treatment be administered.[77] This is quite similar to the pre-*Fleming* system in Ontario. In Manitoba, a similar override of a refusal is available, although only with respect to a refusal made on an incompetent patient's behalf by their substitute decision-maker.

These models involve significantly greater procedural rights for an involuntary patient around treatment decisions than is the case in British Columbia. Nevertheless, the Alberta statute in particular provides for overriding a competent refusal in the patient's best interests. This model is also potentially vulnerable to a Charter challenge on *Fleming*-type grounds.

D. TREATMENT INCAPABILITY: SASKATCHEWAN AND NOVA SCOTIA

As earlier stated, Saskatchewan and Nova Scotia include treatment incompetence in the substantive criteria for involuntary hospitalization. This effectively avoids the consent to treatment dilemma. That is, any person who is treatment competent cannot be involuntarily hospitalized. The question of respecting or overriding a competent refusal does not arise. This model would seem to satisfy any Charter concerns. It does mean that competent persons with mental disorders who present a danger to others will not be committable. Only should they become incompetent, or commit an offence which brings them under the *Criminal Code*, will it be possible to detain them. A potential ambiguity in the approach adopted by Saskatchewan and Nova Scotia exists with respect to an individual committed to hospital on the basis of current incompetence, but who is then discovered to have given a competent refusal of treatment at an earlier, pre-committal time.

E. NON-PSYCHIATRIC AND EXCEPTIONAL TREATMENTS

Statutory provisions that authorize treatment of involuntary patients without consent apply to treatment directed at mental disorder or its symptoms. Medical

---

[76]   [1993] B.C.J. No. 1518, 104 D.L.R. (4th) 391 (B.C.S.C.).

[77]   *Mental Health Act*, C.C.S.M. c. M110, s. 30 and *Mental Health Act*, R.S.A. 2000, c. M-13, s. 29.

treatment for unrelated physiological matters, such as dental surgery, must be provided to an involuntary patient on the same basis as to any other person: with the patient's consent, or if the patient is incompetent, by consent of a substitute decision-maker, or in an emergency. Should this limit not be expressly stated in the statute, it should follow from the fact that both detention and non-consensual treatment are premised on the existence of mental disorder and the need to facilitate its treatment.

Special prohibitions or protections may exist with respect to treatments that are more invasive or controversial than standard psychiatric therapy. These may prevent substitute decision-makers from consenting on a patient's behalf, or impose additional obligations in the authorizing process. For example, Alberta prohibits "psychosurgery" unless both the patient and the review panel agree to it.[78] Ontario's *Health Care Consent Act, 1996* excludes medical procedures done for research or tissue transplant purposes, and non-therapeutic sterilization, from its substitute decision-making provisions.[79] Electro-convulsive therapy (ECT) is not singled out in provincial statutes for particular attention, but hospital and Ministry policy often imposes additional precautions, such as obtaining a second opinion.

F.   COMMUNITY TREATMENT ORDERS

Saskatchewan, Ontario, Nova Scotia, Newfoundland and Labrador, and Alberta have incorporated "community treatment orders" (CTOs) into their mental health statutes.[80] Based on models in several U.S. states, where CTOs are generally referred to as "outpatient committal", this mechanism is intended to impose a duty to comply with psychiatric treatment on mentally ill individuals living in the community. The idea is to break the connection between involuntary hospitalization and non-consensual psychiatric treatment, and by addressing the problem of treatment non-compliance to keep persons healthy and in the community. It is worth asking, however, whether the extension of coercive mental health measures from the hospital into the community is either necessary, or consistent with the idea that the community represents a better alternative to institutional care.

The CTO scheme has its own substantive "committal" criteria. The statutory criteria in Ontario require that in order to issue a CTO:

> (1) the subject of the CTO must have previous involvement with the mental health system;

---

[78] *Mental Health Act*, R.S.A. 2000, c. M-13, s. 29(5).

[79] S.O. 1996, c. 2, Sched. A, s. 6.

[80] *Mental Health Act*, R.S.O. 1990, c. M.7, s. 33.7 (Ontario); *Mental Health Services Act*, S.S. 1984-85-86, c. M-13.1, s. 24.3 (Saskatchewan); *Involuntary Psychiatric Treatment Act*, S.N.S. 2005, 42, s. 47 (Nova Scotia); *Mental Health Care and Treatment Act*, S.N.L. 2006, c. M-9.1, ss. 40-52 (Newfoundland and Labrador); *Mental Health Act*, R.S.A. 2000, c. M-13, s. 9.1 (Alberta).

(2) the subject must meet substantive criteria for mental disorder and risk of harm; and

(3) it must be possible to put a "community treatment plan" in place for the subject.

The target group for CTOs is the "revolving door" or chronic client. In order to be subject to a CTO, a person must have been hospitalized on at least two occasions or for 30 days or more within the preceding three years.[81] The legislation does not limit the previous hospitalizations to involuntary committals. Therefore, individuals who voluntarily admit themselves to psychiatric facilities may make themselves eligible for later CTO committal.

The CTO must include a "community treatment plan". The issuing physician has several responsibilities with respect to the plan. The physician must develop the plan in consultation with the individual and any health practitioners intended to be involved in providing care in the community, ensure that the services set out in the plan are available in the community and assess the individual as being capable of complying with the treatment plan. Further, "the person or his or her substitute decision-maker [must consent] to the community treatment plan in accordance with the rules for consent under the *Health Care Consent Act 1996*".[82] Other provisions set out certain required elements of a community treatment plan. The issuing physician has several additional obligations, such as ensuring that the individual has consulted with a "rights adviser", and that copies of the CTO get to appropriate parties, including any health practitioners named in the plan. Further, the physician is made responsible for "general supervision" of the CTO.[83] The CTO expires after six months unless renewed.

Alberta, the latest province to adopt a CTO mechanism, is the first province to allow for the issuance of a CTO in the case of a person who has not previously been admitted to a psychiatric facility.[84] It has been suggested that this extends the benefit of a less restrictive alternative to hospitalization to a person

---

[81] In Saskatchewan and Nova Scotia, a person is eligible for CTO committal if he or she has been hospitalized in a psychiatric facility for a cumulative total of 60 days in the preceding two years. In Alberta, the figure is 30 days or two admissions within the preceding three years, the lowest threshold in any province.

[82] *Mental Health Act*, R.S.O. 1990, c. M.7, s. 33.1(4)(f).

[83] The attending physician is relieved of liability for any "default or neglect" of other persons providing treatment under the plan (*ibid.*, s. 33.6(1)). By implication, the physician appears not to be relieved of liability for default or neglect in his or her own responsibilities under the plan. Other health practitioners providing treatment under the plan "are responsible for implementing the plan to the extent indicated in it" (*ibid.*, s. 33.5(4)).

[84] Section 9.1(1)(b)(iii) of the Alberta *Mental Health Act*, R.S.A. 2000, c. M.13 sets out the following basis for CTO committal:

... the person has, while living in the community, exhibited a pattern of recurrent or repetitive behaviour that indicates that the person is likely to cause harm to the person or others or to suffer substantial mental or physical deterioration or serious physical impairment if the person does not receive continuing treatment or care while living in the community.

experiencing a first psychotic break.[85] That is true, of course, only if such persons were also committable, and likely to be committed, to hospital. This gives some indication of the difficult judgment call facing a clinician who might consider issuing a CTO in place of a first hospital admission.

The CTO provisions of the five provinces vary as to the way in which they handle the issue of consent. These variations correspond roughly to the rules concerning consent to psychiatric treatment found in each province (see discussion above). While Ontario requires that an individual consent to a CTO, Saskatchewan, Nova Scotia, and Newfoundland and Labrador provide that only persons incompetent to consent to treatment can be the subject of a CTO. Nevertheless, Saskatchewan, like Ontario, makes it a requirement that the issuing physician find the person able to comply with the CTO. In Alberta, the issuing physicians can override the refusal of a competent person to agree to a CTO.[86]

Patients' groups have criticized CTOs as an unnecessary and intrusive mechanism that stigmatizes persons with mental illness as needing to be subject to state control, even in the community.[87] Other criticisms go to whether CTOs are capable of meeting the goals intended by proponents.[88] The problem of non-compliance with psychiatric treatment by persons living in the community is a complex one, and it remains unclear whether the CTO can succeed in addressing it by compulsion. For one thing, the CTO itself is not easily enforced. While it might be thought that non-compliance with a CTO would be sanctioned by involuntary committal to hospital, statutes do not go that far and for good reason. Hospital committal depends on a person's meeting substantive committal criteria related to mental condition and therapeutic need. Committal should not be available as penalty or punishment for failure to comply with an order.

The only sanction for non-compliance with a CTO is the physician's power to issue a form of warrant, authorizing police officers to convey the non-compliant person for purposes of a mental examination. This is not insignificant. A frequent complaint of family members of chronically mentally ill persons is the difficulty they encounter in obtaining help, including from police, to get their unwilling relative to a physician or to hospital when symptoms of acute illness appear. Nevertheless, it is questionable to what degree this authority changes the dynamics of community mental health treatment.

The success of CTOs may largely depend on their being part of a comprehensive plan that puts in place significant treatment resources, including ready

---

[85]   Anita Wandzura, "Community Treatment Orders in Saskatchewan: What Went Wrong?" (2008) 71 Sask. L. Rev. 269.

[86]   *Mental Health Act*, R.S.A. 2000, c. M-13, s. 9.1(1)(f)(ii).

[87]   See, for example, the website of the "No Force Coalition" formed in Ontario to oppose the introduction of CTOs in 2000, online at: <http://www.qsos.ca/qspc/nfc/cto.html>.

[88]   Anita Wandzura, "Community Treatment Orders in Saskatchewan: What Went Wrong?" (2008) 71 Sask. L. Rev. 269 reports that CTOs do not appear to have worked in Saskatchewan. However, she believes the mechanism can be successful if certain legislative changes are made. For a more pessimistic view, see Peter Carver, "Fact or Fashion? Alberta Adopts the Community Treatment" (2010) 19 Health L. Rev. 17.

contact with and support from health care professionals. Planning and support of this kind appears to be intended by the legislation. If CTO schemes work only to the degree that the client is provided with comprehensive treatment and support services, however, it seems reasonable to ask whether similar results could be achieved without issuing a CTO.[89]

The only extensive empirical study yet conducted in Canada on CTO performance suggests that these are valid concerns. The independent consulting group performing a statutorily mandated review for the Ontario government reported in 2007 that CTOs had been infrequently used, especially with those who presented the most difficult problems with treatment compliance:

> It would appear that the neediest individuals, those whose illness is the most severe, those who are the most resistant to care, or those not involved in the formal mental health system, are very unlikely to be put on a CTO. Those who are the most likely appear to be those who are at least somewhat directable or inclined to follow rules.[90]

The Ontario report showed mixed results. While anecdotal evidence from CTO subjects and family members suggested some success had been achieved, the authors were unable to find empirical support for this nor to attribute it to the compulsory features of the CTO itself.[91] The same uncertainty has characterized studies carried out in jurisdictions outside Canada.[92]

A different means of maintaining a person on a treatment program in the community is a leave of absence from hospital for involuntary patients. Several

---

[89] For further discussion of the CTO, see the author's "A New Direction for Mental Health Law: *Brian's Law* and the Problematic Implications of Community Treatment Orders" in T. Caulfield & B. Von Tigerstrom, eds., *Health Care Reform and the Law in Canada: Meeting the Challenge* (Edmonton: University of Alberta Press, 2002) 187; Shelley Trueman, "Community Treatment Orders and Nova Scotia: the Least Restrictive Alternative?" (2003) 11 Health L.J. 1; S. Kisely & L.A. Campbell, "Community Treatment Orders for Psychiatric Patients: The Emperor with No Clothes" (2006) 51 Can. J. Psych. 683; and R.L. O'Reilly, "Community Treatment Orders: This Emperor Is Fully Dressed!" (2006) 51 Can. J. Psych. 691.

[90] "Report on the Legislated Review of Community Treatment Orders, Required under Section 33.9 of the *Mental Health Act*" (Toronto: Ministry of Health and Long-Term Care, 2005) at 115, online at: <http://www.health.gov.on.ca/english/public/pub/ministry_reports/dreezer/dreezer.pdf>.

[91] *Ibid.*, at 124:

> As we travelled the province we heard repeatedly that community treatment orders have profoundly changed many lives and even saved lives. However, it is less than totally clear which factors, or combination of factors, have led to this apparent success. It is difficult to know whether the key is the order itself and the legal control over the patient that it conveys, the services and the treatment team that is frequently assembled to support the patient, or some combination of these factors.

[92] For a particularly useful summary of studies through to 2003, see John Dawson *et al.*, "Ambivalence About Community Treatment Orders" (2003) 26 Int'l J.L. & Psychiatry 243. See also Ann-Marie A. O'Brien & Susan J. Farrell, "Community Treatment Orders: Profile of a Canadian Experience" (2005) 50 Can. J. of Psych. 27; and Richard L. O'Reilly *et al.*, "A Quantitative Analysis of the Use of Community Treatment Orders in Saskatchewan" (2006) 29 Int'l J.L. & Psychiatry 516.

provinces, including Manitoba and British Columbia, have enhanced statutory leave provisions to permit psychiatric facilities to gradually reintroduce involuntary patients into the community while remaining subject to committal and the authority of the facility. Leaves of absence are granted on conditions, often including compliance with a treatment plan. If a patient ceases to comply, or starts to decompensate, he or she can be brought back to hospital under the continuing involuntary status.

The leave of absence approach has advantages over the more complex CTO. The starting place is hospital and inpatient treatment, rather than an effort to enforce compliance on an individual living in the community who may not meet standard committal criteria.

A concern from a civil liberties perspective about leaves of absence is that they might too easily be used as a means of retaining control over individuals who, in fact, no longer meet the criteria for involuntary committal. To date, however, Canadian courts have not been receptive to this argument. In an Alberta case, a patient with an extensive history of self-mutilation argued that repeated leaves which only required him to spend weeknights in hospital were inconsistent with his meeting Alberta's dangerousness criteria for committal. The court disagreed, finding no presumptive inconsistency between a leave of absence and continued certification. The judge commented:

> The granting of leaves of absence on a regular basis allows [the patient] a degree of freedom and human dignity, while at the same time decreasing the likelihood that he will harm himself.[93]

A similar ruling was made in an Ontario case in which a patient argued that because he had received repeated leaves, even though the statute permitted only one leave, he should be declared discharged from involuntary status. The judge described leaves of absence as "a win-win situation", the benefits of which should not be lost by too technical an interpretation of the statute.[94]

V.   THE FORENSIC PSYCHIATRIC SYSTEM

A.   PART XX.1 OF THE CRIMINAL CODE

The forensic psychiatric system deals with persons who commit criminal offences as a consequence of mental illness. As an aspect of criminal law, forensic law in Canada is national in scope. Forensic law was overhauled in 1992 following the Charter decision in *R. v. Swain*.[95] Prior to 1992, the *Criminal Code* provided for a plea of "not guilty by reason of insanity" (NGRI). If found NGRI, the accused individual was automatically and indefinitely detained in hospital on

---

[93]   *Wurfel v. Alberta Hospital (Edmonton)*, [1999] A.J. No. 868 at para. 67 (Alta. Q.B.), *per* Lee J.

[94]   *Lavallie v. Kingston Psychiatric Hospital*, [1999] O.J. No. 4306 at para. 29 (Ont. S.C.J.), *per* Belch J., affd [2000] O.J. No. 3641 (Ont. C.A.).

[95]   [1991] S.C.J. No. 32, [1991] 1 S.C.R. 933 (S.C.C.).

a "Lieutenant Governor's warrant", meaning that release from hospital was ultimately dependent on a decision of the provincial Cabinet.

In *Swain*, the Supreme Court of Canada ruled that the NGRI process violated sections 7 and 9 of the Charter. Parliament responded by introducing a new Part XX.1 to the *Criminal Code* to govern this area.[96] The term "insanity" and the finding of NGRI were replaced by "not criminally responsible by reason of mental disorder" (NCRMD). The legal test is that the accused did not appreciate "the nature and quality of the [criminal] act or omission or [know] that it was wrong".[97] In addition to NCRMDs, Part XX.1 of the *Criminal Code* and forensic psychiatric services also deal with individuals found unfit to stand trial due to mental illness.

A person found NCRMD is not subject to automatic detention in hospital. Rather, section 672.54 of the Code sets out several factors to be taken into consideration with respect to making a disposition of hospital custody, release on conditions or absolute discharge:

> Where a court or Review Board makes a disposition pursuant to subsection 672.45(2) or section 672.47 or 672.83, it shall, taking into consideration the need to protect the public from dangerous persons, the mental condition of the accused, the reintegration of the accused into society and the other needs of the accused, make one of the following dispositions that is the least onerous and least restrictive to the accused:
>
> (a) where a verdict of not criminally responsible on account of mental disorder has been rendered in respect of the accused and, in the opinion of the court or Review Board, the accused is not a significant threat to the safety of the public, by order, direct that the accused be discharged absolutely;
>
> (b) by order, direct that the accused be discharged subject to such conditions as the court or Review Board considers appropriate; or
>
> (c) by order, direct that the accused be detained in custody in a hospital, subject to such conditions as the court or Review Board considers appropriate.

Following initial disposition, ongoing decision-making authority over the individual's continued detention lies with forensic Review Boards established in and by each province. Review Boards must conduct periodic hearings for each patient.

The Supreme Court considered the Charter status of this scheme in *Winko v. British Columbia*.[98] The Court ruled that "dangerousness", in terms of posing "a significant threat to public safety", is the appropriate basis for forensic committal. This standard corresponds to the federal government's constitutional juris-

---

[96] R.S.C. 1985, c. C-46, Part XX.1.

[97] *Ibid.*, s. 16(1).

[98] *Winko v. British Columbia (Forensic Psychiatric Services)*, [1999] S.C.J. No. 31, [1991] 2 S.C.R. 625 (S.C.C.).

diction over the criminal law. The Court ruled that an NCRMD person is entitled to an absolute discharge from custody when he or she is determined to no longer pose a significant threat to public safety. Short of an absolute discharge, Review Boards may order conditional discharges from hospital detention, which permit a return to the community on conditions, such as working with a treatment team.

The *Criminal Code* provisions do not authorize psychiatric treatment of NCRMD persons. Therefore, the authority to treat, including any authority to treat where the individual is unable or unwilling to consent to psychiatric treatment, falls to be determined by the provincial mental health law in the province where the individual is detained. For this reason, forensic patients are often certified under mental health statutes as well as being detained pursuant to the *Criminal Code*. Forensic psychiatric facilities are provincially operated, either as free-standing hospitals or as forensic units in mental health hospitals.

Winko also argued that as an NCRMD person, he remained subject to indefinite detention, and might well be detained beyond the maximum sentence he could have received had he been found guilty of the criminal offence. This, he claimed, constituted discrimination based on mental disability contrary to section 15 of the Charter. The Court ruled, however, that because the system is based on individualized assessment of the person's mental condition, it does not rely on stereotypes of mental illness and so is not discriminatory.

In 2005, Parliament amended various aspects of Part XX.1 of the *Criminal Code*. Most of the amendments were of a housekeeping nature. They included repealing the capping provision, and a dangerous offender sentencing provision linked to capping. Submissions to a Parliamentary committee had recommended extending the powers of Review Boards with respect to ordering psychiatric assessments of patients, and making more detailed orders concerning therapeutic matters. The Senate Committee made similar recommendations.[99] Parliament did not act on these recommendations. Nevertheless, a case concerning the interpretation of Review Board powers under section 672.54 came before the Supreme Court in 2006, and the Court effectively expanded Board authority in ways not unlike those proposed. The case, *Mazzei v. British Columbia (Director of Adult Forensic Psychiatric Services)*,[100] contains an interesting discussion about the nature of psychiatric treatment, and the responsibility of an administrative tribunal charged with supervising treatment plans.

B.   THE ROLE OF FORENSIC REVIEW BOARDS

The issue of forensic Review Boards' powers to intervene in matters going to treatment, has arisen repeatedly in the jurisprudence emerging from Review Board decisions. The argument has generally aligned forensic hospitals and

---

[99]   *Out of the Shadows at Last: Transforming Mental Health, Mental Illness and Addiction Services in Canada*, Final Report of the Standing Committee on Social Affairs, Science and Technology (Ottawa: Senate of Canada, May 2006), Section 4.3, "The Mental Disorder Provisions of the *Criminal Code*".

[100]   [2006] S.C.J. No. 7, [2006] 1 S.C.R. 326 (S.C.C.).

governments on one side, arguing for restricted Board jurisdiction, against Boards and patients on the other. That was true in two cases decided by the Supreme Court in late 2003: *Penetanguishene Mental Health Centre v. Ontario (Attorney General)*[101] and *Pinet v. St. Thomas Psychiatric Hospital.*[102] In both instances, the principal issue concerned whether the duty placed on Review Boards by section 672.54 to ensure that its dispositions are "the least onerous and least restrictive to the accused" extends to the entirety of a Board's order, including any conditions placed on an accused's release into the community or hospital detention. In *Penetanguishene,* the Ontario Review Board ordered that the accused be detained in hospital, but added the conditions that he be held in a medium security rather than a maximum security facility, and that he have certain grounds privileges.

The Government of Ontario appealed, arguing that the Board had erred in ordering the added conditions based on its understanding of what would be least restrictive of the accused's liberty, within the context of hospital detention. The Government argued that the liberty interest pertained only to the Board's choice of "bare" disposition between an absolute discharge, a conditional discharge, and hospital detention. Once having made that decision, the Board was not obliged to take the accused's liberty interests into account.

The Court unanimously rejected the government's interpretation of section 672.54. Justice Binnie stated:

> The heart of the Crown's argument is that a "least onerous and least restrictive" requirement may undermine treatment needs. The Crown argues the "least onerous and least restrictive" requirement would impose undue rigidity, whereas the "appropriateness" test guarantees flexibility. With respect, these arguments do not do justice to the wording of s. 672.54. Just as the Crown is wrong, I think, to try to detach the word "appropriate" from the factors listed in s. 672.54 in order to give Review Boards greater "flexibility", so, too, the Crown is wrong, with respect, to try to detach the "least onerous and least restrictive" requirement from its statutory context. Section 672.54 directs the Review Board to have regard to "the other needs of the accused". At the forefront of these "other needs" is the need for treatment.[103]

This implies that Review Boards may include in their orders conditions that enter with some detail into the planning of the context within which forensic psychiatric treatment is provided to the NCRMD accused. That question arose again in *Mazzei v. British Columbia (Director of Adult Forensic Psychiatric Services).*[104]

Vernon Mazzei had been a forensic patient in British Columbia since 1986. Over the years, the B.C. Review Board granted Mazzei several conditional releases from the province's major forensic hospital facility. On every occasion

[101] [2003] S.C.J. No. 67, [2004] 1 S.C.R. 498 (S.C.C.).

[102] [2004] S.C.J. No. 66, [2004] 1 S.C.R. 528 (S.C.C.).

[103] [2003] S.C.J. No. 67 at para. 67, [2004] 1 S.C.R. 498 (S.C.C.) [emphasis omitted].

[104] [2006] S.C.J. No. 7, [2006] 1 S.C.R. 326 (S.C.C.).

Mazzei breached the terms of his release, and was returned to hospital custody. At a Board hearing in 2002, Mazzei's counsel argued that his client, an Aboriginal, wished to attend a First Nations residential rehabilitation program. The hospital treatment team merely sought renewal of the hospital custody order, without suggesting any new therapeutic options for Mazzei. Evidently frustrated at the treatment team's lack of imagination,[105] the Board issued an order concerning Mazzei's continued custodial status that included these three points:

> 8. THAT for the accused's next hearing the Director undertake a comprehensive global review of Mr. Mazzei's diagnostic formulations, medications and programs with a view to developing an integrated treatment approach which considers the current treatment impasse and the accused's reluctance to become an active participant in his rehabilitation;
>
> 9. THAT for his next hearing the Board be provided with an independent assessment of the accused's risk to the public in consideration of the above refocussed treatment plan;
>
> 10. THAT the Director undertake assertive efforts to enroll the accused in a culturally appropriate treatment program ... [106]

The Director of Adult Forensic Psychiatric Services appealed from this order. He argued that a bright line should be drawn between the Board's power to make orders concerning an accused's custodial status, and the authority of forensic treatment personnel teams to make decisions concerning treatment matters. The Court agreed that section 672.54 does not grant Review Boards the power to order "a particular course of treatment". This would be inconsistent with the division of powers over health care between the federal and provincial governments. A federal statute such as the Code could not grant a power to make treatment decisions.[107] Nevertheless, the Court distinguished between making treatment decisions, and supervising the overall treatment program of an accused. The Court described the latter as lying within the role of the Review Board. The Court elaborated on the distinction between these two roles in this way:

> In essence, conditions "regarding" medical treatment or its supervision are those conditions that Review Boards may impose to ensure that the NCR accused is provided with opportunities for appropriate and effective medical treatment, in order to help reduce the risk to public safety and to facilitate rehabilitation and community reintegration. The scope of this power would arguably include anything short of actually prescribing that treatment be carried out by hospital authorities. It would therefore include the power to require hospital

---

[105] "The Board expressed concern over the 'late' and inadequate information provided by Mazzei's case manager and treatment team; his supervising psychiatrist's absence at the hearing; and his case manager's inability to answer many of the Board's questions": *ibid.*, at para. 3.

[106] *Ibid.*, at para. 4.

[107] *Ibid.*, at para. 34.

authorities and staff to question and reconsider past or current treatment plans or diagnoses, and explore alternatives which might be more effective and appropriate.[108]

Only by fulfilling such a supervisory role "regarding" treatment can Review Boards properly serve the dual purposes of Part XX.1 — enhancing public safety, while protecting the liberty interests of the accused. To properly perform this role, the Board must be able to "form its own independent opinion of an accused's treatment plan and clinical progress, and ultimately of the accused's risk to public safety and prospects for rehabilitation and reintegration".[109] That is, the Board must be able to assess efficacy of past and proposed treatment plans independently of treating personnel. Its task is not merely to accept what it is told by them about treatment matters. The Supreme Court thereby made it clear that forensic Review Boards should play an active role in addressing problems arising from the therapeutic relationship between the forensic system and the individual patient.

The Supreme Court had further occasion to consider the role of forensic review boards in *R. v. Conway*.[110] Paul Conway has resided in forensic psychiatric hospitals in Ontario since being found not guilty by reason of insanity on a charge of sexual assault with a weapon in 1983. At one of his annual reviews before the Review Board, Conway sought rulings that what he alleged were the poor conditions of the facilities, and the lack of helpful psychotherapy, breached several of his Charter rights. This raised the issue of whether the Review Board had jurisdiction to rule on Charter claims, a vexed question in Canadian administrative law. The Court described the Board as a "quasi-judicial body with significant authority over a vulnerable population" and "a broad power to attach flexible, individualized, creative conditions to the discharge and detention orders it devises".[111] As such, forensic boards have jurisdiction to make Charter rulings. However, the Court added, boards lack the power to grant an absolute discharge as a remedy for a breach of the Charter rights of a patient who remains a significant threat to public safety, as Conway was requesting. The implications of this judgment for the review boards and panels that hear appeals of patients' involuntary status under provincial mental health statutes are unclear.

C. MENTAL ILLNESS AND THE CRIMINAL JUSTICE SYSTEM

The forensic system deals with persons whose mental illness caused their unlawful conduct or who were experiencing an episode of serious illness at the time of that conduct. Many observers are concerned about a different issue: the increasing proportion of inmates in the corrections system who have mental health

---

[108] *Ibid.*, at para. 39.

[109] *Ibid.*, at para. 42.

[110] [2010] S.C.J. No. 22, [2010] 1 S.C.R. 765 (S.C.C.). See case comment by H. Archibald Kaiser, "*Conway*: A Bittersweet Victory for Not Criminally Responsible Accused" (2010) 75 C.R. (6th) 241.

[111] *Ibid.*, at paras. 84 and 94 (*per* Abella J.).

problems. In September 2010, the federal Office of the Corrections Investigator released "Under Warrant: A Review of the Implementation of the Correctional Service of Canada's 'Mental Health Strategy'", which gave figures to support the concern:

> According to the latest available data, at admission 11% of offenders committed to federal jurisdiction had a mental health diagnosis, an increase of 71% since 1997, 21.3% had been prescribed medication for psychiatric concerns and 6.1% were receiving outpatient services prior to incarceration. A further 14.5% of male offenders had previously been hospitalized for psychiatric reasons. ... Female offenders are twice as likely as male offenders to have a mental health diagnosis at admission.[112]

The "Under Warrant" report goes on to analyze measures taken by the Corrections Service to provide enhanced services to offenders with mental health issues.

The larger concern, however, goes to the question of why there has been an increased prevalence of mental illness in the prison population. To many, it represents a "criminalization" of the mentally ill, whereby persons with illness are inappropriately channelled into and through the criminal justice system without ever getting the therapeutic assistance they need to avoid conflicts with the law in the first place. One possible solution to the problem has been the development of "mental health courts" or community courts.[113] The most well-known Mental Health Court in Canada operates in downtown Toronto as a division of the Ontario Court of Justice.[114] The court handles NCRMD and unfit to stand trial matters, but also seeks to divert other accused persons into mental health services and programs where available and appropriate. Crown counsel and mental health workers affiliated with the court cooperate to improve these links. Similar initiatives have started in other Canadian cities, including with the Downtown Community Court in Vancouver.[115] The mental health court phenomenon is much more established in the United States, where it has emerged in part from the work of researchers in the field of "therapeutic jurisprudence".[116]

---

[112] Online at: <http://www.oci-bec.gc.ca/rpt/oth-aut/oth-aut20100923-eng.aspx> (see "Executive Summary").

[113] Richard Schneider, Hy Bloom & Mark Heerema, *Mental Health Courts: Decriminalizing the Mentally Ill* (Toronto: Irwin Law, 2007).

[114] See the website for the Toronto Mental Health Court, online at: <http://www.mentalhealth court.ca/pages/7/Diversions.htm>. A Mental Health Court also operates in Saint John, New Brunswick as part of that province's Provincial Court. See online at: <http://www.mental healthcourt-sj.com/summary.html>.

[115] The Downtown Community Court has a broader mandate than addressing the needs of accused persons with mental illness. In particular, the court seeks to provide links to substance abuse programs. See online at: <http://www.criminaljusticereform.gov.bc.ca/en/justice_reform_projects/ community_court/index.html>.

[116] Bruce Winick & David Wexler, eds., *Judging in a Therapeutic Key: Therapeutic Jurisprudence in the Courts* (Durham, NC: Carolina Academic Press, 2003).

VI. THE HUMAN RIGHTS DIMENSION OF MENTAL DISABILITY

A. EQUALITY RIGHTS AND MODELS OF DISABILITY

Persons with disabilities have emphasized the social dimension of disability, the degree to which disadvantage experienced as disability is not so much a consequence of biological impairment as of the design of mainstream activities and environments. By failing to take broad ranges of (dis)abilities into account, mainstream design effectively excludes and stigmatizes those who fall outside its narrow norms. This insight lies at the heart of the social model of disability that largely defines the equality rights project of the disability rights movement.[117] Canadian law has largely embraced the social model of disability. This is the signal triumph of the disability rights movement in the quarter-century that has passed since the adoption of the *Canadian Charter of Rights and Freedoms* in 1982. The Supreme Court of Canada has approved this approach to understanding disability in the context of anti-discrimination law:

> The true focus of the s. 15(1) disability analysis is not on the impairment as such, nor even any associated functional limitations, but is on the problematic response of the state to either or both of these circumstances. It is the state action that stigmatizes the impairment, or which attributes false or exaggerated importance to the functional limitations (if any), or which fails to take into account the "large remedial component" ... that creates the legally relevant human rights dimension to what might otherwise be a straightforward biomedical condition.[118]

For the purposes of human rights law, the social model generally leads to a broad understanding of the term "disability". Any biological/physiological impairment, whether real or merely perceived, can be disabling given the social response to it, including features of social design that exclude persons with that impairment from participation.

Therefore, anti-discrimination law in Canada employs a broad understanding of disabilities that provides protection to the whole spectrum of impairments, from the most serious to those not generally considered to be serious at all. This serves an important interest of equality by contributing to a sense that all people operate on a single continuum of abilities or (dis)abilities, rather than being divided into the able-bodied and the disabled.

The social model of disability played a significant role in the negotiations and drafting of the *United Nations Convention on the Rights of Persons with*

---

[117] Of the many discussions of the meaning and implications of the social model of disability in scholarly literature, two of the better ones are: Jerome Bickenbach, *Physical Disability and Social Policy* (Toronto and Buffalo: University of Toronto Press, 1993) and Simi Linton, *Claiming Disability: Knowledge and Identity* (New York and London: New York University Press, 1998).

[118] *Granovsky v. Canada (Minister of Employment and Immigration)*, [2000] S.C.J. No. 29 at para. 26, [2000] 1 S.C.R. 703 (S.C.C.).

Disabilities (CRPD).[119] The Convention was opened for signature by member countries in March 2007, and to date, 147 countries including Canada have signed. The Convention defines "disability" as

> an evolving concept and that disability results from the interaction between persons with impairments and attitudinal and environmental barriers that hinders their full and effective participation in society and on an equal basis with others...[120]

Several of the rights specified in the CRPD have particular relevance to persons with mental disabilities. These include the right to "physical and mental integrity on an equal basis with others";[121] the right to live independently, in a place of one's choice, and to have a range of residential and community support services;[122] the right to "individual autonomy, including the freedom to make one's own choices"[123] and, in Article 12, a guarantee that measures dealing with legal capacity incorporate effective safeguards, including regular review by impartial or judicial authorities. Canada ratified the Convention in March 2010, making one reservation to a possible interpretation of Article 12 as prohibiting laws providing for substitute decision-making.[124] International treaties such as the CRPD do not have force of law within Canada. However, the Supreme Court of Canada has stated that international human rights agreements signed and ratified by Canada can be used to interpret domestic Canadian law.[125] As a signatory country, Canada also commits to the regular states' reporting process established under the Convention.

B. SECTION 15 OF THE CANADIAN CHARTER OF RIGHTS AND FREEDOMS

The national advocacy organization representing persons with disabilities intervened in *Law Society of British Columbia v. Andrews*,[126] the first section 15 case to reach the Supreme Court. The case concerned a challenge by a non-citizen to a law that limited the practice of law to citizens. The interventions by disability and other groups into a case that might have appeared unrelated to their interests made a real difference: the Court issued a judgment that adopted an understanding of section 15 as promoting substantive rather than formal equality, that is, as seeking to ameliorate conditions of disadvantage in Canadian society.

---

[119]   A/RES/61/611 (2006), in force May 3, 2008; ratified by Canada March 11, 2010.

[120]   *Ibid.*, Preamble, s. (e).

[121]   *Ibid.*, art. 17.

[122]   *Ibid.*, art. 18.

[123]   *Ibid.*, art. 3.

[124]   See Department of Foreign Affairs and International Trade, Press Release, "Canada Ratifies UN Convention on the Rights of Persons with Disabilities" (March 11, 2010), online at: <http://www.international.gc.ca/media/aff/news-communiques/2010/99.aspx>.

[125]   *Baker v. Canada (Minister of Citizenship and Immigration)*, [1999] S.C.J. No. 39, [1999] 2 S.C.R. 817 (S.C.C.).

[126]   [1989] S.C.J. No. 6, [1989] 1 S.C.R. 143 (S.C.C.).

Eight years later, the Supreme Court elaborated on its substantive understanding of constitutional equality in a case involving persons with disabilities.
In *Eldridge v. British Columbia (Attorney General)*,[127] a deaf couple whose
child was born prematurely and a deaf individual with various illnesses that required frequent medical attention challenged the failure of the province's public
health insurance plan and Vancouver General Hospital to cover the costs of sign
language interpreters for patients. In a unanimous decision, the Court ruled that
section 15 imposes such an obligation on government if needed to ensure that
persons with disabilities receive the same benefits that other citizens receive
under legislated schemes such as public health insurance. The Court identified
the two main objectives of equality rights to be: (1) to prohibit the attribution of
untrue characteristics based on stereotyping attitudes (for example, racist or sexist attitudes); and (2) to take into account true characteristics (for example, mobility or communication impairments) that act as barriers to the equal enjoyment
of rights and benefits available to mainstream society. The latter objective is
particularly important for persons with disabilities. It gives rise to a duty of accommodation. That is, where governments design schemes providing general
benefits, they are under a duty to accommodate persons with disabilities so that
they have equal enjoyment of those benefits. This duty may be subject to a limit
of reasonableness, or undue hardship.[128]

The *Eldridge* reasoning strongly figured in the Supreme Court's 1999 re-
working of its equality rights analysis in *Law v. Canada (Minister of Employment and Immigration)*.[129] There, the Court reiterated that substantive equality,
including the duty to accommodate, lies at the heart of its understanding of
equality. It went on to state, however, that in order to succeed on section 15
claims, plaintiffs would need to show that impugned government action had
offended their human dignity. This introduced a further step into equality analysis, putting claimants in the position of needing to identify a pejorative or stereotyping element in the state's treatment of their interests. Few section 15 claims
based on physical or mental disability have succeeded before the Court since it
developed the *Law* test.[130]

With respect to mental disability specifically, the Supreme Court has held
claims can be made on the basis of differential treatment, or failure to accommodate, and can be based on a comparison with physical disability. This permitted a successful claim concerning a disability benefits plan that provided inferior

---

[127] [1997] S.C.J. No. 86, [1997] 3 S.C.R. 624 (S.C.C.).

[128] In *Eldridge, ibid.*, at para. 95, the Court found that the cost of sign language interpreters in medical services would amount to a tiny fraction of the province's overall health insurance budget. It
therefore ordered the government of British Columbia to administer its health insurance plans in
"a manner consistent with the requirements of section 15(1)" — *i.e.*, to pay for interpretation
service as part of health insurance.

[129] [1999] S.C.J. No. 12, [1999] 1 S.C.R. 497 (S.C.C.).

[130] The only successful challenge was *Martin v. Nova Scotia (Workers Compensation Board)*,
[2003] S.C.J. No. 54, [2003] 2 S.C.R. 504 (S.C.C.), which dealt with a denial of equal Workers
Compensation Board benefits to persons with chronic pain syndrome.

benefits for employees with a mental disorder than for those with physical impairments.[131]

C.   HUMAN RIGHTS LEGISLATION

The *Canadian Charter of Rights and Freedoms* is part of the Constitution and, as such, applies to the laws of Canada (federal and provincial) and to government actors. The Charter is not, however, the only document protecting equality rights. Each province as well as the federal government has passed human rights statutes which extend rights protections into the most important areas of social activity, including services customarily available to the public (a phrase that incorporates most public and commercial activities), tenancy and employment.[132]

Human rights protections have succeeded in producing a mini-revolution in the way in which employers are required to respond to mental illness in the workplace. The key concept in bringing this revolution about is the duty of accommodation. In a 1999 case, *Meiorin*,[133] the Supreme Court elaborated a powerful understanding of the duty to accommodate in employment. In that case, a female forest firefighter challenged newly introduced standard qualifications as being discriminatory on the grounds of gender. The qualifications included a test of aerobic capacity that could be met by most men in good physical condition, but not by most women. The Court stated that where standard qualifications have the effect of denying employment to an individual on the basis of a protected characteristic, the onus shifts to the employer to establish that the impugned work rule is a *bona fide* work requirement. To do so, the employer must prove that the rule is reasonably necessary to work performance,[134] and that it is

---

[131] *Battlefords and District Co-operative Ltd. v. Gibbs*, [1996] S.C.J. No. 55, [1996] 3 S.C.R. 566 (S.C.C.). Benefits for mental disability lasted only so long as the individual was hospitalized, whereas benefits continued indefinitely for employees with physical disabilities.

[132] A typical statement governing employment is found in s. 13 of the B.C. *Human Rights Code*, R.S.B.C. 1996, c. 210:

(1) A person must not

    (a) refuse to employ or refuse to continue to employ a person, or

    (b) discriminate against a person regarding employment or any term or condition of employment

because of the race, colour, ancestry ... physical or mental disability, sex, sexual orientation or age of that person ...

    .....

(4) Subsections (1) and (2) do not apply with respect to a refusal, limitation, specification or preference based on a bona fide occupational requirement.

[133] *British Columbia (Public Service Employee Relations Commission) v. British Columbia Government and Service Employees' Union (Meiorin)*, [1999] S.C.J. No. 46, [1999] 3 S.C.R. 3 (S.C.C.).

[134] The full three-step test set out by the Court in *Meiorin, ibid.*, at para. 54 is:

    1.   The employer adopted the rule for a reason rationally connected to job performance.

    2.   The employer adopted the rule in an honest and good faith belief that it was necessary to work performance.

impossible to accommodate individual employees sharing the characteristics of the claimant without imposing undue hardship upon the employer.[135] There are relatively few circumstances in which individual accommodation is impossible without causing undue hardship.

This concept has been of extraordinary benefit to employees experiencing mental distress or illness. Employers have an obligation to accommodate the employee's illness to the point of undue hardship. This may mean providing leaves of absence, offering counselling programs, providing the opportunity to move to another position where symptoms, such as stress, may be alleviated, or reorganizing work responsibilities. Even if an employer had not previously been aware of an employee's mental health issue prior to becoming concerned about work performance, the duty to accommodate arises once the information is provided. Employers who believe or suspect that emotional or psychological problems lie behind an employee's poor performance or inappropriate conduct may have a duty to make inquiries and offer accommodation.

The defence that a particular accommodation may cause undue hardship to the employer is difficult to establish. Ontario's *Human Rights Code* describes hardships as including only costs incurred by the employer and health and safety reasons may be cited as hardships.[136] An employer may not establish undue hardship by showing that a particular accommodation will lower workplace morale, disturb customers, or interfere with rights set out in a collective agreement, such as seniority provisions.[137]

Most, if not all, collective agreements now either expressly or implicitly incorporate human rights protections into their terms. Therefore, disputes over particular accommodations, and undue hardship, have become routine matters in the grievance and arbitration world of the organized workplace. It is difficult to overstate how influential this push from the labour relations community is to the regularization of these ideas in Canadian society.[138] While unorganized workplaces may not provide the easy access to arbitration and grievance processes that is true of the unionized sector, the same human rights protections apply to both — recourse, however, must be sought through the human rights complaint, investigation and hearing process.

---

3. The rule is reasonably necessary to work performance. To show this, it must be demonstrated that it is impossible to accommodate individual employees sharing the characteristics of the claimant without imposing undue hardship upon the employer.

In practice, the first two steps rarely emerge as issues, other than in those cases where it is alleged that an employer has acted in bad faith.

[135] *British Columbia (Superintendent of Motor Vehicles) v. British Columbia (Council of Human Rights)*, [1999] S.C.J. No. 73, [1999] 3 S.C.R. 868 (S.C.C.).

[136] R.S.O. 1990, c. H.19, s. 17(2).

[137] For an overview of the duty to accommodate under the Ontario legislation, see Ontario Human Rights Commission, "Policy and Guidelines on Disability and the Duty to Accommodate" (2000), online at: <http://www.ohrc.on.ca/en/resources/Policies/PolicyDisAccom2/pdf>.

[138] Michael Lynk, "Accommodating Disabilities in the Canadian Workplace" (1999) 7 C.L.E.L.J. 183.

While these breakthroughs in legal protections of workers on the basis of mental disability have had a significant impact for persons already in the workforce, it is questionable how helpful they have been for persons who have little or no attachment to the workforce in the first place. This group includes, of course, individuals with serious mental illness. One explanation is that anti-discrimination laws most benefit those persons who are already employed over those seeking employment at the entry level. The argument for accommodating an existing employee to permit her to remain at work is generally strong. Employees will often have the resources of experienced union representatives, employer consultants and arbitrators put at their disposal to work out solutions.[139] This is a quite different situation than that faced by the individual who comes cold to an employment opportunity, asking for accommodations of individual needs, and whose only recourse is to pursue a human rights complaint.[140]

D.   THE AUTISM SERVICES LITIGATION

Significant Charter section 15 litigation concerning mental disability occurred with respect to services for children with autism, or autism spectrum disorder (ASD). The litigation was driven by the demand by parents for a particular treatment modality for their children, intensive behavioural intervention (IBI). Proponents of IBI believe it to be the only currently known effective therapy that ameliorates the symptoms of autism.

In British Columbia, families of children with autism argued that IBI therapy should be provided as a "medically necessary service" under the province's public health insurance program. When the B.C. government refused, the parents proceeded to court, alleging that the refusal constituted discrimination against their children on the grounds of mental disability. The families succeeded before the B.C. Supreme Court and Court of Appeal. The Supreme Court of Canada overturned these decisions in *Auton (Guardian ad litem of) v. British Columbia (Minister of Health)*.[141] In a unanimous judgment, the Court determined that Canada's publicly insured health care system does not extend coverage to all therapeutic measures, but only "medically required" physician services and hospital services. Beyond those services, each provincial government retains the discretion to decide which treatments are sufficiently established and cost-effective to be brought under public coverage.[142] Since children with autism

---

[139] See Daryl A. Cukierman, "Accommodating Mental Illness: Recent Decisions of the Human Rights Tribunal of Ontario" (2009) 19 Employment and Labour Law Reporter 25.

[140] For further discussion of this issue, and an empirical overview of disability cases before human rights tribunals in Canada, see Judith Mosoff, "Is the Human Rights Paradigm 'Able' to Include Disability: Who's In? Who Wins? What? Why?" (2000) Queen's L.J. 225.

[141] [2004] S.C.J. No. 71, [2004] 3 S.C.R. 657 (S.C.C.).

[142] Chief Justice McLachlin described the benefit provided by Canada's health care system as follows (*ibid.*, at para. 35):

> In summary, the legislative scheme does not promise that any Canadian will receive funding for all medically required treatment. All that is conferred is core funding for services provided by medical practitioners, with funding for non-core services left to the

received core medical services equally with all other citizens, they were not the subject of discrimination.

The decision in *Auton* has been subject of extensive criticism by equality rights theorists[143] who find it to be an exercise in the kind of formal equality the Court had criticized in *Andrews* and *Eldridge*. The substantive equality issue in the case, going to whether children with ASD were discriminated against by being limited to the same core therapies as everyone else, was not broached by the Court. Instead, the Court found that IBI was an "experimental" therapy which provincial governments were entitled to fund or not fund in their discretion. In the Court's view, this distinguished the claim in *Auton* from that in *Eldridge*:

> *Eldridge* was concerned with unequal access to a benefit that the law conferred and with *applying* a benefit-granting law in a non-discriminatory fashion. By contrast, this case is concerned with access to a benefit that the law has not conferred. For this reason, *Eldridge* does not assist the petitioners.[144]

Equality rights is a comparative concept. Claimants are required to identify a "comparator group" which is advantaged with respect to the benefit or protection provided by the impugned law, *vis-à-vis* the claimant group. In *Auton* the parents argued that one relevant comparator group was that of "adults with mental illness". That is, they argued that children with ASD are disadvantaged in comparison with adults with mental illness with respect to having their most important therapeutic needs met by public health care. This was a rare occasion when adults with mental illness have been argued to be advantaged relative to another group in society. In actuality, many outpatient mental health services, including the cost of medications, are not covered by public health insurance. Not surprisingly, perhaps, the Supreme Court found this comparison unconvincing.

While the *Auton* decision closed the door on constitutional claims to have IBI services provided as a medical service, other claims were made to obtain IBI through educational and social service systems. A series of claims was launched in Ontario against that government's policy of limiting IBI services to children under the age of six. In *Wynberg v. Ontario*, [145] parents of autistic children challenged the policy under Charter section 15 as constituting discrimination on grounds both of mental disability and age. Following a year-long trial in which several of North America's leading experts on ASD and IBI testified, Kiteley J.

Province's discretion. Thus, the benefit here claimed — funding for all medically required services — was not provided for by the law.

[143] See several essays in two recent collections dealing with s. 15 jurisprudence: S. McIntyre & S. Rogers, *Diminishing Returns: Inequality and the Canadian Charter of Rights and Freedoms* (Markham, ON: LexisNexis Canada, 2006) and F. Faraday, M. Denike & M.K. Stephenson, *Making Equality Rights Real: Securing Substantive Equality Under the Charter* (Toronto: Irwin Law, 2006).

[144] [2004] S.C.J. No. 71 at para. 38, [2004] 3 S.C.R. 657 (S.C.C.) [emphasis in original].

[145] [2005] O.J. No. 1228, 252 D.L.R. (4th) 10 (Ont. S.C.J.).

ruled in the parents' favour on both grounds. In July 2006, the Ontario Court of Appeal granted the government's appeal.[146] With respect to the disability discrimination claim, the Court of Appeal ruled that the claimants failed to establish that with respect to the statutory benefit of "special education services", children with autism were differently treated than other "exceptional students" who were eligible for special education. This was largely an evidentiary question that followed from the way in which the case had been structured before the trial court. Concerning the discrimination claim based on age, the Court of Appeal found that the cut-off at age six did not represent stereotyping of older autistic children as being "irredeemable", and further that the targeting of the IBI program to children under age six corresponded to the pre-school age identified by experts as the "window of opportunity" for IBI.[147]

This may be one instance in which the legal outcome of litigation is less important than its role in mobilizing social forces. In the roughly five years that autism services were the subject of Charter claims in British Columbia and Ontario, IBI services for children with autism greatly expanded across Canada. Several provinces amended legislation in order to make the provision of services for children with developmental disabilities and special needs a more routine and fair process, including new levels of administrative appeal.

At the same time, the relationship of the claim in *Auton* to the social model of disability is problematic. One intervener in the case who identified herself as having autism, Michelle Dawson, opposed the petitioners' claim on the basis that IBI represents a therapy directed at ameliorating or curing the symptoms of autism through behavioural methods. Ms. Dawson opposed the idea underlying the litigation that to be a person with autism is to be faced with ineffable tragedy. Such an idea, she argued, is inconsistent with the social model and its emphasis on acceptance and accommodation of disability.

VII. CONCLUSION

To summarize the direction of Canadian mental health law in a few words is to do a complex subject an injustice. If we are willing to be unjust, however, it seems reasonable to suggest that the law is moving in two directions at the same time. While not necessarily opposed, these directions or trends do not always sit

---

[146] [2006] O.J. No. 2732, 269 D.L.R. (4th) 435 (Ont. C.A.), leave to appeal refused [2006] S.C.C.A. No. 441 (S.C.C.).

[147] *Ibid.*, at para. 53:

> Moreover, from its inception, the IEIP was targeted at the two to five age group. It was designed to take advantage of the window of opportunity that all experts agree these children present at that age. It was designed to meet their particular circumstances. The implementation of a program that is so centred on its target group carries no message that would worsen any mistaken preconception that, because of their age, autistic children age six and over are irredeemable compared to the younger group, even if such a pre-existing stereotype existed. In our view, because the focus of the program was entirely on helping the two to five age group, and because it is so tailored to their circumstances, it cannot be taken to say anything demeaning about older autistic children.

comfortably together. The first trend involves greater scope for the intervention of state and medical authorities in the lives of persons with serious mental illness, in the interests both of treatment and public safety. This can be seen in relaxed civil committal criteria, the arrival of CTOs and increased numbers of persons with mental illness in the criminal justice system.

The second trend, however, involves a growing appreciation of the human rights dimension of mental illness and mental disability. This can be observed in initiatives of the Mental Health Commission of Canada, including in the area of law,[148] and in Canada's ratification of the *United Nations Convention on the Rights of Persons with Disabilities*.

Indeed, this chapter might have been presented in reverse order. A signal achievement of disability rights movements in Canada and abroad in the past 30 years has been to refocus thinking about disability, including mental disability, in terms of human rights issues. This has involved questioning the significance of biology in disadvantaging persons with disabilities when compared with the impact of social determinants of disadvantage. However, the area of disability that has been least amenable to this kind of analysis is that of mental disorder. There, state interventions directed at treatment and public protection have continued to predominate. This corresponds to the contemporary understanding of mental disorder as having neurobiological causes calling for pharmacological treatment. This chapter has given pride of place and attention to the legal interventions that follow from and support this understanding. In future, legislation directed at mental disorder may come to place greater emphasis on social supports and access to therapeutic programs sought out by clients themselves, not mandated by Canadian society.[149] We are not there yet.

---

[148] See the initiatives of the Commission's Advisory Committee on Mental Health and the Law, online at: <http://www.mentalhealthcommission.ca/English/Pages/MentalHealthandtheLaw.aspx>.

[149] For thought-provoking attempts to depict what such legislation might look like, see H. Archibald Kaiser, "Imagining an Equality Promoting Alternative to the Status Quo of Canadian Mental Health Law" (2003) Health L.J. 185 (Special Edition) and "Canadian Mental Health Law: The Slow Process of Redirecting the Ship of State" (2009) 17 Health L.J. 139.

Chapter 9

DEATH, DYING AND DECISION-MAKING ABOUT END OF LIFE CARE

Joan M. Gilmour[*]

I. INTRODUCTION

Legal issues involving decision-making at the end of life have long given rise to concern. The Law Reform Commission of Canada noted that when it designed the first in-depth Canadian study on euthanasia, aiding suicide and cessation of treatment in the mid-1970s, "the question of cessation of treatment and, more generally, that of euthanasia, was a constant and urgent concern among members of the medical profession, a number of lawyers and a large proportion of the Canadian public".[1] That observation remains accurate today. While the law has become more settled in some respects over the years, troubling questions still abound. Technological advances, our growing ability to sustain life in circumstances where doing so would have been an impossibility until recently, and new sensitivity to the discriminatory potential in determinations about end of life care mean that decision-making is becoming increasingly complex and difficult, making the need for authoritative guidance more pressing. Even in areas where the law is clear, such as the criminal prohibition on assisted suicide, deep divisions in values and judgment persist, evidenced by strong arguments that the law is failing Canadians and ought to be changed.[2] Other issues remain highly contentious as well. Yet, despite numerous government and law commission reports and substantial academic commentary recommending reform, governments have been slow to respond.[3]

---

[*] I am grateful for the research assistance of Natasha Razack, Gabrielle Cohen and Paul Martin.

[1] Law Reform Commission of Canada, "Euthanasia, Aiding Suicide and Cessation of Treatment", Working Paper 28 (Ottawa: Department of Supply and Services Canada, 1982) at 11.

[2] See, *e.g.*, J. Downie, *Dying Justice: A Case for Decriminalizing Euthanasia and Assisted Suicide in Canada* (Toronto: University of Toronto Press, 2004); B. Sneiderman, "Latimer in the Supreme Court: Necessity, Compassionate Homicide, and Mandatory Sentencing" (2001) 64 Sask. L. Rev. 511.

[3] See, *e.g.*, Law Reform Commission of Canada, *Euthanasia, Aiding Suicide and Cessation of Treatment* (Ottawa: Minister of Supply and Services Canada, 1983); Senate of Canada, *Of Life and Death: Special Senate Committee Report on Euthanasia and Assisted Suicide* (Ottawa: Minister of Supply and Services Canada, 1995); Senate of Canada, Special Subcommittee to Update "Of Life and Death", *Quality End-of-Life Care: The Right of Every Canadian* (Ottawa: Senate of Canada, 2000), online at: <http://www.parl.gc.ca/36/2/parlbus/commbus/senate/com-e/upda-

Given the gravity and difficulty of these issues, and given that they routinely arise in decision-making about end of life care, it is surprising that they have seldom been the subject of legal consideration in Canada. For the most part, there has been little litigation and only limited legislative reform. At the federal level, despite extensive deliberation by a Special Committee of the Senate on euthanasia and assisted suicide, as well as an earlier working paper and report by the Law Reform Commission of Canada, the government has not acted to implement legislative change. Private Members' Bills introduced in the House of Commons over the years have died on the order paper or have been defeated.[4] Provinces and territories have been more active on the legislative front, enacting legislation to govern substitute decision-making in the event of decisional incapacity, and in some jurisdictions, codifying requirements for obtaining consent to health care.[5] These initiatives are a welcome advance because they establish a legislatively sanctioned framework for decision-making about health care, including life-sustaining treatment. However, they still leave important questions unanswered.

Although there is a need to clarify and/or reform the law in some respects, it is important to emphasize that many decisions about end of life care are made every day in Canada, and that the great majority of them are absolutely unexceptional from the point of view of law: they are clearly legal. These decisions are already so difficult for all involved that they ought not be made still more

---

e/rep-e/repfinjun00-e.htm>; S. Carstairs, *Still Not There: Quality End-of-Life Care: A Progress Report* (June 2005), online at: <http://www.sen.parl.gc.ca/scarstairs/PalliativeCare/Still%20Not%20There%20June%202005.pdf>; S. Carstairs, *Raising the Bar: A Roadmap for the Future of Palliative Care in Canada* (June 2010), online at: <http://sen.parl.gc.ca/scarstairs/PalliativeCare/Raising%20the%20Bar%20June%202010%20(2).pdf>; Manitoba Law Reform Commission, *Withholding or Withdrawing Life Sustaining Medical Treatment*, Report #109 (Winnipeg: Manitoba Law Reform Commission, 2003); J. Gilmour, *Study Paper on Assisted Suicide, Euthanasia and Foregoing Treatment* (with additional chapters by K. Capen, B. Sneiderman & M. Verhoef) (Toronto: Ontario Law Reform Commission, 1996); J. Downie, *ibid.* In 2009, the Quebec National Assembly established a Select Committee to examine the issue of dying with dignity; see online: <http://www.assnat.qc.ca/en/travaux-parlementaires/commissions/csmd-39-1/index.html>.

4   The most recent of these, Bill C-384, *An Act to amend the Criminal Code (right to die with dignity)*, introduced in 2009 by MP Francine Lalonde, was defeated. It would have permitted medical practitioners to assist individuals who are terminally ill or experiencing severe physical or mental pain without any prospect of relief to "die with dignity". See C-384, online at: <http://www2.parl.gc.ca/HousePublications/Publication.aspxDocid=308458/&file=4>; see also *Of Life and Death, ibid.*, App. E, "Legislative Proposals Previously Introduced to Parliament" at A-33–A-34.

5   See, *e.g.*, *Substitute Decisions Act, 1992*, S.O. 1992, c. 30; *Health Care Consent Act, 1996*, S.O. 1996, c. 2, Sched. A; *Advance Health Care Directives Act*, S.N.L. 1995, c. A-4.1; *Health Care Directives and Substitute Health Care Decision Makers Act*, S.S. 1997, c. H-0.001; *Health Act*, R.S.Y. 2002, c. 106; *Public Curator Act*, R.S.Q., c. C-81; *Civil Code of Québec*, S.Q. 1991, c. 64, arts. 10-34; *Consent to Treatment and Health Care Directives Act*, R.S.P.E.I. 1988, c. C-17.2; *Personal Directives Act*, R.S.A. 2000, c. P-6; *Representation Agreement Act*, R.S.B.C. 1996, c. 405 (and supplement); *Health Care Directives Act*, C.C.S.M. c. H27; *Personal Directives Act*, S.N.S. 2008, c. 8; *Infirm Persons Act*, R.S.N.B. 2000, c. I-8.

fraught by unwarranted concern about what is and is not legally permissible. While there are issues that urgently require guidance, cases in which the law is unsettled are a minority.

This chapter explains the law governing refusal of treatment by patients who are able to make their own decisions about health care, and the legal principles applicable to decision-making about life-sustaining treatment when patients are not competent to do so. It reviews the criminal prohibitions on assisted suicide and euthanasia, and examines how those laws have been applied. It highlights areas where the law is unclear or contentious, and indicates issues requiring additional clarification or reform. Developments in other jurisdictions where similar issues have arisen, as well as relevant policies that may assist in decision-making are identified as well. This summary of the current state of the law and the controversies and debates that remain outstanding will delineate the legal parameters that govern decision-making, reinforce the standards that patients are entitled to expect as part of adequate end of life care (such as appropriate pain management), and guide decision-makers as new issues arise.

II.   WITHHOLDING AND WITHDRAWING POTENTIALLY LIFE-SUSTAINING TREATMENT

A.   DECISIONALLY CAPABLE PATIENTS

1.   Adults

Health care providers must obtain legally valid consent before treating patients. This requirement is based on individuals' right to bodily integrity, and the respect for autonomy that is basic to the common law. Justice Cardozo's early pronouncement that "Every human being of adult years and sound mind has the right to determine what shall be done with his own body" has become a guiding precept in decision-making in this area.[6] Competent individuals can decide about the treatment to which they will consent, and also what treatment they will refuse. In *Malette v. Shulman*, a physician who knew an unconscious patient carried a Jehovah's Witness card refusing blood under any circumstances was held liable for battery when he administered a blood transfusion needed to save her life.[7] As the Ontario Court of Appeal noted, the patient had chosen to make her refusal to consent to blood transfusions known in the only way she could, and in doing so, had validly restricted the treatment that could be provided. Her directions governed in a later period of incompetence. The court clearly identified the rights to self-determination and bodily integrity as the controlling values in the

---

[6]   *Schloendorff v. Society of New York Hospital*, 105 N.E. 92 at 93 (N.Y. 1914).

[7]   *Malette v. Shulman*, [1990] O.J. No. 450, 72 O.R. (2d) 417 (Ont. C.A.), affg [1987] O.J. No. 1180, 63 O.R. (2d) 243 (Ont. H.C.J.). See also *Hobbs v. Robertson*, [2004] B.C.J. No. 1689, 2004 BCSC 1099 (B.C.S.C.) (release executed by patient refusing blood products because of religious faith relieved physician of liability for death of patient resulting from negligently performed operation when effects of negligence could have been remedied by blood transfusion).

doctor-patient relationship: "the right to determine what shall be done with one's own body is a fundamental right in our society. The concepts inherent in this right are the bedrock upon which the principles of self-determination and individual autonomy are based".[8]

The right to consent to or refuse treatment has constitutional dimensions as well. In *Fleming v. Reid*, the Ontario Court of Appeal held that a statute depriving involuntary patients of any right to have prior competent decisions about medication taken into account during a later period of incompetence breached their constitutionally protected right to security of the person.[9] Writing for the court, Robins J. stated that:

> The common law right to bodily integrity and personal autonomy is so entrenched in the traditions of our law to be ranked as fundamental and deserving of the highest order of protection. This right forms an essential part of an individual's security of the person and must be included in the liberty interests protected by s. 7 [of the *Canadian Charter of Rights and Freedoms*[10]]. Indeed, in my view, the common law right to determine what shall be done with one's own body and the constitutional right to security of the person, both of which are founded on the belief in the dignity and autonomy of each individual, can be treated as co-extensive.[11]

A competent patient's refusal of treatment must be honoured by health care providers regardless of the individual's motive, and regardless of whether others consider it ill advised.[12]

Courts have affirmed that patients have the right to refuse treatment even when doing so will result in death. In *B. (N.) v. Hôtel-Dieu de Québec*, Nancy B., a decisionally capable young woman, sought an injunction requiring the hospital in which she was a patient, its staff and her physicians to refrain from administering treatment without her consent, and to stop treatment in progress at her request.[13] Since developing Guillain-Barré Syndrome (a neurological disease) three years earlier, she had been permanently paralyzed and unable to breathe without assistance. She wanted to be removed from the ventilator that sustained her life, but was physically unable to perform the removal herself. The suit was not contested, but the defendant hospital and her physician were concerned about their potential criminal liability. The Quebec Superior Court af-

---

8   *Malette, ibid.*, at para. 41.
9   *Fleming v. Reid*, [1991] O.J. No. 1083, 4 O.R. (3d) 74 (Ont. C.A.).
10   *Canadian Charter of Rights and Freedoms*, Part I of the *Constitution Act, 1982*, being Schedule B to the *Canada Act 1982* (U.K.), c. 11.
11   *Fleming v. Reid*, [1991] O.J. No. 1083 at para. 39, 4 O.R. (3d) 74 (Ont. C.A.). See also *Conway v. Jacques*, [2002] O.J. No. 2333 at para. 28, 59 O.R. (3d) 735 (Ont. C.A.).
12   *Fleming v. Reid, ibid.*, at paras. 30-36.
13   [1992] Q.J. No. 1, 86 D.L.R. (4th) 385 (Que. S.C.). See also *Manoir de la Pointe Bleue (1978) Inc. c. Corbeil*, [1992] J.Q. no 98, R.J.Q. 712 (Que. C.S.) (granting petition of a long-term care institution for a declaration that it must neither administer treatment nor transfer a patient elsewhere without consent when the patient, a 35-year-old man rendered quadriplegic in an accident, had executed a legal directive requesting that he be allowed to die by starvation).

firmed her right to refuse continued treatment and made an order permitting her physician to stop respiratory support when she so requested, and to ask the hospital for any necessary assistance "so that everything takes place while respecting the dignity of the plaintiff".[14] Several weeks after this decision, Nancy B. requested that ventilator support be discontinued; she died shortly afterwards.[15] While the court based its decision on the Quebec *Civil Code*'s requirement of patient consent to treatment, the Supreme Court of Canada has confirmed that the judgment in *B. (N.) v. Hôtel-Dieu de Québec* correctly states the law in common law provinces as well:

> Canadian courts have recognized a common law right of patients to refuse consent to medical treatment, or to demand that treatment, once commenced, be withdrawn or discontinued (*Ciarlariello v. Schachter* ...). This has been specifically recognized to exist even if the withdrawal or refusal of treatment may result in death (*Nancy B. v. Hotel Dieu de Quebec* ... and *Malette v. Shulman* ...).[16] [citations omitted]

In sum, decisionally capable patients can refuse treatment, even if life-sustaining, can withdraw consent to treatment once commenced and can require that it be discontinued.[17]

2.   Mature Minors

In order to consent to or refuse treatment, an individual must be decisionally capable. The law presumes decisional capacity, that is, that an individual has sufficient ability to understand and appreciate the nature and consequences of treatment and its alternatives to be able to make a decision about whether to proceed with it or not.[18] Obviously, young children cannot satisfy that test. However, many older minors are decisionally capable. Under the "mature minor rule" that is part of common law, when a minor is able to understand and appreciate the nature and consequences of a treatment decision, he or she can give legally valid consent to treatment, and physicians cannot rely on parental consent instead.[19] However, although a mature minor can consent to medically recommended treatment, whether and to what extent he or she can either refuse such treatment, or consent to treatment that is not beneficial or therapeutic has

---

[14]   *B. (N.) v. Hôtel-Dieu de Québec, ibid.*, at 389-90.

[15]   B. Sneiderman, "Decision-Making at the End of Life" in Jocelyn Downie, Timothy Caulfield & Colleen Flood, eds., *Canadian Health Law and Policy*, 2d ed. (Markham, ON: LexisNexis Canada, 2002) at 504.

[16]   *Rodriguez v. British Columbia (Attorney General)*, [1993] S.C.J. No. 94 at para. 156, [1993] 3 S.C.R. 519 (S.C.C.).

[17]   *Ciarlariello v. Schachter*, [1993] S.C.J. No. 46, [1993] 2 S.C.R. 119 (S.C.C.).

[18]   *C. (J.S.) v. Wren*, [1986] A.J. No. 1166, [1987] 2 W.W.R. 669 (Alta. C.A.); *Starson v. Swayze*, [2003] S.C.J. No. 33, [2003] 1 S.C.R. 722 (S.C.C.).

[19]   *Johnston v. Wellesley Hospital*, [1970] O.J. No. 1741, 17 D.L.R. (3d) 139 (Ont. H.C.J.); *C. (J.S.) v. Wren, ibid.*; *Van Mol (Guardian ad litem of) v. Ashmore*, [1999] B.C.J. No. 31, 168 D.L.R. (4th) 637 (B.C.C.A.), leave to appeal refused [2000] B.C.J. No. 1474, 188 D.L.R. (4th) 327 (B.C.C.A.).

been less clear.[20] The argument that a minor can only consent to care that would be of benefit is sometimes referred to as "the welfare principle".[21] It suggests that a mature minor can only make those decisions about medical care that others would consider to be in his or her interests;[22] as such, it challenges the extent to which the law will be guided by a commitment to mature minors' interests in self-determination and autonomy, similar to that which prevails *vis-à-vis* adults.

In some provinces, aspects of this question have been addressed by legislation. Statutory provisions may explicitly incorporate welfare principles into decision-making.[23] Other provinces provide that on reaching a specified age, minors are presumed capable of consenting to treatment.[24] Still others could be understood to obviate the mature minor rule in whole or part, at least when child welfare authorities are involved. In Alberta, British Columbia and Manitoba, provincial appellate courts had held that child welfare legislation displaced the common law mature minor doctrine, such that child welfare authorities could be authorized to consent to treatment considered necessary by treating physicians, even when the minor was decisionally capable and refused treatment.[25]

This interpretation of child welfare legislation was rejected by the Supreme Court of Canada in a 2009 decision, *Manitoba (Director of Child and Family*

---

[20] See, generally, J. Gilmour, "Children, Adolescents and Health Care" in *Canadian Health Law and Policy*, 2d ed. (Markham, ON: LexisNexis Canada, 2007) at 213-19; J. Costello, "If I Can Say Yes, Why Can't I Say No? Adolescents at Risk and the Right to Give or Withhold Consent to Health Care" in R.S. Humm, ed., *Child, Parent and State: Law and Policy Reader* (Philadelphia: Temple University Press, 1994) at 490-503.

[21] Manitoba Law Reform Commission, *Minors' Consent to Health Care* (Report No. 91) (Winnipeg: The Commission, 1995) at 5.

[22] B. Sneiderman, J. Irvine & P. Osborne, *Canadian Medical Law: An Introduction for Physicians, Nurses and Other Health Care Professionals*, 2d ed. (Toronto: Carswell, 1995) at 48-49; Manitoba Law Reform Commission, *ibid.*, at 5-7.

[23] For instance, in Quebec the *Civil Code* provides that while a minor over 14 can consent to care, the consent of the person having parental authority is also necessary if the care sought is not medically required, entails a serious health risk, and may cause grave and permanent effects — art. 17; F. Campeau, "Children's Right to Health under Quebec Civil Law" in B. Knoppers, ed., *Canadian Child Health Law* (Toronto: Thomson Educational Publishing, 1992) at 209-58; see also R. Kouri & S. Philips-Nootens, "Civil Liability of Physicians Under Quebec Law" in Jocelyn Downie, Timothy Caulfield & Colleen Flood, *Canadian Health Law and Policy*, 3d ed. (Markham, ON: LexisNexis Canada, 2007) at 161, 164. In British Columbia, a minor's consent to treatment is effective if the health care provider is satisfied not only that the minor is decisionally capable, but also that the health care is in his or her best interests: *Infants Act*, R.S.B.C. 1996, c. 223, s. 17. New Brunswick has a similar legislative provision governing decisionally capable minors under the age of 16, who can validly consent to medical treatment, provided the medical practitioner or dentist is of the opinion that it is in the best interests of the minor and his or her continuing health and well-being: *Medical Consent of Minors Act*, S.N.B. 1976, c. M-6.1, s. 3.

[24] See, *e.g.*, *Child and Family Services*, C.C.S.M. c. C80, s. 25(2).

[25] *Alberta (Director of Child Welfare) v. H. (B.)*, [2002] A.J. No. 518 (Alta. Q.B.); *U. (C.) v. McGonigle*, [2003] A.J. No. 238 (Alta. C.A.); *B. (S.J.) (Litigation guardian of) v. British Columbia (Director of Child, Family and Community Services)*, [2005] B.C.J. No. 836, 42 B.C.L.R. (4th) 321 (B.C.S.C.); *Manitoba (Director of Child and Family Services) v. C. (A.)*, [2007] M.J. No. 26 (Man. C.A.).

Services v. C. (A.).[26] A.C. was almost 15 years old when she was admitted to hospital because of gastrointestinal bleeding caused by Crohn's Disease. Her physicians concluded blood transfusions were necessary to prevent serious risk to her health, and perhaps her life. She and her parents, who were members of the Jehovah's Witness faith, strongly opposed transfusions on religious grounds. The Manitoba Director of Child and Family Services sought a court order authorizing treatment. The lower courts had held that pursuant to the Manitoba legislation, the court could authorize medically recommended treatment for a child found in need of protection that it concluded was in her best interests, whether she consented or not. A.C. and her parents appealed, asserting a breach of her Charter rights. The Supreme Court of Canada held that a mature minor's decisions about treatment must be taken into account regardless of her age, although it upheld the lower court's decision authorizing transfusions because her capacity to decide about this treatment had never been judicially determined. Thus, although A.C. succeeded on the applicable principle, she lost in fact. The Court held that in child protection proceedings, effect can and should be given to a younger minor's decisions about treatment if he or she is sufficiently mature and independent, but that this should occur through the vehicle of the statutory best interests test. Because child protection authorities are only involved in a limited class of cases where the consequences of refusing treatment will be very grave, then "the ineffability inherent in the concept of 'maturity' ... justifies the state's retaining an overarching power to determine whether allowing the child to exercise his or her autonomy in a given situation actually accords with his or her best interests".[27] Writing for the majority, Abella J. commented:

> The more a court is satisfied that a child is capable of making a mature, independent decision on his or her own behalf, the greater the weight that will be given to his or her views when a court is exercising its discretion under [the statute]...If...the court is persuaded that the necessary level of maturity exists, it seems to me necessarily to follow that the adolescent's views ought to be respected.[28]

By adding this gloss to its interpretation, the Court affirmed both the constitutionality of the statutory best interests test in child welfare legislation and young people's rights to autonomy and bodily integrity.

Questions remain about the applicability of the welfare principle and the extent to which the general regime governing consent to health care in a province or territory will apply to mature minors. The Court's reasoning in *C. (A.)* about mature minors' decision-making abilities and rights would apply beyond the context of child protection proceedings, although it is not yet clear whether in such cases, consideration of a mature minor's decisions about treatment when the consequences will be very grave must still be routed through the best interests test in the absence of a statutory requirement to do so. The tension between

---

[26] [2009] S.C.J. No. 30, [2009] 2 S.C.R. 181 (S.C.C.).

[27] *Ibid.*, at para. 86.

[28] *Ibid.*, at para. 87.

giving effect to the value of autonomy and the importance of protecting a minor's life and health, as one who is still considered vulnerable, is evident. It is mitigated somewhat by judicial recognition that the degree of understanding and appreciation of the consequences of the treatment and its alternatives that is required for a finding of decisional capacity will vary with the gravity of the decision.[29] Refusing treatment that is necessary to preserve life legitimately requires a greater appreciation of the ramifications of the decision than refusing less serious treatment. That is not to say that a mature minor can never reject life-sustaining treatment, but that the minor must have sufficient judgment to do so, and that a conclusion the minor is decisionally capable to make such a choice should be subjected to closer scrutiny. The Supreme Court identified a number of factors relevant to that determination in *C. (A.).*[30]

Decisions by mature minors to refuse life-sustaining treatment have been upheld by the courts in some instances, particularly when the refusal was grounded on religious belief. In *Walker (Litigation guardian of) v. Region 2 Hospital Corp.* and *Re Y. (A.)*, both of which involved 15-year-old boys with cancer who were Jehovah's Witnesses and refused blood needed in connection with chemotherapy, courts concluded that the boys were mature minors and decisionally capable, based on their thoughtful consideration of both their religious beliefs and their decisions about treatment, as well as their experience of living with the disease.[31] However, prognoses in both of these cases were very poor in any event, the treatment was onerous and the boys' physicians advised that the treatment required their patients' support in order for it to have a chance of success.[32] In these circumstances, it would have been difficult to justify the treatment as being in their best interests.

The conjunction of being an adolescent with firmly held religious beliefs and a grave illness is not always sufficient to support a finding of decisional capacity, however. While religious faith is a positive and valued attribute, it cannot be equated with, and does not necessarily imply, a co-existing capacity to decide about treatment and comprehend the reasonably foreseeable consequences of such decisions.[33] A more positive prognosis may also affect a court's determination, or at least, its assessment of whether a minor actually comprehends what the treatment offers, and what refusing it means. In *B. (S.J.) v. British Columbia (Director of Child, Family and Community Services)*, a decision that pre-dates *C. (A.)* in which the British Columbia Supreme Court relied on

---

[29]   *Ibid.*, at paras. 94-96. See also *Children's Aid Society of Metropolitan Toronto v. H. (T.)*, [1996] O.J. No. 2578, 138 D.L.R. (4th) 144 at 171 (Ont. Gen. Div.).

[30]   *Manitoba v. C. (A.), ibid.*, at para. 96.

[31]   *Walker (Litigation guardian of) v. Region 2 Hospital Corp.*, [1994] N.B.J. No. 626, 150 N.B.R. (2d) 362 (N.B.C.A.); *Re Y. (A.)*, [1993] N.J. No. 197, 111 Nfld. & P.E.I.R. 91 (Nfld. U.F.C.). See also *Children's Aid Society of Metropolitan Toronto v. K. (L.D.)*, [1985] O.J. No. 803, 48 R.F.L. (2d) 164 (Ont. Prov. Ct.).

[32]   *Walker, ibid.*, at 382; *Re Y. (A.), ibid.*, at 95, 96.

[33]   *Children's Aid Society of Metropolitan Toronto v. H. (T.)*, [1996] O.J. No. 2578 (Ont. Gen. Div.).

provincial child welfare legislation to order treatment over a mature minor's objections, the estimated survival rate with the treatment proposed (including the administration of blood) was 70 per cent.[34]

In order for consent to treatment to be valid, the person concerned must not only be able to understand and appreciate the necessary information about treatments, alternatives, and consequences, but also able to make a choice that is voluntary. In *Re D. (T.T.)*,[35] the court held that a 13-year-old boy suffering from osteosarcoma (bone cancer) who refused consent to medically recommended chemotherapy and amputation of his leg was not a mature minor. Justice Rothery concluded that the boy was so deeply influenced by his father (who had given him inaccurate information about his condition, the treatment proposed and the likelihood that non-medical alternative therapies could be successful) that he did not understand and appreciate the result of refusing the treatment proposed and, further, that the structure and dynamics of his family were such that he could not make a voluntary decision about treatment in any event. Mental illness can also affect an otherwise decisionally capable individual's ability to understand and appreciate information, and to make an independent judgment.[36]

A final issue that arises in this area concerns the relationship between the courts' *parens patriae* jurisdiction, which is to be exercised to protect those who are vulnerable, and both legislation extending the presumption of capacity to older minors, and the common law rights of a mature minor.[37] The tension between the sometimes contradictory underlying policies is evident, and authorities are few. In New Brunswick, the Court of Appeal suggested in *Walker (Litigation guardian of) v. Region 2 Hospital Corp.* that once it had determined that a minor was mature and decisionally capable, its *parens patriae* jurisdiction was displaced; however, as noted previously, it had also concluded that blood transfusions were not in the minor's best interests in any event.[38] Courts in other provinces have reached the opposite conclusion, holding that in the context of decisions about health care, the common law *parens patriae* jurisdiction is not

---

[34]   [2005] B.C.J. No. 836 at para. 8, 42 B.C.L.R. (4th) 321 (B.C.S.C.).

[35]   [1999] S.J. No. 143, 171 D.L.R. (4th) 761 (Sask. Q.B.). Shortly after the court released its decision, the boy's physicians discovered that the cancer had spread, and the proposed treatment could not help him. His parents tried alternative health therapies and other experimental treatment, but he died a few months later (see J. Gilmour, "Children, Adolescents and Health Care" in Jocelyn Downie, Timothy Caulfield & Colleen Flood, *Canadian Health Law and Policy*, 2d ed. (Markham, ON: LexisNexis Canada, 2002) at 218).

[36]   See, *e.g.*, *Katzman* (1995), Ont. Gen. Div. No. 132/95; R. Geist, D. Katzman & J. Colangelo, "The Consent to Treatment Act and an Adolescent with Anorexia Nervosa" (1996) 16 Health L. Can. 110. But see *Re W. (A Minor)*, [1992] 4 All E.R. 627 (C.A.).

[37]   In Manitoba, for instance, the *Child and Family Services Act*, C.C.S.M. c. C80 was amended to provide that child welfare authorities shall not authorize medical treatment for children apprehended under the Act who are 16 years or older without the consent of the child: S.M. 1995, c. 23, s. 2.

[38]   [1994] N.B.J. No. 626, 150 N.B.R. (2d) 362 (N.B.C.A.); *Kennett Estate v. Manitoba (Attorney General)*, [1998] M.J. No. 337, 129 Man. R. (2d) 244 (Man. C.A.).

ousted by legislation, or that legislation has preserved *parens patriae* powers.[39] Taking these cases as a whole, it is apparent that legislation will seldom be held to have supplanted courts' *parens patriae* powers over minors entirely; rather, the two will co-exist and supplement each other.

3.   Limitations

Obvious limitations on the right to consent to and refuse treatment are found in sections 14 and 241 of the *Criminal Code*, which vitiate the effect of consent to one's own death and prohibit aiding suicide.[40] In *Rodriguez v. British Columbia (Attorney General)*, an unsuccessful challenge to the constitutionality of the prohibition on assisted suicide, the Supreme Court of Canada held that, although Sue Rodriguez had the right to refuse even life-preserving treatment, she did not have a right to assistance in bringing about her own death, either at common law or under the *Canadian Charter of Rights and Freedoms*.[41] The Court maintained the distinction between refusing treatment, which is permissible even when death will result, and assisting in taking a life, which is unlawful. However, the difference between what constitutes assisting a patient to refuse treatment and assisting the patient to die is not always so clear in practice.[42] In the case of Nancy B., for instance, the actions of third persons removing her from the venti-lator were characterized as assisting her to refuse continued treatment. They could equally well have been characterized as assisting her to die, since the re-sult that would follow (and indeed, was intended) was obvious to all. Nonethe-less, whether always logically defensible or not, the difference in legal consequences between the two is clear.

B.   DECISIONALLY INCAPABLE PATIENTS

1.   Patients with Advance Directives

Most Canadian provinces and territories have passed legislation making provi-sion for some form of advance directive. While referred to by different names (personal directive, health care directive, power of attorney for personal care, and others), they are meant to provide people who are decisionally capable with a means to retain some control over decisions about their treatment in the event of a later period of incompetence. The statutory regimes are not uniform, but the types of directives permitted fall into two basic categories. Advance directives may allow a decisionally capable individual either to designate someone to make decisions about health care on his or her behalf (proxy directive) or to specify types of treatment that he or she wants accepted or rejected, should the

---

[39]   *Ney v. Canada (Attorney General)*, [1993] B.C.J. No. 993, 79 B.C.L.R. (2d) 47 at 59 (B.C.S.C.); *B. (R.) v. Children's Aid Society of Metropolitan Toronto*, [1994] S.C.J. No. 24, [1995] 1 S.C.R. 315 (S.C.C.).

[40]   R.S.C. 1985, c. C-46.

[41]   [1993] S.C.J. No. 94, [1993] 3 S.C.R. 519 (S.C.C.).

[42]   B. Sneiderman, "The Rodriguez Case: Where Do We Go from Here?" (1999) 2 Health L.J. 1.

need arise (instructional directive). It may also be possible to combine the two. Some provinces allow for reciprocity as well, such that advance directives executed in other jurisdictions can be honoured.[43]

Since statutory regimes governing advance directives and consent to health care vary from province to province, the specific provisions in the jurisdiction in question should be reviewed to determine what is permitted.[44] Where a patient has executed a legally valid advance directive that is applicable in the circumstances, then the patients' instructions (as to the treatment, decision-maker or both) must be followed. Substitute decision-makers' authority will be limited by applicable statutory provisions.[45]

2.   Patients without Advance Directives: Prior Capable Instructions or Wishes

In many respects, legislation governing advance directives, substitute decision-making and consent to health care has overtaken the common law. However, there are Canadian jurisdictions without legislation on the subject; even where legislation is in place, it may not apply to particular situations, or an individual

---

[43]   S. Carstairs, *Still Not There: Quality End-of-Life Care: A Progress Report* (June 2005), online at: <http://www.sen.parl.gc.ca/scarstairs/PalliativeCare/Still%20Not%20There%20June%202005.pdf>.

[44]   Ontario: *Substitute Decisions Act, 1992*, S.O. 1992, c. 30, *Health Care Consent Act, 1996*, S.O. 1996, c. 2, Sched. A; Newfoundland and Labrador: *Advance Health Care Directives Act*, S.N.L. 1995, c. A-4.1; Saskatchewan: *Health Care Directives and Substitute Health Care Decision Makers Act*, S.S. 1997, c. H-0.001; Yukon: *Health Act*, R.S.Y. 2002, c. 106, *Adult Protection and Decision-Making Act*, S.Y. 2003, c. 21, Sched. A; Northwest Territories: no legislation, although the *Powers of Attorney Act*, S.N.W.T. 2001, c. 15 may support the creation of a living will; Nunavut: no legislation; Quebec: *Public Curator Act*, R.S.Q., c. C-81, *Civil Code of Québec*, S.Q. 1991, c. 64, arts. 10-34; Prince Edward Island: *Consent to Treatment and Health Care Directives Act*, R.S.P.E.I. 1988, c. C-17.2; Alberta: *Personal Directives Act*, R.S.A. 2000, c. P-6; British Columbia: *Representation Agreement Act*, R.S.B.C. 1996, c. 405 (and supplement); Manitoba: *Health Care Directives Act*, C.C.S.M. c. H27; Nova Scotia: *Personal Directives Act*, S.N.S. 2008, c. 8; New Brunswick: *Infirm Persons Act*, R.S.N.B. 2000, c. I-8. In British Columbia, the *Adult Guardianship and Personal Planning Statutes Amendment Act, 2006*, 2nd Sess., 38th Parl. would formalize the status of advance directives (instructional directives), in addition to representation agreements (proxy directives) that are already recognized (first reading April 27, 2006), online at: <http://www.leg.bc.ca/38th2nd/1st_read/gov32-1.htm>.

[45]   For instance, physicians owe an independent duty of care to the patient, not only at common law but pursuant to s. 215 of the *Criminal Code*, R.S.C. 1985, c. C-46: "Everyone is under a legal duty ... to provide necessaries of life to a person under his charge if that person is unable, by reason of ... illness ... to withdraw himself from that charge." If a physician had reason to believe the substitute decision-maker's instructions were not in keeping with the prior capable wishes or, failing that, best interests of the patient, the physician cannot simply comply with such instructions: see, generally, B. Sneiderman, "Decision-Making at the End of Life" in Jocelyn Downie, Timothy Caulfield & Colleen Flood, eds., *Canadian Health Law and Policy*, 2d ed. (Markham, ON: LexisNexis Butterworths, 2002) at 510. For an example of constraints on substitute decision-makers, see the *Health Care (Consent) and Care Facility (Admission) Act*, R.S.B.C. 1996, c. 181, s. 18, limiting the ability of temporary substitute decision-makers to refuse consent to health care necessary to preserve life.

may not have complied with the legislative requirements for a valid advance directive. Outside Quebec, the common law will govern in the absence of legislation. Decisions such as *Malette v. Shulman* establish that at common law, an individual's instructions about future care or the identity of designated decision-makers should prevail in treatment decisions after the onset of incapacity.[46] Both *Malette v. Shulman* and *Fleming v. Reid* suggest that such directions need not have been expressed in any particular manner.[47] Judicial recognition of advance instructions in cases such as these is consistent with the very high value that the law places on self-determination.

In some jurisdictions, that approach is now mandated by legislation as well. In Ontario, for instance, the *Health Care Consent Act, 1996* directs the substitute decision-maker for a decisionally incapable person who has not executed a power of attorney for personal care (the term used to refer to advance directives in that province) to follow the individual's prior capable wishes about health care, if these are known and applicable in the circumstances.[48] "Wishes" need not be contained in a power of attorney to be binding; they can be expressed orally, in writing or in any other manner.[49] Statutory regimes vary; regard should be had to the legislation that governs in the jurisdiction in question.

3.   Patients without Advance Directives: Best Interests

Most people have not executed an advance directive, and their wishes about treatment may not be known. Even existing advance directives may be inapplicable in the circumstances. Where a patient is decisionally incapable and the substitute decision-maker does not know of a preference that applies to the situation and is sufficiently precise to guide treatment decisions, then both at common law and under applicable statutory regimes, determinations about treatment are to be made in the patient's best interests.[50]

---

[46]   [1990] O.J. No. 450, 72 O.R. (2d) 417 (Ont. C.A.), affg [1987] O.J. No. 1180, 63 O.R. (2d) 243 (Ont. H.C.J.). The Canadian Medical Association, Canadian Nurses Association and Canadian Healthcare Association issued a "Joint Statement on Preventing and Resolving Ethical Conflicts Involving Health Care Providers and Persons Receiving Care" that recognizes as one of the principles of the therapeutic relationship that health care decisions should be consistent with the patient's known preferences, either found in an advance directive or communicated orally: (1999) 160:12 CMAJ 1757, 1758, online at: <http://policybase.cma.ca/dbtw-wpd/PolicyPDF/PD99-03.pdf>.

[47]   *Malette v. Shulman, ibid.*, at 431; *Fleming v. Reid*, [1991] O.J. No. 1083, 4 O.R. (3d) 74 at 85-86 (Ont. C.A.). *Malette* was cited with approval in *Rodriguez v. British Columbia (Attorney General)*, [1993] S.C.J. No. 94, [1993] 3 S.C.R. 519 at 598 (S.C.C.).

[48]   S.O. 1996, c. 2, Sched. A, s. 21.

[49]   *Ibid.*, s. 5.

[50]   As to the common law, see *E. (Mrs.) v. Eve*, [1986] S.C.J. No. 60, 31 D.L.R. (4th) 2 (S.C.C.); for an example of a statutory best interests test and its application, see the *Health Care Consent Act, 1996*, S.O. 1996, c. 2, Sched. A, s. 21; *Barbulov v. Cirone*, [2009] O.J. No. 1439 at para. 48 (Ont. S.C.J.) (grantor of power of attorney for personal care must know and approve of its contents); *Conway v. Jacques*, [2002] O.J. No. 2333, 59 O.R. (3d) 735 (Ont. C.A.) (when patient's prior capable wish is not applicable to changed circumstances, substitute decision-maker is to decide in the patient's best interests, and not try to determine what the patient would have de-

Any assessment of an individual's best interests must be based on an under-lying value system, a conception of what constitutes "the good", both for that person and generally. In the past, decisions about the treatment that would be in a patient's best interests have often neither articulated the underlying choice of values on which the determination was made nor justified that choice over other possibilities. Legislation that identifies criteria to guide determinations about best interests makes the values and interests that are to be taken into considera-tion when deciding about treatment on behalf of others much more explicit. In Ontario's *Health Care Consent Act, 1996*, for example, substitute decision-makers are directed to consider *inter alia* consistency with the person's value system formed while capable, his or her preferences, the burdens and benefits of the treatment and alternatives (including non-treatment), and which alternative would be least restrictive or intrusive.[51] Recent cases identify similar factors to be taken into account even when legislation is less specific. For instance, in *Sweiss v. Alberta Health Services*, the court listed matters relevant to determin-ing a patient's best interests: the patient's actual condition, the medical treatment recommended, the patient's wishes and directions, and "what is just and equita-ble in the circumstances".[52] Clearly, if each of these factors were assessed indi-vidually, they might suggest different conclusions about whether to consent to or refuse treatment. It is not always clear how such conflicts should be resolved.[53] However, substitute decision-makers are subject to oversight and intervention; while jurisprudence is scant, it suggests that when challenged in court or before a tribunal, their decisions are evaluated on a standard of correctness.[54] In con-trast, tribunal decisions assessing a patient's best interests are generally re-viewed using a standard of reasonableness.[55]

4.   Types of Treatment Substitute Decision-Makers Can Refuse

A substitute decision-maker must decide about treatment in accordance with the decisionally incapable person's prior capable directions or wishes, or if none are known or applicable, based on his or her best interests. He or she must also

---

cided in light of changed circumstances). See also *Re Grover*, [2009] O.J. No. 1496 (Ont. S.C.J.); *Sweiss v. Alberta Health Services*, [2009] A.J. No. 1303, 2009 ABQB 691 (Alta. Q.B.).

[51]   *Health Care Consent Act, 1996, ibid.*; *Scardoni v. Hawryluck*, [2004] O.J. No. 300, 69 O.R. (3d) 700 (Ont. S.C.J.).

[52]   [2009] A.J. No. 1303 at para. 65, 2009 ABQB 691 (Alta. Q.B.).

[53]   See, *e.g.*, *Scardoni v. Hawryluck*, [2004] O.J. No. 300, 69 O.R. (3d) 700 (Ont. S.C.J.); *Sweiss v. Alberta Health Services*, [2009] A.J. No. 1303, 2009 ABQB 691 (Alta. Q.B.); *Rotaru v. Vancou-ver General Hospital Intensive Care Unit*, [2008] B.C.J. No. 456, 2008 BCSC 318 (B.C.S.C.).

[54]   *B. (R.) v. Children's Aid Society of Metropolitan Toronto*, [1994] S.C.J. No. 24, [1995] 1 S.C.R. 315 (S.C.C.); *M. (A.) v. Benes*, [1999] O.J. No. 4236, 46 O.R. (3d) 271 (Ont. C.A.); *Scardoni v. Hawryluck, ibid.*

[55]   *T. (I.) v. L. (L.)*, [1999] O.J. No. 4237, 46 O.R. (3d) 284 (Ont. C.A.); *Conway v. Jacques*, [2002] O.J. No. 2333, 59 O.R. (3d) 735 (Ont. C.A.). However, when interpreting the law, the standard applied is one of correctness: *Starson v. Swayze*, [2003] S.C.J. No. 33 at para. 5, [2003] 1 S.C.R. 722 (S.C.C.), *per* McLachlin C.J.C.

comply with applicable legislative restrictions. This general framework for decision-making applies to decisions about life-sustaining treatment as well. Absent
any statutory restrictions, a substitute decision-maker can legitimately conclude
that it is not in an incapable person's best interests to consent to or continue
treatment, even if that treatment is necessary to preserve life.[56] There is no distinction drawn in law between withholding and withdrawing treatment. Concluding that a person's best interests lie in foregoing life-sustaining treatment
can be an agonizing decision to make, and it is not a decision that will be taken
lightly. It requires careful consideration of the benefits and burdens of treatment,
as well as the totality of the person's circumstances and welfare.

It is sometimes suggested that the provision of artificial nutrition and hydration (ANH) is in a different category, such that a substitute decision-maker cannot decline this form of treatment. Common bases for this claim are that medical
therapies are invasive in ways that artificial nutrition is not, or that feeding is a
form of care rather than treatment, or that foregoing artificial nutrition differs
from refusing other forms of life-sustaining treatment because death will certainly result, or because of its special symbolic or emotional significance.[57]
These arguments are not well-founded in law. Artificial nutrition and hydration
are forms of medical treatment like other types of life-sustaining treatment that
support or replace normal bodily functions, such as ventilators and dialysis.[58]

Other than a few decisions involving decisionally capable individuals, Canadian courts have seldom addressed the issue of foregoing ANH. One such
case, *Janzen v. Janzen*, involved a 43-year-old man who had collapsed and was
ultimately determined to be in a persistent vegetative state.[59] One month after his
initial collapse, his wife, on the recommendation of his treating physicians, requested that he not be put on a ventilator, that ANH be withdrawn and that a
DNR order be entered. Other family members objected and began guardianship
proceedings. The court appointed the patient's wife as his guardian, holding that
her plan to accept the physicians' recommendations (comfort care and palliative
measures only) was in keeping with the patient's prior capable wishes, and that
there was no evidence other types of care would benefit the patient or improve

---

[56]   *London Health Sciences Centre v. K. (R.) (Guardian ad litem of)*, [1997] O.J. No. 4128, 152
D.L.R. (4th) 724 at 735 (Ont. Gen. Div.). See also *Re C. (L.I.)*, [2006] A.J. No. 190 (Alta. Q.B.)
(Public Trustee appointed to make decisions about an individual's health care can authorize
withdrawal of life support).

[57]   See, *e.g.*, P. Derr, "Why Food and Fluids Can Never Be Denied" (1986) Hastings Center Rep.
28; Senate of Canada *Of Life and Death: Special Senate Committee, Report on Euthanasia and
Assisted Suicide* (Ottawa: Minister of Supply and Services Canada, 1995) at 42.

[58]   The Special Senate Committee also concluded that artificial nutrition and hydration are types of
treatment, and consequently, just as with other forms of life-sustaining treatment, can be with-
held or withdrawn in appropriate circumstances: *Of Life and Death: Special Senate Committee
Report on Euthanasia and Assisted Suicide, ibid.*, at 45. See also D. Casarett, J. Kapo & A.
Caplan, "Appropriate Use of Artificial Nutrition and Hydration — Fundamental Principles and
Recommendations" (2005) 353 New Eng. J. Med. 2607; S. Post, "Tube Feeding and Advanced
Progressive Dementia" (2001) 31 Hastings Center Report 36.

[59]   [2002] O.J. No. 450, 44 E.T.R. (2d) 217 (Ont. S.C.J.).

the quality of the patient's life or his well-being. Courts in the United States and the United Kingdom have consistently held that artificial nutrition and hydration are forms of life-prolonging medical treatment like other types of life support.[60] Patients can refuse ANH and, unless prohibited or restricted by statute, substitute decision-makers can do so on behalf of decisionally incapable persons as well, either pursuant to their prior capable instructions or wishes or, failing that, when doing so is in the patient's best interests.

5.　Disagreement Among Family Members

There are two aspects to decision-making about life-sustaining treatment when a patient is decisionally incapable. Consideration must be given not just to how to decide, but also who decides. Where a statutory framework is in place, it will include a means to identify the appropriate substitute decision-maker. Absent an appointed substitute or someone designated in an advance directive, the substitute decision-maker will be a family member willing and able to act, with priority being determined by the degree of their relation to the person concerned.[61] Legislation usually identifies a default decision-maker such as the Public Trustee if no one in the family can or will take on the responsibility.[62] In jurisdictions without legislation governing consent to health care, Sneiderman explains that for incompetent patients without an advance directive, the physician "should be the central figure in the decision-making process" about life-sustaining treatment; provided the decision is medically reasonable, the law has "refrained from interfering".[63] He concluded that, although the family will and should still be consulted, absent legislated decision-making authority, its role is to facilitate but not control decision-making. However, since the time Sneiderman wrote, growing recognition that such decisions involve more than medical considerations is likely to result in greater weight being accorded to familial and other input, even absent a statutory framework.

Conflict may arise not only between family members and health care providers, but also among family members. While in theory this should be resolved by either the terms of the patient's advance directive, if there is one, or if not, by the operation of the statutory framework that designates which family member(s) are authorized to act as substitute decision-maker, that is not always the case. Even when there is a designated substitute decision-maker, other family members may disagree vehemently with his or her decisions about the person's

---

[60]　See, *e.g.*, *Airedale NHS Trust v. Bland*, [1993] 2 W.L.R. 359 (H.L.); A. Meisel, "Barriers to Foregoing Nutrition and Hydration in Nursing Homes" (1995) 21 Am. J. L. & Med. 334 at 353, listing the many American appellate decisions that have accepted that artificial nutrition and hydration are forms of life-prolonging treatment, and that decisions to cease ANH can be considered in the same way as other forms of such treatment.

[61]　See, *e.g.*, *Health Care Consent Act, 1996*, S.O. 1996, c. 2, Sched. A, s. 20.

[62]　*Ibid.*

[63]　B. Sneiderman, "Decision-Making at the End of Life" in Jocelyn Downie, Timothy Caulfield & Colleen Flood, eds., *Canadian Health Law and Policy*, 2d ed. (Markham, ON: LexisNexis Canada, 2002) at 511-13.

care and, especially, about continuing life-sustaining treatment. Again, few Canadian cases address this issue.[64]

The controversy surrounding the case of Terry Schiavo in the United States raises the question whether such conflicts could arise in Canada as well. Terry Schiavo was a young woman who suffered a cardiac arrest in 1990 that left her in a coma, which evolved into a persistent vegetative state.[65] She was cared for in a nursing home, and although her husband and parents initially agreed on treatment plans, after a few years, disagreements ensued about what treatment to pursue. Her parents urged aggressive therapy, while her husband, who was her legal guardian, wanted basic care because her prognosis for neurological recovery was hopeless. Her parents began a 10-year series of legal challenges to her husband's guardianship and his attempts to refuse medical treatment. The courts concluded there was clear and convincing evidence of Terry's prior capable wishes that she did not want to be "kept alive on a machine".[66] When Terry's parents were unsuccessful in the courts, they turned to political intervention. In 2003, following a second, court-ordered removal of Terry's feeding tube, the Florida legislature passed what came to be known as "Terry's law", which gave the state governor the prerogative of having it re-inserted, and required the appointment of a special guardian *ad litem* to review her case. Although that law was later determined to be unconstitutional by the Florida Supreme Court, the guardian *ad litem* did complete a comprehensive medical and legal summary of her care, concluding that the process and substance of proceedings had conformed with the guidelines in Florida law.[67] During the last week of her life, the U.S. Congress passed legislation to move the case from the Florida state courts to the federal court system, but the Florida District Court and the 11th Circuit Court of Appeals held that the evidence submitted by her parents was insufficient to justify a new trial or review.[68] The case sparked immense national and international interest. Media attention was intense and unrelenting during the last year of Terry's life. Right to life groups and disability rights activists staged sit-ins outside the nursing home, with Terry's parents and other members of her

---

[64] See, *e.g.*, *Janzen v. Janzen*, [2002] O.J. No. 450, 44 E.T.R. (2d) 217 (Ont. S.C.J.), described above.

[65] The description and chronology of events are described in R. Cranford, "Facts, Lies and Videotapes: The Permanent Vegetative State and the Sad Case of Terry Schiavo" (2005) 33 J.L. Med. & Ethics 363 at 364-70.

[66] *In re Guardianship of Schiavo*, 780 So. 2d 176 (Fla. 2d DCA 2001); *In re Schiavo*, 2002 WL 31817960 (Fla. Cir. Ct. Nov. 22, 2002); *In re Guardianship of Schiavo*, 800 So. 2d 640 (Fla. 2d Dist. Ct. App. 2003); *Schiavo ex rel. Schindler v. Schiavo*, 2005 U.S. Dist. LEXIS 4265 (Fla. 2d Dist. Ct. 2005).

[67] J. Wolfson, "Erring on the Side of Theresa Schiavo: Reflections of the Special Guardian ad Litem" (2005) 35 Hastings Center Report 16.

[68] *Schiavo ex re. Schindler v. Schiavo*, 358 F. Supp. 2d 1161 (M.D. Fla. 2005), affd *Schiavo ex rel. Schindler v. Schiavo*, 403 F.3d 1298 (11th Cir. (Fla.) 2005), rehearing en banc denied *Schiavo ex rel. Schindler v. Schiavo*, 404 F.3d 1270 (11th Cir. (Fla.) 2005), rehearing denied *Schiavo ex rel. Schindler v. Schiavo*, 404 F.3d 1282 (11th Cir. (Fla.) 2005), stay denied *Schiavo ex rel. Schindler v. Schiavo*, 544 U.S. 957, 125 S. Ct. 1722 (2005).

family pleading to save her life. Finally, after again being authorized by court order and pursuant to her husband's instructions, artificial nutrition and hydration were discontinued and Terry died in April 2005.

The *Schiavo* case gave rise to extensive debate and reflection in the United States. It called into question the basis on which decisions about end of life care are made in that country, highlighting concerns about the sufficiency of the evidence relied on in applying the substituted judgment standard typically used to guide substitute decision-making (which aims to identify the decision the patient would make if able to do so). It is not that the law could not respond to Terry Schiavo's situation — it did, repeatedly — but that its application gave rise to serious second thoughts in some quarters about the framework that had been legislated. Some commentators suggested that by demonstrating the shortcomings in living wills and substituted judgment, the case may have shattered the consensus about end of life care built up over years through a series of state laws and court decisions.[69] However, as Carl Schneider points out, even if Terry Schiavo had expressed her wishes more clearly or had executed an advance directive, it would not have made a difference; her parents had indicated that "they would have fought to have it voided because they did not believe it was consistent with their and her beliefs".[70] Others argue that *Schiavo* will not lead to lasting changes in decision-making about end of life care, particularly given the courts' rulings and the well-established rights of incompetent patients.[71]

The framework that governs substitute decision-making in the United States is not identical to those employed in Canada. However, there are similarities, and developments in American case law on issues that arise in end of life care have informed many of our conclusions about what is and is not acceptable. The attempted political interventions by state and federal governments in Terry Schiavo's care are reflective of a very different political environment in the United States as well, and unlikely to find any counterpart in Canada. However, we are not immune to family disagreements. While Americans have been far more litigious about end of life care than Canadians, serious conflicts among family members have certainly arisen in this country as well and will again, potentially resulting in litigation.

The *Schiavo* controversy also brought evolving views about end of life care and disability to the fore. Commenting on the role of the disability community as events unfolded towards the end of Terry Schiavo's life, Adrienne Asch emphasized that:

> ... the apprehension in the disability community, apprehension about societal indifference and neglect, is more understandable after reviewing a few of the

---

[69] See, *e.g.*, R. Dresser, "Schiavo's Legacy: The Need for an Objective Standard" (2005) 35 Hastings Center Report 20.

[70] C. Schneider, "Hard Cases and the Politics of Righteousness" (2005) 35 Hastings Center Report 24, quoting Terry Schiavo's guardian *ad litem*, 358 F. Supp. 2d 1161 (M.D. Fla. 2005).

[71] L. Hampson & E. Emmanuel, "The Prognosis for Change in End-of-Life Care After the Schiavo Case" (2005) 24 Health Affairs 972.

many instances in which law, medicine, bioethics and government programs failed to help traumatically disabled patients discover the financial, technological, social, and psychological resources that could sustain them and provide the opportunity for rewarding life. When people with relatively intact cognitive and emotional capacities are neglected, neglect is even more likely for those with greatly diminished cognitive and emotional function.[72]

She urges incorporation of a disability equality perspective into assessments of both family decision-making and patients' "supposedly autonomous" decisions about ending life-sustaining treatment, as well as increased support to enable people with disabilities to live their lives, rather than simply endorsing treatment withdrawal. However, as Martha Minow has noted, while one may undervalue the life of an individual who cannot speak for himself, on the other hand, "one may also in unconscious and well-meaning cruelty greatly underestimate the extent of the suffering and deprivations experienced".[73] There are occasions when it is in a person's best interests not to continue to fight death. In the United States, *Blouin, Administratrix of the Estate of Pouliot v. Spitzer* is a case in point.[74] It demonstrates the damage that can result when a surrogate's ability to avoid harmful treatment at the end of an incompetent patient's life is inappropriately limited. In that case, New York law precluded a surrogate from terminating life-sustaining treatment without clear proof of the incapacitated person's intent. Sheila Pouliot was a terminally ill and severely developmentally disabled 42-year-old woman who was admitted to hospital with gastrointestinal bleeding and pain, associated with what the examining physicians concluded was a terminal illness. They advised that further treatment would likely prolong her suffering. Her family, after meeting with her treating physicians, the hospital ethics committee and clergy, asked that treatment, including ANH, be withheld and only palliative treatment be provided. Even a guardian *ad litem* appointed at the instance of the hospital petitioned the court to terminate all nutrition and hydration. The state's insistence on continuing artificial nutrition and hydration against all medical advice and against the wishes of her family, until finally halted by court order after numerous court proceedings, demonstrated a misguided effort to avoid discriminating against a dying patient on the basis of disability. It resulted in a death that has been described as "torturous".[75] The governing legislation has since been amended to permit the guardian of a developmentally disabled person to decide to withhold life-sustaining treatment, including ANH, where there is no reasonable hope of maintaining life, or it poses

---

[72] A. Asch, "Recognizing Death While Affirming Life: Can End of Life Reform Uphold a Disabled Person's Interest in Continued Life?" (2005) 35:6 Hastings Center Special Report S31-S36 at S32.

[73] M. Minow, "Beyond State Intervention in the Family: Baby Jane Doe" (1985) U. Mich. J.L. Reform 933 at 961.

[74] 356 F.3d 348 (2nd Cir. 2002). See also *In re Matthews*, 225 A.D. 2d 142, 650 N.Y.S. 2d 373, 1996 N.Y. App. Div. LEXIS 12210 (N.Y.S.C. App. Div. 1996).

[75] A. Ouellette, "When Vitalism is Dead Wrong: The Discrimination Against and Torture of Incompetent Patients by Compulsory Life-Sustaining Treatment" (2004) 79 Indiana L.J. 1.

an extraordinary burden. While Asch raises the possibility of setting limits on the law's commitment to patient autonomy in end of life care to counteract the constant devaluation of the lives of people with disabilities, cases like that of Sheila Pouliot are a reminder that any proposal to do so must take real account of the potential that such measures could do great harm as well.

6.   Minors Not Yet Able to Decide About Treatment

Parents are recognized as the substitute decision-makers for their decisionally incapable children at common law, and absent an express appointment of someone else, are also designated as such in provincial statutes governing consent to health care. Parents are under a legal duty to ensure their children are provided with needed medical care, and when making decisions about their child's health care, must act in his or her best interests.[76] However, although allowed considerable latitude, they are not entirely free to choose or refuse medical treatment for their child in accordance with their own beliefs, no matter how conscientiously held.

Both at common law and under the *Canadian Charter of Rights and Freedoms*, protecting a child's life and promoting his or her well-being are recognized as important functions of the state; it will intervene when necessary to protect the child's life or health.[77] For instance, in *B. (R.) v. Children's Aid Society of Metropolitan Toronto*, the Supreme Court of Canada held that a temporary wardship order was appropriate to permit the Children's Aid Society to consent to treatment when Jehovah's Witness parents had refused consent to a blood transfusion needed to prevent serious injury to their daughter's health.[78] Thus, although parents are accorded a "protected sphere" of parental decision-making, their ability to depart from medical recommendations in determining what is in their child's best interests is circumscribed.

More difficult issues arise when the appropriate course of treatment is less clear, as is often the case when considering withholding or requiring other types of potentially life-prolonging treatment that are not as widely accepted, or that impose serious burdens on the recipient, or offer physically beneficial effects that are less apparent, or entail serious risk of other harmful effects. Courts reject basing decisions about withholding life-preserving treatment on judgments about the quality of an individual's life. In *British Columbia (Superintendent of Child and Family Services) v. Dawson*, the British Columbia Supreme Court reversed a Provincial Court decision and authorized surgical intervention to replace a shunt in an institutionalized child with severe disabilities over the opposition of his parents.[79] The surgery was medically recommended and would

---

[76]   *B. (R.) v. Children's Aid Society of Metropolitan Toronto*, [1994] S.C.J. No. 24, [1995] 1 S.C.R. 315 (S.C.C.).

[77]   *Ibid.*

[78]   *Ibid.*

[79]   [1983] B.C.J. No. 38, 145 D.L.R. (3d) 610 (B.C.S.C.), revg (*sub nom. Re D. (S.)*) [1983] B.C.J. No. 663, 42 B.C.L.R. 153 (B.C. Prov. Ct.). See also *New Brunswick (Minister of Health and*

improve the child's condition. Non-treatment would have significant deleterious effects. The court concluded that no one could judge the quality of life of the child's life to be so low as not to be worth continuing; decisions about treatment could not be made on that basis.

This is not to say that life-sustaining treatment can never be withheld from a child; there have been instances where courts have upheld parents' decisions not to pursue aggressive treatment. In *Saskatchewan (Minister of Social Services) v. P. (F.)*, the Saskatchewan Provincial Court denied the government's application to have an infant declared in need of protection when his parents decided not to seek a liver transplant for him.[80] While the child's chances of survival with the transplant were good, and death was certain and imminent without it, the court noted that the child would always suffer serious side effects, some of which were themselves potentially life-threatening, that the decision necessarily involved not just medical considerations but important psychological, social and emotional components as well, and most significantly in the court's view, that the parents' decision was "made totally within the bounds of current medical practice" and "did not depart" from values that society expects from thoughtful, caring parents of a terminally ill child. Although medical opinion is highly significant, it will not always be determinative. In *Couture-Jacquet v. Montreal Children's Hospital*, the court supported the family's decision not to have their young child undergo another course of chemotherapy, despite medical recommendations.[81] The burden the treatment would impose on her, the damage it would cause and the very small chance of benefit, justified the decision to forego treatment.

To summarize, while the cases recognize a permitted sphere of parental decision-making about children's health care, their discretion is subject to boundaries, defined by the courts and by societal expectations of those charged with the care of those who are most vulnerable. It is not always clear from the limited jurisprudence when parental decision-making will cross the line, particularly when the treatment is risky and burdensome, and the benefits few or unlikely. Where the burden of continued treatment significantly exceeds the benefits, parents and the health care team may agree that it is appropriate to withdraw life-sustaining treatment, and there is no need for the involvement of child welfare authorities or courts. Withdrawing life-sustaining therapies is an accepted part of end of life care in Canadian hospitals, and proceeds in accordance with accepted medical practice and parental consent. It is in cases of disagreement over a proposed plan of treatment by parents or health care providers, with serious consequences for the life or health of the child, that courts or specialized tribunals may become involved. The law is strongly oriented towards preserving life and protecting those who are vulnerable, especially children. Although courts have

Community Services) v. B. (R.), [1990] N.B.J. No. 404, 106 N.B.R. (2d) 206 (N.B.Q.B.); *In re Goyette: Centre de Services Sociaux du Montréal*, [1983] C.S. 429 (Que. C.S.).

80   [1990] S.J. No. 708, 69 D.L.R. (4th) 134 at 143 (Sask. Prov. Ct.).

81   [1986] Q.J. No. 258, 28 D.L.R. (4th) 22 (Que. C.A.).

on occasion concluded it is in a child's best interests to withdraw or withhold life-sustaining treatment,[82] they seldom do so.

III. PAIN AND SYMPTOM CONTROL AT THE END OF LIFE

Palliative care is "care aimed at alleviating suffering — physical, emotional, psychosocial, or spiritual — rather than curing. It is concerned with the comfort of the suffering individual".[83] It is widely acclaimed as a treatment option for patients with diseases that are not responsive to curative options. In its 1995 report, *Of Life and Death*, the Special Senate Committee on Euthanasia and Assisted Suicide found that access to palliative care was seriously inadequate. A member of that committee, Senator Sharon Carstairs, has tabled reports in the Senate every five years since, reviewing progress on implementing the Committee's recommendations, and making additional recommendations to improve end of life care. Her 2010 report noted that while "there have been significant improvements in providing quality palliative care", at least 70 per cent of Canadians do not have access to palliative care, and many people are still "needlessly dying in pain and with unnecessary suffering".[84] Significant disparities exist

---

[82] See, *e.g.*, *Child and Family Services of Manitoba v. Lavallee*, [1997] M.J. No. 568, 154 D.L.R. (4th) 409 (Man. C.A.), and *In the Matter of EJG* (September 30, 2007), Ont. Consent and Capacity Board, HA-07-2284, HA-07-2285. In *EJG*, the Board concluded it was in the best interests of EJG, an 8-month-old infant who was left in a persistent vegetative state following significant oxygen deprivation prior to birth, and who suffered numerous associated sequelae, including quadriplegia, recurrent respiratory arrests, chronic lung disease and other infections and injuries, to accept a treatment plan proposed by his physicians that involved discontinuing mechanical breathing support, not attempting resuscitation in the event of respiratory failure, and limiting his treatment to comfort care. The Board held that the focus in determining his best interests must be on the expected effects on EJG of the treatment plan and any alternatives, and on his well-being, since he was too young to have values and beliefs of his own. It concluded his parents had been wrong in basing their decisions solely on their own values and beliefs. In a decision upheld on appeal, the Board ordered his parents to consent to the treatment plan proposed, or be replaced as his substitute decision-makers; see P. Hawkins, "Withdrawal of Life Support in Infants", Borden Ladner Gervais, *Health Law Report* (Fall 2008) at 13-15. In Alberta, the parents of Isaiah May, an infant born with severe brain injuries, commenced legal proceedings to stop doctors and the hospital from removing life support from their son. However, after four months of struggle with the decision, and assisted by an expert opinion from an independent neonatologist, Isaiah's parents agreed that he should be removed from life support. He died shortly thereafter. See J. Cotter, "Baby Isaiah taken off life support" *The Globe and Mail* (March 12, 2010) at A11; "May family's statement on Baby Isaiah" *Edmonton Journal* (March 12, 2010), online at: <http://www.edmontonjournal.com/story_print.html?id=2672448&sponsor=>; "Doctor's statement on Baby Isaiah" *Edmonton Journal* (March 11, 2010), online at: <http://www.edmonton journal.com/story_print.html?id=2672404&sponsor=>. See also *Children's Aid Society of Ottawa-Carleton v. C. (M.)*, [2008] O.J. No. 3795 (Ont. S.C.J.).

[83] Senate of Canada, *Of Life and Death: Special Senate Committee Report on Euthanasia and Assisted Suicide* (Ottawa: Minister of Supply and Services Canada, 1995) at 14.

[84] S. Carstairs, *Raising the Bar: A Roadmap for the Future of Palliative Care in Canada* (June 2010), online at: <http://sen.parl.gc.ca/scarstairs/PalliativeCare/Raising%20the%20Bar%20June %202010%20(2).pdf> at 3, 5.

across the country not only in access, but also in quality of care and cost to the patient.

An important part of palliative care is the management of pain and disease symptoms. Although adequate pain control can be achieved for all but a minority of patients, reality often falls short. The Supreme Court of Canada has clearly accepted that the administration of drugs for pain control in dosages that the physician knows may hasten death where it is necessary to achieve the therapeutic purpose of relieving suffering is acceptable medical practice.[85] Yet as the Special Senate Committee noted in *Of Life and Death*, despite the medical profession's ability to control pain, physicians frequently do not administer the medication required because of misplaced concern about the possibility of addiction, or because of potentially life-shortening effects.[86] This is problematic because it leaves patients to face unnecessary pain and suffering, and also because there are strong arguments that both the common law duty of care health professionals owe to their patients and professional standards of practice require practitioners to provide patients with adequate pain management to relieve suffering. Physicians' legal, ethical and professional obligations require them to ensure appropriate relief of pain and other symptoms.

Palliative care may include the use of total sedation; that is, "the practice of rendering a person totally unconscious through the administration of drugs without potentially shortening life".[87] It is sometimes employed to support terminally ill patients suffering intolerable pain that cannot be relieved by other forms of treatment; patients with dyspnea (shortness of breath) and delirium with agitation may also require such sedation.[88] As the Senate Committee noted, "the legal status of this practice is clear. If the sedation is done with the informed consent of the patient or the patient's surrogate, it is legal".[89] For some patients, achieving symptom relief may require terminal sedation, which refers to deep sedation to the point of unconsciousness in order to relieve intractable and intolerable patient suffering, continued until the patient's death, and may also include non-provision of artificial nutrition and hydration after the patient becomes uncon-

---

[85] *Rodriguez v. British Columbia (Attorney General)*, [1993] S.C.J. No. 94, [1993] 3 S.C.R. 519, 607 (S.C.C.).

[86] Senate of Canada, *Of Life and Death: Special Senate Committee Report on Euthanasia and Assisted Suicide* (Ottawa: Minister of Supply and Services Canada, 1995) at 28-29. See also D. Hoffman & A. Tarzian, "Dying in America — An Examination of Policies that Deter Adequate End-of-Life Care in Nursing Homes" (2005) 33 J.L. Med. & Ethics 294.

[87] Senate of Canada, *Of Life and Death: Special Senate Committee Report on Euthanasia and Assisted Suicide, ibid.*, at 14.

[88] E. Latimer, "Euthanasia, Physician-Assisted Suicide and the Ethical Care of Dying Patients" (1994) 151 CMAJ 1133 at 1134. For an example of policy governing use of palliative sedation, see Alberta Health Services, Calgary Zone, "Clinical Practice Guidelines for Palliative Sedation" (2009), online at: <http://www.calgaryhealthregion.ca/clin/cme/cpg/cpg_PalliativeSedation Guidelines2009v4-2.pdf>.

[89] Senate of Canada, *Of Life and Death: Special Senate Committee Report on Euthanasia and Assisted Suicide* (Ottawa: Minister of Supply and Services Canada, 1995) at 33.

scious.[90] Justifications for this practice are based on informed consent, proportionality and the principle of double effect; that is, the intent is to terminate the patient's symptoms, not the patient's life.[91] Terminal sedation in order to achieve symptom relief is consistent with the logic underlying the approval of other practices that may shorten life. Clinicians employ it when needed to achieve symptom relief.[92] However, the practice is not uncontentious, and has not been the subject of judicial consideration in Canada.

IV. DENYING TREATMENT: THE FUTILITY DEBATES

Sometimes, it is not substitute decision-makers who decide treatment is not in a patient's best interests and should be discontinued, but rather health care providers who wish to end treatment while the family wants it continued. Physicians may conclude that treatment is useless (futile) and even harmful, because the patient cannot benefit and may be significantly burdened, while families urge that basic life functions can be maintained or restored, and that this patient's life, even if one of biologic existence only, should be preserved. Difficult decisions must be made about where decision-making power lies in these instances, and also about whether and how concerns about access to resources by this patient and others should be taken into account in decision-making. The issues are not just economic; health care providers raise legitimate concerns about the morality of being required to provide what they consider ineffective and sometimes dam-

---

[90]   N. Cantor, "On Hastening Death Without Violating Legal and Moral Prohibitions" (2005-2006) 37 Loy. U. Chi. L.J. 407 at 418-22, examining legality of different types of terminal sedation; see also American Medical Assn. Council on Ethical and Judicial Affairs, CEJA Report 5-A-08, "Sedation to Unconsciousness in End-of-Life Care"; T. Quill, D. Brock & A. Meisel, "Justifying Different Levels of Palliative Sedation" (2010) 152 Ann. Intern. Med. 333; "AAHPM Position Statements" (2007) 10 J. Palliative Medicine 851; J. Berger, "Rethinking Guidelines for the Use of Palliative Sedation" (2010) 40 Hastings Center Report 32.

[91]   D. Sulmasy & E. Pellegrino, "The Rule of Double Effect: Clearing Up the Double Talk" (1999) 159:6 Arch. Intern. Medicine 545 (on ethical acceptability). But see *contra* H. Kuhse, "From Intention to Consent: Learning from Experience with Euthanasia" in M. Battin, R. Rhodes & A. Silvers, eds., *Physician Assisted Suicide: Expanding the Debate* (New York: Routledge, 1998), at 252, 258-59; D. Orentlicher, "The Supreme Court and Terminal Sedation: An Ethically Inferior Alternative to Physician-Assisted Suicide" in M. Battin, R. Rhodes & A. Silvers, eds., *ibid.*, at 301; R. Magnusson, "The Devil's Choice: Re-Thinking Law, Ethics and Symptom Relief in Palliative Care" (2006) 34 J.L. Med. & Ethics; M. Battin, "Terminal Sedation: Pulling the Sheet Over Our Eyes" (2008) 38 Hastings Center Report 27.

[92]   H.C. Muller-Busch, I. Andres & T. Jehser, "Sedation in Palliative Care – A Critical Analysis of 7 Years Experience" (2003) 2 BMC Palliat. Care; A. De Graaf & M. Dean, "Palliative Sedation Therapy in the Last Weeks of Life: A Literature Review and Recommendations for Standards" (2007) 20 J. Palliative Medicine 67. In Canada, a working group has formed to develop consensus-based clinical guidelines: see Canadian Bioethics Society Newsletter, "Canadian Palliative Sedation Therapy Guidelines – Moving Forward" (January 2010) at 12, online at: <http://www.bioethics.ca/january2010.pdf>.

aging therapy to a patient contrary to their own beliefs and those of the medical profession generally.[93]

A.   DEVELOPMENTS IN THE UNITED STATES AND ENGLAND

The debate about futile treatment began in the early 1980s in the United States, sparked by studies demonstrating the ineffectiveness of cardiopulmonary resuscitation (CPR) for certain categories of patients.[94] Although the issue has been addressed in a number of lawsuits in the United States, it cannot be said there is a consensus on the issue comparable to the one recognizing a patient's right to refuse life-sustaining treatment. However, American courts have generally not been prepared to both go against family wishes and authorize a step that would result in a patient's life ending, at least in circumstances where it is apparent that family members are actively involved and trying conscientiously to determine the patient's best interests.[95] Further, a number of states have enacted legislation restricting circumstances in which life-sustaining treatment can be withheld from a decisionally incapable person at the instance of a substitute decision-maker, even if all involved in the patient's care agree that treatment ought not be continued.[96] Other states, however, have enacted statutes that allow for the uni-

---

[93]   See, generally, J. Gilmour, *Study Paper on Assisted Suicide, Euthanasia and Foregoing Treatment* (Toronto: Ontario Law Reform Commission, 1996) at 229-35; J. Gilmour, "Death and Dying" in Borden Ladner Gervais LLP, ed. (original editor M.J. Dykeman), *Canadian Health Law Practice Manual* (Markham, ON: LexisNexis Canada, 2000, incl. service issues to 2010) at 8.62-8.79; J. Skerritt, "Doctor quits over battle to save patient" *National Post* (June 4, 2008); T. Thanh Ha, "Two more doctors resign over life-support order" *The Globe and Mail* (June 19, 2008) at A5, recounting refusal of critical care specialists to continue working at hospital when required by court order to continue to provide care to a patient, Samuel Golubchuk, that they considered "tantamount to torture". See also *Scardoni v. Hawryluck*, [2004] O.J. No. 300, 69 O.R. (3d) 700 (Ont. S.C.J.).

[94]   J. Paris, "Pipes, Colanders and Leaky Buckets: Reflections on the Futility Debate" (1993) 2 Cambridge Q. Healthcare Ethics 147; M. Gordon, "Cardiopulmonary Resuscitation in the Elderly Long-Term Care Population: Time to Reconsider" (1994) 27 Ann. R.C.P.S.C. at 81-83.

[95]   The issue first came to the fore in ethical debate in the 1990s in the U.S., with the case of Helga Wanglie, an elderly woman in a persistent vegetative state who was dependent on a respirator. The hospital where she was a patient wished to remove her from the ventilator; her husband and family did not. Although the only issue before the court was determining who should act as substitute decision-maker (it settled on the husband), the question of futile treatment was clearly the subtext that prompted the hospital to commence the application in court. Helga Wanglie died three days after the court made its order, still on a ventilator: M. Angell, "The Case of Helga Wanglie: A New Kind of 'Right to Die' Case" (1991) 325 New Eng. J. Med. 511-12. See, *e.g.*, *Baby K*, 382 F. Supp. 1022 (E.D. Va. 1993), aff'd 16 F.3d 590 (4th Cir. 1994), cert. denied 115 S. Ct. 91 (1994) and, generally, J. Gilmour, *Study Paper on Assisted Suicide, Euthanasia and Foregoing Treatment* (Toronto: Ontario Law Reform Commission, 1996) at 231, and references cited therein.

[96]   A. Ouellette, "When Vitalism is Dead Wrong: The Discrimination Against and Torture of Incompetent Patients by Compulsory Life-Sustaining Treatment" (2004) 79 Indiana L.J. 1.

lateral withdrawal or withholding of life-sustaining treatment by health care providers when it is deemed medically inappropriate.[97]

English courts have been both more deferential to medical opinion and willing to acknowledge financial constraints on the health care system as a factor that can be taken into account by a health authority in decision-making.[98] Yet, the issue of how decisions are to be made about futile treatment is not settled in that country either, except to the extent that courts have confirmed a significant, ongoing role for the judiciary in decision-making.[99] Thus, in *An NHS Trust v. B.*, an application by a hospital seeking approval for the withdrawal of life support from an infant with a serious, disabling and fatal degenerative neuromuscular condition, the court held that, although both the views of the child's parents and the treating physicians about treatment required careful consideration in its deliberations, determining the child's "objective best interests" remained its responsibility.[100] It ordered that ventilator support must be continued, but did not require that CPR or antibiotic therapy be repeated. Despite the generally deferential attitude to medical judgment in England, courts have increasingly recognized that these decisions engage more than medical considerations.

The issue of decision-making authority as between a decisionally capable patient and physicians was raised in *R. (Ex p. Burke) and the General Medical Council*.[101] The claimant, a decisionally capable 44-year-old man, had a degenerative neurological condition similar to multiple sclerosis that left him severely disabled; he would eventually require artificial nutrition and hydration (ANH), although he would retain his full cognitive faculties even during the end stages of the disease. He brought an application challenging guidelines about life-prolonging treatment developed by the physicians' regulatory body, the General Medical Council (GMC). Burke was concerned the guidelines would permit a

---

[97]   T. Pope, "Medical Futility Statutes: No Safe Haven to Unilaterally Refuse Life-Sustaining Treatment" (2007) 71 Tenn. L. Rev. 1.

[98]   *Airedale NHS Trust v. Bland*, [1993] W.L.R. 359 (H.L.); *R. v. Cambridge Health Authority, ex p. B.*, [1995] 2 All E.R. 129 (C.A.); *Re G.*, [1995] 2 F.C.R. 46 (Fam. Div.) (application by hospital to withdraw life support; patient's wife not opposed but patient's mother opposed — application granted).

[99]   *Glass v. United Kingdom*, [2004] 1 F.L.R. 1019, 77 B.M.L.R. 120 (Application No. 61827/00), [2004] 1 F.C.R. 553.

[100]   [2006] EWHC 507 (Fam.) (requiring continuation of ventilator support, but authorizing hospital and physicians to refrain from providing certain other forms of life support). See also *Wyatt v. Portsmouth Hospital NHS Trust*, [2005] EWCA Civ. 1181, [2005] 3 F.C.R. 263 (C.A.) for a similar analysis of the decision-making process. And see *An NHS Trust v. D.*, [2005] EWHC 2439 (Fam.), [2006] 1 F.L.R. 638, holding that it was not in the best interests of D., a 32-year-old woman suffering from a terminal genetic neurological illness who was in a vegetative state (likely with no awareness) and no prospect of improvement, to try to prolong her life. Accordingly, over the opposition of D.'s parents and relatives but with the support of the Official Solicitor acting on behalf of D., the court granted the NHS Trust's application for a declaration that it need not take invasive steps to treat her, should she contract a potentially life-threatening condition or her breathing fail.

[101]   [2005] EWCA Civ. 1003, [2006] Q.B. 273 (C.A. (Civ. Div.), revg [2004] EWHC 1879 (Admin.), 79 B.M.L.R. 126.

physician to withdraw ANH from him against his will, and wanted to ensure he would be provided with ANH until he died of natural causes, and that the decision remained his, rather than a physician's.[102] The initial determination in Burke's favour was overturned by the Court of Appeal, which held that the GMC's guidance was lawful and could not in fact be applied in the way the applicant feared. The House of Lords denied leave to appeal, and Burke's application to the European Court of Human Rights was unsuccessful.[103]

B.   CANADA

In Canada, while the issue has come before the courts in an increasing number of cases in recent years, the law remains unsettled.[104] In *Child and Family Services of Manitoba v. Lavallee*, an infant had been left in a persistent vegetative state following a savage attack three months after birth, and had been immediately taken into care by child welfare authorities.[105] There was no hope that his condition would improve; it was only a matter of time until he contracted a life-threatening illness. His physician recommended a "Do Not Resuscitate" order be placed on the boy's chart; his parents refused consent.[106] The Manitoba Court of Appeal agreed that a DNR order was appropriate, but concluded that because a DNR order authorizes *non*-treatment, rather than treatment, neither parental nor judicial consent was required. It considered the decision to write such an order purely a matter of medical judgment. It approved of the order indirectly, however, noting that while it seemed counter-intuitive, the best interests of a child could lie in being permitted to die:

> ... it is in no one's interest to artificially maintain the life of a terminally-ill patient who is in an irreversible vegetative state. That is unless those responsible for the patient being in that state have an interest in prolonging life to avoid criminal responsibility for the death.[107]

The court's analysis of the meaning of "treatment" and the ambit of the physician's authority in *Lavallee* is troubling, and in my view, incorrect. Part of the difficulty arises from the convention that has developed with respect to CPR

---

[102] *Ibid.*, at para. 6.

[103] [2006] 1 W.L.R. 327 (H.L.), EHCR Application No. 19807/06.

[104] *London Health Sciences Centre v. K. (R.) (Guardian ad litem of)*, [1997] O.J. No. 4128, 152 D.L.R. (4th) 724 (Ont. Gen. Div.) was the first of these cases. It began as an application by a hospital for a declaration that it could lawfully discontinue all life-support measures to a patient in a persistent vegetative state, despite his spouse's refusal to consent. However, since she did eventually consent during the course of the proceedings, it was not necessary for the court to determine the issue.

[105] [1997] M.J. No. 568, 154 D.L.R. (4th) 409 (Man. C.A.).

[106] The *Child and Family Services Act*, C.C.S.M. c. C80, s. 25 provided that where a child has been apprehended by child welfare authorities and parents refuse to consent to recommended medical treatment, the agency can apply to the court for authorization to treat, a determination to be made in the best interests of the child.

[107] *Child and Family Services of Central Manitoba v. Lavallee*, [1997] M.J. No. 568 at para. 8, 154 D.L.R. (4th) 409 (Man. C.A.).

— that consent is presumed unless it has been specifically refused, leading to the expectation that CPR will always be performed in the event of cardiac arrest even when inappropriate as a treatment modality.[108] It follows logically that in order not to administer CPR, consent is required to depart from the norm. This is not true of other treatments. The court's conclusion that "treatment" must refer to some positive intervention is not tenable in light of this background.[109] A DNR order is generally one part of a plan for treatment; a treatment plan cannot sensibly be accepted or rejected if an integral part of it is carved out by an artificial distinction between the positive and negative aspects of the plan. Consequently, it should be considered "treatment", and subject to the generally applicable provisions regarding substitute decision-making. In some provinces, "treatment" is explicitly defined to include a "treatment plan", which in turn includes withholding and withdrawing treatment.[110] There is an important role for a substitute decision-maker in determining whether such an order is appropriate for the person concerned; this is not purely a medical decision.

The argument that competent patients and substitute decision-makers have a continuing role in decision-making when health care providers consider life support unwarranted finds support in other cases as well. In *Sawatzky v. Riverview Health Centre Inc.*, a Manitoba physician had entered a DNR order in the case of an elderly patient (a man for whom he considered CPR futile), first without the knowledge of the patient's wife, and then in the face of her opposition.[111] The Public Trustee had earlier been appointed the patient's guardian, but, relying on *Lavallee*, had refused to take any position with respect to the DNR order. On application by the patient and his wife, an interlocutory injunction was issued withdrawing the DNR order pending receipt of medical reports respecting the patient's condition. The presiding judge urged that the matter be

---

[108] Canadian Medical Association, Canadian Nurses Association, Canadian Healthcare Association, Catholic Health Association of Canada, "Joint Statement on Resuscitative Interventions" (1995) 153 CMAJ 1652A-C at 1652A.

[109] J. Gilmour, *Study Paper on Assisted Suicide, Euthanasia and Foregoing Treatment* (Toronto: Ontario Law Reform Commission, 1996) at 57-60. The claim that DNR orders are not "treatment" was rejected by the President's Commission for the Study of Ethical Problems in Medicine and Biomedical and Behavioral Research, *Deciding to Forego Life-Sustaining Treatment* (Washington, DC: U.S. Government Printing Office, 1983) at 241, note 39, and the New York State Task Force on Life and the Law: see R. Baker, "The Legitimation and Regulation of DNR Orders" in R. Baker, M. Strosberg & J. Bynum, eds., *Legislating Medical Ethics: A Study of the New York State Do-Not-Resuscitate Law* (Dordrecht: Kluwer Academic Publishers, 1995) at 50-51. See also J. Downie, "Unilateral Withholding and Withdrawal of Potentially Life-Sustaining Treatment: A Violation of Dignity Under the Law in Canada" (2004) 20 J. Palliative Care 143. Requiring consent is grounded not only on the law regarding liability for battery, but also on the rights to autonomy and bodily integrity. Barney Sneiderman, "Decision-Making at the End of Life" in Jocelyn Downie, Timothy Caulfield & Colleen Flood, eds., *Canadian Health Law and Policy*, 2d ed. (Markham, ON: LexisNexis Canada, 2002) at 517 suggests that whether one agrees with the reasoning in *Lavallee* or not, it reflects reality for many incompetent patients, because families typically accept the judgment and recommendations of the attending physician.

[110] See, *e.g.*, *Health Care Consent Act, 1996*, S.O. 1996, c. 2, Sched. A.

[111] [1998] M.J. No. 506, 167 D.L.R. (4th) 359 (Man. Q.B.).

resolved out of court if possible. She also ordered the Public Trustee to represent the interests of the patient on the application, strongly criticizing her "complete abdication of her responsibility to Mr. Sawatzky, for whom she is responsible".[112] Mediation involving all parties ensued but without a final resolution; Mr. Sawatzky died several months following the initial decision.[113] In *Jin v. Calgary Health Region*, the family of a 66-year-old man who suffered serious head injuries in a fall sought an injunction to prevent the hospital and health care providers from acting on a DNR order.[114] Within a week of his hospitalization, his physicians had concluded he was likely to be left in a persistent vegetative state, and that a DNR order was in his best interests. The court noted it was unclear who had the right to make a DNR order when the family and physicians disagreed. It granted an interim injunction. Within a few months, Mr. Jin had recovered sufficiently to be moved to a rehabilitation facility.[115] In another Manitoba decision, *Golubchuk v. Salvation Army Grace Hospital*, the court continued an interim injunction that the patient's adult children had obtained *ex parte*, preventing the hospital and physicians from withdrawing life support care, ventilation, tube feeding and medication from their 84-year-old father.[116] In this case, too, the court noted that "it is not settled law that, in the event of disagreement between a physician and his patient as to withdrawal of life supports, the physician has the final say".[117] His treating physicians resigned from the hospital staff rather than treat their patient in ways they considered harmful and inhumane.[118] Mr. Golubchuk died before the legal proceedings were resolved. In *Scardoni v. Hawryluck*, the court overturned a decision of the Ontario Consent and Capacity Board that the patient's daughters, whom she had appointed as her substitute decision-makers, were not acting in her best interests when they insisted on continuing life support for their seriously ill and debilitated mother against medical advice.[119] The court held the Board had erred in focusing too heavily on the effects of continued treatment on the patient, and failed to give proper consideration to all the statutory factors to be considered in assessing her "best interests" and, in particular, the patient's values and belief systems.[120]

Yet, families do not necessarily have final decision-making authority either. Courts in a number of provinces have upheld physicians' and hospitals' conclusions that for some patients, continuing life-sustaining treatment is no longer in

---

[112] *Ibid.*, at para. 52.

[113] N. Moharib, "Victor in resuscitation — Issue case dies, wife had battled successfully for court decision" *Winnipeg Sun* (October 28, 1999) at 6.

[114] [2007] A.J. No. 1100 (Alta. Q.B.).

[115] P. Beauchamp, "No regrets over court fight for fall victim's family: Calgary senior on road to recovery after coma" *Calgary Herald* (December 30, 2007) at B3.

[116] [2008] M.J. No. 54, 2008 MBQB 49 (Man. Q.B.).

[117] *Ibid.*, at para. 25.

[118] J. Skerritt, "Doctor quits over battle to save patient" *National Post* (June 4, 2008); T. Thanh Ha, "Two more doctors resign over life-support order" *The Globe and Mail* (June 19, 2008).

[119] [2004] O.J. No. 300 (Ont. S.C.J.).

[120] However, these were not sufficiently explicit to constitute a "wish"; under Ontario legislation, a patient's prior capable wishes must be followed, and would have been controlling.

their best interests. In *Re V. (I.H.)*, an Alberta decision, the court determined it was in the best interests of the patient, a Métis woman terminally ill with cancer, and in keeping with her previously expressed wishes, to proceed with medically recommended palliative care and discontinue ICU interventions, rather than grant the interim injunction requiring more aggressive interventions that some family members had sought.[121] In *Rotaru v. Vancouver General Hospital Intensive Care Unit*, the British Columbia Supreme Court declined a petition brought by the adult daughter of a terminally ill patient with global, irreversible vascular disease and progressive renal failure, seeking an order that previous treatment levels be resumed, rather than medically recommended comfort care.[122] Nor was a DNR order held in abeyance pending resolution of legal proceedings in Nova Scotia in the case of Moorix Yeung, a 46-year-old immunologist with stomach cancer that had metastasized. His physicians considered further treatment of his cancer futile, given its advanced stage. His wife, who wanted the hospital to use whatever means were necessary to keep her husband alive long enough to allow a traditional Chinese healer to try to save him, commenced legal proceedings seeking to have the DNR order rescinded. Mr. Yeung died before the hearing could be concluded, with the DNR order still in place.[123]

Sweiss v. Alberta Health Services also involved a family's fight to have the DNR order to which their 64-year-old father was subject removed, and mechanical ventilation continued.[124] He had suffered severe brain damage as a result of a cardiac arrest. Physicians concluded he had no chance of meaningful recovery, and that the appropriate treatment was palliative care and comfort measures. The court declined to grant the interim injunction that the family

---

[121] [2008] A.J. No. 545, 2008 ABQB 250 (Alta. Q.B.).

[122] [2008] B.C.J. No. 456, 2008 BCSC 318 (B.C.S.C.).

[123] *Yeung v. Capital District Health Authority* (December 15, 2006), Halifax HFX273970 (N.S.T.D.), referenced in J. Downie & K. McEwen, "The Manitoba College of Physicians and Surgeons Position Statement on Withholding and Withdrawal of Life-Sustaining Treatment (2008): Three Problems and a Solution" (2009) 17 Health L.J. 115 at 119, n. 14; T. Blackwell, "Who says doctors know best?" *National Post* (December 11, 2006) at A1, A7. In Ontario, the family of 46-year-old cancer patient, Mann Kee Li, commenced legal proceedings against his physicians and the Sunnybrook Health Sciences Centre seeking to have a DNR order withdrawn. While still competent, Mr. Li had made a power of attorney for personal care and a videotaped statement in which he indicated he wanted all medical measures to save him in the event of a life-threatening emergency, but as his illness worsened, his physicians concluded there had been a material change in circumstances, and that further interventions would be of no benefit to him. Justice Conway made an interim order, effectively revoking Mr. Li's DNR status, but leaving the decision whether to resuscitate him in the event of an emergency to his physicians' judgment, rather than compelling them to do so, and referring the matter to the provincial Consent and Capacity Board (CCB) for determination: R. Cribb, "Family, doctors battle over 'do not resuscitate' order" *The Toronto Star* (October 25, 2010). By the time of the tribunal hearing three days later, the family had concluded Mr. Li's suffering was so great that his previous wishes were never meant to apply to such circumstances, and that aggressive life-saving interventions were not in his best interests. They agreed to a DNR order, and the CCB agreed it was acceptable to depart from Mr. Li's previously expressed wishes: R. Cribb, "Family withdraws request for CPR" *The Toronto Star* (October 26, 2010).

[124] [2009] A.J. No. 1303, 2009 ABQB 691 (Alta. Q.B.).

sought. In a persuasive judgment, Ouellette J. concluded that the traditional test for granting an injunction that had been relied on in *Jin* and *Golubchuk* (which canvasses the potential for irreparable harm and weighs the "balance of convenience"), was poorly suited to cases involving urgent life-threatening situations. As he pointed out, in most of these cases, there is no intent that the matter will proceed to trial and a final resolution; the decision to grant an interim injunction "often determines whether an individual lives or dies".[125] Instead, he concluded that the best interests of the patient, understood more broadly than "the issue of sustaining life v. quality-of-life" (which would always justify "herculean medical efforts"), should govern the inquiry.[126] The court granted an interim injunction preventing the removal of ventilation for a few days to allow the family time to obtain an independent assessment, but refused to remove the DNR order, concluding on the basis of medical evidence that it was in the patient's best interests that no attempts be made to resuscitate him, and that the court should not force his physician to contravene the primary medical principle of doing no harm.

Health care providers' associations have developed policy statements to guide decision-making on this issue. The Canadian Medical Association, Canadian Nurses Association, Canadian Healthcare Association and the Catholic Healthcare Association of Canada issued a Joint Statement on Resuscitative Interventions.[127] Relative to CPR, it distinguishes between treatment that is medically futile or non-beneficial, and instances where the benefit of treatment can only be determined "with reference to the person's subjective judgment about his or her overall wellbeing". Although the policy states that physicians determine questions of medical futility, and that there is no obligation to offer futile or non-beneficial treatment, it adds that: "As a general rule, a person should be involved in determining futility in his or her own case."

Shortly after *Sawatzky* was decided, the same organizations released a "Joint Statement on Preventing and Resolving Ethical Conflicts Involving Health Care Providers and Persons Receiving Care".[128] It provides that the primary goal of care is benefit to the recipient, and that persons who are competent have the right to determine what constitutes a benefit. However, it also affirms that health care providers should not be required to participate in procedures contrary to their professional judgment or values, or those of the treating facility (referencing the earlier Joint Statement on Resuscitative Interventions and Futility). The potential for conflict between the two approaches (patient and provider autonomy) is apparent. The College of Physicians and Surgeons of Ontario approved a policy on "Decision-Making for the End of Life" in 2002 (updated 2006).[129] It states that patients have the right to receive life-sustaining treatment

---

[125] *Ibid.*, at para. 53.

[126] *Ibid.*, at paras. 63, 57. See also *Re V. (I.H.)*, [2008] A.J. No. 545 at para. 31, 2008 ABQB 250 (Alta. Q.B.).

[127] (1995) 153 CMAJ 1652A-C.

[128] (1999) 160:12 CMAJ 1757.

[129] Online at: <http://www.cpso.on.ca/policies/default.aspx?ID=1582>.

that may be of benefit to them, but that physicians are not obliged to provide treatment that almost certainly will not benefit the patient, and should not begin or maintain treatment that will almost certainly not be of benefit or may be harmful to a patient. If conflicts about treatment cannot be resolved, the physician may offer to transfer care. If the patient is incapable, the policy refers physicians to the "structure for managing conflicts" set out in the *Health Care Consent Act, 1996*. Under that statute, application can be made to a tribunal to resolve disputes about substitute decision-making. While these policy statements do not have legal force, courts do rely on and defer to institutional policies and standards of practice. It is difficult to know what message they should or would draw from these; the concepts of benefit and harm remain contested, and the division of power among patients, families, physicians and health care providers remains unclear.

Concerns about continuing treatment that is in fact harmful to a patient, and about allocating scarce resources to costly therapies that are ineffective are legitimate. However, using the language of futility without addressing the assumptions underlying that terminology can give the illusion that the characterization of futility is not and cannot be contested.[130] There are two different emphases in definition among the many writers on this topic. One focuses on probability of success of the treatment in order to divide decision-making power between physicians and patients or substitute decision-makers; the other focuses on the overarching decision-making model in health care (which, in this context, becomes the stronger claim of patient or substitute decision-maker choice of or demand for treatment, rather than simply informed consent to treatment proposed).[131] Still others meld the two, proposing that questions of physiologic futility (treatment cannot achieve the goal) be determined by physicians and qualitative futility (goal is evaluated) be determined by patients or their representatives.[132]

Arguments for physician determination of futility rest on unproven assumptions of unanimity (at least, among physicians): first, about the goals of treatment; and second, about the likelihood of achieving those goals.[133] It is also

---

[130] M.Z. Solomon, "How Physicians Talk About Futility" (1993) 21 J.L. Med. & Ethics 231 at 235, suggesting "the tendency to cloak value judgments in technical, medical jargon may serve a psycho-social function: the terms used may allow all involved to avoid discussing difficult value questions".

[131] Contrast N. Jecker & L. Schneiderman, "Medical Futility: The Duty Not to Treat" (1993) 2 Cambridge Q. Healthcare Ethics 151, and R.D. Truog, A.S. Brett & J. Frader, "The Problem with Futility" (1992) 326 New Eng. J. Med. 1560.

[132] See, *e.g.*, K. Christiansen, "Applying the Concept of Futility at the Bedside" (1992) 1 Cambridge Q. Healthcare Ethics 242 at 244.

[133] Contrast D. Cook, "Determinants in Canadian Health Care Workers of the Decision to Withdraw Life Support from the Critically Ill" (1995) 273 JAMA 703 at 706, finding wide disparity in health care providers (projected) decision-making about withdrawing life support from critically ill patients in the same condition), and R. Sibbald, J. Downar & L. Hawryluck, "Perceptions of 'Futile Care' Among Caregivers in Intensive Care Units" (2007) 177:10 CMAJ 1201 (identifying significant consensus among all types of practitioners in intensive care units about how to de-

important to recognize that unilateral physician decision-making about questions of futility is a departure from the model of shared decision-making in consent to health care, which assumes that patients and substitute decision-makers are capable of making reasonable choices with good information. That model originated, at least in part, to address the power imbalance that exists between doctors and patients, which remains an ongoing concern. The tension between the two has not yet been resolved. Picard and Robertson point out that, although "there is no legal duty to perform treatment the doctor reasonably believes to be medically futile, that is, treatment which offers no prospect of therapeutic benefit for the patient ... many commentators have emphasized the potential dangers and problems underlying the concept of medical futility, particularly if it is interpreted broadly and used to justify withholding treatment for socio-economic and value-laden reasons".[134]

Manitoba has continued to give this issue careful attention at the policy level, first in a 2003 Report by the Manitoba Law Reform Commission, and more recently, in a policy established by that province's College of Physicians and Surgeons.[135] The Law Reform Commission distinguished between the well-recognized right of a competent patient to refuse treatment, and the question of whether patients have a positive right to require life-sustaining or life-prolonging treatment, concluding that although there were no Canadian cases on point, and that a variety of potential arguments may be raised based on constitutional grounds and federal and provincial legislation, "as a general proposition ... the physician has the ultimate power to withhold or withdraw life sustaining treatment *without the consent of the patient*".[136] Recognizing the contentious nature of the issue, it proposed policies and principles to guide decision-making. They are meant to ensure fairness to the patient and family and encourage consensus, but at the same time, to affirm the physician's right to withhold or withdraw life-sustaining treatment where such treatment would be "medically inappropriate or professionally unethical".[137] Despite the importance of autonomous decision-making and personal control in health care, it rejected the idea of a "right to indefinite life sustaining medical treatment", because of concern that it could result in unreasonable demands for unlimited and inappropriate treatment, and that such demands could and would be extended well beyond end of life care.[138]

---

fine and resolve cases of medically futile care and how to limit its impact on intensive care units).

[134] E. Picard & G. Robertson, *Legal Liability of Doctors and Hospitals in Canada*, 4th ed. (Toronto: Thomson Carswell, 2007) at 346.

[135] Manitoba Law Reform Commission, *Withholding or Withdrawing Life Sustaining Medical Treatment*, Report #109 (Winnipeg: Manitoba Law Reform Commission, 2003); College of Physicians and Surgeons of Manitoba, "Withholding and Withdrawing Life-Sustaining Treatment", Statement No. 1602, online at: <http://www.cpsm.mb.ca/statements/st1602.pdf>.

[136] *Ibid.*, at 4 [emphasis in original].

[137] *Ibid.*, at 12.

[138] *Ibid.*, at 13.

Following the Law Commission's lead, and beginning from the premise that in Manitoba, aspects of the law regarding who has legal authority to decide these matters is "ambiguous", in 2006 the provincial College of Physicians and Surgeons proposed a process for physicians to follow when considering withholding or withdrawing life-sustaining treatment,[139] which it finalized in a 2008 policy.[140] In addition to situations where a patient refuses treatment or there is consensus, it provides additional guidance for physicians when "life-sustaining treatment should be withheld or withdrawn because the minimum goal of life-sustaining treatment [defined] is not realistically achievable".

Recent writing on this subject in Canada avoids using the language of "futility" in an attempt to avoid becoming mired in intractable disputes. The Manitoba Law Reform Commission eschewed the term because of both its "pejorative connotation", and its undue emphasis on evaluating the life of the person concerned. Jocelyn Downie, too, has suggested that because there is so little agreement about what "futility" means, different terminology should be employed:[141] unilateral withholding and withdrawal of potentially life-sustaining treatment. Both are deliberate efforts to distance their proposals from the unproductive and circular arguments that have typically marked discussion of the issue, in effect concluding that the language of futility has itself become futile, at least as a basis for policy development.[142] Unlike the Manitoba Law Reform Commission, however, Downie argues that in cases of irreconcilable disagreement between health care providers and the patient or surrogate, the matter must be resolved by a court, rather than through unilateral physician action if informal dispute resolution has been unsuccessful. In her view, there is no room for a health care provider to unilaterally withhold treatment outside clear cases where the treatment demanded cannot succeed at any level. The two are at opposite poles on this issue.

There are few Canadian cases addressing the question of boundaries on either the decision-making authority of patients and substitute decision-makers to

---

[139] Online at: <http://www.cpsm.mb.ca/about/news/2006/10/16/38189_0610160758-046?pageNumber=1>.

[140] College of Physicians and Surgeons of Manitoba, "Withholding and Withdrawing Life-Sustaining Treatment", Statement No. 1602, online at: <http://www.cpsm.mb.ca/statements/st1602.pdf>. For critical analysis, see J. Downie & K. McEwen, "The Manitoba College of Physicians and Surgeons Position Statement on Withholding and Withdrawal of Life-Sustaining Treatment (2008): Three Problems and a Solution" (2009) 17 Health L.J. 115.

[141] Manitoba Law Reform Commission, *Withholding or Withdrawing Life Sustaining Medical Treatment*, Report #109 (Winnipeg: Manitoba Law Reform Commission, 2003) at 12; J. Downie, "Unilateral Withholding and Withdrawal of Potentially Life-Sustaining Treatment: A Violation of Dignity Under the Law in Canada" (2004) 20 J. Palliative Care 143.

[142] A Consultation Document released by the Select Committee of the Quebec National Assembly on Dying with Dignity (May 2010) refers to the concept of "therapeutic obstinacy" as one issue within its purview, online at: <http://www.assnat.qc.ca/en/actualites-salle-presse/nouvelle/actualite-21205.html> at 9. The term is more common in European and theological writing, and while its meaning is not without controversy, seems to connote taking measures to prolong life that are excessive in the sense of not benefitting the patient, and even causing harm. The prejudgment inherent in the language is likely to limit wide adoption of the term in Canada.

require treatment, or on the power of health care providers, institutions and health insurance plans to deny it when it is claimed that treatment is futile.[143] Courts in *Jin* and *Golubchuk* noted, but did not determine, the constitutional dimensions of this issue. While there have been a few lawsuits about access to health care, they are of limited assistance.[144] The legality of denying access to publicly funded treatment to particular individuals because of a judgment that it cannot assist, given the gravity of their underlying disease or disability, or because of ethical concerns, has rarely been judicially considered.[145] The issue has ramifications under the *Canadian Charter of Rights and Freedoms*, as well as human rights legislation, the *Canada Health Act*, and other federal and provincial legislation. It raises societal concerns, not just medical considerations, and entails questions about the designation of decision-makers, boundaries on their authority, resource allocation and access that would better be addressed at the level of policy, and not just in individual cases.

V.   SUBSTITUTE DECISION-MAKING AND ORGAN DONATION AFTER CARDIAC DEATH

Consent to organ donation when a patient has died has not been controversial in Canada for years. Following the lead of the 1968 Report of the Ad Hoc Committee of the Harvard Medical School to Examine the Definition of Brain Death, Canadian organizations such as the Canadian Medical Association and others clearly accepted the concept of brain death as a valid basis for determining death.[146] Legislation governing organ and tissue transplantation for the most part

---

[143] Lawsuits raising this issue are underway, however. Parents of Annie Farlow, a baby who died at the Hospital for Sick Children in Toronto are suing, alleging that their severely ill daughter's death was hastened, and a DNR order entered without parental consent: see T. Boyle, "The death of baby Annie" *The Toronto Star* (October 16, 2010) at GT1, 4. Joy Wawrzyniak, the adult daughter and substitute decision-maker for Douglas DeGuerre, is suing Sunnybrook Hospital and her father's physicians, alleging they changed her father's status from full code to DNR contrary to her instructions, and did not provide treatment needed to save his life: see R. Cribb, "Who decides when you die?" *The Toronto Star* (September 4, 2010) at A1, 17.

[144] See, *e.g.*, *Auton (Guardian ad litem of) v. British Columbia (Attorney General)*, [2004] S.C.J. No. 71, 2004 SCC 78 (S.C.C.); *Cameron v. Nova Scotia (Attorney General)*, [1999] N.S.J. No. 297 (N.S.C.A.) (unsuccessful claims to have state fund treatment (for autism and IVF respectively) that is not included in the public health plan); *Chaoulli v. Quebec (Attorney General)*, [2005] S.C.J. No. 33, 1 S.C.R. 791 (S.C.C.) (successful constitutional challenge to prohibition on purchasing private health insurance if services cannot be accessed in a timely manner in the publicly funded system); *Eldridge v. British Columbia (Attorney General)*, [1997] S.C.J. No. 86, 3 S.C.R. 624 (S.C.C.) (successful claim that the support (sign language interpreters) needed to extend the benefit of publicly funded health services to people not able to access them because of disability (hearing impairment) must be provided).

[145] See *Flora v. Ontario (Health Insurance Plan, General Manager)*, [2008] O.J. No. 2627 (Ont. C.A.).

[146] "Report of the Ad Hoc Committee of the Harvard Medical School to Examine the Definition of Brain Death" (1968) 205 JAMA 85; Canadian Medical Association, "A C.M.A. Position – Guidelines for the Definition of Brain Death" (1987) 136 CMAJ 200A-B; S.D. Shemie, C. Doig, E.B. Dickens *et al.*, "Severe Brain Injury to Neurological Determination of Death: Canadian Fo-

does not define death, but rather, accepts medical determination of death as authoritative, typically providing that for the purposes of post-mortem transplant, death must be determined by at least two physicians "in accordance with accepted medical practice".[147] Until recently in Canada, post-mortem organ donations were only considered when individuals met the criteria for brain death (donation after brain death, or DBD).[148] However, changing practices in the United States and a number of European countries led the Canadian Council for Donation and Transplantation to sponsor a national forum in 2005 to consider proceeding with organ donation after cardiac death (DCD, also known as non-heart-beating organ donation). The report of its Forum Recommendations Group was published in 2006.[149] It proposed principles, procedures and practice related to DCD, and recommended that individual programs be developed beginning with controlled DCD (*i.e.*, in circumstances where death is anticipated but has not yet occurred) within the intensive care unit, after a consensual decision to

---

rum Recommendations" (2006) 174:6 CMAJ S1-S12. Definitions of death may vary depending on the context; for instance, medicine and the civil law may differ from the criminal law: *R. v. Green*, [1988] B.C.J. No. 1807, 43 C.C.C. (3d) 413 (B.C.S.C.). On developments in the legal definition of death generally, see J. Gilmour, *Study Paper on Assisted Suicide, Euthanasia and Foregoing Treatment* (Toronto: Ontario Law Reform Commission, 1996) at 35-40 and J. Gilmour, "Death and Dying" in Borden Ladner Gervais LLP, ed (original editor M.J. Dykeman), *Canadian Health Law Practice Manual* (Markham, ON: LexisNexis Canada, 2000, incl. service issues to 2010) at paras. 8.5-8.11. The use of a neurological standard to determine death — *i.e.*, that "whole brain death — but no other sort of injury that leaves circulation and respiration intact — is an appropriate standard for determining the death of a human being" has become controversial in recent years, to such an extent that in the U.S., the President's Council on Bioethics released a White Paper on the subject, *Controversies in the Determination of Death* (Washington, DC: 2008). As it noted, among the considerable academic commentary on the subject, some argue the neurological standard is "too restrictive to meet the need for transplantable organs, others fear that 'whole brain death' may not be the equivalent of ... death; still others believe that in the face of uncertainty, it is ethically prudent to re-examine the concept and the evidence critically" (*ibid.*, at ix-x).

147 For example, *Trillium Gift of Life Network Act*, R.S.O. 1990, c. H.20, s. 7(1). Of all the provinces and territories, only Manitoba specifically recognizes brain death: *Vital Statistics Act*, R.S.M. 1987, c. V60, s. 2. In *Criteria for the Determination of Death* (Report No. 15) (Ottawa: Supply and Services Canada, 1981) at 25, the Law Reform Commission of Canada recommended legislation recognizing that a person is dead when an irreversible cessation of all that person's brain function occurs, determined on the basis of prolonged absence of spontaneous circulatory and respiratory functions, or when this is impossible because of the use of artificial means of support, by any means recognized by the ordinary standards of current medical practice.

148 C. Doig, "Is the Canadian Health Care System Ready for Donation after Cardiac Death? A Note of Caution" (2006) 175:8 CMAJ 905.

149 S. Shemie, A. Baker, G. Knoll *et al.*, "Donation after Cardiocirculatory Death in Canada" (2006) 175:8 CMAJ S1-S23 [hereinafter "DCD in Canada"]. See also Gouvernement du Québec, *Rapport de consultation sur les enjeux éthiques du don et de la transplantation d'organes : résultats des entrevues de groupes et du mini-sondage réalisé dans le cadre de l'Enquête Statmédia du printemps 2004* (Sainte-Foy, QC: Commission de l'éthique de la science et de la technologie, 2004).

withdraw life-sustaining therapies.[150] In June 2006, the Ottawa Hospital announced organ donation from a patient following cardiac arrest, and by the end
of 2009, organs were being retrieved for donation after cardiac death in four
provinces: British Columbia, Ontario, Quebec and Nova Scotia.[151] With these
developments, an area that had been settled is becoming newly contentious, and
raises new questions for substitute decision-makers.

As Robert Truog points out, there are concerns about conflicts of interest
both when decisions are made about whether to withdraw life support, and when
counselling families about DCD.[152] Delaying the withdrawal of life support may
enhance prognostic certainty for the patient concerned, but damage the quality
of the organs. Difficulties in decision-making are exacerbated because there is
often no consensus among physicians about end of life practices, including pre-
dicting outcome and in particular, irreversibility after a short cessation of cardiac
and respiratory functions.[153] The risk that public trust and confidence will be
eroded is real.

One of the key differences between controlled donation after cardiac death
and donation after brain death is that with DCD, once a decision has been made
to withdraw life support, the option of donation is presented, and if accepted,
then life-sustaining therapies are withdrawn, death is diagnosed using cardiac
criteria and the organs are procured. This differs from common practice with
neurological determination of death, where death is first diagnosed using neu-
rologic criteria, then the option of donation is presented, and if consent is obtained, then the organs are procured. In some DCD programs, it is permissible to
perform interventions on the patient prior to death to maximize the potential for

---

[150] "Consensual decision to withdraw life-sustaining therapies" is defined as "a decision that has been
agreed to by the patient, family and the treating health care team": DCD in Canada, *ibid.*, at S4.

[151] U. Gandhi, "With death, the saving of two lives" *The Globe and Mail* (June 28, 2006) at A21
(the deceased, a 32-year-old woman, had clearly indicated to her parents that she wanted to be an
organ donor if she died); Canadian Institute for Health Information, "Organ donations increasing
in Canada but not keeping pace with demand" (December 22, 2009), online at:
<http://www.cihi.ca/CIHI-ext-portal/internet/en/document/types+of+care/specialized+services/organ
+replacements/release_22dec2009>.

[152] R. Truog, "Donation After Cardiac Death: The Next Great Advance in Organ Transplantation"
(Toronto) Hospital for Sick Children (November 8, 2006); R. Truog & F. Miller, "Re-thinking
the Ethics of Vital Organ Donations" (2008) 38 Hastings Center Report 38.

[153] C. Doig, "Is the Canadian Health Care System Ready for Donation After Cardiac Death? A Note
of Caution" (2006) 175:8 CMAJ 905, citing D.J. Cook, G. Guyatt, R. Jaeschke *et al.*, "Determinants in Canadian Health Care Workers of the Decision to Withdraw Life Support from the Critically Ill. Canadian Critical Care Trials Group" (1995) 273 JAMA 703-708. (Doig was a member
of the Forum Recommendation Group and the CCDT but resigned, believing these issues so significant that he did not endorse the report or support proceeding with DCD based solely on one
forum.) See also J. Downie, M. Kutcher, C. Rajotte & A. Shea, "Eligibility for Organ Donation:
A Medico-Legal Perspective on Defining and Determining Death" (2009) 56:11 Can J. Anesthesia 851; D. Marquis, "Are DCD Donors Dead?" (2010) 40 Hastings Center Report 24; T. Blackwell, "Families of donors misled on death: MDs" *National Post* (September 14, 2010).

usable organs or improve the function of organs once transplanted.[154] While the Forum Report identifies optimal end of life care for the dying patient as the primary responsibility of health care providers, and support for family and loved ones about to be bereaved as a core value, it envisages interventions prior to death that may include vessel cannulation, as well as administration of vasodilators, anticoagulants and thrombolytic agents, and other procedures, raising the prospect that quality end of life care will be compromised by interventions performed not for the benefit of the dying patient, but in order to preserve organs for transplantation.[155]

Interventions to facilitate donation that occur before death, such as vessel cannulation or the administration of medication, require consent — either that of the patient, if competent, or, more likely, that of the substitute decision-maker.[156] This can raise questions about whether substitute decision-makers are even entitled to make such determinations, particularly if there is no indication that the person concerned wanted to be an organ donor. First, absent prior capable wishes or directions, decisions are to be made in the best interests of the patient, and it is difficult to argue that these procedures are meant to benefit this patient; indeed, the "benefit" the Forum Report identifies is to the eventual recipient of the organs.[157] Second, substitute decision-makers are authorized to consent to or refuse "treatment", a term that may be defined in terms focused on measures taken for the good of that patient, raising questions about whether these procedures fall within the definition of "treatment" at all.[158] While some statutes include an exception from the requirement to obtain consent when the treatment poses little or no risk of harm to the patient, and the Forum Recommendations state that interventions undertaken before death to facilitate DCD should pose "no more than minimal risk", it is not clear that the two concepts of minimal risk are the same.[159]

Statutes governing organ donation may authorize substitute consent to post-mortem donation when a patient is decisionally incapable and death is imminent.[160] However, they do not address substitute consent to invasive procedures performed on the patient prior to his death; they were not drafted with that possibility in mind. To confuse matters further, the substitute decision-maker identi-

---

[154] DCD in Canada at S12. See also J. Downie, C. Rajotte & A. Shea, "Pre-Mortem Transplantation Optimizing Interventions: The Legal Status of Consent" (2008) 55:7 Can. J. Anesthesia 458.

[155] *Ibid.*, at S3, S12. R. Truog, "Donation After Cardiac Death: The Next Great Advance in Organ Transplantation" (Toronto) Hospital for Sick Children (November 8, 2006).

[156] Doig notes in "Is the Canadian Health Care System Ready for Donation After Cardiac Death? A Note of Caution" (2006) 175:8 CMAJ 905 that the patients primarily considered for DCD are patients with severe brain injury.

[157] DCD in Canada at S12.

[158] In Ontario, for instance, the *Health Care Consent Act, 1996*, S.O. 1996, c. 2, Sched. A, s. 2(1) defines "treatment" as "anything done for a therapeutic, preventive, palliative, diagnostic, cosmetic or other health-related purpose".

[159] DCD in Canada at S12.

[160] See, *e.g.*, *Trillium Gift of Life Network Act*, R.S.O. 1990, c. H.20, s. 5(2).

fied in human tissue legislation may not be the same as the substitute decision-maker authorized to consent to or refuse treatment while the patient is alive.

DCD raises significant legal and ethical issues. They are of concern to the wider community and engage more than just medical considerations. Broader consideration of this practice is essential.

VI. CRIMINAL LAW

The *Criminal Code* prohibits assisted suicide and euthanasia.[161] It includes a number of other provisions that can impact on medical treatment, failure to treat or cessation of treatment as well. For the most part, they are of general application and were not framed with a view to modern medical realities.[162] Consequently, determining when and how they apply to health care is not always straightforward, nor are the standards that govern decision-making about life-sustaining treatment always clear or uncontentious.[163] Decisions about enforcement are also significant. Administration of the criminal justice system falls within provincial jurisdiction; this includes formulating policies about charging decisions.[164] Accepted medical practice is very influential in deciding whether to lay criminal charges, particularly in cases involving health care providers. However, medical norms will not always be sufficient to resolve issues that arise. Physicians have serious disagreements among themselves about many of these issues. More importantly, decisions about the provision of life-sustaining treatment are not entirely medical; they engage broader values and ethical concerns as well, and these are not areas in which doctors necessarily have special expertise.

With increasing challenges to medical authority, there is less certainty about what norms will prevail; this in turn can affect practice. Concerns over potential criminal liability underlay the refusal of the hospital and treating physician in *B. (N.) v. Hôtel-Dieu de Québec* to accede to her demand that she be removed from the ventilator that sustained her life.[165] Such hesitation is not an isolated occurrence; it arises in other areas as well, such as ensuring patients receive adequate pain management. Legal commentators and the Law Reform Commission of

---

[161] R.S.C. 1985, c. C-46, ss. 222, 241.

[162] Law Reform Commission of Canada, "Euthanasia, Aiding Suicide and Cessation of Treatment", Working Paper 28 (Ottawa: Department of Supply and Services, 1982).

[163] For a more extensive discussion of the ways in which provisions in the *Criminal Code* could affect end of life decision-making and care, see J. Gilmour, *Study Paper on Assisted Suicide, Euthanasia and Foregoing Treatment* (Toronto: Ontario Law Reform Commission, 1996) at chapters 5, 6 and 12; and J. Gilmour, "Death and Dying" in Borden Ladner Gervais LLP, ed. (original editor M.J. Dykeman), *Canadian Health Law Practice Manual* (Markham, ON: LexisNexis Canada, 2000, incl. service issues to 2010) at paras. 8.80-8.116.

[164] See, *e.g.*, B.C. Crown Counsel Policy Guidelines with respect to active euthanasia and assisted suicide, Policy 11-3-93, File No. 56880-01 (Eut 1), reproduced in Senate Special Committee, *Of Life and Death: Special Senate Committee Report on Euthanasia and Assisted Suicide* (Ottawa: Minister of Supply and Services Canada, 1995) at A-59.

[165] [1992] Q.J. No. 1, 86 D.L.R. (4th) 385 (Que. S.C.).

Canada have stressed that criminal proceedings arising out of end of life care are unlikely.[166] They point out that there have been very few criminal prosecutions for assisted suicide or euthanasia, and even fewer arising from the medical treatment involved. Further, where charges have been laid against medical personnel, there has historically been a high acquittal rate. Nonetheless, as the circumstances of particular cases capture public attention and highlight the splintered and fluid nature of societal perceptions and expectations, not only about the use of life-sustaining medical technologies, but also about appropriate decision-making processes and standards, concern about what is and is not permitted in decision-making about end of life care intensifies.

A. ASSISTED SUICIDE

Assisted suicide is "the act of intentionally killing oneself with the assistance of another who provides the knowledge, means or both".[167] The *Criminal Code* makes counselling, aiding or abetting suicide an offence, punishable by up to 14 years' imprisonment.[168] In *Rodriguez v. British Columbia (Attorney General)*, the Supreme Court of Canada considered a constitutional challenge to the prohibition on assisted suicide brought by Sue Rodriguez, a 42-year-old woman who suffered from amyotrophic lateral sclerosis, who claimed that it violated her right to liberty and security of the person under section 7 of the *Canadian Charter of Rights and Freedoms*, to equality under section 15, and to be free from cruel and unusual treatment or punishment under section 12.[169] A narrow majority of the Court rejected her challenge and upheld the law. It held that the law did not breach section 7, and that even if one assumed a breach of section 15 (a point it did not decide), the provision would be saved under section 1 of the Charter, since it was a reasonable limit demonstrably justified in a free and democratic society.[170]

---

[166] Law Reform Commission of Canada, "Euthanasia, Aiding Suicide and Cessation of Treatment" Working Paper 28 (Ottawa: Department of Supply and Services, 1982) at 8, 20; J. Gilmour, "Death and Dying" in Borden Ladner Gervais LLP, ed. (original editor M.J. Dykeman), *Canadian Health Law Practice Manual* (Markham, ON: LexisNexis Canada, 2000, incl. service issues to 2010) at paras. 8.119-8.126.

[167] Special Senate Committee, *Of Life and Death: Special Senate Committee Report on Euthanasia and Assisted Suicide* (Ottawa: Minister of Supply and Services, 1995) at 14.

[168] R.S.C. 1985, c. C-46, s. 241. Attempted suicide itself was decriminalized in 1972; J. Gilmour, *Study Paper on Assisted Suicide, Euthanasia and Foregoing Treatment* (Toronto: Ontario Law Reform Commission, 1996) at 91, note 13.

[169] [1993] S.C.J. No. 94, [1993] 3 S.C.R. 519 (S.C.C.).

[170] A later attempt to revisit the issue after the Senate Committee released *Of Life and Death* in 1995, because of the Report's findings about both the inadequacy of palliative care available in Canada and a lack of societal consensus on the issue of assisted suicide, was rejected: *Wakeford v. Canada (Attorney General)*, [2001] O.J. No. 390 (Ont. S.C.J.). For an argument that developments in the interpretation of s. 7 since *Rodriguez* would support a finding that the *Criminal Code* prohibition on assisting suicide does breach the Charter, see J. Downie & S. Bern, "Rodriguez Redux" (2008) 16 Health L.J. 27.

While prosecutions for assisted suicide are infrequent, they do occur. Family members have been convicted of assisting suicide.[171] In Quebec, for instance, Marielle Houle was charged with assisting suicide when she helped her 36-year-old son to kill himself in 2004. He suffered from multiple sclerosis and as his condition deteriorated, had repeatedly asked her for help in taking his own life.[172] She pleaded guilty and was sentenced to three years' probation. Evidence before the court on sentencing was that the 60-year-old Houle, who was in ill health herself, had lived as a virtual recluse in a nursing home since her son's death. In passing sentence, Laramée J. emphasized that Houle was not able to judge her son's competence, and that considering the sacred nature of life and the possible abuses and lack of proper safeguards to protect the vulnerable, the prohibition on assisted suicide was neither arbitrary nor unreasonable. However, he concluded that although her actions "remained reprehensible and unlawful ... Considering the life Ms. Houle now leads ... punitive conditions are pointless", adding that what she experienced as she helped her son die was enough of a punishment.[173] In other cases in Ontario and Quebec, juries acquitted family members charged with assisting suicide.[174] In Ontario, the accused was alleged to have test-fired the gun his father later used to take his own life, having reportedly told friends he would rather kill himself than live in a nursing home. In the Quebec case, the nephew of a man severely disabled by polio acceded to his uncle's repeated requests to help him die, and set up the apparatus that enabled him to hang himself. In Nova Scotia, police investigated the circumstances surrounding the death of a woman suffering from multiple sclerosis whose husband accompanied her to Switzerland, where she took her own life with the assistance

---

[171] Cases involving charges of assisted suicide and their disposition are summarized in J. Gilmour, "Death and Dying" in Borden Ladner Gervais LLP, ed. (original editor M.J. Dykeman), *Canadian Health Law Practice Manual* (Markham, ON: LexisNexis Canada, 2000, incl. services issues to 2010) at paras. 8.87-8.89. See also A. Mullens, *Timely Death: Considering Our Last Rights* (Toronto: Knopf, 1996) at 52; J. Downie, *Dying Justice* (Toronto: University of Toronto Press, 2004) at 34-35. See also G. Oakes, "B.C.'s top court upheld a conviction for counselling or aiding a person to commit suicide" *Lawyers Weekly* (November 5, 2004) at 2, reporting that the British Columbia Court of Appeal upheld a nine-month conditional sentence and 18 months' probation in the case of Juliana Zsiros, found guilty of aiding suicide by a jury after the body of Linda Whetung was found in her car, which had been left with the motor running and a hose leading from the exhaust pipe into the car: *R. v. Zsiros*, [2004] B.C.J. No. 2099, 203 B.C.A.C. 298 (B.C.C.A.).

[172] T. Thanh Ha, "Mother charged in son's death" *The Globe and Mail* (September 28, 2004) at A9; I. Peritz, "Assisting in her son's suicide was final act of compassion, court told" *The Globe and Mail* (January 24, 2006) at A24.

[173] *R. c. Houle*, [2006] J.Q. no 481, 38 C.R. (6th) 242 (Que. C.S.); T. Thanh Ha, "Mother spared jail in son's assisted suicide" *The Globe and Mail* (January 28, 2006) at A5.

[174] R. Avery, "Man's son 'test-fired' suicide gun, Trial told father feared going into nursing home" *The Toronto Star* (April 19, 2000) at A4; "Quebec man acquitted on assisted suicide charge" CBC News (December 12, 2008), online at: <http://www.cbc.ca/health/story/2008/12/12/mtl-assistedsuicide1212.html>. The Quebec decision was upheld on appeal: *Canadian Broadcasting Corp. v. The Queen*, [2011] S.C.J. No. 3, 2011 SCC 3 at para. 15 (S.C.C.).

of a right to die organization, but reportedly concluded charges were not warranted, since no crime had been committed in Canada.[175]

Others have sought help in ending their lives from non-family members, especially right to die organizations, and this, too, has led to criminal charges being laid for assisting suicide. Evelyn Martens, a 71-year-old member of the Canadian Right to Die Society, was charged with assisting suicide in the deaths of two British Columbia women. The women, aged 64 and 57, both ended their own lives in 2002. They were reported to have been terminally ill and to have requested Marten's assistance in dying. It was alleged that she provided them with "exit bags", helium and sleep-inducing drugs.[176] Following a jury trial, Martens was found not guilty of the charges.[177]

Health care providers have rarely been prosecuted for assisting suicide.[178] In 1996, Dr. Maurice Genereux, a Toronto physician, pleaded guilty to aiding and abetting suicide after prescribing lethal doses of barbiturates to two suicidal patients who were HIV-positive (but not suffering from AIDS). He knew neither was terminally ill, and that treatment could have helped both. One patient did take his own life with the medication, while the other failed in the attempt. The sentence imposed — two years less a day's imprisonment, and three years' probation — was affirmed on appeal.[179] In British Columbia, Dr. Ramesh Sharma pleaded guilty to charges of attempting to assist a 93-year-old patient to commit suicide. She had requested his help to die, and he provided a prescription for drugs that would end her life. The court imposed a conditional sentence of two years less a day, to be served in the community.[180]

---

[175] "No charges in assisted suicide case" CBC News (July 3, 2007), online at: <http://www.cbc.ca/news/canada/nova-scotia/story/2007/07/03/rcmp-macdonald.html>.

[176] D. Meissner, "Woman present at death, trial hears" *The Globe and Mail* (October 13, 2004) at A14; D. Girard, "Suicide debate back in spotlight" *The Toronto Star* (October 12, 2004) at A8.

[177] "Martens not guilty in assisted suicide case" CTV.ca News Staff (November 5, 2004), online at: <http://www.ctv.ca/servlet/ArticleNews/story/CTVNews/1099621315012_6/?hub=Canada%20>.
More recently, it has been reported that two Canadians took their own lives following workshops and instructions offered by right-to-die advocates in Canada: see L. Perreaux, "Canadians followed Australian doctor's suicide instructions" *The Globe and Mail* (September 28, 2010).

[178] Professional discipline proceedings are also rare. See generally J. Gilmour, "Death and Dying" in Borden Ladner Gervais LLP, ed. (original editor M.J. Dykeman), *Canadian Health Law Practice Manual* (Markham, ON: LexisNexis Canada, 2000, incl. services issues to 2010) at paras. 8.128-8.134.1. In an unusual turn of events, a member of the Ontario College of Psychologists complained that another psychologist had contravened its standards of practice by conspiring with a right to die organization, Dignitas, to violate the *Criminal Code* prohibition on assisting suicide, by accompanying a seriously ill friend to Switzerland (where assisted suicide without self-interest is legal), where a Dignitas representative assisted her to take her own life. The complaint was triggered when the psychologist wrote a letter to a newspaper about the experience. The College rejected the complaint, as did the Health Professions Appeal and Review Board: H. Levy, "Doctor's role in assisted suicide probed" *The Toronto Star* (May 16, 2006) at A1; H. Levy, "One complains about role of other in assisted suicide" *The Toronto Star* (May 17, 2006) at A4, online at: <http://www.thestar.com>.

[179] *R. v. Genereux*, [1999] O.J. No. 1387, 44 O.R. (3d) 339 (Ont. C.A.).

[180] Police said the attempted suicide was interrupted by a staff member at the care facility where the patient was a resident: G. Preston, "Doctor charged in attempted suicide" *Vancouver Sun* (Au-

The infrequency of prosecution does not mean that assisted suicides do not occur. The Special Senate Committee on Assisted Suicide and Euthanasia concluded that while it could not ascertain how often assisted suicide is requested or happens, or under what conditions, it had "heard sufficient evidence to suspect it is being requested and provided".[181] The most well-known case is that of Sue Rodriguez. She ultimately ended her own life, reportedly with medical assistance.[182] A special prosecutor appointed to determine whether charges should be laid against a Member of Parliament present at her death concluded that charges were not warranted under British Columbia's charge approval process, as conviction was unlikely in the circumstances, given that others, reportedly including a physician, were present at the time of her death as well.[183] On the other hand, it should not be thought that suicide assistance is freely available despite the law. The Special Senate Committee heard moving testimony from surviving family members of a number of individuals whose last illnesses were pain-wracked, who had endured great suffering, and who had attempted to find a health care practitioner who would help them to die but were unable to do so.[184]

A review of developments in the law governing assisted suicide outside Canada is beyond the scope of this chapter. It is of note, however, that over the last 15 years, a number of jurisdictions have legalized some forms of assisted suicide in restricted circumstances. In the United States, the *Oregon Death with Dignity Act* was passed in 1994, and implemented in 1998. It protects physicians

---

gust 2, 2006); CanWest News Service, "Doctor who offered to assist in suicide accepts suspension" *National Post* (April 3, 2007) at A8; D. Wylie, "Doc who prescribed suicide by pills gets conditional sentence" *Ottawa Citizen* (June 11, 2007).

[181] Senate of Canada, *Of Life and Death: Special Senate Committee Report or Euthanasia and Assisted Suicide* (Ottawa: Minister of Supply and Services Canada, 1995) at 55. See also R. Ogden, *Euthanasia, Assisted Suicide and AIDS* (Pitt Meadows, BC: Perreault/Goedmann Publishing, 1994); Proceedings of the Special Senate Committee on Euthanasia and Assisted Suicide, Testimony of Dr. Ted Boadway, Director of Health Policy, Ontario Medical Association (October 17, 1994) at 20, 82-83.

[182] D. Wilson & D. Downey, "Patient fought to die on her own terms" *The Globe and Mail* (February 14, 1994) at A4.

[183] Canadian Press, "Role of MP in Rodriguez suicide to be probed" *The Toronto Star* (January 11, 1995) at A2; T. Harper, "MP not charged in aided suicide" *The Toronto Star* (June 29, 1995) at A2.

[184] Senate of Canada, *Of Life and Death: Special Senate Committee Report on Euthanasia and Assisted Suicide* (Ottawa: Minister of Supply and Services Canada, 1995) at 65. The stories of many of these families are expanded on in A. Mullens, *Timely Death: Considering Our Last Rights* (Toronto: Knopf, 1996). Fifteen years after the Senate Committee's report, public consultations held by the Quebec National Assembly's Select Committee on Dying with Dignity (which has been charged with examining what options are appropriate in end of life care) revealed agonizing experiences, including that of Laurent Rouleau, a man severely disabled by multiple sclerosis who had decided to end his life before he was completely incapacitated. He shot himself in the stomach, called 911 to avoid having his wife find his body, and was then taken to hospital by emergency responders. Doctors would not honour his refusal of treatment because they concluded he was suicidal. Eventually, a psychiatrist confirmed he was capable of refusing treatment, and he was allowed to die, 14 hours after firing the shots. See L. Perreaux, "Gruelling suicide makes case for euthanasia" *The Globe and Mail* (September 8, 2010) at A10.

in that state from civil or criminal liability when they dispense or prescribe a lethal dose of drugs on the request of a terminally ill patient, provided certain safeguards and conditions are met.[185] The law withstood numerous court challenges, including an attempt by the U.S. Attorney-General to interpret federal legislation regulating controlled substances so as to effectively criminalize physician-assisted suicide under federal law. *Gonzalez v. Oregon* largely bypassed the debate about "the legality and morality and practicality of physician-assisted suicide" and turned instead on administrative law questions, and an analysis of the division of powers between the federal government and states. The United States Supreme Court held that the federal legislation would not bear the interpretation for which the federal Attorney-General argued.[186] In 2009, Washington became the second state to pass legislation making assisted suicide legal in prescribed circumstances. Annual reports by each state indicate that a total of 460 Oregon patients had died from ingesting medications prescribed pursuant to the legislation by the end of 2009, while in Washington, 47 patients died after ingesting lethal doses of medication prescribed during the first 10 months after its law took effect.[187] In Montana, a 2009 ruling by the state Supreme Court concluded that state law did not prevent patients from seeking medical assistance to commit suicide.[188] In 2002, the Netherlands became the first country to pass a law decriminalizing voluntary euthanasia, giving statutory force to an accommodation that had prevailed in that country for a number of years, which allowed voluntary euthanasia under certain conditions.[189] Belgium decriminalized assisted suicide and euthanasia in limited circumstances in 2002, and Luxembourg did so in 2008.[190] In Switzerland, suicide assistance has not been legally

---

[185] B. Bostrom, "Gonzales v. Oregon" (2006) 21 Issues L. & Med. 203.

[186] *Oregon v. Ashcroft*, 126 S. Ct. 904 (2006), affg 368 F.3d 1118 (9th Cir. 2004), affg 192 F. Supp. 2d 1077 (D. Or. 2002); Kennedy J. was citing *Washington v. Glucksberg*, 521 U.S. 702, 735 (1997).

[187] Oregon, *2009 Summary of Oregon's Death with Dignity Act*, online at: <http://www.oregon.gov/DHS/ph/pas/docs/year12.pdf?ga=t>; Washington State Department of Health, "Washington State Department of Health 2009 Death with Dignity Act Report", online at: <http://www.doh.wa.gov/dwda/forms/DWDA_2009.pdf>.

[188] *Baxter v. State of Montana*, 2009 MT 449, 224 P.3d 1211 (S.C.).

[189] T. Sheldon, "Holland decriminalises voluntary euthanasia" (2001) 322 B.M.J. 322, online at: <http://www.bmj.com>; J. De Haan, "The New Dutch Law on Euthanasia" (2002) 10 Med. L. Rev. 57; A. Janssen, "The New Regulation of Voluntary Euthanasia and Medically Assisted Suicide in the Netherlands" (2002) Int'l J.L. Pol'y & Fam. 260.

[190] E. Vermeersch, "The Belgian Law on Euthanasia. The Historical and Ethical Background" (2002) 102 Acta chir. belg. 394; H. Nys, "Recent Developments in the Law in Belgium" (2006) 13:2 Eur. J. Health Law 95; J. Ponthus, "Luxembourg parliament adopts euthanasia law" Reuters, online at: <http://www.reuters.com/assets/print?aid=USL2011983320080220>. One year after euthanasia was legalized in Belgium, the government reported that 203 such deaths had been officially recorded: "In Belgium, 203 chose euthanasia" *Medical Post* (December 9, 2003) at 58.

penalized for almost 100 years, provided it is without self-interest.[191] Of the jurisdictions that allow the practice, it appears to be the least restrictive in the conditions imposed.[192]

In most countries, however, assisted suicide remains illegal.[193] Even so,
there are some indications of change, as states become more explicit in delineat-
ing (and limiting) circumstances in which charges will be laid.[194] In England, the
House of Lords ordered the Director of Public Prosecutions (DPP) to promul-
gate a policy identifying the facts and circumstances considered in decisions to
prosecute for aiding and abetting suicide.[195] Debbie Purdy, a 46-year-old woman
with multiple sclerosis, had challenged the DPP's refusal to advise what factors
would be considered in deciding whether to prosecute her husband if he helped
her travel to a country where assisted suicide was lawful and she took her own
life there. The court held that the lack of guidance about the law and its application breached her rights under the *Convention for the Protection of Human
Rights and Fundamental Freedoms*.[196] The DPP released its policy on assisted
suicide in 2010, describing it as changing the focus of its assessment in charging
decisions to the motivation of the suspect more than the characteristics of the
victim, while leaving the law unchanged.[197]

The pervasive influence of the internet raises new questions for criminal
law in this area. Following the 2008 suicide of a teenaged university student in
Ontario, prosecutors in Minnesota charged a middle-aged male nurse resident in
that state with aiding her suicide and that of others, reportedly by entering into
online suicide pacts with them.[198] The case, and the legal issues it raises, remained unresolved at the time of writing.

---

[191] G. Bosshard, D. Jermini, D. Eisenhart & W. Bar, "Assisted Suicide Bordering on Active Euthanasia" (2002) 117 Int. J. Legal Med. 106 (commenting on the expansive understanding of assisted suicide employed in Switzerland).

[192] G. Bosshard, L. Fischer & W. Bar, "How Switzerland Compares with the Netherlands and Oregon" (2002) 132 Swiss Med. Wkly. 527; A. Frei, T. Schenker, A. Finzen, K. Krauchi, V. Ditt-
mann & U. Hoffmann-Richter, "Assisted Suicide as Conducted by a 'Right-to-Die' Society in
Switzerland: A Descriptive Analysis of 43 Consecutive Cases" (2001) 131 Swiss Med. Wkly
375; S. Hurst & A. Mauron, "Assisted Suicide and Euthanasia in Switzerland: Allowing a Role
for Non-Physicians" (2003) 326 B.M.J. 271.

[193] C. MacKellar, "Laws and Practices Relating to Euthanasia and Assisted Suicide in 34 Countries
of the Council of Europe and the USA" (2003) 10 Eur. J. Health L. 63. In *Pretty v. United Kingdom* (2002), 35 E.H.R.R. 1, [2002] 1 A.C. 800 (C.A.), the European Court of Human Rights and
courts in England rejected a challenge to English law criminalizing assisted suicide.

[194] MacKellar, *ibid.*

[195] *R (Purdy) v. Director of Public Prosecutions*, [2009] UKHL 45, [2009] W.L.R. (D) 271.

[196] (November 4, 1950), 213 U.N.T.S. 221.

[197] United Kingdom, Crown Prosecution Service, "DPP publishes assisted suicide policy" (February
25, 2010), online at: <http://www.cps.gov.uk/news/press_releases/109_10/>.

[198] R. Doolittle, "Minnesota man charged in Brampton teen's suicide" *The Toronto Star* (April 24,
2010) at A3; J. Wingrove, "Man charged with aiding suicide of Ottawa student over the Internet"
The Globe and Mail (April 24, 2010) at A3; Associated Press, "Accused in suicides waives jury
trial" *The Globe and Mail* (February 5, 2011) at A21.

B.   EUTHANASIA

The *Criminal Code* provides that a person commits homicide when he or she causes the death of another human being by any means, whether directly or indirectly.[199] Not all homicides are culpable, and only culpable homicides are criminal offences. Culpable homicide is murder, manslaughter or infanticide, and includes causing death by means of an unlawful act, or by criminal negligence.[200] Culpable homicide is murder, *inter alia*, where the person meant to cause the death or to cause bodily harm that he or she knows is likely to result in death, and is reckless as to whether death ensues or not.[201] Culpable homicide that is not murder — that is, where the agent lacks the necessary subjective mental element (degree of intent) — is manslaughter.[202] The penalties for each differ greatly. Manslaughter is subject to a maximum of life imprisonment, but no mandatory minimum sentence.[203] A conviction for murder carries a mandatory life sentence with a minimum period prior to parole eligibility of 25 years for first degree murder, and 10 years (or such greater time as may be imposed) for second degree murder.[204]

Clearly, euthanasia that involves the deliberate taking of a life can constitute murder.[205] The most well-known case in Canada is that of Robert Latimer. He was charged with first degree murder and convicted of second degree murder when he intentionally asphyxiated his severely disabled young daughter.[206] He was sentenced to life imprisonment, with a minimum period of parole ineligibility of 10 years. The case created a furor, for some because they believed the application of the mandatory minimum sentencing law for murder to be unjust in the circumstances, and for others, because both the crime and the public support for Latimer were seen as not only an affront to the equality and dignity of people with disabilities, but a real threat to their lives.

In one of the few cases in which criminal charges have been laid against a health professional, Dr. Nancy Morrison was charged with first degree murder in connection with the death of one of her patients, a 65-year-old terminally ill man suffering from cancer. His family had consented to the withdrawal of all life support. The charge was based on her intravenous administration of potassium chloride to him after all attempts to relieve the significant pain he was suffering had proved ineffective. She was discharged following a preliminary

---

[199]   R.S.C. 1985, c. C-46, s. 222.

[200]   *Ibid.*

[201]   *Ibid.*, s. 229.

[202]   *Ibid.*, s. 234.

[203]   *Ibid.*, s. 236.

[204]   *Ibid.*, ss. 235, 742.

[205]   In a recent example, retired Quebec Court of Appeal judge Jacques Delisle was charged with murder in the 2009 shooting death of his wife, which police had initially thought to be suicide. See J. Montpetit & S. Banerjee, "Historic murder case involving Quebec judge prompts steps to ensure impartiality" *The Toronto Star* (June 16, 2010); M. White, "Unprecedented murder case of former judge" *National Post* (June 17, 2010).

[206]   *R. v. Latimer*, [1997] S.C.J. No. 11, [1997] 1 S.C.R. 217 (S.C.C.).

inquiry. The presiding judge concluded that no properly instructed jury could convict her, since credible evidence established that the intravenous tip may have been dislodged and the patient may not have received the lethal medication at all, given the massive amount of pain medication that had previously been delivered intravenously, with no effect.[207] The Nova Scotia College of Physicians and Surgeons conducted its own investigation of the events; it issued a letter of reprimand to Dr. Morrison, which she signed, acknowledging that she gave the injection.[208]

Crown attorneys have reduced charges of murder to manslaughter or some other lesser offence because of the accused's compassionate motive. Difficulties in proof can also play a role in decisions to reduce charges. In 2005, André Bergeron in Quebec was charged with attempted murder in the death of his 44-year-old wife, Marielle Houle.[209] She suffered from Friedrich's ataxia, a progressively degenerative neurological disorder that caused her intense pain; she had repeatedly asked to die. Bergeron had been her primary caregiver for more than two decades. He was deeply depressed at the time of her death. Members of her family were quoted as saying that he was mentally and physically exhausted, having done everything for her for many years, and that, while the family did not condone his actions, "we cannot hold it against him".[210] He pleaded guilty to a reduced charge of aggravated assault, and was sentenced to three years' probation.[211] In imposing this sentence, Côté J. said that she would have ordered a jail term, but for "the exceptional and particular tragic circumstances in his case, such as the devotion André Bergeron displayed throughout his shared life with Marielle Houle ... His act was taken not because the accused had come to consider his duty a burden but as a gesture of love for the victim, to free her of her sufferings and preserve her dignity".[212]

In Quebec, the Collège des médecins du Québec released a policy paper in 2009 which recognized "there are exceptional situations where euthanasia could be considered by patients and their loved ones and by doctors and other caregivers as a final step necessary to assure quality care at the very end", and concluded that the *Criminal Code* sometimes prevents physicians from exercising appropriate medical care at the end of life.[213] Soon after, the Quebec National Assembly established an all-party committee, the Select Committee on Dying with Dignity, to inquire broadly into euthanasia, assisted suicide and dying with

---

[207] *R. v. Morrison*, [1998] N.S.J. No. 75 (N.S. Prov. Ct.). The Crown's application for *certiorari* failed, affd [1998] N.S.J. No. 41 (N.S.S.C.).

[208] J. Downie, *Dying Justice* (Toronto: University of Toronto Press, 2004) at 42-43.

[209] R. Marowits, "Case spurs debate on assisted suicide" *The Toronto Star* (July 12, 2005) at A11.

[210] T. Thanh Ha, "A death that 'had to happen'" *The Globe and Mail* (July 15, 2005) at A1, A7.

[211] *R. c. Bergeron*, [2006] J.Q. no 11329, 43 C.R. (6th) 148 (Que. C.Q.); T. Thanh Ha, "Husband avoids jail in assisted-suicide case" *The Globe and Mail* (October 20, 2006) at A9.

[212] T. Thanh Ha, *ibid.*

[213] Collège des médecins du Québec, "Physicians, Appropriate Care and the Debate on Euthanasia" (October 16, 2009) and "The Collège des médecins du Québec Reveals Its Reflections on End-of-Life Care" (November 3, 2009), online at: <http://www.cmq.org/en/EtudiantsResidents/Profil/Commun/Nouvelles/2009/2009-11-03/communique.aspx>.

dignity.[214] At the time of writing, it had consulted with experts, and was undertaking public consultations.

C.   PRINCIPLE OF DOUBLE EFFECT

In Canadian criminal law, the deceased's consent to his or her own death is not a defence to criminal liability.[215] Nor is motive a constituent of the *mens rea* or *actus reus* of an offence, although it can be relevant to both.[216] However, in a departure from the general rules governing criminal liability, health care providers' motives are taken into account in certain instances. The principle of double effect, a long-standing feature of moral argument, has been incorporated into the law when analyzing the actions of health care professionals treating patients. Courts have accepted the legality in medical practice of taking actions with good and bad effects, as long as the actor intended only the good effects. Providing large doses of pain medication to relieve suffering, but with the known likelihood of hastening death, is a good example of this, and one the Supreme Court of Canada explicitly accepted as appropriate in *Rodriguez v. British Columbia (Attorney General)*.[217] Although both legal scholars and philosophers have criticized reliance on the principle of double effect,[218] in law, it functions as a limited exception to the refusal to take motive into account that otherwise prevails in criminal law.

D.   PROSECUTORIAL DISCRETION

Both ending treatment and administering it can come under one or more additional intersecting and overlapping provisions of the criminal law, including causing bodily harm by criminal negligence, failing to provide the necessaries of life to someone under one's charge, administering a noxious thing, failing to use reasonable knowledge, care and skill in administering surgical or medical treatment, causing bodily harm to another person, and others.[219] Prosecutions, however, remain very rare, particularly for the most serious offences. Part of the explanation for this lies in the exercise of prosecutorial discretion. Such discretion is important and properly allows extenuating circumstances to be taken into

---

[214] See, generally, Select Committee on Dying with Dignity of the Quebec National Assembly, online at: <http://www.assnat.qc.ca/en/travaux-parlementaires/commissions/csmd>.

[215] *Criminal Code*, R.S.C. 1985, c. C-46, s. 14.

[216] See, generally, *Lewis v. R.*, [1979] S.C.J. No. 73, [1979] 2 S.C.R. 821 at 833 (S.C.C.).

[217] [1993] S.C.J. No. 94, [1993] 3 S.C.R. 519 at 607 (S.C.C.). See also *B. (N.) v. Hôtel-Dieu de Québec*, [1992] Q.J. No. 1, 86 D.L.R. (4th) 385 (Que. S.C.) (ventilator withdrawal).

[218] See, *e.g.*, J. Rachels, "From 'Letting Die' to Active Killing" in J. Arras & N. Rhoden, eds., *Ethical Issues in Modern Medicine*, 3d ed. (Mountain View, CA: Mayfield Publishing, 1989) at 241-44; J. Fletcher, "The Courts and Euthanasia" (1987-1988) 15 Law, Med. & Health Care 223; J. Gilmour, *Study Paper on Assisted Suicide, Euthanasia and Foregoing Treatment* (Toronto: Ontario Law Reform Commission, 1996) at 243-46.

[219] *Criminal Code*, R.S.C. 1985, c. C-46, ss. 215-221, 245, 269. The applicability of these provisions of the Code to these issues is examined in detail in J. Gilmour, *ibid.*, at 69.

account. However, the lack of predictability and certainty in the charging process is particularly problematic in this context, because characterizations of conduct and circumstances can and do vary so widely, and are sometimes diametrically opposed.[220] Testifying before the Special Senate Committee on Euthanasia and Assisted Suicide, Dr. James Cairns, then Deputy Chief Coroner for Ontario, recounted that 60 senior Crown attorneys attending an educational session sponsored by the Ontario Coroner's office in the aftermath of several criminal prosecutions involving end of life care and assisted deaths "were as divided as anyone else" as to the appropriate charge to be laid should similar circumstances arise again.[221] Even the policy guidelines about charging issued in British Columbia in the wake of Sue Rodriguez's death are expressed at such a level of generality that they ultimately give little direction, beyond confirming what is already clearly accepted law.[222] As is evident from the English Department of Public Prosecution's policy and decision to focus on the motivation of the suspect more than the victim's characteristics in deciding whether to lay charges of assisting suicide,[223] shaping the "law in action" by guiding prosecutorial discretion has the potential to effect change without altering the "law on the books". Given the reality of divided constitutional jurisdiction over criminal law in Canada, this presents one way that provinces, which are responsible for the administration of justice, could affect federal criminal law — through its enforcement.[224]

E. EVALUATING THE LIKELIHOOD OF CRIMINAL PROSECUTION

That said, the reality is that no charges have gone forward in Canada for withholding or withdrawing treatment. Courts have consistently drawn a distinction

---

[220] Commenting on charges of criminal negligence causing death laid against an Ontario man, Peter Fonteece, in the suicide of his wife (to which he pleaded guilty), a *Globe and Mail* editorial stated: "Prosecuting a suicidal, impoverished, blind man ... for failing to stop his wife from killing herself is an almost sadistic use of state power" *The Globe and Mail* (February 27, 2010) at A24).

[221] Proceedings of the Special Senate Committee on Euthanasia and Assisted Suicide, testimony of Dr. James Cairns (October 17, 1994) at 20:8, referenced in J. Gilmour, *Study Paper on Assisted Suicide, Euthanasia and Foregoing Treatment* (Toronto: Ontario Law Reform Commission, 1996) at para. 8.97.

[222] B.C. Crown Counsel Policy Guidelines, Policy 11-3-93, File No. 56880-01 (Eut 1), reproduced in Senate of Canada, *Of Life and Death: Special Senate Committee Report on Euthanasia and Assisted Suicide* (Ottawa: Minister of Supply and Services Canada, 1995) at A-59.

[223] See note 197 and accompanying text. See also S. Doughty, "Husband who helped wife die is spared prosecution" *Daily Mail* (May 25, 2010), online at: <http://www.dailymail.co.UK/news/article-1280836/Husband-helped-wife-kill-UK-face-charges.html>, reporting on the first case in which the DPP's new policy was applied. Michael Bateman helped his 62-year-old wife, who had endured chronic pain for years and had a clear and settled wish to commit suicide, to use a plastic bag and gas to end her life. No charges were laid.

[224] K. Laidlaw, "Euthanasia hearings spark questions over Ottawa's role" *National Post* (September 6, 2010).

between allowing a patient to die from an underlying disease or condition, and causing that death. The former is non-culpable; the latter is culpable conduct. It has also been accepted that where the patient's condition requires it, a physician can prescribe medication in doses sufficient to ensure the patient's comfort, even where such doses may have the secondary effect of shortening the patient's life, provided the intent is symptom relief and not bringing about the patient's death.[225] Courts have accorded a determinative role to health care providers' primary motivation. Against this background, the likelihood of criminal liability following on decisions made in good faith to withhold or withdraw treatment or to provide needed pain medication is small indeed. Nonetheless, the lack of clear guidelines continues to give rise to concerns about potential criminal liability. Whether warranted or not, this uncertainty can impede health care providers and families acting as substitute decision makers in their efforts to ensure that the best care possible is provided at the end of a patient's life.

VII. CONCLUSION

Canada has seen a transformation in the paradigm governing decision-making about health care in the last several decades, accomplished in large part with little litigation, and limited legislative activity. Patient autonomy and self-determination are now key in treatment decisions. That transformation has marked our thinking about care at the end of life as well. Thus, it is now clear that a decisionally capable individual can forego life-sustaining treatment, including nutrition and hydration.[226] The right to refuse treatment is rooted in the common law as well as the Constitution.[227] People can make advance directives setting out their instructions about health care decision-making, to be followed in a later period of incompetence. These, too, are recognized at common law; most provinces and territories have adopted statutory regimes to govern them as well.[228] There is also general recognition that, in the event a person is not competent to make his or her own decisions about health care and there are no known wishes or instructions that are applicable in the circumstances, then health care decisions must be made in the person's best interests.[229]

Many difficult issues remain, however. The *Schiavo* case in the United States raised concerns about substitute decision-makers (for some, that their decisions would, and for others, that they would not be honoured) and about

---

[225] *Rodriguez v. British Columbia (Attorney General)*, [1993] S.C.J. No. 94, [1993] 3 S.C.R. 519 (S.C.C.).

[226] *Ibid.*; *B. (N.) v. Hôtel-Dieu de Québec*, [1992] Q.J. No. 1, 86 D.L.R. (4th) 385 (Que. S.C.); *Manoir de la Pointe Bleue (1978) Inc. c. Corbeil*, [1992] J.Q. no 98, [1992] R.J.Q. 712 (Que. S.C.).

[227] *Fleming v. Reid*, [1991] O.J. No. 1083, 4 O.R. (3d) 74 (Ont. C.A.); *Conway v. Jacques*, [2002] O.J. No. 2333, 59 O.R. (3d) 735 (Ont. C.A.).

[228] *Malette v. Shulman*, [1990] O.J. No. 450, 72 O.R. (2d) 417 (Ont. C.A.), affg [1987] O.J. No. 1180, 63 O.R. (2d) 243 (Ont. H.C.J.); *Fleming v. Reid, ibid.*

[229] *B. (R.) v. Children's Aid Society of Metropolitan Toronto*, [1994] S.C.J. No. 24, [1995] 1 S.C.R. 315 (S.C.C.).

whether advance instructions should be binding.[230] Turning to the best interests test, when a patient's prior wishes are unknown or inapplicable, it can be difficult to determine where a patient's best interests lie or how that should be decided, especially when the burdens and benefits of treatment, and even of continued life, are contested or unclear. Questions about whether and when life-sustaining treatment should be discontinued, and who should make such decisions, complicate matters still further. There may be disagreements among family members, or among family members and health care providers and institutions, or among all those involved and the courts. The decision-making environment in individual cases can also be affected by the reality of public scrutiny, involvement and judgment enabled by the Internet and social networking. Uncertainties about the application of the criminal law add to the difficulty of decision-making, and may increase instances where pain is undertreated or patients receive less than adequate care at the end of life. While there are many areas of consensus about end of life decision-making, we are sharply divided on other questions. Recent criminal prosecutions for assisted suicide and euthanasia, as well as changes in the law in some other countries to allow both in limited circumstances have led to renewed calls for legislative reform to decriminalize one or both in Canada.[231] Others, however, argue that sympathy for the accused in these cases is misplaced, and that regardless of personal tragedies and pressures, such conduct cannot be tolerated; the accused took the life of someone immensely vulnerable, or set the stage for that to occur.[232] They urge that strong legal prohibitions be maintained, in order to protect those who are vulnerable because of illness, disability or age. Despite greater certainty in some areas of the law, more needs to be done. The present state of the law regarding end of life care can impede proper care in dying, as well as efforts to ensure that people can live their lives to the fullest. It is time for a careful examination of current practices and law, as well as proposals for reform, disengaged from the focus on the compelling circumstances of an individual case

---

[230] Contrast, *e.g.*, C. Levine, "The President's Commission on Autonomy: Never Mind!" (2006) 36 Hastings Center Report 46, and R. Dresser, "Schiavo's Legacy: The Need for an Objective Standard" (2005) 35 Hastings Center Report 20.

[231] Collège des médecins du Québec, "The Collège des médecins du Québec reveals its reflections on End-of-Life Care" (November 3, 2009), online at: <http://www.cmq.org/en/Etudiants Residents/Profil/Commun/Nouvelles/2009/2009-11-03/communique.aspx>; B. Jang, "B.C. charges renew debate on euthanasia" *The Globe and Mail* (July 3, 2002) at A7; M. Gordon, "Physician-assisted suicide: Is it time to reconsider?" *Medical Post* (February 14, 2006); Editorial, "For assisted suicide" *The Globe and Mail* (July 12, 2005) at A12; Editorial, *The Globe and Mail* (August 15, 2005) at A12.

[232] See, *e.g.*, R. Matas, "Couple kill disabled son, themselves" *The Globe and Mail* (January 4, 2002) at A1; R. Matas, "Sympathy misplaced, advocates say" *The Globe and Mail* (January 5, 2002) at A4 (recounting both the public dismay and response of disability advocates after a couple in their mid-50s took their own lives and that of their 34-year-old developmentally disabled son. They died of carbon monoxide poisoning. The couple, who were reported to have pressed the government unsuccessfully for years to help them care for their son at home, left a note referring to their financial and health problems, and saying they did not trust anyone else to care for their son, who lived with them).

characteristic of the adversarial process and judicial decision-making. Although there is no great political will for such an undertaking (with the exception of Quebec), it would allow consideration of both the extent to which the principles that guide decision-making accord with and assist us in realizing our goals and values as a society, where there are gaps and deficiencies, and what reforms are needed to better achieve those ends.

Chapter 10

THE REGULATION OF HUMAN BIOMEDICAL RESEARCH IN CANADA

Michael Hadskis[*]

I.   INTRODUCTION

On September 13, 1999, researchers at the University of Pennsylvania Institute for Human Gene Therapy injected a gene enclosed in a dose of attenuated cold virus[1] into 18-year-old Jesse Gelsinger's hepatic artery.[2] Four days later, Jesse died as a result of a severe immune reaction to the injected agent.[3] Jesse's estate later commenced a lawsuit against the researchers, their institutions and the boards within these institutions that reviewed and approved the study in which Jesse had enrolled. A pretrial settlement was struck between the parties within weeks.[4]

Prior to Jesse's involvement in the gene-therapy study, he had experienced a life-long struggle with a partial ornithine transcarbamylase deficiency. This inherited disorder causes toxic levels of ammonia to build up in a person's body. Although the condition is chronic, for some individuals it can be managed by controlling ammonia levels through drug therapy and dietary regimes.[5] This was so for Jesse. He made the decision to enroll in the research project knowing that, even if the genes worked, the positive effects would last a maximum of six weeks. Jesse's participation was motivated by his desire to assist with the development of a treatment for others who might acquire the disorder in the future. However, before deciding to participate, he had not been made aware of serious (but nonfatal) adverse events experienced by prior research participants or of

---

[*]   The author would like to thank Mary-Elizabeth Walker for her truly expert research assistance.
[1]   An attenuated virus is a virus that has been weakened or made less virulent.
[2]   This artery distributes blood into a person's liver.
[3]   Barbara Sibbald, "Death But One Unintended Consequence of Gene-Therapy Trial" (2001) 164 CMAJ 1612.
[4]   Paul L. Gelsinger, "Uninformed Consent: The Case of Jesse Gelsinger" in Trudo Lemmens & Duff R. Waring, eds., *Law and Ethics in Biomedical Research: Regulation, Conflict of Interest and Liability* (Toronto: University of Toronto Press, 2006) 12 at 30.
[5]   See emedicine, "Ornithine Transcarbamylase Deficiency", online at: <http://www.emedicine.com/PED/topic2744.htm>.

adverse reactions encountered during preclinical testing on animals.[6] Also, financial conflicts of interest involving the principal researcher had not been disclosed — he held patents covering aspects of the technology as well as stock in Genovo, a biotechnology company that was collaborating in the research.[7] There were other noteworthy circumstances related to the research project. At the time Jesse received the viral vector, his ammonia levels exceeded the predetermined safe baseline limit for the study. The researchers had also not fulfilled their obligations to report adverse events to the United States Food and Drug Administration and other oversight bodies.[8]

The Gelsinger case is by no means the only human biomedical research scandal that has shaken the research community and raised public concern over the conduct of research. Notorious scandals such as the studies conducted under the Nazi regime, the Tuskegee Syphilis Study and the Tudor (Monster) Study constitute only some of the other research atrocities that have occurred in Europe and the United States.[9] Canada has not been immune from controversial research, as exemplified by the mind-altering studies in the 1950s carried out by Dr. Ewen Cameron at Montreal's Allen Memorial Hospital, research involving the administration of LSD to inmates at Kingston's Prison for Women, the death of James Dent during his participation in gene transfer research in Toronto,[10] and the substantial pressure put on Dr. Nancy Olivieri by the commercial sponsor of a drug study being conducted at a Toronto hospital to not disclose her concerns about the potential toxicity of the drug to the research participants.[11] Though it is not difficult to identify instances of research scandal, the many benefits of biomedical research can also be recited with ease. Better understanding of disease processes, the development of new or improved diagnostic devices and tests, and the creation of effective therapies have all sprung from

---

[6] Paul L. Gelsinger, "Uninformed Consent: The Case of Jesse Gelsinger" in Trudo Lemmens & Duff R. Waring, eds., *Law and Ethics in Biomedical Research: Regulation, Conflict of Interest and Liability* (Toronto: University of Toronto Press, 2006) 12 at 28.

[7] Julian Savulescu, "Harm, Ethics Committees and the Gene Therapy Death" (2001) 27 J. Med. Ethics 148.

[8] Paul L. Gelsinger, "Uninformed Consent: The Case of Jesse Gelsinger" in Trudo Lemmens & Duff R. Waring, eds., *Law and Ethics in Biomedical Research: Regulation, Conflict of Interest and Liability* (Toronto: University of Toronto Press, 2006) 12 at 28.

[9] These studies are described in Jocelyn Downie, "Contemporary Health Research: A Cautionary Tale" (2003) Health L.J. (Special Edition) 1 at 3-5. See also: H.K. Beecher, "Ethics and Clinical Research" (1966) 274 New Eng. J. Med. 1354; Simon Verdun-Jones & David N. Weisstub, "The Regulation of Biomedical Research Experimentation in Canada: Developing An Effective Apparatus for the Implementation of Ethical Principles in a Scientific Milieu" (1996-1997) 28 Ottawa L. Rev. 297 at 307-308; R. Levine, *Ethics and Regulation of Clinical Research*, 2d ed. (New Haven, CT: Yale University Press, 1988) at 69-72.

[10] Kathleen Cranley Glass, "Questions and Challenges in the Governance of Research Involving Humans: A Canadian Perspective" in Trudo Lemmens & Duff R. Waring, eds., *Law and Ethics in Biomedical Research: Regulation, Conflict of Interest and Liability* (Toronto: University of Toronto Press, 2006) 35 at 36-37.

[11] The Olivieri case is discussed in greater detail in the "Conflicts of Interest Involving Researchers" section of this chapter.

biomedical research. This research is also increasingly being used to confirm whether therapies already in use are actually efficacious.[12] In view of the substantial potential benefits and risks that attend human biomedical research, the mechanisms that shape or control this critical human endeavour warrant scrutiny.

This chapter will examine the regulation of human biomedical research in Canada. Part II discusses the importance of distinguishing clinical practice from human biomedical research. Part III outlines the legal and extra-legal instruments that directly or indirectly regulate Canadian biomedical research. With that as a backdrop, the procedural and substantive aspects of the research ethics review mechanisms established by the key regulatory instruments are addressed in Part IV. Part V explores the prospect of legal liability for the main actors in biomedical research when research participants sustain research-related injuries. The chapter concludes, under Part VI, with some general remarks about the need to reform Canada's current regulatory framework for biomedical research.

II.   DISTINGUISHING HUMAN BIOMEDICAL RESEARCH FROM CLINICAL PRACTICE

Much has been written about the distinction between clinical practice and human biomedical research and the murky border that divides the two. In 1979, the United States National Commission for the Protection of Human Subjects of Biomedical and Behavioral Research Practice issued a report, *The Belmont Report: Ethical Principles and Guidelines for the Protection of Human Subjects of Research*,[13] that in part addressed the boundaries between practice and research. The report defined clinical practice as "interventions that are designed solely to enhance the well-being of an individual patient or client and that have a reasonable expectation of success" and research as "an activity designed to test an hypothesis, permit conclusions to be drawn, and thereby to develop or contribute to generalizable knowledge (expressed, for example, in theories, principles, and statements of relationships)". Simply put, the gaze of health professionals engaged in the former activity is to be fixed on diagnosing and treating individual patients' health conditions, while those embarking on biomedical research aim to advance scientific knowledge and develop methods to diagnose and treat future patients.[14]

---

[12] Jocelyn Downie, "Contemporary Health Research: A Cautionary Tale" (2003) Health L.J. (Special Edition) 1 at 1-2.

[13] National Commission for the Protection of Human Subjects of Biomedical and Behavioral Research, *The Belmont Report: Ethical Principles and Guidelines for the Protection of Human Subjects of Research* (1979), online at: <http://ohsr.od.nih.gov/guidelines/belmont.html>.

[14] Kathleen Cranley Glass, "Questions and Challenges in the Governance of Research Involving Humans: A Canadian Perspective" in Trudo Lemmens & Duff R. Waring, eds., *Law and Ethics in Biomedical Research: Regulation, Conflict of Interest and Liability* (Toronto: University of Toronto Press, 2006) 35.

The release of *The Belmont Report* did little to put an end to the struggle to meaningfully clarify the complex interplay that often exists between the delivery of medical care and the conduct of research.[15] A major contributor to this struggle is the reality that research and clinical practice frequently occur in conjunction since many medical interventions are delivered by physician-researchers and form the subject of formal research projects into the interventions' safety and efficacy. Real or apprehended conflicts may exist between physician-researchers' distinct commitments to their patients and to answering the research questions they have posed. The trend toward evidence-based therapies is likely to see a significant rise in this type of research. Interventions considered new or innovative in the sense that they deviate from standard medical practice have also been fodder for the clinical practice versus research debate, particularly with respect to surgical innovation.[16] Confusion in this area has been fostered by the imprudent use of the word "experimental" to describe this activity. As *The Belmont Report* clarifies: "The fact that a procedure is 'experimental,' in the sense of new, untested or different, does not automatically place it in the category of research."[17] In other words, the innovative nature of the activity is not a necessary or sufficient condition for it to be labelled research. As will become apparent further on in this chapter, the application or non-application of regulatory instruments can turn on whether an activity is considered clinical practice or research. Therefore, the need for clarity around the use of the word "research" is of considerable importance.

In the context of this chapter, research will be defined as "an undertaking intended to extend knowledge through a disciplined inquiry or systematic investigation" — this definition is being adopted for reasons of expediency since it is employed by the *Tri-Council Policy Statement: Ethical Conduct for Research Involving Humans* (TCPS), a document that plays a central role in the regulation of biomedical research in Canada.[18] It is, however, not the hallmark of clarity or

---

[15]   Margaret A. Somerville, "Clarifying the Concepts of Research Ethics: A Second Filtration" (1981) 29 Clinical Research 101; Benjamin Freedman, Abraham Fuks & Charles Weijer, "Demarcating Research and Treatment: A Systematic Approach for the Analysis of the Ethics of Clinical Research" (1992) 40 Clinical Research 653; Simon Verdun-Jones & David N. Weisstub, "Consent to Human Experimentation in Québec: The Application of the Civil Law Principles of Personal Inviolability to Protect Special Populations" (1995) 18 Int'l J. L. & Psychiatry 163 at 178-79; Bernard M. Dickens, "What is a Medical Experiment?" (1975) 113 CMAJ 635.

[16]   For example, see: M. McKneally & D. Abdallah, "Introducing New Technologies: Protecting Subjects of Surgical Innovation and Research" (2003) 27 World Journal of Surgery 930; S. Strasberg & P. Ludbrook, "Who Oversees Innovative Practice? Is There a Structure That Meets the Monitoring Needs of New Techniques?" (2003) 196 Journal of the American College of Surgeons 938; and G. Agich, "Ethics and Innovation in Medicine" (2001) 27 J. Med. Ethics 295.

[17]   National Commission for the Protection of Human Subjects of Biomedical and Behavioral Research, *The Belmont Report: Ethical Principles and Guidelines for the Protection of Human Subjects of Research* (1979), online at: <http://ohsr.od.nih.gov/guidelines/belmont.html>.

[18]   TCPS, "Application" commentary under art. 2.1, available online at: <http://www.pre.ethics.gc.ca/eng/policy-politique/initiatives/tcps2-eptc2/Default/>.

precision, thus leaving uncertainty about what activities are caught in its grasp.[19] It is also important to be aware that other definitions of research are beginning to emerge in Canada, particularly in the context of health information legislation.[20]

III. THE REGULATORY LANDSCAPE

The Canadian regulatory landscape for biomedical research involving humans consists of a complex patchwork of diverse forms of regulatory instruments. It has been characterized by some commentators as a "confusing" and "complex, decentralized, and multi-sourced arrangement for regulating research".[21] Others have remarked that its unwieldy nature stems from the reality that the law "applies almost inadvertently to the enterprise of biomedical research"[22] and that "the Canadian regulatory approach to research involving humans ... is an incomplete mosaic of rules that range from formal legal regulations, to administrative policies and voluntary guidelines".[23] The confusing nature of the regulatory landscape may, at least in part, explain the results of Health Canada's 2003–2004 inspections of 45 clinical drug trials, which revealed 292 deviations from

---

[19] For instance, see Michael Yeo, *Biobank Research: The Conflict Between Privacy and Access Made Explicit*, prepared for the Canadian Biotechnology Advisory Council (February 10, 2004), online at: <http://www.laurentian.ca/NR/rdonlyres/C31AFD9B-0E36-4378-ACD8-05E0A39B3F C6/0/PrivacyandBiobankingNationalAdvisoryCouncilonBiotechn.pdf>, where this issue is addressed in the health information context. Yeo asks at footnote 17:

> Where does one draw a line between research and health surveillance or monitoring? ... What distinguishes a disease registry from a research database? How does one distinguish a patient from a research subject in the context of a health information network? At what point does the patient or the research subject vanish into bits or bytes or pieces or strands such that one no longer speaks of research involving human subjects? How do we differentiate clinical care and research in the context of drug utilization and feedback systems? At what point does a collection of information become a database, and at what point does a database become a business, or the activity of research a commercial activity?

However, the TCPS does provide some guidance on distinguishing research from "non-research activities that have traditionally employed methods and techniques similar to those employed in research" (preamble to art. 2.5). For instance, "quality assurance and quality improvement studies, program evaluation activities, and performance reviews, or testing within normal educational requirements when used exclusively for assessment, management or improvement purposes, do not constitute research for the purposes of" the TCPS (art. 2.5).

[20] For example, see *Personal Health Information Protection Act, 2004*, S.O. 2004, c. 3, Sched. A, s. 2, where "research" is defined as "a systematic investigation designed to develop or establish principles, facts or generalizable knowledge, or any combination of them, and includes the development, testing and evaluation of research".

[21] Jocelyn Downie & Fiona McDonald, "Revisioning the Oversight of Research Involving Humans in Canada" (2004) 12 Health L.J. 159 at 174.

[22] B. Dickens, "Governance Relations in Biomedical Research" in M. McDonald, ed., *The Governance of Health Research Involving Human Subjects* (Ottawa: Law Commission of Canada, 2000) 93 at 93.

[23] M. Hirtle, "The Governance of Research Involving Human Participants in Canada" (2003) 11 Health L.J. 137 at 139-40.

regulatory requirements.[24] The outline of the chief regulatory instruments that follows is intended to assist the reader in navigating Canada's research governance framework.

A. OVERVIEW OF THE PRINCIPAL REGULATORY INSTRUMENTS

1. *Tri-Council Policy Statement: Ethical Conduct for Research Involving Humans* (TCPS)

In December 2010, the Canadian Institutes of Health Research (CIHR), the Natural Sciences and Engineering Research Council of Canada (NSERC), and the Social Sciences and Humanities Research Council of Canada (SSHRC), hereinafter "the Tri-Agencies", issued the second edition of the TCPS.[25] Like the first edition, this document establishes an ethical framework for the conduct of human participant research, including studies involving living human participants and "research involving human biological materials, as well as human embryos, fetuses, fetal tissue, reproductive materials and stem cells",[26] whether or not this material is derived from living or deceased persons.

The TCPS requires research institutions to establish or appoint multidisciplinary research ethics boards (REBs) to review and make decisions about the ethical acceptability of research involving humans that takes place within the institutions' jurisdiction or under their auspices.[27] These boards are empowered to approve, propose modifications to, or reject proposed studies. REBs may also require ongoing studies to be altered or terminated.[28] REB decision-making is to be informed by the national norms set out in the TCPS on such issues as participant consent, conflicts of interest, the protection of participants' privacy and confidentiality, and ensuring that the potential harms of research do not outweigh the potential benefits.

Determining when a particular activity is captured by the TCPS is not always a straightforward matter. An important preliminary question to answer is whether the relevant activity meets the TCPS definition of "research" that was discussed above. If not, the TCPS does not apply to it. However, even if the activity constitutes research under that definition, it does not necessarily follow that the TCPS will apply. Being a policy statement, the TCPS lacks the inherent legal authority of a legislative instrument. Instead, the scope and extent of its

---

[24] Health Products and Food Branch Inspectorate, *Summary Report of the Inspections of Clinical Trials Conducted in 2003/2004*, Report to Health Canada (December 14, 2004), online at: <http://www.hc-sc.gc.ca/dhp-mps/compli-conform/clini-pract-prat/report-rapport/2003-2004_tc-tm_e.html>.

[25] The first edition of the TCPS was issued in 1998 and can be found online at: <http://www.pre.ethics.gc.ca/eng/archives/tcps-eptc/Default/>.

[26] TCPS, art. 2.1. The human biological material referenced in this article includes, among other things, tissues, organs, blood, plasma, serum, DNA and RNA: see "Application" commentary under art. 2.1.

[27] TCPS, art. 6.1.

[28] TCPS, art. 6.3.

regulatory impact rests on other factors. One such factor is that, in order to be eligible to receive and administer funding from the Tri-Agencies, institutions must agree to abide a number of Tri-Agency policies referenced in a Memorandum of Understanding (MOU) that each institution enters into with the Tri-Agencies; included within these policies is the TCPS.[29] Additionally, the Tri-Agencies' grant applications require applicant researchers to certify compliance with all of the Tri-Agencies' policies regarding the ethical conduct of research, including the TCPS, if the research will involve human participants. As a result, Tri-Agency-funded researchers and their institutions must comply with the TCPS.

In 2010, the Tri-Agencies published a document entitled *Tri-Agency Process for Addressing Allegations of Non-compliance with Tri-Agency Policies*, which details the process for reviewing allegations of non-compliance with the TCPS (and other Tri-Agency policies) and enumerates the sanctions that can be imposed on institutions and researchers for breaching TCPS requirements. In addition to the possibility of researchers and institutions being ineligible for continued funding, CIHR may require researchers to refund all or part of the funds already paid under the grant. Other funding bodies, both federal[30] and provincial,[31] also require compliance with the TCPS as a condition for the receipt of research funds.

The regulatory impact of the TCPS is not necessarily dependent on the presence of public funding for research. Members of some professional organizations may be required to seek ethics review from a TCPS-compliant REB before conducting human research or risk being subject to disciplinary action by their regulatory bodies. For instance, the College of Physicians and Surgeons of Alberta requires physicians to seek the approval of its own TCPS-compliant REB (the Research Ethics Review Committee) unless the project is otherwise subject to the authority of another research ethics review agency that the College deems appropriate.[32]

In addition to the circumstances already outlined, other factors may serve to promote compliance with the TCPS. Ethics review of the kind provided for in

---

[29] The Memorandum of Understanding is available online at: <http://www.nserc-crsng.gc.ca/ NSERC-CRSNG/Policies-Politiques/MOURoles-ProtocolRoles/index_eng.asp>. The TCPS is referenced in Sched. 2 of the MOU and Sched. 8 of this document deals with the "Investigation and Resolution of Breaches of Agency Policies".

[30] For example, National Research Council, *NRC Policy for Research Involving Human Subjects* (last modified April 15, 2009), online at: <http://www.nrc-cnrc.gc.ca/eng/ethics/policy-human-subjects.html>.

[31] For example, the Nova Scotia Health Research Foundation (see *2010-11 Nova Scotia Health Research Foundation Competition Requirements*, online at: <http://www.nshrf.ca/AbsPage. aspx?siteid=1&lang=1&id=1>) and the Manitoba Health Research Council (see *Manitoba Health Research Council 2011 Competition - General Guidelines*, online at: <http://mhrc.mb.ca/ programs/competition asp>).

[32] Michael Hadskis & Peter Carver, "The Long Arm of Administrative Law: Applying Administrative Law Principles to Research Ethics Boards" (2005) 13:2 & 3 Health L.R. 19 at 23.

the TCPS is often a condition of publication in peer-reviewed journals.[33] Additionally, as discussed below, courts may invoke non-legal instruments such as the TCPS when determining the liability of researchers, REB members and research institutions in tort actions arising from personal injuries or some other actionable harm sustained by research participants as a result of their participation in research. Of course, the impact of this factor on promoting compliance very much depends on researchers appreciating how these instruments may be used by the courts.

2. Clinical Trial Regulations under the *Food and Drugs Act* and the Good Clinical Practice: Consolidated Guidelines

This section provides a thumbnail sketch of two of the key instruments that regulate drug research in Canada: Part C, Division 5 of the Food and Drug Regulations[34] (hereinafter the "Clinical Trial Regulations") and the *Good Clinical Practice: Consolidated Guidelines*[35] (the *GCP Guidelines*). The Clinical Trial Regulations, passed pursuant to the federal *Food and Drugs Act*,[36] establish legal requirements concerning the conduct of clinical drug trials. A "clinical trial" is defined in the regulations as an investigation regarding a drug for use in humans that involves human participants and that is intended to "discover or verify the clinical, pharmacological or pharmacodynamic effects of the drug, identify any adverse events in respect of the drug, study the absorption, distribution, metabolism and excretion of the drug, or ascertain the safety or efficacy of the drug".[37] The Clinical Trial Regulations apply to all clinical drug trials in Canada, irrespective of how this research is being funded.

The Clinical Trial Regulations require trial sponsors to apply to Health Canada for authorization to sell or import a drug for the purposes of conducting a clinical trial.[38] Typically, trials are sponsored by pharmaceutical companies, although the regulations also govern trials that do not have commercial sponsorship. Clinical trial applications must include, among other items, a copy of the trial protocol (*i.e.*, a document describing "the objectives, design, methodology, statistical considerations and organization"[39] of the trial) and the name of the researcher responsible to the sponsor for the conduct of the clinical trial at each

---

[33] Jocelyn Downie & Fiona McDonald, "Revisioning the Oversight of Research Involving Humans in Canada" (2004) 12 Health L.J. 159 at 163. See also International Committee of Medical Journal Editors, *Uniform Requirements for Manuscripts Submitted to Biomedical Journals: Protection of Human Subjects and Animals in Research* (updated February 2006), online at: <http://www.icmje.org/ethical_6protection.html>.

[34] Food and Drug Regulations, C.R.C., c. 870, Part C, Division 5, "Drugs for Clinical Trials Involving Human Subjects".

[35] This is documented on Health Canada's website, online at: <http://www.hc-sc.gc.ca/dhp-mps/prod pharma/applic-demande/guide-ld/ich/efficac/e6_e.html>.

[36] *Food and Drugs Act*, R.S.C. 1985, c. F-27, s. 30.

[37] Clinical Trial Regulations, s. C.05.001.

[38] *Ibid.*, s. C.05.003.

[39] *Ibid.*, s. C.05.001.

clinical site. In order to secure Health Canada's authorization to sell or import a drug for the purposes of a clinical trial, the sponsor must satisfy a number of conditions, one of which requires the sponsor to obtain approval of the REB at each clinical trial site.[40] The REB must attest, in writing, that it reviewed and approved the protocol and informed consent forms and that it carries out its functions in a manner consistent with "good clinical practices",[41] which are defined as "generally accepted clinical practices that are designed to ensure the protection of the rights, safety and well-being of clinical trial subjects and other persons, and the good clinical practices referred to in section C.05.010".[42] Section C.05.010 lists, in very general terms, a sponsor's obligations including, among others, ensuring that the trial is scientifically sound and clearly described in the protocol, that the trial is conducted in accordance with the protocol and regulations, that individuals involved in the conduct of the trial are appropriately qualified, and that the written informed consent of participants is obtained.

The lack of specificity in the Clinical Trial Regulations around what represents good clinical practices is somewhat ameliorated through Health Canada's "endorsement"[43]/ "adoption"[44] of the principles and practices provided for in the *GCP Guidelines*, an international guideline developed by the International Conference on Harmonization of Technical Requirements for Registration of Pharmaceuticals for Human Use. The *GCP Guidelines* provide greater detail than the Clinical Trial Regulations respecting the duties and responsibilities of REBs,[45] investigators, and sponsors,[46] and to some degree reflect the substantive and procedural norms in the TCPS. While Health Canada has taken the position that the *GCP Guidelines* are meant to assist investigators and sponsors in how to comply with the Clinical Trial Regulations and has noted that they do not have the force of law,[47] it is critical to note that it has relied on the *GCP Guidelines* to interpret section C.05.010 when carrying out its inspections and investigations to assess compliance with these regulations[48] pursuant to the *Food and Drugs Act*.[49]

---

[40]   *Ibid.*, ss. C.05.006(*c*) and C.05.010(*d*).

[41]   *Ibid.*, s. C.05.012(*h*).

[42]   *Ibid.*, s. C.05.001.

[43]   See Health Canada's website, online at: <http://www.hc-sc.gc.ca/dhp-mps/prodpharma/applic-demande/guide-ld/ich/efficac/e6_e.html>.

[44]   *Ibid.*

[45]   The *GCP Guidelines* do not actually refer to Research Ethics Boards. Instead, they use the terms "Institutional Review Boards" or "Independent Ethics Committees", which mean the same thing.

[46]   *GCP Guidelines*, ss. 3-5.

[47]   This is documented on Health Canada's website, online at: <http://www.hc-sc.gc.ca/dhp-mps/prodpharma/applic-demande/guide-ld/ich/efficac/e6_e.html>.

[48]   See Health Products and Food Branch Inspectorate, *Summary Report of the Inspections of Clinical Trials Conducted in 2003/2004*, Report to Health Canada (December 14, 2004), online at: <http://www.hc-sc.gc.ca/dhp-mps/compli-conform/clini-pract-prat/report-rapport/2003-2004_tc-tm_e.html>.

[49]   A reasonable argument can be made that Health Canada is enforcing the *GCP Guidelines* by way of its inspections. See Trudo Lemmens, "Federal Regulation of REB Review of Clinical Trials:

Health Canada has implemented a *Compliance and Enforcement Policy*[50] that addresses the measures it may take in response to contraventions of the *Food and Drugs Act* and Clinical Trial Regulations. Examples of the types of actions that may be pursued are warning letters, suspension or cancellation of an authorization to sell or import a drug for the purposes of a clinical trial, injunctions, and criminal prosecutions.[51]

3. Quebec and Newfoundland and Labrador Instruments

Quebec and Newfoundland and Labrador have enacted legislation which directly deals with the conduct of human research. The *Civil Code of Québec*[52] addresses the risk-benefit ratio to which incompetent adults may be exposed,[53] clarifies that "innovative care required by the state of health of the person concerned does not constitute [research]",[54] establishes requirements for the use of human tissue in research,[55] and sets conditions precedent for the participation of minors and incompetent adults in research, including the requirement for such research to be approved and monitored by an REB formed by the Minister of Health and Social Services or another REB designated by the Minister.[56] The Fonds de la recherche en santé du Québec (FRSQ) is tasked with supporting health research in Quebec and plays a critical role in regulating human participant research in the province. All research involving humans that takes place in Quebec's public institutions requires approval and monitoring of an REB.[57] REBs affiliated with institutions that host FRSQ-funded research must comply with FRSQ's regulatory framework and standards[58] which mandate, among other things, adherence to the TCPS.[59]

In 2006, Newfoundland and Labrador enacted the *Health Research Ethics Authority Act*.[60] This Act, which has not been brought into force to date, will

---

A Modest But Easy Step Towards an Accountable REB Review Structure in Canada" (2005) 13:2 & 3 Health L. Rev. 39 at 44.

[50] Health Canada, Health Products and Food Branch Inspectorate, *Compliance and Enforcement Policy*, Policy-0001 (May 31, 2005), online at: <http://www.hc-sc.gc.ca/dhp-mps/alt_formats/hpfb-dgpsa/pdf/compli-conform/pol_1_e.pdf>.

[51] *Ibid.*

[52] S.Q. 1991, c. 64.

[53] *Ibid.*, art. 20.

[54] *Ibid.*, art. 21.

[55] *Ibid.*, arts. 22-24.

[56] *Ibid.*, art. 21.

[57] Fonds de la recherche en santé du Québec (FRSQ), Press Release, "The FRSQ reassures Québecers: Québec keeps close watch" (January 23, 2003), online at: <http://www.muhc.ca/files/research/fiches_media_english.pdf>.

[58] *Ibid.*

[59] FRSQ, *Guide d'éthique et d'intégrité scientifique de la recherché (Research Ethics and Scientific Integrity Guidelines)*, 2e ed. (Montreal: FRSQ, 2003) at 35. Also, FRSQ Research Funding Contracts Stipulate Compliance with the TCPS (Personal Communication, Johane de Champlain, FRSQ Ethics Coordinator, to Mary-Elizabeth Walker, Research Assistant, June 30, 2006).

[60] *Health Research Ethics Authority Act*, S.N.L. 2006, c. H-1.2 [not yet proclaimed in force].

require all persons to obtain the approval of the Health Research Ethics Board established by the province's Health Research Ethics Authority, or another research ethics body approved by the Authority,[61] before conducting "health research involving human subjects"[62] in Newfoundland and Labrador.[63] The TCPS and other relevant regulatory instruments will be applied when deciding whether to approve research projects.[64] Failure to comply with the *Health Research Ethics Authority Act* will be considered an offence; the Act allows for fines of up to $50,000 (for a first conviction) to be imposed for such offences.[65] As well, individuals who hold a licence with a professional regulatory body could face disciplinary action by this body if they do not comply with a determination or direction of the relevant research ethics board.[66]

4.   International Instruments

(a)   United States

The growing involvement of Canadian researchers in multi-national health research requires these researchers to familiarize themselves with the relevant regulatory frameworks adopted by other countries. The United States is one such country. There, Title 45, Part 46 of its *Code of Federal Regulations* prescribes legal standards for the protection of human research participants that apply to research funded by the United States Department of Health and Human Services (DHHS), which includes the National Institutes of Health, or research that is conducted in an institution that receives federal (U.S.) funding for research. Subpart A of the regulations provides the basic rules for the protection of human participants. Other subparts of the regulations set out additional protections for: pregnant women, human fetuses and neonates;[67] prisoners;[68] and children.[69] Under these regulations, Institutional Review Boards (the United States equivalent of Canadian REBs) must review research involving humans according to norms that broadly resemble those found in the TCPS.

Other American instruments also regulate research. For instance, Parts 40 and 56 of Title 21 of the *Code of Federal Regulations*,[70] which fall under the auspices of the United States Food and Drug Administration, apply to human

---

[61]   *Ibid.*, s. 8.
[62]   *Ibid.*, s. 2(d) defines this term as "activities whose primary goal is to generate knowledge in relation to human health, health care and health care systems, and involving human beings as research subjects, health care information respecting human beings and human biological material".
[63]   *Ibid.*, s. 9(1).
[64]   *Ibid.*, s. 9(5).
[65]   *Ibid.*, s. 29.
[66]   *Ibid.*, s. 26(1).
[67]   Title 45 *Code of Federal Regulations*, Part 46, Subpart B.
[68]   *Ibid.*, Subpart C.
[69]   *Ibid.*, Subpart D.
[70]   Title 21 *Code of Federal Regulations*, Parts 40 and 56.

research that uses drugs, medical devices and biological products, regardless of whether the research is federally funded. A multitude of other federal and state laws may also be relevant depending on the research activities being pursued.[71]

Canadian researchers who carry out research supported by DHHS funding must comply with the *Code of Federal Regulations*, even if the research is conducted outside the United States. Canadian institutions that host such research are required to file an "assurance" of compliance with these regulations with the United States Office for Human Research Protections.[72]

(b)   The Nuremberg Code and the Declaration of Helsinki

Two international documents, the *Nuremberg Code*[73] and the *Declaration of Helsinki*,[74] have played a fundamental role in the formulation and evolution of international, regional and national regulatory instruments for the protection of human research participants. The *Nuremberg Code*, which was introduced to the international community in 1948, sets out standards for physicians to follow when carrying out experiments on human participants. It was developed in response to the Military War Crimes Tribunal's condemnation of the atrocities committed by Nazi physicians on concentration camp prisoners in the name of human experimentation.[75] The *Declaration of Helsinki*, developed by the World Health Association and adopted by the 18th World Medical Assembly in Helsinki in 1964, also establishes guidelines regarding human biomedical research. This document, which has undergone a number of revisions, most recently in 2008, has expressly shaped other important international instruments such as the *International Ethical Guidelines for Biomedical Research Involving Human Subjects*, prepared by the Council for International Organizations of Medical Sciences (CIOMS) in collaboration with the World Health Organization.[76] The CIOMS Guidelines are "designed to be of use, particularly to low-resource countries, in defining national policies on the ethics of biomedical research, applying ethical standards in local circumstances, and establishing or redefining

---

[71] For an overview of the United States regulatory regime for research involving humans, see Richard M. Wagner, "Ethical Review of Research Involving Human Subjects: When and Why is IRB Review Necessary?" (2003) 28 Muscle & Nerve 27. See also, Ken Gatter, "Fixing Cracks: A Discourse Norm to Repair the Crumbling Regulatory Structure Supporting Clinical Research and Protecting Human Subjects" (2005) 73 U.M.K.C. L. Rev. 581 at 587-89.

[72] Title 45 *Code of Federal Regulations*, § 46.103(a). For a discussion of the application of United States laws and policy to research conducted outside the United States, see National Institutes of Health, United States Department of Health and Human Services, *Human Participant Protections Education for Research Teams*, National Cancer Institute (2002), online at: <http://cme.cancer.gov/clinicaltrials/learning/humanparticipant-protections.asp>.

[73] Available online at: <http://ohsr.od.nih.gov/guidelines/nuremberg.html>.

[74] Available online at: <http://www.wma.net/en/30publications/10policies/b3/index.html>.

[75] G. Annas & M. Grodin, "Introduction" in G. Annas & M. Grodin, eds., *The Nazi Doctors and the Nuremberg Code* (New York: Oxford University Press, 1992) 3 at 3-4.

[76] Council for International Organizations of Medical Sciences, *International Ethical Guidelines for Biomedical Research Involving Human Subjects* (Geneva, 2002).

adequate mechanisms for ethical review of research involving human subjects".[77]

The *Nuremberg Code* and the *Declaration of Helsinki* continue to influence
the regulation of research in Canada. For example, the *GCP Guidelines* expressly provide that clinical trials "should be conducted in accordance with the
ethical principles that have their origin in the Declaration of Helsinki, and that
are consistent with the [*GCP Guidelines*] and the applicable regulatory require-
ment(s)".[78] Additionally, in part relying on the principles set out in the *Declaration of Helsinki*, in 1989 a Canadian court found a physician liable for not
adequately disclosing the risks involved in taking part in a biomedical research
project to a participant who had died as a result of his participation in the project.[79] Also noteworthy is FRSQ's statement that it "subscribes to the principles"
contained in the *Nuremberg Code* and the *Declaration of Helsinki*.[80]

5.   Other Canadian Regulatory Instruments

The instruments described above are by no means the only instruments that impact the conduct of health research activities in Canada. Medical codes of ethics,
judge-made law on matters such as informed consent,[81] provincial/territorial
legislation on post-mortem gifts of bodies or body parts for research,[82] and legislation restricting research involving psychiatric patients[83] can also exert direct or
indirect regulatory control.[84] Researchers and REBs must also be aware of pro-
vincial/territorial[85] and federal[86] legislation relating to personal information that

---

[77]   Council for International Organizations of Medical Sciences, *International Ethical Guidelines
for Biomedical Research Involving Human Subjects* (Geneva, 2002) at 10.

[78]   *GCP Guidelines*, s. 2.1.

[79]   *Weiss c. Solomon*, [1989] J.Q. no 312, [1989] R.J.Q. 731 (Que. S.C.). This case is discussed
more fully later in the chapter.

[80]   Fonds de la recherche en santé du Québec (FRSQ), Press Release, "The FRSQ reassures Québecers: Québec keeps close watch" (January 23, 2003), online at: <http://www.muhc.
ca/files/research/fiches_media_english.pdf>.

[81]   See *Halushka v. University of Saskatchewan*, [1965] S.J. No. 208, 53 D.L.R. (2d) 436 (Sask.
C.A.) and *Weiss c. Solomon*, [1989] J.Q. no 312, [1989] R.J.Q. 731 (Que. S.C.). Both cases are
discussed later in the chapter.

[82]   For example, see: *Human Organ and Tissue Donation Act*, S.N.S. 2010, c. 36 [not yet in force],
ss. 2(m), 11(1), 21(1) and 21(3); *Human Tissue Donation Act*, R.S.P.E.I. 1988, c. H-12.1, ss.
5(1), 12(1); *Human Tissue Gift Act*, R.S.Y. 2002, c. 117, s. 5(1).

[83]   For example, see: *Mental Health Act*, C.C.S.M. c. M110; *Mental Health Act*, R.S.N.W.T. 1988,
c. M-10.

[84]   Bartha Knoppers, "Ethics and Human Research: Complexity or Confusion?" in Michael
McDonald, ed., *The Governance of Health Research Involving Human Subjects* (Ottawa: Law
Commission of Canada, 2000) 109.

[85]   For example, see *Personal Health Information Act*, S.N.S. 2010, c. 41 [not yet in force], ss. 52-
60; *Health Information Act*, R.S.A. 2000, c. H-5, s. 49; *Personal Health Information Protection
Act, 2004*, S.O. 2004, c. 3, Sched. A. Also see Chapter 6, "Health Information: Confidentiality
and Access".

[86]   *Personal Information Protection and Electronic Documents Act*, S.C. 2000, c. 5.

may have enormous implications for the collection, use and disclosure of personal health information in the research context.

Other instruments can also exert control. For instance, the *Criminal Code*[87] (*e.g.*, the provisions respecting assault[88] and criminal negligence[89]), and the Medical Devices Regulations[90] (passed under the *Food and Drugs Act*) which regulate the use of unlicensed medical devices in clinical investigations and the use of already licensed devices outside the terms of their respective licences.

B.   REGULATORY GAPS

The patchwork nature of Canada's regulatory framework for biomedical research falls short of offering a comprehensive research oversight system. As Downie and McDonald observe, "excepting clinical trials, research conducted in private physician's offices, community-based organizations, charitable organizations, industry, and [some] government departments ... is largely free of regulation".[91] Similarly, in 2008, the Experts Committee for Human Research Participant Protection in Canada issued a report indicating that there "are many gaps in the current [research governance] arrangements, including much unfunded research, some industry sponsored non-drug studies, some community-based research, and some government and private sector research".[92] While there is an absence of empirical data to precisely define the size of the regulatory gap, the gap is estimated to be a "significant problem".[93] This is disconcerting for several reasons, the most significant of which is that research participants are exposed to increased risk of harm since the checks and balances that are available through the application of research ethics review mechanisms are absent. Another concern relates to the need to develop and maintain public trust and confidence in the research governance system. If the public perceives that adequate safeguards are missing for the protection of the rights, safety and well-being of participants, whatever public confidence presently exists will swiftly erode. Loss of public support for research funding initiatives and difficulty re-

---

[87]   R.S.C. 1985, c. C-46.

[88]   *Ibid.*, s. 265.

[89]   *Ibid.*, s. 219.

[90]   SOR/98-282.

[91]   Jocelyn Downie & Fiona McDonald, "Revisioning the Oversight of Research Involving Humans in Canada" (2004) 12 Health L.J. 159 at 164.

[92]   The Experts Committee for Human Research Participant Protection in Canada, *Moving Ahead: Final Report* (Ottawa, 2008), online at: <http://www.hrppc-pphrc.ca/english/movingaheadfinal report2008.pdf>.

[93]   Jocelyn Downie & Fiona McDonald, "Revisioning the Oversight of Research Involving Humans in Canada" (2004) 12 Health L.J. 159 at 165. Kathleen Cranley Glass, "Questions and Challenges in the Governance of Research Involving Humans: A Canadian Perspective" in Trudo Lemmens & Duff R. Waring, eds., *Law and Ethics in Biomedical Research: Regulation, Conflict of Interest and Liability* (Toronto: University of Toronto Press, 2006) 35 at 43 also expresses concern regarding the fact that ethics review is not mandatory for all research conducted in Canada.

cruiting participants are just two of the reasonably foreseeable byproducts of such erosion.[94]

IV. RESEARCH REVIEW

It is clear from the preceding discussion that the main regulatory instruments governing biomedical research involving humans have established REBs[95] as the workhorses of the governance regime. REBs are charged with a number of roles and responsibilities in relation to the reviews they conduct. The Clinical Trial Regulations define the principal mandate of REBs as being "to approve the initiation of, and conduct periodic reviews of, biomedical research involving human subjects in order to ensure the protection of their rights, safety and well-being".[96] The TCPS observes that REBs have "two main goals"; namely, "providing the necessary protection of participants and serving the legitimate requirements of research".[97] It also acknowledges the reality that the dual goals of protecting participants and answering research questions are not always in harmony. To "navigate a sometimes difficult course"[98] between these goals, the TCPS outlines three core principles: respect for persons, concern for welfare, and justice. Regarding concern for welfare, the TCPS indicates that REBs "should aim to protect the welfare of participants, and, in some circumstances, to promote that welfare in view of any foreseeable risks associated with the research".[99]

Speaking to the relationship between research ethics review and scholarly review, the TCPS states that REBs must assess the ethical implications of the methods and design of the research.[100] Another role assigned to TCPS-compliant REBs is to serve as a consultative body on research ethics for the research community.[101] It has also been suggested that REBs serve to protect their host insti-

---

[94] Jocelyn Downie & Fiona McDonald, *ibid.*, at 165-66.

[95] This chapter will concentrate on REBs affiliated with public research institutions such as public hospitals and universities. While not specifically addressed here, the reader should be aware of the presence of private (for-profit) REBs that can be retained to review human research being carried out by private-sector organizations, typically pharmaceutical companies. For a discussion about private REBs, see T. Lemmens & A. Thompson, "Non-institutional Commercial Review Boards in North America: A Critical Appraisal and Comparison with IRBs" (2001) 13:2 IRB: A Review of Human Subjects Research 1.

[96] Clinical Trial Regulations, s. C.05.001.

[97] TCPS, Chapter 1, Section B.

[98] TCPS, Chapter 1, Section B.

[99] TCPS, Chapter 1, Section B.

[100] TCPS, art. 2.7. The "Application" commentary under this article cautions against REBs duplicating previous professional peer-review assessments in the absence of compelling reasons to do so. Where scholarly review is in order, this commentary recommends several mechanisms for the conduct of such reviews.

[101] The educational role of REBs is alluded to in several parts of the TCPS. For example, the "Introduction" to Chapter 3 states that REBs "can play an educational and consultative role in determining the appropriate process for seeking and maintaining consent". In the context of

tutions against liability by ensuring that unlawful or unethical research does not commence or continue.[102] However, on this front, the TCPS appropriately advises: "Legal liability is a separate issue for institutions to handle through mechanisms other than the REB."[103]

Part IV is divided into two sections. The first will focus on procedural features of research ethics review, and the second will examine some of the substantive aspects of the review. Procedural matters include "the process or mechanism of research review, including the way in which the REB functions as a committee and how protocols make their way from the investigator's hands through"[104] the review process, whereas substantive matters concern "the content of research ethics review, particularly the principles or criteria used by REBs to assess the ethical acceptability of research protocols".[105]

A. PROCEDURAL ASPECTS OF RESEARCH ETHICS REVIEW

Much of the attention that has been given to the regulation of biomedical research has concentrated on the substantive aspects of research ethics review. While such rules are of doubtless importance, no less crucial are the procedures that are employed throughout the REB decision-making process. Decision outcomes, parties' perceptions about whether they have been treated fairly and public confidence in the research governance regime are all potentially affected by the procedures REBs follow. As will be seen, the regulatory instruments establish inconsistent procedures, there are procedural gaps and some of the procedural norms may not be optimized to achieve the primary objective of research ethics review.

1. Research Ethics Board Composition

The regulatory instruments typically set parameters around the number of members that REBs must have as well as the kinds of backgrounds and expertise that the REB membership needs to collectively possess. Article 6.4 of the TCPS requires that, for biomedical research, an REB must consist of at least five members, including both men and women, of whom at least two members "have expertise in relevant research disciplines, fields and methodologies covered by the REB", at least one member who is "knowledgeable in ethics", another who is "knowledgeable in the relevant law", and at least "one community member who has no affiliation with the institution". The stated rationale for this membership requirement is to ensure "the necessary basic background, expertise and

---

researcher participation in REB discussions, the TCPS states that these "discussions are an essential part of the educational role of the REB" (see "Application" commentary under art. 6.13).

[102] Eric M. Meslin, "Ethical Issues in the Substantive and Procedural Aspects of Research Ethics Review" (1993) 13:3 Health L. Can. 179 at 179.

[103] TCPS, "Application" commentary under art. 6.4.

[104] Eric M. Meslin, "Ethical Issues in the Substantive and Procedural Aspects of Research Ethics Review" (1993) 13:3 Health L. Can. 179 at 179.

[105] *Ibid.*

perspectives to allow informed independent reflection and decision making on the ethics of research involving humans".[106]

Variability in REB membership requirements exists among the instruments. The Clinical Trial Regulations and *GCP Guidelines*, although not in direct conflict with the TCPS, contain somewhat different membership requirements. The Clinical Trial Regulations require the majority of the REB to be Canadian citizens or permanent residents[107] and there must be one member whose primary experience and expertise is in a non-scientific discipline.[108] These requirements are not expressly stated in the TCPS.[109] Even the Clinical Trial Regulations and *GCP Guidelines* are not entirely consistent; for instance, the former instrument provides that there must be a member knowledgeable in Canadian laws relevant to the biomedical research to be approved[110] and the latter is silent on the matter of legal expertise on the REB. In Quebec, the composition of REBs established under article 21 of the *Civil Code of Québec* is set out under Part 1 of the *Gazette officielle du Québec*[111] and essentially mirrors the TCPS membership requirements.

Research participant representation on REBs is not mandated under the TCPS or any of the other regulatory instruments. However, the TCPS states that the primary role of the community member "is to reflect the perspective of the participant".[112] The TCPS also indicates that "it is highly desirable that institutions seek to appoint former participants on REBs [since their] experience as participants provides the REB with a vital perspective and an important contribution to the ethics review process".[113] While the encouragement to appoint former participants is laudable, it falls short of requiring institutions to make all reasonable efforts to appoint former research participants to their REBs. Moreover, the mere presence of an individual on an REB who is knowledgeable about research participants may not furnish sufficient comfort that the interests and perspectives of research participants will be heard. To further promote the chance of achieving an effective voice for research participants, some commentators have called for requiring equal numbers of science and participant members on REBs[114] and, in appropriate cases, even granting research participant

---

[106] TCPS, "Application" commentary under art. 6.4.
[107] Clinical Trial Regulations, s. C.05.001.
[108] *Ibid.*, s. C.05.001; *GCP Guidelines*, s. 3.2.1.
[109] The TCPS acknowledges that, in the context of clinical trials, the applicable federal regulations may contain membership requirements in addition to those specific in the TCPS (see "Application" commentary under art. 6.4). Regarding community members, the TCPS indicates that it is "advisable" (*i.e.*, not mandatory) that they not be "currently engaged in research or legal work as their principal activities" ("Application" commentary under art. 6.4).
[110] Clinical Trial Regulations, s. C.05.001.
[111] Conditions d'exercice des comités d'éthique de la recherche désignés ou institués, *Gazette officielle du Québec*, 29 août 1998.I.no35.1039.
[112] TCPS, "Application" commentary under art. 6.4.
[113] TCPS, "Application" commentary under art. 6.4.
[114] Paul M. McNeill, *The Ethics and Politics of Human Experimentation* (New York: Cambridge University Press, 1993) at 207-36; and Duff Waring & Trudo Lemmens, "Integrating Values in

representatives (*i.e.*, persons other than REBs' community members) the opportunity to make submissions to REBs on particular research proposals, together
with other procedural rights.[115]

Mechanisms exist under the TCPS[116] and the *GCP Guidelines*[117] for an REB
to consult with experts if adequate expertise on a particular matter is lacking
within the REB's membership. Article 6.5 of the TCPS states that the "REB
should have provisions for consulting ad hoc advisors in the event that it lacks
the specific expertise or knowledge to review the ethical acceptability of a research proposal competently". The commentary under this article elaborates on
the matter of ad hoc advisors: "In the event that the REB is reviewing a project
that requires particular community or participant representation or specific disciplinary or methodological expertise not available from its members, it should
have provisions for consulting ad hoc advisors."[118] The use of the permissive
word "should"[119] in the article and relevant commentary is ill-conceived. If an
REB cannot competently review a given study because of a lack of proper representation or expertise, it should have an unqualified obligation to make provision for appropriate consultation. This deficiency is somewhat remedied in the
context of the review of "clinical trials"[120] since the TCPS states: "If an REB
does not have members with the appropriate expertise to review a particular
trial, then it shall seek out someone with the necessary expertise to consult as an
ad hoc advisor."[121] However, the TCPS advises that, even when ad hoc advisors
are consulted, their input does not have to be considered in the REB's final decision and these advisors should not be allowed to vote on REB decisions.[122]

Risk Analysis of Biomedical Research: The Case for Regulatory and Law Reform" in Law
Commission of Canada, *Law and Risk* (Vancouver: University of British Columbia Press, 2006).

[115] Michael Hadskis, "Giving Voice to Research Participants: Should IRBs Hear from Research
Participant Representatives?" (2007) 14:3 Accountability in Research 155.

[116] TCPS, art. 6.5.

[117] *GCP Guidelines*, s. 3.2.6.

[118] In a subsequent chapter of the TCPS (Chapter 5, "Privacy and Confidentiality"), it is noted that if
the secondary use of identifiable information for research purposes is in relation to very sensitive
information — such as genetic information — REBs may be moved to require researchers to
"engage in discussion with people whose perspectives can help identify the ethical implications
of the research, and suggest ways to minimize any associated risk" (see "Application" commentary under art. 5.5).

[119] According to the TCPS, mandatory provisions are signified by the use of the word "shall"; in
contrast, the word "should" is used to only denote guidance (Chapter 1, Section C).

[120] The TCPS uses the term "clinical trials" to cover much more than just clinical drug trials. Specifically, the TCPS states (at Chapter 11, Introduction):

> For the purposes of this Policy, a clinical trial, a form of clinical research (also known as
> patient-oriented research), is any investigation involving participants that evaluates the
> effects of one or more health-related interventions on health outcomes. Interventions in-
> clude, but are not restricted to, drugs, radiopharmaceuticals, cells and other biological
> products, surgical procedures, radiologic procedures, devices, genetic therapies, natural
> health products, process-of-care changes, preventive care, manual therapies and psycho-
> therapies.

[121] TCPS, "Application" commentary under art. 11.1.

[122] TCPS, "Application" commentary under art. 6.5.

2.   The Application of Administrative Law to Research Ethics Boards

Before discussing some of the specific processes REBs follow in discharging their decision-making role, it is appropriate to first address whether REBs must conduct this function in accordance with administrative law precepts. This is an issue of considerable significance given the direct impact this body of law can have on the decision-making process and the resultant effects on the interests of those who hold a stake in the outcome of REB decisions. REB members and researchers have a particular interest in the application of administrative law to the REB decision-making process. Resort can be had to this body of law to clarify ambiguous or vague procedural requirements in the relevant regulatory instruments, or to obtain guidance where these instruments are entirely silent on a procedural matter. Moreover, legal recourse (in the form of judicial review proceedings) for researchers who are aggrieved by an REB decision would be made possible by virtue of the application of administrative law.

The TCPS states that REBs "shall function impartially, provide a fair hearing to the researchers involved, and provide reasoned and appropriately documented opinions and decisions".[123] This statement gestures toward the importance of REBs' adherence to basic administrative law principles when exercising their decision-making functions. It has been argued that university and hospital-based REBs may fall within the purview of administrative law given that "they derive their authority from parent statutes [*i.e.*, the legislative instruments relating to the establishment and operation of universities and hospitals] which permit university and hospital boards to create internal bodies with mandatory powers; they operate at least indirectly under government control, through research-funding arrangements; and they serve important public purposes within a statutory context".[124] Additionally, the express mandates given to REBs in the context of the statutory regimes relating to clinical drug trials,[125] personal health information,[126] research involving minors or incompetent adults,[127] and the regulation of physicians might very well attract administrative law obligations.[128] Other commentators have also raised the prospect of REBs being subject to administrative law.[129] As of the writing of this chapter, there have been no

---

[123]   TCPS, art. 6.13 and "Application" commentary under art. 6.20.

[124]   Michael Hadskis & Peter Carver, "The Long Arm of Administrative Law: Applying Administrative Law Principles to Research Ethics Boards" (2005) 13:2 & 3 Health L. Rev. 19 at 20.

[125]   That is, the Clinical Trial Regulations (found under the Food and Drug Regulations, C.R.C., c. 870).

[126]   For example, the *Health Information Act*, R.S.A. 2000, c. H-5, s. 49 and *Personal Health Information Act, 2004*, S.O. 2004, c. 3, Sched. A, s. 44.

[127]   *Civil Code of Québec*, S.Q. 1991, c. 64, art. 21.

[128]   Michael Hadskis & Peter Carver, "The Long Arm of Administrative Law: Applying Administrative Law Principles to Research Ethics Boards" (2005) 13:2 & 3 Health L. Rev. 19 at 20.

[129]   Sana Halwani, "Her Majesty's Research Subjects: Liability of the Crown in Research Involving Humans" in Trudo Lemmens & Duff R. Waring, eds., *Law and Ethics in Biomedical Research:*

reported cases of administrative law remedies being sought from a Canadian court in respect of an REB decision. Thus, definitive guidance on the applicability of administrative law to REB decision-making in Canada is lacking. In the United States[130] and England,[131] there are reported cases involving judicial review of decisions made by the equivalent decision-making bodies in those countries, and legal commentators in New Zealand have opined that New Zealand courts may well be open to such proceedings, although this has yet to be tested.[132]

3.   Initiating Research Ethics Board Review

Prior to participant recruitment, access to data or the collection of human biological material, researchers must have their research proposals (including pilot studies) approved by the relevant REB(s).[133] Therefore, the researcher will need to identify the REB or REBs from which he or she will need to seek approval. This was more straightforward in the past because research was typically carried out at only one institution. Now, it is commonplace for research to be conducted at multiple centres within and between provinces, as well as in centres in different countries.[134] Since, according to the TCPS, "[e]ach institution is accountable for the research carried out in its own jurisdiction or under its auspices",[135] the REB approval process can become extremely cumbersome where a research project involves multiple institutions and/or multiple REBs. If researchers who are conducting multi-centred research must seek ethics approval from each relevant institutional REB, this carries with it the possibility of variance in review outcomes between REBs. For example, a consent form acceptable to one may not be so to another because of different disclosure norms that may be applicable to institutions located in separate provinces/territories, or perhaps because of differing interpretations between institutions of a disclosure norm applicable to both. There is also the potential for gross inefficiency as starkly demonstrated by a national epidemiological study in the United Kingdom that required ethics

---

Regulation, Conflict of Interest and Liability (Toronto: University of Toronto Press, 2006) 228 at 235-36.

[130] For example, see *Halikas v. University of Minnesota*, 856 F.Supp. 1331 (D. Minn. 1994). Also see Lars Noah, "Deputizing Institutional Review Boards to Police (Audit?) Biomedical Research" (2004) 25:3 J. Legal Med. 267 for a discussion about the possibility of administrative law remedies only being available in respect of Institutional Review Boards (the U.S. equivalent of REBs) that operate within public institutions.

[131] For example, see *R. v. Ethical Committee of St. Mary's Hospital, ex parte Harriott*, [1988] 1 F.L.R. 512, [1988] Fam. Law 165 (Q.B. Div.), where judicial review was sought in regards to the decision of an infertility services ethical committee of a hospital.

[132] John Dawson, Mary Foley & Nicola Peart, "Research Ethics Committees" in John Dawson & Nicola Peart, eds., *The Law of Research: A Guide* (Dunedin, NZ: University of Otago Press, 2003) 47 at 57-58.

[133] TCPS, art. 6.11.

[134] Jocelyn Downie & Fiona McDonald, "Revisioning the Oversight of Research Involving Humans in Canada" (2004) 12 Health L.J. 159 at 175.

[135] TCPS, "Application" commentary under art. 6.1. See also TCPS, art. 8.1.

approval from 176 REBs. By the end of this laborious process, 50 hours of photocopying time had been used to copy 60,000 sheets of paper.[136]

In an effort to facilitate ethics review processes and minimize the kinds of inefficiencies noted above, Chapter 8 of the TCPS sets out several ethics review models for multi-jurisdictional research. Institutions remain responsible for approving alternative review models for use by their REBs and researchers.[137] Some of the review models involve institutions, by means of "official agreements" containing certain "minimum components",[138] authorizing their REBs to accept the ethics reviews conducted by an external REB. For instance, institutions may allow rescarch ethics review to be delegated to an external, specialized or multi-institutional REB. Alternatively, institutions may permit reciprocal REB review (*i.e.*, official reciprocity agreements between multiple institutions that provide for the acceptance of each other's REB reviews).[139] The TCPS indicates that REBs and researchers should select the most appropriate model from among those authorized by their institution and furnishes some considerations for making such selections.[140] Despite the availability of arrangements such as reciprocity agreements, some institutions have been indisposed to entering into these agreements due to the potential liability they think they might be exposed to should the other institutions' REBs fail to meet applicable standards.[141]

Chapter 8 of the TCPS also deals with the topic of ethics review of research conducted outside the institution. Institutions remain accountable for the ethical conduct and ethical acceptability of research carried out by its faculty, staff or students irrespective of where the research takes place.[142]

The application or submission materials that researchers must provide to REBs can vary according to the specific demands of the relevant REB and the particular type of research being proposed. The required documentation can include research summaries that must follow the format adopted by the REB(s), consent forms, participant recruitment tools (*e.g.*, draft advertisements, letters of invitation/introduction, and telephone scripts), questionnaires, interview guidelines, contracts entered into with sponsors (including confidentiality agreements) and the researchers' *curriculum vitae*. Although the TCPS does not detail the documents that must be reviewed by an REB, the *GCP Guidelines* do.[143]

---

[136] Jocelyn Downie & Fiona McDonald, "Revisioning the Oversight of Research Involving Humans in Canada" (2004) 12 Health L.J. 159 at 176.

[137] TCPS, art. 8.1.

[138] TCPS, "Application" commentary under art. 8.1.

[139] TCPS, "Application" commentary under art. 8.1.

[140] TCPS, art. 8.2.

[141] Kathleen Cranley Glass, "Questions and Challenges in the Governance of Research Involving Humans: A Canadian Perspective" in Trudo Lemmens & Duff R. Waring, eds., *Law and Ethics in Biomedical Research: Regulation, Conflict of Interest and Liability* (Toronto: University of Toronto Press, 2006) 35 at 41.

[142] See TCPS, Section B of Chapter 8.

[143] *GCP Guidelines*, ss. 3.1.2 and 3.1.3.

4.   Level of Research Ethics Board Review

The TCPS puts forward two levels of REB review: full board and delegated. Full board review is the "default requirement" under the TCPS.[144] That is, unless it is appropriate to proceed by way of delegated review, a full board review is necessary. Before setting out the basis for deciding whether to hold a delegated or full board review, each form of review will be described.

Under the TCPS, full board reviews normally involve regularly scheduled, face-to-face REB meetings[145] during which each research project before the REB is discussed with the aim of reaching a decision as to whether to approve, reject or propose modifications to proposed research, or to terminate any ongoing research.[146] The REB must "provide a fair hearing to the researchers involved"[147] and must "accommodate reasonable requests from researchers to participate in discussions about their proposals"[148] before it reaches a decision; however, researchers cannot be present at the meeting when the REB deliberates on their proposals.[149] In terms of quorum requirements for full board review meetings, the TCPS states that institutions must "establish quorum rules for REBs that meet the minimum requirements of membership outlined in Article 6.4".[150] When "there is less than full attendance, decisions requiring full review should be adopted only when the members in attendance at that meeting have the specific expertise, relevant competence and knowledge necessary to provide an adequate research ethics review of the proposals under consideration".[151] The TCPS cautions: "Decisions without a quorum are not valid or binding."[152]

On completing its discussion of a research proposal, the REB must reach a reasoned, well-documented decision[153] in accordance with the decision-making process that it has adopted. If the majority of the REB members determine that a given research project is acceptable, but a minority of the REB membership considers the project unethical, the TCPS states that an effort should be made to reach consensus. If consensus cannot be achieved, "a decision should be made in

---

[144] TCPS, "Application" commentary under art. 6.12.
[145] TCPS, art. 6.10. In "exceptional cases", it is acceptable for an REB member who cannot attend the meeting to provide his or her input by means of technology, such as phone or video link. It is also acknowledged that the use of technology may be necessary for REB meetings when members are "geographically dispersed and there is no other way of holding an effective REB meeting, or when exceptional or exigent circumstances significantly disrupt or limit the feasibility of face-to-face REB meetings (e.g., during a public emergency)": see "Application" commentary under art. 6.10.
[146] TCPS, art. 6.3.
[147] TCPS, art. 6.13.
[148] TCPS, "Application" commentary under art. 6.13; *GCP Guidelines*, s. 3.2.5.
[149] TCPS, "Application" commentary under art. 6.13; *GCP Guidelines*, s. 3.2.5.
[150] TCPS, art. 6.9.
[151] TCPS, art. 6.9.
[152] TCPS, "Application" commentary under art. 6.9.
[153] TCPS, art. 6.13.

accordance with the process agreed upon, and documented by the REB".[154] For example, REBs may decide to grant approvals on a simple majority vote or may require the achievement of some greater majority.

Delegated review usually involves the REB delegating the research ethics review to one or more members of the REB ("delegates").[155] In practice, this may well mean that those conducting the delegated review will not possess the full range of expertise and experience that exists within the REB as a whole. As well, fewer people will pore over the research documentation submitted to the REB. Therefore, delegates must be carefully selected. Delegates can seek the assistance of other reviewers within the REB or refer the project to the full REB if they are of the view that full board review is appropriate. If a delegate is considering rejecting the project, this matter must "be referred to the full REB for review and endorsement before communicating the decision to the researcher".[156] The decisions of delegates must be well-documented and formally reported to the full REB, thus permitting the entire REB to satisfy itself that its participant protection mandate is being met through this process.[157]

Pursuant to the TCPS, decisions about the level of REB review required for a particular study are to be made in accordance with the concept of "proportionate review". This requires consideration of "the level of foreseeable risks to participants: the lower the level of risk, the lower the level of scrutiny (delegated review); the higher the level of risk, the higher the level of scrutiny (full board review)".[158] Foundational to the proportionate approach is the TCPS conception of "minimal risk". If the research involves no more than minimal risk, it "should normally receive delegated review", whereas "above-minimal risk research shall receive full REB review".[159] As will be seen later in the chapter, the application of the minimal risk standard extends beyond its use in determining what type of REB review is to be held.[160] Minimal risk research is defined as "research in which the probability and magnitude of possible harms implied by participation in the research is no greater than those encountered by participants in those aspects of their everyday life that relate to the research".[161] In the context of bio-

---

[154] TCPS, "Application" commentary under art. 6.13. See also the "Application" commentary under art. 6.10.

[155] Ethics review of student course-based research is an exception to the rule that delegates are to be selected from among the REB membership. For such research, ethics review can be undertaken by non-REB members at the institution's department, faculty or equivalent level (see "Application" commentary under art. 6.12).

[156] TCPS, "Application" commentary under art. 6.12.

[157] TCPS, "Application" commentary under art. 6.12.

[158] TCPS, arts. 2.9 and 6.12.

[159] TCPS, "Application" commentary under art. 2.9.

[160] For example, the minimal risk standard is also used in determining: whether consent requirements can be altered (art. 3.7); the extent of scholarly review that is required ("Application" commentary under art. 2.7); whether incompetent persons can be enrolled in research (arts. 3.9 and 4.6); and the type of continuing review process that research is to be subjected to ("Application" commentary under art. 6.14).

[161] TCPS, Chapter 2, Section B.

medical research, any risk of harm that participants would have been exposed to as a consequence of undergoing medical treatment irrespective of their participation in the study, is not considered in the minimal risk calculus. However, those interventions that serve only the needs of the study are included.[162]

Possible harms are to be assessed according to the chance that they will unfold (the probability variable) and the gravity of the consequences should the harm come to pass (the magnitude variable).[163] The TCPS identifies several potential categories of harm that need to be considered in terms of their probability and magnitude: physical; psychological; behavioural; social (*e.g.*, stigmatization); and economic.[164] To the extent that legal consequences (*e.g.*, exposure to civil or criminal liability) and privacy violations are not captured in any of these harm categories, they should nonetheless be considered. If the aggregate risks of harm associated with the research interventions[165] exceed the "everyday life" risks threshold, the research does not meet the minimal risk definition and should not proceed by way of delegated review. The TCPS provides some examples of research that may qualify for delegated review, including: "research that is confidently expected to involve minimal risk; minimal-risk changes to approved research; annual renewals of approved minimal risk research; [and] annual renewals of more than minimal risk research where the research will no longer involve new interventions to current participants, renewal does not involve the recruitment of new participants, and the remaining research activities are limited to data analysis".[166]

The minimal risk standard has sparked vigorous debate in Canada and the United States, which has adopted a similar standard.[167] Some claim that the shifting everyday life threshold is impractical and unjust. It is claimed that individuals and communities vary widely regarding the risks they encounter in the ordinary course of a day and that it would be morally wrong for the minimal risk standard to be more likely met for research involving sick people or persons living in high-crime, low-income communities (*e.g.*, some inner cities) than healthy people or persons living in safer, more affluent areas.[168] Moreover, at the research approval stage, how are REBs going to prospec-

---

[162] TCPS, art. 11.5. This article deals with clinical trials. It states, in part, as follows: "In their evaluation of risk, REBs should ensure that they are evaluating only those risks that are attributable to the research (including cumulative risks), and not compounding them with the risks attributable to clinical care."

[163] TCPS, Chapter 2, Section B.

[164] TCPS, Chapter 2, Section B.

[165] As distinct from the risks connected with the therapeutic interventions to which the patient would otherwise be exposed.

[166] TCPS, "Application" commentary under art. 6.12.

[167] The TCPS minimal risk standard is similar, but not identical, to its counterpart in the relevant American instrument: Title 45 *Code of Federal Regulations*, § 46.102(i). However, its use of the "everyday life" threshold (or the equivalent "daily life" threshold in the United States) opens it to the same criticisms lodged against the American instrument.

[168] Loretta Kopelman, "Estimating Risk in Human Research" (1981) 29 Clinical Research 1; and Loretta Kopelman, "Moral Problems in Assessing Research Risk" (2000) 22:5 I.R.B. 3.

tively evaluate individuals' everyday risks when they have yet to be recruited?[169] Even if the potential participants are known, how are REBs going to go about the task of quantifying the risks?[170]

In defence of the minimal risk standard, others claim that the standard "provides a sound normative basis for the assessment of nontherapeutic research risk".[171] They argue that the standard refers to risks common to us all (*e.g.*, driving a car and crossing the street) not just specific individuals or communities and, regarding the quantification problem, they assert that it can be averted by relying on qualitative/categorical determinations.[172] Nonetheless, other difficulties may persist, such as inconsistent determinations by REBs due to nebulous qualitative criteria.[173] To resolve the debate, one author proposes the elimination of the everyday life threshold; instead, research should be found to pose no more than minimal risk where "the probability and magnitude of the harm or discomfort anticipated in research are no greater than those encountered during the performance of routine physical or psychological examinations or tests".[174] This too may be problematic, since it would likely invite endless debate and inconsistent decisions about what counts as a routine test.

It may be inappropriate to only consider the minimal risk standard in deciding whether to proceed by way of delegated or full board review because some minimal risk research should undergo full review.[175] An example of this would be a minimal risk research project involving long-term care facility residents with Alzheimer's Disease that is being conducted by facility caregivers. Ethical concerns about the recruitment of participants who may be highly dependent on their caregivers and about how competency assessments will be conducted would render delegated review inappropriate. Quebec has addressed this issue, at least for certain persons who may be vulnerable. In that province, delegated reviews cannot be held in relation to research involving incompetent minors and

---

[169] This is a concern attributed to Chris Levy in James A. Anderson & Charles Weijer, "Minimal Risk and its Implications" (2001) 11:1 N.C.E.H.R. Communiqué 15 at 19.

[170] Loretta Kopelman, "Estimating Risk in Human Research" (1981) 29 Clinical Research 1; and Loretta Kopelman, "Moral Problems in Assessing Research Risk" (2000) 22:5 I.R.B. 3.

[171] Paul Miller & Charles Weijer, "Moral Solutions in Assessing Research Risk" (2000) 22:5 I.R.B. 6 at 6.

[172] Benjamin Freedman, Abraham Fuks & Charles Weijer, "*In Loco Parentis*: Minimal Risk as an Ethical Threshold for Research upon Children" (1993) 23:2 Hastings Center Report 13; Charles Weijer, "The Ethical Analysis of Risk" (2000) 28 J.L. Med. & Ethics 344; Charles Weijer, "The Analysis of Risks and Potential Benefits in Research" (1999) 9:2 N.C.E.H.R. Communiqué 16; James A. Anderson & Charles Weijer, "Minimal Risk and its Implications" (2001) 11:1 N.C.E.H.R. Communiqué 15.

[173] See Jennifer Marshall & Michael Hadskis, "Canadian Research Ethics Boards: MRI Research Risks, and MRI Risk Classification" (2009) 31:4 IRB: Ethics & Human Research 9 for a discussion of the difficulties of minimal risk classification in the context of MRI research. Also see David B. Resnik, "Eliminating the Daily Life Risks Standard from the Definition of Minimal Risk" (2005) 31 J. Med. Ethics 35 at 35.

[174] David B. Resnik, "Eliminating the Daily Life Risks Standard from the Definition of Minimal Risk" (2005) 31 J. Med. Ethics 35 at 37-38.

[175] Charles Weijer, "The Ethical Analysis of Risk" (2000) 28 J.L. Med. & Ethics 344 at 358.

adults, even if it presents only minimal risks.[176] The TCPS gestures briefly to the relationship between minimal risk and vulnerability when it notes: "In their assessment of the acceptable threshold of minimal risk, REBs have special ethical obligations to individuals or groups whose situations or circumstances make them vulnerable in the context of a specific research project, and to those who live with relatively high levels of risk on a daily basis. Their inclusion in research should not exacerbate their vulnerability."[177]

Delegated reviews have a very limited role in clinical drug trials.[178] The *GCP Guidelines* state that REBs should have written procedures that provide for delegated reviews for "minor change(s) in ongoing trials", but this is noted to be subject to "applicable regulatory requirements".[179] The Clinical Trial Regulations do not speak to the use of delegated review mechanisms. Assuming this void can be filled by the *GCP Guidelines*, it would seem that delegated reviews of proposed drug trials cannot be undertaken and, with respect to ongoing trials, such reviews can only be conducted in the context of minor changes in the trials. No guidance is provided regarding what counts as a minor change.

5.　Impartiality and Independence

The integrity of the ethics review system and the maintenance of the public's confidence in it rests on REBs and their individual members being unencumbered by extraneous influences during the decision-making process. The imperative for impartial decision-makers and independent decision-making bodies is a longstanding element of natural justice[180] and is partially voiced in some of the relevant regulatory instruments for biomedical research. The policy that underscores this imperative is reflected in the frequently rehearsed legal maxim: "Justice must not only be done, but must manifestly and undoubtedly be seen to be done."[181] This maxim should have no less purchase in the context of REB decision-making.

As a matter of administrative law, individual decision-makers can be disqualified on the basis of actual bias or a reasonable apprehension of bias, the latter form of bias may be found "where a reasonable person, knowing the facts concerning the member, would suspect that the member may be influenced, albeit unintentionally, by improper considerations to favour one side in the matter to be decided".[182] Similarly, the TCPS indicates that in order to "maintain the

---

[176] Fonds de la recherche en santé du Québec, *Guide d'éthique et d'intégrité scientifique de la recherche (Research Ethics and Scientific Integrity Guidelines)*, 2d ed. (Montreal: FRSQ, 2003) at 57.

[177] TCPS, Chapter 2, Section B.

[178] The *GCP Guidelines* actually use the term "expedited reviews". Expedited reviews are, for all intents and purposes, the same thing as delegated reviews.

[179] *GCP Guidelines*, s. 3.3.5.

[180] David Phillip Jones & Anne S. De Villars, *Principles of Administrative Law*, 4th ed. (Scarborough, ON: Carswell, 2004) at 366.

[181] *Ibid.*, at 366.

[182] Sara Blake, *Administrative Law in Canada*, 3d ed. (Markham, ON: Butterworths, 2001) at 94.

independence and integrity of research ethics review, members of the REB must identify, eliminate, minimize or otherwise manage real, potential or perceived conflicts of interest".[183] Although the TCPS uses the term "conflict of interest", for all intents and purposes, the existence of a conflict of interest constitutes "bias" in the decision-making context. The TCPS does not contain a general test for determining whether an apparent conflict of interest exists on the part of REB members. Nonetheless, this instrument contains more direction on the issue of conflicts of interest than the Clinical Trial Regulations, which are entirely silent on the matter, or the *GCP Guidelines*, which provide only scant direction.[184] If administrative law applies to REBs, it can fill the void by furnishing the judicial definition of a reasonable apprehension of bias and a rich body of case law interpreting the rule against bias in a variety of decision-making contexts.

Administrative law is rife with examples of situations where courts have found a reasonable apprehension of bias. Such findings have been made where familial, personal, employment or business relationships prevail between the decision-maker and a party to the proceeding.[185] A financial interest in the outcome of the proceeding is another common example.[186] Given that REB members are largely drawn from the staff and professionals (many of whom are biomedical researchers themselves) from the host institution, strong potential exists for the research ethics review process to be tainted by bias.

The TCPS definitively states that REB members are in a conflict of interest "when their own research projects are under review by their REB, when they are a co-investigator, or when they are in a supervisory or mentoring relationship with a graduate student applicant".[187] Less definitively, the TCPS states that REB members "*may* also be in a conflict of interest situation when they have interpersonal or financial relationships with the researchers, or personal or financial interests in a company ... that may be the sponsor of the research project, or that may be substantially affected by the research".[188] It is further acknowledged that conflicts of interest can exist based on REB members' "collaborations or disputes with colleagues".[189]

It is likely that REB members from many research institutions, particularly those of modest size, will have engaged in academic collaboration or otherwise have significant connections with the researchers whose studies are under review. Therefore, the TCPS wisely recommends that institutions' "conflict of

---

[183] TCPS, "Application" commentary under art. 7.3.

[184] The direction under the *GCP Guidelines* consists of one sentence in s. 3.2.1 advising that only those REB members "who are independent of the investigator and the sponsor of the trial should vote/provide opinion on a trial-related matter".

[185] David Mullan, *Administrative Law*, 3d ed. (Scarborough, ON: Carswell, 1996) at 295.

[186] David Phillip Jones & Anne S. De Villars, *Principles of Administrative Law*, 4th ed. (Scarborough, ON: Carswell, 2004) at 373.

[187] TCPS, Chapter 7, Section A.

[188] TCPS, Chapter 7, Section A [emphasis added].

[189] TCPS, Chapter 7, Section A.

interest policies should determine a reasonable time period during which an REB member is not allowed to review a proposal involving a recent collaborator, supervisor, student or other colleague".[190] Of some note is the TCPS' failure to acknowledge the direct or indirect pressure some REB members may feel to approve a research project due to the financial implications of the study for their institution.[191] Some REB members who work at the host institution may feel that their prospects for tenure and promotion would be damaged if they are considered responsible for mounting barriers to the productivity of the institution's research program.

A conflict of interest may come to the REB's attention by virtue of self-disclosure by a member (as mandated by the TCPS[192]) or by way of a researcher's allegation of bias stemming from, for example, personal animosity or professional rivalry between the member and the researcher. On being presented with a possible conflict of interest, the REB needs to gather information relevant to the matter and then make a ruling on the presence or absence of a conflict of interest before proceeding with the review. This may be relatively straightforward when dealing with a clear conflict of interest. In other instances, such as the case where the REB member not infrequently collaborates in the clinical setting with a colleague whose project is the subject of the review, REBs should apply the facts to the legal test outlined above. The absence of any reported Canadian jurisprudence respecting judicial proceedings being brought against REBs makes it difficult to predict how stringently this test should be applied. It bears highlighting that "the standard of scrutiny of an adjudication by a 'domestic' tribunal may be somewhat less intense than in other contexts",[193] as has been seen in litigation involving allegations of bias against members of university tenure committees and like peer review bodies.[194] On the other hand, the imposition of a less exacting standard in the REB context may well be inappropriate since REB decisions may have profound adverse consequences for the rights, safety and well-being of research participants, who do not have an effective voice in the review process.

Where a conflict of interest is found to exist, the REB member concerned must absent him or herself from any discussion or decision respecting the relevant project and must not have any further involvement in the matter. The TCPS requires that such action be taken[195] and administrative law precepts also de-

---

[190] TCPS, art. 7.3.

[191] Kathleen Cranley Glass & Trudo Lemmens, "Conflict of Interest and Commercialization of Biomedical Research: What is the Role of Research Ethics Review?" in Timothy Caulfield & Bryn Williams-Jones, eds., *The Commercialization of Genetic Research: Ethical, Legal and Policy Issues* (New York: Kluwer Academic/Plenum Publishers, 1999) 79 at 90.

[192] TCPS, art. 7.3.

[193] David Mullan, *Administrative Law*, 3d ed. (Toronto: Carswell, 1996) at 303.

[194] For example, see *Paine v. University of Toronto*, [1981] O.J. No. 3187, 131 D.L.R. (3d) 325 (Ont. C.A.), leave to appeal refused [1982] S.C.C.A. No. 239 (S.C.C.).

[195] TCPS, art. 7.3 and the "Application" commentary under it.

mand the adoption of this approach.[196] Parenthetically, it should be noted that the review of the relevant project must be postponed until an appropriate replacement member is obtained in those instances where the removal of the member possessing the conflict would result in a loss of quorum.[197]

In addition to the requirement that individual REB members be impartial, the structure and operation of a particular REB must not give rise to a reasonable apprehension of bias. Again, the law demands this of administrative adjudicators[198] and this requirement finds some expression in the TCPS,[199] which notes that for "the integrity of the research ethics review process, and to safeguard public trust in that process, institutions shall ensure that REBs are able to operate effectively and independently in their decision making".[200] This means that institutions must provide their REBs with adequate ongoing financial and administrative resources (*e.g.*, sufficient human resources, a research ethics office) to carry out their responsibilities.[201] It also means that REBs are to be free from inappropriate influence.[202] For instance, the independence of the REB would reasonably be brought into question if the institution's legal counsel or risk management staff were to serve on the REB as such individuals could be viewed as being too closely aligned with the institution's financial or legal interests.[203] Similarly, the senior administrators of the institution (*e.g.*, the vice-president of research) should not sit on the REB "or directly or indirectly influence the REB decision-making process".[204]

6.   Review of Ongoing Research

Once a research project has received REB approval and is underway, there is a continuing need to safeguard research participants. Regarding the importance of ongoing ethics review, one author observes: "Continuing review of approved research is essential to ensure that research is conducted as planned, that research subjects comprehend the information given to them in the consent process, and that the potential benefits and risks of the study participation remain acceptable."[205] Others have identified the purposes of continuing review as including education of research staff, quality assurance and prevention of miscon-

---

[196] Sara Blake, *Administrative Law in Canada*, 3d ed. (Markham, ON: Butterworths, 2001) at 107.

[197] The TCPS recommends that a substitute member be in attendance at such meetings so that quorum will not be lost (see "Application" commentary under art. 7.3).

[198] David Phillip Jones & Anne S. De Villars, *Principles of Administrative Law*, 4th ed. (Scarborough, ON: Carswell, 2004) at 387.

[199] Articles 7.1 and 7.2 and their respective "Application" commentaries deal with real, potential or perceived institutional conflicts of interest.

[200] TCPS, "Application" commentary under art. 6.2.

[201] TCPS, art. 6.2.

[202] TCPS, "Application" commentary under art. 6.2.

[203] TCPS, "Application" commentary under art. 6.4.

[204] TCPS, "Application" commentary under art. 6.4.

[205] C. Weijer, "Continuing Review of Research Approved by Canadian Research Ethics Boards" (2001) 164 CMAJ 1305 at 1305.

duct on the part of researchers and their staff.[206] These reasons provide strong support for the implementation of appropriate oversight and review mechanisms.

The key regulatory instruments impose some ongoing review obligations. The TCPS states that continuing ethics review is a collective responsibility involving a number of actors, including institutions, REBs and researchers.[207] While continuing research ethics review is mandatory,[208] the TCPS allows for a considerable degree of latitude respecting REBs' decisions about the nature and frequency of these reviews. Pursuant to the TCPS, the review must, at a minimum, consist of an annual status report to the REB for projects with lifespans exceeding one year and end-of-study reports for projects of less than one year duration.[209] Beyond this, the rigour of the review is to be determined according to the "proportionate approach",[210] with greater-than-minimal risk studies potentially requiring more extensive continuing ethics review, such as "more frequent reporting to the REB, monitoring and review of the consent process, review of participant records, and site visits".[211]

Researchers are required to report to the REB "any unanticipated issue or event that may increase the level of risk to participants, or has other ethical implications that may affect participants' welfare".[212] In its chapter on clinical trials, the TCPS requires researchers to "promptly report new information that may affect the welfare or consent of participants, to the REB"[213] and others (*e.g.*, an unexpected side effect of a study drug or information about a study drug's lack of efficacy). Furthermore, researchers must "promptly inform all participants to whom the information applies (including former participants)".[214]

Data safety monitoring boards can be established for monitoring the safety of participants. Biostatisticians, scientists, bioethicists and clinicians knowledgeable about the relevant research project usually sit on these committees.[215] They are most commonly used in the context of clinical drug trials, where the possibility that trial participants may experience adverse reactions to the study agent is often a concern. These boards typically analyze adverse events with the goal of determining the likelihood that a relationship exists between an adverse occurrence in the health of a participant and his or her participation in the research. They may also perform interim analyses of clinical outcome data to determine if there is sufficient "evidence that one treatment has greater efficacy or

---

[206] J. McCusker *et al.*, "Monitoring Clinical Research: Report of One Hospital's Experience" (2001) 164 CMAJ 1321 at 1321.

[207] TCPS, "Application" commentary under art. 6.14.

[208] TCPS, art. 2.8.

[209] TCPS, art. 6.14.

[210] TCPS, art. 6.14.

[211] TCPS, "Application" commentary under art. 6.14.

[212] TCPS, art. 6.15.

[213] TCPS, art. 11.8.

[214] TCPS, art. 11.8.

[215] A. Slutsky & J. Lavery, "Data Safety and Monitoring Boards" (2004) 350 New Eng. J. Med. 1143 at 1143.

causes greater harm than another".[216] As well, a safety monitoring committee may request additional information from researchers, require revisions to research documentation (*e.g.*, informed consent forms) or recommend the early termination of the research.[217] In the context of clinical trials, the TCPS requires researchers to provide REBs "with an acceptable plan for monitoring the safety of participants";[218] however, the establishment of a data safety monitoring board is not mandatory.[219]

Despite the existence of regulatory requirements for ongoing monitoring, there is overwhelming evidence that REBs are investing the vast majority of their resources in the ethics approval phase,[220] leaving their monitoring responsibilities largely unfulfilled.[221] Senator Michael Kirby's 2002 report, *The Health of Canadians — The Federal Role*, remarks that "few [REBs] monitor the conduct of research once a research protocol has been approved [and therefore] ... often have limited knowledge of what happens after they have approved a research protocol".[222] This is not surprising in light of REBs' substantial research approval workloads and the finite resources (financial and human) at their disposal.[223] Nonetheless, with no or limited knowledge of what happens to partici-

---

[216] *Ibid.*

[217] *Ibid.*

[218] TCPS, art. 11.7.

[219] TCPS, "Application" commentary under art. 11.7.

[220] Michael McDonald, "Ethics and Governance" in Michael McDonald, ed., *The Governance of Health Research Involving Human Subjects* (Ottawa: Law Commission of Canada, 2000) 19 at 61.

[221] Jocelyn Downie & Fiona McDonald, "Revisioning the Oversight of Research Involving Humans in Canada" (2004) 12 Health L.J. 159 at 177-78; Charles Weijer, "Continuing Review of Research Approved by Canadian Research Ethics Boards" (2001) 164 CMAJ 1305 at 1305-1306; Charles Weijer, "Continuing Review of Clinical Research Canadian-Style" (2002) 25:3 Clinical and Investigative Medicine 92 at 92-93; Charles Weijer, Stanley Shapiro, Abraham Fuks, Kathleen Cranley Glass & Myriam Skrutkowska, "Monitoring Clinical Research: An Obligation Unfulfilled" (1995) 152 CMAJ 1973; Eric M. Meslin, "Ethical Issues in the Substantive and Procedural Aspects of Research Ethics Review" (1993) 13:3 Health L. Can. 179 at 185-86; Marie Hirtle, "The Governance of Research Involving Human Participants in Canada" (2003) 11 Health L.J. 137 at 144; Catherine Miller, "Protection of Human Subjects of Research in Canada" (1995) 4:1 Health L. Rev. 8 at 10; Michael McDonald, "Canadian Governance of Health Research Involving Human Subjects: Is Anybody Minding the Store?" (2001) 9 Health L.J. 1 at 10-11; and Jane McCusker *et al.*, "Monitoring Clinical Research: Report of One Hospital's Experience" (2001) 164:9 CMAJ 1321.

[222] The Standing Senate Committee on Social Affairs, Science and Technology, *The Health of Canadians — The Federal Role*, vol. 6, Final Report (Ottawa: The Senate, 2002) (Kirby Report) at s. 12.7.2, online at: <http://www.parl.gc.ca/37/2/parlbus/commbus/senate/com-e/SOCI-E/rep-e/repoct02vol6p-e.htm>.

[223] Jocelyn Downie & Fiona McDonald, "Revisioning the Oversight of Research Involving Humans in Canada" (2004) 12 Health L.J. 159 at 180; and Abbyann Lynch, "Research Ethics Boards — Operational Issues I" (1999) 9:2 & 10:1 N.C.E.H.R. Communiqué 9 at 12-13. On the issue of furnishing REBs with sufficient resources, the TCPS states: "Institutions have a responsibility to provide necessary resources to REBs to assist them in fulfilling their continuing ethics review responsibilities" (see "Application" commentary under art. 6.14).

pants after they are enrolled in studies, how much confidence can reasonably be placed in the research ethics review process?

B.   SUBSTANTIVE ASPECTS OF RESEARCH ETHICS REVIEW

After being presented with the information pertaining to a particular research project through the ethics review process, TCPS-compliant REBs must deliberate on a number of substantive issues. Regarding applications for approval of a proposed study, these issues include: whether the most favourable balance of risks and potential benefits in a research proposal has been achieved;[224] whether risks to participants have been minimized;[225] whether "net benefits" of the research (*e.g.*, benefits for participants and other individuals, benefits for society as a whole and the advancement of knowledge) have been maximized; whether participant selection criteria are fair and equitable;[226] whether the recruitment process is appropriate; whether the proposed consent process is ethically and legally valid; whether vulnerable persons will be respected; whether the privacy of participants and the confidentiality of identifiable personal information being collected for research purposes are properly protected;[227] whether a real, perceived or potential conflict of interest exists on the part of the researchers and, if so, how it should be dealt with;[228] and whether the methods and design of the research are ethically sound.[229] Where ongoing research is under review, REBs most often entertain issues concerning whether the harm-benefit balance has remained unchanged and, if it has changed, what action needs to be taken (*e.g.*, consent form amendments or the immediate termination of the study).

The *GCP Guidelines* also set out substantive norms that are to inform REB decision-making. In addition to the requirement that they comply with the ethical principles in the *Declaration of Helsinki*,[230] REBs are to: weigh foreseeable risks and inconveniences against anticipated benefits for individual trial participants and society;[231] evaluate the scientific "soundness" of the protocol;[232] ensure "freely given informed consent" is obtained from participants;[233] ensure compliance with applicable privacy and confidentiality rules;[234] and pay "special attention" to trials that include "vulnerable subjects".[235] The *GCP Guidelines*, on the whole, offer less guidance than the TCPS on many of these substantive norms.

---

[224]   TCPS, Chapter 1, Section B.
[225]   TCPS, Chapter 1, Section B.
[226]   TCPS, Chapter 4.
[227]   TCPS, Chapter 5.
[228]   TCPS, Chapter 7, Section D.
[229]   TCPS, art. 2.7.
[230]   *GCP Guidelines*, s. 2.1.
[231]   *Ibid.*, s. 2.2.
[232]   *Ibid.*, s. 2.5.
[233]   *Ibid.*, s. 2.9.
[234]   *Ibid.*, s. 2.11.
[235]   *Ibid.*, s. 3.1.1. The term "vulnerable subjects" is defined in s. 1.61.

Substantive issues related to consent, privacy and confidentiality, and conflicts of interest on the part of researchers have received the greatest attention by legal commentators, research ethicists and policy-makers. They will form the focus of this section of the chapter.

1.   Consent

In order for consent to participate in research to be legally and ethically valid, three conditions must be satisfied: the consent must be informed; the consent must be voluntarily given; and the person giving consent must possess decisional capacity. Each of these conditions is discussed below.

(a)   Consent to Participate in Research Must Be Informed

In the medical treatment context, the Supreme Court of Canada[236] has, on multiple occasions, expressed its view that commitments to dignity and autonomy require that individuals have the right to determine whether and to what extent they will accept medical interventions. As detailed in Chapter 4, "Informed Consent", a robust body of law on the issue of informed consent exists in Canada. Comparatively, reported case law expounding on the doctrine of informed consent in the area of human biomedical research is limited. For the most part, researchers and REB members have relied on extra-legal documents to obtain direction on the matter of informed consent. This section will address the modest body of case law on informed consent in the research context and will then outline the relevant norms found in the TCPS, Clinical Trial Regulations and *GCP Guidelines*.

The 1965 Saskatchewan Court of Appeal case of *Halushka v. University of Saskatchewan*[237] is one of two influential judicial decisions in Canada on the issue of informed consent in biomedical research. In this case, a University of Saskatchewan student was offered $50 to participate in a study that was intended to investigate individuals' circulatory response while under general anaesthesia. The study was being conducted by medical researchers employed by the University of Saskatchewan. During the consent process, the student participant was verbally instructed that his participation would involve having a catheter or tube inserted into a vein in his left arm and that he would receive a "new" anaesthetic agent. He was also told that this was a "safe test and there was nothing to worry about". The participant signed a brief consent form containing a clause releasing the researchers and others from liability for "any untoward effects or accidents" arising from his participation.

The next day, he underwent the research interventions that had been explained to him, with the exception that after inserting the catheter into the vein in his left arm, the researchers advanced it toward his heart. At this point, the

---

[236] For example, see *Ciarlariello v. Schacter*, [1993] S.C.J. No. 46, [1993] 2 S.C.R. 119 (S.C.C.) and *Starson v. Swayze*, [2003] S.C.J. No. 33, [2003] 1 S.C.R. 722 (S.C.C.).

[237] [1965] S.J. No. 208, 53 D.L.R. (2d) 436 (Sask. C.A.).

participant experienced discomfort and the anaesthetic agent was administered. The catheter was then put through the chambers of his heart. Concerned that the anaesthesia level was too light, the researchers increased the amount of the anaesthetic agent and the participant experienced complete cardiac arrest that was caused by the agent. Although successfully resuscitated, he had sustained damage and brought a tort action against the researchers. A central issue in the case was whether the consent given by the participant was adequately informed. Finding against the researchers, the court determined that they had failed to inform the participant about, among other things, the risks associated with the use of an anaesthetic and the fact that the catheter would be advanced through his heart.

Several important common law principles arise from the decision. In terms of the researchers' disclosure obligation, the court opined that "the duty imposed upon those engaged in medical research ... to those who offer themselves as subjects for experimentation ... is at least as great as, if not greater than, the duty owed by the ordinary physician or surgeon to his patient".[238] The court also noted that a subject "is entitled to a full and frank disclosure of all the facts, probabilities and opinions which a reasonable man might be expected to consider before giving his consent".[239] Even putting aside the court's unfortunate use of equivocal language respecting the differences between the disclosure standards for medical treatment and research, this case provides limited guidance on defining the contemporary disclosure standard in research. This is largely due to the fact that it was decided 15 years before the Supreme Court of Canada, in *Hopp v. Lepp*[240] and *Reibl v. Hughes*,[241] established the so-called modified objective patient test for disclosure in the context of medical treatment. That test requires disclosure of information a reasonable person *in the patient's position* would require to make an informed decision. The *Reibl* standard is higher than that which existed for medical treatment when *Halushka* was decided[242] (*i.e.*, according to the *Halushka* court, patients were merely entitled to a reasonably clear explanation of the treatment and of the natural and expected outcome of it).

Therefore, subject to the below remarks about therapeutic privilege, it would be difficult to sustain a claim that *Halushka* provides definitive judicial support for a higher standard in research than the medical treatment standard established in *Reibl*. While it may be argued that the *Halushka* court intended to make a general claim that, whatever the treatment standard might be from time to time, the research standard will always be higher, it could also reasonably be contended that the court's decision was inextricably linked to the relatively low

---

[238] *Ibid.*, at 443-44.

[239] *Ibid.*, at 444.

[240] [1980] S.C.J. No. 57, [1980] 2 S.C.R. 192 (S.C.C.).

[241] [1980] S.C.J. No. 105, [1980] 2 S.C.R. 880 (S.C.C.) [*Reibl*].

[242] The elevated standard flowing from *Reibl* is acknowledged in Ellen Picard & Gerald Robertson, *Legal Liability of Doctors and Hospitals in Canada*, 3d ed. (Scarborough, ON: Carswell, 1996) at 150.

disclosure standard for treatment that existed in 1965. In any event, the rationale behind the genesis of the modified objective patient test should have equal purchase in the medical research realm, thus the *unmodified* objective participant standard in *Halushka* is unlikely to be applied in the future.

Importantly, the court found that the failure to inform subjects about a relevant aspect of the study is actionable, even if this information does not relate to the ultimate cause of the damage, provided that the participant would have decided not to participate if it had been disclosed during the consent process. Therefore, it mattered not in *Halushka* that advancing the catheter through the participant's heart did not contribute to the damage he sustained, because the court had found that he may well have refused to participate if such an intervention had been disclosed by the researchers. A final point of significance arising from *Halushka* is the court's pronouncement that there "can be no exceptions to the ordinary requirements of disclosure in the case of research as there may well be in ordinary medical practice", including the therapeutic privilege exception.[243] This is because researchers do "not have to balance the probable effect of lack of treatment against the risk involved in the treatment itself".[244]

The second influential decision in Canada, *Weiss c. Solomon*,[245] was issued in 1989, some 24 years after *Halushka*. In *Weiss*, the Quebec Superior Court was called upon to decide whether a recruiting physician, a physician-researcher, the hospital in which the two worked and the hospital's REB bore legal liability in connection with the death of a research participant (Weiss) during an eye drops study. After undergoing cataract surgery, Weiss was approached by his surgeon about participating in a research study being conducted by a physician-researcher concerning the effectiveness of certain eye drops at reducing a particular negative side effect of cataract surgery. Weiss was told that he would receive no therapeutic benefit through his participation. Information about the eye drops (including its side effects) was also provided, and he was further informed that fluorescein angiography would be performed in order to verify the impact of the drops. Weiss signed a consent form containing the following statement respecting the fluorescein agent: "Some patients may develop a minor allergic reaction to this injection, but the majority of patients have no side effects."[246] Above his signature, the form read: "I have been told of the possible side effects and unfavourable reactions that can happen and what my alternatives are. I have had a chance to ask questions to the doctor and have received acceptable answers."[247] Soon after receiving the fluorescein injection, Weiss, who had a pre-existing asymptomatic heart condition (hypertrophic cardio-

---

[243] *Halushka v. University of Saskatchewan*, [1965] S.J. No. 208, 53 D.L.R. (2d) 436 at 444 (Sask. C.A.). Therapeutic privilege is discussed in Chapter 4, "Informed Consent".

[244] *Ibid.*

[245] [1989] J.Q. no 312, [1989] R.J.Q. 731 (Que. S.C.).

[246] This passage from the consent form is set out in Benjamin Freedman & Kathleen Cranley Glass, "*Weiss v. Solomon*: A Case Study in Institutional Responsibility for Clinical Research" (1990) 18 Law Med. Health Care 395 at 395-96.

[247] See Benjamin Freedman & Kathleen Cranley Glass, *ibid.*, at 396.

myopathy), suffered cardiac failure and died. Weiss' family commenced an action based, in part, on their allegation that Weiss had not been informed about the risk of heart failure from fluorescein injection.

The Quebec Superior Court found that Weiss' cardiac failure was an adverse reaction to the fluorescein injection, that his heart condition was a contraindication to fluorescein angiography, that he had not been informed of the slight risk of cardiac arrest from such injections, and that he likely would have declined to participate in the study had he been so informed. The hospital (through its REB) and the researcher were held liable in negligence for the failure to properly inform Weiss. On the road to making this determination, the court relied on *Halushka, Reibl v. Hughes*,[248] the *Civil Code of Québec*, the *Declaration of Helsinki* and other authorities. According to this case, "the duty to inform in [research involving no anticipated health benefits to participants] is the most exacting possible. All risks must be disclosed, even those which are rare or remote, especially if they entail serious consequences".[249] The extent of the disclosure obligation by researchers was not qualified by an objective participant construct, modified or unmodified, and thus this case would seemingly support the presence of differing disclosure standards for research and treatment. The court also found that the defendants could not seek shelter under the clause in the consent form inviting Weiss to ask clarifying questions. In the court's opinion, all of the risks had to be disclosed, with or without prompting by participants. Since *Weiss* has not received relevant judicial consideration in Quebec or elsewhere in Canada, it remains to be seen whether the case will be followed in the common law provinces or even by a higher court in Quebec.

It bears highlighting that *Halushka* and *Weiss* dealt with research presenting no anticipated health benefits for the participants. There are no reported cases in Canada that discuss the applicable disclosure standard for research with anticipated health benefits for participants where the research had undergone an ethics or peer review process.[250] It therefore remains unresolved whether the *Reibl* standard for medical therapy or a more rigorous one would be imposed by a court in such instances.

Some of the regulatory instruments already referenced in this chapter also establish disclosure standards. For example, the TCPS provides that researchers "shall provide to prospective participants, or authorized third parties, full disclosure of all information necessary for making an informed decision to participate

---

[248] [1980] S.C.J. No. 105, [1980] 2 S.C.R. 880 (S.C.C.).

[249] Ellen Picard & Gerald Robertson, *Legal Liability of Doctors and Hospitals in Canada*, 3d ed. (Scarborough, ON: Carswell, 1996) at 150.

[250] Benjamin Freedman & Kathleen Cranley Glass, "*Weiss v. Solomon*: A Case Study in Institutional Responsibility for Clinical Research" (1990) 18 Law Med. Health Care 395 note that there are Canadian cases dealing with "experimental" treatment (*i.e.*, treatment that deviates from the standard of care for the medical intervention in question), but they "do not deal with instances of research in the sense of a formal protocol that sets forth an objective and a set of procedures designed to reach that objective, as in the *Weiss* case" (at 397).

in a research project".[251] It also advises researchers that they are responsible for adhering to all applicable legal and regulatory requirements regarding consent.[252] The Clinical Trial Regulations indicate that consent must be "given in accordance with the applicable laws governing consent" and that participants must be informed of all "aspects of the clinical trial that are necessary for that person to make the decision to participate".[253] Similar to *Weiss*, none of these instruments expressly require the employment of a modified or unmodified objective participant standard when determining the specific research-related information falling within the scope of their disclosure requirements.

The *GCP Guidelines* list, in some detail, information that is to be disclosed to participants during the consent process. The TCPS sets out a similar list; however, it notes that the listed information is "*generally required* for informed consent"[254] and leaves it "up to the REB to consider whether all elements listed, or additional elements, are necessary to the consent process of the [particular] research project".[255] The information listed in the TCPS and the *GCP Guidelines* includes, among other things: the reasonably foreseeable risks,[256] the research purpose and procedures,[257] the benefits that may arise from participation,[258] a person's right not to participate in the research and their freedom to withdraw at any time without prejudice to pre-existing entitlements,[259] and how participants' confidentiality will be protected and any limits regarding such protections.[260] Although the TCPS also explicitly lists information respecting "the possibility of commercialization of research findings, and the presence of any real, potential or perceived conflicts of interest on the part of the researchers, their institutions or the research sponsors",[261] the Clinical Trial Regulations and *GCP Guidelines* are noticeably silent on these matters.

---

[251] TCPS, art. 3.2.

[252] TCPS, Chapter 3, Introduction.

[253] Clinical Trial Regulations, s. C.05.010(h), found in the Food and Drug Regulations, C.R.C., c. 870. Similarly, the *GCP Guidelines* state that participants are to be "informed of all aspects of the trial that are relevant to the subject's decision to participate" (see s. 1.28).

[254] TCPS, "Application" commentary under art. 3.2 [emphasis added].

[255] TCPS, "Application" commentary under art. 3.2. This commentary also states: "If a researcher does not include some of the listed disclosure requirements, they should explain to the REB why these requirements do not apply to that particular project."

[256] TCPS, "Application" commentary under art. 3.2; *GCP Guidelines*, s. 4.8.10(g).

[257] TCPS, "Application" commentary under art. 3.2.

[258] TCPS, "Application" commentary under art. 3.2; *GCP Guidelines*, s. 4.8.10(h).

[259] TCPS, "Application" commentary under art. 3.2; *GCP Guidelines*, s. 4.8.10(m).

[260] TCPS, "Application" commentary under art. 3.2 and art. 5.2, which states: "Researchers shall describe measures for meeting confidentiality obligations and explain any reasonably foreseeable disclosure requirements ... (b) during the consent process with prospective participants"; *GCP Guidelines*, s. 4.8.10(n) and (o).

[261] TCPS, "Application" commentary under art. 3.2. Also see TCPS, Chapter 7, Introduction, where it is noted: "Failure to disclose and manage conflicts may impede the informed and autonomous choices of individuals to participate in research. Prospective participants need to know about real, potential or perceived conflicts of interest in order to make an informed decision about whether or not to participate."

Also noteworthy is the TCPS requirement that researchers disclose to participants any "material incidental findings" that are made in the course of research.[262] These findings are defined in the TCPS as "unanticipated discoveries made in the course of research but that are outside the scope of the research ... that have been interpreted as having significant welfare implications for the participant, whether health-related, psychological or social".[263] For instance, an individual may participate as an apparently healthy control in a study that involves undergoing an MRI scan of the participant's brain. If the scan unexpectedly reveals a possible brain tumour, very serious legal and ethical issues arise concerning the communication of this discovery to the participant.[264]

The TCPS and *GCP Guidelines* offer additional direction on the subject of informed consent. The TCPS allows REBs to approve research projects that do not involve the researcher obtaining participants' consent if certain conditions are met;[265] however, two of these conditions are that "the research involves no more than minimal risk to the participants"[266] and that "the research does not involve a therapeutic intervention, or other clinical or diagnostic interventions".[267] In view of these conditions, participant consent must be sought in the vast majority of biomedical research projects. A notable consent exception exists for research carried out in the context of medical emergencies; again, some rather demanding conditions must be satisfied before researchers are permitted to proceed in the absence of participant consent.[268] Understandably, the *GCP Guidelines* do not allow for the possibility that its informed consent requirements can be waived given the significant risks associated with drug trials.

---

[262] TCPS, art. 3.4.

[263] TCPS, "Application" commentary under art. 3.4.

[264] Ethical and legal issues concerning incidental findings have attracted the attention of research ethics scholars. For example, see: Michael R. Hadskis & Matthias H. Schmidt, "Pediatric Neuro-imaging Research" in Judy Illes & Barbara J. Sahakian, eds., *Oxford Handbook of Neuroethics* (New York: Oxford University Press, forthcoming 2011); Jocelyn Downie *et al.*, "Paediatric MRI Research Ethics: The Priority Issues" (2007) 4 Bioethical Inquiry 85; J. Illes *et al.*, "Practical Approaches to Incidental Findings in Brain Imaging Research" (2008) 70 Neurology 384; S. Wolf *et al.*, "Managing Incidental Findings in Human Subjects Research: Analysis and Recommendations" (2008) 36 J.L. Med. & Ethics 219.

[265] These conditions are set out in art. 3.7, and include:
    (a)   the research involves no more than minimal risk to the participants;
    (b)   the lack of the participant's consent is unlikely to adversely affect the welfare of the participant;
    (c)   it is impossible or impracticable to carry out the research and to answer the research question properly, given the research design, if the prior consent of the participant is required;
    (d)   whenever possible and appropriate, after participation, or at a later time during the study, participants will be debriefed and provided with additional pertinent information in accordance with Articles 3.2 and 3.4, at which point they will have the opportunity to refuse consent in accordance with Article 3.1; and
    (e)   the research does not involve a therapeutic intervention, or other clinical or diagnostic interventions.

[266] TCPS, art. 3.7(a).

[267] TCPS, art. 3.7(e).

[268] See TCPS, art. 3.8.

The TCPS requires consent to be evidenced in writing.[269] Typically, participants sign a consent form, but in some instances they may orally consent, in which case this form of consent must be documented by the researcher in some fashion.[270] Regarding drug trials, the *GCP Guidelines* state that an informed consent form must be signed by participants or their substitute decision-makers[271] and special procedures are outlined for persons who are unable to read the consent form.[272]

Before leaving the topic of informed consent, a couple of additional matters should be emphasized. Researchers' obligations extend beyond merely disclosing information to participants and/or their substitute decision-makers; they must also ensure the person giving consent understands and appreciates the information provided. Picard and Robertson take the position that the researcher's duty in this regard should be at least as demanding as that for therapeutic interventions.[273] Accordingly, "the researcher must take reasonable steps to ensure that the subject actually understands the information presented, and must be sensitive to any signs or circumstances suggesting a lack of understanding".[274] Reports that between 20 and 40 per cent of persons possessing decisional-capacity do not understand one or more important aspects of research participation (*e.g.*, the attendant risks and the right to withdraw)[275] suggest that significant numbers of researchers are not taking such steps.

The informed consent process must not be rushed or treated as a perfunctory routine. Potential participants must be given the opportunity to ask questions and be provided with ample time[276] to contemplate whether they want to participate.[277] Furthermore, the language used during the process, both oral and written, should be straightforward, devoid of technical jargon[278] and fixed at an appropriate comprehension level for the particular participant. This is something

---

[269] TCPS, art. 3.12.

[270] TCPS, "Application" commentary under art. 3.12.

[271] *GCP Guidelines*, s. 4.8.8. Similarly, s. C.05.010(h) of the Clinical Trial Regulations, found under the Food and Drug Regulations, C.R.C., c. 870, provides that a written informed consent must be obtained.

[272] *GCP Guidelines*, s. 4.8.9.

[273] Ellen Picard & Gerald Robertson, *Legal Liability of Doctors and Hospitals in Canada*, 4th ed. (Toronto: Thomson Carswell, 2007) at 177.

[274] *Ibid.*

[275] David Wendler, "Can We Ensure That All Research Subjects Give Valid Consent?" (2004) 164 Archives of Internal Medicine 2201 at 2202.

[276] See David N. Weisstub & Simon N. Verdun-Jones, "Biomedical Experimentation Involving Elderly Subjects: The Need to Balance Limited, Benevolent Protection with Recognition of a Long History of Autonomous Decision-Making (Part I)" (1998) 18:3 Health L. Can. 95 at 100, where the authors note that the elderly need more time to process complex information and, therefore, research involving this population should use "information sessions tailored to suit the time requirements of the prospective participant" so as to maximize "the ability of individuals to engage meaningfully in the decision to participate in research".

[277] TCPS, "Application" commentary under art. 3.2; *GCP Guidelines*, s. 4.8.7.

[278] *GCP Guidelines*, s. 4.8.6.

that many researchers fail to achieve.[279] In some instances, consideration should be given to supplementing the consent process with such things as plain language pamphlets and DVDs demonstrating study procedures.[280] The time devoted to this process can depend on many variables, such as the emotional state of the potential participant, the setting in which the information is provided (*e.g.*, unsettling clinical environments) and the complexity of the information to be imparted.[281]

(b)   Consent to Participate Must Be Given Voluntarily

The TCPS and the *GCP Guidelines* highlight the need for informed consent to be given voluntarily.[282] The "voluntariness" and "informed" elements of consent should not be conflated. That is, individuals can be informed of all relevant information about a study and fully understand and appreciate this information, yet their agreement to participate may be ethically and legally invalid because it was not voluntarily given. According to the TCPS, consent cannot be considered voluntary if it was coerced, unduly influenced or given as a result of an excessive incentive.[283] *The Belmont Report* defines coercion as "an overt threat of harm [that] is intentionally presented by one person to another in order to obtain compliance".[284] Similarly, the TCPS states that coercion involves "a threat of harm or punishment for failure to participate". Although the *GCP Guidelines* note that a participant's consent should not be coerced,[285] it does not define this term.

Much attention has been dedicated to undue influence[286] and the various forms it can take. The TCPS speaks of undue influence in terms of the impact that power relationships can have on prospective participants. This concern arises where researchers exercise or appear to exercise control over the prospec-

---

[279] See Alan R. Tait, Terri Voepel-Lewis, Shobha Malviya & Sandra J. Philipson, "Improving the Readability and Processability of a Pediatric Informed Consent Document" (2005) 159 Archives of Pediatrics & Adolescent Medicine 347 at 347; J. Flory & E. Emanuel, "Interventions to Improve Research Participants' Understanding in Informed Consent for Research: A Systemic Review" (2004) 292 JAMA 1593 at 1599; James R.P. Ogloff & Randy K. Otto, "Are Research Participants Truly Informed? Readability of Informed Consent Forms Used in Research" (1991) 1:4 Ethics & Behavior 239 at 241-42.

[280] See Michael R. Hadskis & Matthias H. Schmidt, "Pediatric Neuroimaging Research" in Judy Illes & Barbara J. Sahakian, eds., *Oxford Handbook of Neuroethics* (New York: Oxford University Press, forthcoming 2011).

[281] TCPS, "Application" commentary under art. 3.2.

[282] TCPS, art. 3.1; *GCP Guidelines*, s. 2.9.

[283] TCPS, "Application" commentary under art. 3.1.

[284] National Commission for the Protection of Human Subjects of Biomedical and Behavioral Research, *The Belmont Report: Ethical Principles and Guidelines for the Protection of Human Subjects of Research* (1979), online at: <http://ohsr.od.nih.gov/guidelines/belmont.html>.

[285] *GCP Guidelines*, s. 4.8.3.

[286] For a discussion about what constitutes undue inducement (influence) and the distinction between undue inducement and coercion, see Ezekiel J. Emanuel, "Ending Concerns About Undue Inducement" (2004) 32 J.L. Med. & Ethics 100-105.

tive participants, leading the participants to feel compelled to abide by the wishes of the researchers.[287] For instance, elderly patients in long-term care facilities can be extremely dependent on caregivers for fulfillment of their basic physical, social and emotional needs, which tends to promote passivity and unquestioned compliance with instructions and can threaten "the psychological ability of older persons to contradict someone, such as a physician, upon whom they are dependent".[288] Prisoners[289] and civilly committed persons[290] are also markedly dependent on persons in authority within the custodial institution and, therefore, are ripe for being unduly influenced to participate in research. Moreover, voluntary choice can be influenced by other power imbalances that can reside in relationships between employers and employees, and instructors and students.[291] Concerns about voluntariness are extremely acute when the consent of desperately ill patients is being sought in relation to studies (usually drug trials) that hold the last hope of rescue.[292]

Incentives, monetary or otherwise, are used "to encourage participation in a research project"[293] and can undermine the voluntariness of participants' consent. The use of incentives is a common recruitment strategy on the part of researchers, and REBs frequently must wrestle with difficult issues associated with them. Remarkably, the *GCP Guidelines* are silent on the issue of monetary payments and the TCPS, in stating that it "neither recommends nor discourages the use of incentives",[294] goes out of its way to make clear that the Tri-Agencies wish to remain largely non-committal on this important matter. However, the TCPS does indicate that, where incentives are used, "they should not be so large or attractive as to encourage reckless disregard of risks".[295] It also places the onus on researchers to justify their proposed incentive plans to the REB which, before making its decision on whether to approve such plans, is encouraged to consider prospective participants' age, capacity, and economic circumstances, as well as "the customs and practices of the community, and the magnitude and probability of harms".[296] The TCPS further states that participants' guardians

---

[287] TCPS, "Application" commentary under arts. 3.1, 4.7 and 7.4.

[288] Kathleen Cranley Glass, "Informed Decision-Making and Vulnerable Persons: Meeting the Needs of the Competent Elderly Patient or Research Subject" (1993) 18 Queen's L.J. 191 at 208 and 231.

[289] Julio Arboleda-Florez, "The Ethics of Biomedical Research on Prisoners" (2005) 18 Current Opinion in Psychiatry 514.

[290] Julio Arboleda-Florez & David N. Weisstub, "Ethical Research with the Mentally Disordered" (1997) 42 Can. J. Psychiatry 485 at 486-87.

[291] TCPS, commentary under art. 3.1.

[292] For a discussion of such research, see Charles L. Bosk, "Obtaining Voluntary Consent for Research in Desperately Ill Patients" (2002) 40:9 Medical Care V64 and Sarah Hewlett, "Consent to Clinical Research — Adequately Voluntary or Substantially Influenced?" (1996) 22 J. Med. Ethics 232 at 234.

[293] TCPS, "Application" commentary under art. 3.1.

[294] TCPS, "Application" commentary under art. 3.1.

[295] TCPS, "Application" commentary under art. 3.1.

[296] TCPS, "Application" commentary under arts. 3.1 and 4.7.

and authorized third parties "should not receive incentives" for arranging the participants' involvement in the study.[297]

Two additional matters should be noted about the TCPS' position on incentives. First, the much higher threshold of unacceptability (*i.e.*, encouraging reckless disregard of risks) in the current version of the TCPS stands in contrast to the considerably lower threshold of unacceptability in the previous edition of this document (*i.e.*, encouraging participants "to undertake actions that they would not ordinarily accept"[298]). The rationale for the Tri-Agencies' attitude change on incentives is not clear. Second, REBs are left to struggle with serious unanswered questions: If it is permissible to compensate participants for such things as inconvenience[299] and assumption of risk, then how can the compensation for each be properly calibrated so as to not encourage reckless disregard of risks (the present higher threshold of unacceptability) or to undertake actions they would otherwise avoid (the former and arguably more defensible lower threshold of unacceptability)? In order to take into account relative economic circumstances, should wealthier people receive higher payments than people of lesser financial means for their participation in the same study?[300] As a practical matter, how are REB members going to apprise themselves of the financial wherewithal of all individuals within economically diverse pools of potential participants? Some authors have argued that these perplexing issues could be resolved if research participation by healthy individuals were characterized as a kind of labour relation, thereby warranting labour-type legislation.[301]

(c)   *Consent to Participate Must Be Given by Persons Possessing Decisional Capacity*

Serious ethical issues arise when persons with diminished decisional capacity are involved in research. The incomplete cognitive development that exists during various phases of childhood, the impact of mind-altering substances, or the presence of a disorder that results in temporary or permanent cognitive impairment, may account for a research participant's diminished capacity. Enormous care must be exercised in the proper conduct of capacity determinations, since erroneous findings of incompetence[302] can seriously infringe a participant's right to self-determination. This may occur if researchers assume persons with mental

---

[297] TCPS, "Application" commentary under art. 3.1.

[298] TCPS 1st edition (1998), commentary under art. 2.4.

[299] This question has been answered for the Province of Quebec. Under art. 25 of the *Civil Code of Québec*, S.Q. 1991, c. 64, participants can be paid "an indemnity as compensation for the loss and inconvenience suffered" through their participation in research. No other "financial reward" can be given.

[300] Trudo Lemmens & Carl Elliott, "Justice for the Professional Guinea Pig" (2001) 1:2 American Journal of Bioethics 51 at 52.

[301] *Ibid.*

[302] In this chapter, the terms "incompetence" and "incapacity" are used interchangeably and should be taken to have the same meaning.

disabilities lack capacity.[303] At the same time, a mistaken finding of capacity may foreclose the engagement of safeguards for the protection of persons who are vulnerable by reason of their diminished capacity.

The capacity test for participation in research set out in the TCPS applies to all individuals regardless of their age. This test is similar to many provincial/territorial statutory tests for determining whether a patient is competent to consent to medical treatment,[304] though the TCPS[305] rightly cautions that the law on competence can vary between jurisdictions. According to the TCPS, individuals must possess two distinct competencies: the ability to *understand* the relevant information about the specific study and the ability to *appreciate* the potential consequences of making a decision to participate or not participate in the study.[306] The first competency involves the cognitive ability of participants to process and retain information about matters relevant to participation such as the potential harms and benefits that might be occasioned if they are enrolled in the study. That is, they must understand the relevant facts concerning the study.[307] The second calls for the ability to evaluate the information about the research project that they have acquired. This demands the ability to apply the relevant information to a person's individual circumstances and to weigh the potential consequences of participating or not participating in the study.[308]

Competence should not be viewed as being global or static.[309] An individual may have the capacity to consent to participate in one study (*e.g.*, the completion of a questionnaire that solicits non-sensitive information) but not another (*e.g.*, a clinical trial involving a new chemotherapy agent). Moreover, a particular person's ability to consent to participate in a study may fluctuate, even over short time intervals.[310]

---

[303] Julio Arboleda-Florez & David N. Weisstub, "Ethical Research with the Mentally Disordered" (1997) 42 Can. J. Psychiatry 485 at 488; Paddi O'Hara & Ineke Neutel, "A Shadow of Doubt: Ethical Issues in the Use of Proxy Consent in Research. Part I: When are Proxies Needed and How Do They Make Their Decisions?" (2004) 9:1 Canadian Bioethics Society Newsletter 7 at 7.

[304] See Chapter 4, "Informed Consent" and Chapter 11, "Death, Dying and Decision-Making about End of Life Care".

[305] TCPS, Chapter 3, Section C.

[306] TCPS, Chapter 3, Section C. The Supreme Court of Canada in *Starson v. Swayze*, [2003] S.C.J. No. 33, [2003] 1 S.C.R. 722 (S.C.C.) interpreted a similar capacity test set out in Ontario's *Health Care Consent Act, 1996*, S.O. 1996, c. 2, Sched. A.

[307] This statement is made on the basis of a broad application of the legal analysis from *Starson v. Swayze, ibid.*, to the research context.

[308] This statement is also made on the basis of a broad application of the legal analysis from *Starson v. Swayze, ibid.*, to the research context.

[309] TCPS, Chapter 3, Section C. See also Julio Arboleda-Florez & David N. Weisstub, "Ethical Research with the Mentally Disordered" (1997) 42 Can. J. Psychiatry 485 at 486.

[310] See Paddi O'Hara & Ineke Neutel, "A Shadow of Doubt: Ethical Issues in the Use of Proxy Consent in Research. Part I: When are Proxies Needed and How Do They Make Their Decisions?" (2004) 9:1 Canadian Bioethics Society Newsletter 7. The authors comment that some persons with Alzheimer's Disease tend to be less able to make decisions in the evening (a phenomenon known as "sundown").

The TCPS expressly states that researchers should be aware of all relevant legal and regulatory capacity requirements.[311] Chapter 4, "Informed Consent", Chapter 8, "Mental Health Law in Canada" and Chapter 9, "Death, Dying and Decision-Making about End of Life Care" discuss the legal presumption of capacity that exists for adults in Canada under statutory instruments and the common law. The implications of finding an adult competent or incompetent are also discussed. Suffice it to say here that competent adults can legally consent to participate in research, irrespective of whether it holds any potential benefits for them.

However, the situation is not as clear for minors, at least as far as the common law is concerned. As discussed in Chapter 9, the majority of the Supreme Court of Canada in *C. (A.) v. Manitoba (Director of Child and Family Services)*[312] found that, even if a minor has the intellectual capacity to understand the information relevant to making a medical treatment decision and to appreciate the potential consequences of such a decision, this does not necessarily mean the minor has decisional capacity. If the minor is not sufficiently mature and others (*e.g.*, physicians, judges, child welfare authorities) do not consider the minor's decision to be in his or her best interests, then the minor's decision does not have to be respected. While it is unclear whether the common law principles applicable to minors' consent to treatment also apply to their participation in biomedical research because no court (including the Supreme Court of Canada in *C. (A.)*) has been asked to rule on this matter,[313] the courts may well hold that it does.[314] If so, in some circumstances, researchers may not be able to legally rely on minors' consent to study participation, even if the researchers are satisfied that the minors are able to understand the information that is relevant to making a decision about participating in the study and are able to appreciate the potential consequences of making a decision to participate or not participate in the study.

Significant ethical and legal issues arise when considering whether persons lacking capacity can be enrolled in a specific study. Including only competent participants in research can unfairly exclude certain groups, such as children and persons with mental disabilities, from the benefits of research. Thus, automatic exclusion of prospective research subjects based on mental disability is inconsistent with the TCPS[315] or conceptions of distributive justice, inclusiveness and equality. However, there are ethical and legal restrictions on the inclusion of

---

[311] TCPS, Chapter 3, Section C.

[312] [2009] S.C.J. No. 30, 2009 SCC 30 (S.C.C.).

[313] F. Baylis, J. Downie & N. Kenny, "Children and Decision-making in Health Research" (2000) 8:2 Health L. Rev. 3 at 4.

[314] Erin L. Nelson, "Legal and Ethical Issues in ART 'Outcomes' Research" (2005) 13 Health L.J. 165 at 182; and Claire Bernard & Bartha Maria Knoppers, "Legal Aspects of Research Involving Children in Canada" in Bartha Maria Knoppers, ed., *Canadian Child Health Law* (Toronto: Thompson Educational Publishing, 1992) 259 at 299.

[315] TCPS, Chapter 3, Section C and Chapter 4.

persons lacking capacity in research. The balance of this section is devoted to outlining these limitations.

The TCPS and the *GCP Guidelines* state that persons lacking capacity cannot be enrolled in research unless certain conditions are met.[316] Both instruments require that the research question can be addressed only with participants within the identified group.[317] For example, this may be met where it cannot be presumed that a particular treatment will be safe and efficacious for young children purely on the basis of research outcomes regarding adult populations. History has shown that dangerous consequences can result from erroneous assumptions respecting the generalizability of adult data.[318] However, if competent persons would make equally fitting participants for a given study, incompetent persons cannot be enrolled.

The TCPS and the *GCP Guidelines* also require that consent be sought and maintained from authorized third parties.[319] Where incompetent minors are involved, the legally authorized third parties are the minors' parents or guardians[320] but, as addressed below, their powers are substantially constrained. The situation is less clear with incompetent adults, as it is doubtful that the person's next-of-kin can lawfully consent to medical interventions (whether the intervention is undertaken for therapeutic or research purposes) unless this is authorized by a court, a legislative instrument or an advance directive.[321] Alarmingly, evidence suggests that researchers and REB members lack knowledge of who is legally authorized to consent to research on behalf of an incompetent adult participant.[322]

---

[316] In addition to the conditions mentioned below, the TCPS sets out some other conditions: the researcher involves participants who lack the capacity to consent on their own behalf to the greatest extent possible in the decision-making process (art. 3.9(a)); the authorized third party is not the researcher or any other member of the research team (art. 3.9(c)); and when authorization for participation was granted by an authorized third party, and a participant acquires or regains capacity during the course of the research, the researcher shall promptly seek the participant's consent as a condition of continuing participation (art. 3.9(e)).

[317] TCPS, art. 4.6(a); *GCP Guidelines*, s. 4.8.14(a). See also Christy Simpson, "Children and Research Participation: Who Makes What Decisions" (2003) 11:2 Health L. Rev. 20 at 22; Paddi O'Hara & Ineke Neutel, "A Shadow of Doubt: Ethical Issues in the Use of Proxy Consent in Research. Part I: When are Proxies Needed and How Do They Make Their Decisions?" (2004) 9:1 Canadian Bioethics Society Newsletter 7 at 8.

[318] Some examples are provided in Paul B. Miller & Nuala P. Kenny, "Walking the Moral Tightrope: Respecting and Protecting Children in Health-Related Research" (2002) 11 Cambridge Quarterly of Healthcare Ethics 217 at 218.

[319] TCPS, art. 3.9(b) (this article also indicates that the third parties' consent must be based on the best interests of the participants); *GCP Guidelines*, s. 4.8.14.

[320] Erin L. Nelson, "Legal and Ethical Issues in ART 'Outcomes' Research" (2005) 13 Health L.J. 165 at 176.

[321] Lorne E. Rozovsky, *The Canadian Law of Consent to Treatment*, 3d ed. (Markham, ON: LexisNexis Canada, 2003) at 73. Several examples of statutes relevant to the issue of whether a proxy under an advance directive can authorize research participation are discussed below.

[322] G. Bravo *et al.*, "Research with Decisionally Incapacitated Older Adults: Practices of Canadian Research Ethics Boards" (2010) 32:6 IRB: Ethics & Human Research 1; G. Bravo, M. Paquet & M -F. Dubois, "Knowledge of the Legislation Governing Proxy Consent to Treatment and Re-

Additionally, under the TCPS and the *GCP Guidelines*, research cannot expose persons who are incompetent to more than minimal risks without the potential for direct benefits for them.[323] The TCPS also states that, where "the research entails only minimal risk, it should at least have the prospect of providing benefits to participants or to a group that is the focus of the research and to which the participants belong";[324] if the latter is the case, the participants can also only be exposed to "minimal burden".[325] The *GCP Guidelines* require that, for non-therapeutic trials, "unless an exception is justified, [these trials] should be conducted in patients having a disease or condition for which the investigational product is intended".[326]

Both the TCPS and the *GCP Guidelines* state that their approval of non-beneficial minimal risk research involving individuals who lack capacity is subject to applicable legal requirements.[327] This is an extremely important caveat because such research may run afoul of the common law as well as relevant legislative prohibitions that exist in some provinces/territories. Regarding the common law, the Supreme Court of Canada's decision in *E. (Mrs.) v. Eve*[328] has been interpreted by some to be relevant to this issue. In *Eve*, the Supreme Court of Canada dealt with an application that had been brought by "Mrs. E." for court approval (under its *parens patriae* jurisdiction) to give her consent to sterilize "Eve", her incompetent adult daughter, because of a concern that if Eve became pregnant Mrs. E. would have to assume sole responsibility for the care of her daughter's child. The Court denied Mrs. E.'s application on the basis that a court's *parens patriae* jurisdiction can only be exercised for the protection and benefit of the person with the disability. In the Court's view, the sterilization was being sought for the benefit of Mrs. E., not Eve.

---

search" (2003) 29 J. Med. Ethics 44-50; G. Bravo, M.-F. Dubois & M. Paquet, "The Conduct of Canadian Researchers and Institutional Review Boards Regarding Substituted Consent for Research" (2004) 26:1 IRB: Ethics & Human Research 1; G. Bravo *et al.*, "Quebec Physicians' Knowledge and Opinions Regarding Substitute Consent for Decisionally Incapacitated Older Adults" (2004) 26 IRB: Ethics & Human Research 12; and G. Bravo *et al.*, "Substitute Consent for Research Involving the Elderly: A Comparison Between Quebec and France" (2008) 23 Journal of Cross-Cultural Gerontology 239.

[323] TCPS, art. 4.6(b). More precisely, the *GCP Guidelines*, s. 4.8.14(b) and (c) state that the foreseeable risks to the participants must be low and the negative impact on the participant's well-being must be minimized and low.

[324] TCPS, art. 4.6(c).

[325] TCPS, art. 3.9(d).

[326] Section 4.8.14. This section also states that participants "in these trials should be particularly closely monitored and should be withdrawn if they appear to be unduly distressed".

[327] TCPS, art. 4.6 and *GCP Guidelines*, s. 4.8.14.

[328] [1986] S.C.J. No. 60, [1986] 2 S.C.R. 388 (S.C.C.).

While *Eve* did not involve biomedical research, Dickens[329] and others[330] have argued that, in the absence of constitutionally valid legislative authority, its principles can reasonably be extended to impede substitute decision-makers from being able to lawfully consent to the inclusion of incompetent persons in medical research that poses any risks if there is no immediate medical benefit to the incompetent individuals. It has been contended that this would mean that parents cannot even consent to interventions such as heel or finger-prick blood testing of their children that is being conducted for research purposes alone.[331] It is immaterial that the research might benefit other children.[332] Taking a less restrictive slant on *Eve*, other commentators have argued that the decision can be read as indicating that parents can authorize research with no direct medical benefit, provided there is potential for other benefits, such as psychological, social and religious benefit.[333] It has been speculated that the uncertainty around how future courts may interpret *Eve* "has probably had a chilling effect on research involving children in Canada".[334] If the more restrictive interpretation is ultimately judicially embraced, it is feared that important research will not involve incompetent persons and the groups to which they belong will be deprived the benefits of medical advancements, thus becoming "therapeutic orphans".[335]

As previously alluded to, a province/territory can attempt[336] to legislatively authorize substitute consent for the research participation of persons lacking

---

[329] Bernard M. Dickens, "The Legal Challenge of Health Research Involving Children" (1998) 6 Health L.J. 131-48.

[330] Erin L. Nelson, "Legal and Ethical Issues in ART 'Outcomes' Research" (2005) 13 Health L.J. 165 at 177; Julio Arboleda-Florez & David N. Weisstub, "Ethical Research with the Mentally Disordered" (1997) 42 Can. J. Psychiatry 485 at 488; Robert S. Williams, "Pediatric Research and the Parens Patriae Jurisdiction in Canada and England" (1999) 18 Medicine & Law 525-46; Sonja Grover, "On the Limits of Parental Proxy Consent: Children's Right to Non-Participation in Non-Therapeutic Research" (2003) 1 Journal of Academic Ethics 349 at 371.

[331] Bernard M. Dickens, "The Legal Challenge of Health Research Involving Children" (1998) 6 Health L.J. 131 at 135.

[332] *Ibid.*, at 133-34.

[333] This alternative interpretation of *Eve* is canvassed in Françoise Baylis, Jocelyn Downie & Nuala Kenny, "Children and Decision-making in Health Research" (2000) 8:2 Health L. Rev. 3 at 7-8 and Françoise Baylis & Jocelyn Downie, "An Ethical and Criminal Law Framework for Research Involving Children in Canada" (1993) 1 Health L.J. 39.

[334] *Ibid.*, at 8.

[335] Françoise Baylis & Jocelyn Downie, "An Ethical and Criminal Law Framework for Research Involving Children in Canada" (1993) 1 Health L.J. 39. See also David N. Weisstub & Simon N. Verdun-Jones, "Biomedical Experimentation Involving Elderly Subjects: The Need to Balance Limited, Benevolent Protection with Recognition of a Long History of Autonomous Decision-Making (Part I)" (1998) 18:3 Health L. Can. 95 at 99.

[336] This can be attempted, but the legislative instrument could be challenged under the *Canadian Charter of Rights and Freedoms*, Part I of the *Constitution Act, 1982*, being Schedule B to the *Canada Act 1982* (U.K.), 1982, c. 11. See Bernard M. Dickens, "The Legal Challenge of Health Research Involving Children" (1998) 6 Health L.J. 131 at 145-46. For a thorough analysis of the provincial/territorial and federal governments' legislative competence regarding research involving humans, see Jennifer Llewellyn, Jocelyn Downie & Robert Holmes, "Protecting Human Research Subjects: A Jurisdictional Analysis" (2003) Health L.J. 207.

capacity. Quebec has done so under article 21 of its *Civil Code of Québec.*[337] Pursuant to that provision, substitute consent can be given for the participation of incompetent minors and adults in research that exposes them to risk of harm without the potential to benefit them, but there are important limitations. Consent cannot be given if the incompetent person will be exposed to "serious risk" to his or her health or where he or she understands the nature and consequences of the experiment and objects to participation. As well, if the incompetent person is the only subject of the research, it must have "the potential to produce benefit to the person's health or only if, in the case of [research] on a group, it has the potential to produce results capable of conferring benefit to other persons in the same category or having the same disease or handicap". However, such research must be approved and monitored by an REB formed or designated by the Minister of Health and Social Services.[338]

It has been suggested that advance directives are a viable means of avoiding the legal and ethical quagmire concerning the involvement of incompetent persons in research.[339] Specifically, it has been put forward that presently competent individuals whose cognitive capacity is decreasing or fluctuating could issue a directive specifying their wishes to consent to or refuse future participation in non-therapeutic research.[340] Several Canadian jurisdictions have advance health care directives legislation that addresses the power of a substitute decision-maker to consent to the participation of the maker of the directive (the "director") in medical research. For example, such instruments in Newfoundland and Labrador[341] and Manitoba[342] prohibit a proxy appointed under an advance directive from consenting to "medical treatment for the primary purpose of research" unless express authorization for this is given in the directive. Prince Edward Island[343] allows substitute consent for medical research in the absence of express authorization in the directive if the research is likely to benefit the director. In Alberta, without clear instructions in the directive, substitute consent is barred if the participation in the research "offers little or no potential benefit to the maker" of the directive.[344] Other provinces also have relevant legislation.[345]

---

[337] S.Q. 1991, c. 64.

[338] A detailed explanation of art. 21 of the *Civil Code of Québec* is set out in Simon Verdun-Jones & David N. Weisstub, "Consent to Human Experimentation in Québec: The Application of the Civil Law Principles of Personal Inviolability to Protect Special Populations" (1995) 18 Int'l J. L. & Psychiatry 163 at 176-79.

[339] George F. Tomossy & David N. Weisstub, "The Reform of Adult Guardianship Laws: The Case of Non-Therapeutic Experimentation" (1997) 20:1 Int'l J. L. & Psychiatry 113.

[340] This would require detailed instructions regarding critical details, such as the type of research that the makers of these directives wished to participate in, as well as the research interventions and levels of risk of harm that would be acceptable to them. See George F. Tomossy & David N. Weisstub, "The Reform of Adult Guardianship Laws: The Case of Non-Therapeutic Experimentation" (1997) 20 Int'l J. L. & Psychiatry 113 at 131.

[341] *Advance Health Care Directives Act*, S.N.L. 1995, c. A-4.1, s. 5(3).

[342] *Health Care Directive Act*, C.C.S.M. c. H27, s. 14(a).

[343] *Consent to Treatment and Health Care Directives Act*, R.S.P.E.I. 1998, c. C-17.2, s. 12.

[344] *Personal Directive Act*, R.S.A. 2000, c. P-6, s. 15(d).

The TCPS has an article that deals with the subject of "research directives", which may be of relevance in the context of legislative frameworks regarding advance directives. This article reads: "Where individuals have signed a research directive indicating their preferences about future participation in research in the event that they lose capacity or upon death, researchers and authorized third parties should be guided by these directives during the consent process."[346] In the face of uncertainty regarding the practical and legal implications of research directives, the TCPS cautions: "The efficacy of research directives is unknown and their legal status has not been recognized or tested."[347]

It does not necessarily follow from a determination of incapacity that the person cannot take part in the decision to participate in research. Article 3.10 of the TCPS requires researchers to ascertain the wishes of the individual who lacks legal capacity if that person "has some ability to understand the significance of the research". If such a person "dissents", his or her participation is precluded.[348] This position on dissent has been criticized. When the prospective participant is a child, allowing his or her "dissent to function as the moral equivalent of a refusal by a person with decision making capacity, without first having determined that the child has decisional capacity, is to seriously undermine parental responsibility for promoting children's interests".[349] The only province that has provided direct guidance on the legal implications of assent/dissent in research is Quebec. Article 21 of the *Civil Code of Québec* states that a minor or adult who is incapable of giving consent cannot be enrolled in research if he or she "objects" to participation.

2.   Privacy and Confidentiality

Recall that the general regulatory framework for human research has widely been characterized as a complex, confusing patchwork of legal and extra-legal instruments. This description is also apt for those aspects of the framework that establish privacy and confidentiality norms regarding the collection, use and disclosure of personal information for health research. This particular "unwieldy hodgepodge of laws and regulations"[350] reflects history's piecemeal treatment of

---

[345] For British Columbia, see the *Health Care (Consent) and Care Facility (Admission) Act*, R.S.B.C. 1996, c. 181, s. 18(1) and the *Representation Agreement Act*, R.S.B.C. 1996, c. 405, s. 9. For the Northwest Territories (including Nunavut), see the Health Care Regulations, N.W.T. Reg. 050-97, s. 1 under the *Guardianship and Trusteeship Act*, S.N.W.T. 1994, c. 29. For New Brunswick, see the *Nursing Homes Act*, S.N.B. 1982, c. N-11, s. 13.

[346] TCPS, art. 3.11.

[347] TCPS, preamble to art. 3.11.

[348] TCPS, art. 3.10.

[349] Françoise Baylis, Jocelyn Downie & Nuala Kenny, "Children and Decision-making in Health Research" (2000) 8:2 Health L. Rev. 3 at 4. See also David C. Flagel, "Children as Research Subjects: New Guidelines for Canadian REBs" (2000) 22:5 I.R.B. 1 at 3.

[350] Patricia Kosseim, "The Landscape of Rules Governing Access to Personal Information for Health Research: A View from Afar" (2003) Health L.J. (Special Edition) 113 at 115.

privacy and confidentiality issues in the health sector generally.[351] Chapter 6, "Health Information: Confidentiality and Access", addresses the panoply of instruments of which researchers and REBs must take heed when discharging their legal and ethical responsibilities and will not be further explained in any detail here. As demonstrated in that chapter, the applicability of such instruments to the proposed research may depend on many factors, some of which include: the type of personal information to be collected, used or disclosed in the research; the nature of the research institution involved in the research (*e.g.*, public or private); the presence of research funding from certain granting agencies (*e.g.*, CIHR); whether the research constitutes a commercial activity; and the geographic location where the research is being carried out.

The *GCP Guidelines*[352] include respect for privacy and confidentiality in its guiding principles and the TCPS acknowledges that "privacy and the control of information about the person" form part of the core principle "Concern for Welfare".[353] The former instrument directs that applicable regulatory requirements regarding privacy and confidentiality are to be met, but provides scant guidance on how these interests are to be protected. In contrast, the TCPS has a chapter on privacy and confidentiality[354] that, in its opening article, establishes the following general duty of confidentiality: "Researchers shall safeguard information entrusted to them and not misuse or wrongfully disclose it. Institutions shall support their researchers in maintaining promises of confidentiality."[355] Subsequent articles elaborate on this duty. Researchers must advise the REB and inform participants during the consent process about how they will comply with confidentiality obligations and must explain to the REB and participants any reasonably foreseeable disclosure requirements.[356] Examples of disclosure requirements that may be reasonably foreseeable in the context of some biomedical research projects include mandatory reporting of suspected child abuse to child welfare agencies pursuant to provincial/territorial child welfare legislation,[357] and reporting of persons having certain communicable diseases to public health officials under public health legislation.[358] Care must also be taken to ensure that participants are advised of the possibility of disclosure of their personal information to other individuals or groups (*e.g.*, research sponsors, such as pharmaceutical companies and CIHR; REBs; and regulatory bodies).[359]

---

[351] *Ibid.*

[352] *GCP Guidelines*, s. 2.11.

[353] See TCPS, Chapter 1, Section B.

[354] TCPS, Chapter 5.

[355] TCPS, art. 5.1.

[356] TCPS, art. 5.2.

[357] For example, see: *Children and Family Services Act*, S.N.S. 1990, c. 5, ss. 23 and 24; *Child and Family Services Act*, R.S.O. 1990, c. C11, s. 72; and *Child, Family and Community Service Act*, R.S.B.C. 1996, c. 46, s. 14.

[358] For example, see: *Public Health Act*, C.C.S.M. c. P210, s. 41; *Health Protection and Promotion Act*, R.S.O. 1990, c. H.7, s. 25; and *Health Protection Act*, S.N.S. 2004, c. 4, s. 31.

[359] TCPS, "Application" commentary under art. 5.2.

The TCPS obligates researchers to provide REBs with details concerning "their proposed measures for safeguarding information, for the full life cycle of information: its collection, use, dissemination, retention and/or disposal".[360] REBs are provided with factors for assessing the adequacy of these proposed measures.[361] The safeguarding responsibilities on institutions that hold research data are also prescribed in the TCPS.[362]

The secondary use of "identifiable information"[363] for research purposes presents serious privacy issues in the biomedical research realm. The TCPS defines the term "secondary use" as "the use in research of information originally collected for a purpose other than the current research purpose".[364] Therefore, researchers setting out to conduct research using health care records compiled in the clinical context or biological specimens collected for therapeutic purposes are engaging in secondary use activities. The same is true where researchers collect information or biological specimens for one research project and subsequently want to use the same information or specimens in another research project. The TCPS advises that "[p]rivacy concerns and questions about the need to seek consent arise ... when information provided for secondary use in research can be linked to individuals, and when the possibility exists that individuals can be identified in published reports, or through data linkage".[365] Therefore, it imposes a number of mandatory conditions on the secondary use of identifiable information in instances where researchers have not obtained consent from participants for such use of their information. If these conditions are met, an REB may approve the research without requiring consent from the persons to whom the information relates.[366] Among these conditions is the requirement that the

---

[360] TCPS, art. 5.3.

[361] TCPS, "Application" commentary under art. 5.3.

[362] TCPS, art. 5.4 and associated "Application" commentary.

[363] Regarding the term "identifiable information", Chapter 5, Section A, of the TCPS states: "Information that may reasonably be expected to identify an individual, alone or in combination with other available information, is considered identifiable information (or information that is identifiable) for the purposes of this Policy. Where the term 'personal information' appears in this Policy, it refers to identifiable information."

[364] TCPS, Chapter 5, Section D.

[365] TCPS, Chapter 5, Section D.

[366] These conditions are listed in TCPS, art. 5.5, which states:

Researchers who have not obtained consent from participants for secondary use of identifiable information shall only use such information for these purposes if the REB is satisfied that:

(a) identifiable information is essential to the research;

(b) the use of identifiable information without the participants' consent is unlikely to adversely affect the welfare of individuals to whom the information relates;

(c) the researchers will take the appropriate measures to protect the privacy of individuals, and to safeguard the identifiable information;

(d) the researchers will comply with any known preferences previously expressed by individuals about any use of their information;

(e) it is impossible or impracticable to seek consent from individuals to whom the information relates; and

researchers respect "any known preferences previously expressed by individuals about any use of their information".[367] Thus, at the time of initial collection such individuals may have articulated a preference regarding future uses of their information that is inconsistent with the proposed research use[368] (*e.g.*, individuals who explicitly refuse to allow the use of their clinical information for any type of future research use); if so, the proposed secondary use of that information is impermissible. Researchers who subsequently want to contact the individuals to whom the information relates in order to acquire additional information from them must seek the approval of the REB before doing so;[369] in such cases, consideration will need to be given to the possibility that the proposed contact might be unduly distressing to these individuals. The complexities related to secondary use issues are nicely illustrated by the fact that the TCPS has several articles devoted solely to the topic of secondary use of information or human biological materials identifiable as originating from Aboriginal communities or peoples,[370] and an entire section elsewhere in the document pertaining to secondary use of identifiable human biological materials for research purposes that is not directed at such materials from any particular community or population.[371]

There are many other significant privacy issues that surface in biomedical research. For instance, data linkage studies, which are now blossoming as society becomes fully ensconced in the electronic era, can raise the prospect of re-identification of individuals when de-identified or "anonymized"[372] databases are brought together. The TCPS addresses this issue in article 5.7. The storage and banking of human biological materials is another area that implicates privacy issues and which is addressed by the TCPS.[373]

Before leaving the subject of privacy and confidentiality in research, another important document in this area warrants attention. In 2005, CIHR released *CIHR Best Practices for Protecting Privacy in Health Research*[374] ("Best Practices"), which was intended to provide guidance for health researchers and REBs on substantive matters relating to research involving personal information. According to CIHR, this document is "intended as voluntary guidance for the health research community",[375] yet it also indicates that the practices "are based

---

    (f)   the researchers have obtained any other necessary permission for secondary use of information for research purposes.

[367] TCPS, art. 5.5(d).

[368] TCPS, "Application" commentary under art. 5.5.

[369] TCPS, art. 5.6 and its associated "Application" commentary.

[370] See TCPS, arts. 9.20 to 9.22.

[371] TCPS, Chapter 12, Section C.

[372] The TCPS states that information has been anonymized where "the information is irrevocably stripped of direct identifiers, a code is not kept to allow future re-linkage, and risk of re-identification of individuals from remaining indirect identifiers is low or very low" (Chapter 5, Section A).

[373] See TCPS, Chapter 12, Section D and art. 13.7.

[374] CIHR, *CIHR Best Practices for Protecting Privacy in Health Research* (Ottawa: Public Works and Government Services Canada, 2005).

[375] *Ibid.*, at 18.

on and are consistent with the TCPS, and they are designed to assist in the interpretation of the TCPS by offering additional detail and practicality".[376] A couple of points need to be highlighted at this juncture. First, the Best Practices document was issued prior to the release of the second edition of the TCPS in 2010; therefore, it must be read and interpreted accordingly.[377] Second, if the Best Practices document is to be used to determine what various mandatory provisions of the second edition of the TCPS actually mean, it is difficult to grasp how compliance could be viewed as voluntary for those members of the research community who are obligated to adhere to the TCPS by virtue of having entered into a contractual agreement with CIHR (or some other funding body) that requires compliance with the TCPS.

The Best Practices are organized around 10 elements:

(1)   determining the research objectives and justifying the data needed to fulfill these objectives;

(2)   limiting the collection of personal data;

(3)   determining if consent from individuals is required;

(4)   managing and documenting consent;

(5)   informing prospective research subjects about the research;

(6)   recruiting prospective research subjects;

(7)   safeguarding personal data;

(8)   controlling access and disclosure of personal data;

(9)   setting reasonable limits on retention of personal data; and

(10)   ensuring accountability and transparency in the management of personal data.

Importantly, the Best Practices delineate researchers' and REBs' privacy-related responsibilities. For researchers, these responsibilities include, among other things, "being aware of all applicable policies and laws in the jurisdictions in which the research is conducted and conducting their research in accordance with such requirements".[378] REBs' responsibilities involve, but are not limited to, "reviewing any proposed and ongoing research involving humans in accordance with the TCPS and its principles, as well as other applicable laws and policies, including: ... federal, provincial and territorial legislation; and relevant laws, regulations, policies and/or research contexts of other countries, when re-

---

[376]   *Ibid.*, at 18.

[377]   The second edition of the TCPS does reference the Best Practices (see the "Application" commentary regarding the word "impracticable" under art. 5.5).

[378]   CIHR, *CIHR Best Practices for Protecting Privacy in Health Research* (Ottawa: Public Works and Government Services Canada, 2005) at 88.

search is to be conducted in those countries".[379] The sheer breadth and complexity of the potentially relevant regulatory instruments outlined in Chapter 6, "Health Information: Confidentiality and Access", gives some idea of how tall an order this really is, particularly for already resource-strapped REBs. While REBs may find some assistance in the REB member "knowledgeable in the relevant law",[380] it is critical to remember that this person's role is merely "to alert REBs to legal issues and their implications (*e.g.*, privacy issues), not to provide formal legal opinions or to serve as legal counsel for the REB".[381] So, for example, she may inform her fellow REB members that there is an issue surrounding the possible application of the federal *Personal Information Protection and Electronic Documents Act*[382] to the research project at hand and that, if it applies, there is some issue regarding whether the research proposal is consistent with the Act's consent provisions. However, it is beyond the scope of her responsibilities to actually resolve these and like issues as this would likely constitute a formal legal opinion.

Although the Best Practices document can aid in the interpretation of the TCPS, it is of limited value in traversing the maze of privacy law. This is because adherence to the document does not necessarily ensure compliance with other relevant regulatory instruments. On this point, the document states in bold-face type: "These Privacy Best Practices do not replace existing laws, policies and professional codes of conduct that apply to certain types of personal information, designated organizations and/or specific kinds of activity. Researchers, REBs and institutions should be aware of, and continue to comply with, the relevant laws, policies and codes, including the TCPS, that govern research in their respective jurisdictions."[383] Tables of concordance containing references to some Canadian privacy legislation are appended to the document;[384] however, CIHR notes that they are to "only be used as preliminary guidance"[385] and then advises: "The application of the legal provisions in the tables to a particular research project must be determined in consultation with a legal advisor."[386] It remains to be seen whether REBs and researchers will take it upon themselves to seek independent legal advice respecting such issues.

3.   Conflicts of Interest Involving Researchers

The presence of a conflict of interest in the research setting can severely compromise the integrity and effectiveness of the Canadian research governance

---

[379] *Ibid.*, at 89.

[380] TCPS, art. 6.4(c).

[381] TCPS, "Application" commentary under art. 6.4.

[382] S.C. 2000, c. 5.

[383] CIHR, *CIHR Best Practices for Protecting Privacy in Health Research* (Ottawa: Public Works and Government Services Canada, 2005) at 18.

[384] *Ibid.*, Appendix A-7 at 114.

[385] *Ibid.*, at 21.

[386] *Ibid.*

regime by undermining the trust relationship between researchers and research participants, research sponsors, research institutions, and the public. Although the existence of such conflicts is not confined to biomedical research, "the special value placed on health, and the special trust placed in universities make health care centres and universities particularly vulnerable to public scrutiny and accountability".[387] Thompson defines a conflict of interest as "a set of conditions in which professional judgment concerning a primary interest (such as a patient's welfare or the validity of research) tends to be unduly influenced by a secondary interest (such as financial gain)".[388] As discussed in Part II, the primary interest of all researchers "should be valid answers to research questions, since scientific progress which contributes to improved health care is the final goal of research".[389] Where the researchers "are also treating physicians, the well-being of individual patients is a concurrent primary interest".[390] Secondary interests of researchers may include, among others: career advancement through the publication of study results in reputable journals; peer recognition; pleasing research sponsors; financial gain arising from funding acquisition, honoraria, subsidized overhead and patents; satisfaction of intellectual curiosity; and scientific development.[391]

The interests of research participants and researchers can coincide or conflict.[392] The expanding body of literature devoted to exposing the negative impacts of the commercialization of biomedical research on researchers' design and conduct of studies as well as study results, offers a bountiful supply of examples of clashing interests.[393] In order to meet the demand for participants for

---

[387] Kathleen Cranley Glass & Trudo Lemmens, "Conflict of Interest and Commercialization of Biomedical Research: What is the Role of Research Ethics Review?" in Timothy Caulfield & Bryn Williams-Jones, eds., *The Commercialization of Genetic Research: Ethical, Legal and Policy Issues* (New York: Kluwer Academic/Plenum Publishers, 1999) 79 at 79.

[388] Dennis F. Thompson, "Understanding Financial Conflicts of Interest" (1993) 329 New Eng. J. Med. 573 at 573. This definition has been quoted with approval by numerous authors. For examples, see: Kathleen Cranley Glass & Trudo Lemmens, *ibid.*, at 83; Sheldon Krimsky, "The Ethical and Legal Foundations of Scientific 'Conflict of Interest'" in Trudo Lemmens & Duff R. Waring, eds., *Law and Ethics in Biomedical Research: Regulation, Conflict of Interest and Liability* (Toronto: University of Toronto Press, 2006) 63 at 63; Lorraine E. Ferris & C. David Naylor, "Promoting Integrity in Industry-Sponsored Clinical Drug Trials: Conflict of Interest Issues for Canadian Health Sciences Centres" in Trudo Lemmens & Duff R. Waring, eds., *Law and Ethics in Biomedical Research: Regulation, Conflict of Interest and Liability* (Toronto: University of Toronto Press, 2006) 95 at 96.

[389] Kathleen Cranley Glass & Trudo Lemmens, *ibid.*, at 86.

[390] *Ibid.*

[391] *Ibid.*, at 86-87.

[392] Gerald S. Schatz, "Are the Rationale and Regulatory System for Protecting Human Subjects of Biomedical and Behavioral Research Obsolete and Unworkable, or Ethically Important but Inconvenient and Inadequately Enforced?" (2003-2004) 20 J. Contemp. Health L. & Pol'y 1 at 17. The potential for conflicting interests is well described in Kathleen Cranley Glass & Trudo Lemmens, *ibid.*

[393] See Jonathan Kimmelman, Françoise Baylis & Kathleen Cranley Glass, "Stem Cell Trials: Lessons from Gene Transfer Research" (2006) 36:1 Hastings Center Report 23-26 and Kathleen Cranley Glass & Trudo Lemmens, *ibid.*

clinical drug trials, sponsoring companies have used participant recruitment strategies such as the payment of handsome recruitment fees to researchers, researcher recruitment bonuses, competitive enrolment schemes and completion fees for retaining participants in the study. These practices have been criticized for encouraging researchers not to strictly apply inclusion and exclusion criteria, for causing them to put pressure on people to agree to participate in and not to withdraw from the study, and for encouraging them to deviate from informed consent standards.[394]

The circumstances in which Dr. Nancy Olivieri found herself illustrate how conflicts of interest problems can creep into research projects.[395] During the course of a clinical trial that was being conducted by Olivieri and others in order to evaluate the use of a drug in treating persons with a blood disorder, Olivieri became concerned about evidence that, in her opinion, pointed to the study drug's loss of efficacy and to its potential toxicity. She told the commercial sponsor (Apotex Research Inc.) and the REB affiliated with her hospital about these issues. The REB instructed Olivieri to, among other things, inform participants about these concerns but Apotex, who disagreed with the validity of Olivieri's concerns, responded by terminating the trial at Olivieri's study site and by threatening to vigorously pursue all legal remedies against her if she breached a confidentiality agreement she had entered into with the sponsor.[396] Although Olivieri ultimately decided to disclose her concerns to the participants, the powerful interest she had in complying with the confidentiality agreement (and not

---

[394] Timothy Caulfield, "Legal and Ethical Issues Associated with Patient Recruitment in Clinical Trials: The Case of Competitive Enrolment" (2005) 13:2 & 3 Health L. Rev. 58-61; Lorraine E. Ferris & C. David Naylor, "Promoting Integrity in Industry-Sponsored Clinical Drug Trials: Conflict of Interest Issues for Canadian Health Sciences Centres" in Trudo Lemmens & Duff R. Waring, eds., *Law and Ethics in Biomedical Research: Regulation, Conflict of Interest and Liability* (Toronto: University of Toronto Press, 2006) 95 at 96; Trudo Lemmens & Paul B. Miller, "The Human Subjects Trade: Ethical and Legal Issues Surrounding Recruitment Incentives" (2003) 31 J.L. Med. & Ethics 398; Timothy Caulfield & Glenn Griener, "Conflicts of Interest in Clinical Research: Addressing the Issue of Physician Remuneration" (2002) 30 J.L. Med. & Ethics 305; and P. Saradhi Puttagunta, Timothy A. Caulfield & Glenn Griener, "Conflicts of Interest in Clinical Research: Direct Payment to the Investigators for Finding Human Subjects and Health Information" (2002) 10:2 Health L. Rev. 30.

[395] For a thorough description and an excellent analysis of the Olivieri case, see Jocelyn Downie, Patricia Baird & Jon Thompson, "Industry and the Academy: Conflicts of Interest in Contemporary Health Research (2002) 10 Health L.J. 103.

[396] A letter to Olivieri from Dr. Michael Spino, Vice President of Scientific Affairs, Apotex Research Inc., reads in part:

As you now [sic], paragraph 7 of the [research contract] provides that all information whether written or not, obtained or generated by you during the term of the [contract] and for a period of three years thereafter, shall be and remain secret and confidential and shall not be disclosed in any manner to any third party except with the prior written consent of Apotex. Please be aware that Apotex will take all possible steps to ensure that these obligations of confidentiality are met and will vigorously pursue all legal remedies in the event that there is any breach of these obligations.

This excerpt is set out in Robert A. Phillips & John Hoey, "Constraints of Interest: Lessons at the Hospital for Sick Children" (1998) 159 CMAJ 955 at 955.

being mired in a protracted, costly legal battle) plainly conflicted with the safety and well-being of the participants.[397]

Canada does not have a legislative scheme to deal with conflicts of interest involving biomedical researchers. The Clinical Trial Regulations[398] (and the *GCP Guidelines*[399]) are almost entirely silent on the issue of conflicts of interest. REBs and researchers that govern their affairs according to the TCPS are given some direction on this issue. Chapter 7 of the TCPS is committed to the topic of conflicts of interest. Article 7.4 requires researchers to "disclose in research proposals they submit to the REB any real, potential or perceived individual conflicts of interest, as well as any institutional conflicts of interest of which they are aware that may have an impact on their research". Lamentably, the TCPS lacks a general conflicts of interest test to assist researchers or REB members.[400] However, it does mention some situations that may give rise to a conflict of interest:

- "pressures on researchers ... to delay or withhold dissemination of research outcomes or to use inappropriate recruitment strategies";[401]

- researchers' partnerships with "organizations whose primary motive is profit";[402]

- financial "incentives for researchers to recruit quickly, at the expense of a careful review of the suitability of prospective participants";[403]

- "[u]nreasonable payments or undue inducements ... [that] place the researcher ... in a conflict between maximizing financial remuneration on the one hand and protecting participants and meeting the scientific requirements of the project on the other";[404]

---

[397] Jon Thompson, Patricia Baird & Jocelyn Downie, *The Olivieri Report: The Complete Text of the Report of the Independent Inquiry Commissioned by the Canadian Association of University Teachers* (Toronto: James Lorimer & Co., 2001).

[398] Clinical Trial Regulations, s. C.05.001 of the Food and Drug Regulations, C.R.C., c. 870.

[399] *GCP Guidelines*, s. 3.2.1.

[400] Interestingly, the first edition of the TCPS indicated that the presence or absence of a conflict of interest could be determined by asking "whether an outside observer would question the ability of the individual to make a proper decision despite possible considerations of private or personal interests" or, alternatively, "whether the public would believe that the trust relationship between the relevant parties could reasonably be maintained if they had accurate information on the potential sources of conflict of interest" (s. 4A). The first edition of the TCPS can be found online at: <http://www.pre.ethics.gc.ca/eng/archives/tcps-eptc/Default/>.

[401] TCPS, Chapter 7, Section A.

[402] TCPS, "Application" commentary under art. 7.4.

[403] TCPS, "Application" commentary under art. 7.4.

[404] TCPS, "Application" commentary under art. 7.4.

- researchers' "[c]onsideration for the profitability of the research may threaten the ethical integrity of research design and conduct";[405]

- "spin-off companies in which researchers have stakes or private contract research outside of the academic realm";[406] and

- "[d]ual roles of researchers and their associated obligations (*e.g.*, acting as both a researcher and a therapist, health care provider, caregiver ...) may create conflicts, undue influences, power imbalances or coercion that could affect relationships with others and affect decision-making procedures (*e.g.*, consent of participants)".[407]

The TCPS also addresses essentially the same information set out above in its chapter on clinical trials.[408] Importantly, this chapter also discusses the need for provisions in clinical trial contracts, including those related to confidentiality and the publication of scientific findings, to be examined to ensure compliance with institutional policy standards. Some guidance is provided on what should be contained in these policies; for example, it is noted "that the welfare of participants takes precedence over the interests of both researchers and sponsors"[409] and that all confidentiality and publication clauses "be consistent with the researcher's duty to share new information from clinical trials with REBs and trial participants in a timely manner".[410]

An REB, in conducting its ethics review of proposed or ongoing research, is required to assess whether the researcher has a conflict of interest and, if so, to decide what action, if any, is needed to address the situation.[411] In order to properly discharge this responsibility, the REB must acquire adequate knowledge about the research project. Thus, researchers are required to "disclose all kinds and amounts of payment (financial or in-kind) to the researchers by sponsors,

---

[405] TCPS, "Application" commentary under art. 7.4.
[406] TCPS, Chapter 7, Section A.
[407] TCPS, "Application" commentary under art. 7.4. According to the TCPS, the dual roles of clinician-researchers can cause them to "conflate their clinical practice with their clinical trial research. Some may be overly optimistic about the prospects of an experimental intervention and overstate potential benefits or understate foreseeable risks to prospective participants. This can foster therapeutic misconception among patients and influence the recruitment and consent process" (Chapter 11, Section A). The TCPS indicates that "therapeutic misconception occurs when trial participants do not understand that research is aimed primarily at producing knowledge and may not provide any therapeutic benefit to them" (Chapter 11, Section A). See also TCPS, art. 11.6 and associated "Application" commentary. For an exploration of issues pertaining to therapeutic misconception in the context of pediatric neuroimaging research, see Michael Hadskis, Nuala Kenny, Jocelyn Downie, Matthias Schmidt, & Ryan D'Arcy, "The Therapeutic Misconception: A Threat to Valid Parental Consent for Pediatric Neuroimaging Research" (2008) 15 Accountability in Research 133.
[408] TCPS, Chapter 11, Section D.
[409] TCPS, "Application" commentary under art. 11.12.
[410] TCPS, "Application" commentary under art. 11.12.
[411] TCPS, art. 7.4.

commercial interests, and consultative or other relationships, as well as any other relevant information that may affect the project (*e.g.*, donation to an institution by a research sponsor)".[412] The REB also needs details about the research budget[413] and the nature of the relationship between the researcher and the research participants. Only if it is in possession of this type of information can the REB properly decide whether a potential concern exists.

If the REB concludes that a conflict exists, it will next need to decide how to deal with this situation.[414] Once again, the TCPS relies on the proportionate approach to set out a number of possible REB dispositions, including requiring the researcher to disclose this conflict to prospective participants during the consent process[415] or to others (*e.g.*, research sponsors, institutions and relevant professional bodies), prohibiting some forms of payment, requiring the researcher to withdraw from the project (or require other non-conflicted members of the research team to make relevant decisions) or, in "exceptional cases", refusing to approve the project "where the REB decides that the conflict of interest has not been avoided or cannot be properly managed".[416] The REB may also do nothing where the conflict does not warrant specific action.[417] Unfortunately, the TCPS provides little guidance on when a conflict justifies doing nothing. One author has contended that the concept of autonomy and legal disclosure standards demand complete disclosure of a conflict of interest in every case.[418]

V. CIVIL LIABILITY FOR PERSONAL INJURIES SUSTAINED BY RESEARCH PARTICIPANTS

Researchers, REB members, research institutions and others[419] may be exposed to legal liability for personal injuries sustained by individuals as a result of their participation in research studies. Thomson, a pre-eminent Canadian practitioner in pharmaceutical and health law, has predicted an increased likelihood of litigation in Canada in connection with adverse events from clinical trials and other

---

[412] TCPS, "Application" commentary under art. 7.4.
[413] TCPS, "Application" commentary under art. 7.4, and in the specific context of clinical trials, art. 11.11.
[414] TCPS, art. 7.4.
[415] TCPS, art. 3.2(e) and "Application" commentary under art. 7.4.
[416] TCPS, "Application" commentary under art. 7.4.
[417] TCPS, "Application" commentary under art. 7.4.
[418] David T. Marshall, *The Law of Human Experimentation* (Markham, ON: Butterworths, 2000) at 106.
[419] Others that may be included in such lawsuits include research staff that are employed by researchers and research sponsors, including the Crown. For a detailed examination of Crown liability, see Sana Halwani, "Her Majesty's Research Subjects: Liability of the Crown in Research Involving Humans" in Trudo Lemmens & Duff R. Waring, eds., *Law and Ethics in Biomedical Research: Regulation, Conflict of Interest and Liability* (Toronto: University of Toronto Press, 2006) 228. A discussion of liability of sponsors in general can be found in Mary M. Thomson, "Bringing Research into Therapy: Liability Anyone?" in Trudo Lemmens & Duff R. Waring, eds., *Law and Ethics in Biomedical Research: Regulation, Conflict of Interest and Liability* (Toronto: University of Toronto Press, 2006) 183 at 195-96.

research activities.[420] Legal actions are most likely to sound in the torts of negligence and/or battery, although other causes of action may be pleaded.[421] The elements of a negligence action have been detailed in Chapter 3, "Medical Negligence". In sum, a negligence action is made out by a plaintiff on establishing that the defendant owed them a legal duty of care, that the defendant breached the duty by not meeting the requisite standard of care, and that the defendant's failure to meet the standard of care caused the plaintiff to suffer legally recognized damage. A battery action involves a "direct, intentional, and physical interference with the person of another that is either harmful or offensive to a reasonable person".[422]

There is little doubt that researchers owe a duty of care to the individuals that they enroll in their studies.[423] Their liability in negligence will most likely hinge on whether they met the applicable standard of care, which would likely require researchers to exercise the care and skill of a "reasonable researcher" under similar circumstances[424] in designing and conducting the study, including the provision of proper care during any medical intervention. Additionally, regarding informed consent, researchers must meet the applicable disclosure standard as discussed earlier in this chapter or risk being held negligent if the "court is satisfied that a reasonable person in the research subject's position would probably not have agreed to participate in the research if full disclosure of information had been made"[425] (*i.e.*, the causal element of a negligence action). As previously stated, it is generally accepted that extra-legal documents that speak to ethical research norms such as the TCPS, *GCP Guidelines* or *Declaration of Helsinki*,[426] though not binding on the courts, may well be used in negligence actions to define the legal standards against which researchers will be measured.[427]

---

[420] Mary M. Thomson, *ibid.*, at 185.

[421] Such actions include breach of contract. See Mary M. Thomson, *ibid.*, at 185.

[422] Philip H. Osborne, *The Law of Torts*, 2d ed. (Toronto: Irwin Law, 2003) at 226.

[423] Susan Zimmerman, "Translating Ethics into Law: Duties of Care in Health Research Involving Humans" (2005) 13:283 Health L. Rev. 13 at 15.

[424] David T. Marshall, *The Law of Human Experimentation* (Markham, ON: Butterworths, 2000) at 46; and Medical Research Council of Canada ("MRC"), *Report of the Working Group on Liability* (Ottawa: MRC, undated) at 7.

[425] Gerald B. Robertson, "Report on Liability in Research" (Ottawa: MRC, 2000) at 17.

[426] Recall the earlier discussion regarding the *Weiss* court's use of this instrument when establishing the applicable disclosure standard. See Section IV(B)(1)(a) of this chapter.

[427] Angela Campbell & Kathleen Cranley Glass, "The Legal Status of Clinical and Ethics Policies, Codes, and Guidelines in Medical Practice and Research" (2001) 46 McGill L.J. 473 at 480; Mary M. Thomson, "Bringing Research into Therapy: Liability Anyone?" in Trudo Lemmens & Duff R. Waring, eds., *Law and Ethics in Biomedical Research: Regulation, Conflict of Interest and Liability* (Toronto: University of Toronto Press, 2006) 183 at 187; Medical Research Council of Canada (MRC), *Report of the Working Group on Liability* (Ottawa: MRC, undated) at 7; Susan Zimmerman, "Translating Ethics into Law: Duties of Care in Health Research Involving Humans" (2005) 13:2 & 3 Health L. Rev. 13 at 17.

Weiss is illustrative of the care and skill that must be exercised in the design and conduct of a study. The court in that case determined that the participant's heart condition (hypertrophic cardiomyopathy) should have excluded his involvement in the study, or at least required careful monitoring if he were permitted to participate. This obligated the researchers to screen prospective participants for the presence of the condition, which they failed to do. Interestingly, in making this finding, the court did not reference any standard of the profession on the issue of screening for cardiac disease.[428]

Researchers could also be exposed to a battery action if they undertake a medical intervention on a participant on the basis of a consent that is legally vitiated because it was not given voluntarily or the person lacked decisional capacity.[429] A researcher's reliance on a non-mature minor's consent to a blood draw for the purpose of a genetic study is an example of the latter situation. The former is exemplified by a situation where a researcher/treating physician coerced a competent adult's consent to a blood draw by implying that the person would not receive the medical care they would otherwise be entitled to if they did not agree to participate in the genetic study.

Researchers may be tempted to shield themselves from lawsuits by seeking liability waivers from participants. However, the *GCP Guidelines* specify that the consent process cannot contain oral or written statements to the effect that participants are waiving any legal rights or are releasing the researcher or others from liability for negligence.[430] The TCPS addresses this matter by "generally requiring" the informed consent process to contain "a statement to the effect that, by consenting, participants have not waived any rights to legal recourse in the event of research-related harm".[431]

REB members can also be held directly liable for damage sustained by research participants. Since the REB itself does not have legal personality,[432] plaintiffs would be required to commence proceedings against each of its individual members and not the board as a collective. Legal action is likely to be cast in terms of the negligent performance of their mandate as members of the REB. Since REB members are charged with protecting the rights, safety and well-being of research participants, the existence of a duty of care would unquestionably follow.[433] Individuals serving on the REB are likely to be held to the standard of care of a "reasonable REB member" holding the same expertise,

---

[428] Kathleen Cranley Glass & Benjamin Freedman, "Legal Liability for Injury to Research Subjects" (1991) 14 Clinical and Investigative Medicine 176 at 178.

[429] This is in contrast to an action based on a lack of informed consent, which according to the law must be framed in negligence not battery. See *Ciarlariello v. Schacter*, [1993] S.C.J. No. 46, [1993] 2 S.C.R. 119 at 132 (S.C.C.) and *Reibl v. Hughes*, [1980] S.C.J. No. 105, 114 D.L.R. (3d) 1 at 11 (S.C.C.).

[430] *GCP Guidelines*, s. 4.8.4.

[431] TCPS, art. 3.2(k).

[432] Gerald B. Robertson, "Report on Liability in Research" (Ottawa: MRC, 2000) at 30.

[433] Mary M. Thomson, "Bringing Research into Therapy: Liability Anyone?" in Trudo Lemmens & Duff R. Waring, eds., *Law and Ethics in Biomedical Research: Regulation, Conflict of Interest and Liability* (Toronto: University of Toronto Press, 2006) 183 at 198.

thereby allowing for the possibility that members possessing greater expertise in a relevant area (*e.g.*, law, ethics and medicine) will be held to a higher standard than other board members (*e.g.*, community members).[434] A breach of the standard of care might be alleged to have occurred if, for example, the REB member approves an informed consent form that does not adequately inform participants of a risk of harm[435] or approves a protocol that does not provide for adequate safeguards during the research,[436] including screening mechanisms for possible contraindications to their participation.[437] As outlined above, under the TCPS, REBs are responsible for ensuring that ongoing research studies have an appropriate continuing ethics review process, the rigour of which is to be proportionate to the risk of harm that attends the study. In view of the limited amount of ethics oversight that is taking place for ongoing research, this may be another area in which REB members are at legal peril.[438] The TCPS would be just as relevant in defining the legal standard of care for REB members as it would for researchers,[439] a daunting prospect given the myriad of obligations it rests on REB members' shoulders.

Research institutions, including universities and hospitals, may be directly or vicariously liable for a research participant's injuries. Direct liability may be occasioned where the institution has itself acted negligently. As is the case for researchers and REB members, it is accepted that research institutions owe a duty of care to participants and that, in connection with establishing the standard of care, the "reasonable research institution" yardstick would be utilized by the courts. To meet this standard, research institutions would, at a minimum, need "to take reasonable care to hire competent researchers, to have adequate research facilities, to appoint competent people to its REB, and (through its REB) to conduct protocol reviews according to Canadian and international codes and guidelines governing such research".[440] In *Weiss*, the defendant hospital was liable, through its REB,[441] for the inadequate review of the ophthalmic drops research

---

[434] Linda M. Bordas, "Tort Liability of Institutional Review Boards" (1984-85) 87 W. Va. L. Rev. 137 at 148; and B. Robertson, "Report on Liability in Research" (Ottawa: MRC, 2000) at 30.

[435] Linda M. Bordas, *ibid.*, at 143; Jennifer L. Gold, "Watching the Watchdogs: Negligence, Liability, and Research Ethics Boards" (2003) 11 Health L.J. 153 at 161-71; and Ruth Scheuer, "Research in the Hospital Setting on Human Subjects: Protecting the Patient and the Institution" (1993) 60 Mount Sinai J. Med. 391 at 394.

[436] Ruth Scheuer, *ibid.*

[437] Jennifer L. Gold, "Watching the Watchdogs: Negligence, Liability, and Research Ethics Boards" (2003) 11 Health L.J. 153 at 161-71.

[438] Mary M. Thomson, "Bringing Research into Therapy: Liability Anyone?" in Trudo Lemmens & Duff R. Waring, eds., *Law and Ethics in Biomedical Research: Regulation, Conflict of Interest and Liability* (Toronto: University of Toronto Press, 2006) 183 at 199; and Linda M. Bordas, "Tort Liability of Institutional Review Boards" (1984-85) 87 W. Va. L. Rev. 137 at 146.

[439] Gerald B. Robertson, "Report on Liability in Research" (Ottawa: MRC, 2000) at 34.

[440] *Ibid.*, at 33.

[441] The court did not discuss the specific rationale for holding the hospital liable for the actions of the REB. There are speculations that it was because the REB members were appointed by the hospital in furtherance of its legislative obligation regarding research. See Kathleen Cranley

protocol and the consent forms, and for not having a defibrillator on hand. Research institutions could also be held vicariously liable for tortuous acts or omissions of researchers, despite not having engaged in any wrongdoing itself. The nature of the employment relationship for many university faculty members and hospital staff will satisfy the test for vicarious liability, thus making their institutions potentially liable for injuries sustained by participants in their studies. Although the situation is less clear with physician-researchers who have merely been granted privileges by their host hospitals because they are generally considered to be independent contractors and not employees of the hospital, one commentator has opined that hospitals may nonetheless be vicariously liable for physicians conducting research within the hospital.[442]

VI. CONCLUSION

Canada's regulatory framework for human biomedical research is marred by complexity and inefficiency. As this chapter has demonstrated, what, if any, regulatory instruments apply to a given study depends on a great many variables: the particular country or countries, province or provinces, and institution or institutions that will host the research; the type of research being conducted; the professional and institutional affiliations of the researchers; the age and mental status of the participants; the type of information and material collected from or about the participants; and the funding sources for the research. The confusion and frustration biomedical research stakeholders experience when attempting to navigate the current regulatory regime is not difficult to appreciate. REB members find the multiplicity of regulatory instruments to be "extremely confusing"[443] and, worse yet, others are simply unaware of all the major standards.[444] There is certainly no reason to assume researchers are faring any better. This state of affairs is particularly troublesome given that the rights and well-being of research participants and the credibility of the research governance system hang in the balance. Observing that much would be gained from the revision

---

Glass & Benjamin Freedman, "Legal Liability for Injury to Research Subjects" (1991) 14 Clinical and Investigative Medicine 176 at 179.

[442] Gerald B. Robertson, "Report on Liability in Research" (Ottawa: MRC, 2000) at 33; Medical Research Council of Canada (MRC), *Report of the Working Group on Liability* (Ottawa: MRC, undated) at 28.

[443] Brenda Beagan, "Ethics Review for Human Subjects Research: Interviews With Members of Research Ethics Boards and National Organizations" in M. McDonald, ed., *The Governance of Health Research Involving Human Subjects* (Ottawa: Law Commission of Canada, 2000) 173 at 229.

[444] Jocelyn Downie & Fiona McDonald, "Revisioning the Oversight of Research Involving Humans in Canada" (2004) 12 Health L.J. 159.

and harmonization of the current system, commentators are increasingly calling for an effective, efficient, accountable and fair national[445] or provincial[446] regulatory framework that encompasses all health research involving humans.

---

[445] Jocelyn Downie, "The Canadian Agency for the Oversight of Research Involving Humans: A Reform Proposal" (2006) 13 Accountability in Research 75; Jocelyn Downie, "Contemporary Health Research: A Cautionary Tale" (2003) Health L.J. (Special Edition) 1 at 8; and Kathleen Cranley Glass, "Questions and Challenges in the Governance of Research Involving Humans: A Canadian Perspective" in Trudo Lemmens & Duff R. Waring, eds., *Law and Ethics in Biomedical Research: Regulation, Conflict of Interest and Liability* (Toronto: University of Toronto Press, 2006) 35 at 44.

[446] Daryl Pullman, "Research Governance, Bio-politics and Political Will: Recent Lessons from Newfoundland and Labrador" (2005) 13:2 & 3 Health L. Rev. 75-79.

Chapter 11

EMERGING HEALTH TECHNOLOGIES[*]

Ian Kerr, Jennifer Chandler and Timothy Caulfield

I.   THE ELIXIR OF THEUTH

It is not uncommon for a given society to perceive itself as perched on the cusp of radical transformation in the fields of health and medicine. Steeped in mathematics and the natural sciences, the ancient Pythagoreans developed a careful and rigorous diet with the belief that, by understanding the four archetypal elements and keeping the body free of its base "Titanic" nature, they could achieve immortality.[1] Several centuries later, following numerous advances in the science of chemistry, Paracelsus radically transformed medicine[2] by advancing the theory that illness was not caused by an imbalance in the composition of natural elements or the four humours (as the ancients had believed), but that disease must be understood in terms of chemical causes that could be treated with chemical cures. He and other alchemists believed that the principles behind the transmutation of base metals into gold and silver might furnish a similar technique to create an "elixir of life".

With increasing optimism at the wake of the new millennium, many members of the medical community emphasized their quest for a universal panacea. Articulating its vision for the 21st century, the World Health Organization (WHO) proclaimed that:

---

[*]   This chapter was originally written for the third edition of this book by Ian Kerr and Timothy Caulfield with much appreciated research support from the Canada Research Chairs program. Those authors extend continuing gratitude to Angela Long and Alethea Adair for their significant contributions to the original chapter. Ian Kerr and Jennifer Chandler also wish to thank Kristen Thomasen and Dara Jospe for their extraordinary efforts in assisting with the current edition, and for the high quality of research assistance that they so regularly and reliably provide.

[1]   BBC, "Pythagoras, c. 580 – c. 500 BC", Historic Figures, online at: <http://www.bbc.co.uk/history/historic_figures/pythagoras.shtml>.

[2]   Debates raged in Paris in the mid to late 16th century over the place of alchemy within the field of medicine. As Moran notes in Bruce T. Moran, *Distilling Knowledge: Alchemy, Chemistry, and the Scientific Revolution* (Cambridge, MA: Harvard University Press, 2005) at 74-75:

> The real question being asked in the Parisian debate was this: Should alchemy be accepted as an independent discipline, which, because of its powers of understanding the operations of nature and the body, was not merely a part of medicine but *reigned over* medicine and provided medicine with a new, chemical, rationality? ... The real problem was whether alchemy provided a better overall understanding of the workings of the body and better ways to maintain health than other, more ancient forms of medical wisdom.

Now, as we near the end of one century and enter the next, our past achievements and technological advances make us more optimistic about our future
than perhaps at any stage in recent history.[3]

Canadian health agencies expressed similar optimism. Consider the following
remarks made by Dr. Alan Bernstein[4] in an address to the Senate Standing
Committee on Social Affairs, Science and Technology:

> It would not be an understatement to state that the current revolution in health
> research will be one of the drivers, if not the single largest driver, of change in
> the health care system in the next 10 to 20 years. This scientific revolution is
> being fueled by our rapidly emerging understanding of the molecular basis of
> life, of human biology and human disease, and the recent and ongoing advances
> in genetics and genomics, together with an appreciation that our health and sus-
> ceptibility to disease is really the summation of a complex interplay between
> environmental factors, genetics and social factors. That appreciate [*sic*] will
> transform our health care system in the next 10 to 20 years.[5]

In light of the optimism that is practically embedded into the design of emerging
health technologies, it is perhaps instructive to commence this chapter with a
brief retelling of an ancient myth about an inventor and the King of Egypt.

As the story goes,[6] King Thamus was once visited by an inventor named
Theuth. Seeking fame and fortune, Theuth hoped that the king would make his
inventions widely available to the people of Egypt. In reference to one of his
very best discoveries, Theuth promised the king that his new technology "will
make the Egyptians wiser and will improve their memories; for it is an *elixir* of
memory and wisdom that I have discovered".[7] Much to his chagrin, rather than
praising him for the elixir, the king chided the inventor:

> Theuth, my paragon of inventors, the discoverer of an art is not the best judge
> of the good or harm which will accrue to those who practice it. So it is in this;
> you ... have out of fondness for your off-spring attributed to it quite the oppo-
> site of its real function. Those who acquire it will cease to exercise their mem-
> ory and become forgetful; they will rely on [the elixir] to bring things to their
> remembrance by external signs instead of by their own internal resources. What
> you have discovered is a receipt for recollection, not for memory. And as for
> wisdom, your pupils will have the reputation for it without the reality: they will
> receive a quantity of information without proper instruction, and in conse-
> quence be thought very knowledgeable when they are for the most part quite

---

[3]   World Health Organization, *The World Health Report 1998 — Life in the 21st Century: A Vision for All* (Geneva: World Health Organization, 1998) at v.
[4]   Then President of the Canadian Institutes of Health Research.
[5]   Standing Senate Committee on Social Affairs, Science and Technology, *The State of the Health Care System in Canada*, 1st Sess., 37th Parl., Issue 9 (April 26, 2001).
[6]   The most famous retelling of the myth of Theuth is found in Plato's *Phaedrus*.
[7]   Plato, *Phaedrus*, R. Hackforth, trans. (Cambridge: Cambridge University Press, 1972) at para. 274e.

ignorant. And because they are filled with the conceit of wisdom instead of real wisdom they will be a burden to society.[8]

So, what are we to learn from this exchange?

On one level, the myth of Theuth's elixir provides a succinct articulation of the two sides in the debate about memory enhancers. Although an ancient debate, it is one that recurs in modern times.[9] The judgment of King Thamus also reminds us that we are often not well suited to evaluate emerging technologies because their future use may be subject to unintended consequences. A technology created for one purpose can be used for another: the stethoscope can be used to monitor a beating heart in crisis or to crack a safe.

But the story of Theuth's elixir is not just about opposing views on the social value of particular technological artifacts or their potential for misuse; it is not just about whether Theuth's memory elixir is good *or* bad for society. Carefully crafted by Plato,[10] the moral of the story hinges on the indeterminacy of the word "elixir". Like the Greek word *pharmakon*, the notion of an "elixir" carries a duality of meaning. As Jacques Derrida points out in an essay titled "Plato's Pharmacy",[11] the word *pharmakon* refers to an undulating word-play in the practically invisible quantum between "poison" and "cure". In this sense, the story of Theuth's elixir challenges us to consider what happens when a technology is both good *and* bad; when it is at one and the same time the solution and the problem.

As the philosopher of technology, Langdon Winner, once warned:

> [i]n our accustomed way of thinking technologies are seen as neutral tools that can be used well or poorly, for good, evil, or something in between. But we usually do not stop to inquire whether a given device might have been designed and built in such a way that it produces a set of consequences logically and temporally *prior to any of its professed uses. ...* technologies, however, encompass purposes far beyond their immediate use. If our moral and political language for evaluating technology includes only categories having to do with tools and uses, if it does not include attention to the meaning of the designs and

---

[8]   Plato, *Phaedrus and Letters VII and VIII* (New York: Penguin Books, 1973) at 96.

[9]   One might just as easily replace Theuth's elixir with modern cogniceuticals such as Prozac, Ritalin or other nootropic drugs and then imagine a reply by Francis Fukuyama not dissimilar to the judgment of King Thamus. See Francis Fukuyama, *Our Posthuman Future* (New York: Farrar, Straus and Giroux, 2002); and Ronald Bailey, "The Battle for Your Brain", Reasononline (February 2003), online at: <http://www.reason.com/0302/fe.rb.the.shtml>.

[10] Plato's presentation of the myth of Theuth's elixir is rich in irony. It is told through the voice of Socrates, the philosopher most famous for never having written anything. Plato used the character of Socrates in Plato's own writing as the vehicle for the delivery of Plato's own philosophy, written in prose so intriguing and influential that it has been said that "[t]he safest general characterization of the European philosophical tradition is that it consists of a series of footnotes to Plato": Alfred North Whitehead, *Process and Reality* (New York: Free Press, 1979) at 39.

[11] Jacques Derrida, "Plato's Pharmacy" in *Dissemination*, Barbara Johnson, trans. (Chicago: University of Chicago Press, 1981).

arrangements of our artifacts, then we will be blinded to much that is intellectually and practically crucial.[12]

In this chapter, we briefly survey four emerging technologies that are likely
to have a significant impact on Canadian health law and policy in the coming
years as both problems *and* solutions, as political artifacts that draw our attention to the meaning of their designs and arrangements. Our aim is not so much to
prioritize or predict as it is to offer a new lens through which to consider various
fundamental legal and ethical principles and their application to health law and
policy in novel situations. Rather than providing comprehensive coverage of all
known technologies or every issue that might possibly arise, we have chosen to
sample a particular array of current and future technologies, presenting each
alongside a core health law precept or principle.

We commence with a consideration of the Human Genome Project and how
social policy might contend with the possibility of genetic discrimination. Then,
we examine the medical uses of human implantable Radio Frequency Identification (RFID) technology and the potential privacy implications associated with
implanted RFID microchips. Next, we investigate stem cell research and the
questions it raises about the challenges associated with making policy in a morally contested area. Finally, we contemplate issues not yet articulated in a field
not yet defined: nanotechnology and how to regulate against potentially catastrophic harms that are not yet understood. After surveying these four emerging
technologies and the issues they raise, we end the chapter with a brief consideration of issues associated with how science and technology are transferred from
the laboratory to the community through the process of commercialization.

II.   EMERGING TECHNOLOGIES

A.   HUMAN GENETICS

The Human Genome Project (HGP), the international effort to map the entire
human genome, was completed in 2003.[13] This research initiative is one of the
largest and most significant research efforts in human history. It has already
generated a tremendous amount of new scientific knowledge[14] and has laid the
foundation for the development of new health care technologies and therapies,
including genetic tests to assist in the diagnosis and prevention of disease and
drug therapies that are tailored to the genetic characteristics of individual patients, thus maximizing the benefits while, at the same time, minimizing the side

---

[12]   Langdon Winner, *The Whale and the Reactor: The Search for Limits in an Age of High Technology* (Chicago: University of Chicago Press, 1988) at 25.

[13]   The official website for the Human Genome Project declares: "The Human Genome Project was
completed in 2003." The work actually continued past this point with the publication of anno-
tated sequences for all 23 human chromosomes. See Human Genome Project Information, "Major Events in the U.S. Human Genome Project and Related Projects", online at:
<http://www.ornl.gov/sci/techresources/Human_Genome/project/timeline.shtml>.

[14]   Francis Collins, "The Heritage of Humanity" (2006) S1, Nature 9.

effects.[15] While we need to be careful not to succumb to the hype that has surrounded genetics (in fact, many of the promised breakthroughs have been slow to materialize),[16] there is little doubt that this is an area of research that will, one day, have a significant impact on human health. Indeed, as Francis Collins puts it:

> The promise of a revolution in human health remains quite real. Those who somehow expected dramatic results overnight may be disappointed, but should remember that genomics obeys the First Law of Technology: we invariably overestimate the short-term impacts of new technologies and underestimate their longer-term effects.[17]

However, the advances in the area of human genetics have also generated a variety of concerns.[18] Indeed, almost from the start of the HGP there has been concern that the scientific revolution in human genetics would result in new forms of genetic discrimination and the stigmatization of certain communities.[19] In particular, there was concern that the information would be used in the context of employment decisions, health care and life insurance.[20] Shortly after the start of the HGP, Professor O'Hara summarized the concerns as follows:

---

[15] For a useful overview of the uses of genetic testing technologies, see Government of Canada BioPortal, "Genetic Testing", online at: <http://biobasics.gc.ca/english/View.asp?x=780>.

[16] Commenting on the achievements in the 10 years since the release of the draft human genome in 2000, the editors of Nature suggest that the tremendous complexity of the biology involved has made it hard to move from the sequenced genome to the hoped-for therapeutic applications. "The Human Genome at Ten" (2010) 464:7289 Nature 649-50.

[17] Francis Collins, "Has the Revolution Arrived?" (2010) 464:7289 Nature 674-75.

[18] There is a vast literature on the ethical, legal and social issues associated with human genetics, including work on the issues associated with the patenting process, concerns about potential eugenic applications, and its impact on health care systems. For example, see Tom Murray, Mark Rothstein & Robert Murray, eds., *The Human Genome and the Future of Health Care* (Bloomington: Indiana University Press, 1997); Glenn McGee, *The Perfect Baby: A Pragmatic Approach to Genetics* (New York: Rowman and Littlefield, 1997); Therese Marteau & Marin Richards, eds., *The Troubled Helix* (Cambridge: Cambridge University Press, 1996); Phillip Kitcher, *The Lives to Come: The Genetic Revolution and Human Possibilities* (Toronto: Simon & Schuster, 1996); Lori B. Andrews *et al., Assessing Genetic Risks: Implications for Health and Social Policy* (Washington, DC: National Academic Press, 1994); R. Hubbard & E. Wald, *Exploding the Gene Myth* (Boston: Beacon Press, 1993); Tom Wilkie, *Perilous Knowledge: The Human Genome Project and Its Implications* (Boston: Faber & Faber, 1993); George Annas & Susan Elias, eds., *Gene Mapping: Using Law and Ethics* (Oxford: Oxford University Press, 1992); Richard C. Lewontin, *Biology as Ideology: The Doctrine of DNA* (New York: Harpers Perennial, 1992); Danial Kevles & L. Hood, *The Code of Codes* (Cambridge: Harvard University Press, 1992).

[19] For example, see C. Lee, "Creating a Genetic Underclass: The Potential for Genetic Discrimination by the Health Insurance Industry" (1993) 13 Pace L. Rev. 227: "The single most effective way to prevent abuse is a ban on the use of genetic information in health insurance underwriting."

[20] Trudo Lemmens, "Selective Justice, Genetic Discrimination, and Insurance: Should We Single Out Genes in Our Laws?" (2000) 45 McGill L.J. 347-412.

The use of genetic testing or test results has many adverse social and ethical problems leading to social stigmatization as well as a potential for creating an entire population of uninsurable individuals. In addition, genetic testing by insurers can lead to serious psychological damage to those who test positive.[21]

The possible social, economic and psychological risks associated with genetic tests may have implications for physicians as well as patients. Some authors have speculated that these risks must be disclosed by physicians as part of the process of obtaining informed consent where genetic testing is recommended for health reasons,[22] and others debate the ethics and legality of excluding test results from patients' medical records as a response to these risks.[23]

As a result of concerns regarding potential genetic discrimination, many jurisdictions throughout the world have legislated prohibitions against the use of genetic information for anything other than health reasons and research.[24] In the U.S., for example, most states have enacted some form of "anti-genetic discrimination" law.[25] The laws differ greatly in the types of discrimination that they protect against. Some, for example, prohibit discrimination against individuals with specific genetic traits or disorders while others "regulate both the use of genetic testing in employment decisions and the disclosure of genetic test results".[26] All, however, were enacted as a result of the concerns over genetic discrimination. At the federal level, the U.S. enacted the *Genetic Information Nondiscrimination Act of 2008* (GINA), which provides asymptomatic individuals some protections from discrimination in the contexts of employment and health insurance, but not in the context of other forms of insurance such as life

---

[21] S. O'Hara, "The Use of Genetic Testing in the Health Insurance Industry: The Creation of a 'Biologic Underclass'" (1993) 22 Cambridge SW. U. L. Rev. 1227. See also P. Billings *et al.*, "Discrimination as a Consequence of Genetic Testing" (1992) 50 Am. J. Hum. Genet. 476.

[22] See, *e.g.*, Anita Silvers, "Primary Care Physicians and the Duty to Inform about Genetic Discrimination" (2001) 1:3 Am. J. Bioethics 1-2.

[23] Robert Klitzman, "Exclusion of Genetic Information from the Medical Record: Ethical and Medical Dilemmas" (2010) 304:10 JAMA 1120-21.

[24] Bartha Knoppers & Yann Joly, "Physicians, Genetics and Life Insurance" (2004) 170 CMAJ 1421: "In Europe, the Convention on Human Rights and Biomedicine ratified by 17 countries unambiguously states that genetic testing can be used only for health reasons and for research." For an example of relevant legislation see also P. Kossiem, M. Letendre & B. Knoppers, "Protecting Genetic Information: A Comparison of Normative Approaches" (2000) 2 GenEdit, online at: <http://www.humgen.org/int/GE/en/2004-1.pdf>.

[25] Human Genome Project Information, "Genetics Privacy and Legislation", online at: <http://www.ornl.gov/sci/techresources/Human_Genome/elsi/legislat.shtml#II>. See also National Conference of State Legislatures, "State Genetic Privacy Laws", State Genetic Table on Privacy Law, online at: <http://www.ncsl.org/programs/health/genetics/prt.htm>:

> The majority of state legislatures have taken steps to safeguard genetic information beyond the protections provided for other types of health information. This approach to genetics policy is known as genetic exceptionalism, which calls for special legal protections for genetic information as a result of its predictive, personal and familial nature and other unique characteristics.

[26] Human Genome Project Information, "Genetics Privacy and Legislation", online at: <http://www.ornl.gov/sci/techresources/Human_Genome/elsi/legislat.shtml#II>.

and disability insurance.[27] As for those who are actually symptomatic, rather than only carrying a particular gene related to a health condition, the recent reforms to the U.S. health care system made in the *Patient Protection and Access to Care Act* (PPACA) provide some assistance, since the Act takes steps to prevent discrimination on the basis of pre-existing conditions in the context of health insurance.[28]

No province in Canada has enacted a specific anti-genetic discrimination law, but there has been some federal legislative interest in the topic. A recently introduced federal private members' bill proposes to amend the federal *Canadian Human Rights Act*[29] to include "genetic characteristics" among the grounds of impermissible discrimination in employment or service provision.[30] Because of our publicly funded health care system, there is less concern about the impact of genetic testing on health care insurance and access to the health care system than has been the case in the U.S. It is important to note, however, that not all health care services are insured in Canada and, as Pullman and Lemmens point out, erosion in the public health care system may increase the importance of access to private health insurance for Canadians.[31] Another source of concern is the possibility of genetic discrimination in the context of employment. One of the reasons put forward for discrimination in this context in the U.S. is that employers may have an economic incentive to avoid employees considered likely to become ill and thus raise the cost of employer-provided group health plans.[32] It is possible that the recent enactment of GINA may address, to some extent, this issue in the U.S.[33] A recent Australian study suggests that genetic discrimination in employment is not common in Australia, and we may expect Canada to be more like Australia than the U.S. due to the latter's linkage between health

---

[27] H.R. 493, 110th Congress, Second Session (2008) Pub. L. No. 110-223, 122 Stat. 881.

[28] *Patient Protection and Affordable Care Act*, (2010) Pub. L. No. 111-148, online at: <http://docs.house.gov/energycommerce/ppacacon.pdf>. In addition to the immediate creation of an insurance plan for those currently uninsurable due to a pre-existing condition, the Act prohibits (from 2014) the denial of coverage on the basis of pre-existing conditions as well as (in individual and small group markets) premium increases on the basis of pre-existing conditions. For a useful summary of the provisions and a timeline for their coming into effect, see U.S. Dept. of Health and Human Services, "Provisions of the Affordable Care Act, by year", online at: <http://www.healthcare.gov/law/about/order/byyear.html>.

[29] R.S.C. 1985, c. H-6.

[30] Bill C-508, *An Act to Amend the Canadian Human Rights Act (genetic characteristics)*, 3rd Sess., 40th Parl., 2010 (first reading on April 14, 2010), online at: <http://www2.parl.gc.ca/Sites/LOP/LEGISINFO/index.asp?Language=E&query=6981&Session=23&List=toc>.

[31] Daryl Pullman & Trudo Lemmens, "Keeping the GINA in the Bottle: Assessing the Current Need for Genetic Non-Discrimination Legislation in Canada" (2010) 4:2 Open Medicine, online at: <http://www.openmedicine.ca/article/view/339/322>.

[32] Jared A. Feldman & Richard J. Katz, "Genetic Testing & Discrimination in Employment: Recommending a Uniform Statutory Approach" (2002) 19 Hofstra Lab. & Emp. L. J. 289 at 397-98.

[33] A claim of genetic discrimination in the employment context has recently been made under GINA; see Stephanie Reitz, "Conn. woman alleges genetic discrimination at work" ABCNews.com (April 28, 2010), online at: <http://abcnews.go.com/Business/wireStory?id=10500701>.

insurance and employment.[34] As for the life insurance marketplace, there is some evidence that genetic information, drawn from family history rather than genetic testing, is used in the context of Huntington's Disease in Canada.[35] It is difficult to conclude from this evidence that genetic information is generally used in relation to conditions other than Huntington's Disease in the life insurance context in Canada, given that the genes relevant to other conditions may be less predictive than with Huntington's Disease.[36] Nevertheless, these concerns have led to calls for policy reform in Canada,[37] including limiting the use of genetic information in the context of insurance and employment, strengthening privacy laws, and mandating an entitlement to a minimum amount of life, disability and health insurance.[38]

The concern about genetic discrimination and the ensuing regulatory response raises some interesting policy questions. First, to what degree is genetic discrimination really a social problem worthy of legislative action?[39] The public certainly seems worried about it, particularly in the U.S., where access to health insurance is a profound issue.[40] In fact, there is some evidence that concerns about discrimination may deter participation in research and therapy, and "influence access to care".[41] In one study, it was found that 52.4 per cent of U.S. clinicians believed that mutation carriers have difficulty obtaining health insurance and "13% would not encourage genetic testing, despite a family history of can-

---

[34] Margaret Otlowski *et al.*, "Practices and Attitudes of Australian Employers in Relation to the Use of Genetic Information: Report on a National Study" (2010) 31 Comp. Lab. L. & Pol'y J. 637

[35] Yvonne Bombard *et al.*, "Perceptions of Genetic Discrimination Among People at Risk for Huntington's Disease: A Cross Sectional Survey" (2009) British Medical Journal, online at: <http://www.bmj.com/content/338/bmj.b2175.abstract>.

[36] Huntington's Disease is a fully penetrant, single-gene disorder. As a result, carriers of the gene are highly likely to develop the condition. The predictive value (or clinical validity) of genetic tests for more complex conditions is far less clear. C. Erwin *et al.*, "Perception, Experience, and Response to Genetic Discrimination in Huntington Disease: The International RESPOND-HD Study" (2010) 153B:5 American Journal of Medical Genetics, Part B: Neuropsychiatric Genetics 1081 at 1083; Wylie Burke, "Genetic Testing" (2002) 347:23 New Eng. J. Med. 1867-75, discussing clinical validity or the "accuracy with which a test predicts a clinical outcome".

[37] Ontario Law Reform Commission, *Report on Genetic Testing* (Ontario: 1996); Privacy Commissioner of Canada, *Genetic Testing and Privacy* (Ottawa: 1992); Canadian Coalition for Genetic Fairness, online at: <http://www.ccgf-cceg.ca/en>.

[38] For a review of possible policy options, see Bartha Knoppers *et al.*, "Genetics and Life Insurance in Canada: Points to Consider" (2003) 170 CMAJ 1 at 2.

[39] See, for example, T. Lemmens, "Selective Justice, Genetic Discrimination, and Insurance: Should We Single Out Genes in Our Laws?" (2000) 45 McGill L.J. 347. The author provides an interesting critique of the anti-discrimination legislation, arguing that it does not address the underlying inequities associated with health disparities and access to health care.

[40] Amy Harmon, "Insurance fears lead many to shun DNA tests" NYTimes.com (February 24, 2008), online at: <http://www.nytimes.com/2008/02/24/health/24dna.html>.

[41] R. Nedelcu *et al.*, "Genetic Discrimination: The Clinician Perspective" (2004) 66 Clin. Gen. 311. See also Steve Mitchell, "Public Fears Genetic Discrimination", American Assoc. of People with Disabilities (May 26, 2005), online at: <http://www.aapd-dc.org/News/disability/fearsgenetic.html>.

cer".[42] Another study of almost 90,000 patients in the U.S. and Canada found that 40 per cent agreed with the statement: "Genetic testing is not a good idea because you might have trouble getting or keeping your insurance."[43]

Despite these perceptions, some commentators have questioned the existence of the genetic discrimination problem — or, at least, its magnitude.[44] Nonetheless, studies have more recently emerged that suggest that it does occur from time to time in the context of life insurance, and that it may be fairly substantial in that context if the gene in question is highly predictive of the eventual development of the condition.[45] However, only a few genetic tests have high predictive value, while the meaning and actuarial significance of many genetic tests is much less clear.[46]

Where genetic data is predictive, others have asked whether genetic discrimination is necessarily always to be decried. Joly *et al.* note that insurers have long used family history in assessing risk for life insurance purposes, and within an insurance model based on the mutual sharing of roughly equivalent risks, a shift to using genetic information may be an improvement that more accurately links premium levels and risk.[47] Otlowski *et al.* document the use of negative test results by Australian applicants for life insurance to displace the adverse decisions drawn by life insurance companies on the basis of a family history of particular diseases.[48]

---

[42]   *Ibid.* See also K.J. Lowstuter *et al.*, "Influence of Genetic Discrimination Perceptions and Knowledge on Cancer Genetics Referral Practice Among Clinicians" (2008) 10:9 Genetics in Medicine 691-98, reporting that 11 per cent of their survey respondents cited the risk of genetic discrimination as a reason not to refer patients for genetic testing.

[43]   Mark Hall *et al.*, "Concerns in a Primary Care Population about Genetic Discrimination by Insurers" (2005) 7 Genet. Med. 311. See also Peter Neuman, James Hammitt, Curt Mueller *et al.*, "Public Attitudes about Genetic Testing for Alzheimer's Disease" (2001) 20 Health Affairs 252.

[44]   See, *e.g.*, Hank Greely, "Banning Genetic Discrimination" (2005) 353 New Eng. J. Med. 865.

[45]   C. Erwin *et al.*, "Perception, Experience, and Response to Genetic Discrimination in Huntington Disease: The International RESPOND-HD Study" (2010) 153B:5 American Journal of Medical Genetics Part B: Neuropsychiatric Genetics 1081-93; K. Barlow-Stewart *et al.*, "Verification of Consumers' Experiences and Perceptions of Genetic Discrimination and its Impact on Utilization of Genetic Testing" (2009) 11:3 Genetics in Medicine 193-201; M. Otlowski *et al.*, "Investigating Genetic Discrimination in the Australian Life Insurance Sector: The Use of Genetic Test Results in Underwriting 1999-2003" (2007) 14:3 Journal of Law and Medicine 367-96. Yvonne Bombard *et al.*, "Perceptions of Genetic Discrimination Among People at Risk for Huntington's Disease: A Cross Sectional Survey" (2009) British Medical Journal, online at: <http//www.bmj.com/content/338/bmj.b2175.abstract>, reporting that Canadian life insurance applicants with a family history of Huntington's Disease face elevated levels of discrimination.

[46]   Bartha Knoppers *et al.*, "Genetics and Life Insurance in Canada: Points to Consider" (2002) 170 CMAJ Online 1. See also Trudo Lemmens *et al.*, "Genetics and Life Insurance: A Comparative Analysis" (2004) GenEdit 2: "Only a limited number of predictive tests are sufficiently reliable to be of real use to the insurers."

[47]   Yann Joly, Bartha Knoppers & Beatrice Godard, "Genetic Information and Life Insurance: A 'Real' Risk?" (2003) 11 European Journal of Human Genetics 561-64.

[48]   M. Otlowski *et al.*, "Investigating Genetic Discrimination in the Australian Life Insurance Sector: The Use of Genetic Test Results in Underwriting 1999-2003" (2007) 14:3 Journal of Law and Medicine 367-96.

This controversy provides the opportunity to ask whether genetic information is truly special. In other words, should the law be treating genetic information as distinct from other forms of health information? Survey research has shown that Canadians do, rightly or not, think that genetic information is worthy of special protection.[49] Such views accord with a number of international policy documents, such as Article 4 of UNESCO's 2003 *International Declaration on Human Genetic Data* that declares that human genetic information *is* special because it can be used to predict genetic predispositions, has relevance to biological relatives and may have cultural significance for persons or groups. As a result, the Declaration recommends that "[d]ue consideration ... be given to the sensitivity of human genetic data and an appropriate level of protection for these data and biological samples ... be established".[50]

However, in many ways, even the genetic information that is relatively predictive has similarities to other forms of health information (information that is not afforded special legislative treatment). For example, a cholesterol test provides predictive information (that is, information about risks for cardiovascular disease) and has relevance to one's biological relatives (cholesterol levels have a strong genetic component). Likewise, HIV status, a non-genetic condition, is also highly sensitive and predictive of future health concerns.

This line of reasoning has led some groups, such as the Nuffield Council on Bioethics, to conclude that genetic information is not significantly different from other forms of sensitive health information.[51] The Council goes on to recommend that given the "similarities between genetic and other forms of personal information, it would be a mistake to assume that genetic information is qualitatively different in some way".

The debate around genetic discrimination is far from over. With new applications on the horizon, such as nutrigenomics,[52] the profiling of athletes,[53] not to

---

[49]   Pollara & Earnscliffe, "Public Opinion Research into Biotechnology Issues: Presented to the Biotechnology Assistant Deputy Minister Coordinating Committee (BACC), Government of Canada" (Ottawa: Earnscliffe Research & Communications, December 2000).

[50]   United Nations Educational, Scientific and Cultural Organization (UNESCO), *International Declaration on Human Genetic Data* (October 16, 2003), 32nd Session, Official Records (Paris: UNESCO, 2003) at art. 4(b).

[51]   Nuffield Council on Bioethics, *Pharmacogenetics: Ethical Issues* (London: Nuffield Council on Bioethics, 2003) at 6. See also Timothy Caulfield, "Popular Media, Biotechnology and the 'Cycle of Hype'" (2005) 5 J. Health L. & Pol'y 213 at 232.

[52]   Nutrigenomics is an emerging field that involves the tailoring of nutrition to meet individual genetic characteristics, see Nola Ries & Timothy Caulfield, "First Pharmacogenomics, Next Nutrigenomics: Genohype or Genohealthy?" (2006) 46 Jurimetrics 281. A recent example of a large-scale nutrigenomics initiative was the University of California, Berkeley's controversial plan to test incoming freshmen students voluntarily in 2010 for three gene variants that regulate the ability to metabolize alcohol, lactose and folates; see Tamar Lewin, "College Bound, DNA Swab in Hand" NYTimes.com (May 18, 2010), online at: <http://www.nytimes.com/2010/05/19/education/19dna.html>.

[53]   "Controversy over genetic test for athletic ability" *BioNews* (December 23, 2004), online at: <http://www.bionews.org.uk/page_12208.asp>: "An Australian company is offering a genetic test it claims can identify children who have the potential to excel at either sprinting and 'power'

mention the potential non-medical applications under consideration,[54] it seems likely that genetic testing technologies will continue to generate regulatory challenges. Genetic information can be used to individuate, providing natural identifiers that could become a basis for discrimination. Should we treat genetic information as special, and worthy of unique regulatory protection? Or, should we treat it as simply another form of sensitive health information? For the purposes of this chapter, the concerns raised about genetic discrimination stand as an example of how uncertainty and social angst about an emerging technology can trigger legal reform, such as the anti-discrimination laws in the U.S., before it is clear what the best long-term regulatory response might be.

In the section that follows, we turn our investigation to an identification technology that promises an array of useful applications in various medical treatments.

B.   RADIO FREQUENCY IDENTIFICATION

Radio Frequency Identification (RFID) connotes a set of information technologies that enable the remote and automatic identification of physical entities by way of radio signals. Although best known for its ability to manage product inventory through a supply chain,[55] RFID has many valuable applications in health care delivery. For example, RFID can be used to track the whereabouts of a mobile cardiac unit or other life-saving emergency care equipment in real-time.[56] It can be used to help prevent child abduction in neonatal units,[57] and to monitor hand-

---

sports or endurance events." Regarding nutrigenomics, an emerging field that involves the tailoring of nutrition to meet individual genetic characteristics, see Nola Ries & Timothy Caulfield, "First Pharmacogenomics, Next Nutrigenomics: Genohype or Genohealthy?" (2006) 46 Jurimetrics 281.

[54]   One controversial non-medical application is the use of behavioural genetics, the study of the role of genes in behaviour, in the criminal justice system. See, *e.g.*, Emiliano Feresin, "Lighter sentence for murderer with 'bad genes'" Nature.com (October 30, 2009), online at: <http://www.nature.com/news/2009/091030/full/news.2009.1050.html>, where an Italian court reduced a jail term after tests identify genes linked to violent behaviour.

[55]   AME Info, "How RFID Can Optimize Supply Chain Management" (August 21, 2005), online at: <http://www.ameinfo.com/66090.html>. See also Intermec, "Supply Chain RFID: How it Works and Why it Pays" White Paper (2007), online at: <http://epsfiles.intermec.com/eps_files/eps_wp/SupplyChainRFID_wp_web.pdf>.

[56]   RFID systems that track equipment are said to improve the quality of health care, as locating equipment, especially in emergency situations, is made easier. In addition, such technology saves money, as less equipment is lost. See Les Chappell, "RFID Can be a Matter of Life and Death in the Medical World" Wisconsin Technology Network (October 19, 2005), online at: <http://wistechnology.com/article.php?id=2383>. RFID systems can even monitor whether medical equipment has been cleaned before it is reused on new patients. See Claire Swedberg, "Hospital RTLS Tracks Pumps' Status and Movement" RFID J. (July 9, 2010), online at: <http://www.rfidjournal.com/article/view/7713>.

[57]   Stanley Healthcare Solutions markets the Hugs system for tracking infants in hospitals. RFID tags are attached to the infants to track their whereabouts and match them with their mothers. See Stanley Healthcare Solutions: Hugs Infant Protection, online at: <http://www.stanleyhealthcare.com/solutions/patient-security/hugs-infant-protection/how-it-works>. The technology was her-

washing compliance by hospital staff and visitors.[58] And, as we shall see, it can be incorporated into the human body for a variety of informational, and potential therapeutic, purposes including identifying unconscious patients, monitoring blood glucose levels and ensuring patient compliance with pharmaceutical treatment.[59]

Unlike the larger and more costly anti-theft devices that we regularly encounter in clothing and department stores, the signals generated by an RFID tag not only announce their presence, they also announce their unique identities. RFID signals can pass through clothing, knapsacks, body parts and even buildings to communicate with reader devices some distance away. When associated with a database, RFID systems allow computers to recognize and distinguish between physical objects that have been tagged and to collect and integrate a myriad of information about those objects and the people using them.[60]

An RFID system is comprised of two main components: (1) the tag, which emits a signal that carries a unique identifier through radio waves;[61] and (2) the reader, which receives the signal and identifies the object. RFID readers operate by constantly emitting radio waves until a tag is detected. When a tag comes within range, its antenna amplifies the signal and sends the information stored on the chip back to the reader. The reader usually links the information stored on the tag to a database, thus correlating potentially scads of information about the object identified by the tag. The read range depends on the power, efficiency

---

alded worldwide as a bastion of security when the Hugs system foiled the abduction of an infant in a North Carolina hospital. See John Leyden, "Security Bracelet Foils Child Abduction" The Register (July 21, 2005), online at: <http://www.theregister.co.uk/2005/07/21/child_abduction_foiled/>.

[58] Hospital staff and visitors wear an RFID enabled name-tag or wristband that monitors their movement around the hospital, including into and out of patient rooms and washrooms. Likewise, the system monitors use of soap dispensers and can alert administrators to non-compliance. See HandGiene Corp., online at: <http://www.handgienecorp.com/pdf/handGiene_Healthcare.pdf>.

[59] The VeriMed system from PositiveID Corporation is the first to implant RFID chips into human beings for the purpose of identifying unconscious patients in emergency medicine. See PositiveID, online at: <http://www.positiveidcorp.com/health-id.html>. Potential future uses of implantable RFID technology also include: monitoring blood glucose levels, see: PositiveID, "Glucose Sensing Microchip", online at: <http://www.positiveidcorp.com/glucose_sensing.html>; and tracking pharmaceuticals from the manufacturer, through the supply chain, to the end destination within the patient's body. See Erick Jones et al., "RFID Pharmaceutical Tracking: From Manufacturer Through In Vivo Drug Delivery" (2010) 4 J. Med. Devices 015001-2.

[60] There is a significant difference between objects that merely announce their presence and objects that can also identify themselves in the process. For example, consider the difference between knowing that: (1) there is "a tagged object" hidden in that knapsack; and (2) there is a 1 kg bag of fertilizer EPC no. 016 37221 654321 2003004000, which was bought at the Home Depot on Merivale Road in Ottawa on February 26, 2006 at 09:06:17 by CIBC credit card holder no. 4408 0412 3456 XXXX and is hidden in the knapsack beside Ottawa Library book call no. 662.2014 B679 (titled: *Explosives*) signed out by library cardholder no. 11840003708286 on February 20, 2006 along with call no. 921 H6755 (*Mein Kampf*), call no. 320.533 H878 (*Les skinheads et l'extrême droite*), and call no. 296.6509 D288 (*Synagogue Architecture*).

[61] Also known as a "transponder".

and data integrity requirements of both the tag and the reader.[62] The radio frequency employed resides within the unlicensed portion of the broadcast spectrum and will be further determined by industry standards.

To date, only one RFID tag has received approval for human implantation in the U.S.: the VeriMed microchip marketed by PositiveID.[63] This microchip is a passive, unencrypted short-range RFID. Along with a reader and online medical record database, the chip forms part of the VeriMed system. When an implanted individual comes in proximity with a reader, the tag emits a unique subscriber number corresponding to its own proprietary patient registry database. This number can then be used by health care providers as a password to gain access to the online VeriMed patient registry, thus linking patients to their electronic health record. The microchip will "speak on the patient's behalf" — even if the patient is unconscious or otherwise incapacitated — enabling access to vital health information in emergency situations.

As of September 25, 2009, 616 people had received VeriMed microchips and had enrolled in the VeriMed patient registry.[64] Recently, however, PositiveID has suspended its active marketing of the VeriMed system, though it does continue to support existing patients and healthcare facilities.[65]

Despite recent setbacks in the VeriMed patient identification application, RFID is sure to be an important emerging health technology, especially as it becomes integrated into a variety of diagnostic and therapeutic uses. PositiveID, for example, is adapting its RFID technology for use in diabetes treatment.[66] This new biosensing microchip — still under development — will consist of a radio frequency-powered molecular sensor that can assess glucose levels in the body and communicate this data to a handheld reader. The technology will provide 24/7 monitoring and real-time updates of glucose levels, allowing implan-

---

[62] Simson Garfinkel & Henry Holtzman, "Understanding RFID Technology" in Simson Garfinkel & Beth Rosenberg, eds., *RFID: Applications, Security, and Privacy* (Upper Saddle River, NJ: Addison-Wesley, 2005) at 24.

[63] On October 12, 2004, the U.S. Food and Drug Administration (FDA) approved the human implantable device created by VeriChip, as the company was then called, as a Class II medical device. See FDA, online at: <http://www.accessdata.fda.gov/scripts/cdrh/cfdocs/cfPMN/pmn.cfm?ID=13508>.

[64] PositiveID Corporation, *Form S-4/A (Registration Statement for securities to be issued in business combination transactions),* (October 2, 2009) at 112, online: <http://investors.positiveid corp.com/secfiling.cfm?filingID=950123-09-48034>.

[65] The company itself has remained silent on the specific reason for terminating VeriMed marketing. Lower than expected sales of the product may be to blame. See Amy Keller, "A Chip Off the Old Block: Update on Implanted Microchips" *Florida Trend* (July 1, 2010), PDF accessible through PositiveID Corporation, "Press Releases & Media", online at: <http://investors.positiveidcorp. com/common/download/download.cfm?companyid=ABEA-3Y7P8E&fileid=390842&filekey=b885 bd17-aca9-492d-becf-661d7af3e820&filename=69263_eprint.pdf>. See also generally Kenneth R. Foster & Jan Jaeger, "Ethical Implications of Implantable Radiofrequency Identification (RFID) in Humans" (2008) 8:8 Am. J. of Bioethics 44-48.

[66] PositiveID will of course require additional FDA approvals prior to marketing these new products in the United States.

tees to better manage their diabetes.[67] Future variations of the sensor chip may also allow for the release of insulin, serving an added therapeutic function.[68]

Medical researchers are also investigating the potential use of a similar RFID technology to enhance the effectiveness of pharmaceutical treatment. An ingestible RFID tag could be attached to a pharmaceutical and, when ingested, could alert the caregiver that the drug has entered the patient's digestive tract. The hope is that this technology may even monitor internal body conditions, such as pH levels and temperature, allowing for close surveillance of the patient's drug treatment.[69]

These and other potential applications of implantable RFID technology[70] raise a number of important issues for health ethics, law and policy. We will briefly canvass three issues: (1) regulating the sale of implantable RFID microchips as medical devices; (2) informational privacy in the context of ubiquitous health monitoring; and (3) the broader implications of ICT-based medicine.[71]

Some RFID applications tend to serve a rather simple communicative purpose: to transmit information from a chip to a reader. One might therefore expect such applications to be administrative in nature, like the VeriMed patient identification system. Identifying an unconscious patient and linking her to the appropriate medical records could be an extremely useful and perhaps even a life-saving administrative application. Still, it is not therapeutic; it will not repair damaged tissue or treat an infection.

However, when an RFID device is used as part of a treatment plan — for example, to monitor blood glucose levels in a diabetic — it can take on a therapeutic role. Given its potential medical function, how will its sale be regulated?

[67]   PositiveID Corporation, Press Releases & Media, "PositiveID Corporation Files Patent for its Implantable Glucose Sensor to Continuously Monitor Glucose Levels Over an Extended Period of Time" (May 12, 2010), online at: <http://investors.positiveidcorp.com/releasedetail.cfm?ReleaseID=468996>.

[68]   See Amy Keller, "A Chip Off the Old Block: Update on Implanted Microchips" *Florida Trend* (July 1, 2010), PDF accessible through PositiveID Corporation, "Press Releases & Media", online at: <http://investors.positiveidcorp.com/common/download/download.cfm?companyid=ABEA-3Y7P8E&fileid=390842&filekey=b885bd17-aca9-492d-becf-661d7af3e820&filename=69263_eprint.pdf>.

[69]   Erick Jones *et al.*, "RFID Pharmaceutical Tracking: From Manufacturer through In Vivo Drug Delivery" (2010) 4 J. of Med. Devices 015001-1-015001-8; Hong Yu, Chun-Ming Tang & R. Bashirullah, "An Asymmetric RF Tagging IC for Ingestible Medication Compliance Capsules" (June 2009) 2009 IEEE Radio Frequency Integrated Circuits Symposium 101-104.

[70]   For example, RFID chips can be used to pinpoint lesions for biopsy in breast cancer treatment. See SenoRX, Inc. "SenoRx to Conduct Market Research on Its New Radio Frequency Identification (RFID) Tag Device at Annual Congress of the Radiological Society of North America (RSNA)" (November 27, 2009), online at: <http://investor.senorx.com/releasedetail.cfm?ReleaseID=426807>. RFID tags may also be included into surgical sponges to ensure that no sponges accidentally remain within a patient following surgery. See, *e.g.*, A. Rogers, E. Jones & D. Oleynikov, "Radio Frequency Identification (RFID) Applied to Surgical Sponges" (2007) 21 Surg. Endosc. 1235-37.

[71]   ICT is a well-known acronym for "Information and Communication Technology", a term used to capture the convergence of information technology, telecommunications and data networking into a single technology.

In Canada, the regulation of medical devices is carried out by the Therapeutic Products Directorate (TPD).[72] Like the Food and Drug Administration (FDA), the TPD ensures that all medical devices offered for sale meet basic safety and efficacy requirements. It does so by ensuring that no apparatus that falls within the definition of a "medical device" under the *Food and Drugs Act*[73] can be sold in Canada without prior approval and a corresponding licence based on the classification of the device.[74] However, prior to reaching the classification stage, RFID-enabled devices must first fall within the definition of a "medical device".

It is instructive to look at the definition set out in section 2 of the *Food and Drugs Act*:

"device" means any article, instrument, apparatus or contrivance, including any component, part or accessory thereof, manufactured, sold or represented for use in

(a) the diagnosis, treatment, mitigation or prevention of a disease, disorder or abnormal physical state, or its symptoms, in human beings or animals,

(b) restoring, correcting or modifying a body function or the body structure of human beings or animals,

(c) the diagnosis of pregnancy in human beings or animals, or

(d) the care of human beings or animals during pregnancy and at and after birth of the offspring, including care of the offspring,

and includes a contraceptive device but does not include a drug;

The various proposed and existing implantable microchips appear to fall within the first part of the definition of a "device". It is less clear, however, whether each and every RFID application would satisfy any of the second part of the definition's four disjuncts. While the VeriMed patient identification system appears to fall outside of the definition (since it is not designed to serve a therapeutic purpose),[75] PositiveID's more recently proposed glucose sensor chip

---

[72] Pursuant to a licence under the Medical Devices Regulation, SOR/98-282 established pursuant to the *Food and Drugs Act*, R.S.C. 1985, c. F-27, s. 30(*a*)(iii).

[73] R.S.C. 1985, c. F-27.

[74] Medical Devices Regulation, SOR/98-282, Sched. 1.

[75] For this determination, it is useful to turn to the description of the device in the original FDA application:

An implantable radiofrequency transponder system for patient identification and health information is a device intended to enable access to secure patient identification and corresponding health information. This system may include a passive implanted transponder, inserter, and scanner. The implanted transponder is used only to store a unique electronic identification code that is read by the scanner. The identification code is used to access patient identity and corresponding health information stored in a database.

U.S. Department of Health and Human Services, Food and Drug Administration, 21 CFR Part 880 (Docket No. 2004N-0177) "Medical Devices; General Hospital and Personal Use Devices; Classification of Implantable Radiofrequency Transponder System for Patient Identification and

would appear to meet the requirements of subsection 2(a), since the purpose of the chip is to mitigate an abnormal state of high or low insulin.

Nevertheless, the FDA approved the use of the VeriMed patient identification chip as a medical device under similar legislation in the U.S. If PositiveID were to market the VeriMed patient identification system in Canada, it would be necessary to determine whether its sale could be regulated under Canadian legislation.[76]

Determining whether an RFID is a medical device is also difficult when the technology is integrated into pharmaceuticals. After all, it is the drug, and not the chip, that treats a patient, though the microchip is meant to facilitate this treatment. Though these RFID technologies have yet to be introduced to the Canadian market, their development raises questions about how such devices will be regulated. Will Canadian legislation be equipped to deal with emerging RFID health products? Is the current regulatory regime sufficient to accommodate the merger of ICT and medicine? Such questions will gain increasing significance as the development of RFID-enabled devices progresses.

The use of implantable RFID technology to maintain ongoing communication with a patient's body also raises several privacy concerns. In particular, how will a patient ensure privacy in the information contained on the chip itself and in the data that can be generated as a result of a chip's ubiquitous monitoring of the patient's internal health?

Informational privacy is concerned with "the claim of individuals ... to determine for themselves when, how, and to what extent information about them is communicated to others".[77] While an implanted patient has voluntarily chosen to enable the chip to "communicate" information about herself with emergency care workers, a passive, unencrypted chip, like the VeriMed microchip, can be easily read by inexpensive and commercially available scanners. This undermines the implanted individual's ability to control the collection, use or disclosure of identifiable information. Though it may seem odd, easy access to the information on the implanted RFID may in fact be a feature in the design of the chip, rather than a bug.[78] However, with the strategic placement of RFID readers in door portals and other locations, this could not only allow locational tracking of implanted individuals in real-time, but also the ability to collect associated

Health Information" (December 10, 2004), online at: <http://www.fda.gov/ohrms/dockets/98fr/04-27077.htm> (FDA Classification).

[76] It remains unclear whether Canadian health legislation would regulate the sale of the VeriMed chip, given its non-therapeutic function.

[77] Alan F. Westin, *Privacy and Freedom* (New York: Atheneum, 1967) at 7.

[78] From a design perspective, those involved in testing of the VeriMed chip have expressly stated that it should be made to be easily cloned, so that another person can cause a device to imitate the signal emitted by the chip, thus "spoofing" its identity and enabling unauthorized access to the patient's health care record or whatever privileges or permissions are assigned to the *no-longer-unique* subscriber identification number. An attacker will then have less incentive to coerce victims or extract microchips from victims' bodies: John Halamka *et al.*, "The Security Implications of VeriChip Cloning", Privacy and Security in RFID Systems (March 10, 2006), online: <http://www.rsa.com/rsalabs/staff/bios/ajuels/publications/verichip/Verichip.pdf>.

information that would facilitate aggregated profiling and surveillance.[79] Security concerns also arise when an unauthorized disclosure of that identifier leads to unauthorized access to an associated health record or other health data. From an information security perspective, an unencrypted chip like the VeriMed chip is therefore not well suited as an "access control" device.[80] It is not yet clear whether the proposed, therapeutic RFID technologies will also provide implantees with the option to link their medical records to their microchips. This possibility may be particularly relevant to any therapeutic RFID products developed by PositiveID, given the company's existing interest in patient identification systems.

While it is tempting to think that obtaining an initial consent to implantation would satisfy privacy concerns, in Canada the fair information practices[81] underlying federal and provincial privacy legislation generally require those who collect information about an identifiable individual to specify before or at the time of collection the purpose for doing so, and that the information collected cannot be disclosed to or otherwise used by others without fresh consent from the data subject.[82] Fair information practice principles also require that personal data be protected by reasonable security safeguards against unauthorized access or disclosure. PositiveID's current VeriMed system for patient identification does not seem to be in accord with either of these core privacy principles, especially when one considers that the unencrypted chip allows easy collection and use of personal information without consent. Will future RFID technologies be designed in a more privacy friendly manner, or will a Privacy Commissioner launch an investigation?

The convergence of biosensors with RFID communication technology in the various proposed therapeutic RFID systems raises a second privacy concern for the patient, whose internal physical condition is continuously monitored as part of a ubiquitous health care system.[83] A detailed log of the patient's internal

---

[79] See, *e.g.*, M.G. Michael, Sarah Jean Fusco & Katina Michael, "A Research Note on Ethics in the Emerging Age of Überveillance" (2008) 31 Computer Communications 1192-99; Amelia Masters & Katina Michael, "Lend Me Your Arms: The Use and Implications of Humancentric RFID" (2007) 6 Electronic Commerce Research and Applications 29-39 at 35-6; Yang Xiao *et al.*, "Security and Privacy in RFID and Applications in Telemedicine" (2006) 44:4 IEEE Communications Magazine 64-72.

[80] J. Halamka *et al.*, "The Security Implications of VeriChip Cloning", online at: <http://www.rsa.com/rsalabs/staff/bios/ajuels/publications/verichip/Verichip.pdf>.

[81] OECD, *Guidelines on the Protection of Privacy and Transborder Flows of Personal Data* (1980); *Personal Information Protection and Electronic Documents Act*, S.C. 2000, c. 5, Sched. 1 (PIPEDA).

[82] PIPEDA, Principle 4.3.1.

[83] Ubiquitous health care systems utilize ICT in combination with sensors that monitor a patient's vitals such as pulse, temperature or compounds in the blood, to enable continuous observation of the patient. See Joowong Kim, Alastair R. Beresford & Frank Stajano, "Towards a Security Policy for Ubiquitous Health Care Systems (Position Paper)" in Frank Stajano *et al.*, eds., *Ubiquitous Convergence Technology: First International Conference, ICUCT 2006, Jeju Island, Korea, December 5-6, 2006: Revised Selected Papers* (New York: Springer, 2007) at 263-72. For an overview of ubiquitous sensor technologies, see Alexandros Pantelopoulos & Nikolaos G. Bour-

health data is created when an RFID sensor is used to perpetually monitor and report a patient's vitals, such as blood glucose levels. In this context, data collection is continuous and no longer ceases when a patient leaves the hospital, or when the patient no longer requires the data for the maintenance of his or her health.[84] The detailed logs collected by biosensors can also allow data recipients to make inferences about the activities in which the patient is engaged. Though data is not collected for this purpose, it may be impossible to avoid collecting irrelevant, but telling information about the patient's activities without compromising the function of the sensor chip.[85] From an information privacy perspective, this raises concerns about the security of the chip and whether the patient will be able to limit access to the information it generates. The potential expansion of RFID-enabled monitoring raises some critical questions for manufacturers and legislators. Will patients maintain any control over when and what information is communicated to a caretaker or others? How will such information be protected?[86]

Finally, the emerging uses of implantable RFID technology reflect a shift from its current administrative purposes (*e.g.*, identifying patients and linking them to their medical records; tracking hospital equipment) to applications that are therapeutic in nature (*e.g.*, replacing lost function in the pancreas by linking a sensor device to an internal insulin pump). In some cases, emerging applications go even further, shifting toward the development of medical technologies that not only treat but enhance the human body.[87] For example, cochlear implants are gaining in popularity among those with hearing impairments, and it is not difficult to imagine that they will one day enhance rather than merely restore human hearing.[88] While repairing hearing function, why not include within such devices the capability to stream voice transmissions wirelessly so that one does not have to carry or wear phones or portable music players? Such devices are already being marketed in this way.[89]

In the context of a surveillance society that may soon require all telecommunications service providers to build a global intercept capability into all

---

bakis, "A Survey on Wearable Sensor-Based Systems for Health Monitoring and Prognosis" (2010) 40 IEEE Transactions on Systems, Man, and Cybernetics — Part C: Applications and Reviews 1-12.

[84] Kim *et al.*, "Towards a Security Policy for Ubiquitous Health Care Systems (Position Paper)", *ibid.*, at 265.

[85] *Ibid.*, at 266.

[86] Protection of information may be especially relevant given the potential value that insurance companies will see in mining the data and the potential implications this may have for patients. *Ibid.*

[87] See, *e.g.*, Ian Kerr & James Wishart, "A Tsunami Wave of Science": How the Technologies of Transhumanist Medicine are Shifting Canada's Health Research Agenda" (2008) Special Ed. Health L.J. 13-40.

[88] One of the better currently available products is in fact marketed as "HiResolution Bionic Ear System", online at: <http://www.advancedbionics.com/CMS/Products/Harmony-System.aspx>.

[89] See, *e.g.*, Advanced Bionics, "Harmony HiResolution Bionic Ear System", online at: <http://www.advancedbionics.com/UserFiles/File/3-01131-A_ConsumerReliabilty_Report-FNL.pdf>.

communications devices (so that law enforcement can "listen in" under certain circumstances),[90] the myriad of issues that arise transcend health law and policy. As we continue to experiment with implantable devices,[91] and as medicine becomes more and more dependent on wireless and network technologies to manage these devices, there will be an increasing need to understand the human-machine merger, the question of technological enhancement and all of the ethical and legal issues that are bound to ensue as a result of implantable radio frequency microchips.

In the section that follows, we turn our focus to a very different technology that also strikes at the core of what it means to be human, one that has stirred much controversy while, at the same time, generated tremendous potential for treating many serious illnesses.

C.   EMBRYONIC STEM CELLS

Few areas of research have generated as much controversy as embryonic stem cell research. It is a topic that has received an incredible amount of media attention and policy analysis. It has been the subject of legislative debates throughout the world and it has divided the United Nations.[92] But despite almost a decade of intense policy deliberations, there remains little international consensus about how this area should be regulated.[93]

Why has stem cell research caused so much controversy? The focal issue is clearly the moral status of the embryo. While there are a variety of complex issues associated with this field of study — including concern about the consent processes used to obtain embryos for research;[94] the potential risks to women of

---

[90]   Though it died on the Order Page with the fall of the Liberal government in 2005, Bill C-74, *An Act regulating telecommunications facilities to facilitate the lawful interception of information transmitted by means of those facilities and respecting the provision of telecommunications subscriber information*, 1st Sess., 38th Parl., 2005 (not passed) has been resurrected. Bill C-285, of the same name, underwent its first reading on March 3, 2010 (3rd Sess., 40th Parl., 2010).

[91]   For example, see the AbioCor, an implantable replacement heart manufactured by AbioMed, online at: <http://www.abiomed.com/products/heart_replacement.cfm>.

[92]   "UN gives up cloning ban" CBC News (November 19, 2004), online at: <http://www.cbsnews.com/stories/2005/02/18/tech/main675124.shtml>.

[93]   Timothy Caulfield *et al.*, "International Stem Cell Environments: A World of Difference" (2009) Nature Reports Stem Cells doi:10.1038/stemcells.2009.61; A. Elstner *et al.*, "The Changing Landscape of European and International Regulation of Embryonic Stem Cell Research" (2009) 2:2 Stem Cell Research 101-107; Rosario Isasi & Bartha Knoppers, "Mind the Gap: Policy Approaches to Embryonic Stem Cell and Cloning Research in 50 Countries" (2006) 13 Euro. J. Health L. 9-26. See also Shaun Pattinson & Timothy Caulfield, "Variations and Voids: The Regulation of Human Cloning Around the World" (2004) 5 B.M.C. Medical Ethics 9; Lori P. Knowles, "A Regulatory Patchwork – Human ES Cell Research Oversight" (2004) 22 Nature Biotech. 157.

[94]   See Bernard Lo *et al.*, "Informed Consent in Human Oocyte, Embryo, and Embryonic Stem Cell Research" (2004) 82 Fertility and Sterility 559; Henry Greely, "Moving Human Embryonic Stem Cells from Legislature to Lab: Remaining Legal and Ethical Questions" (2006) Public Library of Science Medicine e143; and Margaret Munro, "Ethicist Repeats Call to Halt Embryo Donations" *National Post* (June 28, 2006) at A7.

lines of research, like human cloning, that could require a large supply of oo-cytes;[95] and the patenting of embryonic stem cell lines[96] — the issues related to the moral status of the embryo have been the primary cause of the regulatory patchwork that now exists throughout the world.[97]

Since 1998, when the first human embryonic stem cell lines were created,[98] there has been a great deal of excitement about the scientific and therapeutic potential of stem cells. Embryonic stem cells have the capacity to form almost any tissue in the body (and are, therefore, known as "pluripotent").[99] It is hoped that scientists will one day be able to coax them into becoming tissues that could be used to treat a wide variety of serious illnesses, including Parkinson's disease, diabetes and heart disease. The speculation about prospective benefits has, no doubt, been fuelled by the large degree of hype that has surrounded the entire area.[100] Nevertheless, few would disagree with the suggestion that the therapeutic potential is real, albeit uncertain and, perhaps, a long way off.

However, for those who believe that a human embryo has full moral status, regardless of how early its stage of biological development,[101] no amount of therapeutic potential will justify its destruction. As such, they remain steadfastly opposed to embryonic stem cell research. To cite just one example, the Catholic Church has taken a consistent position against this work. Indeed, a prominent Cardinal has stated: "Destroying an embryo is equivalent to abortion. ... Ex-

---

[95]   Research that depends upon human oocytes will likely require a large supply of oocytes from women, exposing them to pressure to undergo the hormonal and surgical treatment to retrieve those oocytes. Francoise Baylis, "For Love or Money? The Saga of Korean Women Who Provided Eggs for Stem Cell Research" (2009) 30:5 Theoretical Medicine and Bioethics 385-96.

[96]   Timothy Caulfield, "Stem Cell Patents and Social Controversy: A Speculative View From Canada" (2006) 7 Medical L. Int'l 219-32.

[97]   Lori P. Knowles, "A Regulatory Patchwork" – Human ES Cell Research Oversight (2004) 22 Nature Biotech. 157.

[98]   James Thomson *et al.*, "Embryonic Stem Cell Lines Derived from Human Blastocysts" (1998) 282 Science 1145; Abdallah S. Daar & Lorraine Sheremeta, "The Science of Stem Cells: Some Implications for Law and Policy" (2002) 11 Health L. Rev. 5.

[99]   See Oonagh Corrigan *et al.*, *Ethical Legal and Social Issues in Stem Cell Research and Therapy* (briefing paper, Cambridge Genetics Knowledge Park, March 2006) at 1:

   Stem cells are cells that have the potential both for self-renewal and to differentiate into specialized cell types. Stem cells found in the early mammalian embryo, at around 5-7 days after fertilisation, are able to give rise to all the different cell types of the organism. These embryonic stem (ES) cells are said to be "pluripotent."

[100] See, *e.g.*, N. Theise, "Stem Cell Research: Elephants in the Room" (2003) 78 Mayo Clinic Proceedings 1004-1009. The hype surrounding stem cell therapies risks raising unrealistic public expectations, which may generate a backlash against public investment in the science. See, *e.g.*, Timothy Caulfield, "Stem Cell Research and Economic Promises" (2010) 38:2 J.L. Med. & Ethics 303-13. In addition, there is growing concern over stem cell tourism and the vulnerability of patients to unproven and possibly risky stem cell therapies. See D. Lau *et al.*, "Stem Cell Clinics Online: The Direct-to-Consumer Portrayal of Stem Cell Medicine" (2008) 3 Cell Stem Cell 591-94; Aaron D. Levine, "Stem Cell Tourism: Assessing the State of Knowledge" (2010) 7:2 Scripted, online at: <http://www.law.ed.ac.uk/ahrc/script-ed/vol7-2/levine.pdf>.

[101] Stem cells are generally removed from the embryo at a very early stage of development, when the embryo is only a cluster of cells called a "blastocyst".

communication is valid for the women, the doctors and researchers who destroy embryos."[102]

Despite the enduring presence of such sentiments, they seem to represent a minority position in Canada where a majority of the public supports embryonic stem cell research.[103] More significantly, a majority approve of stem cell research *under any circumstance*, as long as it is appropriately regulated.[104] Nevertheless, it seems likely that there will always remain a sector of society that will not endorse the use of human embryos for research purposes, thus making it impossible to craft policy that will be entirely satisfactory to all.

Indeed, it has been noted that individuals with extreme positions at either end of the continuum have done their best to try to portray the debate in terms that will help their cause.[105] For those who favour the work, this means emphasizing the potential scientific and health benefits. For those who oppose the work, the moral issues have remained the focus of debate. In the U.S., for example, some have speculated that a religious agenda has played a role in the tone of

---

[102] News, "Prominent Cardinal Attacks Science Behind Stem Cell Research" *New Scientist* (July 14, 2006) at 5. See also Elisabeth Rosenthal, "Excommunication is sought for stem cell researchers" *The New York Times* (July 1, 2006), online at: <http://www.nytimes.com/2006/07/01/world/europe/01vatican.html?ex=1309406400&en=0e0de4c51c312ccb&ei=5088&partner=rssnyt&emc=rss>. Techniques that use embryos but do not destroy them (such as the removal and use of single cells from early-stage embryos) are also controversial: see, *e.g.*, Nicholas Wade, "Stem cell news could intensify debate" *The New York Times* (August 24, 2006).

[103] Decima Research and the Canadian Biotechnology Secretariat, "A Canada-U.S. Public Opinion Research Study on Emerging Technologies, Report of Findings" (March 31, 2005), online at: <http://www.bioportal.gc.ca/CMFiles/E-Wave13FG49REA-5202005-3052.pdf>; Linda Lyons, "Stem Cell Research Morally OK in Britain, Canada *and* U.S." Gallup (October 19, 2004), online at: <http://www.gallup.com/poll/13681/stem-cell-research-morally-britain-canada-us.aspx>.

[104] Norma Greenway, "Canadians embrace stem cell research" *Ottawa Citizen* (October 14, 2003). See also Jeff Walker, "Report on a Study of Emerging Technologies in Canada and the U.S. 'Prevailing Views, Awareness and Familiarity'" in *First Impressions: Understanding Public Views on Emerging Technologies* (Genome Prairie, September 2005) at 6-19. This finding is consistent with U.S. data: see, *e.g.*, Kathy L. Hudson, Joan Scott & Ruth Faden, *Values in Conflict: Public Attitudes on Embryonic Stem Cell Research* (Genetics and Public Policy Center, October 2005). The emphasis on tighter regulations is attributed to concerns over the efficacy of existing regulatory agencies and processes, and the potential influence of corporate interests. For an interesting comparison of Canadian and U.S. views, see Edna Einsiedel, *First Impressions: Understanding Public Views on Emerging Technologies* (Genome Alberta, Prepared for the Canadian Biotechnology Secretariat, 2005). For a comprehensive review of European public opinion, see George Gaskell *et al.*, "Europeans and Biotechnology in 2005: Patterns and Trends" (May 2006) 64.3 Eurobarometer (a report to the European Commission's Directorate-General for Research).

[105] Matthew Nisbet, "The Competition for Worldviews: Values, Information, and Public Support for Stem Cell Research" (2005) 17 Int'l J. Public Opinion Research 92:

[A] scientifically literate public is assumed [to] be more appreciative of science and technology, and more supportive of science as an institution. In contrast, religious research opponents have sought to mobilize the public by attempting to define stem cell research in the media coverage as a moral issue, emphasizing certain considerations that are likely to promote public opposition to research.

the national bioethics discourse, skewing it toward a neo-conservative ethos.[106] Though not as dominant as in the U.S., religion has also played a role in the direction of policy development in Canada and the United Kingdom.[107] We are left, then, with a seemingly irreconcilable polarity of positions on the issue of embryonic stem cell research.

In 2007, researchers announced the creation of induced pluripotent stem (IPS) cells.[108] The technique involved reprogramming adult somatic cells (such as skin cells) so that they returned to a pluripotent state. The discovery of IPS cells was met with great excitement, in part because it seemed to offer a way to obtain pluripotent stem cell lines without destroying embryos. In addition, it represented a possible way to create self-compatible cell lines for transplanting into patients without engaging in therapeutic cloning and consuming large numbers of the human oocytes that must be obtained at some risk from women.[109] Nonetheless, cautionary voices pointed out that research on embryonic stem cells ought to continue in tandem with research on IPS cells given that the two forms of cell may have unknown and possibly important differences.[110] Furthermore, it is not entirely clear that IPS cells fully resolve the division over the morality of embryonic stem cell research from the perspective of those objecting to that research. For example, IPS cells have been successfully used to create live mouse pups, raising questions about whether they attract the same moral status as embryonic stem cells based on their potentiality.[111] In addition, another possible objection is that IPS cell research is complicit in embryonic stem cell research given its historical and continuing reliance on embryonic stem cell research.[112] The development of IPS cells illustrates the way in which the ethical debate around a particular science or technology can both influence the direction

---

[106] R.A. Charo, "Passing on the Right: Conservative Bioethics is Closer Than It Appears" (2004) 2 J.L. Med. & Ethics 307-14.

[107] A. Plomer, "Beyond the HFE Act 1990: The Regulation of Stem Cell Research in the U.K." (2002) 10 Med. L. Rev. 132-63; M. Deckha, "The Gendered Politics of Embryonic Stem Cell Research in the USA and Canada: An American Overlap and Canadian Disconnect" (2008) 16:1 Med. L. Rev. 52-84.

[108] K. Takahashi *et al.*, "Induction of Pluripotent Stem Cells from Adult Human Fibroblasts by Defined Factors" (2007) 131:5 Cell 861-72.

[109] Herbert Gottweis & Stephen Minger, "IPS Cells and the Politics of Promise" (2008) 26:3 Nature Biotechnology 271-72; C.T. Scott & R.A. Reijo Pera, "The Road to Pluripotence: The Research Response to the Embryonic Stem Cell Debate" (2008) 17(R.1) Hum. Molecular Genetics R3-R9.

[110] Gottweis & Minger, "IPS Cells and the Politics of Promise", *ibid.* As time goes on, researchers are bringing to light ways in which IPS cells do indeed differ in potentially important ways from embryonic stem cells. See Jose M. Polo *et al.*, "Cell Type of Origin Influences the Molecular and Functional Properties of Mouse Induced Pluripotent Cells" (2010) 28 Nature Biotechnology 848-855; K. Kim *et al.*, "Epigenetic Memory in Induced Pluripotent Stem Cells" (July 19, 2010) Nature doi:10.1038/nature09342.

[111] See, *e.g.*, K. Devolder, "To Be, or Not To Be? Are Induced Pluripotent Stem Cells Potential Babies, and Does it Matter?" (2009) 10:12 EMBO Reports 1285-87.

[112] Mark T. Brown, "Moral Complicity in Induced Pluripotent Stem Cell Research" (2009) 19:1 Kennedy Inst. Ethics J. 1-22.

of scientific research as well as itself be transformed by novel developments in the science or technology.

This underlying division on the morality of embryonic stem cell research has led to a diversity of regulatory approaches.[113] For example, some countries, such as Ireland, Italy, Germany and Austria, do not allow the use of human embryos for the purpose of stem cell research.[114] Other jurisdictions, such as the U.K., Sweden, California and Israel have a more permissive environment, allowing a wide range of research activities, including the creation of embryos for research purposes and "therapeutic cloning".[115]

Where does Canada sit on the spectrum of regulatory responses? In 2004, the Canadian Parliament passed the *Assisted Human Reproduction Act*.[116] It contains significant criminal sanctions against a number of scientific activities that are permitted in some jurisdictions, including the creation of embryos specifically for research purposes and "therapeutic cloning".[117] The Act also contained a structure for the regulation of assisted reproductive services in Canada, which was, in some ways, a cautious middle ground approach that allowed research on embryos that had already been created via *in vitro* fertilization (IVF) for the purposes of reproduction.[118] The regulatory scheme contemplated that as long as the regulatory requirements had been satisfied, which included compliance with specific consent guidelines, research on these human embryos could occur.[119] In late 2010, the Supreme Court of Canada ruled in a split decision that much of the regulation of assisted reproductive services (including those provisions regulating the research use of surplus human embryos created for reproductive pur-

---

[113] "[T]he determination of the moral status of the human embryo influences possible responses to questions of the permissibility of, restrictions on, and prohibitions on embryonic research": Rosario Isasi & Bartha Knoppers, "Mind the Gap: Policy Approaches to Embryonic Stem Cell and Cloning Research in 50 Countries" (2006) 13 Euro. J. Health L.9 at 24.

[114] Many of these countries have a religious or historical precedent that, in part, informed the adoption of a more restrictive research environment — such as the role of the Catholic Church in Ireland and Italy. See, *e.g.*, Shaun Pattinson & Timothy Caulfield, "Variations and Voids: The Regulation of Human Cloning Around the World" (2004) 5 B.M.C. Medical Ethics 9.

[115] For a detailed description of regulatory positions throughout the world, see generally Rosario Isasi & Bartha Knoppers, "Mind the Gap: Policy Approaches to Embryonic Stem Cell and Cloning Research in 50 Countries" (2006) 13 Euro J. Health L.9 at 13; and Pattinson & Caulfield, "Variations and Voids: The Regulation of Human Cloning Around the World", *ibid.*, at 9.

[116] S.C. 2004, c. 2. In December 2010, the Supreme Court of Canada ruled that several key sections of the Act are unconstitutional on the basis that the subject matter is a matter of provincial rather than federal jurisdiction (*Reference re Assisted Human Reproduction Act*, [2010] S.C.J. No. 61, 2010 SCC 61 (S.C.C.)).

[117] *Assisted Human Reproduction Act*, S.C. 2004, c. 2, s. 5.

[118] *Ibid.* Prior to being struck down as unconstitutional, s. 40(2) empowered the Assisted Human Reproduction Agency to issue licences authorizing the use of *in vitro* embryos for research if the Agency determined that the use was necessary for the purpose of the research.

[119] *Ibid.*, s. 40(3.1), which has now been struck down, provided: "The Agency shall not issue a licence under subsection (1) for embryonic stem cell research unless it has received the written consent of the original gamete providers and the embryo provider in accordance with the *Human Pluripotent Stem Cell Research Guidelines* released by the Canadian Institutes of Health Research in March, 2002, as specified in the regulations."

poses) was an unconstitutional incursion into provincial legislative jurisdiction. The criminal prohibitions on the creation of *in vitro* embryos for research purposes and on cloning were not challenged, and so remain intact.

But even a middle ground approach of the type that was attempted in the federal *Assisted Human Reproduction Act* is, for some, less than satisfactory. When immutable moral convictions are engaged, compromise is not always an option. The scientific advances that have occurred in the area of stem cell research force us to confront the question of what type of consensus is required as a prerequisite to the development of social policy.[120] To what degree should a particular view of the moral status of embryonic life dictate national policy on the use of stem cells?[121] When is it appropriate for the government to pass laws that may restrict academic research?[122]

In the section that follows, we will investigate the law and policy implications of scientific rather than moral uncertainty. What are the appropriate regulatory responses to the development of technologies so powerful that we are not currently in a position to predict or evaluate their potential danger?

D. NANOMEDICINE

What would happen if modern science were capable of healing the body at the molecular level, one atom at a time? When Nobel physicist Richard Feynman first posed a generalized version of this question to the American Physical Society in his famous 1959 address,[123] he dreamed of "the great future", challenging his colleagues to think big by thinking small:

> The principles of physics, as far as I can see, do not speak against the possibility of maneuvering things atom by atom. [I]t would be, in principle, possible (I think) for a physicist to synthesize any chemical substance that a chemist writes down. How? Put the atoms down where the chemist says, and so you make the substance.[124]

---

[120] See Rosario Isasi & Bartha Knoppers, "Mind the Gap: Policy Approaches to Embryonic Stem Cell and Cloning Research in 50 Countries" (2006) 13 Euro. J. Health L.9 at 25: "Can we address such divisive issues while holding intact our democratic principles and socio-cultural values?"

[121] See, *e.g.*, Norma Greenway, "Jewish, Islamic Faiths Support Controversial Stem Cell Research" (February 29, 2003) at A3.

[122] For an interesting debate about academic freedom in the context of "therapeutic cloning", see Jocelyn Downie, Jennifer Llewellyn & Françoise Baylis, "A Constitutional Defence of the Federal Ban on Human Cloning for Research Purposes" (2005) 31 Queen's L.J. 353; and Barbara Billingsley & Timothy Caulfield, "The Regulation of Science and the Charter of Rights: Would a Ban on Non-Reproductive Human Cloning Unjustifiably Violate Freedom of Expression?" (2004) 29 Queen's L.J. 647-79.

[123] Richard Feynman, "There's Plenty of Room at the Bottom: An Invitation to Enter a New Field of Physics" (lecture, American Physical Society, California Institute of Technology, December 29, 1959) (1960) Engineering and Science 22, online at: <http://www.zyvex.com/nanotech/feynman.html>.

[124] *Ibid.*

Feynman's vision inspired in the subsequent five decades theoretical, experimental and applied scientists from various disciplines to conduct research collectively known today as *nanotechnology*.

Although Feynman's bottom-up approach, subsequently elaborated by Drexler and others,[125] focuses on developing an ability to program and manipulate matter with molecular precision, the term "nanotechnology" has broadened to include top-down[126] technologies that operate on the nano-scale.[127] Debates concerning the feasibility of the bottom-up approach linger.[128] If achievable,

> [f]ull fledged nanotechnology promises nothing less than complete control over the physical structure of matter — the same kind of control over the molecular and structural make-up of physical objects that a word processor provides over the form and content of a text. The implications of such capabilities are significant: to dramatize only slightly, they are comparable to producing a 747 or an ocean liner from the mechanical equivalent of a single fertilized egg.[129]

However, most publicly funded nanotechnology research involves a much less grandiose, much more traditional, top-down model of science (only done on the nano-scale). Even if the "assembler breakthrough" never occurs, many governments are investing heavily in nanotechnology,[130] expecting that it will address a

---

[125] See, *e.g.*, K. Eric Drexler, *Engines of Creation: The Coming Era of Nanotechnology* (New York: Anchor Press/Doubleday, 1986); Eric Drexler, Chris Peterson & Gayle Pergamit, *Unbounding the Future: The Nanotechnology Revolution* (New York: William Morrow and Co., 1991).

[126] .A top-down approach builds things by taking existing matter and reducing or removing unwanted material, *e.g.*, sawing a piece of wood or using a chemical reagent. A bottom-up approach would build matter atom by atom, or cell by cell. According to Drexler's vision, nanomachines known as "assemblers" would be programmed to build larger, more complex materials similar to the manner in which a human being results from a single cell: see K. Eric Drexler, *Engines of Creation: The Coming Era of Nanotechnology* (New York: Anchor Press/Doubleday, 1986) at 14.

[127] Which is an order of magnitude smaller than microtechnology. A nanometer (nm) is one-billionth of a meter, which is about 3 to 6 atoms in length; the thickness of a human hair is said to be 50,000 to 100,000 nm. See Center for Responsible Nanotechnology, "Nanotechnology Glossary", online at: <http://www.crnano.org/crnglossary.htm>.

[128] See, *e.g.*, Ian Kerr & Goldie Bassi, "Not Much Room? Nanotechnology, Networks and the Politics of Dancing" (2004) 12 Health L.J. 103.

[129] Glen Harlan Reynolds, "Forward to the Future: Nanotechnology and Regulatory Policy" (November 2002) Pacific Research 4, online at: <http://www.pacificresearch.org/docLib/2002_Forward_to_Nanotech.pdf>.

[130] It is estimated that, as of 2008, global funding for nanotechnology amounted to approximately USD $25 billion. See AZoNanotechnology, "Global Funding for Nanotechnology Amounts to over $25 Billion in 2008", online at: <http://www.azonano.com/news.asp?newsID=6688>. Worldwide investments are expected to grow, given that nanotechnology accounted for approximately $50 billion in spending worldwide in 2006. The U.S. National Science Foundation has estimated that nanotechnology will be a trillion-dollar market by 2015. See The Nanoethics Group, "The Nanotech Market", online at: <http://www.nanoethics.org/investments.html>. In the United States, according to the National Nanotechnology Initiative, "the Federal funding for nanotechnology has increased from approximately $464 million in 2001 to nearly $1.5 billion for the 2009 fiscal year. Private industry is investing at least as much as the government, according to estimates": see National Nanotechnology Initiative, "FAQ's: Nanotechnology", online at:

broad range of environmental issues, drastically reduce energy consumption, increase food production, create new and better information technologies and consumer products, amplify the precision and efficacy of military devices and weapons, and dramatically advance medicine's ability to cure and prevent diseases.[131] Indeed, the latter area of research is where some of the most prolific and high profile uses of nanotechnology to date are taking place.

Nanomedicine, as it is sometimes called,[132] aims to develop molecular tools that will diagnose, treat and prevent diseases or traumatic injuries. With significantly enhanced levels of control, it promises to eclipse the profit potential of modern pharmaceuticals. Research and development will focus on novel forms of therapy, new methods of drug delivery,[133] and techniques for improving imaging and other medical diagnostics.[134] Nanotechnology is being particularly lauded for its potential to advance the treatment of cancer.[135] The merger of nanotechnology with personalized medicine also holds promise for future bio-

---

<http://www.nano.gov/html/facts/faqs.html>. The European Commission earmarked €3.5 billion for nanotechnology research between 2007 and 2013, up from €1.3 billion between 2003 and 2006: see European Commission "FP7: Tomorrow's Answers Start Today" (2006) at 9, online at: <http://ec.europa.eu/research/fp7/pdf/fp7-factsheets_en.pdf>. In Canada, over $83 million in federal funds were spent or committed for expenditure on projects related to nanotechnology in the 2008–2009 fiscal year. This amount includes $746,000 allocated by Environment Canada to facilitate the development and implementation of a regulatory program to manage nanomaterials, research on the ecological effects of nanomaterials, and investigation of the sustainable use of nanotechnology. Likewise, the Industry Sector of Industry Canada allocated $49,504.30; the National Research Council Canada (NRC) allocated $34,981,000; the Natural Sciences and Engineering Research Council of Canada (NSERC) awarded close to $39 million to researchers and institutions across Canada; the Canada Foundation for Innovation (CFI) Nanotech Award allocated $5,146,177; and Natural Resources Canada (NRCan) allocated $3,257,000 to various nanotechnology related research and development projects. For a more detailed accounting of this expenditure, see House of Commons of Canada, 40th Parl., 3rd Sess., No. 49, Sessional Paper No. 8555-403-177 (2010).

[131] See, *e.g.*, Robert A. Freitas, Jr., "What is Nanomedicine?" (2005) 51 Disease a Month 325; The Nanoethics Group, "The Good", online at: <http://www.nanoethics.org/good.html>.

[132] For a comprehensive introduction to various applications in nanomedicine, see Robert A. Freitas, Jr., "What is Nanomedicine?", *ibid.* See also Kewal K. Jain, *Handbook of Nanomedicine* (Totowa, NJ: Humana Press, 2008).

[133] Including methods that have the ability to target selected cells or receptors within the body: U. Pison *et al.*, "Nanomedicine for Respiratory Diseases" (2006) 533 Eur. J. Pharmacology 343-44. See also Raj Bawa, "Nanoparticle-based Therapeutics in Humans: A Survey" (2008) 5 Nanotech L. & Bus. 135-56.

[134] European Science Foundation (ESF), *Nanomedicine: An ESF European Medical Research Councils (EMRC) Forward Look Report* (ESF, 2005) at 7, online at: <http://www.esf.org/publications.html>. For a discussion of nano-diagnostics in a respiratory context, see U. Pison *et al.*, "Nanomedicine for Respiratory Diseases" (2006) 533 Eur. J. Pharmacology 342-43.

[135] See, *e.g.*, K.K. Jain, "Nanomedicine: Application of Nanobiotechnology in Medical Practice" (2008) 17 Medical Principles and Practice 89-101. For an example of Canadian research in this area, see Zhichao Fang *et al.*, "Direct Profiling of Cancer Biomarkers in Tumor Tissue using a Multiplexed Nanostructured Microelectrode Integrated Circuit" (2009) 3 ACS Nano 3207-13. See also "Microchip Uses Nanotechnology to Detect Cancer" CBC News (September 29, 2009), online at: <http://www.cbc.ca/health/story/2009/09/28/tech-nanotechnology-cancer-chip.html#ixzz0v2YOhRRG>.

medical advancement.[136] Personalized medicine involves the use of molecular biomarkers, such as genes, to tailor medical treatments specifically for an individual patient.[137] These unique biomarkers typically occur at the nano-scale. Nanotechnologies therefore allow for more precise targeting and tailoring of diagnostics and treatments to the individual. For example, imagine using microscopic delivery molecules to transport healthy versions of defective genes to ailing cells in order to facilitate gene therapy, administered through a skin cream or adhesive patch, thus eliminating the need for painful injections. Such technology is currently being investigated by Canadian researchers.[138]

Nanomedicine technologies are not only theoretical, some have already been put to use in hospitals. For example, the medical dressing ACTICOAT, originally created in Canada, is one of the world's first commercially successful applications of nanomedicine.[139] ACTICOAT medical bandages contain silver nanoparticles that work to heal wounds by killing bacteria, reducing inflammation and preventing further infection.[140] The nano-scale of these particles allows them to dissolve in liquid, such as wound fluid, and release pure silver atoms and highly oxidized silver atoms — something that would not be possible with regular silver.[141] These atoms are thought to have strong anti-inflammatory and anti-microbial properties.[142] Both Health Canada and the FDA have approved the ACTICOAT for commercial sale.[143] ACTICOAT serves as an example of the challenge of regulating nanotechnology products. While silver has long been thought to have medicinal properties,[144] we do not know exactly how these silver nanoparticles might affect the body, or what their long-term consequences might be.[145]

---

[136] G.E. Marchant, "Small is Beautiful: What Can Nanotechnology Do for Personalized Medicine?" (2009) 7 Current Pharmacogenomics and Personalized Medicine 231 at 232.

[137] *Ibid.*

[138] Canadian Institutes of Health Research, *Regenerative Medicine and Nanomedicine: Investing Today in the Promise of Tomorrow*, 2d ed. (Ottawa: CIHR, 2009) at 16, online at: <http://www.cihr-irsc.gc.ca/e/documents/regenerative_medicine_2_e.pdf>.

[139] Claudia Sammer & Donald Rumball, "Nanotechnology and Advanced Materials Companies 2008" *Cool Companies Special Issue: Nanotechnology in Alberta* 4:1 (2008-2009) 10-34, online at: <http://www.coolcompaniesmag.com/wp/wp-content/uploads/2008/05/cc41_albertananoand advancedmaterialcompanies_72pdi.pdf>.

[140] Smith & Nephew, "ACTICOAT: Product Information", online at: <http://wound.smith-nephew.com/ca_en/node.asp?NodeId=3114>; Sammer & Rumball, "Nanotechnology and Advanced Materials Companies 2008", *ibid.*, at 22.

[141] Sammer & Rumball, "Nanotechnology and Advanced Materials Companies 2008", *ibid.*, at 22; Bishara S. Atiyeh *et al.*, "Effect of Silver on Burn Wound Infection Control and Healing: Review of the Literature" (2007) 33 Burns 139 at 142.

[142] Sammer & Rumball, "Nanotechnology and Advanced Materials Companies 2008", *ibid.*, at 22.

[143] Smith & Nephew, "Smith & Nephew Announces Launch of ACTICOAT Flex Wound Care Products in the USA" (July 29, 2009), online at: <http://global.smith-nephew.com/master/30020.htm>.

[144] Bishara S. Atiyeh *et al.*, "Effect of Silver on Burn Wound Infection Control and Healing: Review of the Literature" (2007) 33 Burns 139 at 139.

[145] The particles may have consequences for the patient: see, *e.g.*, Atiyeh *et al.*, "Effect of Silver on Burn Wound Infection Control and Healing: Review of the Literature", *ibid.*, at 145; Marija Trop

Like the elixir of Theuth, nanomedicine offers much promise but also potential peril. The unpredictability of nano-scale products and applications raise numerous health and safety issues. This is not uncommon since, by definition, new technologies have not been subject to long-term clinical trials. But there seems to be a crucial distinction between nano and other new technologies. Given their size, nanomaterials are governed not by the laws of gravity but the laws of quantum mechanics.[146] Quantum mechanics in some cases require a non-intuitive understanding of various scientific relationships:

> Some of these dependencies are scientifically intuitive such as the relationship between properties of nanomaterials and their size, composition, impurities (both internally and superficially), the surface chemistry (including passivating agents) and degree of agglomeration. Other dependencies such as shape, change, zeta potential and phase seem less intuitive. And this is just the tip of the iceberg. To complicate matters further, many of the dependencies are intrinsically linked.[147]

One, therefore, cannot always extrapolate from existing knowledge about the behaviour of material properties on a macro-scale. For example, some materials that are inert at the macro-scale are reactive at the nano-scale.[148] A similar difficulty exists when it comes to the relationship between size and phase.[149] Here, nanotechnology is *pharmakon* in the Derridean sense discussed at the outset of this chapter: the remedy may become the poison.[150] The inability to accurately predict what will transpire at the nano-scale can be further exacerbated by changes in temperature, pressure, humidity and the like.

Given its currently unpredictable nature, there is an ongoing debate about the need for a unique regulatory scheme for nanotechnology. In the U.S. context, some have argued that the FDA is not particularly well-equipped to deal with many of the forthcoming challenges of nanotechnology. In addition to lacking the necessary complement of FDA scientists with sufficient expertise to evaluate new products, many nano-applications do not easily fit within existing FDA categories.[151] Others, however, see no need for a new regulatory schema. They

---

et al., "Silver-Coated Dressing Acticoat Caused Raised Liver Enzymes and Argyria-like Symptoms in Burn Patient" (2006) 60 J. Trauma. 648-52; or consequences for the environment: see, e.g., P.V. Asharani et al., "Toxicity of Silver Nanoparticles in Zebrafish Models" (2008) 19 Nanotechnology 255102.

146 Mutaz B. Habal, "Nanosize, Mega-Impact, Potential for Medical Applications of Nanotechnology" (2006) 17 J. Craniofacial Surgery 3.

147 Amanda S. Barnard, "Nanohazards: Knowledge is our First Defence" (2006) 5 Nature Materials 245.

148 *Ibid.*, at 246.

149 *Ibid.*

150 Jacques Derrida, "Plato's Pharmacy" in *Dissemination*, Barbara Johnson, trans. (Chicago: University of Chicago Press, 1981).

151 See, e.g., John Miller, "Beyond Biotechnology: FDA Regulation of Nanomedicine" (2003) 4 Columbia Sci. & Tech. L. Rev. 1. See also Kevin Rollins, "Nanobiotechnology Regulation: A Proposal for Self-Regulation with Limited Oversight" (2009) 6 Nanotech. L. & Bus. 221-49. Because nanomedical research is often highly specialized, it may be difficult for regulatory bodies

point out that, despite the recent buzz, research in nanomedicine is not new. Various such applications have obtained FDA approval for more than a decade.[152] The FDA recently developed a task force to consider nanotechnology regulation.[153] The Task Force has recommended adapting the current regulatory regime to new nanotechnologies, rather than creating nanotechnology-specific legislation.[154]

The same debate, of course, applies in Canada. On March 10, 2010, New Democratic Party Member of Parliament Peter Julian tabled Bill C-494, *An Act to Amend the Canadian Environmental Protection Act, 1999 (Nanotechnology).*[155] This amendment would begin to define a national strategy to guide the development of nano products.[156] It includes precautionary measures, such as the establishment of a national nanotechnology inventory and the development of risk assessment procedures for new nanotechnology products entering the market.[157] The Government Standing Committee on Health has also been tasked with studying the benefits and risks of nanotechnology in Canada.[158] It remains to be seen whether any regulatory amendments will be adopted.[159]

---

to find independent experts with the appropriate knowledge-base to oversee the regulation of new technologies. The researcher may be the only person qualified to make regulatory assessments. For this reason, Rollins proposes developing a legislative framework that places liability for unknown hazards on the manufacturers and distributers of nanomedicine, thus encouraging a regime of self-regulation.

[152] See, *e.g.*, Nuala Moran, "Nanomedicine Lacks Recogniton in Europe" (2006) 24 Nature Biotech. 121, where she quotes Mike Eaton of UCB Celltech as stating: "I'm not sure you need new regulation. Nanomedicines are not new; they have been getting regulatory approval for ten years."

[153] Nanotechnology Task Force, online at: <http://www.fda.gov/ScienceResearch/SpecialTopics/Nanotechnology/NanotechnologyTaskForce/default.htm>.

[154] FDA, "Nanotechnology: A Report of the U.S. Food and Drug Administration Nanotechnology Task Force" (July 25, 2007), online at: <http://www.fda.gov/ScienceResearch/SpecialTopics/Nanotechnology/NanotechnologyTaskForceReport2007/default.htm>.

[155] Bill C-494, *An Act to Amend the Canadian Environmental Protection Act, 1999 (Nanotechnology)*, 3d Sess., 40th Parl., 2010 (first reading on March 10, 2010), online at: <http://www2.parl.gc.ca/HousePublications/Publication.aspx?DocId=4339032&File=30&Language=e&Mode=1>. See also New Democratic Party, Press Release, "New Democrat Tables Nanotechnology Bill for the 21st Century" (March 10, 2010), online at: <http://www.ndp.ca/press/new-democrats-tables-nanotechnology-bill-for-21st-century>.

[156] New Democratic Party, Press Release, "New Democrat Tables Nanotechnology Bill for the 21st Century" (March 10, 2010), online at: <http://www.ndp.ca/press/new-democrats-tables-nano technology-bill-for-21st-century>.

[157] Bill C-494, ss. 4-5.

[158] At the time of writing, the Committee is undertaking a study titled *The Potential Risks and Benefits of Nanotechnology*. Included in this investigation is a consideration of the appropriate regulatory framework for nanotechnology in Canada. Upon completion of the study, a report will be released with details available online at: <http://www2.parl.gc.ca/CommitteeBusiness/Study ActivityHome.aspx?Cmte=HESA&Language=E&Mode=1&Parl=40&Ses=3&Stac=3189363>.

[159] For further reports on Canada's nanotechnology regulatory challenges, see generally Canadian Council of Academies, "Report in Focus, Small is Different: A Science Perspective on the Regulatory Challenges of the Nanoscale" (July 2008), online at: <http://www.scienceadvice.ca/uploads/eng/assessments%20and%20publications%20and%20news%20releases/nano/%282008_07_10%29_nano_report_in_focus.pdf>.

It is perhaps too early to tell whether nanomedicine will be evolutionary or revolutionary. However, given its nascent state of development, its inherent (scientific) unpredictability and the potential risks attendant in more general uses of nanotechnology,[160] it is difficult to imagine a completely unregulated program of research and development. Like genetically modified foods in the U.K., the likely rationale for such regulation will be the precautionary principle, an approach to managing threats of serious or irreversible harm in situations of scientific uncertainty.

Although referred to as though it were a singular, unified and coherent concept, the precautionary principle has in fact seen many different formulations ranging from Hippocrates's "First, do no harm"[161] to the 1992 Rio Declaration on Environment and Development statement that, "[w]here there are threats of serious or irreversible damage, lack of full scientific certainty shall not be used as a reason for postponing cost-effective measures to prevent ... degradation".[162] Though there are divergent views, core elements of the precautionary approach are usually thought to entail that: (1) there exists a duty to take anticipatory action to prevent harm; (2) the burden of proof of harmlessness for an unproven technology lies with its proponents, not the general public; (3) prior to its adoption, there exists an obligation to examine a full range of alternatives (including the alternative of doing nothing); and (4) applying the precautionary principle requires a process that is open, informed, democratic and inclusive of all affected parties.[163]

---

[160] To mention a few, these risks include: (1) catastrophic environmental damage due to unanticipated or uncontrollable consequences of its use; (2) economic oppression by patent owners that would deny those in need of otherwise cheap lifesaving technologies; (3) an unstable arms race as nanotechnology applications are developed for military or terrorist ends; and (4) ubiquitous surveillance of citizens by corporations and governments with the further miniaturization of devices. See generally David Williams, "The Risks of Nanotechnology" (2005) 16 Med. Device Tech. 6; The Nanoethics Group, "The Bad", online at: <http://www.nanoethics.org/bad.html>; European Commission, *Nanotechnologies: A Preliminary Risk Analysis, on the Basis of a Workshop Organized in Brussels on 1-2 March 2004 by the Health and Consumer Protectorate General of the European Commission* (European Commission, March 2004), online at: <http://www.ec.europa.eu/health/ph_risk/documents/ev_20040301_en.pdf>.

[161] While not part of the Hippocratic Oath itself, the maxim "First, do no harm" was reflected within Hippocrates' Corpus at *Epidemics*, Bk. I, Sect. V., where he states, "to help, or at least to do no harm".

[162] United Nations Environment Programme, *Rio Declaration on Environment and Development* (1992), Principle 15, online at: <http://www.unep.org/Documents.multilingual/Default.asp?DocumentID=78&ArticleID=1163>. This approach was subsequently particularized to include health concerns in the *Wingspread Statement on the Precautionary Principle*: "When an activity raises threats of harm to human health or the environment, precautionary measures should be taken even if some cause-and-effect relationships are not fully established scientifically": Global Development Research Center, *Wingspread Statement on the Precautionary Principle* (January 1998), online at: <http://www.gdrc.org/u-gov/precaution-3.html>.

[163] See Rachel's Environment & Health News, "#586 The Precautionary Principle" (February 19, 1998), online at: <http://rachel.org/files/rachel/Rachels_Environment_Health_News_532.pdf>.

There are divergent views on how the precautionary principle ought to apply to nanomedicine. For example, the Action Group on Erosion, Technology and Concentration (ETC), has recommended that

> [g]iven the concerns raised over nanoparticle contamination in living organisms ... governments [must] declare an immediate moratorium on commercial production of new nanomaterials and launch a transparent global process for evaluating the socioeconomic, health and environmental implications of the technology.[164]

Others, including the Center for Responsible Nanotechnology, offer a different perspective, drawing an important distinction between the "strict form" of precaution, which calls for inaction (usually by banning, prohibiting or restricting scientific research and development), and an "active form" of precaution, which requires that we choose "less risky alternatives when they are available ... taking responsibility for potential risks".[165] Concerned that a moratorium would simply result in inaction on the part of responsible and law-abiding people and institutions, while the development and use of dangerous nanotechnologies would continue underground or offshore by less responsible people and institutions, their interpretation of the precautionary principle would call for appropriate efforts to mitigate the risks of nanotechnology, rather than automatically forbid risky activities.[166] This approach suggests that it is "imperative to find and implement the least risky plan that is realistically feasible".[167] These authors further suggest that the safest option is to create a single research and development program for nanotechnology with widespread, though regulated, use of its outputs.[168]

In July 2003, the Government of Canada announced its view that "the application of precaution is a legitimate and distinctive decision-making approach within risk management".[169] The government enumerated a set of guiding principles aimed at improving "the predictability, credibility and consistency of the federal government's application of precaution", as well as strengthening public

---

[164] ETC Group, *The Big Down: Atomtech — Technologies Converging at the Nano-scale* (January 30, 2003) at 72, online at: <http://www.etcgroup.org/upload/publication/171/01/thebigdown. pdf>. ETC Group's call for a moratorium on the use of nanotechnology was recently renewed: see ETC Group, "Nanotech Product Recall Underscores the Need for Nanotech Moratorium: Is the Magic Gone?" (April 1, 2006), online at: <http://www.etcgroup.org/en/materials/publications. html?pub_id=14>.

[165] Chris Phoenix & Mike Treder, "Applying the Precautionary Principle to Nanotechnology" (Center for Responsible Nanotechnology, January 2003; revised December 2003, January 2004), online at: <http://www.crnano.org/precautionary.htm>.

[166] *Ibid.*

[167] *Ibid.*

[168] *Ibid.*

[169] Privy Council Office, *A Framework for the Application of Precaution in Science-based Decision Making about Risk* (Privy Council Office, July 25, 2003), Principle 1, online at: <http://www. pcobcp.gc.ca/index.asp?lang=eng&page=information&sub=publications&doc=precaution/preca ution_e.htm#five1www.pco-bcp.gc.ca/raoicssrdc/docs/Precaution/Discussion/discussion_e.pdf> at para. 4.1. The document uses "precaution" interchangeably with "the precautionary principle".

and stakeholder confidence in federal precautionary decision-making and improving Canada's international influence on the application of precaution.[170] However, the Government of Canada has not yet articulated how its precautionary approach might be applied to nanomedicine. Bill C-494 would give the precautionary principle force in the regulatory framework; however, it remains to be seen what will become of this Bill. For now, the future abounds with question marks.

III. THE CHALLENGE OF COMMERCIALIZATION

When contemplating the appropriate regulatory responses to emerging health technologies, an important factor to remember is that the research environment is becoming ever more closely tied to private industry. Biomedical researchers are increasingly expected to obtain research funding from private sources and to justify research goals in terms of economic development. Even the Canadian Institutes of Health Research (CIHR), the federal public funding agency for health research, has a mandate, explicitly stated in its enabling legislation, to "encourag[e] innovation, facilitat[e] the commercialization of health research in Canada and promot[e] economic development through health research in Canada".[171] Other funding agencies, such as Genome Canada, are charged with similar commercial goals.[172]

There are, of course, numerous benefits to working with industry, including increasing the funds available for research and providing an essential knowledge translation function. Arguably, many of the therapeutic benefits associated with emerging technologies could not be realized in our society without a partnership between academic researchers and industry. For example, new drug therapies or diagnostic technologies can cost hundreds of millions of dollars to produce and disseminate. The infrastructure and funding for this aspect of the research development process must come largely from industry, as universities and other public research institutions do not have the requisite public funding or support to do it on their own. As noted by DeAngelis:

> The discovery of new medications, devices, and techniques is funded primarily by for-profit companies; testing new modalities of treatment is funded primarily by for-profit companies; and the manufacture and the profitable marketing aspects of these modalities appropriately falls in the purview of this industry.[173]

That said, there are also profound concerns that flow from the commercialization of biomedical research. Indeed, some of the greatest challenges associated with the use and integration of emerging technologies can be traced to the influ-

---

[170] *Ibid.*, Foreword at para. 1.0.
[171] *Canadian Institutes of Health Research Act*, S.C. 2000, c. 6.
[172] See Genome Canada, online at: <http://www.genomecanada.ca>.
[173] Catherine D. DeAngelis, "The Influence of Money on Medical Science" (2006) 296 JAMA 996.

ence and role of commercial forces.[174] Here, we will briefly consider the role of patents.[175]

Patent legislation provides the inventor with an exclusive, 20-year monopoly over new inventions. Patents are meant to encourage innovation by providing a clear incentive to invent. The patenting of biomedical inventions, however, has long been a source of social concern — particularly when the "invention" involves human biological substances, such as genetic material and human embryonic stem cell lines.[176] For example, there are those who believe that such patents are unethical or contrary to notions of human dignity.[177] On a practical level, it has been suggested that the push toward patents skews the direction of research away from needed basic science toward research that focuses on commercializable products. There is also speculation that patenting pressure leads to a more secretive research environment, thus inhibiting collaborations and the free flow of valuable research data.[178] Patents may also drive up the cost of emerging technologies, adding to the overall costs of our health care system.[179] In addition to concerns over cost, there is also concern that the practice of granting exclusive licences to single laboratories to offer genetic testing may impede access to second opinions and undermine quality control.[180]

---

[174] See, *e.g.*, D. Chalmers & D. Nicol, "Commercialisation of Biotechnology: Public Trust in Research" (2004) 6 Int'l J. Biotech. 116-33.

[175] There are, of course, many other important social issues associated with commercialization and the involvement of industry not covered in this chapter. For example, see J. Thompson, P. Baird & J. Downie, *Report of the Committee of Inquiry on the Case Involving Dr. Nancy Olivieri, the Hospital for Sick Children, the University of Toronto and Apotex Inc.* (Toronto: James Lorimer & Co., 2001).

[176] See, *e.g.*, Gina Kolata, "Who owns your genes?" *The New York Times* (May 15, 2000) at A-1 and Timothy Caulfield, Richard Gold & Mildred Cho, "Patenting Human Genetic Material: Refocusing the Debate" (2000) 1 Nature Rev. Genetics 227-31. See also Mark Lemley, "Patenting Nanotechnology" (2005) 58 Stanford L. Rev. 601.

[177] For discussions, including critiques, of the ethical objections to human gene patents, see, *e.g.* Arthur Caplan, "What's So Special About the Human Genome?" (1998) 7:4 Cambridge Q. of Healthcare Ethics 422-24; D.B. Resnik, "DNA Patents and Human Dignity" (2001) 29 J.L. Med. & Ethics 152.

[178] P.A. David, "Can 'Open Science' be Protected from the Evolving Regime of IPR Protections?" (2004) 160 Journal of Theoretical and Institutional Economics 1-26; David Blumenthal, "Withholding Research Results in Academic Life Science: Evidence From a National Survey of Faculty" (1997) 277 JAMA 1224.

[179] See Jon Merz *et al.*, "Diagnostic Testing Fails the Test" (2002) 415 Nature 577-79; and Timothy Caulfield, "Policy Conflicts: Gene Patents and Health Care in Canada" (2005) 8 Community Gen. 223-27. For recent case studies on the impact of patents on access to genetic tests in the United States, see the case studies collected at Robert Cook-Deegan & Christopher Heaney, "Gene Patents and Licensing: Case Studies Prepared for the Secretary's Advisory Committee on Genetics, Health & Society" (2010) 12:4 Supp. Genetics in Medicine S1.

[180] See the introductory letter from Stephen Teutsch at the beginning of the recent report to the U.S. Secretary of Health and Human Services: U.S. Department of Health and Human Services, Secretary's Advisory Committee on Genetics, Health, and Society, *Gene Patents and Licensing Practices and Their Impact on Patient Access to Genetic Tests* (April 2010), online at: <http://oba.od nih.gov/oba/sacghs/reports/SACGHS_patents_report_2010.pdf>; James P. Evans, "Putting Patients Before Patents" (2010) 12:4 Supp. Genetics in Medicine S3.

This latter concern received considerable attention in the summer of 2001 when Myriad Genetics attempted to enforce its patents over the BRCA1/2 mutations (genetic mutations that, if present, increase the likelihood that an individual will get breast or ovarian cancer).[181] Through cease and desist letters sent to most provincial health ministries, Myriad Genetics tried to force all testing to be done through the Myriad laboratory in Utah, at a cost of approximately $3,800 — considerably more than the cost of doing the test through available processes at existing provincial laboratories. The dispute catalyzed a Canadian policy debate over genetic patents and the exclusive licensing of gene patents, which has raged for over seven years without coming to a clear resolution at the policy level.[182]

Litigation over Myriad's BRCA1/2 patents continues. In March 2010, the District Court for the Southern District of New York invalidated seven of Myriad's U.S. patents relating to BRCA1/2 and the associated diagnostic tests, on the basis that the genes and tests are unpatentable subject matter.[183] This decision is now under appeal and is expected to be overturned, at least in part.[184]

Despite such issues, the patenting of biomedical inventions, including human genes, has continued, relatively unfettered, for decades. In general, so long as an invention meets the basic statutory requirements for a patent — it must be new, useful and have a clear utility — it can be patented.[185] Indeed, it has been estimated that over 20 per cent of all human genes are associated with at least one patent.[186] That said, the concerns associated with biotechnology patents, particularly those regarding the impact of patents on access, continue to stir debate and have led to a variety of policy recommendations from provincial governments,[187] bioethics and science policy entities,[188] and international

---

[181] Bryn Williams-Jones, "History of a Gene Patent: Tracing the Development and Application of Commercial BRCA Testing" (2002) 10 Health L.J. 123-46. For a discussion of the role of these mutations in the development of cancer, see M.C. King, J. Marks & J. Mandell, "Breast and Ovarian Cancer Risk Due to Inherited Mutations in BRCA1 and BRCA2" (2003) 302 Science 643-46.

[182] For a thorough history of the Myriad controversy, see E. Richard Gold & Julia Carbone, "Myriad Genetics: In the Eye of the Policy Storm" (2010) 12:4 Supp. Genetics in Medicine S39-S70. The Canadian situation is discussed at S49-S54.

[183] *Association for Molecular Pathology et al. v. United States Patent and Trademark Office et al.*, 2010 U.S. Dist. LEXIS 30629, 94 U.S.P.Q.2D (BNA) 1683 (S.D.N.Y. 2010), now under appeal to the U.S. Court of Appeals, Federal Circuit.

[184] See the discussion of the case in E. Richard Gold & Julia Carbone, "Myriad Genetics: In the Eye of the Policy Storm" (2010) 12:4 Supp. Genetics in Medicine S39-S70.

[185] See, generally, *Diamond v. Chakrabarty*, 447 U.S. 303 (1980). Since this landmark decision by the United States Supreme Court, there have been few legal obstacles to the patenting of biologically based "inventions". It should be noted, however, that Canada is the only country with a high court decision that explicitly rejects the patenting of "higher life forms" (*Harvard College v. Canada (Commissioner of Patents)*, [2002] S.C.J. No. 77, [2002] 4 S.C.R. 45 (S.C.C.)).

[186] K. Jensen & F. Murray, "Enhanced: Intellectual Property Landscape of the Human Genome" (2005) 310 Science 239-40.

[187] Ontario Ministry of Health, *Genetics, Testing and Gene Patenting: Charting New Territory in Healthcare* (Toronto: Government of Ontario, 2002).

organizations.[189] The options considered have ranged from clarifying the research exemptions (so researchers can access patented inventions without fear of infringing a patent) to a consideration of compulsory licensing (so provincial health care systems can control the cost of patented inventions).[190]

To date, there have been no major reforms to the Canadian patent system, although there is some evidence that the public is becoming increasingly uncomfortable with biotechnology patents[191] and that the patenting of controversial emerging technologies, including embryonic stem cell lines and nanotechnologies, might stir more interest in policy reform.[192] For example, because the source of embryonic stem cell lines remains controversial, there may be those who believe that the patenting of stem cell lines is morally inappropriate.

Another major concern associated with the commercialization process is that marketing pressure, inextricably tied with the involvement of industry, will lead to an inappropriate increase in the utilization of a given technology.[193] There is evidence that this may be happening in a variety of domains, such as with imaging technologies,[194] genetic testing[195] and pharmaceuticals.[196] Industry has a natural and understandable desire to increase profits by increasing demand.

---

[188] See Canadian Biotechnology Advisory Committee, *Human Genetic Materials, Intellectual Property and the Health Sector* (Ottawa: CBAC, 2006); U.S. National Institutes of Health, Secretary's Advisory Committee on Genetics, Health, and Society, *Gene Patents and Licensing Practices and Their Impact on Patient Access to Genetic Tests* (April 2010), online at: <http://oba.od.nih.gov/oba/sacghs/reports/SACGHS_patents_report_2010.pdf>; The Nuffield Council on Bioethics, *The Ethics of Patenting DNA: A Discussion Paper* (London: Nuffield Council of Bioethics, 2002); and National Academy of Sciences, *Reaping the Benefits of Genomic and Proteomic Research: Intellectual Property Rights, Innovation, and Public Health* (Washington, DC: National Academies Press, 2005).

[189] Organisation for Economic Cooperation and Development (OECD), "Genetic Inventions, Intellectual Property Rights and Licensing Practices: Evidence and Policies" (2002), online at: <http://www.oecd.org/dataoecd/42/21/2491084.pdf>; OECD, *Guidelines for the Licensing of Genetic Inventions* (2006), online at: <http://www.oecd.org/dataoecd/39/38/36198812.pdf>.

[190] Ontario Ministry of Health, *Genetics, Testing and Gene Patenting* (Toronto: Government of Ontario, 2002).

[191] E. Einsiedel & J. Smith, "Canadian Views on Patenting Biotechnology" (Canadian Biotechnology Advisory Committee, June 2005).

[192] See, for example, Timothy Caulfield, "Stem Cell Patents and Social Controversy: A Speculative View From Canada" at 219-32; and Mark Lemley, "Patenting Nanotechnology" (2005) 58 Stanford L. Rev. 601.

[193] See, *e.g.*, Patti Peppin, "The Power of Illusion and the Illusion of Power" in Colleen Flood, ed., *Just Medicare: What's In, What's Out, How We Decide* (Toronto: University of Toronto Press, 2005) at 355.

[194] Richard Smith, "The Screening Industry" (2003) 326 B.M.J.: "Simple minded enthusiasm for screening, combined with the industrial opportunity to make fat profits, may mean that soon none of us will be normal."

[195] J.T. Lowery *et al.*, "The Impact of Direct-to-Consumer Marketing of Cancer Genetic Testing on Women According to their Genetic Risk" (2008) 10:12 Genetics in Medicine 888-94; Stacy Gray & Olufunmilayo I. Olopade, "Direct-to-Consumer Marketing of Genetic Tests for Cancer: Buyer Beware" (2003) 21 J. Clin. Oncology 3191-93.

[196] See Steven Woloshin & Lisa Schwartz, "Giving Legs to Restless Legs: A Case Study of How the Media Makes People Sick" (2006) 3 PloS Med. 452.

But, this inclination may result in marketing strategies that create inappropriate expectations, patient anxiety and more utilization than might be considered ideal. What is ideal utilization can be a difficult judgment to make, of course. The pejorative term "disease-mongering" has been used to suggest that the pharmaceutical industry attempts to convince the public that it is afflicted by spurious diseases or conditions in order to sell treatments for them. While there are examples that do seem to fit that description, there are also reasonable arguments that sufferers from conditions that have been under-diagnosed or under-treated may benefit from the recognition of their conditions and the availability of treatments.[197] Nonetheless, the view that commercialization leads to inappropriate uptake of medical treatments has led to the proposal of various regulatory strategies, including independent technology assessment and controls on marketing approaches.[198]

Finally, the impact of commercialization on that most valuable of assets — public trust — should be considered. Indeed, many scholars have noted that public trust is an essential element of the research infrastructure and, if lost, is tremendously difficult to regain.[199] There is at least some evidence that close ties with industry have the potential to compromise public trust. For example, university researchers funded by public sources are one of the most trusted voices in the area of biotechnology. However, those funded by industry are among the least trusted.[200] The source of funding, and its perceived impact on the impartiality of researchers, seems to be the critical element. And, given the evidence that industry funding impacts the nature and tone of research findings, the public's skepticism is not without foundation.[201] Ghost-writing (the practice of recruiting

---

[197] See, *e.g.*, E. Doran & D. Henry, "Disease Mongering: Expanding the Boundaries of Treatable Disease" (2008) 38:11 Internal Med. J. 858-61; R. Moynihan, I. Heath & D. Henry, "Selling Sickness: The Pharmaceutical Industry and Disease Mongering" (2002) 324:7342 British Medical Journal 886-91. For contrary views, see R. Tiner, "The Pharmaceutical Industry and Disease-Mongering: The Industry Works to Develop Drugs not Diseases" (2002) 325:7357 British Medical Journal 216; and J.L. LaMattina, "Disease Mongering is a Myth" (2009) 15:2 Nature Medicine 134.

[198] Barbara Mintzes, "Disease Mongering in Drug Promotion: Do Governments Have a Regulatory Role?" (2006) 3 PLoS Med. 461. An additional concern, not considered in this brief overview, is the impact that commercialization pressure will have on the direction of research — skewing it toward commercializable objectives and away from basic research and less profitable public health initiatives: see Timothy Caulfield, "Sustainability and the Balancing of the Health Care and Innovation Agendas: The Commercialization of Genetic Research" (2003) 66 Sask L. Rev. 629. See also Paul Nightingale & Paul Martin, "The Myth of the Biotech Revolution" (2004) 565 Trends in Biotech 566-67.

[199] Marcia Angel, "Is Academic Medicine for Sale?" (2000) 342 New Eng. J. Med. 1516-18.

[200] Government of Canada BioPortal, "A Canada-US Public Opinion Research Study on Emerging Technologies" at 55 (see slide no. 110).

[201] Council on Scientific Affairs, American Medical Association, *Influence of Funding Source on Outcome, Validity, and Reliability of Pharmaceutical Research* (C.S.A. Report 10, 2004 A.M.A. Annual Meeting, June 2004), where the authors summarize the research in the area:

Studies with positive findings are more likely to be published than studies with negative or null results and an association exists between pharmaceutical industry sponsorship of

and listing independent academics as authors on papers planned and prepared by those affiliated with economically interested private sector companies) obscures the commercial sector's involvement in the medical literature. This controversial practice takes advantage of the public belief in the impartiality of university researchers and puts that trust at risk.[202] In areas like stem cell research, nanotechnology and human genetics, where the public may already have concerns about the use and implications of the technology,[203] a loss of public trust could be particularly damaging.

If industry is going to continue to play an ever-increasing role in the funding of biomedical research, policies must be developed to ensure that the integrity of the research enterprise is maintained and that public trust is respected and engaged.[204]

IV. CONCLUSION

In this chapter, we have examined four emerging health technologies. We have seen that each has significant potential health benefits. Each also has various ethical and legal controversies associated with its proposed use. In this chapter, we have limited our brief survey to a single health law and policy precept for each: genetics requires us to think about equality and equal treatment; radio frequency identification poses new challenges for informational privacy and security; embryonic stem cell techniques revive debates about the moral limits of human experimentation; nanotechnology raises questions about the practice of precaution; and the issue of commercialization asks us to consider the economic context within which many of these controversies and regulatory challenges arise.

As we continue to think about these new elixirs, it is instructive to recall King Thamus and his admonition to the inventor: "Theuth, my paragon of inventors, the discoverer of an art is not the best judge of the good or harm which will accrue to those who practice it."

---

clinical research and publication of results favoring the sponsor's products. Additionally, the publication of negative results may be delayed compared with the time to publication of studies with positive results.

[202] Virginia Barbour, "How Ghost-Writing Threatens the Credibility of Medical Knowledge and Medical Journals" (2010) 95:1 Haematologica 1-2.

[203] In a 2005 study, only 49 per cent of Canadians surveyed (compared with 57 per cent of Americans) thought that biotechnology was being developed with consideration to their interests, values and beliefs: Government of Canada BioPortal, "A Canada-US Public Opinion Research Study on Emerging Technologies".

[204] See, *e.g.*, Timothy Caulfield, Edna Einsiedel, Jon Merz & Dianne Nicol, "Trust, Patents and Public Perceptions: The Governance of Controversial Biotechnology Research" (2006) 24 Nature Biotechnology 1352-54, where the use of patent pools is recommended as a way of managing the commercialization.

When we consider the governance of science and the proper place of technology in our health care system, it is important to recognize that the technologiesthat science enables are not neutral and that it is therefore not always appropriate to leave science to its own devices. As one team of scholars put it:

> ...values; science alone cannot answer them. The public expect and want science and technology to solve problems, but they also want a say in deciding which problems are worth solving. This is not a matter of attracting public support for an agenda already established by science and scientists, but rather of seeing the public as participants in science policy with whom a shared vision of socially viable science and technological innovation can be achieved.[205]

Likewise, bioethicists, lawyers, policy-makers and other relevant experts all have a crucial role to play in determining the best way to harness emerging technologies that are both good *and* bad; at one and the same time the solution and the problem.

---

[205] George Gaskell *et al.*, "Social Values and the Governance of Science" (2005) 310 Science 1909.

Chapter 12

PUBLIC HEALTH

Barbara von Tigerstrom[*]

I.   INTRODUCTION

Public health law is a rapidly growing area of research and practice. Events like the 2009–2010 H1N1 influenza pandemic and the 2003 SARS outbreak have focused public attention on public health powers and responsibilities and the legal framework within which they are exercised. Less dramatic but equally deadly threats like tobacco consumption and unhealthy diets have provoked debate about legal strategies to promote public health. Underlying many issues in public health law are central questions about the limits of personal freedom and responsibility, the role of government and collective decisions about confronting the risks of contemporary society.

II.   PUBLIC HEALTH AND PUBLIC HEALTH LAW

A much-quoted definition states that public health is "what we, as a society, do collectively to assure the conditions for people to be healthy".[1] It is "public" in the sense both of collective action (primarily, though not exclusively, government action) and of concern with the health of a population rather than specific individuals.[2] Contemporary public health practice aims to use evidence about the risk factors, determinants and incidence of disease, generated from surveillance and epidemiological analysis, to design interventions that will promote population health and prevent disease.

Public health law has been defined as the "study of legal powers and duties of the state to promote the conditions for people to be healthy ... and the limitations on the power of the state to constrain the autonomy, privacy, liberty, proprietary, or other legally protected interests of individuals for the protection or promotion of community health".[3] Whereas medical law is chiefly concerned

---

[*]   The author would like to acknowledge research assistance provided by Ms. Joanne Colledge (J.D. student, University of Saskatchewan).
[1]   Institute of Medicine, *The Future of Public Health* (Washington, DC: National Academies Press, 1988) at 1.
[2]   Lawrence O. Gostin, "Health of the People: The Highest Law?" (2004) 32 J.L. Med. & Ethics 509 at 510.
[3]   *Ibid.*, at 509-10.

with rights and obligations in the relationship between health care provider and patient, in public health many questions involve the powers and duties of government to protect the health of its population. The law is often called on to resolve the tensions that may arise between individual rights and interests, on the one hand, and the common interest of the community, on the other.

Public health and public health law cover a broad range of subjects. Most people associate public health with infectious disease control and sanitation, but its scope extends to such diverse matters as environmental hazards, chronic diseases and injuries.[4] An even broader conception of public health law would encompass the role of law in relation to determinants of health and the causes of disparities in health status, such as poverty and discrimination. Without discounting the importance of these matters, this chapter will focus on a more limited set of issues as an introduction to the field. It will provide an overview of the legal framework for public health in Canada, and then discuss the law relating to infectious disease control and surveillance, chronic disease surveillance and screening, tobacco control, and healthy eating, physical activity and obesity.

III.   THE LEGAL FRAMEWORK FOR PUBLIC HEALTH IN CANADA

Health or public health is not assigned as a single subject matter under the Canadian Constitution but is spread among several heads of power, both federal and provincial.[5] Relevant federal heads of power include trade and commerce, quarantine and marine hospitals, criminal law, and the peace, order and good government (POGG) power;[6] provincial heads of power include hospitals, municipal institutions, property and civil rights, and local and private matters.[7] The federal government has enacted legislation to deal with potentially hazardous consumer products,[8] food and drug safety,[9] and quarantine of goods and persons at border crossings.[10] Both levels of government have legislation relating to

---

[4]   For further details and discussion on many of these topics, see Tracey M. Bailey, Timothy Caulfield & Nola M. Ries, eds., *Public Health Law & Policy in Canada*, 2d ed. (Markham, ON: LexisNexis Canada, 2008).

[5]   For general discussion, see, *e.g.*, Martha Jackman, "Constitutional Jurisdiction Over Health in Canada" (2000) 8 Health L.J. 95; regarding jurisdiction over public health matters, see, *e.g.*, Nola M. Ries, "Legal Foundations of Public Health Law in Canada" in *Public Health Law & Policy in Canada, ibid.*, at 7*ff.*; National Advisory Committee on SARS and Public Health, *Learning from SARS: Renewal of Public Health in Canada* (Ottawa: Health Canada, 2003) at 166*ff.*

[6]   *Constitution Act, 1867* (U.K.), 30 & 31 Vict., c. 3, s. 91(2), (11), (27), reprinted in R.S.C. 1985, App. II, No. 5.

[7]   *Ibid.*, s. 92(7), (8), (13), (16).

[8]   *Hazardous Products Act*, R.S.C. 1985, c. H-3.

[9]   *Food and Drugs Act*, R.S.C. 1985, c. F-27.

[10] *Quarantine Act*, S.C. 2005, c. 20.

emergency management,[11] tobacco control[12] and environmental hazards.[13] Provincial legislation covers most aspects of infectious disease surveillance and control,[14] other health surveillance (such as vital statistics and cancer surveillance) and provincial health care systems.

The overlapping responsibilities of various levels of government in public health have sometimes led to difficulties. In some cases, parties adversely affected by public health legislation have challenged their provisions on the basis that the government lacked jurisdiction to enact them. This has occurred particularly with tobacco control legislation, but the courts have confirmed the shared jurisdiction of federal and provincial governments to legislate in this area.[15] The courts have also upheld municipal bylaws regulating pesticides as potential public health hazards.[16]

All legislation in Canada must be consistent with the *Canadian Charter of Rights and Freedoms*,[17] and may be challenged if affected persons believe their Charter rights have been violated. For example, the tobacco industry has been partly successful in challenging legislation that restricts the marketing of tobacco products.[18] Restrictions on personal liberty, such as quarantine or detention for public health reasons, and intrusions into personal privacy, such as mandatory reporting of diseases, may also be challenged under the Charter.[19] However, decisions of Canadian courts to date suggest that the public health objectives of these provisions will be given considerable weight.[20] The government will be permitted to infringe rights and freedoms protected under the Charter where it can demonstrate that the limit is one which is "reasonable",

---

[11] See, *e.g.*, *Emergencies Act*, R.S.C. 1985 (4th Supp.), c. 22; *Emergency Management and Civil Protection Act*, R.S.O. 1990, c. E.9; *Emergency Measures Act*, S.N.B. 1978, c. E-7.1; *Emergency Planning Act*, S.S. 1989-90, c. E-8.1.

[12] See, *e.g.*, *Tobacco Act*, S.C. 1997, c. 13; *Tobacco Act*, R.S.Q., c. T-0.01; *Tobacco Control Act*, S.S. 2001, c. T-14.1; *Smoke-Free Ontario Act*, S.O. 1994, c. 10 (formerly the *Tobacco Control Act*).

[13] See, *e.g.*, *Canadian Environmental Protection Act, 1999*, S.C. 1999, c. 33; *Environmental Protection and Enhancement Act*, R.S.A. 2000, c. E-12; *Environmental Management Act*, S.B.C. 2003, c. 53.

[14] See, *e.g.*, *Public Health Act*, S.B.C. 2008, c. 28; *Public Health Act*, R.S.A. 2000, c. P-37; *Communicable Diseases Act*, R.S.N.L. 1990, c. C-26.

[15] *RJR-MacDonald Inc. v. Canada (Attorney General)*, [1995] S.C.J. No. 68, [1995] 3 S.C.R. 199 (S.C.C.); *Rothmans, Benson & Hedges Inc. v. Saskatchewan*, [2005] S.C.J. No. 1, [2005] 1 S.C.R. 188 (S.C.C.). See also *Siemens v. Manitoba (Attorney General)*, [2003] S.C.J. No. 69, [2003] 1 S.C.R. 6 (S.C.C.) (regulation of gambling).

[16] *114957 Canada Ltée (Spraytech, Société d'arrosage) v. Hudson (Town)*, [2001] S.C.J. No. 42, [2001] 2 S.C.R. 241 (S.C.C.).

[17] Part I of the *Constitution Act, 1982*, being Schedule B to the *Canada Act 1982* (U.K.), 1982, c. 11 [Charter].

[18] *RJR-MacDonald Inc. v. Canada (Attorney General)*, [1995] S.C.J. No. 68, [1995] 3 S.C.R. 199 (S.C.C.); but see *Canada (Attorney General) v. JTI-Macdonald Corp.*, [2007] S.C.J. No. 30, [2007] 2 S.C.R. 610 (S.C.C.).

[19] *Toronto (City, Medical Officer of Health) v. Deakin*, [2002] O.J. No. 2777 (Ont. C.J.); *Canadian AIDS Society v. Ontario*, [1995] O.J. No. 2361, 25 O.R. (3d) 388 (Ont. Gen. Div.).

[20] See, *e.g.*, *Canadian AIDS Society v. Ontario, ibid.*

"prescribed by law" and "demonstrably justified in a free and democratic society".[21] Decisions of public health authorities may also be challenged on the basis that they breached common law duties owed to affected persons, although plaintiffs have had little success with such actions to date.[22]

Finally, a range of international legal obligations are relevant to Canadian public health law. These include human rights treaties that guarantee the right to health,[23] as well as rights to liberty, personal security, freedom of movement, privacy and freedom of expression that must be respected in public health interventions.[24] International trade agreements may also need to be taken into account; for example, the *General Agreement on Tariffs and Trade* prohibits various types of trade barriers, subject to an exception for measures that are "necessary to protect human ... life or health",[25] and the *Agreement on the Application of Sanitary and Phytosanitary Measures* sets out substantive and procedural requirements for measures relating to food safety and health risks from plant or animal pests and diseases.[26] The International Health Regulations (IHR) provide a framework for responses by states and the World Health Organization (WHO) to outbreaks of disease.[27] The IHR, which were substantially revised in 2005, received their first major test in the 2009–2010 H1N1 influenza pandemic. In some respects the experience was positive, with generally good monitoring and reporting believed to have helped the international community to mitigate

---

[21]   Charter, s. 1. The framework for evaluating whether this s. 1 test has been met was set out in the case of *R. v. Oakes*, [1986] S.C.J. No. 7, [1986] 1 S.C.R. 103 (S.C.C.).

[22]   See, *e.g.*, *Eliopoulos (Litigation trustee of) v. Ontario (Minister of Health and Long-Term Care)*, [2006] O.J. No. 4400, 82 O.R. (3d) 321 (Ont. C.A.), leave to appeal refused [2006] S.C.C.A. No. 514 (S.C.C.); *Laroza Estate v. Ontario*, [2009] O.J. No. 1820, 2009 ONCA 373, 95 O.R. (3d) 764 (Ont. C.A.); *Abarquez v. Ontario*, [2009] O.J. No. 1814, 2009 ONCA 374, 95 O.R. (3d) 414, leave to appeal refused [2009] S.C.C.A. No. 297 (S.C.C.); *Henry Estate v. Scarborough Hospital – Grace Division*, [2009] O.J. No. 1821, 2009 ONCA 375, 66 C.C.L.T. (3d) 184, leave to appeal refused [2009] S.C.C.A. No. 306 (S.C.C.); *Jamal Estate v. Scarborough Hospital – Grace Division*, [2009] O.J. No. 1822, 2009 ONCA 376, 95 O.R. (3d) 760, leave to appeal refused [2009] S.C.C.A. No. 308 (S.C.C.). In all of these actions, the statement of claim was struck on the grounds that Ontario did not owe a private law duty of care to individuals with respect to its efforts to control West Nile Virus and SARS outbreaks.

[23]   *International Covenant on Economic, Social and Cultural Rights* (December 16), 1966, 993 U.N.T.S. 3, art. 12; *Convention on the Rights of the Child* (November 20, 1989), G.A. Res. 44/25, art. 24.

[24]   *International Covenant on Civil and Political Rights* (December 16, 1966), 999 U.N.T.S. 171, arts. 9, 12, 19, 17.

[25]   (October 30, 1947), 58 U.N.T.S. 187, art. XX(b).

[26]   Annex 1A to the *Marrakesh Agreement Establishing the World Trade Organization* (April 15, 1994), 1867 U.N.T.S. 3.

[27]   International Health Regulations (2005), WHA Res. 58.3 (May 23, 2005; in force 2007). See Lawrence O. Gostin, "International Infectious Disease Law: Revision of the World Health Organization's International Health Regulations" (2004) 291 JAMA 2623; Barbara von Tigerstrom, "The Revised International Health Regulations and Restraint of National Health Measures" (2005) 13 Health L.J. 35.

the impact of the pandemic.[28] However, allegations of conflicts of interest and lack of transparency have prompted a review of governance structures in the WHO.[29] Another landmark international instrument in public health law, the *Framework Convention on Tobacco Control* (FCTC), was negotiated under the auspices of the WHO and adopted by the World Health Assembly on May 21, 2003.[30] The Convention came into force in 2005 and as of September 2010 had 168 parties, including Canada.[31] The FCTC commits state parties to a comprehensive range of tobacco control measures, including smoking bans, marketing restrictions and preventing sales to minors.

IV. INFECTIOUS DISEASE SURVEILLANCE AND CONTROL

Public health authorities work to prevent and contain infectious diseases through surveillance and control activities that are supported by a legal framework, typically a provincial public health statute and associated regulations. Surveillance and control are closely related, since surveillance — the systematic collection and analysis of data about the incidence of disease in the population — allows the authorities to prevent and respond to outbreaks through an understanding of patterns and determinants of disease. Mandatory reporting of infectious diseases is used to facilitate comprehensive and timely collection of information. Disease control is achieved through a range of measures including vaccination, testing and treatment of affected individuals, and, where necessary, isolation. Public health authorities also possess a range of coercive powers to respond to a disease outbreak or public health emergency.

A. MANDATORY REPORTING

Public health legislation requires designated persons to report cases of certain diseases. The list of notifiable or reportable diseases is usually prescribed by regulation, but there may also be a general requirement to report any case of a disease that is unusual or part of a suspected outbreak,[32] or provision for the medical officer to require reporting of any other disease that needs to be kept

---

[28] Dr. Margaret Chan, Director-General, World Health Organization, Press Release, "World now at the start of the 2009 influenza pandemic" (June 11, 2009), online at: <http://www.who.int/mediacentre/news/statements/2009/h1n1_pandemic_phase6_20090611/en/print.html>.

[29] Deborah Cohen & Philip Carter, "WHO and the Pandemic Flu 'Conspiracies'" (2010) 340 British Medical Journal 1274; Dr. Margaret Chan, "WHO Director-General Replies to the *BMJ*" (2010) 341 British Medical Journal 7.

[30] (June 16, 2003), 2302 U.N.T.S. 166, online at: WHO <http://whqlibdoc.who.int/publications/2003/9241591013.pdf>.

[31] WHO, "Parties to the WHO Framework Convention on Tobacco Control" (2010), online at: WHO FCTC <http://www.who.int/fctc/signatories_parties/en/index.html>.

[32] See, *e.g.*, Reporting of Diseases and Conditions Regulation, Man. Reg. 37/2009, s. 7; *Public Health Act*, R.S.A. 2000, c. P-37, s. 26; *Health Protection Act*, S.N.S. 2004, c. 4, s. 31(5).

under surveillance.[33] The duty to report is imposed on physicians and other health care practitioners,[34] and may also extend to others such as school teachers and principals,[35] or persons in charge of a laboratory or hospital.[36] These mandatory reporting requirements override the legal or ethical obligations of confidentiality that health care providers would otherwise owe to their patients, but the information reported is protected from further disclosure.[37]

Although mandatory reporting is important to enable public health authorities to track and respond to cases of infectious disease, there is a risk that individuals may be deterred from seeking testing and treatment if they know that their personal health information will be reported. This concern has been especially important in the case of HIV/AIDS, because of the serious consequences and social stigma attached to a positive HIV diagnosis. As a result, many jurisdictions have special provisions that allow anonymous or non-nominal testing for HIV/AIDS.[38] Under these provisions, cases must still be reported but the individual's name and contact information will not be included in the report unless the individual voluntarily agrees to this disclosure. More limited personal information such as the individual's initials, gender and/or birth date will be required.[39] These requirements represent a compromise between protecting confidentiality and minimizing the chance of duplicate reports which would compromise the accuracy of surveillance data.

The mandatory reporting provisions in the Ontario public health legislation were challenged in *Canadian AIDS Society v. Ontario* as being contrary to sections 7 (life, liberty and security of the person) and 8 (freedom from unreasonable search and seizure) of the Charter.[40] The case involved the HIV testing of blood that had been donated up to 10 years previously. The testing identified 22 HIV-positive donors, of whom 13 had not previously been identified as being HIV-positive; the issue was whether the positive tests had to be reported to public health authorities as provided under the *Health Protection and Promotion*

---

[33] See, *e.g.*, *Public Health Act*, R.S.A. 2000, c. P-37, s. 15.

[34] See, *e.g.*, *Health Protection and Promotion Act*, R.S.O. 1990, c. H.7, s. 25; *Communicable Diseases Act*, R.S.N.L. 1990, c. C-26, s. 4; *Public Health Act*, R.S.Q., c. S-2.2, s. 82(1).

[35] See, *e.g.*, *Public Health Act, 1994*, S.S. 1994, c. P-37.1, s. 32(1)(c); *Health Protection and Promotion Act*, R.S.O. 1990, c. H.7, s. 28; *Health Protection Act*, S.N.S. 2004, c. 4, s. 31(2).

[36] See, *e.g.*, Health Act Communicable Disease Regulation, B.C. Reg. 4/83, ss. 2(3), 3; *Public Health Act, 1994*, S.S. 1994, c. P-37.1, s. 32(1)(b); *Public Health Act*, R.S.A. 2000, c. P-37, ss. 22(1), 23; *Public Health Act*, R.S.Q., c. S-2.2, s. 82(2).

[37] See, *e.g.*, *Public Health Act*, R.S.A. 2000, c. P-37, s. 53. Where specific provision is not made, the information may nevertheless be protected by provincial privacy or health information legislation.

[38] Mary Anne Bobinski, "HIV/AIDS and Public Health Law" in Tracey M. Bailey, Timothy Caulfield & Nola M. Ries, eds., *Public Health Law & Policy in Canada*, 2d ed. (Markham, ON: LexisNexis Canada, 2008) at 213-14.

[39] See, *e.g.*, Disease Control Regulations, R.R.S. 2000, c. P-37.1, Reg. 11, ss. 14(3), 15; Health Act Communicable Disease Regulation, B.C. Reg. 4/83, s. 4(5); Reporting Requirements for HIV Positive Persons Regulations, N.S. Reg. 197/2005, s. 9.

[40] [1995] O.J. No. 2361, 25 O.R. (3d) 388 (Ont. Gen. Div.), affd [1996] O.J. No. 4184, 31 O.R. (3d) 798 (Ont. C.A.), leave to appeal dismissed [1997] S.C.C.A. No. 33 (S.C.C.).

Act,[41] and the donors contacted to notify them of the test results.[42] The applicant Canadian AIDS Society argued that under these circumstances the mandatory reporting requirements infringed sections 7 and 8 of the Charter. The court found that the psychological stress caused by reporting could infringe donors' rights to security of the person but that this did not amount to a violation of section 7 because it was in accordance with principles of fundamental justice. The legislation struck an appropriate balance between individual rights and important public health objectives, and it incorporated protections for individuals such as a requirement that information reported under the Act be kept confidential.[43] In coming to this conclusion, Wilson J. stated that in this context, "although due consideration will be given to the privacy rights of individuals, the state objective of promoting public health for the safety of all will be given great weight".[44] The challenge based on section 8 also failed, since although there was a "seizure" of information, it was not unreasonable, again taking into account the public health purpose of the reporting requirement.[45]

B. CONTACT TRACING

Once a case of an infectious disease has been identified and reported, one way of preventing the further spread of the disease is to contact other individuals who may have been exposed to the disease, so that they can be tested and treatment or containment measures carried out if necessary. This is referred to as contact tracing, or alternatively, especially in the case of sexually transmitted infections (STIs), partner notification. It may be done on a voluntary basis but is also provided for by statute in some jurisdictions and may be mandatory, at least for certain diseases, most commonly STIs.[46] Public health legislation may require individuals who are infected with designated diseases to provide a list of names and contact information for individuals with whom they have been in contact.[47] The individual himself or herself, health care provider or medical officer will then communicate with these contacts to inform them that they have been exposed and should be tested and take precautions against further transmis-

---

[41] R.S.O. 1990, c. H.7, s. 29.

[42] It was agreed that the Red Cross was entitled to test the samples for the purpose of tracing recipients of blood from infected donors: *Canadian AIDS Society v. Ontario*, [1995] O.J. No. 2361 at para. 59, 25 O.R. (3d) 388 (Ont. Gen. Div.), affd [1996] O.J. No. 4184, 31 O.R. (3d) 798 (Ont. C.A.), leave to appeal dismissed [1997] S.C.C.A. No. 33 (S.C.C.).

[43] *Ibid.*, at paras. 131-32.

[44] *Ibid.*, at para. 133.

[45] *Ibid.*, at para. 159.

[46] For a useful summary of the variation among Canadian jurisdictions, see Elaine Gibson, "Public Health Information Privacy and Confidentiality" in Tracey M. Bailey, Timothy Caulfield & Nola M. Ries, eds., *Public Health Law & Policy in Canada*, 2d ed. (Markham, ON: LexisNexis Canada, 2008) at 117-19.

[47] See, *e.g.*, *Public Health Act*, R.S.A 2000, c. P 37, s. 56(1); *Public Health Act, 1994*, S.S. 1994, c. P-37.1, s. 33(4)(b); Communicable Disease Regulations, N.S. Reg. 196/2005, s. 11.

sion.[48] In addition to any statutory obligation to carry out contact tracing, health care providers may have legal and ethical duties to warn contacts of their exposure to an infectious disease, particularly if they also have a therapeutic relationship with those individuals.

C. INDIVIDUAL OBLIGATIONS

Public health legislation, as well as empowering public health authorities to take certain measures, may explicitly impose specific obligations on individuals who are or may be infected. These obligations, where they are provided for in legislation, exist independently of any order that may be made by public health authorities (see below). The diseases to which these obligations apply may include all communicable or infectious diseases covered by the legislation, or some subset of them, such as STIs.[49] An individual who suspects that she or he is infected with one of the prescribed diseases has an obligation to seek medical advice and/or testing, and if the test is positive, to submit to prescribed treatment until no longer infectious and take measures to prevent transmission of the disease.[50] If an infected individual refuses or neglects to submit to treatment, the physician may be required to report this to the medical officer,[51] and compulsory orders may be issued.[52] Federal quarantine legislation requires travellers to answer questions and provide information upon request from screening officers, comply with "reasonable measures" ordered by those officers, and notify screening or quarantine officers if they suspect that they have or have come into contact with one of the designated communicable diseases.[53]

Apart from these legislative provisions, it is possible that an individual with an infectious disease who puts others at risk of infection may be liable in tort (for example, for negligence or battery). There have apparently been few cases litigated on this basis in Canada,[54] though there have been some successful ac-

---

[48] See, *e.g.*, *Public Health Act, 1994*, S.S. 1994, c. P-37.1, ss. 33, 34, 35; Disease Control Regulations, R.R.S. 2000, c. P-37.1, Reg. 11, ss. 6, 7, 8.

[49] See, *e.g.*, *Public Health Act*, R.S.A. 2000, c. P-37, s. 20 (prescribed communicable diseases and prescribed STDs); *Minister's Regulation under the Public Health Act*, R.Q. c. S-2.2, r. 2, s. 9 (tuberculosis prescribed as disease for which treatment is mandatory); Disease Control Regulations, R.R.S. 2000, c. P-37.1, Reg. 11, Table 2 (category II diseases to which obligations apply, including HIV, hepatitis, STDs and tuberculosis); *Public Health Act*, S.B.C. 2008, c. 28, s. 15 (any "health hazard").

[50] See, *e.g.*, *Public Health Act*, R.S.A. 2000, c. P-37, s. 20; *Public Health Act, 1994*, S.S. 1994, c. P-37.1, s. 33; *Public Health Act*, S.B.C. 2008, c. 28, ss. 16-17.

[51] Communicable Disease Regulations, N.S. Reg. 196/2005, s. 10(1); Reporting of Diseases and Conditions Regulation, Man. Reg. 37/2009, s. 19; *Health Protection and Promotion Act*, R.S.O. 1990, c. H.7, s. 34; *Public Health Act*, R.S.Q., c. S-2.2, s. 86 (this applies only for prescribed diseases for which treatment is compulsory).

[52] *Public Health Act*, R.S.A. 2000, c. P-37, ss. 39-52. See also the discussion of coercive powers below.

[53] *Quarantine Act*, S.C. 2005, c. 20, s. 15.

[54] See, *e.g.*, *Fitzgerald v. Tin*, [2003] B.C.J. No. 203 (B.C.S.C.) (liability of a taxi company for a needle stick injury); *Healey v. Lakeridge Health Corp.*, [2010] O.J. No. 417, 2010 ONSC 725

tions in the United States.[55] In 2007, a lawsuit was initiated against Andrew Speaker, an American lawyer infected with drug-resistant tuberculosis who took a flight from Prague to Montreal despite being advised not to travel. Nine individuals who were on the flight filed an action in the Quebec Superior Court.[56] The prospects of successfully obtaining substantial damages in this case are limited by the fact that none of the plaintiffs appear to have been infected with tuberculosis, though other damages are alleged.[57]

The Supreme Court of Canada has also held that an individual who does not disclose his or her HIV-positive status and exposes another person to a significant risk of infection (for example, through unprotected sexual contact) may be convicted of aggravated assault.[58] Even if the complainant is not actually infected with the virus, her or his life is put at significant risk through the possibility of infection and this establishes the first element of aggravated assault, endangering the life of the complainant.[59] The majority also held that the second element, the application of force without consent, was established since withholding information about one's HIV status from a potential sexual partner amounts to fraud which vitiates their consent.[60] Interveners in the case had argued that criminal law is not an effective or appropriate way of addressing the risk of HIV transmission, which should be dealt with through public health statutes; they also argued that criminalization could deter people from seeking HIV testing and further stigmatize HIV-positive individuals.[61] However, these arguments were rejected by Cory J. (writing for the majority of the Court), who noted that public education about the risk of HIV transmission did not appear to be effective in all cases and thus argued that the criminal law could have an important supplementary role in deterring particularly risky conduct and thereby providing some protection.[62] Since this decision, a number of individuals have

---

(Ont. S.C.J.) (attempted class actions against the operator of a hospital for transmission of tuberculosis by two infected patients). Note that both cases involve actions against a third party, rather than liability of the infected individual himself or herself.

[55] See the brief discussion in Mary Anne Bobinski, "HIV/AIDS and Public Health Law" in Tracey M. Bailey, Timothy Caulfield & Nola M. Ries, eds., *Public Health Law & Policy in Canada*, 2d ed. (Markham, ON: LexisNexis Canada, 2008) at 233. The decision in *Fitzgerald v. Tin*, [2003] B.C.J. No. 203 at paras. 46-50 (B.C.S.C.) discusses approaches to damages assessment in such cases in the U.S. jurisprudence.

[56] "Canadians launch lawsuits against TB-infected flyer" CBC News (July 12, 2007), online at: <http://www.cbc.ca/canada/story/2007/07/12/tb-lawsuit.html>.

[57] See the discussion in Yann Joly & Gillian Nycum, "The Tuberculosis Scare in Retrospect" (2007) 35 J.L. Med. & Ethics 734 at 735. As of the date of writing, no decision in this case has been reported.

[58] *R. v. Cuerrier*, [1998] S.C.J. No. 64, [1998] 2 S.C.R. 371 (S.C.C.). Subsequently, in *R. v. Williams*, [2003] S.C.J. No. 41, [2003] 2 S.C.R. 134 (S.C.C.), the Court held that the accused could only be convicted of attempted aggravated assault where it could not be established that he infected his partner after he learned of his HIV-positive status.

[59] *R. v. Cuerrier, ibid.*, at para. 95 (*per* Cory J., for the majority).

[60] *Ibid.*, at paras. 125-139 (*per* Cory J., for the majority).

[61] *Ibid.*, at paras. 140-145.

[62] *Ibid.*, at paras 146-147.

been prosecuted and convicted for concealing their HIV status (or other disease, for example, hepatitis C) and exposing others to a risk of infection.[63]

D.   COERCIVE POWERS

Public health legislation also confers on public authorities, such as the medical officer and/or the Minister of Health, a range of powers to prevent and contain the spread of infectious diseases and to deal with other public health threats. These include, for example, the authority to require individuals to submit to testing or treatment, to order the quarantine or isolation of individuals, to inspect premises and order them to be closed or disinfected, to require the production of information, or to require persons to take measures to prevent transmission.[64] Additional powers may be exercised during an epidemic or public health emergency, including the power to limit travel, to close public places, to procure or confiscate essential supplies, to take possession of premises, or any other necessary measure.[65] Federal quarantine officers may require travellers to undergo a health assessment or medical examination if there are reasonable grounds to believe that they have or may have, or have been in contact with, a communicable disease.[66] They may also order travellers to comply with treatment "or any other measure" to prevent the spread of disease.[67] Failure to comply may result in detention.[68]

An order for detention and treatment under Ontario public health legislation was unsuccessfully challenged in *Toronto (City, Medical Officer of Health) v. Deakin*.[69] Mr. Deakin, a "recalcitrant" tuberculosis patient, had consented to an order of detention but objected to treatment and to restraints that had been used to prevent his escape from detention. When the medical officer sought to extend the order, Deakin challenged it on the basis that it infringed his rights under sections 7 and 9 of the *Canadian Charter of Rights and Freedoms*. The Court accepted that the Charter applied to the actions of the medical centre and the doctor, who were acting under statutory authority, but held that any infringement of the patient's rights was justified under section 1 of the Charter. Isolation becomes even more problematic in the case of extensively drug-resistant tuber-

---

[63]   See, *e.g.*, *R. v. Smith*, [2007] S.J. No. 116 (Sask. Prov. Ct.), affd [2008] S.J. No. 283, 2008 SKCA 61 (Sask. C.A.); *R. v. Mabior*, [2008] M.J. No. 277, 2008 MBQB 201 (Man. Q.B.), vard [2010] M.J. No. 308 (Man. C.A.); *R. v. McGregor*, [2008] O.J. No. 4939, 94 O.R. (3d) 500 (Ont. C.A.); *R. v. Wright*, [2009] B.C.J. No. 2785, 2009 BCCA 514 (B.C.C.A.), leave to appeal refused [2010] S.C.C.A. No. 22 (S.C.C.).

[64]   See, *e.g.*, *Health Protection Act*, S.N.S. 2004, c. 4, s. 32; *Health Protection and Promotion Act*, R.S.O. 1990, c. H.7, ss. 22, 41; *Public Health Act*, R.S.A. 2000, c. P-37, ss. 29-52; *Public Health Act, 1994*, S.S. 1994, c. P-37.1, s. 38; *Public Health Act*, S.B.C. 2008, c. 28, ss. 28-29.

[65]   See, *e.g.*, *Health Protection Act*, S.N.S. 2004, c. 4, s. 53(2); *Public Health Act*, R.S.A. 2000, c. P-37, ss. 29(2.1), 52.6; *Public Health Act, 1994*, S.S. 1994, c. P-37.1, s. 45.

[66]   *Quarantine Act*, S.C. 2005, c. 20, ss. 20, 22.

[67]   *Ibid.*, s. 26.

[68]   *Ibid.*, s. 28.

[69]   [2002] O.J. No. 2777 (Ont. C.J.).

culosis (XDR-TB), due to the potentially indefinite period of detention that could be required for a patient whose disease cannot effectively be treated.[70] Nevertheless, an Ontario court approved the extension of a detention order for an individual with XDR-TB on the basis that the individual's plan to return to the community was unrealistic and the risk to the community was too significant.[71]

In addition to the powers provided for in public health legislation, as noted above, both federal and provincial/territorial levels of government have legislation relating to emergency management, which could apply to a public health emergency. Provincial legislation allows provincial ministers and municipal authorities to declare provincial or local states of emergency,[72] and to exercise broad powers to protect public health and safety in an emergency, including implementation of emergency plans, restrictions on movement, and regulation of essential goods and services.[73] Emergency powers may include the power to require qualified persons to provide assistance,[74] which would allow provincial or local authorities to compel medical or other health care professionals to provide services in a public health emergency.

Under the federal *Emergencies Act*, a "public welfare emergency" may include an emergency caused by an actual or imminent disease that "results or may result in a danger to life or property, social disruption or a breakdown in the flow of essential goods, services or resources, so serious as to be a national emergency".[75] A "national emergency" is defined as "an urgent and critical situation of a temporary nature" that, among other things, "seriously endangers the lives, health or safety of Canadians", if it exceeds the capacity or authority of a province and "cannot effectively be dealt with under any other law of Canada".[76] A serious epidemic of infectious disease could fall within this definition. A public welfare emergency may be declared by the Governor in Council to

---

[70] Jerome Amir Singh, Ross Upshur & Nesri Padayatchi, "XDR-TB in South Africa: No Time for Denial or Complacency" (2007) 4:1 PLoS Medicine e50; Jason Andrews *et al.*, "XDR-TB in South Africa: Theory and Practice" (2007) 4:4 PLoS Medicine e163.

[71] *Toronto (City) Medical Officer of Health v. McKay*, [2007] O.J. No. 3802, 2007 ONCJ 444 (Ont. C.J.).

[72] See, *e.g.*, *Emergency Management Act*, S.N.S. 1990, c. 8, s. 12; *Civil Emergency Measures Act*, R.S.N.W.T. 1988, c. C-9, ss. 11, 14; *Emergency Measures Act*, C.C.S.M. c. E80, ss. 10-11; *Emergency Planning Act*, S.S. 1989-90, c. E-8.1, ss. 17, 20; *Emergency Management and Civil Protection Act*, R.S.O. 1990, c. E.9, ss. 4, 7.0.1.

[73] See, *e.g.*, *Emergency Management Act*, S.N.S. 1990, c. 8, s. 14; *Civil Emergency Measures Act*, R.S.N.W.T. 1988, c. C-9, ss. 12, 17; *Emergency Measures Act*, C.C.S.M. c. E80, s. 12; *Emergency Planning Act*, S.S. 1989-90, c. E-8.1, ss. 18, 21; *Emergency Management and Civil Protection Act*, R.S.O. 1990, c. E.9, s. 7.0.2(4).

[74] See, *e.g.*, *Emergency Management Act*, S.N.S. 1990, c. 8, s. 14(c); *Civil Emergency Measures Act*, R.S.N.W.T. 1988, c. C-9, s. 12(d); *Emergency Measures Act*, C.C.S.M. c. E80, s. 12(c); *Emergency Planning Act*, S.S. 1989-90, c. E-8.1, s. 18(1)(m). Compare the *Emergency Management and Civil Protection Act*, R.S.O. 1990, c. E.9, s. 7.0.2(4)12, which provides for orders authorizing, but not requiring, qualified persons to render services.

[75] R.S.C. 1985 (4th Supp.), c. 22, s. 5.

[76] *Ibid.*, s. 3.

exist in all or part of Canada.[77] While the declaration of emergency is in effect, the Governor in Council has the authority to make orders and regulations reasonably believed to be necessary to deal with it, including, for example, restricting travel, regulating essential goods or services, or establishing emergency hospitals.[78]

One of the key challenges is striking the right balance between respect for provincial and local jurisdiction and ensuring coordinated, timely and effective action in an emergency situation. In most situations, measures at the local level will be of primary importance and broader action can be achieved through cooperation. The emergency powers of the Governor in Council under the federal *Emergencies Act* are to be used in a way that does not interfere with provincial emergency measures and "with the view of achieving, to the extent possible, concerted action" with affected provinces.[79] The Governor in Council is required to consult with affected provinces and is not to declare a public welfare emergency where the direct effects of the emergency are limited to a single province, unless that province's Lieutenant Governor in Council has indicated that the emergency exceeds the province's capacity or authority.[80] The limits established by these provisions are designed to avoid federal encroachments on provincial jurisdiction, but might prove to be unduly restrictive in a public health emergency.[81] Among the concerns raised in inquiries following the SARS outbreak were questions about the consistency and interoperability of federal and provincial territorial legislative frameworks for emergency response and the lack of clarity about the allocation of jurisdiction in emergencies.[82]

E.   VACCINATION

Although provincial legislation provides for mandatory immunization to be ordered as well as testing and treatment, individuals may be permitted to refuse immunization on conscientious or other grounds.[83] However, legislation may also provide that children can be excluded from school or day care facilities if

---

[77] *Ibid.*, s. 6.

[78] *Ibid.*, s. 8(1).

[79] *Ibid.*, s. 8(3).

[80] *Ibid.*, s. 14.

[81] For an argument in favour of more extensive federal emergency powers, see Amir Attaran & Kumanan Wilson, "A Legal and Epidemiological Justification for Federal Authority in Public Health Emergencies" (2007) 52 McGill L.J. 381.

[82] National Advisory Committee on SARS and Public Health, *Learning from SARS: Renewal of Public Health in Canada* (Ottawa: Health Canada, 2003) at 6-7, 98-102, 108.

[83] See, *e.g.*, *Public Health Act*, R.S.A. 2000, c. P-37, s. 38(3); *Public Health Act, 1994*, S.S. 1994, c. P-37.1, s. 64; *Immunization of School Pupils Act*, R.S.O. 1990, c. I.1, s. 3. The new British Columbia *Public Health Act*, S.B.C. 2008, c. 28, s. 16(4) is unusual in that it provides for objections on health or conscientious grounds (where permitted by regulation) for any preventive measure, not just vaccination. However, in an emergency, a person may be ordered to take preventive measures notwithstanding an objection (s. 56(1)), unless the person can provide documentation showing that this would seriously jeopardize his or her health (s. 56(2)).

they have not been immunized against designated diseases,[84] and a few jurisdictions specifically provide for mandatory immunization of school children against specified diseases.[85] There have been a number of instances in which students have been suspended from Canadian schools, amid growing concerns about low rates of immunization and the resurgence of previously dormant diseases such as pertussis (whooping cough).[86] Debate continues in Canada and elsewhere about the merits of mandatory vaccination for children;[87] other means of encouraging parents to consent to have their children vaccinated have been discussed, including education, improved adverse event reporting and compensation programs to address concerns about risks.[88]

Vaccines for human papilloma virus (HPV) have been at the centre of recent controversies about immunization programs. Widespread vaccination for HPV has been promoted on the basis that the disease is highly prevalent and poses a serious public health threat given its link to cervical cancer. However, mandatory or publicly funded vaccination for HPV has faced a range of objections, on grounds of religion (since most HPV infections are sexually transmitted), health (given concerns about the risks of the vaccine in proportion to its benefits) and equity (given the focus on girls).[89] Some U.S. states now require HPV vaccination as a condition for school entry for girls, though they allow parents to opt out.[90] In Canada, the National Advisory Committee on Immunization recommended the vaccine for all girls between 9 and 13 years of age, and with some qualifications for females aged 14 to 26.[91] The vaccine is offered on a

---

[84] *Public Health Act, 1994*, S.S. 1994, c. P-37.1, s. 45(2)(d)(ii) (in the case of a serious public health threat); *Communicable Diseases Act*, R.S.N.L. 1990, c. C-26, s. 25.

[85] *Immunization of School Pupils Act*, R.S.O. 1990, c. I.1, s. 6; Reporting and Diseases Regulation, N.B. Reg. 2009-136, s. 12. Note, however, that these are subject to medical or conscientious objection exceptions. Under the *Public Health Act*, R.S.A. 2000, c. P-37, s. 29(2)(b)(ii)(A), the medical officer of health may, by order, prohibit any person from attending a school if the presence of communicable disease is confirmed.

[86] "Kingston students suspended until immunized" CBC News (September 25, 2006), online at: <http://www.cbc.ca/health/story/2006/09/25/immunizations.html>; "More than 1,000 Waterloo students suspended from school" CBC News (May 4, 2006), online at: <http://www.cbc.ca/canada/toronto/story/2006/05/04/immunization-schools20060504.html>.

[87] See Patricia Peppin, "Vaccines and Emerging Challenges for Public Health Law" in Tracey M. Bailey, Timothy Caulfield & Nola M. Ries, eds., *Public Health Law & Policy in Canada*, 2d ed. (Markham, ON: LexisNexis Canada, 2008) at 154-64.

[88] Kumanan Wilson *et al.*, "Addressing the Emergence of Pediatric Vaccination Concerns: Recommendations from a Canadian Policy Analysis" (2006) 97 Can. J. Public Health 139.

[89] See *e.g.*, Gail Javitt, Deena Berkowitz & Lawrence O. Gostin, "Assessing Mandatory HPV Vaccination: Who Should Call the Shots?" (2008) 36 J.L. Med. & Ethics 384; Joanna N. Erdman, "Health Equity, HPV and the Cervical Cancer Vaccine" (2008) Health L.J. 127.

[90] Gail Javitt, Deena Berkowitz & Lawrence O. Gostin, "Assessing Mandatory HPV Vaccination: Who Should Call the Shots?" (2008) 36 J.L. Med. & Ethics 384; Alexandra Stewart, "Childhood Vaccine and School Entry Laws: The Case of HPV Vaccine" (2008) 123 Public Health Reports 801.

[91] National Advisory Committee on Immunization, "Statement on Human Papillomavirus Vaccine" (2007) 33 Canada Communicable Disease Report 1 at 23.

voluntary basis in school-based programs in all provinces and territories, supported by some public funding.[92]

Mandatory vaccination for health care workers has been the subject of on-going debate in the context of seasonal influenza,[93] and was the focus of protests and litigation in the U.S. during the 2009–2010 H1N1 influenza pandemic.[94] The pandemic also brought other vaccine law and policy issues to the fore. The process for testing and approval of the vaccine had to balance the need for adequate safety testing against the urgency of an imminent outbreak.[95] Then, governments faced a range of challenges in designing and implementing fair and efficient policies to deliver limited supplies of vaccines to priority groups and the general public.[96]

V.   CHRONIC DISEASE SURVEILLANCE AND PREVENTION

Chronic diseases are non-communicable diseases (although infectious agents may play a role in their development) that develop and cause disability over an extended time period.[97] These diseases, including heart disease, stroke, cancer and diabetes, account for the majority of deaths and of the burden of disease in Canada and worldwide.[98] Prevention and control of chronic disease present

---

[92] Gina Ogilvie *et al.*, "A Population-Based Evaluation of a Publicly Funded, School-Based HPV Vaccine Program in British Columbia, Canada: Parental Factors Associated with HPV Vaccine Receipt" (2010) 7:5 PLoS Medicine e1000270 at 2. Public funding varies from province to province: see, *e.g.*, Ogilvie, *ibid.*; Ontario Ministry of Health and Long-Term Care, "Human Papillomavirus (HPV) Vaccination Program for Grade 8 Females: What You Need to Know" (2008), online at: <http://www.health.gov.on.ca/en/ms/hpv/docs/hpv_factsheet_english.pdf>; Government of Alberta Health and Wellness, "Human Papillomavirus Vaccine" (2008), online at: <http://www.health.alberta.ca/documents/immunize-HPV-vaccine.pdf>.

[93] Ian Gemmill, "Mandatory Immunization of Health Care Providers: The Time Has Come" (2006) 97 Can. J. Public Health 86; Rebecca Rodal, Nola Ries & Kumanan Wilson, "Influenza Vaccination for Health Care Workers: Towards a Workable and Effective Standard" (2009) 17 Health L.J. 297.

[94] Steve Gorman, "Medical workers balk at mandatory flu vaccines" Reuters (November 13, 2009), online at: <http://uk.reuters.com/article/idUKTRE5AC57F20091113>.

[95] "H1N1 vaccine won't be rushed: Aglukkaq" CBC News (October 16, 2009), online at: <http://www.cbc.ca/health/story/2009/10/16/h1n1-vaccine.html>.

[96] Public Health Agency of Canada, "Guidance on H1N1 Vaccine Sequencing" (September 16, 2009), online at: <http://www.phac-aspc.gc.ca/alert-alerte/h1n1/vacc/pdf/vacc-eng.pdf>; Jason Fekete, "Alberta auditor to probe troubled H1N1 vaccine rollout" *Calgary Herald* (November 19, 2009), online at: <http://www.calgaryherald.com/health/Alberta+auditor+probe+troubled+H1N1+vaccine+rollout/2238524/story.html>; "First Nations need better access to swine flu vaccine: AFN" CBC News (July 17, 2009), online at: <http://www.cbc.ca/health/story/2009/07/17/first-nations-swine-flu-help.html>; Amy Mehler Paperny, "Private clinic doles out vaccine" *The Globe and Mail* (October 31, 2009), online at: <http://www.theglobeandmail.com/life/health/h1n1-swine-flu/private-clinic-doles-out-vaccine/article1346617/>.

[97] WHO, *Preventing Chronic Diseases: A Vital Investment* (Geneva: WHO, 2005) at 35.

[98] Statistics Canada, "Leading Causes of Death, 2007" (November 30, 2010) *The Daily* 11 at 11-13; WHO, *Preventing Chronic Diseases: A Vital Investment* (Geneva: WHO, 2005) at 37

some distinct challenges as compared to infectious diseases. Because these diseases may take years and even decades to develop and may have multiple causes, long-term, multi-faceted prevention strategies are required. The risk factors associated with a large proportion of the chronic disease burden are common and easily recognized — unhealthy diet, insufficient physical activity and smoking — but the interventions required to change them are challenging.

In part due to these challenges, the legal framework relating to chronic disease is more fragmented and difficult to analyze than that of infectious diseases. This section will focus on two main aspects: surveillance of chronic disease and cancer screening programs. The following sections will explore in some detail the range of legal interventions to reduce tobacco consumption and to encourage physical activity and healthier eating as measures to prevent chronic disease.

A. CHRONIC DISEASE REPORTING AND REGISTRIES

As discussed, mandatory reporting under public health legislation applies to many communicable diseases. In contrast, few chronic or non-communicable diseases are subject to mandatory reporting requirements. In 2006, New York City broke new ground (and provoked some controversy) by instituting mandatory reporting from laboratories for diabetes surveillance.[99] In Canada, some statutory reporting requirements could apply to prescribed non-communicable diseases, though these provisions have been little used.[100] Obligations to report work-related diseases and conditions may also exist under occupational health and safety legislation. The most common mandatory reporting provisions for chronic disease are for cancer. Eight provinces and territories have legislation requiring health care providers, laboratories or others to report cases of cancer, and a few others have general provisions under which information, including reports of cancer cases, must be provided on request.[101] Where reporting is compulsory, the obligation to report will override legal or ethical duties of confidentiality, just as for reporting of notifiable infectious diseases.

(chronic disease accounts for 60 per cent of global deaths and is the leading cause of death and burden of disease in all regions except Africa).

[99] Robert Steinbrook, "Facing the Diabetes Epidemic – Mandatory Reporting of Glycosylated Hemoglobin Values in New York City" (2006) 354 New Eng. J. Med. 545; Harold J. Krent *et al.*, "Whose Business is Your Pancreas? Potential Privacy Problems in New York City's Mandatory Diabetes Registry" (2008) 17 Annals Health L. 1.

[100] See, *e.g., Public Health Act, 1994*, S.S. 1994, c. P-37.1, s. 31. No non-communicable diseases have yet been prescribed by regulation for the purpose of this section. See also *Health Protection Act*, S.N.S. 2004, c. 4, s. 4(m): notifiable diseases and conditions are any that are prescribed by regulation, and are not restricted to communicable diseases. To date, only "vaccine associated adverse events" have been prescribed as notifiable non-communicable diseases or conditions: Reporting of Notifiable Diseases and Conditions Regulations, N.S. Reg. 195/2005, Sched. A, Part II.

[101] Barbara von Tigerstrom & Nola Ries, "Cancer Surveillance in Canada: Analysis of Legal and Policy Frameworks and Tools for Reform" (2009) 17 Health L.J. 1 at 14-15.

Each Canadian province and territory has a cancer registry, and all of these provide data to the Canadian Cancer Registry (CCR), which is maintained by Statistics Canada[102] and governed by the *Statistics Act*.[103] Once information is collected in the registry, it is governed by freedom of information and protection of privacy legislation applicable to public bodies, health information legislation and/or confidentiality provisions in the legislation governing the registry.[104] These will allow the information to be used or disclosed only for certain purposes, such as for research, compilation of statistics, designing prevention programs, and treatment or care of the individual who is the subject of the information.[105]

The variation and gaps in legislative frameworks across Canada create some challenges for cancer surveillance.[106] When reporting obligations are not consistent, the data collected cannot easily be compiled and compared. Cancer surveillance could also be more effective if registries had consistent and timely access to more information (*e.g.*, vital statistics data and information in electronic health records).[107] Furthermore, there are some differences and ambiguities in the ways in which legislation and registry policies attempt to enable valuable uses of cancer registry data for surveillance and research while ensuring adequate privacy protection.[108]

B.   SCREENING PROGRAMS

Screening involves testing asymptomatic members of a population or, more commonly, a target sub-population, for a disease or condition (or some precursor, risk factor, or indictor of a disease or condition). Because screening programs mean that many people will be tested who show no symptoms of a disease and may never develop it, the benefits of implementing a screening program must be carefully weighed against its costs and possible risks. Furthermore, our growing knowledge about the relationship between genetics and risks of disease raises the prospect of genetic screening as a public health strategy, carrying with it concerns about protection of genetic information and the use of racial categories to identify at-risk populations.[109]

---

[102]   Statistics Canada, "Canadian Cancer Registry: Detailed Information for 2008" (July 27, 2010), online at: <http://www.statcan.gc.ca/cgi-bin/imdb/p2SV.pl?Function=getSurvey&SDDS=3207& lang=en&db=imdb&adm=8&dis=2>.

[103]   R.S.C. 1985, c. S-19.

[104]   Barbara von Tigerstrom & Nola Ries, "Cancer Surveillance in Canada: Analysis of Legal and Policy Frameworks and Tools for Reform" (2009) 17 Health L.J. 1 at 9-12, 19-22.

[105]   *Ibid.*, at 20-22.

[106]   *Ibid.*, at 28-32.

[107]   *Ibid.*, at 19, 36-37.

[108]   *Ibid.*, at 21-22, 30, 34-36.

[109]   Muin J. Khoury, "From Genes to Public Health: The Applications of Genetic Technology in Disease Prevention" (1996) 86 Am. J. Public Health 1717; Michael J. Fine, Said A. Ibrahim & Stephen B. Thomas, "The Role of Race and Genetics in Health Disparities Research" (2005) 95

The most common chronic disease screening programs in Canada are for cervical cancer and breast cancer.[110] These programs are found in all provinces and territories, and are administered by the health department or provincial cancer agency. The programs involve the provision of screening tests to individuals in the identified target population on a voluntary basis, collection of the results in a centralized database, communication of results to the individual and her physician, and other communications with participants (for example, to remind them when they are due for a test). Although the primary aim of screening is detection and prevention of disease, information collected through organized screening programs also contributes to surveillance.[111]

The cervical cancer screening programs in Saskatchewan and Alberta were investigated by the respective provincial Information and Privacy Commissioners following complaints from women about privacy concerns associated with the programs.[112] Both investigations found that the collection, use and disclosure of information in the screening programs were consistent with provincial health information legislation, but raised concerns about the mandatory nature of the programs and the lack of an opt-out for women who did not wish to participate. The programs allowed women to opt out of receiving reminder letters as part of the program but did not permit them to withdraw from the program entirely. The Alberta report found that the lack of a full opt-out meant that the Alberta Cancer Board "did not implement a program that complied with the duty to consider an expressed wish as an important factor in deciding how much 'health information' to disclose".[113] Prior to the report being released, the Alberta Cancer Board decided to implement a full opt-out.[114] There is no equivalent provision in the Saskatchewan health information legislation,[115] and the Commissioner there found that the legislation had been complied with; he nevertheless recommended

---

Am. J. Public Health 2125; Sandra Soo-Jin Lee, "Racializing Drug Design: Implications of Pharmacogenomics for Health Disparities" (2005) 95 Am. J. Public Health 2133.

[110] Screening programs for newborns, especially for metabolic diseases, are common and may be mandatory in some jurisdictions: see Sheila Wildeman & Jocelyn Downie, "Genetic and Metabolic Screening of Newborns: Must Health Care Providers Seek Explicit Parental Consent?" (2001) 9 Health L.J. 61.

[111] In Manitoba, a specific regulation requires reporting of cervical cancer screening tests: Cervical Cancer Screening Registry Regulation, Man. Reg. 31/2009. In other jurisdictions, general cancer reporting requirements and collection of information by the cancer registry would apply.

[112] Saskatchewan Office of the Information and Privacy Commissioner, *Prevention Program for Cervical Cancer* (April 27, 2005), Investigation Report H-2005-002, online at: <http://www.oipc.sk.ca/Reports/H-2005-002.pdf>; Alberta Information and Privacy Commissioner, *Report on the Collection, Use and Disclosure of Health Information for the Alberta Cervical Cancer Screening Program* (December 12, 2005), Investigation Report H2005-IR-002, online at: <http://www.oipc.ab.ca/ims/client/upload/H2005_IR_002.pdf>.

[113] *Ibid.*, at para. 78. This duty is found in the *Health Information Act*, R.S.A. 2000, c. H-5, s. 58(2).

[114] *Ibid.*, at paras. 86-87.

[115] *Health Information Protection Act*, S.S. 1999, c. II-0.021.

that a full opt-out be available as a matter of policy and best practice.[116] He also found that greater transparency was required and that neither the Saskatchewan Cancer Agency nor many physicians in the province had taken adequate steps to inform women about the operation of the program.[117]

VI. TOBACCO CONTROL

Tobacco-related disease is the leading cause of preventable death in Canada and in the world.[118] Half of all habitual smokers will die of tobacco-related causes such as cardiovascular disease, respiratory diseases, strokes and cancer, losing an estimated average of 15 to 25 years of life expectancy.[119] Approximately 17 per cent of Canadians aged 15 or older, including 14 per cent of youth aged 15-19 years, are current smokers.[120] Recent studies show that about 40,000 deaths in Canada are attributable to tobacco consumption.[121]

Given the serious impact of tobacco consumption on public health, many governments have designed and implemented a broad range of measures to reduce this consumption and the harm it causes. Comprehensive tobacco control policies pursue a number of intermediate goals with the ultimate aim of reducing the human and economic cost of tobacco consumption. Common strategies include: reducing demand through marketing restrictions and price increases; restricting the supply of tobacco products, particularly to young people; and smoking bans to minimize harm from second-hand smoke (SHS). Finally, judicial and other measures can be used to impose accountability, deter harmful conduct and recover costs associated with tobacco consumption.

A. REDUCING DEMAND

One of the objectives of tobacco control is to prevent people from taking up smoking, since the addictive properties of tobacco make it difficult for most

---

[116] Saskatchewan Office of the Information and Privacy Commissioner, *Prevention Program for Cervical Cancer* (April 27, 2005), Investigation Report H-2005-002, online at: <http://www.oipc.sk.ca/Reports/H-2005-002.pdf> at 12, 159*ff.*, 180.

[117] *Ibid.*, at 10-11.

[118] Eva M. Makomaski Illing & Murray J. Kaiserman, "Mortality Attributable to Tobacco Use in Canada and its Regions, 1998" (2004) 95 Can. J. Public Health 38 at 42-43; WHO, *The World Health Report 2003* (Geneva: WHO, 2003) at 91.

[119] International Agency for Research on Cancer, Press Release No. 141 (June 19, 2002), online at: <http://www.iarc.fr/en/media-centre/pr/2002/pr141.html>.

[120] Health Canada, "Canadian Tobacco Use Monitoring Survey (CTUMS): CTUMS 2009 Wave 1 Survey Results" (2010), online at: <http://www.hc-sc.gc.ca/hc-ps/tobac-tabac/research-recherche/stat/_ctums-esutc_2009/w-p-1_sum-som-eng.php>.

[121] Eva M. Makomaski Illing & Murray J. Kaiserman, "Mortality Attributable to Tobacco Use in Canada and its Regions, 1998" (2004) 95 Can. J. Public Health 38 at 42-43 (47,000 deaths or 22 per cent of all deaths in 1998); Dolly Baliunas *et al.*, "Smoking-attributable Mortality and Expected Years of Life Lost in Canada 2002: Conclusions for Prevention and Policy" (2007) 27 Chronic Diseases in Canada 154 at 160 (approximately 40,000 deaths or 16.6 per cent of all deaths in 2002).

people to quit.[122] Many of the same interventions also aim to encourage existing smokers to reduce (and hopefully eliminate) their consumption. The most common legal strategies include marketing restrictions, control over packaging and labelling tobacco products, and increasing the price of tobacco products through taxation. These are implemented alongside other interventions such as public education and "countermarketing" to reduce demand.

1. Marketing Restrictions

The marketing of tobacco, like other consumer products, is subject to general prohibitions on misleading advertising, and these have been the subject of some of the litigation against the tobacco industry, as will be seen below. In addition, governments increasingly restrict the ability of tobacco companies to market their products with the aim of preventing advertising and other marketing activities from increasing demand for these harmful products. In particular, they seek to eliminate marketing that is likely to influence young people; since most smokers become addicted before the age of 18, tobacco marketing campaigns directed at children and youth are a particular concern.[123]

In Canada, both federal and provincial legislation restricts tobacco marketing in a variety of ways. Part IV of the federal *Tobacco Act*[124] sets out restrictions on promotion, which is broadly defined to include any direct or indirect "representation about a product or service by any means, ... including any communication of information about a product or service and its price and distribution, that is likely to influence and shape attitudes, beliefs and behaviours about the product or service".[125] The Act prohibits the promotion of tobacco products or related brand elements except as authorized by the Act and regulations, and proscribes the publication, broadcasting or other dissemination of prohibited promotions.[126] In addition, certain forms of promotion are specifically prohibited, including promotion by any means that are "false, misleading or deceptive or that are likely to create a false impression about the characteristics, health effects or health hazards of the tobacco product or its emissions", testimonials or endorsements (including by fictional characters), or the use of to-

---

[122] U.S. Department of Health and Human Services, *Reducing Tobacco Use: A Report of the Surgeon General* (Atlanta, GA: U.S. Department of Health and Human Services, Centers for Disease Control and Prevention, National Center for Chronic Disease Prevention and Health Promotion, Office on Smoking and Health, 2000), online at: Centers for Disease Control and Prevention <http://www.cdc.gov/tobacco/data_statistics/sgr/2000/complete_report/index.htm> at 97, 129.

[123] See, *e.g.*, Paul J. Chung *et al.*, "Youth Targeting by Tobacco Manufacturers Since the Master Settlement Agreement" (2002) 21 Health Affairs 254.

[124] S.C. 1997, c. 13.

[125] *Ibid.*, s. 18(1). Section 18(2) exempts certain activities from the operation of Part IV, such as literary, artistic or scientific works or reports, commentaries or opinions depicting or referring to tobacco products or brands, provided that no consideration is given by a tobacco retailer or manufacturer for these works.

[126] *Ibid.*, ss. 19, 31(1).

bacco manufacturer names or brand elements in sponsorship or in naming of sports or cultural events or facilities.[127] Sales promotions such as gifts with purchase, cash rebates, games and contests, and the distribution of free tobacco products or accessories are prohibited.[128] Advertisements depicting or evoking tobacco products, packages or brand elements are prohibited.[129] An exception is made for informational and brand preference advertising in direct mail addressed to an adult or places where young persons are not permitted, provided that it is not "lifestyle advertising" or reasonably interpreted as appealing to young people.[130] "Lifestyle advertising" is advertising that "associates a product with, or evokes a positive or negative emotion about or image of, a way of life such as one that includes glamour, recreation, excitement, vitality, risk or daring".[131] The sale and promotion of non-tobacco products displaying a tobacco brand element is also prohibited if they have similar "lifestyle" associations or are associated with or appealing to young persons.[132]

These provisions represent the federal government's attempt to tailor marketing restrictions in a way that would avoid unjustifiable infringements of the right to freedom of expression as interpreted by the Supreme Court of Canada in the 1995 decision of *RJR-MacDonald*.[133] In that case the former federal tobacco legislation, the *Tobacco Products Control Act*[134] was challenged as being outside Parliament's jurisdiction and a violation of the *Canadian Charter of Rights and Freedoms*. The Supreme Court found the legislation to be a valid exercise of the federal government's criminal law power,[135] but some of the provisions were struck down as contrary to the Charter. The Attorney General conceded that the prohibition on tobacco advertising and promotion infringed section 2(*b*) of the Charter, and the majority of judges also found that the requirement of unattributed health warnings infringed this section.[136] By a narrow majority, the Court decided that some of the provisions could not be justified as reasonable limits under section 1 of the Charter. The Act's prohibition on tobacco advertising, ban on the use of tobacco trademarks on non-tobacco products and requirement of unattributed health warnings on tobacco packages were struck down (along with several other sections that could not be severed from these provisions). Despite a strong dissenting judgment by La Forest J. (with whom three other members of

---

127 *Ibid.*, ss. 20, 21, 24, 25.
128 *Ibid.*, s. 29.
129 *Ibid.*, s. 22(1).
130 *Ibid.*, s. 22(2), (3).
131 *Ibid.*, s. 22(4).
132 *Ibid.*, s. 27.
133 *RJR-MacDonald Inc. v. Canada (Attorney General)*, [1995] S.C.J. No. 68, [1995] 3 S.C.R. 199 (S.C.C.).
134 S.C. 1988, c. 20 [repealed by S.C. 1997, c. 13, s. 64].
135 All members of the Court agreed that the provisions requiring health warnings were valid criminal law; all but Major and Sopinka JJ. held that advertising bans could also fall within the criminal law power; and the majority held that the entire Act was validly enacted as criminal law.
136 *RJR-MacDonald v. Canada (Attorney General)*, [1995] S.C.J. No. 68, 3 S.C.R. 199 at para. 124 (S.C.C.).

the Court concurred), the majority concluded that these provisions were not a minimal impairment of freedom of expression since the government had not demonstrated that less stringent measures would not be just as effective. Although both the majority and dissent stated that the necessity of such measures need not be established by definitive, scientific proof but could be supported by logic or common sense, they applied this test quite differently and thereby came to opposite conclusions on these provisions.[137]

The new provisions of the *Tobacco Act* were considered by the Supreme Court in *Canada (Attorney General) v. JTI-Macdonald Corp.*, another challenge on constitutional grounds.[138] The plaintiffs argued that the *Tobacco Act* unjustifiably infringed their freedom of expression in five different respects,[139] and that the regulation increasing the size of mandatory warning labels on tobacco packages was also an unjustifiable infringement.[140] The Court rejected these arguments and upheld all of the impugned provisions, finding that when they were properly interpreted, any violations of freedom of expression were justified under section 1 of the Charter.

Federal authorities have also taken some steps to prevent the use of descriptors such as "light" and "mild" in cigarette marketing, due to concerns that many consumers mistakenly believe these cigarettes are not as harmful and are less likely to quit smoking if they switch to brands marketed as light or mild.[141] The use of these descriptors has been alleged to be misleading or deceptive in litigation and in complaints to the federal Competition Bureau.[142] The Bureau reached agreements with several major cigarette manufacturers in which they would stop using these descriptors.[143] Proposed regulations banning the use of the terms by all manufacturers were published in 2007,[144] but have not yet been adopted. Similar bans have already been adopted in many jurisdictions, including Europe and, more recently, the United States.[145]

---

[137] For discussion, see Barbara von Tigerstrom, "Healthy Communities: Public Health Law at the Supreme Court of Canada" in Jocelyn Downie & Elaine Gibson, eds., *Health Law at the Supreme Court of Canada* (Toronto: Irwin Law, 2007).

[138] *Canada (Attorney General) v. JTI-Macdonald Corp.*, [2007] S.C.J. No. 30, [2007] 2 S.C.R. 610 (S.C.C.).

[139] The challenged provisions in the *Tobacco Act*, S.C. 1997, c. 13 were: ss. 18-19, 20, 22(3), 24-25.

[140] Tobacco Product Information Regulations, SOR/2000-272.

[141] M.J. Ashley, J. Cohen & R. Ferrence, "'Light' and 'Mild' Cigarettes: Who Smokes Them? Are They Being Misled?" (2001) 92 Can. J. Public Health 407; H.A. Tindle *et al.*, "Switching to 'Lighter' Cigarettes and Quitting Smoking" (2009) 18 Tobacco Control 485.

[142] See the discussion of class action litigation on this issue below.

[143] Competition Bureau, News Release, "Competition Bureau Reaches Further Agreements with Six Cigarette Companies to Stop Using 'Light' and 'Mild' on Cigarette Packages" (July 31, 2007), online at: <http://www.competitionbureau.gc.ca/epic/site/cb-bc.nsf/en/02383e.html>.

[144] *Promotion of Tobacco Products and Accessories Regulations (Prohibited Terms)*, C. Gaz. 2007.I.2239.

[145] EC, *Directive 2001/37/EC of the European Parliament and of the Council of 5 June 2001 on the approximation of the laws, regulations and administrative provisions of the Member States concerning the manufacture, presentation and sale of tobacco products*, O.J. L. 194/26, art. 7; *Federal Food, Drug, and Cosmetic Act*, 21 U.S.C. § 387k.

Provincial legislation also restricts tobacco marketing in various ways. Some restrictions duplicate the federal *Tobacco Act* provisions, such as prohibiting sponsorship and endorsements.[146] However, in some cases provincial restrictions may be more stringent than the federal provisions. For example, all provinces and territories prohibit or significantly restrict retail displays of tobacco products,[147] although retail display is specifically permitted by the federal legislation.[148] In *Rothmans, Benson & Hedges Inc. v. Saskatchewan*,[149] a challenge was brought against the retail display prohibition in the Saskatchewan *Tobacco Control Act*[150] on the grounds that it was inoperative because of the doctrine of federal legislative paramountcy. The Court upheld the provincial legislation, noting that a retailer could comply with both federal and provincial provisions, and the federal provisions did not create an *entitlement* to display tobacco products, but merely defined the scope of its promotion prohibition.[151] Both the federal and provincial statutes have the same purposes, so there is no inconsistency between their provisions merely because one is stricter.[152]

2.   Packaging, Labelling and Warnings

Legal requirements with respect to the packaging of tobacco products aim to ensure that consumers are adequately informed about the health risks of these products. The federal *Tobacco Act* requires packages to display warnings as prescribed by the Tobacco Products Information Regulations.[153] The prescribed warnings contain short statements in bold lettering about the health effects of tobacco products and full-colour graphic images, and must cover at least 50 per cent of the principal display surfaces of the package.[154] The regulations also require prescribed health information to be printed on leaflet inserts or on another part of the package, covering 60 per cent to 70 per cent of the surface area

---

[146] *Tobacco Act*, R.S.Q., c. T-0.01, ss. 22, 24(4).

[147] *Tobacco Control Act*, R.S.B.C. 1996, c. 451, s. 2.4; *Tobacco Reduction Act*, S.A. 2005, c. T-3.8, s. 7.1; *Tobacco Control Act*, S.S. 2001, c. T-14.1, s. 6; *Non-Smokers Health Protection Act*, C.C.S.M. c. N92, ss. 7.2, 7.3; *Smoke-Free Ontario Act*, S.O. 1994, c. 10, s. 3.1(1); *Tobacco Act*, R.S.Q., c. T-0.01, s. 20.2; *Tobacco Sales Act*, S.N.B. 1993, c. T-6.1, s. 6.4(2); *Tobacco Access Act*, S.N.S. 1993, c. 14, s. 9AA(1); *Tobacco Sales and Access Act*, R.S.P.E.I. 1988, c. T-3.1, s. 5.1; *Tobacco Control Act*, S.N.L. 1993, c. T-4.1, s. 4.2; *Smoke-Free Places Act*, S.Y. 2009, c. 8, s. 8; *Tobacco Control Act*, S.N.W.T. 2006, c. 9, s. 4(b); *Tobacco Control Act*, S.Nu. 2003, c. 13, s. 8.

[148] *Tobacco Act*, S.C. 1997, c. 13, s. 30.

[149] *Rothmans, Benson & Hedges Inc. v. Saskatchewan*, [2005] S.C.J. No. 1, [2005] 1 S.C.R. 188 (S.C.C.).

[150] *Tobacco Control Act*, S.S. 2001, c. T-14.1, s. 6.

[151] *Rothmans, Benson & Hedges Inc. v. Saskatchewan*, [2005] S.C.J. No. 1, [2005] 1 S.C.R. 188 at paras. 17-18 (S.C.C.).

[152] *Ibid.*, at paras. 25-26.

[153] *Tobacco Act*, S.C. 1997, c. 13, s. 15(1); Tobacco Products Information Regulations, SOR/2000-272, ss. 5-6.

[154] Tobacco Products Information Regulations, *ibid.*, s. 5(2), (3).

in each case,[155] and the amounts of toxic emissions or constituents to be displayed on the package.[156] Some provincial statutes also enable regulations to be adopted prescribing warnings to be carried on tobacco packages.[157] Both federal and provincial legislation require health warnings to be displayed where tobacco products are sold.[158]

3. Taxation

The taxation of tobacco products is an important part of tobacco control, because raising the price of tobacco has been shown to reduce consumption, especially by young people.[159] In Canada, both the federal and provincial governments impose duties and taxes on tobacco products.[160] Federal duties are payable by the manufacturer or importer, while provincial taxes are payable at the point of sale (or upon import, if tobacco products are brought into the province by consumers). Federal and provincial legislation controls the manufacture, sale and import or export of tobacco products, and requires that these products be stamped to indicate that the duty has been paid.[161] Such measures aim to curtail smuggling of tobacco products, which has been an ongoing problem especially where there is significant variation in taxation rates between jurisdictions. Lawsuits in several jurisdictions including Canada have accused major tobacco companies of collusion with smuggling.[162]

B. RESTRICTIONS ON SUPPLY

In most Canadian jurisdictions, sales of tobacco products are prohibited in certain specified locations, such as schools, child care and health care facilities, and

---

[155] *Ibid.*, s. 7.

[156] *Ibid.*, ss. 9-11.

[157] See, *e.g.*, *Smoke-Free Ontario Act*, S.O. 1994, c. 10, ss. 5(1), 19(1)(d); *Tobacco Control Act*, R.S.B.C. 1996, c. 451, s. 11(2)(a); *Tobacco Act*, R.S.Q., c. T-0.01, s. 28; *Non-Smokers Health Protection Act*, C.C.S.M. c. N92, s. 9(1)(e). Ontario has adopted regulations which require packages to carry the warnings prescribed by federal legislation: General, O. Reg. 48/06, s. 9.

[158] *Tobacco Act*, S.C. 1997, c. 13, s. 9 and see, *e.g.*, *Smoke-Free Ontario Act*, S.O. 1994, c. 10, s. 6; Tobacco Control Regulation, B.C. Reg. 232/2007, s. 5(1)(a), Sched. 1; Tobacco Access Regulations, N.S. Reg. 9/96, s. 3, Scheds. A-E; *Tobacco Act*, R.S.Q., c. T-0.01, s. 20.4.

[159] U.S. Department of Health and Human Services, *Reducing Tobacco Use: A Report of the Surgeon General* (Atlanta, GA: U.S. Department of Health and Human Services, Centers for Disease Control and Prevention, National Center for Chronic Disease Prevention and Health Promotion, Office on Smoking and Health, 2000), online: Centers for Disease Control and Prevention <http://www.cdc.gov/tobacco/data_statistics/sgr/2000/complete_report/index.htm> at 337; Frank J. Chaloupka, Melanie Wakefield & Christina Czart, "Taxing Tobacco: The Impact of Tobacco Taxes on Cigarette Smoking and Other Tobacco Use" in Robert L. Rabin & Stephen Sugarman, eds., *Regulating Tobacco* (Oxford: Oxford University Press, 2001) at 39.

[160] See, *e.g.*, *Excise Act, 2001*, S.C. 2002, c. 22, ss. 42-48; *Tobacco Tax Act*, R.S.O. 1990, c. T.10; *Tobacco Tax Act*, R.S.A. 2000, c. T-4; *Tobacco Tax Act*, R.S.B.C. 1996, c. 452.

[161] See, *e.g.*, *Excise Act, 2001*, S.C. 2002, c. 22, ss. 25.1-41; *Tobacco Tax Act*, R.S.B.C. 1996, c. 452; Tobacco Tax Act Regulation, B.C. Reg. 66/2002.

[162] See the discussion in the section on tobacco litigation below.

pharmacies.[163] Vending machines selling cigarettes may be prohibited or limited to certain locations.[164]

Legislation at the federal level and in almost every province and territory prohibits the supply of tobacco products to persons under a prescribed age (18 or 19).[165] The provisions prohibit both direct sales to minors and other forms of supply, such as purchasing tobacco on behalf of a minor (or selling to someone for this purpose).[166] A supplier will have a defence to a charge under these provisions if he or she attempted to verify the minor's age, was shown proof of age and reasonably believed that the minor was of age.[167] However, the mere fact that a minor appeared to be over the prescribed age is not a defence.[168]

The broad prohibitions, including supply as well as sale and sales to someone buying on behalf of a minor, attempt to cover non-commercial sources such as friends and family members who give or sell cigarettes to minors, which are an important source of supply to young people.[169] However, a few jurisdictions exempt private supply by parents or legal guardians from the prohibition.[170] Several statutes also exempt gifts of tobacco for cultural or spiritual use, to accommodate traditional uses of tobacco by Aboriginal peoples.[171]

Alberta, Nova Scotia and the Northwest Territories prohibit the possession, consumption and/or purchase of tobacco products by minors.[172] When these

---

[163] See, *e.g.*, *Tobacco Reduction Act*, S.A. 2005, c. T-3.8, s. 7.3; *Tobacco Control Act*, S.S. 2001, c. T-14.1, s. 8; *Tobacco Access Act*, S.N.S. 1993, c. 14, s. 9B; *Smoke-Free Ontario Act*, S.O. 1994, c. 10, s. 4; *Tobacco Act*, R.S.Q., c. T-0.01, ss. 17, 18.

[164] See, *e.g.*, *Tobacco Act*, S.C. 1997, c. 13, s. 12; *Smoke-Free Ontario Act*, S.O. 1994, c. 10, s. 7; *Tobacco Act*, R.S.Q., c. T-0.01, s. 16.

[165] Alberta's legislation does not, although it prohibits possession or use of tobacco by young persons (see below) and the federal prohibition would apply in Alberta.

[166] See, *e.g.*, *Tobacco Act*, S.C. 1997, c. 13, s. 8(1); *Tobacco Control Act*, R.S.B.C. 1996, c. 451, s. 2(2); *Smoke-Free Ontario Act*, S.O. 1994, c. 10, s. 3(1); *Tobacco Act*, R.S.Q., c. T-0.01, ss. 13, 14.3; *Tobacco Access Act*, S.N.S. 1993, c. 14, s. 5.

[167] See, *e.g.*, *Tobacco Act*, S.C. 1997, c. 13, s. 8(2); *Tobacco Control Act*, R.S.B.C. 1996, c. 451, s. 2(2.1); *Non-Smokers Health Protection Act*, C.C.S.M. c. N92, s. 7(3). The maritime provinces take a slightly different approach and provide that where a purchaser appears to be underage, proof of age in a prescribed form must be provided before the product can be sold: see, *e.g.*, *Tobacco Sales Act*, S.N.B. 1993, c. T-6.1, s. 5(2).

[168] See, *e.g.*, *Tobacco Access Act*, S.N.S. 1993, c. 14, s. 5(3).

[169] Nancy A. Rigotti, "Reducing the Supply of Tobacco to Youths" in Robert L. Rabin & Stephen Sugarman, eds., *Regulating Tobacco* (Oxford: Oxford University Press, 2001) at 146-47; J. Forster *et al.*, "Social exchange of cigarettes by youth" (2003) 12 Tobacco Control 148.

[170] *Non-Smokers Health Protection Act*, C.C.S.M. c. N92, s. 7(2)(a); *Tobacco Control Act*, S.S. 2001, c. T-14.1, s. 4(4).

[171] See *Smoke-Free Ontario Act*, S.O. 1994, c. 10, s. 13(2); *Non-Smokers Health Protection Act*, C.C.S.M. c. N92, s. 7(2)(b); *Tobacco Control Act*, S.S. 2001, c. T-14.1, s. 4(5); *Smoke-free Places Act*, S.N.B. 2004, c. S-9.5, s. 2(2).

[172] *Prevention of Youth Tobacco Use Act*, R.S.A. 2000, c. P-22, s. 2; *Smoke-free Places Act*, S.N.S. 2002, c. 12, s. 11(1); *Tobacco Control Act*, S.N.W.T. 2006, c. 9, s. 3(4.1).

prohibitions are violated, the tobacco in possession of a minor may be confiscated or the minor may be fined.[173]

Several jurisdictions, including Canada, have recently moved to prohibit the use of flavourings (such as fruit or chocolate flavours) in tobacco products, in part because these products are particularly appealing to young people.[174] Bans on flavoured cigarettes took effect in 2010 both in Canada[175] and in the U.S.[176]

C.   PROTECTION FROM SECOND-HAND SMOKE

Second-hand smoke (SHS, also known as environmental tobacco smoke, passive smoking or involuntary smoking) has been found to cause lung cancer and cardiovascular disease, and to have serious health effects on children; a 2006 report of the U.S. Surgeon General concluded that there is no "safe level" of exposure to second-hand smoke.[177] As awareness has spread that SHS is not just a nuisance but a serious health hazard, smoking bans in federal, provincial/territorial and local legislation have been extended progressively to include workplaces, many public places and, most recently, some private spaces. There is a clear trend toward increasingly comprehensive smoking bans, adopted in response to evidence that restricting smoking to designated areas does not effectively minimize the harm from SHS exposure.[178]

The federal *Non-smokers' Health Act* restricts smoking in workplaces within the jurisdiction of the federal government, which include government offices and federally regulated industries.[179] The provinces and territories have imposed a range of restrictions on smoking, as have many municipalities.[180] Non-smoking bylaws are classified according to their level of protection: bronze

---

[173] *Prevention of Youth Tobacco Use Act*, R.S.A. 2000, c. P-22, ss. 3, 4; *Smoke-free Places Act*, S.N.S. 2002, c. 12, s. 11(2); *Tobacco Control Act*, S.N.W.T. 2006, c. 9, s. 28(1).

[174] M. Jane Lewis & Olivia Wackowski, "Dealing with an Innovative Industry: A Look at Flavored Cigarettes Promoted by Mainstream Brands" (2006) 96 Am. J. Public Health 244; G.N. Connolly, "Sweet and Spicy Flavours: New Brands for Minorities and Youth" (2004) 13 Tobacco Control 211.

[175] *Tobacco Act*, S.C. 1997, c. 13, s. 5.1 (applies to cigarettes, little cigars and blunt wraps: see Schedule); *Smoke-Free Ontario Act*, S.O. 1994, c. 10, s. 6.1.

[176] *Federal Food, Drug, and Cosmetic Act*, 21 U.S.C. § 387g(a)(1).

[177] U.S. Department of Health and Human Services, *The Health Consequences of Involuntary Exposure to Tobacco Smoke: A Report of the Surgeon General* (Atlanta, GA: U.S. Department of Health and Human Services, Centers for Disease Control and Prevention, Coordinating Center for Health Promotion, National Center for Chronic Disease Prevention and Health Promotion, Office on Smoking and Health, 2006) at 11.

[178] See, *e.g.*, T. Cains *et al.*, "Designated 'No Smoking' Areas Provide from Partial to No Protection from Environmental Tobacco Smoke" (2004) 13 Tobacco Control 17; M. Pion & M.S. Givel, "Airport Smoking Rooms Don't Work" (2004) 13 Tobacco Control 37.

[179] *Non-smokers' Health Act*, R.S.C. 1985 (4th Supp.), c. 15.

[180] For information on municipal bylaws, see Health Canada, "Canadian Municipal By-laws Banning Smoking in Public Places" (2008), online at: <http://www.hc-sc.gc.ca/hc-ps/tobac-tabac/about-apropos/role/municip/ban-interdiction-eng.php>; Non-Smokers' Rights Association, "Compendium of Smoke-free Workplace and Public Place Bylaws" (2011), online at: <http://www.nsra-adnf.ca/cms/file/Compendium_Winter_2011.pdf>.

standard laws ban smoking in most public places, including restaurants, but allow two or more exemptions for places like bars or billiard halls, and allow the use of designated smoking rooms; silver standard laws are similar but allow only one exemption; and gold standard laws do not allow exemptions or designated smoking rooms.[181] Most provincial and territorial legislation now includes fairly comprehensive bans on smoking in workplaces and public places. They still vary in scope somewhat; for example, whether they include some outdoor spaces, such as restaurant patios and sporting venues, in the definition of public places where smoking is prohibited.[182] A few municipalities have gone further and banned smoking in outdoor spaces such as parks.[183]

Bans on smoking in bars and restaurants have been contentious, with some restaurant and bar owners (in some cases supported by tobacco companies) opposing them on the grounds that they are harmful to their businesses, though the evidence supporting such claims is at best equivocal.[184] Several lawsuits have tried unsuccessfully to challenge municipal bylaws.[185] In a recent Manitoba case,[186] a motel owner who operated a bar and restaurant unsuccessfully challenged a provision in the province's smoke-free legislation which excluded its application to reserve lands.[187] The owner, Mr. Jenkinson, and his company (Creekside Hideaway Motel Ltd.) appealed convictions for multiple breaches of the Act on the basis that differential application of the ban on and off reserve was discriminatory. Justice Clearwater agreed that section 15 had indeed been violated and that

---

[181] Health Canada, *ibid.*

[182] See, *e.g.*, *Tobacco Reduction Act*, S.A. 2005, c. T-3.8, s. 1(c), (h) (outdoor areas part of the definition of restaurants and licensed premises, which are covered by the prohibition); *Smoke-Free Places Act*, S.Y. 2008, c. 8, s. 4(2)(b) (outdoor eating or drinking area); *Smoke-Free Ontario Act*, S.O. 1994, c. 10, s. 9(2)6 (reserved seating area of a sporting or entertainment venue).

[183] See, *e.g.*, City of Vancouver, By-law No. 10077, *A By-law to amend Health By-law No. 9535 regarding regulation of smoking in parks* (June 22, 2010), online at: <http://vancouver.ca/blStorage/10077.PDF>.

[184] M. Scollo *et al.*, "Review of the Quality of Studies on the Economic Effects of Smoke-Free Policies on the Hospitality Industry" (2003) 12 Tobacco Control 13; Rita Luk, Roberta Ferrence & Gerhard Gmel, "The Economic Impact of a Smoke-Free Bylaw on Restaurant and Bar Sales in Ottawa, Canada" (2006) 101 Addiction 738.

[185] See, *e.g.*, *Restaurant and Food Services Assn. of British Columbia v. Vancouver (City)*, [1998] B.C.J. No. 53, 155 D.L.R. (4th) 587 (B.C.C.A.); *Albertos Restaurant v. Saskatoon (City)*, [2000] S.J. No. 725, 2000 SKCA 135 (Sask. C.A.); *Pub and Bar Coalition of Ontario v. Ottawa (City)*, [2002] O.J. No. 2240 (Ont. C.A.); *Filos Restaurant Ltd. v. Calgary (City)*, [2007] A.J. No. 159, 2007 ABQB 97 (Alta. Q.B.).

[186] *R. v. Jenkinson*, [2006] M.J. No. 250, 2006 MBQB 185 (Man. Q.B.).

[187] *Non-Smokers Health Protection Act*, C.C.S.M. c. N92, s. 9.4, which provides that the Act does not apply to "penitentiaries, federally regulated airports, Canadian Forces bases or to any other place or premises occupied by a federal work, undertaking or business, or on lands reserved for Indians". A number of statutes exempt traditional uses of tobacco by Aboriginal peoples from smoking bans, though Manitoba is alone in exempting reserve lands generally: *Tobacco Control Act*, R.S.B.C. 1996, c. 451, s. 2.3(2); *Tobacco Reduction Act*, S.A. 2005, c. T-3.8, s. 2(1); *Tobacco Control Act*, S.S. 2001, c. T-14.1, s. 11(3)(c); *Non-Smokers Health Protection Act*, C.C.S.M. c. N92, s. 5.1; *Smoke-Free Ontario Act*, S.O. 1994, c. 10, s. 13(3), (4); *Smoke-free Places Act*, S.N.B. 2004, c. S-9.5, s. 2(2).

the infringement could not be saved by section 1. However, this decision was overturned by the Court of Appeal, which held that the exemption was based on geography, not race, and Mr. Jenkinson had not been discriminated against on the grounds of any personal characteristic.[188]

Even the most comprehensive smoking bans provide for some exemptions, though increasingly only in designated areas that are limited in size, enclosed and have separate ventilation. Common exemptions include designated areas in residential care facilities and hotels rooms.[189] Some of the most contentious current issues involve the prohibition of smoking in areas that are traditionally seen as private, or at the boundary of public and private spaces. For example, residential care facilities and correctional facilities are workplaces but are also the short-term or long-term home for residents or inmates, so the rights and interests of these groups need to be balanced. Smoking bans in correctional facilities have been particularly contentious, and have been the subject of litigation both by correctional workers and inmates demanding protection and by inmates opposed to bans.[190] Most recently, several provinces have followed the growing international trend to ban smoking in private vehicles when children below a certain age are present.[191] These bans have been prompted by evidence that SHS levels in vehicles, even when the smoker attempts to provide some ventilation, are very high and present a significant health risk, especially to children.[192] However, critics have argued that these bans are an intrusion into private spaces,[193] and that they will be difficult to enforce.[194]

---

[188] *R. v. Jenkinson*, [2008] M.J. No. 78, 2008 MBCA 28 (Man. C.A.).

[189] See, *e.g.*, *Tobacco Reduction Act*, S.A. 2005, c. T-3.8, s. 5 (designated areas in a group living facility); *Tobacco Control Act*, S.S. 2001, c. T-14.1, s. 11(3)(a) (enclosed rooms in a special care home or personal group home); *Non-Smokers Health Protection Act*, C.C.S.M. c. N92, s. 3(1) (designated areas in group living facilities), s. 3(2) (hotel rooms); *Smoke-Free Ontario Act*, S.O. 1994, c. 10, s. 9(7) (residential care homes, where conditions are met), s. 9(10) (hotel rooms); *Tobacco Control Act*, S.N.W.T. 2006, c. 9, s. 8(2)(c) (part of a residential facility that meets prescribed requirements).

[190] See, *e.g.*, *Mercier v. Canada (Correctional Service)*, [2010] F.C.J. No. 816, 2010 FCA 167 (F.C.A.); *Union of Canadian Correctional Officers v. Canada (Attorney General)*, [2008] F.C.J. No. 683, 2008 FC 542 (F.C.). See also the discussion and cases cited in Barbara von Tigerstrom, "Tobacco Control and the Law in Canada" in Tracey M. Bailey, Timothy Caulfield & Nola M. Ries, eds., *Public Health Law & Policy in Canada*, 2d ed. (Markham, ON: LexisNexis Canada, 2008) 247 at 290-91.

[191] *Smoke-Free Ontario Act*, S.O. 1994, c. 10, s. 9.2(1) (passenger under 16 years); *Smoke-free Places Act*, S.N.B. 2004, c. S-9.5, s. 3(*d*.1) (under 16 years); *Smoke-Free Places Act*, S.N.S. 2002, c. 12, s. 5(2A) (under 19 years); *Smoke-Free Places Act*, R.S.P.E.I. 1988, c. S-4.2, s. 4(2) (under 19 years); *Smoke-Free Places Act*, S.Y. 2008, c. 8, s. 4(1)(q) (under 18 years).

[192] Ontario Medical Association, "Exposure to Second-Hand Smoke: Are We Protecting Our Kids?" (2004), online at: <https://www.oma.org/Resources/Documents/2004ExposureToSecond HandSmoke.pdf>; Ontario Medical Association, "Backgrounder – Tobacco Smoke Concentrations in Cars" (2008), online at: <https://www.oma.org/Resources/Documents/TobaccoSmoke ConcentrationsInCars.pdf>.

[193] Note, however, that some private vehicles are already subject to smoking bans if they are considered to be part of a workplace: see, *e.g.*, *Non-Smokers' Health Act*, R.S.C. 1985 (4th Supp.),

D. TOBACCO LITIGATION

One way of trying to hold the tobacco industry accountable for the harms caused by tobacco products and deter the most harmful marketing behaviours is through the use of litigation. Though the value of litigation in this context has been a matter of debate,[195] it has been pursued by governments as well as consumers with the aim of seeking compensation for past harms and furthering public health goals. Proponents have argued that litigation has also contributed indirectly to tobacco control efforts by increasing access to industry information, influencing public opinion, and providing funds for research and control efforts.[196] By far the most litigation has taken place in the United States,[197] but actions have also been attempted in other jurisdictions including Canada.[198] This litigation includes individual actions, class actions and suits by government.

Individual and class actions have used various claims and theories to recover for damage caused to the plaintiffs by tobacco products. Possible claims include negligence (failure to warn and/or negligent product design), misrepresentation, fraud, product liability, express or implied warranty, unjust enrichment, or deceptive advertising (under consumer protection or advertising statutes).[199] Usually, this involves the health consequences of smoking, though

---

c. 15, s. 3(2); *Tobacco Act*, R.S.Q., c. T-0.01, s. 2(10); *Smoke-free Places Act*, S.N.S. 2002, c. 12, s. 5(1)(m).

[194] For summaries of these arguments, see Legislative Library of British Columbia, "Smoking in Cars with Children (Background Brief 2008:01)" (2008), online at: <http://www.llbc.leg.bc.ca/public/background/200801bb_smoking.pdf> at 5; Jennifer L. Strange, "Kicking the Butt of Secondhand Smoke: Why Indiana Should Ban Smoking in Vehicles Carrying Minors" (2009) 6 Ind. Health L. Rev. 291.

[195] See, *e.g.*, Peter D. Jacobson & Soheil Soliman, "Litigation as Public Health Policy: Theory or Reality?" (2002) 30 J.L. Med. & Ethics 224; Benedickt Fischer & Jurgen Rehm, "Some Reflections on the Relationship of Risk, Harm and Responsibility in Recent Tobacco Lawsuits, and Implications for Public Health" (2001) 92 Can. J. Public Health 7; Roberta Ferrence *et al.*, "Tobacco Industry Litigation and the Role of Government: A Public Health Perspective" (2001) 92 Can. J. Public Health 89.

[196] Roberta Ferrence *et al.*, *ibid.*; R. Daynard, "Why Tobacco Litigation? Just How Important Is Litigation in Achieving the Goals of the Tobacco Control Community?" (2003) 12 Tobacco Control 1; Robert L. Rabin, "The Third Wave of Tobacco Tort Litigation" in Robert L. Rabin & Stephen Sugarman, eds., *Regulating Tobacco* (Oxford: Oxford University Press, 2001) at 198-203.

[197] For useful overviews of tobacco litigation in the United States, see Robert L. Rabin, "The Third Wave of Tobacco Tort Litigation" in Robert L. Rabin & Stephen Sugarman, eds., *ibid.*, at 176.

[198] For a recent overview of Canadian litigation, see Trevor Haché, "Tobacco-Related Litigation in Canada" (Smoking and Health Action Foundation & Non-Smokers' Rights Association, March 2010), online at: Non-Smokers' Rights Association <http://www.nsra-adnf.ca/cms/file/pdf/Tobacco-related_Litigation_in_Canada_2010.pdf>. For overviews of litigation in other countries, see D. Douglas Blanke, *Towards Health with Justice: Litigation and Public Inquiries as Tools for Tobacco Control* (Geneva: World Health Organization, 2002) at 33-43; Richard A. Daynard, Clive Bates & Neil Francey, "Tobacco Litigation Worldwide" (2000) 320 British Med. J. 111.

[199] D. Douglas Blanke, *Towards Health with Justice: Litigation and Public Inquiries as Tools for Tobacco Control*, *ibid.*, at 55-56.

an action was brought in Ontario against Imperial Tobacco Canada for negligence and product liability in relation to fires caused by cigarettes.[200] A few individual claims have been attempted in Canada, so far without success and facing numerous procedural challenges.[201]

Class actions have been initiated both in Canada and elsewhere in an attempt to improve the prospects of plaintiffs taking on large corporate defendants that are typically able and willing to devote large resources to fighting litigation.[202] Many such actions have been attempted in the United States, although few have been successful.[203] Certification of the class often presents difficulties in tobacco litigation due to the potential size and diversity of the class of individuals involved.[204] The first major tobacco class action to be filed in Canada was discontinued after an Ontario court refused to certify the class in 2004.[205] Class proceedings have also been ongoing in Quebec since 1998, and two classes were certified in 2005.[206] A class action against Imperial Tobacco for false and misleading marketing of "light" and "mild" cigarettes was commenced in British Columbia in 2003 and certified in 2005.[207] The defendant added the Government of Canada as a third party, alleging that it should bear a share of any liability due to the alleged roles of Health Canada and Agriculture Canada in the development and regulation of "light" and "mild" cigarettes; the third party notice was initially struck out, but on appeal a portion of the third party

---

[200] *Ragoonanan Estate v. Imperial Tobacco Canada Ltd.*, [2000] O.J. No. 4597 (Ont. S.C.J.) (dismissing defendant's application to strike out the plaintiff's pleadings); [2005] O.J. No. 4697 (Ont. S.C.J.) (refusing certification of class for class action), affd [2008] O.J. No. 1644 (Ont. Div. Ct.) (dismissing appeal of refusal of certification of class for class action).

[201] *Perron v. RJR Macdonald Inc.*, [1996] B.C.J. No. 2093 (B.C.C.A.); *Battaglia v. Imperial Tobacco*, [2001] O.J. No. 5541 (Ont. S.C.J.); [2002] O.J. No. 5074 (Ont. S.C.J.); [2003] O.J. No. 4360 (Ont. S.C.J.); *Spasic Estate v. Imperial Tobacco Ltd.*, [2003] O.J. No. 1797 (Ont. S.C.J.); [2003] O.J. No. 824 (Ont. S.C.J.); [2002] O.J. No. 2152 (Ont. S.C.J.); [2001] O.J. No. 4985 (Ont. S.C.J.); [2000] O.J. No. 2690, 188 D.L.R. (4th) 577 (Ont. C.A.); [2000] S.C.C.A. No. 547 (S.C.C.); [1998] O.J. No. 4906 (Ont. Gen. Div.); [1998] O.J. 6529 (Ont. Gen. Div.); *Spasic v. Imperial Tobacco Ltd.*, [1998] O.J. No. 125 (Ont. Gen. Div.).

[202] D. Douglas Blanke, *Towards Health with Justice: Litigation and Public Inquiries as Tools for Tobacco Control* (Geneva: World Health Organization, 2002) at 18, 30.

[203] Stephen D. Sugarman, "Mixed Results from Recent United States Tobacco Litigation" (2002) 10 Tort L. Rev. 94 at 105-10.

[204] *Ibid.*, at 106.

[205] *Caputo v. Imperial Tobacco Ltd.*, [2004] O.J. No. 299, 236 D.L.R. (4th) 348 (Ont. S.C.J.).

[206] *Conseil québécois sur le tabac et la santé c. JTI-MacDonald Corp.*, [2005] J.Q. no 4161 (Que. S.C.). One class is to be represented by the Conseil (at para. 128), and the second by Cécilia Létourneau (at para. 138). This litigation is ongoing and has been the subject of numerous reported decisions, including most recently: *JTI-MacDonald Corp. c. Conseil québécois sur le tabac et la santé*, [2010] J.Q. no 699 (Que. C.A.); *JTI-MacDonald Corp. c. Létourneau*, [2009] J.Q. no 3798 (Que. C.A.).

[207] *Knight v. Imperial Tobacco*, [2005] B.C.J. No. 216, 2005 BCSC 172 (B.C.S.C.), vard [2006] B.C.J. No. 1056, 2006 BCCA 235 (B.C.C.A.) (class limited to those whose claims arose in May 1997 or later). A similar proceeding was commenced in Newfoundland and Labrador in 2004 but certification was refused in 2008: *Sparkes v. Imperial Tobacco Canada Ltd.*, [2008] N.J. No. 379, 2008 NLTD 207 (N.L.T.D.), affd [2010] N.J. No. 108, 2010 NLCA 21 (N.L.C.A.).

claim was allowed to proceed.[208] Several other class actions have been initiated but the classes have not been certified.[209]

Governments in Canada and other countries have also brought actions against tobacco companies on several grounds. In proceedings brought by the United States government against tobacco companies, a federal court found that the companies knowingly deceived the public about the risks and addictiveness of smoking, and ordered them to publish corrective statements and to stop using terms such as "light" and "low tar" because they mislead consumers.[210] Criminal and civil proceedings have also been brought on the basis of tobacco companies' alleged participation or collusion in cigarette smuggling. In 2008 and 2010, agreements were concluded between the federal, provincial and (in 2010) territorial governments and several major tobacco companies in Canada, under which the companies would plead guilty to offences under the *Excise Act*[211] and the *Criminal Code*,[212] and pay a total of $1.7 billion in fines and civil settlements for their role in tobacco smuggling in the 1990s.[213]

In addition, governments have brought claims against tobacco companies to recover health care costs alleged to be attributable to tobacco consumption. In Canada, British Columbia has been at the forefront of these efforts. It enacted specific legislation to address this issue, the *Tobacco Damages and Health Care Costs Recovery Act*,[214] and has brought an action under the Act against a group of Canadian and related foreign companies. The legislation establishes a direct action by the government "against a [tobacco] manufacturer to recover the cost of health care benefits caused or contributed to by a tobacco related wrong", on an individual or aggregate basis.[215] It also provides for certain presumptions of causation, the use of statistical evidence to establish causation and damages, the assignment and apportionment of liability according to each defendant's contribution to risk, based on market share and other considerations, and retroactive

---

[208] *Knight v. Imperial Tobacco Canada Ltd.*, [2007] B.C.J. No. 1461, 2007 BCSC 964 (B.C.S.C.), var'd [2009] B.C.J. No. 2445, 2009 BCCA 541 (B.C.C.A.), leave to appeal granted [2010] S.C.C.A. No. 41 (S.C.C.).

[209] See Trevor Haché, "Tobacco-Related Litigation in Canada" (Smoking and Health Action Foundation & Non-Smokers' Rights Association, March 2010) at 15, online: Non-Smokers' Rights Association <http://www.nsra-adnf.ca/cms/file/pdf/Tobacco-related_Litigation_in_Canada_2010.pdf>.

[210] *United States v. Philip Morris USA Inc.*, 449 F. Supp. 2d 1 (2006), aff'd 566 F.3d 1095 (D.C.C.A. 2009).

[211] R.S.C. 1985, c. E-14.

[212] R.S.C. 1985, c. C-46.

[213] Office of the Minister of National Revenue, News Release, "Federal and Provincial Governments Reach Landmark Settlement with Tobacco Companies" (July 31, 2008), online at: <http://www.cra-arc.gc.ca/nwsrm/rlss/2008/m07/nr080731-eng.pdf>; Canada Revenue Agency, News Release, "Federal, Provincial, and Territorial Governments Conclude Landmark Settlements with Tobacco Companies" (April 13, 2010), online at: <http://www.cra-arc.gc.ca/nwsrm/rlss/2010/m04/nr100413-eng.pdf>.

[214] S.B.C. 2000, c. 30 (formerly *Tobacco Damages Recovery Act*, S.B.C. 1997, c. 41).

[215] *Ibid.*, s. 2. A "tobacco related wrong" is defined in s. 1(1) as "a breach of a common law, equitable or statutory duty or obligation owed by a manufacturer to persons in British Columbia who have been exposed or might become exposed to a tobacco product".

application of the Act's provisions.[216] This legislation was unsuccessfully challenged by tobacco manufacturers, who argued that several of its provisions have extraterritorial application, and that the provisions on presumptions and retroactive application undermine judicial independence and the rule of law. The Supreme Court of Canada in 2005 rejected these arguments and upheld the legislation.[217] The British Columbia claim has proceeded following this decision.[218] Several other provinces have enacted similar legislation,[219] and the New Brunswick government initiated its cost recovery action in 2008.[220]

VII. HEALTHY EATING, PHYSICAL ACTIVITY AND OBESITY

More than half of adults and about 25 per cent of children and youth in Canada are overweight or obese,[221] and rates of obesity have increased substantially in recent years.[222] Excess weight is associated with chronic diseases such as cardiovascular disease, type II diabetes, gallbladder disease, osteoarthritis and certain cancers.[223] It has been estimated that the economic cost of obesity, including health care costs and lost productivity, is $4.3 billion per year in Canada.[224]

---

[216] *Ibid.*, ss. 3(2)-(4), 5, 7-8, 10.

[217] *British Columbia v. Imperial Tobacco Canada Ltd.*, [2005] S.C.J. No. 50, 2005 SCC 49 (S.C.C.).

[218] See *British Columbia v. Imperial Tobacco Canada Ltd.*, [2005] B.C.J. No. 1400, 2005 BCSC 946 (B.C.S.C.), affd [2006] B.C.J. No. 2080, 2006 BCCA 398 (B.C.C.A.) (application to set aside service *ex juris* or to decline jurisdiction dismissed). The defendants issued a third party notice against the federal government similar to that in the *Knight* class action (see above at note 208): *British Columbia v. Imperial Tobacco Canada Ltd.*, [2008] B.C.J. No. 609, 2008 BCSC 419 (B.C.S.C.), vard [2009] B.C.J. No. 2444, 2009 BCCA 540 (B.C.C.A.), leave to appeal granted [2010] S.C.C.A. No. 43 (S.C.C.).

[219] *Crown's Right of Recovery Act*, S.A. 2009, c. C-35, Part 2 [not yet proclaimed in force]; *Tobacco Damages and Health Care Costs Recovery Act*, S.S. 2007, c. T-14.2 [not yet proclaimed in force]; *Tobacco Damages and Health Care Costs Recovery Act*, C.C.S.M. c. T70 [not yet proclaimed in force]; *Tobacco Damages and Health Care Costs Recovery Act, 2009*, S.O. 2009, c. 13; *Tobacco-Related Damages and Health Care Costs Recovery Act*, R.S.Q., c. R-2.2.0.0.1; *Tobacco Damages and Health Care Costs Recovery Act*, S.N.B. 2006, c. T-7.5; *Tobacco Damages and Health-care Costs Recovery Act*, S.N.S. 2005, c. 46 [not yet proclaimed in force]; *Tobacco Damages and Health Care Costs Recovery Act*, S.P.E.I. 2009, c. 22 [not yet proclaimed in force]; *Tobacco Health Care Costs Recovery Act*, S.N.L. 2001, c. T-4.2 [not yet proclaimed in force].

[220] This action has been the subject of a number of pre-trial motions and appeals, especially regarding the contingency fee arrangements used by the province; see, *e.g.*, *New Brunswick v. Rothmans Inc.*, [2010] N.B.J. No. 160, 2010 NBCA 35 (N.B.C.A.).

[221] Michael Tjepkema, "Adult Obesity" (August 2006) 17:3 Health Reports 9; Margot Shields, "Overweight and Obesity Among Children and Youth" (August 2006) 17:3 Health Reports 27.

[222] Shields, *ibid.*; M.S. Tremblay, P.T. Katzmarzyk & J.D. Willms, "Temporal Trends in Overweight and Obesity in Canada, 1981-1996" (2002) 26 International Journal of Obesity 538; Margot Shields & Michael Tjepkema, "Trends in Adult Obesity" (2006) 17:3 Health Reports 53.

[223] Michael Tjepkema, "Adult Obesity" (August 2006) 17:3 Health Reports 9 at 9; Wei Luo *et al.*, "The Burden of Adult Obesity in Canada" (2007) 27:4 Chronic Diseases in Canada 135.

[224] P.T. Katzmarzyk & I. Janssen, "The Economic Costs Associated with Physical Inactivity and Obesity in Canada: An Update" (2004) 29:1 Canadian Journal of Applied Physiology 90.

Changes in both diet and physical activity are believed to be contributing to this public health problem. Typical portion sizes have increased significantly in recent years, and this is believed to have contributed to higher rates of obesity.[225] Many children and adults fall far short of meeting dietary recommendations.[226] Unhealthy eating patterns affect health in many ways in addition to contributing to overweight and obesity: there are recognized links between diet and risks of chronic diseases such as cardiovascular disease and cancer.[227] Only a small proportion of Canadian children and youth meet current guidelines for physical activity,[228] and fitness levels of both children and adults have declined significantly in recent decades.[229] Physical activity has been shown to have important health benefits, both in helping to maintain healthy weights and independent of weight status.[230]

There have been some attempts to address these issues through litigation,[231] but most legal strategies to date have involved legislation and policies at various levels of government. Designing and implementing effective regulatory approaches to influence diet, physical activity and (indirectly) obesity has proven to be challenging. The risk factors influencing the development of chronic diseases are many and complex, so it is difficult to predict which interventions are likely to be effective.[232] Furthermore, the behaviours involved — such as eating

---

[225] Lisa R. Young & Marion Nestle, "The Contribution of Expanding Portion Sizes to the US Obesity Epidemic" (2002) 92 American Journal of Public Health 246.

[226] Didier Garriguet, "Canadians' Eating Habits" (2007) 18:2 Health Reports 17.

[227] Dariush Mozaffarian, Peter W.F. Wilson & William B. Kannel, "Beyond Established and Novel Risk Factors: Lifestyle Risk Factors for Cardiovascular Disease" (2008) 117 Circulation 3031; World Cancer Research Fund/American Institute for Cancer Research, *Policy and Action for Cancer Prevention. Food Nutrition, and Physical Activity: A Global Perspective* (Washington, DC: American Institute for Cancer Research, 2009) at 18; *Sodium Reduction Strategy for Canada: Recommendations of the Sodium Working Group* (July 2010) at 4-5, online: Health Canada <http://www.hc-sc.gc.ca/fn-an/alt_formats/pdf/nutrition/sodium/strateg/index-eng.pdf>.

[228] Canadian Fitness and Lifestyle Research Institute, *Kids CAN PLAY!*, "Bulletin 1: Activity levels of Canadian children and youth" (2009) at 3, online at: <http://www.cflri.ca/eng/statistics/surveys/documents/CANPLAY2009_Bulletin01_PA_levelsEN.pdf>.

[229] Margot Shields *et al.*, "Fitness of Canadian Adults: Results from the 2007-2009 Canadian Health Measures Survey" (2010) 21:1 Health Reports 1; Mark S. Tremblay *et al.*, "Fitness of Canadian Children and Youth: Results from the 2007-2009 Canadian Health Measures Survey" (2010) 21:1 Health Reports 1.

[230] D.E.R. Warburton, C.W. Nicol & S.S.D. Bredin, "Health Benefits of Physical Activity: The Evidence" (2006) 174 Can. Med. Assn. J. 801; G. Egger & J. Dixon, "Obesity and Chronic Disease: Always Offender or Often Just Accomplice?" (2009) 102 Brit. J. Nutrition 1238.

[231] See, *e.g.*, Nola M. Ries & Barbara von Tigerstrom, "Obesity and the Law" in Tracey M. Bailey, Timothy Caulfield & Nola M. Ries, eds., *Public Health Law & Policy in Canada*, 2d ed. (Markham, ON: LexisNexis Canada, 2008) 363 at 388-91; Jess Alderman & Richard A. Daynard, "Applying Lessons from Tobacco Litigation to Obesity Lawsuits" (2006) 30 Am. J. Preventive Medicine 8.

[232] See, *e.g.*, Kenneth Resnicow & Scott E. Page, "Embracing Chaos and Complexity: A Quantum Change for Public Health" (2008) 98 American Journal of Public Health 1382; Ross A. Hammond, "Complex Systems Modeling for Obesity Research" (2009) 6:3 Preventing Chronic Disease 1.

and leisure-time activities — are both resistant to change and generally considered to be private matters. Government intervention to influence these behaviours is therefore difficult and often contentious.[233] Nevertheless, legislation has been enacted or proposed in several areas.[234]

A. LEGISLATIVE APPROACHES

One role for legislation is to help ensure that consumers have accurate information about food products, so that they can make healthier choices. Nutrition labelling on most packaged foods is mandatory in Canada, and the claims that can be made about the nutrient content or health benefits of food products are regulated.[235] It has been proposed to supplement the mandatory nutrition information panels with a simpler front-of-package label,[236] in order to address concerns that many people do not read or understand the information panels and some are misled or confused by commonly used labels.[237] Other jurisdictions have been moving toward voluntary or mandatory schemes for front-of-package labels.[238] Another recent development has seen the extension of limited mandatory labelling to restaurant foods. Several U.S. cities and states passed legislation requiring chain restaurants to post calorie information,[239] and recent federal legislation in the U.S. will impose similar requirements nationwide.[240] In Canada, restau-

---

[233] Nola M. Ries & Barbara von Tigerstrom, "Roadblocks to Laws for Healthy Eating and Activity" (2010) 182 Can. Med. Assn. J. 687 at 688-89.

[234] For more detailed discussions of these issues, see Nola M. Ries & Barbara von Tigerstrom, "Obesity and the Law" in Tracey M. Bailey, Timothy Caulfield & Nola Ries, eds., *Public Health Law and Policy in Canada*, 2d ed. (Markham, ON: LexisNexis Canada, 2008) 363; Nola M. Ries & Barbara von Tigerstrom, "Roadblocks to Laws for Healthy Eating and Activity" (2010) 182 Can. Med. Assn. J. 687.

[235] Food and Drug Regulations, C.R.C. c. 870, Part B, Div. 1.

[236] Canada, Standing Committee on Health, *Healthy Weights for Healthy Kids* (Ottawa: Communication Canada, 2007) at 22-23, online at: Canadian Council of Food and Nutrition <http://www.ccfn.ca/pdfs/HealthyWeightsForHealthyKids.pdf>.

[237] Barbara von Tigerstrom & Tristan Culham, "Food Labelling for Healthier Eating: Is Front-of-Package Labelling the Answer?" (2009) 33 Man. L.J. 87 at 96-97, 99-100; U.S. Food and Drug Administration, "Guidance for Industry: Letter Regarding Point of Purchase Food Labeling" (October 2009), online at: <http://www.fda.gov/Food/GuidanceComplianceRegulatoryInformation/GuidanceDocuments/FoodLabelingNutrition/ucm187208.htm>.

[238] U.K. Food Standards Agency, "Front of pack (FOP) nutrition labelling for pre-packed foods sold through retail outlets in the UK" (2009), online at: <www.food.gov.uk/multimedia/pdfs/consultation/fopnutritionlabelling.pdf>; U.S. Food and Drug Administration, "Front-of-pack and shelf tag nutrition symbols; Establishment of docket; Request for comments and information" (2010) 75:82 Federal Register 22602-22606; EC, *Proposal for a Regulation of the European Parliament and of the Council on the provision of food information to consumers* (Brussels: January 30, 2008), 2008/0028 (COD), online at: <http://ec.europa.eu/food/food/labellingnutrition/foodlabelling/publications/proposal_regulation_ep_council.pdf>.

[239] See Barbara von Tigerstrom, "Mandatory Nutrition Labelling for Restaurants: Is Menu Labelling Coming to Canada?" (2010) 28 Windsor Rev. Legal Soc. Issues 139 at 145-47.

[240] *Patient Protection and Affordable Care Act of 2010*, Pub. L. No. 111-148, § 4205.

rant labelling bills have been introduced in Parliament[241] and in the Ontario legislature,[242] but none has yet been passed. Finally, public health advocates and reports have called for more stringent restrictions on food advertising, especially to children.[243] In the U.K., recent standards prohibit television advertisements for foods high in fat, salt or sugar during or near children's programs.[244]

Legislation can also be used to regulate the content of food products themselves. Food safety has long been an important area of public health legislation.[245] More recently, it has been proposed that legislation be used to limit food ingredients that have been linked to chronic disease risks. To date, the federal government has taken a voluntary approach to trans fats,[246] though this approach has not yielded the desired reductions.[247] A few provincial governments have legislated to limit trans fat content in restaurant or school foods.[248] Voluntary or mandatory reductions in sodium content have also been the subject of much recent discussion.[249]

There are fewer examples of legislation to promote physical activity, though proposed legislation in several provinces would institute or increase mandatory physical education in schools.[250] In addition, the federal government and several provincial/territorial governments have created tax credits that aim to promote

---

[241] Bill C-398, *An Act to amend the Food and Drugs Act (food labelling)*, 37th Parl., 2nd Sess., 2003; Bill C-398, *An Act to amend the Food and Drugs Act (food labelling)*, 37th Parl., 3rd Sess., 2004; Bill C-379, *An Act to amend the Food and Drugs Act (food labelling)*, 38th Parl., 1st Sess., 2005; Bill C-283, *An Act to amend the Food and Drugs Act (food labelling)*, 39th Parl., 1st Sess., 2006.

[242] Bill 156, *Healthy Decisions for Healthy Eating Act, 2009*, 1st Sess., 39th Leg., Ontario, 2009; Bill 90, *Healthy Decisions for Healthy Eating Act, 2010*, 2nd Sess., 39th Leg., Ontario, 2010.

[243] Martin Caraher, Jane Landon & Kath Dalmeny, "Television Advertising and Children: Lessons from Policy Development" (2005) 9 Public Health Nutrition 596; Nola M. Ries & Barbara von Tigerstrom, "Roadblocks to Laws for Healthy Eating and Activity" (2010) 182 Can. Med. Assn. J. 687 at 688-89 (Table 1).

[244] Office of Communications, "Television Advertising of Food and Drink Products to Children: Final Statement" (2007), online at: <http://stakeholders.ofcom.org.uk/binaries/consultations/foodads_new/statement/statement.pdf>.

[245] See Ron Doering, "Foodborne Illness and Public Health" in Tracey M. Bailey, Timothy Caulfield & Nola M. Ries, eds., *Public Health Law & Policy in Canada*, 2d ed. (Markham, ON: LexisNexis Canada, 2008) 483.

[246] Health Canada, "Trans Fat" (2009), online at: <http://www.hc-sc.gc.ca/fn-an/nutrition/gras-trans-fats/index-eng.php>.

[247] "Trans fat rules needed, groups say" CBC News (December 23, 2009), online at: <http://www.cbc.ca/health/story/2009/12/23/trans-fat-ban.html>.

[248] Public Health Impediments Regulation, B.C. Reg. 50/2009, s. 3; *Public Schools Act*, C.C.S.M. c. P250, s. 47.2; Trans Fat Standards, O. Reg. 200/08.

[249] See, *e.g.*, *Sodium Reduction Strategy for Canada: Recommendations of the Sodium Working Group* (July 2010), online at: Health Canada <http://www.hc-sc.gc.ca/fn-an/alt_formats/pdf/nutrition/sodium/strateg/index-eng.pdf>; Institute of Medicine, *Strategies to Reduce Sodium Intake in the United States: Report Brief* (Washington, DC: National Academies Press, 2010).

[250] For a summary of proposals, see Nola M. Ries & Barbara von Tigerstrom, "Roadblocks to Laws for Healthy Eating and Activity" (2010) 182 Can. Med. Assn. J. 687 at 690-91 (Table 2).

physical activity for children.[251] For example, the federal Children's Fitness Tax Credit allows parents of children under 16 years to claim up to $500 per child for the cost of enrolling in eligible physical activity programs, resulting in a non-refundable credit of up to $75 per child.[252] Questions have been raised about the equity and effectiveness of this approach.[253]

VIII. CONCLUSION

Public health law is a rapidly evolving area that continues to face new challenges. The legislative frameworks that have existed for many years to address the threat of infectious diseases are under review as countries and provinces attempt to deal with the impact of globalization on the emergence and spread of infectious disease. Both within Canada and internationally, we have also seen the re-emergence of disease threats that were once thought to have been rendered obsolete by modern medical science. At the same time, the burden of disease attributable to chronic diseases continues to grow and present new challenges for the law. Addressing multiple and complex causes of ill-health like diet and environmental factors requires public health lawyers to re-examine and adapt legal strategies that have been used to deal with other threats to health. However, these analogies have sometimes been controversial,[254] and the expansion of regulatory strategies to new areas has even raised more fundamental questions about the proper role and scope for public health law.[255] All of these developments are taking place within a context of public debate about the rights and responsibilities of governments, corporations and individuals, and shifting perceptions and attitudes about risks to health. These challenges assure that public health will continue to be a dynamic and growing area of health law.

---

[251] *Income Tax Act*, R.S.C. 1985 (5th Supp.), c. 1, s. 118.03; *Active Families Benefit Act*, S.S. 2008, c. A-4.01; *Income Tax Act*, C.C.S.M. c. 110, s. 4.6(10.2)-4.6(10.4); *Income Tax Act*, R.S.N.S. 1989, c. 217, s. 12A; *Income Tax Act*, R.S.Y. 2002, c. 118, s. 6(59).

[252] Canada Revenue Agency, "Children's Fitness Tax Credit" (2008), online at: <http://www.cra-arc.gc.ca/whtsnw/fitness-eng.html>. There are different age limits and additional amounts available for children eligible for the disability tax credit (*ibid.*).

[253] J.C. Spence, "Uptake and Effectiveness of the Children's Fitness Tax Credit in Canada: The Rich Get Richer" (2010) 10 BMC Public Health 356.

[254] See, *e.g.*, Joseph P. McMenamin & Andrea D. Tiglio, "Not the Next Tobacco: Defenses to Obesity Claims" (2006) 61 Food & Drug L.J. 445.

[255] Richard A. Epstein, "In Defense of the 'Old' Public Health: The Legal Framework for the Regulation of Public Health" (2004) 69 Brooklyn L. Rev. 1421.

Chapter 13

INDIGENOUS PEOPLES AND HEALTH LAW AND POLICY: RESPONSIBILITIES AND OBLIGATIONS

Constance MacIntosh[*]

I. INTRODUCTION

According to a 2010 Environics Survey, 80 per cent of urban Canadians believe that Aboriginal people in Canada have the same or a better experience with health care than do non-Aboriginal Canadians. As acknowledged in the survey report, this belief reflects a "significant gap" between "reality and perceptions".[1] Indeed, every comprehensive study that has considered the health situation of Indigenous peoples in Canada has identified urgent unmet needs. For example, the Royal Commission on Aboriginal Peoples characterized the health status of Aboriginal people as being in "crisis".[2] The Kirby Report reached the complementary conclusion that "the state of health of Aboriginal Canadians and the socio-economic conditions in which they live remain deplorable",[3] rendering their health situation a "national disgrace".[4] In the Romanow Report's survey of health in Canada, the disparities between the health status of the Aboriginal and non-Aboriginal population was described as "simply unacceptable".[5] The data which is presented in this chapter indicates that while some of the specifics have changed, there is little to suggest that these characterizations have lost their accuracy.

Although this book explores the role of laws and policies in engaging health-related issues across Canada, much of the description and analysis in its

---

[*]   I express my appreciation to Jocelyn Downie both for her encouragement and support in authoring this chapter, and for her meticulous and thoughtful review of the chapter while in draft form.
[1]   Environics Institute, *Urban Aboriginal Peoples Study: Main Report* (Toronto: Environics Institute for Survey Research, 2010) at 162.
[2]   Canada, Royal Commission on Aboriginal Peoples, *Report of the Royal Commission on Aboriginal Peoples*, vol. 3: *Gathering Strength* (Ottawa: Minister of Supply and Services, 1996) at 119.
[3]   Canada, Senate Standing Committee on Social Affairs, Science and Technology, *The Health of Canadians: The Federal Role – Interim Report*, vol. 4: *Issues and Options* (Ottawa: Senate of Canada, 2002) at 129.
[4]   *Ibid.*, at 130.
[5]   Canada, Commission on the Future of Health Care in Canada, *Building on Values: The Future of Health Care in Canada* (Ottawa: Canadian Government Publishing, 2002) at 211.

chapters bear limited relevance for understanding how laws and policies engage with the health of Indigenous peoples in Canada, and how they are entangled with the current unacceptable situation. Several reasons for this limitation are introduced below. They are returned to at various points in this chapter.

First, there is a fundamentally different foundation for the health care relationships between the state and Indigenous peoples than there is for state relationships with the general population. For the purposes of this chapter, it is sufficient to point out the starting point for Canada's health care relationship with the general population is arguably the *Canada Health Act*, and that the health laws and policies that affect most of the Canadian population are more or less under provincial jurisdiction.[6] In each case, the laws and policies are products of political discretion. The basis for the state-Indigenous health care relationship, and for many of the health laws and policies that affect most Indigenous Canadians, do not fit this description. The constitutional division of powers, combined with obligations that have been articulated as originating in treaties, or else as a result of fiduciary law, put Canada — not the provinces — into a leading role. There are also questions over whether Canada has legal discretion to not address the health care needs of Indigenous peoples.

Second, the health policies and practices that have developed in most provinces, and which may have been endorsed through incorporation into legislation or the common law, presume a universal acceptance of a certain set of norms about values such as autonomy and privacy. This presumption may be in error. Norms arising out of non-Indigenous values may be alien and disruptive, if not harmful, to some Indigenous communities. They may be alien because of distinctions between Indigenous and non-Indigenous cultural values and ways of understanding personhood, relationships between individuals, and between individuals and the collective. The specter of harm arises because the imposition of non-Indigenous norms may both perpetuate the conceptual devaluing of Indigenous world views,[7] and have the practical outcome of forcing people to align important decisions with values that are not their own.

A final and related reason for the limited relevance is that the health status of Indigenous peoples, and what is required for laws or policies to support their health, cannot be understood without a deep appreciation of how state-Indigenous history informs the current situation. Indigenous peoples have been subjected to government laws and policies that were systematic attempts to destroy their cultures, families and connections with land,[8] and to disrupt their po-

---

[6] *Cf.* William Lahey, Chapter 1 of this volume, especially Part III.

[7] As discussed below, such a devaluation was an explicit part of the colonial assimilation project. See Gerald Taiaiake Alfred, "Colonialism and State Dependency" (2009) J. of Aboriginal Health 42 at 48-49.

[8] The most well-known example of this initiative is the residential school system, under which children were forcibly removed from their families and required to attend schools operated by the state or churches, with the hope that upon graduation the children would not return to their families but would rather integrate into the market economy. See Constance MacIntosh, "From Judging Culture to Taxing 'Indians': Tracing the Legal Discourse of the 'Indian Mode of Life'"

litical, economic and legal orders through the imposition of governance regimes that displaced traditional governance and authority structures.[9] It is essential to recall that these laws and policies found their legitimacy in part though casting Indigenous peoples and their practices as inferior and in need of realignment with Euro-Canadian practices and values.[10] George Henry Erasmus, one of the commissioners for the Royal Commission on Aboriginal Peoples, recently offered the following comment on one outcome of these state practices:

> When one considers the material consequences of Canada's century-long policy of state-sponsored, forcible assimilation, a simple fact emerges: for generations, opportunities to live well *as an Aboriginal person* have been actively frustrated.[11]

It is widely held that these laws, policies and practices had and continue to have complex and detrimental impacts upon all aspects of life, including health matters.[12] This conclusion is widely subscribed to. For example, the collective conclusion that was reached at the 2007 International Symposium on the Social Determinants of Indigenous Health was as follows:

> The colonization of Indigenous Peoples was seen as a fundamental underlying health determinant. This process continues to impact health and well being and must be remedied if the health disadvantages of Indigenous Peoples are to be overcome. One requirement for reversing colonization is self determination, to help restore to Indigenous Peoples control over their lives and destinies.[13]

Thus, colonialism has created a social determinant of health that is unique to the Indigenous population within the Canadian context, although it is shared by Indigenous peoples and populations in countries such as New Zealand and

---

(2009) 47 Osgoode Hall L.J. 399. The practice of relocating Indigenous populations onto reserves so as to enable settlers to access land and resources is well-known. However, the 1950s practice of moving Inuit populations to the far north to support Canada's claim to northern sovereignty is less well-known, although the federal government did issue a formal apology for these relocations in August 2010. These families experienced deep hardship, having been moved to areas where the average temperature was 20 degrees lower than what they were used to. See Canada, Royal Commission on Aboriginal Peoples, *The High Arctic Relocation: A Report on the 1953-55 Relocation* (Ottawa: 1994); Indian and Northern Affairs Canada, *Backgrounder: Apology for Inuit High Arctic Relocation* (August 18, 2010), online at: <http://www.ainc-inac.gc.ca/ai/mr/nr/m-a2010/23398bk-eng.asp>.

9   *E.g.*, see the band council system and the banning of political ceremonies such as the Sundance.

10   Constance MacIntosh, "From Judging Culture to Taxing 'Indians': Tracing the Legal Discourse of the 'Indian Mode of Life'" (2009) 47 Osgoode Hall L.J. 399.

11   George Henry Erasmus, "Forward" in Laurence Kirmayer & Gail Valaskakis, eds., *Healing Traditions: The Mental Health of Aboriginal People in Canada* (Vancouver: UBC Press, 2009) at xi [emphasis in original].

12   *E.g.*, see Gerald Taiaiake Alfred, "Colonialism and State Dependency" (2009) J. of Aboriginal Health 42.

13   International Symposium on the Social Determinants of Indigenous Health, "Social Determinants and Indigenous Health: The International Experience and its policy implications", online at: <http://www.who.int/social_determinants/resources/indigenous_health_adelaide_report_07.pdf> at 2.

Australia.[14] As a result, responses to their health situation which are not informed by a decolonizing ethic that is responsive to factors such as political identity, cultural needs and historic wrongs may in many cases be of limited utility because it will not assuage the underlying conditions of political marginalization, alienation and poverty.[15] That is to say, although the frequency of a specific disease or condition can be alleviated by a targeted initiative, the persistence of the underlying social, psychological, economic and political conditions arising out of a century of colonial policy means that ill health will continue to be manifested.

This chapter first provides some baseline information on the Indigenous population and their health situation. It then canvasses the constitutional and legislative framework, before turning to arguments regarding whether health care support arises as a matter of federal discretion or as a lawful obligation. The next section addresses contemporary health policies, practices and protocols. The chapter concludes by considering how health laws and policies may be shaped to counter the legacy of colonialism.

II.   CONTEXT

This section provides some contextual information. It first describes the Indigenous population in Canada. It then surveys their health situation in terms of epidemiological data as well as findings on social determinants of health.

A.   THE INDIGENOUS POPULATION IN CANADA

Indigenous peoples in Canada descended from the populations of humans who first migrated to these lands in waves between 10,000 to 50,000 years ago.[16] Their commonalities are their long presence here, the persistence of their political and cultural communities over time, and the association between specific Indigenous peoples and a territory. These populations now represent 11 distinct language groups with more than 65 dialects. This fact flags the diversity of their cultures and the depth of the distinctive histories of various groups.

It is important to observe that the manner in which Indigenous peoples identify themselves and their political collectives does not necessarily align with categories that are reflected in statutes, the Constitution, or health laws and policies. For example, section 91(24) of the *Constitution Act, 1867*[17] assigns the

---

[14]   Janet Smylie & Paul Adomako, "Executive Summary" in Janet Smylie & Paul Adomako, eds., *Indigenous Children's Health Report: Health Assessment in Action* (Toronto: Centre for Research on Inner City Health, 2010) 1 at 8.

[15]   *Ibid.*, at 4. See also Gerald Taiaiake Alfred, "Colonialism and State Dependency" (2009) J. of Aboriginal Health 42 at 44, who writes: "It is evident to anyone who has experience living or working within First Nation communities that conventional approaches to health promotion and community development are not showing strong signs of success."

[16]   Olive Patricia Dickason, *Canada's First Nations: A History of Founding Peoples from Earliest Times*, 3d ed. (Don Mills, ON: Oxford University Press, 2002) at 3.

[17]   (U.K.), 30 & 31 Vict., reprinted in R.S.C. 1985, App. II, No. 5.

federal government jurisdictional responsibility over "Indians". The term "Indian" is a colonial invention, which presupposed (or imposed) the political and cultural homogeneity of the Indigenous population to facilitate administrative and other state purposes.[18]

The number of constitutionally recognized categories tripled with section 35 of the *Constitution Act, 1982*.[19] Section 35(1) "recognizes and affirms" the rights of the "Aboriginal peoples of Canada". (The term "Aboriginal" is unique to Canada and Australia. Their state governments use it when referring to Indigenous peoples generally.) Section 35(2) further specifies that Aboriginal peoples "includes the Indian, Inuit and Métis peoples of Canada". Although the use of the word "includes" indicates that this list does not purport to exhaust the categories of Aboriginal or Indigenous[20] people in Canada, the Canadian state organizes much of its activities as though these constitutionally cited labels fill the field. This in turn shapes the identification categories which the Canadian state uses to collect data (which is in turn used to organize and deliver health programs). For example, this approach is reflected in the 2006 federal census. The survey instruments asked Indigenous respondents to self-identify in one of just three ways: as "North American Indian", "Métis" or "Inuit".

As to the socio-legal understandings of the terms with which Canada works, the label "Inuit" has come to be a blanket term referring to a number of Indigenous peoples of the Canadian far north who have considerable cultural similarities and share a language group, although there are many different dialects. The label "Métis" has come to refer to peoples whose ancestors were both Indigenous and non-Indigenous and who formed unique cultural communities prior to the Crown having effective control in a territory.[21] As to "North American Indian", Canada uses it synonymously with the term "First Nation",[22] which is a more common term used to refer to "all Aboriginal people in Canada who are

---

[18]   See Wendy Cornet, "Aboriginality: Legal Foundations, Past Trends, Future Prospects" in Joseph Magnet & Dwight Dorey, eds., *Aboriginal Rights Litigation* (Markham, ON: LexisNexis Canada, 2003).

[19]   Being Schedule B to the *Canada Act 1982* (U.K.), 1982, c. 11.

[20]   There are many terms which are or have been used when referring generally to this population. These terms include "Native", "Indian", "Aboriginal" and "Indigenous". For the most part, this chapter will use the term "Indigenous", unless the article, legal instrument, policy, *etc.*, under discussion uses a different term. In such cases, the context-specific term is used. The term "Indigenous" is used because this term is the one which is drawn upon most frequently by Indigenous peoples when they write or speak in generalizations about themselves.

[21]   Although the Supreme Court of Canada purported to define who is Métis for the purposes of s. 35(1) in *R. v. Powley*, [2003] S.C.J. No. 43, 2003 SCC 43 (S.C.C.), the term remains highly contested. See John Giokas & Paul L.A.H. Chartrand, "Who Are the Métis in Section 35? A Review of the Law and Policy Relating to Métis and 'Mixed-Blood' People in Canada" in Paul Chartrand, ed., *Who Are Canada's Aboriginal Peoples? Recognition, Definition and Jurisdiction* (Saskatoon: Purich Publishing, 2002) at 83.

[22]   *E.g.*, see Statistics Canada, "Aboriginal People in Canada in 2006: Inuit, Métis and First Nations, 2006 Census" (Ottawa: Minister of Industry, 2008). Despite the fact that this is a report that describes the findings of the 2006 census, it substitutes the term "First Nation" for the term of "North American Indian", which was used in the Census.

not Inuit or Métis".[23] First Nation individuals are often members of an Indigenous community who calls itself a First Nation. First Nations persons may be registered as "Indians" under the *Indian Act*, or may have ancestors who were registered.[24]

According to the 2006 census, 1,172,790 people in Canada self-identified under one of these three categories.[25] This constitutes about 4 per cent of the Canadian population. Of these individuals, 60 per cent identified as "North American Indian", 4 per cent identified as "Inuit", and 33 per cent identified as "Métis".[26]

As acknowledged by Statistics Canada, these numbers under-represent the actual population of persons who self-identify as Aboriginal,[27] even pursuant to Canada's categories. The size of the under-representation is partially captured by considering the number of persons who indicated on the 2006 census that they were registered Indians. Although the census reported that 564,870 persons self-identified as registered Indians, this figure is about 200,000 less than the number of people who were listed on the federal Indian registry as of 2006. Some of these individuals were undoubtedly not counted by the survey due to being homeless. Indigenous peoples in Canada are over-represented within the homeless population. In Edmonton, for example, 3.8 per cent of the population is Indigenous, but Indigenous people count for 35 per cent of the homeless population, and a disproportionate number of homeless people who sleep on the street (as opposed to shelters) are Indigenous.[28] However, in many instances these individuals were not missed by the survey — instead either these individuals or their communities refused to participate.[29] The refusal to participate highlights ongoing political tensions between the state and some Indigenous peoples about whether or how various state activities perpetuate colonial presumptions. In particular, some Indigenous people reject the right of Canada to impose categories or labels upon them. There are also issues about who has the right to determine how information about Indigenous peoples is collected, stored, shared

---

[23]   Judith Bartlett *et al.*, "Framework for Aboriginal-guided Decolonizing Research Involving Metis and First Nations Persons with Diabetes" (2007) 65 Social Science and Medicine 2371.

[24]   The matter of "registration" and being a "registered" or "status Indian" is returned to below.

[25]   Statistics Canada, "Aboriginal People in Canada in 2006: Inuit, Métis and First Nations, 2006 Census" (Ottawa: Minister of Industry, 2008) at 6.

[26]   *Ibid.*, at 9.

[27]   *Ibid.*, at 18.

[28]   Steven Hwang, "Homelessness and Health" (2001) 164:1 CMAJ 229 at 230. Various studies have concluded that the federal Census undercounts the Indigenous population by 20 per cent to 40 per cent. See Calvin Hanselmann, *Urban Aboriginal People in Western Canada: Realities and Policies* (Calgary: CanadaWest Foundation, 2001) at 3.

[29]   As reported by Statistics Canada, "[u]ndercoverage in the 2006 Census was considerably higher among Aboriginal people than among other segments of the population due to the fact that enumeration was not permitted, or was interrupted before it could be completed, on 22 Indian reserves and settlements": Statistics Canada, "Aboriginal People in Canada in 2006: Inuit, Métis and First Nations, 2006 Census" (Ottawa: Minister of Industry, 2008) at 18.

and used.[30] Given that programming is financed and arranged around state-recognized categories, in practical terms a failure to "fit" into a category and be willing to be counted can have quite significant consequences.

There have been some state-funded initiatives that are responsive to the tensions described above. In particular, mechanisms have and are being developed to support First Nations in conducting survey activities.[31] Such practices are argued to enable a decolonizing practice. For example, they enable the values of Indigenous people to inform the research design, thus making it more likely that culturally relevant information will be collected, and that this information will be collected in a culturally respectful fashion. This approach also provides for Indigenous control at all stages, thus answering some concerns about ownership and ensuring that Indigenous peoples make the decisions about how the information will be shared and used.

B.   THE HEALTH OF INDIGENOUS PEOPLES

The health situation of Indigenous peoples has long been considered by those who study health to be in crisis. The extent and nature of the failure is often conveyed through comparative epidemiological data. More recently, it has also come to often be conveyed through considering how Indigenous peoples fare with the social determinants of health, given the connection between factors or "determinants" outside of the health care system and health status.[32] For example, in 2009 Health Canada published a statistical profile of social determinants of health for First Nations,[33] in which they presented data on education, labour force characteristics, income, personal health practices, culture and physical environment. Whether one surveys epidemiological data, or social determinants information, the picture is stark.

Three key social determinants of health are education, employment and income. A 2010 survey found that the majority of non-Aboriginal urban Canadians think that Aboriginal people are equally likely to earn a good income and have meaningful employment, and have considerably better opportunities to get a good education, than non-Aboriginal Canadians.[34] Once again, the data on

---

[30] See, *e.g.*, "The First Nations Principles of OCAP", online at: <http://www.rhs-ers.ca/english/ocap.asp>.

[31] For example, the First Nations Information Governance Committee has conducted the first phase of a survey, the *First Nations Regional Longitudinal Health Survey (RHS) 2002/2003* (Ottawa: Assembly of First Nations), and is in the process of conducting a second one. See online at: <http://www.rhs-ers.ca/english/>.

[32] Health Canada, *Taking Action on Population Health: A Position Paper for Health Promotions and Programs Branch Staff* (Ottawa: Health Canada, 1988) at 1.

[33] Health Canada, *A Statistical Profile on the Health of First Nations in Canada: Determinants of Health, 1999 to 2003* (Ottawa: Minister of Health, 2009).

[34] Environics Institute, *Urban Aboriginal Peoples Study: Main Report* (Toronto: Environics Institute for Survey Research, 2010) at 162. In particular, 56 per cent thought Aboriginal people earned as good or a better income; 64 per cent thought Aboriginal people had the same or better

these factors does not support these perceptions. According to Health Canada's reports, almost half of First Nation individuals never achieve a high school graduation certificate (48.6 per cent),[35] and almost a quarter (22.9 per cent) have an income of under $5,000 a year. The median income of First Nation people sits at $10,631, which is $11,643 less than the Canadian median of $22,274.[36] The unemployment rate for status Indians is about three times higher than the Canadian average, although for status youth between 15 and 24 years of age, the rate is more than four times higher, at 41 per cent.[37] Given that social inequality is considered to be "the single leading condition for poor health",[38] these figures suggest that Indigenous peoples are living in circumstances where poor health is a predictable outcome.

Inequalities are also manifested through living conditions. Whereas 3 per cent of the non-Aboriginal population live in crowded conditions, 11 per cent of the Aboriginal population does so.[39] As well as being crowded, the homes of Aboriginal peoples are in disrepair, with almost a quarter living in housing that requires major repairs. This contrasts with the non-Aboriginal population, of which 7 per cent live in such housing.[40] Inadequate housing is directly associated with health problems, including heightened transmission rates of infectious diseases such as tuberculosis and hepatitis A, as well as increased likelihood of mental health problems, family violence and risk of injuries.[41] Compounding these problems are inadequate levels of community services. Nearly one-quarter of First Nation on-reserve households have water that is deficient in either quality or quantity,[42] nearly one-fifth have deficient sewage effluent systems[43] and 29 per cent have *no fire protection services* (a further 17 per cent have inadequate fire protection services).[44] As Health Canada has observed, "[w]ater and sanitation services are considered an essential part of preventing occurrences of communicable diseases, and a lack of these basic services is a risk factor for disease outbreaks".[45] A lack of, or inadequate, fire protection services obviously

---

opportunities for meaningful employment; and 77 per cent thought Aboriginal people had the same or better opportunities to get a good education.

[35] Health Canada, *A Statistical Profile on the Health of First Nations in Canada, Determinants of Health, 1999 to 2003* (Ottawa: Ministry of Health, 2009) at 12-13.

[36] *Ibid.*, at 18.

[37] First Nations and Inuit Health Branch, Health Canada, *A Statistical Profile on the Health of First Nations in Canada* (Ottawa: Health Canada, 2003) at 64.

[38] *E.g.*, see discussion in J. Reading, *The Crisis of Chronic Disease Among Aboriginal Peoples: A Challenge for Public Health, Population Health and Social Policy* (Victoria: Centre for Aboriginal Health Research, 2010) at 10.

[39] Statistics Canada, "Aboriginal Peoples in Canada in 2006: Inuit, Métis and First Nations, 2006 Census" (Ottawa: Ministry of Industry, 2008) at 17.

[40] *Ibid.*

[41] Health Canada, *A Statistical Profile on the Health of First Nations in Canada, Determinants of Health, 1999 to 2003* (Ottawa: Ministry of Health, 2009) at 33.

[42] *Ibid.*, at 35.

[43] *Ibid.*, at 36.

[44] *Ibid.*

[45] *Ibid.*, at 38.

puts 46 per cent of First Nation households on-reserve at heightened risk of death or injury due to fire — a situation which is likely exacerbated by factors such as crowding and ill repair.

The impact of social inequalities on individual and collective health and well-being is sadly exemplified by some of the data which was collected as part of the 2006 Aboriginal Peoples Survey. Among other matters, it considered how Aboriginal peoples experience food security. The Survey reports that 30 per cent of Inuit children experience hunger due to their families being unable to afford or otherwise obtain food. Half of these children, so 15 per cent of Inuit children, report having this experience at least once a month. This latter figure contrasts with the non-Aboriginal population, of which 3 per cent are reported to experience similarly severe levels of food insecurity.[46] A study that was reported upon in 2010, which focused on Inuit families in Nunavut, presents even more dire findings. The survey authors found that 70 per cent of children resided in homes that are considered food insecure,[47] and that 15 per cent of all respondents responded affirmatively to the question: "In the last 12 months, did your children ever not eat for a whole day because there wasn't enough money for food?"[48]

The epidemiological data presents a similarly stark picture. For example:

- the rate of infant mortality in First Nation families is nearly twice that of the Canadian population;[49]

- the rate of HIV infection in Saskatchewan First Nations is double that of the Canadian average;[50]

- Métis experience chronic conditions such as asthma and diabetes at close to twice the rate in the general Canadian population;[51]

- viral hepatitis A cases on First Nation reserves in British Columbia are double the rate for the general population of the province;[52]

---

[46]   See the discussion of these figures in Janet Smylie & Paul Adomako, eds., *Indigenous Children's Health Report: Health Assessment in Action* (Toronto: Centre for Research on Inner City Health, 2010) at 24-25.

[47]   Grace Egeland *et al.*, "Food Insecurity Among Inuit Preschoolers: Nunavut Inuit Child Health Survey, 2007-2008" (2010) 182:3 CMAJ 243 at 247.

[48]   *Ibid.*, at 245.

[49]   Janet Smylie & Paul Adomako, "Executive Summary" in Janet Smylie & Paul Adomako, eds., *Indigenous Children's Health Report: Health Assessment in Action* (Toronto: Centre for Research on Inner City Health, 2010) 1 at 4.

[50]   Canadian Press, "Saskatchewan First Nations HIV rate double the national average" *The Globe and Mail* (May 7, 2010).

[51]   Asthma is reported as a chronic condition for 14 per cent of the Métis adult population, compared to 8 per cent for the Canadian population. Diabetes is experienced at 7 per cent, as compared to the Canadian population at 5 per cent. (Statistics Canada, Social and Aboriginal Statistics Division, "Aboriginal Peoples Survey, 2006: An Overview of the Health of the Métis Population" at 11.)

[52]   Janet Smylie & Paul Adomako, eds., *Indigenous Children's Health Report: Health Assessment in Action* (Toronto: Centre for Research on Inner City Health, 2010) at 32.

- the hospital admission rate for infant bronchiolitis in the hospitals serving the majority of the Inuit population "is the highest reported rate of hospitalization of respiratory tract infections in the world";[53] and

- the incidence rate for tuberculosis in the general Canadian population in 2000 was 5.2 per 100,000 people. The incident rate for 2002 in Nunavut was almost 18 times higher, at 93.4 per 100,000.[54]

Many scholars argue that this disproportionate burden of ill health reflects the legacy of the dislocation, disempowerment and community and cultural fragmentation and poverty that was inflicted both intentionally and unintentionally through colonial practices. As simply stated in a recent article in *The Lancet*, "colonialism adversely affected physical, social, emotional, and mental health and wellbeing".[55] This data is also indicative of what can only be a continuing failure of Canadian law and policy to enable and support a systemic remedy.

This chapter now turns to describing how law and policy intersect with the health of Indigenous peoples.

III. THE CONSTITUTIONAL AND LEGISLATIVE FRAMEWORK

This section first considers the Constitutional division of powers and jurisdictional assignment. It then turns to the question of how state responsibilities may arise in law due to treaty or fiduciary obligations, or pursuant to obligations assumed under international law.

The Supreme Court of Canada has determined that pursuant to the *Constitution Act, 1867*, "general jurisdiction over health matters is provincial", with federal jurisdiction being limited to that which is "ancillary to the express heads of power in section 91".[56] However, as noted above, section 91(24) of the *Constitution Act, 1867* identifies a federal head of power of "Indians and lands reserved to the Indians". Together these provisions create some jurisdictional uncertainty. Key issues include whether section 91(24) creates the basis for the federal government having jurisdiction over the health of "Indians" (either directly or as an ancillary matter), and who *is* an "Indian" for the purposes of section 91(24). These two questions are explored below.

The issue of whether section 91(24) assigns jurisdictional responsibility for the health of "Indians" to the federal Crown has not been directly litigated. The most on-point judicial commentary arises in the 1999 decision of *Wuskwi Sipihk*

---

[53] *Ibid.*, at 38.

[54] *Ibid.*

[55] Michael Gracey & Malcolm King, "Indigenous Health Part 1: Determinants and Disease Patterns" (2009) 374 The Lancet 65.

[56] *Schneider v. British Columbia*, [1982] S.C.J. No. 64, [1982] 2 S.C.R. 112 (S.C.C.).

Cree Nation v. Canada (Minister of National Health and Welfare).[57] In this motion, Prothonotary Hargrave was asked by Canada to stay an action against it. The action alleged Canada had breached the constitutional division of powers through delegating responsibility for the health care of the Indigenous litigants to the Province of Manitoba. One of the grounds for which Canada sought the stay was that "the obligation at stake is ... health care which ... is a provincial matter"[58] and so outside the jurisdiction of the federal court. Prothonotary Hargrave found the federal court retained jurisdiction. He wrote: "I look upon the apparent federal excursion into health relating to First Nations as coming within section 91(24) of the *Constitution Act, 1867.*"[59] This action was never heard on its merits, nor was the decision to refuse a stay appealed. It seems highly unlikely that section 91(24) could be interpreted as not authorizing federal jurisdiction over the health of "Indians", either directly or as an ancillary matter. A more contentious question, which remains outstanding, is the extent to which provincial law and policy can lawfully occupy this field.

As to the second issue, "Indian" is not defined in the *Constitution Act, 1867*. As a matter of federal policy, Canada has taken the position that section 91(24) refers to those Indigenous peoples in Canada who have met the statutory criteria set out in the federal *Indian Act* to be registered as an "Indian", and have in fact been registered. In effect, the federal government purports to have the authority to create a statutory definition that limits its constitutional responsibilities.

As has been documented elsewhere, the federal government has changed the statutory criteria for being registered as an "Indian" many times. In its early forms it included (1) persons who were treaty beneficiaries; (2) persons who lived on reserves and had "Indian blood"; (3) persons who had married and were residing with someone of "Indian blood"; or (4) persons who had "Indian blood" and lived the "Indian mode of life" off of a reserve.[60] The motivation for defining "Indians" within the statutory regime was tied in with the colonial assimilation project.[61]

The colonial project took as a premise the idea that Indigenous peoples as a whole were inferior and in need of evolutionary assistance so that they could learn to live as "whites" and be capable of shouldering the responsibilities of citizens, such as owning real property and voting in provincial and federal elections.[62] This premise is captured by the preamble of the 1857 *Act to Encourage the Gradual Civilization of Indians*:

---

[57] [1999] F.C.J. No. 82 (F.C.T.D.).
[58] *Ibid.*, at para. 4.
[59] *Ibid.*, at para. 17.
[60] Constance MacIntosh, "From Judging Culture to Taxing 'Indians': Tracing the Legal Discourse of the 'Indian Mode of Life'" (2009) 47 Osgoode Hall L.J. 399 at 406-407.
[61] *Ibid.*, at 411-14.
[62] The bar against "registered" Indians being allowed to vote remained in place until March 31, 1960.

> Whereas it is desirable to encourage the progress of Civilization among the Indian Tribes...and the gradual removal of legal distinctions between them and Her Majesty's other Canadian subjects, and to facilitate the acquisition of property and of the rights accompanying it, by such Individual Members of said Tribes as shall be found to desire such encouragement and to have deserved it.[63]

Legislation and policies directed to categorizing Indigenous peoples "was integral to one-way assimilation. ... Being defined as Indian ... was intended to determine to whom assimilationist social policies should be applied".[64] The goal of cultural eradication was explicitly expressed by the Superintendent of Indian Affairs in 1920, Duncan Campbell Scott. In reference to introducing revisions to the *Indian Act*, under which all "Indian" children would be required to attend residential schools, he said:

> I want to get rid of the Indian problem ... Our object is to continue until there is not a single Indian in Canada that has not been absorbed into the body politic, and there is no Indian questions, and no Indian Department, that is the whole object of this Bill.[65]

Thus the *Indian Act* identified a specific legal regime for "Indians", with unique rights and restrictions that were shaped around the state's ideas of what was necessary to enable "evolution". While this civilizing process was ongoing, their presumed lessor status required that "Indians" be protected as "wards".[66] For example, "protective" rights included defining Indians as the only persons permitted to live on reserve lands, being unable to alienate reserve land except through the Crown, having their assets protected from garnishment and historically being prohibited from possessing alcohol. Protective practices came to include financing on-reserve housing, infrastructure and health and community services, as well as education (through the notorious residential school system).

One of the consequences of the right to live on a reserve being tied to registered status[67] was that family unity could be shattered when registered status is lost or not obtained by a family member. These latter consequences were realized with greater frequency as the criteria for being registered changed in response to Canada having concerns about the number of individuals for whom it was providing services. Canada came to base registered status upon biological

---

[63]   *An Act to Encourage the Gradual Civilization of Indian Tribes in this Province, and to Amend the Laws Relating to Indians*, 3rd Sess., 5th Parl., c. 26.

[64]   Andrew Armitage, *Comparing the Policy of Aboriginal Assimilation: Australia, Canada, and New Zealand* (Vancouver: University of British Columbia Press, 1995) at 86.

[65]   As cited in John Borrows, "Aboriginal Rights: Indian Agency and Taking What's Not Yours" (2003) 22 Windsor Y.B. Access Just. 253 at note 26. This article considers how control was extended over many aspects of the lives of Indigenous peoples.

[66]   Constance MacIntosh, "From Judging Culture to Taxing 'Indians': Tracing the Legal Discourse of the 'Indian Mode of Life'" (2009) 47 Osgoode Hall L.J. 399 at 411-13.

[67]   To be specific, the right to live on a reserve is limited by the *Indian Act* to members of the "Indian band" for whom Canada holds the land in reserve. However, until 1985, Canada controlled band membership, and only gave it to people who were registered.

parentage, with the right to registration passing through the male line. Assuming that a woman's identity was subsumed in that of her spouse, Canada added the criteria that women who were born with the right to be registered would lose this right if they married someone who was not registered.[68] These sorts of criteria resulted in many people who self-identified as Indigenous either losing the ability to register under the *Indian Act* or else refusing to be registered as a matter of political protest against the registration system.[69] In either case, such individuals would be required to leave reserve communities and would be excluded from most of the health, economical and educational support programs that Canada delivers to registered "Indians". Such individuals are often called "non-status Indians". Although the criteria in the *Indian Act* was modified in 1985[70] and again in 2011[71] to address sexual discrimination issues, the bottom line is that the criteria create an inherited status that rests upon biological parentage and not cultural or political affiliation. As a result, the population of those who are "registered" Indians leaves out many people with strong ancestral, cultural or other ties to First Nation communities.

Many Indigenous peoples have a very conflicted relationship with the *Indian Act* and its registration regime. Despite being a foreign term ("Indian") that conceptually erased their political communities and homogenized their cultures for the purposes of facilitating assimilation, some observers have noted that *Indian Act* definitions and their consequences have become internalized and thus normalized for some Indigenous peoples.[72] As well, Canada has tied the provision of many social and health services of considerable value to a person being registered, making status a commodity.

Canada has assumed that section 91(24)'s jurisdictional assignment of "Indians" can be limited to those persons who have been registered under the *Indian Act*. The defensibility of Canada's presumptions have only been directly challenged before the Supreme Court of Canada once. In *Re Eskimos*, the Court determined that "Inuit" are also "Indians" for the purposes of section 91(24) on the basis that Inuit had been classified with "Indians" in government records

---

[68] For a critical overview, see Wendy Cornet, "Aboriginality: Legal Foundations, Past Trends, Future Prospects" in Joseph Magnet & Dwight Dorey, eds., *Aboriginal Rights Litigation* (Markham, ON: LexisNexis Canada, 2003) at 121-45.

[69] *E.g.*, see discussion *Lovelace v. Ontario*, [2000] S.C.J. No. 36 at paras. 14-17, [2000] 1 S.C.R. 950 (S.C.C.).

[70] The first major attempt to address sexual discrimination was Bill C-31, *An Act to Amend the Indian Act*, in 1985. Its central modification was to make the marital status of women irrelevant for determining whether they qualified for registration as an "Indian".

[71] Bill C-3, *An Act to Promote Gender Equity in Indian Registration*, is Canada's response to a decision of the B.C. Court of Appeal that provisions of the *Indian Act* continue to violate women's equality rights, contrary to the *Canadian Charter of Rights of Freedoms*. See *McIvor v. Canada (Registrar, Indian and Northern Affairs)*, [2009] B.C.J. No. 669, 2009 BCCA 153 (B.C.C.A.). This Act came into force on January 31, 2011.

[72] Val Napoleon, "Extinction by Number: Colonialism Made Easy" (2001) 16:1 Can. J. of L. & Soc. 111.

prior to 1867 (when section 91(24) came into force).[73] So the federal Act — and its definition — does not exhaust the jurisdictional consequences of section 91(24). This opens the door to arguments that *all Indigenous persons* could fall within section 91(24). However, Canada does not accept this possibility. With a few exceptions, Canada assumes responsibility for the health of Indigenous peoples who are Inuit or are registered Indians, and expects the provinces to be responsible for the health of the remainder of the Indigenous population.

This approach to health care programming and delivery is blind to whether individuals live in the same community and share significant cultural and social commonalities, or whether they share the same extreme health challenges. The branch of Health Canada which currently delivers health programming to Aboriginal peoples, the First Nations and Inuit Health Branch ("FNIHB"), has recognized this shortfall in a few instances. For example, FNIHB now makes a limited number of programs, including the Aboriginal Diabetes Initiative, Suicide Prevention and Indian Residential Schools Counselling available to all Aboriginal peoples, including Métis.[74]

IV.   INDIGENOUS HEALTH NEEDS: FEDERAL DISCRETION OR OBLIGATION

As noted above, the Canadian government has programming which addresses some of the health needs of at least part of the Indigenous population. Indigenous communities have long claimed that Canada has broad legal obligations in this area, either due to treaty promises or arising as a feature of Canada's fiduciary obligations to Indigenous peoples. They have more recently begun to draw upon international law as a source of obligations. Canada rejects the claim based on domestic law, taking the position that "there is no constitutional obligation or treaty that requires the Canadian government to offer health programs or services to Aboriginal peoples".[75] Canada does not yet seem to have responded to the arguments draw on international law. If Canada's position is correct, that any health or social services that it provides are exercises of discretion, then Canada would presumptively be within its rights to limit the population to whom it provides services (as long as Canada does not violate the equality guarantees of the Charter) and to dictate the extent of those services. These arguments are canvassed below.

---

[73] *Reference re British North America Act, 1867 (U.K.), s. 91*, [1939] S.C.J. No. 5, [1939] S.C.R. 104 (S.C.C.).

[74] Health Canada, "First Nations and Inuit Health Branch" (January 2009) at 9, online at: <http://www.fnhealthmanagers.ca/docs/e/Intro%20to%20Health%20Determinants%20and%20Funding%202%20How%20FNIHB%20Works.pdf> (Powerpoint slides authored by Eric Costen, Director, Mental Health and Addictions, Community Programs Directorate, FNIHB).

A. TREATY-BASED RIGHTS TO HEALTH CARE OR SERVICES

From the late 19th century and through to the early 1920s, Canada aggressively pursued treaty agreements across much of the prairies. At this time, many Indigenous communities were also being decimated by diseases that had been introduced by European settlers. Although co-terminus documentary evidence indicates health care or medical services were discussed when at least three of these treaties were negotiated,[76] only one of them includes terms that specifically refer to medical matters. This is Treaty 6,[77] which contains two relevant clauses. The first clause reads:

> That in the event hereafter of the Indians ... being overtaken by any pestilence, or by a general famine, the Queen ... will grant to the Indians assistance of such character and to such extent as her Chief Superintendent of Indian Affairs shall deem necessary and sufficient to relieve the Indians from the calamity that shall have befallen them.

The treaty also promises "[t]hat a medicine chest shall be kept at the house of each Indian Agent for the use and benefit of the Indians, at the discretion of such agent". The background for these terms is reflected in the notes of Alexander Morris, the Chief Treaty Commissioner. He recorded that the Indigenous signatories "dreaded that ... they would be swept off by disease ... already they have suffered terribly from the ravages of measles, scarlet fever and small pox".[78]

The meaning of these specific treaty promises has been litigated on several occasions.[79] The first action was brought in 1935, in the case of *Dreaver v. The King*.[80] At issue was whether the treaty promise to provide a "medicine chest" precluded Canada from debiting band funds for the costs of medications issued to band members (all of whom were treaty beneficiaries). The court found that the treaty promise extended to "all the medicines, drugs or medical supplies which they might need entirely free of charge".[81] The court explicitly rejected

---

[75]   As described in the Commission on the Future of Health Care in Canada's report, *Building on Values: The Future of Health Care in Canada* (Ottawa: Canadian Government Publishing, 2002) at 212.

[76]   James Waldram, D. Ann Herring & T. Kue Young, *Aboriginal Health in Canada: Historical, Cultural and Epidemiological Perspectives* (Toronto: University of Toronto Press, 1997) at 142-45.

[77]   *Treaty 6, Between Her Majesty the Queen and the Plain and Wood Cree Indians and Other Tribes of Indians at Fort Carlton, Fort Pitt and Battle River with Adhesions*, 1876, 1889. A copy of this treaty is reproduced by Indian and Northern Affairs Canada as IAND publication no. QS-0574-000-EE-A-1, cat. no. R33-0664.

[78]   James Waldram, D. Ann Herring & T. Kue Young, *Aboriginal Health in Canada: Historical, Cultural and Epidemiological Perspectives* (Toronto: University of Toronto Press, 1997) at 175.

[79]   The Supreme Court of Canada has verified that treaties between the Crown and Aboriginal peoples are enforceable agreements. *Cf. R. v. Badger*, [1996] S.C.J. No. 39 at para. 76, [1996] 1 S.C.R. 771 (S.C.C.).

[80]   (1935), 5 C.N.L.R. 92 (Ex. Ct.).

[81]   *Ibid.*, at 115.

the argument that under the Treaty the Crown had retained discretion to charge for the cost of medications.[82]

This decision stood until 1966, when the Saskatchewan Court of Appeal overturned it in *R. v. Johnson.*[83] In this case, a treaty beneficiary had refused to pay a provincial hospital tax, arguing that Treaty 6 granted him a right to medical care without charge. This argument was accepted at the Magistrate's Court, where, based on *Dreaver*, the Magistrate found the treaty right extended beyond medications to also encompass medical services including hospital care. At the Court of Appeal, however, Culliton C.J.C. found that on a "plain reading" the treaty's text made the "medicine chest" promise subject to the discretion of the administering Indian agent, and that in any case it did not extend to hospital care. He wrote:

> Again, on the plain reading of the 'medicine chest' clause, it means no more than the words clearly convey: An undertaking by the Crown to keep at the house of the Indian agent a medicine chest for the use and benefit of the Indians *at the direction of the agent.*[84]

Chief Justice Culliton heard another case on the scope of the "medicine chest" clause in 1970, in *R. v. Swimmer.*[85] This time the argument was over whether treaty beneficiaries were exempted from being required to pay provincial health care taxes. Chief Justice Culliton affirmed his earlier finding that the "medicine chest" clause was to be interpreted as discretionary, and not in any case to go beyond providing medications.

These decisions are all several decades old. Their value as precedents is questionable. In particular, they were all decided by lower courts *prior to* the Supreme Court of Canada determining that historic treaties attract unique rules of interpretation due to the circumstances in which they were entered into. These circumstances often include the terms being "constituted by an exchange of verbal promises reduced to writing in a language many of the Aboriginal signatories did not understand".[86] This rendered the Indigenous signatories unable to independently affirm that the written terms accurately reflected their understanding of what was agreed to. Given this negotiating context, the rules for interpretation include that treaty terms be interpreted liberally, with any ambiguities interpreted in favour of the Aboriginal signatories. They also require interpreting courts to canvass the context in which treaties were entered into, to try to determine the common intentions of the parties when the agreement was made.[87]

The most recent action based on Treaty 6's health-related clauses was never heard on its merits. Rather, all that was determined was a preliminary motion for

---

82 *Ibid.*
83 [1966] S.J. No. 220, 56 D.L.R. (2d) 749 (Sask. C.A.).
84 *Ibid.*, at para. 14 [emphasis in original].
85 [1970] S.J. No. 272, 17 D.L.R. (3d) 476 (Sask. C.A.).
86 *Quebec (Attorney General) v. Moses*, [2010] S.C.J. No. 17 at para. 7, 2010 SCC 17 (S.C.C.).
87 The principles are summarized in *R. v. Marshall*, [1999] S.C.J. No. 55 at para. 78, [1999] 3 S.C.R. 456 (S.C.C.).

a stay, which was denied. In the 1999 decision of *Wuskwi Sipihk Cree Nation v. Canada (Minister of National Health and Welfare)*,[88] the Wuskwi Sipihk Cree Nation had brought an action against Canada, arguing that its delegation of health responsibilities to Manitoba breached the constitutional order, and also violated their rights under Treaty 6. Canada argued that the federal court had no jurisdiction to hear the action, as health care was within provincial jurisdiction. The prothonotary found that the treaty promise, coupled with section 91(24), clearly had the effect of bringing the health of Indigenous peoples within federal jurisdiction.[89]

In the course of his reasons, the prothonotary canvassed the previous interpretations of Treaty 6. He observed that the Court of Appeal in *Johnson* had taken a literal approach to interpreting its terms. Given the interpretive principles which were subsequently identified by the Supreme Court, the prothonotary concluded that the *Dreaver* decision was correct and *Johnson* "took what is now a wrong approach".[90] The prothonotary went on to observe that "the clause may well require a full range of contemporary medical services",[91] and thus the application for a stay of action was denied.

In light of the current principles for treaty interpretation, with its focus upon the common intention of the parties and the negotiating context, the obiter commentary in *Wuskwi* is likely predictive of the outcome if the medicine chest provisions were to be litigated today. The historic record is replete with examples of how the communities of the various Indigenous signatories were being decimated by introduced diseases, and of their requests for assistance with these "pestilences".[92] Evidence exists that treaty commissioners provided some sort of health-related assurances during negotiations for Treaties 7, 8, 10 and 11.[93]

If these treaty arguments have merit, then there are considerable consequences. One of the principles for interpreting treaties is that their promises evolve to maintain relevancy. In *R. v. Marshall*, the Supreme Court of Canada wrote that treaty rights must be updated "to provide for their modern exercise",

---

[88] [1999] F.C.J. No. 82 (F.C.T.D.).

[89] *Ibid.*, at para. 14.

[90] *Ibid.*

[91] *Ibid.*

[92] See, *e.g.*, James Waldram, D. Ann Herring & T. Kue Young, *Aboriginal Health in Canada: Historical, Cultural and Epidemiological Perspectives* (Toronto: University of Toronto Press, 1997) at 141-46. Waldram *et al.* have extensively canvassed the documentation surrounding the negotiation and signing of several numbered treaties. These documents, ranging from the notes of persons who accompanied the treaty commissioners to the journals of the commissioners themselves, indicated that disease was a pressing issue for the Indigenous signatories, and that promises were made to supply medicines.

[93] Canada, Report of an Interdepartmental Working Group to the Committee of Deputy Ministers on Justice and Legal Affairs, *Fiduciary Relationship of the Crown with Aboriginal Peoples: Implementation and Management Issues – A Guide for Managers* (Ottawa: 1995) at 13, as cited in Yvonne Boyer, "Aboriginal Health: A Constitutional Rights Analysis" (Ottawa: National Aboriginal Health Organization, 2003) at 20.

including "determining what modern practices are reasonably incidental to the core treaty rights in its modern context".[94]

This principle has supported dramatic results. For example, one case involved an Aboriginal right to build shelters from trees harvested from Crown lands. Historically, this right manifested in the form of building wigwams with hand axes. The Crown argued that the current manifestation of the right was limited to small homes that, like wigwams, were built from timber that was hand harvested. The Crown therefore argued the right could not extend to "[l]arge permanent dwellings, constructed from multi-dimensional wood, obtained by modern methods of forest extraction and milling of lumber".[95] The Court rejected the Crown's argument. The historic right to harvest trees to build shelters was found to translate into a right to build shelters that is consistent with current approaches to home design and construction and that utilizes the latest lumbering technology.

It is clear that in its historic form a right to assistance with health needs may have only manifested itself through a right to medications or to avoid health care related taxes. However, given the jurisprudence, the updated and modern form of this right would likely be a robust one with significant consequences for federal obligations. And so it is evident that a generous right to health services and products may well be constitutionally entrenched — at least for the beneficiaries of these numbered treaties.[96] Not all Indigenous peoples entered into one of these treaties. Nonetheless, a lawful obligation to address their health needs has been argued to arise pursuant to fiduciary law.

B.   FIDUCIARY ARGUMENTS

As noted, Canada takes the position that any medical assistance it provides to Indigenous peoples is a discretionary exercise of its jurisdiction under section 91(24). An early statement of this position was given in 1946, when the Superintendent of Indian Health Services asserted that "Although neither law nor treaty imposes such a duty, the Federal Government has, for humanitarian reasons, for self-protection, and to prevent spread of disease to the white population, accepted responsibility for health services to the native population."[97]

Regardless of whether Canada *intended* to bind itself, the historic decision to have "accepted responsibility" supports an argument that Canada is indeed subject to lawful obligations to provide for the health of Indigenous peoples. This is because of the unique way in which fiduciary law operates in Crown-

---

[94]   [1999] S.C.J. No. 55 at para. 78, [1999] 3 S.C.R. 456 (S.C.C.).

[95]   *R. v. Sappier; R. v. Gray*, [2006] S.C.J. No. 54, [2006] 2 S.C.R. 686 at para. 49 (S.C.C.).

[96]   It has been suggested that the strength of this argument is behind Canada's policy of the "generous provision of ... medicines, drugs and medical supplies free of charge": *Duke v. Puts*, [2001] S.J. No. 156 at para. 2, 2001 SKQB 130 (Sask. Q.B.), affd [2004] S.J. No. 60 (Sask. C.A.).

[97]   As cited in James Waldram, D. Ann Herring & T. Kue Young, *Aboriginal Health in Canada: Historical, Cultural and Epidemiological Perspectives* (Toronto: University of Toronto Press, 1997) at 146.

Aboriginal relations. In particular, the Supreme Court of Canada has found that Canada is at times a fiduciary to Indigenous peoples, and that the fiduciary obligations are in the nature of a *private — not public —* law duty, and these are actionable.[98] These fiduciary obligations arise partially as a consequence of the way Canada has assumed control over aspects of Indigenous people's lives. The Court writes:

> The fiduciary duty, where it exists, is called into existence to facilitate supervision of the high degree of discretionary control gradually assumed by the Crown over the lives of aboriginal peoples.[99]

The Court identified a test for when Canada has binding fiduciary obligations to Indigenous people. The test first requires the identification "of a cognizable Indian interest" and then "the Crown's undertaking of discretionary control thereto in a way that invokes responsibility 'in the nature of a private law duty'".[100]

The provision and protection of the health needs of Aboriginal peoples could be argued to be a "cognizable Indian interest". Determining whether Canada assumed discretionary control over this interest is a matter of reviewing the historic record. A brief overview of federal practices would seem to support a *prima facie* conclusion that Canada stands as a fiduciary.

The federal government has involved itself with the health of many Indigenous peoples and communities for over 100 years. For example, it was a consistent practice of the federal government to have physicians accompany Indian agents on their annual visit to Indigenous communities to pay treaty annuities.[101] This practice was common for *all* treaty beneficiaries, not just those whose treaties included health-related clauses. Medical services were also made available to some extent for *all* reserve communities through medical officers who worked under local Indian agents.[102] The federal government formalized its role in health delivery in the early 1900s, when it created a bureaucratic structure to support and oversee these activities.

In 1904, Dr. Peter Bryce joined the Department of Indian Affairs as the General Medical Superintendent responsible for Indian health.[103] Bryce brought about a number of reforms to how health care was delivered to First Nation communities, including placing nursing stations on various reserves[104] and pro-

---

[98] *Wewaykum Indian Band v. Canada*, [2002] S.C.J. No. 79 at para. 77, 2002 SCC 79 (S.C.C.). The Court has taken pains to point out that "potential relief by way of fiduciary remedies is not limited" to situations where there have been violations of rights that have constitutional protection under s. 35, or where land is involved (at para. 79).

[99] *Ibid.*, at para. 79.

[100] *Ibid.*, at para. 85.

[101] James Waldram, D. Ann Herring & T. Kue Young, *Aboriginal Health in Canada: Historical, Cultural and Epidemiological Perspectives* (Toronto: University of Toronto Press, 1997) at 149-56.

[102] *Ibid.*, at 154-56.

[103] *Ibid.*, at 156.

[104] *Ibid.*, at 157.

ducing a "Book of Regulations" to guide the government's local representatives, Indian agents, who were expected to deliver some of the medical services.[105] By the time Bryce's replacement, Stone, was hired in 1927, Indian Affairs had expanded its bureaucracy to include a Medical Branch. Like Bryce, Stone spearheaded a number of initiatives that were directed at improving the health of Indigenous peoples. These included opening health units that targeted "Indian" persons with tuberculosis.[106] By 1935, the Medical Branch of Indian Affairs employed 11 medical officers, and had eight Indian agents with medical training as well. The Medical Branch also employed 250 physicians on a part-time basis who provided care to reserve based communities, and covered the costs of Indian persons seeing private physicians on occasion.[107] By the mid-1940s, the office had 27 full-time physicians employed by what was now called the Indian and Northern Health Service, and 700 part-time physicians providing services on demand.

During these decades, health services expanded far beyond physician, nurse and hospital care. They came to include medical transportation, medication, mental health and communicable disease. In 1945, responsibility for providing these services was transferred to the federal "Department of Health and Welfare", which later became Health Canada. Since then, Canada has continued to play a robust role in financing, administering and providing health services.

These historic initiatives were undoubtedly in part a humanitarian response to the extremely poor health status that many Indigenous communities came to experience through exposure to highly contagious diseases while being required to live on reserves, as well as having been cast into situations of severe food insecurity as traditional sources of food became inaccessible.[108] The need for such aid was taken to affirm the colonial presumption that the Indigenous population was evolutionarily inferior, both on "moral" and "physical" terms.[109]

The other branch of the colonial project, of devaluing and eradicating Indigenous cultural practices, was also served by the federal government taking a dominant role in administering health care services. Indigenous peoples had health care practices that pre-date contract (and which have survived in some form to the current day). Research into this area suggests that while their prac-

---

[105] *Ibid.*, at 158.

[106] *Ibid.*, at 158-59.

[107] *Ibid.*, at 160.

[108] Food insecurity arose in many communities, although often due to different factors. For example, communities on the plains suffered enormously as a result of the loss of the buffalo population. In British Columbia, much suffering arose due to Indigenous peoples having their access to water-based resources, such as fish, severely limited in some instances as settlers claimed land abutting waterways. In many cases, Indigenous peoples were prevented from simply moving themselves to where food resources could be obtained, as they had done for centuries, due to being confined to reserved lands.

[109] James Waldram, D. Ann Herring & T. Kue Young, *Aboriginal Health in Canada: Historical, Cultural and Epidemiological Perspectives* (Toronto: University of Toronto Press, 1997) at 163.

tices had strengths,[110] they failed them in the face of diseases introduced from Europe. As documented by the Royal Commission on Aboriginal Peoples, European-style medical treatment was sought and gratefully received in many instances, especially when it came to infectious diseases. However, when providing these needed services, those at the Medical Branch of Indian Affairs sought to discredit Indigenous practices. They saw all Indigenous health traditions as inferior and based in superstition, and worked to instill the same belief in Indigenous peoples.[111] The Royal Commission describes the complicated "price" of receiving state-provided physician assistance as including the following:

- Aboriginal people with serious illnesses were often sent, unaccompanied, to distant medical facilities for treatment in strange and sometimes hostile environments.

- In their own communities, Aboriginal people were offered health care services that had no foundation in local values, traditions or conditions. At worst, a few were forced (or convinced) to suffer invasive medical procedures, including sterilization.

- Virtually all providers of health and social services were non-Aboriginal, many with little interest in the cultural practices or values of their Aboriginal clients. Encounters were often clouded by suspicion, misunderstanding, resentment and racism.

- Indigenous healing skills and knowledge of herbal medicines and other traditional treatments were devalued by medical personnel and hidden by those who still practised or even remembered them. Much knowledge was eventually lost.[112]

The Royal Commission found that the majority of traditional healers came to abandon their practices "because of persecution by Canadian governments and Christian churches and contempt on the part of bio-medical practitioners for their ceremonies, herbal treatments, and other therapies".[113] This part of Crown-Indigenous history is relevant because fiduciary obligations arise in part due to "the degree of economic, social and proprietary control and discretion asserted by the Crown [that] also left aboriginal populations vulnerable to the risks of government misconduct or ineptitude".[114] The examples above may be consid-

---

[110] Canada, Royal Commission on Aboriginal Peoples, *Report of the Royal Commission on Aboriginal Peoples*, vol. 3: *Gathering Strength* (Ottawa: Minister of Supply and Services, 1996) at 103-104.

[111] James Waldram, D. Ann Herring & T. Kue Young, *Aboriginal Health in Canada: Historical, Cultural and Epidemiological Perspectives* (Toronto: University of Toronto Press, 1997) at 161.

[112] Canada, Royal Commission on Aboriginal Peoples, *Report of the Royal Commission on Aboriginal Peoples*, vol. 3: *Gathering Strength* (Ottawa: Minister of Supply and Services, 1996) at 105-106.

[113] *Ibid.*, at 193.

[114] *Wewaykum Indian Band v. Canada*, [2002] S.C.J. No. 79 at para. 80, 2002 SCC 79 (S.C.C.).

ered to illustrate the extent to which the Canadian government asserted control, and the vulnerability and dependency which many Indigenous peoples experienced as healing knowledge and practice were intentionally displaced (instead of complemented).

To conclude the overview of this argument, on the level of policy and practice, Canada has long asserted a right to oversee or engage with the health of at least some segment of the Indigenous population. By virtue of fiduciary law, these practices may have crystallized into lawful obligations. Although the obligations of a fiduciary vary, at a minimum they include "the obligations of loyalty, good faith, full disclosure appropriate to the matter at hand and acting in what it reasonably and with diligence regards as the best interest of the beneficiary".[115] If fiduciary law does operate here, the consequences are significant because it would require the federal government to make programming decisions based on "best interests", and with far less emphasis upon financial constraints.

C.   OBLIGATIONS UNDER INTERNATIONAL LAW

Both the treaty based argument and the fiduciary law argument are based in domestic law. There are also arguments under international law that Canada is required to bring about considerable improvements to the health of Indigenous peoples.[116] One of these arguments is triggered by the epidemiological and social determinants data that was surveyed above, and how that data engages with the terms of the *International Covenant on Economic, Social and Cultural Rights* (ICESCR).[117]

Canada ratified the ICESCR in 1976. Its binding articles recognize the right "to the highest attainable standard of physical and mental health", and specifically call upon states to address infant mortality, hygiene and the prevention, treatment, and control of epidemic and endemic diseases.[118] To fulfil these legal commitments, and others under the ICESCR, the Committee overseeing the ICESCR has confirmed that governments are required

> to ensure access to the minimum essential food which is nutritionally adequate and safe, to ensure freedom from hunger to everyone; [and] ... [t]o ensure access to basic shelter, housing and sanitation, and an adequate supply of safe and potable water.[119]

---

[115] *Ibid.*, at para. 94.

[116] For a general discussion of international law obligations, see Yvonne Boyer, *The International Right to Health for Indigenous Peoples in Canada* (Ottawa: National Aboriginal Health Organization, 2004) at 22-27.

[117] (December 16, 1966), 993 U.N.T.S. 3, Can. T.S. 1976 No. 46, 6 I.L.M. 360 (entered into force January 3, 1976).

[118] *Ibid.*, art. 12.

[119] Committee on Economic, Social and Cultural Rights, General Comment 14 (2000), *The Right to the Highest Attainable Standard of Health*, 22nd Session, 2000, UN Doc. E/C.12/2000/4 at para. 43.

The ICESCR requires states to meet their obligations pursuant to their re-sources.[120] The data presented above regarding Indigenous peoples' rates of in-fant mortality and epidemic diseases, as well as food insecurity and lack of access to safe housing, adequate sanitation and water, suggests Canada is in breach of its obligations under international law. That is, it is not meeting the standards for health that it has the resources to obtain when it comes to the entire Indigenous population.

The Committee to which signatory countries report on implementation has implied that Canada is not meeting its obligations *vis-à-vis* the Indigenous popu-lation on numerous occasions. For example, in its 2006 report it wrote that:

> The Committee is also concerned by the significant disparities still remaining between Aboriginal people and the rest of the population in areas of employ-ment, access to water, health, housing and education.[121]

Although the Committee receives and replies to reports from signatory countries on compliance, the Committee does not have mechanisms to enforce the ICESCR. Rather, signatory states are expected to act on the obligation in the ICESCR to create domestic mechanisms that guide implementation and provide for enforcement. The Committee urged Canada in 2006 to act upon these out-standing obligations. In particular, the Committee requested Canada take steps to ensure that Covenant rights are directly enforceable through either legislation or policy measures, and to establish "effective" mechanisms to oversee the im-plementation of the ICESCR.[122] Canada has not yet acted upon these requests. Canada was scheduled to deliver a report in June 2010. However, at press time, this report did not yet seem to have been delivered. It remains to be seen how the Committee will respond to the continuing situation.

This chapter now turns to some of the elements of the current federal strate-gies for addressing the health of Indigenous peoples.

V.   CONTEMPORARY HEALTH POLICIES AND PROGRAMS

This section considers Canada's dominant set of contemporary practices and policies for supporting the health of Indigenous peoples. It starts by briefly reviewing the 1979 *Federal Indian Health Policy*, then moves to the Health Transfer Policy and Canada's Non-insured Health Benefits Program. As well as describing some of the strengths and limitations of these strategies, it also offers

---

[120]   ICESCR, art 2.

[121]   Committee on Economic, Social and Cultural Rights (CESCR), *Review of 4th and 5th Periodic Reports: Concluding Observations of the Committee on Economic, Social and Cultural Rights: Canada*, 36th Session; 2006, UN Doc. E/C.12/CAN/CO/4, E/C.12/CAN/CO/5 at para.15, online at: <http://www.unhchr.ch/tbs/doc.nsf/898586b1dc7b4043c1256a450044f331/87793634eae60c00c125 71ca00371262/$FILE/G0642783 pdf>.

[122]   *Ibid.*, at para. 35.

comments on whether the various strategies (or their implementation) appear to enable a decolonizing approach.

A. THE 1979 INDIAN HEALTH POLICY

In the late 1970s, Canada sought to reduce its spending on Indigenous health. In particular, Canada proposed to withdraw funding in such areas as medications and eyeglasses.[123] This provoked forceful protests, and assertions by Aboriginal political organizations that Canada did not have the right to unilaterally withdraw such services.[124] The debate which this dispute engendered ultimately led to Canada adopting its 1979 *Indian Health Policy.* The Policy represented a significant turning point in how Canada conceived of addressing Indigenous health. Its stated goal was to increase "the level of health in Indian communities, generated and maintained by Indian communities themselves".[125] For the first time, Canada acknowledged that Indigenous peoples as communities had a role to play in ameliorating the situation. This conceptual turn clearly opened the door to mediating some aspects of historic Indigenous disempowerment. The policy identified three pillars for success. One pillar, which refers to socio-economic, cultural and spiritual development, was described as the most important one for improving health. The two other pillars were that the federal government maintain "an active role in the Canadian health system as it affects Indians", and that the federal government serve "as an advocate of the interests of Indian communities ... and promote the capacity of Indian communities to achieve their aspirations".[126]

B. THE HEALTH TRANSFER POLICY

The pillars of the 1979 policy are to some extent reflected in the 1988 Health Transfer Policy, which, when announced, was described as the key initiative for supporting Indigenous health.[127] The Federal Cabinet approved the framework for this policy in March 1988, and the Treasury Board approved the required

---

[123] Canada, Royal Commission on Aboriginal Peoples, *Report of the Royal Commission on Aboriginal Peoples*, vol. 3: *Gathering Strength* (Ottawa: Minister of Supply and Services, 1996) at 106.

[124] *Ibid.*, at 114-15.

[125] Health Canada, *Indian Health Policy 1979* (Canada: Health Canada Medical Services Branch, 1979), online at: <http:www.hc-sc.gc.ca/ahc-asc/branch-dirgen/fnihb-dgspni/poli_1979-eng.php>.

[126] This approach is also consistent with addressing the social determinants of health. For a robust discussion of social determinants of health and Indigenous peoples, see Constance MacIntosh, "Law and Policy Regarding the Population Health of Aboriginal Canadians" in Tracey M. Bailey, Timothy Caulfield & Nola M. Ries, eds., *Public Health Law & Policy in Canada*, 2d ed. (Markham, ON: LexisNexis Canada, 2008) at 395-439.

[127] See Josée Lavoie *et al.*, *The Evaluation of the First Nations and Inuit Health Transfer Policy: Final Report: Volume 2, Report* (Winnipeg: Centre for Aboriginal Health Research, 2005) at 36-46.

financial arrangements in 1989.[128] This policy centers around developing contractual agreements, called "Contribution Agreements", under which administrative control over specific community health programs is transferred from the hands of federal departments to certain types of Indigenous communities. These programs include, among others, Aboriginal Head Start On-Reserve, Communicable Disease Control, Prenatal Nutrition, Building Healthy Communities, and the National Native Alcohol and Drug Abuse Program.[129] On a conceptual level, the devolution of control over such programs is clearly consonant with enabling a de-colonialized approach to health care, and with enabling the revitalization of Indigenous communities.

There has been tremendous buy-in to the health transfer program by First Nation communities. As of March 2008, Health Canada reports that 83 per cent of eligible First Nations had entered into one of the three types of transfer agreements.[130] Some of these communities have entered into a "Consolidated Contribution Agreement – General". These are agreements under which the Indigenous community administers specific programs for a one-year term, each of which have an assigned budget. The majority of participating First Nations have entered into a "Consolidated Contribution Agreement-Transfer/Targeted". These contracts have terms that may range from three to five years, and they offer communities a bit more control. The First Nation can select which of the programs they wish to deliver, have some limited room to design new programs, and receive a single budget that they are able to then assign to the various programs. The caveat on control, however, is that communities who enter into these agreements are required to administer the Communicable Disease Control, Environmental/Occupation Health and Safety, and Treatment Services programs, and are assigned a specific budget for each of these. These are potentially quite onerous programs to deliver, as they require considerable capacity. The third type of arrangement is a "Consolidated Contribution Agreement – Integrated/Targeted", which requires the community to develop an overarching health management and delivery scheme, and also includes designing and delivering some of the specified programs.[131] Quite often, the health transfer arrangements are embedded within overarching contracts under which the administration and operation of capital projects such as water treatment infrastructure as well as other services are also devolved to the First Nation.

---

[128] Health Canada, *Ten Years of Health Transfer: First Nations and Inuit Control* (1999) at 3, online at: <http://www.hc-sc.gc.ca/fniah-spnia/pubs/finance/_agree-accord/10_years_ans_trans/2_intro-eng.php#history_of_transfer>.

[129] Josée Lavoie *et al.*, *The Evaluation of the First Nations and Inuit Health Transfer Policy: Final Report: Volume 2, Report* (Winnipeg: Centre for Aboriginal Health Research, 2005) at 5-7.

[130] Health Canada, First Nations, Inuit and Aboriginal Health, "Transfer Status as of March 2008", online at: <http://www.hc-sc.gc.ca/fnih-spni/finance/agree-accord/trans_rpt_stats_e.html>.

[131] The Health Transfer Agreement Policy is discussed in more depth in Constance MacIntosh, "Envisioning the Future of Aboriginal Health under the Health Transfer Process" (2008) Health L.J. 67 at 68-73.

Regardless of what model an Indigenous community chooses to participate in, they face restrictions and fiscal complications that go back to the way that Canada has historically conceptualized its relationship with, and power over, Indigenous peoples. Thus, although the policy is liberating in some respects, in others it retrenches back into a colonial framework.

In particular, the transfer programs are only available to Indigenous communities of First Nations people who are reserve-based. This necessarily excludes any Métis communities. It also excludes any communities of Indigenous peoples who formed as a result of themselves or their ancestors having been forced off of reserves (*i.e.*, due to losing registered status, or due to resisting the whole reserve system).[132] Furthermore, the budget for administering most of these programs is calculated not according to the number of residents of a reserve community, but according to the number of registered Indians who are residents of the reserve community. This calculation reflects the fact that Canada only intends much of the programming to benefit this state-defined population, consistent with Canada's interpretation of its jurisdictional responsibilities.

This creates some obvious practical problems with programs meeting their goals. For example, Health Canada intends the program clients for the Communicable Disease Control Program focused on tuberculosis to only be "First Nations people living on-reserve and Inuit in Labrador".[133] Given its highly contagious character, the astonishing rates of tuberculosis within Indigenous communities are not likely to be controlled as long as a program only serves select residents of reserves instead of the whole community. Such an approach also erodes the meaningfulness of the power that was granted to First Nation bands to determine their own membership criteria. According to the *Indian Act*, with membership comes the right to live on reserve land. Up until 1985, Canada assigned band membership to all persons with status. When Canada amended the *Indian Act* in 1985, one key change was granting bands the power to decide who their members were. Under this funding regime, First Nations have a fiscal motivation to align their membership criteria with the federally determined criteria for status. As funds are not provided or intended to be spent on community members who live off-reserve, nor for band members who are not First Nations (*e.g.*, they may be members and live on-reserve due to "marrying in"), those communities whose political identity deviates from Canada's status criteria will be administering programs that perpetuate the very distinctions which they have rejected.

There are also numerous practical challenges that First Nations take on when they sign these agreements, which are somewhat analogous to the challenges that provinces face in their health care delivery operations. These include

---

[132] A discussion of the complicated decisions that such communities face, and the fiscal consequences of such decisions, is canvassed in *Lovelace v. Ontario*, [2000] S.C.J. No. 36, [2000] 1 S.C.R. 950 (S.C.C.), as well as in *Corbiere v. Canada (Minister of Indian and Northern Affairs)*, [1999] S.C.J. No. 24, [1999] 2 S.C.R. 203 (S.C.C.).

[133] Health Canada, "First Nations, Inuit and Aboriginal Health: Funded Health Programs and Services", online at: <http://www.hc-sc.gc.ca/fniah-spnia/finance/agree-accord/prog/index-eng.php>.

"merging program administrations and creation of more efficient management structures; [developing] effective governance models, recruitment and retention strategies; integration, mergers and other collaborative relationships with neighbouring First Nations; and primary care reform".[134] Recruitment and retention of health care personnel has proven particularly problematic for many First Nations. This is due both to their often isolated locations, and to the financing formulas within the transfer agreements which may leave them unable to compete with the salaries on offer from other communities within a given region or province.[135] A 2005 evaluation of the health transfer program characterized the personnel problem as "becoming insurmountable".[136] A 2009 evaluation of transfers of the Home and Community Care Program found that "wage disparity was a critical issue"[137] as provinces pay more per hour for the same work.[138]

The financing formula contributes directly to this problem because it is insensitive to actual costs. All health transfer agreements include "non-enrichment clauses". These clauses operate to calibrate funding against various fixed and non-responsive factors such as the actual expenditures the year before the community entered into the transfer agreement. So, for many programs historical expenditure determines future funding, not actual costs of delivering the same level of service. This problem is known to Health Canada. In its 2009 evaluation of transfers of the Home and Community Care Program, one of the recommendations was that the funding formula be updated. The specific suggestion was that "[t]he formula should be re-designed so as to be more needs-based, taking into account the increased burden of chronic illness and injuries".[139] The response of the Senior Management Board for Finance, Evaluation and Accountability within Health Canada to this recommendation was that "[c]urrent funding levels do not permit a change in the way that funding is distributed to communities".[140] Obviously, if health care is only supported pursuant to federal discretion and not as a lawful obligation, such an answer is a final one that reflects current funding priorities. And Indigenous communities, like all communities across Canada, must make due. However, if the fiduciary law arguments surveyed above have merit, then such a response may be actionable.

The current approach to funding, which usually links it to funds expended the year prior to the transfer taking place, also engenders inequities across Abo-

---

[134] Laurel Lemchuk-Favel & Richard Jock, "Aboriginal Health Systems in Canada: Nine Case Studies" (2004) 1:1 J. of Aboriginal Health 28 at 40.

[135] See Constance MacIntosh, "Envisioning the Future of Aboriginal Health under the Health Transfer Process" (2008) Health L.J. 67 at 74-75.

[136] Josée Lavoie *et al.*, *The Evaluation of the First Nations and Inuit Health Transfer Policy: Final Report: Volume 2, Report* (Winnipeg: Centre for Aboriginal Health Research, 2005) at 90.

[137] Health Canada, "First Nations, Inuit and Aboriginal Health: Summative Evaluation of the First Nations and Inuit Home and Community Care", online at: <http://www.hc-sc.gc.ca/fniah-spnia/pubs/services/fnihcc-psdmcpni/index-eng.php> at 36.

[138] *Ibid.*, at 37.

[139] *Ibid.*, at 41.

[140] Health Canada, *Management Action Plan – First Nations and Inuit Home and Community Care Summative Evaluation – March 2009* (October 16, 2009) at 1.

riginal communities. This is because federal funding levels are themselves inconsistent over the years. There are analogous health centres whose funding ranges from $430 to $1,418 per capita. The only significant difference between these communities is the year when they entered the health transfer program — not the scope of programs delivered, nor other factors such as remoteness.[141] In general, the later a community enters transfer, the higher their funding level. This obviously has repercussions not just for competing for personnel, but also for delivering any of the transferred programs at a satisfactory level.

There are also serious gaps in services. For example, the community health programs do not include palliative/end of life care or caregiver respite, and so no funding is allocated to address these needs. The transferred community health program also does not include supporting mental health and addiction services in the home. In the program evaluation it was noted that

> high addiction rates and high acquired brain injury rates (either drug or alcohol induced) have led to both acute and chronic mental health issues which remain unrecognized and untreated. Suicide intervention is urgently needed. The gaps in services are much greater than what the FNIHCC [First Nations and Inuit Home and Community Care] programs provide and mental health services pose one of the greatest challenges to effectively deliver within FNIHCC.[142]

The response to recommendations to provide funding in these areas, so that the communities who administer these programs can offer programming that is analogous to provincial services, was met by the assertion that "current funding levels" do not permit this expansion of services.[143]

In practice this approach to financing requires a transferred First Nation to generate funding to address shortfalls, or else have a reduced level of service and be unable to meet many needs that fall outside of Health Canada's vision of community health. Where First Nations do not make up the shortfall and instead over-spend to meet need, or cannot account for their spending, or their members' health is "compromised", they are at risk of the federal government imposing third party management. This is authorized pursuant to the standard terms in the transfer agreement contracts.[144]

---

[141] Josée Lavoie, Evelyn Forget & John O'Neil, "Why Equity in Financing First Nations On-Reserve Health Services Matters: Findings from the 2005 National Evaluation of the Health Transfer Policy" (2007) 2:4 Healthcare Policy 79 at 93.

[142] Health Canada, "First Nations, Inuit and Aboriginal Health: Summative Evaluation of the First Nations and Inuit Home and Community Care", online at: <http://www.hc-sc.gc.ca/fniah-spnia/pubs/services/fnihcc-psdmcpni/index-eng.php> at 22.

[143] Health Canada, *Management Action Plan – First Nations and Inuit Home and Community Care Summative Evaluation – March 2009* (October 16, 2009) at 2.

[144] Standard terms were introduced following a June 2000 Treasury Board policy that called for developing more robust accountability mechanisms. Consultation on the standardized agreements "included input and cooperation from Treasury Board, Indian and Northern Affairs Canada, Justice Canada, other Health Canada branches, and Human Resources Development Canada". See Health Canada, "First Nations, Inuit and Aboriginal Health: Introduction of New Standard Agreements, March 2001", online at: <http://www.hc-sc.gc.ca/fniah-spnia/finance/

As indicated above, health transfers are typically contained within Comprehensive Funding Agreements (CFAs). Most of the terms in CFAs are non-negotiable. Among other things, they set out a number of circumstances where the First Nation will be in default. For all CFAs that are entered into in 2010–2011, these include where the Band Council "defaults in any of its obligations" in the agreement, where an audit shows "a cumulative operating deficit equivalent to eight (8) per cent or more" of annual revenues, or if "the health, safety or welfare of First Nations members is being compromised".[145] If such a situation is present, Indian and Northern Affairs Canada (INAC) has a range of options open to it. These include requiring the band to develop a remedial management plan or to enter into a co-management agreement, as well as imposing third party management. INAC may also terminate the agreement, withhold funds and take "any such other reasonable action as the Minister deems necessary to remedy the default". There are numerous reported cases where a decision by the Minister to impose third party management was judicially reviewed. From these cases, it appears that INAC's approach is typically to exercise its rights in an escalating fashion where the defaults persist.

This contractual right appears to have been drawn upon in many instances when accounting statements do not satisfy INAC.[146] However, the exercise of this contractual right has also been justified by more troubling circumstances. In particular, where the First Nation in question has debts.

The relationship between a First Nation having debts and its ability to deliver transferred programming was illustrated in the Supreme Court of Canada decision of *McDiarmid Lumber Ltd. v. God's Lake First Nation.*[147] In this case, a First Nation had entered into a CFA. Their funds to deliver all of the services and programming, including health, were deposited into a nearby bank. A third party creditor, McDiarmid Lumber, sought to garnish their account for a sizable debt. The Supreme Court of Canada found that the funds were available for garnishing. Presumably, after the funds were seized, Canada provided the funding a second time, given the essential character of the services in question.

---

agree-accord/prog/index-eng.php>. The consultation activities did not seem to engage any Aboriginal organizations.

[145] See INAC's "Comprehensive Funding Arrangement National Model for Use with First Nations and Tribal Councils for 2010–2011", clause 4.1(c) and (d), online at: <http://www.ainc-inac.gc.ca/ai/arp/trp/pubs/cfafn/cfafn-eng.asp>. For agreements entered into prior to 2010–2011, standard terms also include finding default where "the Minister has a reasonable belief, based on material evidence, that the health, safety or welfare of the Members or Recipients is being compromised": see, *e.g.*, INAC's "DIAND/First Nations Funding Agreement National Model for Use with First Nations and Tribal Councils for 2008–2009" at clause 9.1(d), online at: <http://www.ainc-inac.gc.ca/ai/arp/trp/pubs/dfnfa/dfnfa-eng.asp>.

[146] *E.g.*, see *Tobique Indian Band v. Canada*, [2010] F.C.J. No. 60 (F.C.); *Elders Council of Mitchikanibikok Inik v. Canada (Minister of Indian Affairs and Northern Development)*, [2009] F.C.J. No. 478, 2009 FC 374 (F.C.); *Ermineskin Tribe v. Canada*, [2008] F.C.J. No. 933, 2008 FC 741 (F.C.).

[147] [2006] S.C.J. No. 58, 2006 SCC 58 (S.C.C.).

The irony of the situation is that since the Crown cannot be garnished, the health care funding is shielded as long as the Crown delivers the programming. But if a community takes control over administering the programming, then the funds become vulnerable despite the fact that the funding is contractually dedicated to essential services (*i.e.*, the transferred band cannot *choose* to use its transfer funding to pay its debts). The Supreme Court found the only exception to such funding being vulnerable to seizure would be if the funding is held at an on-reserve banking institution. This is because of provisions in the *Indian Act* that shield property when located on a reserve.

This jurisprudence played prominently in the 2010 case of *Tobique Indian Band v. Canada*,[148] where a band sought the judicial review of INAC's decision to impose third party management of their transferred programmes. The First Nation suffered from a billowing state of debt. Justice Beaudry concluded as follows:

> I find that it was realistic to fear that some type of seizure or garnishment proceedings could start at anytime and that the consideration of protection of public funds and trying to insure the future availability of services was a reasonable ground in reaching the decision to implement third party management in order to protect the funds.[149]

Given that payments from the Crown to First Nations that are given under treaties are expressly shielded by legislation against being available for garnishment by third parties, it is obvious that this vulnerability could be addressed through extending the legislated protection to embrace such dedicated funds. However, Parliament has not chosen to make the required legislative amendments. In practical terms, this choice means that First Nations who carry a debt load may not be able to count on being able to plan and administer their own health services under transfer agreements.

The Health Transfer Policy is described by FNIHB as "the best way to deal with the [health] inequalities existing between Aboriginal Peoples and the rest of Canada".[150] It may not be the best way, but despite the criticisms described above it appears to have made a difference. One comprehensive study of First Nation communities in Manitoba and British Columbia that tracked certain health conditions from 1985 to 2005 was described as proving "that First Nation control of health care leads to better health".[151] The study authors specifically considered the rates of hospitalization for ambulatory care sensitive conditions (*i.e.*, medical conditions for which hospitalization is likely avoidable through

---

[148] [2010] F.C.J. No. 60 (F.C.).

[149] *Ibid.*, at para. 61.

[150] Josée Lavoie, "Governed by Contracts: The Development of Indigenous Primary Health Services in Canada, Australia and New Zealand" (2004) 1:1 J. of Aboriginal Health 6 at 12.

[151] Paul Webster, "Local Control Over Aboriginal Health Care Improves Outcome, Study Indicates" (2009) 181:11 CMAJ e249. This article describes the findings of a study by Josée Lavoie and John O'Neil. For one report arising out of this study, see Josée Lavoie *et al.*, "The *Where to Invest Project*" (Centre for Aboriginal Health Research, 2010).

effective primary care). After controlling for a number of factors, they found that the "rates of avoidable hospitalization decreased with each year" following entering into a transfer agreement.[152] The report authors conclude that they have empirically demonstrated a correlation between self-determination and health outcomes.[153]

Other studies have also suggested empirically assessable links between communities participating in health transfer initiatives and health outcomes. One particularly notable study found associations between participating in various self-governance activities including health transfer and reductions in youth suicide.[154]

A final point about this policy is to query how it may be limited due to op-erating largely under the assumption that Canada has correctly identified what Indigenous communities need. It focuses primarily on downloading the *existing set* of community health programmes and categories into the hands of the com-munity. The question which this raises is whether and how programming that supports community health would be differently conceptualized at a fundamen-tal level if it was generated by the community itself. Ensuring that programming that is intended to address Indigenous health is in Indigenous hands is obviously one important aspect of enabling political restoration and facilitating culturally relevance. However, as long as the very nature and categories of the programs is pre-determined there is a risk of misalignment. As well, such an approach may perpetuate the perception that Indigenous communities are not able to make such decisions for themselves, and may not foster building internal capacity.

C. NON-INSURED HEALTH BENEFITS

Another major initiative that FNIHB manages is called the "Non-Insured Health Benefits" ("NIHB") program. NIHB provides a portion of the Indigenous popu-lation with select medically necessary "health-related goods and services" that are not covered by provincial or privately held medical plans.[155] For 2008–2009, these include:

- Pharmacy benefits (including prescription and over-the-counter drugs as well as medical supplies and equipment);

- Dental services;

---

[152] Josée Lavoie *et al.*, "The *Where to Invest Project*" (Centre for Aboriginal Health Research, 2010) at v.

[153] See Josée Lavoie *et al.*, "Have Investments in On-Reserve Health Services and Initiatives Pro-moting Community Control Improved First Nations' Health in Manitoba?" (2010) 17 Soc. Sci. & Med. 717 at 723.

[154] Michael Chandler & Christopher Lalonde, "Cultural Continuity as a Moderator of Suicide Risk Among Canada's First Nations" in Laurence Kirmayer & Gail Valaskakis, eds., *Healing Tradi-tions: The Mental Health of Aboriginal Peoples in Canada* (Vancouver: University of British Columbia Press, 2009) 221 at 238-40.

[155] Health Canada, First Nations and Inuit Health Branch, *Non-Insured Health Benefits Program: Annual Report 2008/2009* (Ottawa: Minister of Health, 2010) at 5.

- Transportation to access medically necessary services;

- Eye and vision care services;

- Provincial health care premiums; and

- Other health care services such as "short-term crisis intervention mental health counseling".[156]

This initiative accounts for nearly half of Health Canada's expenditures for First Nations and Inuit health,[157] with total NIHB expenditures for 2008–2009 being $934.6 million.[158] To put this figure in perspective, Health Canada reports that the national per capita expenditure for all NIHB claims was $1,081 for 2008–2009 and $1,061 for 2007–2008.[159] The figures do vary by age, with the average claimant between 0 and 4 years of age having incurred $158 per year in NIHB benefits in 2008–2009, while claimants over 65 years of age made average claims of $2,119 per year.[160]

Of the total sum expended in 2008–2009, the largest proportion (44.8 per cent) was categorized as pharmacy costs.[161] Pharmacy costs is a broad category, including medications as well as medical supplies and equipment including wheelchairs, audiology items, orthotics and respiratory equipment.[162] The next highest spending category was medical transportation, which accounted for almost 30 per cent of expenditures.[163]

Health Canada describes this initiative as a discretionary one, whose purpose is to "support First Nations and Inuit in reaching the overall health status that is comparable with other Canadians".[164] This goal would seem to be consonant with Canada's obligations under international law as described above. However, like the funding formula for aspects of the health transfer program, only those members of First Nations *who are also registered as "Indians"* under the *Indian Act*, or who are Inuit, count. As of March 31, 2009, a total of 815,800 individuals were deemed eligible for these benefits.[165] Of this population, 95.2 per cent were First Nation persons, while 4.8 per cent were Inuit.[166] Aboriginal

---

[156] *Ibid.*

[157] Assembly of First Nations, "First Nations Action Plan for Non-Insured Health Benefits" (April 25, 2005).

[158] Health Canada, First Nations and Inuit Health Branch, *Non-Insured Health Benefits Program: Annual Report 2008/2009* (Ottawa: Minister of Health, 2010) at 17.

[159] *Ibid.*, at 26.

[160] *Ibid.*, at 34.

[161] *Ibid.*, at 17.

[162] *Ibid.*, at 29. Within this category, the largest spending component was prescription drugs, at 74.4 per cent of all pharmacy expenditures. The second largest category was over-the-counter drugs (for which a prescription has been issued), at 12 per cent. Medical supplies and equipment came in third, at 5.9 per cent. *Ibid.*, at 30-31.

[163] *Ibid.*, at 17.

[164] *Ibid.*, at 5.

[165] *Ibid.*, at 7.

[166] *Ibid.*, at 9.

peoples who are members of First Nation bands but who are non-status do not qualify. Although FNIHB extends the benefits to all children of eligible adults at birth, this eligibility expires when the child is one year old, unless the child also qualifies for status or is an Inuit.[167] Given these criteria for participation, it is challenging to understand how the stated policy objective — of supporting First Nations in obtaining a health status that compares to other Canadians — can be obtained unless Canada is using the term "First Nation" to only mean people who fit *Indian Act* registration criteria.

There are also challenges arising from how the program is delivered. For example, in its 2005 audit of the NIHB program, the Assembly of First Nations (AFN) found that many dentists and orthodontists were requiring individuals to pay for their treatment in advance, due to delays involved in receiving payment from NIHB. Indeed, the Canadian Association of Orthodontists advised its members to follow this course of action.[168] Obviously, the burden of paying for such services and then seeking reimbursement constitutes a deterrent to receiving necessary care. Given Health Canada's finding that the median income of First Nation individuals from 1999–2003 was $10,631,[169] such practices can be expected to effectively undermine the ability of many eligible individuals to access these benefits.

Practical problems also arise because the funding system presumes a certain infrastructure that is not always present. To continue with the example of dental health, dental hygienists are usually charged with addressing basic prevention and health promotion. However, the NIHB scheme requires dental hygienists to be paid through dentists. As a result, communities that lack regular outreach dental services are unable to have dental hygienists visit, resulting in their dental care being largely dental treatment and restoration, instead of being preventative oral health care.[170] Although the AFN brought concerns on this issue forward in 2005, it was only in July 2010 that a pilot project was launched in Alberta to permit dental hygienists to bill NIHB directly for their services.[171] It is hard to understand why it would take five years to begin a pilot program of offering far less expensive preventative health maintenance.

Some other concerns that the AFN identified in a 2005 report were addressed through more immediate changes to the NIHB program. For example, one of the AFN's concerns had been that where a service costs $800 or more, it automatically required pre-approval, engendering treatment delay, a prolonga-

---

[167] *Ibid.*, at 7.

[168] Assembly of First Nations, "First Nations Action Plan for Non-Insured Health Benefits" (April 25, 2005) at 7.

[169] Health Canada, *A Statistical Profile on the Health of First Nations in Canada, Determinants of Health, 1999 to 2003* (Ottawa: Ministry of Health, 2009) at 18.

[170] Assembly of First Nations, "First Nations Action Plan for Non-Insured Health Benefits" (April 25, 2005) at 12.

[171] This pilot program, and the memorandum of understanding under which it is to operate, is described in "Non-Insured Health Benefits Pilot Project in Alberta" (2010) In Touch 1 (College of Registered Dental Hygienists of Alberta).

tion of poor health and additional expenses for secondary visits.[172] This threshold was removed in 2005.[173] As a result, the requirement for pre-approval is now only formally linked to the nature of the proposed service. However, there is nothing to suggest that the issue of delays in receiving payment — and so the practice of requiring payment upfront — has been addressed.

In contrast to Canada's position that NIHB is a discretionary policy-driven initiative, Indigenous organizations characterize the NIHB program as a manifestation of Canada's lawful obligations to Indigenous Canadians emanating from treaty rights and the federal fiduciary obligation.[174] As this argument has been reviewed above, it is not repeated here. If this argument is correct, one obvious consequence is that Canada's criteria for coverage and the scope of programming may be unsustainable. Another consequence would be that changes to the program, and the manner in which it is delivered, could become actionable in a way that provincial decisions regarding health care coverage are not.

There has been some innovation with the NIHB program. On June 21, 1994, a Cabinet decision authorized the creation of pilot programs to experiment with transferring administration of most aspects of NIHB programming to Aboriginal communities or organizations, with the exclusion of the Pharmaceutical and Dental programs.[175] In 1997, Cabinet authorized including all programs within the pilot projects. A total of 16 communities were selected for pilot programs, which commenced in 1996. The expectation was that the results from the pilot projects would then be used to develop a NIHB Transfer Policy.[176] Of these original 16 communities, by 2007 three had left the project because they entered self-government agreements. Of the remaining 13, all but one had withdrawn. The AFN Health Bulletin reports that the communities who withdrew did so because they lacked "the support to build-up infrastructure and capacity",[177] although Health Canada simply describes their withdraw as reflecting a decision to revert to Contribution Agreements.[178] The remaining community, Bigstone Cree First Nation, is characterized in FNIB's 2008–2009 Annual Report as successful. Despite having operated for 13 years, it continues as a pilot project, likely reflecting the fact that while the pilot projects were not successful enough to shape a formal NIHB transfer plan, the Bigstone Cree First Nation's operations ought to continue.

---

[172] Assembly of First Nations, "First Nations Action Plan for Non-Insured Health Benefits" (April 25, 2005) at 19.

[173] See Health Canada, "Dental Bulletin: Non-Insured Health Benefits" (June 2005), online at: <http://www.hc-sc.gc.ca/fniah-spnia/alt_formats/fnihb-dgspni/pdf/pubs/dent/2005-06-bull-lebull-eng.pdf>.

[174] Assembly of First Nations, "First Nations Action Plan for Non-Insured Health Benefits" (April 25, 2005) at 1.

[175] Health Canada, First Nations and Inuit Health Branch, *Non-Insured Health Benefits Program Annual Report, 2002/2003* (Ottawa: Minister of Health, 2003) at 102.

[176] Health Canada, *Transferring Control of Health Programs to First Nations and Inuit Communities: Handbook 2 – The Health Services Transfer* (Ottawa: March 2004 (revised)) at 36.

[177] Assembly of First Nations, "Health Bulletin" (Winter 2007) at 8.

[178] Health Canada, First Nations and Inuit Health Branch, *Non-Insured Health Benefits Program Annual Report, 2002/2003* (Ottawa: Minister of Health, 2003) at 102.

Finally, administrative responsibilities for limited control over some aspects of NIHB programming has been transferred to some Aboriginal communities, as aspects of Contribution Agreements. For example, as of March 2010, eight First Nation or Inuit communities or organizations had entered contracts to administer the Medical Supplies and Equipment claims.[179]

VI. CHALLENGES AND TRANSFORMATIONS

Many of the health inequalities that are experienced by Indigenous peoples arise from social inequalities. As flagged at the opening of this chapter, these social inequalities are themselves associated with the cultural, social, economic and political disruptions that were and are fostered through law, policy and practices which reflect a colonial approach.[180] As simply put by Kelly McShane, Janet Smylie and Paul Adomako, "[t]he colonization of Indigenous peoples globally has been increasingly recognized as a fundamental underlying determinant of health".[181] A recent example of this recognition can be found in a study of the 2009–2010 pandemic influenza (H1N1) virus that sought to identify factors that correlated with severe infection.[182] They were particularly interested in assessing why First Nation peoples experienced a disproportionately high rate of severe infection. After the report authors accounted for all the other factors that were associated with severe infection — including interval between onset of symptoms and treatment, age and underlying comorbidities — they still found that the severity of illness was disproportionately high among the First Nation population.[183] Observing that there is a similar pattern of over-representation of Indigenous peoples in the severe disease cohort for the 2009–2010 H1N1 pandemics in both New Zealand and Australia, and of all three populations for the 1918 Spanish influenza pandemic, the report authors conclude that the severity cannot be the result of genetic predisposition, as these populations do not share common ancestry. Instead, they find that "[w]hat they do have in common is a history of colonization, combined with historic and continuing social inequities that have led to significant health disparities".[184]

---

[179] The Akwesasne Band, Bigstone Cree Nation, Nunatsiavut Government, Nisga'a Valley Health Board, and the Gingolx, Gitakdamix, Lakalzap, and Gitwinksilkw First Nations. See ESI Canada, "NIHB Medical Supplies and Equipment Claims Submission Kit" (effective date: April 9, 2010) (Mississauga, ON: ESI Canada, 2010) at 18.

[180] Malcolm King *et al.*, "Indigenous Health Part 2: The Underlying Causes of the Health Gap" (2009) 374 The Lancet 76 at 76; Judith Bartlett *et al.*, "Framework for Aboriginal-Guided Decolonizing Research Involving Métis and First Nations Persons with Diabetes" (2007) 65 Soc. Sci. & Med. 2371 at 2371-72.

[181] Kelly McShane, Janet Smylie & Paul Adomako, "Health of First Nations, Inuit and Metis Children in Canada" in Janet Smylie & Paul Adomako, eds., *Indigenous Children's Health Report: Health Assessment in Action* (Toronto: Centre for Research on Inner City Health, 2010) 11 at 19.

[182] Ryan Zarychanski *et al.*, "Correlates of Severe Disease in Patients with 2009 Pandemic Influenza (H1N1) Virus Infection" (2010) 182:3 CMAJ 257. I thank Jocelyn Downie and Francois Baylis for drawing this study to my attention.

[183] *Ibid.*, at 262.

[184] *Ibid.*, at 263.

Even Canadian Senate Committees have reached analogous conclusions. For example, one Senate committee that was charged with reporting on mental health in Canada made the following observations:

> ... while many of the causes of mental illness, addiction and suicidal behaviour in Aboriginal and non-Aboriginal communities may be similar, there are added cultural factors in Aboriginal communities that affect individual decision-making and suicidal ideation. These cultural factors include past government policies, creation of the reserve system, the change from an active to a sedentary lifestyle, the impact of residential schools, racism, marginalization and the projection of an inferior self-image.[185]

The International Symposium on the Social Determinants of Indigenous Health composed a similar list of associations, linking colonial policies with forced dislocation from traditional lands, cultural suppression, political marginalization, and forced assimilation and then linking these in turn to an continuing excessive burden of specific health disparities.[186] This complex set of factors, and their manifestation in health inequalities, can likely only be addressed through measures that are informed and shaped by an ethic of enabling decolonization.

This closing section now turns to offering a few comments upon, and highlighting, some examples which have not yet been raised in this chapter of how health law and policy can contribute to a decolonizing process.

One essential decolonizing practice is enabling culturally relevant health education. Such practices can both target a specific health factor, as well as transform some of the underlying conditions that devalue or alienate Indigenous peoples and their cultural and knowledge practices. For example, the lack of culturally appropriate public health education is cited as one of the reasons why tuberculosis rates continue to be shockingly high among the Inuit population in Nunavut, with 30 times more active cases of tuberculosis than the rest of Canada.[187] Ethnographic research has documented that existing public health information is insensitive to Inuit beliefs, as well as ways of learning and transmitting knowledge.[188] Not surprisingly, then, Inuit participants in a 2010 study reported "not noticing or finding relevant public health information"[189] despite there having been a vigorous information campaign. The use of culturally insensitive

---

[185] Interim Report of the Senate Standing Committee on Social Affairs, Science and Technology, "Mental Health, Mental Illness and Addiction: Issues and Options for Canada: Report 1, Mental Health, Mental Illness and Addiction: Overview of Policies and Programs in Canada" (Ottawa: Parliament of Canada, 2004) at 97.

[186] International Symposium on the Social Determinants of Indigenous Health, "Social Determinants and Indigenous Health: The International Experience and its Policy Implications", online at: <http://www.who.int/social_determinants/resources/indigenous_health_adelaide_report_07.pdf>.

[187] Public Health Agency of Canada, "TB in Canada 2005" (2005), online at: <http://www.phac-aspc.gc.ca/publicat/2008/tbcan05/index-eng.php>.

[188] Helle Moller, "Tuberculosis and Colonialism: Current Tales about Tuberculosis and Colonialism in Nunavut" (2010) J. of Aboriginal Health 38 at 43-45.

[189] *Ibid.*, at 44.

health information is both likely to be ineffective for addressing the specific health inequity, and it also "reinforces the historical message that Inuit ways of doing things are inferior".[190]

Obviously, initiatives to decolonize public health care education will be far more likely to succeed if supported by policies to engage Inuit and other Indigenous peoples as health care professionals. Such policies would marry well with addressing the outstanding need for the development of a robust awareness and promotion of Indigenous perspectives on health. There are copious sources that assert that Indigenous peoples have holistic perspectives on health, which is to say that they conceptualize "health" as embracing an embedded network of emotional, spiritual, social and physical aspects.[191] This description risks being too broad to work with in an applied fashion, especially given that these concepts may themselves resonate differently for different Indigenous peoples. Support for more specialized work is therefore required. One example of such work was reported upon in 2010, where the Indigenous scholars sought to clarify how ideas of holistic health resonate with the specific health beliefs of Plains Cree people.[192]

This sort of work is complementary to developing culturally appropriate clinical health care, a goal which is typically approached as a matter of understanding how Indigenous and non-Indigenous health practices can be successfully brought into a partnership. As Maar and Shawande explain, "western-based knowledge frameworks are still generally inadequate to engage with and make sense of wholistic [*sic*] aspects of traditional healing. In addition, western-trained researchers often have difficulties collaborating across different knowledge systems such as traditional Aboriginal healing".[193] This difficulty may help explain the results of a 2005 survey in a Mi'kmaq community health clinic, where 92.4 per cent of patients who used Mi'kmaq medicines did not tell their physician about this usage, and almost a third believed that Mi'kmaq medicine was more effective than "Western" medicine. This led the researcher to conclude that "conventional medical advice may not be accepted or followed by patients", in turn leading to the physician being inhibited in his or her ability "to provide effective care".[194]

---

[190] *Ibid.*

[191] *E.g.*, see Constance MacIntosh, "Law and Policy Regarding the Population Health of Aboriginal Canadians" in Tracey M. Bailey, Timothy Caulfield & Nola M. Ries, eds., *Public Health Law & Policy in Canada*, 2d ed. (Markham, ON: LexisNexis Canada, 2008) 395-439 at 399; National Aboriginal Health Organization, *Ways of Knowing: A Framework for Health Research* (Ottawa: National Aboriginal Health Organization, 2003) at 5.

[192] Holly Graham & Lynnette Stamler, "Contemporary Perceptions of Health from an Indigenous (Plains Cree) Perspective" (2010) J. of Aboriginal Health 6.

[193] Marion Maar & Marjory Shawande, "Traditional Anishinabe Healing in a Clinical Setting: The Development of an Aboriginal Interdisciplinary Approach to Community-Based Aboriginal Mental Health Care" (2010) J. of Aboriginal Health 18 at 20.

[194] Sarah Cook, "Use of Traditional Mi'kmaq Medicine Among Patients at a First Nations Community Health Centre" (2005) 10:2 Can. J. Rural Med. 95.

However, the challenges go beyond trying to find ways to support holistic approaches to health. A holistic approach is in many ways congruent with the general turn that has taken place under which many aspects of health are understood and addressed through a social determinants framework. Greater challenges are created by normative divergences in conceptualizations of matters such as autonomy and its derivative rules regarding consent.

For example, law- and policy-makers, as well as professional regulatory bodies in Canadian provinces, have worked hard in recent years to codify how consent for advance directives is obtained and how it may direct treatment decisions. Nova Scotia recently passed such legislation.[195] These laws start with the individual, and are predicated upon individuals having the ultimate choice as to their treatment path as an aspect of respecting their autonomy. This centralization of the individual is potentially at tension with the more relational sense of self that many Indigenous peoples may hold, which may embrace a legitimate role for a larger group of people to participate in such decisions. Clearly, opportunities must be created to consider whether and how health laws and policies ought to be shaped in response to these different sets of values.

An analogous challenge has been identified as arising in health research, where the traditional models of obtaining consent have been rejected as inappropriate for research that targets obtaining information about Indigenous peoples or communities. Whereas a researcher who sought information on diabetes as experienced by persons of Jewish, Acadian or historic black communities of Nova Scotia could collect information from any individual who chose to participate, such an approach is unacceptable to many Indigenous communities. The rejection of such approaches reflects several issues. For one, there are many examples of situations where Indigenous community knowledge and genetic materials have been taken by medical researchers who failed to obtain proper consent for their ultimate commercial uses.[196] One recent American case, which was resolved in April 2010, included a $700,000 settlement as well as the return of the collected information/materials.[197]

On a more fundamental level, however, an individualized approach to consent may be at odds with the collective sense that is common to many Indigenous peoples, and disregards the jurisdiction which Indigenous communities claim over research that is conducted within their community.[198] The recognition

---

[195]   *Personal Directives Act*, S.N.S. 2008, c. 8.

[196]   *E.g.*, See discussion in Constance MacIntosh, "Indigenous Self-Determination and Research on Human Genetic Material: A Consideration of the Relevance of Debates on Patents and Informed Consent, and the Political Demands on Researchers" (2005) 13 Health L.J. 213 at 214-15 and in Canadian Institutes of Health Research, *CIHR Guidelines for Health Research Involving Aboriginal People* (Ottawa: Canadian Institutes of Health Research, 2007) at 23.

[197]   Amy Harmon, "Indian tribe wins fight to limit research of its DNA" (April 21, 2010) *The New York Times*, online at: <http://www.nytimes.com/2010/04/22/us/22dna.html?pagewanted=1&_r=1>.

[198]   These political rights are acknowledged in Canadian Institutes of Health Research, *CIHR Guidelines for Health Research Involving Aboriginal People* (Ottawa: Canadian Institutes of Health Research, 2007) at 11 and 18.

of these differences is partially captured in the CIHR *Guidelines for Health Research Involving Aboriginal People*, which state that Aboriginal "social norms and values tend to be organized around an operative principle of collective Aboriginal knowledge, ownership and decision-making".[199] As a result, CIHR requires anyone receiving funding from it to obtain both individual and community consent for research regarding "community members as Aboriginal people" as well as any research touching on traditional knowledge.[200] Importantly, these Guidelines acknowledge that Aboriginal communities may have specific research ethics protocols, and require researchers employed at institutions that receive funding from any of the three national funding agencies[201] to comply with whatever protocol has "the more stringent requirements".[202] This requirement is also in theory consistent with a de-colonizing ethic, although it assumes that the formal voice for an Indigenous community — often a Band Council — will always act in the best interest of community members in its decision of whether to permit the research to take place. Although one would hope that this is the case, there is the potential for abuse as community leaders may disallow research that questions power structures or oppressive practices that influential members of the community may be inculcated in.[203] This raises com-

---

[199] Canadian Institutes of Health Research, *CIHR Guidelines for Health Research Involving Aboriginal People* (Ottawa: Canadian Institutes of Health Research, 2007) at 11.

[200] *Ibid.*, at 20.

[201] The *Tri-Council Policy Statement: Ethical Conduct for Research Involving Humans* (TCPS) requires researchers at all institutions which receive funding from the Canadian Institutes of Health Research, the Natural Sciences and Engineering Research Council of Canada, and the Social Sciences and Humanities Research Council of Canada to comply with the TCPS (Interagency Advisory Panel on Research Ethics, *Tri-Council Policy Statement: Ethical Conduct for Research Involving Humans (TCPS) Revised (December 2009)* at 1). Not unlike the CIHR Guidelines, the TCPS also requires researchers to obtain consent from Indigenous communities, and to collaborate, where appropriate (Chapter 9).

[202] Canadian Institutes of Health Research, *CIHR Guidelines for Health Research Involving Aboriginal People* (Ottawa: Canadian Institutes of Health Research, 2007) at 19.

[203] The concern that a community's political representative may not protect the interests of vulnerable sub-groups within that community has been raised in the context of decisions about whether sentencing circles ought to be used to advise a judge in sentencing Indigenous offenders. When sentencing circles are held, community representatives describe the appropriateness of an offender serving their sentence in the community, instead of being incarcerated. The outcome rests largely on the community openly showing their willingness and ability to supervise the terms of the conditional sentence. The potential for dominant groups to abuse this process, and for victims to have the relevance of their experience discounted by the majority, is apparent. For example, in the case of *R. v. Morris*, [2004] B.C.J. No. 1117, 2004 BCCA 305 (B.C.C.A.), women members of an Indigenous community opposed the use of a sentencing circle for a community member who had been convicted of assaulting his spouse. The women spoke of domestic violence as endemic within their community, and they were concerned that their tribal council would not protect their interests. They wrote: " ... Kaska women fear that the decision makers within these political offices are too close to the issue to maintain objectivity. Furthermore, Kaska women fear that the Aboriginal Leadership will use their power and authority to retaliate against those who find the courage to speak out against violence. Kaska women fear that the political leadership and their involvement in this case will only serve to further ostracize, isolate and subject our families to further oppression" (at para. 27). In this case, the court found that a sentencing circle

plex questions about consent processes in Indigenous communities, and whether sub-groups within communities ought to be recognized as authorizing entities for research questions which specifically engage their interests.

Irrespective of this potential problem, research that is privately funded or that takes place outside of a university context is generally not bound to seek community consent. The exceptions arise in jurisdictions such as the Yukon, where there have been legislative interventions that impose obligations on researchers to obtain community consent if they seek to work with in Indigenous communities.[204]

Addressing the health disparities of Indigenous peoples requires strategies to be pursued on multiple levels. There are obviously some social inequalities that affect health which can be resolved through an influx of resources. These would include matters such as substandard housing, inadequate water supplies and a lack of fire protection services. There are also health inequities that obviously would benefit from simply receiving programming, such as in-home mental health and community palliative care. There are also identified gaps between actual need and the level of service possible given funding formulas. Examples that were surveyed in this chapter include inadequate resources to address the burden of chronic illness, chronic mental health and injuries. Addressing these sorts of issues will go a long way towards improving the health status of Indigenous peoples in Canada.

Another tier of strategies is necessary to support the planning and delivery of culturally relevant and sufficient health care. This strategy requires revisiting existing practices and policies, and attempting to discern whether or how they are responsive and effective given the specific situation of Indigenous peoples. It is hard to see how health care can be culturally relevant and enable community revitalization as long as the Indigenous population continues to be splintered into jurisdictionally or legislatively justified health service groups that do not reflect communities or health situation commonalities.

Given the connections between health status and broader issues of disempowerment, displacement, poverty and alienation, it is evident that health strategies are more likely to be successful if they are crafted to address some of these underlying factors, and that such a crafting has compounded benefits. It is equally evident that simultaneous and complementary efforts must also be undertaken in other areas, including education and employment opportunities.

---

was inappropriate. See also Christine Adams, "Ethics, Power and Politics in Aboriginal Health Research" (2002) 3:2 Asia Pacific J. of Anth. 44; C. Weijer & E. Emanuel, "Protecting Communities in Biomedical Research" (2000) 289:5482 Science 1142; Status of Women Canada Report, *Aboriginal Women's Roundtable on Gender Equality* (Ottawa: Status of Women Canada, 2000).

[204] *E.g., Scientists and Explorers Act,* R.S.Y. 2002, c. 200. Also, there have been 11 land claims agreements finalized in the Yukon. In all cases, these agreements recognize the jurisdiction of the Indigenous signatories over research activities. For an overview, see Cultural Services Branch, Department of Tourism and Culture, Government of Yukon, *Guidebook on Scientific Research in the Yukon* (revised April 2008; updated October 2008).

Chapter 14

CHARTER CHALLENGES

Nola M. Ries

I. INTRODUCTION

After the *Canadian Charter of Rights and Freedoms*[1] came into force in 1982, litigants seized on this new legal tool to assert constitutional rights in controversial areas of health policy such as access to physician-assisted suicide and abortion. Later in the 1990s, Charter claims concerning public funding for novel therapies for infertility and autism began working their way through the courts. In the first decade of the 21st century, the highly divisive subject of private health care came before the Supreme Court of Canada in the form of a Charter challenge, resulting in a controversial and split decision that some viewed as the beginning of the end of Medicare. As this chapter discusses, the Charter has been — and continues to be — an important legal tool for asserting fundamental rights and freedoms in a wide range of health law topics, and many laws that aim to achieve health goals have been subject to constitutional challenges. Examples of the types of laws that may implicate Charter rights include mental health laws and public health laws that authorize involuntary treatment of patients;[2] laws restricting activities of health care professionals;[3] and laws that regulate food, drugs and tobacco.[4] Many of these topics are discussed in detail elsewhere in this text, so this chapter focuses primarily on the use of Charter challenges to influence the allocation of health care resources and the structure of our system of publicly insured health services.

This chapter begins with a brief overview of the Canadian health care system and an explanation of Charter provisions that are most often argued in

---

[1] Part I of the *Constitution Act, 1982*, being Schedule B to the *Canada Act 1982* (U.K.), 1982, c. 11.

[2] See, *e.g.*, *Fleming v. Reid*, [1991] O.J. No. 1083, 4. O.R. (3d) 74 (Ont. C.A.) (challenge to involuntary treatment of psychiatric patients) and *Toronto (City, Medical Officer of Health) v. Deakin*, [2002] O.J. No. 2777 (Ont. C.J.) (challenge to mandatory detention and treatment of a person with tuberculosis).

[3] See, *e.g.*, *Waldman v. British Columbia (Medical Services Commission)*, [1999] B.C.J. No. 2014, 1999 BCCA 508 (B.C.C.A.) (billing restrictions for new physicians held to violate mobility rights under s. 6 of the Charter) and *Rombaut v. New Brunswick (Minister of Health and Community Services)*, [2001] N.B.J. No. 243, 2001 NBCA 75 (N.B.C.A.) (physician resource management plan held not to violate s. 6 mobility rights).

[4] See, *e.g.*, *RJR-MacDonald Inc. v. Canada (Attorney General)*, [1995] S.C.J. No. 68, [1995] 3 S.C.R. 199 (S.C.C.).

health care cases — namely, section 7 rights to life, liberty and personal security, and section 15 equality rights. It traces an evolution in the types of claims made under these sections of the Charter in regard to health care, beginning with cases that assert negative conceptions of rights — the freedom to make health decisions without unwarranted state intrusion — and then turning to cases involving positive claims in which litigants ask courts to compel governments to provide specific health care services.

The chapter next analyzes the contest between dollars and rights: when can fiscal constraints justify limits on constitutionally protected rights and freedoms, and when should courts defer to government policy choices? The Supreme Court of Canada's guidance on these questions is examined and problems in evaluating costs and benefits of health care services are highlighted. Finally, the chapter concludes with a discussion of approaches to improve transparency and accountability in health policy choices, since more open and participatory decision-making models may mitigate costly, time-consuming and divisive legal challenges.

II.   THE CANADIAN HEALTH CARE SYSTEM

Chapter 1 in this volume explains in detail the structure and governance of the Canadian health care system, so just a brief overview is provided here. Under the terms of the *Canada Health Act*,[5] the Canadian health care system provides universal public insurance for medically necessary physician and hospital services. Because the provision of health care is primarily an area of provincial authority under the Canadian Constitution,[6] each province operates a public health insurance plan in which patients and care providers participate. As there is no uniform definition of what constitutes a "medically necessary" health care service,[7] there is some variation across the country regarding the types of services that are publicly insured and the circumstances under which patients and providers can opt out of the public system.

Much contemporary debate focuses on the sustainability of the publicly funded health care system in Canada. Spending on health care is an expanding proportion of provincial government budgets, and a 2010 report contends that "[i]f current trends prevail, health care expenditures would make up 80 per cent of total program spending by 2030, up from 46 per cent today. All other programs, such as education, would be funded out of the remaining 20 per cent.

---

[5]   R.S.C. 1985, c. C-6.

[6]   *Constitution Act, 1982*, being Schedule B to the *Canada Act 1982* (U.K.), 1982, c. 11. For further discussion, see, *e.g.*, Martha Jackman, "Constitutional Jurisdiction Over Health in Canada" (2000) 8 Health L.J. 95.

[7]   For analysis of the challenges of defining the concept of medical necessity, see, *e.g.*, Cathy Charles *et al.*, "Medical Necessity in Canadian Health Policy: Four Meanings and ... a Funeral?" (1997) 75:3 Millbank Q. 365, Timothy A. Caulfield, "Wishful Thinking: Defining 'Medically Necessary' in Canada" (1996) 4 Health L.J. 63 and Glenn Griener, "Defining Medical Necessity: Challenges and Implications" (2002) 10 Health L. Rev. 6.

This is not feasible".[8] Factors driving health care spending include population growth and aging, increasing demand for services, growing incidence of chronic diseases, and costs of human resources, new technologies, and drugs.[9] According to the Canadian Institute for Health Information (CIHI), health care spending exceeds $170 billion annually — equivalent to spending half a billion dollars every day.[10] Yet, the CIHI points out that this level of spending is "about the same as other developed countries in our economic league" but "[w]here Canada did appear to lead the pack in the last decade was in the amount of energy focused on the discussion of cost and sustainability".[11] This observation presents two competing interpretations: either Canadians fret too much about health care sustainability or, more troubling, Canada and its economic peers cannot maintain growing demands for health care spending without cutting other public services.

Despite Canada's reputation for having a comprehensive, universal public health care system, private sources (out-of-pocket payments and private insurance) account for around 30 per cent of health care expenditures, primarily for dental and vision care and prescription drugs.[12] Out-of-pocket costs have been increasing by about 6 per cent per year since the late 1990s. The CIHI points out that the private health care sector in Canada "is growing, with the bulk of activity concentrated in the four largest provinces (Ontario, Quebec, B.C. and Alberta)".[13] Private clinics offer access to non-insured services, but some include a mix of non-insured and insured services, leading to concerns about user fees and extra billing and the draining from the public system of skilled medical professionals to service private-pay patients.

A publicly funded health care system cannot provide all services to all people, so rationing is inevitable. Rationing may occur in various ways, such as excluding a service from the public system entirely, providing access only to limited populations (generally based on predicted benefit from receiving the service) or imposing waits for access to publicly insured treatment. All forms of rationing may be subject to Charter challenges. Indeed, frustration over lack of public coverage for specific services or wait lists to access insured services has motivated important Charter challenges in recent years.

---

[8] TD Bank Financial Group, *Charting a Path to Sustainable Health Care in Ontario – 10 proposals to restrain cost growth without compromising quality of care* (TD Economics Group, May 2010) at Foreword, online at: <http://www.td.com/economics/special/db0510_health_care.pdf>.

[9] Conference Board of Canada, *Understanding Health Care Cost Drivers and Escalators* (Ottawa: Conference Board of Canada, 2004).

[10] Canadian Institute for Health Information, *Health Care in Canada 2009: A Decade in Review* (Ottawa: Canadian Institute for Health Information, 2009) at 47. In real terms, health care expenditures have increased by nearly 60 per cent over the past decade.

[11] *Ibid.*

[12] Canadian Institute for Health Information, *National Health Expenditure Trends, 1975-2009* (Ottawa: Canadian Institute for Health Information, 2009).

[13] Canadian Institute for Health Information, *Health Care in Canada 2009: A Decade in Review* (Ottawa: Canadian Institute for Health Information, 2009) at 63.

III. APPLICATION OF THE CHARTER

The Charter was enacted as part of Canada's Constitution in 1982 and protects various rights and freedoms against unjustified governmental infringements. Importantly, the Charter applies only to government[14] so, in the health context, it may be used to challenge health-related laws and actions of governmental bodies such as federal or provincial/territorial health departments or local health authorities. Publicly funded hospitals are only subject to the Charter in their application of government laws or policies.[15] In their general daily operations (for example, with respect to employment issues), hospitals are not subject to the Charter.[16] In 2010, an Ontario court ruled that Canadian Blood Services is not subject to the Charter, since it is a private corporation and its policy development and operational activities are not controlled by the government.[17] As a result, a gay male blood donor was unsuccessful in his discrimination claim concerning the CBS policy of permanently deferring donations from men who have sex with men. This decision underscores the point that private bodies are not subject to the Charter and the growing number of private health care facilities do not owe constitutional obligations to their clients, though they must com-

---

[14] Section 32(1) of the Charter is the application provision and states:

This Charter applies

    (a)   to the Parliament and government of Canada in respect of all matters within the authority of Parliament including all matters relating to the Yukon Territory and Northwest Territories; and

    (b)   to the legislature and government of each province in respect of all matters within the authority of the legislature of each province.

For background on judicial interpretation of the scope of "government", see Robert J. Sharpe, Katherine E. Swinton & Kent Roach, *The Charter of Rights and Freedoms*, 2d ed. (Toronto: Irwin Law, 2002) at 85-96.

[15] See *Eldridge v. British Columbia (Attorney General)*, [1997] S.C.J. No. 86, [1997] 3 S.C.R. 624 (S.C.C.).

[16] For discussion of the Charter's application to hospitals, see *Stoffman v. Vancouver General Hospital*, [1990] S.C.J. No. 125, [1990] 3 S.C.R. 483 (S.C.C.).

[17] *Canadian Blood Services v. Freeman*, [2010] O.J. No. 3811, 2010 ONSC 4885 (Ont. S.C.J.). On the s. 32 Charter analysis, Aitken J. concluded (at para. 343):

CBS is an autonomous private corporation whose governance structure does not include government control. The fact that it performs an important public function, its activities are highly regulated by the federal government, and it is funded in great measure by the provincial and territorial governments does not mean that CBS is a governmental entity for the purposes of s. 32.

This reasoning attracted some immediate criticism. The *Globe and Mail* quoted Professor Bruce Ryder of Osgoode Hall Law School as saying the ruling "is very dangerous because it makes it so easy for governments to avoid their Charter responsibilities. All they have to do is create an arms-length body and refrain from dictating policy. Presto! Charter-free zone." See Kirk Makin, "Ruling on gay blood donors stirs fear of 'Charter-free zone'" *The Globe and Mail* (September 9, 2010).

ply with provincial human rights codes that, for example, prohibit discrimination in services offered to the public.[18]

Unlike constitutions in some other countries, the Canadian Constitution does not explicitly protect a right to health care. However, the Supreme Court of Canada has instructed that "where the government puts in place a scheme to provide health care, that scheme must comply with the *Charter*".[19] In the health care context, sections 7 and 15(1) of the Charter are most often relied on to bring legal challenges to government action. These sections state:

> 7. Everyone has the right to life, liberty and security of the person and the right not to be deprived thereof except in accordance with the principles of fundamental justice.

> . . . . .

> 15(1) Every individual is equal before and under the law and has the right to the equal protection and equal benefit of the law without discrimination and, in particular, without discrimination based on race, national or ethnic origin, colour, religion, sex, age or mental or physical disability.

These rights are not absolute and infringements of them may be justified under section 1 of the Charter if the State has legitimate and compelling reasons. Section 1 states:

> The *Canadian Charter of Rights and Freedoms* guarantees the rights and freedoms set out in it subject only to such reasonable limits prescribed by law as can be demonstrably justified in a free and democratic society.

In its 1986 decision in *R. v. Oakes*,[20] the Supreme Court of Canada set out the framework for analyzing whether a limitation on a Charter right is justified under section 1. In accordance with the so-called *Oakes* test, the following questions must be addressed:

(1) Is the objective of the law or government action based on concerns that are sufficiently pressing and substantial to warrant overriding a Charter right?

(2) Is there a rational connection between the limit on the Charter right and the governmental objective?

(3) Does the limitation constitute a minimum impairment of the Charter right?

(4) Is there proportionality between the benefits of the limitation and its harmful impact?

---

[18] See, *e.g.*, British Columbia's *Human Rights Code*, R.S.B.C. 1996, c. 210 and Ontario's *Human Rights Code*, R.S.O. 1990, c. H.19.

[19] *Chaoulli v. Quebec (Attorney General)*, [2005] S.C.J. No. 33, [2005] 1 S.C.R. 791 at para. 104 (S.C.C.), *per* McLachlin C.J.C. and Major J.

[20] [1986] S.C.J. No. 7, [1986] 1 S.C.R. 103 (S.C.C.).

The principle challenge under section 1 is to balance the rights of individuals with the competing interests of society as expressed through government action.[21] As Dickson C.J.C. (as he then was) stated in *Oakes*, "[i]t may become necessary to limit rights and freedoms in circumstances where their exercise would be inimical to the realization of collective goals of fundamental importance".[22] It is important to note that section 7 has its own internal balancing test: a limit on life, liberty or security of the person will not offend section 7 unless the limit violates principles of fundamental justice. A limitation may be fundamentally unjust on procedural or substantive grounds if it violates basic tenets of our justice system that stress "dignity and worth of the human person and the rule of law".[23] If government action affects section 7 rights but still respects principles of fundamental justice, there is no Charter violation and, consequently, no need to evaluate the impugned action under the section 1 *Oakes* test.

The following section discusses key cases in Canadian health law jurisprudence that apply these sections of the Charter in the health care context.

IV. SECTION 7 OF THE CHARTER

One important category of Charter claims in health care addresses freedom to make decisions about one's health and medical treatment without unwarranted state-imposed restrictions. In early cases, Charter challenges attacked criminalization of certain conduct related to health care choices. More recently, as the scope of section 7 has expanded through judicial interpretation, courts are now willing to apply section 7 in situations where government action outside the realm of criminal regulation has the effect of diminishing rights to life, liberty and personal security.

R. v. Morgentaler[24] involved a section 7 challenge to the *Criminal Code* provisions that criminalized abortion unless the patient obtained a certificate of permission from a hospital therapeutic abortion committee. Many women with unwanted pregnancies experienced barriers in obtaining access to an abortion committee, especially if they lived outside major urban centres. Moreover, the requirement to seek approval from a committee of at least three medical practitioners removed a highly personal decision from the woman and placed it in the hands of third parties.

---

[21] As Joseph E. Magnet notes in *Constitutional Law of Canada*, 8th ed. (Edmonton: Juriliber, 2001) at 225, there is "a tension inherent in s. 1: the Court must strike a balance between the collective interests of the community as expressed by representative legislatures and the rights of individuals. It is not surprising that there is, so far, no quick and easy method, that flows from constitutional doctrine, to deal with this tension".

[22] *R. v. Oakes*, [1986] S.C.J. No. 7, [1986] 1 S.C.R. 103 at 136 (S.C.C.).

[23] *Reference re Motor Vehicle Act (British Columbia), Section 94(2)*, [1985] S.C.J. No. 73 at para. 61, [1985] 2 S.C.R. 486 (S.C.C.), *per* Lamer J.

[24] [1988] S.C.J. No. 1, [1988] 1 S.C.R. 30 (S.C.C.); R.S.C. 1985, c. C-46.

The majority of the Supreme Court of Canada[25] held the *Criminal Code* provision violated section 7 of the Charter and could not be justified under section 1. The judges who found a breach of section 7 held that the right to security of the person protected a woman's physical and mental integrity from serious state interference in the criminal law context. As Beetz J. expressed it, "security of the person must include a right of access to medical treatment for a condition representing a danger to life or health without fear of criminal sanction".[26] Although this case involved a criminal prohibition, the court did not foreclose a wider application of section 7.

Rodriguez v. British Columbia (Attorney General)[27] also involved a section 7 challenge in the health care context. Sue Rodriguez, who had the fatal, progressive condition amyotrophic lateral sclerosis (commonly known as ALS or Lou Gehrig's Disease), challenged the constitutionality of the *Criminal Code* prohibition against assisted suicide. Ms. Rodriguez wanted to have the ability to end her life when her suffering became intolerable. However, when that time came, she would physically be unable to commit suicide without assistance and wanted a physician to help her to die, but any physician who aided her risked criminal sanction.

Ms. Rodriguez sought an order, based on sections 7, 12 and 15 of the Charter, declaring unconstitutional the *Criminal Code* prohibition against assisted suicide.[28] She argued the impugned law deprived her of the right to live the last of her life in dignity and the right to be free from state interference in making fundamental personal decisions. In a closely divided decision, the Supreme Court of Canada dismissed her claim.[29] Justice Sopinka, writing for the majority of the Court, held that though the *Criminal Code* prohibition abridged Ms. Rodriguez's right to security of the person under section 7, that infringement accorded with principles of fundamental justice. With regard to the nature of the interest captured by the right to security of the person under section 7, Sopinka J. stated:

> There is no question then, that personal autonomy, at least with respect to the right to make choices concerning one's own body, control over one's physical and psychological integrity, and basic human dignity are encompassed within security of the person, at least to the extent of freedom from criminal prohibitions which interfere with these.[30]

---

[25] Chief Justice Dickson, Lamer, Beetz, Estey and Wilson JJ. all found an unjustifiable s. 7 violation. Justices McIntyre and La Forest dissented and found no breach of s. 7.

[26] *R. v. Morgentaler*, [1988] S.C.J. No. 1, [1988] 1 S.C.R. 30 at 428 (S.C.C.).

[27] [1993] S.C.J. No. 94, [1993] 3 S.C.R. 519 (S.C.C.).

[28] Section 12 of the Charter is the prohibition against cruel and unusual punishment.

[29] Justices Sopinka, La Forest, Gonthier, Iacobucci and Major constituted the majority. Chief Justice Lamer, L'Heureux-Dubé, Cory and McLachlin JJ. dissented.

[30] *Rodriguez v. British Columbia (Attorney General)*, [1993] S.C.J. No. 94, [1993] 3 S.C.R. 519 at 588 (S.C.C.). As in the *Morgentaler* decision, Sopinka J.'s reference to criminal prohibitions limits the scope of the s. 7 right.

Although Sopinka J. found Ms. Rodriguez's interests under section 7 were engaged, he held she was not deprived of her rights contrary to the principles of fundamental justice, so she could not establish a section 7 violation. He held that the state's interest in protecting vulnerable individuals and safeguarding human life justified the prohibition on assisted suicide.

In her dissent, McLachlin J. (as she then was) held the impugned law violated Ms. Rodriguez's right to security of the person in a manner inconsistent with principles of fundamental justice. Justice McLachlin stated that security of the person "has an element of personal autonomy, protecting the dignity and privacy of individuals with respect to decisions concerning their own body".[31] She further stated that the prohibition against assisted suicide was marked by arbitrariness and lack of respect for individual choice and, in her view, this violation could not be justified under section 1 of the Charter.[32]

R. v. Parker[33] involved a challenge to provisions of the federal *Controlled Drugs and Substances Act* (CDSA) prohibiting possession of marijuana. Mr. Parker suffered from a severe form of epilepsy and grew marijuana for his own use to control his seizures. Upon being charged with possession of marijuana, an offence punishable by imprisonment, Mr. Parker argued the offence provisions violated his rights under section 7 of the Charter because he faced criminal sanction for using marijuana to meet a medical need.

The trial court agreed with Mr. Parker and granted a stay of the possession charge.[34] On appeal, the Ontario Court of Appeal agreed Mr. Parker's rights to liberty and personal security were violated by the untenable choice between protecting his health and risking imprisonment. With respect to the scope of section 7, the Court of Appeal stated that the threat of prosecution and imprisonment engaged Mr. Parker's liberty interests. In the circumstances of this case, the Court held the risk of deprivation of liberty did not accord with principles of fundamental justice, nor could it be justified under section 1 of the Charter. Regarding the right to security of the person, the Court reiterated the *Morgentaler* reasoning that state interference with an individual's physical and psychological integrity violates personal security. Further, the Court emphasized that "[d]eprivation by means of a criminal sanction of access to medication reasonably required for the treatment of a medical condition that threatens life or health also constitutes a deprivation of security of the person".[35] Following the ruling,

---

[31]   *Ibid.*, at 618.

[32]   At the time of writing, the topic of assisted suicide is the subject of active debate in Quebec. A provincial legislative commission began a public consultation process in autumn of 2010 after hearing from expert witnesses at hearings earlier in the year. The committee acknowledges that changing the *Criminal Code* is a matter of federal responsibility but suggested that the province could use its authority over the administration of justice to exercise discretion in not pursuing charges in assisted suicide cases. See CBC News, "Quebec euthanasia hearings seek public input" (September 6, 2010), online at: <http://www.cbc.ca/canada/montreal/story/2010/09/06/quebec-euthanasia-public-hearings.html>.

[33]   [2000] O.J. No. 2787, 49 O.R. (3d) 481 (Ont. C.A.); S.C. 1996, c. 19.

[34]   *R. v. Parker*, [1997] O.J. No. 4550 (Ont. Prov. Div.).

[35]   *R. v. Parker*, [2000] O.J. No. 2787 at para. 97, 49 O.R. (3d) 481 (Ont. C.A.).

the federal government enacted the Marihuana Medical Access Regulations[36] to create a legal framework to grant approvals for production and possession of marijuana for medical purposes only.[37]

Litigation concerning Vancouver's supervised injection facility, Insite, also involved section 7 claims.[38] The federal Minister of Health granted an exemption under the CDSA to allow Insite to operate, thus protecting users and staff within Insite from possession and trafficking charges. When the federal government indicated it would not renew the CDSA exemption, several plaintiffs, including two injection drug users, launched a constitutional challenge. At trial, Pitfield J. ruled that criminalization of controlled substances in the context of Insite's services threatens all three section 7 rights in an arbitrary and disproportionate manner. By criminalizing activities within Insite that seek to reduce the hazards of drug addiction and encourage rehabilitation, the CDSA "contributes to the very harm it seeks to prevent".[39] On appeal, two justices agreed with the trial judge's conclusion on section 7, while the third justice opined that the CDSA provisions infringe the section 7 rights, but that insufficient evidence was produced at trial to show that the deprivation did not accord with the principles of fundamental justice.

While the cases summarized above all involved the threat of criminal sanction, the Supreme Court of Canada has interpreted section 7 to apply outside the criminal justice system, but debate persists over the proper scope of section 7 protection. As Smith J.A. noted in the Insite case, section 7 litigation "has provided some of the most challenging issues in our *Charter* jurisprudence. These issues often arise in the context of social policy legislation upon which reasonable people may have principled differences".[40]

The dispute in *Chaoulli v. Quebec (Attorney General)*[41] brought into high relief divergent viewpoints on the contentious policy issue of private health care in Canada. In that case, Dr. Chaoulli, a physician, and George Zéliotis, a retiree awaiting hip replacement surgery, challenged the provisions of Quebec's health care and hospital insurance legislation that prohibit physicians from delivering

---

36 SOR/2001-227.

37 For more information, see Government of Canada, Health Canada, "Medical Use of Marihuana", online at: <http://www.hc-sc.gc.ca/dhp-mps/marihuana/index-eng.php>.

38 *PHS Community Services Society v. Canada (Attorney General)*, [2008] B.C.J. No. 951, 293 D.L.R. (4th) 392 (B.C.S.C.). In addition to the s. 7 issues, this litigation addresses significant division of powers issues.

39 *Ibid.*, at para. 152.

40 *PHS Community Services Society v. Canada (Attorney General)*, [2010] B.C.J. No. 57 at para. 246, 314 D.L.R. (4th) 209 (B.C.C.A.), leave to appeal granted [2010] S.C.J. No. 49 (S.C.C.). For cases that address the scope of s. 7 outside adjudicative proceedings, see, *e.g.*, *New Brunswick (Minister of Health and Community Services) v. G. (J.)*, [1993] S.C.J. No. 47, [1993] 3 S.C.R. 46 (S.C.C.); *Blencoe v. British Columbia (Human Rights Commission)*, [2000] S.C.J. No. 43, [2000] 2 S.C.R. 307 (S.C.C.); and *Gosselin v. Quebec (Attorney General)*, [2002] S.C.J. No. 85, [2002] 4 S.C.R. 429 (S.C.C.).

41 [2000] J.Q. no 479 (Que. S.C.), affd [2002] J.Q. no 759 (Que. C.A.), revd [2005] S.C.J. No. 33, [2005] 1 S.C.R. 791 (S.C.C.).

private care in publicly funded hospitals and also prevents patients from purchasing insurance privately to pay for health care services otherwise covered through the public system. Mr. Zéliotis asserted that the legislative ban on private insurance jeopardized his life and personal security by requiring him to wait for surgery within the public system. In effect, the claimants sought a ruling that would permit a second tier of private health care; as Mr. Zéliotis' counsel stated: "I argue for the right of wealthier individuals to have access to a parallel system of health care services."[42] The government respondents and interveners argued that such a ruling would have detrimental impacts on accessibility and cost of health care.

The trial judge ruled that the prohibition against private insurance implicated section 7 rights, but accorded with principles of fundamental justice as the public health care scheme aims to provide equal access to care regardless of ability to pay. The Quebec Court of Appeal dismissed the appeal but with differing reasons on the application of section 7.

The Supreme Court of Canada released a divided judgment in *Chaoulli* in June 2005 that instigated much debate over the implications of the Court's ruling.[43] Of the seven judges who heard the appeal, three[44] ruled the legislative prohibition was an unjustifiable violation of the Charter as well as Quebec's *Charter of Human Rights and Freedoms*, three[45] ruled it did not violate the Charter, and the remaining judge[46] restricted her analysis to the Quebec Charter and found it unnecessary to consider the Canadian Charter.

The three judges who found that the ban on private health insurance violated section 7 of the Charter likened the situation to that in *Morgentaler*. A monopolistic public health care system that fails to provide timely access to care triggers section 7 rights. Further, a prohibition on private medical insurance is arbitrary and cannot be justified in circumstances where the public system fails to provide quality care in a timely manner.

In contrast, the three judges who dismissed the section 7 challenge said the case involved "complex fact-laden policy"[47] that governments are best suited to address. They were reticent to apply the Charter in a manner that would precipitate a "seismic shift"[48] in health care policy by permitting a second tier of private health care and concluded that wait list delays do not violate legal principles of fundamental justice under section 7. Due to this judicial division, the end result was a ruling that Quebec's prohibition on private health insurance violates Quebec's Charter but the Court was split on the issue of whether the

---

[42] *Ibid.*, at para. 8 (Que. S.C.) [translated by author].
[43] For extensive analysis of the *Chaoulli* litigation, see Colleen M. Flood, Kent Roach & Lorne Sossin, eds., *Access to Care, Access to Justice: The Legal Debate Over Private Health Insurance in Canada* (Toronto: University of Toronto Press, 2005).
[44] Chief Justice McLachlin, Major and Bastarache JJ.
[45] Justices Binnie, LeBel and Fish.
[46] Justice Deschamps.
[47] *Chaoulli v. Quebec (Attorney General)*, [2005] S.C.J. No. 33 at para. 164 (S.C.C.).
[48] *Ibid.*, at para. 176.

legislative regime violated section 7 rights under the Canadian Charter. In response to the ruling, the Quebec government enacted legislation to establish maximum wait times for specified procedures and permitted private insurance for procedures that had historically longer wait times (*e.g.*, hip, knee and cataract surgeries).[49] The government has also allowed significant growth and reliance on for-profit clinics within the public health care system. Professor Prémont observes that "[t]he political fallout of *Chaoulli* in Québec shows that the focus of public interest has been shifted and drastically redefined in order to make public regulation more friendly and supportive of private healthcare markets".[50]

Despite the nationwide controversy the case generated, outside Quebec, "the actual impact of *Chaoulli* on Medicare has been rather limited in comparison to the transformative potential of the case that many had anticipated".[51] As the Supreme Court ruling had no application in other provinces, litigants in Alberta, British Columbia and Ontario have filed constitutional challenges to legislative restrictions that allegedly impede timely access to care in those provinces.[52] Unless governments can demonstrate that the public system offers

---

[49] For discussion of the Quebec government's responses post-*Chaoulli*, see Marie-Claude Prémont, "Wait-time Guarantees for Health Services: An Analysis of Quebec's Reaction to the *Chaoulli* Supreme Court Decision" (2007) 15 Health L.J. 43.

[50] Marie-Claude Prémont, "Clearing the Path for Private Health Markets in Post-*Chaoulli* Quebec" (2008) Health L.J. Spec. Ed. 237 at 239.

[51] Colleen M. Flood & Y.Y. Brandon Chen, "Charter Rights and Health Care Funding: A Typology of Health Rights Litigation" (2010) 19 Annals Health L. 479. The authors suggest (at 505) that "the greatest impact that has resulted from the *Chaoulli* decision to-date is the transformation of the two-tier system from a largely discounted proposition into a legitimate policy option for Canadian health care reform". See also Daniel Cohn, "*Chaoulli* Five Years On: All Bark and No Bite?" (Paper presented at the 2010 Annual Meeting of the Canadian Political Science Association, Concordia University, Montreal), online at: <http://www.cpsa-acsp.ca/papers-2010/Cohn.pdf>. Cited with the author's permission.

[52] See Lindsay McCreith and Shona Holmes and the Attorney General for the Province of Ontario, Statement of Claim filed at Ontario Superior Court of Justice September 5, 2007. Mr. McCreith and Ms. Holmes sought life-saving care in the United States and argue that the Ontario "health-care monopoly" prevents residents from "accessing essential medically necessary services outside of the system" thus forcing them to "endure significant financial, emotional and physical hardship to access such services" outside the country. See Statement of Claim, paras. 5 and 6. In Alberta, *Murray v. Alberta (Calgary Health Region)*, [2007] A.J. No. 428 at para. 22, 76 Alta. L.R. (4th) 118 (Alta. Q.B.) William Murray claimed that Albertans over the age of 55 have been denied

... access to necessary hip replacement surgery in various ways. This includes first, for denying public access to individuals seeking [a specific hip replacement] procedure if they are over the age of 55. Second, by requiring private facilities to comply with the same standard in their facilities and deny such procedures to those over the age of 55. Third, for failing to reimburse individuals who obtain such procedure outside the publicly funded system in Alberta for the costs so incurred. Fourth, by disallowing Alberta residents from purchasing private health insurance for basic health services.

In British Columbia, several litigants are "seeking to require the Medical Services Commission and the British Columbia government to enforce the *Medicare Protection Act* [internal citation omitted] with respect to its restrictions on the private billing of fees for medical services in the

reasonable access to care and that wait lists do not jeopardize health, statutory impediments to private sector care may be struck down in these post-*Chaoulli* cases. The consequences of such legal outcomes — and the policy shifts that would result — remain open to debate but it is unlikely that any improvements in access to care would be shared equitably among Canadians. As Professor Flood argues: "The well-heeled will get more timely treatment, public resources [*i.e.*, health care providers trained at taxpayer expense] will be redistributed to the wealthy and middle-class from those in greater need, and taxes [that support health, education, social and other programs] need not increase."[53]

V.   SECTION 15 AND HEALTH CARE

Section 15(1) of the Charter provides a constitutional guarantee of equality and prohibits discrimination on grounds such as race, sex and disability.[54] The Supreme Court of Canada had explained that section 15(1) is aimed at "preventing governments from making distinctions based on the enumerated or analogous grounds that: have the effect of perpetuating group disadvantage and prejudice; or impose disadvantage on the basis of stereotyping".[55] The Court emphasizes that not all distinctions amount to unconstitutional discrimination:

> It is not every distinction or differentiation in treatment at law which will transgress the equality guarantees of s. 15 of the Charter. It is, of course, obvious that legislatures may — and to govern effectively — must treat different individuals and groups in different ways. Indeed, such distinctions are one of the main preoccupations of legislatures. The classifying of individuals and groups, the making of different provisions respecting such groups, the application of different rules, regulations, requirements and qualifications to different persons is necessary for the governance of modern society.[56]

The discrimination analysis under section 15(1) of the Charter requires an assessment of the situation of the claimant(s) in relation to an appropriate comparator group. For example, a person with a disability who does not enjoy similar access to health care compared to persons without that disability may argue this denial of access amounts to discrimination. To substantiate this assertion, the claimant must demonstrate that the denial compromises their human dignity,

---

Province. They argue that their *Charter* rights, statutory legal rights, and financial interests have been infringed": see *Canadian Independent Medical Clinics Assn. v. British Columbia (Medical Services Commission)*, [2010] B.C.J. No. 1323 at para. 3, 2010 BCSC 927 (B.C.S.C.).

[53]   Colleen M. Flood, "*Chaoulli*: Political Undertows and Judicial Riptides" (2008) Health L.J. Spec. Ed. 211 at 235.

[54]   The Charter also prohibits discrimination on grounds that are analogous to those listed. The Supreme Court of Canada has defined analogous grounds as "characteristics that we cannot change or that the government has no legitimate interest in expecting us to change to receive equal treatment under the law": see *Corbiere v. Canada (Minister of Indian and Northern Affairs)*, [1999] S.C.J. No. 24 at para. 13, [1999] 2 S.C.R. 203 (S.C.C.).

[55]   *R. v. Kapp*, [2008] S.C.J. No. 42 at para. 25, [2008] 2 S.C.R. 483 (S.C.C.).

[56]   *Andrews v. Law Society of British Columbia*, [1989] S.C.J. No. 6, [1989] 1 S.C.R. 143 at 168 (S.C.C.).

by "perpetuating or promoting the view that the individual is less capable or worthy of recognition or value as a human being or as a member of Canadian society, equally deserving of concern, respect and consideration".[57] It is rarely obvious when denial of public funding for health care violates fundamental human dignity and contravenes equality rights. As a result, section 15(1) cases have often been litigated through many levels of appeal, with rare judicial unanimity.

To date, Canadian courts have had several opportunities to consider Charter cases in which litigants challenged government decisions not to fund specific services in the health care context. While the initial trend suggested section 15 could be used to claim a right to public funding for health care, that trend has now been reversed, but questions remain regarding the application of constitutionally protected equality rights in the health care context.

Eldridge v. British Columbia (Attorney General)[58] was an early success — from the perspective of Charter claimants — in using section 15 to challenge health care resource allocation. In *Eldridge*, three deaf individuals challenged the decision of the government of British Columbia not to fund sign language interpreters as an insured benefit under the B.C. Medical Services Plan. The claimants argued that, without publicly funded interpreter services, they did not have equal access to the health care system as compared to non-deaf individuals. The claim was dismissed at trial and on appeal but in a unanimous decision, the Supreme Court of Canada agreed with the claimants and held the government's failure to fund sign language interpreters, when necessary for effective communication in the health care context, violated the claimants' rights under section 15(1) of the Charter.[59]

The Court of Appeal ruling reveals a strong reticence to interfere with government resource allocation decisions. Justice Lambert found that the funding decision violated section 15(1) but was justified under section 1.[60] In his reasoning, he elaborated on the daunting task of choosing among competing demands for health care dollars:

> In the allocation of scarce financial resources each Province will be required to make choices about spending priorities. Will medical equipment be bought for city hospitals or for small rural hospitals? Will the health care services in re-

---

[57] *Law v. Canada (Minister of Employment and Immigration)*, [1999] S.C.J. No. 12 at para. 88, [1999] 1 S.C.R. 497 (S.C.C.).

[58] [1992] B.C.J. No. 2229, 75 B.C.L.R. (2d) 68 (B.C.S.C.), affd [1995] B.C.J. No. 1168, 125 D.L.R. (4th) 323 (B.C.C.A.), revd [1997] S.C.J. No. 86, [1997] 3 S.C.R. 624 (S.C.C.).

[59] Access to publicly funded sign language interpretation services was litigated in *Canadian Assn. of the Deaf v. Canada*, [2006] F.C.J. No. 1228, 2006 FC 971 (F.C.). The Federal Court ruled that the Government of Canada violated s. 15 of the Charter by not providing sign language interpretation services on request when a deaf person attempted to access federal government services. The court did not address justification arguments because the government did not see "fit to submit evidence or submissions that the failure to provide accommodation is justified under section 1 of the *Charter*" (at para. 116).

[60] Justices Hollinrake and Cumming found there was no s. 15(1) violation.

mote communities or in First Nations communities be improved? Is the best form of expenditure to raise the scale of payment for doctors and other health care workers? Should improved public facilities be provided for detection of cervical cancer, prostate cancer or breast tumours?

Some of the limits imposed [by] ... financial allocation choices ... will result in adverse effects discrimination against people suffering from disabilities, including serious illness itself. ... How can we say, in those circumstances, that expenditure of scarce resources on services that remedy infringed constitutional rights under s. 15, on the one hand, are more desirable than expenditures of scarce resources on things that cure people without affecting constitutional rights, on the other? And, indeed, how can we prefer the allocation of scarce resources to services that remedy the infringed constitutional rights of one disadvantaged group over the allocation of scarce resources to services that remedy the infringed constitutional rights of a different disadvantaged group.

In my opinion the kind of adverse effects discrimination which I consider has occurred in this case should be rectified, if at all, by legislative or administrative action and not by judicial action. ...I have concluded that this is a case for judicial restraint and for deference under the Constitution and under s. 1 of the Charter to legislative and administrative expertise.[61]

The Supreme Court of Canada was not so convinced and ruled the government's funding decision discriminated against deaf patients and could not be justified under section 1. Writing for a unanimous Court, La Forest J. disagreed with the government's characterization of sign language interpretation as a "non-medical 'ancillary' service"[62] that was outside the scope of public funding. Rather, the Court viewed the service as essential for ensuring adequate access to the health care system for deaf persons. In the immediate wake of *Eldridge*, some viewed the Court's decision as a precedent for using section 15 Charter claims to expand the scope of public funding for health care services.[63] The decision is, however, much narrower; it imposes an obligation on governments to fund a service to ensure deaf patients have the means to access the same basket of publicly insured services available to all, but does not require governments to add to that basket. An analogy to a public library helps explain this principle: the *Eldridge* claim is like a wheelchair user asking a library to build a ramp so she may gain access to the books in the library that are available to patrons who can

---

[61] *Eldridge v. British Columbia (Attorney General)*, [1995] B.C.J. No. 1168 at paras. 57-59, 125 D.L.R. (4th) 323 (B.C.C.A.).

[62] *Eldridge v. British Columbia (Attorney General)*, [1997] S.C.J. No. 86 at para. 68, [1997] 3 S.C.R. 624 (S.C.C.).

[63] In a 2005 review of Supreme Court of Canada equality rights jurisprudence, Bruce Porter comments on *Eldridge*, noting that "[t]he Court could have chosen to affirm more clearly in *Eldridge* a positive obligation on governments to provide appropriate health-care ... The right to equality could thus have been framed around a consensus in Canada that appropriate health-care is a social right, linked to equal citizenship. ... there were indications that this might be the direction that the Court was headed": Bruce Porter, "Twenty Years of Equality Rights: Reclaiming Expectations" (2005) 23 Windor Y.B. Access Just. 145.

walk up the stairs. In contrast, *Eldridge* is not like the disabled patron asking the library to purchase new books to put on the shelves.

The next case to raise similar issues was *Cameron v. Nova Scotia (Attorney General)*,[64] which involved an infertile male and his wife who argued the Province of Nova Scotia discriminated against them by not funding fertility treatments, *in vitro* fertilization (IVF) and intracytoplasmic sperm injection (ICSI), that could assist infertile couples (suffering from male-factor infertility) to have a biologically related child. They argued fertile people have access to publicly funded health care services, such as prenatal and childbirth care, to assist them in having children, but the infertile are denied the chance of having a child because they are denied funding for IVF and ICSI.

The trial judge dismissed the claim on the grounds that infertility treatments are not medically necessary since infertile people have other options for becoming parents (such as adoption), the success rate of having a child through IVF and ICSI is low (around 15 per cent to 20 per cent), and there are health risks associated with the procedures.[65] On appeal, the majority found the government's funding decision contravened the claimants' rights under section 15(1). The justices held that IVF and ICSI are medically necessary services for infertile individuals, the denial of which offended their dignity in a manner contrary to the Charter's equality protection, but the violation was justified under section 1. The third justice ruled differently, finding that infertility does not constitute a disability for the purposes of section 15(1) but, even if it did, the denial of funding for IVF and ICSI would not demean the claimants' dignity. The Supreme Court of Canada denied leave to appeal.

The next significant section 15 Charter case is *Auton (Guardian ad litem of) v. British Columbia (Attorney General)*,[66] a case in which parents of children with autism challenged the B.C. government's refusal to fund therapy known as early intensive behavioural intervention (EIBI), which can be effective in reducing autistic behaviour in children. The parents argued that "by failing to fund effective treatment for autism, the government has misinterpreted its legislative mandate to provide health care services".[67] Further, they argued that lack of funding for autism therapy "neglects to take into account the disadvantaged position of autistic children and results in substantively different treatment, placing an additional burden on them"[68] that those without the disease do not face. The trial and appeal courts in B.C. ruled in the claimants' favour.

---

[64] [1999] N.S.J. No. 297, 177 D.L.R. (4th) 611 (N.S.C.A.), affg [1999] N.S.J. No. 33, 172 N.S.R. (2d) 227 (N.S.S.C.), leave to appeal refused [1999] S.C.C.A. No, 531 (S.C.C.).

[65] *Cameron v. Nova Scotia (Attorney General)*, [1999] N.S.J. No. 33 at paras. 95 and 96, 172 N.S.R. (2d) 227 (N.S.S.C.).

[66] [2004] S.C.J. No. 71, [2004] 3 S.C.R. 657 (S.C.C.), revg [2002] B.C.J. No. 2258, 6 B.C.L.R. (4th) 201 (B.C.C.A.), related proceedings [2000] B.C.J. No. 1547, 78 B.C.L.R. (3d) 55 (B.C.S.C.).

[67] *Ibid.*, at para. 125 (B.C.S.C.).

[68] *Ibid.*

The trial judge adopted an expansive view of the medically necessary services that the Medicare system should cover: "Canadians are entitled to expect medical treatment for their physical and mental diseases. This is so, even when a disease cannot be 'cured'."[69] On appeal, Saunders J.A.[70] stated that the fact children with autism did not receive the health care service they most needed to address their disease constituted differential treatment in the section 15(1) analysis and she rejected the government's argument that a finding of discrimination was not warranted because the "health care system does not serve all health care needs and is not designed to do so".[71] In her view, the government discriminated against the children with autism by withholding funding for a treatment that held real promise of mitigating the effects of their devastating condition. She also noted that no alternative therapy was available and the health care system funds services to address other, less serious ailments.

In a surprisingly short and unanimous ruling (in contrast with *Chaoulli*), the Supreme Court of Canada overturned the lower court decisions. Chief Justice McLachlin explicitly stated that Canadians cannot expect the publicly funded health care system to cover every service that may be of some benefit. Rather, she emphasized the relatively narrow boundaries of the system: "In summary, the legislative scheme does not promise that any Canadian will receive funding for all medically required treatment. All that is conferred is core funding for services provided by medical practitioners, with funding for non-core services left to the Province's discretion."[72] Provinces may choose to cover services of non-core practitioners, but have no legal obligation to do so and, further, courts have no legal jurisdiction to entertain a discrimination claim in regard to non-core services that governments exclude from the Medicare basket. However, where the government decides to enter the field and fund a service, it must do so in a manner that does not discriminate on grounds protected under the Charter.

Auton was received with disappointment by those who shared the trial judge's view that the health care system should respond to a broader range of health needs. The Supreme Court's acceptance in *Auton* that the health care system provides "a partial health plan",[73] limited to "core physician-provided benefits plus non-core benefits at the discretion of the Province",[74] stands in contrast to the Court's earlier censure of a narrow conception of the health care system in *Eldridge*, where the government characterized sign language interpretation as an "ancillary" service. The McLachlin Court's depiction of funding for autism

---

[69] *Ibid.*, at para. 109.
[70] Justice Hall concurred. Justice Lambert agreed that s. 15(1) was violated and could not be justified under s. 1, but he dissented in part on a cross-appeal issue regarding remedy.
[71] *Auton (Guardian ad litem of) v. British Columbia (Attorney General)*, [2002] B.C.J. No. 2258 at para. 46, 6 B.C.L.R. (4th) 201 (B.C.C.A.).
[72] *Auton (Guardian ad litem of) v. British Columbia (Attorney General)*, [2004] S.C.J. No. 71 at para. 35, [2004] 3 S.C.R. 657 (S.C.C.).
[73] *Ibid.*, at para. 43.
[74] *Ibid.*, at para. 44.

therapy as a discretionary policy choice that is outside Charter purview has been criticized as formalistic:

> In *Auton*, the Supreme Court claims that section 15 only protects against discrimination where a benefit has been conferred by law. Why would this be so? The *Charter* protects against discrimination by government action, and the government may confer benefits through a wide spectrum of means, including legislation, regulation, program criteria, and spending decisions. ... Should governments that wish to consign an increasing amount of decision-making over benefits to discretionary realms be able to immunize such benefits from *Charter* scrutiny as a result? In our view, such a result would be fundamentally inconsistent with the purpose of the *Charter*.[75]

As it stands, *Auton* leaves open the prospect of using the Charter to challenge alleged underinclusiveness in benefit regimes where a government provides publicly funded services but only to limited categories of beneficiaries. However, the first appeal court decision to address this issue post-*Auton* further restricts section 15's application. *Wynberg v. Ontario*[76] involved a challenge to Ontario's program for children with autism. In 2000, the Ontario government implemented early intensive behavioural therapy for children under age six but resource shortages meant that some children turned six before receiving any therapy. The *Wynberg* claim alleged that the age cut-off constituted unjustified age-based discrimination and the trial court agreed. The appeal court overturned this ruling, finding that the government's autism program is a targeted, ameliorative program designed to meet the needs and circumstances of pre-school age children who are most likely to benefit from intensive autism therapy and exclusion of children aged six and older "does not deny their human dignity or devalue their worth as members of Canadian society".[77] As a result, the government's implementation of an age cut-off for access to publicly funded autism therapy did not violate the children's constitutional rights to equality.

In a similar ruling, the British Columbia Supreme Court rejected a section 15 challenge concerning support services for children and adults with autism.[78] The petitioner, a young man with severe autism and other disabilities, became ineligible for certain children's services upon reaching the age of 20 and was placed on a waiting list for adult programs. Justice Sewell ruled: "In my view *Auton* provides full answer ... The support services at issue are non-core services provided under discretionary statutory authority of the provincial government. The petitioner is on a waiting list, and thus not currently receiving the

---

[75] Laura Pottie & Lorne Sossin, "Demystifying the Boundaries of Public Law: Policy, Discretion, and Social Welfare" (2005) 38 U.B.C. L. Rev. 147 at para. 56.

[76] [2006] O.J. No. 2732 (Ont. C.A.), revg [2005] O.J. No. 1228, 252 D.L.R. (4th) 10 (Ont. S.C.J.), leave to appeal refused [2006] S.C.C.A. No. 441 (S.C.C.).

[77] *Ibid.*, at para. 80 (Ont. C.A.).

[78] *Mendoza v. Community Living British Columbia*, [2009] B.C.J. No. 1370, 2009 BCSC 932 (B.C.S.C.).

services sought, because of financial constraints on the government, a legitimate and non-discriminatory reason according to *Auton.*"[79]

Auton and subsequent decisions mark a retreat from the early prospect that *Eldridge* would open the door for successful Charter challenges to denials of public funding for health care services. Section 15 jurisprudence regarding access to health care services now emphasizes the limits of the publicly funded health care system. Monique Bégin, who served as federal Minister of National Health and Welfare during the drafting and enactment of the *Canada Health Act*,[80] has stated that our public health care system includes more than "a basic level of care. The words of the *Canada Health Act* are generally taken to imply entitlement to a complete health care system".[81] Judicial authority in Canada reveals a divergent conclusion: our system of publicly insured health care cannot provide funding for all services, even those that are medically indicated, and Charter claims are an increasingly unlikely means to influence government funding choices.

Moreover, analyses of the practical outcomes of "successful" Charter challenges reveals an even more discouraging picture of the effectiveness of section 7 and section 15 claims in facilitating health care access. For example, availability of abortion services is limited or even non-existent in some regions of Canada today, despite the ruling in *Morgentaler* that struck down the *Criminal Code* restrictions. Legal scholars Rodgers and Downie describe the persistent problems of inequitable access:

> For many teenaged girls and women, particularly those who are poor, live in rural areas, are young, disabled, Aboriginal, are in a racial minority, are immigrants, or who do not speak English or French — those who are the most vulnerable — access to abortion is limited. In some provinces, abortions are not available at all. Only 17.8% of all general hospitals provide abortion services, a decrease from 20.1% in 1977. Some hospitals require physician referrals, have waiting periods of up to 6 weeks, impose gestational limits or allow abortions only as a "last resort".[82]

Similarly, the plaintiffs' victory in *Eldridge* belies the current reality that many deaf patients across Canada have poor access to medical sign language interpretation. The Canadian Association for the Deaf says that "implementation

---

[79] *Ibid.*, at para. 52.
[80] For Bégin's account of the process leading to the enactment of the *Canada Health Act*, R.S.C. 1985, c. C-6, see Monique Bégin, *Medicare: Canada's Right to Health* (Montreal: Optimum Publishing International, 1988).
[81] Margaret A. Somerville, ed., *Do We Care? Renewing Canada's Commitment to Health. Proceedings of the First Directions for Canadian Health Care Conference* (Montreal: McGill-Queen's University Press, 1999) at 105.
[82] Sanda Rodgers & Jocelyn Downie, "Abortion: Ensuring Access" (2006) 175:1 CMAJ 9 at 9. See also Joanna Erdman, "In the Back Alleys of Health Care: Abortion, Equality and Community in Canada" (2007) 56 Emory L.J. 1093.

of this decision [*Eldridge*] has been, for the most part, disappointing".[83] Patients in provinces that have medical sign language programs, like British Columbia and Ontario, face delays in access and other provinces never implemented interpretation programs. The legal victory has proved largely illusory: "The failure of some provinces to respond to *Eldridge* in the years that have elapsed ... suggests that it may not be safe to assume that governments that are not direct parties to a dispute will promptly, voluntarily and in good faith comply with the Supreme Court's declaration in [a] *Charter* case."[84]

Removal of a legal impediment is clearly only one step in obtaining access to health services. Other constraints, especially fiscal limitations and political unresponsiveness, may prove to be more intractable barriers to access.[85]

VI. OTHER BASES FOR LEGAL CHALLENGES

Litigants may pursue legal mechanisms other than Charter claims to assert rights of access to care. These include complaints to administrative agencies such as health service appeal boards and human rights tribunals or other types of legal claims that may be pursued through the court system. Several Canadian provinces have administrative bodies created and empowered by statute to review certain decisions regarding the provision of health care services. In Ontario, for instance, the Health Services Appeal and Review Board may hear appeals of decisions regarding health insurance benefits made by the General Manager of the Ontario Health Insurance Plan (OHIP).[86] In British Columbia, the Medical Services Commission has authority to determine insured benefits under the provincial health plan.[87] The Régie de l'assurance maladie du Québec is responsible for administering and implementing the provincial health insurance plan and may control eligibility for insured services.[88] Patients in some provinces who experience barriers in accessing care in their province of residence — either because the service is not insured provincially or because of long wait lists — may seek funding (including reimbursement for privately purchased out-of-

---

[83] Canadian Association for the Deaf, *Deaf Issues – Health Care* (May 26, 2007), online at: <http://www.cad.ca/en/issues/health_care.php>.

[84] Kent Roach, "Remedial Consensus and Dialogue Under the Charter: General Declarations and Delayed Declarations of Invalidity" (2002) 35 U.B.C. L. Rev. 211 at 230.

[85] For further discussion of legal victories and failed implementation, see Colleen M. Flood & Y.Y. Brandon Chen, "Charter Rights and Health Care Funding: A Typology of Health Rights Litigation" (2010) 19 Annals Health L. 479.

[86] See *Health Insurance Act*, R.S.O. 1990, c. H.6 and *Ministry of Health Appeal and Review Boards Act, 1998*, S.O. 1998, c. 18, Sched. H.

[87] The Medical Services Commission is composed of nine members: three government representatives; three representatives from the British Columbia Medical Association (BCMA); and three public members jointly nominated by the BCMA and the government: *Medicare Protection Act*, R.S.B.C. 1996, c. 286, s. 3(1). Section 5 sets out the powers and duties of the Medical Services Commission and stipulates it must act in accordance with the principles of the *Canada Health Act*.

[88] See *An Act respecting the Régie de l'assurance-maladie du Québec*, R.S.Q., c. R-5 and the *Health Insurance Act*, R.S.Q., c. A-29.

country care) through appeal to a provincial health services board or commission. These administrative bodies vary in their degree of independence, the scope of their review jurisdiction, expertise of members, and accessibility to the public.[89]

While the Charter applies only to government, provincial human rights laws apply to both public and private entities. Human rights laws across Canada prohibit discrimination in the provision of public services, including health care services, on the basis of characteristics such as disability, sex, religion and race.[90] For example, the British Columbia Human Rights Tribunal found that a physician who specialized in fertility treatments discriminated unfairly against a lesbian couple by refusing to provide artificial insemination to them on the basis of their sexual orientation.[91] Human rights tribunals have also dealt with cases regarding government funding for gender reassignment surgery,[92] autism therapy,[93] cancer screening[94] and infertility treatments.[95] It is important to note that the

---

[89]   For further discussion of provincial health care appeal bodies, see, *e.g.*, Caroline Pitfield & Colleen M. Flood, "Section 7 'Safety Valves': Appealing Wait Times Within a One-Tier System" in Colleen M. Flood, Kent Roach & Lorne Sossin, eds., *Access to Care, Access to Justice: The Legal Debate Over Private Health Insurance in Canada* (Toronto: University of Toronto Press, 2005).

[90]   For example, s. 1 of the Ontario *Human Rights Code*, R.S.O. 1990, c. H.19 states: "Every person has a right to equal treatment with respect to services, goods and facilities, without discrimination because of race, ancestry, place of origin, colour, ethnic origin, citizenship, creed, sex, sexual orientation, age, marital status, same-sex partnership status, family status or disability." Likewise, s. 8(1) of the British Columbia *Human Rights Code*, R.S.B.C. 1996, c. 210 states:

   A person must not, without a bona fide and reasonable justification,

   (a)   deny to a person or class of persons any accommodation, service or facility customarily available to the public, or
   (b)   discriminate against a person or class of persons regarding any accommodation, service or facility customarily available to the public
   because of the race, colour, ancestry, place of origin, religion, marital status, family status, physical or mental disability, sex or sexual orientation of that person or class of persons.

[91]   *Korn v. Potter*, [1996] B.C.J. No. 692, 134 D.L.R. (4th) 437 (B.C.S.C.).

[92]   *Hogan v. Ontario (Health and Long-Term Care)*, [2006] O.H.R.T.D. No. 34, 2006 HRTO 32 (O.H.R.T.); *Waters v. British Columbia (Ministry of Health Services)*, [2003] B.C.H.R.T.D. No. 11, 2003 BCHRT 13 (B.C.H.R.T.). An application for judicial review of this case was filed in the B.C. Supreme Court but has not proceeded.

[93]   *Newfoundland and Labrador v. Sparkes*, [2004] N.J. No. 34 (N.L.S.C.).

[94]   The B.C. Human Rights Tribunal heard a claim in late 2006 alleging that the provincial Ministry of Health discriminates in the provision of cancer screening services by funding mammography screening for breast cancer but does not fund prostate specific antigen (PSA) testing for prostate cancer in men. See *Armstrong v. British Columbia (Ministry of Health)*, [2006] B.C.H.R.T.D. No. 588, 2006 BCHRT 588 (B.C.H.R.T.). The adjudicator ruled that the complainant failed to establish a *prima facie* case of discrimination under the *Human Rights Code*. The complainant was initially successful on judicial review to the B.C. Supreme Court; however, the B.C. Court of Appeal reinstated the dismissal of the complaint. See *Armstrong v. British Columbia (Ministry of Health)*, [2010] B.C.J. No. 216, 2010 BCCA 56 (B.C.C.A.), revg [2009] B.C.J. No. 1279, 2009 BCSC 856 (B.C.S.C.), leave to appeal refused [2010] S.C.C.A. No. 128 (S.C.C.). The Human Rights Tribunal of Ontario dismissed an analogous claim regarding PSA testing in that

Supreme Court of Canada has not yet had occasion to rule on the question of whether human rights adjudicators ought to apply the analytical approach to discrimination claims that has been established under section 15(1) of the Charter.[96]

Administrative law principles, which aim to ensure decision-makers act within the bounds of their legal authority and decision-making processes are fair, may also support legal challenges to government health care decisions. For example, *Stein v. Québec (Régie de l'Assurance-maladie)*[97] involved judicial review of a decision to deny funding for health care services obtained outside Canada. Barry Stein was diagnosed with colon cancer that had spread to his liver. His physicians advised that the liver metastases should be removed as soon as possible but surgery was rescheduled several times, and Mr. Stein ultimately sought surgery in New York to avoid further delay and to obtain a recommended surgical procedure that was considered experimental in Canada. He sought reimbursement from the Régie de l'assurance maladie du Québec for the treatment he underwent in the United States but this request was denied. Mr. Stein then appealed to the Tribunal administratif du Québec, which upheld the Régie's decision. On review, the Quebec Superior Court ruled the Tribunal's

---

province: *Cochrane v. Ontario (Health and Long-Term Care)*, [2010] O.H.R.T.D. No. 1477, 2010 HRTO 1477 (O.H.R.T.).

[95] See, *e.g.*, *Buffett v. Canadian Forces*, [2008] C.H.R.D. No. 4 at para. 4, 2008 CHRT 4 (C.H.R.T.), wherein the adjudicator ordered "the Canadian Forces to take measures ... to amend its policy such that as long as the Canadian Forces continues to fund *in vitro* fertilization (IVF) treatments for its female members, male members shall receive funding for the intracytoplasmic sperm injection (ICSI) portion of their infertility treatments". In 2009, two Ontario couples filed complaints with the Ontario Human Rights Tribunal challenging that province's policy of restricting IVF funding to women with complete fallopian tube blockage: *Ilha v. Ontario (Health and Long-Term Care)*, [2010] O.H.R.T.D. No. 618, 2010 HRTO 594 (O.H.R.T.). For commentary in support of the claim for funding, see, *e.g.*, Jeff Nisker, "Socially Based Discrimination against Clinically Appropriate Care" (2009) 181:10 CMAJ 764.

[96] See discussion of jurisprudence in *Vancouver Rape Relief Society v. Nixon*, [2005] B.C.J. No. 2647 at paras. 28-42, 262 D.L.R. (4th) 360 (B.C.C.A.), leave to appeal refused [2006] S.C.C.A. No. 365 (S.C.C.); *Armstrong v. British Columbia (Ministry of Health)*, [2010] B.C.J. No. 216, 2010 BCCA 56 (B.C.C.A.); *Ball v. Ontario (Community and Social Services)*, [2010] O.H.R.T.D. No. 316, 2010 HRTO 360 (O.H.R.T.); *Cochrane v. Ontario (Health and Long-Term Care)*, [2010] O.H.R.T.D. No. 1477, 2010 HRTO 1477 (O.H.R.T.); and *Hogan v. Ontario (Health and Long-Term Care)*, [2006] O.H.R.T.D. No. 34, 58 C.H.R.R. D/317 (O.H.R.T.). For scholarly commentary, see, *e.g.*, Leslie A. Reaume, "Postcards from *O'Malley*: Reinvigorating Statutory Human Rights Jurisprudence in the Age of the *Charter*" in M. Denike, F. Faraday & M.K. Stephenson, eds., *Making Equality Rights Real: Securing Substantive Equality under the Charter* (Toronto: Irwin Law, 2006) at 373. She argues:

> There is considerable promise in maintaining distinct analytical frameworks between the *Charter* and the statutory human rights arenas. The challenge will be to find ways to develop analytical concepts which give life to the purposes which underlie these important instruments, appreciating that they are linked by the grander purpose of eradicating discrimination. The goal should be an interactive framework which provides opportunities for enriching equality rights jurisprudence and advancing substantive equality without supplanting the principles developed specifically for the issues which arise in these two distinct contexts.

[97] [1999] Q.J. No. 2724, [1999] R.J.Q. 2416 (Que. S.C.).

decision was "irrational, unreasonable and contrary to the purpose of the *Health Insurance Act*"[98] and it ordered the Régie to accept the reimbursement claim.

In contrast with *Stein*, an Ontario man, Adolfo Flora, failed in his attempt to seek reimbursement for a life-saving liver transplant procedure carried out in England after he was deemed ineligible for a transplant at home.[99] The Ontario Health Insurance Plan (OHIP) subsequently rejected his reimbursement claim on the basis that the surgery he had in England was not generally accepted in Ontario. The court ruled that it was reasonable for OHIP to apply an Ontario-based standard: "There is no internationally or globally recognized standard of health care. OHIP relies upon the opinions of Ontario physicians ... [and this provincial] standard ensures that out-of-country funding is provided only to those treatments that are regarded in Ontario as safe and effective."[100] Additionally, the court opined that "[l]imiting the funding of out-of-country medical treatments to those that are 'generally accepted in Ontario' ensures that public funds are not spent on treatments that are inconsistent with the ethics and values of the Ontario medical profession and the Ontario public. This safeguards the integrity of the health care system".[101] In dismissing the appeal, a unanimous Court of Appeal cited *Auton* and *Cameron* in concluding that Mr. Flora had overly broad expectations of the publicly funded health care system; indeed, in words that directly echo *Auton*, the Ontario health insurance legislation does not "promise that insured Ontarians will receive public funding for all medically beneficial treatments".[102]

VII. RESOURCE ALLOCATION, THE ROLE OF COURTS AND CHARTER CHALLENGES

> The fact that the matter is complex, contentious or laden with social values does not mean that the courts can abdicate the responsibility vested in them by our Constitution to review legislation for Charter compliance when citizens challenge it.[103]
>
> . . . . .
>
> What, then, are constitutionally required "reasonable health services"? What is treatment "within a reasonable time"? What are the benchmarks? How short a waiting list is short enough? How many MRIs does the Constitution require?[104]

---

[98]   *Ibid.*, at para. 32.

[99]   *Flora v. Ontario (Health Insurance Plan, General Manager)*, [2007] O.J. No. 91, 83 O.R. (3d) 721, 278 D.L.R. (4th) 45 (Ont. Div. Ct.), affd [2008] O.J. No. 2627, 295 D.L.R. (4th) 309 (Ont. C.A.).

[100] *Ibid.*, at para. 103 (Ont. Div. Ct.).

[101] *Ibid.*, at para. 105 (Ont. Div. Ct.).

[102] *Flora v. Ontario (Health Insurance Plan, General Manager)*, [2008] O.J. No. 2627 at para. 80, 295 D.L.R. (4th) 309 (Ont. C.A.).

[103] *Chaoulli v. Quebec (Attorney General)*, [2005] S.C.J. No. 33 at para. 107 (S.C.C.), *per* McLachlin C.J.C. and Major J.

[104] *Ibid.*, at para. 163, *per* Binnie, LeBel and Fish JJ.

Charter litigation that seeks to assert rights in regard to health care raises thorny legal issues regarding the appropriate scope of the Charter and the roles of courts and legislatures in policy-making and resource allocation. Charter cases can have the effect of "constitutionalizing" a right of access to services and force governments to redistribute resources to fund specific programs (with a consequent reduction in funds available for other services)[105] or change legislative regimes governing access to care.

Much constitutional law literature debates the impact of the Charter on the respective roles of courts and legislatures, with some commentators arguing the Charter allows judges to "interfere" in political matters, while others assert that judges have a legitimate role in superintending government action for compliance with the Constitution.[106] This debate has manifested itself very clearly in Charter health care litigation. In the appeal court ruling concerning Vancouver's supervised injection facility, Rowles J. commented that controversy surrounding a law "is not a reason to cause the court to fail to carry out its constitutional function and duty. There are many cases where the courts have intervened to invalidate laws that might be described as controversial: laws pertaining to abortion, gay and lesbian rights, private health care, collective bargaining and any number of criminal laws such as constructive murder. The fact that a law may be controversial law does not, for that reason alone, bar judicial review and invalidation".[107]

This final section analyzes broader questions of judicial review in cases involving contentious health policy and resource allocation issues. It discusses how courts have weighed arguments of government financial constraint against individual claims for access to health care — what the Supreme Court of Canada has described as the "'dollars versus rights' controversy"[108] — and the degree of deference courts are willing to give governments in reviewing the constitutionality of policy choices.

---

[105] Joel Bakan notes the Supreme Court of Canada decisions in *Tétreault-Gadoury v. Canada (Employment and Immigration)*, [1991] S.C.J. No. 41, [1991] 2 S.C.R. 22 (S.C.C.) and *Schachter v. Canada*, [1992] S.C.J. No. 68, [1992] 2 S.C.R. 679 (S.C.C.) provide an example of governments restricting benefits levels to address a successful Charter claim. These cases required the federal government to extend unemployment insurance benefits to certain groups who had previously been ineligible. However, Bakan notes that, to comply with the Court's ruling, the federal government "raised revenue for these extensions by increasing the number of weeks that a person must work before being eligible for UI benefits, reducing the number of weeks a person can receive benefits, and stiffen[ed] penalties for workers who quit without just cause or refused to take suitable jobs or are fired for misconduct": Joel Bakan, *Just Words: Constitutional Rights and Social Wrongs* (Toronto: University of Toronto Press, 1997) at 59.

[106] For discussion of the legitimacy of the judicial role under the Charter, with a summary of key literature on point, see, *e.g.*, Kent Roach & The Honourable Mr. Justice Robert J. Sharpe, *The Charter of Rights and Freedoms*, 4th ed. (Toronto: Irwin Law, 2009), Chapter 2, "The Legitimacy of Judicial Review".

[107] *PHS Community Services Society v. Canada (Attorney General)*, [2010] B.C.J. No. 57 at para. 61, 2010 BCCA 15 (B.C.C.A.).

[108] *Newfoundland (Treasury Board) v. Newfoundland and Labrador Assn. of Public and Private Employees*, [2004] S.C.J. No. 61 at para. 65, [2004] 3 S.C.R. 381 (S.C.C.).

VIII. JUDICIAL REVIEW OF GOVERNMENT POLICY CHOICES

The Supreme Court of Canada has typically not been receptive to financial constraint arguments, and it has repeatedly warned against courts being too deferential in reviewing government action that violates Charter rights. Despite this general position, the Court has instructed that judges ought to apply a more lenient standard of review in situations where government has acted to protect a vulnerable group, where it mediates among groups with competing interests, where complex social science evidence is involved, and where it must allocate scarce resources.[109] Greschner points out that "[l]aws regulating the health care system usually possess all four of these characteristics".[110]

In cases where courts have found a Charter breach stemming from a government's decision not to fund a particular health care service, the government's justification argument has often rested on considerations of cost. Government respondents argue they face competing claims on public resources (and health care is just one of many), so courts must give governments latitude to establish priorities. To date, cost arguments have met with varied judicial response. The B.C. appellate court in *Eldridge* held it would be too expensive to fund sign language interpreters yet, on appeal, the Supreme Court of Canada rejected the cost justification.

In *Cameron*, the Nova Scotia Court of Appeal accepted the government's cost argument. In *Auton*, both the B.C. Supreme Court and Court of Appeal rejected cost as a factor that could justify withholding public funds for autism therapy. Since the Supreme Court of Canada dismissed *Auton* by finding no discrimination under section 15(1), it did not consider cost arguments in a section 1 justification analysis. Of course, the Court's narrow view both of the provincial health care system and section 15's application (the government funds only a partial plan and section 15 only applies to benefits provided by law) implicitly acknowledges cost constraints; government has discretion to include or exclude non-core services and cost will inevitably be a factor in those choices.

IX. DOLLARS VERSUS RIGHTS — WHERE TO DRAW THE LINE?

Although the Supreme Court of Canada has cautioned that "budgetary considerations cannot be used to justify a [Charter] violation",[111] it is clear that the state's ability to pay for an increasing array of services is a critical issue in

---

[109] *Irwin Toy Ltd. v. Quebec (Attorney General)*, [1989] S.C.J. No. 36, [1989] 1 S.C.R. 927 (S.C.C.) and Peter W. Hogg, *Constitutional Law of Canada*, Stud. Ed. (Toronto: Thomson Carswell, 2004) at 827.

[110] Commission on the Future of Health Care in Canada, *How Will the Charter of Rights and Freedoms and Evolving Jurisprudence Affect Health Care Costs?: Discussion Paper No. 2* by Donna Greschner (Saskatoon: Commission on the Future of Health Care in Canada, 2002) at 14.

[111] *Schachter v. Canada*, [1992] S.C.J. No. 68, [1992] 2 S.C.R. 679 at 709 (S.C.C.).

health care litigation; financial considerations can and will be raised to justify limits on constitutionally protected rights.

Cost arguments have figured prominently in many Charter cases related to social benefit programs. For example, in *Egan v. Canada*,[112] a homosexual couple argued that the federal *Old Age Security Act* violated section 15(1) of the Charter by discriminating against same-sex partners by limiting spousal allowances to opposite-sex partners.[113] The section 1 analyses in this case revealed divisions in the Court as to the appropriate place of financial considerations in justifying government policy choices. The government argued that the cost of extending benefits to same-sex spouses would be prohibitive, with expert evidence estimating additional expenditures of $12 to $37 million per year.[114] However, Iacobucci J. criticized this evidence as "highly speculative and statistically weak"[115] and based on "guesswork".[116] He went on to say that even assuming the cost evidence was valid, he would still find "as a question of law, that they do not justify the denial of the appellants' right to equality".[117] Further:

> The jurisprudence of this Court reveals, as a general matter, a reluctance to accord much weight to financial considerations under a s. 1 analysis. ... This is certainly the case when the financial motivations are not, as in the case at bar, supported by more persuasive arguments as to why the infringement amounts to a reasonable limit.[118]

In contrast, Sopinka J. ruled the government was justified in limiting spousal benefits to opposite-sex couples. He remarked that "government must be accorded some flexibility in extending social benefits"[119] and

> [i]t is not realistic for the Court to assume that there are unlimited funds to address the needs of all. A judicial approach on this basis would tend to make a government reluctant to create any new social benefit schemes because their limits would depend on an accurate prediction of the outcome of court proceedings under s. 15(1) of the *Charter*.[120]

In a unanimous 2004 ruling, the Supreme Court of Canada summarized its views on cost justifications as follows:

> ... courts will continue to look with strong skepticism at attempts to justify infringements of *Charter* rights on the basis of budgetary constraints. To do oth-

---

[112] [1995] S.C.J. No. 43, [1995] 2 S.C.R. 513 (S.C.C.).
[113] Section 19 of the *Old Age Security Act*, R.S.C. 1985, c. O-9 provided spousal allowances for spouses between 60 and 65 years of age if the family income was below a certain level. Section 2 of the legislation defined spouses as being of the opposite sex.
[114] *Egan v. Canada*, [1995] S.C.J. No. 43 at para. 193, [1995] 2 S.C.R. 513 (S.C.C.).
[115] *Ibid.*
[116] *Ibid.*
[117] *Ibid.*
[118] *Ibid.*, at para. 194.
[119] *Ibid.*, at para. 104.
[120] *Ibid.*

erwise would devalue the *Charter* because there are *always* budgetary constraints and there are *always* other pressing government priorities.[121]

As noted above, judicial responses to cost arguments have varied in Charter
health care cases. In *Eldridge*, the Court assumed "without deciding ... that the
objective of this decision — controlling health care expenditures — is 'pressing
and substantial', and that this decision is rationally connected to the objective".[122] Although reiterating Sopinka J.'s statement in *Egan* that courts must
afford governments latitude when making resource allocation decisions, La Forest J. concluded in *Eldridge* that even with a deferential approach to reviewing
the government's decision, the choice to exclude funding for sign language interpretation failed the minimal impairment aspect of the *Oakes* test.[123] The most
persuasive factor was the relatively small magnitude of the cost, since "the estimated cost of providing sign language interpretation for the whole of British
Columbia was only $150,000 [per annum] or approximately 0.0025 percent of
the provincial health care budget at the time".[124] Ultimately, the Court emphasized "the central place of good health in the quality of life of all persons in our
society" and concluded that "the government has simply not demonstrated that
this unpropitious state of affairs must be tolerated in order to achieve the objective of limiting health care expenditures".[125]

In *Cameron*, the Nova Scotia Court of Appeal faced the challenge of evaluating cost implications of insuring IVF and ICSI therapies. The court considered
an expert report estimating an annual expenditure of $1.6 million to insure the
services, not including the cost of drugs required during the process. On cross-
examination, the expert reduced this estimate in half to approximately $800,000
per year.[126] The court also considered the evidence of an executive director with
the Nova Scotia Department of Health who testified at trial that provincial health
care expenditures were increasing while the federal government was reducing
transfer payments for health care, leading to increased pressure on the provincial
budget.[127]

In arguing that IVF and ICSI ought to be covered, the claimants pointed out
that the provincial health care insurance plan covers many expensive treatments,
including organ transplants that can cost the health care system close to
$100,000 per surgery.[128] Their argument suggests that a simple calculation of the

---

[121] *Newfoundland (Treasury Board) v. Newfoundland and Labrador Assn. of Public and Private Employees*, [2004] S.C.J. No. 61 at para. 72, [2004] 3 S.C.R. 381 (S.C.C.).

[122] *Eldridge v. British Columbia*, [1997] S.C.J. No. 86 at para. 84, [1997] 3 S.C.R. 624 (S.C.C.).

[123] *Ibid.*, at para. 85. Although the Court canvassed arguments in support of judicial deference, it ruled (at para. 85) that it was "unnecessary to decide whether in this 'social benefits' context, where the choice is between the needs of the general population and those of a disadvantaged group, a deferential approach should be adopted".

[124] *Ibid.*, at para. 87.

[125] *Ibid.*, at para. 94.

[126] *Cameron v. Nova Scotia*, [1999] N.S.J. No. 297 at para. 227, 177 D.L.R. (4th) 611 (N.S.C.A.).

[127] *Ibid.*, at paras. 219-221.

[128] *Ibid.*, at para. 233.

total annual cost of insuring a new service is relatively meaningless without comparing that expense with the cost of other services that are already publicly funded. The government's expert witness referred to a method of assessing the value of a health care service by calculating its cost in relation to years of life gained. Though the expert "had difficulty translating this [method] to fertility treatments because yet another life becomes part of the picture ... he agreed that $145.00 a year would represent the cost of IVF and ICSI",[129] much less than the cost of providing other insured services.[130] Taking only cost into account, then, a claimant could argue that funding fertility treatments would be relatively inexpensive compared to many other health care services, though certainly the benefit and risks of the service — for example, whether it saves a life or addresses a non-life-threatening problem — must be part of the calculus. Interestingly, recent calls for IVF funding argue that governments would save money by funding IVF for single embryo transfers.[131] If infertile persons pay privately for IVF, they may be more likely to have multiple embryo implantation, leading to a higher risk of giving birth prematurely to infants with disabilities, such as cerebral palsy and blindness, that will require costly medical interventions and social supports.

In *Cameron*, Chipman J.A. ultimately decided that "[t]he best we can do in these circumstances ... is to arrive at an approximate figure for costs which I would estimate to be in the order of a million dollars annually".[132] This response indicates much more tolerance for the "guesswork" involved in estimating costs of insuring new health care services, a view that contrasts sharply with that of Iacobucci J. in *Egan*. Justice Chipman also took judicial notice that limited governmental resources "have been a major concern for some years"[133] and commented that such limits "have threatened, in the minds of most people, the very foundation of health care. It is the general perception that it will take a great deal of effort to make do with what we have".[134] Overall, the decision in *Cameron* seems to reveal a less exacting standard of proof on the government to present evidence regarding the cost implications of expanding public coverage for new health care services. Ultimately, Chipman J.A. adopts a deferential approach:

> The evidence makes clear the complexity of the health care system and the extremely difficult task confronting those who must allocate the resources among a vast array of competing claims.

. . . . .

---

[129] *Ibid.*, at para. 232.

[130] For example, evidence before the Court indicated that cardiac artery bypass grafts cost $50,000 per year of life saved. *Ibid.*

[131] See, *e.g.*, Jeff Nisker, "Socially Based Discrimination Against Clinically Appropriate Care" (2009) 181:10 CMAJ 764.

[132] *Cameron v. Nova Scotia*, [1999] N.S.J. No. 297 at para. 228, 177 D.L.R. (4th) 611 (N.S.C.A.).

[133] *Ibid.*, at para. 218.

[134] *Ibid.*

The policy makers require latitude in balancing competing interests in the constrained financial environment. We are simply not equipped to sort out the priorities. We should not second guess them, except in clear cases of failure on
their part to properly balance the *Charter* rights of individuals against the overall pressing [governmental] objective ....[135]

In *Auton*, the lower courts recognized that "[t]he Crown is entitled to judicial deference in performing its difficult task of making policy choices and allocating scarce resources among myriad vulnerable groups".[136] Yet, where the
fundamental needs of disabled children are at stake, the lower courts were willing to impose a constitutional obligation to fund therapy. As Saunders J.A.
commented, "the age-old reluctance of the courts to allocate the scarce resources
of the taxpayer ... is not without weight. However, the principle that government monies should be allocated only by the legislature, while strong, does not
always prevail when the issue is compliance with the Constitution".[137]

In *Wynberg*, the Ontario Court of Appeal addressed the section 1 analysis
and concluded the trial judge erred in finding that the government did not have
pressing and substantial reasons for limiting autism therapy to children under
age six. The appeal court accepted the evidence of a senior government official
that "there is fierce competition for the resources that exist in government"[138]
and noted that courts are not in a position to make difficult public policy choices
that involve balancing competing demands for scarce resources. Adopting a deferential approach, the appellate justices stated that "[f]or the court to choose a
different option than that selected by the legislature would be to replace one
imprecise evaluation with another".[139]

X.   DIFFERENT PERSPECTIVES ON COSTS AND BENEFITS

Much of the debate between claimants and the government regarding resource
allocation has turned on differing conceptions of costs and benefits. Governments tend to focus on the immediate cost impacts of funding new programs, as
well as the financial liability they may face by setting a precedent for other funding requests. Individuals who seek to expand health care coverage often emphasize the wider cost savings that may result from funding a service, as well as
psychological and social costs incurred when some groups are excluded from
accessing an important benefit. In *Eldridge*, for example, the government focused on the expense of a medical sign language interpretation program, and
was particularly concerned with the possible long-term financial impact of re-

---

[135]   *Ibid.*, at paras. 234, 236.
[136]   *Auton (Guardian ad litem of) v. British Columbia (Minister of Health)*, [2000] B.C.J. No. 1547
        at para. 143, 78 B.C.L.R. (3d) 55 (B.C.S.C.).
[137]   *Auton (Guardian ad litem of) v. British Columbia (Attorney General)*, [2002] B.C.J. No. 2258 at
        paras. 56-57, 6 B.C.L.R. (4th) 201 (B.C.C.A.).
[138]   *Wynberg v. Ontario*, [2006] O.J. No. 2732 at para. 169 (Ont. C.A.).
[139]   *Ibid.*, at para. 184.

quests for language interpretation services by other groups.[140] However, the Supreme Court criticized the government for its lack of evidence to substantiate this speculative concern.[141]

Looking at the issue through a different cost lens, the claimants focused on the broader medical, social and psychological costs that could result from a failure to ensure deaf patients could communicate effectively with their health care practitioners. These include the risk of misdiagnosis, failure to follow a prescribed treatment, and feelings of fear, anxiety and exclusion that deaf patients may experience when they are unable to communicate effectively regarding their health care needs.[142]

Similarly, in *Auton*, the claimants and the government viewed the question of costs and benefits from very different perspectives. While the government argued it could not afford the cost of funding autism therapy, the parents argued the government could not afford *not* to fund it. Without appropriate therapy, the parents argued, many children with autism are likely to "drain" public resources for their entire lives by requiring state-funded income and housing assistance as adults. The trial judge accepted this reasoning, stating that "it is apparent that the costs incurred in paying for effective treatment of autism may well be more than offset by the savings achieved by assisting autistic children to develop their educational and societal potential rather than dooming them to a life of isolation and institutionalization".[143] The government also contended that the lack of empirical evidence proving the effectiveness of autism therapy also justified its funding refusal, but the trial judge rejected this argument: "the fact that autism can't be 'cured' is no reason to withhold treatment. Often cancer cannot be cured but it is unthinkable that treatment designed to ameliorate or delay its effects would not be forthcoming".[144]

Governments also often emphasize the broader tradeoffs or opportunity costs that are involved in choosing to fund one service over another. Justice Lambert's comments in *Eldridge*, excerpted at length earlier, clearly demonstrate the challenge in choosing among competing health funding priorities. In *Auton*, the trial judge noted that "[t]he Crown makes the irrefragable statement that its health care resources are limited and argues that the effect of funding treatment for autistic children would direct resources away from other children with special needs".[145] On appeal, the government argued further that:

---

[140] *Eldridge v. British Columbia (Attorney General)*, [1992] B.C.J. No. 2229 at para. 22, 75 B.C.L.R. (2d) 68 (B.C.S.C.).

[141] *Eldridge v. British Columbia (Attorney General)*, [1997] S.C.J. No. 86 at paras. 92 and 94, [1997] 3 S.C.R. 624 (S.C.C.).

[142] *Ibid.*, at paras. 56, 57, 69.

[143] *Auton (Guardian ad litem of) v. British Columbia (Minister of Health)*, [2000] B.C.J. No. 1547 at para. 147, 78 B.C.L.R. (3d) 55 (B.C.S.C.). However, after considering an economic cost-benefit analysis of the autism therapy tendered into evidence by the claimants, the trial judge opined (at para. 145) that "it is not possible to estimate accurately either the additional immediate costs of a treatment programme or the inevitable savings in the long run".

[144] *Ibid.*, at para. 136.

[145] *Ibid.*, at para. 145.

a decision in favour of the petitioners will impel the necessarily complex administrative choices required to be made in the course of balancing the myriad
and competing demands for health care, into the courts for decision on the allocation of scarce resources on a case by case basis, rather than on a comprehensive and systematic basis.[146]

The last part of this statement — the reference to a comprehensive and systematic basis for making health care funding decisions — is significant.[147] Since
courts must assess the justifiability of a governmental act that violates Charter
rights, governments would do well to have evidence that their choice was based
on a cogent analysis of costs and benefits, including immediate and long-term
financial impacts, as well as broader social impacts of their policy decisions.
This will not be an easy challenge to meet as it takes substantial resources —
time, money, people — and expertise to evaluate the growing number of health
interventions and technologies and make decisions about funding coverage.[148]
The challenge of evaluating new treatments and therapies is especially daunting
when one considers the lack of evidence to substantiate the benefit of many currently insured services, and examples of health care "practices that were once
accepted without doubt [that turned] out to be worthless or even harmful".[149]

XI. DECISION-MAKING CHALLENGES

The assertion that courts ought to defer to the policy choices of governments
rests on the principle that democratically elected legislators are in the best position to consider various options and make decisions based on their expertise and
ability to respond to the needs of the public that voted them into office. This

---

[146] *Auton (Guardian ad litem of) v. British Columbia (Attorney General)*, [2002] B.C.J. No. 2258 at
para. 56, 6 B.C.L.R. (4th) 201 (B.C.C.A.).

[147] Greschner and Lewis make this observation: see Donna Greschner & Steven Lewis, "Medicare
in the Courts: *Auton* and Evidence-Based Decision-Making" (2003) 82 Can. Bar Rev. 501.

[148] For an overview of some of the challenges associated with technology assessment, economic
evaluation and policy development in health care, see, *e.g.*, Deidre DeJean, Mita Giacomini, Lisa
Schwartz & Fiona A. Miller, "Ethics in Canadian Health Technology Assessment: A Descriptive
Review" (2009) 25 International Journal of Technology Assessment in Health Care 463; Jean-
Eric Tarride *et al.*, "Economic Evaluations Conducted by Canadian Health Technology Assessment Agencies: Where Do We Stand?" (2008) 24 International Journal of Technology Assessment in Health Care 437; and Pascale Lehoux, Myriam Hivon, Jean-Louis Denis & Stéphanie
Tailliez, "Health Technology Assessment in the Canadian Health Policy Arena: Evaluating Relationships between Evaluators and Stakeholders" (2008) 14:3 Evaluation 295.

[149] David M. Eddy, "The Use of Evidence and Cost Effectiveness by the Courts: How Can It Help
Improve Health Care?" (2001) 26 J. Health Pol. 387 at 396. Eddy points out (at 396):

We were wrong about diethylstilbestrol [DES], radical mastectomies, ... hormone replacement therapy for heart disease. ... Experts from top universities with the most experience testified under oath that high-dose chemotherapy for late-stage breast cancer
would produce 20 to 30 percent long-term cure rates. Randomized controlled trials later
proved them wrong. This is not to say that all experts are always wrong. It is to say that
we cannot assume they are right, and there is no easy way to tell when they are and when
they are not from their credentials or enthusiasm.

argument, however, falls down in the health care context because a full legislative process, involving opportunities for public debate, input and consultation, is usually not employed to make health care policy choices.

The *Canada Health Act* sets out a requirement for provincial governments to fund medically necessary hospital and physician services on a first-dollar basis in order to attract a federal contribution. However, decisions about what services to include and exclude from the definition of "medically necessary" (and thus from the Medicare basket) have typically been made through negotiation between provincial health ministries and provincial medical associations. The shortcoming of a decision-making process that is largely limited to input from physicians and health ministry officials is that, as Colleen Flood notes, it "rel[ies] upon governments to sufficiently represent public values, and for physicians to bring their technical expertise to the determination of what is 'medically necessary'".[150]

Eldridge provides an example of the somewhat *ad hoc* and variable way in which health care funding decisions may be made. In that case, the Western Institute for the Deaf and the Hard of Hearing, an organization that provided some medical interpreting services for deaf patients in the B.C. Lower Mainland, approached the provincial government for funding in 1989 and 1990. The first request was "declined out of hand"[151] but the second request was given some consideration by Ministry of Health staff. The trial judgment notes that the executive director who initially reviewed the funding request "was sympathetic to the request because he has an understanding of many of the problems encountered by the deaf through his experience with deaf people, including his deaf nine year old daughter".[152] He recommended that the Ministry ought to fund the program but the Ministry Executive Committee decided to reject the request because "it was felt to fund this particular request would set a precedent that might be followed up by further requests from the ethnic communities where the language barrier might also be a factor".[153] The trial decision noted that "[i]f a declined request has sufficient merit in the opinion of a Ministry of Health representative, it will be reconsidered when the budget for the next fiscal year is being formulated",[154] but the Ministry did not reconsider the funding request for medical interpretation services. The description of this process in *Eldridge* highlights a somewhat crude method of decision-making process that appears to de-

---

[150] Colleen M. Flood, "The Anatomy of Medicare" in Jocelyn Downie, Timothy Caulfield & Colleen Flood, eds., *Canadian Health Law & Policy*, 2d ed. (Markham, ON: LexisNexis Canada, 2002) 1 at 23. See also Colleen M. Flood, Mark Stabile & Carolyn Hughes Tuohy, "The Borders of Solidarity: How Countries Determine the Public/Private Mix in Spending and the Impact on Health Care" (2002) 12 Health Matrix 297 at 303.

[151] *Eldridge v. British Columbia (Attorney General)*, [1992] B.C.J. No. 2229 at para. 21, 75 B.C.L.R. (2d) 68 (B.C.S.C.).

[152] *Ibid.*

[153] *Ibid.*, at para. 22. This quotation comes from an internal Ministry of Health memorandum that was entered into evidence at trial.

[154] *Ibid.*

pend largely on chance (will the bureaucrat who initially reviews the request have sympathy because of personal experience?) and speculation (if the government approves this request, will the floodgates then open?).

More transparent government decision-making processes — and opportunities for public involvement in those processes — have long been advocated,[155] but examples of meaningful public engagement in Canadian health policy-making are few. "Worse yet", some contend, "there is evidence of neglect of public input".[156] It is asserted that "increasing the transparency and perceived legitimacy of funding and major priority decisions at all levels should be a foremost concern for our health care leaders. Providing more opportunities for public involvement and clearly reporting how input is used would reduce cynicism" and add the public's voice "to aid in making difficult choices".[157]

Governments have sporadically attempted to solicit public views on health care services or implemented advisory committees to give advice on resource allocation. In 2010, an Alberta government health care committee, tasked with developing recommendations for new health legislation, sought input from 29 community consultations, a survey of 1,500 Albertans and 85 written submissions. The resulting report offered 15 recommendations for a new *Alberta Health Act*, with such legislation including provisions for "a health charter for Alberta, and public engagement with respect to future changes in legislation, regulation, and policy".[158] The report also recommended "the development of an independent entity to support evidence-based decision-making ... [and a] possible framework for ongoing public engagement on broader health system is-

---

[155] For example, the 1994 Canadian Bar Association Task Force on Health Care Reform addressed concerns with governmental processes for making funding choices:

> The impact of provincial health care resource allocation decisions is so important ... that it would be desirable to have public input into these decisions. Currently, these decisions are vulnerable to attack because the lack of an open and consultative process leaves the public only one option — to protest resource allocation decisions after they have been made. This can lead to public outcries which cause the government to retreat from a decision — not a desirable way to make public policy.

Canadian Bar Association Task Force on Health Care, *What's Law Got To Do With It? Health Care Reform in Canada* (Ottawa: Canadian Bar Association, 1994) at 101 [footnote omitted].

[156] Roger Chafe, Wendy Levinson & Paul C. Hébert, Editorial, "The Need for Public Engagement in Choosing Health Priorities" (2011) 183:2 CMAJ 165. As examples of neglect, the authors cite the "mothballing" of the Romanow Report on the future of Canadian health care and the federal Health Minister's disregard of advice concerning appointments to the board of the assisted human reproduction agency.

[157] *Ibid.*

[158] Alberta Advisory Committee on Health (Chair: Fred Horne, MLA), *Putting People First: Part One – Recommendations for an Alberta Health Act* (September 15, 2010), online at: <http://www. health.alberta.ca/documents/Alberta-Health-Act-Report-2010.pdf>, at page 1 of the transmittal letter from MLA Horne to the Minister of Health and Wellness.

sues".[159] Critics panned the report as "light on details" and just another health care report that "lacks substance and likely won't lead to many changes".[160]

The lacklustre outcome of a 2002 Alberta initiative suggests the sceptical response may be warranted. At that time, the government established an Expert Advisory Panel to Review Publicly Funded Health Services to recommend procedures to base health funding decisions on criteria of transparency, rigor, openness and timeliness.[161] The Advisory Panel recommended appointment of board, with expert and lay members, that would review funding for existing and new services.[162] This review process would involve independent assessments by experts (*e.g.*, in health technology assessment) and would include opportunities for "stakeholder participation". The government ultimately rejected this proposal and made a fuzzy commitment to strengthen "[e]xisting processes ... to improve the rigor and timeliness of decisions on whether or not to fund new services" and, concerned that a new board might usurp power, stated that the government "will retain its authority to make decisions on whether or not to fund new procedures".[163]

As another example, in 2006 and 2007 the British Columbia government conducted the "Conversation on Health", a process that involved townhall-style meetings in communities throughout the province and an online discussion forum. The government-stated objective was to engage citizens "to better understand their priorities for health care and their recommendations for how to improve health-care services while ensuring they are sustainable".[164]

Like the earlier Alberta process, little came of the Conversation on Health. One analyst contends that the B.C. government had an ulterior motive of pursuing a privatization agenda:

> it was clear from the context not only what the government thought the problem was – excessive and rising public expenditure on healthcare – but also the

---

[159] *Ibid.*

[160] Josh Wingrove & Gloria Galloway, "Alberta eyes 'People First' overhaul of health care" *The Globe and Mail* (September 16, 2010), online at: <http://www.theglobeandmail.com/news/politics/alberta-eyes-people-first-overhaul-of-health-care/article1710793/>, quoting Michael McBane, Canadian Health Coalition, and David Eggen, Friends of Medicare.

[161] Alberta, Expert Advisory Panel to Review Publicly Funded Health Services, *The Burden of Proof: An Alberta Model for Assessing Publicly Funded Health Services* (Edmonton: Alberta Health and Wellness, 2003) at 5. The report describes the role of the panel as follows: "To review and make recommendations on public funding for the current basket of health services and to recommend an appraisal process for reviewing new and existing health services on an ongoing basis. The objective is to ensure that Alberta's publicly funded health services remain comprehensive and sustainable for the future, and provide the best value" (at 1).

[162] This review would take into account the following factors: safety; demonstrated benefits in treating or preventing health problems; impact of the funding decision on public access to the service; ethical concerns; impact of the funding decision on the health system; availability of other health care options; and financial costs and implications. *Ibid.*, at 1, 9.

[163] See Government of Alberta, News Release, "Government Funding Right Health Services Now, Focus on New Process for Funding Future Services" (July 18, 2003).

[164] Government of British Columbia, *Strategic Plan 2007/08-2009/10* (February 2007), online at: <http://www.bcbudget.gov.bc.ca/2007/pdf/2007_Strategic_Plan.pdf> at 7.

solution: privately financed care supplementing or replacing publicly funded services. In short, an expanded private role in healthcare was to be the topic of conversation. In the end, however, the Conversation on Health provided fresh opportunity for those enamoured of universal, single-tier medicare to restate their case. Instead of *rapprochement*, a meeting of minds between government and its public, the Conversation illustrates the depth of the divide – a government from Mars and a public from Venus.[165]

Some international jurisdictions have implemented expert advisory bodies to provide governments with guidance on health funding decisions. In the United Kingdom, the National Institute for Health and Clinical Excellence (NICE) was established in 1999 as an independent body to make recommendations to the National Health Service (NHS) regarding medicines and treatments, and develop practice and quality standards.[166] NICE technology appraisals may be appealed on three grounds: (1) NICE did not act fairly in its process; (2) the appraisal results cannot reasonably be justified based on available evidence; and (3) NICE exceeded its statutory jurisdiction. While the NICE process has been lauded as a model of independent review of health care therapies that attempts to be more evidence-based, transparent and open to appeal, the organization has been criticized for tardy appraisals that delay availability of recommended therapies and alleged unfairness in restricting or rejecting funding for some life-saving treatments.[167] As one commentator puts it: "NICE can be viewed as either a heartless rationing agency or an intrepid and impartial messenger for the need to set priorities in health care."[168] In either case, the NICE experience can serve as an instructive example of practices to emulate or to avoid.[169]

XII. CONCLUSION

The Charter has been part of the Canadian legal landscape for over a quarter century, but its application in many areas of governmental action — especially public benefit programs such as health care — continues to be the topic of evolution and debate. Inevitably, Charter challenges in the health care context will

---

[165] Alan Davidson, "Sweet Nothings? The BC Conversation on Health" (2008) 3:4 Health Policy 33.

[166] For more information, see online at: <http://www.nice.org.uk/>.

[167] Robert Steinbrook, "Saying 'No' Isn't NICE: The Travails of Britain's National Institute for Health and Clinical Excellence" (2008) 359 New Eng. J. Med. 1977.

[168] *Ibid.*, at 1978. For a spirited critique and defence of NICE, see, *e.g.*, John Harris, "It's not NICE to Discriminate" (2005) 31 Journal of Medical Ethics 373 (critique) and M. Rawlins & A. Dillon, "NICE Discrimination" (2005) 31 Journal of Medical Ethics 683 (defence).

[169] For discussion of other jurisdictions that are experimenting with more transparent and participatory resource allocation mechanisms, see Norman Daniels & James E. Sabin, "Accountability for Reasonableness: An Update" (2008) 338 British Medical Journal a1850 (for discussion of NICE, as well as initiatives in Mexico and Oregon). Note that at the time of writing, the future role of the NICE is subject to change in light of far-reaching budget cuts within the U.K. public sector. For further background, see Alan Maynard & Karen Bloor, "The Future Role of NICE" (2010) 341 British Medical Journal c6286 and Adrian O'Dowd, "Government Halves Number of NHS Quangos to Save £180M" (2010) 341 British Medical Journal c4074.

involve a complex balancing of fundamental individual rights against (usually) pressing governmental objectives. Early cases like *Morgentaler* and *Rodriguez* addressed very controversial social issues, but within a sphere of government activity — criminal regulation — that is clearly subject to Charter review. Subsequent cases — exemplified by *Auton* and *Chaoulli* — have delved into contentious areas of resource allocation and the structure of the overall health care system, areas which are not as susceptible to resolution through constitutional litigation.

While "[t]here may have been a time when it was believed that a commitment to provide the best health care available at whatever cost was all that was needed to make it a reality",[170] that idealistic scenario no longer exists. Although our health care system may be comprehensive in the sense that it covers more than strictly basic care, it does not promise an "unconstrained right to healthcare services, except within available resources".[171] Canadian courts recognize the difficult task legislators face in allocating scarce resources and in regulating the health care system to safeguard the fundamental principles on which Medicare is built. Nonetheless, judges hesitate to accept cost constraints as a sole justification for limiting individual rights; as the Supreme Court of Canada did not address the section 1 analysis in *Auton*, questions remain about how significant a cost impact must be before a government is justified in limiting funding for a "core" medical service. The differing reasons in *Chaoulli* highlight enduring institutional tensions between courts and legislators over the appropriateness of judicial deference to government policy choices. Some Supreme Court rulings have been very critical of "theoretical contentions"[172] and "purely speculative"[173] arguments advanced by governments to justify limits on Charter rights. If a government finds itself in a courtroom defending health care policy choices, it would do well to have solid evidence to substantiate its position; indeed, improved decision-making processes may help avoid journeys to judges' chambers in the first place.

Where does the future of health care lie in Canada and how will the current state of Charter jurisprudence influence health policy changes? Without doubt, the Supreme Court dismissal of *Auton* led to a collective sigh of relief among Canadian health ministers and bureaucrats who are ever concerned with cost pressures and the spectre of courts instructing governments that they have a constitutional obligation to fund specific services. The *Chaoulli* result, in contrast, instigated serious discussions about health system reforms to permit and promote greater private sector involvement; indeed, Flood and Chen contend that "the greatest impact that has resulted from the *Chaoulli* decision to-date is the

---

[170] Rino A. Stradiotto & Jacinthe I. Boudreau, "Resource Allocation and Accountability in Health Care" (2000) 20 Health L. Can. 40 at 51.

[171] Pranlal Manga, "Medicare: Ethics versus Economics" (1987) 136 CMAJ 113.

[172] *Chaoulli v. Quebec (Attorney General)*, [2005] S.C.J. No. 33 at para. 149, [2005] 1 S.C.R. 791 (S.C.C.).

[173] *Eldridge v. British Columbia (Attorney General)*, [1997] S.C.J. No. 86 at para. 89, [1997] 3 S.C.R. 624 (S.C.C.).

transformation of the two-tier system from a largely discounted proposition into a legitimate policy option for Canadian health care reform".[174] Politicians remain careful to emphasize the foundational principles of the *Canada Health Act*, but some question the sustainability of clinging to publicly funded health care as a symbol of Canadian identity.[175]

To date, Canadian courts have been more receptive to health-related claims based on negative conceptions of rights, evidenced in cases such as *Morgentaler*, *Parker* and *Chaoulli*. The Ontario court ruling striking down three prostitution-related offences in the *Criminal Code* also underscores protection of negative liberties.[176] Legal provisions that exacerbate risk of harm for sex trade workers could not withstand section 7 scrutiny. In contrast, claims of positive rights have been less successful in the legal arena, though the public attention generated by litigation can keep an issue — such as funding for autism therapy or IVF — on the government agenda, despite an unsuccessful section 15 challenge.[177]

It is worth noting that characterizing a case as involving negative rights does not mean the cost implications for governments are any less important than cases involving assertions of positive rights. Where a court strikes down a law for non-compliance with the Charter, governments may fill the legislative gap with a new set of regulations that bring budgetary demands. As mentioned earlier, after the *Parker* ruling, the federal government established a medical marijuana access program, which requires public resources to contract for production of marijuana products, monitor for quality control and safety, and process applications for possession and use of medical marijuana. Public resources may also be required to offer protection for women who access abortion services and health professionals who work in this area of reproductive health care. For example, in 1995, British Columbia enacted the *Access to Abortion Services Act*[178] to create safe zones around abortion facilities where persons are prohibited from engaging in protests and interfering with or intimidating patients or care providers. This legislation creates enforcement costs for the state, including legal costs

---

[174] Colleen M. Flood & Y.Y. Brandon Chen, "Charter Rights and Health Care Funding: A Typology of Health Rights Litigation" (2010) 19 Annals Health L. 479.

[175] In an analysis of Canadian newspaper editorials following the *Chaoulli* decision, several commentators from McGill University found that an association between Medicare and Canadian identity "was unexpectedly used most by those who favoured private health insurance, as an example of an empty and obsolete argument that should be discounted": Amélie Quesnel-Vallée *et al.*, "In the Aftermath of *Chaoulli v. Quebec:* Whose Opinion Prevailed?" (2006) 175:9 CMAJ 1051 at 1052.

[176] *Bedford v. Canada*, [2010] O.J. No. 4057, 2010 ONSC 4264 (Ont. S.C.J.). This decision ruled as unconstitutional the prostitution-related offences of: keeping a common bawdy house (s. 201); living off the avails of prostitution (s. 212(1)(j)); and communication for the purposes of prostitution (s. 213(1)(c)). The latter offence was also found to violate s. 2(*b*) of the Charter.

[177] For further discussion on this point, see Colleen M. Flood & Y.Y. Brandon Chen, "Charter Rights and Health Care Funding: A Typology of Health Rights Litigation" (2010) 19 Annals Health L. 479.

[178] R.S.B.C. 1996, c. 1.

of defending a section 2 Charter challenge against this statute.[179] Post-*Chaoulli*, the Government of Quebec also created new legislation — with attendant costs of initial implementation and ongoing administration — to address the health care access problems at the root of the constitutional dispute.

Canadians who confront barriers in accessing care will continue to turn to courts for recourse and successful challenges may have dramatic implications for the structure and operation of our health care systems. In *Auton* and *Wynberg*, Canadian courts show increasing reticence to accept section 15 Charter challenges regarding public funding decisions. Since *Auton* seems to preclude further litigation regarding so-called "non-core" services, future cases will likely examine the constitutionality of targeted health care programs that limit access to specific patient groups. The Supreme Court's dissension in *Chaoulli* leaves much scope for future cases to test the boundaries of section 7 rights in the context of access to health care. The post-*Chaoulli* challenges to legal restrictions on private health care in several other provinces signals further potential for greater private sector involvement where the public system fails to meet patient needs in a timely fashion. The outcome of litigation regarding Vancouver's supervised injection facility will also address fundamental questions about Charter rights and constitutional jurisdiction in the health care context.

Charter litigation is a high-profile tool to try to effect changes in health law and policy in Canada. Supreme Court of Canada rulings — whether unanimous victories, defeats or divided decisions — have reverberations through law, politics and society.

---

[179] See *R. v. Spratt*, [2008] B.C.J. No. 1669, 2008 BCCA 340 (B.C.C.A.).

INDEX